SCOTTINI

dicionário escolar inglês

Português - Inglês
Inglês - Português

Rodovia Jorge Lacerda, 5086 - Poço Grande
Gaspar - SC | CEP 89115-100

Compilação
Alfredo Scottini

IMPRESSO NA ÍNDIA

www.todolivro.com.br

Dados Internacionais de Catalogação na Publicação (CIP)
(Câmara Brasileira do Livro, SP, Brasil)

Scottini, Alfredo
Scottini - Dicionário Escolar de Inglês / Gaspar, SC: Todolivro Editora, 2023.

ISBN 978-85-7389-179-9

1. Língua portuguesa - Dicionários.
2. Língua inglesa - Dicionários. I. Título. II. Scottini, Alfredo

CDD 423.69

Índices para catálogo sistemático:

1. Inglês - Dicionários - Português
2. Português - Dicionários - Inglês I. Scottini, Alfredo.

INTRODUÇÃO

Ninguém pode negar a importância do conhecimento e domínio de línguas estrangeiras, principalmente o inglês, que desempenha papel de destaque como instrumento de comunicação entre povos de diversas nacionalidades.

Este minidicionário inglês-português - português-inglês tem o objetivo de servir como fonte de consulta prática e simples, não somente a estudantes, mas a todos os interessados em ter boa noção ou mesmo aprofundar seus conhecimentos da língua inglesa contemporânea. De seus verbetes consta a informação básica necessária para facilitar a tradução e o emprego adequado das palavras.

De fácil transporte e manuseio, é ideal para todos os que procuram incluir, em sua lista de prioridades, a busca incessante de conhecimento e cultura.

Editor

Com a Nova Ortografia da Língua Portuguesa

Atualizado, incorporando as normas do
Acordo Ortográfico da Língua Portuguesa (1990),
em vigor desde 1° de Janeiro de 2009.

RESUMO DAS ALTERAÇÕES EFETUADAS PELO ACORDO ORTOGRÁFICO DA LÍNGUA PORTUGUESA (1990), EM VIGOR DESDE 1º DE JANEIRO DE 2009

1. Alfabeto: Passou a ter 26 letras, com a introdução de **k**, **w** e **y**.

2. Trema: Abolido. Uso mantido apenas em palavras estrangeiras e suas derivadas: Hübner, hübneriano.

3. Acentuação:

3.a) Não se acentuam os ditongos abertos **éi** e **ói** de palavras paroxítonas (que têm acento forte na penúltima sílaba): ideia, plateia, heroico, paranoico. **Exceção:** paroxítonas terminadas em **r**: destróier, Méier.

3.b) Não são acentuados o **i** e o **u** fortes de palavras paroxítonas, quando estiverem depois de um ditongo (encontro de vogais): feiura, cauila, cheiinha.

3.c) Não são acentuadas as formas verbais **creem**, **deem**, **leem**, **veem** e derivadas (descreem, desdeem, releem, reveem).

3.d) Não são acentuadas as palavras terminadas em **ôo**: perdoo, abençoo, voo.

3.e) Abolido o acento agudo na vogal **u**, forte, nas formas do pres. do ind. dos verbos arguir e redarguir: (ele) argui; (tu) arguis; (eles) arguem.

Nota: Verbos terminados em **guar**, **quar** e **quir** (enxaguar, obliquar, delinquir, etc.) admitem duas pronúncias em algumas formas. Pronunciados com **a** ou **i** fortes, recebem acento: (eu) enxáguo; (eles) oblíquam; (tu) delínquas. Do contrário, não levam acento: enxaguo; obliquam; delinquas. No Brasil, é mais comum a pronúncia com o **a** e **o i** fortes.

3.f) Abolido o acento diferencial: para (verbo)/para (preposição); polo (extremidade geográfica)/polo (jogo); pelo (cabelo, penugem)/pelo (preposição); pera (fruta)/pera (preposição arcaica).

Notas: 1. Permanecem os acentos em: **pôde** (do verbo poder), para diferenciar de pode (3ª pessoa sing. pres. indic. do mesmo verbo); **pôr** (verbo), para diferenciar de por (preposição); **vêm** (pl., verbo vir); **têm** (pl., verbo ter). **2.** É facultativo o uso de acento circunflexo em **fôrma** (substantivo) e forma (substantivo e verbo).

PRINCIPAIS ALTERAÇÕES QUANTO AO USO DO HÍFEN

COM HÍFEN

Palavras compostas (por extenso ou reduzidas) →	Decreto-lei; primeiro-ministro; tenente-coronel; joão-ninguém; luso-brasileiro; mãe-d'água; olho-d'água; para-brisa; para-choque. **Mas:** girassol, madressilva, pontapé, paraquedas, paraquedista e afins – **sem hífen** (consagradas pelo uso).
Elementos repetidos	Blá-blá-blá; zigue-zague; tico-tico; lenga-lenga, etc.
Com as formas *além*, *aquém*, *recém*, *bem*, *sem* →	Além-mar, aquém-mar, recém-eleito; bem-casado; bem-estar; bem-humorado; bem-ditoso. Em alguns compostos o advérbio *bem* se aglutina ao segundo elemento iniciado por consoante, quer esse elemento tenha ou não vida à parte: benfazejo; benfeitor; benquerer; etc.
Com o advérbio *mal* seguido de *vogal, h, l,* ou quando se aplica a doença →	Mal-informado; mal-humorado; mal-lavado; mal-francês (ref. a sífilis); etc.
Com os adjetivos *grã, grão,* em forma verbal e ligados ou não por artigo →	Grã-Bretanha; Grão-Pará; Passa-Quatro, Trás-os-Montes, etc.
Somente estas locuções, de uso já consagrado →	Água-de-colônia; arco-da-velha; cor-de-rosa; mais-que-perfeito; pé-de-meia; ao deus-dará; à queima-roupa.

RESUMO DAS ALTERAÇÕES EFETUADAS PELO ACORDO ORTOGRÁFICO DA LÍNGUA PORTUGUESA (1990), EM VIGOR DESDE 1º DE JANEIRO DE 2009

PRINCIPAIS ALTERAÇÕES QUANTO AO USO DO HÍFEN

COM HÍFEN

Em compostos que designem espécies botânicas, zoológicas e afins →	Erva-doce; bem-me-quer (mas malmequer); andorinha-do-mar; couve-flor, feijão-verde, etc.
Com prefixos ou pseudoprefixos →	1. Terminados em vogal, diante de vogal igual: anti-inflamatório; pseudo-orador; micro-onda. 2. Terminados em consoante, diante de consoante igual: ad-digital; sub-básico. 3. Prefixos **pré-**, **pró-**, **pós-**, quando o segundo elemento tem vida à parte: pré-história; pró-ativo; pós-doutorado. 4. Terminados por **–m** ou **–n** diante de vogal, **h**, **m**, **n**: pan-eslavismo; pan-harmônico; circum-navegação; pan-negritude; pan-negritude. 5. Prefixos **ex-**, **sota-**, **soto-**, **vice-**, **vizo-**: ex-prefeito; sota-capitão; soto-general; vice-diretor; vizo-rei. 6. Elementos terminados por **vogal**, **sob-** e **sub-**, diante de elementos iniciados por **h**: geo-história; anti-histórico; sub-hepático; sub-horizonte. 7. Nas formações com os prefixos **hiper-**, **inter-** e **super-**, diante de elementos iniciados por **r**: hiper-requisitado; inter-regional; super-resistente. 8. Terminados por **b-** (ab-, ob-, sob-, sub-), **d-** (ad) diante de elementos iniciados por **b** ou **r**: ab-rupto; sob-rogar; sub-base; ad-referendum. **Nota:** adrenalina, adrenalite e afins estão consagradas pelo uso sem hífen.
Com sufixos de origem tupi-guarani →	**Açu**, **guaçu** e **mirim**, diante de elementos que terminem por vogal acentuada graficamente ou por exigência de pronúncia: Itajaí-Açu; Mogi-Guaçu; anajá-mirim.

SEM HÍFEN

1. Prefixos terminados em vogal, diante de vogal diferente: autoescola, antiaéreo, agroindustrial.
2. Prefixos terminados por consoante, diante de vogal: hiperativo; interescolar; superinteressante.
3. Prefixos **co-**, **pro-**, **pre-** e **re-**: coautor; coedição; procônsul; preeleito; reedição. **Atenção:** coerdeiro (sem "h", cf Ac. Bras. de Letras).
4. Elementos terminados por **vogal** diante de elementos iniciados por **r** ou **s** (dobram-se as consoantes): corréu; cosseno; antirreacionário; multissecular, etc. **Atenção:** *para-raios*.
5. Locuções em geral: juiz de paz; burro de carga; cor de vinho; quem quer que seja; à vontade; dia a dia; visto que, etc.
6. Prefixos **des-** e **in-** quando o segundo elemento perde o **h**: desumano; desumanidade; inumano, inábil, etc.

IMPORTANTE: AS DEMAIS REGRAS DE ACENTUAÇÃO/USO DO HÍFEN CONTINUAM EM VIGOR.

ABREVIAÇÕES USADAS NESTA OBRA

a.C., antes de Cristo
adj., adjetivo
adj. e s. 2 gen., adjetivo e substantivo comum de dois gêneros
adv., advérbio
anat., anatomia
art. def., artigo definido
bot., botânica
ch., chulo
conj., conjunção
dem., demonstrativo
ex., exemplo
expr., expressão
fam., familiar
fem., feminino
fig., figurado
fut., futuro
gal., galicismo
gír., gíria
gram., gramática
indef., indefinido
ingl., inglês
interj., interjeição
linguíst., linguística
lit., literatura
loc., locução
med., medicina
náut., náutica
num., numeral
pl., plural
pop., popular
prep., preposição
pron., pronominal
quím., química
rg.mt., regência múltipla
sing., singular
s.f., substantivo feminino
s.m., substantivo masculino
v.int., verbo intransitivo
v.lig., verbo de ligação
v. pron., verbo pronominal
v.t., verbo transitivo
zool., zoologia

PRONOMES DE TRATAMENTO

Altas Autoridades - Excelência - V. Exa. / S. Exa.
Reitores de Universidade - Vossa Magnificência - V.Mag.ª
Papa - Vossa Santidade - V.S.
Padres e Pastores - Reverendíssimo - V. Revma.
Reis e Rainhas - Vossa Majestade - V.M.
Príncipes - Vossa Alteza - V. A. / S. A.
Pessoas graduadas ou de cerimônia - Vossa Senhoria - V. S.ª

Doutor - Pessoas formadas - Dr. ou Sr. Dr.
Senhor - Todo homem - Sr.
Senhora - Toda mulher - Sra.
Senhorita - Mulher solteira - Srta.
Professor - Pessoa formada ou indivíduo perito - Prof.
Você - Pessoas em geral - V.

ABREVIATURAS E SIGLAS MAIS COMUNS

A. - autor
a - are
AA. - autores
AC - Estado do Acre
a.C. - antes de Cristo
a/c - aos cuidados
a.D. anno Domini (ano do Senhor)
Aids - SIDA - Síndrome da Imunodeficiência Adquirida
AL - Estado de Alagoas
AM - Estado do Amazonas
APAE - Associação de Pais e Amigos dos Excepcionais
AP - Estado do Amapá
Ap. ou apt. - apartamento
Av., aviação ou avenida
BA - Estado da Bahia
B.C.G - Bacilo de Calmette-Guérin
Bel. - Bacharel
BR - Brasil
cap. - capítulo
c/c - conta corrente
CE - Estado do Ceará
Cel. - coronel
CI - Cédula de Identidade
Cia. - Companhia
cm - centímetro ou centímetros
cód. - código
coml. - comercial
CPF - Cadastro de Pessoa Física
cx. - caixa
d. - dom, senhor, digno
dam - decâmetro
d. C. - depois de Cristo
DD. - digníssimo
Del. - delegado
DF - Distrito Federal
dm - decímetro
Dr. - doutor
Dra. - doutora
ed. - edição
ES - Estado do Espírito Santo
ECT - Empresa de Correios e Telégrafos
ECA - Estatuto da Criança e do Adolescente
etc. - e outras coisas
EUA - Estados Unidos da América
ex. - exemplo
Exa. - excelência
FAB - Força Aérea Brasileira
FAO - Organização das Nações Unidas para a Agricultura e Alimentação
FEB - Força Expedicionária Brasileira
FIFA - Federação Internacional de Futebol Associação
fl. - folha
fls. - folhas
FMI - Fundo Monetário Internacional
g - grama ou gramas
Gen. - general
GO - Estado de Goiás
h - hora ou horas
ha - hectare
HP - cavalo a vapor (horsepower)
Ilmo. - Ilustríssimo
INSS - Instituto Nacional do Seguro Social
IPTU - Imposto Predial e Territorial Urbano
IR - Imposto de Renda
JC - Jesus Cristo
kg - quilograma ou quilogramas
km - quilômetro ou quilômetros
kV - quilovolt (s)
kW - quilowatt (s)
l - litro, litros
loc. - locução
Ltda. - limitada (comercialmente)
m - metro, metros
MA - Estado do Maranhão
mg - miligrama ou miligramas
MG - Estado de Minas Gerais
min - minuto ou minutos
mm - milímetro, milímetros
MM. - meritíssimo
MT - Estado do Mato Grosso
MS - Estado do Mato Grosso do Sul
N. - Norte
N.B. - note bem

ABREVIATURAS E SIGLAS MAIS COMUNS

NE - Nordeste
NO - Noroeste
N.S. - Nosso Senhor
N.T. - Novo Testamento
O - Oeste
OEA - Organização dos Estados Americanos
OK - (inglês), certo, isso mesmo
ONU - Organização das Nações Unidas
Pe. - padre
PA - Estado do Pará
pág., p. - página
PB - Estado da Paraíba
PE - Estado de Pernambuco
p. ex. - por exemplo
pg. - pago
PI - Estado do Piauí
pl. - plural
PR - Estado do Paraná
prof. - professor
profa. - professora
P.S. - post scriptum - (escrito depois)
QG - quartel general, sede principal
ql. - quilate
R. - Rua
Revmo. - reverendíssimo
RJ - Estado do Rio de Janeiro
RN - Estado do Rio Grande do Norte
RO - Estado de Rondônia
rpm - rotação por minuto

RR - Estado de Roraima
RS - Estado do Rio Grande do Sul
s - segundo, segundos
S - Sul
S.A. - Sociedade Anônima
S.A. - Sua Alteza
SC - Estado de Santa Catarina
SE - Estado de Sergipe
S. Exa. - Sua Excelência
SO - Sudoeste
SOS - pedido de socorro urgente
SP - Estado de São Paulo
Sr. - Senhor
Sra - Senhora
Srta. - Senhorita
S.S. - Sua Santidade
STF - Supremo Tribunal Federal
t - tonelada, toneladas
TC - Tribunal de Contas
TO - Estado do Tocantins
TV - televisão
USA - *United States of America*
v - volt, volts
V. - você
V.A. - Vossa Alteza
V.Exa. - Vossa Excelência
V.S.ª - Vossa Senhoria
V.T. - Velho Testamento
W.C. - *(water-closet)*, banheiro

EXPRESSÕES E TERMOS DA LÍNGUA INGLESA, DE USO FREQUENTE

ALL RIGHT - tudo certo, tudo bem.
COMPACT DISC - CD - cedê.
CHARTER - voo charter - voo fretado com saída e chegada predeterminadas.
DESIGN - projeto, modelo.
DISQUETE - pequeno disco.
FEELING - sentimento, modo de agir.
FIFTY-FIFTY - metade do negócio.
FINE - ótimo, muito bom.
GAME - jogo, partida.
GO HOME - vá para casa, afaste-se.
HANDICAP - desvantagem, obstáculo.
HOME - casa, lar.
HOT-DOG - cachorro-quente.
INSIGHT - olhada no interior do indivíduo, ideia que surge rapidamente.
JEANS - tipo de tecido.
KNOW-HOW - conhecimento, domínio de uma técnica.
LAYOUT - plano, esquema.
LIGHT - leve, brilhante.
LOBBY - pressão para obter favor.
NICE - agradável, bom.
OK - tudo bem, certo.
ON-LINE - na mesma linha, automático.
OUTLET CENTER - conjunto de lojas para vendas no varejo e atacado.
PAPER - papel, resumo, minuta.
PARTNER - sócio, companheiro.
POINT - local de encontro badalado.
RAFTING - canoagem em corredeiras, rio de montanha.
SKATE - brinquedo para deslizar.
STAND GO - ir para frente, posição de avanço.
STAND BY - espera, aguardo de.
SOFT - leve, suave.
SOFTWARE - conteúdo de carga do micro, todos os recursos técnicos e humanos de um indivíduo ou empresa.
SHOPPING CENTER - centro comercial, centro de vendas.
SHORT - bermuda, calça curta.
SHOW - espetáculo, apresentação.
SHOW-ROOM - mostruário, sala para expor produtos.
SURF - esporte aquático praticado no mar com uma prancha.
TAPE - fita, filme.
TOP - cume, ápice.
TOP MODEL - modelo de alto valor.
TRAVELER'S CHECK - cheque de viagem.
UPGRADE - posição superior, degrau acima.
V-CHIP - consulta para pronta resposta através da própria TV.
VIDEOTAPE - gravação de um programa de televisão em fita.
VIDEOCASSETTE - aparelho para reproduzir fitas.
VIDEO ON DEMAND - filme por pedido.
V.I.P. - (*very important person*) pessoa muito importante.
VERY MUCH - muito, grande.
YANKEE - ianque, americano, designação depreciativa para americano.
WALKIE-TALKIE - aparelho para transmitir e receber mensagens.
WATER-CLOSET - banheiro.
WINDOWS - programa de linguagem para computador.
WINDSURF - tipo de disputa por barco.

REGRAS DE ACENTUAÇÃO

1. Vocábulos oxítonos:

1.a) Devem ser acentuadas as palavras oxítonas e os monossílabos tônicos terminados em - **a, e, o** - seguidos ou não de **s**.
Ex.: atrás, lá, Alá, sofá, ananás, maracujá...
- mês, pé, café, José, Zé, francês, você...
- pó, nós, avô, vovó, paletó, forró, jiló...
Obs.: Não são acentuadas as palavras terminadas em **i** e **u** tônicos, seguidos ou não de **s**.
Ex.: ali, aqui, tatu, urubu, açu ...
Atenção especial: São acentuadas as formas verbais terminadas em - **a, e, o** - quando seguidas dos pronomes - **la, las, lo, los**.
Ex.: amá-la, pintá-las, amarrá-lo, contá-los, vendê-la, vendê-las, metê-lo, contê-los, pô-la, repô-las, dispô-lo, dispô-los.

1.b) São acentuadas as palavras terminadas em - **em** e **ens** - com mais de uma sílaba.
Ex.: alguém, ninguém, armazém, parabéns...
Obs.: As formas verbais do verbo ter e vir são acentuadas quando estão no plural.
Ex.: ele tem, eles têm; ele vem, eles vêm.
Em formas derivadas, no singular há acento agudo; e no plural, circunflexo.
Ex.: ele contém, eles contêm; ele convém, eles convêm.

1.c) Levam acento agudo as palavras oxítonas que contenham os ditongos abertos **éi, éu** ou **ói**, podendo estes últimos ser seguidos ou não de **s**:
Ex.: papéis, céu(s), heróis(s), véu(s), fiéis.

2. Vocábulos Paroxítonos:

2.a) São acentuadas as palavras paroxítonas terminadas em: **r, x, n, l**.
Ex.: açúcar, caráter, ônix, tórax, hífen, sêmen, fácil, móvel... e em **i(s), us, um, uns, ão(s), ã(s), ei(s), ps**. Ex.: júri, lápis, vírus, múnus, álbum, álbuns, sótão, órfãos, ímã, órfãs, afáveis, bíceps.

2.b) São acentuadas as palavras terminadas em ditongos crescentes.

Ex.: códeas, róseo, argênteo, glória, memória, espécie, colégio, régio, mágoa, régua, água, tênue, ingênuo, contíguo...

2.c) Não são acentuados os ditongos abertos **ei** e **oi** em palavras paroxítonas.
Ex.: ideia; assembleia; epopeia; heroico; jiboia; paranoico.

2.d) Não são acentuados o **i** e o **u** tônicos nas palavras paroxítonas quando precedidos de ditongo.
Ex.: feiura; baiuca; boiuno; cheiinho; saiinha.

2.e) Não são acentuadas as formas verbais que têm o acento tônico na raiz, com **u** tônico precedido de **g** ou **q** e seguido de **e** ou **i**.
Ex.: averigue; apazigue; arguem.

2.f) Não recebem acento circunflexo, em palavras paroxítonas, as vogais tônicas fechadas.
Ex.: enjoo (substantivo e flexão do verbo enjoar); voo (substantivo e flexão do verbo voar); povoo (flexão do verbo povoar); perdoo (flexão do verbo perdoar), destoo (flexão do verbo destoar), etc.

2.g) Não levam acento agudo ou circunflexo as palavras paroxítonas que, tendo respectivamente vogal tônica aberta ou fechada, são homógrafas de palavras em próclise.
1. Para, (flexão do v. parar), e para (preposição).
2. Pela (flexão do v. pelar) e pela (combinação da prep. com o artigo).
3. Polo (substantivo) e polo (combinação antiga e popular de "por" e "lo").
4. Pelo (flexão do v. pelar), pelo (substantivo) e pelo (comb. da prep. com o art.).
5. Pera (fruta), pera (substantivo arcaico – pedra) e pera (preposição arcaica).

2.h) Não levam acento circunflexo as formas verbais paroxítonas que contém um e tônico oral fechado em hiato com a terminação –em da 3ª pessoa do plural do presente do indicativo ou do conjuntivo

REGRAS DE ACENTUAÇÃO

dos verbos **crer, dar, ler e ver e seus derivados**.
Ex.: creem, deem, leem, veem.

3. Vocábulos Proparoxítonos:
São acentuadas todas as palavras proparoxítonas da Língua Portuguesa:
Ex.: matemática, erótico, geógrafo, médico, ônibus, perímetro, quilômetro, belíssimo, período...

4. Hiatos:
São acentuados o **i** e o **u** tônicos quando forem a segunda vogal do hiato e não formarem sílaba com **l, m, n, r, x, z, u**, nem forem seguidos de **nh**.
Ex.: país; faísca; saúde; conteúdo; juiz (mas – juízes); raiz (mas – raízes); Itajaí, Jacareí, baú, Jaú.

5. Trema
Coloca-se o trema apenas em palavras derivadas de nomes próprios estrangeiros.
Ex.: Müller, mülleriano: Hübner, hübneriano, etc.

6. Acento Diferencial
Usa-se o acento circunflexo, obrigatoriamente, para distinguir um vocábulo de outro de grafia igual, nos seguintes casos:
Ex.: Pôr (verbo) e por (preposição).
Pode (pres. indic. do v. poder) pôde (pret. perfeito).

CRASE ou ACENTO GRAVE
A palavra crase significa **fusão**, sendo indicada pelo sinal gráfico grave - à - demonstrando que houve a fusão do artigo feminino "a" com a preposição "a".
A crase aparece ante uma palavra feminina e quando se pode substituí-la por um termo masculino, pelo qual aparece o artigo:
Vamos à escola - Vamos ao teatro. Chegamos à fazenda - Chegamos ao sítio. Refiro-me à professora de Português - Refiro-me ao professor de Português.
Venho a Portugal - Venho de Portugal. Venho da Bolívia - Vou à Bolívia.

NB - Deve haver artigo; portanto, a palavra precisa estar determinada.

Nunca Há Crase:
1. Diante de palavras masculinas e verbos.
2. Diante de pronomes indefinidos.
3. Diante de nomes de cidades, a não ser quando estão adjetivados.
4. Diante da palavra casa, a não ser que esteja determinada.
5. Diante de pronomes de tratamento e dos pronomes "cuja", "cujo" e "quem".
6. Antes da palavra casa, com referência a lar, quando não estiver com modificativo.
   Ex.: Voltou a casa. (Mas: Voltou à casa da avó.)

Casos Especiais:
1. É facultativo o uso da crase ante pronomes possessivos e nomes próprios de mulheres.
   Ex.: Dei um livro à (a) minha irmã. Envio um livro à (a) Ana.
2. Inúmeras expressões adverbiais recebem o sinal de crase:
   Ex.: às escuras, às vezes, à tardinha...
3. Na indicação de horas, sempre se usa a crase:
   Ex.: Chegou às 13h30min. Faremos o encontro às nove. Deito-me às 24h.
4. Usa-se a crase diante de palavra masculina quando se subentender o termo "à moda de".
   Ex.: Pedro veste-se à índio (à moda de). Usa os cabelos à Castro Alves (à moda de).
5. A crase também se manifesta com os pronomes demonstrativos: **aquela(s), aquele(s), aquilo**.
   Ex.: Sempre me refiro àquilo tudo. Assistimos àquele filme.
   No uso de a que - Ouvimos a voz - à que - àquela que - à qual - todos se referem.

Observação: No uso da crase, vale sempre o bom senso e sentir se há uma ligação entre os termos ligados pelo "a". Estas normas são básicas, mas não abrangem tudo, pois as variações linguísticas são muitas.

EMPREGO DAS LETRAS INICIAIS MAIÚSCULAS

1. **Ao iniciarmos uma frase, oração ou citação:**
   Ex.: A flor é belíssima.
   Deus disse: Haja luz.

2. **Nos substantivos próprios (nomes de pessoas, países, Estados, bairros ou logradouros públicos):**
   Ex.: Luís Carlos, Canadá, Brasil, Maranhão, São Paulo, Copacabana, Rua Sete de Setembro, etc.

3. **Nos nomes que designam artes, ciências ou disciplinas:**
   Ex.: Matemática, Música, Direito, Arte, Engenharia, Física, etc.

4. **Nos nomes de eras históricas e épocas notáveis:**
   Ex.: Idade Média, Independência do Brasil, Revolução Farroupilha, etc.

5. **Nos nomes que denotem altos conceitos religiosos, políticos ou funções:**
   Ex.: Arcebispo do Rio de Janeiro, Governador do Estado, Presidente, Estado (referindo-se a uma nação), País (referindo-se ao Brasil), Igreja, etc.

6. **Nos nomes dos pontos cardeais quando designam regiões:**
   Ex.: Os conflitos do Oriente.
   O clamor do Nordeste.

7. **Nos nomes de escolas, edifícios, agremiações culturais ou esportivas, empresas ou instituições públicas ou privadas:**
   Ex.: Colégio São José, Condomínio Palace, Clube de Regatas Flamengo, Ministério da Justiça, Teatro Carlos Gomes, etc.

8. **Nos títulos de revistas, jornais, livros, produções artísticas, literárias ou científicas:**
   Ex.: Isto É, O Globo, Brida, etc.

9. **Nas expressões de tratamento:**
   Ex.: Vossa Senhoria, Vossa Excelência, Sua Santidade, etc.

10. **Nos nomes de comemorações religiosas:**
    Ex.: Natal, Páscoa, Finados, etc.

11. **Nos nomes de corpos celestes:**
    Ex.: Lua, Sol, Via-Láctea, etc.

Observação: Os nomes dos meses devem ser escritos com inicial minúscula:
Ex.: agosto, dezembro, etc.

USO DO HÍFEN

A. Em palavras compostas, locuções e encadeamentos vocabulares

1. Emprega-se o hífen em palavras compostas por justaposição que não contêm formas de ligação e cujos elementos, de natureza nominal, adjetival, numeral ou verbal mantenham significado e acento próprio, podendo o primeiro elemento estar reduzido: ano-luz, arco-íris, decreto-lei, alcaide-mor, afro-asiático, guarda-chuva.
Obs.: Certas compostas se aglutinam: madressilva; pontapé; paraquedas; paraquedista; girassol, etc.

2. Nos topônimos compostos iniciados pelos adjetivos grã, grão ou por forma verbal, ou cujos elementos estejam ligados por artigo: Grã-Bretanha; Grão-Pará; Passa-Quatro; Quebra-Dentes; Baía-de-Todos-os-Santos; Entre-os-Rios.

3. Nas palavras compostas que designam espécies botânicas e zoológicas, estejam ou não ligadas por preposição ou qualquer outro elemento: couve-flor; feijão-verde; ervilha-de-cheiro; bem-me-quer; formiga-branca; cobra-d'água; andorinha-do-mar.

4. Nos compostos com os advérbios bem e mal, quando estes se apresentem antes de qualquer palavra que tenha vida própria e este elemento comece por vogal ou h: bem-aventurado; bem-estar; bem-humorado; mal-humorado; mal-estar, mal-afortunado. Mas o advérbio bem (ao contrário de mal) pode não se aglutinar com palavras começadas por consoante: bem-ditoso (malditoso): bem-falante (malfalante); bem-nascido (malnascido); bem-visto (malvisto), etc.
Obs.: Às vezes, o advérbio bem aparece aglutinando com o segundo elemento, mesmo que este não tenha vida própria: benfazejo; benfeitor; benquerença, etc.

5. Nos compostos com os elementos além, aquém, recém e sem: além-mar; além-fronteiras; aquém-fiar; aquém-Pireneus; recém-casado; recém-nascido; sem-cerimônia; sem-vergonha.

6. Para ligar duas ou mais palavras que ocasionalmente se combinam, formando encadeamentos vocabulares: Liberdade-Igualdade-Fraternidade; a ponte Rio-Niterói; a ligação Paris-Londres. E nas combinações históricas ou ocasionais de topônimos: Áustria-Hungria; Alsácia-Lorena; Rio-Nova Iorque, etc.

7. Nas locuções adjetivas, pronominais, adverbiais, prepositivas ou conjuncionais em geral não se emprega o hífen, a não ser em algumas exceções consagradas pelo uso: água-de-colônia; arco-da-velha; cor-de-rosa; mais-que-perfeito; pé-de-meia; ao deus-dará; à queima-roupa.

B. Nas formações por prefixação, recomposição e sufixação

Nestes casos, o hífen somente é usado:

1. Quando o segundo elemento comece por **h**: anti-higiênico; pré-história; geo-história; semi-hospitalar; sub-hepático. **Mas atenção:** coerdeiro (cf. Acad. Bras. de Letras).

2. Nas formações em que o prefixo ou pseudoprefixo termina na mesma vogal com que se inicia o segundo elemento: anti-ibérico; contra-almirante; arqui-irmão; micro-onda; semi-interno; auto-análise.
Obs.: Nas formações com o prefixo **co-**, em geral este se aglutina com o segundo elemento, mesmo quando iniciado por "o": coobrigação, coordenar, cooperar, cooptação, coocupante, cooficiante, etc.

3. Nas formações com os prefixos **circum-** e **pan-**, quando o segundo elemento começa por **vogal, m** ou **n (além de h)**: circum-escolar; circum-murado; circum-navegação; pan-americano; pan-africano; pan-negritude.

4. Nas formações com os prefixos **hiper-**, **inter-** e **super-**, quando combinados com elementos iniciados pela letra **r**: hiper-requintado; inter-resistente; super-revista.

5. Nas formações com os prefixos **ex-** (com o sentido de estado anterior ou cessamento), **sota-**, **soto-**, **vice-** e **vizo-**: ex-diretor; ex-hospedeira; ex-presidente; sota-piloto; soto-mestre; vice-reitor, etc.

USO DO HÍFEN

6. Nas formações com os prefixos tônicos **pós-**, **pré-** e **pró-**, quando o segundo elemento tem vida própria: pós-graduação; pós-tônico; pré-escolar; pré-natal; pró-africano; pró-europeu.

7. Nas formações por sufixação só se emprega o hífen nos vocábulos terminados por sufixos de origem tupi-guarani que representam formas adjetivas, como **açu**, **guaçu** e **mirim**, quando o primeiro elemento acaba em vogal acentuada graficamente ou quando a pronúncia exige a distinção gráfica dos dois elementos: Itajaí-Açu; capim-açu; Mogi-Guaçu; Aimoré-Guaçu; Itajaí-Mirim; Ceará-Mirim.

Atenção: não se emprega o hífen nos seguintes casos:

1. Nas formações em que o prefixo termina em vogal e o segundo elemento começa por **r** ou **s**, devendo estas consoantes duplicar-se: antirreligioso; contrarregra; extrarregular; antissemita; cosseno; minissaia. **Mas atenção:** para-raios.

2. Nas formações em que o prefixo ou pseudoprefixo termina em vogal e o segundo elemento começa por vogal diferente: antiaéreo; coeducação; plurianual; agroindustrial; hidroelétrico; autoaprendizagem.

3. Nas ligações da preposição **de** às formas monossilábicas do presente do indicativo do verbo haver: hei de, hás de, hão de, etc.

4. Nas formações com os prefixos **co-**, **pro-**, **pre-** e **re-** ocorre, em geral, a aglutinação: coabitar, procônsul, preeleito; reedição.

C. Na ênclise, na mesóclise e com o verbo haver

1. Emprega-se o hífen na ênclise e na mesóclise: enviá-lo; enviá-lo-ei; escrever-lhe; escrever-lhe-emos.

2. Nas ligações de formas pronominais enclíticas ao advérbio **eis** (ei-la, eis-me); e também nas combinações de formas pronominais como no-la, vo-las, quando em próclise.

ALGARISMOS ROMANOS E ALGARISMOS ARÁBICOS

ROMANO	ARÁBICO	ROMANO	ARÁBICO	ROMANO	ARÁBICO
I	1	XV	15	CCC	300
II	2	XVI	16	CD	400
III	3	XVII	17	D	500
IV	4	XVIII	18	DC	600
V	5	XIX	19	DCC	700
VI	6	XX	20	DCCC	800
VII	7	XL	40	CM	900
VIII	8	L	50	M	1000
IX	9	LX	60	MM	2000
X	10	LXX	70	MMXC	2090
XI	11	LXXX	80	MMD	2500
XII	12	XC	90	MMCM	2900
XIII	13	C	100		
XIV	14	CC	200		

PAÍSES DO MUNDO, ADJETIVOS PÁTRIOS E MOEDAS

País	Capital	Nacionalidade	Unidade Monetária	Moeda Divisória
Afeganistão	Cabul	afegane	afegane	100 pules
África do Sul	Cidade do Cabo / Pretória	sul-africana	rand	100 centavos
Albânia	Tirana	albanesa	lek novo	quindarca
Alemanha	Berlim	alemã	marco alemão	pfennig (fênig)
Andorra	Andorra la Vella	andorrana	franco francês	100 cêntimos
Angola	Luanda	angolana ou angolense ou angola	novo cuanza	uei
Antigua	St. Johns	antiguana	dólar do Caribe	100 centavos
Arábia Saudita	Riad (sede do reinado) Jedá (capital administrativa)	saudita ou árabe-saudita	rial saudita	100 halalah
Argélia	Argel	argelina ou argeliana	dinar	100 cêntimos
Argentina	Buenos Aires	argentina	peso	centavos
Armênia	Jerevan	armênia	rublo	copeque
Austrália	Camberra	australiana	dólar	100 centavos
Áustria	Viena	austríaca	xelim	groschen
Azerbaidjão ou Azerbaijão	Baku	azerbaidjâni ou azerbeidjana	rublo	100 copeques
Bahamas	Nassau	baamês ou baamense	dólar baamiano	100 centavos
Bangladesh	Dacca	bengalesa ou bengali	taca	piosha
Barbados	Bridgetown	barbadiana	dólar barbadiano	100 centavos
Barein ou Bareine	Manama	barenita ou bareinita	dinar	1.000 fils
Bélgica	Bruxelas	belga	franco belga	100 cêntimos
Belize	Belmopán	belizenha	dólar de Belize	100 centavos
Benin	Porto Novo	beninense	franco CFA	100 cêntimos
Bielo-Rússia ou Belarus	Minsk	bielo-russa	taler	
Bolívia	La Paz	boliviana	boliviano	100 centavos
Bósnia-Herzegovina	Sarajevo	bósnio	novo dinar iugoslavo	100 paras
Botswana	Gaborone	betchuana	pula	100 tebe
Brasil	Brasília	brasileira	real	100 centavos
Brunei	Bandar Seri Begauan	bruneiana ou bruneana	dólar do Brunei	100 sen
Bulgária	Sófia	búlgara	leu	100 stotinki
Burkina	Magadugu	burquinense	franco CFA	100 cêntimos
Burundi	Bujumbura	burundinesa	franco do Burundi	100 cêntimos
Butão	Thimphu	butanesa	ngultrum	100 chetrum
Cabo Verde	Praia	cabo-verdiana	escudo do Cabo Verde	100 centavos
Camarões	Yaoundé	camaronesa	franco CFA	100 cêntimos

PAÍSES DO MUNDO, ADJETIVOS PÁTRIOS E MOEDAS

País	Capital	Nacionalidade	Unidade Monetária	Moeda Divisória
Camboja	Phnom Penh	cambojana ou cambojiana	riel novo	100 sen
Canadá	Ottawa	canadense	dólar canadense	100 centavos
Catar	Doha	catariana	rial do Catar	100 dirhams
Cazaquistão	Alma Atá	cazaque	rublo	100 copeques
Chade	Ndjamena	chadiana	franco CFA	100 cêntimos
Chile	Santiago	chilena	peso chileno	100 centavos
China	Pequim	chinesa	iuan ou iuane	100 fen
Chipre	Nicósia	cipriota ou cípria	libra cipriota lira turca	100 centavos 100 kurush
Cingapura	Cingapura	cingapuriana ou cingapurense	dólar de Cingapura	100 centavos
Colômbia	Bogotá	colombiana	peso colombiano	100 centavos
Congo	Brazzaville	congolesa ou congolense ou conguesa	franco CPA	100 cêntimos
Coreia do Norte	Pieongyang	norte-coreana	uon norte-coreano	100 chon
Coreia do Sul	Seul	sul-coreana	uon sul-coreano	100 chun
Costa do Marfim	Abidjan	ebúrnea ou marfiniana ou marfinense	franco CFA	100 cêntimos
Costa Rica	San José	costarriquense ou costarriquenha	colom costa-riquenho	100 cêntimos
Croácia	Zagreb	croata	dinar croata	
Cuba	Havana	cubana	peso cubano	100 centavos
Dinamarca	Copenhague	dinamarquesa	coroa dinamarquesa	100 ore
Djibuti	Djibuti	djibutiense ou djibutiana	franco do Caribe	100 cêntimos
Dominica	Roseau	dominicana	dólar do Caribe Oriental	100 centavos
Egito	Cairo	egípcia	libra egípcia	100 piastra
El Salvador	San Salvador	salvadorenha ou salvatoriana	colom salvadorenho	100 centavos
Emirados Árabes Unidos	Abu Dabi	árabe	dirrã	100 fils
Equador	Quito	equatoriana	sucre	100 centavos
Eslováquia	Bratislava	eslovaca		
Eslovênia	Liubliana	eslovena	tolar	100 stotins
Espanha	Madri	espanhola	peseta	100 cêntimos
Estados Unidos da América	Washington	americana	dólar	100 centavos
Estônia	Tallinn	estoniana	coroa estoniana rublo	
Etiópia	Adis-Abeba	etíope	dólar etíope	100 centavos
Fiji	Suva	fijiana	dólar de Fiji	100 centavos
Filipinas	Manila	filipina	peso filipino	100 centavos
Finlândia	Helsinki	finlandesa	marca	100 pennia
Formosa	Taipé	formosina ou taiuanesa	dólar	100 centavos

PAÍSES DO MUNDO, ADJETIVOS PÁTRIOS E MOEDAS

País	Capital	Nacionalidade	Unidade Monetária	Moeda Divisória
França	Paris	francesa	franco francês	100 cêntimos
Gabão	Libreville	gabonense ou gabonesa	franco CFA	100 cêntimos
Gâmbia	Banjul	gambiana	dalasi	100 bututi
Gana	Acra	ganense ou ganesa	cedi novo	100 pesewas
Geórgia	Tbilisi	georgiana	rublo	100 copeques
Grã-Bretanha	Londres	britânica	libra esterlina	100 centavos
Granada	St.George	granadina	dólar do Caribe	100 centavos
Grécia	Atenas	grega	dracma	100 leptae
Guatemala	Guatemala	guatemalteca ou guatemalense	quetzal ou quetçal	100 centavos
Guiana	Georgetown	guianense ou guianesa	franco	100 cêntimos
Guiné	Conacri	guineana	franco	100 cêntimos
Guiné-Bissau	Bissau	guineense	peso	100 centavos
Guiné Equatorial	Malabo	guinéu-equatoriana	franco CFA	100 cêntimos
Haiti	Porto Príncipe	haitiana	gurde	100 cêntimos
Holanda	Amsterdã	holandesa	florim	100 centavos
Honduras	Tegucigalpa	hondurenha	lempira	100 centavos
Hungria	Budapeste	húngara	florim	100 fillér
Iêmen	Sanaa	iemenita	rial iemenita	100 fils
Ilhas Comores	Moroni	comorense	franco comorense	100 cêntimos
Ilhas Marshall	Majuro	marshallina	dólar	100 centavos
Ilhas Salomão	Honiara	salomônica	dólar das ilhas de Salomão	100 centavos
Índia	Nova Délhi	indiana ou hindu ou índia	rupia indiana	100 paisa
Indonésia	Jacarta	indonésia	rupia	100 sen
Irã	Teerã	iraniana	rial iraniano ou real	100 dinares
Iraque	Bagdá	iraquiana	dinar iraquiano	100 dirrãs
Irlanda	Dublin	irlandesa	libra irlandesa	100 pence
Islândia	Reikjavik	islandesa	nova coroa irlandesa	100 aurar
Israel	Jerusalém	israelense ou israeliana	shekel ou siclo novo	100 agoras
Itália	Roma	italiana	lira italiana	100 centésimos
Iugoslávia	Belgrado	iugoslava	novo dinar	100 para
Jamaica	Kingston	jamaicana	dólar jamaicano	100 centavos
Japão	Tóquio	japonesa	iene	100 sen
Jordânia	Amã	jordaniana	dinar jordaniano	1.000 fils
Kiribati	Bairik	kiribatiana	dólar australiano	100 centavos
Kuwait	Al Kuwait	kuwaitiana	dinar kuwaiteano	1.000 fils
Laos	Vientiane	laosiana	kip novo	100 at
Lesoto	Maseru	lesota	loti (pl. maloti)	100 lisente
Letônia	Riga	letã ou leta	rublo letão	
Líbano	Beirute	libanesa	libra libanesa	100 piastras
Libéria	Monróvia	liberiana	dólar liberiano	100 centavos
Líbia	Trípoli	líbia	dinar líbio	1.000 dirrãs

PAÍSES DO MUNDO, ADJETIVOS PÁTRIOS E MOEDAS

País	Capital	Nacionalidade	Unidade Monetária	Moeda Divisória
Liechtenstein	Vaduz	liechtensteiniense	franco suíço	100 rappen
Lituânia	Vilnius	lituana	rublo	
Luxemburgo	Luxemburgo	luxemburguesa	franco luxemburguês	100 cêntimos
Macedônia	Skopje	macedônio	dinar	
Madagascar	Antananarivo	malgaxe	franco malgaxe	100 cêntimos
Malásia	Kuala Lumpur	malaísia	dólar malaísio	100 centavos
Malavi ou Malauí	Lilongüe	malaviana ou malauiana	cuacha maldívia	100 tambalas
Maldivas	Malê	maldívia	rupia maldívia	100 laaris
Mali	Bamaco	malinesa	franco CFA	
Malta	Valeta	maltesa	libra maltesa	100 cêntimos
Marrocos	Rabat	marroquina	dirrã	100 cêntimos
Maurício	Port Louis	mauriciana	rupia mauriciana	100 centavos
Mauritânia	Nouakchott	mauritana	uguia	5 khum
México	Cidade do México	mexicana	peso mexicano	100 centavos
Mianmá	Yangum	birmanesa	quiat	100 pias
Micronésia	Kolonia	micronésia	dólar americano	100 centavos
Moçambique	Maputo	moçambicana	metical	100 centavos
Moldova	Kisinev	moldova	rublo	100 copeques
Mônaco	Mônaco-Ville	monegasca	franco francês	100 cêntimos
Mongólia	Ulan-Bator	mongol	tugrik	mongo
Namíbia	Windhoek	namibiana	rand	100 centavos
Nauru	Nauru	nauruana	dólar australiano	100 centavos
Nepal	Katmandu	nepalesa	rupia nepalesa	100 paisas
Nicarágua	Manágua	nicaragüense ou nicaraguana	córdoba novo	100 centavos
Níger	Niamei	nigerana	franco CFA	100 cêntimos
Nigéria	Lagos	nigeriana	naira	100 kobo
Noruega	Oslo	norueguesa	coroa norueguesa	100 ore
Nova Zelândia	Wellington	neozelandesa	dólar da Nova Zelândia	100 centavos
Omã	Mascate	omani ou omaniana	rial omani	1.000 baiza
Panamá	Cidade do Panamá	panamenha	balboa	100 cêntimos
Papua Nova Guiné	Port Moresby	papuásia ou papua	kina	100 toea
Paquistão	Islamabad	paquistanesa	rupée paquistanês	100 paisa
Paraguai	Assunção	paraguaia	guarani	100 cêntimos
Peru	Lima	peruana	inti	100 cêntimos
Polônia	Varsóvia	polonesa	zloty ou sloti	100 groszy
Portugal	Lisboa	portuguesa	escudo	100 centavos
Quênia	Nairobi	queniana	xelim queniano	100 centavos
Quirguízia	Bishkek	quirguiz	rublo	100 copeques
República Centro-Africana	Bangui	centro-africana	franco CFA	100 cêntimos
República Dominicana	São Domingo	dominicana	peso dominicano	100 centavos
República Tcheca	Praga	tcheca		
Romênia	Bucareste	romena	leu	100 bani
Ruanda	Kigali	ruandesa	franco de Ruanda	100 cêntimos

PAÍSES DO MUNDO, ADJETIVOS PÁTRIOS E MOEDAS

País	Capital	Nacionalidade	Unidade Monetária	Moeda Divisória
Rússia	Moscou	russa	rublo	100 copeques
Samoa Ocidental	Ápia	samoana	tala	100 sene
San Marino	San Marino	são-marinense	lira italiana	100 cêntimos
Santa Lúcia	Castries	santa-lucense	dólar do Caribe	100 centavos
São Cristóvão e Neves	Basseterre	são-cristovense	dólar do Caribe	100 centavos
São Tomé e Príncipe	São Tomé	são-tomense	dobra	100 cêntimos
São Vicente e Granadinas	Kingstown	são-vicentina	dólar do Caribe	100 centavos
Senegal	Dacar	senegalesa	franco CFA	100 cêntimos
Serra Leoa	Freetown	serra-leonesa	leone	100 centavos
Seichelas	Vitória	seichelense	rupia de Seichelas	100 centavos
Síria	Damasco	síria	libra síria	100 piastras
Somália	Mogadíscio	somali ou somaliana	xelim somaliano	100 centésimos
Sri Lanka	Colombo	cingalesa	rupia cingalesa	100 centavos
Suazilândia	Mbabane	suazi	lilangueni	100 centavos
Sudão	Cartum	sudanesa	libra sudanesa	100 millèmes
Suécia	Estocolmo	sueca	coroa sueca	100 ore
Suíça	Berna	suíça	franco suíço	100 centavos
Suriname	Paramaribo	surinamesa	florim surinamês	100 centavos
Tadjiquistão	Dusambe	tadjique	rublo	100 copeques
Tailândia	Bangcoc	tailandesa	baht	100 satangs
Tanzânia	Dodoma	tanzaniana	xelim tanzaniano	100 centavos
Togo	Lomé	togolesa	franco CFA	100 cêntimos
Tonga	Nuku Alofa	tonganesa	paanga	100 seniti
Trinidad e Tobago	Port of Spain	trinitina ou tobaguiana	dólar de Trinidad e Tobago	100 centavos
Tunísia	Túnis	tunisiana	dinar tunisiano	100 millièmes
Turquemenistão	Ashkhábad	turcomana	rublo	100 copeques
Turquia	Ancara	turca	lira turca	100 kurush
Tuvalu	Vaiaku	tuvaluana	dólar tuvaluano	100 centavos
Ucrânia	Kiev	ucraniana	rublo	100 copeques
Uganda	Kampala	ugandense	novo xelim	100 centavos
Uruguai	Montevidéu	uruguaia	peso uruguaio	100 centésimos
Uzbequistão	Taskent	uzbeque	rublo	100 copeques
Vanuatu	Porto Vila	vanuatense	vatu	100 cêntimos
Vaticano	Cidade do Vaticano		lira italiana	
Venezuela	Caracas	venezuelana	bolívar	100 cêntimos
Vietnã	Hanói	vietnamita	dong novo	100 xu
Zaire	Kinshasa	zairense	zaire	100 makuta
Zâmbia	Lusaka	zambiana	kuacha zambiana	100 ngui
Zimbábue	Harare	zimbabuana	dólar zimbabuano	100 centavos

PAÍSES E NACIONALIDADES

Português	Inglês	Nacionalidade
Afeganistão	Afghanistan	Aafghan
África do Sul	South Africa	South African
Alemanha	Germany	German
Arábia Saudita	Saudi Arabia	Saudi
Argentina	Argentina	Argentinian
Austrália	Australia	Australian
Áustria	Austria	Austrian
Bélgica	Belgium	Belgian
Bolívia	Bolivia	Bolivian
Brasil	Brazil	Brazilian
Bulgária	Bulgaria	Bulgarian
Canadá	Canada	Canadian
Chile	Chile	Chilean
China	China	Chinese
Colômbia	Colombia	Colombian
Coreia	Korea	Korean
Cuba	Cuba	Cuban
Dinamarca	Denmark	Dane
Egito	Egypt	Egyptian
Equador	Ecuador	Ecuadorian
Escócia	Scotland	Scot, Scottish
Espanha	Spain	Spaniard, Spanish
Estados Unidos da América	United States of America	American
Filipinas	Philippines	Philippine
Finlândia	Finland	Finn
França	France	French
Gales	Wales	Welsh
Grécia	Greece	Greek
Holanda	Holland	Dutch
Hungria	Hungary	Hungarian
Índia	India	Indian
Inglaterra	England	English
Indonésia	Indonesia	Indonesian
Iraque	Iraq	Iraqi
Israel	Israel	Israeli
Itália	Italy	Italian
Jamaica	Jamaica	Jamaican
Japão	Japan	Japanese
Líbano	Lebanon	Lebanese
Marrocos	Morocco	Moroccan
México	Mexico	Mexican
Mônaco	Monaco	Monacan
Noruega	Norway	Norwegian
Nova Zelândia	New Zeland	New Zelander
Panamá	Panama	Panamanian
Paquistão	Pakistan	Pakistani
Paraguai	Paraguay	Paraguayan
Peru	Peru	Peruvian
Polônia	Poland	Pole

PAÍSES E NACIONALIDADES

Português	Inglês	Nacionalidade
Portugal	Portugal	Portuguese
Rússia	Russia	Russian
Suécia	Sweden	Swede
Suíça	Swizerland	Swiss
Tailândia	Thailand	Thai
Turquia	Turkey	Turkish
Venezuela	Venezuela	Venezuelan
Uruguai	Uruguay	Uruguayan
Vietnã	Vietnam	Vietnamese

ESTADOS BRASILEIROS, SUAS CAPITAIS E ADJETIVOS PÁTRIOS

Estado	Capital
Acre: acreano ou acriano	**Rio Branco:** rio-branquense
Alagoas: alagoano	**Maceió:** maceioense
Amapá: amapaense	**Macapá:** macapaense
Amazonas: amazonense	**Manaus:** manauense
Bahia: baiano	**Salvador:** salvadorense e soteropolitano (pouco usado este último)
Ceará: cearense	**Fortaleza:** fortalezense
Espírito Santo: espírito-santense ou capixaba	**Vitória:** vitoriense
Goiás: goiano	**Goiânia:** goianiense
Maranhão: maranhense	**São Luís:** são-luisense
Mato Grosso: mato-grossense	**Cuiabá:** cuiabano
Mato Grosso do Sul: mato-grossense-do-sul	**Campo Grande:** campo-grandense
Minas Gerais: mineiro ou montanhês	**Belo Horizonte:** belo-horizontino
Pará: paraense	**Belém:** belenense
Paraíba: paraibano	**João Pessoa:** pessoense
Paraná: paranaense	**Curitiba:** curitibano
Pernambuco: pernambucano	**Recife:** recifense
Piauí: piauiense	**Teresina:** teresinense
Rio de Janeiro: fluminense (Estado do Rio de Janeiro)	**Rio de Janeiro:** carioca
Rio Grande do Norte: rio-grandense-do-norte, norte-rio-grandense ou potiguar	**Natal:** natalense
Rio Grande do Sul: sul-rio-grandense, rio-grandense-do-sul ou gaúcho	**Porto Alegre:** porto-alegrense
Rondônia: rondoniense	**Porto Velho:** porto-velhense
Roraima: roraimense	**Boa Vista:** boa-vistense
Santa Catarina: catarinense ou barriga-verde	**Florianópolis:** florianopolitano
São Paulo: paulista (Estado de São Paulo)	**São Paulo:** paulistano (cidade de São Paulo)
Sergipe: sergipano	**Aracaju:** aracajuano
Tocantins: tocantinense	**Palmas:** palmense

NOMES QUE ADMITEM FORMA COLETIVA

abelhas - enxame.
acompanhantes - séquito.
alhos - réstia.
alunos - classe.
anjos - coro, falange, legião.
artistas - companhia, elenco.
árvores - arvoredo, bosque.
asnos - manada, récua.
astros - constelação.
atores - elenco.
aves - bando.
aviões - esquadrilha.
balas - saraiva, saraivada.
bois - boiada, manada, rebanho.
burros - tropa.
cabras - malhada, rebanho, fato.
camelos - cáfila.
caminhões - frota.
cães - matilha.
cardeais - conclave.
carneiros - malhada, rebanho.
carros - comboio.
cavaleiros - cavalgada, cavalhada.
cavalos - tropa.
cebolas - réstia.
chaves - molho, penca.
clientes - clientela, freguesia.
cobras - serpentário.
cônegos - cabido.
demônios - legião.
deputados - câmara, assembleia.
desordeiros - corja, malta, súcia, turba.
dinheiro - bolada.
discos - discoteca.
elefantes - manada.
escritos - antologia, coletânea, seleta.

espigas - molho.
estados - federação, nação.
estrelas - miríade, constelação.
filhotes - ninhada.
flores - ramalhete, buquê.
gafanhotos - nuvem, praga.
garotos - bando.
ilhas - arquipélago.
índios - tribo.
insetos - nuvem.
jornais - hemeroteca.
jumentos - récua.
ladrões - bando, malta, quadrilha.
lobos - alcateia.
macacos - bando.
malfeitores - quadrilha, súcia, tropa.
mapas - mapoteca, atlas.
marinheiros - marujada, tripulação.
médicos - junta.
montanhas - cordilheira, serra.
músicos - orquestra.
navios - frota, esquadra, armada.
nomes - lista, rol.
ovelhas - rebanho.
padres - clero.
panteras - alcateia.
papéis - resma.
passarinhos - nuvem, bando.
peixes - cardume.
pessoas - bando, multidão.
porcos - vara.
quadros - pinacoteca, galeria.
selos - coleção.
soldados - tropa, legião, batalhão, pelotão.
vadios - cambada, caterva, corja, súcia.
varas - feixe.

ESCREVA E FALE CORRETAMENTE

Atenção: em negrito, expressão de forma adequada.

* Recebeu uma quantia *vultuosa*.
  Recebeu uma quantia **vultosa**.

* *Houveram* muitas festas.
  Houve muitas festas.

* *Fazem* dez anos que ele se casou.
  Faz dez anos que ele se casou.

* Eventos *beneficientes*.
  Eventos **beneficentes**.

* Espero que você *seje* feliz.
  Espero que você **seja** feliz.

* Ele era *de menor*.
  Ele era **menor**.

* *Devem haver* muitos candidatos ao cargo.
  Deve haver muitos candidatos ao cargo.

* Ocorreu grande *perca* de material.
  Ocorreu grande **perda** de material.

* Estamos na escola *afim* de estudar.
  Estamos na escola **a fim** de estudar.

* Aquela parte da apresentação é para *mim* ler.
  Aquela parte da apresentação é **para eu** ler.

* Graduou-se *há dois anos atrás*.
  Graduou-se **há dois anos**.
  Graduou-se **dois anos atrás**.

* *Aonde* eles estavam estudando?
  Onde eles estavam estudando?

* Prefiro refrigerante *do que* vinho.
  Prefiro refrigerante **a** vinho.

* Ela não encontrou *impecilhos* no trabalho.
  Ela não encontrou **empecilhos** no trabalho.

* Bebeu chá *ao invés* de refrigerante.
  Bebeu chá **em vez de** refrigerante.

* Éramos *em quatro* naquela casa.
  Éramos **quatro** naquela casa.

* Ela após sua *rúbrica* no documento.
  Ela após sua **rubrica** no documento.

* Eles residem *à* Rua São Paulo.
  Eles residem **na** Rua São Paulo.

* O executivo *interviu*.
  O executivo **interveio**.

* Na ocasião, ela agiu como bem *quiz*.
  Na ocasião, ela agiu como bem **quis**.

* Ela deixou *claro* sua ideia.
  Ela deixou **clara** sua idéia.

* *Aluga-se* apartamentos na praia.
  Alugam-se apartamentos na praia.

* Ela acorda *mau-humorada*.
  Ela acorda **mal-humorada**.

* A secretária ficou *ao par* das notícias.
  A secretária ficou **a par** das notícias.

* Ela ficou *meia* aborrecida.
  Ela ficou **meio** aborrecida.

* Não sei *porque* eles partiram cedo.
  Não sei **por que** eles partiram cedo.

* Ela era uma pessoa *à toa*.
  Ela era uma pessoa **à-toa**.

ESCREVA E FALE CORRETAMENTE

* A reunião começará às *9hrs*.
  A reunião começará às **9h**.

* Ela deu a *luz* a uma linda menina.
  Ela deu **à luz** uma linda menina.

* Ela viajou *às* cinco para as oito.
  Ela viajou **aos** cinco para as oito.

* Os preços dos sapatos estavam muito *caros*.
  Os preços dos sapatos estavam muito **altos**.

* Comprei *menas* frutas na quitanda.
  Comprei **menos** frutas na quitanda.

* Comprou *quinhentas* gramas de sal.
  Comprou **quinhentos** gramas de sal.

* Não a encontro *a* algum tempo.
  Não a encontro **há** algum tempo.

* A escolha ficou *entre eu* e ele.
  A escolha ficou **entre mim** e ele.

* O *auto-falante* era muito possante.
  O **alto-falante** era muito possante.

* Nervosa, fiquei fora de *si*.
  Nervosa, fiquei fora **de mim**.

* Estacionamento *grátis*.
  Estacionamento **gratuito**.

* Ela comprou uma saia *em* algodão.
  Ela comprou uma saia **de** algodão.

* *Ao* persistirem os sintomas, procure seu médico.
  A persistirem os sintomas, procure seu médico.

* É *proibido* a entrada de menores.
  É **proibida** a entrada de menores.
  É **proibido** entrar.

* Quem chega antes tem *previlégios*.
  Quem chega antes tem **privilégios**.

* O barulho passou quase *desapercebido*.
  O barulho passou quase **despercebido**.

* Alcançar sucesso na vida *implica em* muito trabalho.
  Alcançar sucesso na vida **implica** muito trabalho.

* O ministro proferiu um discurso *onde* mencionou vários problemas.
  O ministro proferiu um discurso **no qual** (ou **em que**) mencionou vários problemas.

* *Haja visto* os acontecimentos no carnaval.
  Haja vista os acontecimentos no carnaval.

* O teto daquela casa desabara *há* muito tempo.
  O teto daquela casa desabara **havia** muito tempo.

* Para *maiores* informações, consulte o catálogo.
  Para **mais** (ou **outras**) informações, consulte o catálogo.

* Ela lhe desejou bom *final de semana*.
  Ela lhe desejou bom **fim de semana**.

* A medida econômica foi adotada *a* nível estadual.
  A medida econômica foi adotada **em** nível estadual.

* *Ao* meu ver, o filme foi muito bom.
  A meu ver, o filme foi muito bom.

* A viagem ao campo foi *de encontro* aos desejos da menina.
  A viagem ao campo foi **ao encontro** do desejo da menina.

ESCREVA E FALE CORRETAMENTE

* O projeto do deputado recebeu *apoiamento* unânime.
  O projeto do deputado recebeu **apoio** unânime.

* Os telespectadores foram convidados a *conferir* a nova novela.
  Os telespectadores foram convidados a **assistir** à nova novela.

* Antigamente não havia TV *a* cores.
  Antigamente não havia TV **em** cores.

* Eu, *enquanto* ser humano, não aceito qualquer tipo de preconceito.
  Eu, **como** ser humano, não aceito qualquer tipo de preconceito.

* A *estadia* dos alunos naquele hotel foi muito proveitosa.
  A **estada** dos alunos naquele hotel foi muito proveitosa.

* A jovem providenciou a *estada* de seu carro no estacionamento local.
  A jovem providenciou a **estadia** de seu carro no estacionamento local.

* A jovem disse que, *independente* de autorização, fará a viagem.
  A jovem disse que, **independentemente** de autorização, fará a viagem.

* A autoridade de plantão expediu um *mandato* de prisão.
  A autoridade de plantão expediu um **mandado** de prisão.

* A presidente daquela associação tem um *mandado* de dois anos.
  A presidente daquela associação tem um **mandato** de dois anos.

* Machado de Assis foi um escritor *proeminente*.
  Machado de Assis foi um escritor **preeminente**.

* O médico recomendou-lhe fazer um exame de *raio X*.
  O médico recomendou-lhe fazer um exame de **raios X**.

* Ela foi *uma das que ficou* com a vaga.
  Ela foi **uma das que ficaram** com a vaga.

* Se minha amiga me *ver* cantando, estranhará.
  Se minha amiga me **vir** cantando, estranhará.

* Ontem depositei *hum mil reais* no banco.
  Ontem depositei **mil reais** no banco.

* Estava chovendo; *porisso* não fui ao cinema.
  Estava chovendo; **por isso** não fui ao cinema.

* *O Brasil ele é* um país de muitas belezas naturais.
  O Brasil é um país de muitas belezas naturais.

* As crianças revelam *por si só* suas intenções.
  As crianças revelam **por si sós** suas intenções.

* Os Estados Unidos *é* um país de grandes contradições.
  Os Estados Unidos **são** um país de grandes contradições.

* Ele esteve na cidade *antes de ontem*.
  Ele esteve na cidade **anteontem**.

* Sejam todos *benvindos* à reunião!
  Sejam todos **bem-vindos** à reunião!

* Ele tem muito *ciúmes* da esposa.
  Ele tem muito **ciúme** da esposa.
  Ele tem **ciúmes** da esposa.

ESCREVA E FALE CORRETAMENTE

* O *estrupo* é um crime dos mais violentos.
    O **estupro** é um crime dos mais violentos.

* Ele comprou uma camisa de *tons pastéis*.
    Ele comprou uma camisa de **tons pastel**.

* Ela precisou comprar *um óculos* de grau.
    Ela precisou comprar **óculos** de grau.
    Ela precisou comprar **uns óculos** de grau.

* As pesquisas mostram, *a grosso modo*, que o candidato vencerá.
    As pesquisas mostram, **grosso modo**, que o candidato vencerá.

EVITE AS REDUNDÂNCIAS (REPETIÇÕES DE IDEIA): OU AS IMPROPRIEDADES

* Abertura inaugural.
* Abusar demais.
* Amanhecer o dia.
* Breve alocução.
* Certeza absoluta.
* Comparecer em pessoa.
* Compartilhar conosco.
* Completamente vazio.
* Conclusão final.
* Criar novos.
* Detalhes minuciosos.
* Elo de ligação.
* Em duas metades iguais.
* Encarar de frente.
* Escolha opcional.
* Exceder em muito.
* Expressamente proibido.
* Fato real.
* Ganhar grátis.
* Há anos atrás.
* *Habitat* natural.
* Inaugurar a(o) nova(o).
* Interromper de uma vez.
* Juntamente com.
* Lançar novo.
* Monopólio exclusivo.
* Multidão de pessoas.
* Obra-prima principal.
* Outra alternativa.
* Passatempo passageiro.
* Pequenos detalhes.
* Planejar antecipadamente.
* Planos para o futuro.
* Preço barato.
* Preconceito intolerante.
* Regra geral.
* Repetir outra vez.
* Superávit positivo.
* Surpresa inesperada.
* Todos foram unânimes.
* Última versão definitiva.
* Vandalismo criminoso.
* Vereador da cidade.
* Viúva do falecido.
* Voltar atrás.

MEDIDAS INGLESAS E AMERICANAS

LINEAR MEASURE / MEDIDAS DE COMPRIMENTO

		Equivalente Métrico
1 inch		2,54 cm
1 foot	12 inches	30,48 cm
1 yard	3 feet	91,44 cm
1 pole, rod, perch	5 ½ yards	5,03 m
1 chain (ingl.)	4 poles, etc.	20,12 m
1 furlong (200 yards)	10 chains (40 rods)	201,17 m
1 statute mile (1760 yards)	8 furlongs (5280 feet)	1.609 km
1 nautical mile	6080.2 feet	1.853 km
1 league	3 statute miles	4.828 km

SQUARE MEASURE / MEDIDAS DE SUPERFÍCIE

1 square inch		6,45 cm^2
1 square foot		9,29 dm^2
1 square yard		0,84 m^2
1 square pole (Am.: rod)		25,29 m^2
1 perch (Brit.)	10 square poles	252,93 m^2
1 rood (Brit.)	40 square rodes	1011,71 m^2
1 acre (U.S.A.)	160 square rods	0,4047 ha
1 acre (Brit.)	4 roods	0,4047 ha
1 square mile	640 acres	259,00 ha ou 2.590 km^2

CUBIC MEASURE / MEDIDAS DE VOLUME

1 cubic inch		16,39 cm^3
1 cubic foot	1728 cubic inches	28,32 dm^3
1 cubic yard	27 cubic feet	764,53 dm^3
1 barrel bulck shipping	5 cubic feet	
1 ton shipping	40 cubic feet	

LIQUID MEASURE / MEDIDAS DE CAPACIDADE PARA LÍQUIDOS

		Equivalente Métrico
1 minim (Brit.)	0,0592 milliliter	0,0000592 l
1 minim (U.S.A.)		0,0000616 l
1 fluid dram (Brit.)	60 minims	3,552 ml
1 fluid dram (U.S.A.)	60 minims	3,697 ml
1 fluid ounce (Brit.)	8 fluid drams	28,47 ml
1 fluid ounce (U.S.A.)	8 fluid drams	29,57 ml
1 pint (Brit.)	20 fluid ounces	569,4 ml
1 pint (U.S.A.)	16 fluid ounces	473,12 ml
1 pint (Brit.)	4 gills	0,5682 l
1 quart (Brit.)	2 pints	1,1364 l
1 gallon (Brit.)	4 quarts	4,5459 l
1 gallon (U.S.A.)	4 quarts	3,785 l
1 peck (Brit.)	2 gallons	9,092 l
1 bushel (Brit.)	4 pecks	36,368 l
1 quarter (Brit.)	8 bushels	2,909 hl
1 barrel (U.S.A.)	31 ½ gallons	1,43198 hl
1 hogshead (U.S.A.)	2 barrels	2,86396 hl

DRY MEASURE / MEDIDAS DE CAPACIDADE PARA SECOS

1 pint (Brit.; abbr. pt.)	4 gills	568,3 ml
1 pint (U.S.A.)	4 gills	473,2 ml
1 quart (U.S.A.; abbr. qt.)	2 pints	0,9464 l
1 gallon (Brit.; abbr. gal.)	4 quarts	4,546 l
1 gallon (U.S.A.)	4 quarts	4,41 l
1 peck (Brit.; abbr. pk.)	2 gallons	9,092 l
1 peck (U.S.A.)	2 gallons	8,810 l
1 bushel (Brit.; abbr. bu.)	4 pecks	36,37 l
1 bushel (U.S.A.)	4 pecks	35,24 l
1 barrel (Brit.)	36 gallons	1,637 hl
1 barrel (U.S.A.)	36 gallons	1,192 hl
1 quarter (Brit.)	8 bushels	2,909 hl
1 quarter (U.S.A.)	8 bushels	2,421 hl

AVOIRDUPOIS WEIGHT / PESOS AVOIRDUPOIS *

		Equivalente Métrico
1 ounce (Brit.; abbr. oz.)	16 drams 437 ½ grains troy	28,35 g
1 ounce (U.S.A.); abbr. oz.)		31,10 g
1 pound (Brit.; abbr. lb. av.)	16 ounces	453,6 g
1 stone (Brit.)	14 pounds	6,350 kg
1 quarter (Brit.)	28 pounds	12,70 kg
1 quarter ((U.S.A.)	25 pounds	11,34 kg
1 hundredweight cental (Brit. & U.S.A.; abbr. cwt. sh.)	100 pounds	45,36 kg
1 hundredweight long (Brit.)	4 quarters 112 pounds	50,80 kg
1 long ton	2000 pounds	907,2 kg
1 long ton	2240 pounds	1016,064 kg

* Sistema de pesos usado em todos os países da língua inglesa para qualquer material, com exceção de pedras, metais preciosos e drogas.

MARINERS'MEASURE / MEDIDAS NÁUTICAS (OU MARÍTIMAS)

1 fathom	6 feet	1,83 m
1 nautical mile	1000 fathoms (approx.)	1,853 km
1 league	3 nautical miles	5,559 km

SURVEYORS'MEASURE / MEDIDAS DE AGRIMENSOR

1 link	7.92 inches	20,12 cm
1 chain	100 links	20,12 m
1 mile	80 chains	1609,34 m
1 acre	10 square chains	0,4047 ha

NUMERAIS

	CARDINAIS		ORDINAIS
0	zero, nought, nothing, oh	1st	first
1	one	2nd	second
2	two	3rd	third
3	three	4th	fourth
4	four	5th	fifth
5	five	6th	sixth
6	six	7th	seventh
7	seven	8th	eighth
8	eight	9th	ninth
9	nine	10th	tenth
10	ten	11th	eleventh
11	eleven	12th	twelfth
12	twelve	13th	thirteenth
13	thirteen	14th	fourteenth
14	fourteen	15th	fifteenth
15	fifteen	16th	sixteenth
16	sixteen	17th	seventeenth
17	seventeen	18th	eighteenth
18	eighteen	19th	nineteenth
19	nineteen	20th	twentieth
20	twenty	21st	twenty-first
21	twenty-one	22nd	twenty-second
22	twenty-two	23rd	twenty-third
23	twenty-three	24th	twenty-fourth
24	twenty-four	25th	twenty-fifth
25	twenty-five	26th	twenty-sixth
26	twenty-six	27th	twenty-seventh
27	twenty-seven	28th	twenty-eighth
28	twenty-eight	29th	twenty-ninth
29	twenty-nine	30th	thirtieth
30	thirty	31st	thirty-first
40	fourty	40th	fortieth
50	fifty	41st	forty-first
60	sixty	50th	fiftieth
70	seventy	51st	fifty-first
80	eighty	60th	sixtieth
90	ninety	61st	sixty-first
100	a hundred	70th	seventieth
101	a hundred and one	71st	seventy-first

NUMERAIS

CARDINAIS		ORDINAIS	
110	a hundred and ten	80th	eightieth
120	a hundred and twenty	81st	eighty-first
200	two hundred	90th	ninetieth
1000	a thousand	91st	ninety-first
1001	a thousand and one	100th	hundredth
1010	a thousand and ten	101st	hundred and first
2000	two thousand	200th	two hundredth
10.000	ten thousand	1000th	thousandth
100.000	a hundred thousand	1.000.000th	millionth
1.000.000	a million	1.000.000.000th	billionth
2.000.000	two million		
1.000.000.000	a billion		

LISTA DE VERBOS IRREGULARES

PRESENT TENSE	PRETERITE	PAST PARTICIPLE	EM PORTUGUÊS
abide	abode *	abode *	continuar, permanecer
arise	arose	arisen	levantar-se
awake	awoke	awoke, awaked	acordar
be	was	been	ser
bear	bore	borne, born	suportar
beat	beat	beaten, beat	bater, vencer
become	became	become	tornar-se
beget	begot	begotten	procriar, produzir
begin	began	begun	começar
behold	beheld	beheld	ver, observar
bend	bent	bent	dobrar, curvar
bereave	bereft *	bereft	privar de, roubar
beseech	besought	besought	pedir, implorar
bespeak	bespoke	bespoken	reservar, tratar
bet	bet	bet	apostar
bid	bade *	bidden	mandar, ordenar
bind	bound	bound	atar, amarrar
bite	bit	bitten	morder
bleed	bled	bled	sangrar
blow	blew	blown	soprar, ventar
break	broke	broken	quebrar
breed	bred	bred	produzir, dar cria
bring	brought	brought	trazer
build	built	built	construir
burn	burnt *	burnt *	queimar
burst	burst	burst	explodir
buy	bought	bought	comprar
cast	cast	cast	atirar, arremessar
catch	caught	caught	pegar
chide	chid *	chidden *	ralhar, repreender
choose	chose	chosen	escolher
cleave	cleft *	cleft *	rachar(se), fender(se)
cling	clung	clung	agarrar-se
clothe	clad *	clad *	vestir, cobrir
come	came	come	vir, chegar
cost	cost	cost	custar
creep	crept	crept	arrastar-se, mover-se
crow	crew *	crowed	gritar de alegria (bebê), cantar (galo)

LISTA DE VERBOS IRREGULARES

PRESENT TENSE	PRETERITE	PAST PARTICIPLE	EM PORTUGUÊS
cut	cut	cut	cortar
deal	dealt	dealt	negociar, lidar
dig	dug	dug	cavar
do	did	done	fazer
draw	drew	drawn	desenhar
dream	dreamt *	dreamt *	sonhar
drink	drank	drunk, drunken	beber
drive	drove	driven	dirigir, guiar
dwell	dwelt *	dwelt *	habitar, residir
eat	ate	eaten	comer
fall	fell	fallen	cair
feed	fed	fed	alimentar
feel	felt	felt	sentir
fight	fougth	fougth	lutar
find	found	found	encontrar, achar
flee	fled	fled	fugir, escapar
fling	flung	flung	arremessar, lançar
fly	flew	flown	voar
forbear	forbore	forborne	conter, abster-se
forbid	forbade	forbidden	proibir, vetar
forget	forgot	forgotten	esquecer
forsake	forsook	forsaken	renunciar, abandonar
freeze	froze	frozen	congelar
get	got	got	pegar, realizar
gild	gilt *	gilt *	dourar, disfarçar
girt	girt *	girt *	cingir, envolver
give	gaye	given	dar, doar
go	went	gone	ir, andar
grind	ground	ground	triturar
grow	grew	grown	crescer
hang	hung *	hung *	pendurar
have	had	had	ter, deter, possuir
hear	heard	heard	ouvir
hide	hid	hid, hidden	esconder
hit	hit	hit	bater
hold	held	held	segurar
hurt	hurt	hurt	ferir, machucar
keep	kept	kept	guardar, segurar
kneel	knelt *	knelt *	ajoelhar(-se)

LISTA DE VERBOS IRREGULARES

PRESENT TENSE	PRETERITE	PAST PARTICIPLE	EM PORTUGUÊS
knit	knit *	knit *	tricotar
know	knew	known	saber, conhecer
lade	laded	laden	carregar
lay	laid	laid	pôr, colocar
lead	led	led	levar, liderar
lean	leant *	leant *	inclinar-se, tender
leap	leapt *	leapt *	pular, saltar
learn	learnt *	learnt *	aprender
leave	left	left	partir, ir embora
lend	lent	lent	emprestar
let	let	let	deixar
lie	lay	lain	jazer, estar deitado(a)
light	lit *	lit *	acender
lose	lost	lost	perder
make	made	made	fazer
mean	meant	meant	significar
meet	met	met	encontrar, reunir
melt	melted	molten *	fundir, derreter
mow	mowed	mown *	ceifar, sugar
pay	paid	paid	pagar
pen	pent *	pent *	escrever, redigir
put	put	put	pôr, colocar
read	read	read	ler
rend	rent	rent	lacerar, despedaçar
rid	rid *	rid *	libertar, livrar-se
ride	rode	ridden	cavalgar
ring	rang	rung	soar, ressoar
rise	rose	risen	erguer-se
rive	rived	riven *	rachar, rasgar
rot	rotted	rotten *	apodrecer, deteriorar
run	run	run	correr
saw	sawed	sawn *	serrar
say	said	said	dizer
see	saw	seen	ver
seek	sought	sought	procurar
seethe	seethed	sodden *	ferver
sell	sold	sold	vender
send	sent	sent	enviar, remeter
set	set	set	colocar, pôr

LISTA DE VERBOS IRREGULARES

PRESENT TENSE	PRETERITE	PAST PARTICIPLE	EM PORTUGUÊS
sew	sewed	sewn *	costurar
shake	shook	shaken	sacudir
shear	shore *	shorn *	tosquiar, tosar
shed	shed	shed	derramar
shine	shone	shone	brilhar
shoe	shod	shod	ferrar, calçar
shoot	shot	shot	atirar com arma de fogo
show	showed	shown	mostrar, exibir
shred	shred *	shred *	rasgar, cortar em tiras
shrink	shrank	shrunk	encolher
shrive	shrove*	shriven *	confessar
shut	shut	shut	fechar
sing	sang	sung	cantar
sink	sank, sunk	sunk, sunken	afundar, ir a pique
sit	sat	sat	sentar-se
sleep	slept	slept	dormir
slide	slid	slid	escorregar
sling	slung	slung	atirar, lançar
slink	slunk	slunk	dar à luz prematuramente
slit	slit	slit	cortar, quebrar
smell	smelt *	smelt *	cheirar
smite	smote	smitten	bater, golpear
sow	sowed	sown *	semear
speak	spoke	spoken	falar
speed	sped	sped	correr
spell	spelt *	spelt	soletrar
spend	spent	spent	gastar
spill	spilt *	spilt *	derramar, entornar
spin	spun, span	spun	girar
spit	spat, spit	spat, spit	cuspir
split	split	split	partir, rachar
spoil	spoilt *	spoilt *	estragar, arruinar
spread	spread	spread	espalhar
spring	sprang	sprung	saltar, pular
stand	stood	stood	aguentar, manter-se
steal	stole	stolen	furtar, roubar
stick	stuck	stuck	grudar, colar
sting	stung	stung	picar, furar
stink	stank	stunk	exalar mau cheiro

LISTA DE VERBOS IRREGULARES

PRESENT TENSE	PRETERITE	PAST PARTICIPLE	EM PORTUGUÊS
strew	strewed	strewn *	espalhar, espargir
stride	strode	stridden	andar com passos largos
strike	struck	struck	surrar, golpear
string	strung	strung	amarrar, segurar
strive	strove	striven	esforçar-se, trabalhar
swear	swore	sworn	jurar
sweat	sweat *	sweat *	suar
sweep	swept	swept	varrer
swell	swelled	swelled, swollen	crescer, inchar
swim	swam	swum	nadar
swing	swang	swung	balançar
take	took	taken	tomar, pegar
teach	taught	taught	ensinar
tear	tore	torn	rasgar
tell	told	told	contar, narrar
think	thought	thought	pensar, raciocinar
throw	threw	thrown	lançar, atirar
thrust	thrust	thrust	empurrar, impelir
tread	trod	trodden	andar, marchar
understand	understood	understood	entender, compreender
wake	woke	waked	acordar, despertar
wear	wore	worn	vestir, pôr roupas
weave	wove	woven	tecer
wed	wed	wed	casar, casar-se
weep	wept	wept	chorar
wet	wet *	wet *	molhar
win	won	won	vencer
wind	wound	wound	girar, fazer girar
wring	wrung	wrung	retorcer, espremer
write	wrote	written	escrever

* Verbs for which there is also a regular form ending in "ed".
* Verbos que admitem, também, a forma regular terminada em "ed".

dicionário escolar inglês

Português - Inglês

A

A, *s.*, the first letter of the Portuguese alphabet; *art. def.*, the; *prep.*, to, on, according by; *pron.*, that, the one; *contraction of the prep. a with the art. or pron.* A; **À DIREITA**, on the right.

A.BA, *s. f.*, border, edge, extremity, flap.

A.BA.CA.TE, *s. m.*, avocado, alligator-pear.

A.BA.CA.XI, *s. m.*, ananas, pineaple.

Á.BA.CO, *s. m.*, abacus.

A.BA.DE, *s. m.*, abbot.

A.BA.DI.A, *s. f.*, monastery.

A.BA.FA.DO, *adj.*, airless, stuffy, sultry; oppressed, restricted.

A.BA.FA.MEN.TO, *s. m.*, choking, checking, oppression.

A.BA.FAR, *v.*, to choke, to smother, to suffocate, to stifle.

A.BAI.XAR, *v.*, to lower, to pull down, to decrease, to fall.

A.BAI.XO, *adv.*, down, under, inferior, below.

A.BAI.XO-AS.SI.NA.DO, *s. m.*, petition, application with the signature of several petitioners.

A.BA.JUR, *s. m.*, lampshade.

A.BA.LA.DO, *adj.*, shaky, loose, touched, upset.

A.BA.LAN.ÇAR, *v.*, to balance.

A.BA.LAR, *v.*, to shake, to move, to jog, to affect.

A.BA.LI.ZA.DO, *adj.*, authoritative, distinguished, renowned.

A.BA.LI.ZAR, *v.*, to mark out by bounds or buoys; to delimit, to demarcate.

A.BA.LO, *s. m.*, commotion, disturbance, shock, grief, earthquake.

A.BAL.RO.AR, *v.*, collide, to run into, to attack.

A.BA.NA.DOR, *s. m.*, fan, fanner.

A.BA.NAR, *v.*, to fan, to shake, to agitate.

A.BAN.DO.NA.DO, *adj.*, abandoned, forlorn, deserted, helpless, alone.

A.BAN.DO.NAR, *v.*, to abandon, to leave off, to neglect, to forsake, to renounce.

A.BAN.DO.NO, *s. m.*, abandonment, abandoning, forsaking, helplessness, desertion.

A.BA.NO, *s. m.*, fire-fan, ventilator, shake, fan.

A.BAR.CAR, *v.*, to contain, to embrace, to monopolize, to obtain, to include, to comprehend.

A.BAR.RO.TA.DO, *adj.*, overfull, overloaded, overfilled.

A.BAR.RO.TAR, *v.*, to overfill, to overload, to overstock, to satiate.

A.BAS.TA.DO, *adj.*, rich, wealthy.

A.BAS.TE.CER, *v.*, to supply, to provide, to refuel.

A.BAS.TE.CI.DO, *adj.*, well supplied, abundant.

A.BAS.TE.CI.MEN.TO, *s. m.*, supply, provision, provisioning, supplying.

A.BA.TE, *s. m.*, discount, abatement, reduction, felling (trees).

A.BA.TER, *v.*, to abate, to lower, to discount, to lessen, to diminish, to reduce.

A.BA.TI.DO, *adj.*, abated, prostrated, exhausted, low, depressed.

A.BA.TI.MEN.TO, *s. m.*, abatement, lessening, discount, felling, depression, decay.

AB.DI.CA.ÇÃO, *s. f.*, abdication, renunciation.

AB.DI.CAR, *v.*, to abdicate, to renounce, to leave, to abandon.

AB.DO.ME, AB.DÔ.MEN, *s. m.*, abdomen.

AB.DO.MI.NAL, *adj.*, abdominal.

A.BE.CE.DÁ.RIO, *s. m.*, abecedary, alphabet.

A.BE.LHA, *s. f.*, bee, honey bee.

A.BE.LHA-RA.I.NHA, *s. f.*, queen bee.

A.BE.LHU.DO, *adj.*, curious, indiscreet, impudent, nosy.

A.BEN.ÇO.AR, *v.*, to bless, to protect, to give blessings, to consecrate.

A.BER.RA.ÇÃO, *s. f.*, aberration, deviation.

A.BER.TO, *adj.*, open, opened, exposed, frank.

A.BER.TU.RA, *s. f.*, opening, crevice, gap, overture, inauguration.

A.BE.TO, *s. m.*, abies.
A.BIS.MA.DO, *adj.*, stupefied, shocked, astonished.
A.BIS.MAR, *v.*, to throw into an abyss, to stupefy, to stun.
A.BIS.MO, *s. m.*, abyss, vortex, precipice.
AB.JU.RA.ÇÃO, *s. f.*, abjuration.
AB.JU.RAR, *v.*, to abjure, to renounce, to repudiate.
A.BLA.TI.VO, *s. m.*, the ablative case; *adj.*, ablative.
AB.LU.ÇÃO, *s. f.*, ablution, washing.
AB.NE.GA.ÇÃO, *s. f.*, abnegation, self-denial.
AB.NE.GA.DO, *adj.*, unselfish, self-forgetful.
AB.NE.GAR, *v.*, to abnegate, to renounce.
A.BÓ.BA.DA, *s. f.*, arch, vault, arched roof.
A.BÓ.BO.RA, *s. f.*, pumpkin.
A.BO.BRI.NHA, *s. f.*, summer-squash.
A.BO.CA.NHAR, *v.*, to bite, to bite off, to snap.
A.BO.CAR, *v.*, to snap, to catch with the mouth.
A.BO.LE.TAR, *v.*, to lodge, to billet.
A.BO.LI.ÇÃO, *s. f.*, abolition, abolishment, revocation, abrogation.
A.BO.LIR, *v.*, to abolish, to suppress, to abrogate, to revoke.
A.BO.MI.NAR, *v.*, to abominate, to abhor, to detest, to loathe.
A.BO.MI.NÁ.VEL, *adj.*, abominable, detestable.
A.BO.NAR, *v.*, to declare good or true, to bail, to guarantee.
A.BO.NO, *s. m.*, advance-money, loan, remuneration, warranty.
A.BOR.DAR, *v.*, to board, to attack, to approach, to accost.
A.BO.RÍ.GI.NE, *adj. 2 gen.*, aboriginal.
A.BOR.RE.CER, *v.*, to bore, to displease, to disgust, to hassle, to abhor.
A.BOR.RE.CI.DO, *adj.*, disgusted, displeased, weary, bored, annoyed, odious.
A.BOR.RE.CI.MEN.TO, *s. m.*, disgust, annoyance, nuisance, tediousness.
A.BOR.TAR, *v.*, to abort, to miscarry, to fail.
A.BOR.TO, *s. m.*, abortion, miscarriage.
A.BO.TO.A.DU.RA, *s. f.*, set of buttons.
A.BO.TO.AR, *v.*, to button; to pinch.
A.BRA.ÇAR, *v.*, to embrace, to hug, to encircle, to adopt, to follow.
A.BRA.ÇO, *s. m.*, embrace, embracing, hug, embracement.
A.BRAN.DAR, *v.*, to mitigate, to milden, to assuage, to mollify.
A.BRAN.GER, *v.*, to embrace, to enclose, to comprise, to include, to contain.
A.BRA.SA.DOR, *adj.*, burning, scorching, blazing, glowing.
A.BRA.SAR, *v.*, to fire, to burn, to consume by fire, devastate, to glow, to inflame.
A.BRA.SI.LEI.RA.DO, *adj.*, Brazilianized.
A.BRA.SI.LEI.RAR, *v.*, to adopt Brazilian ways and manners.
A.BRA.SI.VO, *adj.*, abrasive.
A.BREU.GRA.FI.A, *s. f.*, roentgenfotography.
A.BRE.VI.A.ÇÃO, *s. f.*, abbreviation, shortening, reduction.
A.BRE.VI.A.DO, *adj.*, abbreviated, shortened, reduced, condensed.
A.BRE.VI.AR, *v.*, to abbreviate, to shorten, to reduce, to summarize.
A.BRE.VI.A.TU.RA, *s. f.*, abbreviation, shortening.
A.BRI.DOR, *s. m.*, opener, tool for opening.
A.BRI.GA.DO, *adj.*, sheltered, well-covered.
A.BRI.GAR, *v.*, to shelter, to protect, to exempt, to cover, to hide.
A.BRI.GO, *s. m.*, shelter, guard, protection, covering, asylum.
A.BRIL, *s. m.*, April.
A.BRIR, *v.*, to open, to break up, to unlock, to unfold, to unfasten.
AB.RO.GAR, *v.*, to abrogate, to repeal, to abolish, to cancel.
AB-RUP.TO, *adj.*, abrupt, sudden, disconnected.
A.BRU.TA.LHA.DO, *adj.*, brutal, brutish, rude.
A.BRU.TA.LHAR, *v.*, to brutify.
ABS.CES.SO, *s. m.*, abscess.
AB.SO.LU.TA.MEN.TE, *adv.*, absolutely, completely, entirely.
AB.SO.LU.TO, *adj.*, absolute, unrestricted, unlimited, unconditional, total.
AB.SOL.VER, *v.*, to absolve, to forgive, to clear, to isent, to excuse.

ABSOLVIÇÃO   43   ACELERADO

AB.SOL.VI.ÇÃO, *s. f.*, absolution, pardoning.
AB.SOR.ÇÃO, *s. f.*, absorption.
AB.SOR.TO, *adj.*, absorbed, distracted.
AB.SOR.VEN.TE, *s. m.*, absorbent, tampon; *adj.*, absorbing.
AB.SOR.VER, *v.*, to absorb, to consume, to assimilate, to captivate.
ABS.TÊ.MIO, *adj.*, abstemious.
ABS.TEN.ÇÃO, *s. f.*, abstention.
ABS.TER, *v.*, to abstain, to forbear, to refrain, to restrain.
ABS.TI.NÊN.CIA, *s. f.*, abstinence, temperance, abstemiousness.
ABS.TRA.IR, *v.*, to abstract, to take from, to separate.
ABS.TRA.TO, *adj.*, abstract, abstracted, separated; *s. m.*, abstract.
AB.SUR.DO, *s. m.*, absurdity, folly, nonsense; *adj.*, absurd, nonsensical.
A.BUN.DÂN.CIA, *s. f.*, abundance, plenty, copiousness.
A.BUN.DAN.TE, *adj.*, abundant, plentiful, copious.
A.BUN.DAR, *v.*, abound, to be rich in.
A.BU.SA.DO, *adj.*, weary, bored.
A.BU.SAR, *v.*, to abuse, to misuse, to delude, to violate, to annoy.
A.BU.SI.VO, *adj.*, abusive.
A.BU.SO, *s. m.*, abuse, misuse, overuse, nuisance, annoyance, abhorrence.
A.BU.TRE, *s. m.*, vulture.
A.CA.BA.DO, *adj.*, finished, accomplished, ready, complete, worn, used, consumed.
A.CA.BA.MEN.TO, *s. m.*, finishing, completion.
A.CA.BAR, *v.*, to finish, to end, to terminate, to conclude, to achieve.
A.CA.BRU.NHAR, *v.*, to oppress, to lessen, to humiliate.
A.CA.DE.MI.A, *s.f.*, accademy, university, college.
A.CA.DÊ.MI.CO, *adj.*, *s. m.*, academician; *adj.*, academic.
A.ÇA.FRÃO, *s. m.*, saffron.
A.CA.JU, *s. m.*, acajou, mahogany.
A.CAL.MAR, *v.*, to calm, to pacify, to appease, to quiet, to silence, to still, to tranquilize.
A.CA.LO.RAR, *v.*, to heat, to warm, to agitate, to excite.
A.CA.MA.DO, *adj.*, abed, lying in bed.
A.CA.MAR, *v.*, stay in bed, to arrange in layers, to lie in bed.
A.ÇAM.BAR.CAR, *v.*, to monopolize, to forestall.
A.CAM.PA.MEN.TO, *s. m.*, camp, camping.
A.CAM.PAR, *v.*, to camp, to encamp, live in a camp.
A.CA.NA.LAR, *v.*, to channel, to groove, to flute.
A.CA.NHA.DO, *adj.*, timid, bashful, shy, awkward, close.
A.CA.NHAR, *v.*, to restrict, to lessen, to ashame, to intimidate.
A.CAN.TO.NAR, *v.*, to canton, to camp.
A.ÇÃO, *s. f.*, action, movement, activity, act, deed, feat, event, operation, engagement, battle.
A.CA.RE.AR, *v.*, to contrast one thing with another, to confront.
A.CA.RI.CI.AR, *v.*, to caress, to fondle, to pet, to cherish.
A.CA.RI.NHAR, *v.*, to caress, to fondle, to pet.
A.CA.SA.LA.MEN.TO, *s. m.*, mating, coupling, joining.
A.CA.SA.LAR, *v.*, to mate, to couple, to join.
A.CA.SO, *s. m.*, chance, hazard, fortune, luck; *adv.*, perhaps.
A.CA.TA.DO, *adj.*, respected.
A.CA.TA.MEN.TO, *s. m.*, deference, reverence, regard, respect.
A.CA.TAR, *v.*, to respect, to venerate, to regard, to revere, to follow, to obey.
A.CAU.TE.LAR, *v.*, to warn, to forewarn, to caution, to avoid, to shun; to be careful.
A.CE.DER, *v.*, to accede, to conform, to comply with, to consent.
A.CEI.TA.ÇÃO, *s. f.*, acceptance, acceptation, reception, approbation.
A.CEI.TAR, *v.*, to accept, to receive, to take, to admit, to acknowledge.
A.CEI.TÁ.VEL, *adj.*, acceptable, admissible, agreeable.
A.CEI.TO, *adj.*, *v. (part. irreg. de aceitar)*, accepted, received, admitted.
A.CE.LE.RA.ÇÃO, *s. f.*, acceleration, speed.
A.CE.LE.RA.DO, *adj.*, accelerated, quick.

A.CE.LE.RA.DOR, *s. m.*, accelerator.
A.CE.LE.RAR, *v.*, to accelerate, to press, to speed up, to quicken, to push on.
A.CE.NAR, *v.*, to beckon, to provoke, to wave.
A.CEN.DE.DOR, *s. m.*, lighter, igniter.
A.CEN.DER, *v.*, to light, to ignite, to kindle, to set on fire.
A.CE.NO, *s.m.*, nodding, calling, invitation, wink.
A.CEN.TO, *s. m.*, accent, emphasis given to a syllable.
A.CEN.TU.A.ÇÃO, *s. f.*, accent, accentuation.
A.CEN.TU.AR, *v.*, to accentuate, to accent, to pronounce.
A.CEP.ÇÃO, *s. f.*, acceptation, meaning, sense, signification.
A.CER.BO, *adj.*, acerb, bitter, tart.
A.CER.CA, *adv.*, near, about, almost; *prep.*, concerning, regarding.
A.CER.CAR, *v.*, to surround, to enclose.
A.CER.TAR, *v.*, to make right, to set right, to adjust, to regulate, to get right.
A.CER.TO, *s. m.*, hit, lucky hit, skill, prudence.
A.CER.VO, *s. m.*, heap, pile, lot, collection.
A.CE.SO, *adj.*, lighted, burning, inflamed.
A.CES.SO, *s. m.*, access, admittance, admission, entrance.
A.CES.SÓ.RIO, *s. m.*, accessory, complement, addition; *adj.*, accessory, additional.
A.CÉ.TI.CO, *adj.*, acetic, acetous.
A.CE.TI.NA.DO, *adj.*, satiny, silky.
A.CE.TO.NA, *s. f.*, acetone.
A.CHA.QUE, *s. m.*, ailment, illness, indisposition, pretext.
A.CHAR, *v.*, to find, to meet with, to meet, to hit on, to discover, to invent.
A.CHA.TAR, *v.*, to flatten, to squash, to crush, to humble; to humiliate.
A.CHE.GA.DO, *adj.*, near, close.
A.CHE.GAR, *v.*, to arrange, to adjust, to aproximate.
A.CHIN.CA.LHAR, *v.*, to ridicule, to jest, to mock.
A.CHO.CO.LA.TA.DO, *adj.*, like chocolate.
A.CI.DAR, *v.*, acidify.
A.CI.DEN.TA.DO, *adj.*, uneven, rough, broken, irregular, bumpy.
A.CI.DEN.TAL, *adj.*, accidental, unexpected, casual, fortuitous, occasional.
A.CI.DEN.TAR, *v.*, to cause an accident, to change.
A.CI.DEN.TE, *s. m.*, accident, misfortune, disaster, mishap, casualty.
A.CI.DEZ, *s. f.*, acidity, sourness.
A.CI.DI.FI.CAR, *v.*, to acidify.
Á.CI.DO, *adj.*, acid, sour, tart.
A.CI.MA, *adv.*, above, up.
A.CIO.NAR, *v.*, to put in action, to incorporate, to gesticulate.
A.CIO.NIS.TA, *s. 2 gen.*, shareholder.
A.CIR.RAR, *v.*, to irritate, to incite, to instigate.
A.CLA.MA.ÇÃO, *s. f.*, acclamation, applause.
A.CLA.MAR, *v.*, to acclaim, to applaud, to cheer.
A.CLA.RAR, *v.*, to clear, to make clear, to brighten, to clarify.
A.CLI.MA.TAR, *v.*, to acclimatize, to acclimate.
A.CLI.VE, *s. m.*, acclivity, slope, ascent.
A.ÇO, *s. m.*, steel.
A.CO.BER.TAR, *v.*, to cover, to cloak, to hide, to conceal, to dissimulate.
A.CO.CO.RAR-SE, *v.*, to squat, to crouch.
A.ÇO.DA.DO, *adj.*, hasty, hurried, diligent.
A.ÇO.DAR, *v.*, to haste, to urge, to speed, to incite, to instigate.
A.ÇOI.TAR, *v.*, to whip, to lash.
A.ÇOI.TE, *s. m.*, whip, lash, scourge.
A.CO.LÁ, *adv.*, there, yonder, over there.
A.COL.CHO.A.DO, *s. m.*, wadding, padding, stuffing.
A.COL.CHO.AR, *v.*, to wad, to pad, to quilt.
A.CO.LHE.DOR, *adj., s. m.*, welcomer; *adj.*, welcoming.
A.CO.LHER, *v.*, to welcome, to receive, to shelter, to lodge.
A.CO.LHI.DA, *s. f.*, reception, welcome.
A.CO.ME.TER, *v.*, to attack, to assail, to assault, to provoke.
A.CO.ME.TI.DA, *s. f.*, attack, onset, assault, enterprise.
A.CO.MO.DA.ÇÃO, *s. f.*, accomodation,

ACOMODADO — ADAPTAÇÃO

arrangement, room, agreement, adaptation.
A.CO.MO.DA.DO, *adj.*, accomodated, settled, adjusted.
A.CO.MO.DAR, *v.*, to accomodate, to arrange, to put in order.
A.COM.PA.NHA.MEN.TO, *s. m.*, retinue, attendance, train, suite, accompaniment.
A.COM.PA.NHAN.TE, *s. 2 gen.*, companion, escort, follower; *adj.*, accompanying, attendant.
A.COM.PA.NHAR, *v.*, to accompany, come or go along with, escort, follow, wait on, attend.
A.CON.CHE.GAR, *v.*, to aproximate, to bring near, to unite.
A.CON.CHE.GO, *s. m.*, shelter, comfort.
A.CON.DI.CIO.NA.MEN.TO, *s. m.*, conditioning, packing.
A.CON.DI.CIO.NAR, *v.*, to condition, to pack, to box, to adapt, to arrange.
A.CON.SE.LHAR, *v.*, to advise, to counsel, to persuade.
A.CON.SE.LHÁ.VEL, *adj.*, advisable.
A.CON.TE.CER, *v.*, to happen, to take place, to occur, to come about.
A.CON.TE.CI.DO, *adj.*, past, done.
A.CON.TE.CI.MEN.TO, *s. m.*, occurrence, happening, incident, event.
A.COR.DA.DO, *adj.*, awake, alert, watchful, agreed, determined.
A.CÓR.DÃO, *s. m.*, sentence, judgement.
A.COR.DAR, *v.*, to wake up, awake, awaken, to agree upon, to harmonize, to resolve, to grant.
A.COR.DE.ÃO, *s. m.*, accordion.
A.COR.DO, *s. m.*, agreement, harmony, accord, accordance, pact.
A.COR.REN.TAR, *v.*, to chain, to fetter, to enslave.
A.COR.RER, *v.*, to run to help, to assist, to succour.
A.COS.SAR, *v.*, to pursue, to chase.
A.COS.TA.MEN.TO, *s. m.*, margin.
A.COS.TU.MA.DO, *adj.*, accustomed, used, customary, habituated.
A.COS.TU.MAR, *v.*, to accustom, to habituate, to inure, to familiarize.
A.CO.TO.VE.LAR, *v.*, to elbow, to thrust with the elbow, to push.
A.ÇOU.GUE, *s. m.*, butchery, butcher shop.
A.ÇOU.GUEI.RO, *s. m.*, butcher.
A.CRE, *adj.*, acre, acrid, sharp, biting, tart; sarcastic, rude.
A.CRE.DI.TA.DO, *adj.*, credited, accredited.
A.CRE.DI.TAR, *v.*, believe, trust, to credit, to give credit, to obtain credit.
A.CRES.CEN.TAR, *v.*, to add, to increase, to raise, to enlarge.
A.CRES.CER, *v.*, to add, to increase, to grow.
A.CRES.CI.DO, *adj.*, added, increased.
A.CRÉS.CI.MO, *s. m.*, addition, increase.
A.CRO.BA.CI.A, *s. f.*, acrobatics, acrobacy.
A.CRO.BA.TA, *s. 2 gen.*, acrobat.
A.CU.AR, *v.*, to encircle, to corner, to recoil, to contract, to retrogress.
A.ÇÚ.CAR, *s. m.*, sugar.
A.ÇU.CA.RA.DO, *adj.*, sugary, sugared, sweet.
A.ÇU.CA.RAR, *v.*, to sugar, to sweeten with sugar.
A.ÇU.CA.REI.RO, *s. m.*, sugar basin, sugar bowl.
A.ÇU.DE, *s. m.*, dam, weir, sluice.
A.CU.DIR, *v.*, to run to help, to succour, to assist.
A.CUI.DA.DE, *s. f.*, acuity, sharpness, perspicacity.
A.CU.MU.LA.ÇÃO, *s. f.*, accumulation, storage, pile, concentration.
A.CU.MU.LA.DOR, *s. m.*, accumulator, battery.
A.CU.MU.LAR, *v.*, to accumulate, to amass, to pile up, to collect.
A.CÚ.MU.LO, *s. m.*, accumulation.
A.CU.SA.ÇÃO, *s. f.*, accusation, charge, impeachment, indictment.
A.CU.SA.DO, *s. m.*, accused, offender, defendant; *adj.*, accused.
A.CU.SAR, *v.*, to accuse, to charge with, to indict, to impeach.
A.CU.SA.TI.VO, *s. m.*, accusative; *adj.*, accusative, accusatory, accusing.
A.CÚS.TI.CA, *s. f.*, acoustics.
A.CÚS.TI.CO, *adj.*, acoustic.
A.DA.GA, *s. f.*, dagger.
A.DÁ.GIO, *s. m.* adage, proverb.
A.DAP.TA.ÇÃO, *s. f.*, adaptation.

ADAPTADO — ADOLESCÊNCIA

A.DAP.TA.DO, *adj.*, adapted, adjusted.
A.DAP.TAR, *v.*, to adapt, to adjust, to suit, to apply, to conform.
A.DAP.TÁ.VEL, *adj.*, adaptable.
A.DE.GA, *s. f.*, cellar, wine cellar.
A.DEL.GA.ÇA.DO, *adj.*, thin, slender, thinned.
A.DEL.GA.ÇAR, *v.*, to thin, to make thin, to diminish.
A.DEN.SAR, *v.*, to densify, to condense, to compact.
A.DEN.TRO, *adv.*, inwards, inwardly.
A.DEP.TO, *s. m.*, adept, follower.
A.DE.QUA.DO, *adj.*, adequate, fit, suitable, proper.
A.DE.QUAR, *v.*, to adjust, to adapt, to accommodate, to appropriate.
A.DE.RE.ÇAR, *v.*, to address.
A.DE.RÊN.CIA, *s. f.*, adherence, adhesion.
A.DE.REN.TE, *s. m.*, adherent, follower; *adj.*, adherent, sticking.
A.DE.RIR, *v.*, to adhere, to approve, to agree, to join.
A.DE.SÃO, *s. f.*, adhesion, adherence, agreement.
A.DE.SI.VO, *adj.*, adhesive, sticker, sticking plaster.
A.DES.TRA.DO, *adj.*, skilled, trained, dextrous.
A.DES.TRA.MEN.TO, *s. m.*, training, teaching.
A.DES.TRAR, *v.*, to train, to teach, to instruct, to coach.
A.DEUS, *s. m.*, good-bye, farewell, adieu; *interj.*, good-bye, bye-bye, so-long.
A.DI.A.MEN.TO, *s. m.*, postponement, delay, adjournment.
A.DI.AN.TA.DO, *adj.*, advanced, forwarded, interfering, fast.
A.DI.AN.TA.MEN.TO, *s. m.*, advancement, advancing, progress.
A.DI.AN.TAR, *v.*, to advance, to move forward, to pay in advance, to accelerate, to hasten.
A.DI.AN.TE, *adv.*, before, in front of, past, forward, further.
A.DI.AR, *v.*, to adjourn, to postpone, to delay.
A.DI.ÇÃO, *s. f.*, addition, sum, increase.
A.DI.CIO.NA.DO, *adj.*, added, increased.
A.DI.CIO.NAL, *s. m.*, extra, supplement; *adj.*, additional, supplementary.
A.DI.CIO.NAR, *v.*, to add.
A.DI.DO, *s. m.*, attaché.
A.DI.PO.SE, *s. f.*, adiposis, obesity.
A.DI.TI.VO, *s. m.*, minuend; *adj.*, additive.
A.DI.VI.NHA.ÇÃO, *s. f.*, puzzle, enigma.
A.DI.VI.NHAR, *v.*, to prophecy, to predict, to vaticinate.
AD.JA.CÊN.CIA, *s. f.*, adjacency, neighbourhood.
AD.JA.CEN.TE, *adj.*, adjacent, adjoining.
AD.JE.TI.VAR, *v.*, to qualify, to accompany as an adjective.
AD.JE.TI.VO, *adj., s. m.*, adjective.
AD.JUN.TO, *s. m.*, adjunct, assistant; *adj.*, annexed, joined, contiguous.
AD.MI.NIS.TRA.ÇÃO, *s. f.*, administration, management, government, direction.
AD.MI.NIS.TRA.DOR, *s. m.*, administrator, manager, executive.
AD.MI.NIS.TRAR, *v.*, manage, direct, govern, conduct.
AD.MI.NIS.TRA.TI.VO, *adj.*, administrative.
AD.MI.RA.ÇÃO, *s. f.*, admiration, wonder, astonishment, surprise.
AD.MI.RA.DO, *adj.*, admired, astonished.
AD.MI.RA.DOR, *s. m.*, admirer, fan, lover.
AD.MI.RAR, *v.*, to admire, to appreciate, to esteem.
AD.MIS.SÃO, *s. f.*, admission, admittance, inlet.
AD.MI.TI.DO, *adj.*, admitted, esteemed.
AD.MI.TIR, *v.*, to admit, to adopt, to acknowledge.
AD.MO.ES.TA.ÇÃO, *s. f.*, admonition, reproof, warning, monition.
AD.MO.ES.TAR, *v.*, to admonish, to reprove, to reprehend.
A.DO.ÇA.MEN.TO, *s. m.*, sweetening, softening.
A.DO.ÇÃO, *s. f.*, adoption.
A.DO.ÇAR, *v.*, to sweeten, to soften, to facilitate.
A.DO.E.CER, *v.*, to become sick or ill, be taken ill.
A.DO.E.CI.DO, *adj.*, sick, ill.
A.DO.EN.TAR, *v.*, to sicken, make sickish.
A.DO.LES.CÊN.CIA, *s. f.*, adolescence, adolescency.

ADOLESCENTE

AFETAÇÃO

A.DO.LES.CEN.TE, *s. 2 gen.*, adolescent; *adj.*, adolescent, youthful.
A.DO.RA.ÇÃO, *s. f.*, adoration, veneration, devotion.
A.DO.RA.DO, *adj.*, adored, venerated.
A.DO.RA.DOR, *s. m.*, admirer, worshipper, lover.
A.DO.RAR, *v.*, to adore, to venerate, to worship, to love.
A.DOR.ME.CER, *v.*, to put to sleep, to fall asleep.
A.DOR.NAR, *v.*, to adorn, to embellish, to dress.
A.DO.TAR, *v.*, to adopt, to accept, to use, to resolve.
A.DO.TI.VO, *adj.*, adoptive.
AD.QUI.RIR, *v.*, to acquire, to obtain, to get.
ADS.TRIN.GIR, *v.*, to astringe, to compel.
A.DU.A.NA, *s. f.*, customs, custom house.
A.DU.A.NEI.RO, *s. m.*, custom house officer.
A.DU.BA.ÇÃO, *s. f.*, fertilization, manuring.
A.DU.BAR, *v.*, to season, to fertilize, to manure.
A.DU.BO, *s. m.*, fertilizer, manure, seasoning, flavouring.
A.DU.LAR, *v.*, to flatter, to adulate, to coax.
A.DÚL.TE.RA, *s. f.*, adulteress.
A.DUL.TE.RA.ÇÃO, *s. f.*, adulteration, falsification.
A.DUL.TE.RA.DO, *adj.*, adulterated, corrupt.
A.DUL.TE.RA.DOR, *s. m.*, adulterator, falsifier, corrupter.
A.DUL.TE.RAR, *v.*, to adulterate, to falsify, to corrupt.
A.DUL.TÉ.RIO, *s. m.*, adultery.
A.DÚL.TE.RO, *s. m.*, adulterer; *adj.*, adulterous, adulterated.
A.DUL.TO, *adj., s. m.*, adult.
A.DU.ZIR, *v.*, to adduce, to expose, to show.
AD.VEN.TO, *s. m.*, coming, arrival, approach, Advent.
AD.VÉR.BIO, *s. m.*, adverb.
AD.VER.SÁ.RIO, *s. m.*, adversary, opponent, enemy; *adj.*, adverse, opposing.
AD.VER.SI.DA.DE, *s. f.*, adversity, misfortune, mishap.
AD.VER.SO, *adj.*, adverse, contrary, opposed.
AD.VER.TÊN.CIA, *s. f.*, admonition, warning, censure.
AD.VER.TIR, *v.*, to warn, to admonish, to censure, to advise.
AD.VO.CA.CI.A, *s. f.*, advocacy, advocateship.
AD.VO.GA.DO, *s. m.*, lawyer, advocate, attorney.
AD.VO.GAR, *v.*, to act as a lawyer.
A.É.REO, *adj.*, aerial, living in the air, airlike.
A.E.RÓ.DRO.MO, *s. m.*, aerodrome, airdrome.
A.E.RO.MO.ÇA, *s. f.*, flight stewardess.
A.E.RO.NÁU.TI.CA, *s. f.*, aviation, aeronautics.
A.E.RO.NA.VE, *s. f.*, aircraft, airship.
A.E.RO.PLA.NO, *s. m.*, airplan.
A.E.RO.POR.TO, *s. m.*, airport.
A.E.RO.VI.Á.RIO, *s. m.*, person employed in the air service.
A.FA.BI.LI.DA.DE, *s. f.*, affability, politeness, kindness, suavity.
A.FA.GAR, *v.*, to caress, to fondle, to pet, to comfort.
A.FA.GO, *s. m.*, caress, allurement.
A.FA.NAR, *v.*, to strive, to obtain laboriously, to steal.
A.FAS.TA.DO, *adj.*, remote, distant, far off, apart.
A.FAS.TA.MEN.TO, *s. m.*, removal, dismissal, separation, retirement, distance.
A.FAS.TAR, *v.*, to remove, to separate, to repel.
A.FÁ.VEL, *adj.*, polite, courteous, affable, pleasant.
A.FA.ZE.RES, *s. m., pl.*, business, affairs.
A.FEI.ÇÃO, *s. f.*, affection, love.
A.FEI.ÇO.A.MEN.TO, *s. m.*, affection, inclination.
A.FEI.ÇO.AR, *v.*, to captivate, to shape, to form, to charm.
A.FE.MI.NA.DO, *adj.*, effeminate.
A.FE.MI.NAR, *v.*, to become effeminate, to make effeminate.
A.FE.RI.ÇÃO, *s. f.*, gauging, calibrating, checking, collation.
A.FE.RI.DO, *adj.*, gauged, calibrated, checked.
A.FE.RI.DOR, *s. m.*, gauger, standard.
A.FE.RIR, *v.*, to gauge, to calibrate, to check.
A.FER.RO.LHAR, *v.*, to bolt, to imprision.
A.FE.TA.ÇÃO, *s. f.*, affectation, affection, pedantism, vanity.

AFETAR — ÁGIO

A.FE.TAR, *v.*, to affect, to feign, to simulate.
A.FE.TI.VO, *adj.*, affective, dedicated, devoted.
A.FE.TO, *s. m.*, friendship, sympathy, passion; *adj.*, affectionate, friendly.
A.FE.TU.O.SO, *adj.*, affectionate, affable, kind.
A.FI.A.DO, *adj.*, sharpened, sharp, whetted.
A.FI.AN.ÇAR, *v.*, to warrant, to bail, to guarantee, to assure.
A.FI.AR, *v.*, to sharpen, to improve, to irritate.
A.FI.LAR, *v.*, to gauge, to standardize.
A.FI.LHA.DA, *s. f.*, goddaughter.
A.FI.LHA.DO, *s. m.*, godson.
A.FI.LHAR, *v.*, to produce offspring.
A.FI.LI.A.ÇÃO, *s. f.*, affiliation, connection.
A.FI.LI.AR, *v.*, to affiliate, to join.
A.FIM, *s. m.*, kinsman, kinswoman.
A.FI.NAL, *adv.*, finally, at last, after all.
A.FI.NAR, *v.*, to fine, to make fine, to refine, to taper.
A.FIN.CO, *s. m.*, attachment, assiduity.
A.FI.NI.DA.DE, *s. f.*, affinity, relation, relationship.
A.FIR.MA.ÇÃO, *s. f.*, affirmation, assertion.
A.FIR.MAR, *v.*, to affirm, to asseverate, to maintain, to assert, to say, to confirm.
A.FIR.MA.TI.VO, *adj.*, affirmative.
A.FI.VE.LAR, *v.*, to buckle, to fasten.
A.FI.XAR, *v.*, to fix, to fasten, to make firm, to post.
A.FLI.ÇÃO, *s. f.*, affliction, trouble, grief, anguish.
A.FLI.GIR, *v.*, to afflict, to trouble, to distress, to torment.
A.FLI.TI.VO, *adj.*, afflicting, afflictive.
A.FLI.TO, *adj.*, afflicted, afflictive.
A.FLU.EN.TE, *s. m.*, tributary; *adj.*, affluent, confluent.
A.FLU.IR, *v.*, to flow to, flow in, to stream towards.
A.FO.BA.ÇÃO, *s. f.*, hurry, bustle, fatigue.
A.FO.BAR, *v.*, to hurry, to bustle, to embarrass.
A.FO.GA.DO, *adj.*, drowned, asphyxiated, watered, soaked.
A.FO.GA.DOR, *s. m.*, choke, throttle; *adj.*, stifling.
A.FO.GAR, *v.*, suffocate, asphyxiate, stifle, to check, to submerge.
A.FOI.TE.ZA, *s. f.*, courage, fearlessness.
A.FOI.TO, *adj.*, fearless, bold, audacious.
A.FO.NI.A, *s. f.*, aphonia, loss of voice.
A.FO.RA, *adv.*, except, save, excepting, besides.
A.FO.RIS.MO, *s. m.*, aphorism, maxim.
A.FOR.TU.NA.DO, *adj.*, lucky, happy, fortunate.
A.FRE.TAR, *v.*, to freight.
A.FRI.CA.NO, *adj.*, *s. m.*, African.
A.FRO.DI.SÍ.A.CO, *adj.*, *s. m.*, aphrodisiac.
A.FRON.TA, *s. f.*, insult, offence, affront.
A.FRON.TAR, *v.*, to affront, to insult, to importune, to tire, exhaust.
A.FROU.XAR, *v.*, to slacken, to relax, to loosen, to release.
AF.TA, *s. f.*, aphtha.
A.FU.GEN.TAR, *v.*, to chase away, to put to flight, to scare away.
A.FUN.DAR, *v.*, to sink, to founder, to submerge, to deepen.
A.GA.CHA.MEN.TO, *s. m.*, crouching, squatting, cowering.
A.GA.CHAR-SE, *v.*, to crouch, to squat, to cower.
A.GAR.RA.DO, *adj.*, stingy, avaricious, miserly, caught.
A.GAR.RA.MEN.TO, *s. m.*, seizing, holding, catching, stinginess.
A.GAR.RAR, *v.*, to catch, to seize, to clasp, to grip, to snap up.
A.GA.SA.LHA.DO, *adj.*, sheltered, covered, lodged.
A.GA.SA.LHAR, *v.*, to shelter, to lodge, to warm, to protect.
A.GA.SA.LHO, *s. m.*, shelter, warm clothing, wrap.
A.GÊN.CIA, *s. f.*, agency, activity, action, bureau.
A.GEN.CI.AR, *v.*, to negotiate, to work as an agent.
A.GEN.DA, *s. f.*, agenda, notebook.
A.GEN.TE, *s. 2 gen.*, agent.
A.GI.GAN.TAR, *v.*, to make gigantic.
Á.GIL, *adj.*, agile, fast.
A.GI.LI.DA.DE, *s. f.*, agility, quickness, vivacity, nimbleness.
Á.GIO, *s. m.*, agio.

AGIOTA — AIPIM

A.GI.O.TA, *s. 2 gen.*, jobber, usurer, moneylender.
A.GI.O.TA.GEM, *s. f.*, agiotage, usury.
A.GIR, *v.*, to act, to proceed, to do.
A.GI.TA.ÇÃO, *s. f.*, agitation, perturbation, trouble, conflict.
A.GI.TAR, *v.*, to agitate, to shake, to shock, to excite, to disturb, to move.
A.GLO.ME.RA.ÇÃO, *s. f.*, agglomeration, mass, heap.
A.GLO.ME.RAR, *v.*, to agglomerate, to accumulate, to join.
A.GLU.TI.NAR, *v.*, to agglutinate, to unite, to join.
A.GO.NI.A, *s. f.*, agony, pangs of death.
A.GO.NI.A.DO, *adj.*, agonizing, uneasy, anxious.
A.GO.NI.ZAR, *v.*, to agonize, to afflict, to distress, to worry.
A.GO.RA, *adv.*, now, at the present time, however; *conj.*, but.
A.GOS.TO, *s. m.*, August.
A.GOU.RAR, *v.*, to omen, to forebode, to presage, to augur.
A.GOU.RO, *s. m.*, omen, foreboding, prediction.
A.GRA.CI.A.DO, *adj.*, honoured, graced.
A.GRA.CI.AR, *v.*, to grace, to reward, to recompense.
A.GRA.DAR, *v.*, to please, to be agreeable.
A.GRA.DÁ.VEL, *adj.*, agreeable, pleasant, enjoyable, nice, good.
A.GRA.DE.CER, *v.*, to thank, to show gratitude.
A.GRA.DE.CI.DO, *adj.*, grateful, thankful, obliged.
A.GRA.DE.CI.MEN.TO, *s. m.*, thanks, thankfulness.
A.GRA.DO, *s. m.*, pleasure, contentment, delight, satisfaction, kindness.
A.GRA.VAN.TE, *s. m.*, culpability.
A.GRA.VAR, *v.*, to aggravate, to worsen, to oppress, to molest, to offend.
A.GRA.VO, *s. m.*, offence, loss, damage, injury.
A.GRE.DIR, *v.*, to attack, to assault, to aggress, to strike.
A.GRE.GA.ÇÃO, *s. f.*, aggregation, association, agglomeration.
A.GRE.GAR, *v.*, to aggregate, to join, to annex, to associate, to add.
A.GRE.MI.A.ÇÃO, *s. f.*, association, fellowship, reunion.
A.GRE.MI.AR, *v.*, to associate, to reunite.
A.GRES.SÃO, *s. f.*, aggression, wound, injury, blow, assault.
A.GRES.SI.VO, *adj.*, aggressive, offensive.
A.GRES.SOR, *s. m.*, aggressor.
A.GRI.ÃO, *s. m.*, water-cress.
A.GRÍ.CO.LA, *adj., s. 2 gen.*, agricultural.
A.GRI.CUL.TOR, *s. m.*, agriculturist, farmer; *adj.*, agricultural.
A.GRI.CUL.TU.RA, *s. f.*, agriculture, farming, cultivation.
A.GRI.MEN.SOR, *s. m.*, surveyor.
A.GRO.NO.MI.A, *s. f.*, agronomy, agronomics.
A.GRO.NÔ.MI.CO, *adj.*, agronomic.
A.GRU.PA.MEN.TO, *s. m.*, grouping, assembly, group.
A.GRU.PAR, *v.*, to group, to cluster, to gather.
Á.GUA, *s. f.*, water.
A.GUA.CEI.RO, *s. m.*, a shower of rain; squall.
Á.GUA-DE-CO.LÔ.NI.A, *s. f.*, Cologne water.
Á.GUA-MA.RI.NHA, *s. f.*, aquamarine.
A.GUAR, *v.*, to water, to dilute.
A.GUAR.DAR, *v.*, to expect, to await, to wait for, to observe.
A.GUAR.DEN.TE, *s. m.*, brandy, fire-water.
Á.GUA-VI.VA, *s. f.*, medusa, jelly-fish.
A.GU.ÇAR, *v.*, to grind, to sharpen, to whet, to taper, to point, to excite.
A.GU.DE.ZA, *s. f.*, sharpness, keenness.
A.GU.DO, *adj.*, sharp, pointed.
A.GUEN.TAR, *v.*, to support, to bear, to sustain, to endure.
Á.GUIA, *s. f.*, eagle.
A.GU.LHA, *s. f.*, needle.
A.GU.LHA.DA, *s. f.*, needle prick.
AI, *s. m.*, groan, moan; *interj.*, ah!
AÍ, *adv.*, there, in that place, in this respect.
AIDS (sida), *s.f.*, AIDS (acquired immune deficiency sindrome).
A.IN.DA, *adv.*, still, yet, again.
AI.PIM, *s.m.*, sweet cassava.

AIPO   **ALEGRE**

AI.PO, *s. m.*, celery.
A.JA.E.ZAR, *v.*, to harness, to adorn.
A.JAR.DI.NA.DO, *adj.*, gardenlike.
A.JAR.DI.NAR, *v.*, to garden, to form into a garden.
A.JEI.TAR, *v.*, to arrange, to dispose, to accomodate, to adapt.
A.JO.E.LHA.DO, *adj.*, kneeling.
A.JO.E.LHAR, *v.*, to kneel, to kneel down.
A.JU.DA, *s. f.*, help, assistance, support, aid, succour.
A.JU.DAN.TE, *s. 2 gen.*, assistant, helper, acolyte.
A.JU.DAR, *v.*, to help, to aid, to assist, to succour, to support.
A.JU.I.ZA.DO, *adj.*, reasonable, discret, judicious.
A.JU.I.ZAR, *v.*, to judge, to form an opinion, to estimate, to suppose.
A.JUN.TA.MEN.TO, *s. m.*, reunion, meeting, assembly.
A.JUN.TAR, *v.*, to gather, to accumulate, to compile, to add, to collect.
A.JUS.TAR, *v.*, to adjust, to regulate, to order, to accord, to adapt.
A.JUS.TE, *s. m.*, agreement, understanding, pact, settlement.
A.LA, *s. f.*, line, row, file, guard.
A.LA.DO, *adj.*, winged.
A.LA.GA.DO, *adj.*, full of water, waterlogged.
A.LA.GAR, *v.*, to inundate, to overflow, to flood.
A.LAM.BI.CAR, *v.*, to distil, to refine.
A.LAM.BI.QUE, *s. m.*, alembic, still.
A.LA.ME.DA, *s. f.*, lane, alley, grove, avenue, park.
A.LA.RAN.JA.DO, *adj.*, orange, like an orange.
A.LAR.DE, *s. m.*, ostentation, vainglory, pomp, vanity.
A.LAR.GA.MEN.TO, *s. m.*, widening, enlargement, dilatation.
A.LAR.GAR, *v.*, to widen, to dilate, to broaden, to enlarge, to amplify.
A.LA.RI.DO, *s. m.*, clamour, row.
A.LAR.MAR, *v.*, to alarm, to frighten, to trouble.
A.LAR.ME, *s. m.*, alarm, signal.
A.LAS.TRA.MEN.TO, *s. m.*, spreading, expansion, diffusion.

A.LAS.TRAR, *v.*, to spread out, to diffuse, to stow.
A.LA.VAN.CA, *s. f.*, lever, handspike, crowbar.
AL.BA.TROZ, *s. m.*, albatross.
AL.BER.GUE, *s. m.*, inn, lodging, hostelry, shelter.
ÁL.BUM, *s. m.*, album.
AL.BU.MI.NA, *s. f.*, albumin.
AL.ÇA, *s. f.*, ring, eye, handle, holder, strap.
AL.CA.CHO.FRA, *s. f.*, artichoke.
AL.ÇA.DA, *s. f.*, competence, jurisdiction.
AL.CAN.ÇAR, *v.*, to reach, to fetch, to attain, to obtain, to get, to catch up.
AL.CAN.CE, *s. m.*, reach, range, grasp, scope, attainment.
AL.ÇA.PÃO, *s. m.*, trapdoor.
AL.CA.PAR.RA, *s. f.*, caper.
AL.ÇAR, *v.*, to raise, to lift, to elevate, to edify, to heave, to exalt.
AL.CA.TEI.A, *s. f.*, pack of wolves; herd.
AL.CA.TRÃO, *s. m.*, tar, pitch.
AL.CE, *s. m.*, moose, elk.
ÁL.CO.OL, *s. m.*, alcohol, spirit.
AL.CO.Ó.LA.TRA, *s. 2 gen.*, alcoholic, drunkard; *adj.*, alcoholic.
AL.CO.Ó.LI.CO, *adj.*, alcoholic.
AL.CO.O.LIS.MO, *s. m.*, alcoholism.
AL.CO.O.LI.ZAR, *v.*, to alcoholize, to intoxicate.
AL.CO.RÃO, *s. m.*, Alcoran, Koran.
AL.CO.VA, *s. f.*, alcove.
AL.CU.NHA, *s. f.*, nickname.
AL.DE.ÃO, *s. m.*, countryman, peasant, villager.
AL.DEI.A, *s. f.*, village.
A.LE.A.TÓ.RIO, *adj.*, aleatoric.
A.LE.CRIM, *s. m.*, rosemary.
A.LE.GA.ÇÃO, *s. f.*, allegation, assertion, exposition.
A.LE.GAR, *v.*, to allege, to cite, to proof, to present, to plead.
A.LE.GO.RI.A, *s. f.*, allegory.
A.LE.GÓ.RI.CO, *adj.*, allegoric.
A.LE.GRAR, *v.*, to make happy, to rejoice, to gladden.
A.LE.GRE, *adj.*, happy, gay, cheerful, glad, joyful.

ALEGRIA — ALINHAMENTO

A.LE.GRI.A, *s. f.*, cheerfulness, happiness, joy, gladness, pleasure, gaiety.
A.LEI.JA.DO, *s. m.*, cripple; *adj.*, crippled, disabled.
A.LEI.JAR, *v.*, to deform, to mutilate.
A.LEI.TAR, *v.*, to nurse, to shuckle, to feed on milk.
A.LÉM, *adv.*, there, in that place, over there, farther on, beyond.
A.LE.MÃO, *adj.*, *s. m.*, German.
A.LÉM-MAR, *s. m.*, oversea country.
A.LEN.TO, *s. m.*, courage, effort, respiration, diligence.
A.LER.GI.A, *s. f.*, allergy.
A.LER.TA, *s. m.*, alert; *adv.*, alert; *interj.*, attention.
A.LER.TAR, *v.*, to alert, to give alarm.
A.LE.TRI.A, *s. f.*, vermicelli.
AL.FA.BE.TI.ZA.ÇÃO, *s. f.*, alphabetization.
AL.FA.BE.TI.ZAR, *v.*, alphabetize.
AL.FA.BE.TO, *s. m.*, alphabet.
AL.FA.CE, *s. f.*, lettuce.
AL.FAI.A.TA.RI.A, *s. f.*, tailor's workshop.
AL.FAI.A.TE, *s. m.*, tailor.
AL.FÂN.DE.GA, *s. f.*, customs, custom house.
AL.FAN.DE.GÁ.RIO, *adj.*, of or referring to customs.
AL.FA.ZE.MA, *s. f.*, lavender.
AL.FI.NE.TA.DA, *s. f.*, pin-prick.
AL.FI.NE.TE, *s. m.*, pin, tiepin.
AL.FOR.JE, *s. m.*, bag or sack with two pouches.
AL.FOR.RI.A, *s. f.*, enfranchisement, libertation, release from slavery.
AL.GA, *s. f.*, alga, seaweed.
AL.GA.RIS.MO, *s. m.*, cipher, figure, numeral, number.
AL.GA.ZAR.RA, *s. f.*, clamour, uproar, bawling, mutiny, tumult.
ÁL.GE.BRA, *s. f.*, algebra.
AL.GÉ.BRI.CO, *adj.*, algebric.
AL.GE.MAS, *s. f.*, manacles, shackles, handcuffs.
AL.GE.MAR, *v.*, to shackle, to fetter, to handcuff, to dominate.
AL.GI.BEI.RA, *s. f.*, pocket.
AL.GO, *adv.*, somewhat, a bit, a little; *pron.*, something, anything.
AL.GO.DÃO, *s. m.*, cotton.
AL.GO.DÃO-DO.CE, *s. m.*, cotton candy.
AL.GOZ, *s. m.*, executioner, hangman, torturer, monster.
AL.GUÉM, *pron.*, somebody, someone, anybody, anyone.
AL.GUM, *pron.*, *adj.*, some, any.
A.LHE.A.MEN.TO, *s. m.*, alienation.
A.LHE.AR, *v.*, to alienate, to deprive, to transfer property.
A.LHEI.O, *adj.*, strange, foreign, alien, distant, contrary.
A.LHO, *s. m.*, garlic.
A.LI, *adv.*, there, in that place; then.
A.LI.A.DO, *s. m.*, ally; *adj.*, allied, associated.
A.LI.AN.ÇA, *s. f.*, alliance, confederation, association, connection.
A.LI.AR, *v.*, to ally, to join, to unite, to combine, to harmonize.
A.LI.ÁS, *adv.*, besides, otherwise, moreover, on the other hand.
Á.LI.BI, *s. m.*, alibi.
A.LI.CA.TE, *s. m.*, pincers, a pair of pliers.
A.LI.CER.ÇAR, *v.*, to lay the foundation, to found, to base.
A.LI.CER.CE, *s. m.*, foundation, base.
A.LI.CI.AR, *v.*, to allure, to bait, to seduce, to attract.
A.LI.E.NA.ÇÃO, *s. f.*, alienation, madness, transfer of ownership.
A.LI.E.NAR, *v.*, to alienate, to cede, to transfer, to madden.
A.LI.E.NÍ.GE.NA, *s. 2 gen.*, alien.
A.LI.JAR, *v.*, to jettison, to lighten.
A.LI.MEN.TA.ÇÃO, *s. f.*, alimentation, nourishment, food.
A.LI.MEN.TAR, *v.*, to nourish, to feed; *adj.*, alimentary, nutritious.
A.LI.MEN.TO, *s. m.*, food, provisions, supply.
A.LÍ.NE.A, *s. f.*, paragraph.
A.LI.NHA.DO, *adj.*, alined, lined up; elegant.
A.LI.NHA.MEN.TO, *s. m.*, alignment, arrangement.

A.LI.NHAR, *v.*, to ali(g)n, to range; to dress up.
A.LÍ.QUO.TA, *s. f.*, aliquot.
A.LI.SAR, *v.*, to make plane, to smooth, to level, to equal.
A.LIS.TAR, *v.*, to enlist, to recruit, to list.
A.LI.TE.RA.ÇÃO, *s. f.*, alliteration.
A.LI.VI.AR, *v.*, to lighten, to ease, to lessen, to soften, to mitigate, to diminish, to comfort.
A.LÍ.VIO, *s. m.*, relief, softening, ease, comfort, lightening.
AL.MA, *s. f.*, soul, spirit.
AL.MA.NA.QUE, *s. m.*, almanac.
AL.ME.JAR, *v.*, to desire, to long for, to intend.
AL.MI.RAN.TE, *s. m.*, admiral, admiral-ship.
AL.MÍS.CAR, *s. m.*, musk.
AL.MO.ÇAR, *v.*, to lunch, to breakfast.
AL.MO.ÇO, *s. m.*, lunch, breakfast.
AL.MO.FA.DA, *s. f.*, cushion, pillow.
AL.MÔN.DE.GA, *s. f.*, minced meat ball.
AL.MO.XA.RI.FA.DO, *s. m.*, warehouse.
A.LÔ!, *interj.*, hallo!, hullo!, hello!
A.LO.CU.ÇÃO, *s. f.*, allocution, speech.
A.LO.JAR, *v.*, to receive, to shelter, to lodge.
A.LON.GA.DO, *adj.*, elongated, away, lengthened.
A.LON.GAR, *v.*, to prolongate, to extend, to lengthen.
A.LO.PA.TI.A, *s. f.*, allopathy.
AL.PEN.DRE, *s. m.*, shed, porch.
AL.PI.NIS.MO, *s. m.*, Alpinism.
AL.PI.NIS.TA, *s. 2 gen.*, Alpinist, mountaineer.
AL.PIS.TE, *s. m.*, canary grass.
AL.QUI.MIS.TA, *s. 2 gen.*, alchemist.
AL.TA, *s. f.*, raising, rise, boom, increase; delay; nobility.
AL.TAR, *s. m.*, altar.
AL.TE.RA.ÇÃO, *s. f.*, alteration, change, modification, decay, degeneration, perturbation.
AL.TE.RAR, *v.*, to change, to modify, to alter, to disturb, to perturbate, to falsify.
AL.TER.CAR, *v.*, to altercate, to dispute, to debate.
AL.TER.NA.DOR, *s. m.*, alternator.
AL.TER.NAR, *v.*, to alternate, to interchange, to reverse.
AL.TER.NA.TI.VA, *s. f.*, alternative.
AL.TE.ZA, *s. f.*, highness, elevation.
AL.TÍ.ME.TRO, *s. m.*, altimeter.
AL.TI.TU.DE, *s. f.*, altitude.
AL.TI.VEZ, *s. f.*, haughtiness, arrogance, pride.
AL.TO, *adj.*, high, elevated, tall, lofty, excellent, magnificent, loud.
AL.TO-FA.LAN.TE, *s. m.*, loudspeaker.
AL.TO-RE.LE.VO, *s. m.*, high-relief.
AL.TRU.ÍS.MO, *s. m.*, altruism, unselfishness.
AL.TRU.ÍS.TA, *s. 2 gen.*, altruist.
AL.TU.RA, *s. f.*, height, highness, tallness, top, summit, size; altitude.
A.LU.CI.NA.ÇÃO, *s. f.*, hallucination, delusion.
A.LU.CI.NAR, *v.*, to hallucinate, to delude.
A.LU.DIR, *v.*, to allude, to mention.
A.LU.GA.DO, *adj.*, hired, let, rented.
A.LU.GAR, *v.*, to rent, to hire, to let, to lease.
A.LU.GUEL, *s. m.*, letting, rent.
A.LU.MI.AR, *v.*, to illuminate, to light.
A.LU.MÍ.NIO, *s. m.*, aluminium.
A.LU.NA, *s. f.*, pupil, schoolgirl.
A.LU.NO, *s. m.*, pupil, schoolboy, scholar, student, disciple.
A.LU.SÃO, *s. f.*, allusion, reference.
A.LU.VI.ÃO, *s. f.*, alluvium, inundation, torrent.
AL.VA.RÁ, *s. m.*, permit, charter, warrant.
AL.VE.NA.RI.A, *s. f.* masonry, the work of a mason.
AL.VÉO.LO, *s. m.*, alveolus, cell of a honeycomb.
AL.VI.TRE, *s. m.*, reminder, hint, proposal, suggestion, opinion.
AL.VO, *s. m.*, white, target, aim, purpose, object; *adj.*, white, pure, limpid.
AL.VO.RA.DA, *s. f.*, dawn (of day).
AL.VO.RE.CER, *s. m.*, dawn (of day), daybreak.
AL.VO.RO.ÇO, *s. m.*, agitation, alarm, fluster, haste.
AL.VU.RA, *s. f.*, whiteness, purity.
A.MA.BI.LI.DA.DE, *s. f.*, amiability, kindness, friendliness, affection.
A.MA.CI.AR, *v.*, to smooth, to soften, to soothe, to ease, to tranquilize.

AMADA — AMIGDALITE

A.MA.DA, *s. f.*, sweetheart, mistress, girl friend; *adj.*, loved.
A.MA.DO, *adj.*, loved, beloved.
A.MA.DOR, *s. m.*, lover, fan, amateur.
A.MA.DU.RE.CER, *v.*, to mature, to ripen, to grow ripe.
A.MA.DU.RE.CI.MEN.TO, *s. m.*, ripening, maturation, ripeness.
A.MAL.DI.ÇO.AR, *v.*, to curse, to execrate, to damn, to abhor, to detest.
A.MAL.GA.MAR, *v.*, to amalgamate, to mix, to blend.
A.MA.MEN.TA.ÇÃO, *s. f.*, nursing, breast-feeding.
A.MA.MEN.TAR, *v.*, to suckle, to nurse, to nourish.
A.MA.NHÃ, *adv.*, tomorrow.
A.MA.NHAR, *v.*, to cultivate, to till, to prepare, to arrange, to dispose.
A.MA.NHE.CER, *s. m.*, break of the day; *v.*, to dawn, to grow day.
A.MA.NHE.CI.DO, *adj.*, dawned, old.
A.MAN.SAR, *v.*, to tame, to domesticate, to break in, to mitigate, to pacify.
A.MAN.TE, *s. 2 gen.*, lover, boyfriend, girlfriend.
A.MAR, *v.*, to love, to be in love, to like, to adore.
A.MA.RE.LAR, *v.*, to yellow, to fade.
A.MA.RE.LO, *adj.*, yellow, pale, faded.
A.MAR.GAR, *v.*, to embitter, to make bitter.
A.MAR.GO, *adj.*, bitter, acrid, acrimonious, sad.
A.MAR.GOR, *s. m.*, bitterness.
A.MAR.GU.RA, *s. f.*, bitterness, acridity; sorrow, affliction.
A.MAR.GU.RAR, *v.*, to cause sorrow, to afflict, to embitter.
A.MAR.RAR, *v.*, to moor, to bind, to fasten, to close, to chain.
A.MA-SE.CA, *s. f.*, dry nurse, baby sitter.
A.MÁ.SIA, *s. f.*, mistress, concubine.
A.MA.SI.AR-SE, *v.*, to live in concubinage.
A.MÁ.SI.O, *s. m.*, lover.
A.MAS.SA.DO, *adj.*, squashed, crushed, flattened.
A.MAS.SAR, *v.*, to knead, to mix, to squash, to crush, to crumple.
A.MÁ.VEL, *adj.*, amiable, kind, lovable.
ÂM.BAR, *s. m.*, amber.
AM.BI.ÇÃO, *s. f.*, ambition.
AM.BI.CI.O.NAR, *v.*, to pursue ambitiously, strive after.
AM.BI.DES.TRO, *adj.*, ambidextrous.
AM.BI.EN.TE, *s. m.*, environment, ambiance, surrounding, sphere, atmosphere.
AM.BI.GUI.DA.DE, *s. f.*, ambiguity, ambiguousness.
AM.BÍ.GUO, *adj.*, ambiguous, doubtful, dubious, equivocal.
ÂM.BI.TO, *s. m.*, ambit, circuit, circumference.
AM.BOS, *num.*, *adj.*, both.
AM.BU.LÂN.CIA, *s. f.*, ambulance.
AM.BU.LAN.TE, *s. 2 gen.*, ambulant, moving.
AM.BU.LA.TÓ.RIO, *s. m.*, ambulatory.
A.ME.A.ÇA, *s. f.*, threat, menace.
A.ME.A.ÇAR, *v.*, to threaten, to menace.
A.ME.DRON.TA.DO, *adj.*, frightened, afraid, scared.
A.ME.DRON.TAR, *v.*, to frighten, to scare, to alarm, to intimidate.
A.MEI.XA, *s. f.*, plum.
A.MÉM, *s. m.*, amen.
A.MÊN.DOA, *s. f.*, almond.
A.MEN.DO.IM, *s. m.*, peanut, groundnut.
A.ME.NI.DA.DE, *s. f.*, amenity, pleasentness, serenity.
A.ME.NI.ZAR, *v.*, to soften, to ease, to soothe.
A.ME.NO, *adj.*, bland, suave, mild, agreeable, delicate.
A.ME.RI.CA.NIS.MO, *s. m.*, Americanism.
A.ME.RI.CA.NI.ZAR, *v.*, to Americanize.
A.ME.RI.CA.NO, *adj.*, *s. m.*, American.
A.MES.QUI.NHAR, *v.*, to depreciate, to disparage, to humble, to humiliate.
A.MES.TRAR, *v.*, to instruct, to teach, to train.
A.ME.TIS.TA, *s. f.*, amethyst.
A.MI.DO, *s. m.*, starch, amylum.
A.MI.GA, *s. f.*, female friend; mistress, concubine.
A.MI.GÁ.VEL, *adj.*, amicable, friendly.
A.MÍG.DA.LA, *s. f.*, amygdala, tonsil.
A.MIG.DA.LI.TE, *s. f.*, amygdalitis.

A.MI.GO, *s. m.*, friend, lover, protector; *adj.*, friendly, favourable, kind.
A.MI.GO DA ON.ÇA, *s. m.*, false-friend.
A.MIS.TO.SO, *adj.*, friendly, amicable.
A.MI.U.DA.DO, *adj.*, frequent, repeated.
A.MI.U.DAR, *v.*, to do, to happen frequently.
A.MI.Ú.DE, *adv.*, frequent, often, repeated.
A.MI.ZA.DE, *s. f.*, friendship, amity, affection, benevolence.
A.MO, *s. m.*, master, master of house.
A.MO.LA.ÇÃO, *s. f.*, grinding, whetting, sharpening, affliction.
A.MO.LAR, *v.*, to whet, to grind, to sharpen, to vex, to annoy, to importune.
A.MO.LE.CER, *v.*, mollify, to soften, to soak, to weaken, to move, to affect.
A.MO.LE.CI.MEN.TO, *s. m.*, mollification, softening.
A.MÔ.NIA, *s. f.*, ammonia.
A.MON.TO.AR, *v.*, to pile up, to heap up, to accumulate, to amass, to gather.
A.MOR, *s. m.*, love, affection, attachment, devotion, passion, enthusiasm.
A.MO.RA, *s. f.*, mulberry.
A.MO.RAL, *adj.*, amoral.
A.MO.RI.CO, *s. m.*, flirt.
A.MOR.NAR, *v.*, to warm up.
A.MO.RO.SO, *adj.*, loving, affectionate, fond, kind, affable, soft.
A.MOR.TE.CE.DOR, *s. m.*, shock absorber, damper; *adj.*, damping.
A.MOR.TE.CER, *v.*, to deaden, to debilitate, to weaken, to lessen.
A.MOR.TE.CI.MEN.TO, *s. m.*, deadening, debilitation, mitigation.
A.MOR.TI.ZA.ÇÃO, *s. f.*, amortization, paying off.
A.MOR.TI.ZAR, *v.*, to amortize, to pay off.
A.MOS.TRA, *s. f.*, sample, specimen, sign, proof, indication.
AM.PA.RAR, *v.*, to support, to prop, to sustain, to protect, to favour, to assist.
AM.PA.RO, *s. m.*, support, protection, shelter, assistance, help.
AM.PE.RA.GEM, *s. f.*, amperage.
AM.PÈ.RE, *s. m.*, ampere.
AM.PLE.XO, *s. m.*, embracement.
AM.PLI.A.ÇÃO, *s. f.*, amplification, enlargement.
AM.PLI.AR, *v.*, to amplify, to enlarge, to increase.
AM.PLI.DÃO, *s. f.*, amplitude, ampleness, wideness.
AM.PLI.FI.CA.DOR, *s. m.*, amplifier, amplificator.
AM.PLI.FI.CAR, *v.*, to amplify, to enlarge, to increase, to widen.
AM.PLI.TU.DE, *s. f.*, amplitude, largeness.
AM.PLO, *adj.*, ample, wide, extensive, spacious.
AM.PU.TA.ÇÃO, *s. f.*, amputation.
AM.PU.TAR, *v.*, to amputate, to cut off, to mutilate, to restrict.
A.MU.AR, *v.*, to make sullen, to disgust, to vex, to annoy.
A.MU.LE.TO, *s. m.*, amulet, talisman.
A.NA.CRO.NIS.MO, *s. m.*, anachronism.
A.NÁ.GUA, *s. f.*, slip, petticoat.
A.NAL, *adj.*, anal; annual, yearly.
A.NAL.FA.BE.TIS.MO, *s. m.*, analphabetism.
A.NAL.FA.BE.TO, *s. m.*, analphabet; *adj.*, analphabet, letterless.
A.NA.LI.SAR, *v.*, to analyse, to separate, to study the facts.
A.NÁ.LI.SE, *s. f.*, analysis.
A.NA.LIS.TA, *s. 2 gen.*, analyst, writer of annals.
A.NA.LO.GI.A, *s. f.*, analogy, conformity, likeness.
A.NÁ.LO.GO, *adj.*, analogous, similar, resembling.
A.NA.NÁS, *s. m.*, pine-apple.
A.NÃO, *s. m.*, dwarf; *adj.*, dwarfish, small.
A.NAR.QUI.A, *s. f.*, anarchy, disorder, confusion.
A.NAR.QUIS.MO, *s. m.*, anarchism.
A.NAR.QUI.ZAR, *v.*, to anarchize.
A.NA.татомиTO.MI.A, *s. f.*, anatomy, morphology, dissection.
A.NA.TO.MI.ZAR, *v.*, to anatomize, to dissect.
AN.CA, *s. f.*, buttock, haunch.
AN.CI.ÃO, *s. m.*, venerable old man; *adj.*, ancient, old.
AN.CI.NHO, *s. m.*, rake.

ÂN.CO.RA, *s. f.*, anchor; refuge, shelter.
AN.CO.RAR, *v.*, to anchor, to cast anchor.
AN.DAI.ME, *s. m.*, scaffold.
AN.DA.MEN.TO, *s. m.*, process, proceeding, course.
AN.DAR, *s. m.*, gait, floor, story, speed, velocity; *v.*, to go, to walk, to wander, to drive, to ride.
AN.DI.NO, *adj.*, Andean.
AN.DO.RI.NHA, *s. f.*, swallow.
AN.DRA.JO, *s. m.*, rag, tatter.
AN.DRA.JO.SO, *adj.*, tattered, ragged.
A.NE.DO.TA, *s. f.*, anecdote, joke.
A.NEL, *s. m.*, ring, circle, link.
A.NE.LAR, *v.*, to curl, to shape like a ring, to pant; *adj.*, annular.
A.NE.LO, *s. m.*, aspiration, anxiety.
A.NE.MI.A, *s. f.*, an(a)emia.
A.NES.TE.SI.A, *s. f.*, an(a)esthesia.
A.NES.TE.SI.AR, *v.*, to an(a)esthetize.
A.NE.XA.ÇÃO, *s. f.*, annexation.
A.NE.XA.DO, *adj.*, annexed, attached.
A.NE.XAR, *v.*, to annex, to join, to attach.
A.NE.XO, *s. m.*, appurtenance, appendage.
AN.FÍ.BIO, *s. m.* amphibian.
AN.FI.TRI.ÃO, *s. m.*, amphitryon, host.
ÂN.FO.RA, *s. f.*, amphora.
AN.GA.RI.AR, *v.*, to recruit, to engage, to allure.
AN.GE.LI.CAL, *adj.*, pure, beautiful.
AN.GLI.CA.NO, *adj.*, *s. m.*, Anglican.
AN.GLI.CIS.MO, *s. m.*, Anglicism, Briticism.
AN.GRA, *s. f.*, bay, creek.
ÂN.GU.LO, *s. m.*, angle, corner, nook.
AN.GÚS.TIA, *s. f.*, anguish, affliction, annoyance, agony.
AN.GUS.TI.A.DO, *adj.*, afflicted, annoyed.
AN.GUS.TI.AR, *v.*, to afflict, to torment, to distress, to annoy.
A.NIL, *s. m.*, anil, blue; *adj.*, blue, senile.
A.NI.MA.ÇÃO, *s. f.*, animation, liveliness, enthusiasm, activity.
A.NI.MA.DO, *adj.*, *s. m.*, animated.
A.NI.MAL, *adj.*, *s. m.*, animal.
A.NI.MA.LI.ZAR, *v.*, to animalize.
A.NI.MAR, *v.*, to animate, encourage, boost, stimulate.
Â.NI.MO, *s. m.*, courage, will, vitality, life, soul, purpose.
A.NI.MO.SI.DA.DE, *s. f.*, animosity.
A.NI.QUI.LA.ÇÃO, *s. f.*, annihilation.
A.NI.QUI.LA.DO, *adj.*, annihilated.
A.NI.QUI.LAR, *v.*, to annihilate, to extinguish.
A.NIS.TI.A, *s. f.*, amnesty.
A.NI.VER.SA.RI.AN.TE, *s. 2 gen.*, person having a birthday.
A.NI.VER.SA.RI.AR, *v.*, to have (celebrate) one's birthday.
A.NI.VER.SÁ.RIO, *s. m.*, anniversary, birthday.
AN.JO, *s. m.*, angel.
A.NO, *s. m.*, year; ano bissexto, leap year; ano novo, New Year, New Year's Day.
A.NOI.TE.CER, *v.*, to darken, to grow dark; *s.m.*, nightfall.
A.NO.NI.MA.TO, *s. m.*, anonimity.
A.NÔ.NI.MO, *s. m.*, anonym; *adj.*, anonymous, nameless, unnamed.
A.NOR.MAL, *s. 2 gen.*, abnormal person; *adj.*, abnormal, anomalous; mentally defective.
A.NOR.MA.LI.DA.DE, *s. f.*, abnormality, anomaly.
A.NO.TA.ÇÃO, *s. f.*, annotation, notation, note.
A.NO.TAR, *v.*, annotate, take note, mark, note down.
AN.SEI.O, *s. m.*, longing, craving, yearning; anxiety.
ÂN.SIA, *s. f.*, anguish, anxiety, trouble, sorrow.
AN.SI.AR, *v.*, to crave, to hanker, yearn.
AN.SI.E.DA.DE, *s. f.*, anxiety, worry, apprehension, fear, anguish.
AN.SI.O.SO, *adj.*, anxious, uneasy, careworn.
AN.TA, *s. f.*, tapir.
AN.TA.GO.NIS.MO, *s. m.*, antagonism, opposition, incompatibility.
AN.TE, *prep.*, before, in the face of, in view of.
AN.TE.BRA.ÇO, *s. m.*, forearm, underarm.
AN.TE.CE.DÊN.CIA, *s. f.*, antecedence, priority, precedence.
AN.TE.CE.DER, *v.*, to antecede, to precede, to anticipate.
AN.TE.CES.SOR, *s. m.*, antecessor, predecessor,

ANTECIPAÇÃO — AONDE

foregoer.
AN.TE.CI.PA.ÇÃO, *s. f.*, anticipation, advance, expectation, forestalling.
AN.TE.CI.PA.DO, *adj.*, anticipated, beforehand.
AN.TE.CI.PAR, *v.*, to anticipate, to forestall, to do in advance.
AN.TE.NA, *s. f.*, antenna.
AN.TE.ON.TEM, *adv.*, the day before yesterday.
AN.TE.PAS.SA.DO, *s. m.*, forefather, ancestor, predecessor.
AN.TE.PE.NÚL.TI.MO, *adj.*, antepenult, the last but two.
AN.TE.POR, *v.*, to set, to put before, to place before.
AN.TE.PRO.JE.TO, *s. m.*, project, plan, draft, preliminary sketch.
AN.TE.RI.OR, *adj.*, *s. 2 gen.*, anterior, former, foregoing, front, previous.
AN.TES, *adv.*, before, formerly, previously, sooner, ahead.
AN.TES.SA.LA, *s. f.*, antechamber, antecabinet, waiting-room.
AN.TE.VER, *v.*, to foresee.
AN.TE.VI.SÃO, *s. f.*, foresight.
AN.TI.A.É.REO, *adj.*, antiaircraft.
AN.TI.BI.Ó.TI.CO, *s. m.*, antibiotic.
AN.TI.CON.CEP.CIO.NAL, *adj.*, *s. m.*, contraceptive.
AN.TI.CONS.TI.TU.CI.O.NAL, *adj.*, anticonstitutional.
AN.TI.CRIS.TO, *s. m.*, Antichrist.
AN.TI.DER.RA.PAN.TE, *adj.*, *s. m.*, antiskid, nonskid.
AN.TÍ.DO.TO, *s. m.*, antidote.
AN.TI.GO, *adj.*, ancient, old, olden, antique, archaic, antiquated.
AN.TI.GUI.DA.DE, *s. f.*, antiquity, antique, oldness, ancientry.
AN.TI-HI.GI.Ê.NI.CO, *adj.*, antihygienic, unsanitary.
AN.TI.MÔ.NIO, *s. m.*, antimony.
AN.TI.PA.TI.A, *s. f.*, antipathy, aversion, dislike, averseness.
AN.TI.PÁ.TI.CO, *adj.*, antipathetic, averse,

unpleasant, unfriendly.
AN.TI.PA.TI.ZAR, *v.*, to dislike, to feel antipathy.
AN.TI.PA.TRI.Ó.TI.CO, *adj.*, unpatriotic.
AN.TI.QUA.DO, *adj.*, antiquated, antique, old, old-fashioned.
AN.TI.QUÁ.RIO, *s. m.*, antiquary, antiquarian, archaist.
AN.TIS.SO.CI.AL, *adj.*, *s. 2 gen.*, antisocial, unsocial.
AN.TÍ.TE.SE, *s. f.*, antithesis, contraposition.
AN.TI.TE.TÂ.NI.CO, *adj.*, antitetanic.
AN.TO.LO.GI.A, *s. f.*, anthology, florilegium.
AN.TÔ.NI.MO, *s. m.*, antonym.
AN.TRO, *s. m.*, antrum, antre, cave, sty.
AN.TRO.PÓ.FA.GO, *s. m.*, anthropophagite, cannibal.
AN.TRO.PO.LO.GI.A, *s. f.*, anthropology.
AN.TRO.PÓ.LO.GO, *s. m.*, anthropologist.
A.NU.AL, *adj.*, annual, yearly.
A.NU.ÊN.CIA, *s. f.*, approvement, approval, acquiescence.
A.NU.I.DA.DE, *s. f.*, annuity, yearly payment.
A.NU.IR, *v.*, to assent, to approve, to agree, to consent.
A.NU.LA.ÇÃO, *s. f.*, annulment, nullification, cancellation, rescission.
A.NU.LA.DO, *adj.*, canceled.
A.NU.LAR, *v.*, to annul, to cancel, to nullify, to make void; to suppress.
A.NUN.CI.A.ÇÃO, *s. f.*, annunciation, announcement.
A.NUN.CI.AN.TE, *s. 2 gen.*, announcer, advertiser.
A.NUN.CI.AR, *v.*, to announce, to annunciate, to advertise, to promulgate, to proclaim.
A.NÚN.CIO, *s. m.*, advertisement, notice, announcement; bill.
Â.NUS, *s. m.*, anus.
A.NU.VI.AR, *v.*, to grow cloudy, cloud, becloud, to darken.
AN.ZOL, *s. m.*, fishhood, hook, angle.
AO, *contr.* of the *prep.*, **A** and the *art.* **O**: in the, for the, to the, by the.
A.ON.DE, *adv.*, where, wherever, whither.

A.OR.TA, *s. f.*, aorta.
A.PA.GA.DO, *adj.*, extinguished, extinct, dark, unlit, erased.
A.PA.GA.DOR, *s. m.*, extinguisher, quencher, eraser.
A.PA.GAR, *v.*, to extinguish, to quench, to damp, to smother, to blot.
A.PAI.XO.NA.DO, *adj., s. m.*, lover, enamoured, passionate, impassioned, flaming.
A.PAI.XO.NAR, *v.*, to impassion, to enamour, to enfatuate, to smite.
A.PAL.PAR, *v.*, to touch, to feel, to palp, to palpate, to finger.
A.PA.NHA.DO, *s. m.*, resumé, summary, abstract.
A.PA.NHAR, *v.*, to pick, to pick out, to pluck, to gather, to collect.
A.PA.RA.DOR, *s. m.*, parer, cropper, parrier, dresser.
A.PA.RAR, *v.*, to clip, to trim, to cut, to part, to chip.
A.PA.RA.TO, *s. m.*, display, apparatus, grandeur, pomp, device.
A.PA.RE.CER, *v.*, to appear, to show up, to turn up, to arise, to emerge, to begin.
A.PA.RE.CI.MEN.TO, *s. m.*, emersion, appearing, coming, emergence.
A.PA.RE.LHA.GEM, *s. f.*, implements, tools, equipments.
A.PA.RE.LHAR, *v.*, to equip, to outfit, to furnish, to prepare, to prim.
A.PA.RE.LHO, *s. m.*, equipment, arrangement, apparatus, implement, gear.
A.PA.RÊN.CIA, *s. f.*, appearance, aspect, semblance, likelihood, likeness.
A.PA.REN.TAR, *v.*, to pretend, to simulate, have the appearance of, to establish kinship.
A.PA.REN.TE, *adj.*, apparent, semblable, evident.
A.PA.RI.ÇÃO, *s. f.*, phantom, ghost, spectre, apparition, vision.
A.PAR.TA.MEN.TO, *s. m.*, flat, apartment.
A.PAR.TAR, *v.*, to separate, to part, to divide, to alienate, to disjoin.
A.PAR.TE, *s. m.*, incidental remark, interruption; an aside.
A.PAR.TE.AR, *v.*, to interrupt an orator.

A.PAS.SI.VAR, *v.*, to change to the passive.
A.PA.TI.A, *s. f.*, apathy, insensibility, indolence.
A.PÁ.TRI.DA, *adj., s. 2 gen.*, war refugee.
A.PA.VO.RA.DO, *adj.*, panic-stricken, scared.
A.PA.VO.RAR, *v.*, terrify, frighten, horrify.
A.PA.ZI.GUA.DO, *adj.*, pacified, calmed.
A.PA.ZI.GUAR, *v.*, to pacify, to appease, to reconcile, to calm, to quiet, to mollify.
A.PE.DRE.JA.MEN.TO, *s. m.*, stoning, lapidation.
A.PE.DRE.JAR, *v.*, to stone, to lapidate.
A.PE.GAR, *v.*, to attach, to infect, to transmit by contagion.
A.PE.GO, *s. m.*, affection, adherence, fondness, adhesion.
A.PE.LA.ÇÃO, *s. f.*, appeal, appellation, recourse.
A.PE.LAR, *v.*, to appeal, to solicit, to plead, to ask.
A.PE.LI.DAR, *v.*, to cognominate, to nickname, to denominate.
A.PE.LI.DO, *s. m.*, surname, byname, family name, cognomen.
A.PE.LO, *s. m.*, appellation, appeal, plea.
A.PE.NAS, *adv.*, scarcely, hardly, only, merely.
A.PÊN.DI.CE, *s. f.*, appendix, supplement, addendum.
A.PEN.DI.CI.TE, *s. f.*, appendicitis.
A.PEN.SO, *s. m.*, enclosure, thing annexed.
A.PER.CE.BER, *v.*, to prepare, to fit, to adapt, to warn, to inform, to notify.
A.PER.FEI.ÇO.A.DO, *adj.*, improved, polished.
A.PER.FEI.ÇO.A.MEN.TO, *s. m.*, perfection, improvement.
A.PER.FEI.ÇO.AR, *v.*, to improve on, to perfect, to meliorate, to better, to amend.
A.PE.RI.TI.VO, *s. m.*, aperitif, appetizer.
A.PER.TA.DO, *adj.*, pressed, narrow, compressed, scarce, tight, close.
A.PER.TAR, *v.*, to squeeze, to press, to compress, to narrow, to constrict, to limit.
A.PER.TO, *s. m.*, squeeze, pressure, stress, tightness, straitness, narrowness.
A.PE.SAR DE, *prep.*, in spite of, despite, although.
A.PE.TE.CER, *v.*, to have an appetite for, to desire,

APETITE / **APRIMORADO**

to hunger for.
A.PE.TI.TE, *s. m.*, appetite, appetence, hunger.
A.PE.TI.TO.SO, *adj.*, appetizing, savoury, desirable.
A.PI.Á.RIO, *s. m.*, apiary.
Á.PI.CE, *s. m.*, apex, vertex, top, summit.
A.PI.CUL.TOR, *s. m.*, apiculturist, beekeeper, apiarist.
A.PI.CUL.TÚ.RA, *s. f.*, apiculture, beekeeping.
A.PI.E.DAR, *v.*, to pity, to feel sorry for.
A.PI.MEN.TAR, *v.*, to pepper, to spice, to season.
A.PI.TAR, *v.*, to whistle, to blow the whistle.
A.PI.TO, *s. m.*, whistle.
A.PLAI.NAR, *v.*, to level, to smooth, to plane.
A.PLAU.DIR, *v.*, to applaud, to clap, to acclaim, to cheer, to laud.
A.PLAU.SO, *s. m.*, applause, acclamation, cheering, laudation.
A.PLI.CAR, *v.*, to apply, to put into pratice, to adapt, to inflict.
A.PO.DRE.CER, *v.*, to putrefy, to rot, to corrupt, to decompose.
A.PO.DRE.CI.MEN.TO, *s. m.*, putrefaction.
A.PO.GEU, *s. m.*, apogee, summit.
A.POI.AR, *v.*, to support, to stay, to sustain, to prop, to make firm.
A.POI.O, *s. m.*, base, basis, foundation, support, stay, rest, protection.
A.PÓ.LI.CE, *s. f.*, policy, bond, stock, share.
A.PO.LO.GI.A, *s. f.*, apology, discourse.
A.PON.TA.DOR, *s. m.*, pencil sharpener.
A.PON.TA.MEN.TO, *s. m.*, annotation, note, notice, reference.
A.PON.TAR, *v.*, to indicate, to show, to mark, to label, to mention; to point, to sharpen.
A.PO.PLE.XI.A, *s. f.*, apoplexy.
A.POR, *v.*, to appose, to put together or above, to attach, to append, to affix.
A.POR.TAR, *v.*, to enter a port, to arrive at a port.
A.PÓS, *adv.*, after, thereafter, behind.
A.PO.SEN.TA.DO, *adj.*, *s. m.*, pensioner.
A.PO.SEN.TA.DO.RI.A, *s. f.*, retirement.
A.PO.SEN.TAR-SE, *v.*, to retire, to pension off.
A.PO.SEN.TO, *s. m.*, residence, room, domicile, apartment.
A.POS.SAR-SE, *v.*, to take possession of, to put in possession.
A.POS.TA, *s. f.*, bet, betting, wager.
A.POS.TAR, *v.*, to bet, to make a bet, to risk.
A.POS.TI.LA, *s. f.*, apostil, postil, annotation to a script, comment.
A.POS.TO, *s.m.*, appositive; *adj.*, apposed, appositive.
A.PÓS.TO.LO, *s. m.*, apostle.
A.PÓS.TRO.FE, *s. f.*, apostrophe, interruption.
A.PO.TE.O.SE, *s. f.*, apotheosis, glorification.
A.PRA.ZAR, *v.*, to convene, to summon, to cite, to mark a day.
A.PRA.ZÍ.VEL, *adj.*, pleasant, delightful, diverting, amusing.
A.PRE.ÇAR, *v.*, to price, to determine the price of, to appraise.
A.PRE.CI.A.ÇÃO, *s. f.*, appreciation, rating, valuation, concept, idea.
A.PRE.CI.AR, *v.*, to appreciate, to rate, to compute, to value, to estimate, to judge.
A.PRE.ÇO, *s.m.*, valuation, estimation, deference.
A.PRE.EN.DER, *v.*, to make apprehension of, to apprehend; to confiscate; to understand.
A.PRE.EN.SÃO, *s. f.*, apprehension, act of apprehending, arrest, capture.
A.PRE.GO.AR, *v.*, to announce by a crier, proclaim, to divulge, to puff, to boom.
A.PREN.DER, *v.*, to learn; to study, to come to know.
A.PREN.DIZ, *s. m.*, apprentice, beginner, novice.
A.PREN.DI.ZA.DO, *s. m.*, apprenticeship, apprenticement.
A.PRE.SEN.TA.ÇÃO, *s. f.*, presentation, introduction, personal appearance.
A.PRE.SEN.TAR, *v.*, to present, to introduce, to show, to display, to expose, to exhibit.
A.PRES.SA.DO, *adj.*, hurried, ready, in a hurry; hasty.
A.PRES.SAR, *v.*, to speed up, to accelerate, to hurry, to quicken, to instigate.
A.PRI.MO.RA.DO, *adj.*, refined, excellent, fine.

A.PRI.MO.RAR, *v.*, to perfect, to improve, to ameliorate, to refine.
A.PRI.SI.O.NA.MEN.TO, *s. m.*, imprisonment, capture.
A.PRI.SI.O.NAR, *v.*, to arrest, to capture, to imprison, to lead captive.
A.PRO.FUN.DAR, *v.*, to deepen, to make deeper, to sink down.
A.PRON.TAR, *v.*, to prepare, to get ready, to put in order, to equip.
A.PRO.PRI.A.ÇÃO, *s. f.*, appropriation, assumption, accommodation.
A.PRO.PRI.A.DO, *adj.*, appropriate, proper, adequate, suitable.
A.PRO.PRI.AR, *v.*, to appropriate, to make suitable, to apt, to accommodate.
A.PRO.VA.ÇÃO, *s. f.*, approval, approbation, agreement, consent, assent, praise.
A.PRO.VAR, *v.*, to approve, to approbe, to approbate, to validate, to ratify.
A.PRO.VEI.TA.DOR, *s. m.*, profiteer.
A.PRO.VEI.TA.MEN.TO, *s. m.*, utilization, use, profit.
A.PRO.VEI.TAR, *v.*, to use to advantage, make good use of, to utilize, to use.
A.PRO.VI.SI.O.NAR, *v.*, to provision, to provide with food, supply.
A.PRO.XI.MA.ÇÃO, *s. f.*, approximation, approach.
A.PRO.XI.MAR, *v.*, to approach, to approximate, to bring near, colligate.
A.PRO.XI.MA.TI.VO, *adj.*, approximative.
A.PRU.MAR, *v.*, to erect, to put in an upright position.
AP.TI.DÃO, *s. f.*, aptness, aptitude, ability, capacity, capability.
AP.TO, *adj.*, able, capable, qualified, apt, fit.
A.PU.NHA.LAR, *v.*, to stab, to kill with a dagger.
A.PU.PAR, *v.*, to scoff, to jeer, to boo, to sneer, to hoot.
A.PU.PO, *s. m.*, hoot, jeer, boo.
A.PU.RA.ÇÃO, *s. f.*, examination, verification, purifying, refinement, purification.
A.PU.RAR, *v.*, to perfect, to improve, to clean, to purify, to refine, to select, to choose.
A.PU.RO, *s. m.*, purifying, refinement, purification, precision, accuracy.
A.QUA.RE.LA, *s. f.*, aquarelle, water colour.
A.QUÁ.RIO, *s. m.*, aquarium; Aquarius (astr.)
A.QUÁ.TI.CO, *adj.*, aquatic.
A.QUE.CE.DOR, *s. m.*, warmer, heater, radiator.
A.QUE.CER, *v.*, to heat, to warm, to make hot, to make warm.
A.QUE.CI.MEN.TO, *s. m.*, heating, warming, calefaction.
A.QUE.DU.TO, *s. m.*, aqueduct.
A.QUE.LA, A.QUE.LE, *pron.*, that, that one, the one.
A.QUE.LAS, A.QUE.LES, *pron.*, those.
À.QUE.LE(S), À.QUE.LA(S), *pron.*, to that, to those.
A.QUÉ.M, *adv.*, on this side, inferiorly, below, beneath; less.
A.QUI, *adv.*, here, herein, in this, on this place.
A.QUI.ES.CER, *v.*, to acquiesce, to consent, to permit, to assent.
A.QUI.E.TAR, *v.*, to quiet, to appease, to pacify, to calm.
A.QUI.LA.TAR, *v.*, to appraise, to make an appreciation, to assay.
A.QUI.LO, *pron.*, that.
À.QUI.LO, *pron.*, to that.
A.QUI.NHO.AR, *v.*, to portion, to share out.
A.QUI.SI.ÇÃO, *s. f.*, acquisition, acquirement, acquest; buy.
A.QUI.SI.TI.VO, *adj.*, acquisitive.
AR, *s. m.*, air, atmosphere, breath, breeze, wind, climate, aspect, look.
Á.RA.BE, *adj., s. m.*, Arab, Arabian, Arabic.
A.RA.DO, *s. m.*, plough, plow.
A.RA.GEM, *s. f.*, whiff, breeze, wind.
A.RA.ME, *s. m.*, wire.
A.RA.NHA, *s. f.*, spider.
A.RA.PU.CA, *s. f.*, bird-trap; pitfall, snare, trap.
A.RAR, *v.*, to plow, to till.
A.RA.RA, *s. f.*, macaw.
A.RA.RU.TA, *s. f.*, arrowroot.
A.RAU.CÁ.RIA, *s. f.*, araucaria.

AR.BI.TRA.GEM, *s. f.*, arbitration, arbitrament.
AR.BI.TRAR, *v.*, to arbitrate, to decide, to umpire, to mediate.
AR.BI.TRÁ.RIO, *adj.*, arbitrary, despotic, discretionary.
AR.BÍ.TRIO, *s. m.*, will, discretion, judgement, choice, expedient.
ÁR.BI.TRO, *s. m.*, arbiter, umpire, judge, judger.
AR.BÓ.REO, *adj.*, arboreal, arboreous, treelike.
AR.BO.RI.ZA.ÇÃO,*s.f.*,arborization, forestation.
AR.BO.RI.ZA.DO, *adj.*, arboreous, arbored, forested.
AR.BO.RI.ZAR, *v.*, to forest, to plant with trees.
AR.BUS.TO, *s. m.*, shrub, bush.
AR.CA, *s. f.*, ark, chest, coffer, trunk.
AR.CAI.CO, *adj.*, archaic, disused, obsolete, antique.
AR.CAR, *v.*, to bend, to curve, to arch, to bow; to struggle, to grapple.
AR.CE.BIS.PO, *s. m.*, archbishop.
AR.CHO.TE, *s. m.*, torch, torch-light, flambeau.
AR.CO, *s. m.*, arc, arch, squinch, bow, hoop.
AR.CO-Í.RIS, *s. m.*, rainbow.
AR.DEN.TE, *adj.*, ardent, burning, torrid, flaming, fervent, violent.
AR.DER, *v.*, to burn, to flame, to blaze, to smoulder, to shine, to fire.
AR.DIL, *s. m.*, cunning, slyness, craftiness, trickiness, trick; trap, snare.
AR.DI.LO.SO, *adj.*, cunning, artful, crafty, subtle, crooked.
AR.DOR, *s. m.*, heat, burning, hotness, ardour, passion.
ÁR.DUO, *adj.*, arduous, difficult, laborious, hard.
A.RE, *s. m.*, are, measure of 119,6 square yards.
Á.REA, *s. f.*, area, surface, space, ground, yard.
A.RE.AL, *s. m.*, beach, sand dune.
A.REI.A, *s. f.*, sand, grit, gravel.
A.RE.JAR, *v.*, to air, to expose to the air, to weather, to ventilate.
A.RE.NI.TO, *s. m.*, sandstone, grit.
A.RE.NO.SO, *adj.*, sandy, gravelly, gritty.
A.REN.QUE, *s. m.*, herring.
A.RÉ.O.LA, *s. f.*, areola, areole.
A.RES.TA, *s. f.*, edge, corner, brim, border.
AR.FAR, *v.*, to heave, to gasp, to palpitate.
AR.GA.MAS.SA, *s. f.*, mortar, building cement, daub, pug.
AR.GE.LI.NO, *adj.*, *s. m.*, Argelian.
AR.GÊN.TEO, *adj.*, silvery, argentine.
AR.GEN.TI.NO, *adj.*, *s. m.*, Argentinean.
AR.GI.LA, *s. f.*, argil, clay.
AR.GO.LA, *s. f.*, ring, hoop, link, door knocker.
AR.GÚ.CIA, *s. f.*, astuteness, smartness, captiousness.
AR.GUIR, *v.*, to accuse, to reprove, to reprehend, to condemn, to infer.
AR.GU.MEN.TA.ÇÃO, *s. f.*, argumentation, reasoning, dispute, debate.
AR.GU.MEN.TAR, *v.*, to argue, to dispute, to debate.
AR.GU.MEN.TO, *s. m.*, argument, subject, reason, topic.
Á.RIA, *s. f.*, aria, air, song, tune, melody.
A.RI.DEZ, *s. f.*, aridity, aridness, dryness.
Á.RI.DO,*adj.*,arid,dry, desert, withered, sterile.
A.RIS.TO.CRA.CI.A,*s.f.*,aristocracy, nobility.
A.RIS.TO.CRA.TA, *s. 2 gen.*, aristocrat, noble, patrician.
A.RIT.MÉ.TI.CA, *s. f.*, arithmetic.
AR.LE.QUIM, *s. m.*, harlequin.
AR.MA,*s.f.*,weapon arm, power, might, gun, arm.
AR.MA.ÇÃO, *s. f.*, equipment, tackle, outfit.
AR.MA.DA, *s. f.*, armada, fleet, navy.
AR.MA.DI.LHA, *s. f.*, snare, gin, net, pitfall, trap.
AR.MA.DO, *adj.*, armed, equipped, prepared.
AR.MA.DOR, *s. m.*, shipowner, trapper.
AR.MA.MEN.TO, *s. m.*, armament.
AR.MAR, *v.*, to arm, to put in arms, to supply with armament.
AR.MÁ.RIO, *s. m.*, cupboard, buffet, case, locker.
AR.MA.ZÉM, *s. m.*, store, shop, warehouse charges.
AR.MA.ZE.NAR, *v.*, to store, to lay up, to stock-pile.
AR.MIS.TÍ.CIO, *s. m.*, armistice, truce, suspension of hostilities.

ARO — ARREMESSO

A.RO, *s. m.*, iron or wooden hoop, rim of wheel.
A.RO.MA, *s. f.*, flavour, smell, scent, bouquet.
A.RO.MÁ.TI.CO, *adj.*, aromatical, balsamic, flavoured.
A.RO.MA.TI.ZAR, *v.*, to aromatize, to scent, to flavour.
AR.PÃO, *s. m.*, harpoon, gaff, fish-gig.
AR.PO.A.DOR, *s. m.*, harpooner.
AR.QUE.A.DO, *adj.*, arch-shaped, arched, bent.
AR.QUE.AR, *v.*, to arch, to vault, to bow, to curve, to warp.
AR.QUE.JAR, *v.*, to puff, to blow, to pant.
AR.QUE.O.LO.GI.A, *s. f.*, archaeology.
AR.QUE.Ó.LO.GO, *s. m.*, archaeologist.
AR.QUÉ.TI.PO, *s. m.*, archetype.
AR.QUI.DI.O.CE.SE, *s. f.*, archdiocese.
AR.QUI.PÉ.LA.GO, *s. m.*, archipelago.
AR.QUI.TE.TAR, *v.*, to build, to construct, to project, to plan.
AR.QUI.TE.TO, *s. m.*, architect, master builder.
AR.QUI.TE.TU.RA, *s. f.*, architectonics, architecture.
AR.QUI.VAR, *v.*, to collect documents, to shelve, to file.
AR.QUI.VO, *s. m.*, archive, register, index book.
AR.RAI.A, *s. f.*, ray, skate.
AR.RAI.AL, *s. m.*, camp, camping ground, country, small village.
AR.RAI.GAR, *v.*, to root, to take root, to irradicate, to grow.
AR.RAN.CAR, *v.*, to pull or tear away violently, to pluck out, to force.
AR.RA.NHA-CÉU, *s. m.*, skyscraper.
AR.RA.NHAR, *v.*, to scratch, to graze, to scrabble, to mangle.
AR.RAN.JAR, *v.*, to arrange, to provide for, to set in order, to adjust, to dispose.
AR.RAN.JO, *s. m.*, arrangement, settling, fixing.
AR.RAN.QUE, *s. m.*, push, thrust, sudden start.
AR.RA.SA.DO, *adj.*, levelled, laid even, demolished.
AR.RA.SAR, *v.*, to demolish, to humiliate, to destroy.
AR.RAS.TAR, *v.*, to drag, to pull, to induce into, to draw.
AR.RA.ZO.AR, *v.*, to plead, to defend, to reason, to argue.
AR.RE.AR, *v.*, to harness, to array, to dress, to adorn.
AR.RE.BA.TA.DOR, *s. m.*, ravishing, charming, ravisher.
AR.RE.BA.TA.MEN.TO, *s. m.*, ravishing, ecstasy.
AR.RE.BA.TAR, *v.*, to snatch, to grab, to take by force, to rash, to rap.
AR.RE.BEN.TA.ÇÃO, *s. f.*, the breaking of the waves.
AR.RE.BEN.TAR, *v.*, to bear, to burst, to crush, to break.
AR.RE.BI.TAR, *v.*, to turn up, to raise, to lift, to rivet.
AR.RE.CA.DA.ÇÃO, *s. f.*, magazine, deposit, depository, collection of taxes.
AR.RE.CA.DAR, *v.*, to collect duties or taxes, to deposit, to demand.
AR.RE.DI.O, *adj.*, withdrawn, far off, lonesome, apart.
AR.RE.DON.DAR, *v.*, to make round, to round, to sphere, to circularize.
AR.RE.DOR, *adj.*, adjacent, near; *adv.*, around, about.
AR.RE.DO.RES, *s. m., pl.*, envirões, environment, adjacency.
AR.RE.FE.CER, *v.*, to cool, to chill, to allay, to moderate.
AR.RE.FE.CI.MEN.TO, *s. m.*, cooling.
AR.RE.GA.ÇAR, *v.*, to tuck up, to pin up, to truss.
AR.RE.GA.LAR, *v.*, to open one's eyes wide, to gogle.
AR.RE.GA.NHAR, *v.*, to grin, to laugh, to snarl.
AR.REI.O, *s. m.*, saddlery, harness, gear, array.
AR.RE.MA.TAR, *v.*, to finish up, to give the final touch to, to accomplish.
AR.RE.ME.DAR, *v.*, to imitate, to mimic, to mock.
AR.RE.ME.DO, *s. m.*, imitation, mimicry; mockery.
AR.RE.MES.SAR, *v.*, to fling, to dart, to throw, to hurl, to cast; to jaculate.
AR.RE.MES.SO, *s. m.*, throw, cast, pitch, act or fact of.

AR.RE.ME.TER, *v.*, to assault, to invade, to attack, to rush violently upon.
AR.REN.DA.DO, *adj.*, rented, leased; laced.
AR.REN.DA.MEN.TO, *s. m.*, renting, lease, tenantry.
AR.REN.DAR, *v.*, to rent, to lease, to hire.
AR.REN.DA.TÁ.RIO, *s. m.*, tenant, renter, leaseholder.
AR.RE.PEN.DER-SE, *v.*, to repent, to be sorry for, to regret, to rue.
AR.RE.PEN.DI.DO, *adj.*, regretful, penitent, rueful.
AR.RE.PEN.DI.MEN.TO, *s. m.*, regret, penitence, repentance, rue, compunction.
AR.RE.PI.AR, *v.*, to ruffle, to fluff up, to bristle, to roughen.
AR.RI.AR, *v.*, to break down, to collapse, to flop, to put down.
AR.RI.MAR, *v.*, to support, to lean against, to prop, to rhime.
AR.RI.MO, *s. m.*, support, prop, help, protection.
AR.RO.BA, *s. f.*, arroba, unit of weight (15 kg).
AR.RO.CHAR, *v.*, to tighten, to compress, to cram.
AR.RO.GÂN.CIA, *s. f.*, arrogance, presumption, pride, haughtiness.
AR.RO.GAN.TE, *adj., s. 2 gen.*, arrogant, superior, disdainful, haughty.
AR.ROI.O, *s. m.*, arroyo, rivulet, brook.
AR.RO.JAR, *v.*, to fling, to throw violently, to drag, to reject, to repel.
AR.RO.JO, *s. m.*, boldness, audacity, fearlessness.
AR.RO.LAR, *v.*, to enroll, to inscribe, to list.
AR.RO.LHAR, *v.*, to corck.
AR.ROM.BA.MEN.TO, *s. m.*, breaking in, inbreak.
AR.ROM.BAR, *v.*, to break into, to burst, to force.
AR.RO.TAR, *v.*, to belch, to burp, to boast.
AR.RO.TO, *s. m.*, eructation, belch.
AR.ROZ, *s. m.*, rice.
AR.RO.ZAL, *s. m.*, rice field, rice paddy.
AR.RU.A.ÇA, *s. f.*, uproar, street riot, tumult.
AR.RU.DA, *s. f.*, rue.
AR.RU.E.LA, *s. f.*, washer, roundel.
AR.RU.I.NA.DO, *adj.*, ruined, spoiled, bankrupt.
AR.RU.I.NAR, *v.*, to ruin, to destroy, to devastate, to blight.
AR.RU.MA.ÇÃO, *s. f.*, arrangement, putting in order, placing, disposition, shipment.
AR.RU.MA.DEI.RA, *s. f.*, housemaid, chamber maid.
AR.RU.MAR, *v.*, to arrange, to dispose, to set in order, to settle, to tidy up, to pack.
AR.SE.NAL, *s. m.*, arsenal, repository of provisions.
AR.SÊ.NI.CO, *s. m.*, arsenic.
AR.TE, *s. f.*, art, skill, craft, workmanship, trade, profession.
AR.TE.FA.TO, *s. m.*, workmanship, artifact; petard.
AR.TE.LHO, *s. m.*, ankle, anklebone.
AR.TÉ.RIA, *s. f.*, artery, blood vessel.
AR.TE.SA.NA.TO, *s. m.*, workmanship, handicraft.
AR.TE.SÃO, *s. m.*, artisan, craftsman.
ÁR.TI.CO, *adj.*, arctic.
AR.TI.CU.LA.ÇÃO, *s. f.*, articulation, joint, link.
AR.TI.CU.LAR, *adj.*, articular; *v.*, to articulate, to join by articulation.
AR.TI.CU.LIS.TA, *s. 2 gen.*, newspaper writter.
AR.TI.FI.CI.AL, *adj., s. 2 gen.*, artificial, artful, unnatural.
AR.TI.FÍ.CIO, *s. m.*, artifice, skilful making, work of art.
AR.TI.GO, *s. m.*, article, commodity, product, chapter, clause of a contract.
AR.TI.LHA.RI.A, *s. f.*, artillery, gunnery.
AR.TIS.TA, *s. 2 gen.*, artist, artisan; *adj.*, artistic, cunning.
AR.TRI.TE, *s. f.*, arthritis.
AR.VO.RAR, *v.*, to hoist colours, to raise, to lift the flag, to set up.
ÁR.VO.RE, *s. f.*, arbor, tree, mast.
AR.VO.RE.DO, *s. m.*, grove, stand of tree.
AS, *art. pl.*, the; *pron.*, those, them; the ones.
ÀS, *contr.* of the *art.* **A** with the *prep.* **A**: to the, for the, by the.
ÁS, *s. m.*, ace, star.

A.SA, *s. f.*, wing.
AS.CEN.DER, *v.*, to ascend, to rise, to climb.
AS.CEN.SÃO, *s. f.*, ascension, ascent, rising.
AS.CEN.SO.RIS.TA, *s. 2 gen.*, lift boy, elevator operator.
AS.CO, *s. m.*, loathing, aversion, disgust.
AS.FAL.TAR, *v.*, to cover with asphalt.
AS.FAL.TO, *s. m.*, asphalt.
AS.FI.XI.A, *s. f.*, asphyxia.
AS.FI.XI.AR, *v.*, to asphyxiate, to suffocate.
A.SI.Á.TI.CO, *adj.*, Asiatic.
A.SI.LAR, *v.*, to shelter, to give shelter, to refuge.
A.SI.LO, *s. m.*, asylum, refuge, place of refuge.
AS.MA, *s. f.*, asthma.
AS.NA.DA, *s. f.*, a drove of asses or donkeys.
AS.NEI.RA, *s. f.*, foolishness, stupidity, folly.
AS.NO, *s. m.*, ass, donkey; stupid, ignorant person.
AS.PAR.GO, *s. m.*, asparagus.
AS.PEC.TO, *s. m.*, aspect, look, appearance, form, shape, feature.
AS.PE.RE.ZA, *s. f.*, asperity, roughness, rudeness.
ÁS.PE.RO, *adj.*, rough, coarse, rude, crude, rugged.
AS.PI.RA.ÇÃO, *s. f.*, breathing, aspiration, longing.
AS.PI.RA.DOR, *s. m.*, aspirator, exhaustor.
AS.PI.RAR, *v.*, to aspirate, to breathe in, to inhale.
AS.PI.RI.NA, *s. f.*, aspirin.
AS.QUE.RO.SO, *adj.*, loathsome, nasty, nauseous, detestable.
AS.SA.DEI.RA, *s. f.*, roasting or baking pan.
AS.SA.DO, *s. m.*, roast; *adj.*, roasted, baked.
AS.SA.LA.RI.A.DO, *s. m.*, employee; *adj.*, employed.
AS.SA.LA.RI.AR, *v.*, to engage, to employ, to take in pay, to subsidize.
AS.SAL.TAN.TE, *s. 2 gen.*, assailant, burglar, waylayer.
AS.SAL.TAR, *v.*, to assault, to attach, to charge, to storm.
AS.SAL.TO, *s. m.*, assault, attack, onset.
AS.SA.NHA.DO, *adj.*, excited, furious, restless, erotic.
AS.SA.NHA.MEN.TO, *s. m.*, excitement, anger.
AS.SA.NHAR, *v.*, to provoke, to excite, to anger.

AS.SAR, *v.*, to roast, to bake, to grill.
AS.SAS.SI.NAR, *v.*, to murder, to assassinate, to kill.
AS.SAS.SI.NA.TO, *s. m.*, assassination, murder, homicide.
AS.SAS.SI.NO, *s. m.*, murderer, killer, assassin.
AS.SE.DI.AR, *v.*, to besiege, to importune, to molest, to annoy.
AS.SÉ.DIO, *s. m.*, siege, insistence, importuneness, molestation.
AS.SE.GU.RA.DO, *adj.*, insured, assured.
AS.SE.GU.RAR, *v.*, to assert, to affirm, to guarantee, to assure, to secure.
AS.SEI.O, *s. m.*, cleanliness, neatness, decency.
AS.SEM.BLEI.A, *s. f.*, assembly, meeting, gathering, congregation.
AS.SE.ME.LHAR, *v.*, to assimilate, to liken to.
AS.SEN.TA.DO, *adj.*, seated, steady, firm.
AS.SEN.TA.MEN.TO, *s. m.*, seating, sitting down, putting into place.
AS.SEN.TAR, *v.*, to seat, to place, to base, to lay, to settle, to fix.
AS.SEN.TI.MEN.TO, *s. m.*, assent, consent, permission.
AS.SEN.TIR, *v.*, to assent, to agree, to consent.
AS.SEN.TO, *s. m.*, seat, place to sit, chair, base, fundaments.
AS.SES.SOR, *s. m.*, assessor, adviser, counsellor.
AS.SES.SO.RA.MEN.TO, *s. m.*, assistance, advise.
AS.SES.SO.RAR, *v.*, to advise, to assist.
AS.SÍ.DUO, *adj.*, assiduous, sedulous, diligent.
AS.SIM, *adv.*, thus, so, in this manner, like this, such.
AS.SI.MI.LA.ÇÃO, *s. f.*, assimilation, absorption.
AS.SI.MI.LAR, *v.*, to assimilate, absorb.
AS.SI.NA.DO, *adj.*, signed, subscribed.
AS.SI.NA.LAR, *v.*, to mark, to provide with a mark, to distinguish.
AS.SI.NAN.TE, *s. 2 gen.*, subscriber, signatory.
AS.SI.NAR, *v.*, to sign, to underwrite, to subscribe, note.
AS.SI.NA.TU.RA, *s. f.*, signature, subscription.
AS.SIS.TÊN.CIA, *s. f.*, presence, attendance,

ASSISTENTE / ATERRORIZADOR

audience, auditory, assistance, aid.
AS.SIS.TEN.TE, *s. 2 gen.*, assistant, helper, right hand.
AS.SIS.TIR, *v.*, to attend, to be present at, to assist, to aid.
AS.SO.A.LHAR, *v.*, to lay a wood floor.
AS.SO.A.LHO, *s. m.*, floor.
AS.SO.AR, *v.*, to wipe or blow one's nose.
AS.SO.BI.AR, *v.*, to whistle, to hiss, to hoot.
AS.SO.BI.O, *s. m.*, whistle, hiss.
AS.SO.CI.A.ÇÃO, *s. f.*, association, community, society, partnership.
AS.SO.CI.A.DO, *s. m.*, associate, partner; *adj.*, associated.
AS.SO.CI.AR-SE, *v.*, to associate with, to join, to unit.
AS.SO.LAR, *v.*, to desolate, to devastate, to destroy, to ravage.
AS.SOM.BRA.ÇÃO, *s. f.*, apparition, ghost, spook, terror.
AS.SOM.BRAR, *v.*, to shade, to shadow, to darken, to terrify, to astonish.
AS.SOM.BRO, *s. m.*, surprise, admiration, astonishment, wonder.
AS.SU.MIR, *v.*, to assume, to take over, to shoulder.
AS.SUN.TO, *s. m.*, subject, topic, theme, affair, matter, proposition.
AS.SUS.TA.DO, *adj.*, frightened, afraid, timid, timorous.
AS.SUS.TAR, *v.*, to frighten, to startle, to alarm, to terrify.
AS.TE.CA, *s. 2 gen.*, Aztec; *adj.*, Aztec, Aztecan.
AS.TE.RIS.CO, *s. m.*, asterisk, star.
AS.TE.ROI.DE, *s. m.*, asteroid.
AS.TIG.MA.TIS.MO, *s. m.*, astigmatism.
AS.TRO, *s. m.*, star.
AS.TRO.LO.GI.A, *s. f.*, astrology.
AS.TRÓ.LO.GO, *s. m.*, astrologer.
AS.TRO.NAU.TA, *s. 2 gen.*, astronaut.
AS.TRO.NO.MI.A, *s. f.*, astronomy.
AS.TRÔ.NO.MO, *s. m.*, astronomer.
AS.TÚ.CIA, *s. f.*, astuteness, sagacity, smartness.
AS.TU.TO, *adj.*, astute, smart, clever.

A.TA, *s. f.*, record, register, writing.
A.TA.CA.DIS.TA, *s. 2 gen.*, wholesaler.
A.TA.CA.DO, *adj.*, attacked, laced, tied; *s. m.*, wholesale business.
A.TA.CAN.TE, *s. 2 gen.*, agressor, assailant; lineman.
A.TA.CAR, *v.*, to attack, to assault, to seize, to strike.
A.TA.DO, *adj.*, tied, bound, hampered, timid.
A.TA.DU.RA, *s. f.*, tie, band, ligature, string.
A.TA.LAI.A, *s. f.*, sentinel, watchtower.
A.TA.LHO, *s. m.*, bypath, sideway, bypass, crosscut.
A.TA.PE.TAR, *v.*, to carpet.
A.TA.QUE, *s. m.*, attack, assault, onset, fit, agression.
A.TAR, *v.*, to tie, to fasten, to lace, to bind, to dress.
A.TA.RE.FA.DO, *adj.*, busy, occupied, engaged.
A.TA.Ú.DE, *s. m.*, coffin, bier, tomb, casket.
A.TA.VI.AR, *v.*, to trim, to array, to embellish.
A.TA.VIS.MO, *s. m.*, atavism.
A.TÉ, *prep.*, till, untill, by, up to, up till.
A.TE.ÍS.MO, *s. m.*, atheism.
A.TE.MO.RI.ZAR, *v.*, to intimidate, to scare, to daunt, to terrify.
A.TEN.ÇÃO, *s. f.*, attention, concentration, carefulness, vigilance.
A.TEN.CI.O.SO, *adj.*, attentive, respectful, considerate, polite, gallant.
A.TEN.DER, *v.*, to attend, to consider, to mind, to pay attention, to listen.
A.TEN.TAR, *v.*, to attempt.
A.TEN.TO, *adj.*, alert, careful, observant.
A.TE.NU.A.ÇÃO, *s. f.*, attenuation, diminishing.
A.TE.NU.AN.TE, *s. f.*, attenuating.
A.TE.NU.AR, *v.*, to attenuate, to extenuate, to lessen, to diminish.
A.TER.RAR, *v.*, to frighten, to terrify; fill or cover with earth; to land.
A.TER.RIS.SA.GEM, *s. f.*, landing.
A.TER.RIS.SAR, *v.*, to land.
A.TER.RO, *s. m.*, embankment, place filled up with earth.
A.TER.RO.RI.ZA.DOR, *s. m.*, frightful, terrifying.

ATERRORIZAR / **ATUALIZAR**

A.TER.RO.RI.ZAR, *v.*, to terrify, to horrify, to frighten, to dismay.
A.TER-SE, *v.*, to lain against, to rely on, to stick to.
A.TES.TA.DO, *s. m.*, certificate, certification, credential.
A.TES.TAR, *v.*, to attest, to vouch, to witness, to certify.
A.TI.ÇAR, *v.*, to poke, to instigate, to incite.
A.TI.NEN.TE, *adj.*, referent, relative.
A.TIN.GIR, *v.*, to reach, to attain, to arrive at, to touch.
A.TI.RA.DOR, *s. m.*, shooter, rifleman, marksman, soldier.
A.TI.RAR, *v.*, to shoot, to fire, to rifle, to discharge.
A.TI.TU.DE, *s. f.*, attitude, posture, pose, mood, position.
A.TI.VAR, *v.*, to activate, to actuate, to push, to bring into action.
A.TI.VI.DA.DE, *s. f.*, activity, energy, stir, bustle, function.
A.TI.VO, *adj.*, active, busy, brisk, dynamic, alert.
A.TLÂN.TI.CO, *s. m.*, Atlantic Ocean; *adj.*, Atlantic.
A.TLAS, *s. m.*, atlas.
A.TLE.TA, *s. 2 gen.*, athlete.
AT.MOS.FE.RA, *s. f.*, atmosphere.
A.TO, *s. m.*, act, performing, function, doing, action, deed.
A.TO.LA.DO, *adj.*, mired.
A.TO.LAR, *v.*, to stick in the dirt, to mud, to mir; to bog, to stall.
A.TÔ.MI.CO, *adj.*, atomic.
Á.TO.MO, *s. m.*, atom, corpuscle.
A.TÔ.NI.TO, *adj.*, astonished, stupefied, aghast, perplexed.
A.TOR, *s. m.*, actor, artist, player; star.
A.TOR.DO.AR, *v.*, to stun, to stupefy, to consternate, to puzzle.
A.TOR.MEN.TA.DO, *adj.*, tormented.
A.TOR.MEN.TAR, *v.*, to torment, to torture, to afflict, to trouble.
A.TRA.ÇÃO, *s. f.*, attraction, interest, affinity.
A.TRAI.ÇO.AR, *v.*, to betray, to deceive, to delude, to play foul.
A.TRA.IR, *v.*, to attract, to captivate, to magnetize, to draw.
A.TRA.PA.LHAR, *v.*, to confuse, to disturb, to upset, to perturb, to muddle.
A.TRÁS, *adv.*, behind, back, after, before, ago.
A.TRA.SA.DO, *adj.*, backward, retrograde, tardy, behind, late, slow.
A.TRA.SAR, *v.*, to set back, to delay, to retard, to defer, to postpone, to put off.
A.TRA.SO, *s. m.*, delay, retardation, tardiness, lateness, latecoming.
A.TRA.VAN.CAR, *v.*, to clutter, to encumber, to embarrass, to obstruct.
A.TRA.VÉS, *adv.*, through, over, cross, across, athwart.
A.TRA.VES.SA.DO, *adj.*, crossed, laid across, athwart, oblique.
A.TRA.VES.SAR, *v.*, to cross, to pass over, to traverse, to overpass, to transit.
A.TRE.VER-SE, *v.*, to dare, to adventure, to venture, to brave.
A.TRE.VI.DO, *adj.*, daring, bold, insolent, cheeky.
A.TRE.VI.MEN.TO, *s. m.*, dare, daring, daringness, boldness, impudence.
A.TRI.BU.I.ÇÃO, *s. f.*, attribution, duty, power, prerogative.
A.TRI.BU.IR, *v.*, to attribute, to impute to, to assign to.
A.TRI.BU.LAR, *v.*, to afflict, to trouble, to vex.
A.TRI.BU.TO, *s. m.*, attribute, predicate, quality.
A.TRI.TO, *s. m.*, attrition, friction, rubbing, dissension.
A.TRIZ, *s. f.*, actress, star.
A.TRO.CI.DA.DE, *s. f.*, atrocity, cruelty, inhumanity.
A.TRO.FI.A, *s. f.*, atrophy.
A.TRO.FI.AR, *v.*, to atrophy.
A.TU.A.ÇÃO, *s. f.*, actuation, performance.
A.TU.AL, *adj.*, actual, present, current, real, absolute.
A.TU.A.LI.DA.DE, *s. f.*, the present, the present time, opportunity.
A.TU.A.LI.ZA.ÇÃO, *s. f.*, modernization.
A.TU.A.LI.ZAR, *v.*, to modernize.

A.TU.AR, *v.*, to actuate, bring into action, put into action, to operate.
A.TU.RAR, *v.*, to support, to suffer, to endure, to tolerate, to bear.
A.TUR.DI.DO, *adj.*, dizzy, stunned, perturbed.
A.TUR.DIR, *v.*, to stun, to din, to daze, to bewilder, to surprise.
AU.DÁ.CIA, *s. f.*, audacity, audaciousness, daring, presumption.
AU.DI.ÇÃO, *s. f.*, audition, reception, hearing.
AU.DI.ÊN.CIA, *s.f.*, audience, audition, assembly.
AU.DI.TI.VO, *adj.*, auditive.
AU.DI.TOR, *s. m.*, auditor.
AU.DI.TÓ.RIO, *s. m.*, audience, listeners, attendance.
AU.FE.RIR, *v.*, to gain, to profit, to make profit, to obtain.
AU.GE, *s. m.*, summit, height, the highest point, culmination, top, zenith.
AU.GU.RAR, *v.*, to augur, to predict, to forebode, to portend.
AU.GÚ.RIO, *s. m.*, augury, foretoken, presage.
AU.LA, *s. f.*, class, lesson.
AU.MEN.TAR, *v.*, to augment, to enlarge, to amplify, to increase, to grow, to develop.
AU.MEN.TO, *s. m.*, augmentation, enlarging, enlargement, amplification, development.
ÁU.REO, *adj.*, aureate, golden, brilliant.
AU.RÉ.O.LA, *s. f.*, aureole, nimbus, glory.
AU.RO.RA, *s. f.*, aurora, dawn, daybreak, begin.
AU.SÊN.CIA, *s. f.*, absence, nonappearance, privation.
AU.SEN.TAR-SE, *v.*, to go away, to depart.
AU.SEN.TE, *adj.*, absent, away.
AUS.TE.RI.DA.DE, *s. f.*, austerity, severity, rigour.
AUS.TE.RO, *adj.*, austere, severe, rigorous, rigid, strict, grave.
AUS.TRÍ.A.CO, *adj., s. m.*, Austrian.
AU.TAR.QUI.A, *s. f.*, autarchy.
AU.TEN.TI.CA.ÇÃO, *s. f.*, authentication.
AU.TEN.TI.CAR, *v.*, to make authentic, authenticate.
AU.TEN.TI.CI.DA.DE, *s. f.*, authenticity, legality.
AU.TÊN.TI.CO, *adj.*, authentic, legitimate.
AU.TO.BI.O.GRA.FI.A, *s. f.*, autobiography.
AU.TO.DI.DA.TA, *s. 2 gen.*, self-taught person.
AU.TO.DO.MÍ.NIO, *s. m.*, self-control.
AU.TO.ES.TRA.DA, *s. f.*, arterial road, auto highway.
AU.TO.GRA.FAR, *v.*, to autograph.
AU.TÓ.GRA.FO, *s. m.*, autograph.
AU.TO.MA.ÇÃO, *s. f.*, automation.
AU.TO.MA.TI.ZAR, *v.*, to automatize.
AU.TÔ.MA.TO, *s. m.*, automaton, robot.
AU.TO.MO.BI.LIS.MO, *s. m.*, automobilism.
AU.TO.MÓ.VEL, *s. m.*, automobile, motor-car, car.
AU.TO.NO.MI.A, *s. f.*, autonomy, self-government.
AU.TÔ.NO.MO, *adj.*, autonomous, independent.
AU.TÓP.SIA, *s. f.*, autopsy.
AU.TOR, *s. m.*, author, writer, composer, creator, maker.
AU.TO.RA, *s. f.*, authoress.
AU.TO.RI.A, *s. f.*, authorship, paternity.
AU.TO.RI.DA.DE, *s. f.*, authority, jurisdiction, influence.
AU.TO.RI.TÁ.RIO, *adj.*, despotic, authoritarian.
AU.TO.RI.ZA.ÇÃO, *s. f.*, authorization, permission, permit.
AU.TO.RI.ZAR, *v.*, to authorize, to permit, to allow, to sanction, to approve.
AU.TOS.SU.FI.CI.EN.TE, *adj., s. 2 gen.*, self-sufficient.
AU.XI.LI.A.DOR, *s. f.*, helper, auxiliary, assistant, supporter.
AU.XI.LI.AR, *s. 2 gen.*, assistant, adjudant; *adj.*, auxiliary, helpful; *v.*, to help, to aid, to assist.
AU.XÍ.LIO, *s. m.*, help, aid, succour, assistance, backing.
A.VA.CA.LHAR, *v.*, to demoralize, to depress, to lower.
A.VA.LAN.CHE, *s. f.*, avalanche.
A.VA.LI.A.ÇÃO, *s. f.*, valuation, estimate, estimation, appraisement.
A.VA.LI.AR, *v.*, to evaluate, to appraise, to prize, to value, to estimate.

A.VA.LIS.TA, *s. 2 gen.*, bondsman.
A.VA.LI.ZAR, *v.*, to guarantee.
A.VAN.ÇAR, *v.*, to attach, to go, to bring forward, to make go on, go, advance.
A.VAN.ÇO, *s. m.*, advance, advancement, progress, progression, improvement.
A.VAN.TA.JAR, *v.*, to ameliorate, to make better, improve, to be superior.
A.VAN.TE, *adv.*, forward, onward, forth, along.
A.VA.REN.TO, *s. m.*, miser, niggard, money-grubber, penny pincher.
A.VA.RE.ZA, *s. f.*, miserliness, avarice, avidity.
A.VE, *s. f.*, bird, fowl.
A.VEI.A, *s. f.*, oat, oats, oatmeal.
A.VE.LÃ, *s. f.*, hazelnut.
A.VE-MA.RI.A, *s. f.*, Ave Mary, Hail Mary.
A.VE.NI.DA, *s. f.*, avenue, alley, parkway.
A.VEN.TAL, *s. m.*, apron, pinafore.
A.VEN.TU.RA, *s. f.*, adventure, venture, hazard, risk.
A.VEN.TU.REI.RO, *s. m.*, adventurer, venturer; *adj.*, venturesome, venturous.
A.VER.BAR, *v.*, to protocol, to annotate, to note, to register, to legalize.
A.VE.RI.GUA.ÇÃO, *s. f.*, inquiry, investigation, finding.
A.VE.RI.GUAR, *v.*, to inquire, to investigate, to verify, to indagate.
A.VER:ME.LHAR, *v.*, to redden, to make red.
A.VER.SÃO, *s. f.*, aversion, averseness, dislike.
A.VES.SO, *s. m.*, contrary, reverse, back, opposite.
A.VES.TRUZ, *s. m.*, ostrich, emu.
A.VI.A.ÇÃO, *s. f.*, aviation, flying.
A.VI.A.DOR, *s. m.*, aviator, flyer, aeronaut.
A.VI.ÃO, *s. f.*, aeroplane, airplane, plane, flying machine.
A.VI.AR, *v.*, to dispatch, to expedit, to ship, to put on the way.
A.VI.CUL.TOR, *s. m.*, aviculturist, breeder.
A.VI.CUL.TU.RA, *s.f.*, aviculture, poultry raising.

A.VI.DEZ, *s. f.*, avidity, greediness, impatience, rapacity.
Á.VI.DO, *adj.*, eager, grasping, greedy, covetous.
A.VIL.TA.MEN.TO, *s. m.*, abasement, abjection, disgrace, dishonour.
A.VIL.TAR, *v.*, to abase, to debase, to disgrace, to vilify, to depress.
A.VI.SAR, *v.*, to advise, to give notice, to inform, to notify.
A.VI.SO, *s. m.*, notice, advice, communication, warning.
A.VIS.TAR, *v.*, to see from a distance, to discover, to espy.
A.VI.VAR, *v.*, to give life to, to revive, to vivify, to awake.
A.VI.ZI.NHAR, *v.*, to approach, to approximate, to bring near, to put near of.
A.VÔ, *s. f.*, grandfather.
A.VÓ, *s. f.*, grandmother.
A.VO.A.DO, *adj.*, dizzy, giddy, senseless.
A.VO.LU.MAR, *v.*, to augment, to increase the volume of, enlarge.
A.VÓS, *s. m., pl.*, grandparents, forefathers.
A.VUL.SO, *adj.*, detached, pulled out, torn off, single.
A.XI.LA, *s. f.*, axilla, armpit.
A.XI.O.MA, *s. m.* axiom.
A.ZÁ.FA.MA, *s. f.*, great haste, hurry, flurry.
A.ZÁ.LEA, *s. f.*, azalea.
A.ZAR, *s. m.*, misfortune, bad luck, mishap.
A.ZE.DAR, *v.*, to acidify, to sour, to make sour.
A.ZE.DU.ME, *s. m.*, sourness, tartness, acidity.
A.ZEI.TE, *s. m.*, olive-oil.
A.ZEI.TO.NA, *s. f.*, olive; fruit of the olive tree.
A.ZI.A, *s. f.*, pyrosis, heartburn.
A.ZO, *s. m.*, occasion, opportunity.
A.ZUL, *adj.*, blue; *s. m.*, the firmament, the sky.
A.ZU.LAR, *v.*, to blue, to make blue.
A.ZU.LE.JO, *s. m.*, wall tile, glazed tile.
A.ZUR.RAR, *v.*, to bray.

B

B, *s. m.*, second letter of the Portuguese alphabet.
BA.BA, *s. f.*, saliva, slaver, bib, spit.
BA.BÁ, *s. f.*, wet nurse, nanny.
BA.BA.ÇU, *s. m.*, babassu, palm, oil palm.
BA.BA.DOR, *s. m.*, bib, dribble, slobbering.
BA.BAR, *v.*, to bib.
BA.BO.SEI.RA, BA.BO.SI.CE, *s. f.*, folly, nonsense, blunder.
BA.BU.Í.NO, *s. m.*, baboon.
BA.CA.LHAU, *s. m.*, cod, codfish.
BA.CA.NA, *adj.*, good, splendid, excellent.
BA.CHA.REL, *s. m.*, bachelor.
BA.CI.A, *s. f.*, basin, wash-basin, lavabo, tray, pot.
BA.CI.LLO, *s. m.*, bacillus, bacterium, bacteria.
BA.ÇO, *s. m.*, spleen, milt.
BÁ.CO.RO, *s. m.*, piglet, pigling, piggy.
BAC.TÉ.RIA, *s. f.*, bacterium, bacillus.
BAC.TE.RI.CI.DA, *s. m.*, bactericide.
BAC.TE.RI.O.LO.GI.A, *s. f.*, bacteriology.
BA.DA.LA.DA, *s. f.*, clang of a bell, toll.
BA.DA.LAR, *v.*, to ring, to toll, to tinkle.
BA.DER.NA, *s. f.*, frolics, riot, conflict, rumpus.
BA.FA.FÁ, *s. m.*, quarrel, strife, bustle, altercation.
BA.FE.JAR, *v.*, to warm (by breathing on), to favour, to protect.
BA.FE.JO, *s. m.*, puff of wind, breath, whiff, air.
BA.FO, *s. m.*, breath, exhalation, respiration.
BA.FO.RAR, *v.*, exhale, blow, to expel.
BA.GA, *s. f.*, berry or berrylike of fruit, drop.
BA.GA.ÇO, *s. m.*, bagasse.
BA.GA.GEI.RO, *s. m.*, loader, carrying luggage.
BA.GA.GEM, *s. f.*, baggage, lug, luggage, equipage, outfit.
BA.GA.TE.LA, *s. f.*, bagatelle, trifle, fleabite, straw.
BA.GO, *s. m.*, each fruit of a bunch of grapes or any grapelike fruit, berry, acinus.
BA.GUN.ÇA, *s. f.*, tumult, disorder, confusion, mess.
BAI.A, *s. f.*, stall, box, bail.
BA.Í.A, *s. f.*, bay.
BAI.LA.DO, *s. m.*, ballet, choreography.
BAI.LAR, *v.*, to dance, to perform a ballet.
BAI.LA.RI.NO, *s. m.*, ballet dancer, dance artist.
BAI.LE, *s. m.*, dance, ball function.
BAI.O.NE.TA, *s. f.*, bayonet.
BAIR.RIS.MO, *s. m.*, regionalism, localism, local patriotism.
BAIR.RO, *s. m.*, district, ward, precinct, quarter, region.
BAI.XA, *s. f.*, reduction, depression, hollow, decrease, decadence, decay.
BAI.XA.DA, *s. f.*, slope, declivity, depression, lowlands.
BAI.XAR, *v.*, to lower, to let down, to shorten, to incline, to stoop.
BAI.XE.LA, *s. f.*, tableware, tableset.
BAI.XE.ZA, *s. f.*, lowness, inferiority, indignity.
BAI.XO, *s. m.*, lower part, depression, hollow; *adj.*, low, shallow, shoal, inferior.
BAI.XO.TE, *s. m.*, basset; *adj.*, somewhat low or short.
BA.JU.LA.ÇÃO, *s. f.*, flattery, fawning, adulation, cajoling.
BA.JU.LAR, *v.*, to flatter, to adulate, to fawn upon, cringe.
BA.LA, *s. f.*, bullet, missile, shot, ball, projectile; bonbon, sweet, candy.
BA.LAI.O, *s. m.*, hamper, basket made of straw.
BA.LAN.ÇA, *s. f.*, balance, scales, pair of scales, weighing-machine, ponderation.
BA.LAN.ÇAR, *v.*, to balance, to counter-balance, equilibrate, to swing, to oscillate.
BA.LAN.CE.A.MEN.TO, *s. m.*, swinging, oscillation, rocking.
BA.LAN.CE.TE, *s. m.*, trial, intermediate balance,

BA.LAN.ÇO, *s. m.*, swinging, swing, sway, balance sheet, oscillation.
BA.LÃO, *s. m.*, balloon, aerostat.
BA.LA.ÚS.TRE, *s. m.*, baluster, rail post.
BAL.BU.CI.A.ÇÃO, *s. f.*, stuttering, stammering, babbling.
BAL.BU.CI.AR, *v.*, to stutter, to stammer, to babble.
BAL.BÚR.DIA, *s. f.*, confusion, disorder, tumult, messiness.
BAL.CÃO, *s. m.*, balcony, projecting terrace; counter, show counter.
BAL.CO.NIS.TA, *s. 2 gen.*, shop assistant, salesman, shopman.
BAL.DE, *s. m.*, bucket, pail, scuttle.
BAL.DE.A.ÇÃO, *s. f.*, transfusion, decantation, transshipment, connection.
BAL.DE.AR, *v.*, to transfer, to change, to connect, to transship.
BAL.DI.O, *adj.*, unused, uncultivated, fallow.
BA.LE.AR, *v.*, to wound with a shot.
BA.LEI.A, *s. f.*, whale.
BA.LE.LA, *s. f.*, false report, lie, rumour.
BA.LÍS.TI.CA, *s. f.*, ballistics.
BA.LI.ZA, *s. f.*, mark, landmark, sign, boundary, limit.
BAL.NE.Á.RIO, *s. m.*, health-resort, spa, watering-place; *adj.*, balneary.
BA.LOU.ÇAR, *v.*, to balance, to swing, to pendulate, to oscillate.
BAL.SA, *s. f.*, husks of grapes, raft, ferryboat.
BÁL.SA.MO, *s. m.*, balm, balsam.
BA.LU.AR.TE, *s. m.*, fortress, stronghold, bulwark, fortification.
BAM.BO.LEI.O, *s. m.*, swinging, oscillation.
BAMBU, *s. m.*, bamboo.
BAM.BU.ZAL, *s. m.*, bamboo ticket, bamboo plantation.
BA.NAL, *adj.*, common, trivial, vulgar.
BA.NA.LI.ZAR, *v.*, to vulgarize, to make common.
BA.NA.NA, *s. f.*, banana.
BA.NA.NEI.RA, *s. f.*, banana plant.
BAN.CA, *s. f.*, table, stall, writing-table, desk, bureau, business office, lawyer's office.
BAN.CAR, *v.*, to keep the bank, to finance, to pay, to dissimulate.
BAN.CÁ.RIO, *s. m.*, employee of a bank, bank clerk; *adj.*, of or concerning bank.
BAN.CAR.RO.TA, *s. f.*, bankruptcy, insolvency, suspension of payments.
BAN.CO, *s. m.*, seat, pew, bench, footstool, stool, bank.
BAN.DA, *s. f.*, side, flank, shore, band, strip.
BAN.DA.GEM, *s. f.*, dressing, bandaging, compress.
BAN.DA.LHEI.RA, *s. f.*, mean action, ridiculous, shabby trick.
BAN.DEI.RA, *s. f.*, flag, banner, colours, ensign.
BAN.DEI.RO.LA, *s. f.*, banderol, streamer, signal-flag.
BAN.DE.JA, *s. f.*, tray, salver, board.
BAN.DI.DO, *s. m.*, bandit, outlaw, gangster, brigand.
BAN.DO, *s. m.*, gang, group, band, faction, multitude.
BAN.GA.LÔ, *s. m.*, bungalow.
BAN.GUE.LA, *s. f.*, toothless.
BA.NHA, *s. f.*, fat, grease, lard, drippings.
BA.NHA.DO, *s. m.*, marsh, swamp, bog.
BA.NHAR, *v.*, to bathe, to bath, to wash, to take a bath, to inundate, to flood.
BA.NHEI.RA, *s. f.*, bathtub, bath.
BA.NHEI.RO, *s. m.*, bathroom, closet, toilet.
BA.NHO, *s. m.*, bathing, bath, bathroom, wash.
BA.NHO-MA.RI.A, *s. m.*, water-bath.
BA.NIR, *v.*, to banish, to expatriate, to exile, to outlaw.
BAN.QUEI.RO, *s. m.*, banker, dealer, croupier, capitalist.
BAN.QUE.TA, *s. f.*, stool, footstool.
BAN.QUE.TE, *s. m.*, banquet.
BA.QUE, *s. m.*, collision, thud, collapse, fall.
BAR, *s. m.*, bar, pub, saloon, beershop.
BA.RA.LHO, *s. m.*, cards, pack of playing cards.
BA.RÃO, *s. m.*, baron.
BA.RA.TA, *s. f.*, cockroach.

BA.RA.TE.AR, *v.*, to sell at a low price, to undervalue.
BAR.BA, *s. f.*, beard.
BAR.BA.DO, *adj.*, bearded, barbed.
BAR.BAN.TE, *s. m.*, thread, twine, string.
BAR.BA.RI.DA.DE, *s. f.*, barbarity, cruelty, inhumanity.
BAR.BA.RIS.MO, *s. m.*, barbarism.
BÁR.BA.RO, *s. m.*, barbarian; *adj.*, barbarous, uncivilized.
BAR.BE.A.DOR, *s. m.*, shaver.
BAR.BE.AR, *v.*, to shave.
BAR.BE.A.RIA, *s. f.*, barbershop.
BAR.BEI.RO, *s. m.*, shaver, barber.
BAR.BU.DO, *adj.*, bearded.
BAR.CA, *s. f.*, flatboat, barge.
BAR.CO, *s. m.*, boat, bark, ship.
BAR.GA.NHA, *s. f.*, barter, exchange; swindle.
BA.RÔ.ME.TRO, *s. m.*, barometer.
BA.RO.NE.SA, *s. f.*, baroness.
BAR.QUEI.RO, *s. m.*, boatman, ferryman.
BAR.RA, *s. f.*, hem, border, fringe, bar; tablet.
BAR.RA.CA, *s. f.*, tent, barrack, hut.
BAR.RA.CO, *s. m.*, cottage, hut.
BAR.RA.GEM, *s. f.*, barrage, crawl, barrier, dam.
BAR.RAN.CO, *s. m.*, rut, groove, bank, ravine, gorge, precipice.
BAR.RAR, *v.*, to clay, to hem, to hinder, to plug, to obstruct.
BAR.REI.RA, *s. f.*, barricade, barrier, palisade, limit, block, obstacle.
BAR.RI.CA, *s. f.*, barrel, keg, cask, tub.
BAR.RI.GA, *s. f.*, belly, tummy, paunch, abdominal cavity.
BAR.RI.GU.DO, *adj.*, pot bellied, paunchy, obese.
BAR.RIL, *s. m.*, cask, barrel, wooden keg, coop.
BAR.RO, *s. m.*, clay, mud, kaolin, loam.
BAR.RO.SO, *adj.*, clayish, loamy.
BA.RU.LHEI.RA, *s. f.*, uproar, racket, clamour, noise.
BA.RU.LHEN.TO, *adj.*, loud, noisy, uproarious, turbulent, tumultuous.
BA.RU.LHO, *s. m.*, noise, uproar, clamour, tumult, confusion.
BAS.BA.QUE, *adj.*, foolish, stupid, jacknapes.
BA.SE, *s. f.*, base, basis, grounds, support, bottom.
BA.SE.AR, *v.*, to base, to form, to serve as a base, found, establish.
BÁ.SI.CO, *adj.*, basic, essential, fundamental.
BAS.QUE.TE.BOL (BASQUETE), *s. m.*, basketball.
BAS.TAN.TE, *adj.*, enough, sufficient; *adv.*, satisfactory, sufficiently.
BAS.TAR, *v.*, to be enough, to be sufficient, to suffice, to satisfy.
BAS.TAR.DO, *adj., s. m.*, bastard.
BAS.TI.DOR, *s. m.*, embroidery frame, tambour frame.
BA.TA.LHA, *s. f.*, battle, combat, action, engagement, conflict, fight.
BA.TA.LHAR, *v.*, to combat, to contend, to fight.
BA.TA.TA, *s. f.*, potato; **BATATA-DOCE**, sweet-potato.
BA.TA.VO, *adj., s. m.*, Dutchman, Batavian.
BA.TE-BO.CA, *s. m.*, quarrel, discussion, bawling.
BA.TE.DEI.RA, *s. f.*, food-mixer, churn, butter vat.
BA.TEL, *s. m.*, small bark, canoe.
BA.TEN.TE, *s. m.*, rabbet, hard work, door-post, door-knocker.
BA.TE-PA.PO, *s. m.*, chat; conversation.
BA.TER, *v.*, to hit, to hang, to beat, to mix, to knock about, to fight, to strike, to collide.
BA.TI.DA, *s. f.*, beat, stroke, police raid, tap.
BA.TIS.MO, *s. m.*, baptism.
BA.TI.ZA.DO, *s. m.*, baptism; *adj.*, baptized.
BA.TI.ZAR, *v.*, baptize, christen.
BA.TOM, *s. m.*, lipstick.
BA.TU.CAR, *v.*, to drum, to hammer.
BA.TU.QUE, *s. m.*, hammering, drumming.
BA.Ú, *s. m.*, trunk, travelling box, chest.
BAU.NI.LHA, *s. f.*, vanilla.
BA.ZAR, *s. m.*, bazaar, oriental market.
BE.A.BÁ, *s. m.*, alphabet, the ABC.
BE.A.TA, *s. f.*, pious woman, bigot.

BE.A.TI.CE, *s. f.*, bigotry.
BE.A.TO, *s. m.*, beatified man; bigot; *adj.*, devot, fanatic, hypocritical.
BÊ.BA.DO, *s. m.*, drunk, drunkard; *adj.*, drunk, tipsy.
BE.BÊ, *s. m.*, baby, babe.
BE.BE.DEI.RA, *s. f.*, spree, drunkenness, drinking bout.
BE.BER, *v.*, to drink, to take a drink, to imbibe, to swallow.
BE.BER.RÃO, *s. m.*, drunkard, boozer, tippler.
BE.BI.DA, *s. f.*, drink, beverage, potion.
BE.CO, *s. m.*, alley.
BE.DEL, *s. m.*, school attendant.
BE.DU.Í.NO, *adj., s. m.*, Bedouin, Arab.
BE.GE, *adj., s. 2 gen.*, beige.
BEI.ÇO, *s. m.*, lip, pout, salience.
BEI.ÇU.DO, *adj., s. m.*, blubber-lipped.
BEI.JA.DO, *adj.*, kissed.
BEI.JA-FLOR, *s. m.*, hummingbird, colibri.
BEI.JAR, *v.*, to kiss, to caress, to osculate.
BEI.JO, *s. m.*, kiss, osculation.
BEI.RA, *s. f.*, edge, shore, rim, proximity, border.
BEI.RA.DA, *s. f.*, margin, border.
BEI.RAL, *s. m.*, weatherboard.
BEI.RA-MAR, *s. m.*, sea-shore, strand, coast, littoral, waterfront.
BEI.SE.BOL, *s. m.*, baseball.
BE.LE.ZA, *s. f.*, beauty, prettiness, gracefulness, handsomeness.
BEL.GA, *adj., s. m.*, Belgian.
BE.LI.CHE, *s. m.*, berth, bunk, sleeping berth, cabin.
BÉ.LI.CO, *adj.*, warlike, bellicose, litigious.
BE.LI.CO.SO, *adj.*, warlike, bellicose, pugnacious.
BE.LI.GE.RÂN.CIA, *s. f.*, belligerence.
BE.LIS.CÃO, *s. m.*, squeeze, nip, pinch.
BE.LIS.CAR, *v.*, to pinch, to squeeze, to peck, to nip.
BE.LO, *adj.*, beautiful, handsome, pretty, fine, harmonious.
BEL.TRA.NO, *s. m.*, Mr. So-and-so; John Doe.
BEM, *s. m.*, good, goodness, benefit, virtue; *adv.*, well, very, right.
BEM-ES.TAR, *s. m.*, comfort, welfare, satisfaction.
BEM-TE-VI, *s. m.*, tyrant flycatcher.
BÊN.ÇÃO, *s. f.*, blessing.
BEN.DI.TO, *adj.*, blessed, praised.
BE.NE.FI.CEN.TE, *adj.*, beneficent, charitable, beneficial.
BE.NE.FI.CI.AR, *v.*, to benefit, to be beneficial to, to improve, to better; to process.
BE.NE.FÍ.CIO, *s. m.*, benefit, service.
BE.NÉ.FI.CO, *adj.*, benefic, beneficient, useful, salutary.
BE.NE.PLÁ.CI.TO, *s. m.*, consent, approval, permission.
BE.NE.VO.LÊN.CIA, *s. f.*, benevolence, goodwill, amity, friendship.
BEN.FEI.TOR, *s. m.*, benefactor, well-doer, amender.
BEN.FEI.TO.RI.A, *s. f.*, improvement, melioration.
BEN.GA.LA, *s. f.*, cane, walking stick.
BE.NIG.NI.DA.DE, *s. f.*, benignity.
BEN.TO, *adj.*, sacred, holy, consecrated.
BEN.ZE.DU.RA, *s. f.*, blessing, benediction.
BEN.ZER, *v.*, to bless, to consecrate, to make happy.
BE.QUE, *s. m.*, beak, prow, head of a ship.
BER.ÇÁ.RIO, *s. m.*, nursery.
BER.ÇO, *s. m.*, cradle, cot, crib, bassinet.
BE.RIN.JE.LA, *s. f.*, aubergine, eggplant.
BER.RAR, *v.*, to cry, to scream, to shout, to roar, to bellow.
BER.RO, *s. m.*, howl, shout, scream, lowing, clamour.
BE.SOU.RO, *s. m.*, beetle.
BES.TA, *s. f.*, beast, quadruped, mare, mule; a stupid person, duffer; *adj.*, stupid.
BES.TEI.RA, *s. f.*, nonsense, absurdity, foolishness, stupidity.
BES.TI.A.LI.DA.DE, *s. f.*, bestiality, atrocity.
BES.TI.A.LI.ZAR, *v.*, to bestialize, to brutalize, to stupefy.
BES.TI.FI.CAR, *v.*, to bestialize, to brutalize.
BE.TER.RA.BA, *s. f.*, beet, beetroot.
BE.TO.NEI.RA, *s. f.*, concret mixer.

BE.XI.GA, *s. f.*, bladder.
BE.ZER.RO, *s. m.*, bull-calf, male calf, bossy.
BÍ.BLI.A, *s. f.*, the Bible, the Holy Scriptures.
BÍ.BLI.CO, *adj.*, biblical, scriptural.
BI.BLI.O.GRA.FI.A, *s. f.*, bibliography.
BI.BLI.O.GRÁ.FI.CO, *adj.*, bibliographic.
BI.BLI.O.TE.CA, *s. f.*, library, collection of books.
BI.CA, *s. f.*, conduit, pipe, fountain, springlet.
BI.CA.DA, *s. f.*, peck, pecking, beakful.
BI.CAR, *v.*, to peck.
BI.CAR.BO.NA.TO, *s. m.*, bicarbonate.
BI.CHA, *s. f.*, worm, leech; gay, homossexual.
BI.CHO, *s. m.*, animal, beast, worm, any animal; ugly, repulsive or unsociable person.
BI.CHO-DE-PÉ, *s. m.*, jigger.
BI.CI.CLE.TA, *s. f.*, bicycle, bike; wheel.
BI.CO, *s. m.*, beak, bill, pecker, peak, spout.
BI.CO.LOR, *adj.*, two-coloured.
BI.DÊ, *s. m*, bidet.
BI.E.NAL, *adj.*, biennial.
BI.Ê.NIO, *s. m.*, biennium.
BI.FE, *s. m.*, beefsteak, steak.
BI.FOR.ME, *adj.*, biform.
BI.FUR.CAR, *v.*, to bifurcate, to fork, to dichotomize.
BI.GA.MI.A, *s. f.*, bigamy.
BÍ.GA.MO, *s. m.*, bigamist.
BI.GO.DE, *s. m.*, moustache.
BI.GOR.NA, *s. f.*, anvil; incus.
BI.JU.TE.RI.A, *s. f.*, bijouterie, trinckets, small jewels.
BI.LHA, *s. f.*, pitcher, monkey jar.
BI.LHÃO, *num.*, billion.
BI.LHAR, *s. m.*, billiards.
BI.LHE.TE, *s. m.*, note, billet, short letter, notice; ticket.
BI.LHE.TE.RI.A, *s. f.*, booking office, box-office, ticket-office.
BI.LÍN.GUE, *s. m.*, bilingual.
BI.LLO.NÁ.RIO, *adj., s. m.*, billionaire.
BÍ.LIS, *s. f.*, bile, gall.
BI.MEN.SAL, *adj.*, bimensal, bimonthly.
BI.MES.TRAL, *adj.*, bimestrial.

BI.MES.TRE, *s. m.*, bimester.
BI.NÁ.RIO, *adj.*, dual, binary.
BI.NÓ.CU.LO, *s. m.*, binocle, binocular, field-glass.
BI.O.GRA.FAR, *v.*, to biographize.
BI.O.GRA.FI.A, *s. f.*, biography.
BI.Ó.GRA.FO, *s. m.*, biographer.
BI.O.LO.GI.A, *s. f.*, biology.
BI.Ó.LO.GO, *s. m.*, biologist.
BI.OM.BO, *s. m.*, folding screen, screen; blind.
BI.Ó.PSIA, *s. f.*, biopsy.
BI.OS.FE.RA, *s. f.*, biospher.
BI.O.TEC.NO.LO.GI.A, *s. f.*, biotechnology.
BI.PAR.TIR, *v.*, to divide into two parts, divide into halves.
BÍ.PE.DE, *s. m.*, two-footed animal, biped.
BIR.RA, *s. f.*, obstinacy, stubbornness.
BIR.REN.TO, *adj.*, stubborn, obstinate, mad.
BI.RU.TA, *adj., s. 2 gen.*, crazy, nuts.
BIS, *adv.*, bis, again, twice.
BI.SÃO, *s. m.*, bison, buffalo.
BI.SAR, *v.*, to repeat, to do once more.
BI.SA.VÔ, *s. m.*, great-grandfather.
BI.SA.VÓ, *s. f.*, great-grandmother.
BIS.BI.LHO.TAR, *v.*, to snoop, to gossip, to complicate.
BIS.CA.TE, *s. m.*, odd job, casual earnings, casual work.
BIS.COI.TO, *s. m.*, biscuit, sugar bread, scone, cookie.
BIS.NA.GA, *s. f.*, tube, squirt.
BIS.NE.TA, *s. f.*, great-granddaughter.
BIS.NE.TO, *s. m.*, great-grandson.
BIS.PA.DO, *s. m.*, bishopric.
BIS.PO, *s. m.*, bishop.
BIS.SEX.TO, *adj.*, bissextile.
BIS.SE.XU.AL, *adj., s. 2 gen.*, bisexed.
BIS.TU.RI, *s. m.*, scalpel, bistoury.
BI.TO.LA, *s. f.*, gauge, standard measure, tread.
BI.VA.LEN.TE, *adj.*, bivalent.
BI.VA.QUE, *s. m.*, bivouac, camp, encampment.
BI.ZAR.RO, *adj.*, gentle, generous, bizarre; extravagant.
BLAS.FE.MAR, *v.*, to blaspheme, to profane,

BLASFÊMIA | **BORBOLETA**

to damn, to curse.
BLAS.FÊ.MIA, *s.f.*, blasphemy, impiety, profanity.
BLE.FE, *s. m.*, bluff, thimblerig.
BLE.NOR.RA.GI.A, *s.f.*, blennorhea, gonorrhea.
BLI.NDAR, *v.*, to armour, to plate, to case, to coat, to protect, to cover.
BLO.CO, *s. m.*, block; writing pad, date block; bloc: a political group.
BLO.QUE.AR, *v.*, to block, to obstruct, to blockade, to stop.
BLU.SA, *s. f.*, blouse, smock.
BO.A, *s. f.*, boa, snake; *adj.*, good, fine.
BO.A.TO, *s. m.*, rumour, report, hearsey.
BO.BA.GEM, *s.f.*, foolery, buffoonery, nonsense, rot, bullshit, stupidity.
BO.BI.NA, *s. f.*, spool, bobbin, reel.
BO.BO, *s. m.*, fool, imbecile, buffoon, clown; *adj.*, foolish, silly, soft.
BO.BO.CA, *adj.*, stupid, fool.
BO.CA, *s. f.*, mouth, whistle, muzzle.
BO.CA.DO, *s. m.*, piece, a mouthful, morsel, small portion.
BO.CE.JAR, *v.*, to gape, to yawn.
BO.CE.JO, *s. m.*, yawn, gaping.
BO.CE.TA, *s. f.*, little box; vulva (vulg.)
BO.CHE.CHA, *s. f.*, cheek.
BO.CHE.CHU.DO, *adj.*, cheeky, fubsy.
BO.DE, *s. m.*, he-goat, goat, buck-goat.
BO.DE.GA, *s. f.*, wine-cellar, trash.
BO.Ê.MIA, *s. f.*, folly, dissipation.
BO.FE.TA.DA, *s. f.*, box on the ear, slap in the face, flap, cuff; insult, injury.
BOI, *s. m.*, ox, bull, any bovine, bullock.
BOI.A, *s. f.*, buoy, seamark, lifebuoy; meal, food.
BOI.A.DA, *s. f.*, herd of oxen, drove.
BOI.A.DEI.RO, *s. m.*, herdsman, cowboy, cattle dealer.
BOI.AR, *v.*, to float, to buoy, to be afloat, to driff.
BOI.CO.TAR, *v.*, to boycott, to restrict.
BOI.NA, *s. f.*, bonnet, berret, cap.
BO.LA, *s. f.*, ball, globe, sphere; round, bowl.
BO.LA.CHA, *s. f.*, biscuit, cracker, cookies, snap.
BOL.CHE.VIS.MO, *s. m.*, bolshevism, communism.

BO.LE.TIM, *s. m.*, bulletin, short notice, report; school report, periodical publication.
BO.LHA, *s. f.*, blister, bubble, pimple, blain.
BO.LI.CHE, *s. m.*, poolroom, bowling, inn.
BO.LI.NAR, *v.*, to excite, to excite anyone sexually.
BO.LI.VI.A.NO, *adj.*, *s. m.*, Bolivian.
BO.LO, *s. m.*, cake.
BO.LOR, *s. m.*, mould, mildrew, mustiness.
BO.LO.REN.TO, *adj.*, mouldy, musty, frowzy, rusty.
BOL.SA, *s. f.*, purse, small bag, burse, pocket.
BOL.SIS.TA, *s. 2 gen.*, stockbroker, broker.
BOL.SO, *s. m.*, pocket, fob.
BOM, *adj.*, good, fine, right, nice; **BOM-DIA**: good morning.
BOM.BA, *s. f.*, bomb, bomshell, pump, siphon, suction-pipe.
BOM.BAR.DE.AR, *v.*, to shell, to bombard, to bomb, to cannon.
BOM.BAR.DEI.O, *s. m.*, bombardment, shelling.
BOM.BAR.DEI.RO, *s. m.*, bombardier, bombarder.
BOM.BEI.RO, *s. m.*, fireman, hoseman.
BO.NA.CHÃO, *s. m.*, good-natured, honest fellow.
BO.NAN.ÇA, *s. f.*, calm, peace, tranquility, lull, calmness.
BON.DA.DE, *s. f.*, goodness, kindness, graciousness, affability, benevolence.
BON.DE, *s. m.*, streetcar, trolley.
BON.DO.SO, *adj.*, good-natured, charitable, kind-hearted, benevolent.
BO.NÉ, *s. m.*, cap, bonnet, kepi.
BO.NE.CA, *s. f.*, doll, toy, baby.
BO.NE.CO, *s. m.*, puppet, marionette, doll.
BO.NI.FI.CA.ÇÃO, *s. f.*, allowance, money grant, bonus, privilege.
BO.NI.TO, *adj.*, pretty, handsome, beautiful, nice, bonny, nifty.
BÔ.NUS, *s. m.*, bonus, bond, paper.
BO.QUI.A.BER.TO, *adj.*, astonished, amazed, agape, gaping.
BOR.BO.LE.TA, *s. f.*, butterfly, moth.

BORBULHAR | BRILHO

BOR.BU.LHAR, *v.*, to bubble.
BOR.DA, *s. f.*, edge, border, brim, lip, rim, skirt, margin.
BOR.DA.DO, *s. m.*, embroidery, needlework; *adj.*, embroidered.
BOR.DAR, *v.*, to embroider, to hem, to garnish.
BOR.DEL, *s. m.*, whore-house, bawdy-house.
BOR.DO.A.DA, *s. f.*, stroke, knock, punch.
BOR.RA.CHA, *s. f.*, rubber, eraser, india-rubber.
BOR.RA.CHEI.RO, *s. m.*, tyre fitter, vulcanizer.
BOR.RA.CHU.DO, *s. m.*, black fly, gnat.
BOR.RÃO, *s. m.*, blot, blemish, dot, stain, spatter.
BOR.RAR, *v.*, to stain, to besmear, to dirty, to smudge.
BOR.RAS.CA, *s. f.*, tempest, storm, hurricane, thunderstorm.
BOR.RI.FAR, *v.*, to sprinkle, to spray, to asperse, to perfuse, to damp.
BOS.QUE, *s. m.*, woods, forest, thicket, grove.
BOS.TA, *s. f.*, cow dropping, cow dung, shit, crap.
BO.TA, *s. f.*, boot, tub, barrel.
BO.TÂ.NI.CA, *s. f.*, botany.
BO.TÂ.NI.CO, *s. m.*, botanist, herbalist; *adj.*, botanic.
BO.TÃO, *s. m.*, bud, button, flower-bud, gemmule.
BO.TAR, *v.*, to throw, to cast, to fling, to put, to lay an egg.
BO.TE, *s. m.*, assault, boat, skiff, cut, stab, blow.
BO.TE.CO, *s. m.*, bar, tavern, stall.
BO.TE.QUIM, *s. m.*, bar, tavern, taphouse.
BO.VI.NO, *adj.*, bovine.
BO.XE, *s. m.*, boxing, pugilism.
BO.XE.A.DOR, *s. m.*, pugilist, boxer.
BRA.ÇA.DA, *s. f.*, armful, stroke.
BRA.ÇA.DEI.RA, *s. f.*, clamp, brace, band.
BRA.CE.LE.TE, *s. m.*, bracelet, armlet.
BRA.ÇO, *s. f.*, arm, branch.
BRA.DAR, *v.*, to cry, to hollo, to shout, to scream, to yell, to bawl.
BRA.DO, *s. m.*, cry, shout, scream, whoop, acclamation, clamour.
BRA.GUI.LHA, *s. f.*, slit of trousers.
BRA.MIR, *v.*, to roar, to bellow, to yell, to howl.
BRAN.CO, *adj.*, white, light, clear.

BRAN.CU.RA, *s. f.*, white, whiteness, hoar.
BRAN.DIR, *v.*, to brandish, to shake, to swing.
BRAN.DO, *adj.*, tender, soft, mild, bland, light, temperate.
BRAN.DU.RA, *s. f.*, softness, tenderness, mildness, lightness, kindness.
BRAN.QUE.AR, *v.*, to whiten, to make white.
BRÂN.QUIAS, *s. f., pl.*, gills.
BRAN.QUI.DÃO, *s. m.*, whiteness, white colour.
BRA.SA, *s. f.*, live or burning coal, incandescence, ember.
BRA.SEI.RO, *s. m.*, brazier, fire remains.
BRA.SIL, *s. m.*, Brazil.
BRA.SI.LEI.RA, *s. f.*, Brazilian woman or girl.
BRA.SI.LEI.RO, *s. m.*, Brazilian: native or inhabitant of Brazil; *adj.*, Brazilian.
BRA.VI.O, *s. m.*, wild country; *adj.*, wild, savage, fierce, unruly.
BRA.VO, *adj.*, brave, valiant, bold, furious, courageous, valorous.
BRA.VU.RA, *s. f.*, bravery, courage, prowess, exploit.
BRE.CA, *s. f.*, cramp.
BRE.CAR, *v.*, to brake, to put on the brake.
BRE.CHA, *s. f.*, gap, fissure, rupture, chasm, rent.
BRE.JEN.TO, *adj.*, marshy, swampy, boggy.
BRE.JO, *s. m.*, swamp, bog, fen, slough, slash, morass.
BREU, *s. m.*, pitch, tar, colophony, darkness.
BRE.VE, *adj.*, brief, short, rapid, quick, concise.
BRE.VI.DA.DE, *adj.*, shortness, conciseness, brevity, briefness.
BRI.GA, *s. f.*, strife, quarrel, fight, broil.
BRI.GA.DEI.RO, *s. m.*, brigadier, brigadier-general.
BRI.GAR, *v.*, to quarrel, to fight, to combat.
BRI.LHAN.TE, *s. m.*, diamond, brilliant; *adj.*, brilliant, bright, sparkling.
BRI.LHAN.TI.NA, *s. f.*, brilliantine.
BRI.LHAR, *v.*, to shine, to glitter, to scintillate, to star, to flash.
BRI.LHO, *s. m.*, brightness, splendor, brilliancy, luminosity, splendour.

BRINCADEIRA — **BUZINAR**

BRIN.CA.DEI.RA, *s. f.*, entertainment, fun, game, play, sport, merrymaking.
BRIN.CAR, *v.*, to play, to joke, to toy, to frolic, to amuse, to divert.
BRIN.CO, *s. m.*, earring, drop, pendant, toy.
BRIN.DAR, *v.*, to toast, to drink to a person's health.
BRIN.DE, *s. m.*, toast, wish of health.
BRIN.QUE.DO, *s. m.*, toy, plaything, joke.
BRI.O, *s. m.*, sense of dignity, valour, pride, character.
BRI.SA, *s. f.*, breeze, light, fresh wind.
BRI.TÂ.NI.CO, *adj.*, *s. m.*, British.
BRO.A, *s. f.*, bread of maize, pone.
BRO.CA, *s. f.*, drill, bit, auger, gimlet.
BRO.CHE, *s. m.*, brooch, pin, breast-pin.
BRO.CHU.RA, *s. f.*, brochure, paperback edition, pamphlet, booklet.
BRON.CO, *adj.*, rude, dull, stupid, rough.
BRON.QUI.TE, *s. f.*, bronchitis.
BRON.ZE, *s. m.*, bronze, gun metal.
BRON.ZE.AR, *v.*, to tan.
BRO.TAR, *v.*, to arise, to produce, to grow, to issue, to originate.
BRO.TO, *s. m.*, bud, shoot, eye; young girl.
BRO.TO.E.JA, *s. f.*, sudamen, skin eruption, vesicular eruption.
BRO.XA, *s. f.*, stock brush.
BRU.MA, *s. f.*, thick fog, haze, vapour, cloud, mist.
BRU.NIR, *v.*, to polish, to burnish, to furbish.
BRU.TAL, *adj.*, brutal, cruel, rough, brutish, bestial, savage.
BRU.TA.LI.DA.DE, *s. f.*, brutality, atrocity, brutishness, wildness, bestiality.
BRU.TA.LI.ZAR, *v.*, to brutalize, bestialize.
BRU.TO, *s. m.*, animal, beast; *adj.*, rude, rough, dull, raw.
BRU.XA, *s. f.*, witch, sorceress, enchantress.
BRU.XA.RI.A, *s. f.*, witchery, sorcery, witchcraft.
BRU.XO, *s. m.*, wizard, sorcerer, conjurer.
BU.CHA, *s. f.*, bush, sleeve, wad.
BU.CHO, *s. m.*, craw, crop, stomach.
BU.CÓ.LI.CO, *adj.*, pastoral, bucolic.
BU.DIS.MO, *s. m.*, Buddhism.
BU.EI.RO, *s. m.*, sewer, drainpipe, gutter.
BÚ.FA.LO, *s. m.*, buffalo.
BU.FAR, *v.*, to puff, to blow, to snuff, to snort.
BU.FO.NA.RI.A, *s. f.*, buffoonery, drollery.
BU.GI.GAN.GA, *s. f.*, trifle, gewgaws, gadgets, trinket.
BU.GI.O, *s. m.*, ape, monkey, simian.
BU.GRE, *s. m.*, Indian, savage, aborigine.
BU.JÃO, *s. m.*, plug, sttoper, stopple.
BU.LA, *s. f.*, bull, papal or imperial edict or letter.
BU.LE, *s. m.*, coffeepot, teapot.
BÚL.GA.RO, *adj.*, *s. m.*, Bulgarian.
BU.LIR, *v.*, to agitate, to move slightly.
BUN.DA, *s. f.*, bum, buttock, posterior.
BU.QUÊ, *s. m.*, bouquet, bunch of flowers.
BU.RA.CO, *s. m.*, hole, gap, hollow, cavity, cave, gully.
BUR.GO, *s. m.*, burgh, borough, village, hamlet, palace.
BUR.GUÊS, *s. m.*, burgher, citizen, bourgeois.
BUR.GUE.SI.A, *s. f.*, bourgeoisie.
BU.RI.LAR, *v.*, to perfect, to chisel, to carve, to adorn.
BUR.LAR, *v.*, to cheat, to fraud, to trick, to jest, to joke.
BU.RO.CRA.CI.A, *s. f.*, bureaucracy, red-tape, officialism.
BU.RO.CRA.TA, *s. 2 gen.*, bureaucrat, red-tapist.
BUR.RA.DA, *s. f.*, foolish act, nonsense, drove of asses, mistake.
BUR.RI.CE, *s. f.*, stupidity, foolishness, nonsense.
BUR.RO, *s. m.*, ass, donkey, mule; stupid, dull, foolish.
BUS.CA, *s. f.*, search, inquiry, quest, research.
BUS.CAR, *v.*, to search, to seek, to inquire, to quest, to investigate, to obtain.
BÚS.SO.LA, *s. f.*, magnetic needle, compass.
BUS.TO, *s. m.*, bust, bosom, sculture.
BU.TU.CA, *s. f.*, gadfly.
BU.ZI.NA, *s. f.*, horn, trumpet, honk, bugle, hooter.
BU.ZI.NAR, *v.*, to sound a horn, to hoot.

C

C, *s. m.*, the third letter of the Portuguese alphabet; one hundred in Roman numerals (**C**).

CÁ, *adv.*, here, in this place, hither, between us.

CA.A.TIN.GA, *s. f.*, a stunted sparse forest, scrub savana.

CA.BAL, *adj.*, complete, whole, full, perfect.

CA.BA.LAR, *v.*, to cabal, to plot, to intrigue.

CA.BA.NA, *s. f.*, hut, cottage, shack.

CA.BA.RÉ, *s. m.*, cabaret, honky-tonk.

CA.BE.ÇA, *s. f.*, head, poll, scalp, top, intelligence, chief, leader, sagacity, judgment.

CA.BE.ÇA.DA, *s. f.*, a bump with the head, headstall.

CA.BE.ÇA.LHO, *s. m.*, letterhead, heading, pillow, head of a bed, title page.

CA.BE.CE.AR, *v.*, to nod, to doze, to head, to deviate.

CA.BE.CEI.RA, *s. f.*, cushion, pillow, head of a bed, headrest.

CA.BE.ÇO.TE, *s. m.*, headstock.

CA.BE.DAL, *s. m.*, stock, funds, capital, means, prosperity.

CA.BE.LEI.RA, *s. f.*, head of hair, hair; tail of a comet.

CA.BE.LEI.REI.RO, *s.m.*, hairdresser, wigmaker.

CA.BE.LO, *s. m.*, hair.

CA.BE.LU.DO, *adj.*, hairy, hirsute, difficult; obscene.

CA.BER, *v.*, to be contained in, to fit in or inside of; to be containable.

CA.BI.DE, *s. m.*, rack, hat-stand, hanger, peg.

CA.BI.MEN.TO, *s. m.*, relevancy, pertinance, acceptance, capacity.

CA.BI.NA, *s. f.*, cabin, box, berth.

CA.BIS.BAI.XO, *adj.*, downcast, depressed.

CA.BO, *s. m.*, corporal, chief; terminal, end, cape; cable, handle, holder.

CA.BO.CLO, *s. m.*, caboclo, civilized Brazilian Indian, rustic, agricultural labourer.

CA.BO.GRA.MA, *s. m.*, cable, cablegram, wire.

CA.BRA, *s. f.*, she-goat.

CA.BRES.TO, *s. m.*, halter, tame lead ox.

CA.BRI.TA, *s. f.*, a little goat; a young woman.

CA.BRI.TO, *s. m.*, a little buck, kid.

CA.BU.LAR, *v.*, to play truant, to cut classes.

CA.CA, *s. f.*, feces, dirt, shit, excrement.

CA.ÇA, *s. f.*, hunt, hunting, chasing, game; the animals chased.

CA.ÇA.DA, *s. f.*, hunting party, hunt, safari.

CA.ÇA.DOR, *s. m.*, hunter, huntsman.

CA.ÇAM.BA, *s. f.*, bucket, pail, well-bucket, dump-car.

CA.ÇA-MI.NAS, *s. m.*, mine-sweeper.

CA.ÇÃO, *s. m.*, shark, dogfish.

CA.ÇAR, *v.*, to hunt, to chase, to pursue, to catch.

CA.CA.RE.JAR, *v.*, to cackle, to cluck, to chatter.

CA.ÇA.RO.LA, *s. f.*, casserole, saucepan.

CA.CAU, *s. m.*, cacao, cocoa, cacao-bean.

CA.CAU.EI.RO, *s. m.*, cacao tree.

CA.CE.TA.DA, *s. f.*, a blow with a club, beating, thrashing.

CA.CE.TE, *s. m.*, club, mace.

CA.CHA.ÇA, *s. f.*, sugar cane brandy, rum.

CA.CHE.COL, *s. m.*, scarf, neck-cloth, muffler.

CA.CHIM.BO, *s. m.*, pipe, tobacco-pipe.

CA.CHO, *s. m.*, curl, cluster, ringlet, raceme.

CA.CHO.EI.RA, *s. f.*, waterfall, river rapids, overfall, cascade, cataract.

CA.CHO.LA, *s. f.*, head, pate, nut.

CA.CHOR.RA.DA, *s. f.*, a pack of dogs, mob, rabble; wickedness.

CA.CHOR.RI.CE, *s. f.*, wickedness, indignity, outrage.

CA.CHOR.RI.NHO, *s. m.*, puppy, whelp.

CA.CHOR.RO, *s. m.*, dog, puppy.

CA.CHOR.RO-QUEN.TE, *s. m.*, hot dog.

CACIMBA — CALÇADEIRA

CA.CIM.BA, *s. f.*, small pool of stagnant water, dewfall.

CA.CI.QUE, *s. m.*, Indian chief, political boss, big shot.

CA.CO, *s. m.*, bit of broken object; trash; shard.

CA.ÇO.A.DA, *s. f.*, mockery, derision.

CA.ÇO.AR, *v.*, to scoff, to sneer, to make fun of, to mock.

CA.CO.E.TE, *s. m.*, nervous tic, a bad habit, cacoethes.

CA.CO.FO.NI.A, *s. f.*, cacophony.

CAC.TO, *s. m.*, cactus.

CA.ÇU.LA, *s. 2 gen.*, baby, the youngest child of a family.

CA.DA, *pron.*, each, every.

CA.DA.FAL.SO, *s. m.*, scaffold, scaffolding.

CA.DAR.ÇO, *s. m.*, tape, ribbon, floss silk, ferret.

CA.DAS.TRAR, *v.*, to make a cadaster, to register.

CA.DAS.TRO, *s. m.*, cadaster, dossier.

CA.DÁ.VER, *s. m.*, dead body, corpse cadaver, defunct.

CA.DA.VÉ.RI.CO, *adj.*, cadaveric, cadaverous.

CA.DE.A.DO, *s. m.*, padlock, snap.

CA.DEI.A, *s. f.*, prison, jail, network, chain.

CA.DEI.RA, *s. f.*, chair, seat, place, stall.

CA.DE.LA, *s. f.*, female dog, bitch, she-dog.

CA.DÊN.CIA, *s. f.*, cadence, rhythm.

CA.DEN.CI.AR, *v.*, to cadence, to harmonize.

CA.DEN.TE, *adj.*, falling.

CA.DER.NE.TA, *s. f.*, notebook, school register.

CA.DER.NO, *s. m.*, copy-book, notebook.

CA.DE.TE, *s. m.*, cadet.

CA.DU.CAR, *v.*, to grow very old, to decay, to become decrepit.

CA.DU.CO, *adj.*, falling, senile, decrepit.

CA.FA.JES.TE, *s. 2 gen.*, boor, churl, common, vulgar, scum.

CA.FÉ, *s. m.*, coffee.

CA.FE.I.CUL.TOR, *s. m.*, coffee planter.

CA.FE.I.CUL.TU.RA, *s. f.*, coffee planting.

CA.FE.Í.NA, *s. f.*, caffeine.

CA.FE.TEI.RA, *s. f.*, coffee-pot.

CA.FE.ZAL, *s. m.*, coffee plantation.

CA.FU.ZO, *adj., s. m.*, the offspring of Negro and Indian.

CA.GA.ÇO, *s. m.*, fright, fear.

CA.GAR, *v.*, to shit, to defecate.

CAI.A.QUE, *s. m.*, kayak.

CAI.AR, *v.*, to whitewash, to whiten, to conceal.

CÃ.I.BRA, *s. f.*, cramp, kink, convulsion.

CA.Í.DA, *s. f.*, fall, falling, decay, decadence.

CAI.PI.RA, *s. 2 gen.*, rustic, backwoodsman, hayseed, redneck, yokel, country dumpkin.

CA.IR, *v.*, to fall, to decline, to decay, to collapse, to fall down, to tumble.

CAIS, *s. m.*, quay, wharf, dock, pier, mole.

CAI.XA, *s. f.*, box, case, chest, cashier, kit, set, casing.

CAI.XÃO, *s. m.*, coffin, great chest, locker.

CAI.XEI.RO, *s. m.*, salesclerk, salesperson, counter clerk, shop-boy.

CAI.XI.LHO, *s. m.*, window-sash, casement.

CAI.XI.NHA, *s. f.*, tip, casket.

CAI.XO.TE, *s. m.*, box, crate, packing-box.

CA.JA.DA.DA, *s. f.*, a blow with a stick.

CA.JA.DO, *s. m.*, shepherd's stick, crook.

CA.JU, *s. m.*, cashew-nut, cashew.

CA.JU.EI.RO, *s. m.*, cashew-tree.

CAL, *s. f.*, whitewash.

CA.LA.BOU.ÇO, *s. m.*, dungeon, prison, jail, calaboose.

CA.LA.DO, *adj.*, silent, quiet, close, reserved, secret.

CA.LA.FE.TA.GEM, *s. f.*, caulking, gasket.

CA.LA.FE.TAR, *v.*, to calk.

CA.LA.FRI.O, *s. m.*, chill, shiver, shakes, fit of cold.

CA.LA.MI.DA.DE, *s. f.*, calamity, calamitousness, disaster, affliction.

CA.LA.MI.TO.SO, *adj.*, calamitous, disastrous, woeful, tragic.

CA.LÃO, *s. m.*, jargon, slang, cant.

CA.LAR, *v.*, not to speak, to shut up, to silence, to stay silent, to conceal, to disguise.

CAL.ÇA.DA, *s. f.*, pavement, sidewalk, paved street.

CAL.ÇA.DEI.RA, *s. f.*, stamper, rammer; shoe-horn.

CALÇADO / **CAMARADA**

CAL.ÇA.DO, *s. m.*, foot-wear, shoe; *adj.*, paved, shod.
CAL.ÇA.MEN.TO, *s. m.*, paving, pavement.
CAL.CA.NHAR, *s. m.*, heel.
CAL.ÇÃO, *s. m.*, trunks, shorts, trousers.
CAL.CAR, *v.*, to step on, to smash, to crush, to squeeze, to oppress, to grind, to crunch.
CAL.ÇAR, *v.*, to shoe, to boot, to put on (any footwear); to pave.
CAL.CÁ.RIO, *s. m.*, limestone; *adj.*, calcareous, limy, chalky.
CAL.ÇAS, *s. f., pl.*, trousers, pants, pantaloons;
CALCINHAS: panties.
CAL.CI.FI.CAR, *v.*, to calcify, to calcinate.
CAL.CI.NA.ÇÃO, *s. f.*, calcination.
CAL.CI.NAR, *v.*, to calcine, to reduce to lime.
CÁL.CIO, *s. m.*, calcium.
CAL.ÇO, *s. m.*, wedge, a piece of wood, chock, skid.
CAL.CU.LA.DO, *adj.*, calculated, figured, rated.
CAL.CU.LAR, *v.*, to calculate, to compute, to reckon, to count, to estimate, to conjecture.
CÁL.CU.LO, *s. m.*, calculation, reckoning, computation, counting.
CAL.DA, *s. f.*, syrup, preserves.
CAL.DEI.RA, *s. f.*, kettle, caldron, boiler, seether.
CAL.DEI.RÃO, *s. m.*, caldron, large kettle.
CAL.DO, *s. m.*, soup, broth, sauce.
CA.LE.FA.ÇÃO, *s. f.*, heating, warming, calefaction.
CA.LE.JA.DO, *adj.*, callous, horny, hardy, hardened, experienced.
CA.LE.JAR, *v.*, to make callous, to harden, to indurate.
CA.LEN.DÁ.RIO, *s. m.*, calendar, diary, almanac.
CA.LHA, *s. f.*, drip, gutter, gutter pipe, channel.
CA.LHA.MA.ÇO, *s. m.*, an old book, a big book.
CA.LHAM.BE.QUE, *s. m.*, a small coasting vessel, jalopy.
CA.LHAR, *v.*, to fit well in, to go into, to be opportune.
CA.LI.BRA.DOR, *s. m.*, gauge, calibrator, caliber rule.
CA.LI.BRA.GEM, *s. f.*, calibration.
CA.LI.BRAR, *v.*, to measure the caliber of, to gauge, to calibrate.
CA.LI.BRE, *s. m.*, caliber, gauge, bore, measurement.
CÁ.LI.CE, *s. m.*, cup, chalice, wineglass; calyx of a flower.
CÁ.LI.DO, *adj.*, hot, burning, heated, ardent.
CA.LI.GRA.FI.A, *s. f.*, handwriting, calligraphy.
CA.LÍ.GRA.FO, *s. m.*, calligrapher, teacher of calligraphy.
CAL.MA, *s. f.*, calm, calmness, serenity, silence, piece, tranquility, repose.
CAL.MAN.TE, *s. m.*, sedative, calmative; *adj.*, sedative, lenitive, calmative.
CAL.MAR, *v.*, to calm, to quiet, to tranquilize.
CAL.MA.RI.A, *s. f.*, calm, lull, becalmed sea.
CAL.MO, *adj.*, hot, calm, still, quiet, sultry, cool, serene.
CA.LO, *s. m.* corn, callus, callosity, callousness.
CA.LOR, *s. m.*, heat, warmth, hotness, warmness, torridness.
CA.LO.RI.A, *s. f.*, calorie, calory, heat.
CA.LO.RÍ.FI.CO, *adj.*, calorific.
CA.LO.RO.SO, *adj.*, warm, hot, sultry, enthusiastic.
CA.LO.TA, *s. f.*, cap, skulcap.
CA.LO.TE, *s. m.*, unpaid debt, swindle, cheat.
CA.LO.TE.AR, *v.*, not to pay a debt, to swindle.
CA.LO.TEI.RO, *s. m.*, swindler, cheat.
CA.LOU.RO, *s. m.*, rookie, new student, freshman, beginner, novice.
CA.LÚ.NIA, *s. f.*, calumny, slander, falsehood, scandal.
CA.LU.NI.A.DOR, *s. m.*, calumniator, detractor.
CA.LU.NI.AR, *v.*, to calumniate, to detract, to defame.
CAL.VÍ.CIE, *s. f.*, baldness.
CAL.VO, *adj.*, bald, bald-headed, hairless, bare.
CA.MA, *s. f.*, bed; sofa, couch, resting place.
CA.MA.DA, *s. f.*, layer, class, stratum.
CA.MA.LE.ÃO, *s. m.*, chameleon.
CÂ.MA.RA, *s. f.*, chamber, camera, room, bedroom.
CA.MA.RA.DA, *s. 2 gen.*, comrade, roommate,

fellow student, mate, fellow, colleague.
CA.MA.RÃO, *s. m.*, shrimp, prawn.
CA.MA.REI.RA, *s.f.*, chambermaid, housekeeper.
CA.MA.RO.TE, *s. m.*, box, box seat, loge, cabin.
CAM.BA.DA, *s. f.*, gang, mob, rabble.
CAM.BA.LE.AR, *v.*, to sway, to reel, to stagger.
CAM.BA.LHO.TA, *s. f.*, caper, skip, somersault, capriole.
CAM.BI.AL, *s. m.*, cambial; *adj.*, cambial, relative to the exchange.
CAM.BI.AR, *v.*, to change, to exchange, to trade, to convert.
CÂM.BIO, *s. m.*, exchange, change, permutation; gear box.
CAM.BIS.TA, *s. 2 gen.*, money-changer, cambist, banker.
CAM.BU.RÃO, *s. m.*, police van.
CA.MÉ.LIA, *s. f.*, camellia.
CA.ME.LO, *s. m.*, camel.
CA.ME.LÔ, *s. m.*, hawker, street peddler.
CA.MI.NHA.DA, *s. f.*, walk, walking, ride, stroll, excursion, journey.
CA.MI.NHAN.TE, *s. 2 gen.*, walker, hiker, pedestrian; *adj.*, walking, travelling.
CA.MI.NHÃO, *s. m.*, lorry, truck.
CA.MI.NHAR, *v.*, to walk, to hike, to march, to journey, to go, to travel.
CA.MI.NHO, *s. m.*, way, road, route, path, trail, track, street, course.
CA.MI.NHO.NE.TE, *s. f.*, pickup, van, truck.
CA.MI.SA, *s. f.*, shirt, chemise.
CA.MI.SA.RI.A, *s. f.*, shirt factory; shirt shop.
CA.MI.SE.TA, *s. f.*, chemisette, undershirt.
CA.MI.SI.NHA, *s. f.*, condom, preservative.
CA.MI.SO.LA, *s. f.*, nightshirt, nightgown.
CA.MO.MI.LA, *s. f.*, camomile.
CAM.PA, *s. f.*, gravestone, tomb.
CAM.PA.I.NHA, *s. f.*, bell, small bell, handbell.
CAM.PA.NHA, *s. f.*, campaign, wide plains, lowland, camp.
CAM.PAR, *v.*, to camp, to pitch a camp.
CAM.PE.Ã, *s. f.*, championess.
CAM.PE.ÃO, *s. m.*, champion, champ; protagonist.

CAM.PEI.RO, *s. m.*, cowboy, wrangler, farmhand, rural worker.
CAM.PE.O.NA.TO, *s. m.*, championship, sporting event, bout.
CAM.PES.TRE, *adj.*, rural, rustic, campestrian, bucolic.
CAM.PI.NA, *s. f.*, prairie, plain, level land.
CAM.PO, *s. m.*, field, corn land, open country, prairie, country-side; space, opportunity.
CAM.PO.NÊS, *s. m.*, peasant, cottager, farmer, yokel, countryman.
CAM.PO.NE.SA, *s. f.*, countrywoman, peasant woman.
CAM.PO-SAN.TO, *s. m.*, cemetery.
CA.MU.FLA.GEM, *s. f.*, camouflage, disguise, disguising.
CA.MU.FLAR, *v.*, to disguise by camouflage, to disguise.
CA.MUN.DON.GO, *s. m.*, mouse.
CA.NA, *s. f.*, cane, reed, sugar-cane; prison, jail.
CA.NA-DE-A.ÇÚ.CAR, *s. f.*, sugar-cane.
CA.NA.DEN.SE, *adj.*, *s. 2 gen.*, Canadian.
CA.NAL, *s. m.*, channel, canal, waterway, stream.
CA.NA.LHA, *s. 2 gen.*, scum, scoundrel, rabble, mob, crook.
CA.NA.LI.ZA.ÇÃO, *s. f.*, drainage, canalization, system of canals, sewerage.
CA.NA.LI.ZAR, *v.*, to channel, to pipe, to canalize, to sluice.
CA.NA.PÉ, *s. m.*, appetizer; sofa.
CA.NÁ.RIO, *s. m.*, canary.
CA.NAS.TRA, *s. f.*, big basket, dorser, dosser; game of cards.
CA.NA.VI.AL, *s. m.*, reed plot, sugar-cane plantation.
CAN.ÇÃO, *s. f.*, song, singing, chant, chanson.
CAN.CE.LA.DO, *adj.*, cancelled, abrogated.
CAN.CE.LAR, *v.*, cancel, to cross out, to bloc out, to annul, to put off.
CÂN.CER, *s. m.*, cancer.
CAN.CE.RA.DO, *adj.*, affected with cancer, cancered.
CAN.CE.RO.SO, *adj.*, cancered, cankered, affected with cancer, cancerous.

CAN.CHA, *s. f.*, football field, court, ground, playground.
CAN.CI.O.NEI.RO, *s. m.*, collection of songs.
CAN.DE.EI.RO, *s. m.*, candle-holder, chandelier, lamp.
CAN.DEI.A, *s. f.*, lamp, candle, light.
CAN.DE.LA.BRO, *s. m.*, chandelier.
CAN.DEN.TE, *adj.*, *s. 2 gen.*, candescent, glowing.
CAN.DI.DA.TAR-SE, *v.*, to be a candidat for, stand for, run for.
CAN.DI.DA.TO, *s. m.*, candidate, applicant, aspirant.
CAN.DI.DA.TU.RA, *s. f.*, candidateship, candidature, claim, aspiration.
CAN.DI.DEZ, *s. f.*, whiteness, pureness.
CÂN.DI.DO, *adj.*, white, pure, innocent, sincere.
CAN.DU.RA, *s. f.*, whiteness, pureness, sincerity.
CA.NE.CA, *s. f.*, mug, cup, tankard.
CA.NE.CO, *s. m.*, beer mug.
CA.NE.LA, *s. f.*, cinnamon, cinnamon tree; shin, shinbone.
CA.NE.LA.DA, *s. f.*, a blow on the shinbone.
CA.NE.TA, *s. f.*, pen, penholder.
CA.NE.TA-TIN.TEI.RO, *s. f.*, fountain-pen.
CÂN.FO.RA, *s. f.*, camphor, gum camphor.
CAN.GA, *s. f.*, a yoke for oxen; oppression.
CAN.GA.CEI.RO, *s. m.*, bandid, brigand.
CAN.GAR, *v.*, to put the oxen into the yoke, to subdue.
CAN.GO.TE, *s. m.*, occipital region.
CAN.GU.RU, *s. m.*, kangaroo.
CÂ.NHA.MO, *s. m.*, hemp, hemp plant.
CA.NHÃO, *s. m.*, cannon, gun, gorge, defile, ravine, canyon.
CA.NHES.TRO, *adj.*, *s. m.*, clumsy, left-handed, awkward.
CA.NHO.TA, *s. f.*, the left hand.
CA.NHO.TO, *s. m.*, left-hander, counterfoil; *adj.*, left-handed, left.
CA.NI.BAL, *s. 2 gen.*, cannibal, anthropophagite, brutal, cruel; *adj.*, cruel, barbarous.
CA.NI.BA.LIS.MO, *s. m.*, cannibalism, man-eating, anthropophagy.
CA.NI.ÇO, *s. m.*, fishing-rod, rod.
CA.NI.CUL.TU.RA, *s. f.*, breeding of dogs.
CA.NIL, *s. m.*, kennel, dog-house.
CA.NI.NO, *s. m.*, canine tooth, eye tooth, fang; *adj.*, canine, doglike.
CA:NI.VE.TE, *s. m.*, pocket-knife, penknife, jack-knife.
CAN.JA, *s. f.*, chicken soup; easy to do, chicken broth.
CA.NO, *s. m.*, tube, pipe, barrel, barrel of a gun.
CA.NO.A, *s. f.*, canoe, boat, skiff, yawl.
CA.NÔ.NI.CO, *adj.*, canonic.
CA.NO.NI.ZA.ÇÃO, *s. f.*, canonization.
CA.NO.NI.ZA.DO, *adj.*, canonized, sainted.
CA.NO.NI.ZAR, *v.*, to canonize, to declare saint.
CA.NO.RO, *adj.*, canorous, pleasant.
CAN.SA.ÇO, *s. m.*, fatigue, weariness, tiredness, lassitude.
CAN.SA.DO, *adj.*, tired, fatigued, weary, spent, outworn.
CAN.SAR, *v.*, tire, weary, to cause fatigue.
CAN.SA.TI.VO, *adj.*, tiresome, tiring, fatiguing, toilsome.
CAN.SEI.RA, *s. f.*, fatigue, weariness, tiredness.
CAN.TAR, *v.*, to sing, to chant, to warble.
CÂN.TA.RO, *s. m.*, jar, jug, pitcher, urn.
CAN.TA.RO.LAR, *v.*, to sing with a low voice, to trill.
CAN.TEI.RO, *s. m.*, stone-cutter, stone-mason, flower-box.
CAN.TI.GA, *s. f.*, ditty, ballad.
CAN.TIL, *s. m.*, canteen, water-bottle.
CAN.TI.NA, *s. f.*, canteen, mess, tavern.
CAN.TO, *s. m.*, corner, angle, edge; song, chant, singing.
CAN.TO.NEI.RA, *s. f.*, a corner shelf or stand, corner cupboard.
CAN.TOR, *s. m.*, singer, crooner, songster, chanter.
CAN.TO.RA, *s. f.*, songstress, singer.
CÃO, *s. m.*, dog, hound; hammer of a gun.
CA.O.LHO, *adj.*, *s. m.*, one-eyed, cross-eyed.
CA.OS, *s. m.*, chaos, mess, under confusion.
CA.Ó.TI.CO, *adj.*, chaotic, confused.
CA.PA, *s. f.*, coat, cloak, overcoat, cover, mantle.

CA.PA.ÇÃO, *s. f.*, castration.
CA.PA.CE.TE, *s. m.*, helmet, helm, headpiece.
CA.PA.CHO, *s. m.*, door-mat, rug; obeying, servile.
CA.PA.CI.DA.DE, *s. f.*, capacity, ability, volume, capability, competence, talent.
CA.PA.CI.TAR, *v.*, to capacitate, to qualify, to enable, to persuade.
CA.PA.DO, *adj.*, castrated.
CA.PAN.GA, *s. m.*, bully, crime associate, mobster; money bag, bag.
CA.PAR, *v.*, to castrate, to emasculate.
CA.PA.TAZ, *s. m.*, foreman, headman.
CA.PAZ, *adj.*, capable, able, apt, fit, good.
CAP.CI.O.SO, *adj.*, catchy, captious, fallacious.
CA.PE.AR, *v.*, to cover with a coat, to hide.
CA.PE.LA, *s. f.*, chapel, sanctuary.
CA.PEN.GA, *s. 2 gen.*, crippled; *adj.*, crippled, lame.
CA.PE.TA, *s. m.*, devil; naughty child.
CA.PIM, *s. m.*, grass, hay, sedge.
CA.PI.NA, *s. f.*, the act of cutting the grass, weeding.
CA.PI.NA.DO, *adj.*, weeded.
CA.PI.NAR, *v.*, to weed, to hoe.
CA.PIN.ZAL, *s. m.*, pasture, hayfield.
CA.PI.TAL, *s. f.*, capital, funds, wealth, metropolis; *adj.*, capitalistic, essencial, vital.
CA.PI.TA.LIS.MO, *s. m.*, capitalism, economic system.
CA.PI.TA.LIS.TA, *s. 2 gen.*, capitalist, stockholder; *adj.*, capitalistic.
CA.PI.TA.LI.ZA.ÇÃO, *s. f.*, capitalization.
CA.PI.TA.LI.ZAR, *v.*, to capitalize, to accumulate, to amass money.
CA.PI.TÃO, *s. m.*, captain, military commander, leader, chief, officer of the army; political boss.
CA.PI.TU.LA.ÇÃO, *s. f.*, capitulation, surrender, rendition.
CA.PI.TU.LAR, *v.*, to capitulate, to surrender, to agree, to enunciate, to compromise.
CA.PÍ.TU.LO, *s. m.*, chapter.
CA.PI.VA.RA, *s. f.*, capybara, capibara.
CA.PÔ, *s. m.*, hood.

CA.PO.EI.RA, *s. f.*, brushwood, coop; technique of sudden fight.
CA.PO.TA, *s. f.*, cap, hood, headdress, capote.
CA.PO.TA.GEM, *s. f.*, capsize, capsizal.
CA.PO.TAR, *v.*, to capsize, to overturn.
CA.PO.TE, *s. m.*, cloak, mantle, overcoat.
CA.PRI.CHAR, *v.*, to perfect, to excel, to elaborate.
CA.PRI.CHO, *s. m.*, caprice, fancy, whim, freakishness, skittishness.
CA.PRI.CHO.SO, *adj.*, fanciful, freakish, capricious, skittish; petulant, obstinate, extravagant.
CA.PRI.CÓR.NIO, *s. m.*, Capricorn.
CA.PRI.NO, *adj.*, caprine, goatlike, hircine.
CÁP.SU.LA, *s. f.*, capsule.
CAP.TA.ÇÃO, *s. f.*, captation, captivation.
CAP.TAR, *v.*, to captivate, to collect, to catch, to ingratiate.
CAP.TU.RAR, *v.*, to capture, to seize, to catch, to occupy, to arrest.
CA.PUZ, *s. m.*, cap, hood, bonnet.
CA.QUI, *s. m.*, kaki: the fruit of the persimmon tree.
CÁ.QUI, *s. m.*, khaki, khaki-coloured cotton cloth; *adj.*, khaki, khaki-coloured.
CA.RA, *s. f.*, face, appearance, look, outward appearance, boldness.
CA.RA.BI.NA, *s. f.*, rifle.
CA.RA.COL, *s. m.*, snail, caracol, spiral, a spiral line.
CA.RAC.TE.RES, *s. m., pl.*, characters, signs, marks; written letters, printing types.
CA.RAC.TE.RÍS.TI.CA, *s. f.*, characteristic(s), trait, mark.
CA.RAC.TE.RÍS.TI.CO, *adj.*, characteristic, peculiar, distinctive, typical, discriminative.
CA.RAC.TE.RI.ZA.ÇÃO, *s. f.*, characterization, making-up, artistic representation, personality.
CA.RAC.TE.RI.ZA.DO, *adj.*, characterized.
CA.RAC.TE.RI.ZAR, *v.*, to characterize, to point out, to describe, to distinguish, to mark.
CA.RA DE PAU, *s. m.*, brazen, straight-faced person; *adj.*, wooden-faced.
CA.RAM.BO.LA, *s. f.*, starfruit, carom.

CARAMELO   **CARNICEIRO**

CA.RA.ME.LO, *s. m.*, caramel, frozen snow, candy.
CA.RA-ME.TA.DE, *s. f.*, wife.
CA.RA.MU.JO, *s. m.*, snail.
CA.RAN.GUE.JO, *s. m.*, crab; Cancer (zod.)
CA.RA.PU.ÇA, *s. f.*, cap, hood, skull cap, hood, cowl.
CA.RA.TÊ, *s. m.*, karate.
CA.RÁ.TER, *s. m.*, character, mark, feature; badge, symbol, type, structure, letter(s).
CA.RA.VA.NA, *s. f.*, caravan.
CA.RA.VE.LA, *s. f.*, caravel, small sailing vessel.
CAR.BO.I.DRA.TO, *s. m.*, carbohydrate.
CAR.BO.NAR, *v.*, to carbonate, to carbonize.
CAR.BO.NA.TO, *s. m.*, carbonate.
CAR.BO.NÍ.FE.RO, *adj.*, carboniferous, carbonaceous.
CAR.BO.NI.ZA.ÇÃO, *s. f.*, carbonization.
CAR.BO.NI.ZAR, *v.*, to carbonize, burn out.
CAR.BO.NO, *s. m.*, carbon.
CAR.BU.RA.ÇÃO, *s. f.*, carburetion, carburation.
CAR.BU.RA.DOR, *s. m.*, carburetor.
CAR.BU.RAR, *v.*, to carburize, to carburet.
CAR.CA.ÇA, *s. f.*, carcass, carcase, skeleton, framework.
CAR.CE.RA.GEM, *s. f.*, incarceration.
CÁR.CE.RE, *s. m.*, prison, jail.
CAR.CE.REI.RO, *s. m.*, prison guard, director of prison, jailer, warden.
CAR.DA.ÇÃO, *s. f.*, carding, combing.
CAR.DÁ.PIO, *s. m.*, menu, carte.
CAR.DE.AL, *s. m.*, cardinal, principal chief; prelate; *adj.*, cardinal, principal.
CAR.DÍ.A.CO, *adj.*, cardiac, patient.
CAR.DI.NAL, *adj.*, cardinal, basic; **NÚMERO CARDINAL**, *s. m.*, cardinal number.
CAR.DI.O.GRA.FI.A, *s. f.*, cardiography, cardiogram.
CAR.DI.O.LO.GIS.TA, *s. 2 gen.*, cardiologist.
CAR.DU.ME, *s. m.*, shoal of fish, run, flock, cluster.
CA.RE.CA, *s. f.*, baldness; *adj.*, bald, bald-headed.
CA.RE.CER, *v.*, to lack, to need, to require, to necessitate.
CA.REI.RO, *adj.*, costly, expensive.
CA.RÊN.CIA, *s. f.*, lack, need, necessity, scarcity.
CA.REN.TE, *adj.*, wanting, destitute, shy.
CA.RES.TI.A, *s. f.*, high prices, dearness, costlines, scarcity, need.
CA.RE.TA, *s. f.*, grimace, mask, scowl; person stupid, person obsolete.
CAR.GA, *s. f.*, load, burden, freight, cargo, loading.
CAR.GO, *s. m.*, load, charge, duty, task, office, employment, responsibility.
CAR.GUEI.RO, *s. m.*, cargo boat, cargo vessel, freighter.
CA.RI.CA.TU.RA, *s. f.*, caricature, exaggeration; parody, ridiculous person.
CA.RI.CA.TU.RIS.TA, *s. 2 gen.*, cartoonist, caricaturist.
CA.RÍ.CIA, *s. f.*, caress, fondling, affection.
CA.RI.DA.DE, *s. f.*, charity, kindliness, benevolence, mercy, generosity.
CA.RI.DO.SO, *adj.*, charitable, kind, gentle, benevolent.
CÁ.RIE, *s. f.*, caries, tooth decay.
CA.RIM.BA.DO, *adj.*, stamped, sealed.
CA.RIM.BAR, *v.*, to stamp, to seal, to imprint.
CA.RIM.BO, *s. m.*, seal, stamp, signet.
CA.RI.NHO, *s. m.*, kindness, gentleness, caress, fondling, love, affection.
CA.RI.NHO.SO, *adj.*, kind, loving, tender, gentle, affectionate.
CA.RI.O.CA, *adj.*, *s. 2 gen.*, carioca, inhabitant of Rio de Janeiro.
CA.RIS.MA, *s. m.*, charism.
CAR.NAL, *adj.*, fleshly, carnal; bodily, libidinous, sensual.
CAR.NA.LI.DA.DE, *s. f.*, carnality, fleshiness, sensuality.
CAR.NA.VAL, *s. m.*, carnival.
CAR.NE, *s. f.*, flesh, meat, the pulp of fruit; sensuality.
CAR.NEI.RO, *s. m.*, sheep, ram, wether, mutton.
CAR.NE-SE.CA, *s. f.*, jerked meat.
CAR.NI.ÇA, *s. f.*, prey, booty.
CAR.NI.CEI.RO, *s. m.*, butcher, slaughterer; *adj.*, carnivorous, sanguinary.

CAR.NI.FI.CI.NA, *s. f.*, bloodshed, massacre, slaughter.
CAR.NÍ.VO.RO, *s. m.*, carnivore; *adj.*, carnivorous.
CA.RO, *adj.*, dear, costly, expensive.
CA.RO.ÇO, *s. m.*, heart, stone, pit, kernel.
CA.RO.LA, *s. 2 gen.*, piety, devotee, religionist; *adj.*, sanctimonious, pietistic.
CA.RO.LI.CE, *s. f.*, religious fanatism, pietism.
CA.RO.NA, *s. f.*, ride, lift.
CAR.PA, *s. f.*, carp.
CAR.PIN.TA.RI.A, *s. f.*, carpenter's art, carpentry.
CAR.PIN.TEI.RO, *s. m.*, carpenter, woodworker.
CAR.RAN.CU.DO, *adj.*, scowling, frowning, grim.
CAR.RA.PA.TO, *s. m.*, tick, louse.
CAR.RAS.CO, *s. m.*, hangman, hanger, executioner, torturer.
CAR.RE.AR, *v.*, to cart, to carry, to transport, to haul.
CAR.RE.GA.DOR, *s. m.*, loader, packer, porter, trucker, freighter.
CAR.RE.GA.MEN.TO, *s. m.*, lading, loading, cargo, load, oppression.
CAR.RE.GAR, *v.*, to burden, to load, to freight, to bear, to carry, to transport, to charge.
CAR.REI.RA, *s. f.*, profession, career, cartway, route, track.
CAR.RE.TA, *s. f.*, cart, waggon, gig.
CAR.RIL, *s. m.*, rail, steel rail.
CAR.RI.NHO, *s. m.*, dim. form of **CARRO**; a child's play car.
CAR.RO, *s. m.*, car, automobile, cart, carriage, motorcar.
CAR.RO.ÇA, *s. f.*, waggon, cart.
CAR.ROS.SEL, *s. m.*, carrousel, roundabout, merry-go-round.
CAR.RU.A.GEM, *s. f.*, carriage, coach, car, cart, chariot.
CAR.TA, *s. f.*, letter, missive, map, chart, epistle, playing card; charter, bill; document.
CAR.TÃO, *s. m.*, card.
CAR.TAZ, *s. f.*, poster, placard.
CAR.TEI.RA, *s. f.*, wallet, purse;

CARTEIRA DE IDENTIDADE, *s. f.*, identity card.
CAR.TEI.RO, *s. m.*, postman, mailman.
CAR.TI.LA.GEM, *s. f.*, cartilage, gristle.
CAR.TI.LHA, *s. f.*, primer, speller, spelling book.
CAR.TO.LI.NA, *s. f.*, cardboard, pasteboard.
CAR.TO.MAN.TE, *s. 2 gen.*, fortuneteller, cartomancer.
CAR.TÓ.RIO, *s. m.*, register office, registry office, registry, archives.
CAR.TU.CHO, *s. m.*, cartridge, shell, cartouche.
CAR.VA.LHO, *s. m.*, oak, oak tree, oak wood.
CAR.VÃO, *s. f.*, coal, charcoal, cinder.
CAR.VO.A.RI.A, *s. f.*, coal-pit, charcoal works.
CÃS, *s. f.*, white hair.
CA.SA, *s. f.*, house, residence, place, habitation, building; home, family.
CA.SA BAN.CÁ.RIA, *s. f.*, bank.
CA.SA.CO, *s. m.*, coat, jacket, overcoat.
CA.SA.DO, *adj.*, married, wedded, united.
CA.SAL, *s. m.*, couple, pair.
CA.SA.MEN.TO, *s. m.*, marriage, wedding, matrimony, match, espousal.
CA.SAR, *v.*, to marry, to wed, to match, to mate, to espouse, to unite.
CA.SA.RÃO, *s. m.*, large house, building.
CAS.CA, *s. f.*, peel, rind, skin, shell, bark, husk.
CAS.CA.LHO, *s. m.*, gravel, pebbles, grit.
CAS.CA.TA, *s. f.*, cascade, waterfall.
CAS.CA.VEL, *s. f.*, rattlesnake, rattle.
CAS.CO, *s. m.*, hoof, hull, skul, scalp, keg, skin.
CA.SE.BRE, *s. m.*, little paltry cottage, shack.
CA.SE.Í.NA, *s. f.*, casein.
CA.SEI.RO, *s. m.*, tenant, farm manager; *adj.*, home-made, domestic.
CA.SER.NA, *s. f.*, barracks, casern.
CA.SI.MI.RA, *s. f.*, cashmere.
CA.SO, *s. m.*, affair, case, event, fact, story, tale, chance, accident, condiction.
CA.SO, *conj.*, if, if so, thus.
CA.SÓ.RIO, *s. m.*, marriage.
CAS.PA, *s. f.*, dandruff, scaly skin, scale.
CAS.SAR, *v.*, to annul, to cancel, to repeal, to revoke.

CAS.SE.TE.TE, *s. m.*, truncheon, billy.
CAS.SI.NO, *s. m.*, cassino (= casino), a game at cards; building or club for dancing or gambling.
CAS.TA, *s. f.*, caste, race, lineage, stock.
CAS.TA.NHA, *s. f.*, chestnut.
CAS.TA.NHA-DO-PA.RÁ, *s. f.*, Brazil nut.
CAS.TA.NHO, *adj.*, brown, chestnut.
CAS.TE.LHA.NO, *adj., s. m.*, Castilian; Spanish.
CAS.TE.LO, *s. m.*, castle, fortress, fort.
CAS.TI.ÇAL, *s. m.*, candlestick, candleholder.
CAS.TI.DA.DE, *s. f.*, chastity, chasteness, purity, continency, virtue.
CAS.TI.GA.DO, *adj.*, punished, chastised.
CAS.TI.GAR, *v.*, to punish, to castigate, to discipline, to chasten.
CAS.TI.GO, *s. m.*, punishment, penalty, chastisement, correction.
CAS.TO, *adj.*, chaste, pure, clean, virginal, virtuous.
CAS.TOR, *s. m.*, beaver, castor.
CAS.TRA.ÇÃO, *s. f.*, castration.
CAS.TRAR, *v.*, to castrate, to geld, to spay.
CA.SU.AL, *adj.*, casual, occasional, incidental.
CA.SU.A.LI.DA.DE, *s. f.*, casualty, fortuity; accident, hazard, contingency, eventuality.
CA.SU.ÍS.MO, *s. m.*, casuistry.
CA.SU.ÍS.TI.CA, *s. f.*, casuistry.
CA.SU.ÍS.TI.CO, *adj.*, casuistic.
CA.SU.LO, *s. m.*, cocoon.
CA.TA.CLIS.MO, *s. m.*, cataclysm; catastrophe, disaster, ruin.
ÇA.TA.CUM.BA, *s. f.*, catacomb.
CA.TA.LEP.SI.A, *s. f.*, catalepsy.
CA.TA.LI.SAR, *v.*, to catalyze.
CA.TÁ.LI.SE, *s. f.*, catalysis.
CA.TA.LO.GAR, *v.*, to catologue, to classify, to make a list of, to register.
CA.TÁ.LO.GO, *s. m.*, catalogue, catalog, roll, register.
CA.TA.PLAS.MA, *s. m.*, cataplasm, plaster.
CA.TA.PO.RA, *s. f.*, chicken pox, varicella.
CA.TAR, *v.*, to collect, to seek, to discover, to scrutinize.
CA.TA.RA.TA, *s. f.*, cataract, waterfall.

CA.TAR.RO, *s. m.*, catarrh.
CA.TAR.SE, *s.f.*, catharsis, purification, purifying.
CA.TÁS.TRO.FE, *s. f.*, catastrophe, calamity.
CA.TE.CIS.MO, *s. m.*, catechism, religious instruction.
CÁ.TE.DRA, *s. f.*, cathedra, chair.
CA.TE.DRAL, *s. m.*, cathedral, dome.
CA.TE.GO.RI.A, *s. f.*, category, class, order, grade, series, character, quality.
CA.TE.GÓ.RI.CO, *adj.*, categorical, explicit, absolute, decisive.
CA.TE.QUE.SE, *s. f.*, catechesis.
CA.TE.QUI.ZAR, *v.*, catechize, to teach, to convince.
CA.TIN.GA, *s. f.*, fetid smell.
CA.TI.VAR, *v.*, to captivate, to capture, to hold captive, to charm, to fascinate, to enchant.
CA.TI.VEI.RO, *s. m.*, captivity, slavery, servitude, prison, preoccupation.
CA.TI.VO, *s. m.*, captive, prisoner, slave; *adj.*, captive, confined, charmed, fascinating.
CA.TO.LI.CIS.MO, *s. m.*, Catholicism, faith.
CA.TÓ.LI.CO, *adj., s. m.*, Roman Catholic, Catholic.
CA.TOR.ZE, *num.*, fourteen.
CA.TRA.CA, *s. f.*, turnstile, ratchet.
CAU.ÇÃO, *s. f.*, security, guarantee, guaranty, pledge, bond.
CAU.CI.O.NAR, *v.*, to bail, to bond, to vouch for, to pledge.
CAU.DI.LHO, *s. m.*, commander, chief, military leader.
CAU.LE, *s. m.*, stalk, stem.
CAU.SA, *s. f.*, cause, motive, reason, ground, origin.
CAU.SAL, *adj.*, causal, causative.
CAU.SAR, *v.*, to cause, to motivate, to occasion, to engender, to provoke.
CAU.SÍ.DI.CO, *s. m.*, lawyer, attorney.
CAU.TE.LA, *s. f.*, caution, vigilance, watchfulness, prudence.
CAU.TE.LO.SO, *adj.*, cautious, careful, prudent, watchful.
CAU.TE.RI.ZA.ÇÃO, *s.f.*, cautery, cauterization.

CAUTERIZAR | **85** | **CENSO**

CAU.TE.RI.ZAR, *v.*, cauterize, to sear, to burn.
CAU.TO, *adj.*, cautious, prudent.
CA.VA.CO, *s. m.*, a chip of wood.
CA.VA.DEI.RA, *s. f.*, hoe.
CA.VA.DOR, *s. m.*, digger, hoer, ploughman, digging tool.
CA.VA.LA.RI.A, *s. f.*, cavalry, chivalry, a group of horsemen.
CA.VA.LEI.RA, *s. f.*, horsewoman.
CA.VA.LEI.RO, *s. m.*, horseman, rider, equestrian, cavalryman.
CA.VAL.GA.DA, *s. f.*, cavalcade, rodeo.
CA.VAL.GA.DU.RA, *s. f.*, beast, saddle animal; stupid, a rude person.
CA.VAL.GAR, *v.*, to ride on horseback, to mount a horse to jockey.
CA.VA.LHEI.RO, *s. m.*, gentleman; *adj.*, noble.
CA.VA.LO, *s. m.*, horse; knight.
CA.VA.LO-MA.RI.NHO, *s. m.*, sea-horse, hippopotamus.
CA.VA.LO-VA.POR, *s. m.*, horse-power.
CA.VA.NHA.QUE, *s. m.*, goatee, goatee beard.
CA.VA.QUI.NHO, *s. m.*, small guitar.
CA.VAR, *v.*, to dig, to delve, to excavate, to burrow, to cave, to hoe.
CA.VEI.RA, *s. f.*, skull, death's-head.
CA.VER.NA, *s. f.*, cave, cavern, grotto, den, crypt.
CA.VI.AR, *s. m.*, caviar.
CA.VI.DA.DE, *s. f.*, cavity; hole.
CA.XUM.BA, *s. f.*, mumps, parotitis.
CE.AR, *v.*, to eat supper, to dine.
CE.BO.LA, *s. f.*, onion.
CE.BO.LA.DA, *s. f.*, onion stew.
CE.BO.LI.NHA, *s. f.*, welsh onion.
CE.DÊN.CIÁ, *s. f.*, cession, transfer.
CE.DER, *v.*, to cede, to assign, to transfer, to submit.
CE.DI.LHA, *s. f.*, cedilla mark.
CE.DI.NHO, *adv.*, very early.
CE.DO, *adv.*, early, soon.
CE.DRO, *s. m.*, cedar, juniper.
CÉ.DU.LA, *s. f.*, note, short letter, ticket.
CE.FA.LI.TE, *s. f.*, cephalitis.

CE.GA.MEN.TO, *s. m.*, blindness, deprivation of sight.
CE.GAR, *v.*, to blind, to fascinate, to charm, to deprive of sight, to dazzle, daze.
CE.GO, *s. m.*, blind man; *adj.*, blind, blunt, sightless, blinded, dazzled.
CE.GO.NHA, *s. f.*, stork.
CE.GUEI.RA, *s. f.*, blindness, passion, fanatism.
CEI.A, *s. f.*, supper, evening meal.
CE.LA, *s. f.*, cell.
CE.LE.BRA.ÇÃO, *s. f.*, celebration, commemoration, solemnity.
CE.LE.BRAN.TE, *s. 2 gen.*, celebrant; *adj.*, celebrative, celebrant.
CE.LE.BRAR, *v.*, to celebrate, to commemorate, to officiate.
CÉ.LE.BRE, *adj.*, famous, renowned, celebrated, eminent.
CE.LE.BRI.DA.DE, *s. f.*, celebrity, fame, renown; idol star.
CE.LE.BRI.ZAR, *v.*, to fame, to render famous.
CE.LEI.RO, *s. m.*, cellar, granary, corn-floor.
CE.LE.RA.DO, *s. m.*, criminal, malefactor, felon.
CÉ.LE.RE, *adj.*, swift, quick.
CE.LES.TE, *adj.*, celestial, heavenly, divine, paradisiac.
CE.LES.TI.AL, *adj.*, celestial.
CE.LEU.MA, *s. f.*, noise, clamour; uproar, tumult.
CE.LI.BA.TO, *s. m.*, celibacy, bachelorhood.
CE.LO.FA.NE, *s. m.*, cellophane.
CÉ.LU.LA, *s. f.*, cell, cellule.
CE.LU.LAR, *adj.*, cellular.
CE.LU.LI.TE, *s. f.*, cellulitis.
CE.LU.LOI.DE, *s. f.*, celluloid.
CE.LU.LO.SE, *s. f.*, cellulose.
CEM, *num.*, one hundred, a hundred.
CE.MI.TÉ.RIO, *s. m.*, cemetery, burial ground, necropolis.
CE.NA, *s. f.*, scene, stage, scenery, picture.
CE.NÁ.RIO, *s. m.*, scenery, set, landscape.
CE.NO.GRA.FI.A, *s. f.*, scenography.
CE.NÓ.GRA.FO, *s. m.*, scenographer.
CE.NOU.RA, *s. f.*, carrot.
CEN.SO, *s. m.*, census, cense, rank, computation,

CENSOR / **CHÁ**

tribute.
CEN.SOR, *s. m.*, censor, critic, censurer, controller.
CEN.SU.RA, *s. f.*, censorship.
CEN.SU.RAR, *v.*, to censure, to control, to subject to censure, to criticize.
CEN.TA.VO, *s. m.*, cent, centavo, penny, pence.
CEN.TEI.O, *s. m.*, rye.
CEN.TE.LHA, *s. f.*, spark, scintilla, flash, sparkle.
CEN.TE.NA, *s. f.*, a hundred.
CEN.TE.NÁ.RIO, *s. m.*, centenarian, centennial, centenary; *adj.*, centennial, centenary.
CEN.TÉ.SI.MO, *s. m.*, centesimal, hundredth.
CEN.TÍ.GRA.DO, *adj.*, *s. m.*, centigrade.
CEN.TÍ.ME.TRO, *s. m.*, centimetre, centimeter.
CEN.TO, *num.*, a hundred.
CEN.TO.PEI.A, *s. f.*, centipede.
CEN.TRAL, *s. f.*, central, headquarters; *adj.*, central, centric.
CEN.TRA.LI.ZA.DO, *adj.*, centralized.
CEN.TRA.LI.ZAR, *v.*, to centralize, to concentrate.
CEN.TRÍ.FU.GA, *s. f.*, centrifuge.
CEN.TRO, *s. m.*, center, centre, focal point, middle; nucleus.
CÉP.TI.CO, *adj.*, sceptic, agnostic, cynical.
CE.RA, *s. f.*, wax.
CE.RÂ.MI.CA, *s. f.*, ceramics, pottery.
CER.CA, *s. f.*, fence, wire fence, railing, hedge;
CERCA DE, *loc. prep.*, approximately, about.
CER.CA, *adv.*, near, close by, approximate.
CER.CA.DO, *s. m.*, enclosure, yard, park; *adj.*, enclosed, hedged in.
CER.CA.NI.AS, *s. f., pl.*, outskirts.
CER.CAR, *v.*, to surround, to fence in, to enclose, to wall.
CER.CE.AR, *v.*, to lessen, to restrict, to cut around, to cut short.
CER.CO, *s. m.*, circle, siege, encirclement, envelopment.
CE.RE.AL, *s. m.*, cereal, corn, grain.
CE.RE.BRAL, *adj.*, cerebral.
CÉ.RE.BRO, *s. m.*, brain; intelligence.
CE.RE.JA, *s. f.*, cherry.
CE.RE.JEI.RA, *s. f.*, cherry tree.

CE.RI.MÔ.NIA, *s. f.*, ceremony, solemnity, rite, civility.
CE.RI.MO.NI.AL, *s. m.*, rites; *adj.*, ceremonial, ritual.
CER.NE, *s. m.*, center, core, pith.
CER.RA.ÇÃO, *s. f.*, fog, mist, haze, fogginess, darkness.
CER.RAR, *v.*, to close, to shut, to join, to clench.
CER.TA.ME, *s. m.*, fight, combat, discussion, argument.
CER.TEI.RO, *adj.*, adequate, right, convenient, correct.
CER.TE.ZA, *s. f.*, certainty, conviction, confidence, security.
CER.TI.DÃO, *s. f.*, certificate, attestation, voucher.
CER.TI.FI.CA.DO, *s. m.*, certification, certificate, attestation, voucher.
CER.TI.FI.CAR, *v.*, to certify, to attest, to confirm, to authenticate, to affirm.
CER.TO, *adj.*, certain, true, exact, evident, sure, correct, assured, positive.
CER.VE.JA, *s. f.*, beer, ale.
CER.VE.JA.RI.A, *s. f.*, beershop, ale-house, beerhouse, brewery.
CER.VO, *s. m.*, deer.
CE.SA.RI.A.NA, *s. f.*, Caesarian, Caesarian operation.
CES.SA.ÇÃO, *s. f.*, cessation, ceasing, interruption, break.
CES.SÃO, *s. f.*, cession, release.
CES.SAR, *v.*, to cease, to stop, to discontinue, to interrupt.
CES.TA, *s. f.*, basket, coop.
CES.TO, *s. m.*, basket.
CE.TI.CIS.MO, *s. m.*, scepticism.
CÉ.TI.CO, *adj.*, sceptic, cynical.
CE.TIM, *s. m.*, satin.
CE.TRO, *s. m.*, scepter, sceptre.
CÉU, *s. m.*, sky, heaven, firmament, paradise, sphere.
CE.VA.DA, *s. f.*, barley.
CE.VAR, *v.*, to make fat, fatten, to bait, to feed, to nourish.
CHÁ, *s. m.*, tea; tea party, tea-plant.

CHÃ, *adj.*, plain, plateau.
CHA.CAL, *s. m.*, jackal.
CHÁ.CA.RA, *s. f.*, country seat, country house, small farm.
CHA.CI.NA, *s. f.*, slaughter, massacre.
CHA.CI.NAR, *v.*, to slaughter, to massacre.
CHA.CO.TA, *s. f.*, mockery, derision, banter, joke.
CHA.FA.RIZ, *s. m.*, fountain.
CHA.GA, *s. f.*, ulcer, sore, fester.
CHA.LA.ÇA, *s. f.*, bon mot, mockery, derision.
CHA.LÉ, *s. m.*, cottage, lodge, chalet.
CHA.LEI.RA, *s. f.*, kettle, tea-kettle.
CHA.LU.PA, *s. f.*, long-boat, shallop, sloop.
CHA.MA, *s. f.*, flame, fire, blaze, light.
CHA.MA.DA, *s. f.*, call, calling, recall, roll-call.
CHA.MA.DO, *s. m.*, call; *adj.*, called.
CHA.MAR, *v.*, to call, to hail, to summon, to invoke, to evoke, to convoke, to name.
CHA.MA.RIZ, *s. m.*, lure, bait, advertisement, attraction.
CHA.MI.NÉ, *s. f.*, chimney, chimney flue.
CHAM.PA.NHE, *s. m.*, champaign.
CHAM.PI.NHOM, *s. m.*, champignon.
CHA.MUS.CA.DO, *adj.*, slightly burned.
CHA.MUS.CAR, *v.*, to singe, to burn slightly, to scorch.
CHAN.CE, *s. f.*, chance, opportunity, vantage.
CHAN.FRAR, *v.*, to chamfer, to groove, to flute.
CHAN.TA.GEM. *s. f.*, extortion.
CHAN.TA.GIS.TA, *s. 2 gen.*, blackmailer, extortionist.
CHÃO, *s. m.*, earth, ground, floor, plot, background; *adj.*, plain.
CHA.PA, *s. f.*, metal sheet, plate, lamina, pane, foil, tag, tablet.
CHA.PE.LA.RI.A, *s. f.*, hattery, hatmaker's shop.
CHA.PÉU, *s. m.*, hat, dregs of wine.
CHA.RA.DA, *s. f.*, charade, riddle, problem.
CHAR.CO, *s. m.*, bog, dirty, stagnant water, slough.
CHAR.LA.TA.NIS.MO, *s. m.*, charlatanism, charlatanry.
CHAR.LA.TÃO, *s. m.*, charlatan, quack, impostor, faker.
CHA.RU.TA.RI.A, *s. f.*, tobacco shop, cigar shop.
CHA.RU.TEI.RA, *s. f.*, cigar case.
CHA.RU.TO, *s. m.*, cigar, cheroot, stogy.
CHAS.SI, *s. m.*, chassis, frame, body.
CHA.TE.AR, *v.*, to annoy, to importune, to bother, to bore.
CHA.TO, *s. m.*, crablouse; *adj.*, smooth, plain; importunate, annoying.
CHAU.VI.NIS.MO, *s. m.*, chauvinism.
CHA.VÃO, *s. m.*, cliché, household word.
CHA.VE, *s. f.*, key; keynote (mus.)
CHA.VEI.RO, *s. m.*, key keeper, doorman, key rack, jailer.
CHÁ.VE.NA, *s. f.*, tea-cup, cup.
CHE.FÃO, *s. m.*, political leader, boss, big shot.
CHE.FE, *s. m.*, chief, leader, boss, manager, principal.
CHE.FI.A, *s. f.*, leadership, managership.
CHE.FI.AR, *v.*, to direct, to manage, to govern, to chief.
CHE.GA.DA, *s. f.*, arrival, approach, coming.
CHE.GAR, *v.*, to come, to arrive, to begin, to start, to border, to be enough.
CHEI.A, *s. f.*, inundation, flood.
CHEI.O, *adj.*, full, filled up, replete, crammed, packed, massive, dense, pregnant.
CHEI.RAR, *v.*, to smell, to sniff, to snuff, to scent, to investigate, to suspect.
CHEI.RO, *s. m.*, smell, scent, odour, perfume, fragrance.
CHE.QUE, *s. m.*, check, cheque.
CHI.AR, *v.*, to creak, to squeak, to hiss.
CHI.CLE.TE, *s. m.*, chewing gum.
CHI.CÓ.RIA, *s. f.*, chicory, endive.
CHI.CO.TE, *s. m.*, whip, lash.
CHI.FRE, *s. m.*, horn.
CHI.LE.NO, *adj.*, *s. m.*, Chilean.
CHI.NE.LO, *s. m.*, slipper, scuff.
CHI.NÊS, *adj.*, *s. m.*, Chinese.
CHI.QUE, *adj.*, elegant, smart, chic, beautiful, handsome.
CHI.QUEI.RO, *s. m.*, pigsty, sty.

CHIS.TE, *s. m.*, jocosity, joke, jest, wit, witty remark.
CHO.ÇA, *s. f.*, hut, hovel, shack.
CHO.CA.DEI.RA, *s. f.*, a broody hen, brooder.
CHO.CA.LHAR, *v.*, to shake, to stir up, to brattle, to chime.
CHO.CAR, *v.*, to shock, brood, incubate.
CHO.CO.LA.TE, *s. m.*, chocolate.
CHO.FER, *s. m.*, driver.
CHO.PA.DA, *s. f.*, beer party.
CHO.PE, *s. m.*, beer.
CHO.QUE, *s. m.*, collision, crash, clash, impact, shock.
CHO.RA.DEI.RA, *s. f.*, weeping, crying.
CHO.RÃO, *s. m.*, weeping-willow (Bot.), whimperer; *adj.*, crying, whimpering.
CHO.RAR, *v.*, to weep, to cry, to sob, to mourn, to bemoan.
CHO.RO, *s. m.*, weeping, crying, sobbing, wail.
CHO.RO.SO, *adj.*, weeping, weepy, tearful.
CHOU.PA.NA, *s. f.*, cottage, hut, hovel, grass shack.
CHOU.RI.ÇO, *s. m.*, sausage, smoked sausage.
CHO.VER, *v.*, to rain, to pour down.
CHU.CHU, *s. m.*, chayote.
CHU.LO, *adj.*, coarse, crude, vulgar, common, jesting.
CHUM.BAR, *v.*, to lead, to fasten, to fix, to plug with lead, to solder with lead.
CHUM.BO, *s. m.*, lead, shot, lead pellet.
CHU.PAR, *v.*, to suck, to absorb, to soak in.
CHU.PE.TA, *s. f.*, pacifier, sucking bag.
CHUR.RAS.CA.RI.A, *s. f.*, grill room.
CHUR.RAS.CO, *s. m.*, barbecue.
CHU.TAR, *v.*, to kick the ball, to boot the ball.
CHU.TE, *s. m.*, a kick.
CHU.TEI.RA, *s. f.*, football boot, football shoe.
CHU.VA, *s. f.*, rain, shower.
CHU.VEI.RO, *s. m.*, shower.
CHU.VIS.CAR, *v.*, to drizzle, to mizzle, to dribble.
CHU.VIS.CO, *s. m.*, mizzle, drizzle.
CHU.VO.SO, *adj.*, rainy, showery.
CI.A.NU.RE.TO, *s. m.*, cyanide.
CI.Á.TI.CA, *s. f.*, sciatica, neuralgia of the sciatic nerve.
CI.CA.TRIZ, *s. f.*, cicatrix, scar.
CI.CA.TRI.ZA.ÇÃO, *s. f.*, cicatrization.
CI.CA.TRI.ZAR, *v.*, to cicatrize, to scar, to heal.
CÍ.CLI.CO, *adj.*, cyclic, regular.
CI.CLIS.MO, *s. m.*, cyclism.
CI.CLIS.TA, *s. 2 gen.*, cyclist, bicyclist.
CI.CLO, *s. m.*, cycle.
CI.CLO.NE, *s. m.*, cyclone, hurricane, tornado, twister.
CI.CU.TA, *s. f.*, cicuta, water hemlock.
CI.DA.DÃ, *s. f.*, citizeness.
CI.DA.DA.NI.A, *s. f.*, citizenhood, citizenship.
CI.DA.DÃO, *s. m.*, citizen.
CI.DA.DE, *s. f.*, city, town, capital, burg.
CI.ÊN.CIA, *s. f.*, science, knowledge, wisdom, learning.
CI.EN.TE, *adj.*, aware, knowing, cognizant.
CI.EN.TI.FI.CAR, *v.*, to inform, to notify, to notice.
CI.EN.TIS.TA, *s. 2 gen.*, scientist, savant.
CI.FRA, *s. f.*, cipher, cypher, naught, figure.
CI.FRÃO, *s. m.*, money sign.
CI.FRAR, *v.*, to cipher, to cypher, to code, to resume, to include.
CI.GA.NO, *s. m.*, gypsy, horse-dealer.
CI.GAR.RA, *s. f.*, cicada, grasshopper.
CI.GAR.RI.LHA, *s. f.*, cigarillo.
CI.GAR.RO, *s. m.*, cigarette.
CI.LA.DA, *s. f.*, ambush, snare, trap, pitfall.
CI.LIN.DRO, *s. m.*, cylinder, roll, roller.
CÍ.LIO, *s. m.*, eyelash, cilium.
CI.MA, *s. f.*, top, summit, apex.
CI.MEN.TAR, *v.*, to cement, to unit, to consolidate.
CI.MEN.TO, *s. m.*, cement, concrete.
CI.MO, *s. m.*, top, summit, apex.
CIN.CO, *num.*, five, the number five.
CIN.DIR, *v.*, to cut, to separate.
CI.NE, *s. m.*, abbr. form of **CINEMA**.
CI.NE.MA, *s. m.*, cinema, movies.
CIN.GIR, *v.*, to gird, to surround, to enclasp, to unite, to constrain.
CÍ.NI.CO, *s. m.*, cynic; *adj.*, cynic, impudent.

CI.NIS.MO, *s. m.*, cynicism, impudence.
CIN.QUEN.TA, *num.*, fifty.
CIN.QUEN.TÃO, *s. m.*, a man in his fifties.
CIN.QUEN.TE.NÁ.RIO, *s. m.*, the fiftieth anniversary.
CIN.TA, *s. f.*, girdle, sash, belt, waistband.
CIN.TI.LA.ÇÃO, *s. f.*, scintillation, sparkle, blink.
CIN.TI.LAR, *v.*, to scintillate, to blink.
CIN.TO, *s. m.*, belt, girdle, buckle, sash.
CIN.TU.RA, *s. f.*, waist, waistline, waisband, belt.
CIN.ZA, *s. f.*, ash, gray, ember, cinder.
CIN.ZEI.RO, *s. m.*, ash-tray, ash-heap.
CIN.ZEN.TO, *s. m.*, gray, gray colour, ash gray; *adj.*, gray, grey, ashen.
CI.O, *s. m.*, rut, heat, oestrus.
CI.PRES.TE, *s. m.*, cypress, cypress tree.
CIR.CEN.SE, *adj.*, circensian.
CIR.CO, *s. m.*, circus, amphitheater, ring.
CIR.CUI.TO, *s. m.*, circle, circumference, circuit, round.
CIR.CU.LA.ÇÃO, *s. f.*, circulation, rotation, flow, transit, route, orbit.
CIR.CU.LAR, *v.*, to circulate, to move, to surround; *s. m.*, circular, bill; *adj.*, circular, cyclic.
CÍR.CU.LO, *s. m.*, circle, ring, strip, ring, circumference.
CIR.CU.NA.VE.GAR, *v.*, to circumnavigate, to sail round.
CIR.CUN.CI.SÃO, *s. f.*, circumcision.
CIR.CUN.DAR, *v.*, to circle, to encompass, to surround, to enclose.
CIR.CUN.FE.RÊN.CIA, *s. f.*, circumference, circle, periphery.
CIR.CUN.FLU.ÊN.CIA, *s. f.*, circumfluence.
CIR.CUNS.CRE.VER, *v.*, to circumscribe, to encircle, to limit.
CIR.CUNS.CRI.ÇÃO, *s. f.*, circumscription, periphery, district.
CIR.CUNS.TÂN.CIA, *s. f.*, circumstance, condition, fact, detail.
CIR.CUN.VA.GAR, *v.*, to wander about, to move in a circle.

CÍ.RIO, *s. m.*, candle, taper.
CIR.RO.SE, *s. f.*, cirrhosis.
CI.RUR.GI.A, *s. f.*, surgery.
CI.RUR.GI.ÃO, *s. m.*, surgeon.
CI.RÚR.GI.CO, *adj.*, surgical.
CI.SAN.DI.NO, *adj.*, *s. m.*, cisandine.
CI.SÃO, *s. f.*, split, scission, dissension.
CIS.MA, *s. m.*, schism, split, division; *s. f.*, daydreaming, doubt, preoccupation.
CIS.MAR, *v.*, to ponder, to meditate, to daydream.
CIS.NE, *s. m.*, swan, cob.
CIS.TER.NA, *s. f.*, cistern, water-tank.
CIS.TO, *s. m.*, cyst.
CI.TA.ÇÃO, *s. f.*, citation, quotation.
CI.TA.DI.NO, *s. m.*, city-bred, civic, citizen, townsman; *adj.*, civic, urban, citizen.
CI.TA.DO, *adj.*, summoned, arraigned, cited.
CI.TAR, *v.*, to cite, to quote, to summon, to mention, to name.
CI.TO.LO.GI.A, *s. f.*, cytology.
CI.TO.LÓ.GI.CO, *adj.*, cytological.
CI.TO.LO.GIS.TA, *s. 2 gen.*, cytologist.
CÍ.TRI.CO, *adj.*, citrus, citrine.
CI.TRI.CUL.TU.RA, *s. f.*, citriculture.
CI.Ú.ME, *s. m.*, jealousy, emulation.
CI.U.MEN.TO, *adj.*, jealous.
CÍ.VEL, *adj.*, civil.
CÍ.VI.CO, *adj.*, civic, civil.
CI.VI.LI.DA.DE, *s. f.*, civility, courtesy.
CI.VI.LI.ZA.ÇÃO, *s. f.*, civilization.
CI.VI.LI.ZA.DO, *adj.*, civilized, cultured, cultivated, civil, courteous, polite.
CI.VI.LI.ZAR, *v.*, to civilize, to reclaim from, to instruct, to educate.
CI.VIS.MO, *s. m.*, civism, patriotism.
CLÃ, *s. m.*, clan, tribe, family, society.
CLA.MAR, *v.*, to cry, to claim, to vociferate, to clamour.
CLA.MOR, *s. m.*, clamour, outcry, vociferation, exclamation.
CLA.RA, *s. f.*, egg white.
CLA.RÃO, *s. m.*, glaring radiance.
CLA.RE.AR, *v.*, to clear, to clarify.
CLA.RE.ZA, *s. f.*, clearness, clarity, explicitness.

CLA.RI.DA.DE, *s. f.*, clarity, brightness, light, shine.
CLA.RI.FI.CAR, *v.*, to clarify, to make clear, to purify.
CLA.RO, *adj.*, clear, luminous, bright, shining, lucid, transparent, limpid.
CLAS.SE, *s. f.*, class, category, group, kind, variety, type, degree.
CLAS.SI.CIS.MO, *s. m.*, classicism.
CLÁS.SI.CO, *s. m., adj.*, classic, classical.
CLAS.SI.FI.CA.ÇÃO, *s. f.*, classification, arrangement, sorting, qualification.
CLAS.SI.FI.CAR, *v.*, to classify, to class, to assort, to catalogue, to label, to qualify.
CLAUS.TRO, *s. m.*, monastery, convent.
CLÁU.SU.LA, *s. f.*, clause, condition, passage.
CLA.VE, *s. f.*, clef (mus.), axle pin.
CLA.VÍ.CU.LA, *s. f.*, clavicle, collar-bone.
CLE.MÊN.CIA, *s. f.*, clemency, indulgence, mercy, kindness.
CLE.MEN.TE, *adj.*, clement, indulgent, merciful.
CLÉ.RI.GO, *s. m.*, cleric, clergyman, churchman.
CLE.RO, *s. m.*, the clergy.
CLI.CHÊ, *s. m.*, cliché, stereotype.
CLI.EN.TE, *s. 2 gen.*, client, dependent; customer, patron.
CLI.EN.TE.LA, *s. f.*, clientele, clients, customers.
CLI.MA, *s. m.*, clime, climate, zone.
CLI.MÁ.TI.CO, *adj.*, climatic.
CLÍ.MAX, *s. m.*, climax, culmination, apex.
CLÍ.NI.CA, *s. f.*, clinic, hospital clinic.
CLI.QUE, *s. m.*, clique, set; *interj.* click!
CLO.A.CA, *s. f.*, sewer, latrine.
CLO.RAR, *v.*, to chlorinate.
CLO.RE.TO, *s. m.*, chloride.
CLO.RO, *s. m.*, chlorine.
CLO.RO.FI.LA, *s. f.*, chlorophyll.
CLO.RO.FÓR.MIO, *s. m.*, chloroform.
CLU.BE, *s. m.*, club, club-house, association, society.
CO.A.BI.TAR, *v.*, to cohabit, to live together.
CO.A.ÇÃO, *s. f.*, coaction, compulsion.
CO.AD.JU.VAN.TE, *s. 2 gen.*, coadjuvant.
CO.A.DO, *adj.*, filtered, strained.

CO.A.DOR, *s. m.*, percolator, filter.
CO.A.DU.NAR, *v.*, to coadunate, to incorporate.
CO.A.GIR, *v.*, to coerce, to constrain, to restrain.
CO.A.GU.LAR, *v.*, to coagulate, to curdle, to clot.
CO.Á.GU.LO, *s. m.*, coagulum, clot.
CO.A.LA, *s. m.*, koala.
CO.A.LHA.DA, *s. f.*, curdled milk.
CO.A.LHAR, *v.*, to curdle, to clot, to curd.
CO.A.LI.ZÃO, *s. f.*, coalition, alliance, union.
CO.AR, *v.*, to filter, to strain, to percolate, to distill, to cast, to found.
CO.AU.TOR, *s. m.*, co-author, collaborator.
CO.A.XAR, *v.*, to croak.
CO.BAI.A, *s. f.*, guinea pig, cavy.
CO.BAL.TO, *s. m.*, cobalt.
CO.BER.TA, *s. f.*, cap, cover, covering, coverlet, bedspread, hood.
CO.BER.TO, *adj.*, covered, protected, hooded.
CO.BER.TOR, *s. m.*, blanket, coverlet, quilt.
CO.BER.TU.RA, *s. f.*, cover, coverage, covering, wrapper.
CO.BI.ÇA, *s. f.*, envy, greediness, avarice.
CO.BI.ÇAR, *v.*, to covet, to lust after, to desire, to envy.
CO.BI.ÇO.SO, *adj.*, covetous, greedy, avaricious.
CO.BRA, *s. f.*, snake, serpent, adder.
CO.BRA.DOR, *s. m.*, bill collector, receiver.
CO.BRAN.ÇA, *s. f.*, collection, encashment, exaction.
CO.BRAR, *v.*, to receive, to charge, to exact.
CO.BRE, *s. m.*, copper; money.
CO.BRIR, *v.*, to cover, to hide, to conceal, to cloak, to hood, to defend, to protect.
CO.CA.Í.NA, *s. f.*, cocain, cocaine.
CÓC.CIX, *s. m.*, coccyx.
CÓ.CE.GAS, *s. f., pl.*, tickle, tickling, titillation.
CO.CEI.RA, *s. f.*, itch, itching.
CO.CHEI.RA, *s. f.*, box, coach-house.
CO.CHI.CHAR, *v.*, to whisper, to murmur, to mutter.
CO.CHI.CHO, *s. m.*, whispering, whisper, buzz.
CO.CHI.LAR, *v.*, to nod off, to nap, to doze.
CO.CHI.LO, *s. m.*, nap, doze, drowse.
CO.CHO, *s. m.*, trug, hod, trough.

CO.CO, *s. m.*, coconut, coconut tree.
CÓ.CO.RAS, *s. f.*, pl. squatting.
CÔ.DEA, *s. f.*, hull, husk, crust, scab.
CO.DI.FI.CA.ÇÃO, *s. f.*, codification.
CO.DI.FI.CAR, *v.*, to codify, to systematize, to classify.
CÓ.DI.GO, *s. m.*, code, systematic colletion of laws.
CO.DOR.NA, *s. f.*, tinamou.
CO.DOR.NIZ, *s.f.*, quail.
COE.DI.TAR, *v.*, to co-edit.
CO.E.FI.CI.EN.TE, *s. m.*, coefficient, factor, rate.
CO.E.LHO, *s. m.*, rabbit.
CO.EN.TRO, *s. m.*, coriander.
CO.ER.ÇÃO, *s. f.*, coercion, repression.
CO.ER.CI.TI.VO, *adj.*, coercitive, coactive.
CO.E.RÊN.CIA, *s. f.*, coherence, cohesion, harmony.
CO.E.REN.TE, *adj.*, coherent, consistent.
CO.E.SO, *adj.*, cohesive, united.
CO.E.XIS.TÊN.CIA, *s. f.*, coexistence.
CO.E.XIS.TIR, *v.*, to coexist, to exist together.
CO.FRE, *s. m.*, strongbox, box, chest.
CO.GI.TAR, *v.*, to cogitate, to ponder, to recollect; to consider.
COG.NI.ÇÃO, *s. f.*, cognition.
COG.NO.ME, *s. m.*, cognomen, surname, nickname.
CO.GU.ME.LO, *s. m.*, mushroom, fungus.
CO.I.BIR, *v.*, to stop, to repress, to cohibit.
COI.CE, *s. m.*, kick, rear, recoil.
CO.IN.CI.DÊN.CIA, *s. f.*, coincidence, concurrence, concurrency.
CO.IN.CI.DIR, *v.*, to coincide, to contemporize.
COI.SA, *s. f.*, thing, object, matter, substance, affair, event.
COI.TA.DO, *s. m.*, underdog; *adj.*, poor, pitiful, miserable.
COI.TO, *s. m.*, coitus, copulation, coupling.
CO.LA, *s. f.*, glue, gum, adhesive.
CO.LA.BO.RA.ÇÃO, *s. f.*, collaboration, co-operation, common work, help, assistance.
CO.LA.BO.RA.DOR, *s. m.*, collaborator, contributor.
CO.LA.BO.RAR, *v.*, to collaborate, to co-operate.
CO.LA.GEM, *s. f.*, gluing, pasting.
CO.LAP.SO, *s. m.*, collapse, break-down, burst-up.
CO.LAR, *v.*, to glue, to conglutinate, to aglutinate, to gum, to graduate; *s. m.*, necklace, collar.
CO.LA.RI.NHO, *s. m.*, collar, shirt collar, neckband.
CO.LA.TE.RAL, *adj., s. m.*, collateral.
COL.CHA, *s. f.*, blanket, bed-spread, coverlet.
COL.CHÃO, *s. m.*, mattress.
CO.LE.ÇÃO, *s. f.*, collection, compilation, gathering, accumulation.
CO.LE.CI.O.NA.DOR, *s. m.*, collector, compiler.
CO.LE.CI.O.NAR, *v.*, to collect, to gather, to accumulate.
CO.LE.GA, *s. 2 gen.*, colleague, associate, schoolmate, friend, fellow.
CO.LE.GI.AL, *s. 2 gen.*, student; *adj.*, collegiate, collegial.
CO.LÉ.GIO, *s. m.*, college, public school, high school.
CO.LE.GUIS.MO, *s. m.*, collegiality, colleagueship, fellowship.
CÓ.LE.RA, *s. f.*, anger, irritation, passion, rage, ira; cholera.
CO.LÉ.RI.CO, *adj.*, choleric, furious, irascible, irate, choleraic (med.)
CO.LES.TE.ROL, *s. m.*, cholesterol.
CO.LE.TA, *s. f.*, collection, levy, tax, contribution.
CO.LE.TAR, *v.*, to collect, to gather, to rate.
CO.LE.TE, *s. m.*, waistcoat, jumper.
CO.LE.TI.VI.DA.DE, *s. f.*, collectivity, community, society.
CO.LE.TI.VO, *s. m.*, tramwaycar, omnibus; collective; *adj.*, collective, social.
CO.LHEI.TA, *s. f.*, harvest, crop, picking.
CO.LHER, *s. f.*, spoon.
CO.LHER, *v.*, to harvest, to pick, to reap, to perceive.
CO.LHE.RA.DA, *s. f.*, spoonful.
CO.LI.BRI, *s. m.*, colibri, hummingbird.
CÓ.LI.CA, *s. f.*, colic, pain, belly-ache.

COLIDIR — **COMISSÁRIA**

CO.LI.DIR, *v.,* to collide, to shock, to dash.
CO.LI.GA.ÇÃO, *s. f.,* colligation, coalition, confederation.
CO.LI.GAR, *v.,* to colligate, to aproximate, to unite, to join, to connect.
CO.LI.NA, *s. f.,* mount, hill, knoll.
CO.LÍ.RIO, *s. m.,* collyrium, eye drops.
CO.LI.SÃO, *s. f.,* collision, crash, shock, clash.
COL.MEI.A, *s. f.,* beehive, hive, skep.
CO.LO, *s. m.,* neck, bosom, lap; colon (anat.)
CO.LO.CA.ÇÃO, *s. f.,* placement, collocation, job, setting, situation.
CO.LO.CAR, *v.,* to place, to dispose, to arrange, to employ, to set, to plant.
CO.LÔ.NIA, *s. f.,* colony, possession, territory.
CO.LO.NI.A.LIS.MO, *s. m.,* colonialism.
CO.LO.NI.ZA.ÇÃO, *s. f.,* colonization.
CO.LO.NI.ZAR, *v.,* to colonize.
CO.LO.NO, *s. m.,* colonist, planter, settler.
CO.LÓ.QUIO, *s. m.,* colloquy, conversation.
CO.LO.RIR, *v.,* to color, to colour, to paint, to dye, to tinge.
CO.LU.NA, *s. f.,* column, pillar; military column, support; section of a newspaper.
CO.LU.NIS.TA, *s. 2 gen.,* columnist, author of a newspaper column.
COM, *prep.,* with.
CO.MA, *s. m.,* coma, torpor.
CO.MA.DRE, *s. f.,* godmother.
CO.MAN.DAN.TE, *s. 2 gen.,* commander, commandant, chief.
CO.MAN.DAR, *v.,* to command, to control, to order, to direct.
CO.MAN.DO, *s. m.,* command, order, mandate, power, control.
CO.MAR.CA, *s. f.,* judiciary district, district, region.
COM.BA.TE, *s. m.,* combat, fight, battle.
COM.BA.TER, *v.,* to combat, to strive against, to contend, to contest.
COM.BI.NA.ÇÃO, *s. f.,* combination, arrangement, aggregation, formation.
COM.BI.NAR, *v.,* to combine, to join together, to connect, to assort, to stipulate.
COM.BOI.O, *s. m.,* convoy.
COM.BUS.TÃO, *s. m.,* combustion, ignition, tumult.
COM.BUS.TÍ.VEL, *s. m.,* fuel, combustible, gasoline, gas.
CO.ME.ÇAR, *v.,* to begin, to commence, to start, to enter on.
CO.ME.ÇO, *s. m.,* beginning, commencement, birth, start.
CO.MÉ.DIA, *s. f.,* comedy, sketch, farce.
CO.ME.DIR, *v.,* to moderate, to contain, to restrain, to regulate.
CO.ME.MO.RA.ÇÃO, *s. f.,* commemoration, celebration.
CO.ME.MO.RAR, *v.,* to commemorate, to remember, to memorialize, to celebrate.
CO.MEN.TA.DOR, *s.m.,* commentator, expositor.
CO.MEN.TAR, *v.,* to comment, to explain, to annotate.
CO.MEN.TÁ.RIO, *s. m.,* comment, commentary, note, interpretation.
CO.MER, *v.,* to eat, to consume, to feed.
CO.MER.CI.AL, *s. m.,* commercial; *adj.,* commercial, mercantile.
CO.MER.CI.A.LI.ZAR, *v.,* commercialize.
CO.MER.CI.AN.TE, *s. 2 gen.,* merchant, trader, businessman.
CO.MER.CI.AR, *v.,* to trade, to deal.
CO.MÉR.CIO, *s. m.,* commerce, trade, trading, business.
CO.MES.TÍ.VEL, *s. m.,* comestible, edible, food; *adj.,* comestible.
CO.ME.TA, *s. f.,* comet.
CO.ME.TER, *v.,* to commit, to practise, to perform, to perpetrate.
CÔ.MI.CO, *adj.,* comic, funny.
CO.MI.DA, *s. f.,* food, aliment, eating, fare, meal, feed, feeding.
CO.MI.GO, *pron.,* with me, in my society.
CO.MI.LÃO, *s. m.,* a heavy eater, glutton.
CO.MI.NHO, *s. m.,* cumin, cummin.
CO.MIS.SÃO, *s. f.,* commission, committee, retribution.
CO.MIS.SÁ.RIA, *s. f.,* stewardess.

CO.MIS.SÁ.RIO, *s. m.*, commissary, commissioner, police officer.
CO.MI.TÊ, *s. m.*, committee.
CO.MO, *adv.*, how, to what degree, by what means, wherein, for what reason; *conj.*, as, while; *pron.*, why.
CO.MO.ÇÃO, *s. f.*, commotion, agitation, ferment, riot.
CO.MO.DI.DA.DE, *s. f.*, comfortableness, cosiness, convenience.
CÔ.MO.DO, *s. m.*, room, accomodation, comfort; *adj.*, commodious, useful, suitable.
CO.MO.VER, *v.*, to move, to affect, to agitate, to stir up.
COM.PAC.TO, *adj.*, compact, close, massy, massive, dense.
COM.PA.DRE, *s. m.*, godfather.
COM.PAI.XÃO, *s. f.*, compassion, pity, comiseration.
COM.PA.NHEI.RA, *s. f.*, female companion, wife.
COM.PA.NHEI.RO, *s. m.*, companion, friend, fellow, consort, colleague.
COM.PA.NHIA, *s. f.*, company, society, firm, corporation.
COM.PA.RA.ÇÃO, *s. f.*, comparison.
COM.PA.RAR, *v.*, to compare, to contrast, to liken.
COM.PA.RE.CER, *v.*, to attend to, to be present at.
COM.PA.RE.CI.MEN.TO, *s. m.*, attendance, appearance, presence.
COM.PAR.TI.LHAR, *v.*, to share, to participate, to partake.
COM.PA.TI.BI.LI.DA.DE, *s. f.*, compatibility, associability.
COM.PA.TRI.O.TA, *s. 2 gen.*, compatriot, countryman.
COM.PE.LIR, *v.*, to compel, to oblige, to coerce.
COM.PÊN.DIO, *s. m.*, compendium, text-book, school-book, manual.
COM.PE.NE.TRAR, *v.*, to compenetrate, to convince, to enroot.
COM.PEN.SA.ÇÃO, *s. f.*, compensation, recompense, remuneration, indemnity.
COM.PEN.SAR, *v.*, to compensate, to recompense, to indemnify, to even.
COM.PE.TÊN.CIA, *s. f.*, competence, ability, aptitude, efficiency.
COM.PE.TI.ÇÃO, *s. f.*, competition, competitiveness.
COM.PE.TIR, *v.*, to compete, to contest, to contend, to match.
COM.PI.LA.ÇÃO, *s. f.*, compilation, collection.
COM.PI.LAR, *v.*, to compile, to unite, to collect.
COM.PLE.MEN.TAR, *v.*, to complement, to complete; *adj.*, supplementary.
COM.PLE.MEN.TO, *s. m.*, complement.
COM.PLE.TAR, *v.*, to complete, to complement, to accomplish, to conclude.
COM.PLE.TO, *adj.*, complete, entire, finished, done, concluded.
COM.PLE.XO, *s. m.*, compound, complex; *adj.*, complex, complicated.
COM.PLI.CA.ÇÃO, *s. f.*, complication, difficulty, complicacy.
COM.PLI.CAR, *v.*, to complicate, to embarass, to confuse.
COM.POR, *v.*, to compose, to arrange, to put together, to set up, to write, to produce.
COM.POR.TA, *s. f.*, flood-gate, sluice-gate, sluice.
COM.POR.TA.MEN.TO, *s. m.*, conduct, behaviour, manner, posture.
COM.POR.TAR, *v.*, to hold, to contain, to admit, to suffer.
COM.PO.SI.ÇÃO, *s. f.*, composition, mixture, compound, disposition.
COM.PO.SI.TOR, *s. m.*, composer, songwriter, typographer.
COM.POS.TO, *adj.*, composed, consisting of, compound, articulate.
COM.POS.TU.RA, *s. f.*, composition, composure, decency.
COM.PRA, *s. f.*, purchase, acquisition, shopping.
COM.PRA.DOR, *s. m.*, purchaser, buyer, shopper, customer.
COM.PRAR, *v.*, to purchase, to buy, to acquire.

COMPREENDER — CONCURSO

COM.PRE.EN.DER, v., to comprehend, to comprise, to include, to contain, to consist.

COM.PRE.EN.DI.DO, adj., included, comprised, understood.

COM.PRE.EN.SÃO, s. f., comprehension, apprehension, understanding.

COM.PRES.SA, s. f., compress, dressing.

COM.PRES.SÃO, s. f., compression, compressure.

COM.PRES.SOR, s. m., compressor.

COM.PRI.MEN.TO, s. m., lenght, dimension, extent.

COM.PRI.MI.DO, s. m., pill, tablet; adj., compressed.

COM.PRO.ME.TER, v., to compromise, to promise, to pledge, to engage.

COM.PRO.MIS.SO, s. m., liability, obligation, promise, pledge, engagement.

COM.PRO.VA.ÇÃO, s. f., proof, evidence, corroboration.

COM.PRO.VAR, v., to prove, to confirm, to aver, to verify.

COM.PUL.SÓ.RIO, adj., compulsive, compulsory, forced.

COM.PU.TA.ÇÃO, s. f., computation, calculation, representation.

COM.PU.TA.DOR, s. m., computer, calculator.

COM.PU.TAR, v., to compute, to calculate, to count, to estimate.

CO.MUM, adj., common, usual, regular, habitual, plain, ordinary.

CO.MUN.GAR, v., to communicate, to commune; to receive the Lord's Supper.

CO.MU.NHÃO, s. f., Communion, Eucharist, participation.

CO.MU.NI.CA.ÇÃO, s. f., communication, message, connection.

CO.MU.NI.CAR, v., to communicate, to impart, to tell, to notify.

CO.MU.NI.DA.DE, s. f., community, commonness, society.

CO.MU.NIS.MO, s. m., communism.

CO.MU.NIS.TA, s. 2 gen., communist.

CON.CE.BER, v., to conceive, to become pregnant, to think out, to ponder.

CON.CE.DER, v., to concede, to grant, to confer, to impact, to permit, to allow.

CON.CEI.TO, s. m., idea, thought, notion, conception, concept.

CON.CEI.TU.AR, v., to judge, to appraise, to evaluate, to repute as.

CON.CEN.TRA.ÇÃO, s. f., concentration.

CON.CEN.TRAR, v., to concentrate, to centralize.

CON.CEP.ÇÃO, s. f., conception, generation, notion, ideation.

CON.CER.NEN.TE, adj., relative to, with regard to, concerning.

CON.CER.TAR, v., to put in order, to adjust, to regulate, to harmonize.

CON.CES.SÃO, s. f., concession, permission, assent.

CON.CHA, s. f., shell, scoop.

CON.CI.LI.A.ÇÃO, s. f., conciliation, compromise, agreement.

CON.CÍ.LIO, s. m., council.

CON.CI.SÃO, s. f., briefness, brevity, conciseness.

CON.CLA.MAR, v., to shout, to yell, to clamour.

CON.CLU.IR, v., to conclude, to end, to decide, to resolve.

CON.CLU.SÃO, s. f., conclusion, closing, end, inference, decision.

CON.CLU.SI.VO, adj., conclusive, illative, final.

CON.COR.DÂN.CIA, s. f., concordance, agreement, consonance, conformity.

CON.COR.DAR, v., to agree, to concord, to assent, to acquiesce, to harmonize.

CON.COR.DA.TA, s. f., concordat, agreement, contract.

CON.CÓR.DIA, s. f., concordance, harmony, peace.

CON.COR.RÊN.CIA, s. f., affluence, competition, emulation.

CON.COR.RER, v., to compete with, to rival, to contest, to concur.

CON.CRE.TI.ZAR, v., to materialize.

CON.CU.BI.NA, s. f., concubine, mistress.

CON.CUR.SO, s. m., concurrence, confluence, concourse, competition.

CON.DE, *s. m.*, count, earl.
CON.DE.NA.ÇÃO, *s. f.*, condemnation, conviction, censure, penalty.
CON.DE.NA.DO, *s. m.*, convict, felon; *adj.*, condemned, damned, reprobate.
CON.DE.NAR, *v.*, to condemn, to sentence, to declare, to censure.
CON.DEN.SAR, *v.*, to condense, to compact, to concentrate.
CON.DES.SA, *s. f.*, countess.
CON.DI.ÇÃO, *s. f.*, condition, circumstance, quality, character.
CON.DI.CI.O.NAL, *adj.*, conditional, conditioned.
CON.DI.CI.O.NAR, *v.*, to stipulate, to condition.
CON.DI.MEN.TAR, *v.*, to season, to spice.
CON.DI.MEN.TO, *s. m.*, seasoning, condiment, spice.
CON.DI.ZER, *v.*, to suit, to fit well, to agree, to match.
CON.DO.LÊN.CIA, *s. f.*, condolence, sympathy, compassion.
CON.DU.ÇÃO, *s. f.*, conduction, conveyance, transport.
CON.DU.TA, *s. f.*, conduct, behaviour, conveyance, procedure, posture.
CON.DU.ZIR, *v.*, to conduct, to lead, to direct, to drive.
CO.NEC.TAR, *v.*, to connect, to tie in, to link.
CO.NE.XÃO, *s. f.*, connection, link, relation.
CO.NE.XO, *adj.*, connected, linked.
CON.FEC.ÇÃO, *s. f.*, making, confection.
CON.FE.DE.RA.ÇÃO, *s. f.*, confederation, alliance.
CON.FEI.TA.RI.A, *s. f.*, candy shop.
CON.FE.RÊN.CIA, *s. f.*, conference, convention, speech, talk.
CON.FE.RIR, *v.*, to confer, to compare, to check, to control.
CON.FES.SAR, *v.*, to confess, to declare, to reveal, to admit, to acknowledge.
CON.FI.A.DO, *adj.*, confident, fiducial.
CON.FI.AN.ÇA, *s. f.*, confidence, trust, assurance, reliability.
CON.FI.AR, *v.*, to confide, to trust, to believe in, to rely on.
CON.FI.DÊN.CIA, *s. f.*, confidence, trust, secret.
CON.FI.GU.RA.ÇÃO, *s. f.*, configuration, form, aspect, figuration.
CON.FIR.MA.ÇÃO, *s. f.*, confirmation, affirmation, homologation.
CON.FIR.MAR, *v.*, to confirm, to affirm, to sustain, to validate.
CON.FIS.CA.ÇÃO, *s. f.*, confiscation, sequestration.
CON.FIS.CAR, *v.*, to confiscate, to sequestrate.
CON.FIS.CO, *s. m.*, confiscation, requisition.
CON.FLI.TO, *s. m.*, conflict, disagreement, discord, skirmish.
CON.FLU.ÊN.CIA, *s. f.*, confluence.
CON.FLU.IR, *v.*, to join, to flow together.
CON.FOR.MAR, *v.*, to form, to adapt, to conform, to accommodate.
CON.FOR.ME, *adj., s. 2 gen.*, conform, accordant, correspondent; *conj.*, how, according to, as per.
CON.FOR.MI.DA.DE, *s. f.*, conformity, accordance, agreement, convenience.
CON.FOR.TAR, *v.*, to comfort, to console, to stimulate.
CON.FOR.TO, *s. m.*, comfort, well-being, ease.
CON.FRA.DE, *s. m.*, comrade, confrere, fellow.
CON.FRA.TER.NI.ZA.ÇÃO, *s. f.*, confraternization.
CON.FRA.TER.NI.ZAR, *v.*, to fraternize with, to forgather.
CON.FRON.TAR, *v.*, to confront, to compare, to collate.
CON.FRON.TO, *s. m.*, confrontation, comparison.
CON.FUN.DIR, *v.*, to confound, to perplex, to mistake, to humble.
CON.FU.SÃO, *s. f.*, confusion, uproar, tumult, perplexity.
CON.FU.SO, *adj.*, confused, disorderly, woolly.
CON.GE.LA.DOR, *s. m.*, freezer.
CON.GE.LA.MEN.TO, *s. m.*, frozenness, congelation, congealment, freezing of prices.

CONGELAR — **CONSOLIDAR**

CON.GE.LAR, *v.*, to freeze, to ice, to ice up.
CON.GES.TÃO, *s. f.*, congestion.
CON.GES.TI.O.NA.DO, *adj.*, congested, crowded; apoplectic.
CON.GES.TI.O.NAR, *v.*, to congest, to crowd.
CON.GLO.ME.RAR, *v.*, to conglomerate, to accumulate.
CON.GRA.TU.LA.ÇÃO, *s. f.*, congratulation.
CON.GRE.GA.ÇÃO, *s. f.*, congregation, reunion, assembly, fraternity.
CON.GRE.GAR, *v.*, to congregate, to assemble, to convene.
CON.GRES.SO, *s. m.*, congress, conference, session.
CO.NHA.QUE, *s. m.*, cognac, brandy.
CO.NHE.CER, *v.*, to know, to perceive, to be familiar with, to judge, to be aware of.
CO.NHE.CI.DO, *adj.*, known, public, famous.
CO.NHE.CI.MEN.TO, *s. m.*, knowledge, cognizance, familiarity, information, understanding.
CO.NÍ.FE.RA, *s. f.*, conifer.
CO.NI.VÊN.CIA, *s. f.*, connivance, connivancy.
CON.JE.TU.RA, *s. f.*, conjecture, supposition, guess.
CON.JU.GA.ÇÃO, *s. f.*, conjugation, conjunction, union.
CON.JU.GAL, *adj.*, *s. 2 gen.*, conjugal, matrimonial, married.
CON.JU.GAR, *v.*, to conjugate, to unite, to coordinate.
CÔN.JU.GE, *s. 2 gen.*, consort, spouse, partner.
CON.JUN.ÇÃO, *s. f.*, conjunction, union.
CON.JUN.TI.VI.TE, *s. f.*, conjunctivitis.
CON.JUN.TO, *s. m.*, whole, set, kit, team, band; *adj.*, conjunct, united, concurrent.
CO.NOS.CO, *pron.*, with us, to us, for us, together with us.
CON.QUAN.TO, *conj.*, although, though.
CON.QUIS.TA, *s. f.*, conquest, acquisition.
CON.QUIS.TAR, *v.*, to conquer, to defeat, to acquire, to win.
CON.SA.GRA.ÇÃO, *s. f.*, consecration, dedication, devotion.
CON.SA.GRAR, *v.*, to consecrate, to sanctify, to devote.
CONS.CI.ÊN.CIA, *s. f.*, conscience, conscientiousness, scruple.
CONS.CI.EN.CI.O.SO, *adj.*, conscientious, scrupulous.
CON.SE.CU.TI.VO, *adj.*, consecutive.
CON.SE.GUIR, *v.*, to obtain, to achieve, to get, to succeed.
CON.SE.LHO, *s. m.*, counsel, council, synod; advice, recommendation.
CON.SEN.SO, *s. m.*, consensus, agreement, consent, accord.
CON.SEN.TI.MEN.TO, *s. m.*, consent, approval, acquiescence, agreement.
CON.SE.QUÊN.CIA, *s. f.*, consequence, result, sequel.
CON.SER.TAR, *v.*, to repair, to mend, to adjust.
CON.SER.TO, *s. m.*, repair, mending, restoration.
CON.SER.VA, *s. f.*, conserve, comfit, preserve.
CON.SER.VA.ÇÃO, *s. f.*, conservation, maintenance.
CON.SER.VAR, *v.*, to maintain, to conserve, to sustain, to keep, to guard.
CON.SI.DE.RA.ÇÃO, *s. f.*, consideration, appreciation, reflection, respect, regard.
CON.SI.DE.RA.DO, *adj.*, considerate, considered.
CON.SI.DE.RAR, *v.*, to consider, to ponder, to esteem, to regard.
CON.SIG.NAR, *v.*, to consign, to seal.
CON.SI.GO, *pron.*, with him, with himself.
CON.SIS.TÊN.CIA, *s. f.*, consistence, consistency.
CON.SIS.TIR, *v.*, to consist in, to rest in, to comprise.
CON.SO.AN.TE, *s. f.*, consonant; *adj. 2 gen.*, consonant, consonantal; *s. m.*, rhyme; *prep.*, conformable, according to, consonant with.
CON.SO.LAR, *v.*, to comfort, to console, to solace, to relieve.
CON.SO.LI.DA.ÇÃO, *s. f.*, consolidation, solidification, combination.
CON.SO.LI.DAR, *v.*, to consolidate, to solidify, to become hard.

CON.SO.NÂN.CIA, *s. f.*, consonance, consonancy, harmony.
CON.SÓR.CIO, *s. m.*, consortium, partnership.
CON.SOR.TE, *s. 2 gen.*, spouse, husband, wife, partner.
CONS.PI.RAR, *v.*, to conspire, to complot, to collude, to machinate.
CONS.TÂN.CIA, *s. f.*, constancy, fidelity, firmness, stability.
CONS.TAN.TE, *adj.*, constant, persistent, invariable, stable.
CONS.TAR, *v.*, to consist of, to be evident.
CONS.TA.TAR, *v.*, to testify, to find out, to verify.
CONS.TE.LA.ÇÃO, *s. f.*, constellation.
CONS.TI.PA.ÇÃO, *s. f.*, constipation.
CONS.TI.TU.CI.O.NAL, *adj.*, constitutional.
CONS.TI.TU.I.ÇÃO, *s. f.*, constitution, formation, organization.
CONS.TI.TU.IN.TE, *s. 2 gen.*, voter, constituent.
CONS.TI.TU.IR, *v.*, to constitute, to form, to put together.
CONS.TRAN.GER, *v.*, to constrain, to urge, to impel, to oblige.
CONS.TRU.ÇÃO, *s. f.*, construction, building, edification, structure.
CONS.TRU.IR, *v.*, to construct, to build, to form.
CONS.TRU.TOR, *s. m.*, constructor, builder.
CÔN.SUL, *s. m.*, consul.
CON.SU.LA.DO, *s. m.*, consulate, consulship.
CON.SUL.TAR, *v.*, to consult, to refer, to seek information.
CON.SUL.TÓ.RIO, *s. m.*, doctor's office.
CON.SU.MAR, *v.*, to terminate, to finish, to consummate, to complete.
CON.SU.MI.DOR, *s. m.*, consumer.
CON.SU.MIR, *v.*, to consume, to eat up, to spend, to use, to destroy, to exhaust.
CON.SU.MO, *s. m.*, consumption, use, absorption.
CON.TA, *s. f.*, account, count, calculation, sum, total, bill, note.
CON.TA.BI.LI.DA.DE, *s. f.*, accountancy.
CON.TA.BI.LIS.TA, *s. 2 gen.*, accountant.
CON.TA.DOR, *s. m.*, bookkeeper, accountant.
CON.TA.GI.AR, *v.*, to infect, to contaminate, to corrupt.
CON.TÁ.GIO, *s. m.*, infection, contagion, pollution.
CON.TA.MI.NA.ÇÃO, *s. f.*, contamination, infection, contagion.
CON.TA.MI.NAR, *v.*, to infect, to contaminate, to corrupt.
CON.TAN.TO QUE, *conj.*, as long as, if, as.
CON.TAR, *v.*, to count, to calculate, to recount, to number, to tell, to rely.
CON.TA.TO, *s. m.*, contact, proximity, touch.
CON.TEM.PLA.ÇÃO, *s. f.*, contemplation, meditation.
CON.TEM.PLAR, *v.*, to contemplate, to regard, to ponder, to admire, to observe.
CON.TEM.PO.RÂ.NEO, *adj.*, contemporaneous.
CON.TEN.TA.MEN.TO, *s. m.*, contentment, contentedness, satisfaction.
CON.TEN.TAR, *v.*, to content, to satisfy, to suffice, to please.
CON.TEN.TE, *adj.*, content, contented.
CON.TER, *v.*, to contain, to enclose, to comprise, to refrain.
CON.TER.RÂ.NE.O, *s. m.*, fellow, citizen, countryman.
CON.TES.TA.ÇÃO, *s. f.*, contestation, plea, defense, disputation.
CON.TES.TAR, *v.*, to contest, to refute, to object, to argue.
CON.TE.Ú.DO, *s. m.*, content, matter contained.
CON.TEX.TO, *s. m.*, context, structure, composition.
CON.TI.GO, *pron.*, with you, in your company.
CON.TI.NEN.TE, *s. m.*, continent, mainland, container; *adj.*, including, continental.
CON.TI.NU.A.ÇÃO, *s. f.*, continuation, continuance, continuity, sequel, sequence.
CON.TI.NU.A.DO, *adj.*, continued, prolonged.
CON.TI.NU.AR, *v.*, to continue, to pursue, to stay, to extend.
CON.TI.NU.I.DA.DE, *s. f.*, continuity.
CON.TO, *s. m.*, narrative, story, tale, fable, invention.

CON.TOR.ÇÃO, *s. f.*, contortion.
CON.TOR.CER, *v.*, to contort, to distort, to twist.
CON.TOR.NAR, *v.*, to profile, to turn round.
CON.TRA, *prep.*, against, contrary to, versus; *adv.*, adversely, contra.
CON.TRA.BAN.DE.AR, *v.*, to contraband, to smuggle.
CON.TRA.BAN.DIS.TA, *s. 2 gen.*, contrabandist, smuggler.
CON.TRA.BAN.DO, *s. m.*, smuggling, smugled goods.
CON.TRA.ÇÃO, *s. f.*, contraction, shrinking, convulsion.
CON.TRA.DI.ÇÃO, *s. f.*, contradiction, incoherence, variance, opposition.
CON.TRA.DI.TÓ.RIO, *s. m.*, contradictory, contradictive, discordant, incoherent.
CON.TRA.DI.ZER, *v.*, to contradict, to contest, to deny.
CON.TRA.GOL.PE, *s. m.*, counterblow, counterplot.
CON.TRA.GOS.TO, *s. m.*, dislike, aversion.
CON.TRA.IR, *v.*, to contract, to tighten, to compress, to reduce.
CON.TRA.POR, *v.*, to put against, to put in front of.
CON.TRA.PRO.DU.CEN.TE, *adj.*, *s. 2 gen.*, counterproductive.
CON.TRA.PRO.VAR, *v.*, to counterprove.
CON.TRA.RI.A.DO, *adj.*, vexed, annoyed, upset.
CON.TRA.RI.AR, *v.*, to counter, to oppose, to contest, to refute, to antagonize.
CON.TRA.RI.E.DA.DE, *s. f.*, opposition, resistance, contrariety.
CON.TRÁ.RIO, *adj.*, opposed, opponent, contrary, adverse.
CON.TRAS.TAR, *v.*, to contrast, to fight against, to defy, to oppose.
CON.TRAS.TE, *s. m.*, contrast, opposition, assay.
CON.TRA.TAR, *v.*, to contract, to agree upon, to hire, to trade, to ideal.
CON.TRA.TEM.PO, *s. m.*, mischance, mishap, accident.
CON.TRA.TO, *s. m.*, contract, covenant, agreement, bargain.
CON.TRA.VEN.ÇÃO, *s. f.*, contravention, infraction.
CON.TRI.BUI.ÇÃO, *s. f.*, contribution, quota, tribute, tax.
CON.TRI.BU.IN.TE, *s. 2 gen.*, contributor, taxpayer; *adj.*, contributory, tributary.
CON.TRI.BU.IR, *v.*, to contribute, to pay taxes, to donate, to concur.
CON.TRO.LA.DOR, *s. m.*, controller.
CON.TRO.LAR, *v.*, to control, to supervise, to dominate.
CON.TRO.LE, *s. m.*, control, controlment, regulation, direction.
CON.TRO.VÉR.SIA, *s. f.*, controversy, contest, contestation, dispute.
CON.TU.DO, *conj.*, however, yet, although.
CON.TUN.DIR, *v.*, to contuse, to bruise, to injure.
CON.TU.SÃO, *s. f.*, contusion, bruise.
CON.VA.LES.CEN.ÇA, *s. f.*, convalescence.
CON.VA.LES.CER, *v.*, to convalesce, to recover, to fortify.
CON.VEN.ÇÃO, *s. f.*, convention, agreement, pact.
CON.VEN.CER, *v.*, to convince, to persuade, to overcome.
CON.VEN.CI.DO, *adj.*, convinced, satisfied, assured.
CON.VEN.CI.O.NAR, *v.*, to stipulate, to contract, to establish, to arbitrate.
CON.VE.NI.ÊN.CIA, *s. f.*, convenience, fittingness.
CON.VE.NI.EN.TE, *adj.*, convenient, suitable, fitting.
CON.VÊ.NIO, *s. m.*, convention, covenant, accord.
CON.VEN.TO, *s. m.*, convent, cloister.
CON.VER.GIR, *v.*, to converge, to approach.
CON.VER.SA, *s. f.*, conversation, talk, talking, speech.
CON.VER.SA.ÇÃO, *s. f.*, conversation, colloquy.
CON.VER.SA.DOR, *s. m.*, converser, proser.
CON.VER.SÃO, *s. f.*, convertion, commutation,

CON.VER.SAR, *v.*, to talk, to converse, to discourse.
CON.VER.TER, *v.*, to convert, to transform, to invert, to reduce, to change.
CON.VÉS, *s. m.*, deck, shipboard.
CON.VIC.ÇÃO, *s. f.*, conviction, certitude, belief.
CON.VI.DA.DO, *s. m.*, guest, visitor; *adj.*, invited.
CON.VI.DAR, *v.*, to invite.
CON.VIN.CEN.TE, *adj.*, convincing, potent, powerful, conclusive.
CON.VIR, *v.*, to suit, to agree to, to befit.
CON.VI.TE, *s. m.*, invitation, call, convocation, engagement.
CON.VI.VÊN.CIA, *s. f.*, acquaintance, living in society.
CON.VI.VER, *v.*, to live together, to cohabit.
CON.VO.CA.ÇÃO, *s. f.*, convocation, invitation, convening.
CON.VO.CAR, *v.*, to convoke, to call together, to call, to convene.
CON.VOS.CO, *pron.*, with you.
CON.VUL.SÃO, *s. f.*, convulsion, convulsive, fit.
CON.VUL.SI.O.NAR, *v.*, to convulse, to agitate, to disturb.
CON.VUL.SI.VO, *adj.*, convulsive, spasmodic.
CO.O.PE.RA.ÇÃO, *s. f.*, co-operation, coaction.
CO.O.PE.RAR, *v.*, to co-operate, to work together.
CO.OR.DE.NA.ÇÃO, *s. f.*, co-ordination.
CO.OR.DE.NA.DOR, *s. m.*, co-ordinator; *adj.*, co-ordinating.
CO.OR.DE.NAR, *v.*, to co-ordenate, to organize, to classify, to arrange.
CO.PA, *s. f.*, cup, chalice; pantry; butler's pantry; pressing vat; top of a tree.
CO.PEI.RO, *s. m.*, butler.
CÓ.PIA, *s. f.*, copy, reproduction, transcript, imitation.
CO.PI.AR, *v.*, to copy, to reproduce, to duplicate.
CO.PI.LO.TO, *s. m.*, copilot.
CO.PO, *s. m.*, cup, glass, drinking glass.
CÓ.PU.LA, *s. f.*, coitus, coition, copulation.
CO.PU.LAR, *v.*, to copulate, to have sexual intercourse.
CO.QUE, *s. m.*, coke.
CO.QUEI.RO, *s. m.*, coconut palm.
CO.QUE.LU.CHE, *s. m.*, whooping-cough.
CO.QUE.TEL, *s. m.*, cocktail.
COR, *s. f.*, colour, color, hue, tint, paint; wish, heart, desire.
CO.RA.ÇÃO, *s. f.*, heart, courage, feeling.
CO.RA.DO, *adj.*, red-faced, ashamed, ruddy, rosy, florid.
CO.RA.GEM, *s. f.*, courage, daring, fearlessness, valour, gut, grit, bravery.
CO.RA.JO.SO, *adj.*, courageous, daring, valiant, bold, brave.
CO.RAL, *s. m.*, coral, coral plant; chorus, choral, coral snake; *adj.*, choric, choral.
CO.RAR, *v.*, to colour, to dye, to paint.
COR.ÇA, *s. f.*, doe, hind.
COR.CO.VA, *s. f.*, hump, hunch.
COR.CUN.DA, *s. f.*, humpback, hunchback, crookback.
COR.DA, *s. f.*, cord, rope, line, string.
COR.DÃO, *s. m.*, string, thread, twist, lace.
COR.DEI.RO, *s. m.*, lamb.
COR-DE-RO.SA, *adj.*, pink, damask, rosy, roseate.
COR.DI.AL, *adj.*, cordial, sincere, kind, amicable, genial.
COR.DI.A.LI.DA.DE, *s. f.*, cordiality, sincerity, affection.
COR.DI.LHEI.RA, *s. f.*, mountain range.
CO.RI.ZA, *s. f.*, coryza, nasal catarrh.
COR.JA, *s. f.*, rabble, mob, multitude.
CÓR.NEA, *s. f.*, cornea.
COR.NE.TA, *s. f.*, cornet, bugle, horn.
COR.NO, *s. m.*, horn.
CO.RO, *s. m.*, choir, chorus.
CO.RO.A, *s. f.*, crown.
CO.RO.A.ÇÃO, *s. f.*, crowning, coronation, antlers.
CO.RO.A.MEN.TO, *s. m.*, coronation, crowning.
CO.RO.AR, *v.*, to crown, to enthrone, to acclaim, to top.
CO.RO.LÁ.RIO, *s. m.*, corollary, deduction, consequence.

CO.RO.NÁ.RIA, *s. f.*, coronary artery.

CO.RO.NEL, *s. m.*, colonel, commander.

COR.PE.TE, *s. m.*, bodice, camisole.

COR.PO, *s. m.*, body, frame, corpus, society, bulk, regiment, brigade, basis.

COR.PO.RA.ÇÃO, *s. f.*, corporation, association, fraternity.

COR.PO.RAL, *adj.*, corporal.

COR.PO.RA.LI.ZAR, *v.*, to materialize, to give a corporeal form to.

COR.PO.RA.TI.VIS.MO, *s. m.*, corporatism, corporativism.

COR.PÓ.REO, *adj.*, corporal, bodily, material, external.

COR.PU.LÊN.CIA, *s. f.*, corpulence, corpulency.

COR.PU.LEN.TO, *adj.*, corpulent, fat, gross, big.

COR.PÚS.CU.LO, *s. m.*, corpuscule, corpuscle.

COR.RE.ÇÃO, *s. f.*, correction, correctness, rectitude, retification.

COR.RE.DOR, *s. m.*, runner, racer, corridor, passage.

COR.RE.GE.DOR, *s. m.*, corregidor.

CÓR.RE.GO, *s. m.*, brook, streamlet, brooklet, runlet.

COR.REI.A, *s. f.*, strap, belt, leash.

COR.REI.O, *s. m.*, mail, mailman, postal service; messenger.

COR.RE.LA.ÇÃO, *s. f.*, correlation.

COR.RE.LA.CIO.NAR, *v.*, to correlate, to connect.

COR.REN.TE, *s. f.*, chain, cable, stream, flow, tie; *adj.*, current, common, fluent.

COR.REN.TE.ZA, *s. f.*, current, stream, watercourse, flow.

COR.RER, *v.*, to run, to hurry, to pursue, to travel.

COR.RE.RIA, *s. f.*, rush, scurry, running.

COR.RES.PON.DÊN.CIA, *s. f.*, correspondence, letters, conformity, agreement.

COR.RES.PON.DEN.TE, *s. 2 gen.*, correspondent, newspaper correspondent; *adj.*, correspondent.

COR.RES.PON.DER, *v.*, to correspond, to reciprocate, reply, to satisfy.

COR.RE.TA.GEM, *s. f.*, brokerage.

COR.RE.TO, *adj.*, correct, right, true, perfect, exact, proper.

COR.RE.TOR, *s. m.*, broker, agent, commission agent, jobber.

COR.RI.DA, *s. f.*, race, scurrying, way, distance.

COR.RI.GIR, *v.*, to correct, to amend, to set right, to reform.

COR.RI.MÃO, *s. m.*, handrail, stair rail.

COR.RO.BO.RA.ÇÃO, *s. f.*, corroboration, confirmation.

COR.RO.ER, *v.*, to erode, to corrode, to destroy, to deprave.

COR.ROM.PER, *v.*, to corrupt, to spoil, to pervert, to adulterate, to seduce.

COR.RO.SÃO, *s. f.*, corrosion, erosion.

COR.RO.SI.VO, *adj.*, corrosive.

COR.RUP.ÇÃO, *s. f.*, corruption, spoiling, putrefaction, deterioration.

COR.RUP.TO, *adj.*, corrupt, depraved, dissolute.

COR.SÁ.RIO, *s. m.*, corsair, privateer, pirate.

COR.TA.DO, *adj.*, cut, interrupted.

COR.TAR, *v.*, to cut, to chop, to slice, to carve, to shut off.

COR.TE, *s. m.*, cut, incision, section; **CORTE(Ô)**, *s. f.*, court, sovereign's residence.

COR.TE.JAR, *v.*, to court, to flirt with, to greet, to salute.

COR.TE.JO, *s. m.*, procession, courtship, homage.

COR.TÊS, *adj.*, courteous, polite.

COR.TE.SI.A, *s. f.*, courtesy, politeness, urbanity, civility.

COR.TI.NA, *s. f.*, curtain, screen.

CO.RU.JA, *s. f.*, owl, owlet.

COR.VO, *s. m.*, raven, crow.

CÓS, *s. m.*, waistband of a garment.

CO.SE.DU.RA, *s. f.*, sewing.

CO.SER, *v.*, to sew, to stitch.

COS.MÉ.TI.CO, *adj., s. m.*, cosmetic.

CÓS.MI.CO, *adj., s. m.*, cosmic.

COS.MO, *s. m.*, cosmos.

COS.MO.LO.GI.A, *s. f.*, cosmology.

COS.MO.PO.LI.TA, *s. 2 gen.*, cosmopolitan, cosmopolite, citizen of the cosmos.

COS.TA, *s. f.*, coast, seashore, declivity; **COSTAS**, back.
COS.TEI.RO, *adj.*, coastal.
COS.TE.LA, *s. f.*, rib.
COS.TE.LE.TA, *s. f.*, chop, cutlet.
COS.TU.MAR, *v.*, to be accustomed, to be used to.
COS.TU.ME, *s. m.*, custom, habit, practice, usage, use, way, common law.
COS.TU.MEI.RO, *adj.*, usual, customary.
COS.TU.RA, *s. f.*, sewing, needlework, seam, juncture.
COS.TU.RAR, *v.*, to sew, to seam.
COS.TU.REI.RA, *s. f.*, needlewoman, dressmaker.
COS.TU.REI.RO, *s. m.*, seamster.
CO.TA, *s. f.*, share, portion, quota.
CO.TA.ÇÃO, *s. f.*, quotation, assessment.
CO.TAR, *v.*, to estimate, to valuate, to tax.
CO.TI.DI.A.NO, *adj.*, daily, everyday, day-to-day, quotidian.
CO.TI.ZAR, *v.*, to tax, to assess, to rate.
CO.TO.NI.FÍ.CIO, *s. m.*, cotton mill.
CO.TO.VE.LA.DA, *s. f.*, nudge, dig.
CO.TO.VE.LO, *s. m.*, elbow.
COU.RO, *s. m.*, leather, hide.
COU.VE, *s. m.*, kale, cabbage.
COU.VE-FLOR, *s. m.*, cauliflower.
CO.VA, *s. f.*, hole, cavity, hollow, pit; grave.
CO.VAR.DI.A, *s. f.*, cowardice.
CO.VEI.RO, *s. m.*, grave-digger.
CO.XA, *s. f.*, thigh.
CO.XO, *adj., s. m.*, limping, halting, lame.
CO.ZER, *v.*, to cook, to boil, to bake.
CO.ZI.NHA, *s. f.*, kitchen, cuisine, cookery.
CO.ZI.NHAR, *v.*, to cook, to boil.
CO.ZI.NHEI.RA, *s. f.*, cook.
CO.ZI.NHEI.RO, *s. m.*, cook.
CRÂ.NIO, *s. m.*, cranium, skull, brainpan.
CRA.PU.LO.SO, *adj.*, crapulous, licentious.
CRA.SE, *s. f.*, crasis, contraction of two vowels.
CRA.TE.RA, *s. f.*, crater, mouth of a volcano.
CRA.VAR, *v.*, to thrust in, to set, to fix.
CRA.VO, *s. m.*, horseshoe nail, shoe tack; carnation, pink.
CRE.CHE, *s. f.*, nursery.
CRE.DI.Á.RIO, *s. m.*, credit system, instalment system.
CRE.DI.TAR, *v.*, to credit, to guarantee.
CRÉ.DI.TO, *s. m.*, credit, trust; good reputation, power; **CARTA DE CRÉDITO**, letter of credit.
CRE.DO, *s. m.*, Credo, Creed, symbol of the apostles.
CRE.DOR, *s. m.*, creditor.
CRE.DU.LI.DA.DE, *s. f.*, credulity.
CRE.MA.ÇÃO, *s. f.*, cremation, incineration.
CRE.MAR, *v.*, to cremate.
CRE.ME, *s. m.*, cream, custard.
CREN.ÇA, *s. f.*, belief, creed, faith, opinion.
CREN.DI.CE, *s. f.*, superstition.
CREN.TE, *s. 2 gen.*, believer; *adj.*, believing.
CRE.PE, *s. f.*, crape, gauzy fabric.
CRE.PI.TAR, *v.*, to crepitate.
CRE.PÚS.CU.LO, *s. m.*, crepuscle, crepusculum, nightfall, twilight.
CRER, *v.*, to believe, to trust, to think, to judge.
CRES.CEN.TE, *s. m.*, crescent, increasing; the first quarter of the moon.
CRES.CER, *v.*, to grow, to grow up, to increase, to develop, to multiply, to augment.
CRES.CI.MEN.TO, *s. m.*, growth, increase, development, augmentation.
CRE.TI.NIS.MO, *s. m.*, cretinism, stupidity.
CRE.TI.NO, *adj.*, idiot, imbecile, cretin, stupid.
CRI.A.ÇÃO, *s. f.*, creation, invention, universe, institution, nurture, establishment.
CRI.A.DO, *s. m.*, servant, man-servant, domestic; *adj.*, created, bred, raised.
CRI.A.DOR, *s. m.*, creator, The Creator.
CRI.AN.ÇA, *s. f.*, child, infant, baby.
CRI.AN.ÇA.DA, *s. f.*, children, fry, bunch of children.
CRI.AN.CI.NHA, *s. f.*, nestling.
CRI.AR, *v.*, to create, to generate, to produce, to originate, to invent.
CRI.A.TU.RA, *s. f.*, creature, being.
CRI.ME, *s. m.*, crime, felony, delinquency.
CRI.MI.NAL, *adj.*, criminal.

CRI.MI.NA.LI.DA.DE, *s. f.,* criminality, culpability.
CRI.MI.NO.SO, *s. m.,* criminal, felon, offender, delinquent, murderer; *adj.,* criminal.
CRI.OU.LO, *s. m.,* creole.
CRIP.TA, *s. f.,* crypt, vault, catacomb.
CRI.SE, *s. f.,* crisis.
CRIS.MA, *s. f.,* confirmation, chrism; *s. m.,* consecrated oil.
CRIS.MAR, *v.,* to chrism.
CRIS.TA, *s. f.,* crest, cockscomb, comb.
CRIS.TAL, *s. m.,* crystal, crystal glass.
CRIS.TA.LI.NO, *adj.,* crystalline, limpid, like crystal.
CRIS.TA.LI.ZAR, *v.,* to crystallize.
CRIS.TAN.DA.DE, *s. f.,* Christianity.
CRIS.TÃO, *adj., s. m.,* Christian.
CRIS.TI.A.NIS.MO, *s. m.,* Christianism.
CRIS.TI.A.NI.ZAR, *v.,* to Christianize.
CRIS.TO, *s. m.,* Christ, Jesus.
CRI.TÉ.RIO, *s. m.,* criterion, rule, discretion.
CRÍ.TI.CA, *s. f.,* criticism, censure, critique.
CRI.TI.CAR, *v.,* to criticize, to judge, to censure.
CRÍ.TI.CO, *s. m.,* critic, reviewer, censurer; *adj.,* critical, crucial, dangerous.
CRI.VO, *s. m.,* sieve, screen, colander.
CRO.CHÊ, *s. m.,* crochet, crochet work.
CRO.CO.DI.LO, *s. m.,* crocodile.
CRO.MAR, *v.,* to chromate.
CRO.MÁ.TI.CO, *adj.,* chromatic.
CRÔ.NI.CA, *s. f.,* chronicle, narrative, event.
CRÔ.NI.CO, *adj.,* chronic, chronical.
CRO.NIS.TA, *s. 2 gen.,* chronicler, historian.
CRO.NO.LO.GI.A, *s. f.,* chronology.
CRO.NÔ.ME.TRO, *s. m.,* chronometer, precision watch.
CRO.QUI, *s. m.,* sketch.
CROS.TA, *s. f.,* crust, rind.
CRU, *adj.,* raw, uncooked, crude, unprocessed.
CRU.CI.AL, *adj.,* crucial, decisive.
CRU.CI.FI.CA.ÇÃO, *s. f.,* crucifixion.
CRU.CI.FI.CA.DO, *s. m.,* the Crucified, Christ; *adj.,* crucifixed.
CRU.CI.FI.CAR, *v.,* to crucify, to torture, to mortify.
CRU.CI.FI.XO, *s. m.,* crucifix.
CRU.EL, *adj.,* cruel, inhuman, fierce, barbarous.
CRU.EL.DA.DE, *s. f.,* cruelty, inhumanity.
CRUS.TÁ.CEO, *s. m.,* crustacean; *adj.,* crustaceous.
CRUZ, *s. f.,* cross; Christian symbol, Cristianism.
CRUZ VER.ME.LHA, *s. f.,* red cross.
CRU.ZA.DA, *s. f.,* cruzade.
CRU.ZA.MEN.TO, *s. m.,* crossing, intersection, street crossing.
CRU.ZAR, *v.,* to cross, to traverse, to pass through.
CU.BA.NO, *adj., s. m.,* Cuban.
CU.BÍ.CU.LO, *s. m.,* cubicle, cubby-hole.
CU.BO, *s. m.,* cube.
CU.CO, *s. m.,* cuckoo; cuckoo-clock.
CU.E.CAS, *s. f., pl.,* briefs, short drawers.
CUI.DA.DO, *s. m.,* care, precaution, caution, attention.
CUI.DAR, *v.,* to care, to consider; to take care of, to look after, to suppose.
CU.JO, *pron.,* whose, of whom, of which.
CU.LA.TRA, *s. f.,* breech.
CU.LI.NÁ.RIA, *s. f.,* cookery, culinary art.
CU.LI.NÁ.RIO, *adj.,* culinary.
CUL.MI.NAR, *v.,* to culminate, to terminate.
CUL.PA, *s. f.,* blame, fault, guilt, offence, delinquency, crime.
CUL.PA.BI.LI.DA.DE, *s. f.,* culpability.
CUL.PAR, *v.,* to accuse, to inculpate, to incriminate.
CUL.TI.VAR, *v.,* to cultivate, to till, to maintain, to develop, to keep up.
CUL.TI.VO, *s. m.,* cultivation, culture.
CUL.TO, *s. m.,* cult, adoration, veneration; *adj.,* cultured, learned, educated, refined.
CUL.TU.RA, *s. f.,* culture, education, civilization, cultivation, breeding.
CU.ME, *s. m.* summit, top, peak.
CU.ME.EI.RA, *s. f.,* roof ridge, ridge beam.
CÚM.PLI.CE, *s. 2 gen.,* accomplice, partner.
CUM.PLI.CI.DA.DE, *s. f.,* complicity.
CUM.PRI.MEN.TAR, *v.,* to salute, to greet, to bow to, to congratulate.

CUM.PRI.MEN.TO, *s. m.*, accomplishment, compliment, execution, performance.
CUM.PRIR, *v.*, to accomplish, to execute, to fulfil, to carry out, to keep.
CU.NHA.DA, *s. f.*, sister-in-law.
CU.NHA.DO, *s. m.*, brother-in-law.
CU.NHAR, *v.*, to coin, to mint, to stamp, to emboss.
CU.NI.CUL.TU.RA, *s. f.*, rabbit breeding.
CU.PIM, *s. m.*, termite; white ant.
CU.POM, *s. m.*, coupon, voucher.
CU.RA, *s. f.*, cure, healing, sanation, recovery, medication; *s. m.*, curate, rector.
CU.RA.DOR, *s. m.*, curator, guardian, tutor.
CU.RAR, *v.*, to cure, to heal, to treat, to remedy, to medicate.
CU.RA.TI.VO, *s. m.*, curative, medication, remedy.
CU.RIN.GA, *s. m.*, joker.
CU.RI.O.SI.DA.DE, *s. f.*, curiosity, indiscretion, rarity.
CU.RI.O.SO, *s. m.*, curious, looker on, by-stander; *adj.*, curious, inquisitive, studious.
CUR.RAL, *s. m.*, corral, stable, pound.
CUR.RÍ.CU.LO, *s. m.*, curriculum.
CUR.SAR, *v.*, to course, to follow a course of study, to cruise, to navigate.
CUR.SO, *s. m.*, course; run, career, sequence, progress, circulation.
CUR.TIR, *v.*, to tan hides, to harden.
CUR.TO, *adj.*, short, brief, scant, scarce.
CUR.TO-CIR.CUI.TO, *s. m.*, short circuit.
CUR.VA, *s. f.*, curve, bend, crook, bow.
CUR.VAR, *v.*, to curve, to incurvate, to bend, to arch, to inflect.
CUR.VA.TU.RA, *s. f.*, curvature, bend, flection.
CUR.VO, *adj.*, curved, bent, arched.
CUS.PE, *s. m.*, spit, saliva, spittle.
CUS.PIR, *v.*, to spit, to expectorate, to eject.
CUS.TAR, *v.*, to cost, to be worth, to be difficult.
CUS.TE.AR, *v.*, to bear the expense, to finance.
CUS.TO, *s. m.*, cost, expense, difficulty, price, worth.
CUS.TO.DI.AR, *v.*, to keep in custody.
CU.TÂ.NEO, *adj.*, cutaneous, of or relating to the skin.
CU.TE.LO, *s. m.*, chopping knife.
CU.TÍ.CU.LA, *s. f.*, cuticle, pellicle.
CÚ.TIS, *s. f.*, cutis, derma, skin.
CU.TU.CÃO, *s. m.*, dig, jab.
CU.TU.CAR, *v.*, to jog, to poke, to dig.
CZAR, *s. m.*, tsar.

D

D, *s. m.*, the fourth letter of the Portuguese alphabet; **D**, Roman numeral: 500.
DA, *contr.* of the *prep.* **DE** with the *art.* **A**.
DÁ.DI.VA, *s. m.*, gift, present, donation, godsend.
DA.DO, *s. m.*, die, small cube for playing; datum, figure; licit, permitted, free; *conj.*, in view of.
DA.Í, *adv.*, thence, from there, therefore.
DA.LI, *adv.*, thence, therefrom, from there.
DÁ.LIA, *s. f.*, dahlia.
DA.MA, *s. f.*, lady, maid, actress, queen.
DA.NA.ÇÃO, *s. f.*, damagement, anger, fury.
DA.NA.DO, *adj.*, damned, condemned, ruined, decayed, furious, angry.
DA.NAR, *v.*, to harm, to hurt, to injure, to damage, to provoke, to annoy.
DAN.ÇAR, *s. f.*, to dance, to turn around, to bob.
DAN.ÇA.RI.NA, *s. f.*, dancer, ballerina, dancing-girl.
DA.NI.FI.CAR, *v.*, to damage, to harm, to injure, to hurt.
DA.NO, *s. m.*, damage, harm, injury, loss.
DA.NO.SO, *adj.*, prejudicial, damaging.
DA.QUE.LE, *contr.* of the *prep.* **DE** and the *pron. dem.* **AQUELE**, from that, of that.
DA.QUI, *contr.* of the *prep.* **DE** and the *adv.*, **AQUI**, from here, within.
DA.QUI.LO, *contr.* of the *prep.* **DE** and the *pron. dem.* **AQUILO**, from that, of that.
DAR, *v.*, to give, to offer, to bestow; to beat, to grant, to concede, to dedicate.
DA.TA, *s. f.*, date.
DA.TAR, *v.*, to date, to start, to reckon from, to persist.
DA.TI.LO.GRA.FAR, *v.*, to typewrite.
DA.TI.LO.GRA.FI.A, *s. f.*, typewriting.
DA.TI.LÓ.GRA.FO, *s. m.*, typist.
DE, *prep.*, of, from, by, to, on, in, with.
DE.BAI.XO, *adv.*, under, beneath, below, inferior.

DE.BAN.DAR, *v.*, to flee, to scatter, to put to flight.
DE.BA.TE, *s. m.*, debate, discussion, contest.
DE.BA.TER, *v.*, to discuss, to dispute, to contend, to contest.
DÉ.BIL, *adj.*, weak, vacillating, feeble, infirm.
DE.BI.LI.DA.DE, *s. f.*, debility, fragility, weakness.
DE.BI.LI.TAR, *v.*, to weaken, to debilitate, to harm.
DÉ.BI.TO, *s. m.*, debt, obligation, debit.
DE.BO.CHE, *s. m.*, mockery.
DE.BRU.ÇAR, *v.*, to stoop, to bend forward, to lean over.
DE.BU.LHAR, *v.*, thrash, to peel.
DÉ.CA.DA, *s. f.*, decade.
DE.CA.DÊN.CIA, *s. f.*, decadence, decline, decay, fall.
DE.CA.Í.DA, *s. f.*, decay, decline.
DE.CA.IR, *v.*, to decay, to decline, to fall away, to slip.
DE.CAL.CAR, *v.*, to trace, to copy, to imitate.
DE.CA.NO, *s. m.*, dean, elder, senior.
DE.CA.PI.TAR, *v.*, to decapitate, to behead.
DE.CÊN.CIA, *s. f.*, decency, neatness, decorum.
DE.CEN.TE, *adj.*, decent, proper, decorous, honest, fair, convenient.
DE.CE.PAR, *v.*, to cut off, to amputate, to sever, to maim, to interrupt, to mutilate.
DE.CEP.ÇÃO, *s. f.*, disappointment, disillusion, fraud.
DE.CI.DI.DO, *adj.*, resolute, decided, courageous.
DE.CI.DIR, *v.*, to decide, to resolve, to determine, to settle.
DE.CI.MAL, *adj., s. m.*, decimal.
DE.CÍ.ME.TRO, *s. m.*, decimeter, decimetre.
DÉ.CI.MO, *num.*, tenth, tenth part.
DE.CI.SÃO, *s. f.*, decision, resolution,

determination, judgment, verdict.
DE.CI.SI.VO, *adj.*, decisive, conclusive, obvious.
DE.CLA.MAR, *v.*, to declaim, to recite, to proclaim.
DE.CLA.RA.ÇÃO, *s. f.*, declaration, assertion, statement.
DE.CLA.RAR, *v.*, to declare, to assert, to state, to announce.
DE.CLI.NAR, *v.*, to reject, to refuse, to declare, to reveal.
DE.CLI.VE, *s. m.*, descending, declivity; *adj.*, declivous.
DE.CO.LAR, *v.*, to take off.
DE.COM.POR, *v.*, to decompose, to separate, to analyse, to modify.
DE.COM.PO.SI.ÇÃO, *s. f.*, decomposition, disintegration, separation, analysis.
DE.CO.RAR, *v.*, to know by heart, to remember; to decorate, to adorn, to embellish.
DE.CO.RO, *s. m.*, decency, honesty, propriety, decorum.
DE.COR.RER, *v.*, to elapse, to pass away, to happen, to occur, to derive.
DE.CO.TAR, *v.*, to cut off, to make low-necked.
DE.CO.TE, *s. m.*, low neck.
DE.CRÉ.PI.TO, *adj.*, decrepit, old, feeble.
DE.CRES.CER, *v.*, to diminish, to decrease, decline.
DE.CRE.TAR, *v.*, to decree, to determine, to proclaim, to order.
DE.CRE.TO, *s. m.*, decree, edict, designation.
DE.DI.CA.ÇÃO, *s. f.*, dedication, devotion, affection, fondness.
DE.DI.CA.DO, *adj.*, dedicated, devoted, consecrated.
DE.DI.CAR, *v.*, to dedicate, to devote, to hallow, to consecrate.
DE.DI.CA.TÓ.RIA, *s. f.*, dedication.
DE.DO, *s. m.*, finger.
DE.DU.ÇÃO, *s. f.*, deduction, abatement, allowance.
DE.DU.ZIR, *v.*, to deduce, to draw or trace from facts, to infer.
DE.FE.CAR, *v.*, to defecate, to shit, to poop.

DE.FEI.TO, *s. m.*, defect, fault, flaw, deformity.
DE.FEI.TU.O.SO, *adj.*, defective, faulty, imperfect.
DE.FEN.DER, *v.*, to defend, to protect, to help, to aid, to support.
DE.FEN.SOR, *s. m.*, defender, protector.
DE.FE.RÊN.CIA, *s. f.*, deference, respect, regard.
DE.FE.RI.MEN.TO, *s. m.*, grant, concession.
DE.FE.RIR, *v.*, to grant, to approve.
DE.FE.SA, *s. f.*, defence, defense, justification, guard, protection.
DE.FI.CI.ÊN.CIA, *s. f.*, deficiency, lack, want, need, imperfection.
DÉ.FI.CIT, *s. m.*, deficit, shortage.
DE.FI.CI.TÁ.RIO, *adj.*, deficient.
DE.FI.NHAR, *v.*, to debilitate, to weaken, to languish.
DE.FI.NI.ÇÃO, *s. f.*, definition, definement, explanation, decision.
DE.FI.NIR, *v.*, to define, to determine, to fix, to decide.
DE.FI.NI.TI.VO, *adj.*, definitive, conclusive.
DE.FLA.ÇÃO, *s. f.*, deflation.
DE.FLA.GRAR, *v.*, to deflagrate, to burn, to excite.
DE.FLO.RAR, *v.*, to deflorate, to deflower, to violate.
DE.FOR.MA.ÇÃO, *s. f.*, deformation, disfigurement, deformity.
DE.FOR.MAR, *v.*, to deform, to disfigure, to misshape, to warp.
DE.FOR.MI.DA.DE, *s. f.*, deformity.
DE.FRON.TAR, *v.*, to confront, to face.
DE.FRON.TE, *adv.*, face to face, in front of.
DE.FUN.TO, *s. m.*, corpse, deceased; *adj.*, dead, extinct.
DE.GE.LAR, *v.*, to defrost, to deice.
DE.GE.LO, *s. m.*, defrosting, thawing.
DE.GE.NE.RA.ÇÃO, *s. f.*, degeneration.
DE.GE.NE.RAR, *v.*, to degenerate, to fall off, to deteriorate.
DE.GO.LAR, *v.*, to decapitate, to behead.
DE.GRA.DAR, *v.*, to degrade, to lower, to decline.
DE.GRAU, *s. m.*, stair, step.

DEGREDAR — **DENUNCIAR**

DE.GRE.DAR, *v.*, to exile, to banish, to deport.
DE.GUS.TAR, *v.*, to taste, to degust.
DEI.TAR, *v.*, to lie, to lay; to lie down, to incline.
DEI.XAR, *v.*, to leave, to quit, to abandon, to let go, to forsake, to release.
DE.LA, *contr.* of the *prep.* **DE** and the *pron.* **ELA**, her, hers, of her, from her.
DE.LA.TAR, *v.*, to delate, to inform against, to denounce.
DE.LE, *contr.* of the *prep.* **DE** and the *pron.* **ELE**, his, of him, from him.
DE.LE.GA.ÇÃO, *s. f.*, delegation, deputation.
DE.LE.GA.CI.A, *s. f.*, delegateship, police station.
DE.LE.GA.DO, *s. m.*, delegate, police officer.
DE.LE.GAR, *v.*, to delegate, to depute, to authorize, to assign, to appoint.
DE.LEI.TAR, *v.*, to delight, to please, to gratify.
DE.LI.BE.RA.ÇÃO, *s. f.*, deliberation, consideration.
DE.LI.BE.RAR, *v.*, to deliberate, to ponder, to reflect upon, to resolve.
DE.LI.CA.DE.ZA, *s. f.*, politeness, courtesy, fineness.
DE.LI.CA.DO, *adj.*, delicate, polite, courteous.
DE.LÍ.CIA, *s. f.*, delicacy, delight, pleasure.
DE.LI.CI.AR, *v.*, to delight, to please.
DE.LI.CI.O.SO, *adj.*, delicious, delightful.
DE.LI.MI.TAR, *v.*, to delimitate, to delimit, to bound.
DE.LI.NE.AR, *v.*, to delineate, to sketch out, to draw, to outline.
DE.LIN.QUEN.TE, *s. 2 gen.*, delinquent, outlaw, felon, transgressor; *adj.*, delinquent.
DE.LI.RAR, *v.*, to rave, to talk nonsense.
DE.LÍ.RIO, *s. m.*, delirium, insanity, derangement.
DE.LI.TO, *s. m.*, delict, fault, crime, transgression.
DEL.TA, *s. m.*, delta.
DE.MA.GO.GI.A, *s. f.*, demagogy, demagogysm.
DE.MA.GO.GO, *s. m.*, demagogue, demagog.
DE.MAIS, *adv.*, too much, excessive, overmuch; besides, moreover.
DE.MAN.DAR, *v.*, to require, to call for, to demand.
DE.MAR.CAR, *v.*, to demarcate, to delimit, to define, to mark out.
DE.MA.SI.A, *s. f.*, surplus, excess, overplus, superabundance.
DE.MA.SI.A.DO, *adj.*, excessive, overmuch, too much, undue.
DE.MÊN.CIA, *s. f.*, dementia, insanity.
DE.MIS.SÃO, *s. f.*, demission, firing, dismissal, abdication.
DE.MI.TIR, *v.*, to dismiss, to discharge, to fire.
DE.MO.CRA.CI.A, *s. f.*, democracy.
DE.MO.CRA.TA, *s. 2 gen.*, democrat.
DE.MO.CRA.TI.ZAR, *v.*, to democratize.
DE.MO.LI.ÇÃO, *s. f.*, demolition, demolishment.
DE.MO.LIR, *v.*, to demolish, to destroy.
DE.MÔ.NIO, *s. m.*, demon, devil.
DE.MONS.TRAR, *v.*, to demonstrate, to prove by reasoning, to evince.
DE.MO.RA, *s. f.*, delay, retardation, lateness.
DE.MO.RAR, *v.*, to delay, to stay, to detain, to retard.
DE.NE.GRIR, *v.*, to denigrate, to blacken.
DEN.GUE, *s. m.*, dengue, breakbone fever.
DE.NO.MI.NA.ÇÃO, *s. f.*, denomination, name, naming, designation.
DE.NO.MI.NAR, *v.*, to denominate, to name, to call, to entitle.
DE.NO.TA.ÇÃO, *s. f.*, denotation, sign.
DEN.SI.DA.DE, *s. f.*, density, thickness, closeness.
DEN.SO, *adj.*, dense, thick, compact.
DEN.TA.DA, *s. f.*, bite, biting, morsel.
DEN.TA.DU.RA, *s. f.*, denture, set of teeth, false teeth.
DEN.TE, *s. m.*, tooth; **DENTE DE LEITE**, milk tooth.
DEN.TI.ÇÃO, *s. f.*, dentition, teething.
DEN.TI.FRÍ.CIO, *s. m.*, dentifrice, tooth paste.
DEN.TIS.TA, *s. 2 gen.*, dentist.
DEN.TRE, *prep.*, among, in the midst of.
DEN.TRO, *adv.*, inside, within, indoors.
DEN.TU.ÇO, *s. m.*, big-toothed.
DE.NU.DAR, *v.*, to denude, to divest.
DE.NÚN.CIA, *s. f.*, accusation, denunciation, delation.
DE.NUN.CI.AR, *v.*, to denounce, to denunciate,

to accuse, to inform.
DE.PAR.TA.MEN.TO, *s. m.*, department, bureau.
DE.PE.NAR, *v.*, to pluck, to deplume, to pick; to strip of money.
DE.PEN.DÊN.CIA, *s. f.*, dependence, pendency, subjection, subordination.
DE.PEN.DER, *v.*, to depend on, to be based on, to be pending.
DE.PLO.RAR, *v.*, to deplore, to regret, to lament, to bewail.
DE.PO.I.MEN.TO, *s. m.*, deposition, testimony.
DE.POIS, *adv.*, after, afterward, later on, then, besides, moreover.
DE.POR, *v.*, to put down, to lay down, to depose, to put aside, to testify, to witness.
DE.POR.TAR, *v.*, to deport, to banish, to exile.
DE.PO.SI.TAR, *v.*, to deposit, to lay, to entrust, to commit to for custody.
DE.PÓ.SI.TO, *s. m.*, deposit, deposition, act of depositing; storehouse, warehouse.
DE.PRE.CI.AR, *v.*, to depreciate, to undervalue, to lessen.
DE.PRE.DAR, *v.*, to depredate, to destroy.
DE.PRES.SA, *adv.*, fast, quickly, swiftly, readily.
DE.PRES.SÃO, *s. f.*, depression, stagnation.
DE.PRI.MIR, *v.*, to depress, to lower, to weaken, to depreciate.
DE.PU.RA.ÇÃO, *s. f.*, debugging, purification.
DE.PU.RAR, *v.*, to purify, to clean, to depurate.
DE.PU.TA.DO, *s. m.*, deputy, delegate, representative, commissioner, congressman.
DE.RI.VAR, *v.*, to derive, to arise from, to deflect, to trace the origin.
DER.MA.TO.LO.GI.A, *s. f.*, dermatology.
DER.MA.TO.LO.GIS.TA, *s. 2 gen.*, dermatologist.
DER.RA.DEI.RO, *adj.*, last, final, conclusive, hindmost.
DER.RA.MAR, *v.*, to shed, to spill, to lop, to strew, to pour out.
DER.RA.ME, *s. m.*, hemorrhage.
DER.RA.PAR, *v.*, to skid, to sideslip.
DER.RE.DOR, *adv.*, around, about.
DER.RE.TER, *v.*, to melt, to dissolve, to soften, to liquefy, to fuse.
DER.RE.TI.MEN.TO, *s. m.*, melting, fusion.
DER.RO.TA, *s. f.*, defeat, overthrow.
DER.RO.TAR, *v.*, to defeat, to vanquish, to beat, to foil.
DER.RU.BA.DA, *s. f.*, felling (of trees), defeat.
DER.RU.BAR, *v.*, to throw down, to throw to the ground.
DE.SA.BA.FAR, *v.*, to uncover, to expose, to reveal, to open.
DE.SA.BA.FO, *s. m.*, ease, relief, alleviation.
DE.SA.BAR, *v.*, to crumble, to fall down, to tumble.
DE.SA.BI.TA.DO, *adj.*, uninhabited, deserted.
DE.SA.BO.TO.AR, *v.*, to unbutton, to open, to spread.
DE.SA.BRI.GAR, *v.*, to unshelter, to uncover.
DE.SA.BRO.CHAR, *v.*, to bloom, to sprout, to unclasp, to loosen.
DE.SA.CA.TO, *s. m.*, disrespect, disregard, discourtesy.
DE.SA.COR.DO, *s. m.*, disagreement.
DE.SA.COS.TU.MAR, *v.*, to disaccustom, to disuse, to dishabituate.
DE.SA.CRE.DI.TA.DO, *adj.*, discredited.
DE.SA.CRE.DI.TAR, *v.*, to discredit, to disparage, to defame.
DE.SA.FI.AR, *v.*, to challenge, to defy, to provoke, to beard.
DE.SA.FI.NAR, *v.*, to sing or play out of tune.
DE.SA.FI.O, *s. m.*, challenge, defiance, provocation, defy.
DE.SA.FO.GAR, *v.*, to relieve, to ease, to disencumber, to disclose.
DE.SA.FO.RA.DO, *adj.*, insolent, impertinent, rude.
DE.SA.FO.RO, *s. m.*, insolence, impudence, insult, injury, affront.
DE.SA.GRA.DAR, *v.*, to displease, to dissatisfy, dislike.
DE.SA.GRA.DO, *s. m.*, unpleasantness, displeasure, disfavour.
DE.SA.JEI.TA.DO, *adj.*, unskillful, clumsy, awkward.

DESAJUIZADO — DESCASO

DE.SA.JU.I.ZA.DO, *adj.*, witless, unwise, thoughtless.

DE.SA.JUS.TAR, *v.*, to disagree, disadjust, to disarrange, to disturbe.

DE.SA.JUS.TE, *s. m.*, disagreement, conflict.

DE.SA.LEN.TAR, *v.*, to discourage, to depress.

DE.SA.LEN.TO, *s. m.*, discouragement, faintness, prostration.

DE.SA.LO.JAR, *v.*, dislodge, to remove, to unhouse, to drive out.

DE.SA.MAR.RAR, *v.*, to untie, to cast off, to unfasten, to loosen.

DE.SAM.PA.RAR, *v.*, to abandon, to leave, to quit, to forsake.

DE.SAM.PA.RO, *s. m.*, abandonment, helplessness, lurch.

DE.SA.NI.MA.DO, *adj.*, discouraged, down, downhearted, depressed.

DE.SA.NI.MAR, *v.*, to discourage, to depress, to dispirit.

DE.SÂ.NI.MO, *s. m.*, discouragement, dispiriteness, dismay, depression.

DE.SA.PA.RE.CER, *v.*, to disappear, to vanish, to die, to be lost.

DE.SA.PA.RE.CI.MEN.TO, *s. m.*, disappearance.

DE.SA.PE.GO, *s. m.*, unattachment, disaffection.

DE.SA.PER.TAR, *v.*, to loosen, to unlace, to unbrace, to unscrew.

DE.SA.PON.TA.MEN.TO, *s. m.*, disappointment.

DE.SA.PRO.PRI.AR, *v.*, to dispossess, to deprive, to expropriate.

DE.SA.PRO.VA.ÇÃO, *s. f.*, disapproval.

DE.SAR.MA.MEN.TO, *s. m.*, disarmament.

DE.SAR.MAR, *v.*, to disarm, to unarm, to unrig, to unship.

DE.SAR.RAN.JO, *s. m.*, disarrangement, disorder, mishap, distemper.

DE.SAR.RO.LHAR, *v.*, to uncork, unplug.

DE.SAR.RU.MAR, *v.*, to disarrange, to displace, to disorder, to dislocate.

DE.SAR.TI.CU.LA.ÇÃO, *s. f.*, disarticulation.

DE.SAR.TI.CU.LAR, *v.*, to disjoint, to disconnect, to dislocate, to luxate.

DE.SAS.SOM.BRO, *s. m.*, frankness, firmness, resolution.

DE.SAS.SOS.SE.GO, *s. m.*, unquietness, uneasiness.

DE.SAS.TRA.DO, *adj.*, disastrous, clumsy, awkward.

DE.SAS.TRE, *s. m.*, disaster, accident, calamity, misfortune, loss.

DE.SAS.TRO.SO, *adj.*, disastrous, hazardous, calamitous.

DE.SA.TAR, *v.*, to unfasten, to untie, to unhind, to release.

DE.SA.TEN.TO, *adj.*, careless, negligent, heedless, forgetful.

DE.SA.TI.VAR, *v.*, to switch off, to turn off, to power down.

DE.SAU.TO.RI.ZAR, *v.*, to disauthorize.

DE.SA.VEN.ÇA, *s. f.*, dissension, disagreement, discord, differ.

DES.BAS.TAR, *v.*, to cut off, to pare, to thin out.

DES.BO.CA.DO, *s. m.*, big-mouth; *adj.*, unrestrained, shocking, indecent.

DES.BRA.VAR, *v.*, to tame, to domesticate, to break, to cultivate.

DES.CA.BE.LA.DO, *adj.*, dishevelled, hairless.

DES.CAL.ÇAR, *v.*, to take or slip off (shoes, stockings, etc.), to unboot.

DES.CAL.ÇO, *adj.*, unshod, shoeless, barefoot.

DES.CAN.SA.DO, *adj.*, quiet, undisturbed, rested, easy, calm, tranquil.

DES.CAN.SAR, *v.*, to rest, to relax, to repose, to pause.

DES.CAN.SO, *s. m.*, break, rest, resting, restfulness, repose, refreshment.

DES.CA.RA.MEN.TO, *s. m.*, shamelessness, impudence.

DES.CAR.GA, *s. f.*, discharge, unloading, unlading.

DES.CAR.RE.GAR, *v.*, to discharge, to unload, to unburden, to disembárk.

DES.CAR.TAR, *v.*, to discard, to reject, to dismiss, to throw aside.

DES.CAS.CAR, *v.*, to peel, to skin, to rind, to bark.

DES.CA.SO, *s. m.*, negligence, disregard, indifference.

DESCENDÊNCIA — DESEMPREGADO

DES.CEN.DÊN.CIA, *s. f.*, descent, family, lineage, generation.

DES.CEN.DER, *v.*, to descend, to proceed, to come from, to be derived.

DES.CER, *v.*, to descend, to go down, to come down, to dismount, to step down.

DES.CI.DA, *s. f.*, descent, descending, going down, fall.

DES.CO.BER.TA, *s. f.*, discovery, invention, finding.

DES.CO.BRI.MEN.TO, *s. m.*, discovery, invention.

DES.CO.BRIR, *v.*, to discover, to uncover, to disclose, to expose, to show.

DES.COM.POR, *v.*, to discompose, to disarrange, to derange.

DES.CON.CER.TAR, *v.*, to disconcert, to disarrange, to disorder.

DES.CON.CER.TO, *s. m.*, disorder, disarrangement, confusion.

DES.CO.NE.XÃO, *s. f.*, disconnection.

DES.CON.FI.A.DO, *adj.*, suspicious, distrustful.

DES.CON.FI.AN.ÇA, *s. f.*, suspicion, suspiciousness, distrust.

DES.CON.FI.AR, *v.*, to suspect, to mistrust, to doubt, to distrust.

DES.CON.FOR.TO, *s. m.*, discomfort, comfortlessness, uncomfortableness.

DES.CO.NHE.CER, *v.*, to ignore, to disown, to dissemble.

DES.CON.SI.DE.RA.ÇÃO, *s. f.*, disrespect, disregard, slight.

DES.CON.SI.DE.RAR, *v.*, to disrespect, to disregard.

DES.CON.SO.LO, *s. m.*, desolation, distress, sorrow.

DES.CON.TAR, *v.*, to discount, diminish.

DES.CON.TEN.TA.MEN.TO, *s. m.*, discontentment, displeasure, disgust.

DES.CON.TEN.TAR, *v.*, to discontent, to displease, to dissatisfy, to disoblige.

DES.CON.TEN.TE, *adj.*, discontent, unsatisfied.

DES.CON.TO, *s. m.*, discount, abatement, deduction, reduction.

DES.COR.TÊS, *adj.*, unkind, impolite, discourteous, rude.

DES.COR.TE.SI.A, *s. f.*, discourteousness, impoliteness, unkindness.

DES.CREN.ÇA, *s. f.*, incredulity, disbelief, doubt.

DES.CREN.TE, *s. 2 gen.*, unbeliever, infidel; *adj.*, incredulous, unbelieving.

DES.CRE.VER, *v.*, to describe, to relate, to portray.

DES.CRI.ÇÃO, *s. f.*, description, report, picture.

DES.CUI.DAR, *v.*, to neglect, to disregard, to overlook, to slight.

DES.CUI.DO, *s. m.*, carelessness, lapse, disregard, incautiousness.

DES.CUL.PA, *s. f.*, excuse, pardon, apology, defence.

DES.CUL.PAR, *v.*, to excuse, to pardon, to apologize, to forgive, to exculpate.

DES.DE, *prep.*, since, from, after.

DES.DÉM, *s. m.*, disdain, disdainfulness, disregard, depreciation.

DES.DE.NHAR, *v.*, to disdain, to scorn, to despise, to condemn.

DES.DI.TA, *s. f.*, misfortune, unluckiness.

DES.DI.ZER, *v.*, to unsay, to deny, to contradict.

DE.SE.JAR, *v.*, to wish, to want, to will, to desire, to covet.

DE.SE.JO, *s. m.*, desire, wish, will, mind.

DE.SE.JO.SO, *adj.*, desirous, wishful, solicitous.

DE.SEM.BA.RA.ÇAR, *v.*, disembarrass, extricate, disentangle.

DE.SEM.BAR.CAR, *v.*, to disembark, to debark, to land.

DE.SEM.BOL.SAR, *v.*, to disburse, to spend, to lay out, to expend.

DE.SEM.BOL.SO, *s. m.*, disbursement.

DE.SEM.BRU.LHAR, *v.*, to unpack, to unroll, to unwrap.

DE.SEM.PA.TAR, *v.*, to decide, to resolve, to give the casting vote.

DE.SEM.PE.NHO, *s. m.*, performance, discharge, practice.

DE.SEM.PRE.GA.DO, *s. m.*, unemployed; *adj.*, unemployed, unengaged, unoccupied.

DE.SEM.PRE.GO, s. m., unemployment.
DE.SEN.CAI.XAR, v., to disjoint, to dislocate, to displace.
DE.SEN.CA.MI.NHAR, v., to misguide, mislead, misdirect.
DE.SEN.CON.TRAR, v., to fail to meet one another.
DE.SEN.CON.TRO, s. m., failure in meeting, disagreement.
DE.SEN.CO.RA.JAR, v., to discourage, to depress.
DE.SEN.FRE.A.DO, adj., unruled, ungoverned, uncontrolled.
DE.SEN.FRE.AR, v., to let loose, to set free, to unbridle.
DE.SEN.GA.NO, s. m., disillusion, disappointment, undeceiving.
DE.SE.NHAR, v., to design, to draw, to trace, to outline, to create.
DE.SE.NHIS.TA, s. 2 gen., sketcher, designer, tracer, drawer.
DE.SE.NHO, s. m., design, sketch, drawing, draft, outline, draught.
DE.SEN.RO.LAR, v., to unroll, to uncurl, to unwind.
DE.SEN.ROS.CAR, v., to untwine, to untwist, to unscrew.
DE.SEN.TEN.DI.MEN.TO, s. m., misunderstanding, disagreement, ignorance.
DE.SEN.TER.RAR, v., to unbury, to dig up, to unearth.
DE.SEN.VOL.TO, adj., agile, nimble, brisk, light, quick.
DE.SEN.VOL.TU.RA, s. f., agility, nimbleness.
DE.SEN.VOL.VER, v., to develop, to explain, to unwrap, to unrol, to unfold.
DE.SEN.VOL.VI.MEN.TO, s. m., development, growth, evolution, improvement.
DE.SE.QUI.LI.BRAR, v., to unbalance, to throw out of balance.
DE.SE.QUI.LÍ.BRIO, s. m., unbalance, instability, distemper.
DE.SER.DAR, v., to disinherit, to deprive of heritage.
DE.SER.TAR, v., to desert, to abandon; to unpeople.
DE.SER.TO, s. m., desert, wilderness; adj., desert, uninhabited, wild.
DE.SER.TOR, s. m., deserter, runaway, fugitive.
DES.FA.LE.CER, v., to faint, to swoon, to decay.
DES.SES.PE.RA.DO, adj., hopeless, desperate.
DES.SES.PE.RO, s. m., despair, hopelessness, desperation.
DES.FA.LE.CER, v., to faint, to swoon, to decay.
DES.FAL.QUE, s. m., defalcation, peculation, misappropriation.
DES.FA.VO.RÁ.VEL, adj., unfavourable, bad, unpropitious.
DES.FA.ZER, v., to undo, to unmake, to unpack, to demolish.
DES.FE.CHO, s. m., outcome, conclusion, solution, issue.
DES.FEI.TA, s. f., affront, insult, outrage.
DES.FEI.TO, adj., undone, dissolved, disfigured.
DES.FI.LA.DEI.RO, s. m., ravine, canyon, gorge, pass, defile, narrow.
DES.FI.LAR, v., to parade, to march, to file, to defile.
DES.FI.LE, s. m., parade, march, pageant, filling off, review.
DES.FO.LHAR, v., to defoliate, to exfoliate.
DES.FOR.RA, s. f., revenge, retaliation, retribution.
DES.FRU.TAR, v., to usufruct, to hold in usufruct.
DES.GAS.TE, s. m., wearing, consuming, wastage.
DES.GOS.TO, s. m., disgust, sorrow, displeasure.
DES.GOS.TO.SO, adj., displeased, dissatisfied.
DES.GRA.ÇA, s. f., misfortune, misadventure, disaster, catastrophe.
DES.GRU.DAR, v., to unglue, to unstick.
DE.SI.DRA.TAR, v., to anhydrate, to dehydrate.
DE.SIG.NA.ÇÃO, s. f., designation, indication, denomination, denotation.
DE.SIG.NAR, v., to designate, to appoint, to determinate, to mark.
DE.SI.GUAL, adj., unequal, unlike, different, irregular.
DE.SI.LU.DIR, v., to disillusion, to disenchant,

DESILUSÃO — **DESPACHAR**

to undeceive.
DE.SI.LU.SÃO, *s. f.*, disillusion.
DE.SIM.PE.DIR, *v.*, disencumber, disengage, disembarrass.
DE.SIN.DE.XAR, *v.*, to deindex.
DE.SIN.FE.TAR, *v.*, to disinfect, to purify, to antisepticize, to deodorize.
DE.SIN.TE.RES.SE, *s. m.*, indifference, disinterest, nonchalance.
DE.SIS.TÊN.CIA, *s. f.*, cessation, desistance, nonsuit.
DE.SIS.TIR, *v.*, to give up, to stop, to renounce, to quit.
DES.LE.AL, *adj.*, disloyal, false, dishonest, perfidious.
DES.LEI.XA.DO, *adj.*, careless, untidy, neglectful, negligent.
DES.LEI.XO, *s. m.*, negligence, carelessness, indifference, disregard.
DES.LI.GAR, *v.*, to untie, to unfasten, to undo, to unlink.
DES.LI.ZAR, *v.*, to slide, to glide, to skid, slip, to overlook.
DES.LI.ZE, *s. m.*, slip, sliding, gliding, skidding.
DES.LO.CAR, *v.*, to dislocate, to disjoint, to displace, to transfer; to luxate.
DES.LUM.BRAN.TE, *adj.*, dazzling, flaring, blinding, fulgent.
DES.LUM.BRAR, *v.*, to dazzle, to blind, to overpower with light, to fascinate.
DES.MAI.AR, *v.*, to faint, to swoon, to fainting.
DES.MAI.O, *s. m.*, swoon, faint, collapse.
DES.MAN.CHAR, *v.*, to undo, to unmake, to break up, to disarrange, to ruffle, to disorder.
DES.MAR.CAR, *v.*, to cancel.
DES.MA.TA.MEN.TO, *s. m.*, deforestation.
DES.MA.TAR, *v.*, to deforest, to clear.
DES.ME.DI.DO, *adj.*, excessive, immense, immoderate.
DES.MEM.BRAR, *v.*, to separate, to dismember, to dislimb.
DES.MEN.TIR, *v.*, to contradict, to belie, to deny.
DES.ME.RE.CER, *v.*, to demerit, not to deserve,
to undeserve.
DES.MON.TAR, *v.*, to disjoint, to disassemble, to pull down; to unhorse.
DES.MO.RA.LI.ZAR, *v.*, to pervert, to deprave, to demoralize, to corrupt, to undermine.
DES.MO.RO.NA.MEN.TO, *s. m.*, collapse, tumbling, falling in.
DES.MO.RO.NAR, *v.*, to demolish, to pull down, to ruin, to undermine.
DES.NA.CI.O.NA.LI.ZAR, *v.*, to denationalize.
DES.NE.CES.SÁ.RIO, *adj.*, unnecessary, needless.
DE.SO.BE.DE.CER, *v.*, to disobey, to transgress, to disregard.
DE.SO.BE.DI.ÊN.CIA, *s. f.*, disobedience, insubordination, rebellion, indiscipline.
DE.SO.BE.DI.EN.TE, *adj.*, disobedient, contumacious, insubordinate.
DE.SOBS.TRU.IR, *v.*, to remove obstructions, to free.
DE.SO.CU.PA.ÇÃO, *s. f.*, inoccupation, leisure, vacancy.
DE.SO.CU.PAR, *v.*, to vacate, to empty, to disoccupy.
DE.SO.DO.RAN.TE, *s. m.*, deodorant.
DE.SO.LA.ÇÃO, *s. f.*, desolation.
DE.SO.LAR, *v.*, to lay waste, to desolate, to depopulate.
DE.SO.NES.TI.DA.DE, *s. f.*, dishonesty, crookedness.
DE.SON.RA, *s. f.*, dishonour, disgrace, defame.
DE.SON.RAR, *v.*, to dishonour, to discredit.
DE.SOR.DEI.RO, *s. m.*, rowdy, ruffian, rioter, hooligan, *adj.*, turbulent, rowdy, rough.
DE.SOR.DEM, *s. f.*, disorder, confusion, disturbance, jumble, disarray.
DE.SOR.GA.NI.ZAR, *v.*, to disorganize, to disorder.
DE.SO.RI.EN.TAR, *v.*, to lead astray, to bewilder.
DE.SO.VA, *s. f.*, spawning.
DES.PA.CHA.NTE, *s. 2 gen.*, dispatcher, forwarder, forwarding agent; *adj.*, forwarding.
DES.PA.CHAR, *v.*, to forward, to dispatch, to send, to discharge, to clear.

DESPACHO
DESTRAVAR

DES.PA.CHO, *s. m.*, dispatch, forwarding, shipping, expedition.

DES.PE.DI.DA, *s. f.*, farewell, departure, adieu, valediction, dismissal.

DES.PE.DIR, *v.*, to discharge, to dismiss, to disband, to discard, to fire.

DES.PE.JAR, *v.*, to spill, to pour, to dump, to effuse.

DES.PE.JO, *s. m.*, pouring out, dump, spilling, eviction.

DES.PE.NHA.DEI.RO, *s. m.*, precipice, cliff, slop, crag.

DES.PER.DI.ÇAR, *v.*, to waste, to throw away, to squander, to scatter, to dissipate.

DES.PER.DÍ.CIO, *s. m.*, wastefulness, waste, wastage.

DES.PER.TA.DOR, *s. m.*, alarm clock; *adj.*, arousing.

DES.PER.TAR, *s. m.*, awakening; *v.*, to awake, to rouse from sleep, to excite.

DES.PE.SA, *s. f.*, disbursement, expense, outgo.

DES.PIR, *v.*, to undress, to strip, to bare, to unclothe, to divest.

DES.PIS.TAR, *v.*, to mislead, to misguide, to foil.

DES.PON.TAR, *v.*, to blunt, to break, to unfold, to rise.

DES.POR.TIS.TA, *s. 2 gen.*, athlete, sportsman.

DES.POR.TI.VO, *adj.*, athletic, sporting.

DES.POR.TO, *s. m.*, sport, play, game.

DES.PO.SAR, *v.*, to marry, to wed, to affiance, to betroth.

DÉS.PO.TA, *s. m.*, despot, tyrant, oppressor.

DES.PO.VO.A.DO, *s. m.*, desert place; *adj.*, unpeopled, desert, depopulated.

DES.PRA.ZER, *s. m.*, displeasure, disgust, dissatisfaction; *v.*, to displease, to disgust, to dissatisfy.

DES.PREN.DER, *v.*, to loosen, to unfasten, to unhood, to unfix.

DES.PREN.DI.DO, *adj.*, loose, unfastened, untied.

DES.PRE.O.CU.PA.DO, *adj.*, carefree.

DES.PRE.O.CU.PAR, *v.*, to ride, to ease, to free from care.

DES.PRES.TÍ.GIO, *s. m.*, discredit, disreputation.

DES.PRE.ZAR, *v.*, to despise, to scorn, to disdain, to contemn, to slight.

DES.PRE.ZÍ.VEL, *adj.*, despicable, pitiable, contemptible.

DES.PRE.ZO, *s. m.*, disdain, disdainfulness, disregard, contempt.

DES.PRO.POR.ÇÃO, *s. f.*, disproportion.

DES.QUA.LI.FI.CAR, *v.*, to disqualify, to unfit, to incapacitate.

DES.QUI.TE, *s. m.*, divorce, separation, disunion.

DES.RES.PEI.TAR, *v.*, to disrespect, to disregard, to affront.

DES.RES.PEI.TO, *s. m.*, disrespect, contempt, affront.

DES.SA, *contr.* of the *prep.* **DE** and the *pron.* **ESSA**, from that, of that.

DES.SE, *contr.* of the *prep.* **DE** and the *pron.* **ESSE**, from that, of that.

DES.SER.VI.ÇO, *s. m.*, desservice.

DES.TA, *contr.* of the *prep.* **DE** and the *pron.* **ESTA**, of this, from this.

DES.TA.CA.MEN.TO, *s. m.*, detachment.

DES.TA.CAR, *v.*, detach, emphatisize, to exceed, to overtop.

DES.TA.QUE, *s. m.*, prominence, eminence, distinction, notability.

DES.TE, *contr.* of the *prep.* **DE** and the *pron.* **ESTE**, of this, from this.

DES.TE.MI.DO, *adj.*, fearless, dreadless, daring, bold.

DES.TI.LA.RI.A, *s. f.*, distillery.

DES.TI.NAR, *v.*, to destine, to apply, to appropriate, to appoint, to doom, to consecrate.

DES.TI.NA.TÁ.RIO, *s. m.*, addressee, receiver, recipient, consignee.

DES.TI.NO, *s. m.*, destiny, fate, fortune, predestination, destination, purpose.

DES.TI.TU.I.ÇÃO, *s. f.*, dismissal, deposing, need, want.

DES.TI.TU.IR, *v.*, to depose, to dismiss, to displace, to fire, to demit.

DES.TO.AR, *v.*, to discord, to sound out of tune, to diverge, to jar.

DES.TRA.VAR, *v.*, to unlock, to unshackle, to

unfetter.

DES.TRE.ZA, *s. f.*, ability, skill, craft, dexterity, handiness, knack.

DES.TRO, *adj.*, desterous, right-handed, habile, skillful, deft.

DES.TRO.ÇO, *s. m.*, destruction, devastation, havock.

DES.TRU.I.ÇÃO, *s. f.*, destruction, devastation, demolition, ruination, ravage.

DES.TRU.IR, *v.*, to destroy, to demolish, to crush, to devastate, to subvert.

DE.SU.MA.NO, *adj.*, inhuman, brutal, cruel, barbarous, savage.

DE.SU.NIR, *v.*, to disunite, to disjoint, to separate, to divide, to disengage.

DES.VA.LO.RI.ZA.ÇÃO, *s. f.*, depreciation, devaluation, discredit.

DES.VA.LO.RI.ZAR, *v.*, to devaluate, to depreciate.

DES.VAN.TA.GEM, *s. f.*, disadvantage, prejudice, handicap, detriment.

DES.VAN.TA.JO.SO, *adj.*, disadvantageous, prejudicial.

DES.VA.RI.O, *s. m.*, derangement, loss of wits, delirium, absurdity.

DES.VEN.TU.RA, *s. f.*, misadventure, misfortune, unhappiness, unluckiness.

DES.VI.AR, *v.*, to turn aside, to deviate, to divert, to remove, to deflect.

DES.VI.O, *s. m.*, deviation, detour, deflection, bypass.

DE.TA.LHAR, *v.*, to detail, to specify.

DE.TA.LHE, *s. m.*, detail, circumstance.

DE.TEN.ÇÃO, *s. f.*, detention, arrest, imprisonment, confinement.

DE.TER, *v.*, to arrest, to hold, to retain, to keep, to stop, to retard.

DE.TER.GEN.TE, *s. m.*, detergent.

DE.TER.MI.NA.ÇÃO, *s. f.*, determination, resolution, decision, order.

DE.TER.MI.NAR, *v.*, to determine, to order, to command, to enjoin.

DE.TES.TAR, *v.*, to detest, to abhor, to abominate, to dislike, to loathe, to execrate.

DE.TE.TI.VE, *s. 2 gen.*, detective.

DE.TRÁS, *adv.*, after, behind, back.

DE.TRI.MEN.TO, *s. m.*, detriment, damage, loss, disadvantage.

DE.TRI.TO, *s. m.*, remains, detritus, debris.

DE.TUR.PAR, *v.*, to disfigure, to falsify, to deform.

DEUS, *s. m.*, God, Lord, divinity, Creator of the Universe, Spirit.

DEU.SA, *s. f.*, goddess.

DE.VA.GAR, *adv.*, slow, slowly, softly.

DE.VAS.SA, *s. f.*, inquiry, inquest.

DE.VAS.SAR, *v.*, to trespass, to invade, to divulgate, to penetrate.

DE.VAS.TAR, *v.*, to devastate, to lay waste, to destruct, to destroy.

DE.VE.DOR, *s. m.*, debtor; *adj.*, in debt, owing.

DE.VER, *s. m.*, obligation, duty, task, business, job; *v.*, to need, to owe, must, shall.

DE.VI.DO, *adj.*, due, just, owing.

DE.VO.ÇÃO, *s. f.*, devotion, adoration, cult, dedication, religion.

DE.VO.LU.ÇÃO, *s. f.*, devolution, restoration, return, restitution, reversion.

DE.VOL.VER, *v.*, to return, to devolve, to remise, to render.

DE.VO.RAR, *v.*, to devour, to ingurgitate, to wolf.

DE.VO.TA.MEN.TO, *s. m.*, devotement, dedication.

DE.VO.TAR, *v.*, to devote, to dedicate, to consecrate.

DE.VO.TO, *s. m.*, devotee, cultist; *adj.*, devoted, pious.

DEZ, *num.*, ten.

DE.ZEM.BRO, *s. m.*, December.

DE.ZE.NA, *s. f.*, ten, a set of ten.

DE.ZE.NO.VE, *num.*, nineteen.

DE.ZES.SEIS, *num.*, sixteen.

DE.ZES.SE.TE, *num.*, seventeen.

DE.ZOI.TO, *num.*, eighteen.

DI.A, *s. m.*, day, daylight, daytime; **DIA DO TRABALHO**, Labor Day; **DIA DE NATAL**, Christmas Day.

DI.A.BE.TE, *s. f., s. m.*, diabetes.
DI.A.BO, *s. m.*, demon, devil, evil spirit, Satan, Beelzebub.
DI.A.BÓ.LI.CO, *adj.*, devilish, hellish.
DI.Á.CO.NO, *s. m.*, deacon.
DI.A.FRAG.MA, *s. m.*, diaphragm.
DI.AG.NOS.TI.CAR, *v.*, to diagnose.
DI.AG.NÓS.TI.CO, *s. m.*, diagnosis; *adj.*, diagnostic.
DI.A.GO.NAL, *adj.*, diagonal, oblique.
DI.A.LE.TO, *s. m.*, dialect.
DI.A.LO.GAR, *v.*, to dialogue.
DI.Á.LO.GO, *s. m.*, dialogue, conversation, talk.
DI.A.MAN.TE, *s. m.*, diamond.
DI.Â.ME.TRO, *s. m.*, diameter.
DI.AN.TE, *adv.*, before, in front.
DI.AN.TEI.RA, *s. f.*, forepart, front, lead, foreside.
DI.Á.RIA, *s. f.*, daily wages.
DI.Á.RIO, *s. m.*, diary, daybook, journal, daily newspaper; *adj.*, diurnal, daily, quotidian.
DI.AR.REI.A, *s. f.*, diarrhea.
DIC.ÇÃO, *s. f.*, diction, expression.
DI.CI.O.NÁ.RIO, *s. m.*, dictionary, wordbook, lexicon.
DI.DÁ.TI.CO, *adj.*, didactic, instructive, pedagogical.
DI.E.TA, *s. f.*, diet, regimen.
DI.FA.MA.ÇÃO, *s. f.*, defamation, libel, calumny.
DI.FA.MAR, *v.*, to defame, to vilify, to blemish.
DI.FE.REN.ÇA, *s. f.*, difference, unlikeness, disparity, divergence, dissimilarity, deviation.
DI.FE.REN.CI.AR, *v.*, to differentiate, to difference, to distinguish.
DI.FE.REN.TE, *adj.*, different, unlike, unequal, dissimilar, distinct.
DI.FE.RIR, *v.*, to differ, to disagree, to postpone, to delay, to retard.
DI.FÍ.CIL, *adj.*, difficult, hard, uneasy, painful, intricate, arduous, laborious.
DI.FI.CUL.DA.DE, *s. f.*, difficulty, hardness, laboriousness, complication.
DI.FI.CUL.TAR, *v.*, to make difficult, to dificultate, to render difficult.
DI.FUN.DIR, *v.*, to diffuse, to spread, to disseminate, to pour out, to scatter.
DI.FU.SÃO, *s. f.*, diffusion, scattering, dissemination, infiltration.
DI.GE.RIR, *v.*, to digest, to assimilate, to tolerate.
DI.GES.TÃO, *s. f.*, digestion, concoction.
DI.GI.TA.DO, *adj.*, digitate, digitiform.
DI.GI.TAL, *adj.*, digital.
DIG.NI.DA.DE, *s. f.*, dignity, nobleness, honourableness.
DIG.NO, *adj.*, worthy, deserving, respectable.
DI.LA.CE.RAR, *v.*, to lacerate, to tear, to dilacerate.
DI.LA.PI.DAR, *v.*, to dilapidate.
DI.LA.TA.ÇÃO, *s. f.*, dilation, expansion.
DI.LA.TAR, *v.*, to dilate, to enlarge, to widen, to expand, to diffuse.
DI.LI.GEN.TE, *adj.*, diligent, assiduous, industrious, active.
DI.LÚ.VIO, *s. m.*, deluge, flood, inundation.
DI.MEN.SÃO, *s. f.*, measurement, dimension, size, extension.
DI.MI.NU.I.ÇÃO, *s. f.*, diminution, decrease, reduction, subtraction, abatement.
DI.MI.NU.IR, *v.*, to diminish, to reduce, to lessen, to abate.
DI.MI.NU.TI.VO, *adj., s. m.*, diminutive.
DI.NA.MAR.QUÊS, *adj., s. m.*, Dane, Danish.
DI.NÂ.MI.CA, *s. f.*, dynamics.
DI.NA.MI.TE, *s. f.*, dynamite, blasting powder.
DÍ.NA.MO, *s. m.*, dynamo, generator.
DI.NHEI.RO, *s. m.*, money, currency, cash, capital.
DI.NOS.SAU.RO, *s. m.*, dinosaur.
DI.PLO.MA, *s. m.*, diploma, certificate, document.
DI.PLO.MA.CI.A, *s. f.*, diplomacy, tact, skill.
DI.PLO.MA.TA, *s. f.*, diplomat, ambassador; tactful person.
DI.QUE, *s. m.*, dike, embankment, flood-gate; obstacle.
DI.RE.ÇÃO, *s. f.*, direction, course, route, run, administration, government.
DI.REI.TA, *s. f.*, right hand, right side; the conservative party.
DI.REI.TO, *s. m.*, right, law, jurisprudence,

DIRETO / **DISTINTO**

justice; *adj.*, right, straight, even, flat.

DI.RE.TO, *adj.*, direct, straight, nonstop, immediate.

DI.RE.TOR, *s. m.*, director, headmaster, manager.

DI.RE.TO.RI.A, *s. f.*, direction, administration, management, directorship.

DI.RI.GEN.TE, *s. 2 gen.*, director, leader, controller.

DI.RI.GIR, *v.*, to direct, to conduct, to govern, to rule, to command, to head.

DIS.CAR, *v.*, to dial.

DIS.CI.PLI.NA, *s. f.*, discipline, order, correction, education, instruction.

DIS.CI.PLI.NAR, *v.*, to discipline, to educate, to train, to instruct, to correct.

DIS.CÍ.PU.LO, *s. m.*, disciple, follower, pupil, scholar, student.

DIS.CO, *s. m.*, disk, disc, record, dial, discus.

DIS.COR.DÂN.CIA, *s. f.*, disagreement, divergence, discordancy.

DIS.CÓR.DIA, *s. f.*, disharmony, variance, discord, strife, dissension.

DIS.CO.TE.CA, *s. f.*, discotheque, record collection.

DIS.CRI.ÇÃO, *s. f.*, discretion, reserve.

DIS.CRI.MI.NAR, *v.*, to discriminate, to distinguish, to select.

DIS.CUR.SAR, *v.*, to discourse, to declaim, to speech.

DIS.CUR.SO, *s. m.*, discourse, speech.

DIS.CUS.SÃO, *s. f.*, discussion, debate, argument, disputation.

DIS.CU.TIR, *v.*, to discuss, to argue, to dispute, to agitate.

DI.SEN.TE.RI.A, *s. f.*, dysentery.

DIS.FAR.CE, *s. m.*, disguise, mask, veil.

DIS.FOR.ME, *adj.*, deformed, defaced.

DIS.PA.RAR, *v.*, to discharge, to shoot, to fire off, to let fly.

DIS.PA.RA.TE, *s. m.*, folly, nonsense, foolishness, absurdity.

DIS.PA.RO, *s. m.*, discharge, shot.

DIS.PÊN.DIO, *s. m.*, expense.

DIS.PEN.SA, *s. f.*, dispense, dispensation, leave.

DIS.PEN.SAR, *v.*, to dispense, to exempt, to excuse, to release.

DIS.PLI.CÊN.CIA, *s. f.*, negligence, carelessness, displeasure, annoyance.

DIS.PO.NI.BI.LI.DA.DE, *s. f.*, availability, disposability.

DIS.POR, *v.*, to dispose, to arrange, to regulate, to adjust, to fit, to place.

DIS.PO.SI.ÇÃO, *s. f.*, disposition, disposal, arrangement, classification, control.

DIS.PO.SI.TI.VO, *s. m.*, gadget, device, appliance.

DIS.PU.TA, *s. f.*, dispute, discussion, controversy, debate, altercation.

DIS.PU.TAR, *v.*, to dispute, to debate, to discuss, to argue.

DIS.QUE.TE, *s. m.*, diskette, floppy disk.

DIS.SA.BOR, *s. m.*, disgust, contrariety, annoyance, insipidity.

DIS.SER.TA.ÇÃO, *s. f.*, dissertation.

DIS.SER.TAR, *v.*, to dissert, to talk, to speech, to write dissertation.

DIS.SI.MU.LAR, *v.*, to dissimulate, to hide, to feign.

DIS.SI.PAR, *v.*, to dissipate, to scatter, to disperse, to waste, to consume.

DIS.SO, *contr.* of the *prep.* **DE** and the *pron.* **ISSO**, of that, thereof, about that, therefrom.

DIS.SO.LU.ÇÃO, *s. f.*, dissolution, breakup, separation.

DIS.SOL.VER, *v.*, to dissolve, to liquefy, to melt.

DIS.SU.A.DIR, *v.*, to dissuade, to bring off, to turn, to discourage.

DIS.TÂN.CIA, *s. f.*, distance, extension, farness, space.

DIS.TAN.CI.AR, *v.*, to distance, to separate, to situate.

DIS.TAN.TE, *adj.*, distant, far, remote, far-away, cool, reserved.

DIS.TIN.GUIR, *v.*, to distinguish, differentiate, to discriminate, to discern.

DIS.TIN.TI.VO, *s. m.*, badge, emblem, symbol; *adj.*, distinctive, characteristic.

DIS.TIN.TO, *adj.*, distinct, different, distinguished, diverse, individual, special.

DIS.TO, *contr.* of the *prep.* **DE** and the *pron.* **ISTO**, of this, of it, at it, hereof, herefrom.

DIS.TRA.ÇÃO, *s. f.*, distraction, pastime, diversion.

DIS.TRA.IR, *v.*, to distract, to draw away.

DIS.TRI.BU.I.ÇÃO, *s. f.*, distribution, delivery, division, parcelling.

DIS.TRI.BU.I.DOR, *s. m.*, distributor; *adj.*, distributing.

DIS.TRI.BU.IR, *v.*, to distribute, to divide, to deliver, to allocate.

DIS.TRI.TO, *s. m.*, district, quarter, county, zone, circuit, territory.

DIS.TÚR.BIO, *s. m.*, disturb, disturbance, riot, trouble, noise.

DI.TA.DO, *s. m.*, dictation, proverb, sentence.

DI.TA.DOR, *s. m.*, dictator, despot, tyrant.

DI.TA.DU.RA, *s. f.*, dictatorship, despotism.

DI.TAR, *v.*, to dictate, to impose, to command.

DI.TO, *s. m.*, ditto, the same, axiom, sentence; *adj.*, said, stated.

DI.TON.GO, *s. m.*, diphthong.

DI.VÃ, *s. m.*, couch, divan.

DI.VA.GAR, *v.*, to divagate, to wander, to deviate.

DI.VER.GÊN.CIA, *s. f.*, divergence, disagreement, divergency.

DI.VER.SÃO, *s. f.*, diversion, entertainment, amusement.

DI.VER.SI.DA.DE, *s. f.*, diversity, variety, dissimilarity, unlikeness.

DI.VER.SO, *adj.*, different, various, unlike, divers, manifold.

DI.VER.TI.DO, *adj.*, deviated, funny, amusing, diverting.

DI.VER.TI.MEN.TO, *s. m.*, diversion, amusement, pastime, entertainment, play.

DI.VER.TIR, *v.*, to divert, to draw away, to turn aside, to distract, to amuse.

DÍ.VI.DA, *s. f.*, debt, duty, due, liability, obligation, arrears, debit.

DI.VI.DIR, *v.*, to divide, to share, to separate, to disjoin, to break, to split, to parcel out.

DI.VIN.DA.DE, *s. f.*, divinity, sanctity.

DI.VI.NI.ZAR, *v.*, to divinize.

DI.VI.NO, *adj.*, divine, holy, deific, excellent.

DI.VI.SA, *s. f.*, symbol, emblem; device, motto, slogan; frontier, boundary.

DI.VI.SÃO, *s. f.*, division, section, segment, category, partition, split.

DI.VI.SI.BI.LI.DA.DE, *s. f.*, divisibility, partibility.

DI.VI.SOR, *s. m.*, divisor, divider.

DI.VOR.CI.AR, *v.*, to divorce, to disunite, to separate.

DI.VÓR.CIO, *s. m.*, divorce.

DI.VUL.GA.ÇÃO, *s. f.*, divulgation, conveyance.

DI.VUL.GAR, *v.*, to divulge, to publish, to make public, to disclose, to betray.

DI.ZER, *v.*, to say, to speak, to tell, to talk, to declare.

DIZ QUE DIZ, *s. m.*, rumour, gossip, report.

DO, *contr.* of the *prep.* **DE** and the *art.* **O**, of the, from the.

DÓ, *s. m.*, do, C (mus.); pity, compassion, empathy.

DO.A.ÇÃO, *s. f.*, donation, bounty, gift, present.

DO.A.DOR, *s. m.*, donor, giver, donator.

DO.AR, *v.*, to donate, to give.

DO.BRA.DI.ÇA, *s. f.*, hinge, joint.

DO.BRAR, *v.*, to double, to bend, to fold, to bow, to ply.

DO.BRO, *s. m.*, double, duplication.

DO.CA, *s. f.*, dock, quay.

DO.CE, *s. m.*, sweets, sweetmeat, comfit, bonbon, candy, cooky.

DO.CEN.TE, *s. 2 gen.*, teacher, professor, instructor, lecturer, prelector.

DÓ.CIL, *adj.*, docile, amenable, teachable, sweet tempered, ductile.

DO.CI.LI.DA.DE, *s. f.*, docility, teachableness.

DO.CU.MEN.TAR, *v.*, to document, to prove, to bring evidence.

DO.CU.MEN.TO, *s. m.*, document, paper, record, writ, act, voucher, bill.

DO.ÇU.RA, *s. f.*, sweetness, honey.

DO.EN.ÇA, *s. f.*, disease, illness, sickness, affection, ailment.

DO.EN.TE, *s. m.*, patient; *adj.*, sick, ill, diseased.

DO.ER, *v.*, to ache, to hurt.

DOG.MA, *s. m.*, dogma, principle, maxim,

doctrine.
DOI.DO, *s. m.*, madman, foolish; *adj.*, mad, crazy, insane.
DO.Í.DO, *adj.*, aching, painful, hurt, troubled.
DOIS, *num.*, two; deuce.
DÓ.LAR, *s. m.*, dollar; buck.
DO.LO, *s. f.*, fraud, deceit, duplicity.
DO.LO.RI.DO, *adj.*, dolorific, dolorous, painful.
DO.LO.RO.SO, *adj.*, dolorous, aching, sore, cruel.
DOM, *s. m.*, gift, talent, ability, present, donation.
DO.MA.DOR, *s. m.*, tamer, horse-breaker; *adj.*, taming.
DO.MAR, *v.*, to tame, to domesticate, to vanquish, to overcome, to subdue.
DO.MES.TI.CAR, *v.*, to domesticate, to tame, to civilize, to break in.
DO.MÉS.TI.CO, *adj.*, domestic, internal, familiar, private, tame.
DO.MI.CÍ.LIO, *s. m.*, domicile, dwelling, residence, home.
DO.MI.NA.ÇÃO, *s. f.*, domination, dominance, command, rule, control.
DO.MI.NAR, *v.*, to dominate, to rule, to command, to control, to govern.
DO.MIN.GO, *s. m.*, Sunday.
DO.MÍ.NIO, *s. m.*, power, control, domain, command, domination.
DO.MI.NÓ, *s. m.*, domino, *pl.* dominos(oes).
DO.NA, *s. f.*, lady, donna, proprietress; woman, wife.
DON.DE, *adv.*, where, from where, wherefrom.
DO.NO, *s. m.*, master, keeper, owner, proprietor, lord, landlord, holder.
DO.PAR, *v.*, to dope, to drug.
DOR, *s. m.*, ache, pain, ail, grief, sorrow, dolour;
DOR DE BARRIGA, bellyache; **DOR DE CABEÇA**, headache.
DO.RA.VAN.TE, *adv.*, from now on, hereafter, henceforth.
DOR.MI.NHO.CO, *s. m.*, sleepyhead; *adj.*, sleepy, drowsy, dozy.
DOR.MIR, *v.*, to sleep, to slumber, to fall asleep, to repose, to lie, to rest.
DOR.MI.TÓ.RIO, *s. m.*, bedroom.
DOR.SO, *s. m.*, back, reverse, dorsum.
DO.SAR, *v.*, to dose, to portion.
DO.SE, *s. f.*, dose, quantity, proportion, measure.
DOS.SI.Ê, *s. m.*, dossier.
DO.TE, *s. m.*, dot, dotal gift, fortune.
DOU.RA.DO, *adj.*, golden, gilt, gilded.
DOU.RAR, *v.*, to gild, to gild over, to embellish.
DOU.TOR, *s. m.*, doctor, lawyer.
DOU.TO.RA, *s. f.*, doctoress, lady doctor.
DOU.TRI.NA, *s. f.*, doctrine, precept, instruction, teaching.
DOU.TRI.NAR, *v.*, to doctrinize, to teach.
DO.ZE, *num.*, twelve.
DRA.GA, *s. f.*, drag, dredger.
DRA.GÃO, *s. m.*, dragon.
DRA.GAR, *v.*, to drag.
DRA.MA, *s. m.*, drama, play, tragedy.
DRA.MA.TI.ZAR, *v.*, to dramatize.
DRE.NAR, *v.*, to drain, to draw off.
DRO.GA, *s. f.*, drug, rubbish.
DRO.GAR, *v.*, to drug, to dope, to store.
DRO.GA.RI.A, *s. f.*, drugstore, pharmacy.
DRO.ME.DÁ.RIO, *s. m.*, dromedary.
DU.A.LI.DA.DE, *s. f.*, duality.
DU.AS, *num.*, two; *adj.*, twain, two.
DU.BI.E.DA.DE, *s. f.*, dubiety.
DU.BLAR, *v.*, to dub.
DU.BLA.GEM, *s. f.*, dubbing.
DU.E.LO, *s. m.*, duel, duetto, single combat.
DU.EN.DE, *s. m.*, dwarf, elf, boglin.
DU.NA, *s. f.*, dune, sand dune, sand hill.
DU.PLA, *adj., s. f.*, couple, pair, two-some.
DU.PLI.CAR, *v.*, to double, to duplicate, to copy, to repeat.
DU.PLI.CA.TA, *s. f.*, duplicate, copy, bill.
DU.PLI.CI.DA.DE, *s. f.*, duplicity, doubleness.
DU.PLO, *s. m.*, the double; *adj.*, double, duplex, twofold, dual, duplicate.
DU.QUE, *s. m.*, duke.
DU.QUE.SA, *s. f.*, duchess.
DU.RA.BI.LI.DA.DE, *s. f.*, durability.
DU.RA.ÇÃO, *s. f.*, duration, lasting, run, continuance, endurance.

DU.RAN.TE, *prep.*, during, while, in the time of, in the course of, for, by.
DU.RAR, *v.*, to last, to continue, to remain, to abide, to be resistent.
DU.RÁ.VEL, *adj.*, durable, lasting.
DU.RE.ZA, *s. f.*, hardness, consistency, solidity, stiffness, severity.
DU.RO, *adj.*, hard, firm, solid, consistent, compact, dense, strong, vigorous, difficult.

DÚ.VI.DA, *s. f.*, doubt, dubiety, incertainty, incertitude, discredit.
DU.VI.DAR, *v.*, to doubt, to be uncertain, to descredit, suspect.
DU.VI.DO.SO, *adj.*, dubious, doubtful, uncertain, questionable, problematic.
DU.ZEN.TOS, *num.*, two hundred.
DÚ.ZIA, *s. f.*, dozen; **ÀS DÚZIAS**, by the dozen; **MEIA DÚZIA**, half a dozen.

E

E, *s. m.*, the fifth letter of the Portuguese alphabet; *conj.*, and.
É.BRIO, *s. m.*, drunkard; bum; *adj.*, drunk.
E.BU.LI.ÇÃO, *s. f.*, ebullition, boiling, ebullience.
E.CLE.SI.ÁS.TI.CO, *adj.*, ecclesiastic, clerical, canonical.
E.CLÉ.TI.CO, *adj.*, eclectic.
E.CLE.TIS.MO, *s. m.*, eclecticism.
E.CLIP.SE, *s. m.*, eclipse.
E.CLU.SA, *s. f.*, floodgate, dam, canal lock, sluicegate.
E.CO, *s. m.*, echo, repetition, ressonance, resound.
E.CO.AR, *v.*, to echo, to reflect the sound, to repeat.
E.CO.LO.GI.A, *s. f.*, ecology.
E.CO.NO.MI.A, *s. f.*, economy, regulation, method, economics.
E.CO.NÔ.MI.CO, *adj.*, economic, cheap, thrifty, frugal.
E.CO.NO.MIS.TA, *s. 2 gen.*, economist.
E.CO.NO.MI.ZAR, *v.*, to save, to spare, to cut corners, to economize, to husband, to be frugal.
E.COS.SIS.TE.MA, *s. m.*, ecosystem.
E.DE.MA, *s. f.*, oedema, edema.
E.DI.ÇÃO, *s. f.*, edition, issue, publication, impression.
E.DI.FI.CA.ÇÃO, *s. f.*, edification, erection, construction, edifying, building.
E.DI.FI.CAR, *v.*, to construct, to build, to elevate, to erect, to found.
E.DI.FÍ.CIO, *s. m.*, building.
E.DI.TAR, *v.*, to edit, to publish.
E.DI.TOR, *s. m.*, publisher, editor.
E.DI.TO.RA, *s. f.*, publishing house, company.
E.DI.TO.RA.ÇÃO, *s. f.*, editorial business, publishing, publication.
E.DU.CA.ÇÃO, *s. f.*, education, instruction, knowledge, teaching, breeding, development.
E.DU.CA.DOR, *s. m.*, educator.
E.DU.CAR, *v.*, to educate, to bring up, to teach, to instruct.
E.FEI.TO, *s. m.*, effect, result, consequence, realization, efficacy, intention.
E.FÊ.ME.RO, *adj.*, ephemeral, short-lived.
E.FE.MI.NA.DO, *adj*, effeminate, fag, queer, fagot, womanlike.
E.FE.TI.VAR, *v.*, to execute, to effect, to accomplish, to realize.
E.FI.CÁ.CIA, *s. f.*, efficacy, efficiency.
E.FI.CAZ, *adj.*, efficacious.
E.FI.CI.ÊN.CIA, *s. f.*, efficiency.
E.FU.SÃO, *s. f.*, effusion.
E.FU.SI.VO, *adj.*, effusive, expressive, gushing, effluent.
E.GÍP.CIO, *adj., s. m.*, Egyptian.
E.GO.ÍS.MO, *s. m.*, egoism, selfishness.
E.GO.ÍS.TA, *adj.*, egoistic, selfish.
É.GUA, *s. f.*, mare.
EIS, *adv.*, here is, this is, here are, these are.
EI.XO, *s. m.*, axis, axle, axle-tree.
E.JA.CU.LA.ÇÃO, *s. f.*, ejaculation.
E.JA.CU.LAR, *v.*, to ejaculate.
E.JE.TAR, *v.*, to eject.
E.LA, *pron.*, she, it, her; **elas**, they, them.
E.LA.BO.RA.ÇÃO, *s. f.*, elaboration, preparation, working up.
E.LA.BO.RAR, *v.*, to elaborate, to organize, to prepare.
E.LÁS.TI.CO, *s. m.*, elastic cord, elastic band, rubber band; *adj.*, elastic, flexible, stringy.
E.LE, *pron.*, he, it, him; **ELES**, they, them.
E.LE.FAN.TE, *s. m.*, elephant.
E.LE.GÂN.CIA, *s. f.*, elegance, grace, smartness.
E.LE.GER, *v.*, to elect, to choose by vote, to select.
E.LEI.ÇÃO, *s. f.*, election, poll, choice, selection.

E.LEI.TO, *s. m.*, elect; *adj.*, elect, elected, selected.
E.LEI.TOR, *s. m.*, elector, voter, constituent.
E.LE.MEN.TAR, *adj.*, *s. m.*, elementary, elemental.
E.LE.MEN.TO, *s. m.*, element, component, ingredient.
E.LEN.CO, *s. m.*, cast, list, catalogue.
E.LE.TRI.CI.DA.DE, *s. f.*, electricity.
E.LE.TRI.CIS.TA, *s. 2 gen.*, electrician.
E.LÉ.TRI.CO, *adj.*, electric.
E.LE.TRI.ZAR, *v.*, to electrize.
E.LE.TRO.CAR.DI.O.GRA.MA, *s. m.*, electrocardiogram.
E.LE.TRO.CU.TAR, *v.*, to electrocute.
E.LE.TRÔ.NI.CA, *s. f.*, electronics.
E.LE.TRÔ.NI.CO, *adj.*, electronic.
E.LE.VA.ÇÃO, *s. f.*, elevation, rise, increase.
E.LE.VA.DO, *adj.*, elevated, high, lifted up, raised.
E.LE.VA.DOR, *s. m.*, elevator, lift.
E.LE.VAR, *v.*, to elevate, to raise, to lift, to exalt, to ennoble.
E.LI.MI.NAR, *v.*, to eliminate, to remove, to expel, to delete.
E.LIP.SE, *s. f.*, ellipsis, ellipse.
E.LI.TE, *s. f.*, elite.
E.LI.XIR, *s. m.*, elixir, panacea.
E.LO, *s. m.*, link, chain, connexion.
E.LO.GI.AR, *v.*, to praise, to compliment, to extol, to commend.
E.LO.GI.O, *s. m.*, praise, compliment, eulogy.
E.LU.CI.DA.ÇÃO, *s. f.*, elucidation, explanation, clearing up, exposition.
E.LU.CI.DAR, *v.*, to elucidate, to explain, to make clear, to illuminate.
EM, *prep.*, in, into, up, at, on, upon, during, within, by, to.
E.MA, *s. f.*, rhea, Brazilian ostrich.
E.MA.GRE.CER, *v.*, to emaciate, to lose weight, to grow thin, to reduce.
E.MA.GRE.CI.MEN.TO, *s. m.*, thinning, slimming.
E.MAN.CI.PAR, *v.*, to emancipate, to liberate.
EM.BAI.XA.DA, *s. f.*, embassy.

EM.BAI.XA.DOR, *s. m.*, ambassador.
EM.BAI.XA.TRIZ, *s. f.*, ambassadress.
EM.BAI.XO, *adv.*, below, beneath, downstairs.
EM.BA.LA.GEM, *s. f.*, package, packaging.
EM.BAL.SA.MAR, *v.*, to embalm.
EM.BA.RA.ÇAR, *v.*, to embarrass, to distress.
EM.BA.RA.ÇO, *s. m.*, embarrassment.
EM.BAR.CA.ÇÃO, *s. f.*, vessel, ship, craft.
EM.BAR.CAR, *v.*, to embark.
EM.BAR.QUE, *s. m.*, embarkment, shipping.
EM.BE.BER, *v.*, to soak up, to steep.
EM.BE.LE.ZA.MEN.TO, *s. m.*, embellishment.
EM.BE.LE.ZAR, *v.*, to embellish, to beautify.
EM.BLE.MA, *s. m.*, emblem, badge, ensign, allegory.
EM.BOL.SAR, *v.*, to pocket, to pouch, to purse.
EM.BO.RA, *adv.*, though, although, even though, albeit, however, in despite of.
EM.BOS.CA.DA, *s. f.*, ambush, ambuscade.
EM.BRE.A.GEM, *s. f.*, clutch.
EM.BRI.A.GA.DO, *adj.*, drunk, drunken, tipsy, intoxicated.
EM.BRI.A.GAR, *v.*, to make drunk, to intoxicate, to alcoholize.
EM.BRI.ÃO, *s. f.*, embryo, germ.
EM.BRU.LHAR, *v.*, to wrap up, to pack up.
EM.BU.TIR, *v.*, to inlay, to incrust.
E.MEN.DAR, *v.*, to correct, to amend, to emend, to ameliorate.
E.MER.GÊN.CIA, *s. f.*, emergency, incident, crisis.
E.MER.GIR, *v.*, to emerge, to appear.
E.MI.GRAR, *v.*, to emigrate, to migrate.
E.MI.NÊN.CIA, *s. f.*, eminence.
E.MI.NEN.TE, *adj.*, eminent, high, prominent, elevated.
E.MIS.SÃO, *s. f.*, emission, issuing.
E.MIS.SO.RA, *s. f.*, broadcasting station.
E.MI.TIR, *v.*, to emit, to issue, to discharge, to send out.
E.MO.ÇÃO, *s. f.*, emotion, thrill, excitement.
E.MO.CI.O.NAL, *adj.*, emotional.
E.MO.CI.O.NAN.TE, *adj.*, exciting, thrilling.
E.MO.CI.O.NAR, *v.*, to thrill, to touch.

EMPACOTAMENTO — **ENCARAR**

EM.PA.CO.TA.MEN.TO, *s. m.*, wrappage.
EM.PA.CO.TAR, *v.*, to pack, to wrap up, to package.
EM.PA.DA, *s. f.*, patty.
EM.PA.LI.DE.CER, *v.*, to pale.
EM.PAN.TUR.RAR, *v.*, to stuff, to glut, to cram, to gorge.
EM.PA.RE.DAR, *v.*, to wall in, to cloister, to shut up between walls.
EM.PA.RE.LHAR, *v.*, to pair, to couple, to match, to unite, to join, to link.
EM.PA.TAR, *v.*, to make equal, to equalize, to tie up.
EM.PA.TE, *s. m.*, equality, draw, tie.
EM.PE.CI.LHO, *s. m.*, impediment, difficulty, obstruction, snag, hitch.
EM.PE.NHA.DO, *adj.*, iredebt, pledged, engaged.
EM.PE.NHAR, *v.*, to pawn, to mortgage, hypothecate, to induce.
EM.PE.NHO, *s. m.*, pledge, pawn, promise.
EM.PI.LHAR, *v.*, to heap up, to pille, to stack, to accumulate.
EM.PI.NAR, *v.*, to raise up, to lift up, to put straight, to tope.
EM.PLA.CAR, *v.*, to supply with a plate.
EM.PLAS.TRO, *s. m.*, plaster.
EM.PO.BRE.CER, *v.*, to make poor, to impoverish, to pauperize.
EM.PO.BRE.CI.MEN.TO, *s. m.*, impoverishment.
EM.PO.EI.RAR, *v.*, to dust.
EM.POS.SAR, *v.*, to give possession to, to put in possession of.
EM.PRE.EN.DER, *v.*, to undertake, to attempt, to enterprise.
EM.PRE.EN.DI.MEN.TO, *s. m.*, undertaking, enterprise.
EM.PRE.GA.DA, *s. f.*, maid, servant-girl, domestic servant.
EM.PRE.GA.DO, *s. m.*, servant, employee; *adj.*, employed.
EM.PRE.GA.DOR, *s. m.*, employer.
EM.PRE.GAR, *v.*, to employ.
EM.PRE.GO, *s. m.*, employment, job, work, occupation.
EM.PREI.TAR, *v.*, to job, to take over on a contract basis.
EM.PRE.SA, *s. f.*, enterprise, firm, business, company.
EM.PRE.SÁ.RIO, *s. m.*, entrepreneur, contractor, manager, undertaker, impresario.
EM.PRES.TA.DO, *adj.*, lent, loaned, borrowed.
EM.PRES.TAR, *v.*, to lend to, to loan to.
EM.PRÉS.TI.MO, *s. m.*, loan, lending, borrowing.
EM.PUR.RÃO, *s. m.*, push, shove, thrust, jostle, poke.
EM.PUR.RAR, *v.*, to push, to thrust, to shove, to hustle.
E.MU.DE.CER, *v.*, to silence, to still.
E.NA.MO.RA.DO, *adj.*, enamo(u)red, in love.
E.NA.MO.RAR, *v.*, to enchant, to enamo(u)r, to fascinate, to charm.
EN.CA.BU.LAR, *v.*, to abash, to constrain, to ashame.
EN.CA.DE.A.MEN.TO, *s. m.*, chaining, linkage, series; enchainment, concatenation.
EN.CA.DE.AR, *v.*, to enchain, to fetter, to link, to connect, to joint.
EN.CA.DER.NAR, *v.*, to bind books.
EN.CAI.XAR, *v.*, to box, to case, to incase, to mortise.
EN.CAI.XO.TAR, *v.*, to box, to incase, to pack (goods) in boxes.
EN.CAL.ÇO, *s. m.*, pursuit, chase, footprint, trail, track.
EN.CA.MI.NHA.MEN.TO, *s. m.*, direction, guiding, leading.
EN.CA.MI.NHAR, *v.*, to conduct, to lead, to guide, to direct, to orient.
EN.CA.NA.DOR, *s. m.*, plumber, drainer.
EN.CA.NA.MEN.TO, *s. m.*, plumbing, piping, canalization.
EN.CA.NAR, *v.*, to channel, to lay pipes, to convey in pipes.
EN.CAN.TAR, *v.*, to enchant, to charm, to delight.
EN.CAN.TO, *s. m.*, enchantment, delight, wonder, marvel.
EN.CA.RAR, *v.*, to look at, to stare at, to face.

ENCARCERAMENTO ENFADO

EN.CAR.CE.RA.MEN.TO, *s. m.*, imprisonment.
EN.CAR.CE.RAR, *v.*, to imprison, to shut up, to confine, to encarcerate.
EN.CAR.DI.DO, *adj.*, dirty, filthy, grimy.
EN.CA.RE.CER, *v.*, to raise the prices, to endear, to grow dear, to exaggerate.
EN.CAR.GO, *s. m.*, responsibility, duty, mission, charge, incumbency.
EN.CAR.NAR, *v.*, to incarnate, to embody, to personify.
EN.CAR.RE.GAR, *v.*, to charge, to intrust, to put in charge in, to take charge of.
EN.CÉ.FA.LO, *s. m.*, brain, encephalon.
EN.CE.NA.ÇÃO, *s. f.*, staging; simulation.
EN.CE.NAR, *v.*, to stage, to show, to exhibit, to display.
EN.CE.RAR, *v.*, to wax, to polish.
EN.CER.RAR, *v.*, to enclose, to bring to an end, to contain, to hold, to include, to conclude, to keep.
EN.CHAR.CAR, *v.*, to flood, to soak, to drench, to form into a puddle, to inundate.
EN.CHEN.TE, *s. f.*, inundation, flood.
EN.CHER, *v.*, to fill, to make full, to satisfy, to saturate, to satiate, to glut, to abound, to stuff.
EN.CÍ.CLI.CA, *s. f.*, encyclic.
EN.CI.CLO.PÉ.DIA, *s. f.*, encyclop(a)edia.
ÊN.CLI.SE, *s. f.*, enclisis.
EN.CO.BER.TO, *adj.*, covered, hidden.
EN.CO.BRIR, *v.*, to cover, to hide.
EN.CO.LE.RI.ZAR, *v.*, to make angry, to enrage, to infuriate, to irritate.
EN.CO.LHER, *v.*, to shrink, to contract, to draw up, to cramp.
EN.CO.MEN.DA, *s. f.*, order, thing ordered, indent, task.
EN.CO.MEN.DAR, *v.*, to order, to ask for, to charge, to command.
EN.CON.TRAR, *v.*, to meet, to encounter, to find, to find out, to discover.
EN.CON.TRO, *s. m.*, meeting, appointment, date, impact, shock, collision.
EN.CO.RA.JAR, *v.*, to encourage, to foster, to hearten, to give courage to, to stimulate.
EN.COR.PAR, *v.*, to thicken, to grow fat, to make thicker, to increase the body.
EN.COS.TA, *s. f.*, hillside, slope, ascent, declivity, acclivity.
EN.COS.TAR, *v.*, to lean, to prop, to place against, to ask for money.
EN.CREN.CA, *s. f.*, obstacle, difficulty, trouble, complication.
EN.CREN.CAR, *v.*, to break down, seize up, to embarrass, to embroil.
EN.CREN.QUEI.RO, *s. m.*, troublemaker.
EN.CRU.ZI.LHA.DA, *s. f.*, cross, crossroad, crossway.
EN.CUR.TAR, *v.*, to shorten, to diminish, to abbreviate, to curtail, to cut short.
EN.DE.MI.A, *s. f.*, endemic disease.
EN.DE.RE.ÇAR, *v.*, to address.
EN.DE.RE.ÇO, *s. m.*, address.
EN.DEU.SA.MEN.TO, *s. m.*, divinization.
EN.DI.A.BRA.DO, *adj.*, devilish, mad, demoniac, impish.
EN.DI.NHEI.RA.DO, *adj.*, moneyed, rich, opulent.
EN.DI.REI.TAR, *v.*, to straighten, to set to right, to rectify, to make straight, to reform.
EN.DI.VI.DAR, *v.*, to indebt, to lay under obligation.
EN.DOI.DE.CER, *v.*, to become insane, to go crazy, to get mad, to madden.
EN.DOS.CÓ.PIO, *s. m.*, endoscope.
EN.DOS.SAR, *v.*, to endorse, to give sanction to, to defend, to protect.
EN.DOS.SO, *s. m.*, endorsement.
EN.DU.RE.CER, *v.*, to harden, to toughen, to stiffen, to become hard.
EN.DU.RE.CI.MEN.TO, *s. m.*, hardening, callosity.
E.NER.GI.A, *s. f.*, energy, power, strenght, force, vigour, soul, zip.
E.NÉR.GI.CO, *adj.*, energetic, powerful, strenuous, vigorous.
E.NER.VAR, *v.*, to enervate, unnerve.
EN.FA.DO, *s. m.*, unpleasantness, annoyance, boredom, displeasure.

EN.FA.DO.NHO, *adj.*, tiresome, irksome, boring, tedious.

EN.FAR.TE, *s. m.*, heart attack, infarct.

ÊN.FA.SE, *s. f.*, emphasis, stress, accent, ostentation.

EN.FÁ.TI.CO, *adj.*, emphatic.

EN.FA.TI.ZAR, *v.*, to emphasize, to stress.

EN.FEI.TAR, *v.*, to adorn, to decorate, to ornament, to trim, to embellish.

EN.FEI.TE, *s. m.*, ornament, decoration, trimming, embellishment.

EN.FEI.TI.ÇAR, *v.*, to bewitch, to charm, to fascinate.

EN.FER.MA.RI.A, *s. f.*, infirmary, ward, sickroom.

EN.FER.MEI.RA, *s. f.*, nurse.

EN.FER.MEI.RO, *s. m.*, male nurse.

EN.FER.MI.DA.DE, *s. f.*, disease, sickness, infirmity, ailment.

EN.FER.MO, *s. m.*, patient, sick person, sufferer; *adj.*, sick, diseased, infirm.

EN.FER.RU.JAR, *v.*, to rust, to become affected with rust.

EN.FI.LEI.RAR, *v.*, to range in a file, to align, to set in a row, to form a line.

EN.FIM, *adv.*, at last, finally, after all.

EN.FOR.CAR, *v.*, to hang, to squander.

EN.FRA.QUE.CER, *v.*, to weaken, to debilitate, to lose courage.

EN.FRA.QUE.CI.MEN.TO, *s. m.*, weakness, feebleness, debility.

EN.FREN.TAR, *v.*, to face, to meet, to brave, to defy, to confront.

EN.FU.RE.CER, *v.*, to infuriate, to enrage, to make furious, to be furious.

EN.GA.JA.MEN.TO, *s. m.*, engagement, involvement, employment.

EN.GA.JAR, *v.*, to engage, to employ, to take an employment.

EN.GA.NAR, *v.*, to deceive, to mislead, to cheat, to trick.

EN.GA.NO, *s. m.*, mistake, error, fault, swindle, fraud, delusion, deception.

EN.GAR.RA.FA.MEN.TO, *s. m.*, bottling, traffic jam.

EN.GAR.RA.FAR, *v.*, to bottle.

EN.GA.TAR, *v.*, to clamp, to leash.

EN.GA.TE, *s. m.*, clamp, leash, hook, coupling gear.

EN.GA.TI.LHAR, *v.*, to cock, to prepare.

EN.GA.TI.NHAR, *v.*, to creep, to crawl.

EN.GA.VE.TAR, *v.*, to put into a drawer, to postpone.

EN.GE.NHA.RI.A, *s. f.*, engineering.

EN.GE.NHEI.RO, *s. m.*, engineer.

EN.GE.NHO, *s. m.*, inventive power, ingeniousness, wit, ability.

EN.GES.SAR, *v.*, to plaster.

EN.GLO.BAR, *v.*, to embody, encompass, to conglobate, to unite.

EN.GO.DO, *s. m.*, allure, decoy.

EN.GO.LIR, *v.*, swallow, ingest, devour, to gulp down, to englut, to absorb.

EN.GOR.DAR, *v.*, to fatten, to grow fat.

EN.GRA.ÇA.DO, *adj.*, funny, amusing, comic, merry, jocose, jolly.

EN.GRA.DA.DO, *s. m.*, crate, packing box.

EN.GRAN.DE.CER, *v.*, to increase, to raise, to enlarge, to augment.

EN.GRA.VI.DAR, *v.*, to make pregnant, to become pregnant, to render pregnant.

EN.GRA.XAR, *v.*, to shine, to polish, to smear.

EN.GRA.XA.TE, *s. m.*, shoeshiner.

EN.GROS.SAR, *v.*, to enlarge, to thicken, to swell, to augment, to increase.

EN.GUI.A, *s. f.*, eel.

E.NIG.MA, *s. m.*, enigma, ridlle, puzzle.

EN.JAU.LAR, *v.*, to jail, to cage, to imprison, to confine.

EN.JEI.TA.DO, *adj.*, abandoned, rejected.

EN.JEI.TAR, *v.*, to despise, to reject, to abandon.

EN.JO.AR, *v.*, to nauseate, to be sick, to cause nausea, to annoy.

EN.JO.O, *s. m.*, nausea, sickness, repugnance.

EN.LA.CE, *s. m.*, interlacing, union, marriage, enlacement, concatenation.

EN.LA.ME.AR, *v.*, to dirty, to soil with mud, to spatter, to stain.

EN.LA.TAR, *v.*, to tin, to can, to trellis.
E.NO.BRE.CER, *v.*, to ennoble.
E.NOR.MI.DA.DE, *s. f.*, enormity, hugeness, enormousness.
EN.QUA.DRAR, *v.*, to frame, to fit.
EN.QUAN.TO, *conj.*, while, as long as, whereas.
EN.RAI.VE.CER, *v.*, to enrage, to irritate, to infuriate, to anger.
EN.RA.I.ZAR, *v.*, to root, to take root, to strike root.
EN.RE.DAR, *v.*, to complicate, to net, to catch in a net, to snarl, to embroil.
EN.RE.DO, *s. m.*, plot of a drama, story, intrigue.
EN.RI.QUE.CER, *v.*, to enrich, to make rich, to embellish, to adorn, to increase.
EN.RI.QUE.CI.MEN.TO, *s. m.*, enrichment.
EN.RO.LAR, *v.*, to roll, to roll up, to coil, to twist.
EN.RU.BES.CER, *v.*, to redden, to blush, to flush.
EN.RU.GA.DO, *adj.*, wrinkled, furrowed.
EN.RU.GAR, *v.*, to wrinkle, to crinkle, to crease.
EN.SA.BO.AR, *v.*, to soap, to wash with soap, to reprove.
EN.SA.CAR, *v.*, to sack, to bag.
EN.SAI.AR, *v.*, to test, to rehearse, to run in to, assay, to analyze, to try.
EN.SAI.O, *s. m.*, assay, an analysis, trial, test, examination.
EN.SAN.GUE.NTAR, *v.*, to stain with blood, to bloody.
EN.SE.A.DA, *s. f.*, inlet, small bay, cove, lagoon.
EN.SE.JO, *s. m.*, opportunity, chance, occasion.
EN.SI.NA.MEN.TO, *s. m.*, teaching, training, instruction, education.
EN.SI.NAR, *v.*, to teach, to instruct, to train, to coach, to drill.
EN.SI.NO, *s. m.*, teaching, instruction, train, education.
EN.SO.LA.RA.DO, *adj.*, sunny.
EN.SOM.BRAR, *v.*, to shadow.
EN.SUR.DE.CE.DOR, *s. m.*, deafening.
EN.SUR.DE.CER, *v.*, to deafen, to make deafen, to stun with noise.

EN.TA.LAR, *v.*, to splint, to put between splints, to put in a tight spot.
EN.TAN.TO, *adv.*, in the meantime, meanwhile.
EN.TÃO, *adv.*, then, at that time, on this occasion, in that case.
EN.TAR.DE.CER, *s. m.*, late afternoon, nightfall; *v.*, to grow dark, to grow night.
EN.TE, *s. m.*, being, person, living creature, life.
EN.TE.A.DA, *s. f.*, stepdaughter.
EN.TE.A.DO, *s. m.*, stepson.
EN.TE.DI.AR, *v.*, to bore, to tire.
EN.TEN.DER, *v.*, to understand, to apprehend, to learn, to figure out, to perceive, to know.
EN.TEN.DI.DO, *s. m.*, expert, knower; *adj.*, understood, learned, erudite.
EN.TEN.DI.MEN.TO, *s. m.*, understanding, agreement, comprehension, perception.
EN.TER.RAR, *v.*, to bury, to inter, to hide.
EN.TER.RO, *s. m.*, burial, interment, entombment.
EN.TI.DA.DE, *s. f.*, entity, being, essence, corporation, existence.
EN.TO.AR, *v.*, to sing, to chant, to tune, to intone, to vocalize.
EN.TOR.NAR, *v.*, to spill, to upset, to overturn.
EN.TOR.PE.CEN.TE, *s. m.*, any narcotic; *adj.*, narcotic.
EN.TOR.PE.CER, *v.*, to torpify, to make torpid, to numb, to paralyse, to weaken.
EN.TOR.PE.CI.MEN.TO, *s. m.*, torpor, numbness, torpid condition.
EN.TOR.TAR, *v.*, to crook, to curve, to bend, to bow, to twist, to warp, to mislead.
EN.TRA.DA, *s. f.*, entrance, entry, inlet, opening, gate, passage, access, admission, ingress.
EN.TRA.NHA, *s. f.*, viscera, entrails, bowels.
EN.TRA.NHAR, *v.*, to pierce, to penetrate.
EN.TRAR, *v.*, to enter, to come in, to go in, to get into, to go inside of, to become a member.
EN.TRA.VAR, *v.*, to obstruct, to block, to impede, to trammel.
EN.TRE, *prep.*, between, among, amongst, during the interval.
EN.TRE.A.BRIR, *v.*, to open partially, to bloom.

ENTREGA   **EPILEPSIA**

EN.TRE.GA, *s. f.*, delivery, surrender, treachery, cession.
EN.TRE.GA.DOR, *s. m.*, deliverer, delivery man, traitor.
EN.TRE.GAR, *v.*, to deliver, to hand over, to remit, to restore, to return.
EN.TRE.LI.NHA, *s. f.*, space between two lines, interlineation.
EN.TRE.ME.AR, *v.*, to intermix, to intermingle, to interpose.
EN.TRE.MEN.TES, *adv.*, meantime, meanwhile.
EN.TRE.POR, *v.*, to interpose, to place between.
EN.TRE.TAN.TO, *adv.*, meantime, meanwhile, in the meantime.
EN.TRE.TE.NI.MEN.TO, *s. m.*, entertainment, diversion.
EN.TRE.TER, *v.*, to entertain, to amuse, to divert, to recreate, to delay.
EN.TRE.VER, *v.*, to see indistinctly, to have a pressentiment.
EN.TRE.VIS.TA, *s. f.*, interview, meeting, conference.
EN.TRE.VIS.TA.DOR, *s. m.*, interviewer.
EN.TRE.VIS.TAR, *v.*, to interview.
EN.TRIS.TE.CER, *v.*, to sadden, to make sad, to afflict, to grieve.
EN.TRIS.TE.CI.MEN.TO, *s. m.*, sadness, sorrow.
EN.TRON.CA.MEN.TO, *s. m.*, crossing point, junction.
EN.TRON.CAR, *v.*, to make a junction, to make robust.
EN.TRO.SAR, *v.*, to gear, to mesh.
EN.TU.PI.DO, *adj.*, obstructed, blocked up.
EN.TU.PIR, *v.*, to block, to choke up, to obstruct, to clog.
EN.TU.SI.AS.MA.DO, *adj.*, excited, ravished, exalted.
EN.TU.SI.AS.MAR, *v.*, to ravish, to enrapture, to excite, to animate.
EN.TU.SI.AS.MO, *s. m.*, enthusiasm, excitement, zeal.
EN.TU.SI.ÁS.TI.CO, *adj.*, enthusiastic.
E.NU.ME.RA.ÇÃO, *s. f.*, enumeration.
E.NU.ME.RAR, *v.*, to enumerate, to count, to number.
E.NUN.CI.AR, *v.*, to enunciate, to state, to utter, to express.
EN.VE.LHE.CER, *v.*, to age, to grow old, to make old.
EN.VE.LO.PE, *s. m.*, envelope.
EN.VE.NE.NA.MEN.TO, *s. m.*, poisoning, intoxication.
EN.VE.NE.NAR, *v.*, to poison, to put poison in, to give poison.
EN.VER.GO.NHA.DO, *adj.*, ashamed, bashful.
EN.VER.GO.NHAR, *v.*, to shame, to make ashamed.
EN.VER.NI.ZAR, *v.*, to varnish, to polish.
EN.VI.A.DO, *s. m.*, messenger, envoy; *adj.*, sent, dispatched.
EN.VI.AR, *v.*, to send, to dispatch, to forward, to depute.
EN.VI.DRA.ÇAR, *v.*, to glaze, to cover with glass.
EN.VI.O, *s. m.*, sending, forwarding, remittance, dispatch; shipment.
EN.VI.U.VAR, *v.*, to widow.
EN.VOL.TO, *adj.*, wrapped, covered, mixed.
EN.VOL.VER, *v.*, to involve, to wrap up, to cover, to envelop, to contain, to hold.
EN.VOL.VI.DO, *adj.*, wrapped up, involved in.
EN.VOL.VI.MEN.TO, *s. m.*, involvement.
EN.XA.DA, *s. f.*, hoe, spade.
EN.XA.ME, *s. m.*, a swarm of bees, hive.
EN.XA.QUE.CA, *s. f.*, migraine, megrim.
EN.XER.GAR, *v.*, to see, to discover, to discern, to descry.
EN.XER.TO, *s. m.*, graft.
EN.XO.FRE, *s. m.*, sulphur, brimstone.
EN.XO.TAR, *v.*, to scare, to frighten away, to chase away, to expel, to banish.
EN.XU.GAR, *v.*, to dry, to wipe, to wipe out.
EN.XUR.RA.DA, *s. f.*, downpour, torrent, rushing stream of water.
EN.XU.TO, *adj.*, dry.
EN.ZI.MA, *s. f.*, enzime.
E.PI.DE.MI.A, *s. f.*, epidemic.
E.PI.DER.ME, *s. f.*, epidermis.
E.PI.LEP.SI.A, *s. f.*, epilepsy.

EPÍLOGO

ESCARPA

E.PÍ.LO.GO, *s. m.*, epilog, epilogue, summary, conclusion.
E.PI.SÓ.DIO, *s. m.*, episode.
E.PÍS.TO.LA, *s. f.*, epistle, a letter.
E.PI.TÁ.FIO, *s. m.*, epitaph.
É.PO.CA, *s. f.*, epoch, era, period, age, season, time, tide, cycle.
E.PO.PEI.A, *s. f.*, epopee, epopoeia.
E.QUA.ÇÃO, *s. f.*, equation.
E.QUA.DOR, *s. m.*, equator.
E.QUA.TO.RI.A.NO, *adj., s. m.*, Ecuadorian.
E.QUES.TRE, *adj., s. m.*, equestrian.
E.QUI.DA.DE, *s. f.*, equity, fairness.
E.QUI.LI.BRAR, *v.*, to equilibrate, to balance.
E.QUI.LÍ.BRIO, *s. m.*, balance, equilibrium, poise.
E.QUI.NO, *adj.*, equine.
E.QUI.NÓ.CIO, *s. m.*, equinox.
E.QUI.PA.MEN.TO, *s. m.*, equipment, apparatus, outfit, takle.
E.QUI.PAR, *v.*, to equip, to fit, to man.
E.QUI.PA.RAR, *v.*, to equal, to equalize, to compare, to make equal.
E.QUI.PE, *s. f.*, team, squad, staff, group.
E.QUI.TA.ÇÃO, *s. f.*, equitation, horsemanship.
E.QUI.VA.LÊN.CIA, *s. f.*, equivalence.
E.QUI.VA.LER, *v.*, to be equivalent to, to amount, to equivale.
E.QUÍ.VO.CO, *s. m.*, mistake, error, ambiguity, equivocation.
E.RA, *s. f.*, era, epoch, period of time.
E.RÁ.RIO, *s. m.*, exchequer.
E.RE.ÇÃO, *s. f.*, erection.
E.RE.TO, *adj.*, erected, erect, raised, upright.
ER.GO.ME.TRI.A, *s. f.*, ergometrics.
ER.GUER, *v.*, to raise, to lift, to elevate, to rear.
ER.MO, *s. m.* hermitage, wilderness, desert; *adj.*, solitary, retired, desert.
E.RO.SÃO, *s. f.*, erosion, corrosion.
E.RÓ.TI.CO, *adj.*, erotic, sensual.
E.RO.TIS.MO, *s. m.*, eroticism.
ER.RA.DI.CA.ÇÃO, *s. f.*, eradication.
ER.RA.DI.CAR, *v.*, to eradicate, to extirpate.
ER.RA.DO, *adj.*, mistaken, wrong, false, erroneous.

ER.RAR, *v.*, to miss, to mistake, to misunderstanding, to fail.
ER.RO, *s. m.*, error, fault, mistake.
ER.RÔ.NEO, *adj.*, erroneous, false.
E.RU.DI.ÇÃO, *s. f.*, erudition, learning.
E.RU.DI.TO, *adj., s. m.*, erudit.
E.RUP.ÇÃO, *s. f.*, eruption, outbreak.
ER.VA, *s. f.*, herb, grass.
ER.VI.LHA, *s. f.*, pea.
ES.BAN.JAR, *v.*, to waste, to squander, to lavish, to dissipate, to misspend.
ES.BAR.RAR, *v.*, to dash, to collide with.
ES.BO.ÇAR, *v.*, to sketch, to roughdraw, to draft, to delineate.
ES.BO.ÇO, *s. m.*, sketch, outline.
ES.BO.FE.TE.AR, *v.*, to slap, to strike.
ES.BRA.VE.JAR, *v.*, to roar, to shout, to cry out.
ES.BU.RA.CA.DO, *adj.*, bored, perfurated, full of holes, broken.
ES.BU.RA.CAR, *v.*, to make holes, to bore, to perforate.
ES.CA.DA, *s. f.*, staircase, stairs, ladder.
ES.CA.DA.RI.A, *s. f.*, a flight of stairs, stairway.
ES.CA.LA, *s. f.*, scale, stopover, ladder.
ES.CAL.DAR, *v.*, to scald, to burn, to parch, to inflame, to heat.
ES.CA.LO.NA.MEN.TO, *s. m.*, assignment.
ES.CA.MA, *s. f.*, scale.
ES.CA.MO.SO, *adj.*, scaly, squamous.
ES.CAN.CA.RAR, *v.*, to set wide open, to open, to show.
ES.CAN.DA.LI.ZAR, *v.*, to scandalize, to offend, to shock, to defame.
ES.CÂN.DA.LO, *s. m.*, scandal, offense, opprobrium.
ES.CAN.DI.NA.VO, *adj., s. m.*, Scandinavian.
ES.CAN.TEI.O, *s. m.*, corner.
ES.CA.PA.MEN.TO, *s. m.*, exhaust pipe, muffler.
ES.CA.PAR, *v.*, to escape, to get out, to run away.
ES.CA.PE, *s. m.*, escape, flight, evasion, leakage.
ES.CAR.LA.TE, *s. m.*, scarlet.
ES.CÁR.NIO, *s. m.*, mockery, derision.
ES.CAR.PA, *s. f.*, scarp, slope, cliff.

ES.CAS.SEZ, *s. f.*, scarcity, scarceness, need, privation, dearth, want, lack, parsimony.
ES.CAS.SO, *adj.*, scarce, sparing, insufficient.
ES.CA.VA.DEI.RA, *s. f.*, digging machine, digger.
ES.CA.VAR, *v.*, to excavate, to hollow, to scoop.
ES.CLA.RE.CER, *v.*, to clear, to elucidate.
ES.CLA.RE.CI.MEN.TO, *s. m.*, clearing up, explanation, elucidation, light, clearness.
ES.CO.A.MEN.TO, *s. m.*, flowing off, drainage, flowage, outlet, filtration.
ES.CO.CÊS, *adj.*, *s. m.*, Scottish, Scotch, Scot.
ES.CO.LA, *s. f.*, school, schoolhouse.
ES.CO.LHA, *s. f.*, choice, election, selection, option.
ES.CO.LHER, *v.*, to choose, to make a choice of, to select.
ES.CO.LHI.DO, *adj.*, chosen, elected.
ES.COL.TA, *s. f.*, guard, escort.
ES.COM.BRO, *s. m.*, rubbish.
ES.CON.DER, *v.*, to hide, to conceal, to put, to occult, to weil.
ES.CO.RA, *s. f.*, prop, stay, support, aid, help, brace.
ES.CÓ.RIA, *s. f.*, dross, slag, dregs, scum, scoria, refuse.
ES.CO.RI.AR, *v.*, to excoriate, to strip off the skin, to fly.
ES.COR.PI.ÃO, *s. m.*, scorpion.
ES.COR.RE.GÃO, *s. m.*, slip, slipping, sliding.
ES.COR.RE.GAR, *v.*, to slide, to slip, to skid, to glide.
ES.COR.RER, *v.*, to let flow off, to drain, to drop, to trickle, to drip.
ES.CO.TEI.RO, *s. m.*, Boy Scout; a scout.
ES.CO.VA, *s. f.*, brush; **ESCOVA DE CABELO**, hairbrush.
ES.CO.VAR, *v.*, to brush.
ES.CRA.VI.DÃO, *s. f.*, slavery, servitude.
ES.CRA.VI.ZAR, *v.*, to enslave, to reduce to slavery.
ES.CRA.VO, *s. m.*, slave; *adj.*, slave, slavish.
ES.CRE.VER, *v.*, to write.
ES.CRI.TA, *s. f.*, writing, handwriting.
ES.CRI.TO, *s. m.*, writing, *adj.*, written, described.

ES.CRI.TOR, *s. m.*, writer, author.
ES.CRI.TO.RA, *s. f.*, writer, authoress.
ES.CRI.TÓ.RIO, *s. m.*, office, bureau, counting-house.
ES.CRI.TU.RA, *s. f.*, deed, legal document, writ, contract.
ES.CRI.TU.RAR, *v.*, keep books, keep account.
ES.CRI.TU.RÁ.RIO, *s. m.*, bookkeeper, clerk, scribe.
ES.CRI.VA.NI.NHA, *s. f.*, desk, writing desk.
ES.CRI.VÃO, *s. m.*, notary, notary public, clerk, copyst.
ES.CRO.TO, *s. m.*, scrotum.
ES.CRÚ.PU.LO, *s. m.*, scruple, susceptibility, remorse.
ES.CRU.TÍ.NIO, *s. m.*, scrutiny, balloting, ballot-box.
ES.CU.DO, *s. m.*, shield, buckler, arms; Portuguese currency.
ES.CUL.TU.RA, *s. f.*, sculpture.
ES.CU.MA.DEI.RA, *s. f.*, skimmer.
ES.CU.RE.CER, *v.*, to darken, to blacken, to obscure, to make dark.
ES.CU.RI.DÃO, *s. f.*, darkness, blackness, obscurity.
ES.CU.RO, *adj.*, dark, shadowy, black, obscure, lightless, tenebrous.
ES.CU.SA, *s. f.*, excuse, pardon, apology.
ES.CU.TAR, *v.*, to hearken, to give ear to, to listen, to hear.
ES.FA.QUE.AR, *v.*, to stab, to knife, to cut with a knife.
ES.FAR.RA.PAR, *v.*, to tear, to rend, to reduce to tatters.
ES.FE.RA, *s. f.*, sphere, globe, ball, orb.
ES.FIN.GE, *s. f.*, sphinx.
ES.FO.LAR, *v.*, to flay, to skin, to scratch, to chafe, to rap, to abrade, to excoriate.
ES.FO.ME.A.DO, *adj.*, hungry, famished, ravenous.
ES.FOR.ÇAR, *v.*, to make strong, to encourage, to incite, to strengthen, to stimulate.
ES.FOR.ÇO, *s. m.*, effort, endeavour, struggle, attempt, exertion, courage, valour.

ESFREGAR | **ESPESSO**

ES.FRE.GAR, *v.*, to rub, to scour, to scrub, to scrape.
ES.FRI.A.MEN.TO, *s. m.*, refrigeration, cooling.
ES.FRI.AR, *v.*, to cool, to chill, to make cool, to refresh, to refrigerate.
ES.GO.TA.DO, *adj.*, drained, emptied, exhausted, finished.
ES.GO.TA.MEN.TO, *s. m.*, prostration, weakness, debility, fatigue.
ES.GO.TAR, *v.*, exhaust, to drain to the last drop, to dry.
ES.GO.TO, *s.m.*, drain, drainage, sewer, sewerage.
ES.GRI.MA, *s. f.*, fencing.
ES.GUI.CHO, *s. m.*, squirt, jet, waterspout.
ES.LA.VO, *adj., s. m.*, Slavonian, Slavic, Slavonic, Slav.
ES.MA.GAR, *v.*, to compress, to squeeze, to press, to crush.
ES.MAL.TE, *s. m.*, enamel.
ES.ME.RAL.DA, *s. f.*, emerald.
ES.ME.RIL, *s. m.*, emery.
ES.ME.RO, *s. m.*, care, diligence, carefulness, perfection.
ES.MI.GA.LHAR, *v.*, to crumb, to crumble, to break into fragments, to triturate.
ES.MO.LA, *s. f.*, alms, charity, almsdeed, benefit.
ES.MO.RE.CER, *v.*, to dismay, to discourage, to depress, to love heart.
ES.MUR.RAR, *v.*, to box, to sock, to beat, to punch, to pummel.
ES.NO.BE, *s. 2 gen.*, snob; snobbish.
E.SÔ.FA.GO, *s. m.*, gullet, esophagus.
ES.PA.CI.AL, *adj., s. m.*, spatial, space.
ES.PA.ÇO, *s. m.*, space, area, place.
ES.PA.DA, *s. f.*, sword.
ES.PÁ.DUA, *s. f.*, shoulder, shoulder blade.
ES.PAI.RE.CER, *v.*, to amuse, to recreate, to entertain, to divert.
ES.PA.LHA.FA.TO.SO, *adj.*, fussy, noisy, ostentatious.
ES.PA.LHAR, *v.*, to spread, to scatter about, to disperse, to dispel, to divulge.
ES.PA.NA.DOR, *s. m.*, duster, feather broom.
ES.PAN.CA.MEN.TO, *s. m.*, spanking, beating.
ES.PAN.CAR, *v.*, to spank, to beat, to drub, to thrash.
ES.PA.NHOL, *adj., s. m.*, Spaniard, Spanish.
ES.PAN.TAR, *v.*, to astonish, to frighten, to terrify, to alarm, to scare, to surprise.
ES.PAN.TO, *s. m.*, fright, terror, scare, fear, astonishment.
ES.PA.RA.DRA.PO, *s. m.*, adhesive tape.
ES.PAR.RA.MAR, *v.*, to scatter about, to spread, to strew, to disperse.
ES.PA.TI.FAR, *v.*, to shatter, to smash, to splinter.
ES.PÁ.TU.LA, *s. f.*, spatula, slice, spattle, trowel.
ES.PE.CI.AL, *adj.*, special, particular, excellent, individual.
ES.PE.CI.A.LI.DA.DE, *s. f.*, speciality, particularity, peculiarity.
ES.PE.CI.A.LI.ZA.ÇÃO, *s. f.*, specialization, speciality.
ES.PE.CI.A.LI.ZAR, *v.*, to specialize, to differentiate, to particularize.
ES.PÉ.CIE, *s. f.*, species, sort, kind, variety, class, order, group.
ES.PE.CI.FI.CAR, *v.*, to specify, to indicate, to particularize, to stipulate.
ES.PEC.TA.DOR, *s. m.*, spectator, looker-on, viewer, observer, onlooker.
ES.PEC.TRO, *s. m.*, ghost, spectre, spirit, apparition, phantom.
ES.PE.CU.LAR, *v.*, to speculate.
ES.PE.LHAR, *v.*, to mirror; to polish, to bright.
ES.PE.LHO, *s. m.*, mirror, looking-glass.
ES.PE.LUN.CA, *s. f.*, honky-tonk, cavern, hole, den.
ES.PE.RA, *s. f.*, expectation, waiting-for, a wait.
ES.PE.RAN.ÇA, *s. f.*, hope, expectation.
ES.PE.RAR, *v.*, to hope for, to wait, to expect, to await.
ES.PER.MA, *s. m.*, sperm, semen.
ES.PER.MA.TO.ZOI.DE, *s. m.*, spermatozoid, spermatozoon.
ES.PER.TE.ZA, *s. f.*, briskness, quickness, smartness, liveliness, vivacity.
ES.PER.TO, *adj.*, brisk, lively, smart, clever.
ES.PES.SO, *adj.*, thick, dense.

ES.PES.SU.RA, *s. f.*, thickness.
ES.PE.TÁ.CU.LO, *s. m.*, spectacle, show, entertainment, view, scene.
ES.PE.TO, *s. m.*, spit, skewer, broach.
ES.PE.ZI.NHAR, *v.*, to trample on, to oppress, to vex.
ES.PI.ÃO, *s. m.*, spy, secret agent, intelligencer.
ES.PI.AR, *v.*, to spy, to watch, to observe, to look at, to dog, to pry into.
ES.PI.NA.FRE, *s. m.*, spinach.
ES.PIN.GAR.DA, *s. f.*, rifle, shotgun.
ES.PI.NHA, *s. f.*, spine, backbone, spinal column.
ES.PI.NHO, *s. m.*, thorn, prickle, sting, spine.
ES.PI.O.NA.GEM, *s. f.*, espionage, spying.
ES.PI.O.NAR, *v.*, to spy, to observe.
ES.PI.RAL, *s. f.*, spiral, wreath.
ES.PÍ.RI.TA, *s. 2 gen.*, spiritist; *adj.*, spiritualistic.
ES.PI.RI.TIS.MO, *s. m.*, spiritism.
ES.PÍ.RI.TO, *s. m.*, spirit, soul, mind, a ghost, spectre; energy.
ES.PI.RI.TU.AL, *adj.*, spiritual, immaterial.
ES.PI.RI.TU.A.LI.DA.DE, *s. f.*, spirituality, immateriality.
ES.PI.RI.TU.A.LIS.MO, *s. m.*, spiritualism.
ES.PI.RI.TU.O.SO, *adj.*, spirituous, alcoholic, witty, spirited.
ES.PIR.RAR, *v.*, to sneeze, to splash, to crepitate.
ES.PLÊN.DI.DO, *adj.*, splendid, brilliant, magnificent, shining, grand, admirable.
ES.PLEN.DOR, *s. m.*, splendor, glory, pomp, refulgence, magnificence.
ES.PON.JA, *s. f.*, sponge.
ES.PON.TA.NEI.DA.DE, *s. f.*, spontaneity, spontaneousness, free will.
ES.PON.TÂ.NEO, *adj.*, spontaneous, voluntary.
ES.PO.RA, *s. f.*, spur.
ES.POR.TE, *s. m.*, sport, sports.
ES.POR.TIS.TA, *s. 2 gen.*, sportsman, sportswoman.
ES.PO.SA, *s. f.*, wife, consort, spouse.
ES.PO.SAR, *v.*, to marry, espouse.
ES.PO.SO, *s. m.*, husband, consort.
ES.PREI.TAR, *v.*, to peep, to watch, to observe, to pry, to spy.
ES.PRE.ME.DOR, *s. m.*, squeezer, smasher.
ES.PRE.MER, *v.*, to press, to squeeze, to compress, to crush, to express, to constrict.
ES.PU.MA, *s. f.*, foam, froth, scum, spume.
ES.PU.MAR, *v.*, to scum, skim, to foam, to bubble, to froth.
ES.QUA.DRA, *s. f.*, squadron, naval fleet.
ES.QUA.DRI.LHA, *s. f.*, squadron, wing, flotilla.
ES.QUA.DRO, *s. m.*, square.
ES.QUE.CER, *v.*, to forget, to disremember, to neglect.
ES.QUE.CI.MEN.TO, *s. m.*, forgetfulness, oblivion.
ES.QUE.LE.TO, *s. m.*, skeleton.
ES.QUE.MA, *s. m.*, scheme, project, plan, model, design.
ES.QUEN.TAR, *v.*, to heat, to warm, to make warm, to overheat, to animate.
ES.QUER.DA, *s. f.*, the left side or hand, the opposition.
ES.QUER.DO, *adj.*, left.
ES.QUI, *s. m.*, ski.
ES.QUI.AR, *v.*, to ski.
ES.QUI.LO, *s. m.*, squirrel.
ES.QUI.MÓ, *adj.*, *s. 2 gen.*, Eskimo.
ES.QUI.NA, *s. f.*, corner, street corner.
ES.QUI.SI.TI.CE, *s. f.*, extravagance, eccentricity.
ES.QUI.SI.TO, *adj.*, exquisite, singular, rare, strange.
ES.QUI.ZO.FRE.NI.A, *s. f.*, schizophrenia.
ES.SA, *pron. dem.*, that; **ESSAS**, those.
ES.SE, *pron. dem.*, that, that one; **ESSES**, those.
ES.SÊN.CIA, *s. f.*, essence, substance.
ES.SEN.CI.AL, *adj.*, essential, main.
ES.TA, *pron. dem.*, this, the latter; **ESTAS**, these, these ones.
ES.TA.BE.LE.CER, *v.*, to establish, to settle, to fix, to set up, to found, to determine.
ES.TA.BE.LE.CI.MEN.TO, *s. m.*, establishment, shop, store, institution.
ES.TA.BI.LI.DA.DE, *s. f.*, stability, stableness, firmness.
ES.TA.BI.LI.ZAR, *v.*, to stabilize, to fix, to fixate.
ES.TÁ.BU.LO, *s. m.*, stall, stable.

ES.TA.ÇÃO, *s. f.*, station, season, term, stand.
ES.TA.CIO.NA.MEN.TO, *s. m.*, parking, parking lot, car park.
ES.TA.CIO.NAR, *v.*, to park, to station.
ES.TÁ.DIO, *s. m.*, stadium.
ES.TA.DIS.TA, *s. 2 gen.*, statesman, stateswoman.
ES.TA.DO, *s. m.*, state, condition, circumstance.
ES.TA.DU.AL, *adj.*, state.
ES.TA.DU.NI.DEN.SE, *s. 2 gen.*, North American; *adj.*, American.
ES.TA.FA, *s. f.*, stress, fatigue, hard work.
ES.TA.GI.Á.RIO, *s. m.*, trainee.
ES.TÁ.GIO, *s. m.*, training, probation.
ES.TA.LEI.RO, *s. m.*, shipyard, dockyard.
ES.TAM.PA, *s. f.*, impression, print, model, picture.
ES.TAM.PAR, *v.*, to print, to imprint, to impress, to stamp.
ES.TÂN.CIA, *s. f.*, stay, ranch, state, country, residence, resort, strophe.
ES.TAN.DE, *s. f.*, stand.
ES.TA.NHO, *s. m.*, tin, pewter.
ES.TAN.TE, *s. f.*, shelf, rack, bookstand, bookcase.
ES.TAR, *v.*, to be, to stay, to remain, to lie, to exist, to be present, to attend.
ES.TAR.RE.CER, *v.*, to frighten, to strike with fear, terrorize.
ES.TA.TÍS.TI.CA, *s. f.*, statistics.
ES.TA.TÍS.TI.CO, *s. m.*, statistician; *adj.*, statistic.
ES.TÁ.TUA, *s. f.*, statue.
ES.TA.TU.RA, *s. f.*, tallness, size, stature.
ES.TA.TU.TO, *s. m.*, statute, decree, rule, law.
ES.TE, *pron. dem.*, this, the latter; **ESTES**, these, these ones.
ES.TEN.DER, *v.*, to extend, to stretch out, to enlarge, to expand, to amplify.
ES.TE.PE, *s. f.*, steppe.
ES.TER.CAR, *v.*, to manure, to dung, to fertilize.
ES.TER.CO, *s. m.*, manure, dung, excrement.
ES.TÉ.RIL, *adj.*, infertile, sterile, unfruitful, barren.
ES.TE.RI.LI.DA.DE, *s. f.*, sterility, infertility.
ES.TE.RI.LI.ZA.ÇÃO, *s. f.*, sterilization.
ES.TE.RI.LI.ZAR, *v.*, to sterilize, to make barren or sterile.
ES.TÉ.TI.CA, *s. f.*, esthetics.
ES.TE.TOS.CÓ.PIO, *s. m.*, stethoscope.
ES.TI.A.GEM, *s. f.*, drought, dryness.
ES.TI.CAR, *v.*, to extend, to stretch out, to dilate.
ES.TIG.MA, *s. m.*, stigma, mark, spot.
ES.TI.LE.TE, *s. m.*, probe, sound, stiletto.
ES.TI.LÍS.TI.CA, *s. f.*, stylistic(s).
ES.TI.LO, *s. m.*, style, method, fashion.
ES.TI.MA, *s. f.*, esteem, respect, regard, affection, fondness.
ES.TI.MAR, *v.*, to esteem, to regard with respect, to prize, to consider.
ES.TI.MU.LAN.TE, *adj., s. m.*, stimulant, incitant.
ES.TI.MU.LAR, *v.*, to stimulate, to incite, to instigate, to excite.
ES.TÍ.MU.LO, *s. m.*, stimulus, incentive, impulse.
ES.TI.PU.LAR, *v.*, to stipulate, to contract, to covenant.
ES.TIR.PE, *s. f.*, race, origin, stock, lineage.
ES.TI.VA, *s. f.*, stowage.
ES.TI.VA.DOR, *s. m.*, stower, docker.
ES.TO.FA.DO, *s. m.*, upholstered.
ES.TO.FAR, *v.*, to stuff, to upholster.
ES.TO.JO, *s. m.*, case, box, kit, set, container.
ES.TÔ.MA.GO, *s. m.*, stomach.
ES.TO.PA, *s. f.*, tow, hards, hurds, oakum.
ES.TO.PIM, *s. m.*, quickmatch, fuse.
ES.TO.QUE, *s. m.*, stock, reserve.
ES.TOR.VAR, *v.*, to hinder, to embarrass, to obstruct, to impede.
ES.TOR.VO, *s. m.*, hindrance, impediment, embarrassment, obstacle.
ES.TRA.BIS.MO, *s. m.*, squint, strabismus.
ES.TRA.DA, *s. f.*, road, highway, main road.
ES.TRA.DO, *s. m.*, mattress, frame, bedframe.
ES.TRA.GAR, *v.*, to destroy, to spoil, to danger, to ruin, to blemish, to damage, to waste.
ES.TRA.GO, *s. m.*, damage, prejudice, harm, injury.
ES.TRAN.GEI.RO, *s. m.*, foreigner, stranger.
ES.TRA.NHAR, *v.*, to find queer, to odd, to strange, to wonder.
ES.TRA.NHE.ZA, *s. f.*, queerness, amazement,

ESTRANHO — EVITAR

surprise, shyness.
ES.TRA.NHO, *s. m.*, stranger, foreigner; *adj.*, foreign, strange, alien, odd, wonderful, exotic.
ES.TRA.TA.GE.MA, *s. m.*, stratagem, cunning, ruse, artifice.
ES.TRA.TÉ.GIA, *s. f.*, strategy.
ES.TRA.TOS.FE.RA, *s. f.*, stratosphere.
ES.TRE.BA.RIA, *s. f.*, horse stable.
ES.TREI.A, *s. f.*, handsel, première, beginning, debut.
ES.TREI.TAR, *v.*, to narrow, to straiten, to crimp.
ES.TREI.TO, *s. m.*, strait; *adj.*, narrow, strait, close.
ES.TRE.LA, *s. f.*, star, guide, fate, fortune, destiny.
ES.TRE.ME.CER, *v.*, to tremble, to shake, to quake, to excite, to affect.
ES.TRE.ME.CI.MEN.TO, *s. m.*, shudder, trembling.
ES.TRES.SAR, *v.*, to wear down.
ES.TRES.SE, *s. m.*, stress, strain.
ES.TRO.FE, *s. f.*, strophe, stanza.
ES.TRON.DO, *s. m.*, noise, cracking, boom, blast, thundering, rumble.
ES.TRU.ME, *s. m.*, dung, manure, fertilizer.
ES.TRU.TU.RA, *s. f.*, structure, framework, framing.
ES.TRU.TU.RAL, *adj.*, structural.
ES.TU.Á.RIO, *s. m.*, estuary.
ES.TU.DAN.TE, *s. 2 gen.*, student, scholar.
ES.TU.DAR, *v.*, to study, to learn, to investigate.
ES.TÚ.DIO, *s. m.*, studio, atelier.
ES.TU.DO, *s. m.*, study, application.
ES.TU.FA, *s. f.*, stove, hothouse, greenhouse.
ES.TU.PE.FA.TO, *adj.*, stupefied.
ES.TU.PI.DEZ, *s. f.*, stupidity, foolishness, silliness, dullness.
ES.TÚ.PI.DO, *adj.*, stupid, dull, silly, idiotic.
ES.TU.PRA.DOR, *s. m.*, raper, violator, deflowerer.
ES.TU.PRAR, *v.*, to rape, to deflower.
ES.VA.ZI.A.MEN.TO, *s. m.*, emptying, exhaustion.
ES.VA.ZI.AR, *v.*, to empty, evacuate.
E.TA.PA, *s. f.*, stage, stopping place.

É.TER, *s. m.*, ether.
E.TER.NI.DA.DE, *s. f.*, eternity.
E.TER.NI.ZAR, *v.*, to eternalize, eternize.
E.TER.NO, *adj.*, eternal, immortal, timeless.
É.TI.CA, *s. f.*, ethics.
É.TI.CO, *adj.*, ethic, moral.
E.TI.MO.LO.GI.A, *s. f.*, etymology.
E.TÍ.O.PE, *adj., s. m.*, Ethiopian.
E.TI.QUE.TA, *s. f.*, etiquette, formality, ticket, tag.
E.TI.QUE.TAR, *v.*, to label, to ticket.
E.TRUS.CO, *adj., s. m.*, Etruscan, Etrurian.
EU, *pron.*, I, the ego, the self-conscious subject; me.
EU.CA.LIP.TO, *s. m.*, eucalyptus.
EU.CA.RÍS.TI.CO, *adj.*, Eucharistic.
EU.FE.MIS.MO, *s. m.*, euphemism.
EU.FO.NI.A, *s. f.*, euphony.
EU.FO.RI.A, *s. f.*, euphoria; a sense of well-being.
EU.NU.CO, *s. m.*, eunuch.
EU.RO.PE.I.ZAR, *v.*, to Europeanize.
EU.RO.PEU, *adj., s. m.*, European.
EU.TA.NÁ.SI.A, *s. f.*, euthanasia.
E.VA.CU.AR, *v.*, to evacuate, to empty, to void, to excrete.
E.VA.DIR, *v.*, to escape, to avoid, to shun, to delude.
E.VAN.GE.LHO, *s. m.*, Evangel, Gospel.
E.VAN.GE.LIS.TA, *s. 2 gen.*, Evangelist.
E.VAN.GE.LI.ZA.DOR, *s. m.*, evangelist, preacher.
E.VAN.GE.LI.ZAR, *v.*, to evangelize.
E.VA.PO.RA.ÇÃO, *s. f.*, evaporation.
E.VA.PO.RAR, *v.*, to evaporate, to vaporize, to exale, to dissipate.
E.VA.SÃO, *s. f.*, evasion, escape, elopement.
E.VEN.TO, *s. m.*, event, ocurrence, happening.
E.VEN.TU.A.LI.DA.DE, *s. f.*, eventuality, event.
E.VI.DÊN.CIA, *s. f.*, evidence, clearness.
E.VI.DEN.CI.AR, *v.*, to evidence, to make evident, to make clear.
E.VI.DEN.TE, *adj.*, evident, clear, plain, obvious.
E.VI.TAR, *v.*, to avoid, to shun, to escape.

E.VO.CAR, *v.*, to evocate.
E.VO.LU.ÇÃO, *s. f.*, evolution.
E.VO.LU.IR, *v.*, to develop, to unfold, to progress.
E.XA.GE.RA.DO, *adj.*, exaggerating, excessive.
E.XA.GE.RAR, *v.*, to exaggerate, to amplify, to magnify.
E.XA.GE.RO, *s. m.*, exaggeration, amplification.
E.XA.LAR, *v.*, to exhale, to emit, to emanate.
E.XAL.TAR, *v.*, to exalt, to glorify, to praise, to magnify.
E.XA.ME, *s. m.*, examination, interrogatory.
E.XA.MI.NA.DOR, *s. m.*, examiner, examinator.
E.XA.MI.NAR, *v.*, to examine, to search, to inquire into, to interrogate, to investigate.
E.XA.TI.DÃO, *s. f.*, exactness, preciseness, precision, punctuality.
E.XA.TO, *adj.*, exact, accurate, precise, correct, right, strict.
E.XAU.RIR, *v.*, to exhaust, to drain, to draw out.
E.XAUS.TO, *adj.*, exhausted, drained, emptied.
EX.CE.ÇÃO, *s. f.*, exception, excepting.
EX.CE.DER, *v.*, to exceed, to overstep, to surpass, to excel.
EX.CE.LÊN.CIA, *s. f.*, excellence, excellency.
EX.CE.LEN.TE, *adj.*, excellent, eminent, admirable.
EX.CEP.CI.O.NAL, *adj.*, exceptional, peculiar, irregular, unusual.
EX.CES.SI.VO, *adj.*, excessive, exceeding, immoderate.
EX.CES.SO, *s. m.*, excess, abuse, outrage, immoderation, exorbitance.
EX.CE.TO, *prep.*, except, excepting, save, unless, but, excluding.
EX.CI.TA.ÇÃO, *s. f.*, excitation, excitement, heat, simulation, agitation.
EX.CI.TAR, *v.*, to excite, to stimulate, to incite, to instigate.
EX.CLA.MA.ÇÃO, *s. f.*, exclamation; **PONTO DE EXCLAMAÇÃO**, exclamation mark.
EX.CLA.MAR, *v.*, to exclaim, to cry out.
EX.CLU.IR, *v.*, to exclude, to preclude, to shut out.
EX.CLU.SÃO, *s. f.*, exclusion, elimination.

EX.CLU.SI.VI.DA.DE, *s. f.*, exclusiveness.
EX.CLU.SI.VO, *adj.*, exclusive, restricted, limited.
EX.CO.MUN.GA.DO, *s. m.*, excommunicate; excommunicated.
EX.CO.MUN.GAR, *v.*, to excommunicate.
EX.CRE.MEN.TO, *s. m.*, excrement, feces, shit, crap, fecal matter.
EX.CUR.SÃO, *s. f.*, excursion, trip, tour, journey, sally, raid.
E.XE.CU.ÇÃO, *s. f.*, execution, performance.
E.XE.CU.TAR, *v.*, to execute, to perform, to realize, to effectuate.
E.XE.CU.TI.VO, *s. m.*, executive; *adj.*, executive, resolute, active, brisk.
E.XEM.PLAR, *s. m.*, exemplar, model, specimen, copy, issue; *adj.*, exemplary.
E.XEM.PLO, *s. m.*, example, model, instance.
E.XER.CER, *v.*, to exercise, to practise, to exert.
E.XER.CÍ.CIO, *s. m.*, exercise, practice, drill, exercitation, work.
E.XÉR.CI.TO, *s. m.*, army, troops.
E.XI.BI.ÇÃO, *s. f.*, exhibition, display, exposition, ostentation.
E.XI.BIR, *v.*, to exhibit, to show, to display, to expose, to show off.
E.XI.GÊN.CIA, *s. f.*, exigence, exigency, request, demand, necessity, need.
E.XI.GIR, *v.*, to claim, to exact, to demand, to require, to urge.
E.XI.LAR, *v.*, to exile, to banish, to deport, to expatriate.
E.XÍ.LIO, *s. m.*, exile, banishment.
E.XÍ.MIO, *adj.*, conspicuous, excellent, extraordinary.
E.XIS.TÊN.CIA, *s. f.*, existence, reality, life.
E.XIS.TEN.CI.A.LIS.MO, *s. m.*, existentialism.
E.XIS.TIR, *v.*, to exist, to be, to live, to subsist.
Ê.XI.TO, *s. m.*, effect, result, outcome, success, triumph.
Ê.XO.DO, *s. m.*, exodus, migration.
E.XO.NE.RA.ÇÃO, *s. f.*, exoneration, dismissal, discharge.
E.XO.NE.RAR, *v.*, to exonerate, to dismiss, to free.

E.XOR.BI.TÂN.CIA, s. f., exorbitance, exorbitancy, extravagance.
E.XOR.BI.TAR, v., to exorbitate, exceed.
E.XOR.CIS.MO, s. m., exorcism.
E.XÓ.TI.CO, adj., exotic, foreign, odd, extravagant.
EX.PAN.DIR, v., to expand, to enlarge, to unfold, to extend.
EX.PAN.SÃO, s. f., expansion, expansiveness.
EX.PA.TRI.AR, v., to expatriate, to exile, to banish, to deport.
EX.PEC.TA.DOR, s. m., expectant, expectator.
EX.PEC.TA.TI.VA, s. f., expectancy, expectation.
EX.PE.DI.ÇÃO, s. f., expedition, despatch; trek, excursion.
EX.PE.DI.EN.TE, s. m., expedient, office hours, working day, business.
EX.PE.DIR, v., to expel, to eject, to dispatch, to express.
EX.PE.LIR, v., to expel, to eject.
EX.PE.RI.ÊN.CIA, s. f., experience, practice, knowledge, proof.
EX.PE.RI.MEN.TA.ÇÃO, s. f., experimentation, experiment, test, trial.
EX.PE.RI.MEN.TAR, v., to experiment, to try, to test.
EX.PE.RI.MEN.TO, s. m., experiment, trial, test, proof.
EX.PI.AR, v., to expiate, to atone for, to pay for a crime.
EX.PI.RAR, v., to expire, to die, to end, to exhale, to conclude.
EX.PLA.NA.ÇÃO, s. f., explanation, explication, elucidation.
EX.PLA.NAR, v., to explain, to elucidate, to explicate.
EX.PLI.CA.ÇÃO, s. f., explication, explanation, elucidation.
EX.PLI.CAR, to explain, to elucidate, to explicate, to interpret.
EX.PLO.DIR, v., to explode, to blast, to detonate, to blow-up.
EX.PLO.RA.ÇÃO, s.f., exploration, investigation.
EX.PLO.RAR, v., to explore, to search, to inquire into.
EX.PLO.SÃO, s. f., explosion, blast, outburst, detonation.
EX.POR, v., to expose, to lay out, to exhibit, to show, to display.
EX.POR.TA.ÇÃO, s. f., exportation, export.
EX.POR.TAR, v., to export.
EX.PO.SI.ÇÃO, s. f., exposition, exhibition, explanation, interpretation.
EX.PRES.SÃO, s. f., expression, utterance, countenance, term, phrase, sentence.
EX.PRES.SAR, v., to express.
EX.PRES.SO, s. m., express, courier; adj., express, plain, explicit.
EX.PRI.MIR, v., to express, to speak, to utter.
EX.PUL.SÃO, s. f., expulsion, exclusion, dismissal.
EX.PUL.SAR, v., to expel, to drive away, to turn out, to dismiss.
ÊX.TA.SE, s. f., ecstasy, rapture, trance.
EX.TEN.SÃO, s. f., extension, stretching, length, range, enlargement.
EX.TEN.SO, adj., extensive, ample, vast.
EX.TE.RI.OR, s. m., exterior, outside; adj., exterior, external, outer.
EX.TE.RI.O.RI.ZAR, v., to express, to utter.
EX.TER.MI.NAR, v., to exterminate, to destroy, to annihilate.
EX.TER.MÍ.NIO, s. m., extermination, extirpation.
EX.TER.NO, adj., external, exterior, outside.
EX.TIN.ÇÃO, s. f., extinction, destruction.
EX.TIN.GUIR, v., to extinguish, to put out, to stifle.
EX.TIN.TO, adj., extinct, extinguished, dead, defunct.
EX.TIN.TOR, s. m., extinguisher.
EX.TOR.SÃO, s. f., extortion, exaction, blackmail, usurpation.
EX.TRA, s. 2 gen., extra; adj., extra, additional, supplementary.
EX.TRA.ÇÃO, s. f., extraction, derivation, drawing.
EX.TRA.IR, v., to extract, to draw out, to

withdraw.
EX.TRA.OR.DI.NÁ.RIO, *adj.*, extraordinary, unusual, extra.
EX.TRA.TER.RE.NO, *adj.*, extraterrestrial.
EX.TRA.TO, *s. m.*, extract, summary.
EX.TRA.VA.GÂN.CIA, *s. f.*, extravagance, garishness, absurdity, folly.
EX.TRA.VA.SAR, *v.*, to flow out, to extravasate.
EX.TRA.VI.A.DO, *adj.*, astray, lost, amiss, depraved, corrupt.
EX.TRA.VI.AR, *v.*, to lead astray, to misplace, to put out of the way.
EX.TRA.VI.O, *s. m.*, misleading, deviation, miscarriage, loss.

EX.TRE.MI.DA.DE, *s. f.*, extremity, edge, end, border; misery.
EX.TRE.MO, *s. m.*, extreme, extremity, end; *adj.*, extreme, last, final, utmost.
EX.TRE.MO O.RI.EN.TE, *s. m.*, Far East.
E.XU.BE.RÂN.CIA, *s. f.*, exuberance, exuberancy.
E.XU.BE.RAN.TE, *adj.*, exuberant, rich, copious, luxuriant.
E.XUL.TAN.TE, *adj.*, exultant.
E.XUL.TAR, *v.*, to exult, to crow, to rejoice, to jubilate.
E.XU.MA.ÇÃO, *s. f.*, exhumation.
E.XU.MAR, *v.*, to exhume, to disinter.

F

F, *s.m.*, the sixth letter of the Portuguese alphabet.
FÃ, *s.2 gen.*, fan, admirer, devotee.
FÁ, *s.m.*, fa, the fourth musical note.
FÁ.BRI.CA, *s.f.*, factory, workshop, mill, plant, industry.
FA.BRI.CA.ÇÃO, *s.f.*, fabrication, manufacture, production.
FA.BRI.CAN.TE, *s.2 gen.*, manufacturer, producer, maker, fabricant.
FA.BRI.CAR, *v.*, to make, to produce, to manufacture, to edify.
FA.BRIL, *adj.*, industrial.
FÁ.BU.LA, *s.f.*, fable, tale, legend.
FA.CA, *s.f.*, knife.
FA.CA.DA, *s.f.*, stab, thrust with a knife.
FA.ÇA.NHA, *s.f.*, achievement, effort, performance, exploit.
FA.CÃO, *s.m.*, large knife.
FAC.ÇÃO, *s.f.*, feat, faction, part, wing, set.
FA.CE, *s.f.*, face, side, look, visage, appearance, surface.
FA.CHA.DA, *s.f.*, front, face, façade.
FÁ.CIL, *adj.*, easy, simple, fluent, ready, flowing, fast.
FA.CI.LI.DA.DE, *s.f.*, facility, easiness, simplicity, readiness, agility.
FA.CI.LI.TAR, *v.*, to facilitate, make easy.
FA.CÍ.NO.RA, *s.m.*, criminal, villain, gangster.
FA.CUL.DA.DE, *s.f.*, faculty, capacity, ability, talent, reach, power.
FA.CUL.TAR, *v.*, to grant, to permit, to facilitate.
FA.CUL.TA.TI.VO, *adj.*, facultative, optional.
FA.DA, *s.f.*, fairy.
FA.DI.GA, *s.f.*, fatigue, tiredness, lassitude.
FA.GU.LHA, *s.f.*, spark, flash.
FAI.NA, *s.f.*, work, labour.
FAI.SÃO, *s.m.*, pheasant.
FA.ÍS.CA, *s.f.*, spark, flashing, gleam, flake, fire.
FA.IS.CAR, *v.*, to spark, to flash, to sparkle, to scintillate, to coruscate.
FAI.XA, *s.f.*, band, banner, strip, range, belt, ribbon, bandage; zone, area.
FA.LA, *s.f.*, speech, talk, conversation, discourse, words, allocution.
FA.LA.DO, *adj.*, talked over, famous.
FA.LA.DOR, *s.m.*, talker, indiscret; *adj.*, talkative, indiscret, communicative.
FA.LAN.GE, *s.f.*, phalanx, phalange, digital bones of the hand or foot.
FA.LAR, *v.*, to speak, to say, to tell, to communicate, to talk, to express.
FAL.CÃO, *s.m.*, falcon, hawk.
FAL.CA.TRU.A, *s.f.*, fraud, imposture.
FA.LE.CER, *v.*, to decease, to die, to expire.
FA.LE.CI.MEN.TO, *s.m.*, death, dying, decease, departure.
FA.LÊN.CIA, *s.f.*, insolvency, bankruptcy, crash, collapse.
FA.LHA, *s.f.*, crack, fissure, rent, error, imperfection, fault.
FA.LHAR, *v.*, to fail, to err, to miss.
FA.LI.DO, *adj.*, broken, bankrupt.
FA.LIR, *v.*, to fail, to break, to be unable to pay.
FAL.SÁ.RIO, *s.m.*, falsifier, forger, perjurer.
FAL.SI.DA.DE, *s.f.*, falseness, falsehood, mendacity, hypocrisy.
FAL.SI.FI.CAR, *v.*, to falsify, to counterfeit, to fake, to forge.
FAL.SO, *adj.*, untrue, false, fraudulent, spurious, fake, wrong, sham, simulate.
FAL.TA, *s.f.*, need, lack, absence, privation, deficiency, failure.
FAL.TAR, *v.*, to miss, to be absent, to fail, to neglect, to omit.
FAL.TO.SO, *adj.*, faulty, delinquent.
FA.MA, *s.f.*, fame, glory, reputation.

FAMÍLIA — FAZER

FA.MÍ.LIA, *s.f.*, family, folk, people, tribe, clan, lineage.
FA.MI.LI.AR, *adj.*, familiar, domestic, familial; known.
FA.MI.LIA.RI.DA.DE, *s.f.*, familiarity, intimacy, frankness.
FA.MI.LIA.RI.ZAR, *v.*, familiarize, to become familiar, to habituate, to vulgarize.
FA.MIN.TO, *adj.*, hungry, starving, famishing, voracious.
FA.MO.SO, *adj.*, famous, renowned, famed, noted.
FA.NÁ.TI.CO, *s.m.*, fanatic, fan, bigot; *adj.*, fanatic, fan, bigoted.
FA.NA.TIS.MO, *s.m.*, fanaticism, bigotry, passion.
FA.NA.TI.ZAR, *v.*, to fanaticize.
FA.NHO.SO, *adj.*, snuffling, nasal.
FAN.TA.SI.A, *s.f.*, fantasy, imagination, fancy, illusion, extravagancy.
FAN.TA.SI.AR, *v.*, to fantasy, to fancy, to daydream.
FAN.TAS.MA, *s.f.*, phantom, ghost, apparition.
FAN.TÁS.TI.CO, *adj.*, fantastic, imaginary, unreal.
FAN.TO.CHE, *s.m.*, puppet, marionette.
FA.QUEI.RO, *s.m.*, knife box.
FA.QUIR, *s.m.*, fakir, fakeer.
FA.RA.Ó, *s.m.*, Pharaoh.
FAR.DA, *s.f.*, uniform, military dress.
FAR.DO, *s.m.*, bundle, pack, package, bale, bunch.
FA.RE.JAR, *v.*, to scent, to smell out, to trace.
FA.RE.LO, *s.m.*, bran, crumb, sawdust, pollard.
FA.RIN.GE, *s.f.*, pharynx.
FA.RI.NHA, *s.f.*, flour, meal, breadstuff, farina; **FARINHA DE AVEIA**, *s.f.*, oatmeal.
FA.RI.SEU, *s.m.*, Pharisee.
FAR.MA.CÊU.TI.CO, *s.m.*, pharmacist, apothecary, druggist.
FAR.MÁ.CIA, *s.f.*, pharmacy, pharmaceutics, drugstore.
FA.ROL, *s.m.*, lighthouse, light, warning light, pharos, seamark.
FAR.PA, *s.f.*, splinter, barb.
FAR.RA, *s.f.*, binge, fun, revelry, bust, bender.
FAR.RA.PO, *s.m.*, rag, ragamuffin, shred, clout, junk.
FAR.SA, *s.f.*, farce, burlesque, satirical composition.
FAR.TO, *adj.*, satiated, full, satisfied, tired, weary.
FAR.TU.RA, *s.f.*, abundance, profusion, wealth, plenty.
FAS.CÍ.CU.LO, *s.m.*, fascicle.
FAS.CI.NA.ÇÃO, *s.f.*, fascination, enchantment, captivation, charm.
FAS.CI.NAR, *v.*, to fascinate, to captivate, to attract, to dazzle.
FAS.CIS.TA, *s.2 gen.*, Fascist.
FA.SE, *s.f.*, phase, stage, period, phasis, aspect, side, angle.
FAS.TI.O, *s.m.*, lack of appetite, disgust, aversion, dislike.
FA.TAL, *adj.*, fatal, fateful, ruinous, deadly.
FA.TA.LI.DA.DE, *s.f.*, fatality, destiny, disaster.
FA.TI.A, *s.f.*, slice, chop, chip, piece, section.
FA.TI.GAR, *v.*, to fatigue, to tire, to bore, to wear out, to exhaust, to flog.
FA.TO, *s.m.*, fact, deed, event, occurence.
FA.TOR, *s.m.*, factor.
FA.TU.RA, *s.f.*, invoice, bill, voucher.
FA.TU.RAR, *v.*, to invoice, to bill.
FAU.NA, *s.f.*, fauna.
FA.VE.LA, *s.f.*, slum, shanty-town.
FA.VO, *s.m.*, honeycomb; sweet.
FA.VOR, *s.m.*, favor, help, benefit, privilege, attention, courtesy, regard, interest.
FA.VO.RÁ.VEL, *adj.*, favourable, suitable, propitious, benefic.
FA.VO.RE.CER, *v.*, to favour, to help, to aid, to support, to patronize.
FA.VO.RI.TIS.MO, *s.m.*, favoritism, preference, nepotism.
FA.VO.RI.TO, *adj.*, favorite, fond, preferred.
FA.XI.NA, *s.f.*, cleaning, fascine.
FA.ZEN.DA, *s.f.*, farm, ranch, estate, property; public finances, treasury; cloth, textile material.
FA.ZEN.DEI.RO, *s.m.*, farmer, landholder.
FA.ZER, *v.*, to make, to do, to build, to produce, to perform, to form, to write.

FÉ, *s.f.*, faith, creed, belief, conviction, persuasion, trust, credit.

FE.BRE, *s.f.*, fever, temperature, pyrexia.

FE.BRIL, *adj.*, febril, feverous, feverish, agitated.

FE.CHA.DO, *adj.*, closed, close, shut, shut in, locked, unopened.

FE.CHA.DU.RA, *s.f.*, lock.

FE.CHAR, *v.*, to close, to shut, to shut up, to lock up, to unite, to finish, to stop, to belt.

FE.CHO, *s.m.*, bolt, latch, clasp, clip, fastener, conclusion, closure.

FE.CUN.DA.ÇÃO, *s.f.*, fecundation, fertilization.

FE.CUN.DAR, *v.*, to fecundate, to fructify, to fertilize, to develop.

FE.CUN.DI.DA.DE, *s.f.*, fecundity, abundance, pregnancy, productivity.

FE.DER, *v.*, to stink, to reek, to smell badly, to bore.

FE.DE.RA.ÇÃO, *s.f.*, federation, union, federacy, confederation, alliance.

FE.DE.RAL, *adj.*, federal, allied.

FE.DE.RA.LIS.MO, *s.m.*, federalism.

FE.DOR, *s.m.* stink, stench.

FE.DO.REN.TO, *adj.*, fetid, stinking, rammy.

FEI.ÇÃO, *s.f.*, feature, aspect, appearance, look, manner, humour.

FEI.JÃO, *s.m.*, bean.

FEI.O, *adj.*, ugly, disagreeable, insightly, haggish.

FEI.RA, *s.f.*, fair, street market.

FEI.TI.ÇA.RI.A, *s.f.*, witchcraft, sorcery, magic, charm.

FEI.TI.CEI.RA, *s.f.*, witch, sorceress.

FEI.TI.CEI.RO, *s.m.*, sorcerer, wizard, enchanter.

FEI.TI.ÇO, *s.m.*, witchcraft, sorcery, enchantment, charm, magic power.

FEI.TI.O, *s.m.*, shape, make, fabric, pattern, manner.

FEI.TO, *s.m.*, fact, deed, act, action; *adj.*, made, done, built, finished, fashioned, ready, prepared.

FEI.TOR, *s.m.*, administrator, manager, foreman.

FEI.U.RA, *s.f.*, ugliness; indignity.

FEI.XE, *s.m.*, sheaf, bundle, faggot, cluster, bunch, handful.

FEL, *s.m.*, bile, gall.

FE.LI.CI.DA.DE, *s.f.*, happiness, bliss, contentment, felicity, luckiness.

FE.LI.CI.TA.ÇÃO, *s.f.*, felicitation, congratulation.

FE.LI.CI.TAR, *v.*, to felicitate, to congratulate, to make happy, to compliment.

FE.LI.NO, *adj.*, feline, felid.

FE.LIZ, *adj.*, happy, lucky, fortunate, blessed, felicitous, fain, sunny, blissful.

FE.LI.ZAR.DO, *adj.*, lucky fellow.

FEL.TRO, *s.m.*, felt.

FÊ.MEA, *s.f.*, female.

FE.MI.NI.LI.DA.DE, *s.f.*, femininity, womanishness, feminineness.

FE.MI.NI.NO, *adj.* female, feminine, womanly, womanlike.

FE.MI.NIS.TA, *s.2 gen.*, feminist.

FÊ.MUR, *s.m.*, femur, thighbone.

FEN.DA, *s.f.*, crack, fissure, chink, chap, gap, cleft.

FE.NÍ.CIO, *adj.*, *s.m.*, Phoenician.

FÊ.NIX, *s.f.*, phoenix.

FE.NO, *s.m.*, hay.

FE.NO.ME.NAL, *adj.*, phenomenal, extraordinary, remarkable, wonderful.

FE.NÔ.ME.NO, *s.m.*, phenomenon.

FE.RA, *s.f.*, wild animal, wild beast.

FÉ.RE.TRO, *s.m.*, funeral, funeral procession, grave, coffin.

FÉ.RIA, *s.f.*, weekday; salary, rest, recreation, repose; **FÉRIAS**, holidays, vacations.

FE.RI.A.DO, *s.m.*, holiday, feast day, vacation.

FE.RI.DA, *s.f.*, wound, sore, trauma, hurt.

FE.RI.MEN.TO, *s.m.*, wound, trauma, injury.

FE.RIR, *v.*, to wound, to hurt, to injure, to bruise, to beat.

FER.MEN.TA.ÇÃO, *s.f.*, fermentation, leavening, working.

FER.MEN.TAR, *v.*, to leaven, to ferment, to yeast.

FER.MEN.TO, *s.m.*, ferment, leaven, yeast.

FE.RO.CI.DA.DE, *s.f.*, ferocity, ferociousness.

FE.ROZ, *adj.*, ferocious, wild, savage, fierce.

FER.RA.GEM, *s.f.*, hardware, iron tools.

FER.RA.MEN.TA, *s.f.*, tool, instrument, utensil, implement.
FER.RÃO, *s.m.*, sting, prickle, ferret.
FER.RA.RI.A, *s.f.*, ironworks, iron mill.
FER.REI.RO, *s.m.*, smith, blacksmith, forger.
FÉR.REO, *adj.*, ferrous, iron, ferric.
FER.RO, *s.m.*, iron; cutting blade; tool, implement; **FERROS**, chains, jail; **FERRO DE PASSAR**, pressing iron.
FER.RO.AR, *v.*, to sting, to prickle.
FER.RO.LHO, *s.m.*, bolt, push bolt, door bolt, latch.
FER.RO.VI.A, *s.f.*, railway, railroad.
FER.RO.VI.Á.RIO, *s.m.*, railway man, railroader.
FER.RU.GEM, *s.m.*, rust, rustiness, ferric oxyde.
FÉR.TIL, *adj.*, fertile, fruitful, fructuous, fecund.
FER.TI.LI.DA.DE, *s.f.*, fertility, fruitfulness, prolificacy.
FER.TI.LI.ZA.ÇÃO, *s.f.*, fertilization.
FER.TI.LI.ZAN.TE, *s.m.*, fertilizer, manure.
FER.TI.LI.ZAR, *v.*, to fertilize, to fecundate, to impregnate, to fructify.
FER.VER, *v.*, to boil, to cook, to seethe.
FER.VOR, *s.m.*, boiling, seething, ebulition, heat, hotness.
FES.TA, *s.f.*, party, feast, feasting, entertainment; **BOAS FESTAS** – Merry Christmas.
FES.TAN.ÇA, *s.f.*, big party, revelry, celebration.
FES.TE.JAR, *v.*, to feast, to celebrate, to entertain, to commemorate.
FES.TE.JO, *s.m.*, feast, festivity, celebration, frolic, entertainment.
FES.TI.VAL, *s.m.*, festival.
FES.TI.VI.DA.DE, *s.f.*, festivity, celebration, feast.
FES.TI.VO, *adj.*, festive, joyful, cheerful.
FE.TO, *s.m.*, fetus.
FEU.DAL, *adj.*, *s.m.*, feudal, feudalistic.
FEU.DA.LIS.MO, *s.m.*, feudalism.
FE.VE.REI.RO, *s.m.*, February.
FE.ZES, *s.f.*, *pl.*, feces, excrement.
FI.A.ÇÃO, *s.f.*, spinning, spinnery.
FI.A.DO, *s.m.*, trusting, trustful; varn, filament; *adj.*, on credit, trusting; spun.
FI.A.DOR, *s.m.*, warrantor, truster, guarantor.
FI.AN.ÇA, *s.f.*, security, bail, pledge, warrant, deposit, responsibility.
FI.AR, *v.*, to spin, to weave, to guarantee, to give security.
FI.AS.CO, *s.m.*, fiasco, failure, washout, fizzle, frost.
FI.BRA, *s.f.*, fibre, fiber, filament, nerve, energy, strength.
FI.CAR, *v.*, to remain, to stay, to stand, to tarry, to rest, to sojourn.
FIC.ÇÃO, *s.f.*, fiction, invention, legend, romance.
FI.CHA, *s.f.*, card, counter, check, chip.
FI.CHAR, *v.*, to register, to annotate, to mark, to note down, to record, to card.
FI.CHÁ.RIO, *s.m.*, card index, card registry, file.
FIC.TÍ.CIO, *adj.*, fictitious, imaginary, unreal, fabulous.
FI.DE.LI.DA.DE, *s.f.*, fidelity, fealty, faithfulness, loyalty, integrity.
FI.EL, *s.m.*, follower, *pl.* (rel.) churchgoers; *adj.*, faithful, loyal, true, trusty.
FÍ.GA.DO, *s.m.*, liver.
FI.GO, *s.m.*, fig.
FI.GUEI.RA, *s.f.*, fig tree.
FI.GU.RA, *s.f.*, figure, form.
FI.GU.RI.NO, *s.m.*, model, fashion plate.
FI.LA, *s.f.*, file, line, row, queue, rank, tier.
FI.LA.MEN.TO, *s.m.*, filament, fibre, string.
FI.LAN.TRO.PI.A, *s.f.*, philanthropy, goodwill.
FI.LAN.TRÓ.PI.CO, *adj.*, philanthropic.
FI.LAN.TRO.PO, *s.m.*, philanthropist.
FI.LÉ, *s.m.*, filet, steak.
FI.LEI.RA, *s.f.*, row, rank, tier, range, line, string.
FI.LHA, *s.f.*, daughter.
FI.LHO, *s.m.*, son, descendant; offspring; **FILHOS** – children.
FI.LHO.TE, *s.m.*, nestling, native, descendant.
FI.LI.A.ÇÃO, *s.f.*, affiliation, filiation, descent, adoption.
FI.LI.AL, *s.f.*, branch, branch office or establishment.
FI.LI.AR, *v.*, to adopt, to affiliate, to branch out.

FILIGRANA — FLIPERAMA

FI.LI.GRA.NA, *s.f.*, filigrane.
FIL.MA.GEM, *s.f.*, filming, motion picture shot.
FIL.MAR, *v.*, to film, to shoot.
FIL.ME, *s.m.*, film, movie, motion picture.
FI.LO.LO.GI.A, *s.f.*, philology.
FI.LO.SO.FI.A, *s.f.*, philosophy.
FI.LÓ.SO.FO, *s.m.*, philosopher.
FIL.TRA.ÇÃO, *s.f.*, filtration.
FIL.TRAR, *v.*, to filter, to filtrate, to percolate.
FIL.TRO, *s.m.*, filter, strainer, percolator.
FIM, *s.m.*, end, conclusion, termination, ending, expiration, closure.
FI.NA.DO, *s.m.*, deceased, dead, defunct; *adj.*, dead, defunct.
FI.NAL, *s.m.*, conclusion, end, finish, terminal; *adj.*, last, terminal, terminative.
FI.NA.LI.DA.DE, *s.f.*, purpose, end, goal, finality, effect.
FI.NA.LI.ZAR, *v.*, to finish, to terminate, to conclude, to accomplish.
FI.NAN.ÇAS, *s.f.*, pl. finances, funds capital.
FI.NAN.CEI.RO, *adj.*, financial.
FI.NAN.CIA.MEN.TO, *s.m.*, financing.
FI.NAN.CI.AR, *v.*, to finance, to provide capital for, to support.
FIN.DAR, *v.*, to finish, to conclude, to complete, to terminate.
FI.NE.ZA, *s.f.*, slimness, thinness, gracefulness, perfection, delicacy.
FIN.GI.DO, *adj.*, insincere, false, feigned.
FIN.GI.MEN.TO, *s.m.*, simulation, hypocrisy, dissimulation.
FIN.GIR, *v.*, to pretend, to simulate, to dissimulate, to feign.
FIN.LAN.DÊS, *adj.*, *s.m*, Finn, Finnish.
FI.NO, *adj.*, thin, slim, slender, thread, string; delicate, gentle, pure.
FI.O, *s.m.*, thread, twine, yarn; file, row, line, string.
FIR.MA, *s.f.*, firm, business; signature, seal.
FIR.MA.MEN.TO, *s.m.*, sky, heaven, firmament.
FIR.MAR, *v.*, to firm, to fix, to set, to secure.
FIR.ME, *adj.*, firm, fixed, strong, rigid, stable.
FIR.ME.ZA, *s.f.*, firmness, steadiness, fortitude, fixedness.
FIS.CA.LI.ZA.ÇÃO, *s.f.*, fiscalization, control, inspection.
FIS.CA.LI.ZAR, *v.*, to fiscalize, to subject to fiscal control, to inspect, to examine.
FIS.CO, *s.m.*, public revenue, public treasury.
FIS.GAR, *v.*, to hook, to catch, to gaff.
FÍ.SI.CA, *s.f.*, physics.
FÍ.SI.CO, *s.m.*, constitution, build, physique, physicist; *adj.*, physical, material, personal, corporeal.
FI.SIO.LO.GI.A, *s.f.*, physiology.
FI.SIO.NO.MI.A, *s.f.*, physio(g)nomy, face, semblance, look, brow, aspect.
FI.SIO.TE.RA.PI.A, *s.f.*, physiotherapy.
FIS.SÃO, *s.f.*, fission.
FIS.SU.RA, *s.f.*, chink, split, crack, rime, fissure.
FI.TA, *s.f.*, ribbon, band, string, snood, ferret; tape.
FI.TAR, *v.*, to stare, to gaze, to eye, to envisage.
FI.VE.LA, *s.f.*, buckle, clasp, loop.
FI.XAR, *v.*, to fasten, to attach, to fix, to firm, affix, to steady.
FI.XO, *adj.*, fixed, firm, stable, steady, durable.
FLA.GE.LA.DO, *s.m.*, flagellate; *adj.*, flagellate, tortured.
FLA.GE.LAR, *v.*, to flagellate.
FLA.GE.LO, *s.m.*, scourge, whip, punishment, calamity, plague.
FLA.GRAN.TE, *s.m.*, moment, instant, chance; *adj.*, flagrant, ardent, pressing, urgent.
FLA.ME.JAR, *v.*, to flame, to blaze, to burn, to glow.
FLAN.CO, *s.m.*, flank, side.
FLAU.TA, *s.f.*, pipe, flute.
FLE.CHA, *s.f.*, arrow, spire, dart, shaft, bolt.
FLER.TAR, *v.*, to flirt.
FLER.TE, *s.m.*, flirt, flirtation.
FLEU.MA, *s.f.*, phlegm, apathy, indifference.
FLE.XI.BI.LI.DA.DE, *s.f.*, flexibility, flexibleness, pliancy.
FLE.XIO.NAR, *v.*, to inflect, to bend, to deflect.
FLE.XÍ.VEL, *adj.*, flexible, versatile, deflective.
FLI.PE.RA.MA, *s.m.*, pinball machine.

FLOR, *s.f.*, flower, bloom, blossom.
FLO.RA, *s.f.*, Flora, the goddess of flowers; flora, botany.
FLO.RA.ÇÃO, *s.f.*, blooming.
FLO.RAR, *v.*, to flower, to bloom, to flourish.
FLO.REI.RA, *s.f.*, flowerpot, flower vase.
FLO.REN.TI.NO, *adj.*, *s.m.*, Florentine.
FLO.RES.CER, *v.*, to blossom, to bud, to flower, to florish, to grow.
FLO.RES.TA, *s.f.*, forest, wood, wildwood.
FLO.RI.CUL.TU.RA, *s.f.*, floriculture.
FLO.RIR, *v.*, to flower, to blossom; to grow.
FLO.RIS.TA, *s.2 gen.*, florist, flower seller; flower girl.
FLU.ÊN.CIA, *s.f.*, fluency, flux, flow.
FLU.EN.TE, *adj.*, fluent, flowing, fluid, liquid, easy.
FLUI.DEZ, *s.f.*, fluidity, fluidness, fluency.
FLUI.DO, *s.m.*, fluid, liquid, gas; *adj.*, fluid, fluent.
FLU.IR, *v.*, to flow, to run, to stream, to emanate.
FLU.TU.A.ÇÃO, *s.f.*, flotation, fluctuation, surging.
FLU.TU.AR, *v.*, to float, to wave, to drift, to fluctuate, to roll.
FLU.VI.AL, *adj.*, fluvial, fluviatic.
FLU.XO, *s.m.*, flow, stream, flood, flux.
FLU.XO.GRA.MA, *s.m.*, flow-chart.
FO.CA, *s.f.*, seal, phoca.
FO.CA.LI.ZAR, *v.*, to focalize, to focus.
FO.CAR, *v.*, to focus, to focalize.
FO.CI.NHO, *s.m.*, muzzle, snout, mouth, trunk.
FO.CO, *s.m.*, focus, focal point.
FO.FO, *adj.*, light, soft, smooth, mild, gentle.
FO.FO.CA, *s.f.*, gossip.
FO.FO.QUEI.RO, *s.m.*, gossiper.
FO.GÃO, *s.m.*, stove, hearth, cooker.
FO.GA.REI.RO, *s.m.*, burner, cooker, little stove.
FO.GO, *s.m.*, fire, blaze, energy, vigor, flame, conflagration; home.
FO.GUEI.RA, *s.f.*, bonfire, fire, pyre.
FO.GUE.TE, *s.m.*, rocket; admonition.
FOI.CE, *s.f.*, scythe, sickle, hedgebill.
FOL.CLO.RE, *s.m.*, folklore.
FOL.CLÓ.RI.CO, *adj.*, folkloric.
FÔ.LE.GO, *s.m.*, breath, wind, respiration, rest, relaxation.
FOL.GA, *s.f.*, pause, leisure, rest, repose, slackness.
FOL.GA.DO, *adj.*, loose, idle, lazy, broad, ample, baggy.
FO.LHA, *s.f.*, leaf, list, sheet, report, journal, paper, newspaper.
FO.LHA.GEM, *s.f.*, foliage.
FO.LHE.A.DO, *adj.*, foliaged, foliate, foliaceous.
FO.LHE.AR, *v.*, to leaf, to turn over the pages of a book.
FO.LHE.TO, *s.m.*, pamphlet, leaflet, prospectus, brochure.
FO.LHI.NHA, *s.f.*, calendar.
FO.ME, *s.f.*, hunger, famine, hungriness, scarcity.
FO.MEN.TA.DOR, *s.m.*, fomenter.
FO.MEN.TAR, *v.*, to foment, to promote, to develop.
FO.MEN.TO, *s.m.*, fomentation, incitement.
FO.NE, *s.m.*, phone, receiver, telephone.
FO.NÉ.TI.CA, *s.f.*, phonetics.
FO:NÉ.TI.CO, *adj.*, phonetic.
FO.NÔ.ME.TRO, *s.m.*, phonometer.
FON.TE, *s.f.*, fountain, font, origin, source, headspring.
FO.RA, *s.m.*, rejection, elimination; *adv.*, out, outside, outdoors, outlying, beyond, abroad, off, away; *prep.*, except.
FO.RA.GI.DO, *s.m.*, fugitive, refugee, absconder, outlaw; *adj.*, fugitive, flighty, erratic.
FO.RAS.TEI.RO, *s.m.*, foreigner, stranger, outlander; *adj.*, foreign, strange.
FOR.CA, *s.f.*, gallows, gibbet, scaffold.
FOR.ÇA, *s.f.*, force, strength, power, energy, vigour; fibre.
FOR.ÇA.DO, *adj.*, compelled, obliged, compulsory.
FOR.ÇAR, *v.*, to force, to oblige, to impel, to compel, to constrain.
FO.REN.SE, *adj.*, forensic, judicial, judiciary.
FOR.JA, *s.f.*, forge, smithy, foundry.
FOR.MA, *s.f.*, form, shape, configuration,

FORMAÇÃO / **FRAMBOESA**

structure, appearance, build; mould, last.
FOR.MA.ÇÃO, *s.f.*, formation, forming, development, origin, forming, arrangement.
FOR.MA.LI.DA.DE, *s.f.*, formality, ceremony, etiquette, conventionalism.
FOR.MA.LIS.MO, *s.m.*, formalism, pedantry.
FOR.MA.LI.ZAR, *v.*, to formalize.
FOR.MÃO, *s.m.*, chisel, former.
FOR.MAR, *v.*, to form, to shape, to model, to instruct, to produce, to establish.
FOR.MA.TAR, *v.*, to format.
FOR.MA.TO, *s.m.*, format, shape, size.
FOR.MA.TU.RA, *s.f.*, formation, development, arrangement, graduation.
FOR.MI.GA, *s.f.*, ant, pismire.
FOR.MI.GUEI.RO, *s.m.*, anthill, ants'nest.
FOR.MOL, *s.m.*, formaldehyde.
FOR.MO.SO, *adj.*, beautiful, handsome, pretty, fair, comely.
FOR.MO.SU.RA, *s.f.*, beauty, handsomeness, prettiness.
FÓR.MU.LA, *s.f.*, formula, form.
FOR.MU.LAR, *v.*, to formulate, to prescribe, to formul, to enounce.
FOR.MU.LÁ.RIO, *s.m.*, formulary, collection, form.
FOR.NE.CE.DOR, *s.m.*, furnisher, supplier, contractor, provisioner.
FOR.NE.CER, *v.*, to furnish, to supply, to provide, to purvey, to stock.
FOR.NI.CAR, *v.*, to fornicate, to afflict, to vex.
FOR.NO, *s.m.*, oven, hearth, stove, kiln.
FO.RO, *s.m.*, forum.
FOR.RA.ÇÃO, *s.f.*, furring.
FOR.RA.GEM, *s.f.*, feed, forage, silage.
FOR.RAR, *v.*, to cover with, to face, to line, to case.
FOR.RO, *s.m.*, covering, doubling, lining, padding, ceiling.
FOR.TA.LE.CER, *v.*, to fortify, to invigorate, to strengthen.
FOR.TA.LE.ZA, *s.f.*, fortress, fort, fortification.
FOR.TE, *s.m.*, fort, fortification, fortress; *adj.*, strong, vigorous, robust, valiant.
FOR.TI.FI.CAR, *v.*, to fortify, to make strong, to encourage.
FOR.TU.NA, *s.f.*, fortune, good luck, destiny, prosperity, success.
FOS.FA.TO, *s.m.*, phosphate.
FÓS.FO.RO, *s.m.*, phosphorus, match.
FOS.SA, *s.f.*, cesspool, cesspit, sinkhole, gully.
FÓS.SIL, *s.m.*, fossil.
FO.TO, *s.f.*, photo.
FO.TO.CÓ.PIA, *s.f.*, photocopy.
FO.TO.GRA.FAR, *v.*, to photograph, to shoot.
FO.TO.GRA.FI.A, *s.f.*, photography, snapshot, photo.
FO.TÓ.GRA.FO, *s.m.*, photographer.
FO.TÔ.ME.TRO, *s.m.*, photometer.
FO.TOS.FE.RA, *s.f.*, photosphere.
FO.TOS.SÍN.TE.SE, *s.f.*, photosynthesis.
FOZ, *s.f.*, estuary, mouth of a river, outfall.
FRA.ÇÃO, *s.f.*, fraction, quantum; rupture, part, fragment.
FRA.CAS.SAR, *v.*, to fail, to break, to shatter, to miscarry.
FRA.CAS.SO, *s.m.*, crash, smash, failure, ruin, disaster.
FRA.CIO.NAR, *v.*, to shatter, to fragment, to divide, to split.
FRA.CO, *adj.*, feeble, weak, faint, fragile, debile, slim, slender.
FRA.DE, *s.m.*, friar, monk.
FRÁ.GIL, *adj.*, fragile, weak, frail, feeble, transitory.
FRA.GI.LI.DA.DE, *s.f.*, fragility, weakness, delicateness.
FRAG.MEN.TA.DO, *adj.*, fragmented.
FRAG.MEN.TAR, *v.*, to fragment, to break up, to shatter, to split.
FRAG.MEN.TO, *s.m.*, fragment, fraction, scrap, piece, part, portion.
FRA.GOR, *s.m.*, crash, loud repport.
FRA.GRÂN.CIA, *s.f.*, fragrance, flavor, perfume, pleasant scent.
FRA.GRA.NTE, *adj.*, fragrant, odoriferous, odorous, balmy.
FRAL.DA, *s.f.*, diaper, nappy, lap, flap, brim.
FRAM.BO.E.SA, *s.f.*, raspberry (fruit).

FRANCÊS — FRUTIFICAR

FRAN.CÊS, *adj., s.m.*, French, Frenchman, Gaul.

FRAN.CIS.CA.NO, *adj., s.m.*, Franciscan; friar of the Franciscan order.

FRAN.CO, *s.m.*, franc; monetary unit in France, Belgium and Switzerland; *adj.*, frank, candid, outspoken.

FRAN.GO, *s.m.*, chicken, young cock.

FRAN.JA, *s.f.*, fringe, edging.

FRAN.QUE.AR, *v.*, to free, to exempt, to facilitate, to clear; to frank (from taxes or duties).

FRAN.QUE.ZA, *s.f.*, frankness, candour, sincerity, liberality.

FRAN.QUI.A, *s.f.*, postage, postage stamp, franchise, exemption, privilege.

FRA.QUE.JAR, *v.*, to weaken, to lose courage, to succumb.

FRA.QUE.ZA, *s.f.*, weakness, debility, powerlessness.

FRAS.CO, *s.m.*, flask, bottle, flagon.

FRA.SE, *s.f.*, phrase, sentence, proposition, expression.

FRAS.QUEI.RA, *s.f.*, bottle rack, cellaret.

FRA.TER.NAL, *adj.*, fraternal, brotherlike, brotherly.

FRA.TER.NI.DA.DE, *s.f.*, fraternity, brotherhood.

FRA.TER.NO, *adj.*, fraternal, brotherly.

FRA.TU.RAR, *v.*, to fracture, to break.

FRAU.DAR, *v.*, to defraud.

FRAU.DE, *s.f.*, swindle, fraud, hoax.

FRE.AR, *v.*, to brake, to repress, to refrain, to control.

FRE.GUÊS, *s.m.*, customer, client, patron.

FRE.GUE.SI.A, *s.f.*, community, customers, parish, clientele.

FREI, *s.m.*, friar, monk.

FREI.O, *s.m.*, bridle, bit, brake, rein, repression.

FREI.RA, *s.f.*, nun, sister, religious.

FRE.NE.SI, *s.m.*, frenzy, madness.

FREN.TE, *s.f.*, front, forefront, façade, face, head, front side, frontage.

FRE.QUÊN.CIA, *s.f.*, frequency, periodicity, concourse.

FRE.QUEN.TAR, *v.*, to frequent, to attend, to visit.

FRES.CO, *adj.*, fresh, new, recent, vigorous, green.

FRES.TA, *s.f.*, slit, opening, gap, aperture.

FRE.TAR, *v.*, to charter, to freight, to rent.

FRE.TE, *s.m.*, freight, freightage, carriage, portage.

FRI.A.GEM, *s.f.*, cold(ness), chill(ness).

FRIC.ÇÃO, *s.f.*, friction, attrition, rub, fret.

FRIC.CIO.NAR, *v.*, to rub, to grit.

FRI.GI.DEI.RA, *s.f.*, frying pan.

FRI.GIR, *v.*, to fry, to cook in hot fat.

FRI.GO.RÍ.FI.CO, *s.m.*, freezer, refrigerator; *adj.*, frigorific, frigorifical.

FRI.O, *s.m.*, cold, coldness, iciness, frost, low temperature; indifference; *adj.*, cold, icy, frosty, algid; indifferent.

FRI.SAR, *v.*, to nap, to curl, to emphasize.

FRI.SO, *s.m.*, frieze.

FRI.TAR, *v.*, to fry, to roast.

FRI.TO, *adj.*, fried.

FRI.TU.RA, *s.f.*, fried food.

FRI.VO.LI.DA.DE, *s.f.*, frivolousness, futility, frivolity, emptiness, lightness.

FRÍ.VO.LO, *adj.*, frivolous, wanton, trivial, futil, light.

FRO.NHA, *s.f.*, pillowcase, pillow.

FRON.TE, *s.f.*, forehead, head, brow.

FRON.TEI.RA, *s.f.*, frontier, border, bound, boundary, limit, mark.

FRON.TEI.RO, *adj.*, frontier, bordering, facing, opposite.

FRO.TA, *s.f.*, fleet, navy, shipping.

FROU.XO, *adj.*, weak, feeble, slack, sluggish, lax.

FRU.GAL, *adj.*, frugal, sparing, moderate.

FRU.GA.LI.DA.DE, *s.f.*, frugality, frugalness, parsimony, economy.

FRUS.TRA.ÇÃO, *s.f.*, frustration, failure, defeat.

FRUS.TRAR, *v.*, to frustrate, to foil, to balk, to baffle, to defeat; to disappoint.

FRU.TA, *s.f.*, fruit, fruitage.

FRU.TEI.RA, *s.f.*, fruit bowl or plate.

FRU.TÍ.FE.RO, *adj.*, fruitful, fructiferous, fecund, fertile.

FRU.TI.FI.CAR, *v.*, to fructify.

FRU.TO, *s.m.*, fruit, fruitage, offspring; produce, result, profit, gain.
FU.BÁ, *s.m.*, flour, maize, corn meal.
FU.GA, *s.f.*, escape, flight, escapement, run, runaway.
FU.GAZ, *adj.*, transitory, rapid, fugacious, fugitive.
FU.GIR, *v.*, to flee, to run away, to escape, to run.
FU.GI.TI.VO, *s.m.*, fugitive, exile, deserter, runaway; *adj.*, fugitive, flying, fleeing.
FU.LA.NO, *s.m.*, (Mr.) So-and-so.
FUL.GOR, *s.m.*, fulgency, effulgence, fulgor.
FU.LI.GEM, *s.f.*, soot, smoke-black.
FUL.MI.NAN.TE, *adj.*, fulminant, sudden, detonating, fulminating, lethal.
FUL.MI.NAR, *v.*, to fulminate, to lighten, to strike, to kill instantaneously.
FU.LO, *adj.*, irritated, furious.
FU.MA.ÇA, *s.f.*, smoke, fume, vapour, steam, reek.
FU.MA.CEI.RA, *s.f.*, dense smoke.
FU.MAN.TE, *s.2 gen.*, smoker; *adj.*, smoking, smoky.
FU.MAR, *v.*, to smoke.
FU.MI.CUL.TOR, *s.m.*, tobacco planter.
FU.MO, *s.m.*, tobacco; smoke, fume, vapour.
FUN.ÇÃO, *s.f.*, function, activity, operation, action, duty, occupation, performance.
FUN.CHO, *s.m.*, fennel.
FUN.CIO.NA.LIS.MO, *s.m.*, functionalism, public functionaries, officialism.
FUN.CIO.NA.MEN.TO, *s.m.*, functioning, action, acting.
FUN.CIO.NAR, *v.*, to function, to work, to perform, to officiate.
FUN.CIO.NÁ.RIO, *s.m.*, employee, official, public functionary.
FUN.DA.ÇÃO, *s.f.*, foundation.
FUN.DA.DOR, *s.m.*, founder.
FUN.DA.MEN.TAL, *adj.*, fundamental, basic.
FUN.DA.MEN.TAR, *v.*, to found, to ground, to base, to establish, to evidence.
FUN.DA.MEN.TO, *s.m.*, basis, foundation, origin, motive, cause.

FUN.DAR, *v.*, to found, to establish, to build, to originate.
FUN.DI.ÇÃO, *s.f.*, foundry, smeltry, forge, melt.
FUN.DI.DOR, *s.m.*, founder, moulder.
FUN.DIR, *v.*, to found, to cast, to fuse, to melt, to liquefy, to unite.
FUN.DO, *s.m.*, bottom, remotest, profoundest, floor, depth, depress; *adj.*, deep, fordless, hollowed.
FUN.DU.RA, *s.f.*, profundity, depth, deepness.
FÚ.NE.BRE, *adj.*, funeral, mortuary, macabre.
FU.NE.RAL, *s.m.*, funeral, obsequies; *adj.*, funeral.
FU.NE.RÁ.RIO, *adj.*, funerary, funereal.
FU.NES.TO, *adj.*, funest, fatal, sinister, disastrous, unlucky.
FUN.GI.CI.DA, *s.f.*, fungicide.
FUN.GO, *s.m.*, fungus, fungal.
FU.NIL, *s.m.*, funnel, filler.
FU.RA.CÃO, *s.m.*, hurricane, ciclone, tornado, whirlwind.
FU.RA.DEI.RA, *s.f.*, drill, drilling machine.
FU.RA.DOR, *s.m.*, awl, bradawl, perforator, bodkin.
FU.RAR, *v.*, to bore, to pierce, to drill, to perforate, to hole, to puncture.
FUR.GÃO, *s.m.*, delivery van.
FÚ.RIA, *s.f.*, fury, furiosity, furiousness, rage, extreme rage, rave.
FU.RI.O.SO, *adj.*, furious, mad, ragefull.
FUR.NA, *s.f.*, cavern, grotto, hole, den.
FU.RO, *s.m.*, hole, bore, boring, perforation, puncture, orifice.
FU.ROR, *s.m.*, furor, fury, rage, passion, tantrum, madness.
FUR.TAR, *v.*, to steal, to thieve, to rob, to pick.
FUR.TI.VO, *adj.*, stealthy, secret, clandestine.
FUR.TO, *s.m.*, theft, stealing, thievery, robbery.
FU.RÚN.CU.LO, *s.m.*, furuncle, boil.
FU.SÃO, *s.f.*, fusion, melting, blend, amalgam, union.
FU.SÍ.VEL, *s.m.*, fuse; *adj.*, fusile, fusible.
FU.SO, *s.m.*, spindle, spool, screw.
FU.TE.BOL, *s.m.*, football, soccer.
FÚ.TIL, *adj.*, futile, heedless, careless.

FU.TI.LI.DA.DE, *s.f.*, futility, triviality, frivolousness.
FU.TU.RO, *s.m.*, future, destiny, fate; *adj.*, future, coming.
FU.XI.CAR, *v.*, to intrigue, to wrinkle, to gossip.
FU.XI.CO, *s.m.*, intrigue, plot.
FU.XI.QUEI.RO, *s.m.*, intriguer, intrigant.
FU.ZIL, *s.m.*, rifle.
FU.ZI.LAR, *v.*, to shoot, to fusillade.
FU.ZI.LEI.RO, *s.m.*, fusileer, rifleman.
FU.ZU.Ê, *s.m.*, noise, clamour, confusion.

G

G, *s.m.*, the seventh letter of the Portuguese alphabet.

GA.BAR, *v.*, to praise, to laud, to eulogize, to flatter.

GA.BA.RI.TO, *s.m.*, mould, form, model, pattern, gauge.

GA.BI.NE.TE, *s.m.*, cabinet, study, closet, office, chamber, room.

GA.BO.LI.CE, *s.f.*, bragging, boast.

GA.DO, *s.m.*, cattle, stock, livestock, herd, drove.

GA.FA.NHO.TO, *s.m.*, grasshopper, locust.

GA.FE, *s.f.*, involuntary indiscretion.

GA.GÁ, *s.2 gen.*, decrepit, senile, enfeebled.

GA.GO, *s.m.*, stutterer, stammerer; *adj.*, stammering, stuttering.

GA.GUE.JAR, *v.*, to stammer, to stutter.

GAI.O.LA, *s.f.*, cage, bird-cage, prison, coop.

GAI.TA, *s.f.*, shepherd's pipe or flute, reed; **GAITA DE FOLE**, bagpipe.

GAI.VO.TA, *s.f.*, gull, sea-gull, pewit-gull.

GA.LÃ, *s.m.*, leading gentleman; lover.

GA.LAN.TEI.O, *s.m.*, gallantry, courtesy, politeness.

GA.LÃO, *s.m.*, galloon, strap; stripe.

GA.LÁ.XIA, *s.f.*, galaxy.

GA.LE.RI.A, *s.f.*, gallery, art gallery, passage.

GA.LÊS, *adj., s.m.*, Welsh.

GAL.GAR, *v.*, to speed along, to climb, to pass over, to ascend, to pass beyond.

GA.LHO, *s.m.*, branch of tree, limb, arm, twig, offshoot.

GA.LI.NHA, *s.f.*, hen, chicken, fowl, biddy.

GA.LI.NHEI.RO, *s.m.*, poultry yard, poulterer, henhouse.

GA.LO, *s.m.*, cock, rooster, chanticleer.

GA.LO.PAR, *v.*, to gallop, to run by leaps.

GA.LO.PE, *s.m.*, gallop.

GAL.PÃO, *s.m.*, hangar, shed, haven, coach house.

GAL.VA.NI.ZA.ÇÃO, *s.f.*, galvanization, plating.

GAL.VA.NI.ZAR, *v.*, to galvanize, to coat with metal, to zinc.

GA.MA, *s.f.*, gamma (third letter of the Greek alphabet), scale, series of theories.

GAM.BÁ, *s.m.*, opossum.

GA.ME.LA, *s.f.*, wooden trough, tray.

GA.MO, *s.m.*, fallow deer, deer, buck, stag.

GA.NA, *s.f.*, hunger, appetite, desire, will, ill will, spite.

GA.NÂN.CIA, *s.f.*, greed, greediness, rapacity, gain, profit.

GA.NAN.CI.O.SO, *adj.*, greedy, avaricious, profitable.

GAN.CHO, *s.m.*, hook, grapple, crook, cramp.

GAN.GOR.RA, *s.f.*, seesaw, teeter, snare.

GAN.GRE.NA, *s.f.*, gangrene, necrosis.

GAN.GRE.NAR, *v.*, to gangrene, to canker, to pervert, to corrupt.

GA.NHAR, *v.*, to acquire, to earn, to get, to obtain, to receive, to procure, to gain.

GA.NHO, *s.m.*, gain, profit, acquisition, advantage, lucre.

GA.NIR, *v.*, to bark, to yelp, to yap.

GAN.SO, *s.m.*, goose, gander.

GA.RA.GEM, *s.f.*, garage.

GA.RA.GIS.TA, *s.2 gen.*, garage man.

GA.RAN.TI.A, *s.f.*, guarantee, guaranty, warranty, bail, pawn, responsibility.

GA.RAN.TIR, *v.*, to guarantee, to warrant, to pledge, to secure.

GAR.BO, *s.m.*, elegance, garb, dress, gracefulness.

GAR.ÇA, *s.f.*, heron.

GAR.ÇOM, *s.m.*, waiter, potman.

GAR.ÇO.NE.TE, *s.f.*, waitress, barmaid.

GAR.FO, *s.m.*, fork, pitchfork.

GAR.GA.LHA.DA, *s.f.*, laughter.

GARGANTA / GEÓLOGO

GAR.GAN.TA, *s.f.*, throat; larynx, weasand; abyss, gulf.
GAR.GA.RE.JO, *s.m.*, gargling, gargle.
GA.RI, *s.2 gen.*, sweeper, street cleaner.
GA.RIM.PEI.RO, *s.m.*, diamond or gold seeker, prospector.
GA.RO.A, *s.f.*, drizzle, mizzle.
GA.RO.AR, *v.*, to drizzle, to mizzle.
GA.RO.TA, *s.f.*, girl, baby, lass.
GA.RO.TO, *s.m.*, boy, lad, kid.
GAR.RA, *s.f.*, claw, courage, talon, pounce.
GAR.RA.FA, *s.f.*, bottle, flask, carboy.
GAR.RA.FÃO, *s.m.*, large bottle, demijohn.
GÁS, *s.m.*, gas, vapour, fume; animation.
GA.SEI.FI.CAR, *v.*, to gasify.
GA.SO.LI.NA, *s.f.*, petrol, gas.
GA.SO.SA, *s.f.*, soda, soda water, fizz.
GA.SO.SO, *adj.*, gaseous, gassy, aeriform.
GAS.TAR, *v.*, to consume, to use up, to spend, to diminish, to deteriorate, to defray, to disburse.
GAS.TO, *s.m.*, expense, disbursement, expenditure, outlay, cost, waste.
GÁS.TRI.CO, *adj.*, gastric.
GAS.TRI.TE, *s.f.*, gastritis, gastric fever.
GAS.TRO.NO.MI.A, *s.f.*, gastronomy.
GA.TA, *s.f.*, cat; beautiful girl.
GA.TI.NHA, *s.f.*, kitten, pussy.
GA.TI.NHO, *s.m.*, pussycat, kitty, cattling.
GA.TO, *s.m.*, cat, tom-cat, miauler.
GA.TU.NO, *s.m.*, thief, stealer, robber, sharper.
GA.TU.RA.MO, *s.m.*, tanager.
GA.VE.TA, *s.f.*, drawer, locker.
GA.VI.ÃO, *s.m.*, hawk, sparrow-hawk.
GA.ZE, *s.f.*, gauze, tissue.
GA.ZE.TA, *s.f.*, gazette, journal, newspaper.
GE.A.DA, *s.f.*, frost, hoar, hoar-frost.
GE.AR, *v.*, to frost, to chill, to freeze, to rime.
GE.LA.DEI.RA, *s.f.*, refrigerator, freezer, cooler, ice-box.
GE.LA.DO, *s.m.*, sherbet, ice-cream; *adj.*, icy, frozen, frosty.
GE.LAR, *v.*, to freeze, to chill, to ice, to congeal.
GE.LA.TI.NA, *s.f.*, gelatin, jelly.
GE.LEI.A, *s.f.*, fruit-jelly, marmalade.
GE.LEI.RA, *s.f.*, ice-cap, glacier, ice-cave.
GE.LO, *s.m.*, ice, chill.
GE.MA, *s.f.*, egg yolk, yellow; shoot, germ.
GÊ.MEO, *s.m.*, twin(s); *adj.*, twin.
GE.MER, *v.*, to groan, to moan; to lament, to wail, to bewail.
GE.MI.DO, *s.m.*, groan, moan, wailing, lamentation.
GE.NE.A.LO.GI.A, *s.f.*, genealogy.
GE.NE.RAL, *s.m.*, general.
GE.NE.RA.LI.DA.DE, *s.f.*, generality, bulk.
GE.NE.RA.LI.ZAR, *v.*, to generalize.
GE.NÉ.RI.CO, *adj.*, generic, general.
GÊ.NE.RO, *s.m.*, class, order, kind, genus, sort, line, style.
GE.NE.RO.SI.DA.DE, *s.f.*, generosity, liberality, freeness.
GE.NE.RO.SO, *adj.*, generous, liberal, noble.
GÊ.NE.SE, *s.f.*, genesis.
GE.NÉ.TI.CO, *adj.*, genetic, genic.
GEN.GI.BRE, *s.f.*, ginger.
GEN.GI.VA, *s.f.*, gum.
GE.NI.AL, *adj.*, ingenious, inspired, brilliant.
GE.NI.A.LI.DA.DE, *s.f.*, geniality, genius.
GÊ.NI.O, *s.m.*, genius, temper, talent, character, spirit.
GE.NI.TAL, *adj.*, genital, reproductive.
GE.NI.TOR, *s.m.*, genitor, father.
GE.NO.CÍ.DIO, *s.m.*, genocide.
GEN.RO, *s.m.*, son-in-law.
GEN.TE, *s.f.*, people, population, humanity, folk, nation.
GEN.TIL, *adj.*, gentle, noble, pleasant, agreeable.
GEN.TI.LE.ZA, *s.f.*, courtesy, kindness, gentility, niceness.
GEN.TI.O, *s.m.*, pagan, heathen; *adj.*, pagan, savage.
GE.NU.I.NI.DA.DE, *s.f.*, genuineness, authenticity.
GE.NU.Í.NO, *adj.*, genuin, authentic.
GE.O.GRA.FIA, *s.f.*, geography.
GE.Ó.GRA.FO, *s.m.*, geographer.
GE.O.LO.GI.A, *s.f.*, geology.
GE.Ó.LO.GO, *s.m.*, geologist.

GE.Ô.ME.TRA, *s.2 gen.*, geometer.
GE.O.ME.TRI.A, *s.f.*, geometry.
GE.RA.ÇÃO, *s.f.*, creation, offspring, generation, lineage, progeny.
GE.RAL, *adj.*, common, generic, general, usual.
GE.RÂ.NIO, *s.m.*, geranium.
GE.RAR, *v.*, to beget, to engender, to father, to generate.
GE.RÊN.CIA, *s.f.*, management, administration, managership.
GE.REN.TE, *s.2 gen.*, manager, administrator, supervisor, director, conductor.
GE.RI.A.TRI.A, *s.f.*, geriatrics.
GE.RIR, *v.*, to manage, to administrate, to direct, to supervise.
GER.MÂ.NI.CO, *adj.*, *s.m.*, Germanic.
GER.MI.NA.ÇÃO, *s.f.*, germination.
GER.MI.NAR, *v.*, to germinate, to bud, to sprout.
GE.RÚN.DIO, *s.m.*, gerund.
GES.SO, *s.m.*, plaster, cast, gypsum.
GES.TA.ÇÃO, *s.f.*, gestation, pregnancy.
GES.TÃO, *s.f.*, management, administration.
GES.TI.CU.LAR, *v.*, to gesticulate, to motion.
GES.TO, *s.m.*, gesture, sign, gesticulation.
GI.GAN.TE, *s.m.*, giant, titan, colossus; *adj.*, giant, gigantic.
GI.GAN.TES.CO, *adj.*, enormous, huge, gigantic, gigantean.
GI.LE.TE, *s.f.*, Gillette; shaving tackle.
GIM, *s.m.*, gin.
GI.NA.SI.AL, *adj.*, gymnasial.
GI.NÁ.SIO, *s.m.*, high school, gymnasium, secondary school.
GI.NÁS.TI.CA, *s.f.*, gymnastics.
GI.NE.CO.LO.GI.A, *s.f.*, gynecology.
GI.NE.CO.LO.GIS.TA, *s.2 gen.*, gynecologist.
GI.RA.FA, *s.f.*, giraffe.
GI.RAR, *v.*, to go, move, swing or turn (a)round, to circle, to rotate.
GI.RAS.SOL, *s.m.*, sunflower.
GÍ.RIA, *s.f.*, slang, dialect, jargon.
GI.RO, *s.m.*, rotation, spin, revolution, circuit, turn, circulation.
GIZ, *s.m.*, chalk, chalk-pencil.

GLA.CÊ, *s.m.*, glacé silk, icing.
GLA.CI.AL, *adj.*, glacial, icy, freezing, frigid.
GLÂN.DU.LA, *s.f.*, glandula, gland, small gland.
GLI.CE.RI.NA, *s.f.*, glycerin, glycerol.
GLI.CO.SE, *s.f.*, glucose, dextrose, grap sugar.
GLO.BAL, *adj.*, global, total, spherical, integral, over-all.
GLO.BO, *s.m.*, sphere, ball, globe.
GLÓ.BU.LO, *s.m.*, globule, little globe.
GLÓ.RIA, *s.f.*, glory, praise, honour, renown, pomp.
GLO.RI.FI.CA.ÇÃO, *s.f.*, glorification, praise, beatification.
GLO.RI.FI.CAR, *v.*, to glorify, to extol, to apotheosize, to make glorious, to exalt.
GLO.RI.O.SO, *adj.*, glorious, illustrious, splendid, bright.
GLO.SAR, *v.*, to gloss, to comment, to annotate.
GLOS.SÁ.RIO, *s.m.*, glossary, vocabulary, dictionary.
GLU.TÃO, *s.m.*, glutton, gormandizer; *adj.*, voracious, gluttonous.
GNOS.TI.CIS.MO, *s.m.*, Gnosticism.
GO.E.LA, *s.f.*, throat, gullet, esophagus.
GOI.A.BA, *s.f.*, guava.
GOL, *s.m.*, goal.
GO.LA, *s.f.*, collar, shirt-collar.
GO.LE, *s.m.*, gulp, sip, draught, swallow.
GO.LEI.RO, *s.m.*, goalkeeper.
GOL.FE, *s.m.*, golf.
GOL.FI.NHO, *s.m.*, dolphin.
GOL.FO, *s.m.*, gulf, large open bay.
GOL.PE, *s.m.*, blow, punch, stroke, wound, injury, hit, knock.
GOL.PE.AR, *v.*, to strike, to beat, to knock, to hit.
GO.MA, *s.f.*, gum, latex, gumma, glue.
GO.MO, *s.m.*, bud, shoot, gemma, button.
GÔN.DO.LA, *s.f.*, gondola; Venetian boat.
GON.GO, *s.m.*, gong.
GO.RAR, *v.*, to miscarry, to go wrong.
GOR.DO, *adj.*, obese, adipose, fat, corpulent.
GOR.DU.RA, *s.f.*, obesity, adiposity; fatness, fat.
GOR.DU.REN.TO, *adj.*, unctuous, fatty.

GOR.DU.RO.SO, *adj.*, greasy, fatty, lardy, oily.
GO.RI.LA, *s.m.*, gorilla.
GOR.JE.AR, *v.*, to warble, to quaver, to trill.
GOR.JE.TA, *s.f.*, tip, gratuity, gratification.
GOR.RO, *s.m.*, cap, bonnet.
GOS.TAR, *v.*, to like, to enjoy, to relish, to find palatable.
GOS.TO, *s.m.*, taste, gustation, flavour, relish, savour.
GOS.TO.SO, *adj.*, tasty, savoury, sapid, flavorous.
GO.TA, *s.f.*, drop, raindrop, dewdrop; minim.
GO.TEI.RA, *s.f.*, gutter, leak, eaves; drain.
GO.TI.NHA, *s.f.*, droplet.
GO.VER.NA.DOR, *s.m.*, governor, commander; *adj.*, governing.
GO.VER.NA.MEN.TAL, *adj.*, governmental, civil.
GO.VER.NAN.TA, *s.f.*, governess, tutoress, nurse.
GO.VER.NAR, *v.*, to govern, to command, to rule, to dominate.
GO.VER.NO, *s.m.*, government, authority, domination, direction.
GO.ZA.DOR, *s.m.*, enjoyer.
GO.ZAR, *v.*, to derive pleasure from, to enjoy oneself, to profit.
GO.ZO, *s.m.*, joy, enjoyment, pleasure, delight, contentment, utility.
GRA.ÇA, *s.f.*, grace, favor, joke, goodwill, benevolence, kindness, charm, mercy.
GRA.CE.JAR, *v.*, to joke, to jest, to banter, to droll, to frolic.
GRA.CE.JO, *s.m.*, joke, jest, mirth, merriness, gracefulness.
GRA.CI.O.SI.DADE, *s.f.*, grace, gracefulness, amenity.
GRA.CI.O.SO, *adj.*, gracious, graceful, elegant, charming, lovely, adorable.
GRA.DA.ÇÃO, *s.f.*, gradation, gradual increase or diminution.
GRA.DE, *s.f.*, grate, grid, grille, barrier.
GRA.DO, *s.m.*, will, wish.
GRA.DU.A.ÇÃO, *s.f.*, gradation, graduation, gradation scale.

GRA.DU.AL, *adj.*, gradual, successive, slow.
GRA.DU.AR, *v.*, to graduate, to calibrate, to gauge, to classify, to divide into grade.
GRA.FI.A, *s.f.*, style of writing; orthography.
GRÁ.FI.CO, *s.m.*, graph, chart, diagram; *adj.*, graphic.
GRA.FO.LO.GI.A, *s.f.*, graphology.
GRA.MA, *s.f.*, grass, grama; *s.m.*, gram, gramme.
GRA.MA.DO, *s.m.*, lawn, turf, grass, green.
GRA.MÁ.TI.CA, *s.f.*, grammar, grammar book.
GRA.MA.TI.CAL, *adj.*, grammatic, grammatical.
GRA.MÁ.TI.CO, *s.m.*, grammarian, grammatist; *adj.*, grammatic, grammatical.
GRAM.PE.A.DOR, *s.m.*, stapler.
GRAM.PE.AR, *v.*, to staple, to clip, to cramp.
GRAM.PO, *s.m.*, cramp, clip, clasp, staple, brace.
GRA.NA, *s.f.*, money.
GRA.NA.DA, *s.f.*, grenade, bomb, shell.
GRAN.DE, *adj.*, great, big, large, bulky, tall, high, vast, ample.
GRAN.DE.ZA, *s.f.*, largeness, greatness, bigness, tallness, height, ampleness.
GRAN.DI.O.SI.DA.DE, *s.f.*, grandiosity.
GRAN.DI.O.SO, *adj.*, grandioso, grand, elevated, lofty, sublime, strong.
GRA.NÍ.TI.CO, *adj.*, granitic.
GRA.NI.TO, *s.m.*, granite.
GRA.NI.ZO, *s.m.*, hail, hailstorm, hailstone.
GRAN.JA, *s.f.*, farm, grange, ranch.
GRAN.JE.AR, *v.*, to cultivate, to acquire, to obtain.
GRA.NU.LA.ÇÃO, *s.f.*, granulation, graining.
GRA.NU.LAR, *v.*, to granulate, to corn.
GRÂ.NU.LO, *s.m.*, granule, corn.
GRÃO, *s.m.*, grain, cereal, corn.
GRAS.SAR, *v.*, to develop gradually; to rage.
GRA.TI.DÃO, *s.f.*, gratitude, gratefulness, thankfulness.
GRA.TI.FI.CA.ÇÃO, *s.f.*, gratification, reward, recompense.
GRA.TI.FI.CAR, *v.*, to gratify, to reward, to recompense.
GRÁ.TIS, *adv.*, gratis, gratuitously, free, costless.
GRA.TO, *adj.*, grateful, thankful, gratified.

GRA.TUI.TO, *adj.*, gratis, gratuitous, free, costless.
GRAU, *s.m.*, step, pace, degree, grade, measure, extent, lenght, dimension.
GRA.Ú.DO, *adj.*, great, distinguished, developed.
GRA.VA.ÇÃO, *s.f.*, engraving, recording, record, aggravation.
GRA.VA.DO, *adj.*, engraved, incised.
GRA.VA.DOR, *s.m.*, tape recorder, engraver, chaser, graver.
GRA.VAR, *v.*, to engrave, to sculpture, to record, to save.
GRA.VA.TA, *s.f.*, tie, neckcloth.
GRA.VE, *adj.*, grave, serious, heavy, weighty, ponderous, solemn.
GRÁ.VI.DA, *adj.*, pregnant, expectant.
GRA.VI.DA.DE, *s.f.*, gravity, seriousness, graveness, solemnity, ponderation.
GRA.VI.DEZ, *s.f.*, pregnancy.
GRA.VI.TA.ÇÃO, *s.f.*, gravitation.
GRA.VI.TAR, *v.*, to gravitate, to be affected by gravitation.
GRA.XA, *s.f.*, grease.
GRÉ.CIA, *s.f.*, Greece.
GRE.GÁ.RIO, *adj.*, gregarious.
GRE.GO, *adj., s.m.*, Greek.
GRE.LAR, *v.*, to sprout, to germinate, to grow.
GRE.LHA, *s.f.*, grill, grate, fire grate.
GRE.LHAR, *v.*, to grill, to fry.
GRÊ.MIO, *s.m.*, bosom, lap, community, club, society, circle.
GRE.TA, *s.f.*, cleft, crack, fissure, hiatus.
GRE.VE, *s.f.*, strike, turn-out.
GRE.VIS.TA, *s.2 gen.*, striker, worker on strike.
GRI.FAR, *v.*, to underline, to curl; to emphasize.
GRI.LO, *s.m.*, cricket.
GRI.NAL.DA, *s.f.*, garland, wreath.
GRIN.GO, *s.m.*, gringo, foreigner, greenhorn.
GRI.PE, *s.f.*, influenza, cold, grip, catarrh.
GRI.SA.LHO, *adj.*, grey, greyish, grizzled.
GRI.TAN.TE, *adj.*, chiding, crying.
GRI.TAR, *v.*, to cry, to shout, to clamour, to bawl, to exclaim.
GRI.TA.RI.A, *s.f.*, crying, shouting, bawling.
GRI.TO, *s.m.*, cry, shout, yell, scream, call, clamour, vociferation.
GRO.GUE, *s.m.*, grog; *adj.*, groggy, toddy.
GRO.SA, *s.f.*, gross, rasp.
GRO.SE.LHA, *s.f.*, gooseberry, currant.
GROS.SEI.RO, *adj.*, gross, impolite, crude, rustic, clumsy.
GROS.SE.RI.A, *s.f.*, roughness, rudeness, uncivility, grossness, indelicacy.
GROS.SO, *s.m.*, main part, bulk; *adj.*, bulky, big, great, dense, compact.
GROS.SU.RA, *s.f.*, thickness, stoutness, bulkiness.
GRO.TÃO, *s.f.*, large cavern.
GRO.TES.CO, *adj.*, grotesque, ridiculous.
GROU, *s.m.*, crane.
GRU.A, *s.f.*, crane.
GRU.DA.DO, *adj.*, glued.
GRU.DAR, *v.*, to glue, to paste, to joint, to unite.
GRU.DE, *s.m.*, glue, size, paste.
GRU.NHIR, *v.*, to grunt.
GRU.PO, *s.m.*, group, class, party, clan, bunch, ring, cluster, collection, gang.
GRU.TA, *s.f.*, grot, grotto, cavern, cave.
GUAR.DA, *s.f.*, guard, vigilance, prudence, caution; *s.m.*, keeper, officer, caretaker.
GUAR.DA-COS.TAS, *s.2 gen.*, bodyguard; coast-guard vessel.
GUAR.DA-JOI.AS, *s.m.*, jewel-case.
GUAR.DA-LI.VROS, *s.m.*, book-keeper, accountant.
GUAR.DA-LOU.ÇA, *s.m.*, cupboard.
GUAR.DA.NA.PO, *s.m.*, napkin, serviette.
GUAR.DA-NO.TUR.NO, *s.m.*, night watchman.
GUAR.DA-PÓ, *s.m.*, dust-coat, smock-frock.
GUAR.DAR, *v.*, to guard, to protect, to defend, to store, to shield, to check, to retain, to keep.
GUAR.DA-ROU.PA, *s.m.*, wardrobe.
GUAR.DA-SOL, *s.m.*, sunshade, parasol, umbrella.
GUA.RI.TA, *s.f.*, lodge, sentry-box.
GUAR.NE.CER, *v.*, to provide, to supply, to furnish, to equip.
GUAR.NI.ÇÃO, *s.f.*, crew, garrison, personnel, post.

GUEL.RA, *s.f.*, gills.
GUER.RA, *s.f.*, war, warfare, conflict, battle, strife.
GUER.RE.AR, *v.*, to war, to make war, to fight, to combat, to struggle.
GUER.REI.RO, *s.m.*, warrior, fighter, soldier, combatant.
GUER.RI.LHA, *s.f.*, guerilla.
GUE.TO, *s.m.*, ghetto.
GUI.A, *s.f.*, guidance, guidebook, manual, guide, courier, pass bill, permit.
GUI.AR, *v.*, to guide, to lead, to conduct, to direct, to drive, to advise, to teach.
GUI.CHÊ, *s.m.*, sliding window, ticket-office window, information counter.
GUI.DÃO, *s.m.*, handle bar.
GUI.LHO.TI.NA, *s.f.*, guillotine.
GUIN.CHAR, *v.*, to scream, to shriek, to screech, to ululate.
GUIN.CHO, *s.m.*, tow-car, squeal, crab.
GUIN.DAS.TE, *s.m.*, crane, hoist, crab.
GUI.SA, *s.f.*, mode, fashion, manner.
GUI.SA.DO, *s.m.*, stew, ragout, hash.
GUI.SAR, *v.*, to stew.
GUI.TAR.RA, *s.f.*, guitar.
GUI.TAR.RIS.TA, *s.2 gen.* guitar player.
GU.LA, *s.f.*, gluttony, voracity, greed, gorge.
GU.LO.DI.CE, *s.f.*, delicacy, dainty, sweetmeat.
GU.LO.SO, *adj.*, gluttonous, greedy, lickerish.
GU.ME, *s.m.*, edge, knife-edge, cutting or sharp edge.
GU.RI, *s.m.*, boy, child.
GU.SA, *s.f.*, cast-iron, pig-iron.
GU.TU.RAL, *adj.*, guttural, throaty.
GU.TU.RA.LI.ZAR, *v.*, to gutturalize.

H

H, *s.m.*, the eighth letter of the Portuguese alphabet.
HÁ.BIL, *adj.*, skilful, skilled, able, dexterous, capable, fit.
HA.BI.LI.DA.DE, *s.f.*, ability, aptitude, capacity, talent, intelligence, skill.
HA.BI.LI.DO.SO, *adj.*, skilful, skilled, handy, dexterous, clever, witty, able.
HA.BI.LI.TA.ÇÃO, *s.f.*, qualification, habilitation, fitness, capacity, competence.
HA.BI.LI.TA.DO, *adj.*, qualified, competent, capable.
HA.BI.LI.TAR, *v.*, to habilitate, to qualify, to entitle, to enable, to prepare, to make ready.
HA.BI.TA.ÇÃO, *s.f.*, habitation, house, residence.
HA.BI.TA.DO, *adj.*, inhabited.
HA.BI.TAN.TE, *s.2 gen.*, inhabitant, resident, habitant, dweller, lodger, colonist.
HA.BI.TAR, *v.*, to inhabit, to reside, to lodge, to live in.
HA.BI.TAT, *s.m.*, habitat.
HÁ.BI.TO, *s.m.*, custom, habit, usage; dress, garment.
HA.BI.TU.AL, *adj.*, habitual, customary, usual, regular, common.
HA.BI.TU.AR, *v.*, to habituate, to familiarize, to accustom, to inure.
HAI.TI.A.NO, *adj., s.m.*, Haitian.
HÁ.LI.TO, *s.m.*, breath, respiration, exhalation.
HAN.GAR, *s.m.*, hangar, shed, dock.
HAN.SE.NI.A.NO, *s.m.*, lazar, leper; *adj.*, leprous.
HA.RAS, *s.m.*, stud, horse breeding farm.
HA.RÉM, *s.m.*, harem, seraglio.
HAR.MO.NI.A, *s.f.*, harmony, accord, consonance, concord.
HAR.MÔ.NI.CO, *adj.*, harmonious, harmonic, consonant, regular.
HAR.MO.NI.O.SO, *adj.*, harmonious, melodious, musical.
HAR.MO.NI.ZA.ÇÃO, *s.f.*, harmonization.
HAR.MO.NI.ZAR, *v.*, to harmonize, to make harmonious, to conciliate.
HAR.PA, *s.f.*, harp.
HAS.TE, *s.f.*, staff, stick, stem, stalk, long stick.
HAS.TE.AR, *v.*, to hoist, to run up, to heave.
HA.VAI.A.NO, *adj., s.m.*, Hawaiian.
HA.VER, *s.m.*, credit, fortune; *v.*, to have, to possess, to own, to occur.
HA.XI.XE, *s.m.*, hashish.
HE.BRAI.CO, *adj., s.m.*, Hebrew, Hebraist.
HE.BREU, *adj., s.m.*, Hebrew.
HEC.TO.LI.TRO, *s.m.*, hectoliter.
HE.DI.ON.DO, *adj.*, hideous, dreadful.
HE.GE.MO.NI.A, *s.f.*, hegemony, predominance.
HÉ.LI.CE, *s.f.*, helix, propeller.
HE.LI.CÓP.TE.RO, *s.m.*, helicopter, chopper.
HEL.VÉ.CIO, *adj., s.m.*, Helvetian, Swiss.
HE.MA.TO.LO.GI.A, *s.f.*, hematology.
HE.MA.TO.MA, *s.m.*, bruise, hematoma.
HE.MIS.FÉ.RIO, *s.m.*, hemisphere.
HE.MO.FI.LI.A, *s.f.*, hemophilia.
HE.MO.FÍ.LI.CO, *adj.*, hemophiliac.
HE.MOR.RA.GI.A, *s.f.*, hemorrhage.
HE.MOR.ROI.DAS, *s.f.*, hemorrhoids.
HE.PA.TI.TE, *s.f.*, hepatitis.
HE.RAN.ÇA, *s.f.*, inheritance, heritage, legacy, heredity, birthright.
HER.BÁ.RIO, *s.m.*, herbarium.
HER.BÍ.VO.RO, *s.m.*, herbivore; *adj.*, herbivorous.
HER.DAR, *v.*, to inherit, to bequeath, to legate.
HER.DEI.RA, *s.f.*, heiress, inheritress.
HER.DEI.RO, *s.m.*, heir, inheritor.
HE.RE.GE, *s.2 gen.*, heretic, dissenter, misbeliever, sectary.
HE.RE.SI.A, *s.f.*, heresy.
HER.MA.FRO.DI.TA, *s.2 gen.*, hermaphrodite.
HER.ME.NÊU.TI.CA, *s.f.*, hermeneutics.
HÉR.NIA, *s.f.*, hernia, rupture.
HE.RÓI, *s.m.*, hero.

HEROICO — HOMOSSEXUAL

HE.ROI.CO, *adj.*, heroic, noble, bold, courageous.
HE.RO.Í.NA, *s.f.*, heroess, heroine; heroin.
HE.RO.ÍS.MO, *s.m.*, heroism, courage, intrepidity, valour.
HER.PES, *s.f., pl.*, herpes.
HE.SI.TA.ÇÃO, *s.f.*, hesitation, hesitance, vacillation.
HE.SI.TAN.TE, *s.2 gen.*, hesitant, wavering, irresolute, indecisive.
HE.SI.TAR, *v.*, to hesitate, to vacillate, to waver, to halt, to doubt.
HE.TE.RO.GÊ.NEO, *adj.*, heterogeneous, unlike, dissimilar, motley.
HE.XÂ.ME.TRO, *s.m.*, hexameter.
HI.A.TO, *s.m.*, hiatus, gap, opening.
HI.BER.NAR, *v.*, to hibernate.
HÍ.BRI.DO, *adj.*, hybrid.
HI.DRAN.TE, *s.m.*, hydrant.
HI.DRA.TAR, *v.*, to hydrate.
HÍ.DRI.CO, *adj.*, hydric.
HI.DRO.A.VI.ÃO, *s.m.*, hydro-airplane.
HI.DRO.FO.BI.A, *s.f.*, hydrophobia, rabies.
HI.DRO.GÊ.NIO, *s.m.*, hydrogen.
HI.DRÔ.ME.TRO, *s.m.*, hydrometer.
HI.DRO.TE.RA.PI.A, *s.f.*, hydrotherapeutics, hydrotherapy.
HI.E.NA, *s.f.*, hyena.
HI.E.RAR.QUI.A, *s.f.*, hierarchy.
HI.E.RÓ.GLI.FO, *s.m.*, hieroglyph.
HÍ.FEN, *s.m.*, hyphen.
HI.GI.E.NE, *s.f.*, hygienics, hygiene, cleanliness.
HI.GI.Ê.NI.CO, *adj.*, hygienic, hygienical, sanitary, clean.
HIN.DU, *s.2 gen.*, Hindu, Hindo; *adj.*, Hindu, Hindoo.
HI.NO, *s.m.*, hymn, anthem.
HI.PÉR.BO.LE, *s.f.*, hyperbole.
HI.PER.TEN.SÃO, *s.f.*, hypertension.
HI.PER.TRO.FI.A, *s.f.*, hypertrophy.
HÍ.PI.CO, *adj.*, hippic, equine.
HIP.NO.SE, *s.f.*, hypnosis, hypnotism.
HIP.NO.TIS.MO, *s.m.*, hypnotism.
HIP.NO.TI.ZAR, *v.*, to hypnotize.
HI.PO.CRI.SI.A, *s.f.*, hypocrisy.
HI.PÓ.CRI.TA, *s.2 gen.*, hypocrite, pretender, dissimulator.
HI.PÓ.DRO.MO, *s.m.*, hippodrome, race-course.
HI.PO.PÓ.TA.MO, *s.m.*, hippopotamus.
HI.PO.TE.CA, *s.f.*, hypothec, mortgage.
HI.PO.TE.CAR, *v.*, to mortgage, to hypothecate, to bond.
HI.PO.TE.NU.SA, *s.f.*, hypotenuse.
HI.PÓ.TE.SE, *s.f.*, hypothesis, supposition, theory.
HIS.PÂ.NI.CO, *adj.*, Hispanic.
HIS.TE.RI.A, *s.f.*, hysteria.
HIS.TÉ.RI.CO, *adj.*, hysteric, excited.
HIS.TÓ.RIA, *s.f.*, history, tale, narration, story, legend, fable.
HIS.TO.RI.A.DOR, *s.m.*, historian, historiographer.
HIS.TÓ.RI.CO, *s.m.*, description, narration, review; *adj.*, historical, true, veracious.
HO.JE, *adv.*, today, this day, actually.
HO.LAN.DA, *s.f.*, Holland, Netherlands.
HO.LAN.DÊS, *adj., s.m.*, Hollander, Netherlander, Dutchman.
HO.LO.FO.TE, *s.m.*, holophote, projector, spotlight.
HO.MEM, *s.m.*, man, human being, mankind, humanity, male, husband.
HO.ME.NA.GE.AR, *v.*, to homage, to honor, to pay tribute to.
HO.ME.NA.GEM, *s.f.*, homage, tribute, allegiance, reverence, respect.
HO.ME.O.PA.TA, *s.2 gen.*, homeopathist.
HO.ME.O.PA.TI.A, *s.f.*, homeopathy.
HO.MI.CI.DA, *s.2 gen.*, murderer, slayer, homicide; *adj.*, murderous, homicidal.
HO.MI.CÍ.DIO, *s.m.*, homicide, murder, assassination.
HO.MO.GE.NEI.DA.DE, *s.f.*, homogeneity.
HO.MO.GÊ.NEO, *adj.*, homogeneous, uniform, smooth.
HO.MO.LO.GA.ÇÃO, *s.f.*, homologation, ratification, confirmation.
HO.MO.LO.GAR, *v.*, to homologate, to ratify, to confirm.
HO.MÓ.LO.GO, *adj.*, homologous.
HO.MÔ.NI.MO, *s.m.*, homonym, namesake.
HO.MOS.SE.XU.AL, *adj., s.2 gen.*, homossexual,

gay, fag.
HON.DU.RE.NHO, *adj.*, *s.m.*, Honduran.
HO.NES.TI.DA.DE, *s.f.*, honesty, honour, integrity, uprightness, truth.
HO.NES.TO, *adj.*, honest, honourable, frank, sincere.
HO.NO.RA.BI.LI.DA.DE, *s.f.*, honourableness, reputability.
HO.NO.RÁ.RIO, *adj.*, honorary, honorific.
HO.NO.RÁ.RI.OS, *s.m.*, *pl.*, honorarium, remuneration, pay.
HON.RA, *s.f.*, honor, reputation, honour, repute, respect, reverence.
HON.RA.DEZ, *s.f.*, honour, probity, honesty, righteousness.
HON.RA.DO, *adj.*, honourable, reputable, honest, sincere, worthy.
HON.RAR, *v.*, to honor, to esteem, to respect, to revere.
HON.RO.SO, *adj.*, honourable, honest, praiseworthy.
HO.RA, *s.f.*, hour, time, opportunity.
HO.RÁ.RIO, *s.m.*, timetable, schedule; *adj.*, hourly; **HORÁRIO DE EXPEDIENTE** - working hours.
HO.RI.ZON.TAL, *adj.*, horizontal.
HO.RI.ZON.TE, *s.m.*, horizon, skyline, sealine.
HOR.MÔ.NIO, *s.m.*, hormone.
HOR.REN.DO, *adj.*, horrendous, fearful, frightful.
HOR.RÍ.VEL, *adj.*, horrible, terrible, horrid, dreadful.
HOR.ROR, *s.m.*, horror, terror, hate, repulsion, aversion.
HOR.RO.RI.ZAR, *v.*, to horrify, to terrify, to frighten.
HOR.RO.RO.SO, *adj.*, horrible, terrible, horrific, fearful.
HOR.TA, *s.f.*, vegetable garden, kitchen garden.
HOR.TA.LI.ÇA, *s.f.*, greens, vegetables.
HOR.TE.LÃ, *s.f.*, mint, spearmint.
HOR.TÊN.SIA, *s.f.*, hortensia.
HOR.TI.CUL.TU.RA, *s.f.*, horticulture.
HOS.PE.DA.GEM, *s.f.*, hospitality, lodging, accomodation.
HOS.PE.DAR, *v.*, to house, to lodge, to accomodate.
HOS.PE.DA.RI.A, *s.f.*, inn, lodging house, hotel, guest house.
HÓS.PE.DE, *s.2 gen.*, guest, visitor, lodger.
HOS.PE.DEI.RO, *s.m.*, host, innkeeper.
HOS.PÍ.CIO, *s.m.*, hospice, hospitium, mental hospital, asylum, mad house.
HOS.PI.TAL, *s.m.*, hospital, clinic, sanatorium.
HOS.PI.TA.LI.DA.DE, *s.f.*, hospitality, hospitableness.
HOS.PI.TA.LI.ZA.ÇÃO, *s.f.*, hospitalization.
HOS.PI.TA.LI.ZAR, *v.*, to hospitalize, to intern in a hospital.
HÓS.TIA, *s.f.*, Host, holy bread, Eucharist.
HOS.TIL, *adj.*, hostile, inimical, adverse, antagonistic, belligerent.
HOS.TI.LI.DA.DE, *s.f.*, hostility, enmity.
HOS.TI.LI.ZAR, *v.*, to hostilize, to antagonize, to persecute, to oppose.
HO.TEL, *s.m.*, hotel, inn, lodging house.
HO.TE.LEI.RO, *s.m.*, hotelkeeper.
HU.MA.NI.DA.DE, *s.f.*, humanity, mankind, human nature.
HU.MA.NI.TÁ.RIO, *s.m.*, humanitarian, philantropist; *adj.*, humanitarian, humane.
HU.MA.NI.ZA.ÇÃO, *s.f.*, humanization.
HU.MA.NI.ZAR, *v.*, to humanize.
HU.MA.NO, *adj.*, *s.m.*, human.
HU.MIL.DA.DE, *s.f.*, humbleness, humility, modesty, submission.
HU.MIL.DE, *adj.*, humble, modest, submissive, poor.
HU.MI.LHA.ÇÃO, *s.f.*, humiliation, abasement.
HU.MI.LHAR, *v.*, to humiliate, to humble, to mortify.
HU.MOR, *s.m.*, humor, mood, moisture, mental state, disposition, temper.
HU.MO.RA.DO, *adj.*, humoured, tempered.
HU.MO.RIS.MO, *s.m.*, humorism.
HU.MO.RIS.TA, *s.2 gen.*, humorist.
HÚ.MUS, *s.m.*, humus, earth.
HÚN.GA.RO, t*adj.*, *s.m.*, Hungarian.

I, *s.m.*, ninth letter of the Portuguese alphabet; number one in the Roman notation (I).
IAN.QUE, *adj.*, *s.m.*, Yankee.
IA.TE, *s.m.*, yacht.
IA.TIS.MO, *s.m.*, yachting.
I.ÇAR, *v.*, to hoist, to hoist up, to lift, to jack.
Í.CO.NE, *s.m.*, icon.
I.DA, *s.f.*, departure, setting out, starting, going, leaving.
I.DA.DE, *s.f.*, age, time, lifetime, epoch, maturity.
I.DE.AL, *s.m.*, ideal, model, example; *adj.*, ideal, imaginary.
I.DE.A.LIS.MO, *s.m.*, idealism.
I.DE.A.LIS.TA, *s.2 gen.*, idealist; *adj.*, idealistic.
I.DE.A.LI.ZAR, *v.*, to idealize, to imagine, to organize.
I.DEI.A, *s.f.*, idea, thought, notion, concept, image, imagination.
I.DEM, *adj.*, ditto, the same.
I.DÊN.TI.CO, *adj.*, identical, equal, similar, analogous.
I.DEN.TI.DA.DE, *s.f.*, identity, identicalness, sameness, exactness, individuality.
I.DEN.TI.FI.CA.ÇÃO, *s.f.*, identification.
I.DEN.TI.FI.CAR, *v.*, to identify, to recognize, to make identical.
I.DE.O.LO.GI.A, *s.f.*, ideology.
I.DÍ.LIO, *s.m.*, idyl, rural poem.
I.DI.O.MA, *s.m.*, idiom, language, tongue.
I.DI.O.TA, *s.2 gen.*, idiot, fool, cretin; *adj.*, idiotic, idiotical, stupid, foolish.
I.DI.O.TI.CE, *s.f.*, foolishness, madness.
I.DO.LA.TRAR, *v.*, to idolize, to adore, to admire, to worship.
I.DO.LA.TRI.A, *s.f.*, idolatry, idolism.
Í.DO.LO, *s.m.*, idol, image, icon, effigy.
I.DO.NEI.DA.DE, *s.f.*, decency, honesty, aptitude, competence.
I.DÔ.NEO, *adj.*, idoneous, apt, competent, fit.
I.DO.SO, *adj.*, *s.m.*, old-aged, elder, advanced in years.
IG.NI.ÇÃO, *s.f.*, ignition, combustion.
IG.NO.MÍ.NIA, *s.f.*, ignominy, dishonour, disgrace.
IG.NO.RA.DO, *adj.*, unknown, obscure.
IG.NO.RÂN.CIA, *s.f.*, ignorance.
IG.NO.RAN.TE, *s.2 gen.*, ignorant, illiterate, idiot, know-nothing, unlearned, stupid.
IG.NO.RAR, *v.*, to ignore, not to know, to be ignorant of.
I.GRE.JA, *s.f.*, church.
I.GUAL, *adj.*, equal, even, identic, equable, uniform, like, alike.
I.GUA.LAR, *v.*, to equalize, to make equal, to equal, to match, to cap.
I.GUAL.DA.DE, *s.f.*, equality, equity, equalness, equation, uniformity.
I.LE.GAL, *adj.*, illegal, illicit, lawless, injudicial, wrong.
I.LE.GA.LI.DA.DE, *s.f.*, illegality, unlawfulness.
I.LE.GÍ.TI.MO, *adj.*, illegitimate, illegal, unlawful, spurious, criminal.
I.LESO, *adj.*, unhurt, uninjured.
I.LE.TRA.DO, *s.m.*, illiterate; *adj.*, illiterate, unlearned, rude, uncultured.
I.LHA, *s.f.*, island, isle, islet.
I.LHÉU, *s.m.*, islander, islet.
I.LÍ.CI.TO, *adj.*, illicit, illegal, unlawful, lawless.
I.LI.MI.TA.DO, *adj.*, unlimited, limitless, free, unrestricted.
I.LU.DIR, *v.*, to deceive, to cheat, to dupe.
I.LU.MI.NA.ÇÃO, *s.f.*, illumination, explication.
I.LU.MI.NA.DO, *adj.*, illuminated, lighted, illustrated.
I.LU.MI.NAR, *v.*, to illuminate, to light up, to illumine, elucidate.
I.LU.SÃO, *s.f.*, illusion, illusiveness, fantasy, fancy.

I.LU.SI.O.NIS.MO, *s.m.*, illusionism.
I.LU.SÓ.RIO, *adj.*, illusory, delusive, deceptive, delusory.
I.LUS.TRA.ÇÃO, *s.f.*, illustration, knowledge, culture, erudition, picture.
I.LUS.TRA.DO, *adj.*, illustrated, erudite, learned, cultured.
I.LUS.TRAR, *v.*, to illustrate, to illuminate, to illumine, to elucidate, to explain.
I.LUS.TRE, *adj.*, *s.2 gen.*, illustrious, eximious, famous, egregious, brilliant.
Í.MÃ, *s.m.*, magnet, loadstone.
I.MA.CU.LA.DO, *adj.*, immaculate, spotless.
I.MA.GEM, *s.f.*, image, drawing, painting, likeness, semblance, picture.
I.MA.GI.NAR, *v.*, to imagine, to suppose, to conjecture, to invent.
I.MA.GI.NÁ.RIO, *adj.*, imaginary, fantastic, fictive.
I.MA.TE.RI.AL, *adj.*, immaterial.
I.MA.TU.RI.DA.DE, *s.f.*, immaturity, precocity, untimeliness.
I.MA.TU.RO, *adj.*, immature, unripe, premature.
IM.BE.CIL, *s.2 gen.*, feeble-minded, imbecile, fool; *adj.*, feeble-minded, idiot, imbecile, silly, stupid.
IM.BE.CI.LI.DA.DE, *s.f.*, imbecility.
I.ME.DI.A.TO, *s.m.*, chief officer; *adj.*, immediate, direct, proximate, near, close.
I.MEN.SO, *adj.*, immense, immeasurable, unlimited, great, huge, vast.
I.ME.RE.CI.DO, *adj.*, gratuitous, unworthy, immerited.
I.MER.GIR, *v.*, to immerse, to immerge, to plunge into, to penetrate.
I.MER.SÃO, *s.f.*, immersion, plunge.
I.MI.GRA.ÇÃO, *s.f.*, immigration.
I.MI.GRAN.TE, *s.2 gen.*, immigrant.
I.MI.GRAR, *v.*, to immigrate, migrate.
I.MI.TA.ÇÃO, *s.f.*, imitation, copy; sham, mock.
I.MI.TA.DO, *adj.*, imitated, imitative, copied, sham.
I.MI.TAR, *v.*, to imitate, to copy, to reproduce, to assume, to pretend.
I.MO, *adj.*, intimate, inmost.
I.MO.BI.LI.Á.RIO, *s.m.*, immovable, real estate, property; *adj.*, of, pertaining to or relative to immovable property.
I.MO.BI.LI.DA.DE, *s.f.*, immobility, immovability.
I.MO.BI.LI.ZA.ÇÃO, *s.f.*, immobilization.
I.MO.BI.LI.ZAR, *v.*, to immobilize, to fix, to impede.
I.MO.DE.RA.DO, *adj.*, immoderate, excessive, intemperate.
I.MO.RAL, *adj.*, immoral, vicious, indecent.
I.MO.RA.LI.DA.DE, *s.f.*, immorality, vice, wickedness.
I.MOR.TAL, *adj.*, immortal, undying, deathless, eternal.
I.MOR.TA.LI.DA.DE, *s.f.*, immortality, eternity.
I.MOR.TA.LI.ZAR, *v.*, to immortalize, to eternalize, to become famous.
I.MÓ.VEL, *s.m.*, real estate, landed property, property, building; *adj.*, immobile, immovable.
IM.PA.CI.ÊN.CIA, *s.f.*, impatience, restlessness, anxiety, irritability.
IM.PA.CI.EN.TE, *adj.*, impatient, eager, restive, hasty, quick.
IM.PAC.TO, *s.m.*, impact, discharge, shot, shock, hit.
ÍM.PAR, *adj.*, odd, uneven, unique.
IM.PAR.CI.AL, *adj.*, impartial, fair.
IM.PAR.CI.A.LI.DA.DE, *s.f.*, impartiality.
IM.PAS.SE, *s.m.*, impasse, predicament, dilemma.
IM.PÁ.VI.DO, *adj.*, impavid, fearless, brave.
IM.PE.DI.DO, *adj.*, hindered, obstructed, blocked.
IM.PE.DI.MEN.TO, *s.m.*, hindrance, obstruction, impediment, impeachment.
IM.PE.DIR, *v.*, to impede, to hinder, to obstruct, to intercept, to deter, to restrain.
IM.PE.LIR, *v.*, to impel, to push on, to throw, to thrust, to incite.
IM.PEN.SA.DO, *adj.*, thoughtless, heedless, wild.
IM.PE.RA.DOR, *s.m.*, emperor.
IM.PE.RAR, *v.*, to reign, to rule, to command, to govern, to dominate.
IM.PE.RA.TI.VO, *s.m.*, imperative, imperative mood; *adj.*, imperative, absolute, obligatory.
IM.PE.RA.TRIZ, *s.f.*, imperatrix, empress.
IM.PER.CEP.TÍ.VEL, *adj.*, imperceptible,

IMPERDOÁVEL / **IMPRENSAR**

insensible.
IM.PER.DO.Á.VEL, *adj.*, unpardonable, inexcusable, unforgivable.
IM.PER.FEI.ÇÃO, *s.f.*, imperfection, fault, defectiveness.
IM.PER.FEI.TO, *s.m.*, imperfect tense; *adj.*, imperfect, defective, deficient.
IM.PE.RIA.LIS.MO, *s.m.*, imperialism.
IM.PE.RÍ.CIA, *s.f.*, unskilfulness, incapacity, incompetence.
IM.PÉ.RIO, *s.m.*, empire, imperium, monarchy.
IM.PE.RI.O.SO, *adj.*, imperious, commanding, urgent.
IM.PER.ME.A.BI.LI.DA.DE, *s.f.*, impermeability.
IM.PER.ME.A.BI.LI.ZAR, *v.*, to render impermeable.
IM.PER.ME.Á.VEL, *s.m.*, raincoat; *adj.*, impermeable, impenetrable, waterproof.
IM.PER.TI.NÊN.CIA, *s.f.*, impertinence, irrelevance, annoyance.
IM.PER.TI.NEN.TE, *adj.*, impertinent, insolent, petulant, importune.
IM.PES.SO.AL, *adj.*, impersonal.
ÍM.PE.TO, *s.m.*, impulse, rashness, emotion.
IM.PE.TRA.ÇÃO, *s.f.*, impetration.
IM.PE.TRAR, *v.*, to impetrate, to supplicate, to petition.
IM.PE.TU.O.SO, *adj.*, impetuous, hasty, furious, vehement.
IM.PIN.GIR, *v.*, to impinge, to strike, to dash, to force.
ÍM.PIO, *s.m.*, impious man; *adj.*, impious, ungodly, profane.
IM.PLA.CÁ.VEL, *adj.*, implacable, inexorable, unappeasable.
IM.PLAN.TA.ÇÃO, *s.f.*, implantation.
IM.PLAN.TAR, *v.*, to introduce, to establish, to implant, to insert, to instil.
IM.PLE.MEN.TO, *s.m.*, implement, accessory.
IM.PLI.CAR, *v.*, to implicate, to involve, to entangle, to imply, to embarrass, to hint, to include.
IM.PLÍ.CI.TO, *adj.*, implicit, implicate, implied, inferred.

IM.PLO.RA.ÇÃO, *s.f.*, imploration.
IM.PLO.RAR, *v.*, to implore, to entreat, to supplicate, to beseech.
IM.PON.DE.RA.DO, *adj.*, inconsiderate, heedless, rash.
IM.PO.NÊN.CIA, *s.f.*, portliness, imposingness, majesty.
IM.PON.TU.A.LI.DA.DE, *s.f.*, impunctuality.
IM.PO.PU.LAR, *adj.*, unpopular.
IM.POR, *v.*, to impose, to burden, to lay on, to encumber, to direct, to command.
IM.POR.TA.ÇÃO, *s.f.*, importation, import(s), entry.
IM.POR.TA.DOR, *s.m.*, importer.
IM.POR.TÂN.CIA, *s.f.*, importance, sum, consideration, regard, emphasis, preciousness.
IM.POR.TAN.TE, *adj.*, important, essential, significant, pretentious.
IM.POR.TAR, *v.*, to import, to interest, to matter, to aggregate, to concern.
IM.POR.TU.NAR, *v.*, to importune, to annoy, to molest, to embarrass.
IM.POR.TU.NO, *s.m.*, annoyer, molester; *adj.*, importunate, importune, worrysome, obstrusive.
IM.PO.SI.ÇÃO, *s.f.*, imposition, assessment, tax, tribute, order.
IM.POS.SI.BI.LI.TAR, *v.*, to make impossible, to weaken, to enfeeble.
IM.POS.SÍ.VEL, *adj.*, impossible, unfeasible, unattainable, impracticable.
IM.POS.TO, *s.m.*, tax, tribute, duty; *adj.*, forced, enforced; **IMPOSTO DE RENDA**, income tax.
IM.POS.TOR, *s.m.*, impostor.
IM.PO.TÊN.CIA, *s.f.*, impotence, impotency.
IM.PRA.TI.CÁ.VEL, *adj.*, impracticable, impossible.
IM.PRE.CAR, *v.*, to imprecate, to invoke.
IM.PRE.CI.SÃO, *s.f.*, imprecision, inexactness.
IM.PREG.NA.DO, *adj.*, impregnated, saturated.
IM.PREG.NAR, *v.*, to impregnate, to permeate, to fecundate, to steep.
IM.PREN.SA, *s.f.*, press, printing press, newspaper, typography.
IM.PREN.SAR, *v.*, to press, to compress, to print,

IMPRESCINDÍVEL — INATIVO

to imprint.
IM.PRES.CIN.DÍ.VEL, *adj.*, necessary, vital, indispensable.
IM.PRES.SÃO, *s.f.*, feeling, idea, impression, printing, imprint, edition.
IM.PRES.SIO.NAN.TE, *adj.*, impressive, impressing, striking.
IM.PRES.SIO.NAR, *v.*, to impress, to mark, to stamp in, to affect, to touch.
IM.PRES.SO, *s.m.*, printed matter; *adj.*, printed.
IM.PRES.SOR, *s.m.*, pressman, printer.
IM.PRES.SO.RA, *s.f.*, printer, printing press.
IM.PRE.TE.RÍ.VEL, *adj.*, unsurpassable, implicit, unconditional, undeclinable.
IM.PRE.VIS.TO, *s.m.*, unforeseen, unexpected, surprising.
IM.PRI.MIR, *v.*, to print, to imprint, to impress, to stamp.
IM.PRO.BI.DA.DE, *s.f.*, improbity.
IM.PRO.DU.TI.VI.DA.DE, *s.f.*, unproductiveness.
IM.PRO.DU.TI.VO, *adj.*, unproductive, barren, nonproductive.
IM.PRO.PÉ.RIO, *s.m.*, affront, insult, outrage.
IM.PRÓ.PRIO, *adj.*, improper, inappropriate, inadequate, inexact, indecorous.
IM.PRO.VI.SA.ÇÃO, *s.f.*, improvisation, extemporization.
IM.PRO.VI.SA.DO, *adj.*, improvised, unprepared, extempore.
IM.PRO.VI.SAR, *v.*, to improvise, to improvisate, to extemporize.
IM.PRO.VI.SO, *s.m.*, improvisation, extemporization.
IM.PRU.DÊN.CIA, *s.f.*, imprudence, rashness, heedlesness, indiscretion.
IM.PRU.DEN.TE, *adj.*, imprudent, rash, precipitate, headless, incautious.
IM.PU.DEN.TE, *adj.*, impudent, shameless, insolent.
IM.PU.DI.CO, *adj.*, shameless, impudent, insolent.
IM.PUG.NAR, *v.*, to refute, to contest, to contradict.
IM.PUL.SIO.NAR, *v.*, to animate, to stimulate, to boast.
IM.PUL.SO, *s.m.*, impulse, impelling force, drive, thrust, push.
IM.PU.NE, *adj.*, unpunished.
IM.PU.NI.DA.DE, *s.f.*, impunity, exemption from penalty.
IM.PU.RE.ZA, *s.f.*, impurity, uncleanness, muddiness, lees.
IM.PU.RO, *adj.*, impure, dirty, foul.
IM.PU.TAR, *v.*, to impute, to attribute, to accuse.
I.MUN.DÍ.CIE, *s.f.*, uncleanness, filthiness, foulness.
I.MUN.DO, *adj.*, dirty, filthy, unclean, foul, impure, feculent.
I.MU.NE, *adj.*, immune, exempt.
I.MU.NI.DA.DE, *s.f.*, immunity, exemption, franchise.
I.MU.NI.ZA.ÇÃO, *s.f.*, immunization.
I.MU.NI.ZAR, *v.*, to immunize.
I.NÁ.BIL, *adj.*, unfit, incapable, unapt, unskilled.
I.NA.BI.LI.DA.DE, *s.f.*, inability, incapacity, incompetence, inaptness.
I.NA.BI.TA.DO, *adj.*, uninhabited, unoccupied, untenanted.
I.NA.CA.BA.DO, *adj.*, unfinished, uncompleted.
I.NA.CEI.TÁ.VEL, *adj.*, unacceptable.
I.NA.CES.SÍ.VEL, *adj.*, inaccessible, impervious, unapproachable, exclusive.
I.NA.CRE.DI.TÁ.VEL, *adj.*, incredible, unbelievable, doubtful.
I.NA.DE.QUA.DO, *adj.*, inadequate, improper, inappropriate, unfit.
I.NAD.MIS.SÍ.VEL, *adj.*, inadmissible, unpermissible.
I.NAD.VER.TI.DO, *adj.*, inadvertent, headless, careless.
I.NA.LA.ÇÃO, *s.f.*, inhalation.
I.NA.LAR, *v.*, to inhale, to breath in.
I.NA.LIE.NÁ.VEL, *adj.*, inalienable.
I.NA.NI.ÇÃO, *s.f.*, inanition, starvation.
I.NA.NI.MA.DO, *adj.*, inanimate, lifeless, dead.
I.NAP.TI.DÃO, *s.f.*, inaptness, inability, inaptitude.
I.NAP.TO, *adj.*, inapt, unfit.
I.NA.TI.VO, *adj.*, inactive, inert, passive, idle, indolent.

I.NA.TO, *adj.*, innate, native, inborn, connate.
I.NAU.GU.RA.ÇÃO, *s.f.*, inauguration, initiation, beginning, opening.
I.NAU.GU.RAR, *v.*, to inaugurate, to initiate.
IN.CA, *s.2 gen.*, Inca; *adj.*, Incan.
IN.CAL.CU.LÁ.VEL, *adj.*, incalculable.
IN.CAN.DES.CÊN.CIA, *s.f.*, incandescence, incandescency.
IN.CAN.DES.CEN.TE, *adj.*, incandescent, red hot, aglow, fervent.
IN.CAN.SÁ.VEL, *adj.*, tireless, unweariable, untiring.
IN.CA.PA.CI.DA.DE, *s.f.*, incapacity.
IN.CA.PAZ, *adj.*, incapable, inapt, unfit, incompetent, inefficient.
IN.CAU.TO, *adj.*, incautious, unwary, heedless, imprudent.
IN.CEN.DI.AR, *v.*, to ignite, to set on fire, to enkindle, to inflame, to excite.
IN.CÊN.DIO, *s.m.*, fire, blaze, burning, conflagration.
IN.CEN.SO, *s.m.*, incense, aromatic fumes, perfume; flattery, adulation.
IN.CEN.TI.VAR, *v.*, to stimulate, to animate, to encourage, to incite.
IN.CEN.TI.VO, *s.m.*, incentive, impulse, incitement, encouragement.
IN.CER.TE.ZA, *s.f.*, uncertainty, uncertainness, dubiety, incertitude, hesitance, hesitation.
IN.CER.TO, *adj.*, uncertain, hesitating, doubtful, dubious, insecure.
IN.CES.SAN.TE, *adj.*, incessant, permanent.
IN.CES.TO, *s.m.*, incest.
IN.CES.TU.O.SO, *adj.*, incestuous.
IN.CHA.ÇÃO, *s.f.*, swelling, tumour, tumefaction.
IN.CHA.DO, *adj.*, swollen, turgid, turgescent, inflated, exalted.
IN.CHAR, *v.*, to swell, to intumesce, to inflate, to bulge, to rise, to belly.
IN.CI.DÊN.CIA, *s.f.*, incidence, incidency.
IN.CI.DEN.TAL, *adj.*, incidental.
IN.CI.DEN.TE, *s.m.*, incident.
IN.CI.DIR, *v.*, to happen, to occur, to fall on or fall upon.

IN.CI.NE.RA.ÇÃO, *s.f.*, incineration.
IN.CI.NE.RAR, *v.*, to incinerate, to cremate.
IN.CI.PI.EN.TE, *adj.*, *s.2 gen.*, incipient.
IN.CI.SÃO, *s.f.*, cut, incision.
IN.CI.SI.VO, *adj.*, incisive, cutting, sharp, keen.
IN.CI.TA.MEN.TO, *s.m.*, incitement, incitation.
IN.CI.TAR, *v.*, to incite, to stimulate, to inspire, to encourage, to excite.
IN.CI.VI.LI.DA.DE, *s.f.*, incivility, discourtesy, disrespect.
IN.CLE.MÊN.CIA, *s.f.*, inclemency.
IN.CLI.NA.ÇÃO, *s.f.*, incline, inclination, bow, nod, bending, vocation, tendency.
IN.CLI.NAR, *v.*, to incline, to recline, to tilt, to slope, to bow, to bend, to be fond.
IN.CLU.IR, *v.*, to include, to enclose, to comprise, to comprehend, to contain, to add in, to involve.
IN.CLU.SÃO, *s.f.*, inclusion, inclosure, enclosure.
IN.CLU.SI.VE, *adv.*, inclusively.
IN.CLU.SO, *adj.*, included, enclosed.
IN.CO.E.REN.TE, *adj.*, incoherent, disjointed.
IN.CÓG.NI.TA, *s.f.*, unknown quantity.
IN.CO.LOR, *adj.*, colourless.
IN.CÓ.LU.ME, *adj.*, unhurt, scarless, entire, whole.
IN.CO.MO.DAR, *v.*, to incommode, to trouble, to disturb, to importune.
IN.CÔ.MO.DO, *s.m.*, indisposition, disease, discomfort, trouble, disturbance, nuisance, fatigue.
IN.COM.PA.RÁ.VEL, *adj.*, incomparable, matchless, peerless.
IN.COM.PA.TI.BI.LI.ZAR, *v.*, to make incompatible, to make irreconcilable.
IN.COM.PE.TÊN.CIA, *s.f.*, incompetence, incapacity, inability.
IN.COM.PE.TEN.TE, *adj.*, incompetent, unfit.
IN.COM.PLE.TO, *adj.*, incomplete, unfinished, uncompleted, fragmentary.
IN.COM.PRE.EN.SÃO, *s.f.*, incomprehension.
IN.COM.PRE.EN.SÍ.VEL, *adj.*, incomprehensible, inconceivable, impenetrable.
IN.CO.MUM, *adj.*, uncommon, unusual, scarce, rare.
IN.CON.CE.BÍ.VEL, *adj.*, inconceivable, incomprehensible, extraordinary.

IN.CON.CLU.SI.VO, *adj.*, inconclusive.
IN.CON.DI.CIO.NAL, *adj.*, unconditional, absolute, categorical.
IN.CON.FES.SO, *adj.*, unconfessed.
IN.CON.FI.DÊN.CIA, *s.f.*, unconfidence, infidelity, treachery, distrust.
IN.CON.FI.DEN.TE, *adj.*, disloyal, unfaithful.
IN.CON.FUN.DÍ.VEL, *adj.*, unconfoundable, unmistakable, distinct.
IN.CON.GRU.ÊN.CIA, *s.f.*, incongruence, incongruity.
IN.CONS.CI.ÊN.CIA, *s.f.*, unconsciousness.
IN.CONS.CI.EN.TE, *s.2 gen.*, unconscious; *adj.*, unconscious, unaware, insensible.
IN.CON.SIS.TEN.TE, *adj.*, inconsistent, flimsy, incongruous.
IN.CON.SO.LÁ.VEL, *adj.*, inconsolable, disconsolate.
IN.CONS.TÂN.CIA, *s.f.*, inconstancy, instability.
IN.CONS.TAN.TE, *adj.*, inconstant, changeable.
IN.CONS.TI.TU.CIO.NAL, *adj.*, unconstitutional.
IN.CON.TES.TÁ.VEL, *adj.*, incontestable, certain.
IN.CON.TI.DO, *adj.*, unrestricted.
IN.CON.TI.NÊN.CIA, *s.f.*, incontinence.
IN.CON.VE.NI.ÊN.CIA, *s.f.*, inconvenience, impoliteness, inconveniency.
IN.COR.PO.RA.DO, *adj.*, incorporated, consolidated.
IN.COR.PO.RAR, *v.*, to incorporate, to embody, to connect.
IN.COR.RER, *v.*, to incur, to run into.
IN.COR.RE.TO, *adj.*, incorrect, faulty, wrong.
IN.COR.RI.GÍ.VEL, *adj.*, incorrigible, incurable, hopeless.
IN.CRE.DU.LI.DA.DE, *s.f.*, incredulity, ungodliness, unbelief.
IN.CRÉ.DU.LO, *s.m.*, sceptic, agnostic, unbeliever: *adj.*, incredulous, ungodly, impious.
IN.CRE.MEN.TAR, *v.*, to develop, to augment, to increase, to swell.
IN.CRE.MEN.TO, *s.m.*, increment, incrementation, development, increase.
IN.CRI.MI.NAR, *v.*, to incriminate, to accuse, to blame, to criminate.
IN.CRÍ.VEL, *adj.*, incredible, unbelievable, extraordinary.
IN.CU.BA.ÇÃO, *s.f.*, incubation.
IN.CU.BAR, *v.*, to incubate, to hatch.
IN.CUL.TI.VÁ.VEL, *adj.*, uncultivable.
IN.CUL.TO, *adj.*, uncultivated, uncultured, fallow, rough.
IN.CUM.BÊN.CIA, *s.f.*, incumbency, task, duty, responsibility.
IN.CUM.BIR, *v.*, to encharge, to charge with, to entrust, to assign a duty.
IN.CU.RÁ.VEL, *adj.*, incurable, irremediable.
IN.CÚ.RIA, *s.f.*, negligence, carelessness.
IN.CUR.SÃO, *s.f.*, incursion, raid, foray, attack.
IN.CU.TIR, *v.*, to infuse, to instil, to inspire, to inculcate, to suggest.
IN.DA.GA.ÇÃO, *s.f.*, searching, search, indagation, quest, inquiry.
IN.DA.GAR, *v.*, to inquire, to investigate, to query, to quest, to scan, to search.
IN.DE.CÊN.CIA, *s.f.*, indecency, indelicacy, immorality, obscenity.
IN.DE.CEN.TE, *adj.*, *s.2 gen.*, indecent, indecorous, vulgar, improper.
IN.DE.CI.SÃO, *s.f.*, indecision, irresolution, vacillation, hesitation, doubt.
IN.DE.CI.SO, *adj.*, undecided, undecisive, hesitant, vacillating, unconfirmed.
IN.DE.CO.RO.SO, *adj.*, indecorous, unseemly.
IN.DE.FE.RI.DO, *adj.*, rejected, refused.
IN.DE.FE.RI.MEN.TO, *s.m.*, denial, refusal, rejection.
IN.DE.FE.RIR, *v.*, to refuse, to reject a demand.
IN.DE.FE.SO, *adj.*, defenceless, unprotected, undefended.
IN.DE.FI.NI.DO, *s.m.*, vagueness, indefiniteness; *adj.*, indefinite, vague, uncertain.
IN.DE.LÉ.VEL, *adj.*, indelible, indeleble.
IN.DE.LI.CA.DE.ZA, *s.f.*, indelicacy, discourtesy, incivility, unkindness.
IN.DE.LI.CA.DO, *adj.*, indelicate, indecent, impolite, rude.
IN.DE.NI.ZA.ÇÃO, *s.f.*, indemnity,

INDENIZAR — INÉRCIA

indemnification, reparation, damage.
IN.DE.NI.ZAR, *v.*, to indemnify, to repay, to reimburse, to compensate.
IN.DE.PEN.DÊN.CIA, *s.f.*, independence, autonomy, freedom, liberty, independency.
IN.DE.PEN.DEN.TE, *adj.*, independent, free, autonomous.
IN.DES.CRI.TÍ.VEL, *adj.*, unspeakable, indescribable.
IN.DE.SE.JA.DO, *adj.*, undesired, unwished.
IN.DES.TRU.TÍ.VEL, *adj.*, undestroyable.
IN.DE.TER.MI.NA.ÇÃO, *s.f.*, undetermination, hesitation.
IN.DE.VI.DO, *adj.*, undue, improper.
IN.DE.XA.ÇÃO, *s.f.*, indexing.
IN.DE.XAR, *v.*, to index.
IN.DI.A.NO, *adj.*, *s.m.*, Indian.
IN.DI.CA.ÇÃO, *s.f.*, indication, nomination, designation, manifestation, sign, evidence.
IN.DI.CAR, *v.*, to indicate, to denote, to appoint, to show, to determine.
IN.DI.CA.TI.VO, *s.m.*, sign, mark, indication, indicative mod; *adj.*, indicative, expressive.
ÍN.DI.CE, *s.m.*, index, catalogue, table.
IN.DI.CI.AR, *v.*, to denounce, to accuse.
IN.DÍ.CIO, *s.m.*, indicium, indication, clue, trace, vestige.
IN.DI.FE.REN.ÇA, *s.f.*, indifference, indifferency, unconcern, negligence, apathy.
IN.DI.FE.REN.TE, *adj.*, indifferent, unconcerned, negligent, careless.
IN.DI.GES.TÃO, *s.f.*, indigestion.
IN.DIG.NA.ÇÃO, *s.f.*, indignation, vexation.
IN.DIG.NAR, *v.*, to cause indignation, to provoke.
IN.DIG.NI.DA.DE, *s.f.*, indignity, unworthiness.
ÍN.DIO, *adj.*, *s.m.*, Indian.
IN.DI.RE.TO, *adj.*, indirect, oblique, disguised, simulated.
IN.DIS.CI.PLI.NA, *s.f.*, indiscipline, insubordination, disorder, unruliness.
IN.DIS.CRE.TO, *adj.*, indiscreet, imprudent, injudicious.
IN.DIS.CRI.MI.NA.DO, *adj.*, indiscriminate.
IN.DIS.FAR.ÇÁ.VEL, *adj.*, undisguisable.

IN.DIS.POR, *v.*, to indispose, disincline, to irritate, to upset, to alienate.
IN.DIS.PO.SI.ÇÃO, *s.f.*, indisposition, ailment, dislike, aversion.
IN.DIS.POS.TO, *adj.*, indisposed, unwell, sick, ailing, disliking.
IN.DI.VI.DU.AL, *adj.*, individual, personal, single, singular.
IN.DI.VI.DUA.LI.DA.DE, *s.f.*, individuality, identity.
IN.DI.VI.DUA.LIS.MO, *s.m.*, individualism.
IN.DI.VI.DUA.LI.ZAR, *v.*, to individualize.
IN.DI.VÍ.DUO, *s.m.*, being, person, fellow, guy.
IN.DI.VI.SÍ.VEL, *adj.*, indivisible.
IN.DÓ.CIL, *adj.*, indocile, unruly, wayward, restive, stubborn.
ÍN.DO.LE, *s.f.*, nature, temper, sort, type, character, propensity.
IN.DO.LÊN.CIA, *s.f.*, indolence.
IN.DO.LEN.TE, *adj.*, indolent, negligent, apathetic.
IN.DO.LOR, *adj.*, painless.
IN.DU.BI.TÁ.VEL, *adj.*, undoubted, certain, assured.
IN.DU.ÇÃO, *s.f.*, induction, suggestion.
IN.DUL.GÊN.CIA, *s.f.*, indulgence, clemency.
IN.DÚS.TRIA, *s.f.*, industry, works, diligence.
IN.DUS.TRI.AL, *s.2 gen.*, manufacturer, producer; *adj.*, industrial, manufacturing.
IN.DUS.TRIA.LI.ZA.ÇÃO, *s.f.*, industrialization.
IN.DUS.TRIA.LI.ZAR, *v.*, to industrialize.
IN.DUS.TRI.Á.RIO, *s.m.*, industrial employer.
IN.DU.ZIR, *v.*, to induce, to prompt, to incite, to persuade, to conclude.
I.NE.BRI.AR, *v.*, to inebriate, to make drunk, to intoxicate.
I.NÉ.DI.TO, *adj.*, inedited, unpublished.
I.NE.FI.CÁ.CIA, *s.f.*, inefficacy.
I.NE.FI.CAZ, *adj.*, inefficacious, inoperative, powerless.
I.NE.FI.CI.ÊN.CIA, *s.f.*, inefficiency.
I.NE.LE.GÍ.VEL, *adj.*, ineligible.
I.NE.QUÍ.VO.CO, *adj.*, inequivocal.
I.NÉR.CIA, *s.f.*, inertness, inactivity, indolence.

I.NE.REN.TE, *adj.*, inherent, intrinsic, native.
I.NER.TE, *adj.*, inert, inactive, lazy.
I.NES.PE.RA.DO, *adj.*, unexpected, unforeseen, sudden, abrupt.
I.NES.QUE.CÍ.VEL, *adj.*, unforgettable.
I.NE.VI.TÁ.VEL, *adj.*, unavoidable, fatal, unpreventable.
I.NE.XA.TO, *adj.*, inexact, incorrect.
I.NE.XIS.TÊN.CIA, *s.f.*, inexistence.
I.NE.XO.RÁ.VEL, *adj.*, inexorable, inflexible, merciless.
I.NEX.PE.RI.ÊN.CIA, *s.f.*, inexperience, rawness.
I.NEX.PE.RI.EN.TE, *s.2 gen.*, rookie; *adj. 2 gen.*, inexperienced, green, raw.
I.NEX.PLI.CÁ.VEL, *adj.*, inexplicable, incomprehensible, obscure.
IN.FA.LÍ.VEL, *adj.*, infallible, certain, sure.
IN.FA.MAR, *v.*, to defame.
IN.FA.ME, *adj., s.2 gen.*, infamous, odious, shameful.
IN.FÂ.MIA, *s.f.*, infamy, dishonour, disgrace.
IN.FÂN.CIA, *s.f.*, infancy, childhood.
IN.FAN.TI.CI.DA, *s.2 gen.*, infanticide.
IN.FAN.TIL, *adj.*, infantile, childish, innocent.
IN.FAN.TI.LI.DA.DE, *s.f.*, childlike nature, childishness.
IN.FEC.ÇÃO, *s.f.*, infection, contamination, contagion.
IN.FEC.CIO.NAR, *v.*, to infect, to contaminate, to corrupt, to taint.
IN.FEC.CI.O.SO, *adj.*, infective, infectious, contagious.
IN.FE.CUN.DO, *adj.*, infecund, sterile.
IN.FE.LI.CI.DA.DE, *s.f.*, infelicity, unhappiness, misfortune, adversity.
IN.FE.LIZ, *adj.*, unhappy, unfortunate, unlucky, disastrous.
IN.FE.RI.OR, *s.2 gen.*, inferior, subordinate; *adj.*, inferior, low.
IN.FE.RIO.RI.DA.DE, *s.f.*, inferiority.
IN.FER.NAL, *adj.*, infernal, hellish, atrocious, diabolic, terrible.
IN.FER.NO, *s.m.*, hell, underworld.
IN.FES.TAR, *v.*, to infest, attack, molest.

IN.FI.DE.LI.DA.DE, *s.f.*, infidelity, disloyalty, falseness.
IN.FI.EL, *adj.*, infidel, unfaithful, disloyal, dishonest, false.
IN.FIL.TRA.ÇÃO, *s.f.*, infiltration.
IN.FIL.TRAR, *v.*, to infiltrate, to infilter, to seep, to penetrate.
ÍN.FI.MO, *adj.*, lowermost, undermost, inferior.
IN.FI.NI.DA.DE, *s.f.*, infinity, infiniteness.
IN.FI.NI.TO, *s.m.*, infinite, infinity; *adj.*, infinite, infinitive, boundless, timeless, eternal.
IN.FLA.ÇÃO, *s.f.*, inflation, swelling, pride.
IN.FLA.CIO.NAR, *v.*, to inflate.
IN.FLA.MA.ÇÃO, *s.f.*, inflammation, ignition.
IN.FLA.MA.DO, *adj.*, inflamed.
IN.FLA.MAR, *v.*, to inflame, to ignite, to kindle, to excite, to stimulate.
IN.FLA.MÁ.VEL, *adj.*, inflammable.
IN.FLE.XÃO, *s.f.*, inflection, inflexion, variation.
IN.FLE.XÍ.VEL, *adj.*, inflexible, unpliant, stiff, rigid.
IN.FLI.GIR, *v.*, to inflict, to impose.
IN.FLU.ÊN.CIA, *s.f.*, influence, hold, influx, action, power.
IN.FLU.EN.CI.AR, *v.*, to influence, to sway over, to modify, to affect.
IN.FLU.IR, *v.*, to influence, to excite, to implant, to impel, to actuate.
IN.FOR.MA.ÇÃO, *s.f.*, information, intelligence, report.
IN.FOR.MA.DO, *adj.*, informed, aware, knowing.
IN.FOR.MA.DOR, *s.m.*, informer.
IN.FOR.MAN.TE, *s.2 gen.*, informer; *adj.*, informant, informative.
IN.FOR.MAR, *v.*, to inform, to teach, to instruct, to confirm, to tell, to notify.
IN.FOR.MÁ.TI.CA, *s.f.*, informatics, computer science.
IN.FOR.TU.NA.DO, *adj.*, unfortunate, fortuneless, unhappy.
IN.FOR.TÚ.NIO, *s.m.*, misfortune, infelicity, adversity, unhappiness, misery.
IN.FRA.ÇÃO, *s.f.*, infraction, infringement, breach, transgression.

IN.FRA.TOR, *s.m.*, infractor, transgressor, violator, offender.
IN.FRIN.GIR, *v.*, to infringe, to infract, to violate, to transgress, to break.
IN.FU.SÃO, *s.f.*, infusion, maceration.
IN.GE.NU.I.DA.DE, *s.f.*, ingenuity, simplicity, naiveness, frankness.
IN.GÊ.NUO,*adj.*,naïve, simple, ingenuous, frank.
IN.GE.RIR, *v.*, to ingest, to swallow, to introduce, to interfere in.
IN.GLÊS, *adj.*, *s.m.*, English, British.
IN.GRA.TI.DÃO,*s.f.*,ingratitude, ungratefulness.
IN.GRA.TO, *adj.*, ungrateful, thankless, ingrate.
IN.GRE.DI.EN.TE, *s.m.*, ingredient, element.
ÍN.GRE.ME, *adj.*, steep, sheer, abrupt.
IN.GRES.SAR, *v.*, to enter, to go in, to ingress.
IN.GRES.SO, *s.m.*, ingress, entry, entrance, admission, admittance, ticket.
I.NHA.ME, *s.m.*, yam.
I.NI.BI.ÇÃO, *s.f.*, inhibition, prohibition.
I.NI.BIR, *v.*, to inhibit, to check, to forbid, to prohibit, to interdict.
I.NI.CIA.ÇÃO, *s.f.*, initiation, start.
I.NI.CI.A.DO, *adj.*, initiate, adept.
I.NI.CIA.DOR, *s.m.*, initiator, founder.
I.NI.CI.AR, *v.*, to initiate, to begin, to start, to commence, to introduce, to induct.
I.NI.CIA.TI.VA, *s.f.*, iniciative, enterprise, activity.
I.NÍ.CIO, *s.m.*, beginning, start, commencement, outset, opening.
I.NI.MI.GO, *s.m.*, enemy, adversary, foe, opponent, antagonist; *adj.*, averse, inimical.
I.NI.MI.ZA.DE, *s.f.*, enmity, hostility, animosity.
I.NIN.TER.RUP.TO, *adj.*, uninterrupted, unbroken.
I.NI.QUI.DA.DE, *s.f.*, iniquity.
IN.JE.ÇÃO, *s.f.*, injection, shot.
IN.JE.TAR, *v.*, to inject, to introduce, to insert.
IN.JÚ.RIA, *s.f.*, injury, offense, harm, affront, wrong, insult, outrage.
IN.JU.RI.AR, *v.*, to injure, to do harm, to hurt, to affront, to offend.
IN.JUS.TI.ÇA, *s.f.*, injustice, wrong, inequity, iniquity.
IN.JUS.TO, *adj.*, unfair, unjust, dishonest.
I.NOB.SER.VÂN.CIA, *s.f.*, inobservance.
I.NO.CÊN.CIA, *s.f.*, innocence, innocency, harmlessness.
I.NO.CEN.TAR, *v.*, to pronounce not guilty, acquit.
I.NO.CEN.TE, *adj.*, innocent, inoffensive, chaste.
I.NO.CU.LAR, *v.*, to inoculate, to insert, to transmit.
I.NÓ.CUO, *adj.*, innocuous, harmless.
I.NO.DO.RO, *adj.*, inodorous, scentless.
I.NO.FEN.SI.VO, *adj.*, inoffensive, harmless, unoffending.
I.NOL.VI.DÁ.VEL, *adj.*, unforgettable.
I.NOR.GÂ.NI.CO, *adj.*, inorganic.
I.NÓS.PI.TO, *adj.*, inhospitable, wild.
I.NO.VA.ÇÃO, *s.f.*, innovation, change, alteration, newness.
I.NO.VAR, *v.*, to innovate, to renew.
I.NO.XI.DÁ.VEL, *adj.*, inoxidable, rustproof, stainless.
IN.QUÉ.RI.TO, *s.m.*, inquiry, investigation, question, examination.
IN.QUI.E.TA.ÇÃO, *s.f.*, inquietude, unrest, disquiet, anxiety, disturbance.
IN.QUI.E.TAR, *v.*, to disquiet, to disturb, to alarm, to worry.
IN.QUI.E.TO, *adj.*, unquiet, disturbed, uneasy, anxious.
IN.QUIE.TU.DE, *s.f.*, unquietness.
IN.QUI.LI.NO, *s.m.*, tenant, lodger, occupant.
IN.QUI.RI.ÇÃO, *s.f.*, inquest, inquiry, investigation.
IN.QUI.RIR,*v.*,to inquire,to query, to interrogate.
IN.QUI.SI.ÇÃO, *s.f.*, inquisition.
IN.QUI.SI.TI.VO, *adj.*, inquisitive.
IN.SA.CI.Á.VEL, *adj.*, insatiable, insatiate, voracious.
IN.SA.LU.BRE, *adj.*, insalubrious.
IN.SA.LU.BRI.DA.DE, *s.f.*, insalubrity.
IN.SA.NI.DA.DE, *s.f.*, insanity, insaneness.
IN.SA.NO, *adj.*, insane, crazy, mad, demented, foolish.
IN.SA.TIS.FA.ÇÃO, *s.f.*, dissatisfaction.

INSATISFEITO / **INSTRUÇÃO**

IN.SA.TIS.FEI.TO, *adj.*, dissatisfied, unhappy, discontented.
INS.CRE.VER, *v.*, to inscribe, to engrave, to register.
INS.CRI.ÇÃO, *s.f.*, inscription, lettering, legend, matriculation, registry.
INS.CRI.TO, *adj.*, inscribed, registered.
IN.SE.GU.RAN.ÇA, *s.f.*, insecurity, unsafeness.
IN.SE.GU.RO, *adj.*, insecure, unsafe, unsure.
IN.SE.MI.NA.ÇÃO, *s.f.*, insemination.
IN.SEN.SA.TEZ, *s.f.*, folly, nonsense, madness, stupidity.
IN.SEN.SA.TO, *adj.*, senseless, insensate, irrational, foolish.
IN.SEN.SÍ.VEL, *adj.*, unfeeling, insensitive, hard, unaffected.
IN.SE.PA.RÁ.VEL, *adj.*, inseparable.
IN.SER.ÇÃO, insertion.
IN.SE.RIR, *v.*, to insert, to introduce, to put in, to implant.
IN.SER.TO, *adj.*, insert, put in.
IN.SE.TI.CI.DA, *s.m.*, insecticide; *adj.*, insecticidal.
IN.SE.TO, *s.m.*, insect.
IN.SÍ.DIA, *s.f.*, ambush, treachery.
IN.SÍG.NIA, *s.f.*, sign, mark, emblem, symbol.
IN.SIG.NI.FI.CÂN.CIA, *s.f.*, insignificance.
IN.SIG.NI.FI.CAN.TE, *adj.*, insignificant, trivial, unimportant.
IN.SI.NU.A.ÇÃO, *s.f.*, insinuation, hint, allegation.
IN.SI.NU.AR, *v.*, to insinuate, to suggest, to imply, to allege.
IN.SÍ.PI.DO, *adj.*, insipid, tasteless, flat.
IN.SI.PI.EN.TE, *adj., s.2 gen.*, insipient.
IN.SIS.TÊN.CIA, *s.f.*, insistence, perseverance, persistence.
IN.SIS.TIR, *v.*, to insist, to persist, to stand upon.
IN.SO.CI.AL, *adj.*, unsocial.
IN.SO.LA.ÇÃO, *s.f.*, insolation, sunstroke.
IN.SO.LÊN.CIA, *s.f.*, insolence, impertinence, arrogance.
IN.SO.LEN.TE, *adj., s.2 gen.*, insolent, arrogant.
IN.SO.LU.BI.LI.DA.DE, *s.f.*, insolubility.
IN.SO.LÚ.VEL, *adj.*, insoluble, unsolvable.

IN.SOL.VÊN.CIA, *s.f.*, insolvency, bankruptcy.
IN.SOL.VEN.TE, *adj., s.2 gen.*, insolvent.
IN.SÔ.NIA, *s.f.*, insomnia, restlessness, sleeplessness.
IN.SOS.SO, *adj.*, saltless, tasteless, dull.
INS.PE.ÇÃO, *s.f.*, inspection, survey, check, controlment, review.
INS.PE.CIO.NAR, *v.*, to inspect, to examine, to survey, to control.
INS.PE.TOR, *s.m.*, inspector, supervisor, overseer.
INS.PI.RA.ÇÃO, *s.f.*, inspiration, creative impulse, instinct.
INS.PI.RAR, *v.*, to inspire, to inhale, to breathe in, to imbue.
INS.TA.BI.LI.DA.DE, *s.f.*, instability, instableness.
INS.TA.BI.LI.ZAR, *v.*, to unsettle.
INS.TA.LA.ÇÃO, *s.f.*, installation, instalment, facilities, construction.
INS.TA.LA.DOR, *s.m.*, installer, fitter.
INS.TA.LAR, *v.*, to instal, to place in a seat.
INS.TÂN.CIA, *s.f.*, instance, instancy, urgency, law court.
INS.TAN.TÂ.NEO, *adj.*, instantaneous, rapid.
INS.TAN.TE, *s.m.*, instant, moment, minute, second, flash.
INS.TAR, *v.*, to press, to urge.
INS.TAU.RA.ÇÃO, *s.f.*, instauration.
INS.TAU.RAR, *v.*, to begin, to initiate, to establish, to start.
INS.TÁ.VEL, *adj.*, unstable, unsteady, changeable.
INS.TI.GA.DO, *adj.*, instigated, induced.
INS.TI.GAR, *v.*, to instigate, to goad on, to urge, to spur.
INS.TIN.TI.VO, *adj.*, instinctive, conative, natural.
INS.TIN.TO, *s.m.*, instinct, intuition, flair.
INS.TI.TU.I.ÇÃO, *s.f.*, institution, establishment, constitution.
INS.TI.TU.IR, *v.*, to institute, to establish, to found, to instruct.
INS.TI.TU.TO, *s.m.*, institute, institution, order.
INS.TRU.ÇÃO, *s.f.*, instruction, education, schooling, coaching, knowledge.

INS.TRU.Í.DO, *adj.*, learned, educated, wise, initiate.

INS.TRU.IR, *v.*, to instruct, to teach, to educate, to train, to inform.

INS.TRU.MEN.TA.ÇÃO, *s.f.*, instrumentation.

INS.TRU.MEN.TAL, *s.m.*, instruments.

INS.TRU.MEN.TO, *s.m.*, instrument, means, agency, tool, implement.

INS.TRU.TI.VO, *adj.*, instructive, informative, instructional.

INS.TRU.TOR, *s.m.*, instructor, teacher, trainer, coach, tutor.

IN.SU.BOR.DI.NA.ÇÃO, *s.f.*, insubordination, subversion, mutiny, rebellion.

IN.SU.BOR.DI.NA.DO, *adj., s.m.*, insubordinate.

IN.SU.BOR.DI.NAR, *v.*, to revolt, to rebel.

IN.SUBS.TI.TU.Í.VEL, *adj.*, irreplaceable.

IN.SU.CES.SO, *s.m.*, ill success, failure.

IN.SU.FI.CI.EN.TE, *adj.*, insufficient, meager, deficient, scanty.

IN.SU.FLAR, *v.*, to insufflate.

IN.SU.LI.NA, *s.f.*, insulin.

IN.SUL.TAR, *v.*, to insult, to abuse, to affront, to offend.

IN.SUL.TO, *s.m.*, insult, abuse, affront, offence.

IN.SU.POR.TÁ.VEL, *adj.*, intolerable, unbearable.

IN.SUS.TEN.TÁ.VEL, *adj.*, unsustainable, baseless.

IN.TAC.TO, *adj.*, intact, untouched, whole.

ÍN.TE.GRA, *s.f.*, totality, completeness.

IN.TE.GRA.ÇÃO, *s.f.*, integration.

IN.TE.GRAL, *adj.*, integral, complete, entire, total, whole.

IN.TE.GRA.LI.ZAR, *v.*, to integrate.

IN.TE.GRAR, *v.*, to integrate, to complete, to form.

IN.TE.GRI.DA.DE, *s.f.*, integrity, entireness.

ÍN.TE.GRO, *adj.*, complete, entire, intact, inviolable, honest, righteous.

IN.TEI.RAR, *v.*, to complete, to integrate, to inform, to acquaint.

IN.TEI.RO, *s.m.*, whole number, integer; *adj.*, entire, whole, exact, perfect, complete.

IN.TE.LEC.TO, *s.m.*, intellect, intelligence, mind.

IN.TE.LEC.TU.AL, *adj., s.m.*, intellectual.

IN.TE.LEC.TUA.LIS.MO, *s.m.*, intellectualism.

IN.TE.LI.GÊN.CIA, *s.f.*, intelligence, knowledge, intellect.

IN.TE.LI.GEN.TE, *adj.*, clever, intelligent, acute, sagacious.

IN.TE.LI.GÍ.VEL, *adj.*, intelligible, comprehensible, clear, plain.

IN.TEM.PÉ.RIE, *s.f.*, bad weather, inclemency.

IN.TEN.ÇÃO, *s.f.*, intention, intent, purpose, aim.

IN.TEN.CIO.NA.DO, *adj.*, intentioned, affected, disposed.

IN.TEN.CIO.NAL, *adj.*, intentional, intended.

IN.TEN.DÊN.CIA, *s.f.*, intendency, administration.

IN.TEN.SÃO, *s.f.*, intensity.

IN.TEN.SI.DA.DE, *s.f.*, intensity.

IN.TEN.SI.FI.CAR, *v.*, to intensify, to amplify, to enhance.

IN.TEN.SI.VO, *adj.*, intensive.

IN.TEN.SO, *adj.*, intense, intensive, active, vivid.

IN.TEN.TO, *s.m.*, intention, intent, plan, project, aim.

IN.TER.CÂM.BIO, *s.m.*, exchange, interchange, barter, reciprocity.

IN.TER.CE.DER, *v.*, to intercede, to mediate, to plead for, to intervene.

IN.TER.CEP.TA.ÇÃO, *s.f.*, interception, interruption, obstruction.

IN.TER.CEP.TAR, *v.*, to intercept, interrupt, obstruct.

IN.TER.CES.SÃO, *s.f.*, intercession.

IN.TER.CES.SOR, *s.m.*, intercessor, interceder.

IN.TER.CON.TI.NEN.TAL, *adj.*, intercontinental.

IN.TER.DI.TAR, *v.*, to interdict, to forbid, to prohibit.

IN.TE.RES.SA.DO, *adj.*, interested, concerned, biased.

IN.TE.RES.SAN.TE, *adj.*, interesting.

IN.TE.RES.SAR, *v.*, to interest, to concern, to affect.

IN.TE.RES.SE, *s.m.*, interest, benefit, advantage,

profit, gain, regard.
IN.TE.RES.TA.DU.AL, *adj.*, *s.2 gen.*, interstate.
IN.TER.FE.RÊN.CIA, *s.f.*, interference, intervention.
IN.TER.FE.RIR, *v.*, to interfere, to intervene, to interpose, to restrict.
IN.TER.FO.NE, *s.m.*, interphone.
ÍN.TE.RIM, *s.m.*, meantime, interim.
IN.TE.RI.NO, *adj.*, interim, temporary, conditional.
IN.TE.RI.OR, *s.m.*, interior, inland, countryside, inside, province; *adj.*, interior, inner, inward, internal.
IN.TE.RIO.RA.NO, *adj.*, provincial, upcountry.
IN.TER.JEI.ÇÃO, *s.f.*, interjection.
IN.TER.LO.CU.TOR, *s.m.*, interlocutor, speaker.
IN.TER.LO.CU.TO.RA, *s.f.*, interlocutress.
IN.TER.ME.DI.Á.RIO, *s.m.*, intermediate, intermediary, broker; *adj.*, intermediate, interposed.
IN.TER.MÉ.DIO, *s.m.*, intermediary, agent, mediator, way; *adj.*, intervening, intermediate.
IN.TER.MI.NÁ.VEL, *adj.*, interminable, endless, limitless.
IN.TER.MUN.DI.AL, *adj.*, intercontinental, intermundane.
IN.TER.MUS.CU.LAR, *adj.*, intermuscular.
IN.TER.NA.ÇÃO, *s.f.*, internation, internment.
IN.TER.NA.CIO.NAL, *adj.*, international.
IN.TER.NA.CIO.NA.LIS.MO, *s.m.*, internationalism.
IN.TER.NA.CIO.NA.LI.ZAR, *v.*, to internationalize.
IN.TER.NA.DO, *adj.*, interned.
IN.TER.NAR, *v.*, to intern, to confine, to introduce, to insert.
IN.TER.NA.TO, *s.m.*, boarding school, orphanage.
IN.TER.NO, *s.m.*, internee; *adj.*, internal, intern, interior, inside, inner.
IN.TER.PE.LA.ÇÃO, *s.f.*, interpellation, questioning.
IN.TER.PE.LAN.TE, *s.2 gen.*, interpellant.
IN.TER.PE.LAR, *v.*, to interpellate, to question, to interrogate.
IN.TER.POR, *v.*, to interpose, to place between, to interrupt, to intervene.

IN.TER.PRE.TA.ÇÃO, *s.f.*, interpretation, explanation, explication, version.
IN.TER.PRE.TAR, *v.*, to interpret, to expound, to elucidate.
IN.TÉR.PRE.TE, *s.2 gen.*, interpreter, translator, performer, artist.
IN.TER.RO.GA.ÇÃO, *s.f.*, interrogation, questioning, interrogatory, inquiry.
IN.TER.RO.GA.DO, *adj.*, questioned, interrogated.
IN.TER.RO.GAR, *v.*, to interrogate, to inquire, to examine, to ask.
IN.TER.RO.GA.TÓ.RIO, *s.m.*, interrogatory, hearing, interrogation, questioning.
IN.TER.ROM.PER, *v.*, interrupt, discontinue, cease, break off, stop, desist.
IN.TER.RUP.ÇÃO, *s.f.*, interruption, cessation, intermission, suspension, break.
IN.TER.RUP.TOR, *s.m.*, circuit breaker, switch; *adj.*, interrupting.
IN.TE.RUR.BA.NO, *adj.*, interurban; between cities.
IN.TER.VA.LO, *s.m.*, interval, space, intermission, interact.
IN.TER.VEN.ÇÃO, *s.f.*, intervention, interference.
IN.TER.VEN.TOR, *s.m.*, interventor, temporary governor.
IN.TER.VIR, *v.*, to intervene, to interfere, to interpose, to intermediate.
IN.TES.TI.NAL, *adj.*, intestinal.
IN.TES.TI.NO, *s.m.*, intestine, bowel, entrails; *adj.*, intestine, internal, inward.
IN.TI.MA.ÇÃO, *s.f.*, notification, citation, announcement, summons, writ.
IN.TI.MAR, *v.*, to summon, to cite, to convoke, to notify, to inform.
IN.TI.MI.DA.ÇÃO, *s.f.*, intimidation.
IN.TI.MI.DA.DE, *s.f.*, intimacy, privacy, familiarity, nearness, friendship.
IN.TI.MI.DAR, *v.*, to intimidate, to frighten, to discourage, to bully.
ÍN.TI.MO, *adj.*, intimate, inner, internal, innermost, inmost, close, near.
IN.TI.TU.LA.ÇÃO, *s.f.*, intitulation.

IN.TI.TU.LAR, v., to intitule, to give a right to, to entitle, to name.
IN.TO.CÁ.VEL, adj., untouchable.
IN.TO.LE.RÂN.CIA, s.f., intolerance, bigotry, intolerancy, impatience.
IN.TO.LE.RAN.TE, s.2 gen., intolerant, intransigent.
IN.TO.LE.RÁ.VEL, adj., intolerable, unbearable, insupportable.
IN.TO.XI.CA.ÇÃO, s.f., intoxication, poisoning.
IN.TO.XI.CA.DO, adj., intoxicated.
IN.TO.XI.CAR, v., to poison, to intoxicate.
IN.TRA.GÁ.VEL, adj., unpalatable, uneatable.
IN.TRA.MUS.CU.LAR, adj., intramuscular.
IN.TRAN.QUI.LI.DA.DE, s.f., intranquility.
IN.TRAN.SI.GÊN.CIA, s.f., intransigence.
IN.TRAN.SI.TÁ.VEL, adj., impassable, untransitable, pathless.
IN.TRAN.SI.TI.VO, adj., intransitive.
IN.TRANS.PO.NÍ.VEL, adj., unsurmountable.
IN.TRA.TÁ.VEL, adj., intractable, stubborn, dogged, haughty.
IN.TRA.VE.NO.SO, adj., intravenous.
IN.TRÉ.PI.DO,adj.,intrepid,bold,fearless, brave.
IN.TRI.GA, s.f., intrigue, plot, scheme, conspiracy, snare, trap.
IN.TRI.GAR, v., to intrigue, to involve, to entangle, to plot for, to scheme.
IN.TRÍN.SE.CO, adj., intrinsic, inherent, inward.
IN.TRO.DU.ÇÃO, s.f., introduction, importation, preface.
IN.TRO.DU.TOR, s.m., introducer.
IN.TRO.DU.ZIR, v., to introduce, to lead in, to bring in, to import, to insert.
IN.TRO.ME.TER, v., to introduce, to intrude, to insert, to intromit.
IN.TRO.ME.TI.DO, s.m., intruder; adj., intrusive, importunate, meddlesome.
IN.TRO.MIS.SÃO, s.f., intromission, interference, introduction.
IN.TRO.VER.SÃO, s.f., introversion.
IN.TRU.SO, s.m., intruder, trespasser; adj., intruded, intrusive.
IN.TU.I.ÇÃO, s.f., intuition, feeling.
IN.TU.I.TI.VO, adj., intuitive.
IN.TUI.TO, s.m., design, intention, plan, scheme, aim.
I.NU.MA.NO, adj., inhuman, cruel, brutal.
I.NU.ME.RÁ.VEL, adj., innumerable, unnumbered.
I.NUN.DA.ÇÃO, s.f., inundation, flood, overflow, cataclysm.
I.NUN.DA.DO, adj., flooded, awash.
I.NUN.DAR, v., to inundate, to flood, to overflow, to deluge.
I.NÚ.TIL, adj., worthless person; adj., inutile, useless, unnecessary, superfluous, hopeless, needless.
I.NU.TI.LI.DA.DE, s.f., inutility, uselessness, worthlessness.
I.NU.TI.LI.ZAR, v., to nullify, to make useless, to frustrate.
IN.VA.DIR, v., to invade, to conquer, to encroach.
IN.VA.LI.DEZ, s.f., invalidity, infirmity, disability, invalidism.
IN.VÁ.LI.DO, s.m., invalid; adj., infirm, disabled, invalid.
IN.VA.RI.Á.VEL, adj., invariable, unchangeable, unalterable, constant.
IN.VA.SÃO, s.f., invasion, incursion, inroad.
IN.VA.SOR, s.m., invader, forayer.
IN.VE.JA, s.f., envy, jealousy, enviousness, emulation.
IN.VE.JAR, v., to envy, to feel envious of, to grudge, to desire.
IN.VE.JO.SO, s.m., envier, grudger; adj., envious, jealous.
IN.VEN.ÇÃO, s.f., invention, creation, discovery.
IN.VEN.CI.BI.LI.DA.DE, s.f., invincibility, invincibleness, insuperability.
IN.VEN.CÍ.VEL, adj., invincible, insuperable.
IN.VEN.TA.DO, adj., invented.
IN.VEN.TAR, v., to invent, to create.
IN.VEN.TÁ.RIO, s.m., inventory, schedule, register, stock.
IN.VEN.TO, s.m., invention.
IN.VEN.TOR, s.m., inventor, discoverer, author, fabricator.
IN.VER.NAL, adj., hibernal, winterly.

INVERNO — **IRREVOGÁVEL**

IN.VER.NO, *s.m.*, winter, winter season, winter time.
IN.VE.ROS.SÍ.MIL, *adj.*, improbable, unlikely.
IN.VER.SÃO, *s.f.*, inversion, reversion, reversal.
IN.VER.SO, *s.m.*, contrary, reverse, inverse; *adj.*, inverse, reciprocal.
IN.VER.TE.BRA.DO, *s.m.*, invertebrate animal; *adj.*, invertebrate.
IN.VER.TER, *v.*, to invert, to reverse, to transpose, to change, to modify.
IN.VÉS, *s.m.*, reverse side, opposite.
IN.VES.TI.DA, *s.f.*, attack, assault, charge, rush.
IN.VES.TI.DO, *adj.*, vested.
IN.VES.TI.GA.ÇÃO, *s.f.*, investigation, inquiry, research.
IN.VES.TI.GA.DOR, *s.m.*, investigator, detective, researcher; *adj.*, investigating.
IN.VES.TI.GAR, *v.*, to investigate, examine, to search into.
IN.VES.TI.MEN.TO, *s.m.*, investment, attack, assault.
IN.VES.TIR, *v.*, to invest, to attack, to assault.
IN.VI.Á.VEL, *adj.*, unviable.
IN.VIC.TO, *adj.*, unvanquished, unconquered.
IN.VI.SI.BI.LI.DA.DE, *s.f.*, invisibility.
IN.VI.SÍ.VEL, *adj.*, invisible, unseen.
IN.VO.CA.ÇÃO, *s.f.*, invocation.
IN.VO.CAR, *v.*, to invoke, to implore, to call for protection or aid.
IN.VÓ.LU.CRO, *s.m.*, involucre, wrapping, cover, wrappage.
IN.VO.LUN.TÁ.RIO, *adj.*, *s.m.*, involuntary.
IN.VUL.GAR, *adj.*, invulgar, rare, unusual, exceptional.
IN.VUL.NE.RÁ.VEL, *adj.*, invulnerable.
IO.DO, *s.m.*, iodine.
IO.GA, *s.f.*, yoga.
IO.IÔ, *s.m.*, yo-yo.
IO.GUR.TE, *s.m.*, yoghurt.
ÍP.SI.LÃO, *s.m.*, wye, upsilon.
IR, *v.*, to go, to move, to depart, to go away, to proceed, to row, to sail, to travel.
I.RA, *s.f.*, ranger, rage, wrath, ire, passion, exasperation.

I.RA.DO, *adj.*, irate, ireful, angry, wrathful, furious.
I.RA.NI.A.NO, *adj.*, *s.m.*, Iranian.
I.RA.QUE, *s.m.*, Iraq.
I.RA.QUI.A.NO, *adj.*, *s.m.*, Iraqi, Iraki.
I.RAR, *v.*, to make angry, to enrage, to irritate, to provoke.
Í.RIS, *s.f.*, iris.
IR.LAN.DÊS, *adj.*, *s.m.*, Irish, Irishman.
IR.MÃ, *s.f.*, sister.
IR.MA.NAR, *v.*, to fraternize, to fellow, to couple.
IR.MAN.DA.DE, *s.f.*, brotherhood, sisterhood, fraternity.
IR.MÃO, *s.m.*, brother, twin.
I.RO.NI.A, *s.f.*, irony, mockery, sarcasm.
I.RÔ.NI.CO, *adj.*, ironic, sarcastic.
IR.RA.CIO.NAL, *adj.*, irrational, illogical.
IR.RA.CIO.NA.LI.DA.DE, *s.f.*, irrationality, unreason.
IR.RA.DI.A.ÇÃO, *s.f.*, irradiation, irradiance.
IR.RA.DI.AR, *v.*, to irradiate, to emit rays, to radiate.
IR.RE.AL, *adj.*, unreal, illusive, visionary.
IR.RE.A.LI.DA.DE, *s.f.*, unreality, unsubstantiality.
IR.RE.CO.NHE.CÍ.VEL, *adj.*, irrecognizable.
IR.RE.CU.PE.RÁ.VEL, *adj.*, irretrievable, irrecoverable.
IR.RE.FU.TÁ.VEL, *adj.*, irrefutable, unquestionable.
IR.RE.GU.LAR, *adj.*, irregular, illegal, lawless.
IR.RE.GU.LA.RI.DA.DE, *s.f.*, irregularity.
IR.RE.PA.RÁ.VEL, *adj.*, irreparable.
IR.RE.QUIE.TO, *adj.*, unquiet, restless, fussy, turbulent.
IR.RE.SIS.TÍ.VEL, *adj.*, irresistible, resistless, overpowering.
IR.RES.PON.SA.BI.LI.DA.DE, *s.f.*, irresponsibility.
IR.RES.PON.SÁ.VEL, *adj.*, irresponsible.
IR.RES.TRI.TO, *adj.*, unrestricted, unrestrained.
IR.RE.VE.RÊN.CIA, *s.f.*, irreverence, disrespect.
IR.RE.VE.REN.TE, *adj.*, *s.2 gen.*, irreverent.
IR.RE.VER.SÍ.VEL, *adj.*, irreversible.
IR.RE.VO.GÁ.VEL, *adj.*, irrevocable, unchangeable.

IR.RI.GAR, *v.*, to irrigate, to water.
IR.RI.SÃO, *s.f.*, irrision, derision, sneering.
IR.RI.SÓ.RIO, *adj.*, derisive, scornful.
IR.RI.TA.ÇÃO, *s.f.*, irritation, anger, enragement.
IR.RI.TAR, *v.*, to irritate, to anger, to annoy, to enrage.
IR.RI.TÁ.VEL, *adj.*, irritable.
IR.ROM.PER, *v.*, to rush in, to urge forward, to break out, to emerge.
IS.CA, *s.f.*, bait, lure, tinder, allurement.
I.SEN.ÇÃO, *s.f.*, exemption, freedom, immunity.
I.SEN.TAR, *v.*, to exempt, to free from, to release, to relieve.
I.SEN.TO, *adj.*, exempt, free, immune.
IS.LÃ, *s.m.*, Islam.
IS.LÂ.MI.CO, *adj.*, *s.m.*, Islamic.
IS.LAN.DÊS, *adj.*, *s.m.*, Icelander, Icelandic.
I.SO.LA.DO, *adj.*, isolated, separate, alone, segregate.
I.SO.LA.MEN.TO, *s.m.*, isolation, separation, insulation.
I.SO.LAN.TE, *s.m.*, isolating, insulating material; *adj.*, isolating.
I.SO.LAR, *v.*, to isolate, to detach, to separate, to insulate.
IS.QUEI.RO, *s.m.*, lighter, fire-lighter.
IS.RA.EL, *s.m.*, Israel.
IS.RA.E.LEN.SE, *adj.*, *s.2 gen.*, Israeli.
IS.RA.E.LI.TA, *adj.*, *s.2 gen.*, Israelite, Hebrew.
IS.SO, *pron.*, that; **ISSO MESMO** - exactly.
IS.TO, *pron.*, this.
I.TÁ.LIA, *s.f.*, Italy.
I.TA.LI.A.NO, *adj.* *s.m.*, Italian.
Í.TA.LO, *adj.*, *s.m.*, Italian.
I.TEM, *s.m.*, item, article.
I.TE.RA.ÇÃO, *s.f.*, iteration, repetition.
I.TE.RA.TI.VO, *adj.*, iterative.
I.TI.NE.RAN.TE,*s.2 gen.*,itinerant; *adj.*, itinerary.
I.TI.NE.RÁ.RIO, *s.m.*, itinerary, route, schedule.
IU.GOS.LA.VO, *adj.*, *s.m.*, Yugoslav.

J

J, *s.m.*, tenth letter of the Portuguese alphabet.
JÁ, *adv.*, now, at once, immediately, then, presently; conj., already, since, once.
JA.BU.TI, *s.m.*, land turtle.
JA.CA.RÉ, *s.m.*, alligator, jacare, cayman.
JA.CIN.TO, *s.m.*, hyacinth.
JA.EZ, *s.m.*, harness, quality, sort.
JA.GUAR, *s.m.*, jaguar.
JA.GUA.TI.RI.CA, *s.f.*, leopard cat.
JA.MAI.CA.NO, *adj.*, *s.m.*, Jamaican.
JA.MAIS, *adv.*, never, ever, at no time.
JA.NEI.RO, *s.m.*, January.
JA.NE.LA, *s.f.*, window.
JAN.GA.DA, *s.f.*, raft.
JÂN.GAL, *s.m.*, jungle.
JAN.TA, *s.f.*, dinner.
JAN.TAR, *s.m.*, dinner; *v.*, to dine.
JA.PO.NA, *s.f.*, short jacket.
JA.PO.NÊS, *adv.*, *s.m.*, Japanese.
JA.QUE.TA, *s.f.*, jacket, jumper.
JAR.DA, *s.f.*, yard (36 inches; 0,9144m).
JAR.DIM, *s.m.*, garden, flower-garden; **JARDIM DE INFÂNCIA** - kindergarten.
JAR.DI.NEI.RO, *s.m.*, gardener.
JAR.GÃO, *s.m.*, jargon, slang, gibberish.
JAR.RA, *s.f.*, jar, pitcher, jug, vase, flowerpot.
JAR.RO, *s.m.*, pitcher, jar.
JAS.MIM, *s.m.*, jasmin, jessamin.
JA.TO, *s.m.*, gush, jet, outpour, stream.
JAU.LA, *s.f.*, cage.
JA.VA.LI, *s.m.*, wild pig, wild boar.
JA.VA.NÊS, *adj.*, *s.m.*, Javanese.
JA.ZER, *v.*, to lie, to be stretched out, to rest.
JA.ZI.DA, *s.f.*, resting-place, couch, natural deposit of ores.
JA.ZI.GO, *s.m.*, grave, sepulcher, tomb, burial monument.
JEI.TO, *s.m.*, aptitude, aptness, way, knack, skill, dexterity.
JEI.TO.SO, *adj.*, skilful, adroit, dexterous, clever, handy.
JE.JU.AR, *v.*, to fast, to be ignorant.
JE.JUM, *s.m.*, fast(ing), abstinence.
JE.RI.MUM, *s.m.*, pumpkin.
JE.SU.Í.TA, *s.m.*, Jesuit; *adj.*, jesuitical.
JI.BOI.A, *s.f.*, boa constrictor.
JI.PE, *s.m.*, jeep.
JO.A.LHEI.RO, *s.m.*, jeweler.
JO.A.LHE.RI.A, *s.f.*, jewelry store; jeweller's shop.
JO.ÃO-NIN.GUÉM, *pron.*, nobody.
JO.E.LHO, *s.m.*, knee, joint.
JO.GA.DA, *s.f.*, play, game, move, stroke, cast.
JO.GA.DOR, *s.m.*, player, gambler.
JO.GAR, *v.*, to play, to take part in a game, to gamble, to stake.
JO.GO, *s.m.*, game, match, play, gamble.
JO.GRAL, *s.m.*, jester, scoffer.
JOI.A, *s.f.*, jewel, trinket, gem.
JÓ.QUEI, *s.m.*, jockey.
JOR.NA.DA, *s.f.*, journey, treck, a day's work, expedition.
JOR.NAL, *s.m.*, newspaper, journal, diary.
JOR.NA.LEI.RO, *s.m.*, newsboy, newspaper boy, newsdealer; *adj.*, daily.
JOR.NA.LIS.MO, *s.m.*, journalism, press.
JOR.NA.LIS.TA, *s.2 gen.*, journalist, reporter, newspaperman.
JOR.RAR, *v.*, to gush, to spur, to spout out, to pour, to belly out.
JOR.RO, *s.m.*, outpour, gush, jet, spurt, spate, stream.
JO.VEM, *s.2 gen.*, young person; *adj.*, young, youthful.
JO.VI.AL, *adj.*, jovial, merry, gay, jolly.
JO.VI.A.LI.DA.DE, *s.f.*, joviality, merriment,

jollity, gaiety, good humour.
JU.BI.LEU, *s.m.*, jubilee.
JÚ.BI.LO, *s.m.*, jubilation, exultation, joy, rejoicing, satisfaction.
JU.DAI.CO, *adj.*, Jewish, Judaic.
JU.DA.ÍS.MO, *s.m.*, Judaism.
JU.DEU, *s.m.(f.-IA)*, Jew; *adj.*, Jewish.
JU.DI.CI.AL, *adj.*, judicial, juridical.
JU.GO, *s.m.*, yoke, submission, servitude.
JU.IZ, *s.m.*, judge, referee, arbiter.
JU.Í.ZO, *s.m.*, judgement, trial, brains, reason, opinion.
JUL.GA.MEN.TO, *s.m.*, judgement, verdict, sentence, opinion, court session, trial.
JUL.GAR, *v.*, to judge, to try, to pass sentence on, to think, to deem, to believe.
JU.LHO, *s.m.*, July.
JU.MEN.TO, *s.m.*, ass, donkey.
JUN.ÇÃO, *s.f.*, junction, connection, joint, linking.
JUN.GIR, *v.*, to yoke, to unite, to couple, to join, to link.
JU.NHO, *s.m.*, June.
JÚ.NIOR, *adj.*, junior, younger.
JUN.TA, *s.f.*, junction, board, juncture, union, pair, yoke, team.
JUN.TAR, *v.*, to join, to connect, to associate, to collect, to adjoin.
JUN.TO *adj.*, united, jointed, next to, near, close, together.
JU.RA.DO, *s.m.*, member of the jury; *adj.*, sworn to.
JU.RA.MEN.TO, *s.m.*, swearing, oath, vow, imprecation.
JU.RAR, *v.*, to swear, to vow, to pledge.
JÚ.RI, *s.m.*, jury.
JU.RÍ.DI.CO, *adj.*, juridical, forensic, legal.
JU.RIS.DI.ÇÃO, *s.f.*, jurisdiction, power, authority.
JU.RIS.PRU.DÊN.CIA, *s.f.*, jurisprudence, the science of law.
JU.RIS.TA, *s.2 gen.*, lawyer, jurist.
JU.RO, *s.m.*, interest, right.
JUS, *s.m.*, right.
JUS.TA.MEN.TE, *adv.*, just, justly, fairly.
JUS.TI.ÇA, *s.f.*, justice, rightness, justness, equity.
JUS.TI.FI.CAR, *v.*, to justify, to prove, to warrant, to vindicate.
JUS.TI.FI.CÁ.VEL, *adj.*, justifiable.
JUS.TO, *s.m.*, fair, correct; *adj.*, just, fair, equitable, right, righteous, honest.
JU.TA, *s.f.*, jute.
JU.VE.NIL, *adj.*, juvenile, youthful, young.
JU.VEN.TUDE, *s.f.*, youth, young people.

K, *s.m.*, letter not included in the Portuguese alphabet; used only in foreign words (internationally known symbols and abbreviations).
KAN.TIS.MO, *s.m.*, Kantism.

KG, *s.m.*, kg, kilogram.
KM, *s.m.*, km, kilometer.
KW, *s.m.*, kw, kilowatt.

L

L, *s.m.*, the eleventh letter of the Portuguese alphabet; Roman numeral for fifty (**L**).
LÁ, *s.m.*, la, a (musical note); *adv.*, there, beyond.
LÃ, *s.f.*, wool.
LA.BA.RE.DA, *s.f.*, flame, blaze, flare, fire.
LÁ.BIO, *s.m.*, lip, labium.
LA.BI.O.DEN.TAL, *adj.*, *s.2 gen.*, labiodental.
LA.BI.RIN.TO, *s.m.*, labyrinth, embarrassment.
LA.BO.RA.TÓ.RIO, *s.m.*, laboratory.
LA.BO.RI.O.SO, *adj.*, laborious, toilsome.
LA.BU.TAR, *v.*, to struggle, to drudge, to labour.
LA.ÇA.DA, *s.f.*, bowknot, tie, loop.
LA.CAI.O, *s.m.*, lackey, valet.
LA.ÇAR, *v.*, to lace, to tie, to bind.
LA.ÇO, *s.m.*, bowknot, bond, bow, tie, loop.
LA.CÔ.NI.CO, *adj.*, Laconian, laconic, curt, brief, succinct, concise.
LA.CRAR, *v.*, to seal, to plumb.
LA.CRE, *s.m.*, sealing wax.
LA.CRI.MAL, *adj.*, lachrymal, lacrimal.
LA.CRI.ME.JAN.TE, *adj.*, tearful.
LA.CRI.ME.JAR, *v.*, to shed tears.
LA.CRI.MO.GÊ.NEO, *adj.*, lachrymatory.
LA.CRI.MO.SO, *adj.*, lachrymose, tearful.
LÁC.TEO, *adj.*, milky.
LA.CU.NA, *s.f.*, gap, blank, omission.
LA.CUS.TRE, *adj.*, lacustrine.
LA.DA.I.NHA, *s.f.*, litany.
LA.DEI.RA, *s.f.*, declivity, hill, steep street, slope, ascent.
LA.DO, *s.m.*, side, flank.
LA.DRÃO, *s.m.*, thief, burglar, robber, bandit, gansgter.
LA.DRAR, *v.*, to bark, to bay.
LA.DRI.LHAR, *v.*, to tile.
LA.DRI.LHO, *s.m.*, tile, floor tile, brick.
LA.DRO.A.GEM, *s.m.*, thievery, robbery.
LA.GAR.TA, *s.f.*, caterpillar; track.
LA.GAR.TI.XA, *s.f.*, gecko, hiker.
LA.GAR.TO, *s.m.*, lizard.
LA.GO, *s.m.*, lake, pool, pond.
LA.GO.A, *s.f.*, lagoon, pond, pool, marsh.
LA.GOS.TA, *s.f.*, lobster.
LÁ.GRI.MA, *s.f.*, tear, teardrop, drop.
LA.GU.NA, *s.f.*, lagoon.
LAI.A, *s.f.*, quality, kind, sort, nature, race, ilk.
LAI.VO, *s.m.*, spot, blot, speck.
LA.JE, *s.f.*, flag, flagstone, flagging.
LA.JO.TA, *s.f.*, small flagstone.
LA.MA, *s.f.*, mud, dirt, sludge, mire, slime.
LA.MA.ÇAL, *s.m.*, slough, muddy place, bog, swamp.
LAM.BA.DA, *s.f.*, blow, stroke, lash, rap.
LAM.BE.DOR, *s.m.*, licker; flatterer, wheedler.
LAM.BER, *v.*, to lick, to touch slightly, to polish.
LAM.BI.DA, *s.f.*, licking, lick; flattery.
LAM.BRE.TA, *s.f.*, scooter.
LAM.BU.JA, *s.f.*, sweetmeat, gain.
LAM.BU.JEM, *s.f.*, sweetmeat, dainty; gain.
LAM.BU.ZAR, *v.*, to dirty, to stain.
LA.MEN.TA.ÇÃO, *s.f.*, lamentation, wailing, outcry.
LA.MEN.TAR, *v.*, to lament, to regret, to pity.
LA.MEN.TÁ.VEL, *adj.*, lamentable, doleful, mournful, grievous.
LA.MEN.TO, *s.m.*, lament, moan, groan, complaint.
LÂ.MI.NA, *s.f.*, blade, sheet, platter, strip.
LA.MI.NA.ÇÃO, *s.f.*, lamination.
LA.MI.NAR, *v.*, to laminate, to roll.
LÂM.PA.DA, *s.f.*, lamp, bulb; light.
LAM.PA.RI.NA, *s.f.*, oil lamp, small lamp.
LAM.PE.JAR, *v.*, to sparkle, to coruscate.
LAM.PI.ÃO, *s.m.*, lantern, large lamp.
LA.MÚ.RIA, *s.f.*, lamentation, complaint.
LAN.ÇA, *s.f.*, lance, spear, javelin.

LANÇAMENTO   **LAVRAR**

LAN.ÇA.MEN.TO, *s.m.*, cast, casting, throw, pitch, release, publication, edition.
LAN.ÇA-PER.FU.ME, *s.m.*, perfume squirter.
LAN.ÇAR, *v.*, to cast, to throw, to release, to pitch, to fling, to launch.
LAN.CE, *s.m.*, throw, cast, casting, hurl, conjuncture, risk.
LAN.CHA, *s.f.*, motorboat, launch, barge.
LAN.CHAR, *v.*, to take a snack, to eat.
LAN.CHE, *s.m.*, snack.
LAN.CHO.NE.TE, *s.f.*, snack bar.
LA.NHAR, *v.*, to wound, to hurt, to injure, to bruise.
LA.NÍ.FE.RO, *adj.*, lanigerous.
LAN.TER.NA, *s.f.*, lantern.
LA.PE.LA, *s.f.*, lapel.
LA.PI.DA.ÇÃO, *s.f.*, stone-cutting, refining, lapidation.
LA.PI.DAR, *v.*, to lapidate, to polish gems, to polish.
LÁ.PI.DE, *s.f.*, gravestone, tombstone, ledger.
LÁ.PIS, *s.m.*, pencil.
LAP.SO, *s.m.*, lapse, slip, error.
LAR, *s.m.*, home, residence.
LA.RAN.JA, *s.f.*, orange.
LA.RAN.JA.DA, *s.f.*, orangeade.
LA.RAN.JAL, *s.m.*, orangery.
LA.RAN.JEI.RA, *s.f.*, orange (tree).
LA.RÁ.PIO, *s.m.*, pilferer, filcher, thief.
LA.REI.RA, *s.f.*, fireplace.
LAR.GA.DA, *s.f.*, start, departure, prowess.
LAR.GA.DO, *adj.*, abandoned, despised.
LAR.GAR, *v.*, to release, to let go, to free, to relax, to leave, to ease, to abandon.
LAR.GO, *s.m.*, breadth, width, plaza, public square, high sea; *adj.*, broad, large, wide, ample.
LAR.GU.RA, *s.f.*, breadth, width, wideness, broadness.
LA.RIN.GE, *s.f.*, larynx.
LA.RIN.GI.TE, *s.f.*, laryngitis.
LAR.VA, *s.f.*, larva, worm.
LAS.CAR, *v.*, to splinter, to chip, to crack, to cleave.
LAS.CI.VO, *adj.*, lascivious, wanton, lewd.

LA.SER, *s.m.*, laser.
LÁS.TI.MA, *s.f.*, pity, pain, grief, sorrow, lamentation, compassion.
LAS.TI.MAR, *v.*, to lament, to regret, to grieve, to deplore, to commiserate.
LAS.TI.MO.SO, *adj.*, pitiful, doleful.
LA.TA, *s.f.*, tin, can, tin plate, canister.
LA.TÃO, *s.m.*, brass.
LA.TE.JAR, *v.*, to pulsate, to throb, to palpitate, to pulse.
LA.TEN.TE, *adj.*, latent, hidden, concealed.
LA.TE.RAL, *adj.*, lateral, transversal.
LA.TI.CÍ.NIO, *s.m.*, dairy, creamery.
LA.TI.DO, *s.m.*, bark, barking, yelp, baying.
LA.TI.FUN.DI.Á.RIO, *s.m.*, the owner of a latifundium.
LA.TI.FÚN.DIO, *s.m.*, latifundium, a large farm.
LA.TIM, *s.m.*, Latin.
LA.TI.NI.ZAR, *v.*, to Latinize.
LA.TI.NO, *adj.*, *s.m.*, Latin.
LA.TI.NO-A.ME.RI.CA.NO, *adj.*, *s.m.*, Latin-American.
LA.TIR, *v.*, to bark, to yap, to yelp, howl.
LA.TI.TU.DE, *s.f.*, latitude, breadth, scope.
LA.TRI.NA, *s.f.*, latrine, privy.
LA.TRO.CÍ.NIO, *s.m.*, armed robbery, hold-up.
LAU.DO, *s.m.*, report, award, report of experts.
LÁU.REA, *s.f.*, laurel.
LAU.RE.AR, *v.*, to laureate, to praise, to applaud.
LAU.TO, *adj.*, sumptuous, splendid, abundant.
LA.VA, *s.f.*, lava, torrent, fire.
LA.VA.BO, *s.m.*, any wash-basin.
LA.VA.DEI.RA, *s.f.*, laundress, washing-machine.
LA.VA.DO, *adj.*, washed.
LA.VA.GEM, *s.f.*, wash, cleansing, ablution.
LA.VAN.DA, *s.f.*, lavender.
LA.VAN.DE.RI.A, *s.f.*, laundry.
LA.VAR, *v.*, to wash, to bathe, to cleanse, to purify, to purge.
LA.VA.TÓ.RIO, *s.m.*, lavatory, wash-basin.
LA.VOU.RA, *s.f.*, farming, agriculture, tillage.
LA.VRA.DOR, *s.m.*, farmer, tiller, peasant.
LA.VRAR, *v.*, to cultivate, to till, to plough, to plow.

LAXANTE   174   **LER**

LA.XAN.TE, *s.m.*, purgative, laxative; *adj.*, laxative, purgative.

LA.XA.TI.VO, *adj.*, laxative, purgative.

LÁ.ZA.RO, *s.m.*, lazar.

LA.ZER, *s.m.*, leisure, spare time, recreation.

LE.AL, *adj.*, loyal, true, devoted, sincere.

LE.AL.DA.DE, *s.f.*, loyalty, faithfulness, fidelity.

LE.ÃO, *s.m.*, lion.

LE.ÃO DE CHÁ.CA.RA, *s.m.*, bouncer.

LE.ÃO-MA.RI.NHO, *s.m.*, sea-lion.

LE.BRE, *s.f.*, hare.

LE.CI.O.NAR, *v.*, to teach, to lecture, to doctrinate, to instruct, to study.

LE.GA.ÇÃO, *s.f.*, legation, diplomacy, legacy.

LE.GA.DO, *s.m.*, legate, envoy, legacy, bequest.

LE.GAL, *adj.*, legal, lawful, right.

LE.GA.LI.DA.DE, *s.f.*, legality, lawfulness.

LE.GA.LI.ZA.ÇÃO, *s.f.*, legalization.

LE.GA.LI.ZAR, *v.*, to legalize, to authenticate, to validate, to legitimate.

LE.GEN.DA, *s.f.*, story, inscription, legend, caption.

LE.GI.ÃO, *s.f.*, legion, multitude, host.

LE.GIS.LA.ÇÃO, *s.f.*, legislation.

LE.GIS.LA.DOR, *s.m.*, legislator, lawgiver.

LE.GIS.LAR, *v.*, to legislate, to make laws.

LE.GIS.LA.TI.VO, *s.m.* legislative, the legislative power; *adj.*, legislative.

LE.GIS.LA.TU.RA, *s.f.*, legislature.

LE.GIS.TA, *s.2 gen.*, legist, jurist, lawyer; doctor-legist.

LE.GI.TI.MA.ÇÃO, *s.f.*, legitimation.

LE.GI.TI.MAR, *v.*, to legitimate, to make legitimate, to legalize.

LE.GI.TI.MI.DA.DE, *s.f.*, legitimacy, legality.

LE.GÍ.TI.MO, *adj.*, legitimate, lawful, legal, rightful, true, genuine, authentic.

LE.GÍ.VEL, *adj.*, readable, legible.

LÉ.GUA, *s.f.*, league, measure of 6,000 meters.

LE.GU.ME, *s.m.*, legume, vegetables.

LEI, *s.f.*, law, rule, commandment.

LEI.GO, *s.m.*, layman, outsider, laic; *adj.*, laic, lay, secular, unprofessional.

LEI.LÃO, *s.m.*, auction, outcry.

LEI.LO.AR, *v.*, to auction, to sell by auction.

LEI.LO.EI.RO, *s.m.*, auctioneer.

LEI.TÃO, *s.m.*, piglet, shoat.

LEI.TE, *s.m.*, milk; **LEITE CONDENSADO**, condensed milk; **DENTE DE LEITE**, milk tooth.

LEI.TEI.RA, *s.f.*, milk jug, milkpot; dairy woman.

LEI.TEI.RO, *s.m.*, milkman.

LEI.TE.RI.A, *s.f.*, dairy, creamery, milkshop.

LEI.TO, *s.m.*, bed, berth; couch, bunk.

LEI.TOR, *s.m.*, reader, lecturer.

LEI.TU.RA, *s.f.*, read, read out, reading, lecture.

LE.MA, *s.m.*, lemma, motto, slogan, premise.

LEM.BRA.DO, *adj.*, mindful.

LEM.BRAN.ÇA, *s.f.*, remembrance, recollection, souvenir, keepsake, recall, memory, mind.

LEM.BRAR, *v.*, to recall, to remember, to remind, to suggest.

LEM.BRE.TE, *s.m.*, reminder, note, memorandum.

LE.ME, *s.m.*, rudder, government, direction, helm.

LEN.ÇO, *s.m.*, handkerchief.

LEN.ÇOL, *s.m.*, sheet.

LEN.DA, *s.f.*, legend, folk tale, myth, fable, fiction.

LEN.DÁ.RIO, *adj.*, legendary, mythical.

LE.NHA, *s.f.*, firewood, fuel.

LE.NHA.DOR, *s.m.*, woodcutter, lumberman.

LE.NHO, *s.m.*, xylem, wood, log.

LE.NI.TI.VO, *adj.*, lenitive, palliative.

LE.NO.CÍ.NIO, *s.m.*, panderage.

LEN.TE, *s.f.*, lens; *s.m.*, university professor, teacher.

LEN.TI.DÃO, *s.f.*, slowness, lentitude, sluggishness, delay, indolence.

LEN.TO, *adj.*, slow, sluggish, tardy.

LE.O.A, *s.f.*, lioness.

LE.O.PAR.DO, *s.m.*, leopard.

LE.PO.RI.NO, *adj.*, leporine.

LE.PRA, *s.f.*, leprosy.

LE.PRO.SÁ.RIO, *s.m.*, leprosery.

LE.PRO.SO, *s.m.*, leper, lazar; *adj.*, leprous.

LE.QUE, *s.m.*, fan.

LER, *v.*, to read, to peruse, to interpret, to recite.

LER.DE.ZA, *s.f.*, slowness, sluggishness.
LER.DO, *adj.*, slow, sluggish, laggard, dull, stupid.
LE.SA.DO, *adj.*, injured, wounded, hurt, damaged.
LE.SÃO, *s.f.*, lesion, hurt, wound, injury.
LE.SAR, *v.*, to injure, to hurt, to wound, to damage, to bruise, to wrong.
LÉS.BI.CA, *s.f.*, Lesbian.
LÉS.BI.CO, *adj.*, Lesbian.
LE.SI.VO, *adj.*, injurious, offensive.
LES.MA, *s.f.*, snail, slug.
LES.TE, *s.m.*, east, the Orient.
LE.TAL, *adj.*, lethal, deadly, mortal, fatal.
LE.TI.VO, *adj.*, concerning school or a period of learning.
LE.TRA, *s.f.*, letter, character, type, inscription.
LE.TREI.RO, *s.m.*, lettering, label, ticket, inscription.
LÉU, *s.m.*, time, leisure, opportunity, occasion, chance.
LEU.CE.MI.A, *s.f.*, leukemia.
LE.VA.DI.ÇO, *adj.*, mobile, movable.
LE.VAN.TA.DO, *adj.*, upright, erect, up.
LE.VAN.TA.MEN.TO, *s.m.*, survey, elevation, lifting, raising, rise, erection.
LE.VAN.TAR, *v.*, to lift, to raise, to elevate, to rise up, to upload.
LE.VAR, *v.*, to carry, to lead, to remove, to convey, to run, to transport, to lead.
LE.VE, *adj.*, light, slight, nimble, quick, agile.
LE.VE.DAR, *v.*, to leaven, to yeast.
LE.VE.DU.RA, *s.f.*, yeast, leaven.
LE.VI.TA.ÇÃO, *s.f.*, levitation.
LÉ.XI.CO, *s.m.*, lexicon, dictionary.
LE.XI.CO.LO.GI.A, *s.f.*, lexicology.
LHE, *pron.*, him, her, it, to him, to it, her, to her.
LI.BA.ÇÃO, *s.f.*, libation.
LI.BA.NÊS, *adj.*, *s.m.*, Lebanese.
LI.BÉ.LU.LA, *s.f.*, dragonfly.
LI.BE.RA.ÇÃO, *s.f.*, liberation, release, liquidation, discharge.
LI.BE.RAL, *adj.s.2 gen.*, liberalist; *adj.*, liberal, munificent, befitting.
LI.BE.RA.LI.DA.DE, *s.f.*, liberality, generosity.
LI.BE.RA.LIS.MO, *s.m.*, liberalism.
LI.BE.RA.LI.ZAR, *v.*, to liberalize, to lavish.
LI.BE.RAR, *v.*, to discharge, to liquidate, to settle.
LI.BER.DA.DE, *s.f.*, liberty, freedom, permission, frankness, exemption.
LI.BER.TA.ÇÃO, *s.f.*, liberation, relief, release, delivery.
LI.BER.TAR, *v.*, to liberate, to set free, to free, to deliver, to release.
LI.BER.TI.NO, *adj.*, libertine, licentious, dissolute.
LI.BI.DI.NO.SO, *adj.*, libidinous.
LI.BRA, *s.f.*, pound, the weight and the monetary unit.
LI.ÇÃO, *s.f.*, lesson, example, task, school-work, explanation.
LI.CEN.ÇA, *s.f.*, license, permission, consent, liberty.
LI.CEN.CI.A.MEN.TO, *s.m.*, licensing, permission, discharge.
LI.CEN.CI.AR, *v.*, to license, to authorize, to discharge.
LI.CEU, *s.m.*, lyceum, a secondary school.
LÍ.CI.TO, *adj.*, licit, lawful.
LI.COR, *s.m.*, liqueur, liquor.
LI.DA, *s.f.*, work, toil, chore.
LÍ.DER, *s.m.*, leader, chief, commander, guide.
LI.DE.RAN.ÇA, *s.f.*, leadership, lead.
LI.DE.RAR, *v.*, to lead, to guide, to conduct.
LI.GA.ÇÃO, *s.f.*, ligation, joining, junction, connection, bond, binding.
LI.GA.DO, *adj.*, joint, connected, intimate, close.
LI.GA.MEN.TO, *s.m.*, ligament, bandage, bond.
LI.GAR, *v.*, to tie, to bind, to link, to fasten, to attach, to connect, to pay attention to.
LI.GEI.RE.ZA, *s.f.*, quickness, lightness, swiftness.
LI.GEI.RO, *adj.*, quick, swift, fast, speedy, rapid, light, alert.
LI.MA, *s.f.*, file, steel instrument; sweet lime.
LI.MÃO, *s.m.*, lemon.
LI.MAR, *v.*, to sand, to file, to polish.
LIM.BO, *s.m.*, limb, edge, border.

LIMINAR LIVRAR

LI.MI.NAR, *s.f.*, preliminary, introductory.
LI.MI.TA.ÇÃO, *s.f.*, limitation, restriction, check.
LI.MI.TAR, *v.*, to limit, to delimit, to circumscribe, to border.
LI.MI.TE, *s.m.*, limit, bound, border, frontier, end.
LI.MÍ.TRO.FE, *adj.*, adjacent, limitrophe.
LI.MO.EI.RO, *s.m.*, lemon tree.
LI.MO.NA.DA, *s.f.*, lemonade.
LIM.PA.DOR, *s.m.*, cleaner, wiper; **LIMPADOR DE PARA-BRISA**, windshield wiper.
LIM.PAR, *v.*, to clarify, to clean, to purify, to wash.
LIM.PE.ZA, *s.f.*, cleanness, neatness, cleaning.
LÍM.PI.DO, *adj.*, limpid, clear, transparent, lucid, bright.
LIM.PO, *adj.*, clean, neat, trim, tidy, clear, pure, clearly, immaculate.
LIN.CE, *s.m.*, lynx.
LIN.CHAR, *v.*, to lynch.
LIN.DO, *adj.*, pretty, beautiful, handsome, nice, fine, elegant, graceful, good.
LI.NE.AR, *adj.*, linear, lineal.
LIN.GO.TE, *s.m.*, ingot.
LÍN.GUA, *s.f.*, tongue, speech, language, idiom; interpreter.
LIN.GUA.GEM, *s.f.*, language, idiom, dialect.
LIN.GUA.JAR, *s.m.*, talk, speech, dialect.
LIN.GUA.RU.DO, *s.m.*, gossipy, chatterbox, gabbler.
LIN.GUI.ÇA, *s.f.*, sausage.
LIN.GUÍS.TI.CA, *s.f.*, linguistics.
LIN.GUÍS.TI.CO, *adj.*, linguistic.
LI.NHA, *s.f.*, line, thread, string, lineage, cord, rail; **LINHA FÉRREA**, railway.
LI.NHA.GEM, *s.f.*, lineage, genealogy, race, pedigree.
LI.NO.TI.PO, *s.m.*, linotype.
LI.PÍ.DIO, *s.m.*, lipid.
LI.QUE.FA.ÇÃO, *s.f.*, liquefaction.
LI.QUE.FA.ZER, *v.*, to liquefy, to reduce to a liquid.
LI.QUI.DA.ÇÃO, *s.f.*, liquidation, sale, clearing.
LI.QUI.DA.DO, *adj.*, liquidated, finished.
LI.QUI.DAR, *v.*, to liquidate, to settle, to adjust, to shut down.
LI.QUI.DEZ, *s.f.*, liquidness.
LI.QUI.DI.FI.CA.DOR, *s.m.*, mixer, blender, liquidizer, liquifier.
LI.QUI.DI.FI.CAR, *v.*, to liquefy.
LÍ.QUI.DO, *s.m.*, liquid; *adj.*, liquid, fluid, net, clear, evident.
LI.RA, *s.f.*, lyre; Italian monetary unit.
LÍ.RI.CO, *adj.*, lyric; sentimental.
LÍ.RIO, *s.m.*, lily.
LIS, *s.m.*, lily.
LI.SO, *adj.*, smooth, even, sleeky, lank, soft, flat, sincere.
LI.SON.JA, *s.f.*, flattery, adulation, coaxing, cajolery.
LI.SON.JE.AR, *v.*, to flatter, to court, to fawn, to adulate, to cajole, to please.
LI.SON.JEI.RO, *adj.*, flattering, pleasing, adulatory, satisfactory.
LIS.TA, *s.f.*, list, roll, roster, catalogue; ribbon, band, slip.
LIS.TRA, *s.f.*, stripe.
LI.SU.RA, *s.f.*, smoothness, softness, sincerity, frankness.
LI.TE.RAL, *adj.*, literal, exact, true.
LI.TE.RÁ.RIO, *adj.*, literary.
LI.TE.RA.TO, *s.m.*, literate.
LI.TE.RA.TU.RA, *s.f.*, literature, letters, learning, literary profession.
LI.TI.GAN.TE, *adj.*, *s.2 gen.*, litigant, litigator.
LI.TI.GAR, *v.*, to litigate, to contend.
LI.TÍ.GIO, *s.m.*, litigation, lawsuit, dispute.
LI.TO.GRA.FI.A, *s.f.*, lithography.
LI.TO.GRÁ.FI.CO, *adj.*, lithographical.
LI.TO.RAL, *s.m.*, coast, littoral, seaside, seaboard; *adj.*, littoral, coastal.
LI.TO.RÂ.NEO, *adj.*, littoral, coastal.
LI.TRO, *s.m.*, liter, litre.
LI.TU.A.NO, *adj.*, *s.m.*, Lithuanian.
LI.TUR.GI.A, *s.f.*, liturgy, ritual.
LI.TÚR.GI.CO, *adj.*, liturgical.
LÍ.VI.DO, *adj.*, livid, ashy.
LI.VRAR, *v.*, to liberate, to free, to release, to

LIVRARIA   LOUVAR

save, to deliver.
LI.VRA.RI.A, *s.f.*, bookshop, bookstore.
LI.VRE, *adj.*, free, independent, at liberty, exempt, absolved, released.
LI.VREI.RO, *s.m.*, bookseller.
LI.VRES.CO, *adj.*, bookish.
LI.VRO, *s.m.*, book.
LI.XA, *s.f.*, sandpaper, glasspaper.
LI.XAR, *v.*, to sandpaper, to paper, to sand, to polish.
LI.XEI.RA, *s.f.*, garbage can.
LI.XEI.RO, *s.m.*, garbage man, dustman.
LI.XÍ.VIA, *s.f.*, lixivium.
LI.XO, *s.m.*, trash, garbage, waste, rubbish, sweepings, dirtiness.
LO.BA, *s.f.*, she-wolf.
LÓ.BI, *s.m.*, lobby.
LO.BI.NHO, *s.m.*, a little wolf, boy scout.
LO.BIS.TA, *s.2 gen.*, lobbyist.
LO.BO, *s.m.*, wolf.
LO.CA.ÇÃO, *s.f.*, location, situation, place, hiring, lease.
LO.CA.DOR, *s.m.*, lessor, landlord, hirer.
LO.CAL, *s.m.*, place, spot, site, locality.
LO.CA.LI.DA.DE, *s.f.*, locality, place, settlement, situation.
LO.CA.LI.ZA.ÇÃO, *s.f.*, localization, location, position.
LO.CA.LI.ZAR, *v.*, to localize, to locate, to place.
LO.CA.TÁ.RIO, *s.m.*, lodger, tenant, lessee.
LO.CO.MO.ÇÃO, *s.f.*, locomotion.
LO.CO.MO.TI.VA, *s.f.*, locomotive, train engine.
LO.CO.MO.VER-SE, *v.*, to move about.
LO.CU.ÇÃO, *s.f.*, locution, expression, phrase, phraseology.
LO.CU.PLE.TAR, *v.*, to enrich, to satiate.
LO.CU.TOR, *s.m.*, speaker, radio announcer.
LO.DO, *s.m.*, mud, mire, clay, slime, dirt, slop, slush.
LO.DO.SO, *adj.*, muddy, miry, slimy, sloppy.
LO.GA.RIT.MO, *s.m.*, logarithm.
LÓ.GI.CA, *s.f.*, logic.
LÓ.GI.CO, *adj.*, logical, rational, coherent.

LO.GO, *adv.*, immediately, at once, right away, soon, before long.
LO.GRAR, *v.*, to cheat, to trick, to deceive, to defraud, to swindle.
LO.GRO, *s.m.*, cheat, swindle, fraud, trick.
LOI.RO, *adj., s.m.*, blond.
LO.JA, *s.f.*, shop, store, baz(a)ar, workshop.
LO.JIS.TA, *s.2 gen.*, shopkeeper, storekeeper.
LOM.BA.DA, *s.f.*, range of hills, mountain-ridge.
LOM.BI.NHO, *s.m.*, tenderloin.
LOM.BO, *s.m.*, loin, reins, back, pork loin.
LOM.BRI.GA, *s.f.*, roundworm, ringworm.
LO.NA, *s.f.*, canvas, sailcloth, tarpaulin.
LON.GE, *adj.*, remote, distant; *adv.*, far, far-off.
LON.GE.VI.DA.DE, *s.f.*, longevity, long life.
LON.GÍN.QUO, *adj.*, distant, far-away, far-off.
LON.GI.TU.DE, *s.f.*, longitude.
LON.GO, *adj.*, long, lenghty, prolix.
LON.JU.RA, *s.f.*, distance, great distance.
LON.TRA, *s.f.*, otter.
LO.QUA.CI.DA.DE, *s.f.*, loquacity.
LOR.DE, *s.m.*, lord.
LO.RO.TA, *s.f.*, lie, idle, fib, nonsense.
LOS.NA, *s.f.*, wormwood.
LO.TA.ÇÃO, *s.f.*, allotment, capacity, a little bus.
LO.TA.DO, *adj.*, replete, full.
LO.TE, *s.m.*, lot, allotment, portion, parcel, share.
LO.TE.A.MEN.TO, *s.m.*, division of land into lots.
LO.TE.AR, *v.*, to divide land into lots.
LO.TE.RI.A, *s.f.*, lottery.
LOU.ÇA, *s.f.*, chinaware, dishware, dishes, ceramics.
LOU.CO, *s.m.*, madman, lunatic; *adj.*, mad, lunatic, crazy, insane, bold.
LOU.CU.RA, *s.f.*, madness, craziness, insanity, folly, extravagance.
LOU.RO, *s.m.*, laurel, parrot; laurel tree.
LOU.SA, *s.f.*, blackboard, gravestone.
LOU.VA A DEUS, *s.m.*, grasshopper.
LOU.VA.DO, *adj.*, praised.
LOU.VAR, *v.*, to praise, to laud, to extol, to exalt, to glorify.

LOU.VOR, *s.m.*, praise, laud, laudation, glorification.
LU.A, *s.f.*, moon.
LU.AR, *s.m.*, moonlight, moonshine.
LÚ.BRI.CO, *adj.*, lubricous, slippery.
LU.BRI.FI.CA.ÇÃO, *s.f.*, lubrification.
LU.BRI.FI.CAN.TE, *adj.*, *s.m.*, lubricant.
LU.BRI.FI.CAR, *v.*, to lubricate, to grease, to oil.
LU.CI.DEZ, *s.f.*, lucidity, brightness, perspicacity.
LÚ.CI.DO, *adj.*, lucid, shining, bright, clear.
LU.CRAR, *v.*, to profit, to benefit, to gain.
LU.CRA.TI.VO, *adj.*, lucrative, profitable, gainful.
LU.CRO, *s.m.*, profit, gain, returns, earning, utility.
LU.CU.BRAR, *v.*, to lucubrate.
LU.FA.DA, *s.f.*, gust of wind, flurry.
LU.GAR, *s.m.*, place, space, room, site, locality, seat, spot.
LU.GAR CO.MUM, *s.m.*, commonplace.
LU.GA.RE.JO, *s.m.*, hamlet, small village.
LÚ.GU.BRE, *adj.*, lugubrious, doleful, sad.
LU.ME, *s.m.*, fire, flame, light, candle.
LU.MI.NÁ.RIA, *s.f.*, luminary.
LU.MI.NO.SI.DA.DE, *s.f.*, luminosity.
LU.MI.NO.SO, *adj.*, luminous, shining, bright, brilliant, radiant.
LU.NAR, *adj.*, lunar.
LU.NÁ.TI.CO, *s.m.*, madman, lunatic; *adj.*, lunatic, mad.
LU.NE.TA, *s.f.*, field-glass, spyglass, lunette, eye-glass.
LU.PA, *s.f.*, lens, magnifying glass.
LUS.CO-FUS.CO, *s.m.*, dusk, nightfall, twilight.
LU.SI.TA.NO, *adj.*, *s.m.*, Lusitanian, Portuguese.
LUS.TRAR, *v.*, to polish, to shine, to burnish.
LUS.TRE, *s.m.*, chandelier, gloss, shine; luster.
LUS.TRO, *s.m.*, gloss, sheen, shine; lustrum, quinquennium.
LU.TA, *s.f.*, fight, contest, combat, conflict, war, battle.
LU.TA.DOR, *s.m.*, fighter, wrestler, boxer, contender.
LU.TAR, *v.*, to fight, to combat, to wrestle, to contend.
LU.TE.RA.NO, *adj.*, *s.m.*, Lutheran.
LU.TO, *s.m.*, mourning, sorrow, grief, affliction.
LU.VA, *s.f.*, glove, socket.
LU.XA.ÇÃO, *s.f.*, luxation, dislocation.
LU.XAR, *v.*, to luxate, to dislocate, to disjoint.
LU.XO, *s.m.*, luxury, splendour, magnificence, ostentation, pomp.
LU.XU.O.SO, *adj.*, luxurious, sumptuous.
LU.XÚ.RIA, *s.f.*, luxury, luxuriance, lust, libertinism.
LU.XU.RI.AN.TE, *adj.*, luxuriant, copious, plenty, sensual.
LUZ, *s.f.*, light, luminosity, illumination, radiance, clearness.
LU.ZER.NA, *s.f.*, light, flash, skylight.
LU.ZI.DI.O, *adj.*, bright, shining.
LU.ZIR, *v.*, to shine, to light, to glitter, to glisten, to radiate.

M

M, *s.m.*, twelfth letter of the Portuguese alphabet; **M** 1,000 in Roman numerals.
MA.CA, *s.f.*, stretcher, litter.
MA.ÇA, *s.f.*, bat, mace, club.
MA.ÇÃ, *s.f.*, apple; **MAÇÃS DO ROSTO**, cheek.
MA.CA.BRO, *adj.*, macabre, gruesome.
MA.CA.CO, *s.m.*, monkey, ape, hoist, jack.
MA.CA.DA.ME, *s.m.*, macadam.
MA.ÇA.NE.TA, *s.f.*, knob, pommel, door handle, doorknob.
MA.CA.QUI.CE, *s.f.*, foolishness, foolery, apishness.
MA.ÇA.RI.CO, *s.m.*, torch, blowtorch, blowpipe.
MA.CAR.RÃO, *s.m.*, macaroni, pasta.
MA.CAR.RÔ.NI.CO, *adj.*, macaronic, burlesque.
MA.CE.RAR, *v.*, to macerate; to mortify.
MA.CHA.DI.NHA, *s.f.*, hatcher.
MA.CHA.DO, *s.m.*, ax, axe, hatchet.
MA.CHÃO, *s.m.*, fearless, bossy.
MA.CHIS.TA, *s.m.*, male chauvinist.
MA.CHO, *s.m.*, male, tough guy.
MA.CHU.CA.DU.RA, *s.f.*, wound, injury, bruise, contusion.
MA.CHU.CAR, *v.*, to wound, to hurt, to injure, to crush.
MA.CI.EI.RA, *s.f.*, apple tree.
MA.CI.EZ, *s.f.*, softness, smoothness, sleekness.
MA.CI.LEN.TO, *adj.*, emaciated, pale, lean.
MA.CI.O, *adj.*, soft, smooth, sleek, supple, flexible.
MA.ÇO, *s.m.*, mallet, bundle, bunch, wad, pile, pack.
MA.ÇOM, *s.m.*, mason, Freemason.
MA.ÇO.NA.RI.A, *s.f.*, Freemasonry.
MA.CO.NHA, *s.f.*, marijuana, marihuana.
MA.ÇÔ.NI.CO, *adj.*, masonic.
MÁ-CRI.A.ÇÃO, *s.f.*, ill breeding, bad manners, discourtesy.
MA.CRO.BI.Ó.TI.CA, *s.f.*, macrobiotics.
MA.CRO.COS.MO, *s.m.*, macrocosm.
MÁ.CU.LA, *s.f.*, macula, spot, stain, blemish.
MA.CU.LA.DO, *adj.*, maculate, spotted, stained, impure.
MA.CU.LAR, *v.*, to maculate, to stain, to spot, to blemish.
MA.DA.ME, *s.f.*, madam, lady, mistress.
MA.DEI.RA, *s.f.*, wood, timber, lumber.
MA.DEI.RA.MEN.TO, *s.m.*, framework, framing, timberwork.
MA.DEI.REI.RO, *s.m.*, wood merchant, woodworker, logger.
MA.DEI.XA, *s.f.*, tress, lock of hair.
MA.DRAS.TA, *s.f.*, stepmother.
MA.DRE, *s.f.*, mother, professed nun.
MA.DRE.PÉ.RO.LA, *s.f.*, nacre, mother-of-pearl.
MA.DRI.NHA, *s.f.*, godmother.
MA.DRU.GA.DA, *s.f.*, dawn, day-break, early morning.
MA.DRU.GA.DOR, *s.m.*, early riser.
MA.DRU.GAR, *v.*, to get up early in the morning.
MA.DU.RE.ZA, *s.f.*, ripeness, maturity.
MA.DU.RO, *adj.*, ripe, mature, seasoned, mallow.
MÃE, *s.f.*, mother, Mummy.
MA.ES.TRO, *s.m.*, maestro, composer.
MÁ-FÉ, *s.f.*, bad faith.
MA.GA.ZI.NE, *s.m.*, magazine.
MA.GI.A, *s.f.*, magic, sorcery, witchcraft, fascination.
MÁ.GI.CA, *s.f.*, magic, sorcery.
MÁ.GI.CO, *s.m.*, magician, juggler; *adj.*, magic.
MA.GIS.TÉ.RIO, *s.m.*, professorship, mastership, teaching profession.
MA.GIS.TRA.DO, *s.m.*, magistrate, judge.
MA.GIS.TRA.TU.RA, *s.f.*, magistrature, magistracy, function of a magistrate.
MAG.MA, *s.m.*, magma.

MAGNÉSIA   **MALTRATAR**

MAG.NÉ.SIA, *s.f.*, magnesia.
MAG.NÉ.TI.CO, *adj.*, magnetic, magnetical.
MAG.NE.TIS.MO, *s.m.*, magnetism.
MAG.NE.TI.ZAR, *v.*, to magnetize, to influence, to attract, to enchant.
MAG.NÍ.FI.CO, *adj.*, magnificent, magnific, superb.
MAG.NI.TU.DE, *s.f.*, magnitude, size, extent.
MAG.NÓ.LIA, *s.f.*, magnolia.
MA.GO, *s.m.*, magus, sorcerer, magician.
MÁ.GOA, *s.f.*, bruise, sore, hurt, sorrow, grief.
MA.GO.AR, *v.*, to hurt, to injure, to bruise, to wound, to afflict, to upset.
MA.GRE.ZA, *s.f.*, slenderness, thinness, slimness.
MA.GRO, *adj.*, thin, skinny, lean, meager, slim, bony.
MAI.O, *s.m.*, May.
MAI.Ô, *s.m.*, bathing suit.
MAI.O.NE.SE, *s.f.*, mayonnaise.
MAI.OR, *s.m.*, adult, major; *adj.*, comparative of **GRANDE**, larger, higher, bigger.
MAI.O.RI.A, *s.f.*, majority, the greater number.
MAI.O.RI.DA.DE, *s.f.*, majority, full legal age.
MAIS, *adv.*, more, also, besides, over, preferentially, further.
MAIS-QUE-PER.FEI.TO, *s.m.*, pluperfect.
MAI.ÚS.CU.LO, *adj.*, capital.
MA.JES.TA.DE, *s.f.*, majesty, magnificence.
MA.JES.TO.SO, *adj.*, majestic, august, regal.
MA.JO.RAR, *v.*, to rise, to raise, to increase.
MAL, *s.m.*, evil, illness, disease, pain, maleficence, wrong, harm; *adj.*, bad, ill; *adv.*, scarcely, hardly, badly.
MA.LA, *s.f.*, bag, handbag, suitcase, valise, box.
MA.LA.BA.RIS.MO, *s.m.*, juggling.
MAL-A.GRA.DE.CI.DO, *adj., s.m.*, ungrateful.
MA.LA.GUE.TA, *s.f.*, malagueta pepper.
MA.LAN.DRA.GEM, *s.f.*, roguery, trickery.
MA.LAN.DRO, *s.m.*, scoundrel, rascal, swindler.
MA.LÁ.RIA, *s.f.*, malaria.
MAL.BA.RA.TAR, *v.*, to sell at a loss, to dissipate.
MAL.CHEI.RO.SO, *adj.*, stinking, stinky.
MAL.CRI.A.DO, *adj.*, ill-bred, impolite, rude.
MAL.DA.DE, *s.f.*, badness, wickedness, malice, iniquity, cruelty.
MAL.DI.ÇÃO, *s.f.*, imprecation, spell, curse.
MAL.DI.TO, *adj.*, devil, damned, cursed.
MAL.DI.ZER, *v.*, to curse, to slander, to defame, backbite, to execrate.
MAL.DO.SO, *adj.*, wicked, bad, spiteful, malign, nasty, pernicious.
MA.LE.A.BI.LI.DA.DE, *s.f.*, malleability, ductility.
MA.LE.DI.CÊN.CIA, *s.f.*, slander, calumny.
MAL-E.DU.CA.DO, *adj.*, ill-bred, impolite.
MA.LE.FÍ.CIO, *s.m.*, harm, misdeed, malefaction.
MA.LÉ.FI.CO, *adj.*, evil, malign, malefic, harmful.
MA.LEI.TA, *s.f.*, malaria.
MAL-ES.TAR, *s.m.*, indisposition, unrest.
MA.LE.TA, *s.f.*, handbag, small suitcase.
MAL.FA.ZE.JO, *adj.*, maleficent, malignant.
MAL.FEI.TO, *adj.*, ill-done, badly-finished, deformed; bad.
MAL.FEI.TOR, *s.m.*, malefactor, evil-doer, criminal, villain.
MAL.GRA.DO, *prep.*, in spite of.
MA.LHA, *s.f.*, mesh, stich in knitting, spot, speckle.
MA.LHO, *s.m.*, sledgehammer, flail, maul.
MAL-HU.MO.RA.DO, *adj.*, ill-humoured, tempered.
MA.LÍ.CIA, *s.f.*, malice, evil intention, spite.
MA.LI.CI.AR, *v.*, to impute malice to somebody.
MA.LI.CI.O.SO, *adj.*, malicious, malevolent, artful, crafty, catty, foxy.
MA.LIG.NO, *s.m.*, the devil; *adj.*, malign, pernicious, baleful, bad, harmful.
MA.LO.GRAR, *v.*, to frustrate, to fail, to spoil, to wreck, to overthrow, to waste.
MA.LO.GRO, *s.m.*, frustration, failure.
MAL.QUE.RER, *s.m.*, animosity, aversion, enmity.
MAL.TA, *s.f.*, rabble, mob, gang, pack.
MAL.TRA.TA.DO, *adj.*, maltreated, abused, hurt.
MAL.TRA.TAR, *v.*, to mishandle, to receive badly, to insult, to vex.

MA.LU.CO, *s.m.*, nut, crackpot, fool; *adj.*, wacky, nutty, mad, crazy, insane.
MA.LU.QUI.CE, *s.f.*, craziness, madness, wackiness.
MAL.VA, *s.f.*, mallow.
MAL.VA.DO, *adj.*, mean, wicked, perverse.
MA.MA, *s.f.*, breast, teat, udder.
MA.MA.DEI.RA, *s.f.*, nursing bottle.
MA.MÃE, *s.f.*, mamma, mammy, mother.
MA.MÃO, *s.m.*, papaya.
MA.MAR, *v.*, to suck.
MA.MA.TA, *s.f.*, shady business, theft.
MA.MÍ.FE.RO, *s.m.*, mammifer, mammal; *adj.*, mammalian, mammiferous.
MA.MI.LO, *s.m.*, nipple.
MA.NA, *s.f.*, sister.
MA.NÁ, *s.m.*, manna.
MA.NA.DA, *s.f.*, herd of cattle.
MA.NAN.CI.AL, *s.m.*, fountainhead, spring, source.
MAN.CAL, *s.m.*, bearing, pillow.
MAN.CAR, *v.*, to fail, to limp, to hobble, to go lame, to cripple.
MAN.CHA, *s.f.*, stain, spot, speck, fleck, blotch; disgrace, reproach.
MAN.CHA.DO, *adj.*, stained, spotted, mottled, soiled.
MAN.CHAR, *v.*, to spot, to blot, to stain, to soil, to blemish.
MAN.CHE.TE, *s.f.*, headline.
MAN.CO, *s.m.*, lame person, cripple; *adj.*, lame, hobbling, mutilated, unable.
MAN.DA.DO, *s.m.*, order, command, court order, commission, message; *adj.*, ordered, sent.
MAN.DA.MEN.TO, *s.m.*, command, order, commandment, jurisdiction.
MAN.DAN.TE, *s.2 gen.*, commander, boss; *adj.*, commanding.
MAN.DAR, *v.*, to order, to command, to rule, to govern, to dominate, to send.
MAN.DA.TÁ.RIO, *s.m.*, mandatory, executive, attorney, person holding a mandate.
MAN.DA.TO, *s.m.*, mandate, commission, power of attorney.
MAN.DÍ.BU.LA, *s.f.*, mandible, jaw, jawbone.
MAN.DI.O.CA, *s.f.*, cassava, manioc.
MAN.DO, *s.m.*, power, authority, command, right.
MA.NEI.RA, *s.f.*, way, manner, form, fashion, kind, opportunity.
MA.NEI.RO.SO, *adj.*, mannered, mannerly.
MA.NE.JAR, *v.*, to handle, to carry out, to direct, to move, to manage, to govern.
MA.NE.JO, *s.m.*, management, administration, handling, attendance.
MA.NE.QUIM, *s.m.*, model, dummy, mannequin.
MAN.GA, *s.f.*, mango(fruit), sleeve(clothes).
MAN.GA.NÊS, *s.m.*, manganese.
MAN.GUE, *s.m.*, swamp, bayou, mangrove, marsh.
MAN.GUEI.RA, *s.f.*, rubber or canvas hose, mango tree.
MA.NHA, *s.f.*, slyness, cunningness, malice, dexterity, trick.
MA.NHÃ, *s.f.*, morning, forenoon, dawn.
MA.NHO.SO, *adj.*, foxy, cunning, crafty, smart, whimsical, vicious.
MA.NI.A, *s.f.*, mania, excentricity, obsession, whim, kink.
MA.NÍ.A.CO, *adj.*, *s.m.*, maniac.
MA.NI.CÔ.MIO, *s.m.*, asylum, bedlam, madhouse.
MA.NI.CU.RE, *s.2 gen.*, manicurist.
MA.NI.FES.TA.ÇÃO, *s.f.*, manifestation, gathering, meeting.
MA.NI.FES.TAR, *v.*, to manifest, to make public, to reveal, to disclose, to show.
MA.NI.FES.TO, *s.m.*, manifest, public declaration; *adj.*, manifest, evident, obvious, clear.
MA.NI.LHA, *s.f.*, armlet, shackle, fetter.
MA.NI.PU.LA.ÇÃO, *s.f.*, manipulation, handling.
MA.NI.PU.LA.DO, *adj.*, manipulated, processed.
MA.NI.PU.LAR, *v.*, to manipulate, to handle, to process, to work.
MA.NI.VE.LA, *s.f.*, handle, crank.
MAN.JAR, *s.m.*, any foodstuff, tidbit, dainty.
MAN.JE.RI.CÃO, *s.m.*, basil.
MA.NO, *s.m.*, brother, friend.

MA.NO.BRA, *s.f.*, maneuver, a skillful move, scheme.
MA.NO.BRAR, *v.*, to maneuver, to manipulate, to handle, to conduct.
MA.NÔ.ME.TRO, *s.m.*, manometer.
MAN.SÃO, *s.f.*, mansion.
MAN.SI.DÃO, *s.f.*, tameness, meekness, gentleness, docility.
MAN.SO, *adj.*, tame, domesticated, meek, gentle, docile.
MAN.TA, *s.f.*, blanket, travelling rug, shawl.
MAN.TEI.GA, *s.f.*, butter.
MAN.TEI.GUEI.RA, *s.f.*, butter dish.
MAN.TER, *v.*, to maintain, to sustain, to keep, to support, to pay for, to conserve.
MAN.TI.MEN.TO, *s.m.*, maintainance, provisions, supply, food.
MAN.TO, *s.m.*, mantle, cloak, robe, veil.
MA.NU.AL, *s.m.*, manual, handbook; *adj.*, manual.
MA.NU.FA.TU.RA, *s.f.*, manufacture, factory.
MA.NU.FA.TU.RAR, *v.*, to manufacture, to make by hand, to produce.
MA.NUS.CRI.TO, *s.m.*, manuscript, document, letter; *adj.*, handwritten.
MA.NU.SE.AR, *v.*, to handle, to manage, to touch, to feel, to soil.
MA.NU.TEN.ÇÃO, *s.f.*, maintenance, keeping, support, administration, management.
MÃO, *s.f.*, hand, side, each of the directions of the traffic, help.
MÃO DE FER.RO, *s.f.*, iron hand.
MÃO DE O.BRA, *s.f.*, manual work on a job.
MA.O.ME.TA.NO, *adj.*, *s.m.*, Mohammedan, Mahometan.
MA.PA, *s.f.*, map, chart, graph.
MA.QUE.TE, *s.f.*, maquette.
MA.QUI.AR, *v.*, to make up.
MA.QUI.A.VÉ.LI.CO, *adj.*, astute, sly, Machiavellian.
MÁ.QUI.NA, *s.f.*, machine, engine, car, automobile.
MA.QUI.NA.RI.A, *s.f.*, machinery.
MA.QUI.NIS.TA, *s.2 gen.*, engine driver, machinist, locomotive driver.

MAR, *s.m.*, sea, ocean; **MAR MORTO**, the Dead Sea.
MA.RA.CU.JÁ, *s.m.*, passion fruit; maracock.
MA.RA.JÁ, *s.m.*, maharaja(h).
MA.RAS.MO, *s.m.*, marasmus, moral apathy, indifference.
MA.RA.VI.LHA, *s.f.*, wonder, marvel, prodigy.
MA.RA.VI.LHAR, *v.*, to marvel, to amaze, to cause admiration.
MA.RA.VI.LHO.SO, *adj.*, wonderful, marvellous, amazing, admirable.
MAR.CA, *s.f.*, mark, brand, type, seal, stamp, token, signature, impression, limit.
MAR.CA.ÇÃO, *s.f.*, act of marking.
MAR.CAR, *v.*, to mark, to brand, to seal, to label, to book, to stamp.
MAR.CE.NEI.RO, *s.m.*, joiner.
MAR.CHA, *s.f.*, march, progress, walk, route, gear, journey.
MAR.CHAR, *v.*, to march, to run, to turn, to work.
MAR.CO, *s.m.*, mark, limit, boundary, landmark, demarcation, sign, mark.
MAR.ÇO, *s.m.*, March.
MA.RÉ, *s.f.*, tide; **MARÉ ALTA**, high tide, floodtide.
MA.RE.CHAL, *s.m.*, marshal.
MA.RE.MO.TO, *s.m.*, seaquake.
MA.RE.SI.A, *s.f.*, rollers, whitecaps.
MAR.FIM, *adj.*, *s.m.*, ivory.
MAR.GA.RI.DA, *s.f.*, daisy.
MAR.GA.RI.NA, *s.f.*, margarine.
MAR.GE.AR, *v.*, to marginate, to border.
MAR.GEM, *s.f.*, margin, border, limit, edge, shore, bank, rim.
MAR.GI.NAL, *s.m.*, delinquent; *adj.*, marginal.
MA.RI.CAS, *s.m.*, sissy, coward.
MA.RI.DO, *s.m.*, husband, spouse.
MA.RIM.BON.DO, *s.m.*, wasp.
MA.RI.NHA, *s.f.*, navy, marine, naval force, naval service.
MA.RI.NHEI.RO, *s.m.*, sailor, seaman, mariner, seafarer.
MA.RIS.CO, *s.m.*, shellfish.

MARÍTIMO — **MATRÍCULA**

MA.RÍ.TI.MO, *adj.*, maritime, marine.
MAR.ME.LA.DA, *s.f.*, quince jam.
MAR.ME.LO, *s.m.*, quince.
MAR.MI.TA, *s.f.*, metal pan with a lid.
MAR.MO.RA.RI.A, *s.f.*, marble industry, marble work.
MÁR.MO.RE, *s.m.*, marble.
MA.RO.TO, *s.m.*, scoundrel, rascal, rogue; *adj.*, malicious, artful, lascivious.
MAR.QUÊS, *s.m.*, marquis.
MAR.QUE.SA, *s.f.*, marchioness, marquise.
MAR.RE.CO, *s.m.*, wild duck, teal.
MAR.RE.TA, *s.f.*, hammer, mallet.
MAR.RE.TA.DA, *s.f.*, blow.
MAR.ROM, *s.m.*, brown colour; *adj.*, brown, hazel.
MAR.SU.PI.AL, *adj.*, *s.m.*, marsupial.
MAR.TE.LA.DA, *s.f.*, blow with a hammer.
MAR.TE.LAR, *v.*, to hammer, to pound, to beat, to bother, to annoy.
MAR.TE.LO, *s.m.*, hammer.
MÁR.TIR, *s.m.*, martyr, sufferer.
MAR.TÍ.RIO, *s.m.*, martyrdom, suffering, torment.
MAR.TI.RI.ZAR, *v.*, to martyrize, to torment.
MA.RU.JO, *s.m.*, sailor, seaman, marine.
MAR.XIS.MO, *s.m.*, Marxism.
MAR.XIS.TA, *s.2 gen.*, Marxist.
MAS, *conj.*, but, however, still, yet, even, only.
MAS.CAR, *v.*, to chew, to mumble, to mutter, to grumble.
MÁS.CA.RA, *s.f.*, mask.
MAS.CA.RA.DO, *s.m.*, masqued, mask; *adj.*, masked, disguised.
MAS.CA.RAR, *v.*, to mask, to disguise, to hide.
MAS.CA.TE, *s.m.*, peddler, hawker.
MAS.CO.TE, *s.m.*, mascot.
MAS.CU.LI.NI.ZAR, *v.*, to make masculine.
MAS.CU.LI.NO, *adj.*, masculine, male, manly, virile.
MÁS.CU.LO, *adj.*, pertaining to the male sex, virile, manly, masculine, gender.
MAS.MOR.RA, *s.f.*, dungeon, subterraneous prison.
MAS.SO.QUIS.MO, *s.m.*, masochism.
MAS.SA, *s.f.*, mass, pasta; totality.
MAS.SA.CRAR, *v.*, to massacre, to kill.
MAS.SA.CRE, *s.m.*, massacre, slaughter, butchery.
MAS.SA.GEM, *s.f.*, massage.
MAS.SA.GIS.TA, *s.2 gen.*, masseur, masseuse.
MAS.TI.GA.DO, *adj.*, masticated, chewed.
MAS.TI.GAR, *v.*, to chew, to masticate, to crunch, to munch, to ponder.
MAS.TIM, *s.m.*, mastiff, cur, tyke.
MAS.TO.DON.TE, *s.m.*, mastodon.
MAS.TRO, *s.m.*, flagstaff, flagpole.
MAS.TUR.BA.ÇÃO, *s.f.*, masturbation, onanism.
MAS.TUR.BAR, *v.*, to masturbate.
MA.TA, *s.f.*, wood, forest, jungle, thicket.
MA.TA.DOR, *s.m.*, killer, assassin, murderer.
MA.TA.GAL, *s.m.*, jungle, bush, thicket.
MA.TAN.ÇA, *s.f.*, killing, massacre, slaughter, butchery.
MA.TAR, *v.*, to kill, to assassin, to murder, to slaughter, to extinguish, to eliminate.
MA.TE, *s.m.*, checkmate, Paraguay tea.
MA.TE.MÁ.TI.CA, *s.f.*, mathematics.
MA.TE.MÁ.TI.CO, *s.m.*, mathematician; *adj.*, mathematical.
MA.TÉ.RIA, *s.f.*, matter, substance; stuff, material, subject, topic.
MA.TE.RI.AL, *s.m.*, material, stuff, matter, substance; *adj.*, material, solid, crude, raw.
MA.TE.RI.A.LI.ZAR, *v.*, to materialize, to become crude, to stupid.
MA.TÉ.RIA-PRI.MA, *s.f.*, raw material.
MA.TER.NAL, *adj.*, maternal, motherlike.
MA.TER.NI.DA.DE, *s.f.*, maternity, motherhood, maternity hospital.
MA.TER.NO, *adj.*, maternal, motherly, kind.
MA.TI.LHA, *s.f.*, pack of hounds or wolves.
MA.TI.NAL, *adj.*, matutinal, matutine, morning.
MA.TI.NÊ, *s.f.*, matinée.
MA.TIZ, *s.m.*, nuance, tone, tint, tincture.
MA.TI.ZAR, *v.*, to variegate, to adorn.
MA.TO, *s.m.*, wood, forest, brushwood.
MA.TRA.CA, *s.f.*, rattle.
MA.TREI.RO, *adj.*, sly, smart, shrewd, crafty.
MA.TRÍ.CU.LA, *s.f.*, registration, enrollment,

MATRICULADO — **MEIO**

matriculation fee.
MA.TRI.CU.LA.DO, *adj.*, matriculated, registered.
MA.TRI.CU.LAR, *v.*, to matriculate, to register, to enroll.
MA.TRI.MO.NI.AL, *adj.*, matrimonial, nuptial, conjugal, spousal.
MA.TRI.MÔ.NIO, *s.m.*, matrimony, marriage.
MA.TRIZ, *s.f.*, matrix, source, mold; *adj.*, original, primitive, primordial.
MA.TRO.NA, *s.f.*, matron, woman.
MA.TU.RA.ÇÃO, *s.f.*, maturation.
MA.TU.RAR, *v.*, to mature, to ripen, to season.
MA.TU.RI.DA.DE, *s.f.*, maturity, matureness, ripeness.
MA.TU.TI.NO, *adj.*, matutinal, early.
MAU, *s.m.*, evil, bad; *adj.*, bad, evil, harmful, noxious, pernicious, perverse.
MAU.SO.LÉU, *s.m.*, mausoleum.
MA.VI.O.SO, *adj.*, affectionate, suave, compassionate.
MA.XI.LA, *s.f.*, maxilla, jaw, jawbone.
MA.XI.LAR, *s.m.*, jaw, jawbone.
MÁ.XI.MA, *s.f.*, maxim, precept, aphorism.
MÁ.XI.ME, *adv.*, principally.
MÁ.XI.MO, *adj.*, maximum, greatest, utmost.
MA.ZE.LA, *s.f.*, wound, sore, bruise.
ME, *pron.*, me, to me, myself, to myself.
ME.CÂ.NI.CA, *s.f.*, mechanics.
ME.CÂ.NI.CO, *s.m.*, mechanic; *adj.*, mechanical.
ME.CA.NIS.MO, *s.m.*, mechanism, device, gear, machinery.
ME.DA.LHA, *s.f.*, medal.
ME.DA.LHÃO, *s.m.*, medallion, locket.
MÉ.DIA, *s.f.*, mean, medium, average.
ME.DI.A.ÇÃO, *s.f.*, mediation, intervention, interposition.
ME.DI.A.DOR, *s.m.*, mediator, intermediary, interposer, arbiter.
ME.DI.AN.TE, *prep.*, by means of, by, through, against.
ME.DI.AR, *v.*, to halve, to mediate, to intervene, to interpose, to interfere.
ME.DI.CA.ÇÃO, *s.f.*, medical treatment, medication.
ME.DI.CAL, *adj.*, medical.
ME.DI.CA.MEN.TO, *s.m.*, medicine, remedy, medicament.
ME.DI.ÇÃO, *s.f.*, measurement.
ME.DI.CAR, *v.*, to medicate.
ME.DI.CI.NA, *s.f.*, medicine, medicament.
ME.DI.CI.NAL, *adj.*, medicinal.
MÉ.DI.CO, *s.m.*, physician, doctor, medico, practitioner, surgeon.
ME.DI.DA, *s.f.*, measure, dimension, size.
ME.DI.DOR, *s.m.*, measurer, meter.
ME.DI.E.VAL, *adj.*, medieval.
MÉ.DIO, *adj.*, mean, medium, middle, median.
ME.DÍ.O.CRE, *adj.*, mediocre, ordinary, commonplace.
ME.DI.O.CRI.DA.DE, *s.f.*, mediocrity, commonness.
ME.DIR, *v.*, to measure, to gauge, to mete, to survey, to consider.
ME.DI.TA.ÇÃO, *s.f.*, meditation, thought, cogitation, ponderation, reflection.
ME.DI.TAR, *v.*, to meditate, to cogitate, to think, to ponder.
ME.DI.TER.RÂ.NEO, *s.m.*, Mediterranean; *adj.*, mediterranean.
ME.DO, *s.m.*, fear, fright, awe, terror.
ME.DO.NHO, *adj.*, awful, frightful, horrible, dreadful, terrible.
ME.DRO.SO, *adj.*, fearful, frightful, timid, timorous.
ME.DU.LA, *s.f.*, medula, marrow.
ME.GA.FO.NE, *s.m.*, megaphone.
ME.GA.LO.MA.NI.A, *s.f.*, megalomania.
ME.GE.RA, *s.f.*, Megaera, cruel woman, shrew.
MEI.A, *s.f.*, sock, stocking, hose.
MEI.A-Á.GUA, *s.f.*, one plane roof.
MEI.A-LU.A, *s.f.*, half-moon, crescent.
MEI.A-NOI.TE, *s.f.*, midnight.
MEI.GO, *adj.*, sweet, tender, gentle, loving, kind, mild, amiable.
MEI.GUI.CE, *s.f.*, tenderness, gentleness, sweetness, affability.
MEI.O, *s.m.*, middle, centre, medium, expedient,

MEIO AMBIENTE — MERCÊ

means; *adj.*, half, mean, middle, undecided.
MEI.O AM.BI.EN.TE, *s.m.*, environment, milieu.
MEL, *s.m.*, honey.
ME.LA.ÇO, *s.m.*, molasses.
ME.LAN.CI.A, *s.f.*, watermelon.
ME.LAN.CO.LI.A, *s.f.*, melancholy, melancholia, gloom, dismalness.
ME.LAN.CÓ.LI.CO, *adj.*, melancholic, gloomy, dreary.
ME.LÃO, *s.m.*, melon.
ME.LE.NA, *s.f.*, long hair.
ME.LHOR, *s.m.*, the best; *adj.*, better, superior, preferable, best; *adv.*, better, preferably.
ME.LHO.RA, *s.f.*, improvement, amelioration.
ME.LHO.RA.MEN.TO, *s.m.*, advance, progress, enrichment, profit, improvement.
ME.LHO.RAR, *v.*, to improve, to get better, to ameliorate, to reform, to amend.
ME.LHO.RI.A, *s.f.*, advance, improvement, amelioration, superiority.
ME.LÍ.FLUO, *adj.*, mellifluous, mellifluent.
ME.LIN.DRAR, *v.*, to hurt the feelings of, to wound, to pique, to scandalize.
ME.LIN.DRE, *s.m.*, politeness, sensitivity, susceptibility, coyness, prudery.
ME.LO.DI.A, *s.f.*, melody, tune, air, sweetness.
ME.LO.DI.O.SO, *adj.*, melodious, harmonious.
ME.LO.SO, *adj.*, sticky, syrupy, sweet.
MEL.RO, *s.m.*, blackbird, ouzel.
MEM.BRA.NA, *s.f.*, membrane.
MEM.BRO, *s.m.*, member, limb; fellow, associate.
ME.MO.RAN.DO, *s.m.*, memorandum, memorial, notification, note.
ME.MO.RAR, *v.*, to memorize, to remind.
ME.MO.RÁ.VEL, *adj.*, memorable, notable, remarkable.
ME.MÓ.RIA, *s.f.*, memory, storage, remembrance, reminescence.
ME.MO.RI.ZAR, *v.*, to memorize.
MEN.ÇÃO, *s.f.*, mention, reference, citation, notice.
MEN.CIO.NAR, *v.*, to mention, to refer to, to cite, to name, to narrate.
MEN.DI.GAR, *v.*, to beg, to go begging, to cadge.
MEN.DI.GO, *s.m.*, beggar, mendicant, cadger, pauper.
ME.NEI.O, *s.m.*, wagging, waggling, shaking.
ME.NI.NA, *s.f.*, girl, maiden, young woman.
ME.NIN.GI.TE, *s.f.*, meningitis.
ME.NI.NI.CE, *s.f.*, childhood, infancy.
ME.NI.NO, *s.m.*, boy, infant, lad.
ME.NIS.CO, *s.m.*, meniscus.
ME.NO.PAU.SA, *s.f.*, menopause.
ME.NOR, *s.2 gen.*, minor, person under legal age; *adj.*, smaller, lesser, younger, minor.
ME.NOS, *s.m.*, the least; *adv.*, less, least; *conj.*, but, save, except, less.
ME.NOS.PRE.ZAR, *v.*, to despise, to scorn, to contemn, to disdain, to disparage.
MEN.SA.GEI.RO, *s.m.*, messenger, courier, bellboy, emissary, announcer, herald.
MEN.SA.GEM, *s.f.*, message, communication, dispatch, summons.
MEN.SAL, *adj.*, monthly.
MEN.SA.LI.DA.DE, *s.f.*, monthly fee, allowance.
MEN.SA.LIS.TA, *s.2 gen.*, temporary worker, monthly paid employee.
MENS.TRU.A.ÇÃO, *s.f.*, menstruation, menses.
MENS.TRU.AL, *adj.*, menstrual.
MENS.TRU.AR, *v.*, to menstruate.
MEN.TA, *s.f.*, mint.
MEN.TAL, *adj.*, mental.
MEN.TA.LI.DA.DE, *s.f.*, mentality.
MEN.TE, *s.f.*, mind, intellect, spirit, intention, intent.
MEN.TIR, *v.*, to lie, to tell a lie, to illude, to deceive.
MEN.TI.RA, *s.f.*, lie, untruth, falsehood, deceit, falseness, illusion.
MEN.TI.RO.SO, *s.m.*, liar, false; *adj.*, lying, untruthful, false.
MEN.TOR, *s.m.*, mentor, guide.
MER.CA.DO, *s.m.*, market, market place, fair, emporium.
MER.CA.DOR, *s.m.*, merchant, trader, dealer.
MER.CA.DO.RI.A, *s.f.*, merchandise, goods, commodity.
MER.CÊ, *s.f.*, indult, grace, mercy, favour.

MER.CE.A.RI.A, *s.f.*, grocery, grocery store.
MER.CE.NÁ.RIO, *s.m.*, mercenary, hireling.
MER.CÚ.RIO, *s.m.*, mercury, quicksilver.
MER.DA, *s.f.*, shit, crap.
ME.RE.CE.DOR, *adj.*, meritorious, worthy.
ME.RE.CER, *v.*, to earn, to deserve, to merit.
ME.RE.CI.DO, *adj.*, merited, deserved, just, due.
ME.RE.CI.MEN.TO, *s.m.*, merit, desert, worthiness.
ME.REN.DAR, *v.*, to have a snack.
ME.RE.TRIZ, *s.f.*, prostitute, harlot, whore, hooker.
MER.GU.LHA.DOR, *s.m.*, diver, plunger.
MER.GU.LHAR, *v.*, to dive, to plunge, to sink, to duck, to immerse.
MER.GU.LHO, *s.m.*, dive, plunge, dip.
ME.RI.DI.A.NO, *s.m.*, meridian.
ME.RI.DIO.NAL, *adj.*, meridional, austral, southern.
ME.RI.TÍS.SI.MO, *adj.*, most worthy, Your Honor.
MÉ.RI.TO, *s.m.*, aptitude, superiority.
ME.RI.TÓ.RIO, *adj.*, meritorious, worthy.
ME.RO, *adj.*, mere, sheer, simple, pure.
MÊS, *s.m.*, month.
ME.SA, *s.f.*, table, board.
ME.SA.DA, *s.f.*, monthly allowance.
MES.CLAR, *v.*, to mix, to add, to intercalate, to variegate.
MES.MO, *s.m.*, the same, *adj.*, same, like, equal, identical; *adv.*, exactly, precisely, even.
MES.QUI.NHA.RI.A, *s.f.*, avarice, stinginess.
MES.QUI.NHO, *adj.*, stingy, paltry, skimpy, mean, little.
MES.TI.ÇO, *s.m.*, half-breed, mongrel; *adj.*, mestizo, crossbred.
MES.TRA, *s.f.*, mistress, teacher.
MES.TRE, *s.m.*, master, expert, principal, instructor.
ME.TA, *s.f.*, aim, goal, purpose, mark.
ME.TA.BO.LIS.MO, *s.m.*, metabolism.
ME.TA.DE, *s.f.*, half, moiety.
ME.TA.FÍ.SI.CA, *s.f.*, metaphysics.

ME.TA.FÍ.SI.CO, *s.m.*, metaphysician; *adj.*, metaphysical, supernatural.
ME.TÁ.FO.RA, *s.f.*, metaphor, trope.
ME.TAL, *s.m.*, metal, brass.
ME.TÁ.LI.CO, *adj.*, metallic.
ME.TA.LUR.GI.A, *s.f.*, metallurgy.
ME.TA.LÚR.GI.CO, *s.m.*, metallurgist, metalworker; *adj.*, metallurgic.
ME.TE.O.RI.TO, *s.m.*, meteorite, fallen meteor.
ME.TE.O.RO, *s.m.*, meteor, bolide, fireball.
ME.TE.O.RO.LO.GI.A, *s.f.*, meteorology.
ME.TE.O.RO.LÓ.GI.CO, *adj.*, meteorologic.
ME.TER, *v.*, to put, to put into, to introduce, to place, to lay, to set, to deposit.
ME.TI.CU.LO.SO, *adj.*, meticulous, overcareful.
ME.TI.DO, *adj.*, meddling, busy.
ME.TÓ.DI.CO, *adj.*, methodic, sistematical, orderly.
MÉ.TO.DO, *s.m.*, method, mode, system, form.
ME.TO.DO.LO.GI.A, *s.f.*, methodology.
ME.TRA.GEM, *s.f.*, lenght, lenght in meters.
ME.TRA.LHA.DO.RA, *s.f.*, machine gun.
ME.TRI.CO, *adj.*, metric, relating to the meter.
ME.TRO, *s.m.*, meter, meter stick.
ME.TRÔ, *s.m.*, subway, underground, tube.
ME.TRO.LO.GI.A, *s.f.*, metrology.
ME.TRÓ.PO.LE, *s.f.*, metropolis, capital, town.
ME.TRO.PO.LI.TA.NO, *s.m.*, metropolitan, subway, underground railway.
MEU, *pron.*, my, mine.
ME.XER, *v.*, to move, to stir, to shuffle, to shake, to fidget, to touch.
ME.XE.RI.CA, *s.f.*, tangerine.
ME.XE.RI.CO, *s.m.*, gossip, intrigue.
ME.XI.CA.NO, *adj.*, *s.m.*, Mexican.
ME.XI.LHÃO, *s.m.*, mussel, muscle.
ME.ZA.NI.NO, *s.m.*, mezzanine, entresol.
MI, *s.m.*, mi or E: third note of the diatonic scale.
MI.A.DO, *s.m.*, mew, mewing of a cat.
MI.AR, *v.*, to mew, to miaul.
MI.AU, *s.m.*, mew, miaow.
MI.CO, *s.m.*, name for several species of monkeys.
MI.CRO, *s.m.*, micron.
MI.CRÓ.BIO, *s.m.*, microbe, germ, microorganism.

MI.CRO.BI.O.LO.GI.A, *s.f.*, microbiology.
MI.CRO.COM.PU.TA.DOR, *s.m.*, micro, microcomputer, personal computer.
MI.CRO.COS.MO, *s.m.*, microcosm.
MI.CRO.FO.NE, *s.m.*, microphone.
MI.CRO.LO.GI.A, *s.f.*, micrology.
MI.CRO.ME.TRI.A, *s.f.*, micrometry.
MI.CRÔ.ME.TRO, *s.m.*, micrometer.
MI.CRO-ON.DAS, *s.m.*, microwaves.
MI.CRO-OR.GA.NIS.MO, *s.m.*, microorganism, microbe.
MI.CROS.CÓ.PIO, *s.m.*, microscope.
MIC.TÓ.RIO, *s.m.*, urinal, public convenience.
MÍ.DIA, *s.f.*, media, mass communication.
MI.GA.LHA, *s.f.*, crumb, bit, small portion.
MI.GRA.ÇÃO, *s.f.*, migration, wandering.
MI.GRAN.TE, *s.2 gen.*, migrant.
MI.GRAR, *v.*, to migrate.
MI.GRA.TÓ.RIO, *adj.*, migratory.
MI.JAR, *v.*, to piss, to piddle, to urinate.
MIL, *num.*, thousand; great number.
MI.LA.GRE, *s.m.*, miracle, wonder, marvel.
MI.LA.GRO.SO, *adj.*, miraculous, wonderful, marvelous.
MI.LE.NÁ.RIO, *s.m.*, millenary; *adj.*, millenial, millenarian.
MI.LÊ.NIO, *s.m.*, millenium.
MI.LÉ.SI.MO, *s.m.*, millesimal.
MI.LHA, *s.f.*, mile.
MI.LHAL, *s.m.*, maize field.
MI.LHÃO, *s.m.*, million.
MI.LHAR, *num.*, thousand.
MI.LHA.RAL, *s.m.*, maize field, cornfield.
MI.LHO, *s.m.*, maize, corn.
MI.LI.GRA.MA, *s.f.*, milligramme.
MI.LÍ.ME.TRO, *s.m.*, millimeter.
MI.LI.O.NÁ.RIO, *s.m.*, millionnaire.
MI.LI.TAN.TE, *adj.*, *s.2 gen.*, militant.
MI.LI.TAR, *s.m.*, soldier; *v.*, to fight, to serve as a soldier, to militate.
MI.LI.TA.RIS.TA, *s.2 gen.*, militarist.
MI.LI.TA.RI.ZA.ÇÃO, *s.f.*, militarization.
MIM, *pron.*, me.
MI.MAR, *v.*, to pet, to fondle, to spoil, to pamper, to cocker.
MI.ME.Ó.GRA.FO, *s.m.*, mimeograph.
MÍ.MI.CA, *s.f.*, mime, mimic.
MÍ.MI.CO, *adj.*, mimic, mimical.
MI.MO, *s.m.*, gift, offering, present, tenderness.
MI.MO.SO, *adj.*, tender, sweet, exquisite.
MI.NA, *s.f.*, mine, quarry, pit.
MI.NAR, *v.*, to mine, to excavate, to undermine, to sap, to corrode.
MI.NEI.RO, *s.m.*, miner, collier, native of the State of Minas Gerais; *adj.*, mining.
MI.NE.RA.ÇÃO, *s.f.*, mining.
MI.NE.RAL, *s.m.*, mineral; *adj.*, mineral, inorganic.
MI.NE.RA.LO.GI.A, *s.f.*, mineralogy.
MI.NÉ.RIO, *s.m.*, ore.
MÍN.GUA, *s.f.*, lack, need, scarcity, shortage.
MIN.GUAR, *v.*, to wane, to decrease, to diminish.
MI.NHA, *pron.*, mine, my.
MI.NHO.CA, *s.f.*, earthworm.
MI.NI.A.TU.RA, *s.f.*, miniature, summary.
MÍ.NI.MO, *s.m.*, minimum, the least; *adj.*, minimal, least, remote.
MI.NIS.TÉ.RIO, *s.m.*, ministry, cabinet, state department, charge, office.
MI.NIS.TRA.NTE, *s.m.*, ministrant, acolyte; *adj.*, ministering.
MI.NIS.TRAR, *v.*, to minister, to furnish, to give, to administer, to supply.
MI.NIS.TRO, *s.m.*, minister, minister of state; clergyman.
MI.NO.RI.A, *s.f.*, minority.
MI.NÚ.CIA, *s.f.*, minute, detail, nicety, insignificance.
MI.NU.CI.O.SI.DA.DE, *s.f.*, minuteness, particularity, accuracy, exactness.
MI.NU.CI.O.SO, *adj.*, minute, circumstantial, particular.
MI.NÚS.CU.LO, *adj.*, minuscule, tiny.
MI.NU.TA, *s.f.*, minute, draft of a document.
MI.NU.TO, *s.m.*, minute, moment, instant.
MI.O.LO, *s.m.*, brain, medulla, soft part of bread.
MÍ.O.PE, *s.m.*, myopic person; *adj.*, myopic.
MI.O.PI.A, *s.f.*, myopia, nearsightedness.

MI.O.SÓ.TIS, *s.2 gen.*, myosotis, forget-me-not.
MI.RA, *s.f.*, sight, aim, mark, purpose, scope, end.
MI.RA.CU.LO.SO, *adj.*, miraculous.
MI.RA.GEM, *s.f.*, optical illusion, deception, mirage.
MI.RAR, *v.*, to eye, to examine, to look at, to see.
MI.RÍ.A.DE, *s.f.*, myriad.
MI.RIM, *adj.*, small.
MIR.RA, *s.f.*, myrrh.
MI.SAN.TRO.PO, *s.m.*, misanthrope; *adj.*, misanthropic.
MIS.CE.LÂ.NEA, *s.f.*, miscellanea, miscellany, confusion.
MI.SE.RÁ.VEL, *s.2 gen.*, miserable, miser, skinflint; *adj.*, unhappy, miserable, woeful, pitiful.
MI.SÉ.RIA, *s.f.*, misery, distress, poverty, calamity, unhappiness.
MI.SE.RI.CÓR.DIA, *s.f.*, mercy, compassion, commiseration, pity.
MI.SE.RI.COR.DI.O.SO, *adj.*, merciful, clement.
MÍ.SE.RO, *adj.*, disgraced, miserable, unhappy.
MIS.SA, *s.f.*, mass.
MIS.SÃO, *s.f.*, mission, delegation, commission, vocation, missionary station.
MÍS.SIL, *s.m.*, missile.
MIS.SI.O.NÁ.RIO, *s.m.*, missionary.
MIS.TER, *s.m.*, occupation, employment, office.
MIS.TÉ.RIO, *s.m.*, mystery, enigma, secret.
MÍS.TI.CO, *s.m.*, mystic; *adj.*, mystic, spiritually, allegorical.
MIS.TI.FI.CA.ÇÃO, *s.f.*, mystification.
MIS.TI.FI.CA.DOR, *s.m.*, mystifier; *adj.*, mystifying.
MIS.TI.FI.CAR, *v.*, to mystify, to puzzle, to bewilder.
MIS.TO, *adj.*, mixed, variegated, confused.
MIS.TU.RA, *s.f.*, mixture, blend.
MIS.TU.RA.DOR, *s.m.*, mixer.
MIS.TU.RAR, *v.*, to mix, to blend, to mingle, to shuffle, to confuse.
MI.TI.GAR, *v.*, to mitigate, to alleviate, to moderate.
MI.TO, *s.m.*, myth.
MI.TO.LO.GI.A, *s.f.*, mythology.
MI.TRA, *s.f.*, miter, mitre.
MI.U.DE.ZA, *s.f.*, minuteness, smallness.
MI.Ú.DO, *adj.*, small, little, minute; *s.m.*, pl. giblets.
MI.XÓR.DIA, *s.f.*, confusion, mix-up, medley.
MÓ, *s.f.*, millstone.
MO.BI.LI.AR, *v.*, to furnish.
MO.BÍ.LIA, *s.f.*, furniture.
MO.BI.LI.ZAR, *v.*, to mobilize, to render mobile, to put in motion.
MO.ÇA, *s.f.*, girl, young woman, miss.
MO.ÇA.DA, *s.f.*, youngsters.
MO.ÇÃO, *s.f.*, motion, movement, commotion.
MO.CHI.LA, *s.f.*, backpack, rucksack, haversack.
MO.CI.DA.DE, *s.f.*, youth, youthfulness.
MO.ÇO, *s.m.*, boy, young man; *adj.*, young, youthful.
MO.DA, *s.f.*, fashion, manner, vogue, custom, way, method, song.
MO.DA.LI.DA.DE, *s.f.*, modality, manner, way.
MO.DE.LAR, *v.*, to model, to shape, to mould, to form; *adj.*, model.
MO.DE.LO, *s.m.*, model, mould, standard, example, ideal.
MO.DE.RA.ÇÃO, *s.f.*, moderation.
MO.DE.RAR, *v.*, to moderate, to temper, to diminish, to mitigate, to restrain.
MO.DER.NI.ZAR, *v.*, to modernize, to render modern.
MO.DER.NO, *adj.*, new, modern, actual.
MO.DÉS.TIA, *s.f.*, modesty, humbleness, simplicity.
MO.DES.TO, *adj.*, modest, unpretentious, moderate.
MÓ.DI.CO, *adj.*, small, slight, low.
MO.DI.FI.CA.ÇÃO, *s.f.*, modification, alteration.
MO.DI.FI.CAR, *v.*, to modify, to change, to alter.
MO.DO, *s.m.*, mode, manner, fashion, style, form, custom, method, humour.
MO.DOR.RA, *s.f.*, sleepiness, somnolence, sturdy.
MO.DU.LAR, *v.*, to modulate, to inflect; *adj.*, modular.

MÓ.DU.LO, *s.m.*, module, modulus, coefficient.
MO.E.DA, *s.f.*, coin, currency.
MO.E.DOR, *s.m.*, grinder, pounder; *adj.*, grinding.
MO.E.LA, *s.f.*, gizzard.
MO.ER, *v.*, to grind, to crush, to triturate, to bray, to press.
MO.FA.DOR, *s.m.*, scoffer, mocker.
MO.FAR, *v.*, to mock, to scorn, to deride, to jeer.
MO.FO, *s.m.*, mould, mildew, must.
MO.Í.DO, *adj.*, ground, crushed.
MO.I.NHO, *s.m.*, mill, flour-mill.
MOI.TA, *s.f.*, bush, thicket, scrub, tuft.
MO.LA, *s.f.*, spring, coil, motive, incentive.
MO.LAR, *s.m.*, molar, grinding.
MOL.DA.DO, *adj.*, moulded, mould, moulding.
MOL.DA.GEM, *s.f.*, moulding.
MOL.DAR, *v.*, to mould, to cast, to make moulds, to shape, to model.
MOL.DE, *s.m.*, mould, pattern, norm.
MOL.DU.RA, *s.f.*, frame, borders.
MO.LE, *adj.*, soft, tender, lazy, sluggish.
MO.LÉ.CU.LA, *s.f.*, molecule.
MO.LE.CU.LAR, *adj.*, molecular.
MO.LE.QUE, *s.m.*, young boy; dude; *adj.*, funny, mocking.
MO.LÉS.TIA, *s.f.*, disease, sickness, malady, illness.
MO.LE.ZA, *s.f.*, softness, tenderness, laziness, indolence.
MO.LHA.DO, *adj.*, moist, wet.
MO.LHAR, *v.*, to wet, to dampen, to moisten, to soak.
MO.LHO(ó), *s.m.*, bunch, bundle, faggot, sheaf; *s.m.*, **MOLHO**(ô), sauce, gravy.
MO.LUS.CO, *s.m.*, mollusc, shellfish.
MO.MEN.TÂ.NEO, *adj.*, momentary, instantaneous, transitory.
MO.MEN.TO, *s.m.*, moment, instant, circumstance.
MO.MO, *s.m.*, Momus, pantomine.
MO.NAR.CA, *s.f.*, monarch, sovereign.
MO.NAR.QUI.A, *s.f.*, monarchy, sovereignty.
MO.NAR.QUIS.MO, *s.m.*, monarchism.
MO.NAS.TÉ.RIO, *s.m.*, monastery.
MO.NE.TÁ.RIO, *adj.*, monetary.
MON.GE, *s.m.*, monk, friar.
MO.NI.TOR, *s.m.*, monitor.
MO.NI.TÓ.RIA, *s.f.*, monitory, advice, reproof.
MON.JA, *s.f.*, nun.
MO.NO, *s.m.*, monkey, ape.
MO.NÓ.CU.LO, *s.m.*, monocle, single eyeglass.
MO.NO.GA.MI.A, *s.f.*, monogamy.
MO.NO.GRA.FI.A, *s.f.*, monograph.
MO.NO.GRA.MA, *s.m.*, monogram.
MO.NÓ.LO.GO, *s.m.*, monologue, soliloquy.
MO.NO.PÓ.LIO, *s.m.*, monopoly.
MO.NO.PO.LI.ZA.ÇÃO, *s.f.*, monopolization.
MO.NO.PO.LI.ZAR, *v.*, to monopolize.
MO.NOS.SÍ.LA.BO, *s.m.*, monosyllable; *adj.*, monosyllabic.
MO.NO.TE.ÍS.MO, *s.m.*, monotheism.
MO.NO.TO.NI.A, *s.f.*, monotony, sameness.
MO.NÓ.TO.NO, *adj.*, monotone, tedious, tiresome, irksome.
MONS.TRO, *s.m.*, monster; prodigy.
MONS.TRU.O.SI.DA.DE, *s.f.*, monstrosity, monstrousness.
MONS.TRU.O.SO, *adj.*, monstrous, abnormal, huge.
MON.TA.GEM, *s.f.*, mounting, erecting, erection, assembly.
MON.TA.NHA, *s.f.*, mountain, pile.
MON.TA.NHO.SO, *adj.*, mountainous.
MON.TAR, *v.*, to mount, to ride, to assemble, to erect, to furnish.
MON.TA.RI.A, *s.f.*, riding horse.
MON.TE, *s.m.*, mount, hill, heap, pile, accumulation.
MON.TÊS, *adj.*, montane, rustic, wild.
MO.NU.MEN.TAL, *adj.*, monumental, magnificent, extraordinary.
MO.NU.MEN.TO, *s.m.*, monument, memorial, memory.
MO.RA, *s.f.*, delay, respite.
MO.RA.DA, *s.f.*, residence, habitation, dwelling.
MO.RA.DIA, *s.f.*, residence.
MO.RA.DOR, *s.m.*, resident, lodger, inhabitant, tenant.

MO.RAL, *s.f.*, morals, ethics, morality, morale; *adj.*, moral, ethical.
MO.RA.LI.DA.DE, *s.f.*, morality.
MO.RA.LIS.TA, *s.2 gen.*, moralist.
MO.RA.LI.ZAR, *v.*, to moralize, to censure.
MO.RAN.GO, *s.m.*, strawberry.
MO.RAR, *v.*, to live, to inhabit, to reside, to abide.
MOR.BI.DEZ, *s.f.*, morbidness, morbidity.
MÓR.BI.DO, *adj.*, morbid, diseased, sickly.
MOR.CE.GO, *s.m.*, bat, flickermouse.
MOR.DA.ÇA, *s.f.*, muzzle, gag.
MOR.DER, *v.*, to bite, to nip, to snap, to sink the teeth into.
MOR.DI.DA, *s.f.*, bite, teethmark.
MOR.DO.MO, *s.m.*, butler, majordomo.
MO.RE.NO, *s.m.*, brunet; *adj.*, brunet, brown, dark.
MOR.FI.NA, *s.f.*, morphine.
MOR.FO.LO.GI.A, *s.f.*, morphology.
MO.RI.BUN.DO, *s.m.*, moribund; *adj.*, moribund, dying, expiriting.
MOR.MA.ÇO, *s.m.*, sweltry.
MOR.NO, *adj.*, lukewarm, tepid.
MO.RO.SI.DA.DE, *s.f.*, slowness, tardiness, moroseness.
MO.RO.SO, *adj.*, morose, glum, gloomy.
MOR.RER, *v.*, to die, to perish, to decease, to pass away, to decay.
MOR.RO, *s.m.*, mount, mound, hill.
MOR.TAL, *adj.*, mortal, lethal, deadly, fatal.
MOR.TA.LHA, *s.f.*, hearse cloth.
MOR.TA.LI.DA.DE, *s.f.*, mortality.
MOR.TE, *s.f.*, death, decease, dying, destruction.
MOR.TÍ.FE.RO, *adj.*, mortal, lethal, murderous.
MOR.TO, *s.m.*, dead, deceased, defunct; *adj.*, dead, deceased, killed, wilted, withered.
MOR.TU.Á.RIO, *adj.*, mortuary, funerary.
MO.SAI.CO, *s.m.*, mosaic.
MOS.CA, *s.f.*, fly.
MOS.QUI.TEI.RO, *s.m.*, mosquito-net.
MOS.QUI.TO, *s.m.*, mosquito.
MOS.TAR.DA, *s.f.*, mustard.
MOS.TEI.RO, *s.m.*, monastery, convent.
MOS.TRA, *s.f.*, show, exhibition, display.
MOS.TRAR, *v.*, to show, to display, to present, to signify, to denote.
MOS.TRU.Á.RIO, *s.m.*, showcase, collection.
MO.TE.JO, *s.m.*, scorn, jest, joke.
MO.TEL, *s.m.*, motel.
MO.TIM, *s.m.*, mutiny, revolt, uproar.
MO.TI.VA.ÇÃO, *s.f.*, motivation, argumentation.
MO.TI.VAR, *v.*, to motivate, to incite, to reason.
MO.TI.VO, *s.m.*, motive, ground, cause, reason, intent.
MO.TO.CI.CLE.TA, *s.f.*, motorcycle, bike, motorbike.
MO.TO.CI.CLIS.TA, *s.2 gen.*, motorcyclist.
MO.TOR, *s.m.*, motor, engine; *adj.*, motor, moving.
MO.TO.RIS.TA, *s.2 gen.*, driver, motorist, engineer.
MO.TRIZ, *adj.*, motor, motive.
MOU.RE.JAR, *v.*, to work hard, to toil.
MOU.RO, *s.m.*, Moor, Saracen; *adj.*, Moorish.
MO.VE.DI.ÇO, *adj.*, movable, unstable.
MÓ.VEL, *s.m.*, piece of furniture; *adj.*, movable, moveable, changeable.
MO.VER, *v.*, to move, to put in motion, to advance, to progress.
MO.VI.DO, *adj.*, moved, impelled.
MO.VI.MEN.TAR, *v.*, to move, to stir, to animate.
MO.VI.MEN.TA.DO, *adj.*, lively, busy, active.
MO.VI.MEN.TO, *s.m.*, movement, motion, move, moving.
MU.AM.BA, *s.f.*, smuggling, theft, fraud.
MU.CO, *s.m.*, mucus, slime, phlegm.
MU.ÇUL.MA.NO, *adj., s.m.*, Mussulman, Moslem.
MU.DA, *s.f.*, change, shift, move, moving.
MU.DAN.ÇA, *s.f.*, change, alteration, move, substitution.
MU.DAR, *v.*, to change, to shift, to move, to exchange, to alter.
MU.DO, *s.m.*, speechless, mute; *adj.*, speechless, voiceless, dumb, mute.
MUI.TO, *adj.*, much, plenty, very, a good deal;
MUITOS, many, a great many; *adv.*, very, most, much, too much.

MU.LA, *s.f.*, mule, she-hinny.
MU.LA.TA, *s.f.*, mulatto woman.
MU.LA.TO, *s.m.*, mulatto.
MU.LE.TA, *s.f.*, crutch, support.
MU.LHER, *s.f.*, woman, wife.
MU.LHE.REN.GO, *s.m.*, skirt chaser, milksop; *adj.*, unmanly.
MUL.TA, *s.f.*, fine, penalty, forfeiture.
MUL.TAR, *v.*, to fine, to mulct.
MUL.TI.CO.LOR, *adj.*, multicoloured.
MUL.TI.DÃO, *s.f.*, multitude, crowd, throng.
MUL.TI.MI.LI.O.NÁ.RIO, *s.m.*, multimillionaire.
MUL.TI.PLI.CA.ÇÃO, *s.f.*, multiplication, increase in number.
MUL.TI.PLI.CA.DOR, *s.m.*, multiplier, coefficient.
MUL.TI.PLI.CAR, *v.*, to multiply, to increase in number.
MUL.TI.PLI.CI.DA.DE, *s.f.*, multiplicity.
MÚL.TI.PLO, *adj.*, multiple.
MÚ.MIA, *s.f.*, mummy.
MUN.DA.NA, *s.f.*, dissolute, prostitute, whore.
MUN.DA.NO, *adj.*, mundane, worldly, earthly.
MUN.DI.AL, *adj.*, worldwide, general.
MUN.DO, *s.m.*, world, universe, earth, humanity.
MU.NI.ÇÃO, *s.f.*, munition, supplies.
MU.NI.CI.PAL, *adj.*, municipal.
MU.NI.CÍ.PIO, *s.m.*, municipal district.
MU.NIR, *v.*, to munition, to provide, to supply.
MU.RA.LHA, *s.f.*, wall, rampart, battlement.
MU.RAR, *v.*, to wall, to immure, to enclose, to fence in.
MUR.CHAR, *v.*, to wilt, to dry up, to wither, to wizen.
MUR.CHO, *adj.*, wilted, faded, drooping, wizened.
MUR.MU.RAR, *v.*, to murmur, to whisper, to mumble.
MUR.MÚ.RIO, *s.m.*, murmur, murmur of many voices.
MU.RO, *s.m.*, wall, enclosure.
MUR.RO, *s.m.*, punch, blow, slug.
MU.SA, *s.f.*, muse.
MUS.CU.LAR, *adj.*, muscular.
MUS.CU.LA.TU.RA, *s.f.*, musculature, muscularity.
MÚS.CU.LO, *s.m.*, muscle, brawn.
MUS.CU.LO.SO, *adj.*, muscular, sinewy.
MU.SEU, *s.m.*, museum.
MUS.GO, *s.m.*, moss.
MÚ.SI.CA, *s.f.*, music, melody, harmony.
MU.SI.CAL, *adj.*, musical.
MÚ.SI.CO, *s.m.*, musician, artist, performer; *adj.*, musical, harmonious.
MU.TA.ÇÃO, *s.f.*, mutation, change, alteration, variation.
MU.TÁ.VEL, *adj.*, mutable, changeable.
MU.TI.LA.ÇÃO, *s.f.*, mutilation.
MU.TI.LAR, *v.*, to mutilate, to maim, to cripple, to disable.
MU.TIS.MO, *s.m.*, mutism, muteness.
MU.TU.Á.RIO, *s.m.*, borrower.
MÚ.TUO, *s.m.*, loan, insurance; *adj.*, mutual, reciprocal, interchangeable.
MU.XO.XO, *s.m.*, smack, kiss, caress.

N

N, *s.m.*, thirteenth letter of the Portuguese alphabet.
NA, *contr.* of the art. A with the *prep.* **IN**, in the.
NA.BO, *s.m.*, turnip.
NA.ÇÃO, *s.f.*, nation, country, land, state, people, folk.
NA.CI.O.NAL, *adj.*, national, inlandish.
NA.CI.O.NA.LI.DA.DE, *s.f.*, nationality.
NA.CI.O.NA.LIS.MO, *s.m.*, nationalism.
NA.CI.O.NA.LI.ZA.ÇÃO, *s.f.*, nationalization.
NA.CI.O.NA.LI.ZAR, *v.*, to nationalize, naturalize.
NA.CO, *s.m.*, large piece, lump, chop, portion.
NA.DA, *s.m.*, nothing, nil, nought, insignificance; *adv.*, nothing, not at all.
NA.DA.DEI.RA, *s.f.*, fin, flipper.
NA.DA.DOR, *s.m.*, swimmer; *adj.*, swimming.
NA.DAR, *v.*, to swim, to float, to wallow.
NÁ.DE.GA,*s.f.*,buttock,rump, backside, crupper.
NAF.TA.LI.NA, *s.f.*, naphtalin, naphtalene.
NAI.PE, *s.m.*, suit.
NA.MO.RA.DA,*s.f.*,sweetheart, ladylove, flame.
NA.MO.RA.DO, *s.m.*, sweetheart, boyfriend, lover.
NA.MO.RAR, *v.*, to court, to go out with, to make love, to woo.
NA.MO.RO, *s.m.*, courtship, going out, love-making, wooing.
NA.NI.CO, *s.m.*, dwarfish, stunted.
NÃO, *s.m.*, no, refusal, denial; *adv.*, no, not.
NA.QUE.LE, *contr.* of the *prep.* **EM** and the *pron.* **AQUELE**, in that, thereat, at that, therein, on that.
NAR.CI.SIS.MO, *s.m.*, narcissism.
NAR.CI.SO, *s.m.*, narcissus.
NAR.CÓ.TI.CO, *s.m.*, narcotic, drug, stuff; *adj.*, narcotic.
NAR.CO.TI.ZAR,*v.*,to narcotize, to dope, to drug.
NA.RI.NA, *s.f.*, nostril.
NA.RIZ, *s.m.*, nose; smeller, pecker.
NAR.RA.ÇÃO,*s.f.*,narration,narrative, narrating.
NAR.RA.DOR, *s.m.*, narrator, story-teller; *adj.*, narrative.
NAR.RAR,*v.*,to narrate, to relate, to report, to tell.
NA.SAL, *adj.*, nasal.
NAS.CEN.ÇA,*s.f.*, birth, origin, source, nascency.
NAS.CEN.TE, *s.f.*, fountain, source, origin, beggining, rise, spring; *adj.*, nascent, being born.
NAS.CER, *s.m.*, rising; *v.*, to be born, to see the light, to come to light.
NAS.CI.DO, *adj.*, born.
NAS.CI.MEN.TO, *s.m.*, birth, origin, source, nativity.
NA.TA, *s.f.*, cream, skim.
NA.TA.ÇÃO, *s.f.*, swimming, natation.
NA.TAL, *s.m.*, Christmas, birthday; *adj.*, native, natal.
NA.TA.LÍ.CIO, *s.m.*, natal; **ANIVERSÁRIO**, birthday.
NA.TA.LI.DA.DE, *s.f.*, natality, birth.
NA.TI.VI.DA.DE, *s.f.*, nativity, birth.
NA.TI.MOR.TO, *adj.*, *s.m.*, stillborn.
NA.TI.VO, *s.m.*, native, homeborn; *adj.*, native, indigenous, national.
NA.TO, *adj.*, born, native, alive, innate.
NA.TU.RAL, *adj.*, natural, native, genuine, spontaneous.
NA.TU.RA.LI.DA.DE, *s.f.*, naturalness, simplicity.
NA.TU.RA.LI.ZA.ÇÃO, *s.f.*, naturalization.
NA.TU.RA.LI.ZAR, *v.*, to naturalize, to nationalize, to familiarize.
NA.TU.RE.ZA, *s.f.*, nature, forces of nature, character.
NAU.FRA.GAR,*v.*,to wreck,to shipwreck,to fail.
NAU.FRÁ.GIO, *s.m.*, wreck, failure, shipwreck, failure.

NÁU.FRA.GO, *s.m.*, shipwrecked person.
NÁU.SEA, *s.f.*, nausea, sickness, repugnance, qualm.
NAU.SE.A.DO, *adj.*, nauseated, sick.
NAU.SE.AR, *v.*, to nauseate, to sicken, to repugnate, to disgust.
NÁU.TI.CA, *s.f.*, nautics, navigation.
NÁU.TI.CO, *adj.*, nautical, marine, navigational, naval.
NA.VAL, *adj.*, naval, marine, maritime.
NA.VA.LHA, *s.f.*, razor.
NA.VE.GA.ÇÃO, *s.f.*, navigation, shipping, sailing.
NA.VE.GA.DOR, *s.m.*, navigator.
NA.VE.GAR,*v.*,to navigate,to sail,to travel by sea.
NA.VI.O, *s.m.*, ship, vessel, craft, boat.
NE.BLI.NA, *s.f.*, mist, fog, haze, gauze.
NE.BU.LO.SI.DA.DE, *s.f.*, nebulosity, mistiness.
NE.BU.LO.SO,*adj.*,misty,foggy,hazy, vaporous.
NE.CES.SÁ.RIO, *adj.*, necessary, indispensable, exigent.
NE.CES.SI.DA.DE, *s.f.*, necessity, necessariness, must, need, poverty.
NE.CES.SI.TAR, *v.*, to need, to necessitate, to demand.
NE.CRÓ.PO.LE, *s.f.*, necropolis, cemetery.
NE.CROP.SI.A, *s.f.*, necropsy, autopsy.
NE.CRO.TÉ.RIO, *s.m.*, mortuary, morgue.
NÉC.TAR, *s.m.*, nectar.
NE.FAN.DO, *adj.*, nefarious, abominable.
NE.FAS.TO, *adj.*, disastrous, disgraceful, tragic.
NE.FRI.TE, *s.f.*, nephritis.
NE.GA.ÇÃO, *s.f.*, negation, negative, denial.
NE.GAR, *v.*, to deny, to say no, to negate, to contradict.
NE.GA.TI.VA, *s.f.*, negative, refusal.
NE.GLI.GÊN.CIA,*s.f.*,negligence,neglect, omit.
NE.GLI.GEN.CI.AR, *v.*, to neglect, to disregard, to omit.
NE.GLI.GEN.TE, *adj.*, *s.2 gen.*, negligent, neglectful, lazy; lax.
NE.GO.CI.A.ÇÃO, *s.f.*, negotiation, transaction, deal.

NE.GO.CI.AN.TE, *s.2 gen.*, merchant, merchandiser, trader, businessman.
NE.GO.CI.AR, *v.*, to negotiate, to trade in, to do business.
NE.GO.CI.Á.VEL, *adj.*, negotiable.
NE.GÓ.CIO, *s.m.*, business, trade, commerce, transaction.
NE.GRI.DÃO, *s.f.*, blackness, obscurity.
NE.GRO, *s.m.*, Negro, black; *adj.*, black, dark, negro, African.
NE.GRU.ME, *s.m.*, darkness, obscurity.
NE.LA, *contr.* of the *prep.* **EM** with the *pron.* **ELA**, in her, on her, in it, on it.
NE.LE, *contr.* of the *prep.* **EM** with the *pron.* **ELE**, in him, on him, in it, on it.
NEM, *conj.*, neither, nor, not even.
NE.NÊ, *s.m.*, baby, newborn.
NE.NHUM, *adj.*, null, void, any, neither; *adv.*, none, nobody, not any.
NE.Ó.FI.TO, *s.m.*, neophite, proselite, novice.
NE.O.LA.TI.NO, *adj.*, *s.m.*, Neolatin.
NE.O.LO.GIS.MO, *s.m.*, neologism.
NÉ.ON, *s.m.*, neon.
NE.PO.TIS.MO, *s.m.*, nepotism.
NER.VO, *s.m.*, nerve.
NER.VO.SIS.MO, *s.m.*, nerves, nervousness, excitability.
NER.VO.SO, *adj.*, nervous, energetic, vigorous, irritable, nervy.
NES.SA, *contr.* of the *prep.* **EM** with the *pron.* **ESSA**, in that, on that; **NESSAS**, in those, on those.
NES.SE, *contr.* of the *prep.* **EM** with the *pron.* **ESSE**, in that, on that; **NESSES**, in those, on those.
NES.TA, *contr.* of the *prep.* **EM** with the *pron.* **ESTA**, in this, on this; **NESTAS**, in these, on these.
NES.TE, *contr.* of the *prep.* **EM** with the *pron.* **ESTE**, in this, on this; **NESTES**, in these, on these.
NE.TA, *s.f.*, granddaughter.
NE.TO, *s.m.*, grandson.
NEU.RAS.TE.NI.A, *s.f.*, neurasthenia.

NEU.RO.LO.GI.A, *s.f.*, neurology.
NEU.RO.SE, *s.f.*, neurosis.
NEU.RÓ.TI.CO, *adj.*, neurotic.
NEU.TRA.LI.DA.DE, *s.f.*, neutrality, impartiality.
NEU.TRA.LI.ZAR, *v.*, to neutralize; to kill, to destroy.
NEU.TRO, *s.m.*, neuter; *adj.*, neuter, neutral, impartial.
NE.VAR, *v.*, to snow, to cover with snow.
NE.VAS.CA, *s.f.*, snow-storm, blizzard.
NE.VE, *s.f.*, snow.
NÉ.VOA, *s.f.*, fog, mist.
NE.VO.EI.RO, *s.m.*, fog, mist.
NE.VRAL.GI.A, *s.f.*, neuralgia.
NE.XO, *s.m.*, connection, nexus, link, tie.
NI.CO.TI.NA, *s.f.*, nicotine.
NI.DI.FI.CAR, *v.*, to nidificate, to nidify.
NI.I.LIS.MO, *s.m.*, nihilism.
NI.I.LIS.TA, *s.2 gen.*, nihilist.
NI.NAR, *v.*, to lull to sleep.
NIN.FA, *s.f.*, nymph.
NIN.FE.TA, *s.f.*, nymphet.
NIN.FO.MA.NI.A, *s.f.*, nymphomania.
NIN.GUÉM, *pron.*, nobody, no one, no man, no person.
NI.NHA.DA, *s.f.*, nide, clutch, covery.
NI.NHA.RI.A, *s.f.*, trifle, insignificance.
NI.NHO, *s.m.*, nest, hole, den.
NI.PÔ.NI.CO, *adj., s.m.*, Japanese.
NÍ.QUEL, *s.m.*, nickel.
NI.QUE.LAR, *v.*, to nickel.
NIS.SO, *contr.* of the *prep.* **EM** with the *pron.* **ISSO**, at that, in that, on that, thereat, herein, thereon, thereby.
NIS.TO, *contr.* of the *prep.* **EM** with the *pron.* **ISTO**, at this, in this, on this, hereat, herein, hereon, hereby.
NI.TI.DEZ, *s.f.*, clearness, distinctness, brightness, brilliance.
NÍ.TI.DO, *adj.*, clear, sharp, explicit, neat, fair.
NI.TRO.GÊ.NIO, *s.m.*, azote, nitrogen.
NÍ.VEL, *s.m.*, level; situation; **NÍVEL SOCIAL**, social level.
NI.VE.LA.MEN.TO, *s.m.*, levelling, grading.
NI.VE.LAR, *v.*, to level, to grade, to equalize.
NÓ, *s.m.*, node, knot; problem, difficulty.
NO.BRE, *s.m.*, noble, nobleman, aristocrat; *adj.*, noble, generous, gallant.
NO.BRE.ZA, *s.f.*, nobility, aristocracy, nobleness.
NO.ÇÃO, *s.f.*, notion, conception, impression, idea.
NO.CAU.TE, *s.m.*, knockout.
NO.CI.VO, *adj.*, harmful, bad, noxious, ruinous.
NÓ.DOA, *s.f.*, blot, spot, stain, mark, blur, fleck.
NO.DO.SO, *adj.*, nodose, knotty.
NÓ.DU.LO, *s.m.*, nodule, node, knot.
NOI.TA.DA, *s.f.*, vigil, watch, night's period.
NOI.TE, *s.f.*, night, darkness, obscurity.
NOI.VA, *s.f.*, bride, fiancée.
NOI.VA.DO, *s.m.*, engagement, betrothal.
NOI.VAR, *v.*, to become engaged, to court, to woo.
NOI.VO, *s.m.*, fiancé, bridegroom.
NO.JEN.TO, *adj.*, nauseating, sickening, repulsive.
NO.JO, *s.m.*, nausea, disgust, loathing, qualm, repugnance.
NÔ.MA.DE, *s.2 gen.*, nomad; *adj.*, nomad, nomadic, errant.
NO.ME, *s.m.*, name, designation, denomination, noun, nickname, reputation, renown.
NO.ME.A.ÇÃO, *s.f.*, nomination, appointment.
NO.ME.AR, *v.*, to name, to denominate, to call, to designate.
NO.MEN.CLA.TU.RA, *s.f.*, nomenclature.
NO.MI.NAL, *adj.*, nominal.
NO.MI.NA.TI.VO, *s.m.*, nominative.
NO.NA.GE.NÁ.RIO, *adj., s.m.*, nonagenarian.
NO.NA.GÉ.SI.MO, *num.*, ninetieth.
NO.NO, *num.*, ninth.
NO.RA, *s.f.*, daughter-in-law.
NOR.DES.TE, *s.m.*, northeast; *adj.*, northeastern.
NÓR.DI.CO, *adj., s.m.*, Nordic.
NOR.MA, *s.f.*, norm, principle, rule, direction, precept.
NOR.MAL, *adj.*, normal, regular, natural.
NOR.MA.LI.DA.DE, *s.f.*, normality, normalness.
NOR.MA.LI.ZAR, *v.*, to normalize, to adjust.
NO.RO.ES.TE, *adj., s.m.*, northwest.
NOR.TE, *s.m.*, north, northward; *adj.*, north,

northern.
NOR.TE.AR, *v.*, to guide, to direct, to lead, to indicate the north.
NO.RU.E.GUÊS, *adj.*, *s.m.*, Norwegian.
NOS, *contr. prep.* EM with *art. m. pl.* OS: at the, in the, on the.
NÓS, *pron.*, we; us.
NO.SO.CÔ.MIO, *s.m.*, hospital.
NOS.SO, *pron.*, our, ours.
NOS.TAL.GI.A, *s.f.*, homesickness, nostalgia.
NO.TA, *s.f.*, note, reminder, bill, account, annotation, chit.
NO.TA.ÇÃO, *s.f.*, notation.
NO.TAR, *v.*, to notice, to observe, to note, to remark.
NO.TÁ.RIO, *s.m.*, notary.
NO.TÍ.CIA, *s.f.*, news, information, report, tidings.
NO.TI.CI.AR, *v.*, to inform, to announce, to publish, to advertise.
NO.TI.CI.Á.RIO, *s.m.*, news, news service.
NO.TI.FI.CA.ÇÃO, *s.f.*, notification.
NO.TI.FI.CAR, *v.*, to notify, to inform, to announce, to intimate, to warn.
NO.TO.RI.E.DA.DE, *s.f.*, notoriety, notoriousness, publicity.
NO.TÓ.RIO, *adj.*, notorious, public.
NO.TUR.NO, *adj.*, nocturnal, nightly.
NO.VA.TO, *s.m.*, beginner, apprentice, newcomer, rookie, freshman; *adj.*, inexperienced, raw.
NO.VE, *num.*, nine.
NO.VE.CEN.TOS, *num.*, nine hundred.
NO.VE.LA, *s.f.*, novel, soap opera, tale, story.
NO.VEM.BRO, *s.m.*, November.
NO.VE.NA, *s.f.*, novena, space of nine days.
NO.VEN.TA, *num.*, ninety.
NO.VI.ÇO, *s.m.*, begginer, novice, neophyte.
NO.VI.DA.DE, *s.f.*, newness, recentness, novelty, news.
NO.VI.LHA, *s.f.*, heifer.
NO.VI.LHO, *s.m.*, bullock, steer.
NO.VO, *adj.*, young, new, recent, fresh, novel, green.
NOZ, *s.f.*, nut, walnut.
NOZ-MOS.CA.DA, *s.f.*, nutmeg.
NU, *s.m.*, nude, *adj.*, nude, bare, naked, undressed, uncovered.
NU.AN.ÇA, *s.f.*, nuance, shade.
NU.BLA.DO, *adj.*, cloudy, dark, obscure, somber, skyless.
NU.BLAR, *v.*, to cloud, to darken, to overcloud, to obscure, to shadow.
NU.CA, *s.f.*, nape, scruff, neck.
NU.CLE.AR, *adj.*, nuclear, *v.*, to nucleate.
NÚ.CLEO, *s.m.*, nucleous, center.
NU.DEZ, *s.f.*, nakedness, nudity, bareness.
NU.LI.DA.DE, *s.f.*, nullity, invalidity, voidness.
NU.LO, *adj.*, null, void, zero, none, inept.
NU.ME.RA.ÇÃO, *s.m.*, numbering, numeration.
NU.ME.RAL, *s.m.*, numeral, *adj.*, numeric, numeral.
NU.ME.RAR, *v.*, to number, to enumerate, to expose.
NU.MÉ.RI.CO, *adj.*, numeric, numerical.
NÚ.ME.RO, *s.m.*, number, cypher, mark, quantity.
NU.ME.RO.SO, *adj.*, numerous, plentiful.
NUN.CA, *adv.*, never, at no time, ever.
NÚN.CIO, *s.m.*, nuncio, legate.
NUP.CI.AL, *adj.*, nuptial, bridal.
NÚP.CIAS, *s.f.*, *pl.*, nuptials, marriage, wedding.
NU.TRI.ÇÃO, *s.f.*, nutrition, feed, nourishment, alimentation.
NU.TRI.CI.O.NIS.TA, *s.2 gen.*, nutritionist.
NU.TRI.DO, *adj.*, fed, nourished, robust.
NU.TRIR, *v.*, to nourish, to feed, to maintain, to sustain, to foster.
NU.TRI.TI.VO, *adj.*, nutritious, nutrient.
NU.VEM, *s.f.*, cloud, haze, mist.

O

O, *s.m.*, the fourteenth letter of the Portuguese alphabet; article (m.) the; zero, cypher; *pron.*, it, him, to him; you, to you.
O.Á.SIS, *s.m.*, oasis.
OB.CE.CA.ÇÃO, *s.f.*, blindness, obduracy.
OB.CE.CAR, *v.*, to blind, to obscure, to obfuscate, to obsess.
O.BE.DE.CER, *v.*, to obey, to comply, to execute, to submit.
O.BE.DI.ÊN.CIA, *s.f.*, obedience, submission, compliance, dependence.
O.BE.DI.EN.TE, *adj.*, obedient, submissive.
O.BE.LIS.CO, *s.m.*, obelisk.
O.BE.SI.DA.DE, *s.f.*, obesity, fatness.
O.BE.SO, *adj.*, fat, obese.
Ó.BI.TO, *s.m.*, death, decease, obit.
O.BI.TU.Á.RIO, *s.m.*, obituary.
OB.JE.ÇÃO, *s.f.*, objection, opposition, contestation.
OB.JE.TAR, *v.*, to object, to oppose, to refute.
OB.JE.TI.VAR, *v.*, to objectify, to materialize.
OB.JE.TI.VI.DA.DE, *s.f.*, objectivity.
OB.JE.TI.VO, *s.m.*, objective, end, aim, object.
OB.JE.TO, *s.m.*, object, matter, topic, purpose, motive, reason.
O.BLI.QUI.DA.DE, *s.f.*, obliquity.
O.BLÍ.QUO, *adj.*, oblique, slanting, skew.
O.BLI.TE.RAR, *v.*, to obliterate, to erase, to efface.
O.BLON.GO, *adj.*, oblong, elongated, oval.
O.BRA, *s.f.*, work, job, handwork.
OBRA-PRI.MA, *s.f.*, masterpiece.
O.BREI.RO, *s.m.*, worker, wright, workman.
O.BRI.GA.ÇÃO, *s.f.*, obligation, duty.
O.BRI.GA.DO, *adj.*, obliged, compelled, thankful.
O.BRI.GAR, *v.*, to oblige, to force, to compel, to subject.
O.BRI.GA.TO.RI.E.DA.DE, *s.f.*, obligatoriness.
O.BRI.GA.TÓ.RIO, *adj.*, obligatory, forceable, mandatory.
OBS.CE.NI.DA.DE, *s.f.*, obscenity, indecency.
OBS.CE.NO, *adj.*, obscene, indecent, filthy, impure, sensual.
OBS.CU.RI.DA.DE, *s.f.*, obscurity, obscureness, darkness.
OBS.CU.RO, *adj.*, obscure, dark, dim, cloudy, enigmatic, misty, unknown.
OB.SE.QUI.AR, *v.*, to oblige, to captivate, to do a favour.
OB.SÉ.QUIO, *s.m.*, favour, courtesy.
OB.SER.VA.ÇÃO, *s.f.*, observation, remark, note.
OB.SER.VA.DOR, *s.m.*, observer, watcher, spectator, onlooker.
OB.SER.VÂN.CIA, *s.f.*, observance.
OB.SER.VAR, *v.*, to observe, to watch, to look at, to notice, to perceive.
OB.SER.VA.TÓ.RIO, *s.m.*, observatory.
OB.SES.SÃO, *s.f.*, obsession, mania.
OB.SO.LE.TO, *adj.*, obsolete, archaic, antiquated.
OBS.TÁ.CU.LO, *s.m.*, obstacle, hindrance, obstruction, difficulty.
OBS.TAN.TE, *adj.*, *s.2 gen.*, hindering, obstructive; **NÃO OBSTANTE**, in spite of, despite of, however.
OBS.TAR, *v.*, to oppose, to thwart, to resist.
OBS.TE.TRA, *s.2 gen.*, obstetrician.
OBS.TE.TRÍ.CIA, *s.f.*, obstetrics.
OBS.TI.NA.ÇÃO, *s.f.*, obstinacy, stubbornness, pertinacity.
OBS.TI.NAR, *v.*, to become obstinate, to persevere.
OBS.TRU.ÇÃO, *s.f.*, obstruction, blockage.
OBS.TRU.IR, *v.*, to obstruct, to block up, to engorge, to shut, to close.
OB.TEN.ÇÃO, *s.f.*, obtainment, acquirement, obtention, acquisition.

OB.TER, *v.*, to obtain, to gain, to achieve, to get, to attain, to secure, to bay.
OB.TI.DO, *adj.*, obtained, attained.
OB.TU.RA.ÇÃO, *s.f.*, obturation, filling, stopping.
OB.TU.RAR, *v.*, to obturate, to fill, to close, to stop, to plug.
OB.TU.SO, *adj.*, obtuse, rounded, blunt.
ÓB.VIO, *adj.*, obvious, plain, evident, clear.
O.CA.SI.ÃO, *s.f.*, occasion, time, opportunity, motive, reason, place.
O.CA.SI.O.NAL, *adj.*, occasional, eventual, casual.
O.CA.SI.O.NAR, *v.*, to occasion, to cause, to originate, to provoke.
O.CA.SO, *s.m.*, sunset, west, decline, occident.
OC.CI.PI.TAL, *s.m.*, occipital.
O.CE.A.NO, *s.m.*, ocean, sea.
O.CE.A.NO.GRA.FI.A, *s.f.*, oceanography.
O.CE.A.NÓ.GRA.FO, *s.m.*, oceanographer.
O.CI.DEN.TAL, *adj.*, occidental, western.
O.CI.DEN.TE, *s.m.*, occident, west.
Ó.CIO, *s.m.*, leisure, rest, inactivity, laziness, indolence.
O.CI.O.SI.DA.DE, *s.f.*, laziness, idleness, indolence.
O.CI.O.SO, *s.m.*, laybones, truant, idler; *adj.*, idle, lazy, indolent.
O.CO, *adj.*, hollow, empty, deep, addle.
O.COR.RÊN.CIA, *s.f.*, occurrence, incident, event, fact, chance.
O.COR.RER, *v.*, to occur, happen, befall, to appear, to come out.
OC.TO.GE.NÁ.RIO, *adj.*, *s.m.*, octogenarian.
OC.TO.GÉ.SI.MO, *num.*, eightieth.
OC.TÓ.GO.NO, *s.m.*, octagon; *adj.*, octagonal.
O.CU.LAR, *adj.*, *s.2 gen.*, ocular.
O.CU.LIS.TA, *s.2 gen.*, oculist, optician, eye-doctor.
Ó.CU.LOS, *s.m.*, *pl.*, spectacles, glasses.
O.CUL.TA.ÇÃO, *s.f.*, occultation.
O.CUL.TAR, *v.*, to occult, to hide, to conceal, to cover, to eclipse.
O.CUL.TO, *adj.*, occult, hidden, secret, covered, secret.

O.CU.PA.ÇÃO, *s.f.*, occupation, job, business, employment.
O.CU.PA.DO, *adj.*, occupied, busy, engaged, taken.
O.CU.PAR, *v.*, to occupy, to possess, to live in, to reside, to tenant.
O.DE, *s.f.*, ode, the poem.
O.DI.AR, *v.*, to hate, to detest, to dislike, to abhor, to abominate.
Ó.DIO, *s.m.*, hate, hatred, odium, enmity, aversion.
O.DI.O.SO, *adj.*, hateful, loathsome, abominable, spiteful.
O.DON.TO.LO.GI.A, *s.f.*, odontology, dentistry.
O.DON.TO.LO.GIS.TA, *s.2 gen.*, dentist, odontologist.
O.DOR, *s.m.*, smell, scent, odor, aroma, fragrance.
O.ES.TE, *s.m.*, west, occident; *adj.*, west, western.
O.FE.GAR, *v.*, to pant, to puff, to gasp.
O.FEN.DE.DOR, *s.m.*, offender.
O.FEN.DER, *v.*, to offend, to insult, to hurt, to pique, to displease.
O.FEN.DI.DO, *adj.*, offended, insulted.
O.FEN.SA, *s.f.*, offense, insult, affront, wound, hurt.
O.FEN.SI.VA, *s.f.*, offensive, aggression, assault.
O.FEN.SI.VO, *adj.*, offensive, aggressive, attacking.
O.FEN.SOR, *s.m.*, offender, wounder.
O.FE.RE.CER, *v.*, to offer, to give, to tender, to proffer, to expose.
O.FE.RE.CI.MEN.TO, *s.m.*, offer, proffer, proposal.
O.FE.REN.DA, *s.f.*, offer, proffer.
O.FER.TA, *s.f.*, offer, donation, present.
O.FER.TAR, *v.*, to present, to offer, to proffer.
O.FER.TÓ.RIO, *s.m.*, offertory.
O.FI.CI.AL, *s.2 gen.*, officer; *adj.*, official.
O.FI.CI.A.LI.ZAR, *v.*, to officialize.
O.FI.CI.NA, *s.f.*, workshop, shop, pantry.
O.FÍ.CIO, *s.m.*, profession, service, art, work, job.
O.FÍ.DIO, *s.m.*, ophidian, snake.
OF.TAL.MO.LO.GI.A, *s.f.*, ophthalmology.
OF.TAL.MO.LO.GIS.TA, *s.2 gen.*, ophthalmologist.
O.FUS.CAR, *v.*, to obfuscate, to obscure, to dazzle, to darken, to dim.

O.GI.VA, *s.f.*, ogive.
OH!, *interj.*, ó!, oh!
OI!, *interj.*, hallo!, hello!
OI.TA.VA, *s.f.*, octave.
OI.TA.VO, *num.*, eighth.
OI.TEN.TA, *num.*, eighty.
OI.TO, *num.*, eight.
OI.TO.CEN.TOS, *num.*, eight hundred.
O.JE.RI.ZA, *s.f.*, grudge, ill will, antipathy.
O.LA.RI.A, *s.f.*, pottery, brickyard.
O.LE.AR, *v.*, to oil.
Ó.LEO, *s.m.*, oil.
O.LE.O.DU.TO, *s.m.*, pipeline, oleoduct.
OL.FA.TO, *s.m.*, smell, scent.
O.LHA.DA, *s.f.*, glimpse, glance, look, peep.
O.LHAR, *s.m.*, look, glance; *v.*, to look, to eye, to stare at, to gaze, to view.
O.LHEI.RAS, *s.f., pl.*, shades, shadows around the eyes.
O.LHO, *s.m.*, eye; eyesight, view, look.
O.LI.GAR.QUI.A, *s.f.*, oligarchy.
O.LIM.PÍ.A.DA, *s.f.*, Olympiad, Olympic games.
O.LÍM.PI.CO, *adj.*, Olympic.
O.LI.VA, *s.f.*, olive, olive tree.
O.LI.VEI.RA, *s.f.*, olive tree.
OL.VI.DAR, *v.*, to forget, to omit, to neglect.
OL.VI.DO, *s.m.*, forgetfulness, oblivion.
OM.BRO, *s.m.*, shoulder, dilligence.
O.ME.LE.TE, *s.f.*, omelet.
O.MIS.SÃO, *s.f.*, omission, neglect, oversight, default, negligence.
O.MI.TIR, *v.*, to omit, to overlook, to neglect, to overslip, to fail.
O.MO.PLA.TA, *s.f.*, omoplate, shoulder blade.
ON.ÇA, *s.f.*, jaguar(animal), ounce(unit of weight).
ON.DA, *s.f.*, wave, billow, comber, surge, undulation, vibration, oscillation, fashion.
ON.DE, *adv.*, where; *pron.*, wherein, in which.
ON.DU.LA.ÇÃO, *s.f.*, undulation, fluctuation, waving, vibration.
ON.DU.LA.DO, *adj.*, wavy.
ON.DU.LAR, *v.*, to wave, to undulate.
O.NE.RAR, *v.*, to burden, to tax, to load, to oppress.

O.NE.RO.SO, *adj.*, onerous, oppressive, weighty, heavy.
Ô.NI.BUS, *s.m.*, bus, coach, omnibus.
O.NI.PO.TÊN.CIA, *s.f.*, omnipotence.
O.NI.PO.TEN.TE, *adj.*, omnipotent, almighty.
O.NO.MA.TO.PEI.A, *s.f.*, onomatopoeia.
ON.TEM, *adv.*, yesterday.
ON.TO.LO.GI.A, *s.f.*, ontology.
ON.TO.LÓ.GI.CO, *adj.*, ontological.
Ô.NUS, *s.m.*, onus, burden, charge.
ON.ZE, *num.*, eleven.
O.PA.CO, *adj.*, opaque, dull, obscure, dark.
OP.ÇÃO, *s.f.*, option, choice, selection.
Ó.PE.RA, *s.f.*, opera.
O.PE.RA.ÇÃO, *s.f.*, operation, action.
O.PE.RA.DOR, *s.m.*, operator, surgeon; *adj.*, operative, operating.
O.PE.RAR, *v.*, to produce, to work, to function, to perform.
O.PE.RÁ.RIO, *s.m.*, worker, workman, labourer.
O.PE.RA.TÓ.RIO, *adj.*, operative, operating.
O.PE.RO.SI.DA.DE, *s.f.*, operoseness.
O.PI.NAR, *v.*, to judge, to opine, to consider, to think, to vote.
O.PI.NI.ÃO, *s.f.*, opinion, point of view, idea, judgment.
Ó.PIO, *s.m.*, opium.
O.PO.NEN.TE, *s.2 gen.*, opponent, antagonist, adversary; *adj.*, opponent.
O.POR, *v.*, to oppose, to refuse, to resist, to hinder, to prevent.
O.POR.TU.NI.DA.DE, *s.f.*, opportunity, chance, occasion.
O.POR.TU.NO, *adj.*, opportune, suitable, timely, handy, propitious, convenient.
O.PO.SI.ÇÃO, *s.f.*, opposition, resistance, antagonism.
O.POS.TO, *adj.*, opposite, contrary.
O.PRES.SÃO, *s.f.*, oppression, hardship, pressure, tyranny.
O.PRES.SI.VO, *adj.*, opressive, tyrannical.
O.PRES.SOR, *s.m.*, oppressor, despot, tyrant; *adj.*, oppressive.
O.PRI.MIR, *v.*, to oppress, tyrannize over,

torment, suppress, persecute.
OP.TAR, *v.*, to opt, to choose, to prefer, to select, to make a choice.
ÓP.TI.CA, *s.f.*, optics.
ÓP.TI.CO, *adj.*, optic, optical.
O.PU.LÊN.CIA, *s.f.*, opulence, opulency, riches, wealthiness.
O.PU.LEN.TO, *adj.*, opulent, rich, wealthy, plentiful.
O.RA, *adv.*, now, at present; *conj.*, but, however, nevertheless.
O.RA.ÇÃO, *s.f.*, prayer, supplication, rogation, clause, sentence.
O.RÁ.CU.LO, *s.m.* oracle.
O.RA.DOR, *s.m.*, orator, public speaker.
O.RAL, *adj.*, oral, verbal, vocal, spoken.
O.RAN.GO.TAN.GO, *s.m.*, orangutan, orangoutang.
O.RAR, *v.*, to pray, to supplicate, to beseech, to preach, to orate.
O.RA.TÓ.RIA, *s.f.*, oratory.
O.RA.TÓ.RIO, *s.m.*, oratory.
ÓR.BI.TA, *s.f.*, orbit, eye socket.
OR.ÇA.MEN.TO, *s.m.*, budget, calculation.
OR.ÇAR, *v.*, to calculate, to compute, to estimate, to rate, to apprize, to budget for.
OR.DEM, *s.f.*, order, disposition, method, regularity, tidiness, neatness, rule, regulation.
OR.DE.NA.DO, *s.m.*, salary, wage; *adj.*, in order, orderly, arranged.
OR.DE.NAR, *v.*, to order, to arrange, to organize, to dispose.
OR.DE.NHAR, *v.*, to milk.
OR.DI.NAL, *adj.*, ordinal.
OR.DI.NÁ.RIO, *adj.*, ordinary, habitual, common, usual, customary.
O.RE.LHA, *s.f.*, ear, the organ of earing.
O.RE.LHU.DO, *adj.*, long-eared, stupid, ignorant.
OR.FA.NA.TO, *s.m.*, orphanage, orphan asylum.
ÓR.FÃO, *s.m.*, orphan; *adj.*, orphan, fatherless.
OR.GÂ.NI.CO, *adj.*, organic.
OR.GA.NIS.MO, *s.m.*, organism, body, formation.
OR.GA.NIS.TA, *s.2 gen.*, organist.
OR.GA.NI.ZA.ÇÃO, *s.f.*, organization, arrangement, order, institution.
OR.GA.NI.ZA.DOR, *s.m.*, organizer.
OR.GA.NI.ZAR, *v.*, to organize, to arrange, to systematize, to establish.
OR.GA.NO.GRA.MA, *s.m.*, organization chart.
ÓR.GÃO, *s.m.*, organ, pipe organ, instrument, agency.
OR.GAS.MO, *s.m.*, orgasm.
OR.GI.A, *s.f.*, orgy, revelry, debauch.
OR.GU.LHAR, *v.*, to make proud of.
OR.GU.LHO, *s.m.*, pride, vanity.
O.RI.EN.TA.ÇÃO, *s.f.*, orientation, direction.
O.RI.EN.TAL, *adj.*, oriental, eastern.
O.RI.EN.TAR, *v.*, to orient, to guide, to direct, to orientate.
O.RI.EN.TE, *s.m.*, east, orient.
O.RI.FÍ.CIO, *s.m.*, orifice, hole, opening.
O.RI.GEM, *s.f.*, origin, source, ancestry, cause, ascendance.
O.RI.GI.NAL, *s.m.*, original, archetype, pattern; *adj.*, original, inventive, primitive, primary.
O.RI.GI.NA.LI.DA.DE, *s.f.*, originality.
O.RI.GI.NAR, *v.*, to originate, to cause, to rise, to start, to produce, to create.
O.RI.GI.NÁ.RIO, *adj.*, originary, primitive, derived, descended.
O.RI.UN.DO, *adj.*, derived, native.
OR.LA, *s.f.*, border, edge, margin, rim.
OR.NA.MEN.TA.ÇÃO, *s.f.*, ornamentation.
OR.NA.MEN.TAR, *v.*, to ornament, to adorn, to decorate.
OR.NA.MEN.TO, *s.m.*, ornament, decoration, adornment.
OR.NAR, *v.*, to adorn, to ornament, to decorate, to embellish.
OR.NI.TÓ.LO.GO, *s.m.*, ornithologist.
OR.QUES.TRA, *s.f.*, orchestra.
OR.QUES.TRAR, *v.*, to orchestrate.
OR.QUÍ.DEA, *s.f.*, orchid.
OR.TO.DO.XO, *adj., s.m.*, orthodox, Orthodox.
OR.TO.GRA.FI.A, *s.f.*, orthography.
OR.TO.GRÁ.FI.CO, *adj.*, orthographic.
OR.TO.PE.DI.A, *s.f.*, orthopedics.
OR.TO.PÉ.DI.CO, *adj.*, orthopedic.

OR.VA.LHAR, *v.*, to bedew, to dew, to drop moisture.
OR.VA.LHO, *s.m.*, dew, morning dew, mist.
OS.CI.LA.ÇÃO, *s.f.*, oscillation, vibration, fluctuation, variation.
OS.CI.LAN.TE, *adj.*, *s.2 gen.*, oscillating, oscillatory.
OS.CI.LAR, *v.*, to oscillate, to swing, to sway, to vibrate.
ÓS.CU.LO, *s.m.*, osculum, kiss.
OS.MO.SE, *s.f.*, osmosis, osmose.
OS.SA.DA, *s.f.*, skeleton, ruins, heap of bones.
ÓS.SEO, *adj.*, osseous, bony.
OS.SI.FI.CA.ÇÃO, *s.f.*, ossification.
OS.SO, *s.m.*, bone; difficulty.
OS.TEN.SI.VO, *adj.*, ostensive, demonstrative.
OS.TEN.TA.ÇÃO, *s.f.*, ostentation, show, vanity, display, pomp.
OS.TEN.TAR, *v.*, to exhibit, make a show of.
OS.TRA, *s.f.*, oyster.
OS.TRA.CIS.MO, *s.m.*, ostracism, relegation.
O.TÁ.RIO, *s.m.*, sucker, dull, gull, dupe.
Ó.TI.CA, *s.f.*, otics.
Ó.TI.CO, *adj.*, otic.
O.TI.MIS.MO, *s.m.*, optimism.
O.TI.MIS.TA, *s.2 gen.*, optimist, hopeful.
O.TI.MI.ZA.ÇÃO, *s.f.*, optimization.
O.TI.MI.ZAR, *v.*, to optimize.
Ó.TI.MO, *adj.*, excellent, very good, best, fine.
O.TO.MA.NO, *adj.*, *s.m.*, Ottoman, Turk.
OU, *conj.*, or, either.
OU.RI.ÇO, *s.m.*, hedgehog.
OU.RI.VES, *s.m.*, goldsmith, jeweler.
OU.RI.VE.SA.RI.A, *s.f.*, jewelry, goldsmithery.
OU.RO, *s.m.*, gold.
OU.SA.DI.A, *s.f.*, daring, boldness, courage, audacity, bravery.
OU.SA.DO, *adj.*, bold, audacious, brave, insolent.
OU.SAR, *v.*, to dare, to risk, to attempt.
OU.TEI.RO, *s.m.*, hillock, hill.
OU.TO.NO, *s.m.*, autumn, fall.
OU.TOR.GA, *s.f.*, grant, bestowal.
OU.TOR.GAR, *v.*, to approve, to sanction, to grant, to warrant, to confer.
OU.TREM, *pron.*, somebody else, other people.
OU.TRO, *pron.*, other, another; **OUTROS**, others.
OU.TRO.RA, *adv.*, formerly, of old, long ago.
OU.TROS.SIM, *adv.*, also, likewise.
OU.TU.BRO, *s.m.*, October.
OU.VI.DO, *s.m.*, ear, audition.
OU.VIN.TE, *s.2 gen.*, listener, hearer.
OU.VIR, *v.*, to hear, to listen, to attend to, to pay attention to.
O.VA, *s.f.*, fish ovary, spawn.
O.VA.ÇÃO, *s.f.*, ovation, applause.
O.VA.CI.O.NAR, *v.*, to acclaim, to applaud, to homage.
O.VAL, *adj.*, oval, ovate, oviform.
O.VA.LAR, *v.*, to ovalize, to make oval.
O.VÁ.RIO, *s.m.*, ovary, ovarium.
O.VE.LHA, *s.f.*, ewe, sheep; member of a spiritual flock.
O.VE.LHI.NHA, *s.f.*, lamb.
O.VER.DO.SE, *s.f.*, overdose.
O.VIL, *s.m.*, sheep-cote.
O.VI.NO, *adj.*, ovine, sheeplike.
O.VI.NO.CUL.TU.RA, *s.f.*, sheep raising.
O.VO, *s.m.*, egg; **CLARA DO OVO**, egg white; **GEMA DO OVO**, egg yolk.
O.VOI.DE, *adj.*, ovoid.
O.VU.LA.ÇÃO, *s.f.*, ovulation.
Ó.VU.LO, *s.m.*, ovule, small ovum.
O.XA.LÁ, *interj.*, would to God!
O.XI.DA.ÇÃO, *s.f.*, rust, oxidation, corrosion.
O.XI.DAR, *v.*, to oxidate, to oxidize, to rust.
O.XI.DÁ.VEL, *adj.*, oxidable.
Ó.XI.DO, *s.m.*, oxid.
O.XI.GE.NA.ÇÃO, *s.f.*, oxygenation.
O.XI.GE.NA.DO, *adj.*, oxygenated.
O.XI.GE.NAR, *v.*, to oxygenate, to treat.
O.XI.GÊ.NIO, *s.m.*, oxygen.
O.XÍ.TO.NO, *adj.*, *s.m.*, oxytone.
O.ZÔ.NIO, *s.m.*, ozone.
O.ZO.NI.ZAR, *v.*, to ozonize.

P

P, *s.m.*, fifteenth letter of the Portuguese alphabet.
PÁ, *s.f.*, spade, shovel, scoop, peel.
PA.CA.TEZ, *s.f.*, tranquility, placidity.
PA.CA.TO, *adj.*, quiet, peaceful.
PA.CHOR.RA, *s.f.*, phlegm, sluggishness, apathy.
PA.CI.ÊN.CIA, *s.f.*, patience, solitaire (card game).
PA.CI.EN.TE, *adj.*, *s.2 gen.*, patient.
PA.CI.FI.CA.ÇÃO, *s.f.*, pacification, reconciliation.
PA.CI.FI.CA.DOR, *s.m.*, pacifier, pacificator, pacifist.
PA.CI.FI.CAR, *v.*, to pacify, to pacificate, to tranquilize, to calm, to conciliate.
PA.CÍ.FI.CO, *s.m.*, pacific; *adj.*, pacific, calm, peaceful, tranquil.
PA.CI.FIS.TA, *s.2 gen.*, pacifist; *adj.*, pacifistic.
PA.CO.TE, *s.m.*, package, packet, pack, parcel, bundle.
PAC.TO, *s.m.*, pact, agreement, compact.
PAC.TU.AR, *v.*, to make a pact with.
PA.DA.RIA, *s.f.*, bakery, baker's shop.
PA.DE.CER, *v.*, to suffer, to endure pain, tolerate.
PA.DEI.RO, *s.m.*, baker.
PA.DI.O.LA, *s.f.*, handbarrow, litter.
PA.DRÃO, *s.m.*, standard, gauge, model, pattern.
PA.DRAS.TO, *s.m.*, stepfather.
PA.DRE, *s.m.*, priest, father, clergyman.
PA.DRE-NOS.SO, *s.m.*, Pater Noster.
PA.DRI.NHO, *s.m.*, godfather, protector, sponsor.
PA.DRO.EI.RO, *s.m.*, patron, protector, patron saint.
PA.DRO.NI.ZAR, *v.*, to standardize, to gauge.
PA.GA.DOR, *s.m.*, payer, paymaster.
PA.GA.MEN.TO, *s.m.*, payment, salary.
PA.GÃO, *adj.*, *s.m.*, pagan.
PA.GAR, *v.*, to pay, to remunerate, to reimburse, to compensate, to repay.

PÁ.GI.NA, *s.f.*, page.
PA.GI.NAR, *v.*, to paginate, to page.
PAI, *s.m.*, father; pais, parents.
PAI.NEL, *s.m.*, panel, picture.
PAI.OL, *s.m.*, storehouse, barn.
PAI.RAR, *v.*, to hover, to scud, to hang (over).
PA.ÍS, *s.m.*, country, nation, land, region.
PAI.SA.GEM, *s.m.*, landscape, scenery.
PAI.SA.NO, *s.m.*, compatriot, fellow countryman; *adj.*, compatriot.
PAI.XÃO, *s.f.*, passion, love, infatuation.
PA.JÉ, *s.m.*, peai, shaman.
PA.JEM, *s.m.*, page, attendant, baby sitter.
PA.LA.CE.TE, *s.m.*, a small palace.
PA.LÁ.CIO, *s.m.*, palace.
PA.LA.DAR, *s.m.*, taste, liking, palate.
PA.LAN.QUE, *s.m.*, stand, scaffold.
PA.LA.TO, *s.m.*, palate, taste, savour.
PA.LA.VRA, *s.f.*, word, term, expression, vocable, promise.
PAL.CO, *s.m.*, stage.
PA.LE.O.LÍ.TI.CO, *adj.*, palaeolithic.
PA.LE.O.LO.GIA, *s.f.*, palaeology.
PA.LER.MA, *s.m.*, idiot, fool, imbecile; *adj.*, foolish, idiotic, dull, silly.
PA.LES.TRA, *s.f.*, lecture, talk, conversation.
PA.LE.TA, *s.f.*, shoulder-blade.
PA.LE.TÓ, *s.m.*, coat, jacket.
PA.LHA, *s.f.*, straw, dry grass.
PA.LHA.ÇO, *s.m.*, clown, buffoon, jester.
PA.LHEI.RO, *s.m.*, hayloft, haystack.
PA.LI.A.TI.VO, *s.m.*, a palliative medicine.
PA.LI.DEZ, *s.f.*, paleness, wanness, whiteness.
PÁ.LI.DO, *adj.*, pale, shallow, wan, pallid, whitish.
PA.LI.TO, *s.m.*, stick, toothpick.
PAL.MA, *s.f.*, palm.
PAL.MA.DA, *s.f.*, slap, rap, cuff.
PAL.MA.TÓ.RIA, *s.f.*, ferule, a pandy.

PALMEIRA   **PARAGUAIO**

PAL.MEI.RA, *s.f.*, palm tree.
PAL.MI.LHA, *s.f.*, insole.
PAL.MÍ.PE.DE, *s.m.*, palmiped.
PAL.MI.TO, *s.m.*, heart of palm.
PAL.MO, *s.m.*, span (of the hand), palm.
PAL.PÁ.VEL, *adj.*, palpable, touchable; evident.
PÁL.PE.BRA, *s.f.*, eyelid.
PAL.PI.TA.ÇÃO, *s.f.*, palpitation, throb.
PAL.PI.TAN.TE, *adj., s.2 gen.*, palpitant.
PAL.PI.TAR, *v.*, to palpitate, to throb, to pulsate, to pulse.
PAL.PI.TE, *s.m.*, suggestion, tip.
PAL.PI.TEI.RO, *s.m.*, tipster, tout.
PAL.RAR, *v.*, to jabber, to chatter, to converse.
PA.LUS.TRE, *adj.*, swampy, marshy.
PA.NA.CA, *s.2 gen.*, fool, simpleton; *adj.*, silly, simple, foolish.
PA.NA.ME.NHO, *adj., s.m.*, Panamanian.
PAN-A.ME.RI.CA.NO, *adj., s.m.*, Pan-American.
PAN.ÇA, *s.f.*, rumen; paunch.
PAN.CA.DA, *s.f.*, blow, knock, bang, hit.
PAN.CA.DA.RI.A, *s.f.*, scuffle, fray, brawl, beating, spanking.
PÂN.CREAS, *s.m.*, pancreas.
PAN.DEI.RO, *s.m.*, tambourine.
PAN.DE.MÔ.NIO, *s.m.*, pandemonium.
PA.NE, *s.f.*, failure or breakdown of a motor of an automobile, airplane, etc.
PA.NE.LA, *s.f.*, pot, pan, saucepan.
PA.NE.LA.DA, *s.f.*, potful, panful.
PAN.FLE.TO, *s.m.*, pamphlet, brochure.
PÂ.NI.CO, *s.m.*, panic, terror, alarm; *adj.*, panic.
PA.NI.FI.CA.ÇÃO, *s.f.*, panification, breadmaking.
PA.NI.FI.CA.DO.RA, *s.f.*, bakery.
PA.NO, *s.m.*, cloth.
PA.NO.RA.MA, *s.f.*, panorama, landscape, view, scene.
PAN.QUE.CA, *s.f.*, pancake.
PAN.TA.NAL, *s.m.*, swampland.
PÂN.TA.NO, *s.m.*, swamp, marsh, bog, morass.
PAN.TA.NO.SO, *adj.*, swampy, marshy, boggy.
PAN.TE.ÍS.MO, *s.m.*, pantheism.
PAN.TE.ÍS.TA, *s.2 gen.*, pantheist.

PAN.TE.RA, *s.f.*, panther.
PAN.TÓ.GRA.FO, *s.m.*, pantograph.
PÃO, *s.m.*, bread, loaf, roll; PÃO CASEIRO, home-baked bread.
PÃO DE LÓ, *s.m.*, sponge-cake.
PÃO-DU.RO, *s.m.*, miser, niggard.
PÃO.ZI.NHO, *s.m.*, little bread.
PA.PA, *s.m.*, pope; *s.f.*, pap.
PA.PA.GAI.AR, *v.*, to parrot, to talk idly.
PA.PA.GAI.O, *s.m.*, parrot, kite.
PA.PAI, *s.m.*, dad, daddy, father, pappy.
PA.PÃO, *s.m.*, bugbear, hobgoblin.
PA.PEI.RA, *s.f.*, parotitis.
PA.PEL, *s.m.*, paper, role; **PAPÉIS**, documents;
PAPEL ALMAÇO, foolscap paper.
PA.PE.LÃO, *s.m.*, cardboard.
PA.PE.LA.RI.A, *s.f.*, stationery, stationer's shop.
PA.PEL-MO.E.DA, *s.f.*, paper currency.
PA.PI.RO, *s.m.*, papyrus.
PA.PO, *s.m.*, crop, pouch, craw.
PA.POU.LA, *s.f.*, poppy.
PA.QUE.TE, *s.m.*, packet.
PA.QUI.DER.ME, *s.m.*, pachyderm.
PAR, *s.m.*, pair, couple, peer, brace, partner; *adj.*, equal, like, similar, equivalent.
PA.RA, *prep.*, for, to, toward, in, in(to), in order to, about to.
PA.RA.BÉNS, *s.m.*, pl., congratulations, felicitations.
PA.RÁ.BO.LA, *s.f.*, parable, parabola.
PA.RA.BÓ.LI.CO, *adj.*, parabolic.
PA.RA-BRI.SA, *s.f.*, windshield.
PA.RA-CHO.QUE, *s.m.*, bumper.
PA.RA.DA, *s.f.*, parade, stop, pause, rest, halt.
PA.RA.DIG.MA, *s.m.*, paradigm.
PA.RA.DO.XAL, *adj.*, paradoxical.
PA.RA.DO.XO, *s.m.*, paradox.
PA.RA.FI.NA, *s.f.*, paraffin.
PA.RÁ.FRA.SE, *s.f.*, paraphrase.
PA.RA.FU.SAR, *v.*, to screw, to fasten with a screw.
PA.RA.FU.SO, *s.m.*, screw, bolt.
PA.RÁ.GRA.FO, *s.m.*, paragraph.
PA.RA.GUAI.O, *adj., s.m.*, Paraguayan.

PA.RA.Í.SO, *s.m.*, paradise, heaven, the garden of Eden.
PA.RA-LA.MA, *s.m.*, mudguard, fender, dashboard.
PA.RA.LE.LA, *s.f.*, parallel.
PA.RA.LE.LE.PÍ.PE.DO, *s.m.*, parallelepiped.
PA.RA.LE.LO, *s.m.*, parallel, confrontation, comparison.
PA.RA.LI.SA.ÇÃO, *s.f.*, paralyzation, stoppage, weakness, interruption.
PA.RA.LI.SAR, *v.*, to paralyze, to weaken, to neutralize.
PA.RA.LI.SIA, *s.f.*, paralysis, palsy.
PA.RA.LÍ.TI.CO, *adj.*, *s.m.*, paralytic.
PA.RA.NIN.FO, *s.m.*, sponsor, patron, paranymph.
PA.RA.NOI.A, *s.f.*, paranoia.
PA.RA.NOI.CO, *adj.*, paranoiac.
PA.RA.PEI.TO, *s.m.*, parapet, window sill.
PA.RA.PLÉ.GI.CO, *adj.*, *s.m.*, paraplegic.
PA.RA.PSI.CO.LO.GIA, *s.f.*, parapsychology.
PA.RA.QUE.DAS, *s.m.*, parachute.
PA.RA.QUE.DIS.TA, *s.2 gen.*, parachutist.
PA.RAR, *v.*, to stop, to quit, to pause, to halt, to discontinue, to stay.
PA.RA-RAI.OS, *s.m.*, pl., lightning-rod, lightning-conductor.
PA.RA.SI.TA, *s.2 gen.*, parasite.
PA.RA.SI.TO.LO.GIA, *s.f.*, parasitology.
PAR.CEI.RO, *s.m.*, partner, associate, companion; *adj.*, similar, like, equal.
PAR.CE.LA, *s.f.*, parcel, portion, fragment, quota.
PAR.CE.LA.DO, *adj.*, made in parcels.
PAR.CE.LAR, *v.*, to parcel, to divide into parcels.
PAR.CE.RIA, *s.f.*, partnership, association.
PAR.CI.AL, *adj.*, partial, biased, unfair, prejudiced.
PAR.CI.A.LI.DA.DE, *s.f.*, partiality, unfairness, bias, faction.
PAR.CI.MÔ.NIA, *s.f.*, parsimony, economy.
PAR.CO, *adj.*, economic, frugal, poor.
PAR.DAL, *s.m.*, sparrow.
PAR.DO, *s.m.*, mulatto, pard; *adj.*, brown, dusky.
PA.RE.CER, *s.m.*, aspect, opinion, concept, point of view; *v.*, to appear, to seem, to look, to resemble.
PA.RE.CI.DO, *adj.*, similar, like, resembling.
PA.RE.DE, *s.f.*, wall, barrier, partition.
PA.RE.LHA, *s.f.*, team, yoke, pair, couple.
PA.REN.TE, *s.2 gen.*, relative, kindfolk, kinsman.
PA.REN.TE.LA, *s.f.*, kindred, relations, relatives, kinsfolk.
PA.REN.TES.CO, *s.m.*, kinship, relationship, kinsfolk.
PA.RÊN.TE.SE, *s.m.*, parenthesis, bracket.
PÁ.REO, *s.m.*, horse race, running match.
PA.RI.DA.DE, *s.f.*, parity, equality.
PA.RIR, *v.*, to bring forth, to give birth to, to have a baby; to cause.
PA.RI.SI.EN.SE, *adj.*, *s.2 gen.*, Parisian.
PAR.LA.MEN.TA.ÇÃO, *s.f.*, parleying.
PAR.LA.MEN.TAR, *s.2 gen.*, parliamentary; *v.*, to parley, to treat, to negotiate.
PAR.LA.MEN.TA.RIS.MO, *s.m.*, parliamentarism.
PAR.LA.MEN.TO, *s.m.*, parliament, legislative body.
PAR.ME.SÃO, *s.m.*, Parmesan, Parmesan cheese.
PAR.NA.SI.A.NO, *adj.*, *s.m.*, Parnassian.
PÁ.RO.CO, *s.m.*, parish priest, vicar, curate.
PA.RÓ.DIA, *s.f.*, parody.
PA.RÓ.QUIA, *s.f.*, parish.
PA.RO.QUI.AL, *adj.*, parochial.
PA.RO.QUI.A.NO, *s.m.*, parishioner; *adj.*, parochial.
PA.RO.XIS.MO, *s.m.*, paroxysm.
PAR.QUE, *s.m.*, park, public square, garden.
PAR.REI.RA, *s.f.*, vine, grapevine, trellis.
PAR.RI.CI.DA, *s.2 gen.*, parricide.
PAR.TE, *s.f.*, part, portion, piece, fraction, spot, particle, side, region, place.
PAR.TEI.RA, *s.f.*, midwife, accoucheuse.
PAR.TI.CI.PA.ÇÃO, *s.f.*, participation, notice, communication, notification, advice.
PAR.TI.CI.PAR, *v.*, to communicate, to announce, to report, to take part in, to inform, to share in.
PAR.TI.CÍ.PIO, *s.m.*, participle.
PAR.TÍ.CU.LA, *s.f.*, particle.

PAR.TI.CU.LAR, *s.m.*, private person, particulars; *adj.*, particular, private, individual, special, specific.

PAR.TI.CU.LA.RI.DA.DE, *s.f.*, characteristic, detail.

PAR.TI.CU.LA.RI.ZAR, *v.*, to particularize.

PAR.TI.DA, *s.f.*, departure, leaving, start, party; game, shipment.

PAR.TI.DÁ.RIO, *s.m.*, adherent, sectarian, partisan.

PAR.TI.DO, *s.m.*, party, faction, side, part; *adj.*, broken, fractured.

PAR.TI.LHA, *s.f.*, partition, division, repartition, allotment, share.

PAR.TI.LHAR, *v.*, to partition, to share with, to divide.

PAR.TIR, *v.*, to break, to shatter, to split, to depart, to leave, to go away.

PAR.TO, *s.m.*, parturition, delivery, childbirth.

PAR.TU.RI.EN.TE, *s.f.*, a parturient woman.

PAS.CAL, *adj.*, paschal.

PÁS.COA, *s.f.*, Easter.

PAS.MAR, *v.*, to amaze, to astonish, to surprise, to stupefy.

PAS.MO, *adj.*, amazed.

PAS.SA, *s.f.*, raisin.

PAS.SA.DO, *s.m.*, the past; *adj.*, past, gone, bygone, ended, old-fashioned; last.

PAS.SA.GEI.RO, *s.m.*, passenger, traveller; *adj.*, transitory, temporary, ephemeral.

PAS.SA.GEM, *s.f.*, passage, crossing, ticket.

PAS.SA.POR.TE, *s.m.*, passport.

PAS.SAR, *v.*, to pass, to cross, to traverse, to go, to around, to employ.

PAS.SA.RE.LA, *s.f.*, platform, bridge, runway, ramp.

PAS.SA.RI.NHO, *s.m.*, small bird, birdie, bird.

PÁS.SA.RO, *s.m.*, bird.

PAS.SA.TEM.PO, *s.m.*, pastime, amusement, diversion.

PAS.SE, *s.m.*, pass, permission, pass bill.

PAS.SE.AR, *v.*, to promenade, to walk, to stroll, to journey.

PAS.SE.A.TA, *s.f.*, parade, demonstration, stroll.

PAS.SEI.O, *s.m.*, walk, promenade, stroll, jaunt.

PAS.SI.BI.LI.DA.DE, *s.f.*, passibility.

PAS.SÍ.VEL, *adj.*, passible, susceptible.

PAS.SI.VI.DA.DE, *s.f.*, passivity, passiviness.

PAS.SI.VO, *adj.*, passive, inactive, inert, indifferent.

PAS.SO, *s.m.*, pace, step, footstep, walk, march, passage.

PAS.TA, *s.f.*, paste, dough, pulp, portfolio, folder, briefcase.

PAS.TA.GEM, *s.f.*, pasture, pasturage.

PAS.TAR, *v.*, to pasture, to graze.

PAS.TEL, *s.m.*, pastry, pie.

PAS.TE.LEI.RO, *s.m.*, pastryman, pastry-cook, pastry-maker.

PAS.TEU.RI.ZAR, *v.*, to pasteurize.

PAS.TI.LHA, *s.f.*, pastille, tablet, lozenge.

PAS.TO, *s.m.*, pasture, pasturage.

PAS.TOR, *s.m.*, herdsman, shepherd, priest, clergyman, vicar.

PAS.TO.RAL, *s.f.*, pastoral.

PAS.TO.RIL, *adj.*, pastoral.

PAS.TO.SO, *adj.*, pasty, viscous, gummy, sticky.

PA.TA, *s.f.*, paw, foot; female duck.

PA.TA.DA, *s.f.*, a kick, stamping with the paws or foot.

PA.TA.MAR, *s.m.*, platform, stairhead, landing.

PA.TEN.TE, *s.f.*, patent; *adj.*, patent, evident, manifest, obvious.

PA.TER.NAL, *adj.*, paternal, fatherly.

PA.TER.NA.LIS.MO, *s.m.*, paternalism.

PA.TER.NI.DA.DE, *s.f.*, paternity, fatherhood, fathership.

PA.TER.NO, *adj.*, paternal, fatherly.

PA.TE.TA, *s.2 gen.*, dotard, simpleton, fool.

PA.TÉ.TI.CO, *adj.*, pathetic.

PA.TÍ.BU.LO, *s.m.*, gallows, gibbet.

PA.TI.FE, *s.2 gen.*, rascal, villain, rogue, rotter; *adj.*, scoundrel.

PA.TIM, *s.m.*, roller-skate, ice-skate.

PA.TI.NAR, *v.*, to skate, to skid.

PÁ.TIO, *s.m.*, courtyard, yard, court.

PA.TO, *s.m.*, duck, drake.

PA.TO.LO.GI.A, *s.f.*, pathology.

PA.TRÃO, *s.m.*, master, boss, employer, chief, foreman.
PÁ.TRIA, *s.f.*, native country, home, homeland.
PA.TRI.AR.CA, *s.m.*, patriarch.
PA.TRI.AR.CA.DO, *s.m.*, patriarchate.
PA.TRÍ.CIO, *s.m.*, patrician, aristocrat; *adj.*, distinct, elegant.
PA.TRI.MÔ.NIO, *s.m.*, patrimony, property, inheritance.
PA.TRI.O.TA, *s.2 gen.*, patriot; *adj.*, patriot, patriotic.
PA.TRI.O.TIS.MO, *s.m.*, patriotism.
PA.TRO.A, *s.f.*, mistress, housekeeper.
PA.TRO.CI.NAR, *v.*, to sponsor, to patronize, to support, to defend.
PA.TRO.CÍ.NIO, *s.m.*, patronage, protection, support, aid, sponsorship.
PA.TRU.LHA, *s.f.*, patrol, a patrolling.
PA.TRU.LHAR, *v.*, to patrol.
PAU, *s.m.*, stick, wood, timber, lath; **PAUS**, clubs (cards).
PAU.LA.DA, *s.f.*, a blow with a cudgel.
PAU.SA, *s.f.*, pause, stop, interruption, interval.
PAU.SA.DO, *adj.*, paused.
PAU.SAR, *v.*, to pause, to make a pause.
PAU.TA, *s.f.*, stave, staff; list, roll, agenda.
PAU.TAR, *v.*, to rule, to mark.
PA.VÃO, *s.m.*, peacock.
PA.VI.LHÃO, *s.m.*, pavillion, the external ear, canopy.
PA.VI.MEN.TA.ÇÃO, *s.f.*, paving.
PA.VI.MEN.TAR, *v.*, to pave, to floor, to cover with asphalt.
PA.VI.MEN.TO, *s.m.*, pavement, paving, floor.
PA.VIO, *s.m.*, wick, fuse.
PA.VOR, *s.m.*, fright, dread, terror.
PA.VO.RO.SO, *adj.*, dreadful, terrible, horrific, frightful.
PAZ, *s.f.*, peace, tranquillity, calm, repose, rest.
PÉ, *s.m.*, foot, linear measure (12 in.), foundation, bottom, stalk; **A PÉ**, on foot; **DAR NO PÉ**, run away.
PE.ÃO, *s.m.*, walker, farm hand, footman.
PE.ÇA, *s.f.*, piece, fragment, portion, division, section, play, musical composition.
PE.CA.DO, *s.m.*, sin, offense, misdeed, error, fault, transgression.
PE.CA.DOR, *s.m.*, sinner, offender, wrongdoer.
PE.CA.DO.RA, *s.f.*, sinner, sinful woman.
PE.CAR, *v.*, to sin, to commit sin, to err, to offend.
PE.CHA, *s.f.*, defect, failing.
PE.CHIN.CHA, *s.f.*, bargain.
PE.CHIN.CHAR, *v.*, to bargain, to barter.
PE.ÇO.NHEN.TO, *adj.*, poisonous, venomous.
PE.CU.Á.RIA, *s.f.*, cattle breeding, cattle raising.
PE.CU.LA.TO, *s.m.*, peculation.
PE.CU.LI.AR, *adj.*, peculiar, special, singular, uncommon, individual.
PE.CU.LI.A.RI.DA.DE, *s.f.*, peculiarity, peculiarness.
PE.CÚ.NIA, *s.f.*, money.
PE.CU.NI.Á.RIO, *adj.*, pecuniary, monetary.
PE.DA.ÇO, *s.m.*, piece, bit, fragment, fraction, bite, slice, portion, parcel.
PE.DÁ.GIO, *s.m.*, toll.
PE.DA.GO.GI.A, *s.f.*, pedagogy.
PE.DA.GO.GO, *s.m.*, pedagog, pedagogue.
PE.DAL, *s.m.*, pedal.
PE.DA.LAR, *v.*, to pedal.
PÉ DE CA.BRA, *s.m.*, crowbar.
PE.DES.TAL, *s.m.*, basis, pedestal, socle.
PE.DES.TRE, *s.2 gen.*, pedestrian, a walker; *adj.*, pedestrian, walking.
PE.DI.A.TRA, *s.2 gen.*, pediatrist, pediatrician.
PE.DI.A.TRI.A, *s.f.*, pediatrics.
PE.DI.DO, *s.m.*, petition, demand, request, solicitation, prayer.
PE.DIN.TE, *s.2 gen.*, beggar, mendicant; *adj.*, mendicant.
PE.DIR, *v.*, to ask, to beg, to demand, to claim, to appeal, to pray, to implore.
PE.DRA, *s.f.*, stone, gravel, rock, flint; calculus.
PE.DRA.DA, *s.f.*, throw of a stone.
PE.DRA-SA.BÃO, *s.f.*, soap-stone.
PE.DRE.GO.SO, *adj.*, stony, full of stones.
PE.DREI.RA, *s.f.*, quarry, stone-pit.
PE.DREI.RO, *s.m.*, mason, bricklayer, stonemason.

PE.GA.DA, *s.f.*, footstep, footprint.
PE.GA.DO, *adj.*, near to, close to, next to.
PE.GA.DOR, *s.m.* catcher.
PE.GA.JO.SO, *adj.*, clammy, sticky, viscous, adhesive.
PE.GAR, *v.*, to catch, to hold, to take, to connect, to adhere, to begin.
PEI.TO, *s.m.*, chest, breast, bosom, guts; heart, courage.
PEI.TU.DO, *adj.*, a big chest, valiant.
PEI.XA.RI.A, *s.f.*, fish market, fish store.
PEI.XE, *s.m.*, fish.
PEI.XE-BOI, *s.m.*, manatee, cowfish.
PEI.XEI.RO, *s.m.*, fishmonger.
PE.JO, *s.m.*, encumbrance, embarrassment.
PE.JO.RA.TI.VO, *adj.*, pejorative, depreciative.
PE.LAR, *v.*, to peel, to bark, to make bald, to skin.
PE.LE, *s.f.*, skin, epidermis, hide, fur, leather; hull.
PE.LE.JA, *s.f.*, fight, struggle, battle, combat, conflict, contention, discussion.
PE.LE.JAR, *v.*, to fight, to combat, to struggle with, to contend.
PE.LE-VER.ME.LHA, *s.2 gen.*, Red Indian.
PE.LI.CA.NO, *s.m.*, pelican.
PE.LÍ.CU.LA, *s.f.*, pellicle, cuticle; film, motion picture.
PE.LO, *s.m.*, hair, down, flue.
PE.LO.TÃO, *s.m.*, platoon, troop.
PE.LÚ.CIA, *s.f.*, plush.
PE.LU.DO, *adj.*, hairy, shaggy, shy.
PEL.VE, *s.f.*, pelvis.
PE.NA, *s.f.*, feather, plume, quill; punishment, penalty, pity; style; writer.
PE.NA.DO, *adj.*, feathered; afflicted.
PE.NAL, *adj.*, penal, punitive.
PE.NA.LI.DA.DE, *s.f.*, penalty, punishment, castigation.
PE.NA.LI.ZAR, *v.*, to pain, to afflict, to distress, to grieve, to torment.
PE.NAR, *v.*, to pain, to suffer, to endure, to grieve.
PEN.CA, *s.f.*, stalk, bunch.
PEN.DÊN.CIA, *s.f.*, quarrel, dispute, scuffle, fight.

PEN.DEN.TE, *adj.*, hanging, pending, pendent, imminent, sloping.
PEN.DER, *v.*, to hang, to lean, to slope, to bend, to tend, to incline.
PEN.DOR, *s.m.*, declivity, slope, incline, bent, inclination.
PÊN.DU.LO, *s.m.*, pendulum.
PEN.DU.RAR, *v.*, to hang, to suspend.
PE.NE.DO, *s.m.*, a great stone, stone.
PE.NEI.RA, *s.f.*, bolter, sieve, screen, strainer.
PE.NEI.RAR, *v.*, to sift, to screen, to strain, to sieve.
PE.NE.TRA.ÇÃO, *s.f.*, penetration.
PE.NE.TRAN.TE, *adj.*, penetrant, penetrative, piercing.
PE.NE.TRAR, *v.*, to penetrate, to invade, to enter, to go in.
PE.NHA, *s.f.*, rock, cliff.
PE.NHAS.CO, *s.m.*, cliff, crag, rock.
PE.NHOR, *s.m.*, pawn, pledge, mortgage; proof.
PE.NHO.RA, *s.f.*, distress, seizure, attachment.
PE.NHO.RA.DO, *adj.*, pawned, pledged.
PE.NHO.RAR, *v.*, to pledge, to pawn, to warrant, to oblige, to engage.
PE.NI.CI.LI.NA, *s.f.*, penicillin.
PE.NÍN.SU.LA, *s.f.*, peninsula, spit.
PÊ.NIS, *s.m.*, penis, cock.
PE.NI.TÊN.CIA, *s.f.*, penitence, contrition.
PE.NI.TEN.CI.Á.RIA, *s.f.*, penitentiary, prison.
PE.NI.TEN.TE, *adj., s.2 gen.*, penitent.
PE.NO.SO, *adj.*, painful, hard, difficult.
PEN.SA.DO, *adj.*, thought of, considered, deliberate.
PEN.SA.DOR, *s.m.*, thinker, philosopher.
PEN.SA.MEN.TO, *s.m.*, thought, thinking, imagination, mind, idea, spirit.
PEN.SÃO, *s.f.*, pension, allowance, boarding house.
PEN.SAR, *v.*, to think, to ponder, to meditate, to imagine, to consider, to reflect, to judge.
PEN.SA.TI.VO, *adj.*, thoughtful, meditative; melancholic.
PÊN.SIL, *adj.*, suspended, hanging.
PEN.SI.O.NA.TO, *s.m.*, boarding school,

boarding house.
PEN.TÁ.GO.NO, *s.m.*, pentagon.
PEN.TE, *s.m.*, comb, card.
PEN.TE.A.DO, *s.m.*, hairdressing, coiffure.
PEN.TE.A.DOR, *s.m.*, comber, hairdresser.
PEN.TE.AR, *v.*, to comb, to dress the hair.
PEN.TE.COS.TES, *s.m.*, Pentecost.
PE.NU.GEM, *s.f.*, fluff, down, fuzz.
PE.NÚL.TI.MO, *adj.*, last but one, penultimate.
PE.NUM.BRA, *s.f.*, shade, half-light, partial shadow.
PE.NÚ.RIA, *s.f.*, penury, indigence, extreme poverty, misery, need.
PE.PI.NO, *s.m.*, cucumber.
PE.PI.TA, *s.f.*, nugget, lump.
PE.QUE.NEZ, *s.f.*, smallness, littleness; infancy.
PE.QUE.NI.NO, *s.m.*, young boy; *adj.*, very little.
PE.QUE.NO, *adj.*, small, little, short.
PE.RA, *s.f.*, pear.
PE.RAM.BU.LAR, *v.*, to perambulate, to walk about.
PE.RAN.TE, *prep.*, in the presence of, before, in front of.
PER.CAL.ÇO, *s.m.*, disturbance, trouble.
PER.CE.BER, *v.*, to perceive, to know, to discern, to note, to discry, to hear.
PER.CEN.TA.GEM, *s.f.*, percentage.
PER.CEP.ÇÃO, *s.f.*, perception, feeling, comprehension, perceptivity.
PER.CEP.TÍ.VEL, *adj.*, perceptible, sensible, noticeable.
PER.CE.VE.JO, *s.m.*, bedbug.
PER.COR.RER, *v.*, to go through, to visit, to travel, to traverse.
PER.CUR.SO, *s.m.*, course, route, way, trajectory, journey, circuit.
PER.DA, *s.f.*, loss, damage, casualty, prejudice, detriment, calamity.
PER.DÃO, *s.m.*, pardon, forgiveness, indulgence.
PER.DER, *v.*, to lose, to miss, to fail, to ruin, to deprave, to waste, to squander.
PER.DI.ÇÃO, *s.f.*, perdition, damnation, ruin, destruction, disgrace, eternal death.

PER.DI.DO, *adj.*, lost, dispersed, ruined, gone.
PER.DIZ, *s.f.*, partridge.
PER.DO.AR, *v.*, to pardon, to forgive, to excuse, to absolve, to remit.
PER.DO.Á.VEL, *adj.*, excusable.
PER.DU.LÁ.RIO, *s.m.*, prodigal, lavisher; *adj.*, prodigal, lavish, wasteful.
PER.DU.RAR, *v.*, to last, to persist, to remain, to forever, to persist.
PE.RE.CER, *v.*, to perish, to die, to decay, to end, to finish.
PE.RE.GRI.NA.ÇÃO, *s.f.*, pilgrimage, peregrination, journey.
PE.RE.GRI.NAR, *v.*, to travel, to go on a pilgrimage.
PE.RE.GRI.NO, *s.m.*, pilgrim, traveller, peregrinator; *adj.*, pilgrim.
PE.REI.RA, *s.f.*, pear-tree.
PE.RE.NE, *adj.*, perennial, unceasing, continual, incessant, permanent, eternal.
PE.RE.RE.CA, *s.f.*, tree-frog.
PER.FA.ZER, *v.*, to complete, to finish, to perform.
PER.FEI.ÇÃO, *s.f.*, perfection, excellence, completeness, finishing.
PER.FEI.TO, *adj.*, perfect, completed, finished, correct, entire.
PER.FÍ.DIA, *s.f.*, perfidy, perfidiousness.
PER.FIL, *s.m.*, profile, outline; aspect.
PER.FI.LAR, *v.*, to profile, to stand.
PER.FU.MA.DO, *adj.*, perfumed, odorous, fragrant.
PER.FU.MAR, *v.*, to perfume, to aromatize, to scent.
PER.FU.ME, *s.m.*, perfume, fragrance, scent.
PER.FU.RA.ÇÃO, *s.f.*, perforation, drill.
PER.FU.RAR, *v.*, to perforate, to bore, to drill, to penetrate, to enter.
PER.GA.MI.NHO, *s.m.*, parchment.
PER.GUN.TA, *s.f.*, question, inquiry, enquiry, interrogation.
PER.GUN.TAR, *v.*, to ask, to interrogate, to question, to query, to ask for.
PE.RÍ.CIA, *s.f.*, skill, ability, dexterity, know-

PERICLITAR | **PERTENCENTE**

how, investigation.
PE.RI.CLI.TAR, *v.*, to run a risk, to endanger.
PE.RI.FE.RI.A, *s.f.*, outskirts, suburbs, circumference.
PE.RÍ.FRA.SE, *s.f.*, periphrasis.
PE.RI.GO, *s.m.*, danger, hazard, peril, risk.
PE.RI.GO.SO, *adj.*, dangerous, hazardous, perilous.
PE.RÍ.ME.TRO, *s.m.*, perimeter.
PE.RI.Ó.DI.CO, *s.m.*, periodical, publication; *adj.*, periodic, periodical.
PE.RÍO.DO, *s.m.*, period, cycle, circuit, age, era, lapse of time, term.
PE.RI.PÉ.CIA, *s.f.*, peripetia.
PE.RI.QUI.TO, *s.m.*, paraquito, parrakeet.
PE.RIS.CÓ.PIO, *s.m.*, periscope.
PE.RI.TO, *s.m.*, expert, specialist, tecnician; *adj.*, skilful, expert, proficient, dexterous.
PER.JU.RAR, *v.*, to perjure, to forswear.
PER.JÚ.RIO, *s.m.*, perjury, false oath.
PER.MA.NE.CER, *v.*, to stay, to continue, to stand, to remain, to last, maintain.
PER.MA.NÊN.CIA, *s.f.*, permanence, stableness, durability, stability.
PER.MA.NEN.TE, *s.2 gen.*, perm (abbrev. of permanent wave); *adj.*, permanent, lasting, durable, enduring, constant, fixed.
PER.ME.Á.VEL, *adj.*, permeable.
PER.MIS.SÃO, *s.f.*, permission, allowance, permit, consent, licence.
PER.MIS.SI.VO, *adj.*, permissive.
PER.MI.TIR, *v.*, to permit, to allow, to consent, to authorize, to admit, to tolerate.
PER.MU.TA, *s.f.*, exchange, interchange, barter.
PER.MU.TAR, *v.*, to exchange, to interchange, to truck, to barter.
PER.MU.TÁ.VEL, *adj.*, permutable.
PER.NA, *s.f.*, leg; **BARRIGA DA PERNA**, calf.
PER.NE.TA, *s.2 gen.*, one-legged person.
PER.NI.CI.O.SO, *adj.*, pernicious, destructive, malign, bad, noxious.
PER.NIL, *s.m.*, thighbone, a thin leg.
PER.NI.LON.GO, *s.m.*, mosquito.
PÉ.RO.LA, *s.f.*, pearl, bead.

PE.RÔ.NIO, *s.m.*, fibula.
PER.PAS.SAR, *v.*, to pass-by, to graze, to move.
PER.PE.TRAR, *v.*, to perpetrate.
PER.PE.TU.AR, *v.*, to perpetuate, to immortalize, to propagate.
PER.PÉ.TUO, *adj.*, perpetual, constant, ceaseless, eternal, immortal.
PER.PLE.XI.DA.DE, *s.f.*, perplexity, amazement, bewilderment, hesitation.
PER.PLE.XO, *adj.*, perplexed, uncertain, astonished.
PER.SA, *adj.*, *s.2 gen.*, Persian.
PERS.CRU.TAR, *v.*, to search, to scrutinize, to scan, to examine.
PER.SE.GUI.ÇÃO, *s.f.*, persecution, oppression, pursuit, chase.
PER.SE.GUIR, *v.*, to persecute, pursue, to trace, to chase, to hunt, to oppress, to annoy.
PER.SE.VE.RAN.ÇA, *s.f.*, perseverance, persistence, constancy.
PER.SE.VE.RAR, *v.*, to persevere, to persist, to continue, to remain, to stay, to last.
PER.SIS.TÊN.CIA, *s.f.*, persistence, perseverance, constancy, stability.
PER.SIS.TIR, *v.*, to persist, to continue, to persevere, to insist.
PER.SO.NA.GEM, *s.2 gen.*, personage, character.
PER.SO.NA.LI.DA.DE, *s.f.*, personality, individuality.
PER.SO.NA.LI.ZA.ÇÃO, *s.f.*, personalization.
PER.SO.NA.LI.ZAR, *v.*, to personalize.
PER.SO.NI.FI.CA.ÇÃO, *s.f.*, personification.
PER.SO.NI.FI.CAR, *v.*, to personify, to represent, to typify.
PERS.PEC.TI.VA, *s.f.*, perspective, view, outlook, prospect.
PERS.PI.CAZ, *adj.*, perspicacious, astute, keen, sharp-sighted.
PER.SU.A.DIR, *v.*, to persuade, to influence, to convince, to advise, to counsel.
PER.SU.A.SÃO, *s.f.*, persuasion, conviction.
PER.SU.A.SI.VO, *adj.*, persuasive, persuading.
PER.TEN.CE, *s.m.*, appurtenance, appendage.
PER.TEN.CEN.TE, *adj.*, pertaining, belonging,

proper.
PER.TEN.CER, *v.*, to pertain, to be part of, to belong to, to be owned by, to concern.
PER.TI.NEN.TE, *adj.*, pertinent.
PER.TO, *adj.*, near, close, proximate; *adv.*, near, nearby, nearly, close, towardly.
PER.TUR.BA.ÇÃO, *s.f.*, perturbation, commotion, trouble, disturbance, disorder.
PER.TUR.BA.DO, *adj.*, perturbed, upset, uneasy.
PER.TUR.BAR, *v.*, to perturb, to molest, to disturb, to agitate, to disorder, to confuse.
PE.RU, *s.m.*, turkey.
PE.RUA, *s.f.*, van, station wagon; turkey hen; drunkenness.
PE.RU.A.NO, *adj.*, *s.m.*, Peruvian.
PE.RU.CA, *s.f.*, wig, periwig.
PER.VER.SI.DA.DE, *s.f.*, perversity, perverseness.
PER.VER.SO, *adj.*, perverse, wicked, evil, devilish.
PER.VER.TER, *v.*, to pervert, to make perverse, to corrupt, to distort.
PE.SA.DE.LO, *s.m.*, nightmare.
PE.SA.DO, *adj.*, weighty, heavy, hard, onerous, difficult.
PE.SA.GEM, *s.f.*, weighing, weighage.
PÊ.SA.MES, *s.m.*, *pl.*, condolences.
PE.SAR, *s.m.*, sorrow, regret, grief, sadness; *v.*, to weigh, to ponder, to consider, to balance, to examine.
PE.SA.RO.SO, *adj.*, sorrowful, sorry.
PES.CA, *s.f.*, fishing, fishery.
PES.CA.DOR, *s.m.*, fisherman, fisher.
PES.CAR, *v.*, to fish, to catch fish, to net, to entrap.
PES.CA.RI.A, *s.f.*, fishery, fishing.
PES.CO.ÇO, *s.m.*, neck, throat.
PE.SO, *s.m.*, weight, heaviness, power, burden, load, oppression, onus; **PESO BRUTO**, gross weight.
PES.QUI.SA, *s.f.*, search, inquiry, investigation, examination.
PES.QUI.SAR, *v.*, to search, to inquire, to research, to examine, to investigate.

PÊS.SE.GO, *s.m.*, peach.
PES.SE.GUEI.RO, *s.m.*, peach tree.
PES.SI.MIS.MO, *s.m.*, pessimism.
PES.SI.MIS.TA, *s.2 gen.*, pessimist.
PÉS.SI.MO, *adj.*, very bad.
PES.SO.A, *s.f.*, person, human being, individual.
PES.SO.AL, *adj.*, personnel, folks; *adj.*, personal, individual.
PES.TA.NA, *s.f.*, eyelash.
PES.TE, *s.f.*, plague, pest.
PES.TI.CI.DA, *s.f.*, pesticide.
PE.TA, *s.f.*, lie, story, humbug.
PÉ.TA.LA, *s.f.*, petal.
PE.TAR.DO, *s.m.*, petard, bomb.
PE.TI.ÇÃO, *s.f.*, petition, request, suit, appeal, solicitation.
PE.TI.CI.O.NAR, *v.*, to petition.
PE.TIS.CO, *s.m.*, tidbit, dainty, morsel.
PE.TRI.FI.CAR, *v.*, to petrify, to change to stone, to paralyze.
PE.TRO.LEI.RO, *s.m.*, oil tanker, pétroleur.
PE.TRÓ.LEO, *s.m.*, petroleum, oil.
PE.TU.LÂN.CIA, *s.f.*, petulance, sauciness, insolence.
PE.TÚ.NIA, *s.f.*, petunia.
PEZ, *s.m.*, pitch, resin.
PI.A, *s.f.*, sink, wash-basin.
PI.A.DA, *s.f.*, joke, peep, chirp, bird.
PI.A.NIS.TA, *s.2 gen.*, pianist; piano player.
PI.A.NO, *s.m.*, piano.
PI.CA.DA, *s.f.*, sting, bite; peck.
PI.CA.DI.NHO, *s.m.*, minced meat, hash.
PI.CAN.TE, *s.2 gen.*, whet, appetizer; *adj.*, appetizing, piquant.
PI.CA-PAU, *s.m.*, woodpecker.
PI.CAR, *v.*, to sting, to bite, to prick, to peck.
PI.CA.RE.TA, *s.f.*, pickax.
PI.CHAR, *v.*, to pitch, to tar, to cover, to paint into graffito.
PI.CHE, *s.m.*, pitch, tar, betumen, asphalt.
PI.CLES, *s.m.*, *pl.*, pickles.
PI.CO, *s.m.*, peak, top, summit, apex, sharp point.
PI.CO.TA.GEM, *s.f.*, perforation, punching.
PI.CO.TAR, *v.*, to perforate, to punch.

PI.CO.TE, *s.m.*, picot, purl.
PI.CU.I.NHA, *s.f.*, cheep, chirp, peep, jest.
PI.E.DA.DE, *s.f.*, pity, compassion, mercy, devotion.
PI.E.DO.SO, *adj.*, pious, religious, godly, devout.
PIG.MEN.TA.ÇÃO, *s.f.*, pigmentation, coloration.
PIG.MEN.TAR, *v.*, to pigment.
PIG.MEN.TO, *s.m.*, pigment, colouring matter.
PIG.MEU, *s.m.*, Pigmy; *adj.*, pigmy.
PI.JA.MA, *s.m.*, pyjamas, pajama.
PI.LAN.TRA, *s.2 gen.*, rascal, scamp, scoundrel.
PI.LAR, *s.m.*, pillar, column, post.
PI.LE.QUE, *s.m.*, drunkenness.
PI.LHA, *s.f.*, plunder, pillage.
PI.LHA.GEM, *s.f.*, plunder, sacking, pillage.
PI.LHAR, *v.*, to plunder, to pillage, to sacking, to sack.
PI.LHÉ.RIA, *s.f.*, quip, jest, joke.
PI.LHE.RI.AR, *v.*, to quip, to jest, to joke.
PI.LO.TAR, *v.*, to pilot, to direct, to fly.
PI.LO.TI, *s.m.*, stilt.
PI.LO.TO, *s.m.*, pilot, steersman, flyer, aviator.
PÍ.LU.LA, *s.f.*, pill.
PI.MEN.TA, *s.f.*, pepper; **PIMENTA-DO-REINO**, black pepper.
PI.MEN.TÃO, *s.m.*, pimento, green pepper, red pepper.
PI.MEN.TEI.RA, *s.f.*, pepper tree.
PIN.ÇA, *s.f.*, tweezers, nippers.
PÍN.CA.RO, *s.m.*, apex, pinnacle, summit.
PIN.CEL, *s.m.*, brush.
PIN.CE.LA.DA, *s.f.*, a stroke with a brush.
PIN.CE.LAR, *v.*, to paint with a brush.
PIN.GA, *s.f.*, a drop, rum.
PIN.GAR, *v.*, to drip, to fall in drops, to sprinkle, to drizzle.
PIN.GEN.TE, *s.m.*, pendant, earring, drop.
PIN.GO, *s.m.*, drop, dripping.
PIN.GUE-PON.GUE, *s.m.*, ping-pong.
PIN.GUIM, *s.m.*, penguin.
PI.NHEI.RO, *s.m.*, pine tree.
PI.NHO, *s.m.*, pinewood.
PI.NI.CO, *s.m.*, beak.
PI.NO, *s.m.*, pin, peg, bolt, pivot, top, apex.
PI.NO.TE, *s.m.*, jump, bound, leap.
PIN.TA, *s.f.*, spot, mark.
PIN.TAR, *v.*, to paint, to draw, to set in colours, to tinge.
PIN.TO, *s.m.*, young chicken, kid, cock, penis.
PIN.TOR, *s.m.*, painter.
PIN.TO.RA, *s.f.*, paintress.
PIN.TU.RA, *s.f.*, picture, painting, image.
PI.O, *s.m.*, peep, cheep; *adj.*, pious, godly, devout.
PI.O.LHO, *s.m.*, louse.
PI.O.NEI.RO, *s.m.*, pioneer, precursor, explorer.
PI.OR, *s.m.*, the worst; *adj.*, worse, worst.
PI.O.RAR, *v.*, to worsen, to aggravate, to complicate.
PI.PA, *s.f.*, kite, cask, barrel.
PI.PI, *s.m.*, piss.
PI.PO.CA, *s.f.*, popcorn.
PI.PO.QUEI.RO, *s.m.*, popcorn seller.
PI.QUE.NI.QUE, *s.m.*, picnic.
PI.QUE.TE, *s.m.*, picket.
PI.RA, *s.f.*, pyre.
PI.RÂ.MI.DE, *s.f.*, pyramid.
PI.RA.NHA, *s.f.*, caribe, whore, prostitute.
PI.RA.TA, *s.m.*, pirate, corsair, buccaneer, sea-robber.
PI.RA.TA.RIA, *s.f.*, piracy, fraud, robbery.
PI.RA.TE.AR, *v.*, to pirate, to fraud, to rob.
PI.RES, *s.m.*, saucer.
PI.RI.LAM.PO, *s.m.*, firefly.
PI.RI.TA, *s.f.*, pyrites.
PI.RO.GA, *s.f.*, piragua, pirogue.
PI.RO.TEC.NIA, *s.f.*, pyrotechnics.
PIR.RA.ÇA, *s.f.*, spite, roguish trick.
PI.RU.LI.TO, *s.m.*, lollypop, lollipop.
PI.SA.DE.LA, *s.f.*, treading, stamping.
PI.SAR, *v.*, to tread on, to trample, to step on, to offend.
PIS.CA-PIS.CA, *s.m.*, flasher, blinker, indicator.
PIS.CAR, *v.*, to wink, to blink, to twinkle.
PIS.CI.NA, *s.f.*, swimming pool, basin.
PI.SO, *s.m.*, floor, pavement, gait.
PIS.TA, *s.f.*, track, racecourse, race track, clue.
PIS.TO.LA, *s.f.*, pistol.
PIS.TO.LEI.RO, *s.m.*, gunfighter, bandit, gunman.

PI.TA.DA, *s.f.*, pinch, small quantity.
PI.TAR, *v.*, to smoke.
PÍ.TON, *s.m.*, python, serpent.
PI.TO.RES.CO, *adj.*, picturesque, pictorial.
PI.VÔ, *s.m.*, pivot, pin tooth, central factor.
PLA.CA, *s.f.*, plate, board, card, plaque.
PLA.CAR, *s.m.*, placard, scoreboard, poster bill.
PLA.CEN.TA, *s.f.*, placenta.
PLÁ.CI.DO, *adj.*, placid, quiet, tranquil, calm.
PLA.GI.AR, *v.*, to plagiarize, crib.
PLAI.NA, *s.f.*, plane.
PLA.NA.DOR, *s.m.*, glider.
PLA.NAL.TO, *s.m.*, plateau, upland.
PLA.NAR, *v.*, to plane, to glide.
PLA.NE.JA.MENTO, *s.m.*, projection, planning.
PLA.NE.JAR, *v.*, to plan, to project.
PLA.NE.TA, *s.m.*, planet.
PLA.NE.TÁ.RIO, *s.m.*, planetarium.
PLAN.GER, *v.*, to lament, to mourn, to beat.
PLA.NÍ.CIE, *s.f.*, plain, lowland.
PLA.NI.FI.CA.ÇÃO, *s.f.*, planning.
PLA.NI.LHA, *s.f.*, spreadsheet, worksheet.
PLA.NO, *s.m.*, plan, scheme, project, plane.
PLAN.TA, *s.f.*, plant, plan, blueprint.
PLAN.TA.ÇÃO, *s.f.*, plantation, planting.
PLAN.TÃO, *s.m.*, duty, service.
PLAN.TAR, *v.*, to plant, to cultivate, to sow.
PLAN.TI.O, *s.m.*, plantation.
PLAS.MA, *s.m.*, plasma, protoplasm.
PLAS.MAR, *v.*, to model.
PLÁS.TI.CA, *s.f.*, plastic surgery.
PLÁS.TI.CO, *adj.*, plastic.
PLA.TA.FOR.MA, *s.f.*, platform, programme, political programme.
PLA.TEI.A, *s.f.*, pit, auditorium, audience.
PLA.TI.NA, *s.f.*, platinum.
PLA.TÔ, *s.m.*, plateau.
PLA.TÔ.NI.CO, *adj.*, Platonic, ideal, mental.
PLE.BE, *s.f.*, the common people, mob, rabble.
PLE.BEU, *s.m.*, plebeian.
PLE.BIS.CI.TO, *s.m.*, plebiscite, referendum.
PLEI.TE.AR, *v.*, to plead, to go to law, to demand, to dispute.
PLEI.TO, *s.m.*, lawsuit, process, plea.

PLE.NÁ.RIO, *s.m.*, court, plenary assembly, jury.
PLE.NI.TU.DE, *s.f.*, plenitude, fullness.
PLE.NO, *adj.*, full, absolute, plenary, complete.
PLE.O.NAS.MO, *s.m.*, pleonasm.
PLEU.RA, *s.f.*, pleura.
PLU.MA, *s.f.*, plume, feather.
PLU.MA.GEM, *s.f.*, plumage, feathers, plume, crest.
PLU.RAL, *adj.*, *s.m.*, plural.
PLU.RA.LI.DA.DE, *s.f.*, plurality.
PLU.TO.CRA.CIA, *s.f.*, plutocracy.
PLU.TO.CRA.TA, *s.2 gen.*, plutocrat.
PLU.TÔ.NIO, *s.m.*, plutonium.
PLU.VI.AL, *adj.*, pluvial, rainy.
PLU.VI.Ô.ME.TRO, *s.m.*, pluviometer.
PNEU, *s.m.*, tire; **PNEU FURADO**, a flat tire.
PNEU.MO.NIA, *s.f.*, pneumonia.
PÓ, *s.m.*, powder, dust.
PO.BRE, *s.m.*, pauper, beggar; *adj.*, poor, needy, indigent.
PO.BRE.ZA, *s.f.*, poverty, indigence, need.
PO.ÇA, *s.f.*, plash, pool.
PO.ÇÃO, *s.f.*, potion.
PO.CIL.GA, *s.f.*, sty, pigsty.
PO.ÇO, *s.m.*, well, pit.
PO.DAR, *v.*, to prune, to cut.
PO.DER, *s.m.*, power, might, strenght, authority; *v.*, to be able to, to can, to may, to have power to.
PO.DE.RI.O, *s.m.*, power, might, force.
PO.DE.RO.SO, *adj.*, powerful, mighty, efficacious, potent, intense.
PO.DRE, *adj.*, rotten, putrid, carious.
PO.DRI.DÃO, *s.f.*, rottenness, putridity, putrefaction.
PO.E.DEI.RA, *s.f.*, laying hen.
PO.EI.RA, *s.f.*, dust, powder.
PO.EI.REN.TO, *adj.*, dusty.
PO.E.MA, *s.m.*, poem.
PO.EN.TE, *s.m.*, the west, occident; *adj.*, setting.
PO.E.SI.A, *s.f.*, poetry, poesy.
PO.E.TA, *s.m.*, poet, bard.
PO.É.TI.CO, *adj.*, poetic, poetical.

PO.E.TI.SA, *s.f.*, poetess, poetress.
POIS, *conj.*, since, because, whereas, therefore, as, for.
PO.LA.CO, *s.m.*, Pole; *adj.*, Polish.
PO.LAR, *adj.*, polar.
PO.LA.RI.DA.DE, *s.f.*, polarity.
PO.LA.RI.ZAR, *v.*, to polarize.
POL.CA, *s.f.*, polka.
PO.LE.GA.DA, *s.f.*, inch (2,54 cm).
PO.LE.GAR, *s.m.*, thumb, the big toe.
PO.LEI.RO, *s.m.*, roost, perch, hen-roost.
PO.LÊ.MI.CA, *s.f.*, polemic(s), controversy.
PO.LÊ.MI.CO, *adj.*, polemic, polemical.
PO.LE.MI.ZAR, *v.*, to polemize.
PÓ.LEN, *s.m.*, pollen.
PO.LIA, *s.f.*, pulley, sheave.
PO.LÍ.CIA, *s.f.*, police.
PO.LI.CI.AL, *s.2 gen.*, officer, policeman, cop.
PO.LI.CI.A.MEN.TO, *s.m.*, patrolling.
PO.LI.CI.AR, *v.*, to police, to patrol, to guard.
PO.LI.CLÍ.NI.CA, *s.f.*, polyclinic.
PO.LI.CRO.MIA, *s.f.*, polychromy.
PO.LI.DEZ, *s.f.*, politeness, courtesy, civility.
PO.LI.DO, *adj.*, polished, smoothed, varnished, bright.
PO.LI.GA.MI.A, *s.f.*, polygamy.
PO.LÍ.GA.MO, *s.m.*, polygamist; *adj.*, polygamous.
PO.LI.GLO.TA, *s.2 gen.*, polyglot; *adj.*, polyglot.
PO.LÍ.GO.NO, *s.m.*, polygon.
PO.LI.MEN.TO, *s.m.*, polish, shine, burnish.
PO.LI.MOR.FO, *adj.*, polymorphic.
PO.LI.NI.ZA.ÇÃO, *s.f.*, pollination.
PO.LI.NI.ZAR, *v.*, to pollinate.
PO.LIO.MI.E.LI.TE, *s.f.*, poliomyelitis.
PO.LIR, *v.*, to polish, varnish, civilize.
PO.LIS.SÍ.LA.BO, *s.m.*, polysyllable.
PO.LÍ.TI.CA, *s.f.*, politics, policy, agility.
PO.LI.TI.CA.GEM, *s.f.*, petty politics.
PO.LÍ.TI.CO, *s.m.*, politician, statesman; *adj.*, politic, diplomatic.
PO.LI.TI.QUEI.RO, *s.m.*, petty politician.
PO.LO, *s.m.*, pole, terminal, polar region; polo (sport).

PO.LO.NÊS, *s.m.*, Pole; *adj.*, Polish.
POL.PA, *s.f.*, pulp; the meat of fruits.
POL.PU.DO, *adj.*, pulpy, fleshy.
POL.TRO.NA, *s.f.*, easy chair, armchair; seat.
PO.LU.I.ÇÃO, *s.f.*, pollution, desecration.
PO.LU.Í.DO, *adj.*, polluted, contaminated.
PO.LU.I.DOR, *s.m.*, polluter.
PO.LU.IR, *v.*, to pollute, to defile, to soil.
POL.VI.LHO, *s.m.*, manioc flour.
POL.VO, *s.m.*, octopus.
PÓL.VO.RA, *s.f.*, gunpowder, powder.
PO.MA.DA, *s.f.*, salve, ointment, cream, pomade, unction.
PO.MAR, *s.m.*, orchard.
POM.BA, *s.f.*, pigeon, female dove.
POM.BAL, *s.m.*, pigeon house, dove-cot.
POM.BO, *s.m.*, dove, pigeon.
PO.MI.CUL.TOR, *s.m.*, pomiculturist, orchardist.
PO.MO, *s.m.*, fruit, pome.
POM.PA, *s.f.*, pomp, pagentry, splendour, ostentation.
POM.PO.SO, *adj.*, pompous, ostentatious, grandiose.
PON.DE.RA.ÇÃO, *s.f.*, ponderation, consideration, deliberation.
PON.DE.RAR, *v.*, to ponder, to weigh, to reflect, to think over, to deliberate, to consider.
PÔ.NEI, *s.m.*, pony.
PON.TA, *s.f.*, point, peak, top, extremity, corner, nib, jag.
PON.TA.DA, *s.f.*, jab, stab, pang, twinge.
PON.TA.PÉ, *s.m.*, kick, blow with the foot.
PON.TA.RI.A, *s.f.*, aim, sight, target, sighting.
PON.TE, *s.f.*, bridge, deck, dental bridge; bridgework.
PON.TEI.RO, *s.m.*, pointer, fescue, indicator, point.
PON.TI.A.GU.DO, *adj.*, pointed, sharp, peaky, acerose.
PON.TI.FI.CAR, *v.*, to pontify, to pontificate.
PON.TÍ.FI.CE, *s.m.*, pontiff, pontifex, bishop.
PON.TI.LHAR, *v.*, to stipple, to dot, to baste.
PON.TO, *s.m.*, point, dot, tittle, mark, period, full stop, spot, speck, stitch.

PON.TU.A.ÇÃO, *s.f.*, punctuation, pointing.
PON.TU.A.DO, *adj.*, punctated, dotted.
PON.TU.AL, *adj.*, punctual, precise, exact, strict.
PON.TU.A.LI.DA.DE, *s.f.*, punctuality, punctualness, accuracy.
PON.TU.AR, *v.*, to punctuate, to point, to dot.
PON.TU.DO, *adj.*, pointed, peaked, pricked, spiky.
PO.PA, *s.f.*, poop, stern.
PO.PU.LA.ÇÃO, *s.f.*, population, inhabitants, people, class.
PO.PU.LAR, *adj.*, popular, public, common, communal.
PO.PU.LA.RI.DA.DE, *s.f.*, popularity.
PO.PU.LA.RI.ZAR, *v.*, to popularize, to divulge.
PO.PU.LO.SO, *adj.*, populous, crowded.
PÔ.QUER, *s.m.*, poker.
POR, *prep.*, at, by, for, from, per, to, through, by means of, in behalf of, by order of, in order to, out of.
PÔR, *v.*, to put, to place, to lay, to set, to put on, to include, to deposit, to add, to inculcate.
PO.RÃO, *s.m.*, cellar, basement, stowage.
POR.CA, *s.f.*, sow; nut, screw-nut.
POR.CA.DA, *s.f.*, a herd of swine, dirt.
POR.ÇÃO, *s.f.*, portion, part, piece, snack, bit, slice, share, dose.
POR.CA.RIA, *s.f.*, dirtiness, filthiness, nastiness, rubbish.
POR.CE.LA.NA, *s.f.*, porcelain, chinaware, dishware, earthenware.
POR.CEN.TA.GEM, *s.f.*, percentage.
POR.CO, *s.m.*, swine, pig, hog, porker, grunter; *adj.*, swinish, hoggish, dirty, filthy, obscene.
PO.RÉM, *conj.*, but, yet, however, still, notwithstanding, nevertheless.
POR.FI.A, *s.f.*, discussion, argument.
POR.ME.NOR, *s.m.*, particularity, particular, detail.
POR.ME.NO.RI.ZAR, *v.*, to particularize.
POR.NO.GRA.FIA, *s.f.*, pornography.
PO.RO, *s.m.*, pore.
PO.RO.SI.DA.DE, *s.f.*, porosity.
POR.QUAN.TO, *conj.*, as, when, while, whereby, because.
POR.QUE, *conj.*, because, since, as, in as much as.
POR.QUÊ, *s.m.*, the cause or reason.
POR QUÊ?, *pron.*, why?, for what reason.
POR.QUI.NHO, *s.m.*, piglet.
POR.QUI.NHO-DA-ÍN.DIA, *s.m.*, guinea pig.
POR.RE, *s.m.*, binge, swallow.
POR.TA, *s.f.*, door, entrance, gateway, entry, gate, access.
POR.TA-A.VI.ÕES, *s.m.*, aircraft carrier.
POR.TA-BA.GA.GEM, *s.m.*, parcel rack, rack.
POR.TA-CHA.VES, *s.m.*, key-ring.
POR.TA.DOR, *s.m.*, porter, carrier, messenger.
POR.TA-JOI.AS, *s.m.*, jewel case, jewel box.
POR.TAL, *s.m.*, portal, the main door of a building.
POR.TA-LU.VAS, *s.m.*, glove compartment.
POR.TA-MA.LAS, *s.m.*, boot, trunk.
POR.TAN.TO, *adv.*, therefore, hence, thus; *conj.*, as, in so far as, in as much as.
POR.TÃO, *s.m.*, gate, gateway, portal, entrance.
POR.TAR, *v.*, to carry, to land, to enter a port, to go on.
POR.TA-RE.TRA.TOS, *s.m.*, picture frame.
POR.TA.RI.A, *s.f.*, entrance, reception desk, order, regulation.
POR.TÁ.TIL, *adj.*, portable, handy, small, light.
POR.TA-TO.A.LHAS, *s.m.*, towel rack.
POR.TA-VOZ, *s.m.*, spokesman, megaphone.
POR.TE, *s.m.*, transport fee, importance, carriage, load, burden.
POR.TEI.RO, *s.m.*, doorman, doorkeeper, gatekeeper.
POR.TEN.TO, *s.m.*, marvel, prodigy, miracle.
POR.TO, *s.m.*, port, harbor, haven, refuge.
POR.TO-RI.QUE.NHO, *adj.*, *s.m.*, Puerto Rican.
POR.TU.Á.RIO, *s.m.*, dock worker.
POR.TU.GUÊS, *s.m.*, Portuguese; *adj.*, Portuguese.
POR.VEN.TU.RA, *adv.*, by chance, possibly, perhaps.
POR.VIR, *s.m.*, future, time to come, destiny.
PÓS, *prep.*, post, after, behind; *pref.*, post.

PO.SAR, *v.*, to pose, to posture, to sit for.
PÓS-DA.TA, *s.f.*, postdate.
PO.SE, *s.f.*, pose, position, posture, posing.
PÓS-ES.CRI.TO, *s.m.*, postscript.
PÓS-GRA.DU.A.DO, *s.m.*, postgraduate.
PO.SI.ÇÃO, *s.f.*, position, attitude, posture, rank, disposition.
PO.SI.TI.VI.DA.DE, *s.f.*, positivity.
PO.SI.TI.VIS.MO, *s.m.*, positivism, Comtist.
PO.SI.TI.VO, *adj.*, positive, real, actual, evident, clear, obvious, sure, certain.
POS.POR, *v.*, to postpone, to omit, to neglect.
POS.PO.SI.ÇÃO, *s.f.*, postposition.
POS.SAN.TE, *adj.*, powerful, mighty.
POS.SE, *s.f.*, ownership; posses, possessions, riches, property.
POS.SEI.RO, *s.m.*, leaseholder.
POS.SES.SÃO, *s.f.*, possession, estate, dominion, landed property.
POS.SES.SIVO, *adj.*, possessive, proprietary.
POS.SES.SO, *s.m.*, demoniac; *adj.*, possessed, mad.
POS.SI.BI.LI.DA.DE, *s.f.*, possibility, contingency, chance, odds.
POS.SI.BI.LI.TAR, *v.*, to enable, to make possible, allow.
POS.SÍ.VEL, *adj.*, possible, feasible.
POS.SUIR, *v.*, to possess, to have, to hold, to own, to occupy, to inhabit.
POS.TAL, *s.m.*, postcard; *adj.*, postal; **CAIXA POSTAL**, P.O. Box.
POS.TAR, *v.*, to post, to mail, to dispose.
POS.TE, *s.m.*, stake, stud, post, pillar, mast.
POS.TER.GAR, *v.*, to postpone, to put off, to pass over, to omit.
POS.TE.RI.DA.DE, *s.f.*, posterity, descendants, issue.
POS.TE.RI.OR, *s.m.*, posterior; *adj.*, posterior, later, behind, ulterior.
POS.TI.ÇO, *adj.*, false, artificial, counterfeit.
POS.TO, *s.m.*, post, place, position, station, stand, office; *adj.*, put, disposed, arranged.
POS.TU.LAR, *v.*, to postulate.
PÓS.TU.MO, *adj.*, posthumous.
POS.TU.RA, *s.f.*, posture, position, situation, state attitude, pose.
PO.TÁ.VEL, *adj.*, drinkable, potable.
PO.TE, *s.m.*, pot, vessel, water jug.
PO.TÊN.CIA, *s.f.*, potency, power, might, strength, potence, authority.
PO.TEN.CI.AL, *s.m.*, potential, *adj.*, powerful, potential, mighty.
PO.TEN.TA.DO, *s.m.*, potentate, monarch.
PO.TEN.TE, *adj.*, potent, powerful, mighty, potential, strong.
PO.TRA, *s.f.*, filly, colt.
PO.TRO, *s.m.*, colt, foal, young horse.
POU.CA-VER.GO.NHA, *s.f.*, shamelessness, rascality.
POU.CO, *s.m.*, a little, small quantity; *adj.*, little; *adv.*, little, insufficiently, nearly, rather.
POU.PAN.ÇA, *s.f.*, economy, savings, parsimony.
POU.PAR, *v.*, to spare, to save, to preserve, to economize, to lay up.
POU.SA.DA, *s.f.*, stopping, resting, inn, lodging.
POU.SAR, *v.*, to rest, to lodge, to stop, to lay down, to perch, to repose.
POU.SO, *s.m.*, resting place, landing, slip.
PO.VA.RÉU, *s.m.*, rabble.
PO.VO, *s.m.*, people, folk, nation, race, crowd, mob.
PO.VO.A.ÇÃO, *s.f.*, village, settlement, population.
PO.VO.A.DO, *s.m.*, settlement, village; *adj.*, populated.
PO.VO.AR, *v.*, to populate, to settle, to fill, to colonize.
PRA.ÇA, *s.f.*, square, market-place.
PRA.DA.RIA, *s.f.*, prairie, meadow.
PRA.DO, *s.m.*, meadow, plain, grassy land.
PRA.GA, *s.f.*, curse, malediction, damnation, imprecation, plague, blasphemy.
PRAG.MA.TIS.MO, *s.m.*, pragmatism.
PRA.GUE.JAR, *v.*, to curse, to imprecate, to blaspheme, to swear.
PRAI.A, *s.f.*, beach, seashore, coast, strand.
PRAN.CHA, *s.f.*, plank, board.
PRAN.CHE.TA, *s.f.*, drawing board, small board.

PRAN.TO, *s.m.*, weeping, lamentation, wailing.
PRA.TA, *s.f.*, silver.
PRA.TA.RIA, *s.f.*, silverware.
PRA.TE.A.DO, *adj.*, silvered.
PRA.TE.AR, *v.*, to silver, to cover with silver.
PRA.TE.LEI.RA, *s.f.*, shelf, rack.
PRÁ.TI.CA, *s.f.*, practice, usage, custom, perfomance, habit, function, experience.
PRA.TI.CAR, *v.*, to practice, to practise, to execute, to perform, to profess.
PRÁ.TI.CO, *s.m.*, pilot, practician; *adj.*, practical, skilled.
PRA.TO, *s.m.*, plate, dish, food, meal.
PRA.XE, *s.f.*, practice, praxis, use, habit, custom.
PRA.ZEN.TEI.RO, *adj.*, festive, pleasant, merry, gay.
PRA.ZER, *s.m.*, pleasure, joy, delight, satisfaction
PRA.ZE.RO.SO, *adj.*, joyful, merry.
PRA.ZO, *s.m.*, time, term, stated period, delay.
PRE.A.MAR, *s.f.*, flood, high water, high tide.
PRÉ-A.VI.SO, *s.m.*, advance notice.
PRE.CÁ.RIO, *adj.*, precarious, uncertain, insecure.
PRE.CAU.ÇÃO, *s.f.*, precaution, caution, foresight, care.
PRE.CA.VER, *v.*, to prevent, to obviate, to provide.
PRE.CA.VI.DO, *adj.*, precautious, wary.
PRE.CE, *s.f.*, prayer, petition, invocation.
PRE.CE.DÊN.CIA, *s.f.*, precedence, priority, anteriority.
PRE.CE.DEN.TE, *adj.*, *s.2 gen.*, precedent.
PRE.CE.DER, *v.*, to precede, to go before in time, to anticipate.
PRE.CEI.TO, *s.m.*, precept, principle, maxim, rule.
PRE.CI.O.SO, *adj.*, precious, valuable, splendid, excellent.
PRE.CI.PÍ.CIO, *s.m.*, precipice, abyss, ruin.
PRE.CI.PI.TA.ÇÃO, *s.f.*, precipitation, haste, rush, abruptness, rainfall.
PRE.CI.PI.TA.DO, *adj.*, precipitate, heedless.
PRE.CI.PI.TAR, *v.*, to precipitate, to deposit, to extract.

PRE.CI.SÃO, *s.f.*, precision, exactness, accuracy, need.
PRE.CI.SAR, *v.*, to need, to require, to exact, to fix.
PRE.CI.SO, *adj.*, precise, exact, just, definite, distinct.
PRE.ÇO, *s.m.*, price, cost, value, charge.
PRE.CO.CE, *adj.*, precocious, premature.
PRE.CO.CI.DA.DE, *s.f.*, precocity, prematurity.
PRE.CON.CE.BER, *v.*, to preconceive.
PRE.CON.CEI.TO, *s.m.*, preconceit, preconception, conclusion, prejudice.
PRE.CO.NI.ZAR, *v.*, to preconize, to profess, to proclaim.
PRE.CUR.SOR, *s.m.*, forerunner, pioneer; *adj.*, precursory, preceding.
PRE.DA.DOR, *s.m.*, predator.
PRE.DA.TAR, *v.*, to predate.
PRE.DE.CES.SOR, *s.m.*, predecessor, precursor.
PRE.DES.TI.NA.ÇÃO, *s.f.*, predestination, fate, destiny, election.
PRE.DES.TI.NAR, *v.*, to predestinate, predestine.
PRE.DE.TER.MI.NAR, *v.*, to predetermine, preordain, preorder.
PRE.DI.AL, *adj.*, predial; **IMPOSTO PREDIAL**, house tax.
PRE.DI.CA.DO, *s.m.*, quality, attribute, talent, faculty; predicate.
PRE.DI.ÇÃO, *s.f.*, prediction, presage.
PRE.DI.LE.ÇÃO, *s.f.*, predilection, favour.
PRE.DI.LE.TO, *adj.*, favourite, beloved, dear.
PRÉ.DIO, *s.m.*, estate, landed property, building, edifice.
PRE.DIS.POR, *v.*, to predispose, to prearrange, to prepare.
PRE.DI.ZER, *v.*, to predict, to foretell, to prophesy.
PRE.DO.MI.NÂN.CIA, *s.f.*, predominance, domination, prevalence.
PRE.DO.MI.NAN.TE, *adj.*, predominant, prevailing, superior.
PRE.DO.MI.NAR, *v.*, to predominate, to preponderate, to rule.
PRE.DO.MÍ.NIO, *s.m.*, power, predominancy, supremacy.

PRÉ-E.LEI.ÇÃO, *s.f.*, pre-election.
PRE.EN.CHER, *v.*, to fulfill, to fill in, to perform, to supply.
PRÉ-ES.CO.LAR, *adj.*, preschool.
PRE.ES.TA.BE.LE.CER, *v.*, to pre-establish.
PRÉ-ES.TREI.A, *s.f.*, preview.
PRE.FÁ.CIO, *s.m.*, preface, preamble, introduction.
PRE.FEI.TO, *s.m.*, mayor, prefect.
PRE.FEI.TU.RA, *s.f.*, town hall, city hall, prefecture.
PRE.FE.RÊN.CIA, *s.f.*, preference, choise, selection, favouritism, liking.
PRE.FE.REN.CI.AL, *adj.*, preferential.
PRE.FE.RI.DO, *adj.*, favoured, preferred, elected.
PRE.FE.RIR, *v.*, to prefer, to give preference to, to select, to opt.
PRE.FE.RÍ.VEL, *adj.*, preferable, better.
PRE.FI.XO, *s.m.*, prefix, affix.
PRE.GA, *s.f.*, pleat, crease.
PRE.GA.ÇÃO, *s.f.*, preachment.
PRE.GA.DOR, *s.m.*, preacher, nailer; *adj.*, preaching.
PRE.GAR, *v.*, to nail, to fix, to fasten, to attach, to stick; to predicate, to preach.
PRE.GO, *s.m.*, nail, sprig.
PRE.GUI.ÇA, *s.f.*, sluggishness, laziness, indolence.
PRE.GUI.ÇO.SO, *s.m.*, lazy-bones, idler; *adj.*, lazy, idle, indolent, laggard.
PRÉ-HIS.TÓ.RI.CO, *adj.*, prehistoric.
PRE.JU.DI.CA.DO, *adj.*, prejudiced, damaged.
PRE.JU.DI.CAR, *v.*, to prejudice, to damage, to hurt, to wrong, to injure.
PRE.JU.DI.CI.AL, *adj.*, prejudicial, hurtful, harmful, evil.
PRE.JU.Í.ZO, *s.m.*, prejudice, prejudgement, bias, leaning.
PRE.LE.ÇÃO, *s.f.*, prelection, reading, sermon.
PRE.LI.MI.NAR, *adj., s.f.*, preliminary.
PRE.LO, *s.m.*, printing press.
PRE.MA.TU.RI.DA.DE, *s.f.*, prematureness, precocity.
PRE.MA.TU.RO, *adj.*, premature, immature.
PRE.ME.DI.TA.ÇÃO, *s.f.*, premeditation.
PRE.ME.DI.TAR, *v.*, to premeditate, to plan.
PRE.MEN.TE, *adj.*, pressing, urgent.
PRE.MI.AR, *v.*, to reward, award a prize to.
PRÊ.MIO, *s.m.*, reward, prize, award, remuneration, gain.
PRE.MIS.SA, *s.f.*, premise, reason, supposition.
PRE.MO.NI.ÇÃO, *s.f.*, premonition.
PREN.DE.DOR, *s.m.*, fastener, clip, arrester, seizer.
PREN.DER, *v.*, to fasten, to tie, to fix, to bind, to grip, to gasp.
PRE.NHE, *adj.*, gravid, pregnant.
PRE.NO.ME, *s.m.*, first name, Christian name.
PREN.SA, *s.f.*, press, printing press.
PREN.SAR, *v.*, to press, to compress, to crush.
PRÉ-NUP.CI.AL, *adj.*, antenuptial, premarital.
PRE.O.CU.PA.ÇÃO, *s.f.*, preoccupation, apprehension, anxiety.
PRE.O.CU.PAR, *v.*, to preoccupy, concern.
PRE.PA.RA.ÇÃO, *s.f.*, preparation, preparing, training.
PRE.PA.RA.DO, *adj.*, prepared, ready.
PRE.PA.RAR, *v.*, to prepare, to make ready, to arrange, to provide.
PRE.PA.RA.TI.VOS, *s.m.*, pl., preparatives, preparatories.
PRE.PA.RO, *s.m.*, preparation, education, competence, ability.
PRE.PON.DE.RAR, *v.*, to preponderate, to overbear, to predominate.
PRE.PO.SI.ÇÃO, *s.f.*, preposition.
PRE.POS.TO, *adj.*, preferred.
PRE.PO.TÊN.CIA, *s.f.*, prepotence, prepotency, superiority, despotism.
PRER.RO.GA.TI.VA, *s.f.*, prerogative.
PRE.SA, *s.f.*, prey, fang, capture, catch, tusk.
PRES.CIN.DIR, *v.*, to prescind, to dispense, to leave out, to renounce.
PRES.CRE.VER, *v.*, to prescribe, to order the use of, to ordain, to assign, to fall into desuse.
PRES.CRI.ÇÃO, *s.f.*, prescription, precept, lapse, order, instruction.
PRE.SEN.ÇA, *s.f.*, presence, aspect, appearance.

PRE.SEN.CI.AR, *v.*, to be present, to witness, to observe.
PRE.SEN.TE, *s.m.*, present, actuality, gift, donative; *adj.*, present, actual, current.
PRE.SEN.TE.AR, *v.*, to present, to offer as a gift.
PRE.SÉ.PIO, *s.m.*, stable, stall, crèche.
PRE.SER.VA.ÇÃO, *s.f.*, preservation, conservation.
PRE.SER.VAR, *v.*, to preserve, to protect, to guard, to defend, to save, to retain.
PRE.SER.VA.TI.VO, *s.m.*, preservative, condom; *adj.*, preservative.
PRE.SI.DÊN.CIA, *s.f.*, presidency, chairmanship.
PRE.SI.DEN.TE, *s.m.*, president, chairman, manager; *adj.*, presiding.
PRE.SÍ.DIO, *s.m.*, prison, fortress, garrison, penitentiary.
PRE.SI.DIR, *v.*, to preside, to manage, to direct, to administer, to coordinate.
PRE.SO, *s.m.*, prisoner, captive; *adj.*, captive, imprisoned, arrested.
PRES.SA, *s.f.*, haste, hurry, rush, velocity, urgency.
PRES.SÁ.GIO, *s.m.*, presage, sign, omen, augury.
PRES.SÃO, *s.f.*, pressure, compulsion, stress, strain, pressing, oppression.
PRES.SÃO SANGUÍNEA, *s.f.*, blood pressure.
PRES.SEN.TI.MEN.TO, *s.m.*, presentiment, foreboding, apprehension.
PRES.SEN.TIR, *v.*, to foresee, anticipate, suspect.
PRES.SU.POR, *v.*, to presuppose, to assume.
PRES.SU.POS.TO, *s.m.*, pretext, purpose; *adj.*, presupposed, assumed.
PRES.SU.RO.SO, *adj.*, speedy, swift, quick, prompt.
PRES.TA.ÇÃO, *s.f.*, installment, contribution.
PRES.TAR, *v.*, to lend, to load, to render, to give, to perform, to be useful.
PRES.TA.TI.VO, *adj.*, serviceable, useful, helpful.
PRES.TE.ZA, *s.f.*, quickness, readiness, promptness, rapidity, celerity.
PRES.TI.DI.GI.TA.ÇÃO, *s.f.*, prestidigitation, jugglery, magic.
PRES.TI.DI.GI.TA.DOR, *s.m.*, prestidigitator, magician, wizar, juggler.
PRES.TI.GI.AR, *v.*, to esteem, to give prestige to.
PRES.TÍ.GIO, *s.m.*, fascination, prestige, reputation, influence, charm.
PRÉS.TI.MO, *s.m.*, utility, usefulness, service, fitness.
PRÉS.TI.TO, *s.m.*, cortège, train.
PRE.SU.MI.DO, *adj.*, arrogant, presumptuous.
PRE.SU.MIR, *v.*, to presume, to suppose, to surmise, to suspect.
PRE.SU.MÍ.VEL, *adj.*, presumable, probable, presumptive.
PRE.SUN.ÇÃO, *s.f.*, presumption, supposition, arrogance, guess, pride.
PRE.SUN.ÇO.SO, *adj.*, presumptuous, vainglorious, arrogant.
PRE.SUN.TO, *s.m.*, ham.
PRE.TEN.DÊN.TE, *s.2 gen.*, pretender, candidate; *adj.*, pretending, expecting.
PRE.TEN.DER, *v.*, to claim, to demand, to aspire, to wish, to intend, to contemplate, to expect.
PRE.TEN.SÃO, *s.f.*, pretension, claim, demand, intention, design.
PRE.TEN.SI.O.SO, *adj.*, pretentious, arrogant, ambitious, snobbish.
PRE.TEN.SO, *adj.*, assumed, supposed, presumed, alleged.
PRE.TE.RIR, *v.*, to pretermit, to neglect, to defer, to slight.
PRE.TÉ.RI.TO, *s.m.*, past, The Past Time; *adj.*, past, preterit, bygone.
PRE.TEX.TO, *s.m.*, pretext, excuse, pretension, cloak.
PRE.TO, *s.m.*, Negro, black; *adj.*, black, dark, jet, sombre.
PRE.TU.ME, *s.m.*, darkness.
PRE.VA.LE.CER, *v.*, to prevail, to predominate, to preponderate.
PRE.VA.LE.CI.DO, *adj.*, impertinent, arrogant, snobbish.
PRE.VA.RI.CAR, *v.*, to prevaricate, to transgress.
PRE.VEN.ÇÃO, *s.f.*, prevention, precaution, warning, prejudice.

PREVENIDO | **PROCRIAR**

PRE.VE.NI.DO, *adj.*, advised, forewarmed, cautious, informed.
PRE.VE.NIR, *v.*, to prevent, to avert, to forestall, to alarm, to alert.
PRE.VER, *v.*, to foresee, to calculate.
PRE.VI.DÊN.CIA, *s.f.*, providence, precaution, provision.
PRE.VI.DEN.TE, *adj.*, provident, cautious, prudent.
PRÉ.VIO, *adj.*, previous, precedent, prior, former, foregoing, precedent.
PRE.VI.SÃO, *s.f.*, prevision, foresight, forecast.
PRE.VIS.TO, *adj.*, foreseen, anticipated.
PRE.ZA.DO, *adj.*, dear, esteemed.
PRE.ZAR, *v.*, to esteem, to value, to respect, to honour.
PRI.MA, *s.f.*, cousin.
PRI.MÁ.RIO, *adj.*, basic, primary, primitive, original.
PRI.MA.VE.RA, *s.f.*, spring, springtime; primrose (flower).
PRI.MA.VE.RIL, *adj.*, vernal.
PRI.MA.ZI.A, *s.f.*, primacy, superiority.
PRI.MEI.RO, *s.m.*, the first; *adj.*, first, prime, foremost, main, chief, original, principal.
PRI.MI.TI.VO, *adj.*, primitive, original, early, simple, rude.
PRI.MO, *s.m.*, cousin; *adj.*, prime, excellent, perfect.
PRI.MO.GÊ.NI.TO, *s.m.*, the first-born, the eldest born.
PRI.MOR, *s.m.*, beauty, delicacy.
PRI.MOR.DI.AL, *adj.*, primordial, original, prime.
PRIN.CE.SA, *s.f.*, princess.
PRIN.CI.PAL, *adj.*, principal, main, essential, chief, superior.
PRÍN.CI.PE, *s.m.*, prince.
PRIN.CI.PES.CO, *adj.*, princely, magnificent.
PRIN.CI.PI.AN.TE, *s.2 gen.*, principiant, beginner, novice, tyro; *adj.*, beginning.
PRIN.CI.PI.AR, *v.*, to begin, to initiate, to start.
PRIN.CÍ.PIO, *s.m.*, start, beginning, source, origin, maxim, axiom.

PRI.O.RI.DA.DE, *s.f.*, priority, preference, precedence.
PRI.SÃO, *s.f.*, prison, jail, ward, capture, apprehension, imprisonment.
PRI.SI.O.NEI.RO, *s.m.*, prisoner, captive.
PRIS.MA, *s.f.*, prisma.
PRI.VA.ÇÃO, *s.f.*, privation, want, destitution.
PRI.VA.DA, *s.f.*, privy, water-closet, toilet.
PRI.VAR, *v.*, to prive, to deprive, to prohibit, to forbid.
PRI.VA.TI.VO, *adj.*, privative, peculiar, particular, private.
PRI.VI.LE.GI.A.DO, *adj.*, privileged, favoured.
PRI.VI.LE.GI.AR, *v.*, to privilege, to favour, to exempt, to invest.
PRI.VI.LÉ.GIO, *s.m.*, privilege, advantage, prerogative, immunity.
PRÓ, *adv.*, pro, in favor of.
PRO.A, *s.f.*, stem, prow, bow, nose.
PRO.BA.BI.LI.DA.DE, *s.f.*, probability, likelihood, chance.
PRO.BI.DA.DE, *s.f.*, probity, honesty, integrity.
PRO.BLE.MA, *s.m.*, problem, proposition, trouble, doubt.
PRO.BLE.MÁ.TI.CO, *adj.*, problematic.
PRO.CE.DÊN.CIA, *s.f.*, origin, derivation, provenance, source, genealogy.
PRO.CE.DEN.TE, *adj.*, proceeding, derived, descended.
PRO.CE.DER, *v.*, to procede, to go on, to come, to arise from, to result, to originate.
PRO.CE.DI.MEN.TO, *s.m.*, proceeding, procedure, dealing, transaction.
PRO.CES.SAR, *v.*, to process, to carry on a lawsuit, to law, to prosecute.
PRO.CES.SO, *s.m.*, process, legal proceedings, method, procedure.
PRO.CIS.SÃO, *s.f.*, procession, cortège.
PRO.CLA.MA.ÇÃO, *s.f.*, proclamation, publication, ban, declaration.
PRO.CLA.MAR, *v.*, to proclaim, to promulgate, to announce.
PRO.CRI.A.ÇÃO, *s.f.*, procreation, generation.
PRO.CRI.AR, *v.*, to procreate, to beget, to

engender, to generate.
PRO.CU.RA, *s.f.*, search, pursuit, demand.
PRO.CU.RA.ÇÃO, *s.f.*, procuration, mandate.
PRO.CU.RA.DOR, *s.m.*, procurator, attorney, proxy, proctor, mandatary.
PRO.CU.RA.DO.RI.A, *s.f.*, procuracy, procuratorship.
PRO.CU.RAR, *v.*, to look for, to seek, to search, to try, to attempt, to visit, to call.
PRO.DI.GA.LI.DA.DE, *s.f.*, prodigality, lavishness, profusion.
PRO.DÍ.GIO, *s.m.*, prodigy, marvel, sign.
PRÓ.DI.GO, *s.m.*, prodigal, waster, squanderer.
PRO.DU.ÇÃO, *s.f.*, production, producing, manufacturing, output.
PRO.DU.TO, *s.m.*, product, production, produce, proceeds, output.
PRO.DU.TOR, *s.m.*, producer, creator, manufacturer.
PRO.DU.ZIR, *v.*, to produce, to bear, to yield, to cause, to effect, to afford.
PRO.E.ZA, *s.f.*, prowess, bravery, courage, valor.
PRO.FA.NAR, *v.*, to profane, to pollute, to abuse.
PRO.FA.NO, *s.m.*, profane, layman; *adj.*, profane, secular, irreligious.
PRO.FE.CIA, *s.f.*, prophecy, prediction, forecast.
PRO.FE.RIR, *v.*, to pronounce, utter, speak, say.
PRO.FES.SAR, *v.*, to profess, to avow, to acknowledge, affirm, to teach, to educate.
PRO.FES.SOR, *s.m.*, teacher, professor, master, educator, instructor.
PRO.FES.SO.RA.DO, *s.m.*, professorship, faculty.
PRO.FE.TA, *s.2 gen.*, prophet, predictor, foreteller.
PRO.FE.TI.ZAR, *v.*, to prophetize, to prophesy, to predict.
PRO.FI.CI.ÊN.CIA, *s.f.*, proficiency, skill, adeptness.
PRO.FÍ.CUO, *adj.*, useful, advantageous.
PRO.FI.LA.XIA, *s.f.*, prophylaxis.
PRO.FIS.SÃO, *s.f.*, profession, occupation, career, employment.
PRO.FIS.SI.O.NAL, *adj.*, professional, occupational.
PRO.FUN.DI.DA.DE, *s.f.*, depth, profundity.
PRO.FUN.DO, *s.m.*, profundity, depth; *adj.*, deep, profound, impenetrable.
PRO.FU.SÃO, *s.f.*, profusion, prodigality.
PRO.GE.NI.TOR, *s.m.*, progenitor, forefather.
PROG.NOS.TI.CAR, *v.*, to prognosticate, to foretell, to predict.
PROG.NÓS.TI.CO, *s.m.*, omen, presage, prognostic, prediction, prognosis.
PRO.GRA.MA, *s.m.*, program, programme, plan.
PRO.GRA.MA.ÇÃO, *s.f.*, programming, program.
PRO.GRA.MA.DOR, *s.m.*, programmer.
PRO.GRA.MAR, *v.*, to program, to plan.
PRO.GRE.DIR, *v.*, to progress, to proceed, to advance.
PRO.GRES.SIS.TA, *s.2 gen.*, progressist; *adj.*, progressive.
PRO.GRES.SI.VO, *adj.*, progressive, advancing, gradual.
PRO.GRES.SO, *s.m.*, progress, advancement, improvement, growth, development.
PRO.I.BI.ÇÃO, *s.f.*, prohibition, ban, interdiction, forbidding.
PRO.I.BI.DO, *adj.*, prohibited, forbidden.
PRO.I.BIR, *v.*, to prohibit, forbid, deny.
PRO.JE.ÇÃO, *s.f.*, projection, plan, delineation, scheme.
PRO.JE.TAR, *v.*, to project, to throw out, to design, to cast forth, to shoot.
PRO.JÉ.TIL, *s.m.*, projectile, missile, bullet, shot, bomb.
PRO.JE.TO, *s.m.*, project, plan, scheme, design, sketch.
PRO.JE.TOR, *s.m.*, projector.
PROL, *s.2 gen.*, advantage, benefit.
PRO.LE, *s.f.*, offspring, progeny, descendants.
PRO.LE.TA.RI.A.DO, *s.m.*, proletariat.
PRO.LE.TÁ.RIO, *s.m.*, proletarian.
PRO.LI.FE.RA.ÇÃO, *s.f.*, proliferation.
PRO.LI.FE.RAR, *v.*, to proliferate, reproduce, grow rapidly.
PRO.LI.XI.DA.DE, *s.f.*, prolixity, diffuseness.

PRO.LI.XO, *adj.*, prolix, diffuse, tedious.
PRÓ.LO.GO, *s.m.*, prologue, preamble, introduction.
PRO.LON.GA.DO, *adj.*, prolonged, delayed, protracted.
PRO.LON.GA.MEN.TO, *s.m.*, prolongation, delay.
PRO.LON.GAR, *v.*, to prolong, to lenghten, to extend, to delay.
PRO.MES.SA, *s.f.*, promise, assurance, word.
PRO.ME.TER, *v.*, to promise, to pledge.
PRO.ME.TI.DO, *adj.*, promised.
PRO.MIS.CUI.DA.DE, *s.f.*, promiscuity.
PRO.MÍS.CUO, *adj.*, promiscuous, mixed.
PRO.MIS.SÓ.RIA, *s.f.*, promissory note.
PRO.MO.ÇÃO, *s.f.*, promotion, preference, preferment.
PRO.MO.TOR, *s.m.*, promoter, sponsor, inciter, instigator; **PROMOTOR DE JUSTIÇA**, attorney, prosecutor.
PRO.MO.VER, *v.*, to promote, to foster, to raise.
PRO.MUL.GAR, *v.*, to promulgate, to publish.
PRO.NO.ME, *s.m.*, pronoun.
PRON.TI.DÃO, *s.f.*, promptitude, promptness, readiness.
PRON.TO, *adj.*, ready, prompt, prepared, disposed.
PRON.TO-SO.COR.RO, *s.m.*, first-aid clinic.
PRON.TU.Á.RIO, *s.m.*, dossier, promptuary, record.
PRO.NÚN.CIA, *s.f.*, pronunciation, enunciation.
PRO.NUN.CI.AR, *v.*, to pronounce, to enunciate, to utter.
PRO.PA.GA.ÇÃO, *s.f.*, propagation, diffusion, dissemination.
PRO.PA.GAN.DA, *s.f.*, advertising, publicity, advertisement, propaganda.
PRO.PA.GAR, *v.*, to propagate, to multiply, to reproduce, to diffuse, to spread, to scatter.
PRO.PA.LAR, *v.*, to blab, to divulge.
PRO.PE.LIR, *v.*, to propel, to impel.
PRO.PEN.SÃO, *s.f.*, propensity, propension, tendency, disposition.
PRO.PEN.SO, *adj.*, propense, inclined, prone, ready.
PRO.PI.CI.AR, *v.*, to propitiate, to conciliate.
PRO.PÍ.CIO, *adj.*, propitious, promising, benevolent, kind.
PRO.PI.NA, *s.f.*, propine, gratuity, tip.
PRO.POR, *v.*, to propose, to suggest, to recommend, to offer.
PRO.POR.ÇÃO, *s.f.*, proportion, rate, ratio, symmetry.
PRO.POR.CI.O.NAL, *adj.*, proportional.
PRO.POR.CI.O.NA.LI.DA.DE, *s.f.*, proportionateness.
PRO.POR.CI.O.NAR, *v.*, to proportion, to proportionate, to adjust, to provide.
PRO.PO.SI.ÇÃO, *s.f.*, proposition, proposal.
PRO.PÓ.SI.TO, *s.m.*, purpose, aim, intention, matter.
PRO.POS.TA, *s.f.*, proposal, bid, offer, proposition.
PRO.POS.TO, *adj.*, offered, proposed.
PRO.PRI.E.DA.DE, *s.f.*, propriety, accuracy, quality, real estate.
PRO.PRI.E.TÁ.RIO, *s.m.*, proprietor, owner.
PRÓ.PRIO, *adj.*, proper, peculiar, private, own, fit, suitable, correct, appropriate, right.
PRO.PUL.SÃO, *s.f.*, propulsion.
PROR.RO.GA.ÇÃO, *s.f.*, prorogation, deferment.
PROR.RO.GAR, *v.*, to prorogate, to prorogue, to put off.
PRO.SA, *s.f.*, prose, talk, chatter, courtship.
PRO.SAI.CO, *adj.*, prosaic, dull, commonplace.
PROS.CRI.TO, *s.m.*, outlaw; *adj.*, proscribed, outlawed.
PRO.SÉ.LI.TO, *s.m.*, proselyte, convert.
PRO.SÓ.DIA, *s.f.*, prosody.
PROS.PE.RAR, *v.*, to prosper, to thrive, to flourish.
PROS.PE.RI.DA.DE, *s.f.*, prosperity, success, welfare.
PRÓS.PE.RO, *adj.*, prosperous, successful, propitious.
PROS.SE.GUI.MEN.TO, *s.m.*, pursuit, continuation, following.
PROS.SE.GUIR, *v.*, to follow, to continue, to

proceed, to go on, to pursue.
PRÓS.TA.TA, *s.f.*, prostate, the prostate gland.
PROS.TÍ.BU.LO, *s.m.*, brothel, whore-house.
PROS.TI.TUI.ÇÃO, *s.f.*, prostitution.
PROS.TI.TU.IR, *v.*, to prostitute, to corrupt.
PROS.TI.TU.TA, *s.f.*, prostitute, courtesan, whore.
PROS.TRA.ÇÃO, *s.f.*, prostration, debility.
PROS.TRAR, *v.*, to prostrate, to humiliate, to weaken, to humble.
PRO.TA.GO.NIS.TA, *s.2 gen.*, protagonist.
PRO.TE.ÇÃO, *s.f.*, protection, patronage, support, security, help, favour.
PRO.TE.GER, *v.*, to protect, to defend, to support, shield.
PRO.TE.GI.DO, *adj.*, protected, favoured.
PRO.TE.Í.NA, *s.f.*, protein.
PRO.TE.LAR, *v.*, to delay, to postpone, to prolong.
PRO.TES.TAN.TE, *s.2 gen.*, Protestant; *adj.*, Protestant, protesting.
PRO.TES.TAR, *v.*, to protest, to make a protest against, to object.
PRO.TES.TO, *s.m.*, protest, disapproval, objection, asseveration.
PRO.TE.TOR, *s.m.*, protector, supporter, guardian; *adj.*, protecting, protective, shielding.
PRO.TO.CO.LO, *s.m.*, protocol, ceremony, register, record.
PRO.TÓ.TI.PO, *s.m.*, prototype, model, pattern.
PRO.TU.BE.RÂN.CIA, *s.f.*, protuberance, projection, bulge.
PRO.VA, *s.f.*, proof, experiment, essay, trial, examen, test, demonstration, testimony.
PRO.VA.ÇÃO, *s.f.*, probation, proving, trial.
PRO.VAR, *v.*, to prove, to try, to experiment, to test, to check, to verify, to testify.
PRO.VÁ.VEL, *adj.*, probable, likely, provable.
PRO.VE.DOR, *s.m.*, purveyor.
PRO.VEI.TO, *s.m.*, profit, advantage, gain, benefit, progress.
PRO.VEI.TO.SO, *adj.*, profitable, advantageous, lucrative.
PRO.VE.NI.EN.TE, *adj.*, deriving from, coming, proceeding.
PRO.VER, *v.*, to provide, to furnish, to supply, to give, to grant, to confer.
PRO.VÉR.BIO, *s.m.*, proverb, saying.
PRO.VI.DÊN.CIA, *s.f.*, Providence, God, providence, foresight, precaution.
PRO.VI.DEN.CI.AR, *v.*, to provide, to make arrangement for, to arrange, to prepare.
PRO.VÍN.CIA, *s.f.*, province, region, territory, district.
PRO.VIN.CI.AL, *adj.*, provincial.
PRO.VIR, *v.*, to proceed, to come, to issue.
PRO.VI.SÃO, *s.f.*, provision, supply, store, storage.
PRO.VI.SÓ.RIO, *adj.*, temporary, transitory.
PRO.VO.CA.ÇÃO, *s.f.*, provocation, provoking, affront, challenge.
PRO.VO.CAN.TE, *adj.*, provocative.
PRO.VO.CAR, *v.*, to provoke, to affront, to incite, to insult.
PRO.XI.MI.DA.DE, *s.f.*, proximity, nearness, kinship.
PRÓ.XI.MO, *s.m.*, fellow man, neighbor; *adj.*, next, coming, near, close, adjacent.
PRU.DÊN.CIA, *s.f.*, prudence, caution, circumspection.
PRU.DEN.TE, *adj.*, careful, prudent, discreet, provident.
PRU.MO, *s.m.*, plumb bob, plummet.
PSEU.DÔ.NI.MO, *s.m.*, pseudonym.
PSI.CA.NÁ.LI.SE, *s.f.*, psychoanalysis.
PSI.CA.NA.LIS.TA, *s.2 gen.*, psychoanalyst.
PSI.CO.GRA.FAR, *v.*, to write through spiritual agency.
PSI.CO.GRA.FI.A, *s.f.*, psychography.
PSI.CO.LO.GIA, *s.f.*, psychology.
PSI.CO.LÓ.GI.CO, *adj.*, psychological.
PSI.CÓ.LO.GO, *s.m.*, psychologist.
PSI.CO.PA.TA, *s.2 gen.*, psychopath.
PSI.CO.SE, *s.f.*, psychosis.
PSI.CO.TE.RA.PI.A, *s.f.*, psychotherapy.
PSI.CÓ.TI.CO, *adj.*, psychotic.
PSI.QUE, *s.f.*, psyche, soul, spirit, mind.
PSI.QUI.A.TRA, *s.2 gen.*, psychiatrist.

PSI.QUI.A.TRI.A, *s.f.*, psychiatry.
PSÍ.QUI.CO, *adj.*, psychic.
PU.A, *s.f.*, prick, point, bit.
PU.BER.DA.DE, *s.f.*, puberty.
PU.BLI.CA.ÇÃO, *s.f.*, publication.
PU.BLI.CAR, *v.*, to publish, to announce, to edit, to spread.
PU.BLI.CI.DA.DE, *s.f.*, publicity, advertisement, advertising.
PÚ.BLI.CO, *s.m.*, public, audience, spectators; *adj.*, public.
PU.DE.RA!, *interj.*, small wonder! why!
PU.DIM, *s.m.*, pudding.
PU.DOR, *s.m.*, chastity, shyness, modesty.
PU.E.RIL, *adj.*, puerile, childish.
PU.E.RI.LI.DA.DE, *s.f.*, puerility, childishness, foolishness.
PU.GI.LA.TO, *s.m.*, boxing.
PU.GI.LIS.MO, *s.m.*, pugilism, boxing.
PU.GI.LIS.TA, *s.2 gen.*, pugilist, boxer.
PU.IR, *v.*, to polish, to abrade.
PU.JAN.TE, *adj.*, puissant, strong, powerful.
PU.LAR, *v.*, to leap, to bounce, to hop, to spring.
PUL.GA, *s.f.*, flea.
PUL.MÃO, *s.m.*, lung.
PUL.MO.NAR, *adj.*, pulmonary.
PU.LO, *s.m.*, jump, leap, skip, vault.
PU.LÔ.VER, *s.m.*, pullover.
PÚL.PI.TO, *s.m.*, pulpit.
PUL.SA.ÇÃO, *s.f.*, pulsation, pulse.
PUL.SAR, *v.*, to pulsate, to pulse, to impel, to vibrate.
PUL.SEI.RA, *s.f.*, bracelet, wristband.
PUL.SO, *s.m.*, pulse, wrist, strength, vigor.
PUL.VE.RI.ZA.ÇÃO, *s.f.*, pulverization.
PUL.VE.RI.ZAR, *v.*, to pulverize, to spray, to destroy.
PU.MA, *s.f.*, puma, cougar.
PUN.ÇÃO, *s.f.*, puncture, perforation.
PUN.GIR, *v.*, to prick, to pierce, to hurt.
PU.NHA.DO, *s.m.*, handful, a few, bunch.
PU.NHAL, *s.m.*, dagger, poniard.
PU.NHO, *s.m.*, fist, wrist, handle.
PU.NI.ÇÃO, *s.f.*, punishment, penalty.
PU.NIR, *v.*, to punish, to reprimand.
PU.NI.TI.VO, *adj.*, punitive.
PU.PI.LA, *s.f.*, pupil; the opening of the iris.
PU.PI.LO, *s.m.*, pupil, ward.
PU.RÊ, *s.m.*, purée, pap.
PU.RE.ZA, *s.f.*, pureness, purity, innocence, perfection.
PUR.GAN.TE, *s.m.*, purgative; *adj.*, purgative, laxative.
PUR.GAR, *v.*, to purge.
PUR.GA.TÓ.RIO, *s.m.*, purgatory.
PU.RI.FI.CA.ÇÃO, *s.f.*, purification.
PU.RI.FI.CA.DOR, *s.m.*, purifier, refiner.
PU.RI.FI.CAR, *v.*, to purify, to clean, to clear, to refine.
PU.RIS.MO, *s.m.*, purism.
PU.RI.TA.NO, *s.m.*, Puritan; *adj.*, puritan, prudish.
PU.RO, *adj.*, pure, clear, clean, unmingled, unspoiled, blameless, innocent.
PÚR.PU.RA, *s.f.*, purple; purple cloth.
PU.RU.LEN.TO, *adj.*, purulent, suppurative.
PUS, *s.m.*, pus, matter.
PÚS.TU.LA, *s.f.*, pustule, pimple.
PU.TA, *s.f.*, whore, hooker, prostitute, bitch.
PU.TRE.FA.ÇÃO, *s.f.*, putrefaction, decomposition.
PU.TRE.FA.ZER, *v.*, to putrefy, to rot, to corrupt.
PU.XA!, *interj.*, why!, now!, gee.
PU.XA.DA, *s.f.*, draft, pull.
PU.XA.DOR, *s.m.*, handle, knob.
PU.XÃO, *s.m.*, pull, tug, jerk.
PU.XAR, *v.*, to pull, to draw, to haul, to drag, to tug, to pluck.
PU.XA-SA.CO, *s.m.*, cajoler, flatterer, bootlicker, toady.

Q

Q, *s.m.*, sixteenth letter of the Portuguese alphabet.
QUA.DRA, *s.f.*, square place, court, block, yard.
QUA.DRA.DO, *s.m.*, square; *adj.*, square, quadrate.
QUA.DRA.GE.NÁ.RIO, *adj.*, *s.m.*, quadragenarian.
QUA.DRA.GÉ.SI.MO, *num.*, fortieth.
QUA.DRÂN.GU.LO, *s.m.*, quadrangle.
QUA.DRAN.TE, *s.m.*, quadrant, circle, dial.
QUA.DRA.TU.RA, *s.f.*, quadrature.
QUA.DRI.CU.LA.DO, *adj.*, checkered.
QUA.DRI.CU.LAR, *adj.*, checker; *v.*, to checker, to divide, to crossline.
QUA.DRI.E.NAL, *adj.*, quadrennial.
QUA.DRI.Ê.NIO, *s.m.*, quadrennium.
QUA.DRIL, *s.m.*, hip, haunch.
QUA.DRI.LÁ.TE.RO, *s.m.*, quadrilateral.
QUA.DRI.LHA, *s.f.*, gang, band.
QUA.DRO, *s.m.*, picture, painting, portrait, board, panel, list, staff, image, figure.
QUA.DRÚ.PE.DE, *s.m.*, quadruped, four-footed, animal.
QUAL, *pron.*, which, that which, that one, such as, who, whom.
QUA.LI.DA.DE, *s.f.*, quality, kind, characteristic, class.
QUA.LI.FI.CA.ÇÃO, *s.f.*, qualification.
QUA.LI.FI.CAR, *v.*, to qualify, designate, consider, to classify, to denominate.
QUA.LI.TA.TI.VO, *adj.*, qualitative.
QUAL.QUER, *pron.*, any, some, a, an, every, either, whatever, certain; **A QUALQUER HORA**, any time.
QUAN.DO, *adv.*, when, how soon, at what time; *conj.*, when, at which, as soon as, at the time that.
QUAN.TI.A, *s.f.*, sum, amount, quantity.
QUAN.TI.DA.DE, *s.f.*, quantity, quantum, amount, sum.
QUAN.TO, *adj.*, how much, whatever, as much as; *adv.*, how, as to; *pron.*, how much?, how many?, whatever.
QUÃO, *adv.*, how, as.
QUA.REN.TA, *num.*, forty.
QUA.REN.TÃO, *s.m.*, quadragenarian.
QUA.REN.TE.NA, *s.f.*, quarantine.
QUA.RES.MA, *s.f.*, Lent.
QUAR.TA, *s.f.*, quarter, forth part.
QUAR.TA-FEI.RA, *s.f.*, Wednesday.
QUAR.TEI.RÃO, *s.m.*, block.
QUAR.TEL, *s.m.*, quarter, barrack, caserne.
QUAR.TE.TO, *s.m.*, quartet.
QUAR.TO, *s.m.*, the fourth part, a quarter, room, bedroom.
QUART.ZO, *s.m.*, quartz.
QUA.SE, *adv.*, almost, near, nearly, closely, about.
QUA.TOR.ZE, *num.*, fourteen.
QUA.TRI.Ê.NIO, *s.m.*, quadrennium.
QUA.TRO, *num.*, four.
QUA.TRO.CEN.TOS, *num.*, four hundred.
QUE, *pron.*, that, which, who, whom, what; *adv.*, what, how; *conj.*, as, for, than, however.
QUÊ, *s.m.*, anything, something, difficulty, obstacle.
QUE.BRA, *s.f.*, break, breakage, breaking, fracture, interruption, hillside.
QUE.BRA-CA.BE.ÇA, *s.f.*, puzzle.
QUE.BRA.DO, *adj.*, broken, fragmented.
QUE.BRAR, *v.*, to break, to shatter, to violate, to transgress, to go bankrupt, to interrupt.
QUE.DA, *s.f.*, fall, decadence, destruction, drop, tendency, bent.
QUE.DO, *adj.*, quiet, still, stationary.
QUEI.JEI.RO, *s.m.*, cheese maker.
QUEI.JO, *s.m.*, cheese.
QUEI.MA.DA, *s.f.*, burn.
QUEI.MA.DO, *adj.*, burned, burnt, scorched, carbonized.

QUEI.MA.DU.RA, *s.f.*, burn.
QUEI.MAR, *v.*, to burn, to destroy by fire, to cremate.
QUEI.XA, *s.f.*, complaint, formal accusation, charge, offence, protest.
QUEI.XO, *s.m.*, chin, mandible, lower jaw.
QUEI.XO.SO, *s.m.*, complainant; *adj.*, complaining, querulous, plaintiff.
QUEI.XU.ME, *s.m.*, lamentation, complaint, whine.
QUEM, *pron.*, who, whom, one or anybody who.
QUEN.TE, *adj.*, hot, burning.
QUE.PE, *s.m.*, kepi.
QUER, *conj.*, or, whether or though, notwithstanding.
QUE.RER, *v.*, to wish, to will, to desire, to want, to intend, to aspire.
QUE.RI.DO, *adj.*, dear, darling, beloved, favourite.
QUER.MES.SE, *s.f.*, kermis, kermess.
QUE.RO.SE.NE, *s.m.*, kerosene, oil.
QUE.SI.TO, *s.m.*, inquiry, query, question.
QUES.TÃO, *s.f.*, question, inquiry, query, interrogation.
QUES.TI.O.NA.DOR, *s.m.*, questioner.
QUES.TI.O.NAR, *v.*, to question, to debate, to discuss, to argue.
QUES.TI.O.NÁ.RIO, *s.m.*, questionnaire.
QUI.A.BO, *s.m.*, okra.
QUI.ÇÁ, *adv.*, perhaps, maybe, possibly.
QUI.E.TO, *adj.*, quiet, still, placid, serene, tranquil.
QUI.E.TU.DE, *s.f.*, quietude, peacefulness, calmness, serenity.
QUI.LA.TE, *s.m.*, carat, karat.
QUI.LHA, *s.f.*, keel, bottom, hull.
QUI.LO, *s.m.*, kilo; chyle, kilogram.
QUI.LO.GRA.MA, *s.m.*, kilogram, kilogramme.
QUI.LO.ME.TRA.GEM, *s.f.*, a distance or a measuring in kilometers.
QUI.LÔ.ME.TRO, *s.m.*, kilometer, kilometre.
QUI.LO.WATT, *s.m.*, kilowatt.
QUI.ME.RA, *s.f.*, chimera.
QUÍ.MI.CA, *s.f.*, chemistry.
QUÍ.MI.CO, *s.m.*, chemist; *adj.*, chemic, chemical.
QUI.MO.NO, *s.m.*, kimono.
QUI.NA, *s.f.*, edge, corner, five spots (cards).
QUIN.GEN.TÉ.SI.MO, *num.*, five hundredth.
QUI.NHÃO, *s.m.*, portion, parcel, partition.
QUI.NHEN.TOS, *num.*, five hundred.
QUIN.QUÊ.NIO, *s.m.*, quinquennium.
QUIN.TA-FEI.RA, *s.f.*, Thursday.
QUIN.TAL, *s.m.*, yard, backyard.
QUIN.TE.TO, *s.m.*, quintet.
QUIN.TO, *num.*, fifth, quint; *adj.*, fifth.
QUIN.TU.PLI.CAR, *v.*, to quintuple, to quintuplicate.
QUIN.ZE, *num.*, fifteen.
QUIN.ZE.NA, *s.f.*, fortnight.
QUI.OS.QUE, *s.m.*, kiosk, news stand.
QUI.RO.MAN.CI.A, *s.f.*, chiromancy.
QUI.RO.MAN.TE, *s.2 gen.*, fortuneteller, chiromancer.
QUIS.TO, *s.m.*, cyst, wen.
QUI.TA.ÇÃO, *s.f.*, quittance, repayment.
QUI.TAN.DA, *s.f.*, greengrocery.
QUI.TAR, *v.*, to quit, to exempt, to desist from, to free, to liberate.
QUI.TE, *adj.*, quit, free, settled.
QUI.XO.TES.CO, *adj.*, quixotic.
QUI.XO.TIS.MO, *s.m.*, quixotism.
QUO.CI.EN.TE, *s.m.*, quotient.
QUO.TA, *s.f.*, quota, share.
QUO.TI.DI.A.NO, *adj.*, daily.
QUO.TI.ZAR, *v.*, to parcel out.

R

R, *s.m.*, the seventeenth letter of the Portuguese alphabet.
RÃ, *s.f.*, frog.
RA.BA.DA, *s.f.*, tail, caudal fin, rump.
RA.BA.NE.TE, *s.m.*, radish.
RA.BE.CA, *s.f.*, violin, fiddle.
RA.BI, *s.m.*, rabbi.
RA.BI.CHO, *s.m.*, pigtail, crupper, tail.
RA.BI.NO, *s.m.*, rabbi.
RA.BIS.CAR, *v.*, to scribble, scrawl, to scrabble.
RA.BIS.CO, *s.m.*, scribble, scrawl, doodle.
RA.BO, *s.m.*, tail, brush, handle.
RA.BU.GEN.TO, *adj.*, morose, cross, sullen, ill-humoured, peevish.
RÁ.BU.LA, *s.f.*, pettifogger, shyster.
RA.ÇA, *s.f.*, race, generation, origin, descent, species, pedigree, family.
RA.ÇÃO, *s.f.*, ration, portion.
RA.CHAR, *v.*, to split, to cleave, to splinter, to shiver, to chap.
RA.CIAL, *adj.*, racial.
RA.CI.O.CI.NAR, *v.*, to reason, to ratiocinate, to think, to consider.
RA.CI.O.CÍ.NIO, *s.m.*, ratiocination, reasoning, thought.
RA.CI.O.NAL, *adj.*, rational, reasonable.
RA.CI.O.NA.LIS.MO, *s.m.*, rationalism.
RA.CI.O.NA.LIS.TA, *s.2 gen.*, rationalist.
RA.CI.O.NA.LI.ZA.ÇÃO, *s.f.*, rationalization.
RA.CI.O.NA.MEN.TO, *s.m.*, rationing, ration.
RA.CI.O.NAR, *v.*, to ration.
RA.CIS.MO, *s.m.*, racism.
RA.CIS.TA, *s.2 gen.*, racist.
RA.DAR, *s.m.*, radar.
RA.DI.A.ÇÃO, *s.f.*, radiation.
RA.DI.A.DOR, *s.m.*, radiator.
RA.DI.A.LIS.TA, *s.2 gen.*, broadcaster.
RA.DI.AN.TE, *adj.*, radiant, beautiful, splendid, gleeful.
RA.DI.CAL, *adj.*, radical, basic, fundamental.
RA.DI.CA.LIS.MO, *s.m.*, radicalism.
RA.DI.CAR, *v.*, to radicate, to take root, to root, to settle down.
RÁ.DIO, *s.m.*, radius, radium, radio.
RA.DI.O.A.TI.VI.DA.DE, *s.f.*, radioactivity.
RA.DI.O.A.TI.VO, *adj.*, radioactive.
RA.DI.O.DI.FU.SÃO, *s.f.*, broadcasting.
RA.DI.O.GRA.FAR, *v.*, to radiograph.
RA.DI.O.GRA.FIA, *s.f.*, radiography, roentgenogram.
RA.DI.O.GRA.MA, *s.m.*, radiogram.
RA.DI.O.LO.GIA, *s.f.*, radiology.
RA.DI.O.SO, *adj.*, radiant, brilliant, ecstatic.
RA.DI.OU.VIN.TE, *s.2 gen.*, radio listener.
RAI.A, *s.f.*, line, stroke, streak, race-course, limit.
RAI.AR, *v.*, to break, to dawn, to emit rays, to radiate.
RA.I.NHA, *s.f.*, queen; queen bee.
RAI.O, *s.m.*, ray, beam, thunderbolt, radius, sign, indication.
RAI.VA, *s.f.*, rage, fury, hydrophobia, rabies, hate.
RAI.VO.SO, *adj.*, angry, furious.
RA.IZ, *s.f.*, root, base, bottom, origin.
RA.JÁ, *s.m.*, raja, rajah.
RA.JA.DA, *s.f.*, gust of wind, squall.
RA.LA.DOR, *s.m.*, rasper, grater.
RA.LAR, *v.*, to rasp, to grate, to annoy.
RA.LÉ, *s.f.*, common people, rabble.
RA.LHAR, *v.*, to rail, to scold, to chide.
RA.LO, *s.m.*, grater, rasper, strainer.
RA.MA.GEM, *s.f.*, branches, boughs, foliage.
RA.MAL, *s.m.*, extension line, railroad branch line.
RA.MA.LHE.TE, *s.m.*, bunch of flowers, bouquet, nosegay.

RAMIFICAÇÃO — REAGIR

RA.MI.FI.CA.ÇÃO, *s.f.*, ramification, branching.
RA.MI.FI.CAR, *v.*, to divide into branches, ramify, to furcate.
RA.MI.NHO, *s.m.*, twig.
RA.MO, *s.m.*, branch, bough, twig, sprig.
RAM.PA, *s.f.*, ramp, stage.
RAN.CHO, *s.m.*, fare, ranch, farm; food.
RAN.COR, *s.m.*, rancour, resentment.
RAN.CO.RO.SO, *adj.*, rancorous, resentful.
RAN.GER, *v.*, to screak, to creak, to grit.
RAN.GI.DO, *s.m.*, creaking, screak.
RA.NHO, *s.m.*, snivel, snot.
RA.NHU.RA, *s.f.*, groove, slot, slit, notch.
RAN.ZIN.ZA, *s.f.*, sullen, sulky, ill-humoured, unruly.
RA.PAR, *v.*, to scrape, to scratch, to wear out.
RA.PA.RI.GA, *s.f.*, girl, maiden.
RA.PAZ, *s.m.*, boy, guy, lad, youngster, young man, fellow.
RA.PA.ZI.NHO, *s.m.*, kid, little boy.
RA.PA.ZO.TE, *s.m.*, kid, little boy.
RA.PI.DEZ, *s.f.*, rapidity, quickness, swiftness, speed.
RÁ.PI.DO, *adj.*, rapid, quick, swift, speedy.
RA.PI.NA, *s.f.*, rapine, robbery.
RA.PI.NA.GEM, *s.f.*, robbery, plunder.
RA.PO.SA, *s.f.*, fox, vixen.
RAP.SÓ.DIA, *s.f.*, rhapsody.
RAP.TAR, *v.*, to ravish, to abduct, to kidnap, to rob.
RAP.TO, *s.m.*, abduction, ravishment, kidnapping.
RAP.TOR, *s.m.*, abductor, kidnapper.
RA.QUE.TA, *s.f.*, racket, racquet.
RA.QUÍ.TI.CO, *adj.*, rachitic, richety, scrubby.
RA.RE.AR, *v.*, to rarefy, to diminish.
RA.RE.FA.ÇÃO, *s.f.*, rarefaction, rarefication.
RA.RE.FA.ZER, *v.*, to rarefy, to make thin.
RA.RI.DA.DE, *s.f.*, rareness, rarity, scarcity.
RA.RO, *adj.*, rare, thin, seldom, unusual.
RA.SAN.TE, *adj., s.2 gen.*, levelling, smoothing, skimming.
RAS.CU.NHAR, *v.*, to sketch, to outline.
RAS.CU.NHO, *s.m.*, draft, sketch, rough copy.
RAS.GA.DO, *adj.*, torn, rent, frank, open.

RAS.GAR, *v.*, to tear, to rend, to split, to cleave.
RAS.GO, *s.m.*, rip, tear, split, cleft, scratch.
RA.SO, *s.m.*, plain; *adj.*, level, flat, low, vulgar.
RAS.PA, *s.f.*, scrapings, chip, shaving.
RAS.PA.DEI.RA, *s.f.*, scraper, rasp, eraser.
RAS.PAR, *v.*, to scrape, to scratch, to erase.
RAS.TEI.RA, *s.f.*, trip.
RAS.TE.JA.DOR, *s.m.*, searcher, tracer, tracker; *adj.*, searching, trailing, tracing.
RAS.TE.JAR, *v.*, to trace, to track, to follow the track, to crawl.
RAS.TO, *s.m.*, trace, track.
RAS.TRE.AR, *v.*, to trace, to track, to pursue, to trace down.
RAS.TRO, *s.m.*, trace, track, vestige.
RA.SU.RA, *s.f.*, erasure.
RA.TEI.O, *s.m.*, share, apportionment.
RA.TI.FI.CA.ÇÃO, *s.f.*, ratification.
RA.TI.FI.CAR, *v.*, to ratify, to confirm, to validate.
RA.TO, *s.m.*, mouse, rat.
RA.TO.EI.RA, *s.f.*, mousetrap, rat-trap.
RA.VI.NA, *s.f.*, ravine, mountain steam.
RA.ZÃO, *s.f.*, reason, reasoning, ground, justice, right, rate, proportion, moral law.
RA.ZO.Á.VEL, *adj.*, reasonable, sensible, rational, sane.
RÉ, *s.f.*, female criminal; *s.m.*, re, the second musical note; *s.f.*, **MARCHA À RÉ**, reverse speed.
RE.A.BAS.TE.CER, *v.*, to supply, to replenish, to supply with fresh provisions.
RE.A.BAS.TE.CI.MEN.TO, *s.m.*, replenishment, restocking.
RE.A.BER.TU.RA, *s.f.*, reopening.
RE.A.BI.LI.TA.ÇÃO, *s.f.*, rehabilitation.
RE.A.BI.LI.TAR, *v.*, to rehabilitate, to reinstate.
RE.A.ÇÃO, *s.f.*, reaction, resistance.
RE.A.CI.O.NÁ.RIO, *adj.*, reactionary.
RE.AD.MI.TIR, *v.*, to readmit, to admit again.
RE.A.FIR.MA.ÇÃO, *s.f.*, reaffirmation, reassertment.
RE.A.FIR.MAR, *v.*, to reaffirm, to reassert.
RE.A.GEN.TE, *s.m.*, reagent; *adj.*, reactive.
RE.A.GIR, *v.*, to react, to answer, to resist.

RE.A.GRU.PA.MEN.TO, *s.m.*, reassemblage, rally.
RE.A.JUS.TAR, *v.*, to readjust, rearrange.
RE.A.JUS.TE, *s.m.*, readjustment.
RE.AL, *adj.*, real, actual, factual, genuine, royal, kingly.
RE.AL.ÇAR, *v.*, to enhance, to emphasize, to intensify.
RE.AL.CE, *s.m.*, distinction, enhancement.
RE.A.LE.ZA, *s.f.*, royalty, regality, kingship.
RE.A.LI.DA.DE, *s.f.*, reality, actuality, fact, truth, verity.
RE.A.LIS.MO, *s.m.*, realism; royalism.
RE.A.LI.ZA.ÇÃO, *s.f.*, accomplishment, fulfillment, achievement, attainment.
RE.A.LI.ZAR, *v.*, to accomplish, to consummate, to realize, to achieve.
RE.AL.MEN.TE, *adv.*, really, actually.
RE.A.NI.MA.ÇÃO, *s.f.*, reanimation, revivification.
RE.A.NI.MAR, *v.*, to reanimate, to restore to life, to revive, to revivify.
RE.A.PA.RE.CER, *v.*, to reappear, to appear again.
RE.A.PA.RE.CI.MEN.TO, *s.m.*, reappearance.
RE.AR.MA.MEN.TO, *s.m.*, rearmament.
RE.AS.SU.MIR, *v.*, to reacquire, to retake, to recover.
RE.A.TAR, *v.*, to rebind, to reattach, to renew.
RE.A.TI.VAR, *v.*, to reactivate, to revive, to reanimate, reobtain.
RE.A.TOR, *s.m.*, reactor, reagent.
RE.A.VER, *v.*, to get back, to reobtain, to recover, to recuperate.
RE.A.VI.VAR, *v.*, to revive, to recall, to renew.
RE.BAI.XA.MEN.TO, *s.m.*, lowering, reduction, degradation.
RE.BAI.XAR, *v.*, to lower, to let down, to depreciate.
RE.BA.NHO, *s.m.*, flock of sheep, herd of cattle, drove, cattle.
RE.BA.TE, *s.m.*, repelling, act or effect of striking again.
RE.BA.TER, *v.*, to strike again, to repel, to refute.
RE.BE.LAR, *v.*, to cause to revolt, to rebel, to revolt.
RE.BEL.DE, *s.2 gen.*, rebel, insurgent; *adj.*, rebel, revolutionary.
RE.BEL.DIA, *s.f.*, rebellion, revolt, insurrection, opposition.
RE.BE.LIÃO, *s.f.*, rebellion, revolt, mutiny.
RE.BEN.TAR, *v.*, to burst, to split open, to blow up, to explode, to roar.
RE.BI.TAR, *v.*, to rivet, to clinch.
RE.BI.TE, *s.m.*, rivet, clinch.
RE.BO.CA.DOR, *s.m.*, tug, towboat.
RE.BO.CAR, *v.*, to plaster, to coat with stucco, to tow.
RE.BO.CO, *s.m.*, plaster, roughcast.
RE.BO.LAR, *v.*, to roll, to shake the hips, hipswing.
RE.BO.QUE, *s.m.*, towing, plaster, rough-cast.
RE.BRO.TAR, *v.*, to sprout again.
RE.BUS.CAR, *v.*, to search thoroughly, to refine, to perfect, to search again.
RE.CA.DO, *s.m.*, message, word, information.
RE.CA.IR, *v.*, to fall again, to fall back, to befall.
RE.CAL.CA.DO, *adj.*, depressed, beaten down.
RE.CAL.CA.MEN.TO, *s.m.*, repression, suppression.
RE.CAL.CAR, *v.*, to step on, to press down.
RE.CAL.CU.LAR, *v.*, to recalculate, to recount.
RE.CAL.QUE, *s.m.*, pressing down, repression, suppression.
RE.CAN.TO, *s.m.*, place, corner, hiding place, retreat, recess, nook.
RE.CA.PI.TU.LA.ÇÃO, *s.f.*, recapitulation.
RE.CA.PI.TU.LAR, *v.*, to recapitulate, to repeat.
RE.CAP.TU.RAR, *v.*, to recapture again.
RE.CAR.RE.GAR, *v.*, to reload, to recharge.
RE.CA.TO, *s.m.*, modesty, honesty, bashfulness.
RE.CAU.CHU.TAR, *v.*, to recap, to retread.
RE.CE.AR, *v.*, to fear, to dread, to be apprehensive, to doubt.
RE.CE.BE.DOR, *s.m.*, receiver, gatherer; *adj.*, receiving, gathering.
RE.CE.BER, *v.*, to accept, to take, to get, to

RECEBIMENTO | RECONQUISTAR

receive, to cash in.
RE.CE.BI.MEN.TO, *s.m.*, receiving, reception, receipt.
RE.CEI.O, *s.m.*, fear, dread, terror, apprehension.
RE.CEI.TA, *s.f.*, income, revenue, recipe, prescription, budget.
RE.CEI.TAR, *v.*, to prescribe, to advise, to counsel.
RE.CÉM-CA.SA.DO, *adj.*, married or wed, newly married, just married.
RE.CÉM-NAS.CI.DO, *s.m.*, a newborn baby; *adj.*, newborn.
RE.CEN.SE.A.MEN.TO, *s.m.*, census, survey.
RE.CEN.SE.AR, *v.*, to take a census, to poll, to survey, to verify.
RE.CEN.TE, *adj.*, recent, modern, new, fresh.
RE.CE.O.SO, *adj.*, afraid, fearful, anxious, apprehensive, timid.
RE.CEP.ÇÃO, *s.f.*, reception, receipt, admittance.
RE.CEP.CI.O.NAR, *v.*, to receive guests, to entertain.
RE.CEP.TA.DOR, *s.m.*, fence; *adj.*, receiving, fencing.
RE.CEP.TAR, *v.*, to receive, to conceal.
RE.CEP.TI.VI.DA.DE, *s.f.*, receptivity, receptiveness.
RE.CEP.TOR, *s.m.*, receiver, receptor.
RE.CES.SÃO, *s.f.*, recession.
RE.CES.SIVO, *adj.*, recessive.
RE.CES.SO, *s.m.*, recess, corner, niche, retreat.
RE.CHE.A.DO, *adj.*, stuffed, filled.
RE.CHEI.O, *s.m.*, stuffing, farcing, dressing.
RE.CI.BO, *s.m.*, receipt, voucher, acquittance.
RE.CI.CLA.GEM, *s.f.*, recycling.
RE.CI.FE, *s.m.*, key, skerry.
RE.CI.PI.EN.TE, *s.m.*, recipient, receiver, vessel.
RE.CI.PRO.CI.DA.DE, *s.f.*, reciprocity.
RE.CÍ.PRO.CO, *adj.*, reciprocal, reciprocative, mutual.
RE.CI.TAL, *s.m.*, recital, concert.
RE.CI.TAR, *v.*, to recite, to declaim.
RE.CLA.MA.ÇÃO, *s.f.*, complaint, reclamation, demand.
RE.CLA.MAR, *v.*, to object, to protest, to complain, to oppose, to require.
RE.CLI.NA.DO, *adj.*, reclinate, turned, reclining.
RE.CLI.NAR, *v.*, to lean back, to recline.
RE.CLU.SÃO, *s.f.*, reclusion, recluseness.
RE.CO.BRAR, *v.*, to recover, to recuperate, to regain, to retrieve.
RE.CO.BRIR, *v.*, to cover again, to recover.
RE.CO.LHER, *v.*, to pick up, to collect, to guard, to preserve.
RE.CO.LHI.DO, *adj.*, retired, reserved, solitary.
RE.CO.LHI.MEN.TO, *s.m.*, retiring, retirement, shelter, refuge, home.
RE.CO.LO.CAR, *v.*, to put back, to restore.
RE.CO.ME.ÇAR, *v.*, to begin again, to resume, to continue, to start over, to renew.
RE.CO.ME.ÇO, *s.m.*, recommencement.
RE.CO.MEN.DA.ÇÃO, *s.f.*, recommendation, advice, suggestion.
RE.CO.MEN.DAR, *v.*, to recommend, to commend, to praise.
RE.COM.PEN.SA, *s.f.*, reward, prize, recompense.
RE.COM.PEN.SAR, *v.*, to retribute, to reward, to premiate, to compensate.
RE.COM.POR, *v.*, to recompose, to renew, to reorganize.
RE.CÔN.CA.VO, *s.m.*, deep cave, grotto, hollow.
RE.CON.CI.LI.A.ÇÃO, *s.f.*, reconciliation, reconcilement.
RE.CON.CI.LI.A.DOR, *s.m.*, reconciler, conciliator.
RE.CON.CI.LI.AR, *v.*, to reconcile, to conciliate, to establish peace.
RE.CON.DU.ZIR, *v.*, to lead back, to return, to reconduct.
RE.CON.FOR.TAR, *v.*, to recomfort, to refresh, to stimulate, to console.
RE.CO.NHE.CER, *v.*, to recognize, to acknowledge, to admit, to know again, to verify.
RE.CO.NHE.CI.MEN.TO, *s.m.*, recognition, acknowledgement, cognizance.
RE.CON.QUIS.TA, *s.f.*, reconquest, reconquering.
RE.CON.QUIS.TAR, *v.*, to reconquer, to retake, to conquer again.

RECONSIDERAR   229   **REELEIÇÃO**

RE.CON.SI.DE.RAR, *v.*, to reconsider, to ponder.
RE.CONS.TRU.ÇÃO, *s.f.*, reconstruction, rebuilding.
RE.CONS.TRU.IR, *v.*, to reconstruct, to rebuild, to reorganize.
RE.CON.TAR, *v.*, to recount, to count again.
RE.CON.VA.LES.CER, *v.*, to recover from illness, to get better.
RE.COR.DA.ÇÃO, *s.f.*, remembrance, recollection, reminiscence.
RE.COR.DAR, *v.*, to remember, to recall, to recollect.
RE.COR.DE, *s.m.*, record, feat, special prowess.
RE.COR.RER, *v.*, to run over, to go through again, to search, to scrutinize.
RE.COR.TA.DO, *adj.*, indented, denticulate, crenate.
RE.COR.TAR, *v.*, to cut out, to trim, to clip, to slash, to slice.
RE.COR.TE, *s.m.*, newspaper clipping, press cutting.
RE.COS.TAR, *v.*, to recline, to lean back, to bend, to rest on.
RE.CO.ZI.MEN.TO, *s.m.*, cooking, boiling, overcooking.
RE.CRE.A.ÇÃO, *s.f.*, recreation, entertainment, amusement, enjoyment.
RE.CRE.AR, *v.*, to recreate, to entertain, to divert, to play.
RE.CRE.A.TI.VO, *adj.*, recreative, refreshing, amusing.
RE.CRELO, *s.m.*, recreation, relaxation, diversion, interval.
RE.CRI.MI.NA.ÇÃO, *s.f.*, recrimination, exprobation.
RE.CRI.MI.NAR, *v.*, to recriminate, reproach, to censure.
RE.CRU.DES.CER, *v.*, to recrudesce.
RE.CRU.TA, *s.m.*, recruit, rookie, novice.
RE.CRU.TA.MEN.TO, *s.m.*, recruitment, recruiting, enlistment.
RE.CRU.TAR, *v.*, to recruit, to enlist, to draft.
RE.CUO, *s.m.*, retrocession, recoiling, recoil, recession, retreat.
RE.CU.PE.RA.ÇÃO, *s.f.*, recuperation, recovery.
RE.CU.PE.RAR, *v.*, to recuperate, to recover.
RE.CUR.SO, *s.m.*, appeal, petition, recourse, claim, reclamation, complaint.
RE.CUR.VAR, *v.*, to recurve, to curve again, to curve back.
RE.CU.SA, *s.f.*, denial, refusal, rejection.
RE.CU.SAR, *v.*, to refuse, to deny, to resist, to rebel, to reject, to oppose.
RE.DA.ÇÃO, *s.f.*, redaction, composition, editorship, editorial staff, editorial room.
RE.DA.TOR, *s.m.*, editor, newspaper editor, redactor, writer, journalist.
RE.DA.TO.RA, *s.f.*, editress.
RE.DE, *s.f.*, net, network.
RÉ.DEA, *s.f.*, reins, bridle, control.
RE.DEN.ÇÃO, *s.f.*, redemption, redeeming, ransom.
RE.DEN.TOR, *s.m.*, redeemer, saviour.
RE.DES.CO.BRIR, *v.*, to rediscover, to reveal again.
RE.DI.GIR, *v.*, to write, to write down, to compose.
RE.DI.MIR, *v.*, to redeem, to regain.
RE.DI.ZER, *v.*, to say again.
RE.DO.MA, *s.f.*, glass shade, vial.
RE.DON.DE.ZA, *s.f.*, round, roundness, rotundness, environs.
RE.DON.DO, *adj.*, round, circular, globular, spherical, cylindrical.
RE.DOR, *s.m.*, circle, circuit, contour, outline.
RE.DU.ÇÃO, *s.f.*, reduction, decrease, shortening, reducing.
RE.DUN.DÂN.CIA, *s.f.*, redundance, pleonasm, redundancy.
RE.DU.TO, *s.m.*, redoubt, outwork.
RE.DU.ZIR, *v.*, to reduce, to decrease, to restrict, to compress.
RE.E.DI.ÇÃO, *s.f.*, re-ediction, new edition.
RE.E.DI.FI.CAR, *v.*, to rebuild, to re-edify.
RE.E.DI.TAR, *v.*, to re-edit, to republish, to reprint.
RE.E.LE.GER, *v.*, to re-elect, to elect again.
RE.E.LEI.ÇÃO, *s.f.*, re-election.

RE.EM.BOL.SAR, *v.*, to reimburse, to pay back, to repay.
RE.EM.BOL.SO, *s.m.*, reimbursement, refund.
RE.EN.TRAR, *v.*, to re-enter, to enter again.
RE.ER.GUER, *v.*, to re-erect, to reconstruct, to raise again.
RE.ES.CRE.VER, to rewrite.
RE.FA.ZER, *v.*, to remake, to make over again.
RE.FEI.ÇÃO, *s.f.*, meal, repast.
RE.FEI.TÓ.RIO, *s.m.*, refectory, dining-hall.
RE.FÉM, s.m. hostage.
RE.FE.RÊN.CIA, *s.f.*, reference, indication, allusion, mention, remark.
RE.FE.REN.TE, *adj.*, referring, relating to, relative, concerning, regarding.
RE.FE.RI.MEN.TO, *s.m.*, reference, remark.
RE.FE.RIR, *v.*, to refer, to narrate, to tell, to relate, to report.
RE.FI.NA.DO, *adj.*, pure, purified, polished.
RE.FI.NA.MEN.TO, *s.m.*, refining, refinement, culture.
RE.FI.NAR, *v.*, to refine, to civilize, to cultivate, to perfect.
RE.FI.NA.RI.A, *s.f.*, refinery.
RE.FLE.TIR, *v.*, to reflect; to consider, to ponder.
RE.FLE.TOR, *s.m.*, reflector.
RE.FLE.XÃO, *s.f.*, reflection, meditation, consideration, contemplation.
RE.FLE.XO, *s.m.*, reflection, reaction.
RE.FLO.RES.CER, *v.*, to blossom again, to reflourish, to reflower.
RE.FLO.RES.TA.MEN.TO, *s.m.*, reforestation, reforestment.
RE.FLO.RES.TAR, *v.*, reforest.
RE.FLU.IR, *v.*, to flow back, to reflow, to recede.
RE.FLU.XO, *s.m.*, reflow, refluence.
RE.FOR.ÇA.DO, *adj.*, reinforced, strong, vigorous.
RE.FOR.ÇAR, *v.*, to reinforce, to amplify, to intensify.
RE.FOR.ÇO, *s.m.*, reinforcement, reinforcing, succour, help.
RE.FOR.MA, *s.f.*, reform, reformation; Reforma, the Reformation.
RE.FOR.MA.DO, *adj.*, reformed, retired, converted.
RE.FOR.MA.DOR, *s.m.*, reformer, redresser, remodeller.
RE.FOR.MAR, *v.*, to reform, to remodel, to reconstruct, to rebuild, to renovate.
RE.FOR.MU.LAR, *v.*, to reformulate, to formulate again.
RE.FRA.ÇÃO, *s.f.*, refraction, deflection.
RE.FRÃO, *s.m.*, refrain, adage, proverb.
RE.FRA.TÁ.RIO, *s.m.*, refractory; *adj.*, refractory, intractable, unruly.
RE.FRE.AR, *v.*, to refrain, to restrain, to repress.
RE.FRE.GA, *s.f.*, fight, combat, fray.
RE.FRES.CO, *s.m.*, refreshment, drink.
RE.FRI.GE.RA.ÇÃO, *s.f.*, refrigeration, cooling, chilling.
RE.FRI.GE.RA.DOR, *s.m.*, refrigerator, fridge, freezer, cooler, ice-box.
RE.FRI.GE.RAN.TE, *s.m.*, refreshment, cooling; *adj.*, refrigerant, refreshing.
RE.FRI.GE.RAR, *v.*, to refresh, to cool, to make fresh.
RE.FÚ.GIO, *s.m.*, refuge, rejection.
RE.FU.GO, *s.m.*, refuse, garbage, rejection.
RE.FU.TA.ÇÃO, *s.f.*, refutation, refute.
RE.FU.TAR, *v.*, to refute, to contradict, to disprove.
RE.GA.ÇO, *s.m.*, lap, bosom, breast, shelter.
RE.GA.DOR, *s.m.*, waterer, sprinkler.
RE.GA.LAR, *v.*, to regale, to entertain, to please, to delight.
RE.GA.LI.A, *s.f.*, regal rights, prerogative.
RE.GA.LO, *s.m.*, regalement, pleasure, gift.
RE.GAR, *v.*, to water, to irrigate, to sprinkle, to wash.
RE.GA.TO, *s.m.*, rivulet, rill, creek.
RE.GE.LAR, *v.*, to freeze.
RE.GÊN.CIA, *s.f.*, regency, government, administration.
RE.GE.NE.RA.ÇÃO, *s.f.*, regeneration.
RE.GE.NE.RAR, *v.*, to regenerate, to reproduce, to restore, to reorganize.
RE.GER, *v.*, to reign, to rule, to govern, to manage, to administer, to direct, to guide.

RE.GIÃO, *s.f.*, area, country, province, region, section.
RE.GI.ME, *s.m.*, regime, regimen, political system; diet.
RE.GI.MEN.TO, *s.m.*, regiment, administration, guide, rule.
RE.GIO.NAL, *adj.*, regional, sectional.
RE.GIO.NA.LIS.MO, *s.m.*, regionalism.
RE.GIS.TRAR, *v.*, to register, to book, to list.
RE.GIS.TRO, *s.m.*, register, record, registry;
RE.GIS.TRO CI.VIL, registry office.
RE.GO.ZI.JAR, *v.*, to rejoice, to delight, to please.
RE.GO.ZI.JO, *s.m.*, pleasure, joy, glee, gladness.
RE.GRA, *s.f.*, ruler, norm, standard, rule, principle, law.
RE.GRAR, *v.*, to rule, to control, to regulate.
RE.GRE.DIR, *v.*, to retrograde, to recede.
RE.GRES.SAR, *v.*, to return, to go back, to come back.
RE.GRES.SO, *s.m.*, return, returning.
RÉ.GUA, *s.f.*, ruler, rule.
RE.GU.LA.DO, *adj.*, regulated, regular.
RE.GU.LA.DOR, *s.m.*, regulator, governor, corrector.
RE.GU.LA.MEN.TA.ÇÃO, *s.f.*, regulation.
RE.GU.LA.MEN.TAR, *v.*, to regulate, to arrange, to control, to order.
RE.GU.LA.MEN.TO, *s.m.*, regulation, rule, ordinance, resolution, precept.
RE.GU.LAR, *v.*, to regulate, to direct, to guide; *adj.*, regular, constant, legal, lawful.
RE.GU.LA.RI.ZA.ÇÃO, *s.f.*, regularization.
RE.GU.LA.RI.ZAR, *v.*, to regularize, to regulate, to make uniform.
REI, *s.m.*, king, monarch, sovereign.
RE.IM.PRI.MIR, *v.*, to reprint, to republish.
REI.NA.DO, *s.m.*, reign, govern, rule, supremacy.
REI.NAR, *v.*, to reign, to govern, to rule, to dominate.
RE.IN.CI.DÊN.CIA, *s.f.*, recidivation, reincidence.
RE.IN.CI.DIR, *v.*, to relapse, to repeat once again; to fall back.
RE.I.NI.CI.AR, *v.*, to start over, to begin again.
REI.NO, *s.m.*, kingdom, realm, monarchy, domain.
RE.IN.TE.GRA.ÇÃO, *s.f.*, reintegration, restoration.
RE.IN.TE.GRAR, *v.*, to reintegrate, to restore, to renew, to reinstall.
REI.TE.RA.ÇÃO, *s.f.*, reiteration, repetition.
REI.TE.RAR, *v.*, to reiterate, to repeat, to reaffirm, to renew.
REI.TOR, *s.m.*, rector, head of a university or college, principal, dean.
REI.VIN.DI.CA.ÇÃO, *s.f.*, vindication, claim, demand, reclamation.
REI.VIN.DI.CAR, *v.*, to revindicate, to vindicate, to demand.
RE.JEI.ÇÃO, *s.f.*, rejection, refusal, exclusion.
RE.JEI.TAR, *v.*, to reject, to cast or throw away, to refuse, to repudiate.
RE.JU.BI.LAR, *v.*, to jubilate, to cause great joy.
RE.JU.VE.NES.CER, *v.*, to rejuvenate, to make young again, to renew.
RE.JU.VE.NES.CI.MEN.TO, *s.m.*, rejuvenescence, rejuvenation.
RE.LA.ÇÃO, *s.f.*, report, roll, list, relationship, connection, analogy.
RE.LA.CI.O.NA.DO, *adj.*, related, connected.
RE.LA.CI.O.NA.MEN.TO, *s.m.*, relationship.
RE.LA.CI.O.NAR, *v.*, to relate, to tell, to include in a list, to register, to inscribe, to catalogue, to confront.
RE.LÂM.PA.GO, *s.m.*, lightning, thunderbolt, flash of lightning.
RE.LAN.CE, *s.m.*, glance, glimpse.
RE.LAP.SO, *s.m.*, relapser, recidivist, backslider; *adj.*, relapsing, backsliding, obstinate.
RE.LA.TAR, *v.*, to mention, to tell, to narrate, to refer to, to explain, to report.
RE.LA.TI.VI.DA.DE, *s.f.*, relativity, relativeness, conditionality.
RE.LA.TI.VO, *adj.*, relative, relating to.
RE.LA.TO, *s.m.*, report, account, narration, description.
RE.LA.TOR, *s.m.*, relator, reporter.

RE.LA.TÓ.RIO, *s.m.*, report, account, relation.
RE.LA.XA.DO, *adj.*, loose, slack, relaxed, careless, remiss.
RE.LA.XA.MEN.TO, *s.m.*, slackness, negligence, relax, relaxing, demoralization.
RE.LA.XAN.TE, *s.m.*, relaxing, relaxant.
RE.LA.XAR, *v.*, to relax, to slacken, to loosen, to make less severe, to corrupt.
RE.LE.GAR, *v.*, to relegate, to exile, to banish, to expatriate.
RE.LEM.BRAR, *v.*, to remember again, to put in mind, to recollect.
RE.LEN.TO, *s.m.*, dew, moisture.
RE.LER, *v.*, to reread, to read again.
RE.LES, *adj.*, *s.2 gen.*, despicable, shabby, poor, worthless, feeble.
RE.LE.VÂN.CIA, *s.f.*, prominence, importance, significance, consequence.
RE.LE.VAN.TE, *adj.*, important, considerable, weighty.
RE.LE.VAR, *v.*, to permit, to allow, to exempt, to excuse, to forgive.
RE.LE.VO, *s.m.*, relief, salience, relievo, salience; **ALTO-RELEVO**, high relief; **BAIXO-RELEVO**, low relief.
RE.LI.CÁ.RIO, *s.m.*, reliquary, tabernacle.
RE.LI.GIÃO, *s.f.*, religion, religiousness, piety.
RE.LI.GI.O.SI.DA.DE, *s.f.*, religiosity.
RE.LI.GI.O.SO, *s.m.*, member of a monastic order, monk; *adj.*, religious, pious, devout, spiritual, godly.
RE.LIN.CHO, *s.m.*, neigh, whinny.
RE.LÍ.QUIA, *s.f.*, relic, venerated object.
RE.LÓ.GIO, *s.m.*, watch, clock.
RE.LO.JO.A.RIA, *s.f.*, a watchmaker's shop.
RE.LO.JO.EI.RO, *s.m.*, watchmaker, clockmaker.
RE.LU.TÂN.CIA, *s.f.*, resistance, aversion, reluctance.
RE.LU.TAR, *v.*, to fight again, to struggle against, to resist, to reluct.
RE.LU.ZIR, *v.*, to shine brightly, to sparkle, to glitter, to glow.
REL.VA, *s.f.*, grass, to turf, to lawn, sward.
REL.VA.DO, *s.m.*, grassplot, turf, lawn.

RE.MA.DOR, *s.m.*, rower, boatmann, oarsman.
RE.MA.NES.CER, *v.*, to be leftover, to rest, to remain, to survive.
RE.MAN.SO, *s.m.*, immobility, calmness, stillness.
RE.MAR, *v.*, to row, to paddle, to oar, to swim.
RE.MAR.CAR, *v.*, to re-mark, to give a new designation to, to relabel.
RE.MA.TA.DO, *adj.*, complete, perfect.
RE.MA.TAR, *v.*, finish, to conclude, to achieve, to accomplish, to complete.
RE.MA.TE, *s.m.*, end, conclusion, finish, finishing.
RE.ME.DI.AR, *v.*, to remedy, to relieve, to attenuate, to repair, to amend, to hinder.
RE.MÉ.DIO, *s.m.*, remedy, medicine, medicament, help.
RE.ME.MO.RA.ÇÃO, *s.f.*, remembrance, recollection.
RE.ME.MO.RAR, *v.*, to remember, to recollect, to recall.
RE.MEN.DAR, *v.*, to patch, to mend, to repair.
RE.MEN.DO, *s.m.*, patch, botch, mending.
RE.MES.SA, *s.f.*, remittance, remitting, transmittal, delivery, letter.
RE.ME.TEN.TE, *s.2 gen.*, remitter, forwarder; *adj.*, shipmail, post, remitting, sending.
RE.ME.TER, *v.*, to remit, to send, to forward, to ship, to mail, to post, to expedite, to postpone.
RE.ME.XER, *v.*, to stir or mix again, to move, to shake, to rummage, to jumble, to agitate.
RE.MI.ÇÃO, *s.f.*, redemption, redeeming, ransom.
RE.MIR, *v.*, to redeem, to repurchase, to free, to save, to pay off.
RE.MIS.SÃO, *s.f.*, remission, forgiveness, absolution, mitigation.
RE.MIS.SI.VO, *adj.*, remissive, forgiving, abating.
RE.MIS.SO, *adj.*, remiss, lax, negligent, indolent, lazy.
RE.MI.TIR, *v.*, to remit, to forgive, to pardon, to absolve, to excuse.
RE.MO, *s.m.*, oar, paddle.
RE.MO.ÇÃO, *s.f.*, removal, remotion, transfer.
RE.MO.DE.LA.ÇÃO, *s.f.*, remodelment, recast,

REMODELAGEM — REPETIR

transformation.
RE.MO.DE.LA.GEM, *s.f.*, remodelment.
RE.MO.DE.LAR, *v.*, to remodel, to recast, to reform.
RE.MO.ER, *v.*, to grind again, to grind slowly and thoroughly, to ruminate.
RE.MON.TAR, *v.*, to ascend, to go up, to lift up, to raise.
RE.MOR.SO, *s.m.*, remorse.
RE.MO.TO, *adj.*, remote, distant, out of the way.
RE.MO.VER, *v.*, to move again, to remove, to transfer, to drive away, to displace.
RE.MU.NE.RA.ÇÃO, *s.f.*, remuneration, salary, wages, gratification.
RE.MU.NE.RAR, *v.*, to remunerate, to recompense, to reward, to satisfy.
RE.NA, *s.f.*, reindeer.
RE.NAL, *adj.*, renal.
RE.NAS.CEN.ÇA, *s.f.*, renascence, renascency; Renaissance.
RE.NAS.CEN.TE, *adj.*, renascent.
RE.NAS.CER, *v.*, to be born again, to grow again, to reborn.
RE.NAS.CI.DO, *adj.*, newborn, reborn.
RE.NAS.CI.MEN.TO, *s.m.*, renascence, revival, renewal, rebirth.
REN.DA, *s.f.*, lace, lacework, gains, revenue.
REN.DER, *v.*, to subject, to subjugate, to conquer, to produce, to yield.
REN.DI.ÇÃO, *s.f.*, surrender, capitulation.
REN.DI.DO, *adj.*, rent, split, submissive, obedient.
REN.DI.MEN.TO, *s.m.*, revenue, income, profit, yield.
REN.DO.SO, *adj.*, profitable, lucrative, fruitful, productive, yielding.
RE.NE.GAR, *v.*, to deny, to abjure, to renounce, to betray, to detest, to refute.
RE.NO.MA.DO, *adj.*, renowned, reputed, famous.
RE.NO.ME, *s.m.*, reputation, fame, glory, prestige, renown.
RE.NO.VA.ÇÃO, *s.f.*, renovation, revival.
RE.NO.VA.DOR, *s.m.*, renovator, renewer, reformer.
RE.NO.VAR, *v.*, to renew, to renovate, to furbish.

REN.QUE, *s.m.*, row, rank.
REN.TE, *adj.*, close by, near; *adv.*, closely, even with.
RE.NÚN.CIA, *s.f.*, renunciation, renouncement, rejection, desistance.
RE.NUN.CI.AR, *v.*, to renounce, to resign, to reject, to refuse, to desist.
RE.OR.GA.NI.ZA.ÇÃO, *s.f.*, reorganization, rearrangement, reform.
RE.OR.GA.NI.ZAR, *v.*, to reorganize, to organize anew, to improve, to better.
RE.PA.RA.ÇÃO, *s.f.*, reparation, repair, repairing, reform, indemnity, satisfaction.
RE.PA.RAR, *v.*, to repair, to mend, to observe, to restore, to retouch, to remedy.
RE.PA.RO, *s.m.*, repair, repairing, restoration, notice, remark.
RE.PAR.TI.ÇÃO, *s.f.*, partition, department, division, section.
RE.PAR.TIR, *v.*, to separate, to slice, to share, to split, to distribute.
RE.PAS.SAR, *v.*, to repass, to read over again, to drench, to soak.
RE.PAS.TO, *s.m.*, repast, banquet.
RE.PA.TRI.A.MEN.TO, *s.m.*, repatriation.
RE.PA.TRI.AR, *v.*, to repatriate, to remigrate.
RE.PE.LEN.TE, *s.m.*, repellent, repugnant, repulsive.
RE.PE.LIR, *v.*, to repel, to repulse, to drive, to expulse, to reject.
RE.PEN.TE, *s.m.*, suddenness, impulsive act; **DE REPENTE**, suddenly.
RE.PEN.TI.NO, *adj.*, sudden, abrupt, instantaneous, rapid, acute.
RE.PER.CUS.SÃO, *s.f.*, repercussion, reverberation, echo.
RE.PER.CU.TIR, *v.*, to reverberate, to rebound, to reflect, to deflect.
RE.PER.TÓ.RIO, *s.m.*, repertory, index, list, catalogue.
RE.PE.TI.ÇÃO, *s.f.*, repetition, reiteration, recurrence.
RE.PE.TIR, *v.*, to repeat, to recur, to spread, to do over again.

RE.PI.QUE, *s.m.*, tolling of bells, alarm.
RE.PI.SAR, *v.*, to retread, to trample, to tread over again, to insist on.
RE.PLE.TO, *adj.*, replete, very full, stuffed, congested.
RÉ.PLI.CA, *s.f.*, response, reply, replication.
RE.PLI.CAR, *v.*, to answer, to reply, to rejoin, to rebut, to object.
RE.PO.LHO, *s.m.*, cabbage.
RE.POR, *v.*, to replace, to put back, to restitute, to refund.
RE.POR.TA.GEM, *s.f.*, newspaper report, interview.
RE.POR.TAR, *v.*, to transport, to resolve, to turn back.
RE.PÓR.TER, *s.m.*, reporter, journalist, news writer.
RE.PO.SI.ÇÃO, *s.f.*, replacement, restitution.
RE.POU.SAR, *v.*, to rest, to repose, to calm, to quiet, to sleep.
RE.POU.SO, *s.m.*, rest, repose, tranquility, calmness, ease.
RE.PRE.EN.DER, *v.*, to reprehend, to reprimand, to censure.
RE.PRE.EN.SÃO, *s.f.*, reprehension, reprimand, reproach.
RE.PRE.EN.SÍ.VEL *adj.*, reprehensible, censurable.
RE.PRE.SA, *s.f.*, dam, dike, sluice, weir, reservoir.
RE.PRE.SÁ.LIA, *s.f.*, retaliation, revenge, reprisal.
RE.PRE.SAR, *v.*, to dam up, to dike, to restrain.
RE.PRE.SEN.TA.ÇÃO, *s.f.*, representation, exhibition, presentation.
RE.PRE.SEN.TA.DO, *adj.*, represented.
RE.PRE.SEN.TAN.TE, *s.2 gen.*, representative, minister, ambassador, delegate; *adj.*, representing, representative.
RE.PRE.SEN.TAR, *v.*, to personate, to impersonate, to represent, to play.
RE.PRES.SÃO, *s.f.*, repression, suppression, check.
RE.PRES.SI.VO, *adj.*, repressive.
RE.PRES.SOR, *s.m.*, represser, coercer.
RE.PRI.MEN.DA, *s.f.*, reprimand, reprehension, correction.
RE.PRI.MIR, *v.*, to curb, to check, to stop, to repress, to restrain.
RE.PRI.SAR, *v.*, to replay, to repeat.
RE.PRI.SE, *s.f.*, rerum, replay.
RE.PRO.DU.ÇÃO, *s.f.*, reproduction, copy, replication, propagation, duplicate.
RE.PRO.DU.TI.VO, *adj.*, reproductive.
RE.PRO.DU.TOR, *s.m.*, reproducer, procreator, studhorse.
RE.PRO.DU.ZIR, *v.*, to reproduce, to transcribe, to copy, to multiply, to propagate.
RE.PRO.VA.ÇÃO, *s.f.*, reproving, rejection, reproof, reproach.
RE.PRO.VA.DO, *adj.*, reproved, damned, condemned.
RE.PRO.VAR, *v.*, to disapprove, to reprove, to censure, to reject, to admonish.
RE.PRO.VÁ.VEL, *adj.*, reprovable.
RÉP.TIL, *s.m.*, reptile; *adj.*, crawling, creeping.
RE.PÚ.BLI.CA, *s.f.*, republic, commonwealth.
RE.PU.BLI.CA.NO, *adj., s.m.*, republican.
RE.PU.BLI.CAR, *v.*, to republish.
RE.PU.DI.AR, *v.*, to repudiate, to divorce, to disclaim, to reject.
RE.PUG.NÂN.CIA, *s.f.*, repugnance, aversion, disgust, antipathy, repulsion, averseness.
RE.PUG.NAR, *v.*, to repugn, to react, to reject, to repel.
RE.PUL.SA, *s.f.*, repulse, repellence, aversion.
RE.PUL.SI.VO, *adj.*, repulsive, repugnant, repellent.
RE.PU.TA.ÇÃO, *s.f.*, reputation, renown, fame, credit.
RE.PU.TAR, *v.*, to repute, to consider, to regard.
RE.PU.XAR, *v.*, to pull, to pull violently.
RE.QUE.BRAR, *v.*, to waddle, to walk in a languishing manner.
RE.QUEI.JÃO, *s.m.*, cheesecurds, cottage cheese.
RE.QUEN.TAR, *v.*, to heat or warm up again.
RE.QUE.REN.TE, *s.2 gen.*, petitioner, solicitant, applicant, procurator.
RE.QUE.RER, *v.*, to request, to ask or apply for,

REQUERIMENTO · RESPOSTA

RE.QUE.RI.MEN.TO, *s.m.*, request, requirement, solicitation, demand.
RE.QUIN.TAR, *v.*, to refine, to purify, to perfect.
RE.QUIN.TE, *s.m.*, refinement.
RE.QUI.SI.ÇÃO, *s.f.*, requisition, solicitation, demand.
RE.QUI.SI.TAR, *v.*, to requisition, to require, to order, to request.
RE.QUI.SI.TO, *s.m.*, qualification, requisite, requirement.
RÊS, *s.f.*, cattle, livestock, any quadruped bred.
RÉS, *s.m.*, level, close.
RES.CAL.DO, *s.m.*, reflected heat.
RES.CIN.DIR, *v.*, to break, to dissolve, to sever.
RES.CI.SÃO, *s.f.*, rescission, repeal, annulment, cancellation, revocation.
RE.SE.NHA, *s.f.*, review, summary, abridgement, digest.
RE.SE.NHAR, *v.*, to recount, to write a detailed report.
RE.SER.VA, *s.f.*, reservation, restriction, store, stock.
RE.SER.VAR, *v.*, to reserve, to set apart.
RE.SER.VA.TÓ.RIO, *s.m.*, reservoir, tank, deposit, store.
RE.SER.VIS.TA, *s.2 gen.*, reservist.
RES.FRI.A.DO, *s.m.*, cold, catarrh; *adj.*, cold, chilly, iced, frozen.
RES.FRI.A.MEN.TO, *s.m.*, cooling, cold, chilly.
RES.FRI.AR, *v.*, to cool again, to cool, to freeze, to become chilly.
RES.GA.TAR, *v.*, to ransom, to redeem, to pay off.
RES.GA.TE, *s.m.*, ransom, redemption, deliverance.
RES.GUAR.DAR, *v.*, to guard, to defend, to shelter.
RES.GUAR.DO, *s.m.*, guard, protection, watch.
RE.SI.DÊN.CIA, *s.f.*, residence, residency, dwelling, home.
RE.SI.DEN.CI.AL, *adj.*, residential, residentiary.
RE.SI.DEN.TE, *s.2 gen.*, resident, diplomatic, agent; *adj.*, resident, residential.
RE.SI.DIR, *v.*, to reside, to live, to dwell, to inhabit.
RE.SÍ.DUO, *s.m.*, rest, remainder, residue, refuse.
RE.SIG.NA.ÇÃO, *s.f.*, resignation, abnegation.
RE.SIG.NAR, *v.*, to resign, to give up, to surrender, to abdicate.
RE.SI.NA, *s.f.*, resin, rosin.
RE.SIS.TÊN.CIA, *s.f.*, resistance, opposition, obstacle, reaction.
RE.SIS.TIR, *v.*, to resist, to oppose, to withstand, to endure, to hold out.
RES.MA, *s.f.*, ream, 500 sheets of paper.
RES.MUN.GAR, *v.*, to mumble, to grumble.
RES.MUN.GO, *s.m.*, mutter, mumble.
RE.SO.LU.ÇÃO, *s.f.*, resolution, deliberation, decision, purpose.
RE.SO.LU.TO, *adj.*, resolute, courageous.
RE.SOL.VER, *v.*, to resolve, to decide, to solve, to conclude, to determine, to liquidate.
RE.SOL.VI.DO, *adj.*, resolved, settled, decided.
RES.PEC.TI.VO, *adj.*, respective, concerning.
RES.PEI.TA.DO, *adj.*, respected, considered.
RES.PEI.TAR, *v.*, to respect, to esteem, to honour, to venerate.
RES.PEI.TO, *s.m.*, respect, regard, esteem, consideration, reverence, veneration.
RES.PEI.TO.SO, *adj.*, respectful, dutiful.
RES.PIN.GAR, *v.*, to sprinkle, to spray.
RES.PI.RA.ÇÃO, *s.f.*, respiration, breath.
RES.PI.RAR, *v.*, to breathe, to respire, to be, to live.
RES.PI.RA.TÓ.RIO, *adj.*, respiratory.
RES.PLAN.DE.CER, *v.*, to shine, to glitter, to sparkle.
RES.PLEN.DOR, *s.m.*, resplendence, resplendency.
RES.PON.DER, *v.*, to respond, to reply, to answer, to communicate, to answer back.
RES.PON.SA.BI.LI.DA.DE, *s.f.*, responsibility.
RES.PON.SA.BI.LI.ZAR, *v.*, to make or consider responsible.
RES.PON.SÁ.VEL, *adj.*, responsible.
RES.PON.SO, *s.m.*, antiphon, response.
RES.POS.TA, *s.f.*, response, answer, reply.

RES.QUÍ.CIO, *s.m.*, residue, rest, remainder, trace, mark.
RES.SA.CA, *s.f.*, surf, flux and reflux, hangover.
RES.SAL.TAR, *v.*, to stick out, to stand out, to project.
RES.SAL.VA, *s.f.*, reservation, exception, safety clause.
RES.SAR.CI.MEN.TO, *s.m.*, compensating, compensation.
RES.SEN.TI.MEN.TO, *s.m.*, resentment, offense.
RES.SEN.TIR, *v.*, to resent, to feel again, to feel anew, to take offense.
RES.SE.QUI.DO, *adj.*, dried up, parched.
RES.SO.AR, *v.*, to tune, to intone, to resound.
RES.SO.NÂN.CIA, *s.f.*, resonance, echo.
RES.SO.NAR, *v.*, to resound, to reverberate.
RES.SUR.GI.MEN.TO, *s.m.*, resuscitation, resurgence.
RES.SUR.GIR, *v.*, to resurge, to rise again, to revive.
RES.SUR.REI.ÇÃO, *s.f.*, resurrection, resuscitation.
RES.SUS.CI.TAR, *v.*, to revive, to resuscitate, to resurrect.
RES.TA.BE.LE.CER, *v.*, to restore, to re-establish.
RES.TA.BE.LE.CI.MEN.TO, *s.m.*, re-establishing, restoration.
RES.TAR, *v.*, to rest, to remain.
RES.TAU.RA.ÇÃO, *s.f.*, restoration, restoring, repair.
RES.TAU.RA.DOR, *s.m.*, restorer, liberator.
RES.TAU.RAN.TE, *s.m.*, restaurant.
RES.TAU.RAR, *v.*, to restore, to recuperate, to recapture, to repair, to renovate.
RÉS.TIA, *s.f.*, rope, rope braided from reeds or sedge grass.
RES.TI.TU.I.ÇÃO, *s.f.*, restitution, restoration, returning.
RES.TI.TU.IR, *v.*, to restitute, to restore, to return, to replace.
RES.TO, *s.m.*, rest, remain, residue, end.
RES.TRI.ÇÃO, *s.f.*, restriction, limitation, restraint.
RES.TRIN.GIR, *v.*, to restrict, to restringe, to straiten, to narrow, to restrain.
RES.TRI.TI.VO, *adj.*, restrictive.
RES.TRI.TO, *adj.*, restricted, limited.
RE.SUL.TA.DO, *s.m.*, result, consequence, effect, deliberation.
RE.SUL.TAR, *v.*, to result, to proceed, to spring or arise from, to derive from.
RE.SU.MIR, *v.*, to abbreviate, to abridge, to reduce, to synthetize.
RE.SU.MO, *s.m.*, abridgement, abbreviation, summary.
RES.VA.LAR, *v.*, to let slip or fall, to slide, to slip, to slither.
RE.TA, *s.f.*, straight line, trace or stroke.
RE.TA.GUAR.DA, *s.f.*, rearguard, back.
RE.TA.LHA.ÇÃO, *s.f.*, act of cutting.
RE.TA.LHAR, *v.*, to cut into small pieces, to stab, to slash, to rend.
RE.TA.LI.A.ÇÃO, *s.f.*, retaliation.
RE.TA.LI.AR, *v.*, to retaliate.
RE.TAN.GU.LAR, *adj.*, rectangular, right-angled.
RE.TÂN.GU.LO, *s.m.*, rectangle, square.
RE.TAR.DA.DO, *adj.*, retarded, delayed.
RE.TAR.DA.MEN.TO, *s.m.*, retardation, retarding, delay.
RE.TAR.DAR, *v.*, to retard, to delay, to impede.
RE.TAR.DA.TÁ.RIO, *s.m.*, latecomer, laggard, straggler; *adj.*, tardy, slow.
RE.TEM.PE.RAR, *v.*, to retemper.
RE.TEN.ÇÃO, *s.f.*, retention, retaining, restraint, suppression.
RE.TEN.TOR, *s.m.*, retainer, keeper, retentor.
RE.TER, *v.*, to keep, to hold back, to guard, to detain, to remember.
RE.TI.CÊN.CIA, *s.f.*, reticence, omission points.
RE.TI.CEN.TE, *adj.*, reticent, reserved, silent.
RE.TÍ.CU.LA, *s.f.*, reticle, a small net.
RE.TI.DÃO, *s.f.*, rightness, honesty, integrity.
RE.TI.DO, *adj.*, restrained, curbed.
RE.TI.FI.CA.ÇÃO, *s.f.*, rectification, rectifying, emendation.
RE.TI.FI.CA.DO, *adj.*, rectified, corrected.
RE.TI.FI.CA.DOR, *s.m.*, rectifier.
RE.TI.FI.CAR, *v.*, to rectify, to straighten, to

RETILÍNEO — REVERENDÍSSIMO

correct, to amend.
RE.TI.LÍ.NEO, *adj.*, rectilineal, rectilinear.
RE.TI.NA, *s.f.*, retina.
RE.TIN.TO, *adj.*, redyed, coloured again.
RE.TI.RA.DA, *s.f.*, retreat, evacuation, withdrawal.
RE.TI.RAR, *v.*, to draw back, to withdraw, to remove, to take away, to retract.
RE.TI.RO, *s.m.*, solitary place, seclusion, retreat, privacy, exile, nest.
RE.TO, *s.m.*, rectum; *adj.*, straight, right, direct, plain, just.
RE.TO.CAR, *v.*, to retouch, to finish, to complete, to correct, to ameliorate.
RE.TO.MAR, *v.*, to retake, to take again, to recover.
RE.TO.QUE, *s.m.*, retouching.
RE.TOR.CER, *v.*, to twist again, to retwuist, to wrench, to rewind.
RE.TOR.CI.DO, *adj.*, twisted, winding.
RE.TÓ.RI.CA, *s.f.*, rhetoric, eloquence, oratory.
RE.TÓ.RI.CO, *adj.*, rhetorical, rhetorician, declamatory.
RE.TOR.NAR, *v.*, to return, to turn, to get back.
RE.TOR.NO, *s.m.*, return, regress, coming back.
RE.TOR.TA, *s.f.*, retort.
RE.TRA.ÇÃO, *s.f.*, retractation, retracting.
RE.TRA.Í.DO, *adj.*, retracted, retired, reserved.
RE.TRA.IR, *v.*, to draw back, to withdraw, to retract, to shrink.
RE.TRANS.MIS.SÃO, *s.f.*, retransmission, reconveyance.
RE.TRANS.MI.TIR, *v.*, to retransmit, to transmit again.
RE.TRA.TA.ÇÃO, *s.f.*, retractation.
RE.TRA.TAR, *v.*, to portray, to paint, to draw, to photograph.
RE.TRA.TO, *s.m.*, picture, portrait, photograph.
RE.TRI.BU.I.ÇÃO, *s.f.*, retribution, recompense, payment, remuneration.
RE.TRI.BU.Í.DO, *adj.*, retributed, rewarded.
RE.TRI.BU.IR, *v.*, to retribute, to reward, to repay, to recompense.
RE.TRO.A.ÇÃO, *s.f.*, retroaction.

RE.TRO.A.GIR, *v.*, to retroact, to react, to act backward.
RE.TRO.A.TI.VO, *adj.*, retroactive.
RE.TRO.CE.DER, *v.*, to retrocede, to go back, to decline.
RE.TRO.CES.SO, *s.m.*, retrocession, backspacer, retrogression.
RE.TRÓ.GRA.DO, *s.m.*, retrograde, reactionary; *adj.*, retrograde, backward.
RE.TROS.PEC.ÇÃO, *s.f.*, retrospection, retrospect.
RE.TROS.PEC.TO, *s.m.*, retrospection, retrospect.
RE.TRO.VI.SOR, *s.m.*, rear view mirror.
RE.TRU.CAR, *v.*, to reply, to answer, to retort.
RE.TUM.BAR, *v.*, to resound, to reverberate.
RÉU, *s.m.*, defendant, the accused, respondent.
REU.MÁ.TI.CO, *adj.*, rheumatic.
REU.MA.TIS.MO, *s.m.*, rheumatism, arthritis.
RE.U.NI.ÃO, *s.f.*, reunion, meeting, gathering, meet, party.
RE.U.NIR, *v.*, to reunite, to assemble, to congregate, to meet, to rejoin.
RE.VA.LI.DA.ÇÃO, *s.f.*, revalidation.
RE.VA.LI.DAR, *v.*, to revalidate, to renew.
RE.VA.LO.RI.ZA.ÇÃO, *s.f.*, revalorization.
RE.VA.LO.RI.ZAR, *v.*, to revalorize.
RE.VE.LA.ÇÃO, *s.f.*, revelation, revealment, disclosure, eye-opener, discovery.
RE.VE.LAR, *v.*, to unveil, to unmask, to reveal, to disclose, to divulge, to expose.
RE.VE.LI.A, *s.f.*, default, nonsuit, non-appearance.
RE.VEN.DA, *s.f.*, resale, second sale.
RE.VEN.DER, *v.*, to resale, to resell, to sell again.
RE.VER, *v.*, to see again, to review, to revise.
RE.VER.BE.RA.ÇÃO, *s.f.*, reverberation, repercussion.
RE.VER.BE.RAR, *v.*, to reverberate, to reflect.
RE.VER.DE.CER, *v.*, to make green again.
RE.VE.RÊN.CIA, *s.f.*, reverence, deference, veneration.
RE.VE.REN.CI.AR, *v.*, to treat with reverence, to respect.
RE.VE.REN.DÍS.SI.MO, *s.m.*, Right Reverend.

RE.VE.REN.DO, *s.m.,* Reverend.
RE.VE.REN.TE, *adj.,* reverent, reverential.
RE.VER.SÃO, *s.f.,* reversion, reversal.
RE.VER.SÍ.VEL, *adj.,* reversible.
RE.VER.SO, *s.m.,* backside, opposite; *adj.,* reverse, contrary, opposite.
RE.VER.TER, *v.,* to return, to go back, to revert.
RE.VÉS, *s.m.,* reverse, backside, contrary.
RE.VES.TI.DO, *adj.,* covered, coated.
RE.VES.TI.MEN.TO, *s.m.,* revetment, revetting, coating, facing.
RE.VES.TIR, *v.,* to revest, to dress up, to coat, to cover, to line, to overlay.
RE.VE.ZA.DO, *adj.,* alternate.
RE.VE.ZA.MEN.TO, *s.m.,* alternation, rotation, relay.
RE.VE.ZAR, *v.,* to alternate, to rotate, to relieve, to relay.
RE.VI.DAR, *v.,* to retort, to correspond, to requite, to retribute.
RE.VI.DE, *s.m.,* retaliation, reprisal.
RE.VI.GO.RAR, *v.,* to reanimate, to revive, to revigorate.
RE.VI.RAR, *v.,* to turn, to turn over again, to twist.
RE.VI.RA.VOL.TA, *s.f.,* reversal of position, turn.
RE.VI.SÃO, *s.f.,* revision, revisal, revise, review.
RE.VI.SAR, *v.,* to revise, to review, to check, to recense.
RE.VI.SOR, *s.m.,* reviewer, reviser, proofreader, reader, revisor, correcter.
RE.VIS.TA, *s.f.,* magazine, review, inspection, revisal.
RE.VIS.TA.DO, *adj.,* revised, reviewed, examined.
RE.VIS.TAR, *v.,* to examine, to review, to revise, to search.
RE.VI.TA.LI.ZA.ÇÃO, *s.f.,* revitalization.
RE.VI.TA.LI.ZAR, *v.,* to revitalize, to animate again.
RE.VI.VER, *v.,* to revive, to revivify, to resuscitate.
RE.VI.VI.FI.CA.ÇÃO, *s.f.,* revivification.
RE.VO.AR, *v.,* to fly again, to fly back, to soar.

RE.VO.GA.ÇÃO, *s.f.,* revocation, revokement.
RE.VO.GAR, *v.,* to revoke, to revocate, to annul, to cancel, to recall.
RE.VOL.TA, *s.f.,* revolt, rebellion, uprising.
RE.VOL.TA.DO, *adj.,* revolted.
RE.VOL.TAR, *v.,* to revolt, to rebel, to raise up against, to disgust, to resent.
RE.VOL.TO.SO, *s.m.,* rebel; *adj.,* revolted.
RE.VO.LU.ÇÃO, *s.f.,* revolution, rebellion, circular motion, rotation, insurrection.
RE.VO.LU.CI.O.NAR, *v.,* to revolutionize.
RE.VO.LU.CI.O.NÁ.RIO, *s.m.,* revolutionary, revolutionist.
RE.VÓL.VER, *s.m.,* revolver, gun, pistol.
RE.VOL.VER, *v.,* to revolve, to turn round, to turn over again.
RE.VOL.VI.DO, *adj.,* revolved, stirred.
RE.ZA, *s.f.,* prayer, praying, oration.
RE.ZAR, *v.,* to pray, to supplicate, to mention, to say, to tell.
RI.A.CHO, *s.m.,* brook, creek, rivulet, streamlet.
RI.BAL.TA, *s.f.,* limelight, row of footlights.
RI.BAN.CEI.RA, *s.f.,* ravine, cliff, bank.
RI.BEI.RÃO, *s.m.,* stream, large brook.
RI.BEI.RO, *s.m.,* rivulet, streamlet, brook, creek.
RI.CA.ÇO, *s.m.,* moneygrubber.
RI.CO, *adj.,* rich, wealthy, abundant, fertile.
RI.DI.CU.LA.RI.ZA.ÇÃO, *s.f.,* satire, act of exciting laughter.
RI.DI.CU.LA.RI.ZAR, *v.,* to ridicule, to make fun of, to mock.
RI.DÍ.CU.LO, *adj.,* ridiculous, comic, foolish.
RI.FA, *s.f.,* raffle.
RI.FAR, *v.,* to raffle.
RI.FLE, *s.m.,* rifle, carbine, gun.
RI.GI.DEZ, *s.f.,* rigidity, severity, stiffness.
RÍ.GI.DO, *adj.,* rigid, stiff, severe, austere.
RI.GOR, *s.m.,* rigidity, severity, strictness, hardness.
RI.GO.RO.SO, *adj.,* rigorous, inflexible, rigid, severe, strict.
RI.JE.ZA, *s.f.,* hardness, rigidness.
RI.JO, *adj.,* rigid, hard, inflexible, solid, firm.
RIM, *s.m.,* kidney.

RI.MA, *s.f.*, rhyme.
RI.MA.DO, *adj.*, rhymed, versified.
RI.MAR, *v.*, to rhyme, to versify.
RIN.CÃO, *s.m.*, hidden corner, sylvan retreat, nook.
RIN.GUE, *s.m.*, ring.
RI.NO.CE.RON.TE, *s.m.*, rhinoceros.
RIO, *s.m.*, river, stream, water, watercourse.
RI.QUE.ZA, *s.f.*, wealth, riches, abundance, money.
RIR, *v.*, to laugh, to smile.
RI.SA.DA, *s.f.*, loud laughter, laughter, laughing.
RIS.CAR, *v.*, to scratch out, to rub out, to delete, to cross.
RIS.CO, *s.m.*, scratch, stroke, stripe, danger, hazard, risk.
RI.SO, *s.m.*, laughter, laughing, smile.
RI.SO.NHO, *adj.*, smiling, cheerful.
RI.SO.TO, *s.m.*, risotto.
RIS.PI.DEZ, *s.f.*, roughness, severity, sternness.
RÍS.PI.DO, *adj.*, harsh, rough, severe, stern.
RIT.MA.DO, *adj.*, rhythmic, cadenced.
RIT.MAR, *v.*, to give rhythm to, to cadence.
RIT.MO, *s.m.*, rhythm, cadence.
RI.TO, *s.m.*, ceremony, rite, cult, sect.
RI.TU.AL, *s.m.*, ritual, cerimonial; *adj.*, ritual.
RI.TU.A.LIS.MO, *s.m.*, ritualism.
RI.VAL, *s.2 gen.*, rival, antagonist, opponent.
RI.VA.LI.DA.DE, *s.f.*, rivalry, rivalship, antagonism.
RI.VA.LI.ZAR, *v.*, to rival, to compete, to dispute, to oppose.
RI.XA, *s.f.*, quarrel, dispute, wrangle, brawl.
RI.XAR, *v.*, to quarrel, to wrangle.
RI.ZI.CUL.TOR, *s.m.*, rice grower, rice planter.
RI.ZI.CUL.TU.RA, *s.f.*, rice-growing, rice-planting.
RO.BUS.TE.CER, *v.*, to make strong, to strengthen, to consolidate.
RO.BUS.TEZ, *s.f.*, robustness, burliness.
RO.BUS.TO, *adj.*, robust, strong, vigorous.
RO.ÇAR, *v.*, to clear the land of underwood, to graze.
RO.CHA, *s.f.*, rock, stone.
RO.CHE.DO, *s.m.*, steep, rugged rock, rock, crag.
RO.DA, *s.f.*, wheel, circle, circumference, social group, clique.
RO.DA.DA, *s.f.*, round (of drinks, cards).
RO.DA.PÉ, *s.m.*, footer, skirting board, baseboard.
RO.DAR, *v.*, to roll, to twirl, to gyrate.
RO.DE.AR, *v.*, to surround, to encircle, to circle.
RO.DEI.O, *s.m.*, surrounding, circumlocution, evasion.
RO.DÍ.ZIO, *s.m.*, shift, turn, relay work.
RO.DO, *s.m.*, squeegee, rake, wooden scraper.
RO.DO.PI.AR, *v.*, to whirl about, to twirl, to spin, to circle.
RO.DO.VIA, *s.f.*, highway.
RO.DO.VI.Á.RIO, *adj.*, of, pertaining to or relative to a highway.
RO.E.DOR, *s.m.*, rodent, rodents; *adj.*, rodent.
RO.ER, *v.*, to gnaw, to nibble, to bite, to chew, to corrode.
RO.GA.DOR, *s.m.*, supplicant, intercessor, mediator.
RO.GAR, *v.*, to implore, to supplicate, to beg, to pray for.
RO.Í.DO, *adj.*, corroded, gnawed.
RO.JÃO, *s.m.*, rocket.
ROL, *s.m.*, roll, list, register, file, scroll.
RO.LA, *s.f.*, turtle dove.
RO.LA.MEN.TO, *s.m.*, rolling, welter, bearing.
RO.LAN.TE, *adj.*, rolling, rotating, revolving.
RO.LAR, *v.*, to roll, to move in circle, to tumble.
ROL.DA.NA, *s.f.*, pulley.
RO.LE.TA, *s.f.*, roulette.
RO.LHA, *s.f.*, cork, stopper.
RO.LO, *s.m.*, cylinder, roll, road roller.
RO.MÃ, *s.f.*, pomegranate.
RO.MAN.CE, *s.m.*, novel, fiction, love affair, tale, fable.
RO.MAN.CIS.TA, *s.2 gen.*, romancist, novelist.
RO.MÂ.NI.CO, *adj.*, Romanic.
RO.MA.NO, *adj., s.m.*, Roman.
RO.MÂN.TI.CO, *adj.*, Romantic, dreamy.
RO.MAN.TIS.MO, *s.m.*, romanticism, romantism.

ROMANTIZAR / RUINDADE

RO.MAN.TI.ZAR, *v.*, to romanticize.
RO.MA.RI.A, *s.f.*, pilgrimage, peregrination, procession.
ROM.BO, *s.m.*, hole, gap, rift, split.
RO.MEI.RO, *s.m.*, pilgrim, peregrinator.
RO.ME.NO, *adj.*, *s.m.*, Rumanian.
ROM.PAN.TE, *s.m.*, fury, impetuosity, vehemence; *adj.*, arrogant, proud.
ROM.PER, *v.*, to break, to break up, to destroy, to tear.
ROM.PI.MEN.TO, *s.m.*, breaking, disruption, split, rupture.
RON.CAR, *v.*, to snore.
RON.CO, *s.m.*, snore, snoring.
RON.DA, *s.f.*, patrol, rounds, prowl.
RON.DAR, *v.*, to round, to watch, to walk around.
RO.SA, *s.f.*, rose; *adj.*, rosy, rose-coloured, pink.
RO.SÁ.CEA, *s.f.*, rosette, plant of the rose family.
RO.SA.DO, *adj.*, rose-coloured, rosy, rosate.
RO.SÁ.RIO, *s.m.*, rosary.
ROS.BI.FE, *s.m.*, roast-beef.
ROS.CA, *s.f.*, thread, screw thread, spiral.
RO.SEI.RA, *s.f.*, rosebush.
RO.SEI.RAL, *s.m.*, rosary, rosetum.
RÓ.SEO, *adj.*, rose, rose-coloured.
ROS.MA.NI.NHO, *s.m.*, rosemary.
ROS.NAR, *v.*, to snarl, to growl.
ROS.QUI.NHA, *s.f.*, ring-shaped cooky.
ROS.TO, *s.m.*, face, visage, physiognomy.
RO.TA, *s.f.*, direction, route, course, path.
RO.TA.ÇÃO, *s.f.*, rotation, gyration, rolling.
RO.TA.TI.VA, *s.f.*, rotary press.
RO.TA.TI.VO, *adj.*, rotative, rotational, rotary.
RO.TEI.RO, *s.m.*, itinerary, route, schedule, road-book, norm.
RO.TI.NA, *s.f.*, routine, custom, practice, rut.
RO.TI.NEI.RO, *adj.*, routine, routinish, habitual, customary.
RO.TO, *adj.*, ragged, ratty, shabby.
RÓ.TU.LA, *s.f.*, knee-cap, rotula, grating.
RO.TU.LA.ÇÃO, *s.f.*, labelling.
RO.TU.LAR, *v.*, to label, to mark, to designate.
RÓ.TU.LO, *s.m.*, label, mark, ticket.
RO.TUN.DO, *adj.*, rotund, round, roundish.

ROU.BA.DO, *adj.*, robbed, stolen, despoiled.
ROU.BA.LHEI.RA, *s.f.*, robbery.
ROU.BAR, *v.*, to rob, to steal, to plunder, to hold up.
ROU.BO, *s.m.*, robbery, theft, loot.
ROU.CO, *adj.*, hoarse, raucous, harsh, husky.
ROU.PA, *s.f.*, clothes, clothing, vesture, wear, dress, garment; **ROUPA-BRANCA**, body linen.
ROU.PÃO, *s.m.*, dressing gown, bathing gown.
ROU.PEI.RO, *s.m.*, wardrobe, clothes closet.
ROU.XI.NOL, *s.m.*, nightingale.
RO.XE.AR, *v.*, to purple.
RO.XO, *s.m.*, purple hue; *adj.*, violet, purple.
RU.A, *s.f.*, street, way; **RUA!**, interj., get out!, out you go!
RU.BÉO.LA, *s.f.*, rubeola.
RU.BI, *s.m.*, ruby.
RU.BI.FI.CAR, *v.*, to rubify.
RU.BOR, *s.m.*, redness, shame, modesty.
RU.BO.RI.ZA.ÇÃO, *s.f.*, blushing.
RU.BO.RI.ZAR, *v.*, to redden, to rubify, to become red.
RU.BRI.CA, *s.f.*, rubric, initials, sign.
RU.BRI.CAR, *v.*, to rubricate, to countersign.
RU.BRO, *adj.*, rouge, ruby-red, rubious.
RU.DE, *adj.*, rude, uncultivated, indelicate, rough, harsh.
RU.DEZ, *s.f.*, rudeness, crudity, roughness.
RU.DI.MEN.TAR, *adj.*, rudimental.
RU.DI.MEN.TO, *s.m.*, rudiment, element, beginning.
RU.E.LA, *s.f.*, bystreet, alley.
RU.FI.ÃO, *s.m.*, ruffian, hooligan.
RU.GA, *s.f.*, wrinkle, corrugation.
RU.GI.DO, *s.m.*, roar, bellow, growl.
RU.GIR, *v.*, to bellow, to roar.
RU.GO.SO, *adj.*, rugose, rugous.
RU.Í.DO, *s.m.*, noise, sound, din, hubbub, uproar, clamour, tumult, row.
RU.I.DO.SO, *adj.*, noisy, loud, boisterous.
RU.IM, *adj.*, bad, ill, miserable, wicked.
RU.Í.NA, *s.f.*, ruin, wreck, collapse, downfall, deterioration.
RU.IN.DA.DE, *s.f.*, wickedness.

RU.IR, *v.*, to collapse, to fall into ruins, to crash.
RUI.VO, *s.m.*, redhead; *adj.*, red-haired, rufous.
RUM, *s.m.*, rum.
RU.MAR, *v.*, to steer to, to head for, to set a course.
RU.MI.NAN.TE, *s.2 gen.*, ruminant, ruminator.
RU.MI.NAR, *v.*, to ruminate, to chew the cud.
RU.MO, *s.m.*, route, course, direction, setting, set.
RU.MOR, *s.m.*, rumour, gossip, din, murmur.
RU.MO.RE.JAR, *v.*, to rustle, to buzz, to murmur.
RU.MO.RO.SO, *adj.*, loud, noisy, clamorous.
RUP.TU.RA, *s.f.*, breakage, rupture, breach, disruption.
RU.RAL, *adj.*, rural, rustic.
RU.RA.LIS.MO, *s.m.*, ruralism.
RU.RA.LIS.TA, *s.2 gen.*, ruralist.
RUS.GA, *s.f.*, noise, confusion, brawl, row.
RUS.GUEN.TO, *adj.*, quarrelsome, noisy.
RÚS.SIA, *s.f.*, Russia.
RUS.SI.FI.CAR, *v.*, to Russify, Russianize.
RUS.SO, *adj., s.m.*, Russian.
RUS.TI.CI.DA.DE, *s.f.*, rusticity, rusticalness.
RÚS.TI.CO, *adj.*, rustic, rural, bucolic, rough.
RU.TI.LAR, *v.*, to rutilate, to shine, to glitter, to gleam.

S

S, *s.m.*, eighteenth letter of the Portuguese alphabet.
SÃ, *adj. fem.*, healthy
SÁ.BA.DO, *s.m.*, Saturday.
SA.BÃO, *s.m.*, soap; **SABÃO DE COCO**, coconut soap.
SA.BE.DOR, *s.m.*, learned person; *adj.*, learned, knowing.
SA.BE.DO.RI.A, *s.f.*, wisdom, knowledge.
SA.BER, *s.m.*, knowledge; learning, erudition, wisdom.
SA.BER, *v.*, to know, to be aware or cognizant of, to recognize, to identify.
SA.BI.Á, *s.m.*, song-thrush.
SA.BI.CHÃO, *s.m.*, smarty, wise-guy, egghead; *adj.*, clever, learned, erudite.
SA.BI.DO, *adj.*, known, wise, intelligent, learned.
SÁ.BIO, *s.m.*, scientist, wise, *adj.*, learned, erudite, scholarly.
SA.BO.NE.TE, *s.m.*, toilet soap.
SA.BO.NE.TEI.RA, *s.f.*, soap dish, soap bowl.
SA.BOR, *s.m.*, flavor, taste, savour.
SA.BO.RE.AR, *v.*, to taste, to relish, to savour.
SA.BO.RO.SO, *adj.*, savoury, tasty, palatable.
SA.BO.TA.GEM, *s.f.*, sabotage, intentional damage.
SA.BO.TAR, *v.*, to sabote, to sabotage, to wreck, to sap.
SA.BU.GO, *s.m.*, slough, pith.
SA.CA, *s.f.*, bag, surf.
SA.CA.DA, *s.f.*, balcony, terrace.
SA.CAR, *v.*, to draw out, to tear out, to pull out, to extract, to drag.
SA.CA.RI.NA, *s.f.*, saccharin.
SA.CA-RO.LHAS, *s.m.*, corkscrew.
SA.CER.DÓ.CIO, *s.m.*, priesthood.
SA.CER.DO.TAL, *adj.*, sacerdotal, priestly.
SA.CER.DO.TE, *s.m.*, priest, clergyman.
SA.CER.DO.TI.SA, *s.f.*, priestess.
SA.CI.AR, *v.*, to satiate, to appease, to satisfy, to gratify, to satisfy.
SA.CIE.DA.DE, *s.f.*, satiety.
SA.CO, *s.m.*, sack, bag, ball, sac, sackcloth.
SA.CO.LA, *s.f.*, wallet, knapsack.
SA.CRA.MEN.TO, *s.m.*, sacrament.
SA.CRI.FI.CAR, *v.*, to sacrifice, to offer.
SA.CRI.FÍ.CIO, *s.m.*, sacrifice, self-denial, immolation.
SA.CRI.LÉ.GIO, *s.m.*, sacrilege, profanation, irreverence.
SA.CRIS.TÃO, *s.m.*, sacristan, sexton.
SA.CRO, *s.m.*, sacrum; *adj.*, holy, sacred, venerable.
SA.CU.DI.DA, *s.f.*, shake, toss, tossing, shaking.
SA.CU.DI.DO, *adj.*, shaken, jerked, quick, agile.
SA.CU.DIR, *v.*, to shake, to shake off, to move, to rock, to vibrate.
SÁ.DI.CO, *s.m.*, sadist; *adj.*, sadistic.
SA.DI.O, *adj.*, healthy, healthful, sound.
SA.DIS.MO, *s.m.*, sadism.
SA.FA.DE.ZA, *s.f.*, knavishness, rascality, baseness.
SA.FA.DO, *s.m.*, trickster, rogue; *adj.*, shameless, immoral, roguish.
SA.FAR, *v.*, to take away, to wear out, to steal.
SA.FÁ.RI, *s.m.*, safari.
SA.FI.RA, *s.f.*, sapphire.
SA.FRA, *s.f.*, crop, harvest.
SA.GA, *s.f.*, saga, tale, story.
SA.GA.CI.DA.DE, *s.f.*, sagacity, perspicacity.
SA.GAZ, *adj.*, sagacious, astute, intelligent, apprehensive.
SA.GRA.ÇÃO, *s.f.*, consecration.
SA.GRA.DO, *adj.*, sacred, holy, hallowed.
SA.GRAR, *v.*, to consecrate, to sanctify.
SA.GUÃO, *s.m.*, entrance-hall, lobby, vestibule.
SAI.A, *s.f.*, skirt.

SAI.BRO, *s.m.*, gross sand.
SA.Í.DA, *s.f.*, departure, output, exit, check up.
SA.IR, *v.*, to go, to come or step out, to quit, to leave.
SAL, *s.m.*, salt.
SA.LA, *s.f.*, room, saloon, hall.
SA.LA.DA, *s.f.*, salad, mess, confusion; **SALADA DE FRUTAS**, fruit salad.
SA.LA.DEI.RA, *s.f.*, salad dish.
SA.LA.ME, *s.m.*, salami, sausage.
SA.LÃO, *s.m.*, saloon, salon, ball-room.
SA.LÁ.RIO, *s.m.*, salary, wages.
SAL.DAR, *v.*, to liquidate, to pay.
SAL.DO, *s.m.*, balance, remainder.
SA.LEI.RO, *s.m.*, salt-cellar, salt-shaker.
SA.LE.TA, *s.f.*, small hall, sitting-room.
SAL.GA.DI.NHOS, *s.m.*, pl., appetizers.
SAL.GA.DO, *adj.*, salted, salty.
SAL.GAR, *v.*, to salt, to cure.
SAL.GUEI.RO, *s.m.*, willow.
SA.LI.ÊN.CIA, *s.f.*, salience, prominence.
SA.LI.EN.TAR, *v.*, to point out, to accentuate, to emphasize, to jut out.
SA.LI.EN.TE, *adj.*, salient, prominent.
SA.LI.NO, *adj.*, saline, salt.
SA.LI.TRE, *s.m.*, salpettre, nitre.
SA.LI.VA, *s.f.*, spittle, saliva.
SA.LI.VAR, *v.*, to salivate, to drivel.
SAL.MÃO, *s.m.*, salmon.
SAL.MO, *s.m.*, psalm.
SAL.MOU.RA, *s.f.*, brine, pickle, reproof.
SAL.PI.CAR, *v.*, to besprinkle, splash.
SAL.PI.CO, *s.m.*, sprinkle, splash, speck.
SAL.SA, *s.f.*, garden parsley, sharp sauce.
SAL.SI.CHA, *s.f.*, sausage.
SAL.TAR, *v.*, to leap, to jump, to skip, to spring, to bound.
SAL.TE.A.DOR, *s.m.*, bandit, brigant, footpad.
SAL.TE.AR, *v.*, to assault, to rob.
SAL.TI.CAR, *v.*, to hop, to jump, to digress.
SAL.TO, *s.m.*, leap, bound, hop, jump, vault; shoe heel.
SA.LU.BRE, *adj.*, salutary, salubrious.
SA.LU.TAR, *adj.*, salutary, profitable, healthful.
SAL.VA, *s.f.*, salvia, sage.
SAL.VA.ÇÃO, *s.f.*, salvation, salvage.
SAL.VA.DOR, *s.m.*, savior, rescuer, deliverer, redeemer.
SAL.VA.GUAR.DA, *s.f.*, safeguard, protection.
SAL.VA.MEN.TO, *s.m.*, salvation, rescue.
SAL.VAR, *v.*, to save, to rescue, to free, to deliver.
SAL.VA-VI.DAS, *s.m.*, life-saver, life-belt.
SAL.VE!, *interj.*, hail!
SAL.VO, *adj.*, safe, unhurt, secure, unmolested; *prep.*, save, except, unless.
SA.MAM.BAI.A, *s.f.*, fern.
SA.MA.RI.TA.NO, *adj.*, *s.m.*, Samaritan.
SAM.BA, *s.m.*, samba.
SA.NAR, *v.*, to cure, to heal.
SA.NA.TÓ.RIO, *s.m.*, sanatorium, health resort.
SAN.ÇÃO, *s.f.*, sanction, ratification, decree.
SAN.CIO.NA.DO, *adj.*, sanctioned.
SAN.CIO.NAR, *v.*, to sanction, to confirm, to approbate.
SAN.DÁ.LIA, *s.f.*, sandal.
SAN.DU.Í.CHE, *s.m.*, sandwich.
SA.NEA.MEN.TO, *s.m.*, sanitation, cleaning.
SA.NE.AR, *v.*, to sanitate, to clean.
SAN.FO.NA, *s.f.*, accordion, hurdy-gurdy.
SAN.GRAR, *v.*, to bleed, to open a vein.
SAN.GREN.TO, *adj.*, bloody, sanguinary.
SAN.GRI.A, *s.f.*, bleeding, sangria.
SAN.GUE, *s.m.*, blood; race, lineage.
SAN.GUES.SU.GA, *s.f.*, leech, bloodsucking worm.
SAN.GUI.NÁ.RIO, *adj.*, sanguinary.
SAN.GUÍ.NEO, *adj.*, sanguine, sanguineous.
SA.NHA, *s.f.*, wrath, fury, rage.
SA.NI.DA.DE, *s.f.*, sanity, sanitation, hygiene.
SA.NI.TÁ.RIO, *s.m.*, toilet, *adj.*, sanitary.
SÂNS.CRI.TO, *s.m.*, Sanskrit.
SAN.TI.DA.DE, *s.f.*, holiness, sanctity.
SAN.TI.FI.CA.DO, *adj.*, sanctified, blessed, sacred.
SAN.TI.FI.CAR, *v.*, to sanctify, to hallow, to glorify.
SAN.TO, *s.m.*, saint; *adj.*, saint, saintly, holy, pure; **DIA DE TODOS OS SANTOS**, All

Saints'Day.
SAN.TU.Á.RIO, *s.m.*, sanctuary, a holy place, temple, refuge.
SÃO, *s.m.*, saint; *adj.*, sound, healthy, sane, robust.
SA.PA, *s.f.*, spade, shovel.
SA.PA.TA.RI.A, *s.f.*, shoe store, shoemaking.
SA.PA.TE.AR, *v.*, to tap-dance.
SA.PA.TEI.RA, *s.f.*, shoe closet.
SA.PA.TEI.RO, *s.m.*, shoemaker.
SA.PA.TO, s.m. shoe.
SA.PE.CA, *s.f.*, flirt, coquette.
SA.PO, *s.m.*, toad.
SA.PO.NÁ.CEO, *adj.*, saponaceous.
SA.PO.NI.FI.CAR, *v.*, to saponify.
SA.QUE, *s.m.*, draw, drawing, service, bill; sack, robbery.
SA.QUEA.DOR, *s.m.*, plunderer, pillager.
SA.QUE.AR, *v.*, to sack, to plunder, to pillage, to devastate.
SA.RA.DO, *adj.*, healed, cured.
SA.RAI.VA, *s.f.*, hail, hailstone.
SA.RAM.PO, *s.m.*, measles.
SA.RAR, *v.*, to heal, to cure, to recover.
SA.RAU, *s.m.*, soirée.
SAR.CAS.MO, *s.m.*, sarcasm, bitter irony.
SAR.CÁS.TI.CO, *adj.*, sarcastic, ironical.
SAR.CÓ.FA.GO, *s.m.*, sarcophagus.
SAR.DA, *s.f.*, freckle.
SAR.DEN.TO, *adj.*, freckled, freckly.
SAR.DI.NHA, *s.f.*, sardine.
SAR.GEN.TO, *s.m.*, sergeant.
SAR.JA, *s.f.*, serge.
SAR.JE.TA, *s.f.*, gutter, drain.
SAR.NA, *s.f.*, scabies, itch.
SAR.NEN.TO, *adj.*, scabious, itchy, rancid.
SAR.RA.CE.NO, *adj., s.m.*, Saracen, Moor, Arab.
SAR.RA.FO, *s.m.*, lath, slat.
SA.TÃ, *s.m.*, Satan, devil, Lucifer.
SA.TA.NÁS, *s.m.*, Satan, the devil.
SA.TÂ.NI.CO, *adj.*, satanic.
SA.TÉ.LI.TE, *s.m.*, satellite.
SÁ.TI.RA, *s.f.*, satire, sarcasm, lampoon.
SA.TÍ.RI.CO, *adj.*, satiric.
SA.TI.RI.ZAR, *v.*, to satirize, to lampoon.

SA.TIS.FA.ÇÃO, *s.f.*, satisfaction, pleasure, pride, explanation, compensation.
SA.TIS.FA.TÓ.RIO, *adj.*, satisfactory, satisfying, sufficient.
SA.TIS.FA.ZER, *v.*, to satisfy, to please, to satiate.
SA.TIS.FEI.TO, *adj.*, satisfied, content, contented, happy.
SA.TU.RA.ÇÃO, *s.f.*, saturation.
SA.TU.RA.DO, *adj.*, saturated, intense, deep.
SA.TU.RAR, *v.*, to saturate, to soak, to impregnate, to satiate.
SA.TUR.NO, *s.m.*, Saturn.
SAU.DA.ÇÃO, *s.f.*, salutation, greeting, welcome, salute.
SAU.DA.DE, *s.f.*, longing, yearning, nostalgia.
SAU.DAR, *v.*, to salute, to greet, to hail.
SAU.DÁ.VEL, *adj.*, sound, healthy, wholesome, salutary.
SA.Ú.DE, *s.f.*, health, soundness.
SAU.DO.SO, *adj.*, longing, yearning, ardent.
SÁU.RIO, *s.m.*, saurian.
SA.VA.NA, *s.f.*, savannah.
SA.XÃO, *adj., s.m.*, Saxon.
SA.XO.FO.NE, *s.m.*, saxophone.
SA.ZÃO, *s.f.*, season.
SA.ZO.NAR, *v.*, to season, to ripen, to mellow.
SE, *refl. pers. pron.*, himself, herself, itself, oneself, yourself, yourselves, themselves; *conj.*, if, whether, provided, in case that.
SÉ, *s.f.*, see, cathedral.
SE.A.RA, *s.f.*, cornfield, harvest.
SE.BO, *s.m.*, fat, tallow, suet.
SE.BO.SO, *adj.*, tallowish, tallowy.
SE.CA, *s.f.*, drought, dryness, aridity.
SE.CA.DOR, *s.m.*, dryer, desiccator.
SE.ÇÃO, *s.f.*, section, division, department, partition, (var. secção).
SE.CAR, *v.*, to dry, to drain, to wipe, to desiccate, to evaporate.
SE.CIO.NAR, *v.*, to section, to divide.
SE.CO, *adj.*, dry, arid, droughty.
SE.CRE.ÇÃO, *s.f.*, secretion.
SE.CRE.TA.RI.A, *s.f.*, secretaryship, bureau, office, secretariat, ministry.

SE.CRE.TÁ.RIA, *s.f.*, woman secretary.
SE.CRE.TÁ.RIO, *s.m.*, secretary, minister of state; confidant.
SE.CRE.TO, *adj.*, secret, private, hidden, occult.
SE.CU.LAR, *adj.*, lay, secular, archaic, profane.
SÉ.CU.LO, *s.m.*, century, secular life.
SE.CUN.DAR, *v.*, to second, to assist, to sustain, to aid.
SE.CUN.DÁ.RIO, *adj.*, secondary, subordinate, minor.
SE.DA, *s.f.*, silk; **BICHO-DA-SEDA**, silkworm.
SE.DA.TI.VO, *s.m.*, sedative, depressant; *adj.*, sedative.
SE.DE, *s.f.*, seat, headquarters, ground, place; dryness, thirst, thirstiness.
SE.DEN.TÁ.RIO, *adj.*, sedentary, stationary.
SE.DEN.TO, *adj.*, thirsty.
SE.DI.ÇÃO, *s.f.*, sedition, rebellion.
SE.DI.MEN.TAR, *adj.*, sedimentary, mothery.
SE.DI.MEN.TO, *s.m.*, sediment, settlings, lees.
SE.DO.SO, *adj.*, silken, silky; hairy.
SE.DU.ÇÃO, *s.f.*, seduction, seducement, temptation.
SE.DU.ZIR, *v.*, to seduce, to tempt, to mislead.
SEG.MEN.TAR, *v.*, to segment, to divide.
SEG.MEN.TO, *s.m.*, segment, section, division.
SE.GRE.DAR, *v.*, to confide, to tell in secret.
SE.GRE.DO, *s.m.*, secret, mistery, secrecy.
SE.GRE.GA.ÇÃO, *s.f.*, segregation, apartheid, separation.
SE.GRE.GAR, *v.*, to segregate, to secrete, to isolate.
SE.GUI.DA, *s.f.*, following, pursuing.
SE.GUI.DO, *adj.*, followed, continued, continuous.
SE.GUI.DOR, *s.m.*, follower, sectarian, adherent.
SE.GUI.MEN.TO, *s.m.*, following, pursuance.
SE.GUIN.TE, *s.m.*, the next, the following; *adj.*, next, following, subsequent.
SE.GUIR, *v.*, to follow, to pursue, to chase, to watch, to spy.
SE.GUN.DA-FEI.RA, *s.f.*, Monday.
SE.GUN.DO, *s.m.*, second; *adj.*, second, next, secondary; *adv.*, secondly.
SE.GU.RAN.ÇA, *s.f.*, security, certainty, assurance, safety, safeguard, insurance, sureness.
SE.GU.RAR, *v.*, to secure, to guard, to shield, to support, to hold, to catch, to guarantee.
SE.GU.RO, *s.m.*, insurance, security, guarantee; *adj.*, secure, safe, firm, steady, reliable.
SEI.O, *s.m.*, breast, bosom, tit, core.
SEIS, *num.*, six.
SEIS.CEN.TOS, *num.*, six hundred.
SEI.TA, *s.f.*, sect, faction.
SEI.VA, *s.f.*, sap, juice of a plant.
SEI.XO, *s.m.*, pebble, flint.
SE.LA, *s.f.*, saddle.
SE.LA.DO, *adj.*, stamped, sealed.
SE.LAR, *v.*, to stamp, to saddle, to seal.
SE.LE.ÇÃO, *s.f.*, selection.
SE.LE.CIO.NA.DO, *adj.*, eclectic.
SE.LE.CIO.NAR, *v.*, to select, to sort, to pick, to choose.
SE.LEI.RO, *s.m.*, saddler.
SE.LE.TO, *adj.*, select, selected, choice, picked, different.
SE.LIM, *s.m.*, saddle of a bicycle.
SE.LO, *s.m.*, seal, cachet, postage stamp, stamp.
SEL.VA, *s.f.*, jungle, forest.
SEL.VA.GEM, *s.m.*, a savage, rough fellow; *adj.*, savage, wild, rude, brutal.
SEM, *prep.*, without, lacking, wanting, less.
SE.MÁ.FO.RO, *s.m.*, semaphore, traffic light, ligths.
SE.MA.NA, *s.f.*, week; **FIM DE SEMANA**, week end.
SE.MA.NAL, *adj.*, weekly.
SE.MÂN.TI.CA, *s.f.*, semantics.
SEM.BLAN.TE, *s.f.*, face, look, visage, physiognomy.
SE.ME.AR, *v.*, to sow, to plant, to spread, to disseminate.
SE.ME.LHAN.ÇA, *s.f.*, likeness, resemblance, similarity.
SE.ME.LHAN.TE, *s.2 gen.*, fellow creature; *adj.*, analogous, like, similar.
SE.ME.LHAR, *v.*, to resemble, to be similar.
SÊ.MEN, *s.m.*, semen, sperm.

SE.MEN.TE, *s.f.*, seed, semen, sperm.
SE.MES.TRE, *s.m.*, semester, half-year; *adj.*, semestral.
SE.MI.CIR.CU.LAR, *adj.*, semicircular.
SE.MI.CÍR.CU.LO, *s.m.*, semicircle.
SE.MI.DEUS, *s.m.*, demigod.
SE.MI.MOR.TO, *adj.*, half dead, torpid.
SE.MI.NÁ.RIO, *s.m.*, seminar, seminary.
SE.MI.NA.RIS.TA, *s.m.*, seminarist.
SE.MI.NU, *adj.*, half-naked.
SE.MI.TA, *adj.*, *s.m.*, Semire, *adj.*, Semitic.
SEM.PRE, *adv.*, always, ever, constantly.
SEM-VER.GO.NHA, *adj.*, shameless.
SE.NA.DO, *s.m.*, senate.
SE.NA.DOR, *s.m.*, senator.
SE.NÃO, *s.m.*, fault, defect; *adv.*, except, save, else, otherwise; *conj.*, but, saving.
SEN.DA, *s.f.*, narrow road, footpath.
SE.NHA, *s.f.*, password, signal.
SE.NHOR, *s.m.*, owner, proprietor, possessor, master, sir, mister, lord.
SE.NHO.RA, *s.f.*, lady, wife, housewife; **NOSSA SENHORA**, Our Lady.
SE.NHO.RIL, *adj.*, lordly, lordlike.
SE.NHO.RI.O, *s.m.*, landlord, lordship.
SE.NHO.RI.TA, *s.f.*, miss.
SE.NIL, *adj.*, old, senile.
SE.NI.LI.DA.DE, *s.f.*, senility, old age.
SÊ.NIOR, *s.m.*, senior, older; *adj.*, senior, older, elder.
SEN.SA.ÇÃO, *s.f.*, sensation.
SEN.SA.CIO.NAL, *adj.*, sensational, remarkable.
SEN.SA.TEZ, *s.f.*, sensibleness, judiciousness, understanding.
SEN.SA.TO, *adj.*, judicious, sensible, rational.
SEN.SI.BI.LI.DA.DE, *s.f.*, sensibility, sensitiveness.
SEN.SI.BI.LI.ZAR, *v.*, to sensitize, to penetrate, to touch.
SEN.SI.TI.VO, *adj.*, sensitive, sensory.
SEN.SÍ.VEL, *adj.*, sensitive.
SEN.SO, *s.m.*, sense, sagacity, keenness, wisdom, reasoning, meaning, understanding, signification.
SEN.SOR, *s.m.*, sensor.

SEN.SO.RI.AL, *adj.*, sensorial.
SEN.SU.AL, *adj.*, sensual, luxurious, voluptuous, libidinous.
SEN.SUA.LI.DA.DE, *s.f.*, sensuality, fleshlines.
SEN.SUA.LIS.MO, *s.m.*, sensualism.
SEN.TAR, *v.*, to seat; **SENTAR-SE**, to seat down, to take a seat.
SEN.TEN.ÇA, *s.f.*, sentence, proverb, maxim, verdict, decision, a judicial decision.
SEN.TEN.CI.AR, *v.*, to judge, to convict.
SEN.TI.DO, *s.m.*, each of the five senses, feeling, meaning, sense; *adj.*, sensible, sorry, sad, grieved.
SEN.TI.MEN.TAL, *adj.*, sentimental, emotional, romantic.
SEN.TI.MEN.TO, *s.m.*, sentiment, feeling, emotion, perception, passion.
SEN.TI.NE.LA, *s.f.*, sentinel, watchman, guard.
SEN.TIR, *v.*, to feel, to experience, to suffer, to think, to be moved.
SEN.ZA.LA, *s.f.*, slave house.
SE.PA.RA.ÇÃO, *s.f.*, separation, dissociation, division.
SE.PA.RA.DO, *adj.*, separate, severed, disunited.
SE.PA.RAR, *v.*, to separate, to disconnect, to disunite, to sever.
SEP.TI.CE.MI.A, *s.f.*, septicemia.
SEP.TUA.GÉ.SI.MO, *num.*, seventieth.
SE.PUL.CRO, *s.m.*, sepulchre, grave, tomb.
SE.PUL.TA.MEN.TO, *s.m.*, burial, funeral, sepulture.
SE.PUL.TAR, *v.*, to bury, to inhumate, to sepulchre.
SE.PUL.TU.RA, *s.f.*, sepulture, grave, tomb, sepulchre.
SE.QUAZ, *adj.*, sequacious, following, adherent.
SE.QUÊN.CIA, *s.f.*, sequence, continuation, continuity.
SE.QUER, *adv.*, at least, even, not even, so much as.
SE.QUES.TRAR, *v.*, to sequestrate, to confiscate, to kidnap.
SE.QUES.TRO, *s.m.*, sequestration, kidnapping.
SE.QUI.O.SO, *adj.*, arid, dry, desirous, avid.
SÉ.QUI.TO, *s.m.*, suite, train, attendance.

SER, *s.m.*, being, creature, existence, life, substance; *v.*, to be, to exist, to become, to happen, to belong.
SE.RA.FIM, *s.m.*, seraph.
SE.RÃO, *s.m.*, overtime, soirée.
SE.REI.A, *s.f.*, siren, mermaid.
SE.RE.NAR, *v.*, to serene, to calm, to pacify.
SE.RE.NA.TA, *s.f.*, serenade.
SE.RE.NI.DA.DE, *s.f.*, serenity, tranquility, calmness.
SE.RE.NO, *s.m.*, serene, dew, mist; *adj.*, serene, cheerful, placid, tranquil.
SE.RES.TA, *s.f.*, serenade.
SE.RI.AL, *adj.*, serial.
SÉ.RIE, *s.f.*, series, row, set, continuation, succession.
SE.RIE.DA.DE, *s.f.*, seriousness, integrity, sobriety.
SE.RIN.GA, *s.f.*, syringe, squirt.
SE.RIN.GUEI.RA, *s.f.*, rubber tree.
SÉ.RIO, *adj.*, serious, grave, reliable, earnest.
SER.MÃO, *s.m.*, discourse, sermon, preach, telling-off.
SER.PEN.TE, *s.f.*, serpent, snake.
SER.PEN.TE.AR, *v.*, to coil.
SER.PEN.TI.NA, *s.f.*, coil, worm, serpentin.
SER.RA, *s.f.*, saw, mountain ridge, mountain range, elevation.
SER.RA.GEM, *s.f.*, sawdust, scobs.
SER.RA.LHEI.RO, *s.m.*, locksmith.
SER.RAR, *v.*, to saw.
SER.RA.RIA, *s.f.*, sawframe, sawmill.
SER.RO.TE, *s.m.*, hand-saw.
SER.TA.NE.JO, *s.m.*, inlander, backwoodsman; *adj.*, rude, rough.
SER.TÃO, *s.m.*, interior, midland part, hinterland, heart of the country.
SER.VEN.TE, *s.2 gen.*, servant, attendant, helper, jobber; *adj.*, serving, attendant.
SER.VEN.TIA, *s.f.*, usefulness, utility, service.
SER.VI.ÇO, *s.m.*, service, work, employment, job, performance.
SER.VI.DÃO, *s.f.*, servitude, slavery, vassalage, service.
SER.VI.DO, *adj.*, served, used.
SER.VI.DOR, *s.m.*, servant, server, public functionary; *adj.*, attendant, serving.
SER.VIL, *adj.*, servile, sequacious, slavish.
SER.VI.LIS.MO, *s.m.*, servility, servileness.
SER.VIR, *v.*, to serve, to wait, to supply, to attend on, to help, to benefit.
SER.VÍ.VEL, *adj.*, serviceable.
SER.VO, *s.m.*, servant, slave, drudge.
SES.SÃO, *s.f.*, session, assembly.
SES.SEN.TA, *num.*, sixty.
SES.TA, *s.f.*, siesta.
SE.TA, *s.f.*, arrow, dart, pointer.
SE.TE, *num.*, the number seven, seven.
SE.TE.CEN.TOS, *num.*, seven hundred.
SE.TEM.BRO, *s.m.*, September.
SE.TEN.TA, *num.*, seventy.
SE.TEN.TRIO.NAL, *adj.*, northern, septentrional.
SÉ.TI.MO, *s.m.*, seventh part; *adj.*, seventh.
SE.TOR, *s.m.*, sector, section.
SE.TUA.GE.NÁ.RIO, *s.m.*, septuagenarian; *adj.*, septuagenary.
SEU, *pron.*, his, her, its, your, their, theirs, yours, hers.
SE.VE.RI.DA.DE, *s.f.*, severity, rigidity, harshness, rigorousness.
SE.VE.RO, *adj.*, severe, austere, rigorous, harsh, bitter, grave, accurate, exact.
SE.VÍ.CIAS, *s.f.*, ill-treatment, inhumanity.
SE.XA.GE.NÁ.RIO, *s.m.*, sexagenarian.
SE.XA.GÉ.SI.MO, *num.*, sixtieth.
SE.XO, *s.m.*, sex; **FAZER SEXO**, have sex; **AMBOS OS SEXOS**, man and woman.
SEX.TA-FEI.RA, *s.f.*, Friday; **SEXTA-FEIRA SANTA**, Good Friday.
SEX.TO, *s.m.*, sixth part; *adj.*, sixth.
SE.XU.AL, *adj.*, sexual.
SI, *s.m.* (mus.), si, B; *pron.*, himself, herself, itself, oneself, yourself, yourselves, themselves.
SIA.MÊS, *s.m.*, Siamese.
SI.BE.RI.A.NO, *adj., s.m.*, Siberian.
SI.BI.LAR, *v.*, to sibilate, to hiss, to whistle.
SI.BI.LO, *s.m.*, sibilation, whistle, zip.
SI.CÁ.RIO, *s.m.*, sicarian, criminal.

SI.CI.LI.A.NO, *adj.*, *s.m.*, Sicilian.
SIDA, *s.f.*, AIDS, (Acquired Immune Deficiency Syndrome).
SI.DE.RAL, *adj.*, sideral, astral.
SI.DE.RUR.GI.A, *s.f.*, siderurgy, metallurgy, ironworks.
SI.DE.RÚR.GI.CO, *adj.*, metallurgic, metallurgical, siderurgic.
SI.DRA, *s.f.*, cider, apple-wine.
SI.FÃO, *s.m.*, siphon, syphon.
SÍ.FI.LIS, *s.f.*, syphilis, lues.
SI.GI.LO, *s.m.*, seal, sigil, secret, signet.
SI.GLA, *s.f.*, abbreviature.
SIG.NA.TÁ.RIO, *s.m.*, signatory, signer.
SIG.NI.FI.CA.ÇÃO, *s.f.*, signification, significance.
SIG.NI.FI.CA.DO, *s.m.*, meaning, sense.
SIG.NI.FI.CAN.TE, *adj.*, significant.
SIG.NI.FI.CAR, *v.*, to signify, to mean, to denote, to imply.
SIG.NI.FI.CA.TI.VO, *adj.*, significative, significant.
SIG.NO, *s.m.*, sign.
SÍ.LA.BA, *s.f.*, syllable.
SI.LA.BAR, *v.*, to syllable, to syllabize.
SI.LEN.CI.AR, *v.*, to silence, to keep silent, to hush.
SI.LÊN.CIO, *s.m.*, silence, stillness, calm, quiet.
SI.LEN.CI.O.SO, *adj.*, silent, speechless, still, quiet, noiseless, voiceless, mute.
SI.LHU.E.TA, *s.f.*, silhouette, profile.
SÍ.LI.CA, *s.f.*, silica, silex.
SI.LO, *s.m.*, silo, garner.
SI.LO.GIS.MO, *s.m.*, syllogism.
SIL.VAR, *v.*, to whistle, to sibilate.
SIL.VES.TRE, *adj.*, silvan, savage, woodsy.
SIL.VÍ.CO.LA, *s.2 gen.*, savage, barbarian, aborigine.
SIL.VO, *s.m.*, whistle, hiss.
SIM, *adv.*, yes, yea, all right, absolutely, exactly.
SIM.BI.O.SE, *s.f.*, symbiosis.
SIM.BÓ.LI.CO, *adj.*, symbolic, symbolical.
SIM.BO.LI.ZAR, *v.*, to symbolize, to symbol, to typify.
SÍM.BO.LO, *s.m.*, symbol, figure, image, token, sign.
SI.ME.TRI.A, *s.f.*, symmetry, harmony, proportion.
SI.MÉ.TRI.CO, *adj.*, symmetric, harmonious.
SI.MI.LAR, *adj.*, similar, alike, uniform.
SI.MI.LA.RI.DA.DE, *s.f.*, similarity, likeness, resemblance.
SÍ.MIO, *s.m.*, simian, monkey, ape.
SIM.PA.TI.A, *s.f.*, sympathy, affinity, compatibility, appeal.
SIM.PÁ.TI.CO, *adj.*, friendly, helpful, nice, sympathetic.
SIM.PA.TI.ZAR, *v.*, to like, to sympathize, to feel an affection.
SIM.PLES, *adj.*, simple, plain, clear, ingenuous, unadorned, evident, clear.
SIM.PLI.CI.DA.DE, *s.f.*, simplicity, naturalness.
SIM.PLI.FI.CA.ÇÃO, *s.f.*, simplification, facilitation.
SIM.PLI.FI.CAR, *v.*, to simplify, to facilitate, to clarify.
SIM.PLÓ.RIO, *adj.*, simpleton, simple-minded.
SIM.PÓ.SIO, *s.m.*, symposium, feast.
SI.MU.LA.ÇÃO, *s.f.*, simulation, pretense.
SI.MU.LA.DO, *adj.*, simulate, mock, sham, false.
SI.MU.LAR, *v.*, to simulate, to feign, to camouflage, to imitate.
SI.MUL.TÂ.NEO, *adj.*, simultaneous, synchronous.
SI.NA, *s.f.*, fate, destiny, flag.
SI.NA.GO.GA, *s.f.*, synagogue, Jewish temple.
SI.NAL, *s.m.*, signal, sign, mark, indication, signature, gesture.
SI.NAL DA CRUZ, *s.m.*, act of crossing.
SI.NA.LI.ZA.ÇÃO, *s.f.*, signalizing, traffic signs or signals.
SI.NA.LI.ZAR, *v.*, to signal, to telegraph, to mark.
SIN.CE.RI.DA.DE, *s.f.*, sincerity, frankness, openness.
SIN.CE.RO, *adj.*, sincere, frank, open, honest, truthful, simpled.
SÍN.CO.PE, *s.f.*, syncope, temporary loss of

SIN.CRO.NI.A, *s.f.*, synchronization, synchronicity.
SIN.CRÔ.NI.CO, *adj.*, synchronous, simultaneous.
SIN.CRO.NI.ZA.ÇÃO, *s.f.*, synchronization.
SIN.CRO.NI.ZAR, *v.*, to synchronize, to adjust.
SIN.DI.CAL, *adj.*, syndical.
SIN.DI.CA.LIS.MO, *s.m.*, syndicalism.
SIN.DI.CA.LI.ZA.ÇÃO, *s.f.*, syndicalization.
SIN.DI.CA.LI.ZAR, *v.*, to syndicalize, to syndicate.
SIN.DI.CÂN.CIA, *s.f.*, syndication, inquiry, inquest.
SIN.DI.CAR, *v.*, to investigate, to inquire into.
SIN.DI.CA.TO, *s.m.*, syndicate.
SÍN.DI.CO, *s.m.*, syndic, janitor, lawyer.
SI.NE.TA, *s.f.*, a small bell.
SIN.FO.NI.A, *s.f.*, symphony.
SIN.FÔ.NI.CO, *adj.*, symphonic.
SIN.GE.LE.ZA, *s.f.*, singleness, simplicity.
SIN.GE.LO, *adj.*, simple, plain, sincere, single.
SIN.GU.LAR, *s.m.*, singular, the singular number; *adj.*, single, individual, singular.
SIN.GU.LA.RI.DA.DE, *s.f.*, singularity, uniqueness, oddity, remark.
SIN.GU.LA.RI.ZAR, *v.*, to singularize, to single out, to particularize.
SI.NIS.TRO, *s.m.*, accident, casualty, disaster, damage, ruin, loss; *adj.*, left, sinister, ominous, fatal, evil.
SI.NO, *s.m.*, bell.
SÍ.NO.DO, *s.m.*, synod.
SI.NÔ.NI.MO, *s.m.*, synonym.
SI.NOP.SE, *s.f.*, synopsis, analysis, summary.
SIN.TÁ.TI.CO, *adj.*, syntactic.
SIN.TA.XE, *s.f.*, syntax.
SÍN.TE.SE, *s.f.*, synthesis, composition.
SIN.TÉ.TI.CO, *adj.*, synthetic, synthetical, resumed, abbreviated.
SIN.TE.TI.ZAR, *v.*, to synthesize, to synthetize.
SIN.TO.MA, *s.m.*, sympton, sign, indication.
SIN.TO.NI.A, *s.f.*, syntony.
SIN.TO.NI.ZAR, *v.*, to syntonize, to tune in.
SI.NU.CA, *s.f.*, snooker.
SI.NUO.SI.DA.DE, *s.f.*, sinuosity, flexuosity, tortuosity.
SI.NU.O.SO, *adj.*, sinuous, winding, bending.
SI.NU.SI.TE, *s.f.*, sinusitis.
SI.RE.NE, *s.f.*, siren, syren, alarm.
SÍ.RIO, *adj.*, *s.m.*, Syrian.
SI.SAL, *s.m.*, sisal, sisal-hemp.
SÍS.MI.CO, *adj.*, seismic, seismal, cataclysmic.
SIS.MO, *s.m.*, seismism, move, earthquake.
SI.SO, *s.m.*, judgment, criterion, prudence.
SIS.TE.MA, *s.m.*, system, scheme, organization, structure.
SIS.TE.MÁ.TI.CA, *s.f.*, systematics, taxonomy.
SIS.TE.MÁ.TI.CO, *adj.*, systematic.
SIS.TE.MA.TI.ZAR, *v.*, to systemize, systematize.
SI.SU.DEZ, *s.f.*, circumspection, prudence, wisdom.
SI.SU.DO, *adj.*, serious, judicious, wise, sensible, serious.
SÍ.TIO, *s.m.*, place, locality, soil, farm, ranch, country.
SI.TO, *adj.*, situated, located.
SI.TUA.ÇÃO, *s.f.*, situation, position, location, place, circumstances.
SI.TU.AR, *v.*, to place, to situate, to position.
SÓ, *adj.*, alone, unique, single, sole, lone, solitary.
SO.A.LHO, *s.m.*, floor, flooring, ground.
SO.AR, *v.*, to sound, to clang, to jingle.
SOB, *prep.* sub, under, below, beneath.
SO.BE.JAR, *v.*, to overabound, to superabound.
SO.BE.JO, *s.m.*, refuse, candle-end, excess.
SO.BE.RA.NI.A, *s.f.*, sovereignty, domain, rule, reign.
SO.BE.RA.NO, *s.m.*, sovereign, imperator, monarch.
SO.BER.BO, *adj.*, superb, proud, splendid, sumptuous, prideful.
SO.BRA, *s.f.*, surplus, excess, overplus, overmuch.
SO.BRA.DO, *s.m.*, two-store house.
SO.BRAN.CE.LHA, *s.f.*, brow, eyebrow.
SO.BRAR, *v.*, to overabound, to be in excess of, to be superfluous.
SO.BRAS, *s.f.*, pl., scrap, garbage.

SO.BRE, *prep.*, about, above, concerning, over, across, besides, over and above.
SO.BRE.A.VI.SO, *s.m.*, precaution, forethought, prevention.
SO.BRE.CA.PA, *s.f.*, overcoat, raglan.
SO.BRE.CAR.GA, *s.f.*, overburden, overload, surcharge, overcharge.
SO.BRE.CAR.RE.GAR, *v.*, to overload, to overburden, to overfreight.
SO.BRE-E.XAL.TAR, *v.*, to superexalt.
SO.BRE.LO.JA, *s.f.*, mezzanine.
SO.BRE.MA.NEI.RA, *s.f.*, greatly, extremely, excessively.
SO.BRE.ME.SA, *s.f.*, dessert.
SO.BRE.NA.TU.RAL, *adj.*, supernatural.
SO.BRE.NO.ME, *s.m.*, surname, family name.
SO.BRE.PE.SO, *s.m.*, surcharge, overweight.
SO.BRE.POR, *v.*, to put on or upon, to lean against, to superpose, to juxtapose, to connect.
SO.BRE.PO.SI.ÇÃO, *s.f.*, overlapping, superposing
SO.BRE.PU.JAR, *v.*, to surmount, to raise above, to surpass.
SO.BRES.CRE.VER, *v.*, to superscribe, to address a letter.
SO.BRES.SA.IR, *v.*, to salient, to be projecting, to jut out.
SO.BRES.SAL.TA.DO, *adj.*, jumpy, apprehensive, fearful.
SO.BRES.SAL.TAR, *v.*, to assail, to attack, to surprise, to take by surprise, to jump over.
SO.BRES.SAL.TO, *s.m.*, dread, fear, alarm, start.
SO.BRES.SA.LEN.TE, *s.m.*, surplus, overplus, rest, remainder, spare part.
SO.BRE.TA.XA, *s.f.*, surtax, supercharge, surcharge.
SO.BRE.TU.DO, *adv.*, over all, above all, chiefly, mainly, essencially.
SO.BRE.VIR, *v.*, to befall, to happen, to come to pass.
SO.BRE.VI.VÊN.CIA, *s.f.*, survival.
SO.BRE.VI.VEN.TE, *s.2 gen.*, survivor, outliver; *adj.*, surviving.
SO.BRE.VI.VER, *v.*, to survive, to outlive, to outlast, to continue, to exist.
SO.BRIE.DA.DE, *s.f.*, sobriety, temperance, seriousness, frugality.
SO.BRI.NHA, *s.f.*, niece.
SO.BRI.NHO, *s.m.*, nephew.
SÓ.BRIO, *adj.*, sober, abstinent, temperate, austere.
SO.CAR, *v.*, to strike with the fist, to beat, to bruise, to hurt.
SO.CIA.BI.LI.DA.DE, *s.f.*, sociability, sociality, communicativeness.
SO.CIA.BI.LI.ZAR, *v.*, to make sociable, to form a society.
SO.CI.AL, *adj.*, social, social-minded, sociable.
SO.CIA.LIS.MO, *s.m.*, socialism.
SO.CIA.LIS.TA, *s.2 gen.*, socialist.
SO.CIA.LI.ZA.ÇÃO, *s.f.*, socialization.
SO.CIA.LI.ZAR, *v.*, to socialize.
SO.CI.Á.VEL, *adj.*, social, sociable, urban, associable.
SO.CIE.DA.DE, *s.f.*, society, friendly intercourse, association, corporation.
SÓ.CIO, *s.m.*, member, associate, partner, shareholder.
SO.CIO.LO.GIA, *s.f.*, sociology.
SO.CI.Ó.LO.GO, *s.m.*, sociologist.
SO.CO, *s.m.*, blow, punch.
SO.ÇO.BRAR, *v.*, to subvert, to turn upside down, to founder.
SO.COR.RER, *v.*, to protect, to aid, to help, to assist, to relieve.
SO.COR.RO, *s.m.*, relief, aid, assistance, succour.
SO.DA, *s.f.*, soda, fizzy water.
SÓ.DIO, *s.m.*, sodium.
SO.DO.MI.A, *s.f.*, sodomy, pederasty.
SO.FÁ, *s.m.*, sofa, couch; **SOFÁ-CAMA**, sofa-bed.
SO.FIS.MA, *s.m.*, sophism, fallacy.
SO.FIS.TI.CA.ÇÃO, *s.f.*, sophistication, sophistry.
SO.FIS.TI.CA.DO, *adj.*, sophistecated, falsified.
SO.FIS.TI.CAR, *v.*, to sophisticate, to falsify.
SO.FRE.AR, *v.*, to bridle, to curb, to check, to refrain.
SO.FRE.DOR, *s.m.*, sufferer, endurer.

SO.FRE.GUI.DÃO, *s.f.*, greediness, voraciousness, avidity.

SO.FRER, *v.*, to suffer, to bear, to endure, to sustain, to support, to undergo.

SO.FRI.MEN.TO, *s.m.*, suffering, sufferance, pain, agony, torment.

SO.GRA, *s.f.*, mother-in-law.

SO.GRO, *s.m.*, father-in-law.

SO.JA, *s.f.*, soybean, soja, soy.

SOL, *s.m.*, sun; SOL, the fifth musical note.

SO.LA, *s.f.*, sole-leather, sole of a shoe.

SO.LA.PAR, *v.*, to hollow out, to undermine, to sap.

SO.LAR, *s.m.*, manor-house, manor, mansion; *adj.*, solar; *v.*, to sole a shoe, to play solo.

SOL.DA, *s.f.*, solder, weld, soldering.

SOL.DA.DO, *s.m.*, soldier, private; *adj.*, soldered, welded, joined.

SOL.DAR, *v.*, to solder, to weld, to join, to fasten.

SOL.DO, *s.m.*, soldier's pay.

SO.LE.CIS.MO, *s.m.*, solecism, error, guilt.

SO.LEI.RA, *s.f.*, sill, door-sill.

SO.LE.NE, *adj.*, solemn, pompous, ominous, serious.

SO.LE.NI.DA.DE, *s.f.*, solemnity, celebration, festivity.

SO.LE.NI.ZAR, *v.*, to solemnize, to celebrate.

SO.LE.TRAR, *v.*, to spell, to read badly.

SO.LI.CI.TA.ÇÃO, *s.f.*, solicitation, request, appeal.

SO.LI.CI.TAN.TE, *adj.*, *s.2 gen.*, solicitant.

SO.LI.CI.TAR, *v.*, to solicit, to seek, to search for, to look for, to obtain.

SO.LI.CI.TU.DE, *s.f.*, solicitude, carefulness, diligence.

SO.LI.DÃO, *s.f.*, solitude, seclusion, loneliness.

SO.LI.DA.RIE.DA.DE, *s.f.*, solidarity, sympathy.

SO.LI.DÁ.RIO, *adj.*, sympathetyc, solidary, mutual.

SO.LI.DA.RI.ZAR, *v.*, to solidarize, to make solidary.

SO.LI.DEZ, *s.f.*, solidity, solidness, firmness.

SO.LI.DI.FI.CAR, *v.*, to solidify, to coagulate, to congeal, to set, to settle.

SÓ.LI.DO, *adj.*, solid, consistent, compact, durable.

SO.LIS.TA, *s.2 gen.*, solist.

SO.LI.TÁ.RIA, *s.f.*, tapeworm, solitary cell.

SO.LI.TÁ.RIO, *adj.*, solitary, lonely, secluded.

SO.LO, *s.m.*, soil, solo, earth.

SOLS.TÍ.CIO, *s.m.*, solstice.

SOL.TAR, *v.*, to unfasten, to untie, to unbind, to loosen, to free, to release.

SOL.TEI.RA, *s.f.*, single woman, spinster; *adj.*, single, unmarried.

SOL.TEI.RÃO, *s.m.*, bachelor.

SOL.TEI.RO, *s.m.*, single man, single.

SOL.TEI.RO.NA, *s.f.*, spinster.

SOL.TO, *adj.*, free, slack, loose, released.

SOL.TU.RA, *s.f.*, freeing, liberation.

SO.LU.ÇÃO, *s.f.*, solution, conclusion, answer.

SO.LU.ÇAR, *v.*, to sob, to hiccup, to whimper, to whine.

SO.LU.CIO.NAR, *v.*, to give a solution, to resolve.

SO.LU.ÇO, *s.m.*, hiccup, sob, sobbing, din.

SO.LÚ.VEL, *adj.*, dissoluble, soluble.

SOL.VÊN.CIA, *s.f.*, solvency.

SOL.VER, *v.*, to solve, to explain, to resolve, to pay, to settle a debt.

SOM, *s.m.*, sound, tone.

SO.MA, *s.f.*, sum, addition, total, totality.

SO.MAR, *v.*, to add, to sum up, to total.

SOM.BRA, *s.f.*, shadow, shade, darkness.

SOM.BRE.AR, *v.*, to shade, to shadow, to darken.

SOM.BRI.NHA, *s.f.*, parasol.

SOM.BRIO, *adj.*, shady, shadowy, obscure, dark, sad, dismal, cloudy, moody.

SO.MEN.TE, *adv.*, only.

SO.NÂM.BU.LO, *s.m.*, sleepwalker, somnambulist; *adj.*, somnambulistic.

SO.NAR, *s.m.*, sonar.

SO.NA.TA, *s.f.*, sonata.

SON.DA, *s.f.*, sounding lead, style, catheter.

SON.DA.GEM, *s.f.*, sounding investigation, perforation, drilling, exploration.

SON.DAR, *v.*, to sound, to search, to evaluate, to probe.

SO.NE.CA, *s.f.*, somnolence, nap, doze, sleepiness.

SO.NE.GA.ÇÃO, *s.f.*, defraudation, misappropriation.

SO.NE.GAR, *v.*, to withhold, to defraud, to misapply, to steal.

SO.NE.TO, *s.m.*, sonnet.

SO.NHA.DOR, *s.m.*, visionary, dreamer, dozer.

SO.NHAR, *v.*, to dream, to imagine, to fancy.

SO.NHO, *s.m.*, dream, reverie; SONHO (rosquinha de massa), dough-nut.

SO.NO, *s.m.*, sleep, slumber, rest, repose, sleepiness.

SO.NO.LÊN.CIA, *s.f.*, somnolence, sleepiness.

SO.NO.LEN.TO, *adj.*, somnolent, sleepy, drowsy, inert.

SO.NO.RI.DA.DE, *s.f.*, sonority, loudness.

SO.NO.RI.ZAR, *v.*, to render sonorous, to sound.

SO.NO.RO, *adj.*, sonorous, loud.

SON.SO, *adj.*, sly, artful, cunning, clever, crafty.

SO.PA, *s.f.*, soup, sop, broth.

SO.PA.PO, *s.m.*, slap, wipe.

SO.PEI.RA, *s.f.*, soup dish.

SO.PO.RÍ.FE.RO, *adj., s.m.*, soporific.

SO.PRAR, *v.*, to blow, to puff.

SO.PRO, *s.m.*, puff of air, whiff, exhalation, blowing, blast.

SOR.DI.DEZ, *s.f.*, sordidness, paltriness, dirtiness.

SÓR.DI.DO, *adj.*, dirty, filthy, sordid, vile, base, nasty, repulsive.

SO.RO, *s.m.*, serum.

SO.RO.LO.GI.A, *s.f.*, serology.

SO.ROR, *s.f.*, sister, nun.

SO.RO.TE.RA.PI.A, *s.f.*, serum therapy.

SOR.RI.DEN.TE, *adj.*, smiling, radiant, beaming, genial.

SOR.RIR, *v.*, to smile, to laugh gently.

SOR.RI.SO, *s.m.*, smile, act of smiling, grin.

SOR.TE, *s.f.*, fate, destiny, fortune, chance, luck, doom, lot, hazard, risk.

SOR.TE.AR, *v.*, to choose or pick out by lot, to draw lots.

SOR.TEI.O, *s.m.*, sortition, allotment, raffle, lottery.

SOR.TI.DO, *adj.*, assorted, sorted.

SOR.TI.MEN.TO, *s.m.*, classification, assortment, supply.

SOR.TIR, *v.*, to supply, to furnish, to provide, to variegate.

SOR.VER, *v.*, to sip, to suck, to absorb, to engulf.

SOR.VE.TE, *s.m.*, ice-cream.

SOR.VE.TE.RI.A, *s.f.*, ice-cream shop.

SÓ.SIA, *s.f.*, double, counterpart, second self.

SOS.LAI.O, *s.m.*, obliquity.

SOS.SE.GA.DO, *adj.*, quiet, calm, tranquil, restful, sleepy, drowsy.

SOS.SE.GAR, *v.*, to calm, to quiet, to tranquilize, to soothe, to pacify.

SOS.SE.GO, *s.m.*, tranquility, calmness, calm, peace.

SÓ.TÃO, *s.m.*, attic, garret.

SO.TA.QUE, *s.m.*, accent, brogue.

SO.TER.RA.DO, *adj.*, covered with earth.

SO.TER.RAR, *v.*, to bury, to cover with earth.

SO.VA, *s.f.*, beating, thrashing, caning.

SO.VA.CO, *s.m.*, axilla, armpit.

SO.VAR, *v.*, to knead, to batter, to drub.

SO.VE.LA, *s.f.*, bradawl, awl, pricker, broach.

SO.VI.É.TI.CO, *adj., s.m.*, Russian, soviet, sovietic.

SO.VI.NI.CE, *s.f.*, avariciousness, greediness, parsimony.

SO.ZI.NHO, *adj.*, alone, lonely, solo; *adv.*, all alone, solely, all by oneself.

SU.A, *pron.*, his, her, its, your, their, his, hers, its, yours, theirs.

SU.A.DO, *adj.*, sweaty, perspiring.

SU.AR, *v.*, to sweat, to perspire, to transpire, to exhale, to exude.

SU.A.VE, *adj.*, agreeable, pleasant, mild, gentle, kind, affable, delicate, sweet, lenient.

SUA.VI.DA.DE, *s.f.*, amenity, mildness, suaveness, gentleness.

SUA.VI.ZAR, *v.*, to soothe, to soften, to milden.

SU.BA.LI.MEN.TAR, *v.*, to undernourish, to underfeed.

SU.BAL.TER.NO, *s.m.*, subaltern, subordinate; *adj.*, subaltern, subordinate, inferior, secondary.

SU.BA.LU.GAR, *v.*, to sublet, to underlet.

SUB.CHE.FE, *s.m.*, subchief.

SUB.CONS.CI.EN.TE, *s.m.*, the unconscious, unconsciousness.
SUB.CU.TÂ.NEO, *adj.*, subcutaneous.
SUB.DE.LE.GA.DO, *s.m.*, subdelegate, inspector, controller.
SUB.DE.SEN.VOL.VI.DO, *adj.*, underdeveloped.
SUB.DE.SEN.VOL.VI.MEN.TO, *s.m.*, underdevelopment.
SUB.DI.VI.DIR, *v.*, to subdivide.
SUB.DI.VI.SÃO, *s.f.*, subdivision, suballocation.
SU.BEM.PREI.TAR, *v.*, to subcontract.
SU.BEN.TEN.DER, *v.*, to perceive or interpret correctly an implication, to suppose.
SU.BES.PÉ.CIE, *s.f.*, subspecies.
SU.BES.TI.MAR, *v.*, to underestimate.
SU.BI.DA, *s.f.*, ascension, ascent, raise, rise, rising, acclivity.
SU.BIR, *v.*, to ascend, to rise, to go up, to mount up, to scale, to increase, to lift.
SÚ.BI.TO, *adj.*, sudden, abrupt, unexpected, swift.
SUB.JE.TI.VA.ÇÃO, *s.f.*, subjectiveness, subjectivity.
SUB.JE.TI.VAR, *v.*, to render subjective.
SUB.JE.TI.VO, *adj.*, subjective.
SUB.JU.GA.DO, *adj.*, subjugated, dominated.
SUB.JU.GAR, *v.*, to subjugate, to submit, to subdue.
SUB.JUN.TI.VO, *s.m.*, subjunctive mood, subjunctive; *adj.*, subjunctive.
SU.BLI.MA.ÇÃO, *s.f.*, sublimation.
SU.BLI.ME, *adj.*, sublime, splendid, glorious, divine.
SU.BLI.NHAR, *v.*, to underline.
SUB.LO.CAR, *v.*, to underlet, to sublet.
SUB.MA.RI.NO, *s.m.*, submarine; *adj.* submarine.
SUB.MER.GIR, *v.*, to submerge, to inundate, to overflow, to deluge.
SUB.MER.SÃO, *s.f.*, submergence, submersion.
SUB.MER.SÍ.VEL, *adj.*, submergible.
SUB.MER.SO, *adj.*, submerged.
SUB.ME.TER, *v.*, to submit, to subdue, to subject.
SUB.MIS.SÃO, *s.f.*, submission, submissiveness, subjection.

SUB.MIS.SO, *adj.*, submissive, obedient, dutiful, subordinate.
SUB.NU.TRI.ÇÃO, *s.f.*, underfeeding, undernourishment.
SUB.NU.TRI.DO, *adj.*, underfed, undernourished.
SU.BOR.DI.NA.ÇÃO, *s.f.*, subordination, obedience.
SU.BOR.DI.NA.DO, *adj.*, subordinate.
SU.BOR.DI.NAR, *v.*, to subordinate, to subject, to subdue.
SU.BOR.NAR, *v.*, to suborn, to bribe.
SU.BOR.NO, *s.m.*, subornation, embracery, bribery.
SUB.PRO.DU.TO, *s.m.*, subproduct, byproduct.
SUBS.CRE.VER, *v.*, to subscribe, to underwrite, to sign, to endorse.
SUBS.CRI.ÇÃO, *s.f.*, subscription, subscribing, agreement.
SUB.SE.QUEN.TE, *adj.*, subsequent, sequent, ensuing.
SUB.SI.DI.Á.RIO, *adj.*, subsidiary.
SUB.SÍ.DIO, *s.m.*, subsidy, aid, assistance, help, grant, subvention.
SUB.SIS.TÊN.CIA, *s.f.*, subsistence, sustenance.
SUB.SIS.TIR, *v.*, to subsist, to exist, to survive, to persist.
SUB.SO.LO, *s.m.*, subsoil, substrate, underground.
SUBS.TÂN.CIA, *s.f.*, substance, matter, stuff, essence, amount.
SUBS.TAN.CI.AL, *adj.*, essential, nutritive, nourishing.
SUBS.TAN.CI.O.SO, *adj.*, substantial.
SUBS.TAN.TI.VO, *s.m.*, substantive, noun; *adj.*, substantive.
SUBS.TI.TUI.ÇÃO, *s.f.*, substitution, substituting.
SUBS.TI.TU.IR, *v.*, to substitute, to put, to replace.
SUBS.TI.TU.TO, *s.m.*, substitute, successor, proxy.
SUB.TER.FÚ.GIO, *s.m.*, subterfuge, excuse, shift, text.
SUB.TER.RÂ.NEO, *s.m.*, a subterranean place, cave, basement, cavern; *adj.*, subterranean.
SUB.TÍ.TU.LO, *s.m.*, sub-title, sub-heading.
SUB.TO.TAL, *s.m.*, subtotal.

SUB.TRA.ÇÃO, *s.f.,* subtraction, diminution, deduction.
SUB.TRA.IR, *v.,* to subtract, to withdraw, to defalcate.
SUB.TRO.PI.CAL, *adj.,* subtropical.
SU.BUR.BA.NO, *adj.,* suburban, suburbial, uptown.
SU.BÚR.BIO, *s.m.,* suburb, environs.
SUB.VEN.ÇÃO, *s.f.,* subvention, subsidy.
SUB.VER.SÃO, *s.f.,* subversion, overthrow, revolt.
SUB.VER.TER, *v.,* to subvert, to overturn, to destroy, to ruin, to disturb.
SU.CA.TA, *s.f.,* scrap(s), scrap iron, junk iron.
SUC.ÇÃO, *s.f.,* suction, suck, aspiration.
SU.CE.DER, *v.,* to succeed, to happen, to occur, to follow after.
SU.CE.DI.DO, *adj.,* occurred, successful.
SU.CES.SÃO, *s.f.,* succession, sequence, progression.
SU.CES.SI.VO, *adj.,* successive, succeeding.
SU.CES.SO, *s.m.,* outcome, success.
SU.CES.SOR, *s.m.,* successor, aftercomer.
SÚ.CIA, *s.f.,* gang, mob, rabble.
SU.CIN.TO, *adj.,* succinct, brief, short.
SU.CO, *s.m.,* juice, sap, essence.
SU.CU.LEN.TO, *adj.,* succulent, sappy, pulpy, rich.
SU.CUM.BIR, *v.,* to succumb, to yield, to submit, to perish, to despair.
SU.CU.RI, *s.f.,* anaconda.
SU.DÁ.RIO, *s.m.,* sudarium, sweat cloth.
SÚ.DI.TO, *s.m.,* subject, vassal, liege.
SU.DO.ES.TE, *s.m.,* southwest.
SU.E.CO, *s.m.,* Swede; *adj.,* Swedish.
SU.É.TER, *s.m.,* sweater.
SU.FI.CI.ÊN.CIA, *s.f.,* sufficiency, adequacy, ability, capacity.
SU.FI.CI.EN.TE, *adj.,* sufficient, adequate, enough.
SU.FI.XO, *s.m.,* suffix, postfix, affix.
SU.FO.CA.ÇÃO, *s.f.,* suffocation, choke, strangulation.
SU.FO.CAR, *v.,* to suffocate, to choke, to smother, to strangle.
SU.FRÁ.GIO, *s.m.,* suffrage, vote, voting.
SU.GAR, *v.,* to suck, to absorb, to extort.
SU.GE.RIR, *v.,* to suggest, to insinuate, to inspire, to prompt.
SU.GES.TÃO, *s.f.,* suggestion, proposal, hint, intimation.
SU.GES.TIO.NAR, *v.,* to suggestion, to influence, to inspire.
SU.GES.TI.VO, *adj.,* suggestive, significant.
SU.I.CI.DA, *s.2 gen.,* suicide.
SUI.CI.DAR-se, *v.,* to suicide, to commit suicide.
SUI.CÍ.DIO, *s.m.,* suicide, self-murder.
SU.Í.ÇO, *adj., s.m.,* Swiss.
SU.Í.NO, *s.m.,* swine, pig; *adj.,* swinish.
SU.JAR, *v.,* to dirty, to stain, to spot, to maculate, to blot.
SU.JEI.RA, *s.f.,* dirt, filth, slosh.
SU.JEI.TAR, *v.,* to subject, to submit, to obligate, to dominate.
SU.JEI.TO, *s.m.,* subject, citizen, individual, fellow, chap.
SU.JO, *adj.,* dirty, filthy, sordid, indecorous, greasy, soiled.
SUL, *s.m.,* south, south wind.
SUL-A.ME.RI.CA.NO, *adj., s.m.,* South American.
SUL.CAR, *v.,* to sulcate, to furrow, to ridge.
SU.LIS.TA, *s.2 gen.,* southerner; *adj.,* southern.
SUL.TA.NA, *s.f.,* sultana, sultaness.
SUL.TÃO, *s.m.,* sultan, ruler, sovereign.
SU.MA, *s.f.,* summary, sum, total.
SU.MÁ.RIO, *s.m.,* summary, digest, abbreviation, synopsis; *adj.,* summary, concise, succint.
SU.MI.ÇO, *s.m.,* disappearance, escape, vanishing.
SU.MIR, *v.,* to disappear, to vanish, to lose, to submerge.
SU.MO, *s.m.,* juice, sap, lushness; *adj.,* lofty, superior, supreme.
SÚ.MU.LA, *s.f.,* summula, epitome, summary, compendium.
SUN.TUO.SI.DA.DE, *s.f.,* sumptuosity.
SUN.TU.O.SO, *adj.,* sumptuous, magnificent, luxurious, splendid.

SU.OR, *s.m.*, sweat, perspiration.
SU.PE.RA.BUN.DAR, *v.*, to superabound, overabound.
SU.PE.RA.QUE.CER, *v.*, to superheat, to overheat.
SU.PE.RAR, *v.*, to overcome, to dominate, to subjugate, to subdue.
SU.PE.RÁ.VIT, *s.m.*, superavit, surplus.
SU.PER.CÍ.LIO, *s.m.*, eyebrow.
SU.PE.RES.TRU.TU.RA, *s.f.*, superstructure.
SU.PER.FI.CI.AL, *adj.*, superficial, external, outside.
SU.PER.FI.CIA.LI.DA.DE, *s.f.*, superficiality.
SU.PER.FÍ.CIE, *s.f.*, surface, superficies, outside.
SU.PÉR.FLUO, *adj.*, superfluous, unnecessary.
SU.PER-HO.MEM, *s.m.*, superman.
SU.PE.RIN.TEN.DEN.TE, *s.2 gen.*, superintendent.
SU.PE.RI.OR, *s.m.*, superior, head of a monastery; *adj.*, higher, upper, loftier, greater.
SU.PE.RIO.RI.DA.DE, *s.f.*, superiority.
SU.PER.LA.TI.VO, *s.m.*, superlative; *adj.*, superlative.
SU.PER.LO.TA.ÇÃO, *s.f.*, overcrowding.
SU.PER.LO.TAR, *v.*, to overcrowd, to overload.
SU.PER.MER.CA.DO, *s.m.*, supermarket.
SU.PER.POR, *v.*, to superpose.
SU.PER.PRO.DU.ÇÃO, *s.f.*, overproduction.
SU.PER.SEN.SÍ.VEL, *adj.*, supersensible.
SU.PER.SÔ.NI.CO, *adj.*, supersonic.
SU.PERS.TI.ÇÃO, *s.f.*, superstition.
SU.PERS.TI.CI.O.SO, *adj.*, superstitious.
SU.PER.VA.LO.RI.ZA.ÇÃO, *s.f.*, overvaluation.
SU.PER.VI.SÃO, *s.f.*, supervision.
SU.PER.VI.SIO.NAR, *v.*, to supervise, to oversee.
SU.PER.VI.SOR, *s.m.*, supervisor.
SU.PLAN.TAR, *v.*, to supplant, to supersede.
SU.PLE.MEN.TAR, *v.*, to supplement; *adj.*, supplemental, additional.
SU.PLE.MEN.TO, *s.m.*, supplement, appendix.
SU.PLEN.TE, *s.2 gen.*, substitute; *adj.*, substitutional.
SU.POR, *v.*, to suppose, to assume, to think, to imagine.

SU.POR.TAR, *v.*, to support, to suffer, to endure, to stand.
SU.POR.TÁ.VEL, *adj.*, supportable, tolerable.
SU.POR.TE, *s.m.*, support, stay, prop.
SU.PO.SI.ÇÃO, *s.f.*, supposition, conjecture, presumption.
SU.PO.SI.TÓ.RIO, *s.m.*, suppository.
SU.POS.TO, *adj.*, supposed, presumed, assumed.
SU.PRAS.SU.MO, *s.m.*, top, utmost, highest, ideal.
SU.PRE.MA.CI.A, *s.f.*, supremacy, sovereignty.
SU.PRE.MO, *s.m.*, Supreme Court; *adj.*, supreme, highest, utmost.
SU.PRES.SÃO, *s.f.*, suppression.
SU.PRI.MEN.TO, *s.m.*, supply, subsidy, aid, loan.
SU.PRI.MIR, *v.*, to suppress, to abolish, to omit.
SU.PRIR, *v.*, to supply, to furnish, to help, to aid, to compensate.
SU.PU.RAR, *v.*, to suppurate.
SUR.DEZ, *s.f.*, deafness.
SUR.DI.NA, *s.f.*, mute, sourdine.
SUR.DO, *adj.*, deaf, unable to hear.
SUR.DO-MU.DO, *adj.*, *s.m.*, deaf-mute.
SUR.GIR, *v.*, to arise, to appear, to emerge, to arouse, to well.
SUR.PRE.EN.DEN.TE, *adj.*, surprising, astonishing, amazing.
SUR.PRE.EN.DER, *v.*, to surprise, to astonish, to amaze, to startle.
SUR.PRE.SA, *s.f.*, surprise, surprisal, astonishment.
SUR.PRE.SO, *adj.*, surprised, amazed, startled.
SUR.RA, *s.f.*, thrashing, spanking.
SUR.RA.DO, *adj.*, worn, worn out, curried.
SUR.RAR, *v.*, to beat, to spank, to curry, to tan, to beat, to flog.
SUR.RE.A.LIS.MO, *s.m.*, surrealism.
SUR.TIR, *v.*, to occasion, to result in.
SUR.TO, *s.m.*, outbreak, boom.
SUS.CE.TI.BI.LI.DA.DE, *s.f.*, susceptibility, touchiness.
SUS.CE.TI.BI.LI.ZAR, *v.*, to hurt, to offend, to grieve.

SUS.CI.TAR, *v.*, to suscitate, to excite, to rouse, to cause, to provoke.
SUS.PEI.TA, *s.f.*, suspicion, diffidence, doubt.
SUS.PEI.TAR, *v.*, to suspect, to distrust, to suppose.
SUS.PEI.TO, *adj.*, suspect, suspected, suspicious.
SUS.PEN.DER, *v.*, to hang, to suspend, to hang up, to hoist, to postpone.
SUS.PEN.SÃO, *s.f.*, suspension, interruption, postponement, suspending.
SUS.PEN.SO, *adj.*, suspended, hanging, interrupted.
SUS.PEN.SÓ.RIO, *s.f.*, suspensory, shoulder straps.
SUS.PI.RAR, *v.*, to sigh, to lament.
SUS.PI.RO, *s.m.*, sigh, suspiration; meringue (candy).
SUS.SUR.RAR, *v.*, to whisper, to murmur, to rustle.
SUS.SUR.RO, *s.m.*, rustle, whisper, whispering.
SUS.TE.NI.DO, *s.m.*, sharp.
SUS.TEN.TA.ÇÃO, *s.f.*, sustentation, subsistence, holding.
SUS.TEN.TAR, *v.*, to sustain, to support, to maintain, to uphold, to defend.
SUS.TEN.TO, *s.m.*, maintenance, support.
SUS.TER, *v.*, to support, to prop, to sustain.
SUS.TO, *s.m.*, fright, shock, alarm.
SU.TI.Ã, *s.m.*, brassière, bust bodice.
SU.TIL, *adj.*, subtile, subtle, tenous, rarefied, wily, crafty.
SU.TI.LE.ZA, *s.f.*, subtileness, subtility, subtlety.
SU.TU.RA, *s.f.*, suture, sewing, seam.
SU.TU.RAR, *v.*, to suture, to join by suture or sewing.

T, *s.m.*, the nineteenth letter of the Portuguese alphabet.
TA.BA, *s.f.*, Indian village.
TA.BA.CA.RI.A, *s.f.*, tobacco shop, cigar store.
TA.BA.CO, *s.m.*, tobacco.
TA.BE.FE, *s.m.*, whey, slap.
TA.BE.LA, *s.f.*, table, chart, list, catalogue, schedule, index, roster.
TA.BE.LA.MEN.TO, *s.m.*, control of prices.
TA.BE.LAR, *v.*, to control, to put on the official price list, to regulate.
TA.BE.LI.ÃO, *s.m.*, notary public.
TA.BE.LIO.NA.TO, *s.m.*, office of a notary.
TA.BER.NA, *s.f.*, tavern, pot-house, inn.
TA.BLA.DO, *s.m.*, stage, raised platform.
TA.BLE.TE, *s.m.*, tablet, bar, pastille.
TA.BLOI.DE, *s.m.*, tabloid.
TA.BU, *s.m.*, taboo.
TÁ.BUA, *s.f.*, board; **TÁBUA DE PASSAR ROUPA**, ironing board.
TA.BU.A.DA, *s.f.*, multiplication table.
TA.BU.LEI.RO, *s.m.*, checkerboard, flower bed.
TA.BU.LE.TA, *s.f.*, signboard.
TA.ÇA, *s.f.*, cup.
TA.CA.NHO, *adj.*, short, not tall, avaricious, niggard.
TA.CHA, *s.f.*, tack, sharp.
TA.CHAR, *v.*, to tax, to censure, to brand, to stigmatize.
TA.CHO, *s.m.*, bowl, pot, pan, boiler.
TÁ.CI.TO, *adj.*, tacit, silent, reserved, implicit.
TA.CI.TUR.NO, *adj.*, taciturn, reserved.
TA.CO, *s.m.*, billiard cue, golf club, hockey stick.
TA.CÔ.ME.TRO, *s.m.*, tachometer.
TA.GA.RE.LA, *s.2 gen.*, chatterer, talkative, babbler.
TA.GA.RE.LAR, *v.*, to chatter, to babble, to jabber.
TA.GA.RE.LI.CE, *s.f.*, talkativeness, indiscretion, loquacity, blab.
TA.I.NHA, *s.f.*, mullet.
TAL, *adj.*, such, like, similar; *adv.*, so, thus, accordingly; *pron.*, this, that.
TA.LA, *s.f.*, champ, splice, splint.
TA.LÃO, *s.m.*, coupon stub; **TALÃO DE CHEQUE**, checkbook.
TAL.CO, *s.m.*, talc, talcum powder.
TA.LEN.TO, *s.m.*, talent, ability, ingenuity, aptitude.
TA.LEN.TO.SO, *adj.*, talented, able, smart.
TA.LHAR, *v.*, to cut, to cut off, to cut out, to slice.
TA.LHA.RIM, *s.m.*, noodles.
TA.LHE, *s.m.*, cut, fashion, style, form.
TA.LHER, *s.m.*, set of knife, fork and spoon.
TA.LHO, *s.m.*, cutting, chopping.
TA.LIS.MÃ, *s.m.*, talisman, amulet, charm, fetish.
TA.LO, *s.m.*, stalk, petiole, bind.
TA.LU.DE, *s.m.*, talus, inclination, acclivity.
TAL.VEZ, *adv.*, perhaps, maybe, possibly.
TA.MAN.CO, *s.m.*, clog, sabot.
TA.MAN.DU.Á, *s.m.*, tamandua, anteater.
TA.MA.NHO, *s.m.*, size, bulk, proportion, volume.
TÂ.MA.RA, *s.f.*, date.
TAM.BÉM, *adv.*, also, so, besides, too, likewise, either.
TAM.BOR, *s.m.*, drum, tambour, drummer.
TAM.BO.RI.LAR, *v.*, to drum, to pelt.
TAM.PA, *s.f.*, cover, covering, lid, cap, stopple.
TAM.PAR, *v.*, to cover, to cap, to shut, to top, to stopper.
TAM.PI.NHA, *s.f.*, bottle cap.
TAM.PO.NAR, *v.*, to plug, to bung.
TAM.POU.CO, *adv.*, either, neither, no more.
TAN.GEN.TE, *s.f.*, tangent; *adj.*, tangent, touching.

TAN.GER, *v.*, to play, to sound, to ring.
TAN.GE.RI.NA, *s.f.*, tangerine, mandarin.
TAN.GI.BI.LI.DA.DE, *s.f.*, tangibleness, tangibility.
TAN.GÍ.VEL, *adj.*, tangible, palpable, impressionable.
TAN.GO, *s.m.*, tango.
TAN.QUE, *s.m.*, tank, reservoir, cistern, basin.
TAN.TO, *s.m.*, an indeterminate quantity, sum; *adj.*, as much, so much, as.many; *adv.*, thus, to such a degree.
TÃO, *adv.*, so, such, that, as, so much.
TÃO SO.MEN.TE, *adv.*, only, simply.
TA.PA, *s.m.*, slap, rap, flap.
TA.PAR, *v.*, to close, to plug, to fill up, to block, to cover.
TA.PEA.ÇÃO, *s.f.*, swindle, cheat, trickery, fake.
TA.PE.AR, *v.*, to deceive, to fake, to trick, to humbug.
TA.PE.TE, *s.m.*, carpet, rug, matting.
TA.PI.NHA, *s.f.*, slap, pat.
TA.PU.ME, *s.m.*, hedge, boarding, screen, fence.
TA.QUI.CAR.DI.A, *s.f.*, tachycardia.
TA.QUI.GRA.FI.A, *s.f.*, tachygraphy, shorthand.
TA.RA, *s.f.*, defect, flaw, degeneration.
TA.RA.DO, *adj.*, perverted, sex maniac.
TAR.DA.MEN.TO, *s.m.*, slowness, delay, retardation.
TAR.DAR, *v.*, to delay, to lag, to procrastinate, to postpone.
TAR.DE, *s.f.*, afternoon, evening; *adj.*, late; *adv.*, tardly.
TAR.DIO, *adj.*, slow, late.
TA.RE.FA, *s.f.*, task, duty, assignment, function, job.
TA.RI.FA, *s.f.*, tariff, rate, fare, charge, tax, fee.
TAR.RA.FA, *s.f.*, fishing net, casting net.
TAR.RA.XA, *s.f.*, screw or twist of a screw, wedge, peg, plug.
TAR.TA.RU.GA, *s.f.*, turtle, tortoise.
TAR.TU.FO, *s.m.*, tartuffe, hypocrite.
TA.RU.GO, *s.m.*, wooden pin, slug.
TA.TE.AR, *v.*, to grope, to touch, to feel, to probe.
TÁ.TI.CA, *s.f.*, tactics, method, policy.

TÁ.TI.CO, *adj.*, tactical.
TA.TO, *s.m.*, touch, feeling, tact, sensibility, discretion, prudence, sense.
TA.TU, *s.m.*, armadillo.
TA.TU.A.GEM, *s.f.*, tattooage, tattooing.
TA.TU.AR, *v.*, to tattoo.
TAU.MA.TUR.GO, *s.m.*, thaumaturge, magician.
TA.VER.NA, *s.f.*, tavern, pub, inn, pothouse.
TA.XA, *s.f.*, tribute, tax, tariff, fee, duty, toll.
TA.XA.ÇÃO, *s.f.*, taxation, appraisement, rating.
TA.XAR, *v.*, to rate, to regulate, to fix a value or a price, to tax.
TA.XA.TI.VO, *adj.*, rating, taxing.
TÁ.XI, *s.m.*, taxi, cab, taxicab.
TA.XÍ.ME.TRO, *s.m.*, taximeter.
TE, *pron.*, you, to you.
TEAR, *s.m.*, weaver's loom, clockwork.
TEA.TRAL, *adj.*, theatrical.
TE.A.TRO, *s.m.*, theater, playhouse, stage.
TE.CE.LA.GEM, *s.f.*, textile industry.
TE.CER, *v.*, to weave, to web, to spin.
TE.CI.DO, *s.m.*, tissue, texture, cloth, textile; *adj.*, woven, designed.
TE.CLA, *s.f.*, key.
TE.CLA.DO, *s.m.*, keyboard.
TÉC.NI.CA, *s.f.*, technic, technique, know-how.
TÉC.NI.CO, *s.m.*, technicist, technician, expert; *adj.*, technical.
TEC.NO.LO.GI.A, *s.f.*, technology.
TEC.NO.LÓ.GI.CO, *adj.*, technologic.
TÉ.DIO, *s.m.*, tedium, boredom.
TE.DI.O.SO, *adj.*, tedious, wearisome, dull.
TEI.A, *s.f.*, texture, tissue, cloth, textile, plot, intrigue, scheme.
TEI.MA, *s.f.*, obstinacy, obstinateness, wilfulness.
TEI.MAR, *v.*, to insist, to persist, to persevere.
TEI.MO.SI.A, *s.f.*, obstinacy, stubbornness, pertinacity.
TEI.MO.SO, *adj.*, stubborn, obstinate, insistent.
TE.ÍS.MO, *s.m.*, theism.
TE.LA, *s.f.*, canvas, screen.
TE.LE.FO.NAR, *v.*, to telephone, to phone, to call.
TE.LE.FO.NE, *s.m.*, telephone.
TE.LE.FO.NE.MA, *s.m.*, telephone call.

TE.LE.FÔ.NI.CO, *adj.*, telephonic.
TE.LE.FO.NIS.TA, *s.2 gen.*, telephone operator, operator.
TE.LE.FO.TO, *s.f.*, telephoto.
TE.LE.GRA.FAR, *v.*, to telegraph, to cable, to wire.
TE.LE.GRA.FI.A, *s.f.*, telegraphy.
TE.LE.GRÁ.FI.CO, *adj.*, telegraphic, cabled.
TE.LÉ.GRA.FO, *s.m.*, telegraph.
TE.LE.GRA.MA, *s.m.*, telegram, cable, wire.
TE.LE.JOR.NAL, *s.m.*, TV news.
TE.LÊ.ME.TRO, *s.m.*, telemeter.
TE.LE.NO.VE.LA, *s.f.*, soap opera.
TE.LE.OB.JE.TI.VA, *s.f.*, telephoto lens.
TE.LE.PA.TI.A, *s.f.*, telepathy.
TE.LES.CÓ.PIO, *s.m.*, telescope.
TE.LE.TI.PO, *s.m.*, teletype.
TE.LE.VI.SÃO, *s.f.*, television, telly, video, TV, TV set.
TE.LE.VI.SAR, *v.*, to televise.
TE.LE.VI.SOR, *s.m.*, television receiver.
TE.LEX, *s.m.*, telex.
TE.LHA, *s.f.*, tile, whim, fancy.
TE.LHA.DO, *s.m.*, roof.
TE.LÚ.RI.CO, *adj.*, teluric.
TE.MA, *s.m.*, theme, topic, subject, thesis.
TE.MER, *v.*, to fear, to doubt, to reverence, to respect, to venerate, apprehend.
TE.ME.RÁ.RIO, *adj.*, temerarious, rash, foolhardy.
TE.ME.RO.SO, *adj.*, fearful, dreadful, affraid, terrible.
TE.MI.DO, *adj.*, feared, dreaded.
TE.MOR, *s.m.*, dread, fear, fright, anxiety, awe.
TÊM.PE.RA, *s.f.*, temper, seasoning, flavour, spice.
TEM.PE.RA.DO, *adj.*, temperate, seasoned, spiced.
TEM.PE.RA.MEN.TAL, *adj.*, temperamental.
TEM.PE.RA.MEN.TO, *s.m.*, temperament, mentality, mood, character.
TEM.PE.RAR, *v.*, to season, to flavour, to spice, to moderate, to calm, to soften.
TEM.PE.RA.TU.RA, *s.f.*, temperature.
TEM.PE,RO, *s.m.*, seasoning, spice, condiment.

TEM.PES.TA.DE, *s.f.*, tempest, storm, rainstorm, thunderstorm, tumult.
TEM.PES.TU.O.SO, *adj.*, stormy.
TEM.PLO, *s.m.*, temple.
TEM.PO, *s.m.*, time, period, era, season, weather, tense, duration, opportunity.
TEM.PO.RA.DA, *s.f.*, period, season, era, stay.
TEM.PO.RAL, *s.m.*, tempest, rainstorm, hailstorm; *adj.*, temporary, secular, mundane.
TEM.PO.RA.LI.ZAR, *v.*, to make temporal.
TEM.PO.RÁ.RIO, *adj.*, temporary, provisory.
TEM.PO.RI.ZAR, *v.*, to temporize, to procrastinate.
TE.NA.CI.DA.DE, *s.f.*, tenacity, obstinacy.
TE.NAZ, *s.f.*, tongs, forceps, pliers; *adj.*, tenacious, stubborn, persistent.
TEN.ÇÃO, *s.f.*, intention, purpose, plan, aim.
TEN.DA, *s.f.*, tent, canvas.
TEN.DÃO, *s.m.*, tendon, sinew.
TEN.DÊN.CIA, *s.f.*, tendency, inclination, trend, fall.
TEN.DEN.CI.O.SO, *adj.*, tendentious, partial.
TEN.DER, *v.*, to tend, to incline, to verge, to trend.
TÊN.DER, *s.m.*, tender.
TE.NE.BRO.SO, *adj.*, tenebrous, dark, obscure, gloomy.
TE.NEN.TE, *s.m.*, lieutenant.
TÊ.NIS, *s.m.*, tennis, sneakers.
TE.NIS.TA, *s.2 gen.*, tennis player.
TEN.RO, *adj.*, tender, mild, soft, immature, sensible.
TEN.SÃO, *s.f.*, tension, stress, strain, tensity.
TEN.SO, *adj.*, tense, tight.
TEN.TA.ÇÃO, *s.f.*, temptation, allurement.
TEN.TÁ.CU.LO, *s.m.*, tentacle.
TEN.TA.DO, *adj.*, tempted, incited.
TEN.TA.DOR, *s.m.*, tempter, seducer; *adj.*, tempting, seductive.
TEN.TAR, *v.*, to try, to test, to experiment, to attempt, to tempt.
TEN.TA.TI.VA, *s.f.*, experiment, trial, attempt, effort.
TEN.TO, *s.m.*, caution, attention, maulstick; score, point.

TÊNUE — TÊXTIL

TÊ.NUE, *adj.*, fragile, weak, feeble, insignificant.
TE.NU.I.DA.DE, *s.f.*, tenuousness, weakness.
TE.O.LO.GI.A, *s.f.*, theology.
TE.Ó.LO.GO, *s.m.*, theologian, theologician.
TE.OR, *s.m.*, tenor, text, meaning, style.
TE.O.RI.A, *s.f.*, theory.
TE.Ó.RI.CO, *adj.*, theoretical, abstract.
TE.PI.DEZ, *s.f.*, tepidity, tepidness.
TER, *v.*, to have, to possess, to own, to hold, to keep, to occupy, to retain.
TE.RA.PEU.TA, *s.2 gen.*, therapist, counselor.
TE.RA.PÊU.TI.CA, *s.f.*, therapeutics.
TE.RA.PI.A, *s.f.*, therapy.
TER.ÇA-FEI.RA, *s.f.*, Tuesday.
TER.CEI.RO, *num.*, third, third part; *adj.*, third.
TER.CE.TO, *s.m.*, tercet, triplet, trio.
TER.ÇO, *s.m.*, third part; chaplet, string of beads.
TE.RE.BIN.TI.NA, *s.f.*, turpentine.
TER.MAL, *adj.*, thermal.
TÉR.MI.CO, *adj.*, thermic.
TER.MI.NAL, *s.m.*, terminal; *adj.*, terminal, terminating.
TER.MI.NAR, *v.*, to terminate, to end, to finish, to close, to complete, to expire.
TÉR.MI.NO, *s.m.*, conclusion, ending, expiration.
TER.MI.NO.LO.GI.A, *s.f.*, terminology.
TER.MO, *s.m.*, term, limit, limitation, boundary, landmark, expression, word, vocable.
TER.MÔ.ME.TRO, *s.m.*, thermometer.
TER.MO.NU.CLE.AR, *adj.*, thermonuclear.
TER.MO.QUÍ.MI.CA, *s.f.*, thermochemistry.
TER.MOS.TA.TO, *s.m.*, thermostate.
TER.NO, *s.m.*, man's suit, ternary; *adj.*, tender, delicate, mild.
TER.NU.RA, *s.f.*, tenderness, kindness, love, affection.
TER.RA, *s.f.*, earth, world, globe, land, grand, soil, country, nation, birthplace.
TER.RA.ÇO, *s.m.*, terrace, platform.
TER.RA.PLA.NA.GEM, ter.ra.ple.na.gem, *s.f.*, earthwork, embankment, levelling of the ground.
TER.REI.RO, *s.m.*, yard, square.
TER.RE.MO.TO, *s.m.*, earthquake.
TER.RE.NO, *s.m.*, land, terrain, ground, soil, glebe, site; *adj.*, terrestrial, earthy.
TÉR.REO, *adj.*, ground, earthy; **ANDAR TÉRREO,** ground floor; **CASA TÉRREA,** one-story house.
TER.RES.TRE, *adj.*, terrestrial, wordly.
TER.RI.TÓ.RIO, *s.m.*, territory, land, country, region.
TER.RÍ.VEL, *adj.*, terrible, awful, dreadful.
TER.ROR, *s.m.*, terror, horror, awe, fright, fear, dread.
TER.RO.RIS.MO, *s.m.*, terrorism, reign of terror.
TER.RO.RIS.TA, *s.2 gen.*, terrorist.
TER.RO.RI.ZAR, *v.*, to terrorize, to frighten.
TE.SÃO, *s.f.*, tension, rigidity, rigour.
TE.SE, *s.f.*, thesis, proposition, theory, hypothesis.
TE.SOU.RA, *s.f.*, scissors, a pair of scissors.
TE.SOU.RA.RI.A, *s.f.*, treasury, treasurership.
TE.SOU.REI.RO, *s.m.*, treasurer.
TE.SOU.RO, *s.m.*, treasure, riches, treasury.
TES.TA, *s.f.*, forehead, brow, front.
TES.TA.MEN.TÁ.RIO, *adj.*, testamentarious, testamentary.
TES.TA.MEN.TO, *s.m.*, will, last will, testament.
TES.TAR, *v.*, to test, to try, to legate, to testify.
TES.TE, *s.m.*, test, examination, research, trial.
TES.TE.MU.NHA, *s.f.*, witness, evidence, testimony, proof.
TES.TE.MU.NHAR, *v.*, to bear witness, to testify, to attest.
TES.TE.MU.NHO, *s.m.*, testimony, evidence, proof.
TES.TÍ.CU.LO, *s.m.*, testicle, ball.
TES.TI.FI.CAR, *v.*, to testify, to bear witness, to certify.
TE.TA, *s.f.*, teat, tit, nipple.
TÉ.TA.NO, *s.m.*, lockjaw.
TE.TEI.A, *s.f.*, charm, trinket.
TE.TO, *s.m.*, ceiling, roof, cover, refuge.
TÉ.TRI.CO, *adj.*, sad, gloomy, mournful, sorrowful.
TE.TRO, *adj.*, dark, black, dusky, horrible.
TEU, *pron.*, your, yours.
TEU.TO, *adj.*, Teutonic.
TÊX.TIL, *adj.*, textile.

TEXTO,   **TOLERAR**

TEX.TO, *s.m.,* text.
TEX.TU.AL, *adj.,* literal, textual.
TEZ, *s.f.,* complexion, epidermis, cutis.
TI, *pron.,* you, yourself.
TI.A, *s.f.,* aunt.
TÍ.BIA, *s.f.,* shinbone, tibia.
TI.BI.E.ZA, *s.f.,* lukewarmness, indolence.
TÍ.BIO, *adj.,* tepid, lukewarm.
TI.E.TE, *s.2 gen.,* fan.
TI.FO, *s.m.,* typhoid fever.
TI.GE.LA, *s.f.,* bowl, cup, dish, drinking vessel.
TI.GRE, *s.m.,* tiger.
TI.JO.LO, *s.m.,* brick.
TIL, *s.m.,* tilde, tittle.
TI.MÃO, *s.m.,* tiller, pole, rudder, helm.
TIM.BRAR, *v.,* to stamp, to class, to mark with an emblem.
TIM.BRE, *s.m.,* letterhead, emblem, stamp, seal; expression, tone.
TI.ME, *s.m.,* team.
TI.MI.DEZ, *s.f.,* shyness, timidity, timidness.
TÍ.MI.DO, *adj.,* shy, timid, coy, bashful.
TÍM.PA.NO, *s.m.,* tympanum, eardrum.
TI.NA, *s.f.,* tub, wooden vessel.
TIN.GIR, *v.,* to dye, to stain, to tint, to colour.
TI.NIR, *v.,* to clink, to clank, to ding, to tinkle.
TI.NO, *s.m.,* discernment, good sense, intelligence.
TIN.TA, *s.f.,* paint, ink, tincture.
TIN.TEI.RO, *s.m.,* inkpot, inkwell, inkholder.
TIN.TO, *adj.,* dyed, coloured, red (wine).
TIN.TU.RA, *s.f.,* dyeing, dye, colour, tint, hue.
TIN.TU.RA.RI.A, *s.f.,* dyeing, dye works.
TIO, *s.m.,* uncle.
TÍ.PI.CO, *adj.,* typic, typical, characteristic, symbolic.
TI.PO, *s.m.,* type, kind, sort, variety, fashion, norm.
TI.PO.GRA.FI.A, *s.f.,* typography.
TI.PÓ.GRA.FO, *s.m.,* typographer.
TI.QUE, *s.m.,* tic, twitch, bad habit.
TI.RA, *s.f.,* band, ribbon, strip; *s.m.,* policeman.
TI.RA.GEM, *s.f.,* drawing, circulation, issue, printing, edition, hauling, draft.
TI.RA.NI.A, *s.f.,* tyranny, despotism, oppression.
TI.RA.NO, *s.m.,* tyrant, despot, oppressor; *adj.,* tyrannical, despotic.
TI.RAR, *v.,* to draw, to pull, to remove, to extract, to exclude, to suppress.
TI.RE.OI.DE, *s.f.,* thyroid gland.
TI.RI.TAR, *v.,* to shiver, to quiver, to shake.
TI.RO, *s.m.,* shot, pop, shooting, firing.
TI.RO.CÍ.NIO, *s.m.,* tyrocinium, apprenticeship.
TI.RO.TEI.O, *s.m.,* shooting, firing.
TÍ.SI.CA, *s.f.,* phthisis.
TI.TÃ, *s.m.,* Titan.
TI.TI.A, *s.f.,* auntie.
TI.TU.BE.AR, *v.,* to stagger, to totter.
TI.TU.LAR, *s.m.,* titleholder, office holder; *adj.,* titular, honorary; *v.,* to title, to entitle, to call.
TÍ.TU.LO, *s.m.,* title, heading, caption, denomination, label, top line, inscription, voucher, bond.
TO.A.LE.TE, *s.f.,* toilet.
TO.A.LHA, *s.f.,* towel.
TO.A.LHEI.RO, *s.m.,* towel rack.
TO.AR, *v.,* to sound, to resound, to thunder.
TO.BO.GÃ, *s.m.,* toboggan.
TO.CA, *s.f.,* den, burrow.
TO.CA-DIS.COS, *s.m.,* record player.
TO.CA-FI.TAS, *s.m.,* tape recorder.
TO.CAI.A, *s.f.,* trap, ambush, blind.
TO.CAN.TE, *adj.,* touching, feeling, affecting.
TO.CAR, *v.,* to touch, to feel, to contact, to brush, to play, to perform, to ring.
TO.CHA, *s.f.,* torch, flambeau, firebrand.
TO.CO, *s.m.,* stub, stump.
TO.DA.VI.A, *conj.,* but, yet, still, however, nevertheless, though.
TO.DO, *s.m.,* the whole, totality, mass; **TODOS**, each and every, one and all, every one; *adj.,* all, whole, complete, every, entire. **TODO MUNDO**, everybody.
TOI.CI.NHO, *s.m.,* lard, bacon, pork fat.
TOL.DO, *s.m.,* sun blind, awning.
TO.LE.RÂN.CIA, *s.f.,* tolerance, endurance, toleration, allowance.
TO.LE.RAN.TE, *adj., s.2 gen.,* tolerant, enduring, indulgent.
TO.LE.RAR, *v.,* to tolerate, to endure, to bear,

to stand, to abide, to allow.
TO.LHER, *v.*, to hinder, to hamper, to prevent, to restrain, to stop.
TO.LHI.DO, *adj.*, paralysed, disabled, lame, crippled.
TO.LI.CE, *s.f.*, foolishness, silliness, folly, vanity, stupidity.
TO.LO, *s.m.*, fool, simpleton, idiot; *adj.*, foolish, crazy, daft, ignorant.
TOM, *s.m.*, tone, sound, inflection, key, intonation.
TO.MA.DA, *s.f.*, taking, seizure, conquest; plug, plug socket.
TO.MAR, *v.*, to take, to seize, to catch, to capture, to grasp, to conquer, to gather, to take possession.
TO.MA.TE, *s.m.*, tomato.
TOM.BA.MEN.TO, *s.m.*, act of falling, stumbling.
TOM.BAR, *v.*, to throw or fall down; to register lands.
TOM.BO, *s.m.*, fall, tumble, cropper.
TÔM.BO.LA, *s.f.*, lotto, bingo, tombola.
TO.MO, *s.m.*, tome, volume.
TO.NA, *s.f.*, surface, skin.
TO.NA.LI.DA.DE, *s.f.*, tonality, character of tone.
TO.NE.LA.DA, *s.f.*, ton (weight of 1,000 kg).
TÔ.NI.CO, *s.m.*, tonic, corroborative; *adj.*, tonic, restorative, fundamental, stressed, predominant.
TON.TE.AR, *v.*, to fool, to stupefy.
TO.PAR, *v.*, to meet, to encounter, to find.
TO.PÁ.ZIO, *s.m.*, topaz.
TO.PE, *s.m.*, top, summit.
TO.PE.TE, *s.m.*, topknot, forelock, crest, tuft.
TÓ.PI.CO, *s.m.*, topic, subject, theme, heading, matter, text, argument; *adj.*, topical.
TO.PO, *s.m.*, summit, top, peak, acme.
TO.PO.GRA.FI.A, *s.f.*, topography.
TO.QUE, *s.m.*, touch, contact, feeling, keystroke, call.
TÓ.RAX, *s.m.*, thorax.
TOR.ÇÃO, *s.f.*, torsion, twisting, intorsion.
TOR.CE.DOR, *s.m.*, supporter, twister, throwster; *adj.*, inciting, cheering.
TOR.CER, *v.*, to twist, to turn, to wrench, to distort, to support, to crick.
TOR.CI.DA, *s.f.*, wick, group of cheerers.
TOR.MEN.TA, *s.f.*, tempest, violent storm.
TOR.MEN.TO, *s.m.*, torment, affliction, distress, agony.
TOR.NA.DO, *s.m.*, tornado.
TOR.NAR, *v.*, to return, to go, to turn, to come back, to send back.
TOR.NE.AR, *v.*, to turn, to turn round, to shape, to mold.
TOR.NEI.O, *s.m.*, tournament, tourney, cup.
TOR.NEI.RA, *s.f.*, tap, faucet, cock.
TOR.NO, *s.m.*, lathe, vice, spigot.
TOR.NO.ZE.LO, *s.m.*, ankle, ancle.
TOR.PE, *adj.*, torpid, dirty, vile.
TOR.PE.DE.AR, *v.*, to torpedo, to destroy.
TOR.PE.DO, *s.m.*, torpedo.
TOR.QUÊS, *s.f.*, pincers.
TOR.RA.DA, *s.f.*, toast.
TOR.RA.DEI.RA, *s.f.*, toaster.
TOR.RA.DO, *adj.*, toasted, roasted.
TOR.RAR, *v.*, to toast, to roast, to grill, to brown.
TOR.RE, *s.f.*, tower, pylon, castle, rook.
TOR.RE.FA.ÇÃO, *s.f.*, torrefaction.
TOR.REN.CI.AL, *adj.*, torrential.
TOR.REN.TE, *s.f.*, torrent, stream, flood, flow, cataract.
TOR.RES.MO, *s.m.*, crackling, scrap.
TÓR.RI.DO, *adj.*, torrid, very hot, burning.
TOR.TA, *s.f.*, tart, pie.
TOR.TO, *adj.*, twisted, crooked, bent, curved, oblique, deformed.
TOR.TU.O.SO, *adj.*, tortuous, curved, crooked, sinuous.
TOR.TU.RA, *s.f.*, torture, pain, anguish.
TOR.TU.RAR, *v.*, to torture, to torment, to afflict, to grieve.
TO.SAR, *v.*, to shear, to fleece, to clip.
TOS.QUI.AR, *v.*, to shear, to clip, to fleece, to poll.
TOS.SE, *s.f.*, cough, coughing.
TOS.SIR, *v.*, to cough.
TOS.TAR, *v.*, to toast, to roast.
TO.TAL, *s.m.*, total, totality, whole, sum; *adj.*,

TOTALIDADE   **TRANSCREVER**

total, whole, entire, integral, complete.
TO.TA.LI.DA.DE, *s.f.*, totality, entirety, universality.
TO.TA.LI.TÁ.RIO, *adj.*, totalitarian.
TO.TA.LI.ZAR, *v.*, to totalize.
TOU.CI.NHO, *s.m.*, lard, bacon.
TOU.PEI.RA, *s.f.*, mole, talpa; *adj.*, idiot.
TOU.REI.RO, *s.m.*, bullfighter, torero.
TOU.RO, *s.m.*, bull.
TO.XI.CI.DA.DE, *s.f.*, toxicity.
TÓ.XI.CO, *s.m.*, toxin, poison; *adj.*, toxicant.
TO.XI.CO.MA.NI.A, *s.f.*, drug addiction, toxicomania.
TO.XI.DEZ, *s.f.*, toxicity.
TRA.BA.LHA.DO, *adj.*, worked, laboured, elaborate.
TRA.BA.LHA.DOR, *s.m.*, worker, laborer, toiler; *adj.*, laborious, busy, diligent.
TRA.BA.LHAR, *v.*, to work, to labor.
TRA.BA.LHO, *s.m.*, work, job, service.
TRA.BA.LHO.SO, *adj.*, hard, arduous, difficult.
TRA.ÇA, *s.f.*, moth, clothes moth.
TRA.ÇA.DO, *s.m.*, trace, tracing, drawing, design; *adj.*, drawn, traced, sketchy.
TRA.ÇÃO, *s.f.*, traction, pull, tension, pulling.
TRA.ÇAR, *v.*, to trace, to draw, to delineate, to outline, to sketch.
TRA.ÇO, *s.m.*, trace, line, stroke of a pen, feature, aspect.
TRA.DI.ÇÃO, *s.f.*, tradition; memory.
TRA.DI.CI.O.NAL, *adj.*, traditional, habitual.
TRA.DI.CI.O.NA.LIS.TA, *s.2gen.*, traditionalist.
TRA.DU.ÇÃO, *s.f.*, translation, version.
TRA.DU.TOR, *s.m.*, translator, interpreter; *adj.*, translating.
TRA.DU.ZIR, *v.*, to translate, to express.
TRA.FE.GAR, *v.*, to transit, to pass through, to traffic.
TRÁ.FE.GO, *s.m.*, traffic, transit, transport, business, commerce.
TRA.FI.CAN.TE, *s.2 gen.*, trafficker, dealer, trader; swindler, rascal.
TRA.FI.CAR, *v.*, to traffic, to trade, to swindle, to trick.

TRÁ.FI.CO, *s.m.*, traffic, trade.
TRA.GAR, *v.*, to devour, to swallow, to absorb, to gulp down.
TRA.GÉ.DIA, *s.f.*, tragedy, calamity, disaster, drama, story.
TRÁ.GI.CO, *adj.*, sad, tragic, terrible, mournful.
TRA.GO, *s.m.*, draft, gulp, swallow, drink.
TRAI.ÇÃO, *s.f.*, treason, treachery, perfidy.
TRAI.ÇO.EI.RO, *adj.*, treacherous, perfidious.
TRAI.DOR, *s.m.*, traitor, betrayer; *adj.*, perfidious, treacherous.
TRA.IR, *v.*, to betray, to be false.
TRA.JAR, *v.*, to wear, to dress, to vesture.
TRA.JE, *s.m.*, dress, cloth(es), costume, garb.
TRA.JE.TO, *s.m.*, stretch, distance, course.
TRA.JE.TÓ.RIA, *s.f.*, trajectory.
TRA.MA, *s.f.*, plot, scheme, woof, weft.
TRA.MAR, *v.*, to weave, to plot, to scheme.
TRAM.BO.LHO, *s.m.*, clog.
TRÂ.MI.TE, *s.m.*, path, course, way.
TRA.MOI.A, *s.f.*, chicane, trick, intrigue.
TRAM.PO.LIM, *s.m.*, springboard, diving board.
TRAN.CA, *s.f.*, bar, crossbar, hindrance, obstacle.
TRAN.CAR, *v.*, to fasten, to latch, to lock, to bolt.
TRAN.ÇAR, *v.*, to tress, to interlace, to weave, to braid, to twist.
TRAN.CO, *s.m.*, collision, push, jolt, jog, hump.
TRAN.QUI.LI.DA.DE, *s.f.*, tranquility, peace, serenity, rest, silence.
TRAN.QUI.LI.ZAR, *v.*, to tranquilize, to quiet, to still, to appease, to pacify.
TRAN.QUI.LO, *adj.*, calm, tranquil, peaceful, easy, quiet.
TRAN.SA.ÇÃO, *s.f.*, transaction, dealing, business.
TRAN.SA.TLÂN.TI.CO, *s.m.*, transatlantic.
TRANS.BOR.DA.MEN.TO, *s.m.*, overflow, overflowing.
TRANS.BOR.DAR, *v.*, to overflow.
TRANS.CEN.DER, *v.*, to transcend, overpass, overtop, excel.
TRANS.COR.RER, *v.*, to elapse, to go by, to pass.
TRANS.CRE.VER, *v.*, to transcribe, to copy, to

transfer.
TRANS.CRI.ÇÃO, *s.f.*, transcription, transcribing.
TRANS.CRI.TO, *s.m.*, transcript, copy, translation; *adj.*, transcript.
TRAN.SE, *s.m.*, trance, anguish, trouble, distress, difficulty.
TRAN.SE.UN.TE, *s.2 gen.*, transient, pedestrian; *adj.*, transient, transitory.
TRANS.FE.RÊN.CIA, *s.f.*, transference, transfer.
TRANS.FE.RIR, *v.*, to transfer, to remove, to convey, to transport.
TRANS.FI.GU.RA.ÇÃO, *s.f.*, transfiguration.
TRANS.FOR.MA.ÇÃO, *s.f.*, transformation.
TRANS.FOR.MA.DOR, *s.m.*, transformer; *adj.*, transforming, changing.
TRANS.FOR.MAR, *v.*, to transform, to alter, to change, to modify, to transfigure.
TRANS.FU.SÃO, *s.f.*, transfusion.
TRANS.GRE.DIR, *v.*, to transgress, to infringe, to violate, to infract.
TRANS.GRES.SÃO, *s.f.*, transgression, lawbreaking.
TRAN.SI.ÇÃO, *s.f.*, transition, passage.
TRAN.SI.GÊN.CIA, *s.f.*, compromise, agreement, acquiescence.
TRAN.SI.GIR, *v.*, to compromise, to condescend, to agree.
TRAN.SI.TAR, *v.*, to transit, to pass.
TRAN.SI.TI.VO, *adj.*, transitive, transitional.
TRÂN.SI.TO, *s.m.*, transit, passage, conveyance, traffic.
TRAN.SI.TÓ.RIO, *adj.*, transitory, passing, brief.
TRANS.LA.ÇÃO, *s.f.*, transfer, remove, metaphor.
TRANS.LÚ.CI.DO, *adj.*, translucent, limpid, clear.
TRANS.MI.GRAR, *v.*, to transmigrate.
TRANS.MIS.SÃO, *s.f.*, transmission.
TRANS.MIS.SOR, *s.m.*, transmitter.
TRANS.MI.TIR, *v.*, to transmit, to transfer, to send, to deliver, to pass on, to hand over, to convey.
TRANS.PA.RE.CER, *v.*, to become visible, to be evident.
TRANS.PA.RÊN.CIA, *s.f.*, transparency, pellucidity, diaphaneity.
TRANS.PA.REN.TE, *s.m.*, transparence; *adj.*, transparent, translucent, limpid, clear.
TRANS.PI.RA.ÇÃO, *s.f.*, transpiration.
TRANS.PI.RAR, *v.*, to transpire, to sweat, to perspire, to become known.
TRANS.PLAN.TAR, *v.*, to transplant, to translocate.
TRANS.POR, *v.*, to transpose, to cross over, to overrun.
TRANS.POR.TAR, *v.*, to transport, to carry, to convey, to entrance.
TRANS.POR.TE, *s.m.*, transport, transportation, conduction, vehicle.
TRANS.TOR.NAR, *v.*, to overturn, to disturb, to perturb, to alter.
TRANS.VER.SAL, *adj.*, transverse, transversal.
TRANS.VI.AR, *v.*, to wander, to err, to deviate.
TRA.PA.ÇA, *s.f.*, fraud, knavery, deceit, trick, swindle.
TRA.PA.CEI.RO, *s.m.*, trickster, swindler, crook.
TRA.PÉ.ZIO, *s.m.*, trapezium, trapeze, trapezoid.
TRA.PE.ZIS.TA, *s.2 gen.*, trapezist.
TRA.PO, *s.m.*, rag, tatter, shred, frazzle.
TRA.QUEI.A, *s.f.*, trachea, windpipe.
TRA.QUE.JO, *s.m.*, practice, experience.
TRÁS, *prep.*, behind, after, back.
TRA.SEI.RA, *s.f.*, rear, hinder part, back.
TRA.SEI.RO, *s.m.*, bum, butt, buttocks; *adj.*, back, posterior, rear.
TRAS.LA.DA.ÇÃO, *s.f.*, translation, copy, transcription.
TRAS.LA.DAR, *v.*, to transfer, to remove, to transport.
TRAS.LA.DO, *s.m.*, transfer, removal, copy, transcript, translation.
TRA.TA.DO, *s.m.*, treaty, agreement, pact, accord.
TRA.TA.MEN.TO, *s.m.*, treatment, treating, handling, usage, daily ration.
TRA.TAN.TE *s.2 gen.*, rascal, crook, scoundrel.
TRA.TAR, *v.*, to treat, to deal with, to handle, to transact, to attend.
TRA.TO, *s.m.*, deal, agreement, contract, dealing.
TRA.TOR, *s.m.*, tractor.

TRAUMA 265 **TRIO**

TRAU.MA, *s.m.*, trauma.
TRAU.MÁ.TI.CO, *adj.*, traumatic.
TRA.VA, *s.f.*, block, lock, key bolt.
TRA.VA.DO, *adj.*, connected, joined, linked.
TRA.VAR, *v.*, to join, to connect, to brace, to unite.
TRA.VE, *s.f.*, bar, crossbar.
TRA.VES.SA, *s.f.*, beam, crossbar, crossroad, transom, batten.
TRA.VES.SÃO, *s.m.*, dash, division; cross-wind.
TRA.VES.SEI.RO, *s.m.*, pillow.
TRA.VES.SIA, *s.f.*, crossing.
TRA.VES.SU.RA, *s.f.*, prank, gambol, frisk.
TRA.ZER, *v.*, to bring, to fetch, to carry, to convey, to introduce.
TRE.CHO, *s.m.*, period, space, section, distance, interval.
TRÉ.GUA, *s.f.*, armistice, truce, rest.
TREI.NA.DO, *adj.*, trained, drilled.
TREI.NA.DOR, *s.m.*, trainer, coach.
TREI.NAR, *v.*, to train, to drill, to coach, to exercise, to practise.
TREI.NO, *s.m.*, training, coaching.
TREM, *s.m.*, train.
TRE.MA, *s.m.*, diaresis.
TRE.ME.DEI.RA, *s.f.*, trembling, quaking, fit, shivering.
TRE.MEN.DO, *adj.*, tremendous, terrifying, awful, frightful, terrible.
TRE.MER, *v.*, to tremble, to quake, to shake, to quiver, to vibrate.
TRE.MOR, *s.m.*, tremor, shake, thrill, quiver.
TRE.MU.LA.ÇÃO, *s.f.*, tremble, trembling, flicker.
TRE.MU.LAR, *v.*, to tremble, to quaver, to wave, to flicker, to twinkle, vascillate.
TRÊ.MU.LO, *adj.*, trembling, fearful, hesitant.
TRE.NÓ, *s.m.*, sled, sleigh, sledge, toboggan.
TRE.PA.DEI.RA, *s.f.*, creeper, creeping.
TRE.PAR, *v.*, to climb, to ascend, to rise, to scale.
TRE.PI.DA.ÇÃO, *s.f.*, trepidation, vibration, agitation.
TRE.PI.DAR, *v.*, to tremble, to shake, to oscillate, to vibrate, to vacillate.
TRÊS, *num.*, three.
TRES.LOU.CA.DO, *adj.*, crazy, mad, deranged.
TRE.VAS, *s.f., pl.*, darkness, obscurity, ignorance, gloom, mirkiness.
TRE.VO, *s.m.*, clover, intersection, shamrock.
TRE.ZE, *num.*, thirteen.
TRE.ZEN.TOS, *num.*, three hundred.
TRI.ÂN.GU.LO, *s.m.*, triangle, trigon.
TRI.BAL, *adj.*, tribal.
TRI.BO, *s.m.*, tribe, clan, race, folk, family.
TRI.BU.LA.ÇÃO, *s.f.*, tribulation, grief, trouble.
TRI.BU.NA, *s.f.*, tribune, rostrum, pulpit, gallery.
TRI.BU.NAL, *s.m.*, court of justice, tribunal, council.
TRI.BU.TA.ÇÃO, *s.f.*, taxation, assessment.
TRI.BU.TA.DO, *adj.*, taxed, assessed.
TRI.BU.TAR, *v.*, to lay a tribute on, to tax.
TRI.BU.TÁ.RIO, *s.m.*, tributary; *adj.*, tributary, contributary.
TRI.BU.TO, *s.m.*, tribute, duty, tax, toll, due.
TRI.CEN.TE.NÁ.RIO, *adj.*, tricentenary.
TRI.CÔ, *s.m.*, knitting, tricot.
TRI.CO.LOR, *adj.*, tricolour, tricoloured.
TRI.Ê.NIO, *s.m.*, triennial, a period of three years.
TRI.GAL, *s.m.*, wheat field, cornfield.
TRI.GÊ.MEO, *s.m.*, triplet, trilling.
TRI.GÉ.SI.MO, *adj.*, thirtieth.
TRI.GO, *s.m.*, wheat.
TRI.GO.NO.ME.TRI.A, *s.f.*, trigonometry.
TRI.LHA, *s.f.*, trail, track.
TRI.LHAR, *v.*, to thrash, to flail, to beat.
TRI.LHO, *s.m.*, trail, track, rail.
TRI.LO.GI.A, *s.f.*, trilogy.
TRI.MES.TRAL, *adj.*, trimestrial.
TRI.MES.TRE, *s.m.*, quarter, period of three months.
TRI.NAR, *v.*, to trill, to shake, to quaver.
TRIN.CA, *s.f.*, trine, gang, scratch, crack.
TRIN.CAR, *v.*, to crush, to bite, to crunch.
TRIN.CO, *s.m.*, door latch, latch bolt.
TRIN.DA.DE, *s.f.*, Trinity, triad, trine.
TRIN.TA, *num.*, thirty.
TRI.O, *s.m.*, trio, a set of three.

TRI.PA, *s.f.*, intestine, gut, tripe.
TRI.PÉ, *s.m.*, tripod, trivet, spider.
TRI.PLI.CA.ÇÃO, *s.f.*, triplication.
TRI.PLI.CAR, *v.*, to triplicate, to triple.
TRI.PLO, *s.m.*, triple, triplex; *adj.*, triple, threefold.
TRI.PU.DI.AR, *v.*, to tripudiate, to exult, to rejoice.
TRI.PU.LA.ÇÃO, *s.f.*, crew, personnel.
TRI.PU.LAN.TE, *s.2 gen.*, member of the crew, seaman, sailor.
TRIS.TE, *adj.*, dreary, melancholic, sorrowful, unhappy, depressed.
TRIS.TE.ZA, *s.f.*, sorrow, grief, unhappiness, melancholy, depression.
TRIS.TO.NHO, *adj.*, unhappy, depressed, dejected.
TRI.TI.CUL.TU.RA, *s.f.*, wheat growing.
TRI.TU.RAR, *v.*, to grind, to mill, to triturate.
TRI.UN.FAL, *adj.*, triumphal.
TRI.UN.FAR, *v.*, to triumph, to win, to conquer, to be successful.
TRI.UN.FO, *s.m.*, triumph, victory, conquest, success.
TRI.VI.AL, *adj.*, trivial, common, trifling, banal, petty.
TRI.VI.A.LI.DA.DE, *s.f.*, trivialism, triviality, trivialness.
TRIZ, *s.m.*, moment, trice.
TRO.CA, *s.f.*, change, mutation, conversion, small cash.
TRO.CA.DI.LHO, *s.m.*, pun, quibble, play on words.
TRO.CAR, *v.*, to change, to turn, to alter, to replace, to commute, to substitute.
TROM.BA, *s.f.*, trunk (of an elephant or tapir).
TROM.BE.TA, *s.f.*, trumpet, tuba, horn.
TROM.BO.NE, *s.m.*, trombone.
TRON.CO, *s.m.*, trunk, stem of a tree, body, main body.
TRO.NO, *s.m.*, throne.
TRO.PA, *s.f.*, troop, band, host.
TRO.PE.ÇÃO, *s.f.*, stumbling, stumble, trip, slip.
TRO.PE.ÇAR, *v.*, to stumble, to trip, to slip.

TRO.PE.ÇO, *s.m.*, stumble, false step, obstacle.
TRO.PI.CAL, *adj.*, tropical.
TRÓ.PI.CO, *s.m.*, tropic.
TRO.TAR, *v.*, to trot, to lope.
TRO.VA, *s.f.*, ballad.
TRO.VÃO, *s.m.*, thunder.
TRO.VE.JAN.TE, *adj.*, thundering.
TRO.VE.JAR, *v.*, to thunder, to rumble, to roar, to lighten, to flash.
TRO.VO.A.DA, *s.f.*, thunderstorm.
TRU.CI.DAR, *v.*, to murder, to kill, to slaughter, to savage.
TRU.CU.LÊN.CIA, *s.f.*, truculence, truculentness, truculency.
TRU.CU.LEN.TO, *adj.*, truculent, savage, cruel.
TRU.FA, *s.f.*, truffle.
TRUN.CAR, *v.*, to truncate, to cut off, to ruff.
TRU.QUE, *s.m.*, trick, artifice, dodge.
TRUS.TE, *s.m.*, trust.
TRU.TA, *s.f.*, trout.
TU, *pron.*, you.
TU.A, *pron.*, your, yours.
TU.BA.RÃO, *s.m.*, shark.
TU.BER.CU.LO.SE, *s.f.*, tuberculosis.
TU.BO, *s.m.*, tube, pipe, duct, chute.
TU.BU.LA.ÇÃO, *s.f.*, pipeline, tubulation, piping.
TU.CA.NO, *s.m.*, toucan.
TU.DO, *s.m.*, all, everything, the whole; *pron.*, all, everything.
TU.FÃO, *s.m.*, hurricane, typhoon, tornado, windstorm.
TU.LI.PA, *s.f.*, tulip.
TUM.BA, *s.f.*, tomb, grave, tombstone.
TU.MOR, *s.m.*, tumor, tumour.
TÚ.MU.LO, *s.m.*, tomb, grave, sepulcher, vault.
TU.MUL.TO, *s.m.*, tumult, uproar, turbulence, commotion, clamour, ruckus.
TU.MUL.TU.AR, *v.*, to tumultuate, to riot, to mob, to excite.
TUN.DRA, *s.f.*, tundra.
TÚ.NEL, *s.m.*, tunnel.
TÚ.NI.CA, *s.f.*, tunic.
TUR.BI.LHÃO, *s.m.*, vortex, whirlpool, tornado, whirlwind, tumult, eddy, abyss.

TUR.BI.NA, *s.f.,* turbine.
TUR.BU.LÊN.CIA, *s.f.,* turbulence, disturbance, turmoil, agitation.
TUR.BU.LEN.TO, *adj.,* turbulent, troublesome, inquiet, factious.
TUR.CO, *s.m.,* Turk; *adj.,* Turkish.
TUR.FE, *s.m.,* the turf, race-course.
TUR.GI.DEZ, *s.f.,* turgidity, swelling.
TU.RIS.MO, *s.m.,* tourism, touring.
TU.RIS.TA, *s.2 gen.,* tourist.
TUR.MA, *s.f.,* group, gang, people, division.
TUR.MA.LI.NA, *s.f.,* tourmaline.
TUR.NO, *s.m.,* turn, shift.

TUR.QUE.SA, *s.f.,* turquoise.
TUR.VA.ÇÃO, *s.f.,* perturbation, disturbance, overcasting.
TUR.VAR, *v.,* to darken, to dim, to dazzle, to trouble.
TUR.VO, *adj.,* muddy, cloudy, darkish.
TU.TA.NO, *s.m.,* marrow, medulla.
TU.TE.LA, *s.f.,* tutelage, guardianship, tutorship, custody.
TU.TE.LAR, *adj.,* tutelar, protective; *v.,* to tutor, to protect, to guard.
TU.TOR, *s.m.,* tutor, preceptor, guardian.

U

U, *s.m.*, the twentieth letter of the Portuguese alphabet.
Ú.BE.RE, *s.m.*, udder; dug; *adj.*, abundant, fertile.
U.BÍ.QUO, *adj.*, ubiquitous, omnipresent.
U.CRA.NI.A.NO, *adj.*, *s.m.*, Ukrainian.
U.FA.NAR, *v.*, to render proud, to flatter, to boast.
UÍS.QUE, *s.m.*, whisky.
UI.VAR, *v.*, to howl.
UI.VO, *s.m.*, howl.
ÚL.CE.RA, *s.f.*, ulceration.
UL.CE.RA.DO, *adj.*, ulcerous, ulcerated.
UL.CE.RAR, *v.*, to ulcerate, to suppurate, to rankle.
UL.TI.MA.DO, *adj.*, concluded, finished, completed.
UL.TI.MAR, *v.*, to terminate, to finish, to end, to close.
UL.TI.MA.TO, *s.m.*, ultimatum.
ÚL.TI.MO, *adj.*, last, ultimate, latter, late, latest.
UL.TRA.JAR, *v.*, to revile, to slander, to insult, to affront, to offend.
UL.TRA.JE, *s.m.*, affront, offence, insult, defamation.
UL.TRA.MO.DER.NO, *adj.*, ultramodern.
UL.TRA.PAS.SAR, *v.*, to surpass, to exceed, to pass over or beyond, to outdate, to leave behind.
UL.TRAS.SOM, *s.m.*, supersonic, ultrasonic.
UL.TRA.VI.O.LE.TA, *adj.*, *s.m.*, ultraviolet.
UM, *num.*, one, cardinal number; art., the, a, an, some; **ERA UMA VEZ**, once upon a time.
U.ME.DE.CER, *v.*, to moisten, dampen, to wet, to humidify.
U.ME.DE.CI.DO, *adj.*, wettish, wet, damp.
U.ME.DE.CI.MEN.TO, *s.m.*, moistening, wetting, wetness.
U.MI.DA.DE, *s.f.*, humidity, moistness, dampness.
U.NÂ.NI.ME, *adj.*, unanimous.
U.NA.NI.MI.DA.DE, *s.f.*, unanimity, consensus.
UN.ÇÃO, *s.f.*, unction, anointment.
UN.GUEN.TO, *s.m.*, unguent, balm.
U.NHA, *s.f.*, nail; **UNHA ENCRAVADA**, ingrowing nail.
U.NI.ÃO, *s.f.*, union, alliance, association, junction.
Ú.NI.CO, *s.m.*, unique; *adj.*, unique, single, alone, sole, only, one, one and only.
U.NI.DA.DE, *s.f.*, unity, oneness, unit, union, drive.
U.NI.DO, *adj.*, united, joined, allied.
U.NI.FI.CA.ÇÃO, *s.f.*, unification.
U.NI.FI.CAR, *v.*, to unify, to gather, to standardize, to unite.
U.NI.FOR.ME, *s.m.*, uniform; *adj.*, uniform, identic, same, regular.
U.NI.FOR.MI.DA.DE, *s.f.*, uniformity.
U.NI.FOR.MI.ZAR, *v.*, to uniformize, to make uniform, to unify.
U.NI.LA.TE.RAL, *adj.*, unilateral.
U.NIR, *v.*, to unite, to join, to connect, to adjoin, to unify, to fasten, to attach.
U.NÍS.SO.NO, *s.m.*, unison; *adj.*, unisonant, unisonous.
U.NI.VA.LEN.TE, *adj.*, *s.2 gen.*, univalent, monovalent.
U.NI.VER.SAL, *adj.*, universal.
U.NI.VER.SA.LI.DA.DE, *s.f.*, universality, totality.
U.NI.VER.SA.LI.ZAR, *v.*, to universalize.
U.NI.VER.SI.DA.DE, *s.f.*, university.
U.NI.VER.SI.TÁ.RIO, *adj.*, universitarian, academic.
U.NI.VER.SO, *s.m.*, universe, the solar system, a whole; *adj.*, universal.
U.NO, *adj.*, one, sole, only one, single.
UN.TAR, *v.*, to anoint, to daub, to grease.
UN.TU.O.SI.DA.DE, *s.f.*, unctuosity, greasiness.
U.RÂ.NI.CO, *adj.*, uranic.

U.RÂ.NIO, *s.m.*, uranium.
UR.BA.NI.DA.DE, *s.f.*, urbanity, urbaneness, politeness.
UR.BA.NIS.TA, *s.2 gen.*, urbanist.
UR.BA.NI.ZA.ÇÃO, *s.f.*, urbanization.
UR.BA.NI.ZAR, *v.*, to urbanize, to civilize.
UR.BA.NO, *adj.*, urban, civic, townish.
UR.DIR, *v.*, to warp, to weave, to plot, to intrigue.
U.REI.A, *s.f.*, urea.
U.RE.TER, *s.m.*, ureter.
U.RE.TRA, *s.f.*, urethra.
UR.GÊN.CIA, *s.f.*, urgency, haste, need, exigence.
UR.GEN.TE, *adj.*, urgent, urging, pressing.
U.RI.NA, *s.f.*, urine.
U.RI.NAR, *v.*, to urinate, to piss.
UR.NA, *s.f.*, urn, coffin.
U.RO.LO.GI.A, *s.f.*, urology.
UR.SO, *s.m.*, bear.
U.RU.BU, *s.m.*, vulture.
U.RU.GUAI.O, *adj.*, *s.m.*, Uruguayan.
U.RU.TU, *s.f.*, urutu.
U.SA.DO, *adj.*, usual, used, spent, old.
U.SAR, *v.*, to use, to employ, to accustom, to habituate, to utilize, to spend.
U.SÁ.VEL, *adj.*, usable, wearable.
U.SI.NA, *s.f.*, work, workshop, works, mill, plant, factory.
U.SO, *s.m.*, use, employ, utilization.
U.SU.AL, *adj.*, usual, normal, habitual, customary, commonplace.
U.SU.Á.RIO, *s.m.*, user, usuary.
U.SU.CA.PI.ÃO, *s.m.*, usucapion, udal.
U.SU.FRU.IR, *v.*, to usufruct.
U.SU.FRU.TO, *s.m.*, usufruct, fruition, enjoyment.
U.SU.RA, *s.f.*, usury, interest, avarice, shabbiness.
U.SU.RÁ.RIO, *s.m.*, usurer.
U.SUR.PA.ÇÃO, *s.f.*, usurpation, encroachment, arrogation.
U.SUR.PAR, *v.*, to usurp, encroach, assume, to arrogate.
U.TEN.SÍ.LIO, *s.m.*, utensil, tool, implement, ware.
Ú.TE.RO, *s.m.*, uterus, womb.
Ú.TIL, *adj.*, useful, practical, handy, helpful.
U.TI.LI.DA.DE, *s.f.*, utility, use, convenience.
U.TI.LI.TÁ.RIO, *s.m.*, jeep, station wagon.
U.TI.LI.TA.RIS.MO, *s.m.*, utilitarism.
U.TI.LI.ZA.ÇÃO, *s.f.*, utilization.
U.TI.LI.ZAR, *v.*, to utilize, to make useful, to profit, to apply.
U.TO.PI.A, *s.f.*, Utopia, dream, chimera, fancy.
U.TÓ.PI.CO, *adj.*, Utopian, fanciful, visionary, fantastic.
U.VA, *s.f.*, grape.
Ú.VU.LA, *s.f.*, uvula.

V

V, *s.m.*, the twenty-first letter of the Portuguese alphabet.
VA.CA, *s.f.*, cow, beef.
VA.CI.LA.ÇÃO, *s.f.*, vacillation, hesitation, oscillation.
VA.CI.LAR, *v.*, to vacillate, to hesitate, to waver, to falter.
VA.CI.NA, *s.f.*, vaccine.
VA.CI.NA.ÇÃO, *s.f.*, vaccination, inoculation.
VA.CI.NAR, *v.*, to vaccinate.
VÁ.CUO, *s.m.*, vacuum, hollow, gap, void, vacuity.
VA.DI.A.GEM, *s.f.*, idleness, indolence.
VA.DI.AR, *v.*, to idle, to laze, to loaf, to lounge.
VA.DI.O, *s.m.*, idler, lounger, loafer; *adj.*, vagrant, idle, vagabond.
VA.GA, *s.f.*, vacancy, leisure, wave, billow.
VA.GA.BUN.DA.GEM, *s.f.*, vagabondage, vagrancy.
VA.GA.BUN.DO, *s.m.*, vagabond, vagrant, idler, tramp, bum; *adj.*, idle, lazy, vagrant, roving.
VA.GA-LU.ME, *s.m.*, firefly, glowworm.
VA.GÃO, *s.m.*, railway car, waggon.
VA.GAR, *v.*, to vacate, to become vacant, to rove, to run, to ramble.
VA.GA.RO.SO, *adj.*, slow, sluggish, dull, languid.
VA.GEM, *s.f.*, kidney beans, French beans.
VA.GI.NA, *s.f.*, vagina.
VA.GO, *adj.*, vacant, vacuous, vague, empty, indistinct.
VAI.A, *s.f.*, hiss, catcall, hoot, mockery.
VAI.AR, *v.*, to hoot, to hiss at, to boo.
VAI.DA.DE, *s.f.*, vanity, vainness, pride.
VAI.DO.SO, *adj.*, vain, proud, flatulent, conceited.
VA.LA, *s.f.*, trench, ditch.
VA.LE, *s.m.*, valley, dale, plain; credit note, bill.
VA.LEN.TE, *adj.*, valiant, intrepid, brave, bold.
VA.LEN.TI.A, *s.f.*, valiantness, bravery, valour.
VA.LER, *v.*, to value, to be worth, to be valuable, to cost, to protect, to help.
VA.LE.TE, *s.m.*, knave, jack.
VA.LI.A, *s.f.*, worth, value, price, merit, favour.
VA.LI.DA.ÇÃO, *s.f.*, validation.
VA.LI.DA.DE, *s.f.*, validity, legality, force.
VA.LI.DAR, *v.*, to validate, to legalize, to authenticate, to acknowledge.
VÁ.LI.DO, *adj.*, valid, sound, legal, binding.
VA.LI.O.SO, *adj.*, valuable, worthy, precious, rich.
VA.LI.SE, *s.f.*, valise, gripsack, small suitcase.
VA.LOR, *s.m.*, value, worth, courage, effort, merit, price, force, feck.
VA.LO.RI.ZAR, *v.*, to valorize, to value, to prize, to appraise.
VA.LO.RO.SO, *adj.*, valorous, worthy, valiant, manly.
VAL.SA, *s.f.*, waltz.
VÁL.VU.LA, *s.f.*, valve.
VAM.PI.RO, *s.m.*, vampire.
VÂN.DA.LO, *s.m.*, Vandal; *adj.*, vandalic.
VAN.GLO.RI.AR, *v.*, to puff up, to praise, to flatter.
VAN.GUAR.DA, *s.f.*, vanguard, advance guard, van.
VAN.TA.GEM, *s.f.*, advantage, benefit, profit, boot.
VAN.TA.JO.SO, *adv.*, profitable, advantageous, favourable.
VÃO, *s.m.*, void, vacuum, interspace; *adj.*, vain, void, futile, empty, useless.
VA.POR, *s.m.*, vapour, steam, fume, steamship, ship.
VA.PO.RI.ZA.ÇÃO, *s.f.*, vaporization.
VA.PO.RI.ZAR, *v.*, to vaporize, to evaporate.
VA.QUEI.RO, *s.m.*, cowboy, herdsman.
VA.RA, *s.f.*, stick, rod, cane, switch, staff.
VA.RAN.DA, *s.f.*, balcony, terrace.

VA.RE.JEI.RA, *s.f.*, blowfly.
VA.RE.JIS.TA, *s.2 gen.*, retail dealer, retailer.
VA.RE.JO, *s.m.*, retail.
VA.RI.A.ÇÃO, *s.f.*, change, modification, diversification.
VA.RI.A.DO, *adj.*, varied, diverse, assorted, inconstant.
VA.RI.AR, *v.*, to vary, to change, to alter, to diversify, to alternate, to shade.
VA.RI.CE.LA, *s.f.*, chickenpox, varicella.
VA.RI.E.DA.DE, *s.f.*, variety, diversity, variousness, inconstancy.
VA.RI.E.GA.DO, *adj.*, variegated, varying.
VÁ.RIO, *adj.*, different, various, variegated.
VA.RÍ.O.LA, *s.f.*, variola, smallpox.
VA.RO.NIL, *adj.*, manly, manlike, manful.
VAR.RER, *v.*, to sweep, to broom, to clean, to clear up.
VÁR.ZEA, *s.f.*, lea, plain.
VA.SE.LI.NA, *s.f.*, vaseline.
VA.SEC.TO.MI.A, *s.f.*, vasectomy.
VA.SI.LHA, *s.f.*, vessel, pail, basin.
VA.SI.LHA.ME, *s.m.*, vessels, casks, bottles.
VA.SO, *s.m.*, vase, flowerpot.
VAS.SOU.RA, *s.f.*, broom, besom.
VAS.TI.DÃO, *s.f.*, vastness, wideness, ampleness, amplitude.
VAS.TO, *adj.*, vast, great, colossal, huge, ample.
VA.TI.CA.NO, *s.m.*, Vatican.
VA.TI.CÍ.NIO, *s.m.*, vatication, foretelling, prediction.
VA.ZA.MEN.TO, *s.m.*, leak, leakage, leakiness, seepage.
VA.ZÃO, *s.f.*, flowing out, outflow, emptying.
VA.ZAR, *v.*, to empty, to pour out, to drain, to discharge, to spill.
VA.ZI.O, *s.m.*, emptiness, vaccuum, vacuity; *adj.*, empty, vacant, void, vain.
VE.A.DO, *s.m.*, deer, hart, stag.
VE.DA.ÇÃO, *s.f.*, prohibition, impediment, hindrance, stoppage, closing, barrier, blocking, enclosure.
VE.DAR, *v.*, to hinder, to prohibit, to forbid, to interdict, to stop, to bar.

VE.DE.TE, *s.f.*, star.
VE.E.MÊN.CIA, *s.f.*, vehemence, vehemency, passion.
VE.GE.TA.ÇÃO, *s.f.*, vegetation.
VE.GE.TAL, *adj.*, vegetable.
VE.GE.TA.RI.A.NO, *adj., s.m.*, vegetarian.
VE.GE.TA.TI.VO, *adj.*, vegetative.
VEI.A, *s.f.*, vein, tendency, vocation.
VE.Í.CU.LO, *s.m.*, vehicle.
VE.LA, *s.f.*, sail, canvas, sheet; candle.
VE.LE.JAR, *v.*, to sail.
VE.LHA, *s.f.*, old woman, crone.
VE.LHA.CO, *s.m.*, knave, rogue, villain; *adj.*, knavish, roguish, crafty, foxlike.
VE.LHI.CE, *s.f.*, old age, oldness.
VE.LHO, *s.m.*, old man; *adj.*, old, aged, ancient, obsolete, archaic, worn out, shabby.
VE.LO.CI.DA.DE, *s.f.*, velocity, speed, fastness, swiftness.
VE.LO.CÍ.ME.TRO, *s.m.*, speedometer.
VE.LO.CÍ.PE.DE, *s.m.*, velocipede, bicycle.
VE.LÓ.RIO, *s.m.*, deathwatch.
VE.LOZ, *adj.*, swift, quick, speedy, fast.
VE.LU.DO, *s.m.*, velvet, velveting, velure.
VEN.CER, *v.*, to win, to succeed, to triumph, to vanquish, to overcome, to get, to surpass.
VEN.CI.DO, *adj.*, vanquished, overcome, conquered.
VEN.CI.MEN.TO, *s.m.*, overcoming, deadline, expiring date, expiration, salary.
VEN.DA, *s.f.*, sale, selling, bandage, blindfold.
VEN.DA.VAL, *s.m.*, windstorm, whirlwind.
VEN.DE.DOR, *s.m.*, salesman, seller, vendor, agent.
VEN.DER, *v.*, to sell, to vend, to make sales, to deal in.
VE.NE.NO, *s.m.*, poison, venom, toxine.
VE.NE.NO.SO; *adj.*, poisonous, venomous.
VE.NE.RA.ÇÃO, *s.f.*, veneration, worship.
VE.NE.RAR, *v.*, to venerate, to adore, to worship.
VE.NÉ.REO, *adj.*, venereal.
VE.NE.ZU.E.LA.NO, *adj., s.m.*, Venezuelan.
VÊ.NIA, *s.f.*, leave, permission, bow.
VEN.TA, *s.f.*, nostril.

VEN.TA.NI.A, *s.f.*, windstorm, blow.
VEN.TAR, *v.*, to wind, to blow.
VEN.TI.LA.ÇÃO, *s.f.*, ventilation, airing.
VEN.TI.LA.DOR, *s.m.*, ventilator, aerator, fan.
VEN.TO, *s.m.*, wind, air, drift.
VEN.TRE, *s.m.*, womb, belly, abdomen.
VEN.TU.RO.SO, *adj.*, lucky, fortunate, happy, felicitous.
VÊ.NUS, *s.f.*, Venus.
VER, *v.*, to see, to behold, to look, to watch at, to observe.
VE.RA.NEI.O, *s.m.*, summer resort.
VE.RÃO, *s.m.*, summer.
VER.BA, *s.f.*, available sum or amount, budget, clause.
VER.BAL, *adj.*, verbal, oral.
VER.BA.LI.ZAR, *v.*, to verbalize.
VER.BO, *s.m.*, verb, word, expression.
VER.DA.DE, *s.f.*, truth, reality, fact, true.
VER.DA.DEI.RO, *adj.*, true, veracious, real, actual, exact, certain.
VER.DE, *s.m.*, green colour; *adj.*, green.
VER.DE.JAR, *v.*, to green.
VER.DU.GO, *s.m.*, hangman, executioner.
VER.DU.RA, *s.f.*, greens, vegetable.
VER.DU.REI.RO, *s.m.*, greengrocer.
VE.RE.A.DOR, *s.m.*, town councillor.
VE.RE.DIC.TO, *s.m.*, verdict, judgement, opinion.
VER.GAS.TAR, *v.*, to whip, to flog.
VER.GO.NHA, *s.f.*, shame, ashamedness, bashfulness.
VER.GO.NHO.SO, *adj.*, shameful, disreputable.
VE.RÍ.DI.CO, *adj.*, veracious, veridical, true.
VE.RI.FI.CAR, *v.*, to verify, to examine, to check, to control, to find out, to test.
VER.ME, *s.m.*, worm.
VER.ME.LHO, *adj.*, red, scarlet.
VER.MI.CI.DA, *s.m.*, vermicide, vermifuge.
VER.MU.TE, *s.m.*, vermouth.
VER.NÁ.CU.LO, *s.m.*, vernacular, mother tongue; *adj.*, vernacular, native.
VER.NIZ, *s.m.*, varnish, shellac, lake.
VE.ROS.SÍ.MIL, *adj.*, probable, likely.
VER.RU.GA, *s.f.*, wart.
VER.SÃO, *s.f.*, version, translation.
VER.SAR, *v.*, to versify.
VER.SÁ.TIL, *adj.*, versatile.
VER.SO, *s.m.*, verse, rime, rhyme, poetry; back, reverse.
VÉR.TE.BRA, *s.f.*, vertebra, spondyl.
VER.TE.BRA.DO, *adj.*, *s.m.*, vertebrate.
VER.TER, *v.*, to flow, to gush, to pour, to spout, to spill, to shed, to translate, to overflow.
VER.TI.CAL, *adj.*, vertical, upright.
VER.TI.GEM, *s.f.*, vertigo, giddiness.
VES.GO, *s.m.*, squint-eyed person; *adj.*, cross-eyed, strabismal, squinting.
VE.SÍ.CU.LA, *s.f.*, vesicle, bladder, blister.
VES.PA, *s.f.*, wasp.
VÉS.PE.RA, *s.f.*, eve, evening, afternoon.
VES.PER.TI.NO, *adj.*, vesper, vespertine.
VES.TE, *s.f.*, vest, vestment, clothes, garment, vesture.
VES.TI.BU.LAR, *s.m.*, vestibular.
VES.TI.DO, *s.m.*, dress, garment.
VES.TÍ.GIO, *s.m.*, vestige, footprint, trail, clue, mark, trace.
VES.TIR, *v.*, to dress, to wear, to clothe, to equip, to array.
VES.TU.Á.RIO, *s.m.*, clothes, clothing, garment.
VE.TAR, *v.*, to veto, to refuse, to interpose.
VE.TE.RA.NO, *s.m.*, veteran, vet; *adj.*, veteran, senior.
VE.TE.RI.NÁ.RIO, *s.m.*, veterinarian, veterinary.
VE.TO, *s.m.*, veto, interdiction.
VÉU, *s.m.*, veil, veling, covering.
VE.XA.ÇÃO, *s.f.*, vexation, molestation.
VE.XA.ME, *s.m.*, vexation, shame, blunder.
VEZ, *s.f.*, time, turn, occasion, opportunity.
VI.A, *s.f.*, way, path, street, road, route, means, manner, direction, channel; **VIA LÁCTEA**, The Milky Way.
VI.A.DU.TO, *s.m.*, viaduct, overpass.
VI.A.GEM, *s.f.*, travel, voyage, journey, trip, tour, excursion.
VI.A.JAN.TE, *s.2 gen.*, traveller, voyager; *adj.*, travelling, itinerant, wandering.

VI.A.JAR, *v.*, to travel, to journey, to tour, to voyage, to wander.
VI.A.TU.RA, *s.f.*, vehicle.
VÍ.BO.RA, *s.f.*, viper, adder.
VI.BRA.ÇÃO, *s.f.*, vibration, vibrancy, oscillation.
VI.BRAR, *v.*, to vibrate, to oscillate, to pulse, to pulsate.
VI.CI.A.DO, *adj.*, addicted, addict, vicious.
VI.CI.AR, *v.*, to vitiate, to corrupt, to pervert, to infect, to contaminate.
VÍ.CIO, *s.m.*, vice, addiction, immorality.
VI.DA, *s.f.*, life.
VI.DEN.TE, *s.2 gen.*, visionary, prophet; *adj.*, clairvoyant.
VÍ.DEO, *s.m.*, video, video cassette.
VI.DRA.ÇA, *s.f.*, windowpane, window glass.
VI.DRO, *s.m.*, glass, bottle, flask, phial.
VI.E.LA, *s.f.*, lane, alley, narrow, pass.
VI.GA.MEN.TO, *s.m.*, framework, framing.
VI.GÁ.RIO, *s.m.*, vicar.
VI.GA.RIS.TA, *s.2 gen.*, swindler, bilker, trickster.
VI.GÊN.CIA, *s.f.*, legality, force, validity.
VI.GÉ.SI.MO, *num.*, twentieth; *adj.*, twentieth.
VI.GI.A, *s.f.*, watch, watchman, guard, sentinel.
VI.GI.AR, *v.*, to watch, to guard, to be vigilate.
VI.GI.LÂN.CIA, *s.f.*, vigilance, guard, alertness.
VI.GÍ.LIA, *s.f.*, night-watch, vigil.
VI.GOR, *s.m.*, vigor, force, strenght.
VI.GO.RO.SO, *adj.*, vigorous, robust, active, strong, energetic.
VIL, *adj.*, vile, cheap, worthless.
VI.LA, *s.f.*, villa, small town.
VI.LÃO, *adj.*, villain, rascal, scoundrel, dirty.
VI.ME, *s.m.*, osier, willow, withe.
VI.NA.GRE, *s.m.*, vinegar.
VIN.CU.LA.DO, *adj.*, entailed, bound, linked.
VIN.CU.LAR, *v.*, to entail, to bond, to link, to annex.
VÍN.CU.LO, *s.m.*, entail, entailment, bond, link.
VIN.DA, *s.f.*, coming, arrival, forthcoming.
VIN.DI.MA, *s.f.*, vintage, harvest.
VIN.DO, *adj.*, arrived, come.
VIN.DOU.RO, *adj.*, coming, future, towardly.
VIN.GA.DOR, *s.m.*, avenger, revenger.
VIN.GAN.ÇA, *s.f.*, vengeance, revenge, retaliation.
VIN.GAR, *v.*, to avenge, to revenge, to retaliate, to punish.
VI.NHA, *s.f.*, vine, vineyard.
VI.NHO, *s.m.*, vine.
VI.NÍ.CO.LA, *s.f., adj.*, wine-growing.
VIN.TE, *num.*, twenty.
VI.O.LA, *s.f.*, viola.
VI.O.LA.ÇÃO, *s.f.*, violation, rape, infraction, trespass.
VI.O.LÃO, *s.m.*, guitar.
VI.O.LAR, *v.*, to violate, to transgress, to rape.
VI.O.LÊN.CIA, *s.f.*, violence, impetuosity, ferocity.
VI.O.LEN.TAR, *v.*, to violate, to force, to coerce, to rape.
VI.O.LEN.TO, *adj.*, violent, powerful.
VI.O.LE.TA, *s.f.*, violet.
VI.O.LI.NO, *s.m.*, violin, fiddle.
VI.O.LON.CE.LO, *s.m.*, violoncello, cello.
VIR, *v.*, to come, to arrive, to come from, to result, to happen, to proceed from.
VI.RA-LA.TA, *s.m.*, street-dog.
VI.RAR, *v.*, to turn, to reverse, to invert, to change.
VIR.GEM, *s.f.*; virgin; *adj.*, virginal, innocent, pure, untouched, spotless.
VIR.GIN.DA.DE, *s.f.*, virginity.
VÍR.GU.LA, *s.f.*, comma.
VIR.GU.LAR, *v.*, to punctuate, to insert commas.
VI.RIL, *adj.*, virile, vigorous, energetic, masculine, manlike.
VI.RI.LHA, *s.f.*, groin.
VIR.TU.AL, *adj.*, virtual, practical, actual.
VIR.TU.DE, *s.f.*, virtue, morality, moral action, purity.
VÍ.RUS, *s.m.*, virus.
VI.SÃO, *s.f.*, vision, sight, eyesight, view.
VI.SAR, *v.*, to aim at, to drive at, to seek, to look at.
VÍS.CE.RA, *s.f.*, viscera, entrails.
VI.SI.BI.LI.DA.DE, *s.f.*, visibility.
VI.SI.TA, *s.f.*, visit, visiting, visitation, inspection.
VI.SI.TAN.TE, *s.2 gen.*, visitant, visitor, caller.
VI.SI.TAR, *v.*, to visit, to call on, to see, to pay a visit.
VI.SÍ.VEL, *adj.*, visible, perceptible, manifest.

VI.SOR, *s.m.*, view finder, spy-hole.
VIS.TA, *s.f.*, sight, eyesight, vision, glimpse, view.
VIS.TO, *s.m.*, visa; *adj.*, accepted, seen, known.
VIS.TO.RI.A, *s.f.*, inspection, survey.
VIS.TO.RI.AR, *v.*, to inspect, to examine, to search.
VI.SU.AL, *adj.*, visual.
VI.SU.A.LI.ZAR, *v.*, to visualize.
VI.TAL, *adj.*, vital.
VI.TA.LÍ.CIO, *adj.*, lifelong, for life.
VI.TA.LI.DA.DE, *s.f.*, vitality.
VI.TA.MI.NA, *s.f.*, vitamin.
VI.TE.LA, *s.f.*, heifer, calf, a young of a cow.
VÍ.TI.MA, *s.f.*, victim, prey.
VI.TI.MAR, *v.*, to victimize.
VI.TÓ.RIA, *s.f.*, victory, triumph, conquest.
VI.TO.RI.O.SO, *adj.*, victorious, triumphant.
VÍ.TREO, *adj.*, vitreous, vitric, glassy.
VI.TRI.NA, *s.f.*, window, display window, shopwindow.
VI.Ú.VA, *s.f.*, widow.
VI.U.VEZ, *s.f.*, widowhood.
VI.Ú.VO, *s.m.*, widower.
VI.VA.CI.DA.DE, *s.f.*, vivacity.
VI.VEI.RO, *s.m.*, nursery, aquarium, fishpond.
VI.VER, *v.*, to live, to be alive, to exist, to be, to endure, to last.
VI.VO, *adj.*, alive, living, lively, smart, quick, alert.
VI.ZI.NHAN.ÇA, *s.f.*, neighbourhood, vicinity.
VI.ZI.NHO, *s.m.*, neighbour.
VO.AR, *v.*, to fly, to soar.
VO.CA.BU.LÁ.RIO, *s.m.*, vocabulary.
VO.CÁ.BU.LO, *s.m.*, vocable, word, term, name.
VO.CA.ÇÃO, *s.f.*, vocation.
VO.CA.CI.O.NAL, *adj.*, vocational.
VO.CAL, *adj.*, vocal, oral.
VO.CÁ.LI.CO, *adj.*, vocalic, vowel.
VO.CA.LI.ZA.ÇÃO, *s.f.*, vocalization.
VO.CA.LI.ZAR, *v.*, to vocalize, to vowelize.
VO.CÊ, *pron.*, you.
VOD.CA, *s.f.*, vodka.
VO.GAL, *s.f.*, vowel, vocal, voter.
VO.LAN.TE, *s.m.*, gauze, wheel; *adj.*, movable.
VO.LA.TI.ZA.ÇÃO, *s.f.*, volatization.
VOL.TA, *s.f.*, return, regress, curve, change, recurrency, alteration, replacement, gyre.
VOL.TA.GEM, *s.f.*, voltage, tension.
VOL.TAR, *v.*, to return, to come or go back, to regress, to recur, to devolve.
VO.LU.ME, *s.m.*, volume, capacity, content, book, pack, packet, bundle, extent, size.
VO.LUN.TÁ.RIO, *s.m.* volunteer; *adj.*, voluntary, spontaneous, gratuitous.
VO.LÚ.PIA, *s.f.*, sensuality, voluptuousness.
VO.LÚ.VEL, *adj.*, voluble, inconstant, fickle, fluky.
VO.MI.TAR, *v.*, to vomit, to throw up, to puke, to regurgitate, to spew, to cat.
VÔ.MI.TO, *s.m.*, vomit, spew, puke.
VON.TA.DE, *s.f.*, will, volition, wish, desire, mind, intention, purpose, determination, fancy.
VO.O, *s.m.*, flight.
VO.RA.CI.DA.DE, *s.f.*, voracity, voraciousness.
VO.RAZ, *adj.*, voracious, avid.
VÓS, *pron.*, you.
VOS.SO, *pron.*, your, yours.
VO.TA.ÇÃO, *s.f.*, voting, poll, election.
VO.TAR, *v.*, to vote, to elect, to poll.
VO.TO, *s.m.*, vote, promise, vow, ballot, election.
VO.VÔ, *s.m.*, grandpa.
VO.VÓ, *s.f.*, grandma, granny.
VOZ, *s.f.*, voice, right to speak.
VUL.CÂ.NI.CO, *adj.*, volcanic, vulcanian.
VUL.CA.NI.ZAR, *v.*, to vulcanize, to volcanize.
VUL.CÃO, *s.m.*, volcano.
VUL.GAR, *adj.*, vulgar, common, popular, banal.
VUL.GA.RI.DA.DE, *s.f.*, vulgarity, coarseness, vulgarism, banality.
VUL.GA.RI.ZAR, *v.*, to vulgarize, to make vulgar, to divulge, to propagate.
VUL.NE.RAR, *v.*, to hurt, to wound, to offend.
VUL.NE.RÁ.VEL, *adj.*, vulnerable.
VUL.TO, *s.m.*, shadow, shape, face, body, figure.
VUL.TO.SO, *adj.*, voluminous, bulky, important.
VUL.VA, *s.f.*, vulva.

X

X, *s.m.*, the twenty-second letter of the Portuguese alphabet; Roman numeral for ten (X).
XÁ, *s.m.*, Shah, soberano, na língua persa.
XA.DREZ, *s.m.*, chess, chessboard, check, mosaic, prison.
XA.LE, *s.m.*, shawl, plaid.
XAM.PU, *s.m.*, shampoo.
XA.RÁ, *s.2 gen.*, namesake, homonym.
XA.RO.PE, *s.m.*, syrup.
XE.LIM, *s.m.*, shilling.
XE.NO.FO.BI.A, *s.f.*, xenophobia.
XE.PA, *s.f.*, meal, food.
XE.QUE, *s.m.*, check; sheik.
XE.QUE-MA.TE, *s.m.*, checkmate, mate.
XE.RE.TA, *s.2 gen.*, snoopy, nosy, prying.
XE.RI.FE, *s.m.*, sheriff.
XÍ.CA.RA, *s.f.*, cup.
XI.LIN.DRÓ, *s.m.*, jail, gaol, prison.
XIN.GA.ÇÃO, *s.f.*, chiding, abuse, scolding.
XIN.GA.MEN.TO, *s.m.*, calling names, swearword.
XIN.GAR, *v.*, to chide, to scold, to rail, to offend.
XIS.TO, *s.m.*, schist; xisto argiloso, shale.
XI.XI, *s.m.*, urine.
XO.DÓ, *s.m.*, flirtation, sweetheart.

Z

Z, *s.m.*, the twenty-third and last letter of the Portuguese alphabet.
ZA.GUEI.RO, *s.m.*, back, fullback.
ZAN.GA.DO, *adj.*, angry, vexed, annoyed.
ZAN.GÃO, *s.m.*, drone, humble-bee, male honeybee.
ZAN.GAR, *v.*, to annoy, to make angry, to molest.
ZAN.ZAR, *v.*, to rove, to ramble, to wander.
ZAR.CÃO, *s.m.*, minium, red lead.
ZA.RO.LHO, *adj.*, squint-eyed, cross-eyed.
ZAR.PAR, *v.*, to weigh anchor, to sail.
ZE.BRA, *s.f.*, zebra.
ZEBU, *s.m.*, zebu.
ZÉ.FI.RO, *s.m.*, zephyr, the West wind.
ZE.LA.DOR, *s.m.*, janitor, watcher, keeper, overseer, inspector.
ZE.LA.DO.RA, *s.f.*, janitress.
ZE.LAR, *v.*, to watch over, to administer, to manage.
ZE.LO, *s.m.*, zeal, devotion, dedication, diligence.
ZE.LO.SO, *adj.*, zealous, careful, watchful, diligent, dedicated.
ZÊ.NI.TE, *s.m.*, zenith, vertex.
ZE.RO, *s.m.*, zero, a cipher, nobody, ought.
ZEUG.MA, *s.m.*, zeugma.
ZI.GUE-ZA.GUE, *s.m.*, zigzag.
ZIN.CO, *s.m.*, zinc.
ZÍ.PER, *s.m.*, zipper, slide fastener.
ZO.DI.A.CAL, *adj.*, zodiacal.
ZO.DÍ.A.CO, *s.m.*, zodiac.
ZOM.BA.DOR, *s.m.*, scoffer, jester, jeerer, mocker.
ZOM.BAR, *v.*, to mock, to make jokes, to make fun of, to flout.
ZOM.BA.RI.A, *s.f.*, mockery, sarcasm, ridicule, derision.
ZO.NA, *s.f.*, zone, area, region, country.
ZO.O.LO.GIA, *s.f.*, zoology.
ZO.O.LÓ.GI.CO, *adj.*, zoologic, zoological; **JARDIM ZOOLÓGICO**, zoological garden, zoo.
ZO.O.TEC.NI.A, *s.f.*, zootechny.
ZUM.BI.DO, *s.m.*, hum, buzz.
ZUM.BIR, *v.*, to hum, to buzz, to whir, to whiz.
ZU.NI.DO, *s.m.*, whiz, whir, buzz.
ZUR.RAR, *v.*, to bray, to heehaw.
ZUR.RO, *s.m.*, bray, braying, heehaw, rattle.

dicionário escolar inglês

Inglês - Português

A

A, *s.*, a primeira letra do alfabeto; lá.
A, *art indef.*, um, uma.
ABACK, *adv.*, para trás, atrás.
ABA.CUS, *s.*, ábaco.
ABAN.DON, *v.*, abandonar, largar, ceder; desamparar, conceder.
ABAN.DONED, *adj., part.*, abandonado, largado, cedido.
ABAN.DON.MENT, *s.*, abandono, desamparo.
ABASE, *v.*, humilhar, rebaixar.
ABASE.MENT, *s.*, humilhação, rebaixamento, degradação.
ABASH, *v.*, rebaixar, envergonhar, humilhar.
ABASH.MENT, *s.*, humilhação, rebaixamento.
ABAS.ING, *adj.*, vergonhoso.
ABATE, *v.*, abater, enfraquecer, diminuir, reduzir.
ABATE.MENT, *s.*, abatimento, enfraquecimento.
AB.BEY, *s.*, abadia, mosteiro.
ABBOT, *s.*, abade.
AB.BRE.VI.ATE, *v.*, abreviar, resumir, condensar.
AB.BRE.VI.ATION *s.*, abreviação, resumo, condensação.
AB.DI.CATE, *v.*, abdicar, renunciar, deixar de.
AB.DO.MEN, *s.*, abdome, ventre.
AB.DOM.INAL, *adj.*, abdominal.
AB.DUCT, *v.*, sequestrar, raptar.
AB.DUCTION, *s.*, rapto, sequestro.
ABEAR, *v.*, aguentar, suportar, ajeitar.
ABED, *adj.*, deitado, acamado.
AB.ER.RA.TION, *s.*, aberração, aleijão, desvio.
ABET, *v.*, instigar, estimular, incitar, provocar.
ABEY.ANCE, *s.*, suspensão, inatividade, ócio, pausa.
AB.HOR, *v.*, abominar, odiar, detestar, ter aversão.
AB.HOR.RENCE, *s.*, repugnância, aversão, ódio.
ABIDE, *v.*, continuar, permanecer, suportar.
ABID.ING.LY, *adv.*, fixamente, permanentemente.
ABIL.I.TY, *s.*, habilidade, capacidade, perícia, competência.
AB.JECT, *adj.*, abjeto, desprezível, vil.
AB.JEC.TION, *s.*, abjeção, desprezo, vileza.
AB.JU.RATION, *s.*, abjuração, renúncia.
AB.JURE, *v.*, abjurar, renunciar, renegar, deixar de.
AB.LATIVE, *s.*, *adj.*, ablativo.
ABLAZE, *adj.*, inflamado, queimante, em chamas, brilhante.
ABLE, *adj.*, hábil, perito, capaz, esperto.
ABLOOM, *adj.*, florido, florescente, em flor.
AB.LU.TION, *s.*, ablução, lavagem, limpeza, purificação.
AB.NE.GATE, *v.*, abnegar, negar, renunciar, desistir.
AB.NOR.MAL, *adj.*, anormal, anômalo.
AB.NOR.MAL.I.TY *s.*, anormalidade, defeito.
ABOARD *adv.*, a bordo.
ABODE, *s.*, domicílio, *s.*, residência; *v.*, *part.*, de **ABIDE**.
ABOL.ISH, *v.*, abolir, anular, desfazer.
AB.O.LI.TION, *s.*, abolição, anulamento.
ABOM.I.NA.BLE, *adj.*, abominável, detestável, nojento.
ABOM.I.NATE, *v.*, abominar, detestar.
AB.ORIG.I.NE, *s.*, aborígene, indígena.
ABORT, *v.*, abortar, cancelar, anular.
ABOR.TION, *s.*, aborto, abortamento.
ABOR.TIVE, *adj.*, abortivo.
ABOUND, *v.*, abundar, ser abundante.
ABOUT, *adv.*, quase, em torno, ao redor, na vizinhança, a respeito.
ABOVE, *adv.*, acima, por sobre, em cima.
ABRA.SIVE, *adj., s.*, abrasivo.
ABRIDGE, *v.*, abreviar, resumir, condensar.
AB.RO.GA.TION, *s.*, ab-rogação, anulação.
ABRUPT, *adj.*, abrupto, íngreme, ríspido.

ABRUPT.NESS s., rispidez, brusquidão.
AB.SCESS, s., abcesso.
AB.SENCE, s., ausência, falta, lacuna.
AB.SENT, adj., ausente, faltante, abstrato.
AB.SO.LUTE, adj., absoluto, infinito, total.
AB.SO.LUTE.LY, adv., certamente, absolutamente.
AB.SO.LU.TION, s., absolvição, perdão.
AB.SO.LUT.ISM, s., absolutismo.
AB.SOLVE, v., absolver, perdoar.
AB.SORB, v., absorver, assimilar, apreender.
AB.SORPTION, s., absorção, apreensão.
AB.SORP.TIVE adj., absortivo, absorcível.
AB.STAIN, v., abster-se, deixar de, privar-se.
AB.STE.MI.OUS, adj., abstêmio.
AB.STEN.TION, s., abstenção, abstinência.
AB.STI.NENCE, s., abstinência, renúncia.
AB.STI.NENT, adj., abstinente, abstêmio.
AB.STRACT, adj., abstrato, ideal, extrato, resumo.
AB.STRACT.ED, adj., abstraído, absorto.
AB.STRACT.ED.NESS, s., abstração, distração.
AB.STRAC.TION, s., abstração, divagação, furto.
AB.SURD, adj., absurdo, estúpido, anormal.
AB.SUR.DI.TY, s., absurdidade, disparate, estupidez.
AB.SURD.NESS, s., absurdo, disparate, incongruência.
ABUN.DANCE, s., abundância, copiosidade.
ABUN.DANT, adj., abundante, copioso, farto.
ABUSE, s., abuso, desaforo, engano, maus tratos.
ABUSE, v., abusar, desaforar, enganar, maltratar.
ABU.SIVE, adj., abusivo, desaforado.
ABUT, v., limitar, confinar, restringir.
ABYS.MAL, adj., abismal, fundo; ruim, péssimo.
ABYSS, s., abismo.
AC.A.DEM.IC, adj., acadêmico; universitário.
AC.A.DE.MI.CIAN, s., acadêmico; lente, docente.
ACAD.E.MY, s., academia.
AC.CEDE, v., aceder, alcançar, permitir;
ACCEDE to – conceder.
AC.CEL.ER.ATE, v. acelerar, impulsionar.

AC.CEL.ER.A.TION, s., aceleração, aceleramento.
AC.CEL.ER.A.TOR, s., acelerador.
AC.CENT, s., acento, sotaque, pronúncia; acento gráfico.
AC.CEN.TU.AL, adj., acentuado, destacado, rítmico.
AC.CEN.TU.ATE,v.,acentuar,destacar, enfatizar.
ACCENTUATION, s., acentuação, ênfase.
AC.CEPT, v., aceitar, receber, suportar, adotar.
AC.CEPT.ABIL.I.TY, s., aceitabilidade, aceitação, recepção.
AC.CEP.TANCE, s., aceitação.
AC.CEP.TA.TION, s., aceitação, aceitamento, acepção.
AC.CESS, s., acesso, aproximação, entrada; v., acessar, entrar.
ACCESSORY, s., adj., acessório, suplementar.
AC.CI.DENT, s., acidente, incidente; acaso
AC.CI.DENT.AL, adj., acidental, fortuito.
AC.CLAIM, s., aplauso, aclamação, ovação.
AC.CLA.MA.TION, s., aclamação, ovação.
AC.CLI.MA.TION, s., aclimatação.
AC.CLI.MA.TIZE, v., aclimatar, aclimar.
AC.CLIV.I.TY, s., aclive, ladeira, encosta.
AC.COM.MO.DATE, v., acomodar, abrigar, alojar.
AC.COM.MO.DA.TION, s., acomodação, alojamento.
AC.COM.MO.DA.TIVE, adj., acomodável, acomodativo.
AC.COM.PANI.MENT, s., acompanhamento.
AC.COM.PA.NY, v., acompanhar, seguir junto.
AC.COM.PLICE, s., cúmplice, comparsa.
AC.COM.PLISH, v., concluir, terminar, finalizar.
AC.COM.PLISH.MENT, s., conclusão, finalização.
AC.CORD, s., tratado, acordo, pacto; v., acordar, concordar.
AC.COR.DANCE, s., acordo, concordância.
AC.COR.DANT, adj., conforme, concorde.
AC.CORD.ING, adj., concorde, acordado, de acordo.
AC.COR.DI.ON, s., acordeão, gaita, sanfona.
AC.COUNT, s., conta, soma, cálculo, cômputo;

v., contar, somar, calcular.
AC.COUNT.ABIL.I.TY, *s.*, responsabilidade.
AC.COUN.TANT, *s.*, contabilista, contador.
AC.COUNT.ING, *s.*, contabilidade.
AC.CRED.IT, *v.*, acreditar, aceitar, abonar.
AC.CREDIT.ED, *adj.*, acreditado, aceito.
AC.CRE.TION, *s.*, acréscimo, aumento, crescimento.
AC.CRUE, *v.*, advir, provir, resultar.
AC.CU.MU.LATE, *v.*, acumular, amontoar.
AC.CU.MU.LA.TION, *s.*, acumulação, amontoamento.
AC.CU.MU.LA.TIVE, *adj.*, acumulativo.
AC.CU.RA.CY, *s.*, exatidão, precisão.
AC.CU.RATE, *adj.*, acurado, preciso, exato.
AC.CURSE, *v.*, amaldiçoar, maldizer.
AC.CURSED, *adj.*, amaldiçoado, desgraçado, maldito.
AC.CUS.ABLE, *adj.*, acusável, condenável.
AC.CU.SA.TION, *s.*, acusação.
AC.CU.SA.TIVE, *s.*, acusativo.
AC.CUSE, *v.*, acusar, delatar, denunciar.
AC.CUSED, *s., adj.*, acusado, réu.
AC.CUS.ER, *s.*, acusador, procurador público.
AC.CUS.TOM, *v.*, acostumar, ter por hábito.
AC.CUS.TOMED, *adj.*, acostumado, habituado.
ACE, *s.*, ás; ponto; bagatela.
ACERB, *adj.*, acerbo, duro, rigoroso, amargo.
ACER.BI.TY, *s.*, amargura, acerbidez, acidez.
AC.E.TONE, *s.*, acetona.
ACE.TOUS, *adj.*, acetoso, azedo.
ACHE, *v.*, doer, sofrer; *s.*, dor, sofrimento.
ACHIEV.ABLE, *adj.*, realizável.
ACHIEVE, *v.*, concluir, acabar, terminar, alcançar.
ACHIEVE.MENT, *s.*, acabamento, conclusão, término.
ACH.ING, *s.*, dor, sofrimento: *adj.*, dolorido.
ACH.RO.MAT.IC, *adj.*, acromático.
ACHRO.MA.TISM, *s.*, acromatismo.
ACHRO.MA.TIZE, acromatizar.
AC.ID, *s., adj.*, ácido.
ACID.I.FY, *v.*, acidificar, azedar.
ACID.I.TY, *s.*, acidez.
AC.KNOWL.EDGE, *v.*, reconhecer, conhecer, vir a saber.
AC.KNOWL.EDGE.MENT, *s.*, reconhecimento, conhecimento.
AC.ME, *s.*, cume, pico, culminância.
AC.NE, *s.*, acne.
ACOUS.TIC, *adj.*, acústico.
ACOUS.TICS, *s.*, acústica.
AC.QUAINT, *v.*, comunicar, informar, conhecer.
AC.QUAIN.TANCE, *s.*, conhecimento, habilidade, capacidade.
AC.QUI.ESCE, *v.*, aquiescer, concordar, acordar, aceitar.
AC.QUI.ES.CENCE, *s.*, aquiescência, concordância.
AC.QUIRE, *v.*, adquirir, obter, conquistar.
AC.QUIRE.MENT, *s.*, aquisição; conhecimento.
AC.QUI.SI.TION, *s.*, aquisição, compra.
AC.QUIT, *v.*, absolver, desobrigar-se, inocentar.
ACQUITTANCE, *s.*, recibo, quitação.
AC.QUIT.TER, *s.*, pagador, pagante.
ACRE, *s.*, acre, med. agrária de 4.046,84 m².
AC.RID, *adj.*, acre, azedo.
ACRID.I.TY, *s.*, aspereza.
AC.RO.BAT, *s.*, acrobata.
AC.RO.BAT.ICS, acrobacia.
ACROSS, *prep., adv.*, através de, do outro lado, obliquamente.
ACRYL.IC, *s., adj.*, acrílico.
ACT, *s.*, ação, ato, procedimento; *v.*, agir, proceder, comportar-se.
ACT.ING, *s.*, ação, realização; *adj.*, ativo, efetivo, interino.
AC.TION, *s.*, ação, ato, efeito, atitude.
AC.TION.ABLE, *adj.*, acionável, litigável.
AC.TI.VATE, *v.*, ativar, colocar em movimento.
AC.TIVE, *adj.*, ativo, aplicado, diligente.
AC.TIV.I.TY, *s.*, atividade, ação, presteza.
AC.TOR, *s.*, ator, figurante.
AC.TRESS, *s.*, atriz.
AC.TU.AL, *adj.*, atual, real, verdadeiro.
AC.TU.AL.I.TY, *s.*, atualidade, realidade.
AC.TU.ATE, *v.*, acionar, atuar, movimentar.
AC.TU.A.TION, *s.*, ação, efetivação, acionamento.
ACU.MEN, *s.*, perspicácia, sagacidade.

ACUMINATE / **ADULTERATE**

ACU.MI.NATE, *v.*, afiar, aguçar.
ACU.PUNC.TURE, *s.*, acupuntura.
ACUTE, *adj.*, agudo, pontudo, apontado.
ACUTE.NESS, *s.*, agudez, perspicácia, sagacidade.
AD.AGE, *s.*, adágio, provérbio.
ADAPT, *v.*, adaptar, ajustar, acomodar.
ADAPT.ABIL.I.TY, *s.*, adaptabilidade, acomodação.
ADAPT.ABLE, *adj.*, adaptável, acomodável.
AD.AP.TA.TION, *s.*, adaptação, acomodação.
ADD, *v.*, adir, acrescentar, somar.
AD.DEN.DUM, *s.*, adendo, aditamento.
AD.DIC.TION, *s.*, devoção, inclinação, apego.
AD.DI.TION, *s.*, adição, soma, acréscimo.
AD.DI.TION.AL, *adj.*, adicional.
AD.DI.TIVE, *adj.*, aditivo.
AD.DLE, *v.*, confundir, aturdir.
AD.DRESS, *s.*, endereço, discurso; *v.*, remeter, endereçar.
AD.DUCE, *v.*, aduzir, alegar.
AD.DUC.TION, *s.*, adução, alegação, referência.
AD.EPT, *s.*, especialista, perito; *adj.*, hábil, perito.
AD.E.QUA.CY, *s.*, suficiência.
AD.E.QUATE, *adj.*, adequado.
AD.HERE, *v.*, aderir, optar.
AD.HER.ENCE, *s.*, aderência, colagem, união.
AD.HER.ENT, *adj.*, aderente, unido, ligado.
AD.HE.SION, *s.*, adesão.
AD.HE.SIVE, *adj.*, *s.*, adesivo.
AD.HIBIT, *v.*, aderir, adicionar, juntar.
AD.I.POSE, *adj.*, adiposo, gordo.
AD.JA.CEN.CY, *s.*, adjacência.
AD.JA.CENT, *adj.*, adjacente, próximo.
AD.JEC.TIVE, *s.*, adjetivo.
AD.JOIN, *v.*, achegar, aproximar, ajuntar, acrescer.
AD.JOIN.ING, *adj.*, contíguo, próximo, adjacente.
AD.JOURN, *v.*, adiar, protelar, transferir.
AD.JU.DI.CATE, *v.*, julgar, sentenciar; examinar.
AD.JU.DI.CA.TION, *s.*, julgamento.
AD.JUNCT, *s.*, *adj.*, adjunto, adido, assessor.
AD.JUNC.TION, *s.*, junção, ligação, união.
AD.JURE, *v.*, adjurar, imprecar, esconjurar.
AD.JUST, *v.*, ajustar, conectar, regular, acertar.
AD.JUST.ABLE, *adj.*, ajustável, regulável.

AD.JUST.MENT, *s.*, ajuste, ajustamento, acerto, reajuste.
AD.JU.VANT, *s.*, assistente, adido, ajudante, assessor.
AD.MIN.IS.TER, *v.*, administrar, governar, ministrar.
AD.MIN.IS.TRA.TION, *s.*, administração, direção, orientação.
AD.MIN.IS.TRA.TIVE, *adj.*, administrativo.
AD.MIN.IS.TRA.TOR, *s.*, administrador.
AD.MIN.IS.TRA.TOR.SHIP, *s.*, administração.
AD.MI.RA.BLE, *adj.*, admirável.
AD.MI.RAL, *s.*, almirante.
AD.MI.RA.TION, *s.*, admiração, veneração.
AD.MIRE, *v.*, admirar, venerar, respeitar.
AD.MIR.ER, *s.*, admirador, fã.
AD.MIS.SION, *s.*, entrada, admissão, ingresso.
AD.MIT, *v.*, admitir, aceitar, concordar.
AD.MIX, *v.*, misturar.
AD.MIX.TURE, *s.*, mistura.
AD.MON.ISH, *v.*, admoestar, advertir.
AD.MON.ISH.MENT, *s.*, admoestação, advertência.
AD.NOM.I.NAL, *adj.*, adnominal, adjunto.
AD.O.LES.CENCE, *s.*, adolescência, juventude.
AD.O.LES.CENT, *s.*, adolescente.
ADOPT, *v.*, adotar, aceitar.
ADOPT.ED, *adj.*, adotado, aceito.
ADOP.TION, *s.*, adoção.
ADOP.TIVE, *adj.*, *s.*, adotivo.
ADOR.ABIL.I.TY, *s.*, adorabilidade.
ADOR.ABLE, *adj.*, adorável, divino.
AD.O.RA.TION, *s.*, adoração, respeito, veneração.
ADORE, *v.*, adorar.
ADORN, *v.*, adornar, enfeitar, embelezar.
ADORN.ER, *s.*, adornador, decorador.
ADOWN, *prep.*, *adv.*, para baixo, de cima para baixo; *prep.*, ao longo de ou sobre.
ADREN.A.LIN, *s.*, adrenalina.
ADRY, *adj.*, seco, sedento.
AD.U.LATE, *v.*, adular, bajular, lisonjear.
AD.U.LA.TION, *s.*, adulação, bajulação.
ADULT, *adj.*, *s.*, adulto.
ADUL.TER.ATE, *v.*, adulterar; *adj.*, adulterado.

ADUL.TER.ER, s., adúltero.
ADUL.TER.ESS, s., adúltera.
ADUL.TERY, s., adultério.
AD.UM.BRATE, v., prenunciar, sombrear, eclipsar.
ADUST, adj., queimado, seco, ressecado.
AD.VANCE, s., avanço, antecipação; v., avançar.
AD.VANCE.MENT, s., avanço, progresso.
AD.VAN.TAGE, s., vantagem, superioridade.
AD.VENT, s., advento.
AD.VEN.TURE, s., aventura, ação.
AD.VEN.TUR.ER, s., aventureiro.
AD.VERB, s., advérbio.
AD.VER.BI.AL, adj., adverbial.
AD.VER.SARY, s., adversário.
AD.VER.SA.TIVE, adj., adversativo.
AD.VERSE, adj., adverso, contrário.
AD.VER.SI.TY, s., adversidade; desgraça.
AD.VERT, v., advertir, admoestar.
AD.VER.TENCE, s., advertência.
AD.VER.TISE.MENT, s., anúncio.
AD.VER.TIS.ING, s., propaganda, publicidade.
AD.VICE, s., aviso, conselho, recomendação.
AD.VIS.ABLE, adj., avisável.
AD.VISE, v., avisar, aconselhar, recomendar.
AD.VISED, adj., avisado, advertido.
AD.VIS.ED.NESS, s., prudência, juízo.
AD.VO.CA.CY, s., advocacia.
AD.VO.CATE, v., advogar, defender, litigar.
AD.VO.CATE.SHIP, s., advocacia.
AD.VO.CAT.ESS, s., advogada.
AE.DILE, s., edil.
AERA, s., era, época, tempo.
AERA.A.TION, s., ventilação, arejamento.
AE.RI.AL, s., antena; adj., aéreo.
AERA.O.BICS, s., aeróbica.
AERO.DY.NAM.ICS, s., aerodinâmica.
AERO.NAUT, s., aeronauta.
AERO.NAU.TICS, s., aeronáutica.
AERO.PLANE, s., aeroplano.
AES.THET.ICS, s., estética.
AES.TI.VAL, adj., estival, relativo ao verão.
AES.TI.VATE, v., veranear.
AETHER, s., éter.
AF.FA.BIL.I.TY, s., afabilidade.

AF.FA.BLE, adj., afável.
AF.FA.BLE.NESS, s., afabilidade.
AF.FAIR, s., negócio, assunto, objetivo.
AF.FECT, v., afetar, influir.
AF.FEC.TA.TION, s., afetação, influência.
AF.FECT.ED, adj., afetado, influenciado.
AF.FEC.TION, s., afeto, afeição, apego, carinho.
AF.FEC.TION.AL, adj., afetivo.
AF.FEC.TION.ATE.NESS, s., afetividade, carinho.
AF.FEC.TIVE, adj., afetivo, afeiçoado, emocional.
AF.FINED, adj., afim, ligado.
AF.FIN.I.TY, s., afinidade, parentesco.
AF.FIRM, v., afirmar, assegurar, confirmar.
AF.FIRM.ABLE, adj., afirmável.
AF.FIR.MANCE, s., afirmação, confirmação.
AF.FIR.MA.TION, s., afirmação solene, confirmação.
AF.FIR.MA.TIVE, adj., afirmativo.
AF.FIX, v., afixar, pregar, fixar.
AF.FLA.TION, s., sopro.
AF.FLICT, v., afligir, angustiar.
AF.FLICT.ED, adj., aflito.
AF.FLIC.TION, s., aflição, dor, sofrimento.
AF.FLIC.TIVE, adj., aflitivo.
AF.FLUX, s., afluxo.
AF.FRAN.CHISE, v., liberar, libertar.
AF.FRAN.CHISE.MENT, s., libertação, liberação, emancipação.
AF.FRAY, s., briga, confusão.
AF.FRIGHT, s., pavor, terror.
AF.FRONT, v., ofender, injuriar, insultar; s., ofensa, injúria.
AFIRE, adv., em chamas, que está queimando.
AFOOT, adv., a pé.
AFRESH, adv., novamente, outra vez, de novo.
AF.TER, adv., depois, após, em seguida.
AF.TER.DAYS, s., pl., futuro.
AF.TER.EF.FECT, s., efeitos posteriores, consequências.
AF.TER.lIFE, s., pós-morte.
AF.TER.NOON, s., tarde, período vespertino.
AF.TER.SHAVE, s., loção pós-barba.
AGAIN, adv., novamente, outra vez, de novo.

AGAINST, *prep.*, contra, em oposição, ao contrário.
AGE, *s.*, idade, época, momento, velhice.
AGED, *adj.*, velho, idoso, sazonado, maturado.
AG.ED.NESS, *s.*, idade, velhice.
AGEN.CY, *s.*, agência, repartição, seção, setor.
AGEN.DA, *s.*, agenda, programa, roteiro.
AGENT, *s.*, agente, encarregado, delegado.
AG.GLOM.ER.ATE, *adj.*, aglomerado; *v.*, aglomerar, juntar.
AG.GLOM.ER.A.TION, *s.*, aglomeração, ajuntamento.
AG.GLU.TI.NATE, *v.*, aglutinar, reunir, juntar.
AG.GLU.TI.NA.TION, *s.*, aglutinação, ligação.
AG.GRAN.DIZE, *v.*, engrandecer, tornar grande, aumentar.
AG.GRA.VATE, *v.*, agravar, irritar, provocar.
AG.GRA.VA.TION, *s.*, agravamento, aborrecimento, irritação.
AG.GRE.GATE, *v.*, agregar; *adj., s.*, agregado; *s.*, massa, conjunto aposto.
AG.GRE.GA.TION, *s.*, agregação, ajuntamento, acúmulo.
AG.GRESS, *v.*, agredir, atacar, insultar, ofender.
AG.GRES.SION, *s.*, agressão, ataque, ofensa, insulto.
AG.GRES.SIVE, *adj.*, agressivo, ofensivo.
AG.GRES.SOR, *s.*, agressor, atacante.
AG.GRIEVE, *v.*, agredir, afligir, incomodar, magoar.
AG.GRIEVED, *adj., part.*, agredido, aflito, ofendido.
AG.ILE, *adj.*, ágil, rápido, leve.
AGIL.I.TY, *s.*, agilidade, rapidez.
AGIO, *s.*, ágio.
AG.I.TATE, *v.*, agitar, sacudir, mover, provocar.
AG.I.TA.TION, *s.*, agitação, incômodo, movimento.
AG.I.TA.TOR, *s.*, agitador, provocador.
AG.NO.MEN, *s.*, sobrenome.
AG.NOS.TIC, *adj.*, agnóstico, incrédulo.
AGO, *prep.*, desde, atrás.
AGO.ING, *adv.*, em movimento; *v.*, andando.
AG.O.NIZE, *v.*, agonizar, morrer; massacrar, afligir.
AG.O.NIZ.ING, *adj.*, agonizante, moribundo.
AG.O.NY, *s.*, agonia, dor, sofrimento.
AGREE, *v.*, ceder, corresponder, ser do agrado de.
AGREE.ABLE, *adj.*, agradável, prazeroso.
AGREE.MENT, *s.*, consentimento, acordo, aceitação.
AGRES.TIC, *adj.*, agreste, rústico, bruto.
AG.RI.CUL.TUR.AL, *adj.*, agrícola, relativo a agricultura.
AG.RI.CUL.TURE, *s.*, agricultura.
AG.RI.CUL.TUR.IST, *s.*, agricultor.
AGRON.O.MIST, *s.*, agrônomo.
AGRON.O.MY, *s.*, agronomia.
AGROUND, *adj., adv.*, parado, encalhado.
AHEAD, *adv.*, a frente, para diante; primeiro.
AID, *s.*, auxílio, ajuda, socorro, apoio.
AID.ER, *s.*, o que socorre, dá ajuda.
AIL, *v.*, perturbar, incomodar, afligir.
AIM, *v.*, apontar, mirar; *s.*, mira, pontaria.
AIR, *s.*, ar, atmosfera, céu, espaço, firmamento; jeito, atitude.
AIR-BRAKE, *s.*, freio a ar.
AIR.ING, *s.*, ventilação, arejamento.
AIR.MAN, *s.*, aviador, piloto de avião.
AIR.PORT, *s.*, aeroporto.
AIRY, *adj.*, aéreo, etéreo, leve, arejado.
AITCH, *s.*, h, letra h.
AKIN, *adj., s.*, parente, parecido, consanguíneo.
ALAND, *adv.*, em terra.
ALARM, *s.*, alarme, aviso, sinal de perigo.
ALARM.IST, *s.*, alarmista.
ALATE, *adj.*, alado.
AL.BE.IT, *conj.*, embora, não obstante, todavia.
AL.BI.NISM, *s.*, albinismo.
AL.BI.NO, *adj., s.*, albino.
AL.BUM *s.*, álbum.
AL.BU.MIN, *s.*, albumina.
AL.CHE.MIST, *s.*, alquimista.
AL.CHE.MY, *s.*, alquimia.
ALCOHOL, *s.*, álcool.
AL.CO.HOL.IC, *adj.*, alcoólico.
AL.CO.HOL.ISM, *s.*, alcoolismo.

AL.CO.HOL.I.ZA.TION, *s.*, alcoolização.
AL.CO.HOL.IZE, *v.*, alcoolizar, encher com álcool.
AL.COVE, *s.*, alcova.
ALE, *s.*, cerveja.
ALE.A.TO.RY, *adj.*, aleatório.
ALEM.BIC, *s.*, alambique.
ALERT, *adj.*, alerta, pronto, preparado; alerta; *v.*, alertar.
ALERT.NESS, *s.*, precaução, vigilância, agilidade.
AL.GA, *s.*, alga.
AL.GE.BRA, *s.*, álgebra.
AL.GE.BRA.IC, *adj.*, algébrico.
AL.GID.I.TY, *s.*, frio intenso, algidez.
AL.I.BI, *s.*, álibi.
ALIEN, *s.*, alienígena, estrangeiro, estranho.
ALIEN.ABIL.I.TY, *s.*, alienabilidade.
ALIEN.ABLE, *adj.*, alienável.
ALIEN.ATE, *v.*, alienar, transferir, mandar adiante, vender.
ALIEN.ATION, *s.*, alienação, venda, transferência.
ALIEN.IST, *s.*, alienista.
ALIGHT, *adv.*, iluminado, brilhante, aceso, inflamado.
ALIGN, *v.*, alinhar, colocar em ordem.
ALIKE, *adj.*, semelhante, parecido.
AL.I.MENT, *s.*, alimento; *v.*, alimentar.
AL.I.MENT.AL, *adj.*, nutritivo.
AL.I.MEN.TA.RY, *adj.*, alimentar, nutritivo, alimentício.
AL.I.MEN.TA.TION, *s.*, alimentação.
ALINE.MENT, *s.*, alinhamento.
ALIVE, *adj.*, vivo, alegre, satisfeito, ágil, esperto.
AL.KA.LI, *s.*, álcali.
AL.KAL.I.FY, *v.*, alcalinizar.
AL.KA.LIZE, *v.*, tornar alcalino, alcalinizar.
AL.KOR.AN, *s.*, alcorão, corão.
ALL, *adj.*, todo, tudo; *pl.*, todos, todas; *adv.*, de todo, completamente.
AL.LAY, *v.*, acalmar, aliviar, pacificar.
AL.LAY.ING, *s.*, alívio, consolo, consolação, paz.
AL.LE.GA.TION, *s.*, alegação, desculpa.
AL.LEGE, *v.*, alegar, aduzir, dizer, declarar.
AL.LE.GIANCE, *s.*, lealdade, amizade, fidelidade.
AL.LE.GO.RIZE, *v.*, alegorizar, figurar, metaforizar.
AL.LE.GO.RY, *s.*, alegoria, parábola.
AL.LE.LU.IA, *s.*, aleluia.
AL.LER.GY, *s.*, alergia.
AL.LE.VI.ATE, *v.*, aliviar, diminuir, decrescer.
AL.LE.VI.A.TION, *s.*, alívio, consolo.
AL.LEY, *s.*, aleia, alameda, viela, beco.
AL.LI.ANCE, *s.*, aliança.
AL.LIED, *adj.*, *s.*, aliado.
AL.LI.GA.TOR, *s.*, aligátor, jacaré, crocodilo.
ALL.NIGHT, *adv.*, toda a noite.
AL.LO.CA.TION, *s.*, alocação, localização, situação.
AL.LO.CU.TION, *s.*, alocução, fala, discurso.
AL.LO.PA.THY, *s.*, alopatia.
AL.LOT, *v.*, aquinhoar, lotear, destinar.
AL.LOT.MENT, *s.*, partilha, distribuição.
ALL-OUT, *adj.*, máximo, o maior; *adv.*, com tudo.
AL.LOW, *v.*, permitir, ceder, aceitar, admitir.
AL.LOW.ANCE, *s.*, mesada, ajuda, pensão, diária.
AL.LOY, *v.*, ligar, juntar metais; *s.*, fusão de metais.
AL.LUDE, *v.*, aludir, referir, dizer de.
AL.LU.SION, *s.*, alusão, referência.
AL.LU.SIVE, *adj.*, referente, alusivo.
AL.LU.VI.ON, *s.*, aluvião.
AL.LY, *s.*, aliado; *v.*, aliar-se, juntar-se.
AL.MA.NAC, *s.*, almanaque, calendário, folhinha.
AL.MO.NER, *s.*, esmoleiro.
AL.MOST, *adv.*, quase.
ALMS, *s.*, esmola, dádiva, donativo.
ALONE, *adj.*, sozinho, solitário, só.
ALONG, *prep.*, ao longo de, ao lado de.
ALONG.SHORE, *adv.*, na costa, ao longo da praia.
ALONG.SIDE, *prep.*, ao lado de, junto a.
ALOUD, *adv.*, em voz alta.
ALOW, *adv.*, baixo.
ALP, *s.*, montanha, cume, pico.
AL.PHA, *s.*, alfa; início.
AL.PHA.BET, *s.*, alfabeto, abecê.
AL.PHA.BET.IC, *adj.*, alfabético.
AL.PINE, *adj.*, alpino.

AL.READY, *adv.*, já, agora, neste momento.
AL.SO, *adv.*, também, igualmente, além disso.
AL.TAR, *s.*, altar.
AL.TER, *v.*, alterar, mudar, modificar.
AL.TER.ABLE, *adj.*, alterável, mutável.
AL.TER.ATION, *s.*, alteração.
AL.TER.CATE, *v.*, altercar, litigar, lutar, disputar.
AL.TER.NATE,*v.*,alternar, alterar; *adj.*, alternado.
AL.THOUGH, *conj.*, apesar de, embora, ainda que.
AL.TI.TUDE, *s.*, altitude, altura.
AL.TO.GETH.ER, *adv.*, completamente, de todo.
AL.TRU.ISM, *s.*, altruísmo.
AL.U.MIN.I.UM, *s.*, alumínio.
AL.VE.O.LAR, *adj.*, alveolar.
AL.VE.O.LUS, *s.*, alvéolo.
AL.WAYS, *adv.*, sempre.
AMAIN, *adv.*, com rapidez, com energia.
AMASS, *v.*, juntar, amontoar, acumular.
AM.A.TEUR, *adj., s.*, amador, diletante.
AM.A.TEUR.ISH, *adj.*, amador.
AM.A.TEUR.ISH.NESS, *s.*, amadorismo, diletantismo.
AM.A.TO.RY, *adj.*, amador, erótico, sensual.
AMAZE, *v.*, espantar, assustar.
AM.A.ZON, *s.*, amazona.
AM.BAS.SA.DOR, *s.*, embaixador.
AM.BI.DEX.TER *s.*, ambidestro.
AM.BI.ENT, *s.*, ambiente.
AM.BI.GU.I.TY, *s.*,ambiguidade.
AM.BIT, *s.*, âmbito.
AM.BI.TION, *s.*, ambição.
AM.BI.TIOUS, *adj.*, ambicioso, ganancioso.
AM.BI.TIOUS.NESS, *s.*, ambição, ganância.
AM.BIV.A.LENT, *adj.*, ambivalente.
AM.BU.LANCE, *s.*, ambulância.
AM.BUS.CADE, *s.*, emboscada; *v.*, emboscar, fazer uma cilada.
AM.BUSH, *s.*, emboscada; *v.*, emboscar.
AME.LIO.RATE, *v.*, melhorar, arrumar, aperfeiçoar.
AME.LIO.RA.TION, *s.*, melhoria, melhoramento, aperfeiçoamento.
AMEN, *interj.*, amém.
AME.NI.TY, *s.*, amenidade, afabilidade, suavidade.
AMER.I.CAN, *adj., s.*, americano.
AMER.I.CAN.IZE, *v.*, americanizar.
AMI.A.BLE, *adj.*, amável, afável, bondoso.
AM.I.CA.BIL.I.TY, *s.*, amizade, afeto.
AM.I.CA.BLE.NESS, *s.*, amabilidade, gentileza, cordialidade.
AMID, *prep.*, no meio, entre, de per meio de.
AM.IDE, *s.*, amido.
AMISS, *adj.*, defeituoso, impróprio, errado.
AM.I.TY, *s.*, amizade.
AM.MO.NI.AC, *s.*, amoníaco.
AM.MU.NI.TION, *s.*, munições.
AM.NE.SIA, *s.*, amnésia.
AM.NES.TY, *s.*, anistia; *v.*, anistiar.
AMONG, *prep.*, entre, no meio de.
AM.OR.IST, *s.*, namorador, amante, amador.
AM.O.ROUS, *adj.*, amoroso, afetuoso, carinhoso.
AMOR.PHOUS, *adj.*, amorfo.
AM.OR.TI.ZA.TION, *s.*, amortização.
AM.OR.TIZE, *v.*, amortizar.
AMOUNT, *s.*, soma, quantia, monte, valor; *v.*, importar, elevar.
AMOUR, *s.*, galanteio, amor, namoro.
AM.PHIB.IA, *s., pl.*, anfíbios, batráquios.
AM.PHIB.I.AN, *adj., s.*, anfíbio, batráquio.
AM.PHI.BOL.O.GY, *s.*, anfibologia, ambiguidade.
AM.PHI.THE.ATRE, *s.*, anfiteatro.
AM.PLE, *adj.*, amplo, vasto, extenso.
AM.PLE.NESS,*s.*,amplidão,imensidão, vastidão.
AM.PLI.ATE, *v.*, ampliar, aumentar.
AM.PLI.A.TION, *s.*, ampliação, aumento.
AM.PLI.FY, *v.*, ampliar, aumentar.
AM.PLI.TUDE, *s.*, amplitude, grandeza.
AM.PU.TATE, *v.*, amputar, cortar algo.
AM.PU.TA.TION, *s.*, amputação.
AM.U.LET, *s.*, amuleto.
AMUSE, *v.*, divertir, agradar, distrair.
AMUSE.MENT, *s.*, diversão, divertimento, agrado, folga.
AMUS.ING, *adj.*, agradável, divertido, folgado.
AN, *art. ind.* um, uma – usado antes de vogal ou

ANNOYANCE

AN.NOY.ANCE, s. enjoo, aborrecimento, incômodo.
AN.NU.AL, adj. anual; s. anuário
AN.NU.I.TY, s. anuidade
AN.NU.LAR, v. anelado.
AN.NU.LET, s. anelzinho, pequeno anel.
AN.NUL.MENT, v. anulação, cancelamento
AN.NUN.CI.ATE, v. anunciar, proclamar, declarar.
AN.NUN.CI.A.TION, s. anunciação
ANOINT, v. ungir, untar, azeitar.
ANOINT.MENT, s. unção.
ANOM.A.LOUS, adj. anômalo, diferente.
ANOM.A.LOUS.NESS, s. anormalidade, disformidade.
ANOM.A.LY, s. anomalia, anormalidade
AN.O.NYM, s. anônimo
AN.O.NYM.I.TY, adj. anonimato
ANON.Y.MOUS, adj. anônimo
AN.O.RE.XIA, s. anorexia
AN.OTH.ER, pron. adj. outro, outra.
AN.SWER, v. responder, retrucar; s. resposta, solução.
AN.SWER.A.BLE, adj. responsável, respondível.
ANT, s. formiga.
AN.TAG.O.NISM, s. antagonismo, adversidade.
AN.TAG.O.NIST, s. antagonista, opositor.
AN.TAG.O.NIZE, v. contrariar, antagonizar, opor.
AN.TE.CEDE, v. anteceder, preceder.
AN.TE.CED.ENCE, s. antecedência, preferência.
AN.TE.CED.ENT, adj. antecedente, precedente.
AN.TE.CES.SOR, s. antecessor
AN.TE.CHAM.BER, s. antecâmara.
AN.TE.DI.LU.VI.AN, adj. antediluviano
AN.TE.LOPE, s. antílope.
AN.TEN.NA, s. antena.
AN.TE.NUP.TIAL, adj. antenupcial.
AN.TE.RI.OR, adj. anterior, precedente.
AN.TE.RI.OR.NESS, s. anterioridade.
AN.TE.ROOM, s. antessala
AN.THOL.O.GY, s. antologia
AN.THRO.POID, s. antropoide
AN.THRO.POL.O.GIST, s. antropólogo
AN.THRO.POL.O.GY, s. antropologia.
AN.THRO.PO.MOR.PHOUS, adj. antropomorfo
AN.THRO.POPH.A.GY, s. antropofagia.
AN.TI.BI.OT.IC, adj. s. antibiótico
AN.TI.BODY, s. anticorpo.
AN.TIC.I.PATE, v. prever, prognosticar, vaticinar, prevenir.
AN.TIC.I.PA.TION, s. antecipação, vaticínio, expectativa.
AN.TIC.I.PA.TIVE, adj. antecipado
AN.TI.CLI.MAX, s. anticlímax.
AN.TI.DOTE, s. antídoto
AN.TI.FLU, adj. antigripal
AN.TI.MO.NY, s. antimônio
AN.TI.NA.TION.AL, adj. antinacional
AN.TIN.O.MY, s. antinomia, oposição, contrariedade.
AN.TI.PA.THET.IC, adj. antipático
AN.TIP.A.THY, s. antipatia
AN.TI.PHON, s. antífona
AN.TI.PODE, s. antípoda
AN.TI.QUAR.I.AN, adj. s. antiquário
AN.TI.QUA.RY, s. antiquário
AN.TI.QUATE, adj. antiquado, velho, antigo
AN.TIQUE, adj. antigo; s. antiguidade.
AN.TIQ.UI.TY, s. antiguidade.
AN.TI.SEP.TIC, adj. s. antisséptico
AN.TI.SO.CIAL, adj. antissocial.
AN.TI.SO.CIAL.IST, adj. antissocialista.
AN.TITH.E.SIS, s. antítese.
AN.TI.TOX.IN, s. antídoto, antitóxico, contraveneno.
AN.TO.NYM, s. antônimo.
ANUS, s. ânus.
AN.VIL, s. bigorna.
ANX.I.E.TY, s. inquietação, ansiedade.
ANX.IOUS, adj. ansioso, preocupante, angustiante.
ANX.IOUS.NESS, s. ansiedade, ansiedade.
ANY, adj. pron. algum, alguma, algumas, certo, certos.
AN.Y.BODY, pron. alguém, qualquer um, fulano.
AN.Y.HOW, adv. de qualquer maneira, de qualquer modo.

288

ANYHOW

ANACHRONIC

ANA.CHRON.IC, *adj.* anacrônico.
ANAE.MIA, *s.* anemia.
ANAE.MIC, *adj.* anêmico.
AN.AES.THE.SIA, *s.* anestesia.
AN.AES.THE.TIZE, *v.* anestesiar.
AN.A.GRAM, *s.* anagrama.
anal, *adj.* anal.
AN.AL.GE.SIC, *adj.* analgésico.
AN.A.LOG, *adj.* analógico.
AN.A.LOG.IC, *adj.* analógico.
ANAL.O.GIZE, *v.* analogizar, representar por analogia.
ANAL.O.GOUS, *adj.* análogo, semelhante, parecido.
ANAL.O.GY, *s.* analogia.
AN.AL.PHA.BET.IC, *adj.* analfabeto, iletrado, ignorante.
AN.A.LYSE, *v.* analisar, examinar.
ANAL.Y.SIS, *s.* análise.
AN.A.LYST, *s.* analista.
AN.A.LYT.IC, *adj.* analítico.
AN.AR.CHIC, *adj.* anárquico.
AN.AR.CHISM, *s.* anarquismo.
AN.AR.CHY, *s.* anarquia.
ANATH.E.MA, *s.* anátema.
ANA.TOM.IC, *adj.* anatômico.
ANAT.O.MIZE, *v.* anatomizar.
ANAT.O.MY, *s.* anatomia.
AN.CES.TOR, *s.* antepassado, antenato.
AN.CES.TRAL, *adj.* ancestral.
AN.CES.TRY, *s.* ascendência.
AN.CHOR, *s.* âncora; *v.* fundear, ancorar, atracar.
AN.CHOR.AGE, *s.* ancoragem, porto.
AN.CIENT, *adj.* velho, antigo, vetusto.
AN.CIENT.RY, *s.* antiguidade.
AND, *conj.* bem como; assim como, também, além disso.
AN.DROID, *s.* andróide, robô.
AN.EC.DOTE, *s.* anedota, pilhéria.
ANE.MIA, *s.* anemia, debilidade.
ANE.MIC, *adj.* anêmico, fraco, debilitado.
AN.E.MOM.E.TER, *s.* anemômetro.
ANES.THE.TIZE, *v.* anestesiar.

ANNOY

AN.EU.RISM, *s.* aneurisma.
ANEW, *adv.* de novo, outra vez, novamente.
AN.GEL, *s.* anjo.
AN.GEL.IC, *adj.* angélico, angelical, divino.
AN.GER, *s.* raiva, ira, fúria, cólera.
AN.GLE, *s.* ângulo, esquina, curva.
AN.GLI.CAN, *adj.* anglicano.
ANGLICISM, *s.* anglicismo.
AN.GLI.CIZE, *v.* inglesar.
AN.GLO-SA.XON, *adj.* anglo-saxão.
AN.GRI.LY, *adv.* raivoso, furioso.
AN.GRY, *adj.* irado, zangado, furioso.
AN.GUISH, *s.* dor, sofrimento, desconforto.
AN.GU.LAR, *adj.* angular.
AN.HY.DROUS, *adj.* anídrico.
ANIL, *s.* anil.
AN.I.LINE, *s.* anilina.
AN.I.MAL, *adj., s.* animal.
AN.I.MAL.ISM, *s.* animalismo; carnalidade.
AN.I.MAL.I.TY, *s.* animalidade, sensualidade.
AN.I.MAL.IZE, *v.* animalizar, bestializar.
AN.I.MATE, *v.* animar, avivar, entusiasmar; *adj.* animado, vivo.
AN.I.MA.TION, *s.* animação.
AN.I.MA.TIVE, *adj.* animador, animante.
AN.I.MOS.I.TY, *s.* animosidade.
AN.I.MUS, *s.* ódio, contrariedade, aversão, repulsa.
AN.ISE, *s.* anis, erva-doce.
AN.KLE, *s.* tornozelo.
AN.NAL.IST, *s.* cronista, historiador.
AN.NALS, *s.* anais, crônicas, histórias.
AN.NEX, *v.* anexo, adendo, aditamento; *v.* anexar, conectar, ligar.
AN.NEX.A.BLE, *adj.* anexável.
AN.NEX.A.TION, *s.* anexação, aditamento.
AN.NI.HI.LA.TION, *s.* aniquilação.
AN.NI.VER.SA.RY, *s.* aniversário.
AN.NO.TATE, *v.* anotar, escrever, referir.
AN.NO.TA.TION, *s.* anotação, referência.
AN.NOUNCE, *v.* anunciar, dizer, proclamar.
AN.NOUNCE.MENT, *s.* anúncio, declaração.
AN.NOY, *v.* aborrecer, incomodar, enjoar.

ANY.ONE, *pron.*, alguém, um tipo indeterminado.
ANY.THING, *pron.*, alguma coisa, algo.
ANY.WAY, *adv.*, de qualquer maneira.
ANY.WHEN, *adv.*, de qualquer jeito.
ANY.WHERE, *adv.*, em qualquer lugar, em todo lugar.
AOR.TA, *s.*, aorta.
APACE, *adv.*, depressa, com rapidez.
APART.HEID, *s.*, segregação na África; apartaide.
APART.MENT, *s.*, apartamento.
APART.NESS, *s.*, separação, isolamento.
AP.A.THET.IC, *adj.*, apático, abúlico, indiferente.
AP.A.THY, *s.*, apatia, indiferença.
APE, *s.*, macaco, símio, bugio, mono.
APEAK, *adv.*, a pique, vertical, perpendicular.
APEPSY, *s.*, apepsia.
APER.I.TIF, *s.*, aperitivo.
AP.ER.TURE, *s.*, orifício, buraco, abertura.
APEX, *s.*, ápice, cume, pico.
APHA.SIA, *s.*, afasia, rouquidão.
APHO.NIA, *s.*, afonia.
APHO.NIC, *adj.*, afônico.
APH.O.RISM, *s.*, aforismo.
APH.RO.DI.SI.AC, *adj.*, *s.*, afrodisíaco.
APH.THA, *s.*, afta.
API.A.RIST, *s.*, apicultor.
API.ARY, *s.*, apiário, colmeia.
API.CUL.TURE, *s.*, apicultura.
APIECE, *adv.*, cada, cada um, um por vez.
APLOMB, *s.*, desenvoltura, postura.
APOC.A.LYPSE, *s.*, apocalipse.
APOC.RY.PHA, *s.*, escritos falsos, apócrifos.
APOD, *adj.*, ápode, sem pés.
APO.GEE, *s.*, apogeu, clímax, ápice.
APOL.O.GET.IC, *adj.*, apologético.
APOL.O.GET.I.CAL, *adj.*, apologético.
APOL.O.GET.ICS, *s.*, apologia.
AP.O.LOGUE, *s.*, apólogo, fábula.
APOL.O.GY, *s.*, apologia, defesa.
AP.O.PLEXY, *s.*, apoplexia.
APOS.TA.SY, *s.*, apostasia.
APOS.TA.TIZE, *v.*, apostatar.
APOS.TIL, *s.*, apostila.
APOS.TLE, *s.*, apóstolo.
APOS.TLE.SHIP, *s.*, apostolado.
APOS.TRO.PHE, *s.*, apóstrofo, apóstrofe.
APOS.TRO.PHIZE, *v.*, apostrofar, admoestar.
AP.PAL, *v.*, horrorizar, apavorar, amedrontar.
AP.PALL.ING, *adj.*, terrível, horrorizante, apavorante.
AP.PAR.ENT, *adj.*, aparente, claro, evidente.
AP.PA.RI.TION, *s.*, aparição, fantasmas.
AP.PEAL, *v.*, apelar, chamar a atenção; *s.*, apelo, pedido.
AP.PEAL.ER, *adj.*, *s.*, apelante.
AP.PEAL.ING, *adj.*, atraente, sedutor, fascinante.
AP.PEAR, *v.*, aparecer, parecer.
AP.PEAR.ANCE, *s.*, aparecimento, aparência.
AP.PEASE, *v.*, pacificar, apaziguar, acalmar.
AP.PEASE.MENT, *s.*, apaziguamento, pacificação.
AP.PEND, *v.*, juntar, anexar, conectar, colocar junto.
AP.PEND.AGE, *s.*, apêndice.
AP.PEN.DANT, *adj.*, ligado, unido, junto, conexo.
AP.PEN.DI.CI.TIS, *s.*, apendicite.
AP.PEN.DIX, *s.*, apêndice.
AP.PER.CEP.TION, *s.*, percepção.
AP.PER.TAIN, *v.*, pertencer, ser de.
AP.PER.TI.NENT, *adj.*, pertencente.
AP.PE.TENCE, *s.*, apetite, vontade, desejo.
AP.PE.TITE, *s.*, apetite.
AP.PE.TI.TIVE, *adj.*, apetitivo, apetitoso.
AP.PLAUD, *v.*, aplaudir, ovacionar, aclamar.
AP.PLAUSE, *s.*, aplauso, ovação.
AP.PLE, *s.*, maçã.
AP.PLI.ABLE, *adj.*, aplicável.
AP.PLI.ANCE, *s.*, aparelho.
AP.PLI.CA.BIL.I.TY, *s.*, aplicabilidade.
AP.PLI.CA.BLE, *adj.*, aplicável.
AP.PLI.CA.TION, *s.*, aplicação, requerimento.
AP.PLIED, *adj.*, aplicado, usado, colocado.
AP.PLY, *v.*, aplicar, colocar, usar, praticar.
AP.POINT, *v.*, apontar, indicar, nomear.
AP.POINT.MENT, *s.*, agenda, encontro marcado, nomeação.
AP.POSE, *v.*, observar, analisar, examinar.
AP.PO.SITE, *adj.*, próprio, apropriado, exato,

certo.
AP.PO.SI.TION, *s.*, justaposição, aposição, colocação.
AP.PRAIS.ABLE, *adv.*, apreciável, aprazível.
AP.PRAIS.AL, *s.*, apreciação, análise.
AP.PRAISE, *v.*, apreciar, examinar, observar.
AP.PRE.CI.ATE, *v.*, apreciar, avaliar, estimar, agradecer.
AP.PRE.CI.A.TION, *s.*, apreciação.
AP.PRE.HEND, *v.*, apreender, prender, temer.
AP.PRE.HEN.SION, *s.*, apreensão, temor.
AP.PRE.HEN.SIVE, *adj.*, apreensivo, temeroso.
AP.PREN.TICE.SHIP, *s.*, aprendizagem.
AP.PRISE, *v.*, informar, referir, avisar.
AP.PROACH, *v.*, aproximar, ir para, dirigir-se, achegar-se.
AP.PROACH.ABIL.I.TY, *s.*, ser acessível, acessibilidade.
AP.PROACH.ING, *adj.*, achegado, próximo.
AP.PRO.BATE, *v.*, aprovar, sancionar, deferir.
AP.PRO.BA.TION, *s.*, aprovação, sanção.
AP.PRO.PRI.A.TION, *s.*, apropriação.
AP.PROV.ABLE, *adj.*, aprovável.
AP.PROV.AL, *s.*, aprovação, deferimento, consentimento.
AP.PROVE, *v.*, aprovar, liberar, autorizar, conceder.
AP.PROX.I.MATE, *v.*, aproximar, aproximar-se, avizinhar-se.
AP.PROX.I.MA.TION, *s.*, aproximação.
APRI.COT, *s.*, damasco.
APRIL, *s.*, abril.
APRI.OR.I.TY, *s.*, apriorismo, prioridade.
APRON, *s.*, avental.
APT, *adj.*, apto, capaz, hábil, capacitado.
AP.TI.TUDE, *s.*, aptidão, capacidade, pendor.
APT.NESS, *s.*, aptidão.
AQUA.MA.RINE, *s.*, água-marinha.
AQUA.RELLE, *s.*, aquarela.
AQUA.R.IUM, *s.*, aquário.
AQUAT.IC, *adj.*, aquático.
AQ.EU.DUCT, *s.*, aqueduto.
AR.AB, *adj., s.*, árabe.
ARA.BI.AN, *adj.*, árabe.

AR.A.BLE, *adj.*, arável.
ARACH.NID, *s.*, aracnídeo.
AR.AU.CAR.IA, *s.*, araucária, pinheiro.
AR.BI.TER, *s.*, árbitro, juiz.
AR.BIT.RA.MENT, *s.*, arbitramento.
AR.BI.TRARY, *adj.*, arbitrário.
AR.BI.TRATE, *v.*, arbitrar, julgar, avaliar.
AR.BI.TRA.TION, *s.*, arbitragem.
AR.BOR.I.CUL.TURE, *s.*, arboricultura.
AR.BOR.I.CUL.TUR.IST, *s.*, arboricultor.
AR.BOR.I.ZA.TION, *s.*, arborização.
ARC, *s.*, arco.
AR.CAD.ED, *adj.*, arcado, com arcos.
AR.CAD.I.AN.ISM, *s.*, arcadismo.
ARCH, *s.*, arco; *v.*, arquear, fazer com arcos.
AR.CHAE.OL.O.GY, *s.*, arqueologia.
AR.CHA.IC, *adj.*, arcaico.
AR.CHA.ISM, *s.*, arcaísmo.
AR.CHA.IZE, *v.*, arcaizar.
ARCH.AN.GEL, *s.*, arcanjo, anjo.
ARCH.BISH.OP, *s.*, arcebispo.
ARCH.DI.O.CESE, *s.*, arquidiocese.
ARCH.DUKE, *s.*, arquiduque.
ARCH.EN.E.MY, *s.*, arqui-inimigo.
AR.CHE.TYP.AL, *s.*, arquétipo.
AR.CHE.TYPE, *s.*, arquétipo.
AR.CHI.PEL.A.GO, *s.*, arquipélago.
AR.CHI.TET, *s.*, arquiteto.
AR.CHI.TEC.TON.IC, *adj.*, arquitetônico.
AR.CHI.TEC.TURE, *s.*, arquitetura.
AR.CHIVE, *s.*, arquivo.
ARCH.WAY, *s.*, viaduto.
ARC.TIC, *s.*, Ártico; *adj.*, ártico.
AR.CU.A.TION, *s.*, arqueamento, arqueação.
AR.DEN.CY, *s.*, ardência, calor.
AR.DENT, *adj.*, ardente, quente, caloroso, apaixonado.
AR.E.A, *s.*, área, zona, região, superfície.
AR.E.FY, *v.*, secar, ressecar.
AR.E.O.MET.RY, *s.*, areometria.
AR.GEN.TIN.I.AN, *adj., s.*, argentino.
AR.GIL, *s.*, argila, barro.
AR.GOT, *s.*, calão, linguagem chula.
AR.GU.ABLE, *adj.*, discutível.

AR.GU.ABLY, *adv.*, possivelmente, talvez.
AR.GUE, *v.*, discutir, argumentar, convencer.
AR.GU.MENT, *s.*, argumento, contenda, discussão.
AR.GU.MEN.TA.TION, *s.*, argumentação, discussão.
AR.I.AN.ISM, *s.*, arianismo.
AR.ID, *adj.*, árido, seco, ressecado.
ARID.I.TY, *s.*, aridez, secura.
ARIGHT, *adv.*, corretamente, com acerto.
ARISE, *v.*, levantar-se, subir, alçar-se, erguer-se.
AR.IS.TOC.RA.CY, *s.*, aristocracia.
ARIS.TO.CRAT, *s.*, aristocrata.
ARITH.ME.TIC, *s.*, aritmética.
ARK, *s.*, arca, refúgio, esconderijo.
ARM, *s.*, braço, manga; seção, setor.
AR.MA.MENT, *s.*, armamento.
ARM.CHAIR, *s.*, poltrona.
ARMED, *adj.*, armado.
ARM.FUL, *s.*, braçada.
AR.MI.STICE, *s.*, armistício.
ARM.LET, *s.*, pulseira, bracelete.
ARM.PIT, *s.*, axila, sovaco.
AR.MY, *s.*, exército.
ARO.MA, *s.*, aroma, perfume.
AR.O.MAT.IC, *adj.*, aromático.
ARO.MA.TIZE, *v.*, aromatizar, perfumar.
AROUND, *adv.*, *prep.*, ao redor, em volta, perto.
AROUSE, *v.*, acordar, despertar.
AR.RAIGN, *v.*, processar, levar a juízo, denunciar.
AR.RAIGN.MENT, *s.*, acusação, denúncia, processo.
AR.RANGE, *v.*, arranjar, organizar, ordenar.
AR.RANGE.MENT, *s.*, arranjo, acerto, acordo.
AR.REARS, *s.*, dívida em atraso, dívidas.
AR.REST, *v.*, arrestar, prender, deter; *s.*, arresto, prisão.
AR.REST.A.TION, *s.*, prisão, encarceramento, arresto.
AR.REST.MENT, *s.*, arresto, prisão.
AR.RIV.AL, *s.*, chegada, vinda.
AR.RIVE, *v.*, chegar, vir.
AR.RO.GANCE, *s.*, arrogância, presunção.
AR.RO.GANT, *adj.*, arrogante, presunçoso.

ARSE, *s.*, ânus, traseiro.
AR.SE.NAL, *s.*, arsenal.
AR.SE.NIC, *s.*, arsênico.
ART, *s.*, arte, jeito, habilidade, engenho.
AR.TE.FACT, *s.*, artefato.
AR.TE.RI.AL, *adj.*, arterial.
AR.TERY, *s.*, artéria.
ART.FUL.NESS, *s.*, astúcia, sagacidade.
AR.THRI.TIS, *s.*, artrite.
AR.TI.CLE, *s.*, artigo, cláusula, objeto, peça.
AR.TIC.U.LAR, *adj.*, articular.
AR.TIC.U.LA.TION, *s.*, articulação.
AR.TIC.U.LA.TOR, *s.*, articulador.
AR.TI.FICE, *s.*, artifício, artimanha, engano.
AR.TI.FI.CIAL, *adj.*, artificial.
AR.TIL.LERY, *s.*, artilharia.
AR.TI.SAN, *s.*, artesão, artista.
ART.IST, *s.*, artista.
AR.TIS.TIC, *adj.*, artístico.
AS, *conj.*, quanto, como, tão; *prep.*, como.
AS.CEND, *v.*, ascender, subir, alçar-se.
AS.CEN.DANT, *s.*, ascendência, superioridade.
AS.CEN.DENCE, *s.*, ascendência.
AS.CEN.SION, *s.*, ascensão, subida.
AS.CENT, *s.*, subida, aclive, rampa, ladeira.
AS.CER.TAIN, *v.*, verificar, examinar.
AS.CER.TAIN.MENT, *s.*, investigação, busca, demanda.
AS.CET.IC, *s.*, asceta; *adj.*, ascético.
AS.CET.I.CISM, *s.*, ascetismo.
AS.CRIBE, *v.*, atribuir.
ASEP.TIC, *adj.*, asséptico.
ASEX.U.AL, *adj.*, assexuado.
ASEX.U.AL.I.TY, *s.*, assexualidade.
ASH, *s.*, cinza.
ASHAMED, *adj.*, envergonhado.
ASHAM.ED.NESS, *s.*, vergonha.
ASHORE, *adv.*, em terra.
ASH.TRAY, *s.*, cinzeiro.
ASHY, *adj.*, cinzento, pálido, cor cinza.
ASIA, *s.*, Ásia.
ASIAN, *adj.*, asiático.
ASIDE, *adj.*, à parte, apartado; *s.*, aparte.
AS.I.NINE, *adj.*, asinino, tolo.

AS.I.NIN.I.TY, s., burrice, tolice, estupidez.
ASK, v., perguntar, indagar.
ASKEW, adv., torto.
ASK.ING, s., pedido, petição, súplica.
ASLEEP, adj., dormente, adormecido; v., dormir.
AS.PAR.A.GUS, s., aspargo.
AS.PECT, s., aspecto, aparência, expressão.
AS.PECT.ABLE, adj., visível, admirável.
AS.PER.GE, v., aspergir, benzer.
AS.PER.I.TY, s., aspereza, rispidez.
AS.PERSE, v., difamar, falar mal, caluniar.
AS.PHALT, s., asfalto; v., asfaltar.
AS.PHYX.IA, s., asfixia.
AS.PHYX.I.ATE, v., asfixiar, sufocar.
AS.PI.RA.TION, s., aspiração, ruído; desejo.
AS.PIRE, v., aspirar, desejar, querer.
AS.PI.RIN, s., aspirina.
AS.PIR.ING, adj., desejoso, ganancioso.
AS.PIR.ING.NESS, s., ambição, ganância.
ASS, s., burro, jumento, jegue; idiota, imbecil.
AS.SAIL, v., assaltar, roubar, atacar.
AS.SAIL.ANT, s., assaltante.
AS.SAS.SIN, s., assassino.
AS.SAS.SI.NATE, v., assassinar.
AS.SAS.SI.NA.TION, s., assassínio.
AS.SAS.SI.NA.TOR, s., assassino.
AS.SAULT, s., assalto, ataque; v., assaltar, atacar.
AS.SAY, v., analisar, examinar, verificar; s., análise de metais.
AS.SEM.BLAGE, s., assembleia, coleção.
ASSEMBLE, v., reunir, congregar; colecionar.
AS.SEM.BLY, s., assembleia, reunião, sessão.
AS.SENT, s., aprovação; v., aprovar, consentir.
AS.SERT, v., afirmar, manter, confirmar.
AS.SER.TION, s., afirmação, assertiva.
AS.SESS, v., avaliar, sopesar, taxar, tributar.
AS.SESS.ABLE, adj., tributável.
AS.SESS.MENT, s., avaliação.
AS.SES.SOR, s., assessor; tributarista.
AS.SET, s., bens, haveres, ativos.
AS.SETS, s., espólio; massa falida.
AS.SEV.ER.A.TION, s., asseveração, confirmação, afirmação.
AS.SI.DU.ITY, s., assiduidade, diligência, aplicação.
AS.SID.U.OUS, adj., assíduo, aplicado, atento.
AS.SIG.NA.TION, s., partilha, divisão.
AS.SIGN.MENT, s., designação, indicação.
AS.SIM.I.LATE, v., assimilar, absorver.
AS.SIM.I.LA.TION, s., assimilação.
AS.SIST, v., assistir, auxiliar, socorrer.
AS.SIS.TANCE, s., assistência, socorro, ajuda.
AS.SOCI.A.BIL.I.TY, s., sociabilidade.
AS.SO.CI.ATE, s., companheiro, camarada, sócio; v., associar-se.
AS.SO.CI.A.TION, s., associação, sociedade.
AS.SORT, v., agrupar, classificar.
AS.SORT.MENT, s., sortimento, agrupamento.
AS.SUAGE, v., suavizar, diminuir, mitigar, aliviar.
AS.SUAGE.MENT, s., alívio, suavização.
AS.SUME, v., supor, imaginar, presumir.
AS.SUM.ING, adj., pretensioso, presunçoso.
AS.SUR.ANCE, s., garantia, certeza, segurança, seguro.
AS.SURE, v., assegurar, garantir, afirmar.
AS.SURED.LY, adv., certamente, com certeza.
AS.SURED.NESS, s., certeza, garantia.
AS.TER.ISK, s., asterisco.
AS.TER.OID, s., asteroide.
ASTH.MA s., asma.
ASTH.MA.TIC.AL, adj., asmático.
ASTIG.MA.TISM, s., astigmatismo.
AS.TON.ISH, v., espantar, estontear, maravilhar.
AS.TON.ISH.ED, adj., espantado, maravilhado, pasmado.
AS.TON.ISH.ING, adj., espantoso.
AS.TON.ISH.MENT, s., espanto, admiração.
AS.TOUND, v., espantar, pasmar, surpreender.
AS.TOUND.MENT, s., assombro, terror.
AS.TRAL, adj., astral.
A.STRAY, adv., extraviado, sem rumo.
A.STRICT, v., comprimir, apertar, restringir.
A.STRIC.TION, s., compressão, pressão.
A.TRIN.GE, v., restringir, oprimir, apertar.
AS.TROL.O.GER, s., astrólogo.
AS.TRO.LOG.IC, adj., astrológico.
AS.TRO.LOG.I.CAL, adj., astrológico.
AS.TROL.O.GY, s., astrologia.

AS.TRO.NAUT, *s.*, astronauta.
AS.TRON.O.MER, *s.*, astrônomo.
AS.TRO.NOM.IC, *adj.*, astronômico.
AS.TRON.O.MY, *s.*, astronomia.
AS.TUTE, *adj.*, astuto, esperto, sagaz, vivo.
AS.TUTE.NESS, *s.*, esperteza, sagacidade, astúcia.
ASY.LUM, *s.*, asilo, abrigo, albergue.
ASYM.ME.TRY, *s.*, assimetria.
ASYN.DE.TON, *s.*, assíndeto.
AT, *prep.*, em, a, de, no, na.
AT.A.VIC, *adj.*, atávico.
AT.A.VISM, *s.*, atavismo.
ATHE.ISM, *s.*, ateísmo.
ATHE.IST, *adj., s.*, ateu, ateísta.
ATHE.IS.TIC, *adj.*, ateísta, ateístico, ateu.
ATH.LETE, *s.*, atleta.
ATH.LE.TIC, *adj.*, atlético.
ATH.LET.I.CISM, *s.*, atletismo.
ATH:RONG, *adv.*, em tropel, com pressa.
AT.LAN.TIC, *adj.*, atlântico.
AT.LAS, *s.*, atlas.
AT.MO.SPHERE, *s.*, atmosfera.
ATMO.SPHER.IC, *adj.*, atmosférico.
ATOLL, *s.*, atol, abrolho.
AT.OM, *s.*, átomo.
ATOM.IC, *adj.*, atômico.
AT.OM.IZA.TION, *s.*, atomização.
AT.OM.IZE, *v.*, atomizar.
ATON.IC, *adj.*, atônico, debilitado, fraco.
AT.O.NY, *s.*, atonia, fraqueza, debilidade.
ATOP, *adv., prep.*, no cimo, no tope, na crista.
ATRO.CIOUS, *adj.*, atroz, cruel, perverso, ruim, mau, malvado.
ATROC.I.TY, *s.*, atrocidade, maldade, crueldade.
ATRO.PHIC, *adj.*, atrófico, enfraquecido.
AT.RO.PHY, *v.*, atrofiar, enfraquecer, debilitar; *s.*, atrofia.
AT.TACH, *v.*, prender, afixar, conectar, anexar.
AT.TA.CHÉ, *s.*, adido; *adj.*, ligado.
AT.TACH.MENT, *s.*, ligação, união, anexo.
AT.TACK, *v.*, atacar, agredir; *s.*, ataque, agressão, assalto.
AT.TACK.ABLE, *adj.*, atacável.

AT.TACK.ER, *s.*, agressor, atacante, assaltante.
AT.TAIN, *v.*, alcançar, obter, conseguir, lograr.
AT.TAIN.ABIL.I.TY, *s.*, possibilidade de obter.
AT.TAINT, *s.*, mancha, nódoa, mácula; *v.*, macular, desonrar, manchar.
AT.TEMP.ER, *v.*, condimentar, temperar, moderar.
AT.TEMP.ER.ANCE, *s.*, temperança, comedimento.
AT.TEMPT, *s.*, tentativa; *v.*, tentar, provar.
AT.TEND, *v.*, assistir, participar, estar presente, tratar.
AT.TEN.DANCE, *s.*, comparecimento, frequência, assistência.
AT.TEN.DANT, *s.*, assistente, servidor; *adj.*, assistente.
AT.TEN.TION, *s.*, atenção, cuidado, respeito.
AT.TENUATE, *v.*, atenuar, minorar, suavizar.
AT.TEN.U.A.TION, *s.*, atenuação, suavizamento.
AT.TEST, *v.*, atestar, afirmar, testemunhar.
AT.TES.TA.TION, *s.*, atestado, testemunho.
AT.TEST.OR, *s.*, testemunha.
AT.TIC, *s.*, sótão.
AT.TIRE, *v.*, ornar, enfeitar, ataviar; *s.*, ornato, ornamento, enfeite.
AT.TIRE.MENT, *s.*, ornato, adorno, atavio, enfeite.
AT.TIR.ING, *s.*, enfeite.
AT.TI.TUDE, *s.*, atitude, postura, faceta, comportamento.
AT.TOR.NEY, *s.*, advogado.
AT.TRACT, *v.*, atrair, puxar, seduzir, persuadir.
AT.TRACT.ABIL.I.TY, *s.*, atração, sedução.
AT.TRAC.TION, *s.*, atração, sedução.
AT.TRAC.TIVE, *adj.*, atraente, sedutor, interessante.
AT.TRAHENT, *adj.*, atraente.
AT.TRIB.UTE, *s.*, atributo; *v.*, atribuir, dar, oferecer.
AT.TRI.BU.TION, *s.*, atribuição, dom.
AT.TRIST, *v.*, entristecer, contristar, tornar triste.
AT.TRITE, *adj.*, atritado, gasto, puído.
AT.TRITE.NESS, *s.*, atrito, fricção.
AT.TRITON, *s.*, atrito, fricção.
AT.TUNE, *v.*, harmonizar, acertar, concertar.

AU.BER.GINE, *s.*, berinjela.
AUC.TION, *s.*, leilão; *v.*, leiloar.
AUC.TO.RI.AL, *adj.*, próprio de um autor.
AU.DA.CIOUS, *adj.*, audacioso, ousado, valente.
AU.DA.CIOUS.NESS, *s.*, audácia, valentia, ousadia.
AU.DAC.I.TY, *s.*, audácia, ousadia, valentia.
AU.DI.BLE, *adj.*, audível, ouvível.
AU.DI.ENCE, *s.*, audiência, plateia.
AU.DI.ENT, *adj., s.*, ouvinte.
AU.DIO.VI.SU.AL, *s.*, audiovisual.
AU.DIT, *s.*, auditoria.
AU.DI.TION, *s.*, audição.
AU.DI.TIVE, *adj.*, auditivo.
AU.DI.TOR, *s.*, auditor.
AU.DI.TO.RI.UM, *s.*, auditório.
AU.GER, *s.*, broca, verruma.
AUG.MENT, *v.*, aumentar, ampliar, expandir.
AUG.MEN.TA.TION, *s.*, aumento, acréscimo.
AU.GUR, *s.*, áugure, adivinho; *v.*, vaticinar.
AU.GU.RY, *s.*, augúrio.
AU.GUST, *s.*, agosto.
AU.MAIL, *v.*, esmaltar.
AUNT, *s.*, tia.
AU.RA, *s.*, ar, fisionomia, aparência.
AU.RE.OLA, *s.*, auréola.
AU.RIC, *adj.*, áureo.
AU.RI.CLE, *s.*, aurícula.
AU.RO.RA, *s.*, aurora, madrugada.
AUS.CUL.TA.TION, *s.*, auscultação, busca.
AUS.PI.CIOUS, *adj.*, auspicioso, propício.
AUS.TERE, *adj.*, austero, severo, rigoroso.
AUS.TERE.NESS, *s.*, austeridade.
AUS.TER.I.TY, *s.*, austeridade, rigor, simplicidade.
AUS.TRA.LIAN, *adj., s.*, australiano.
AUS.TRI.AN, *adj., s.*, austríaco.
AU.THEN.TIC, *adj.*, autêntico, real, genuíno.
AU.THEN.TI.CATE, *v.*, autenticar.
AU.THEN.TI.CA.TION, *s.*, autenticação.
AU.THEN.TIC.I.TY, *s.*, autenticidade, realidade.
AU.THOR, *s.*, autor.
AU.THOR.ESS, *s.*, autora.
AU.THOR.I.TAR.I.AN, *adj.*, autoritário.

AU.THOR.I.TA.TIVE.NESS, *s.*, autoritarismo.
AU.THOR.I.TY, *s.*, autoridade, comando, jurisdição.
AU.THOR.IZ.ABLE, *adj.*, autorizável.
AU.THOR.I.ZA.TION, *s.*, autorização.
AU.THO.RIZE, *v.*, autorizar, deferir.
AUTO, *s.*, carro, veículo.
AU.TO.BI.OG.RA.PHER, *s.*, autobiógrafo.
AU.TO.BI.OG.RA.PHY, *s.*, autobiografia.
AU.TO.BUS, *s.*, ônibus.
AU.TOCH.THON, *s.*, autóctone, indígena, silvícola.
AU.TOC.RA.CY, *s.*, autocracia.
AU.TO.CRAT, *s.*, autocrata.
AU.TO.DI.DACT, *s.*, autodidata.
AU.TO.GRAPH, *s.*, autógrafo; *v.*, autografar.
AU.TO.GRAPHY, *s.*, autografia.
AU.TO.MAT.IC, *adj.*, automático; arma automática.
AU.TO.MA.TION, *s.*, automação.
AU.TOM.A.TISM, *s.*, automatismo.
AU.TOM.A.TIZE, *v.*, automatizar.
AU.TO.MO.BILE, *s.*, carro, automóvel.
AU.TON.OMY, *s.*, autonomia.
AU.TOP.SY, *s.*, autópsia.
AU.TO.SUG.GES.TION, *s.*, autossugestão.
AU.TO.TRUCK, *s.*, caminhão.
AU.TUMN, *s.*, outono.
AU.TUM.NAL, *adj.*, outonal.
AVAIL, *s.*, vantagem, benefício, lucro; *v.*, aproveitar-se, beneficiar-se.
AVAIL.ABIL.I.TY, *s.*, viabilidade, disponibilidade.
AVAIL.ABLE, *adj.*, viável, disponível.
AV.A.LANCHE, *s.*, avalanche, alude, avalancha.
AVANT.GARD, *s.*, vanguarda.
AV.A.RICE, *s.*, avareza, usura.
AV.A.RI.CIOUS, *adj.*, avarento, avaro, unha de fome.
AV.A.RI.CIOUS.NESS, *s.*, avareza, usura.
AVENGE, *v.*, vingar.
AVENGE.MENT, *s.*, vingança.
AVENG.ER, *s.*, vingador.
AV.E.NUE, *s.*, avenida, alameda, bulevar.

AVER, *v.*, afirmar, confirmar, asseverar.
AV.ER.AGE, *s.*, média, proporção; avaria, dano; *v.*, calcular, ratear.
AVER.MENT, *s.*, afirmação, asseveramento.
AVERSE, *adj.*, contrário, oposto, ao avesso.
AVERSE.NESS, *s.*, oposição, contrariedade.
AVER.SION, *s.*, aversão.
AVERT, *v.*, advertir, prevenir; desviar.
AVERT.IBLE, *adj.*, advertível, previsível.
AVI.AR.IST, *s.*, avicultor.
AVI.ARY, *s.*, aviário.
AVI.ATE, *v.*, viajar de avião, voar.
AVI.A.TION, *s.*, aviação.
AVI.A.TOR, *s.*, aviador, piloto.
AV.ID, *adj.*, ávido, cobiçoso.
AVID.ITY, *s.*, avidez, cupidez.
AV.O.CA.DO, *s.*, abacate.
AV.O.CA.TION, *s.*, distração, lazer, divertimento, folga.
AVOID, *v.*, evitar, escapar; esquivar-se.
AVOID.ABLE, *adj.*, evitável.
AVOUCH, *s.*, garantia, segurança.
AVOUCH.ABLE, *adj.*, garantível.
AVOW, *v.*, confessar, declarar, proclamar.
AVOW.ABLE, *adj.*, confessável.
AVOW.AL, *s.*, confissão, declaração.
AWAIT, *v.*, esperar.
AWAK.EN, *v.*, acordar.
AWAK.EN.ING, *adj.*, despertante; *s.*, o ato de acordar.
AWARD, *s.*, prêmio, recompensa; *v.*, premiar, recompensar.
AWARE, *adj.*, precavido, avisado.
AWARE.NESS, *s.*, consciência, conhecimento.
AWAY, *adv.*, longe, ao longe.
AWE, *s.*, medo, receio, respeito.
AW.FUL, *adj.*, terrível, medonho, horrendo, horrível.
AW.FUL.LY, *adv.*, muito.
AWHILE, *adv.*, por certo tempo.
AWK.WARD, *adj.*, desajeitado, incômodo, deselegante.
AWK.WARD.ISH, *adj.*, desastrado, incapaz, inepto.
AWK.WARD.NESS, *s.*, inépcia, incapacidade, ignorância.
AWL, *s.*, sovela, pua.
AW.NING, *s.*, toldo, barraca.
AWRY, *adj.*, desleixado, deselegante.
AXE, *s.*, machado; *v.*, abandonar, largar.
AXE.MAN, *s.*, lenhador.
AX.I.AL, *adj.*, axial.
AX.IL, *s.*, axila.
AX.IL.LARY, *adj.*, axilar.
AX.I.OM, *s.*, axioma.
AX.I.OM.AT.IC, *adj.*, axiomático.
AX.IS, *s.*, eixo.
AYAH, *s.*, aia, ama, babá.
AYE, *adv.*, sempre, sem fim; sim, voto afirmativo.
AZA.LEA, *s.*, azaleia, azálea.
AZOTE, *s.*, azoto.
AZURE, *adj.*, azul-celeste.

B

B, segunda letra do alfabeto inglês.
BAB.BLE, *s.*, fala incompreensível, murmúrio; *v.*, balbuciar.
BAB.BLE.MENT, *s.*, balbucio; tolice.
BA.BY, *s.*, bebê, nenê.
BA.BY.HOOD, *s.*, infância, meninice.
BA.BY.ISH, *adj.*, infantil, pueril.
BA.BY.ISH.NESS, *s.*, infantilidade, puerilidade.
BA.BY.NURS.ERY, *s.*, creche.
BA.BY-SIT.TER, *s.*, babá.
BAC.CHA.NAL, *s.*, bacanal, orgia.
BACH.E.LOR, *s.*, solteiro, bacharel.
BACH.E.LOR.HOOD, *s.*, estado de solteiro, bacharelado.
BA.CIL.LA.RY, *adj.*, bacilar.
BA.CIL.LUS, *s.*, bacilo.
BACK, *s.*, costas, dorso, fundos.
BACK.ACHE, *s.*, dor nas costas.
BACK AWAY, *v.*, voltar, recuar.
BACK.BONE, *s.*, espinha dorsal.
BACK DOWN, *v.*, desistir, entregar-se.
BACKER, *s.*, defensor, zagueiro.
BACK.GROUND, *s.*, fundo, motivo; fato; prática, conhecimento.
BACK.HAND, *s.*, caligrafia.
BACK.HAND.ER, *s.*, bofetada, bofetão.
BACK.ING, *s.*, apoio, auxílio, ajuda.
BACK OUT, *v.*, desistir, ir atrás.
BACK.SET, *s.*, revés, retrocesso.
BACK.SIDE, *s.*, traseiro, nádegas.
BACK.UP, *s.*, cópia de segurança, arquivo reserva.
BACK UP, *v.*, reforçar, copiar para segurança.
BACK.WARD, *adj.*, para trás, reverso.
BACK.WA.TER, *s.*, água represada.
BACK.WOODS, *s.*, sertão, região distante e selvagem.
BACK.YARD, *s.*, quintal, jardim.
BA.CON, *s.*, bacon, toucinho.
BACON.IZE, *v.*, transformar em toucinho, engordar.
BAC.TE.RIA, *s.*, bactéria.
BAC.TE.RI.OL.O.GY, *s.*, bacteriologia.
BAD, *adj.*, mau, ruim, maldoso, malvado.
BAD.DISH, *adj.*, menos mau, inferior.
BAD.LY, *adv.*, maldosamente.
BAD.NESS, *s.*, maldade, ruindade.
BAD-TEM.PERED, *adj.*, mal-humorado.
BAF.FLER, *s.*, enganador, falsário.
BAG, *s.*, saco, sacola, bolsa; mala.
BAG.GAGE, *s.*, bagagem.
BAG.GY, *adj.*, largo, folgado, aberto.
BAG.PIPES, *s.*, gaita de foles.
BAG UP, *v.*, ensacar, pôr em sacos.
BAIL, *s.*, fiança, caução; *v.*, liberar sob fiança.
BAI.LEE, *s.*, depositário.
BAIL.OR, *s.*, fiador.
BAIT, *s.*, isca, engodo, engano; *v.*, engodar, enganar.
BAKE, *v.*, cozer no forno, assar.
BA.KE.LITE, *s.*, baquelita.
BAK.ER, *s.*, padeiro.
BAKER.Y, *s.*, padaria.
BAK.ING, *s.*, cozimento.
BAL.ANCE, *s.*, balança, equilíbrio; balanço, saldo.
BAL.ANC.ER, *s.*, acrobata.
BAL.ANCE SHEET, *s.*, balancete; demonstração dos resultados.
BAL.CO.NY, *s.*, balcão, varanda; galeria.
BALD, *s.*, careca, calvo.
BALD.HEAD.ED, *adj.*, calvo, careca.
BALE.FUL, *adj.*, maligno, pernicioso, triste, tristonho.
BALK, *s.*, obstáculo, empecilho; *v.*, obstaculizar, impedir.
BALL, *s.*, bola, novelo.
BAL.LAD, *s.*, balada.

BAL.LAST, *s.*, lastro em navio.
BAL.LE.RI.NA, *s.*, bailarina.
BAL.LET, *s.*, balé, bailado.
BAL.LIS.TICS, *s.*, balística.
BAL.LOON, *s.*, balão.
BAL.LOON.IST, *s.*, balonista, aeronauta.
BAL.LOT, *s.*, voto; *v.*, votar.
BALL.POINT, *s.*, esferográfica.
BALL.ROOM, *s.*, salão de danças.
BALM, *s.*, bálsamo.
BALMY, *adj.*, balsâmico, perfumado.
BAL.SAM, *s.*, bálsamo.
BAL.SAM.IC, *adj.*, balsâmico.
BAM.BOO, *s.*, bambu.
BAM.BOO.ZLE, *v.*, lograr, enganar.
BAN, *s.*, proibição, interdição, veto.
BA.NAL, *adj.*, banal, trivial.
BA.NAL.I.TY, *s.*, banalidade.
BA.NANA, *s.*, banana.
BAND, *s.*, banda, orquestra; banda, faixa; *v.*, ligar, unir.
BAN.DAGE, *s.*, ligadura, bandagem; *v.*, enfaixar, ligar.
BAND.AID, *s.*, curativo rápido, bandeide.
BAN.DIT, *s.*, bandido, delinquente.
BAN.DOG, *s.*, mastim, cão.
BANE, *s.*, veneno, tóxico.
BANE.FUL, *adj.*, venenoso, nocivo, prejudicial.
BANG, *s.*, estalo, estrondo, explosão.
BANG DOWN *v.* atirar no chão, cair.
BAN.GLE, *s.*, bracelete.
BAN.ISH, *v.*, banir, exilar, desterrar.
BAN.ISH.MENT, *s.*, exílio, desterro, deportação.
BAN.IS.TER, *s.*, corrimão.
BAN.JO, *s.*, banjo.
BANK, *s.*, banco, ribanceira; ladeira.
BANK AC.COUNT, *s.*, conta bancária.
BANK.ER, *s.*, banqueiro.
BANK.ING, *s.*, negócio de banco.
BANK.ING.HOUSE, *s.*, casa bancária.
BANK PAPER, *s.*, papel-moeda.
BANK.RUPT, *adj.*, falido, quebrado; *v.*, falir, quebrar.
BANK.RUPT.CY, *s.*, falência, bancarrota.
BAN.NER, *s.*, bandeira, faixa de publicidade.
BAN.QUET, *s.*, banquete; *v.*, banquetear.
BAN.TER, *s.*, gracejo, ironia, sarcasmo.
BANT.ING, *s.*, fedelho, moleque.
BAP.TISM, *s.*, batismo.
BAP.TIS.MAL, *adj.*, batismal.
BAP.TIS.TERY, *s.*, batistério.
BAP.TIZE, *v.*, batizar.
BAR, *s.*, bar; barra, vara; empecilho, tribunal.
BAR.BAR.IAN, *adj.*, bárbaro.
BAR.BAR.IC, *adj.*, bárbaro, barbárico.
BAR.BA.RISM, *s.*, barbarismo, barbaridade.
BAR.BA.RIZE, *v.*, barbarizar, brutalizar.
BAR.BATE, *adj.*, barbado.
BAR.BE.CUE, *s.*, churrasco.
BAR.BER, *s.*, barbeiro; *v.*, barbear.
BARE, *adj.*, nu, despido; deserto.
BARE.FACED, *adj.*, descarado, safado, sem vergonha.
BARE.FOOT, *adj.*, descalço.
BARE.LY, *adv.*, apenas, mal, somente.
BARE.NESS, *s.*, pobreza, miséria, carência.
BAR.GAIN, *s.*, barganha, negócio, acordo; regatear, pechinchar.
BARGE, *s.*, barcaça, chata, barca.
BARG.EE, *s.*, barqueiro.
BARK, *s.*, casca de árvore; *v.*, curtir.
BAR.LEY, *s.*, cevada.
BARM, *s.*, levedura, fermento.
BAR.MAN, *s.*, empregado de bar.
BARN, *s.*, celeiro.
BARNEY, *s.*, discussão, altercação, briga.
BA.ROM.E.TER, *s.*, barômetro.
BAR.ON, *s.*, barão, ricaço, magnata.
BAR.ON.ESS, *s.*, baronesa.
BAR.RACK, *v.*, aquartelar tropas; montar barracas.
BAR.RACKS, *s.*, quartel, caserna, exército.
BAR.RAGE, *s.*, barragem, dique; fogo de artilharia.
BAR.REL, *s.*, barril; *v.*, embarrilar.
BAR.REL OR.GAN, *s.*, realejo.
BAR.REN, *adj.*, infecundo, estéril, seco.
BAR.REN.NESS, *s.*, infertilidade, esterilidade.

BAR.RI.ER, *s.*, barreira, empecilho, obstáculo.
BAR.RING, *prep.*, exceto, salvo, com exceção.
BAR.ROW, *s.*, carrinho de mão.
BAR.TER, *s.*, troca, permuta; *v.*, trocar, cambiar, permutar.
BA.SALT, *s.*, basalto.
BASE, *s.*, base, fundamento, apoio; *v.* embasar, apoiar, basear.
BASE.BALL, *s.*, beisebol.
BASE.BORN, *adj.*, popular, plebeu, vulgar, bastardo.
BASE.LESS, *adj.*, infundado, sem base.
BASE.NESS, *s.*, baixeza, vileza.
BASH, *v.*, soquear, esmurrar, dar socos.
BASH.FUL, *adj.*, acanhado, tímido.
BA.SIC, *adj.*, básico, fundamental, essencial.
BA.SI.CAL.LY, *adv.*, basicamente.
BA.SIL, *s.*, manjericão.
BA.SIL.I.CA, *s.*, basílica.
BA.SIN, *s.*, bacia.
BA.SIS, *s.*, base, fundamento.
BASK, *v.*, aquecer.
BAS.KET, *s.*, cesto, cesta.
BAS.KET.BALL, *s.*, basquete, bola ao cesto.
BAS.RE.LIEF, *s.*, baixo relevo.
BAS.TARD, *adj.*, bastardo, ilegítimo.
BAS.TARD.IZE, *v.*, abastardar.
BAT, *s.*, morcego; bastão; *v.*, usar um bastão.
BATE, *s.*, redução, abatimento.
BATH, *s.*, banho, banheira; *v.*, banhar-se, tomar banho.
BATH CHAIR, *s.*, carrinho para nenê ou deficiente físico.
BATHE, *v.*, banhar-se, tomar banho.
BATH.ER, *s.*, banhista, quem toma banho.
BATH.ING, *s.*, banho.
BATH.ROBE, *s.*, saída de banho; roupão de banho.
BA.TRA.CHIA, *s.*, batráquios.
BA.TRA.CHI.AN, *s.*, batráquio.
BAT.TAL.ION, *s.*, batalhão.
BAT.TEN, *s.*, tábua de assoalho, ripa; *v.*, engordar, tornar-se gordo.
BAT.TER, *v.*, espancar, castigar; *s.*, massa de farinha.
BAT.TERY, *s.*, bateria de carro; trem de cozinha; bateria.
BAT.TERY.CHAR.GER, *s.*, carregador de baterias.
BAT.TLE, *s.*, batalha, combate, guerra, luta.
BAT.TUE, *s.*, batida, diligência, captura.
BAT.TY, *s.*, maluco, pateta.
BAU.BLE, *s.*, bugiganga, ninharia.
BAUX.ITE, *s.*, bauxita.
BAWD, *s.*, alcoviteira.
BAWD.RY, *s.*, linguagem chula, calão.
BAWDY, *adj.*, obsceno, indecente.
BAWDY HOUSE, *s.*, lupanar, bordel, casa de meretrício.
BAWL, *v.*, berrar, gritar.
BAY, *s.*, baía, enseada; latido; *v.*, latir, ladrar.
BAY.O.NET, *s.*, baioneta.
BA.ZAAR, *s.*, bazar, loja.
BE, *v.*, ser, existir, continuar, acontecer, estar.
BEACH, *s.*, praia; *v.*, encalhar, vir para terra firme.
BEACHY, *adj.*, praiano, de praia.
BEA.CON, *s.*, farol, faixa; *v.*, brilhar.
BEA.DLE, *s.*, bedel, atendente, porteiro.
BEA.GLE, *s.*, cão de caça.
BEAK, *s.*, bico; *v.*, bicar, atingir com o bico.
BEAKED, *adj.*, possuidor de bico.
BEA.KER, *s.*, béquer, proveta.
BEAM, *s.*, trave, viga; raio de luz; *v.*, brilhar, sorrir.
BEAM.FUL, *adj.*, luminoso, brilhante.
BEAM.I.NESS, *s.*, brilho, esplendor, luminosidade.
BEAM.ING, *adj.*, brilhante, luminoso.
BEAM.LESS, *adj.*, opaco, sem brilho.
BEAMY, *adj.*, brilhante, luminoso, claro.
BEAN, *s.*, feijão, grão.
BEAN SPROUTS, *s.*, vagem.
BEAR, *s.*, urso; indivíduo que espera a queda de preços.
BEAR.ABLE, *adj.*, suportável, aceitável.
BEAR.ABLE.NESS, *s.*, tolerância, ato de suportar.
BEARD, *s.*, barba; *v.*, pegar pela barba.

BEARD.ED, *adj.*, barbado, barbudo.
BEAR.ING, *s.*, comportamento, postura, porte, contato.
BEAR.ISH, *adj.*, bruto, brutamontes, grosseiro.
BEAR.ISH.NESS, *s.*, brutalidade, grosseria, estupidez.
BEAR OUT, *v.*, apoiar, confirmar, dar forças.
BEAR UP, *v.*, resistir, manter a calma.
BEAST, *s.*, bicho, animal, besta.
BEAST.I.NESS, *s.*, bestialidade, animalidade.
BEAST.LY, *adv.*, bestialmente, brutalmente.
BEAT, *s.*, batida; compasso, ritmo; *v.*, bater em, derrotar, superar.
BEAT.EN, *adj.*, batido, gasto, cansado.
BEAT.ER, *s.*, batedor, martelo, malho.
BE.AT.I.FI.CA.TION, *s.*, beatificação.
BE.AT.I.FY, *v.*, beatificar.
BEAT.ING, *s.*, surra, sova.
BE.AT.I.TUDE, *s.*, beatitude.
BEAT ON, *v.*, surrar, bater em.
BEAT UP, *v.*, espancar, surrar.
BEAU, *adj., s.*, janota, almofadinha, mauricinho.
BEAU.TE.OUS, *adj.*, belo, formoso, elegante.
BEAU.TE.OUS.NESS, *s.*, beleza, formosura, elegância.
BEAU.TI.FUL, *adj.*, belo, formoso, elegante.
BEAU.TI.FUL.LY, *adv.*, formosamente, maravilhosamente.
BEAU.TI.FY, *v.*, embelezar.
BEAU.TY, *s.*, beleza, formosura, elegância, maravilha.
BEA.VER, *s.*, castor.
BE.CALL, *v.*, injuriar, ofender, desrespeitar.
BE.CALM, *v.*, acalmar, aquietar, pacificar.
BE.CAUSE, *conj.*, porque, visto que, porquanto.
BE.CHAM, *v.*, seduzir, persuadir, convencer.
BECK, *s.* aceno, sinal, gesto.
BE.CKON, *s.* aceno, sinal; *v.*, acenar, gesticular.
BE.CLOUD, *v.*, obscurecer, ensombrar.
BE.COME, *v.*, tornar-se, vir a ser, chegar a ser, assentar.
BE.COM.ING, *adj.*, adequado, próprio, conveniente, certo.
BED, *s.*, cama, colchão; canteiro de flores; *v.*, acamar, ajeitar.
BE.DASH, *v.*, molhar, regar.
BE.DAUB, *v.*, sujar, emporcalhar.
BED.CHAMB.ER, *s.*, quarto de dormir, dormitório.
BED.DING, *s.*, roupa de cama.
BED DOWN, *v.*, pôr na casa, deitar-se.
BED.LAM, *s.* confusão, balbúrdia.
BED.ROOM, *s.*, quarto de dormir.
BED.SIDE, *s.* cabeceira.
BED.SPREAD, *s.*, colcha.
BED.TIME, *s.*, hora de dormir; hora de ir para a cama.
BEE, *s.*, abelha.
BEEF, *s.*, bife, carne bovina, bisteca.
BEEF.BUR.GER, *s.*, hambúrguer.
BEEF.STEAK, *s.*, bife, bife pequeno.
BEE.HIVE, *s.*, colmeia.
BEEL.ZE.BUB, *s.*, belzebu, diabo, demônio.
BEER, *s.*, cerveja.
BEER.I.NESS, *v.*, ficar bêbado com cerveja.
BEET, *s.*, beterraba.
BEE.TLE, *s.*, besouro; malho, maço, macete; *v.*, malhar, bater.
BEE.TLE.STOCK, *s.*, cabo de pá.
BE.FALL, *v.*, acontecer, sobrevir.
BE.FIT.TING, *adj.*, próprio, conveniente, adequado.
BE.FOG, *v.*, enevoar, cobrir de nevoeiro, escurecer.
BE.FOOL, *v.*, enganar, iludir, lograr.
BE.FORE, *prep.*, antes de, perante; *conj.*, antes que; *adv.*, anteriormente.
BE.FORE.HAND, *adv.*, de antemão, antecipadamente.
BE.FOUL, *v.*, sujar, emporcalhar, inundar.
BE.FRIEND, *v.*, favorecer, apoiar, auxiliar.
BEG, *v.*, mendigar, esmolar, pedir esmola.
BE.GET.TER, *s.*, progenitor, gerador, criador, provocador.
BEG.GAR, *s.*, mendicante, mendigo, pedinte.
BEG.GAR.LI.NESS, *s.*, pobreza, miséria.
BEG.GARY, *s.*, pobreza, miséria, carência, necessidade.
BE.GIN.NER, *s.*, principiante, iniciante, neófito.

BE.GIN.NING, *s.*, início, começo, princípio.
BE.GONE, *interj.*, fora!, rua!, saia!
BE.GO.NIA, *s.*, begônia.
BE.GRUDGE, *v.*, cobiçar, desejar, querer.
BE.GUILE, *v.*, seduzir, enganar, iludir.
BE.HAVE, *v.*, comportar-se, portar-se.
BE.HAV.IOUR, *s.*, comportamento, postura.
BE.HEAD, *v.*, decapitar, degolar, cortar a cabeça.
BE.HEAD.ER, *s.*, carrasco, verdugo.
BE.HEAD.ING, *s.*, decapitação, degolamento.
BE.HIND, *prep.*, atrás de; *adv.*, para trás, depois; *s.*, traseiro.
BE.HOLD.EN, *adj.*, grato, agradecido.
BE.HOLD.ER, *s.*, espectador.
BEIGE, *adj.*, bege.
BE.ING, *s.*, existência, vida.
BE.KNOWN, *adj.*, reconhecido, grato.
BE.LAT.ED, *adj.*, atrasado, demorado.
BE.LAUD, *v.*, elogiar, louvar.
BE.LAY, *v.*, amarrar, trancar.
BELCH, *s.*, arroto, vômito; *v.*, vomitar, arrotar.
BELCH.ING, *s.*, vômito, arroto.
BEL.FRY, *s.*, campanário, torre.
BEL.GIAN, *adj., s.*, belga.
BE.LIE, *v.*, esconder, ocultar, desmentir.
BE.LIEF, *s.*, fé, credo, ideia, opinião.
BE.LIEV.ABLE, *adj.*, crível, acreditável, verossímil.
BE.LIEVE, *v*, acreditar, crer, confiar.
BE.LIEV.ER, *s.*, crente, fiel, seguidor, partidário.
BE.LIEV.ING, *adj.*, confiante, seguidor, crente.
BE.LIT.TLE, *v.*, decrescer, diminuir, reduzir.
BELL, *s.*, sino, campainha; *v.*, colocar sinos, dar forma de sino.
BELLE, *adj.*, belicoso, guerreiro.
BEL.LIG.ER.ENCE, *s.*, beligerância.
BEL.LIG.ER.ENT, *s.*, beligerante, lutador.
BEL.LOW, *s.*, mugido, grito de dor; mugir, bramir, berrar.
BEL.LY, *v.*, ventre, barriga; pop., pança.
BE.LONG, *v.*, referir-se, pertencer a.
BE.LOVED, *adj.*, amado, querido, quisto.
BE.LOW, *prep.*, sob, por baixo de, embaixo de.
BELT, *s.*, cinto, cinturão; *v.*, amarrar, segurar.
BEL.VE.DERE, *s.*, mirante, belvedere.
BE.MOAN, *v.*, chorar, lamentar, deplorar.
BE.MOCK, *v.*, zombar, escarnecer.
BEND, *s.*, curva, dobra; *v.*, encurvar, dobrar.
BEND.ING, *s.*, curva, dobradura.
BE.NEATH, *prep.*, abaixo de, sob, mais baixo, inferior.
BEN.E.DICK, *s.*, recém-casado.
BENE.DIC.TION, *s.*, bênção.
BEN.E.FAC.TOR, *s.*, benfeitor.
BE.NEF.ICE, *s.*, benefício.
BE.NEF.I.CENCE, *s.*, beneficência.
BE.NEF.I.CENT, *adj.*, beneficente, filantrópico.
BEN.E.FIT, *s.*, benefício, vantagem, proveito.
BE.NEV.O.LENCE, *s.*, benevolência.
BE.NEV.O.LENT, *adj.*, benévolo.
BE.NIGN, *adj.*, benigno, bondoso, amável.
BE.NIG.NI.TY, *s.*, benignidade, bondade.
BE.NUMB, *v.*, entorpecer.
BEN.ZI.NE, *s.*, benzina.
BEN.ZOL, *s.*, benzol.
BE.QUEATH, *v.*, deixar em testamento, legar, testamentar.
BE.RATE, *v.*, repreender, censurar, recriminar.
BE.RET, *s.*, boina, boné.
BER.GA.MOT, *s.*, bergamota, tangerina.
BER.RY, *v.*, produzir bagas; *s.*, baga, semente.
BERTH, *s.*, beliche, camarote, cabina.
BER.THAGE, *s.*, ancoradouro.
BE.SEECH, *v.*, suplicar, pedir, implorar.
BE.SEECH.ING, *s.*, súplica, pedido.
BE.SIDE, *prep.*, ao lado de, junto de.
BE.SIDES, *adv.*, além disso, de qualquer modo; *prep.*, além de.
BE.SMOKE, *v.*, sujar com fumo.
BE.SPEAK, *v.*, pedir com antecedência.
BEST, *adj.*, melhor; *s.*, o melhor.
BE.STAIN, *v.*, macular, manchar, sujar.
BES.TIAL, *adj.*, bestial, animal, brutal, selvagem.
BES.TI.AL.I.TY, *s.*, bestialidade, selvageria.
BES.TIAL.IZE, *v.*, bestializar, brutalizar.
BE.STOW, *v.*, conceder, dar, outorgar, deferir.
BE.STOWAL, *s.*, concessão, graça, favor, mercê.
BEST.SELL.ER, *s.*, bestseler, o livro mais

vendido.
BET, *s.*, aposta, quantia; *v.*, apostar, jogar.
BE.TAKE, *v.* ir para, mudar-se, transladar-se.
BE.TRAY, *v.*, trair, atraiçoar.
BE.TRAY.ER, *s.*, traidor.
BET.TER, *adj., adv.*, melhor; *v.*, melhorar.
BET.TER.MENT, *s.*, melhoria, melhoramento.
BET.TOR, *s.*, apostador.
BE.TWEEN, *prep.*, no meio de, entre.
BEV.ER.AGE, *s.*, bebida.
BEVY, *s.*, revoada, bando de pássaros, grupo.
BE.WAIL, *v.*, chorar, lamentar.
BE.WAIL.ING, *s.*, lamentação, choro.
BE.WARE, *v.*, precaver-se, cuidar-se.
BE.WIL.DER.MENT, *s.*, confusão.
BE.WITCH, *v.*, fascinar, seduzir, encantar.
BE.WITCH.ING, *s.*, encantador, sedutor.
BE.WITCH.MENT, *s.*, encanto, sedução, encantamento.
BE.YOND, *prep.*, além de, acima de, fora de; *adv.*, além.
BIAS, *s.*, preconceito, tendência, inclinação.
BI.AX.I.AL, *adj.*, com dois eixos.
BI.BLE, *s.*, bíblia.
BIB.LI.CAL, *adj.*, bíblico.
BIB.LI.OG.RA.PHER, *s.*, bibliógrafo.
BIB.LI.OG.RA.PHY, *s.*, bibliografia.
BIB.U.LOUS, *adj.*, alcoólatra, viciado em bebida alcoólica.
BI.CAR.BON.ATE *s.*, bicarbonato.
BI.CEN.TE.NA.RY, *s.* bicentenário.
BI.CEPS, *s.*, bíceps.
BICK.ER, *v.*, brigar, altercar.
BICK.ER.ER, *s.*, briguento, brigão.
BI.CY.CLE, *s.*, bicicleta.
BID, *s.*, oferta, lance; *v.*, oferecer.
BI.DET, *s.*, bidê.
BI.FO.CALS, *s.*, óculos bifocais.
BI.FUR.CATE, *v.*, bifurcar.
BI.FUR.CA.TION, *s.*, bifurcação.
BIG, *adj.*, grande, imenso, volumoso.
BIG.A.MIST, *s.*, bígamo.
BIG.A.MOUS, *adj.*, bígamo.
BIG.A.MY, *s.*, bigamia.

BIG.GIN, *s.*, touca.
BIG.NESS, *s.*, grandeza, imensidão, volume.
BIG.OT, *s.*, fanático.
BIG.OT.RY, *s.*, fanatismo.
BIKE; *s.*, bicicleta.
BI.KI.NI, *s.*, biquíni.
BI.LA.BI.AL, *adj., s.*, bilabial.
BI.LAT.ER.AL, *adj., s.*, bilateral.
BILE, *s.*, bílis; mau humor.
BIL.I.ARY, *adj.*, biliar, próprio da bílis.
BI.LIN.GUAL, *adj., s.*, bilíngue.
BI.LIN.GUIST, *s.*, bilíngue.
BILK, *v.*, enganar, iludir, falsear.
BILL, *s.*, conta, fatura, nota; despesa em restaurante.
BIL.LET, *s.*, alojamento.
BIL.LIARDS, *s.*, bilhar.
BIL.LION, *s.*, bilhão.
BIL.LOW, *s.*, onda, vaga.
BI.MAN.U.AL, *adj.*, bímano, feito com as duas mãos.
BIN, *s.*, caixa; *v.*, encaixotar, colocar em caixa.
BI.NA.RY, *adj.*, binário.
BIND, *v.*, atar, amarrar, ligar, unir.
BIND.ING, *s.*, ligadura, cinta; encadernação.
BIND UP, *v.*, ligar.
BIN.GO, *s.*, bingo.
BIN.OC.U.LARS, *s.*, binóculos.
BI.NO.MI.AL, *s.*, binômio.
BIO.GEN.E.SIS, *s.*, biogênese.
BI.OG.RA.PHER, *s.*, biógrafo.
BIOGRAPHY, *s.*, biografia.
BI.O.LOG.IC, *adj.*, biológico.
BI.O.LOG.IST, *s.*, biólogo.
BI.OL.O.GY, *s.*, biologia.
BI.PED, *adj., s.*, bípede.
BIRCH.ING, *s.*, açoite, castigo, pena.
BIRD, *s.*, ave, pássaro.
BI.RO, *s.*, esferográfica.
BIRTH, *s.*, nascimento; linhagem.
BIRTH.DAY, *s.*, aniversário, dia de nascimento.
BIRTH.DOM, *s.*, direito de nascimento.
BIRTH.PLACE, *s.*, local de nascimento; terra natal.

BIS.CUIT, *s.* biscoito, bolacha.
BI.SEX.U.AL, *adj.*, bissexual.
BISH.OP, *s.*, bispo.
BISH.OP.RIC, *s.*, bispado, diocese.
BI.SON, *s.*, bisonte.
BIS.SEX.TILE, *adj.*, bissexto; *s.*, ano bissexto.
BIS.TOU.RY, *s.*, bisturi.
BITCH, *s.*, cadela, cachorra; prostituta, meretriz, rameira.
BITER, *s.*, mordedor.
BIT.ING, *s.*, cortante, mordente, picante, sarcástico.
BIT.LESS, *adj.*, sem freio, desenfreado.
BIT.TER, *s.*, tipo de cerveja; *adj.*, amargo.
BIT.TER.NESS, *s.*, amargura, amargor, rancor.
BIT.TERS, *s.*, licor doce-amargo.
BI.TU.MEN, *s.*, betume.
BIV.OUAC, *s.*, bivaque, acampamento; *v.*, acampar, acantonar.
BI.ZARRE, *adj.*, bizarro, exótico.
BLAB, *v.*, dar com a língua nos dentes, falar demais.
BLAB.BER, *v.*, falar de modo indiscreto.
BLACK, *adj.*, preto, negro, escuro, sinistro, sujo; *s.*, cor preta.
BLACK.A.MOOR, *s.*, negro.
BLACK.BALL, *v.*, votar contra; *s.*, voto contrário.
BLACK BEER, *s.*, cerveja preta.
BLACK.BOARD, *s.*, quadro-negro, lousa.
BLACK.CAT.TLE, *s.*, gado vacum, bovinos.
BLACK.EN, *v.* empretecer, pintar de preto, tingir de preto; difamar.
BLACK.GUARD, *s.*, velhaco, safado, cafajeste.
BLACK.HEARTED, *adj.*, mau, maldoso, perverso.
BLACK.ING, *s.*, graxa.
BLACK.LEAD, *s.*, grafite.
BLACK.LIST, *s.*, lista negra.
BLACK.MAIL, *s.*, chantagem; *v.*, chantagear.
BLACK.NESS, *s.*, escuridão.
BLACK OUT, *v.*, desmaiar, cerrar cortinas, desligar, apagar algo.
BLACK.OUT, *s.*, desmaio, queda geral de luz, escuridão, boicote.

BLACK.SMITH, *s.*, ferreiro.
BLACKY, *s.*, negro *m.*, negra *f.*
BLAD.DER, *s.*, bexiga.
BLAM.ABLE, *adj.*, censurável.
BLAM.ABLE.NESS, *s.*, culpabilidade, censurabilidade.
BLAME, *s.*, culpa; *v.*, culpar, advertir.
BLAME.LESS, *adj.*, inocente.
BLAME.LESS.NESS, *s.*, inocência.
BLANCH, *adj.*, embranquecido; *v.*, embranquecer.
BLANCH.ING, *s.*, branqueamento.
BLAND, *adj.*, suave, brando, meigo.
BLAN.DISH, *v.*, adular, lisonjear.
BLAN.DISH.MENT, *s.*, lisonja, adulação, bajulação.
BLANK, *adj.*, em branco, vazio, com lacuna; *s.*, espaço em branco.
BLANK.NESS, *s.*, palidez.
BLAS.PHEME, *v.*, blasfemar, praguejar, amaldiçoar.
BLAS.PHEM.ER, *s.*, blasfemo, blasfemador.
BLAS.PHEM.ING, *s.*, blasfêmia.
BLAS.PHE.MY, *s.*, blasfêmia.
BLAST, *s.*, rajada de vento, pé de vento, explosão; *v.*, explodir, arrasar.
BLA.TAN.CY, *s.*, barulho, ruído.
BLAZE, *s.*, fogo, incêndio; *v.*, arder, brilhar.
BLAZ.ER, *s.*, casaco, blusa; bleizer.
BLAZ.ING, *adj.*, brilhante, luminoso.
BLEACH, *v.*, branquear; branqueamento.
BLEAK, *adj.*, desolado, sombrio.
BLEAK.NESS, *s.*, frio, frialdade.
BLEAR, *adj.*, turvo, escuro, opaco.
BLEAT, *s.*, balido; *v.*, balir.
BLEED, *v.*, sangrar, tirar o sangue.
BLEED.ING, *adj.*, ensanguentado; *s.*, hemorragia.
BLEEPER, *s.*, bip, aparelho para receber chamadas.
BLEND, *s.*, mistura; *v.*, misturar.
BLEND.ING, *s.*, mistura, combinação.
BLESS, *v.*, abençoar.
BLESS.ED, *s.*, abençoado, santo.
BLIGHT, *v.*, frustrar, impedir.
BLIN, *v.*, suspender, terminar.

BLIND, *adj.*, cego; *v.*, cegar; *s.*, persiana.
BLIND.AGE, *s.*, blindagem.
BLINDY, *adv.*, às cegas, cegamente, às escuras.
BLIND.NESS, *s.*, cegueira.
BLINK, *s.*, cintilação, brilho; *v.*, piscar, cintilar, brilhar.
BLISS, *s.*, felicidade, alegria, ventura.
BLISS.FUL, *adj.*, feliz, gostoso.
BLIS.TER, *s.*, bolha, pústula; farol, sinal luminoso.
BLITHE, *adj.*, alegre, feliz, contente.
BLITHE.NESS, *s.*, felicidade, alegria.
BLITZ, *s.*, ataque aéreo, ataque repentino; vistoria policial.
BLOAT, *v.*, inchar, intumescer; envaidecer.
BLOC, *s.*, bloco, coligação partidária.
BLOCK, *s.*, bloco, laje; obstrução; *v.*, bloquear, obstruir, trancar.
BLOCK.ADE, *s.*, bloqueio.
BLOCK.AGE, *s.*, obstrução.
BLOCK.HEAD, *s.*, cabeça dura; *adj.*, ignorante.
BLOCK.ISH.NESS, *s.*, ignorância.
BLOND, BLONDE *adj.*, e *s.*, louro, loura.
BLOOD, *s.*, sangue, linhagem, descendência; *v.*, sangrar.
BLOOD BROTHER, *s.*, irmão de sangue, irmão; amigo.
BLOOD.GUILTY, *s.*, homicida.
BLOOD PRESSURE, *s.*, pressão sanguínea.
BLOODY, *adj.*, sangrento, ensanguentado.
BLOOM, *s.*, flor, florescência, vigor; juventude; *v.*, florir, ser jovem.
BLOOM.ING, *adj.*, florido, florescente.
BLOT, *s.*, borrão de tinta, mancha, mácula; *v.*, borrar, manchar.
BLOTCH, *s.*, mancha na pele, grande mancha.
BLOTCHY, *adj.*, manchado.
BLOT.TER, *s.*, mata-borrão.
BLOUSE, *s.*, blusa.
BLOW, *s.*, soco, golpe, pancada; *v.*, soprar, ventar, ofegar, bufar.
BLOW BACK, *v.*, trazer de volta.
BLOW.DRY, *s.*, escova.
BLOW.ER, *s.*, ventilador.

BLOW.ING, *s.*, ventilação, hausto, sopro.
BLOW.TORCH, *s.*, maçarico elétrico.
BLUB.BER, *v.*, chorar, prantear.
BLUE, *s.*, azul, cor azul, firmamento; *adj.*, azul; *v.*, pintar de azul.
BLUE BLOOD; *s.*, sangue azul.
BLUFF, *s.*, simulação, blefe; *v.*, fingir, simular.
BLU.ISH, *adj.*, azulado.
BLUN.DER, *s.*, erro, asneira, bobagem; *v.*, fazer tolices, errar.
BLUNGE, *v.*, amassar barro.
BLUNT, *v.*, embotar, cegar; *adj.*, embotado, cego; *s.*, agulha grossa.
BLUNT.NESS, *s.*, embotamento; falta de visão.
BLUR, *s.*, borrão, mácula, obscuridade; *v.*, obscurecer, toldar, turvar.
BLUSH, *v.*, corar, enrubescer; *s.*, enrubescimento, rubor.
BLUSH.FUL, *adj.*, envergonhado, corado, enrubescido.
BLUSH.ING, *s.*, vermelhidão, rubor; *adj.*, envergonhado.
BLUS.TER, *v.*, bramir, roncar, vociferar; *s.*, berro, violência, ruído.
BLUS.TERY, *s.*, gabolice, fanfarronice.
BOA, *s.*, boa, jiboia.
BOAR, *s.*, porco macho; javali.
BOARD, *s.*, tábua, prancha; quadro, tabuleiro; palco; mesa de conselho.
BOARD.ER, *s.*, aluno interno, pensionista.
BOARD.ING HOUSE, *s.*, pensão, casa para pensão.
BOAST, *s.*, ostentação; *v.*, gabar-se, vangloriar-se, jactar-se.
BOAST.FUL, *adj.*, vaidoso, fanfarrão.
BOAT, *s.*, bote, barco, canoa, navio; *v.*, levar em barco.
BOAT.ING, *s.*, passeio em barco.
BOAT.MAN, *s.*, barqueiro.
BOB, *s.*, truque, logro; *v.* enganar, lograr; *s.*, rapaz, pessoa, estudante.
BOCK, *s.*, cerveja.
BODE, *v.*, pressagiar, vaticinar.
BODE.MENT, *s.*, vaticínio, presságio.

BODY, *s.*, corpo, cadáver; tronco; grupo de pessoas; corpo sólido.
BODY.GUARD, *s.*, guarda-costas.
BOG, *s.*, pântano, charco, atoleiro; *v.*, atolar, afundar na lama.
BOG.GLE, *v.*, confundir, enganar.
BOG.GY, *adj.*, pantanoso, lodoso.
BO.GLE, *s.*, fantasma.
BO.GUS, *adj.*, farsante, adulterado; *s.*, falsificação.
BOIL, *s.*, ebulição, fervura; *v.*, ferver, estar inchado, aquecer para ferver.
BOI.LER, *s.*, caldeira.
BOIL.ING, *s.*, fervura, ebulição; fervente.
BOIS.TER.OUS, *adj.*, tumultuoso, barulhento, violento, rude.
BOIS.TER.OUS.NESS, *s.*, truculência, violência, rudeza.
BOLD, *adj.*, corajoso, valente, audaz, arrojado.
BOLD.NESS, *s.*, coragem, valentia, audácia.
BO.LIV.I.AN, *adj.*, *s.*, boliviano.
BOL.STER, *s.*, travesseiro.
BOLT, *s.*, trinco, pino, parafuso; *v.*, trancar, aferrolhar; peneirar.
BOMB, *s.*, bomba, projétil; *v.*, bombardear, atacar.
BOM.BARD, *v.*, bombardear.
BOMB.ER, *s.*, bombardeiro.
BOMB.SHELL, *s.*, bomba.
BOND, *s.*, vínculo, laço, obrigação; bônus; *v.*, ligar, unir, hipotecar.
BOND.AGE, *s.*, cativeiro, escravidão.
BOND.MAID, *s.*, escrava.
BOND.MAN, *s.*, escravo, servo.
BONE, *s.*, osso, espinha, chifre; *v.*, desossar, tirar as espinhas.
BONED, *adj.*, ossudo.
BON.FIRE, *s.*, fogueira.
BO.NUS, *s.*, bônus, bonificação, dividendo.
BONY, *adj.*, ossudo, ósseo, cheio de ossos.
BOO.BY, *s.*, pessoa tola; *adj.*, bobo, ignorante.
BOO.BY HATCH, *s.*, manicômio, hospício.
BOO.BY.ISH, *adj.*, tolo, imbecil, idiota.
BOO.DLE, *s.*, luvas, suborno; cambada; *v.*, subornar, induzir a.
BOOK, *s.*, livro, caderno, obra literária; *v.*, registrar, pôr em livro.
BOOK.BIND.ER, *s.*, encadernador.
BOOK.BIND.ING, *s.*, encadernação; gráfica para encadernar.
BOOK.CASE, *s.*, estante, prateleira.
BOOK.COV.ER, *s.*, capa de livro.
BOOK IN, *v.*, reservar quarto em hotel, anotar.
BOOK.ISH, *adj.*, estudioso, aplicado; livresco.
BOOK.KEEP.ER, *s.*, guarda-livros.
BOOK.LET, *s.*, brochura.
BOOK.MAK.ER, *s.*, agenciador de apostas, bukmeiquer.
BOOK.SELL.ER, *s.*, livreiro, vendedor de livros.
BOOK.SELL.ING, *s.*, venda de livros.
BOOK.SHOP, *s.*, livraria.
BOOM, *s.*, estouro, estrondo; *v.*, soar, ressoar, estourar.
BOO.MER.ANG, *s.*, bumerangue.
BOOR, *s.*, tipo rústico; camponês.
BOOR.ISH, *adj.*, rústico, rude, grosseiro.
BOOR.ISH.NESS, *s.*, rusticidade, grosseria.
BOOST, *s.*, auxílio, estímulo; *v.*, estimular, impulsionar, auxiliar.
BOOT, *s.*, bota, botina, chuteira, pontapé, chute; *v.*, calçar botas, chutar.
BOO.TEE, *s.*, botina.
BOOT.LESS, *adj.*, inútil, imprestável.
BOOT.LESS.NESS, *s.*, inutilidade.
BOR.DER, *s.*, margem, borda, orla, limite; *v.*, limitar, orlar, bordejar.
BOR.DER.ING, *s.*, borda, margem; *adj.*, limítrofe, confinante.
BORE, *v.*, esburacar, cavar, escavar; aborrecer; *s.*, aborrecedor.
BO.RE.AL, *adj.*, boreal.
BOR.ING, *adj.*, aborrecido, enfadonho, enjoativo.
BORN, *part.*, nascido, nato.
BOR.ROW, *v.*, empréstimo; *v.*, pedir emprestado.
BOR.ROW.ING, *s.*, empréstimo.
BOSS, *s.*, chefe, patrão, dono; *v.*, mandar, impor algo.
BOSSY, *adj.*, mandão, metido, autoritário.
BO.TAN.IC, *adj.*, botânico.
BOT.A.NIST, *s.*, botânico.

BOTANY   **BREAKABLE**

BOT.A.NY, *s.*, botânica.
BOTCH, *s.*, remendo, remendão, serviço mal feito; *v.*, remendar mal.
BOTH, *pron.*, ambos, os dois, as duas.
BOTH.ER, *s.*, preocupação, incômodo; *v.*, incomodar, perturbar.
BOTH.ER.ATION, *s.*, aborrecimento, incômodo.
BOT.TLE, *s.*, garrafa, vasilhame, frasco; *v.*, engarrafar.
BOT.TLED, *adj.*, engarrafado.
BOT.TLE.NECK, *s.*, engarrafamento.
BOT.TLE.OPEN.ER, *s.*, abridor de garrafas.
BOT.TOM, *s.*, fundo, parte mais baixa, traseiro, rodapé; *adj.*, ínfimo, baixo; *v.* chegar ao fundo, ir à parte mais baixa.
BOT.TOM.LESS, *adj.*, sem fundo.
BOUGH, *s.*, ramo, galho.
BOUL.DER, *s.*, seixo, pedregulho.
BOUN.TI.FUL, *adj.*, beneficente, generoso.
BOUN.TI.FUL.NESS, *s.*, bondade, generosidade.
BOUN.TY, *adj.*, generoso, bondoso.
BOU.QUET, *s.*, buquê, maço; aroma, perfume.
BOUR.GEOIS, *adj.*, *s.*, burguês.
BOUR.GEOI.SIE, *s.*, burguesia; classe média.
BOUT, *s.*, vez, turno, ataque, golpe.
BO.VINE, *adj.*, bovino.
BOW, *s.*, laço, arco para flechas; desculpa, escusa; *v.*, curvar-se, inclinar.
BOW.EL, *s.*, intestino, tripa.
BOWL, *s.*, tigela, bola; *v.*, atirar uma bola.
BOWL.ER, *s.*, lançador de bola.
BOW.MAN, *s.*, arqueiro.
BOX, *s.*, caixa, camarote; box; *v.*, encaixotar, colocar em caixa, boxear.
BOX.ING, *s.*, boxe, pugilato, luta.
BOY, *s.*, rapaz, moço, menino, garoto.
BOY.COTT, *s.*, boicote; *v.*, boicotar.
BOY.FRIEND, *s.*, namorado.
BOY.HOOD, *s.*, infância, meninice, adolescência.
BOY.ISH, *adj.*, criançola, infantil, pueril.
BOY.ISH.NESS, *s.*, criancice, infantilidade.
BRA, *s.*, sutiã.
BRACE.LET, *s.*, bracelete, pulseira.
BRACK, *s.*, fenda, falha, defeito.

BRACK.ET, *s.*, suporte, classe, faixa, parêntese; *v.*, pôr entre parênteses.
BRAD, *s.*, prego sem cabeça.
BRAH.MAN, *s.*, brâmane.
BRAILLE, *s.*, braile.
BRAIN, *s.*, cérebro, miolos, inteligência, intelecto.
BRAIN FE.VER, *s.*, meningite.
BRAIN.LESS, *adj.*, sem miolos; desmiolado, irresponsável.
BRAINY, *adj.*, inteligente, perspicaz.
BRAKE, *s.*, trava, travão; *v.*, travar.
BRAN, *s.*, farelo.
BRANCH, *s.*, ramo, galho; sucursal, filial; *v.*, ramificar.
BRANCHIA, *s.*, brânquias, guelras.
BRANCH.ING, *s.*, ramagem, ramificação, ramo, galho.
BRANCHY, *adj.*, ramificado, ramado.
BRAND, *s.*, tição, marca de fogo no gado, sinal; *v.*, marcar, manchar.
BRAN.DY, *s.*, conhaque, licor, aguardente.
BRAN.GLE, *s.*, latão; *v.*, cobrir com latão.
BRAS.SARD, *s.*, braçal.
BRAS.SIÈRE, *s.*, sutiã.
BRAVE, *adj.*, bravo, corajoso, valente, atrevido; *v.*, desafiar.
BRAV.ERY, *s.*, coragem, valentia.
BRA.VO, *interj.*, bravo!, muito bem!
BRAWN, *s.*, músculo, força física.
BRAWNY, *adj.*, musculoso, forte, vigoroso.
BRAY, *v.*, zurrar; *s.*, zurro.
BRA.ZEN, *adj.*, descarado; *v.*, ser descarado.
BRA.ZEN.NESS, *s.*, descaramento.
BRA.ZIL, *s.*, Brasil.
BRA.ZIL.IAN, *adj.*, *s.*, brasileiro.
BRA.ZIL.WHOOD, *s.*, pau-brasil.
BREACH, *s.*, brecha, fenda, abertura; *v.*, abrir brecha, fender.
BREAD, *s.*, pão.
BREAD.BOX, *s.*, caixa para pão.
BREADTH, *s.*, largura.
BREAK, *v.*, quebrar, partir, transgredir; *s.*, abertura, fratura, quebra.
BREAK.ABLE, *adj.*, frágil, quebradiço.

BREAK.AGE, s., rotura, fratura, quebradura.
BREAK.FAST, s., desjejum, primeira refeição do dia; v., tomar café.
BREAK.ING, s., fratura, arrombamento.
BREAST, s., peito, tórax; mama, teta; sentimentos; v., peitar, enfrentar.
BREATH, s., respiração, hálito, alento, bafo, fôlego, brisa.
BREATHE, v., respirar, tomar fôlego, descansar, ventar.
BREATH.ER, s., pausa.
BREATH.ING, s., respiração.
BREECH, s., traseiro, nádegas.
BREED.ER, s., reprodutor, produtor.
BREED.ING, s., reprodução, educação.
BREEZE, s., brisa, aragem, vento suave.
BREEZ.I.NESS, s., jovialidade, alegria, contentamento.
BRE.VET, s., patente, licença; v., deferir a patente, licenciar.
BRE.VI.ATE, v., abreviar, resumir; adj., abreviado, resumido; s., resumo.
BREV.I.TY, s., brevidade, resumo, concisão.
BREW, s., bebida fermentada, bebida; v., fazer cerveja.
BREW.AGE, s., fabricação de cerveja, cerveja.
BREW.ER, s., cervejeiro.
BREW.ERY, s., cervejaria.
BRIBE, s., suborno; v., subornar.
BRIBE.LESS, adj., insubornável.
BRIB.ER, s., subornador.
BRIB.ERY, s., suborno.
BRICK, s., tijolo, coisa.
BRICK.LAY.ER, s., pedreiro.
BRICK.LED, adj., frágil, quebradiço.
BRICK.MAK.ER, s., fabricante de tijolos.
BRICK.WORK, s., construção com tijolos.
BRID.AL, adj., nupcial.
BRIDE, s., noiva.
BRIDE.BED, s., leito nupcial, tálamo.
BRIDE.CAKE, s., bolo da noiva, bolo de casamento.
BRIDE.GROOM, s., noivo.
BRIDGE, s., ponte; ponte de comando; jogo de cartas.
BRI.DLE, s., rédea, freio, cabeçada; v., reprimir, sufocar, restringir.
BRIEF, s., sumário, síntese; adj., breve; v., resumir, sintetizar.
BRIEF.ING, s., instruções.
BRIEF.LY, adv., resumidamente, rapidamente.
BRIEF.NESS, s., brevidade, concisão, síntese.
BRIG, s., brigue, navio.
BRIG.A.DIER, s., brigadeiro.
BRIG.AND, s., bandido, criminoso, salteador.
BRIGHT, adj., brilhante, luminoso; inteligente, feliz, alegre.
BRIGHT.EN, v., animar, alegrar, clarear, iluminar.
BRIGHT.NESS, s., brilho, esplendor, luminosidade.
BRIL.LIANCE, s., brilho, esplendor, claridade.
BRIL.LIANT, adj., brilhante; maravilhoso.
BRIM.STONE, s., enxofre.
BRING, v., trazer, transportar, carregar.
BRING ALONG, v., carregar consigo.
BRING BACK, v., devolver, recompor.
BRING.ER, s., portador.
BRING IN, v., introduzir, tirar de dentro, trazer.
BRING.ING, s., transporte.
BRING TO.GETH.ER, v., apresentar pessoas, reconciliar.
BRINK, s., orla, margem.
BRINY, adj., salgado, salobro.
BRISK, v., animar, estimular; adj., vivo, forte, vigoroso.
BRISK.NESS, s., viveza, força, estímulo.
BRIS.TLE, s., pelo, cerda, barba dura; v., irritar-se, enraivar-se.
BRIS.TLY, adj., duro, hirsuto, resistente.
BRIT.AIN, s., Grã-Bretanha.
BRI.TAN.NIC, adj., britânico.
BRIT.I.CISM, s., britanicismo.
BRIT.ISH, adj., britânico.
BRIT.ON, adj., bretão, nativo ou habitante da Grã-Bretanha.
BRIT.TLE, adj., frágil, quebradiço.
BRIT.TLE.NESS, s., fragilidade, fraqueza.
BROACH, v., abordar, começar, iniciar; s., sovela,

furador, mandril.
BROAD, *adj.*, largo, amplo.
BROAD.CAST, *s.*, transmissão de rádio ou TV; *v.*, transmitir.
BROAD.EN, *v.*, alargar, aumentar.
BROAD.MIND.ED, *adj.*, tolerante, compreensivo.
BROAD.NESS, *s.*, largura, amplitude.
BROC.CO.LI, *s.*, brócolos, brócolis.
BRO.CHURE, *s.*, brochura, livreto, folheto.
BROI.DERY, *s.*, bordado.
BROIL, *v.*, grelhar, assar na grelha.
BROIL.ER, *s.*, grelha.
BRO.KEN, *adj.*, *part.*, quebrado, partido.
BRO.KEN-DOWN, *adj.*, falido, arruinado, destruído.
BRO.KER, *s.*, corretor.
BRO.KER.AGE, *s.*, corretagem, ato de fazer a corretagem.
BROKERY, *s.*, corretagem.
BROL.LY, *s.*, guarda-chuva.
BRONCHIA, *s.*, *pl.*, brônquios.
BRON.CHIT.IC, *adj.*, próprio da bronquite.
BRON.CHI.TIS, *s.*, bronquite.
BRONZE, *s.*, bronze; *v.*, bronzear, dar cor de bronze.
BRONZY, *adj.*, bronzeado, revestido de bronze.
BROOCH, *s.*, broche, alfinete.
BROOD, *v.*, pensar, cismar, refletir.
BROOK, *s.*, regato, arroio, ribeiro.
BROOK.LET, *s.*, regato, arroio.
BROOM, *s.*, vassoura.
BROTH, *s.*, caldo.
BROTH.EL, *s.*, bordel, lupanar.
BROTH.ER, *s.*, irmão.
BROTH.ER.HOOD, *s.*, irmandade, fraternidade, família.
BROTH.ER.IN.LAW, *s.*, cunhado.
BROTH.ER.LY, *adj.*, fraternal; *adv.*, fraternalmente.
BROW, *s.*, testa, fronte, sobrancelha; cume, pico; *v.*, estar na orla.
BROWN, *adj.*, castanho, pardo, moreno; *s.*, cor castanha.

BROWN.ISH, *adj.*, acastanhado, amorenado.
BRUCKLE, *adj.*, frágil, fraco.
BRUISE, *s.*, contusão, hematoma, machucadura; *v.*, machucar, magoar.
BRU.MOUS, *adj.*, brumoso, enevoado.
BRUNCH, *s.*, almoço depois da hora.
BRU.NETTE, *s.*, morena.
BRUSH, *s.*, escova, pincel, ato de escovar; *v.*, escovar, varrer, limpar.
BRUSH.ING, *s.*, escovadela, pequena escovada.
BRUSH UP, *v.*, retocar, refazer.
BRU.TAL, *adj.*, brutal.
BRU.TAL.ISM, *s.*, brutalismo, brutalidade.
BRU.TAL.I.TY, *s.*, brutalidade.
BRU.TAL.IZA.TION, *s.*, brutalização, perversidade, animalismo.
BRU.TAL.IZE, *v.*, brutalizar, bestializar.
BRUTE, *adj.*, *s.*, bruto, animal.
BUB.BLING, *s.*, fervura, ebulição.
BUC.CAL, *adj.*, bucal, próprio da boca.
BUCK.ET, *s.*, balde.
BUCK.LE, *s.*, fivela; *v.*, afivelar.
BUCK.SHEE, *s.*, gorjeta, gratificação.
BU.COL.IC, *adj.*, bucólico.
BUD, *s.*, botão, broto: *v.*, brotar, nascer.
BUD.DHISM, *s.*, budismo.
BUDGE, *v.*, mover-se, mexer-se, fazer mover.
BUD.GET, *s.*, orçamento, receita; bolsa de couro; *v.*, fazer orçamento.
BUF.FA.LO, *s.*, búfalo.
BUFF.ER, *s.*, para-choque.
BUF.FOON, *s.*, bobo, tolo, palhaço.
BUF.FOON.ERY, *s.*, tolice, idiotice; palhaçada.
BUG, *s.*, bicho, inseto, besouro.
BUG.GY, *s.*, carrinho para nenê.
BUILD, *s.*, construção, estilo, talhe, manequim; *v.*, construir.
BUILD.ER, *s.*, construtor, empreiteiro.
BUILD.ING, *s.*, construção, edifício.
BUILT, *adj.*, e *part.*, construído, edificado.
BULL, *s.*, touro, macho; bula, escrito.
BULL.DOG, *s.*, buldogue.
BUL.LE.TIN, *s.*, boletim, publicação.
BULL.FIGHT.ER, *s.*, toureiro.

BUM, *s.*, vagabundo, farra; *vulg.*, nádegas, traseiro.
BUMP, *s.*, impacto, batida, choque; *v.*, bater, chocar-se.
BUMP.ER, *s.*, para-choque.
BUN, *s.*, bolo, pãozinho, doce de passas.
BUNCH, *s.*, buquê de flores, maço; molho, feixe, cacho.
BUN.DLE, *s.*, trouxa, pacote, embrulho.
BUNG, *s.*, rolha, tampão, batoque; *v.*, tampar, fechar.
BUN.GA.LOW, *s.*, bangalô, chalé.
BUN.GLE, *s.*, trabalho mal feito; *v.*, estragar, fazer mal um serviço.
BUNK, *s.*, beliche, cama; *v.*, dormir em beliche.
BUN.KER, *s.*, mina de carvão; casamata, búnquer.
BUN.NY, *s.*, coelho.
BUOY, *s.*, boia, salva-vidas; *v.*, boiar, flutuar.
BUOY.ANT, *adj.*, flutuante, que boia.
BUR.DEN.OUS, *adj.*, pesado, difícil.
BU.REAU, *s.*, escrivaninha, cômoda, escritório, agência, departamento.
BU.REAU.CRAT, *s.*, burocrata.
BURG, *s.*, burgo, cidade, vila.
BUR.GESS, *s.*, burguês, cidadão.
BUR.GLAR, *s.*, ladrão, assaltante.
BUR.GLARY, *s.*, roubo, assalto.
BUR.GLE, *v.*, assaltar, roubar.
BURI.AL, *s.*, enterro, sepultamento.
BURI.ER, *s.*, coveiro.
BURN, *v.*, queimar, incendiar, arder.
BURN.ABLE, *adj.*, combustível, queimável.
BUR.ROW, *s.*, toca, esconderijo; *v.*, entocar-se, esconder-se, refugiar-se.
BURSE, *s.*, bolsa de estudos.
BURST, *s.*, estouro, explosão, eclosão, fenda; *v.*, estourar, explodir.
BURY, *v.*, sepultar, enterrar, sepultar.
BURY.ING, *s.*, sepultamento, enterro.
BURY.ING PLACE, *s.*, cemitério, campo santo.
BUS, *s.*, ônibus.
BUSI.NESS, *s.*, negócio, comércio, tema, assunto, objeto.
BUSI.NESS.LIKE, *adj.*, capaz, eficiente, hábil.
BUSI.NESS.MAN, *s.*, homem de negócios.
BUSI.NESS.WO.MAN, *s.*, mulher de negócios.
BUS.STOP, *s.*, parada de ônibus.
BUST, *s.*, busto; explosão, estouro; *v.*, explodir.
BUS.TLE, *s.*, afã, animação, alvoroço; *v.*, animar-se, apressar-se.
BUSY, *adj.*, ocupado, atarefado; *v.*, ocupar, manter-se ocupado, agir.
BUSY.BODY, *s.*, intrometido.
BUT, *conj.*, mas, porém, contudo, todavia.
BUTCH.ER, *s.*, açougueiro, carniceiro; assassino; *v.*, matar, assassinar.
BUTCH.ERY, *s.*, açougue, matadouro.
BUT.LER, *s.*, mordomo.
BUT.LERY, *s.*, despensa.
BUT.TER, manteiga; *v.*, passar manteiga.
BUT.TER.FLY, *s.*, borboleta; mariposa.
BUT.TOCK, *s.*, nádegas.
BUT.TON, *s.*, botão, emblema; *v.*, abotoar.
BUT.TON.HOLE, *s.*, casa de botão.
BUX.OM, *adj.*, gordo, rechonchudo.
BUY, *v.*, comprar; *s.*, compra.
BUY.ABLE, *adj.*, comprável.
BUY.ER, *s.*, comprador.
BUZZ, *s.*, zumbido, zunido; *v.*, zumbir, zunir.
BY, *prep.*, por, de, com, perto de, conforme, segundo.
BY.LAW, *s.*, lei municipal.
BYE, *interj.*, adeus.
BY.GONE, *adj.*, antigo, passado.
BY.PASS, *s.*, via secundária.
BY-PUR.POSE, *s.*, fim secundário.
BYRE, *s.*, abrigo para vacas, estrebaria.
BYROAD, *s.*, via secundária, atalho, vereda, senda.
BY-STREET, *s.*, viela, beco, ruela.
BYTE, *s.*, bite.
BY.WAY, *s.*, via secundária, atalho, vereda.
BY.WORD, *s.*, provérbio, máxima, sentença.

C

C, terceira letra do alfabeto inglês.
C, s., dó (música) 100 C (alg. romano).
CAB, s., táxi, cabina; v., andar de táxi, andar de carro.
CA.BAL, s., cabala, intriga, trama; v., intrigar, tramar.
CAB.BAGE, s., repolho, couve.
CAB.BY, s., taxista, motorista de táxi.
CAB.IN, s., cabana, choupana; camarote de navio, cabina.
CA.BLE, s., cabo, cabograma, telegrama; v., remeter cabograma.
CA.BLE CAR, s., teleférico.
CA.BLE.GRAM, s., cabograma.
CAB.O.TAGE, s., cabotagem.
CA.CAO, s., cacau.
CACK.LE, s., cacarejo; v., cacarejar; tagarelar.
CACK.LING, s., tagarelice.
CA.COPH.O.NY, s., cacofonia.
CAC.TUS, s., cacto.
CAD, s., pessoa grosseira, malcriada.
CA.DAS.TRE, s., cadastro.
CA.DAV.ER.OUS, adj., cadavérico.
CADE, adj., criado à mão (animal).
CA.DENCE, s., cadência, compasso.
CA.DEN.CY, s., cadência.
CA.DET, s., cadete.
CA.DU.CI.TY, s., caducidade.
CA.FÉ, s., café, restaurante.
CAF.E.TE.RIA, s., bar ou restaurante de autosserviço.
CAGE, s., gaiola, viveiro, jaula.
CA.ÏQUE, s., caíque.
CA.JOLE, v., persuadir, convencer; bajular, adular.
CAKE, s., bolo, doce, torta; v., endurecer.
CAL.A.BASH, s., cabaça.
CAL.A.BOOSE, s., calabouço, enxovia, cadeia.
CA.LAM.I.TOUS, adj., calamitoso, desastroso.
CA.LAM.I.TOUS.NESS, s., calamidade.
CA.LAM.I.TY, s., calamidade.
CAL.CAR, s., esporão.
CAL.CAR.E.OUS, s., calcário.
CAL.CI.NA.TION, s., calcinação.
CAL.CINE, v., calcinar.
CAL.CI.UM, s., cálcio.
CAL.CU.LA.BLE, adj., calculável.
CAL.CU.LATE, v., calcular, computar.
CAL.CU.LA.TION, s., cálculo.
CAL.E.FY, v., aquecer, escaldar.
CAL.EN.DAR, s., calendário, folhinha.
CALF, s., bezerro, cria, filhote de bicho.
CAL.I.BRATE, v., calibrar.
CAL.I.BRA.TION, s., calibragem.
CAL.I.BRE, s., calibre, capacidade.
CAL.I.PERS, s., compasso de calibre.
CA.LIX, s., cálice.
CALL, v., chamar, denominar, intitular, apelar; s., chamado, apelo, grito.
CALL BOX, s., cabina telefônica.
CAL.LER, s., visitante, chamador.
CAL.LIG.RA.PHER, s., calígrafo.
CAL.LIG.RA.PHY, s., caligrafia.
CALL.ING, s., vocação, tendência, pendor.
CAL.LOS.I.TY, s., calosidade.
CAL.LOUS.NESS, s., calosidade.
CALL OUT, v., berrar, gritar, chamar.
CALL UP, v., telefonar, evocar, invocar.
CALM, adj., calmo, tranquilo, sereno; s., calma; v., acalmar, sossegar.
CALM.ATIVE, s., calmante.
CALM.NESS, s., calma, serenidade.
CALMY, adj., calmo, sereno, sossegado.
CAL.O.RIE, s., caloria.
CAL.O.RIF.IC, adj., calorífico.
CA.LUM.NI.ATE, v., caluniar, difamar.
CA.LUM.NI.A.TION, s., calúnia.

CA.LUM.NI.A.TOR, *s.*, caluniador.
CAL.UM.NY, *s.*, calúnia.
CALVE, *v.*, parir, gerar.
CA.LIX, *s.*, cálice, cálix.
CAM.BRIC, *s.*, cambraia.
CAM.EL, *s.*, camelo.
CA.MEL.LIA, *s.*, camélia.
CAM.ERA, *s.*, câmara fotográfica, de TV ou cinema.
CAM.O.MILE, *s.*, camomila.
CAM.OU.FLAGE, *s.*, camuflagem; *v.*, camuflar.
CAMP, *s.*, campo, acampamento, setor.
CAM.PAIGN, *s.*, campanha; *v.*, fazer campanha.
CAM.PAIGN.ER, *s.*, soldado, veterano.
CAM.PA.NI.LE, *s.*, campanário.
CAM.PHOR, *s.*, cânfora.
CAMP.ING, *s.*, campismo.
CAM.PUS, *s.*, câmpus universitário.
CAN, *s.*, lata; *v.*, enlatar; *v. aux.*, poder, saber.
CA.NA.DI.AN, *adj., s.*, canadense.
CA.NAL, *s.*, canal; *v.*, canalizar, fazer um canal.
CA.NA.LI.ZA.TION, *s.*, canalização.
CAN.A.LIZE, *v.*, canalizar.
CA.NARY, *s.*, canário.
CAN.CEL, *v.*, cancelar, anular, desfazer.
CAN.CEL.LA.TION, *s.*, cancelamento.
CAN.CEL OUT, *v.*, anular, cancelar.
CAN.CER, *s.*, câncer, cancro.
CAN.CER.OUS, *adj.*, canceroso.
CAN.DE.LA.BRA, *s.*, candelabro.
CAN.DES.CENSE, *s.*, incandescência..
CAN.DI.DA.CY, ou **CANDIDATURE**, *s.* candidatura.
CAN.DI.DATE, *s.*, candidato; *v.*, candidatar-se.
CAN.DID.NESS, *s.*, candidez, sinceridade, boa-fé.
CAN.DLE, *s.*, vela.
CAN.DLE.STICK, *s.*, castiçal.
CAN.DOUR, **CAN.DOR**, *s.*, candura, sinceridade, imparcialidade.
CAN.DY, *s.*, açúcar, bombom, caramelo.
CAN.DY SHOP, *s.*, confeitaria.
CANE, *s.*, cana, junco, taquara, vara, vareta; *v.*, bater com vara.
CANE.BRAKE, *s.*, bambuzal, taqueral.

CA.NINE, *s.*, canino, dente canino, próprio de cão.
CAN.ING, *s.*, tunda, surra, sova.
CAN.KERED, *adj.*, canceroso, chagado.
CAN.KER.OUS, *adj.*, canceroso.
CANNED GOODS, *s., pl.*, enlatados, conservas.
CAN.NI.BAL, *s.*, canibal, antropófago.
CAN.NI.BAL.ISM, *s.*, canibalismo.
CAN.NI.NESS, *s.*, astúcia, esperteza, argúcia.
CAN.NON, *s.*, canhão.
CAN.NON.RY, *s.*, artilharia.
CAN.NY, *adj.*, esperto, astuto, arguto.
CA.NOE, *s.*, canoa.
CA.NON.IC, *adj.*, canônico.
CAN.ON.I.ZA.TION, *s.*, canonização, santificação.
CAN.ON.IZE, *v.*, canonizar.
CA.NO.ROUS, *adj.*, canoro.
CA.NO.ROUS.NESS, *s.*, harmonia, sonoridade, musicalidade.
CAN.TEEN, *s.*, cantina.
CANT.ING, *s.*, hipocrisia; *adj.*, hipócrita.
CAN.TLE, *s.*, fragmento, pedaço; *v.*, fragmentar, despedaçar.
CAN.TON.MENT, *s.*, acantonamento.
CAN.YON, *s.*, desfiladeiro, garganta.
CAP, *s.*, gorro, tampa; *v.*, cobrir, tapar.
CA.PA.BIL.I.TY, *s.*, capacidade.
CA.PA.BLE, *adj.*, capaz, habilitado.
CA.PAC.I.TATE, *v.*, capacitar, tornar capaz.
CA.PAC.I.TY, *s.*, capacidade, lotação.
CAPE, *s.*, capa; cabo.
CA.PER, *s.*, alcaparra.
CAP.I.TAL, *s.*, capital, metrópole, bens, dinheiro.
CAP.I.TAL.ISM, *s.*, capitalismo.
CAP.I.TAL.IZE, *v.*, capitalizar.
CA.PIT.U.LARY, *s.*, capitular.
CA.PIT.U.LA.TION, *s.*, capitulação.
CA.PRI.CIOUS, *adj.*, caprichoso.
CAP.SULE, *s.*, cápsula.
CAP.TAIN, *s.*, capitão; comandante.
CAP.TION, *s.*, captura, prisão, confisco.
CAP.TIOUS, *adj.*, capcioso, malicioso, astuto.
CAP.TIOUS.NESS, *s.*, capciosidade, malícia, fraude.

CAP.TI.VATE, *v.*, cativar, seduzir.
CAP.TI.VA.TION, *s.*, sedução, cativamento, fascinação.
CAP.TIV.I.TY, *s.*, cativeiro.
CAP.TURE, *v.*, capturar, prender, aprisionar; *s.*, captura, prisão.
CAR, *s.*, carro, automóvel.
CAR.A.MEL, *s.*, caramelo, açúcar.
CAR.AT, *s.*, quilate.
CAR.BINE, *s.*, carabina.
CAR.BON, *s.*, carbono.
CAR.BON.IF.ER.OUS, *adj.*, carbonífero.
CAR.BON.IZE, *v.*, carbonizar.
CAR.BU.RE.TOR, *s.*, carburador.
CAR.CASS, *s.*, carcassa.
CARD, *s.*, carta de baralho, cartão, bilhete, cardápio.
CAR.DI.AC, *adj.*, cardíaco.
CAR.DI.GAN, *s.*, casaco aberto na frente, casaco de lã, jaqueta.
CAR.DI.NAL, *adj.*, cardeal, cardinal; *s.*, cardeal.
CARD.ING, *s.*, cardação.
CARE, *s.*, cuidado, preocupação, empenho, guarda; *v.*, cuidar, preocupar.
CARE.FUL, *adj.*, cuidadoso, zeloso, cauteloso.
CARE.LESS, *adj.*, descuidado, negligente, relaxado, desleixado.
CARE.LESS.NESS, *s.*, descuido, negligência, relaxamento.
CA.RESS, *s.*, carícia, afago, carinho, agrado; *v.*, acariciar, afagar.
CARE.TAK.ER, *s.*, zelador, vigia, guarda.
CAR.GO, *s.*, carga, frete.
CA.RIB.BE.AN, *adj.*, *s.*, caribenho.
CAR.I.CA.TUR.AL, *adj.*, caricatural.
CAR.I.CA.TURE, *s.*, caricatura; *v.*, caricaturar.
CAR.IES, *s.*, cárie.
CAR.I.OUS, *adj.*, cariado, carioso.
CAR.MINE, *s.*, carmim, cor vermelha.
CAR.NAGE, *s.*, mortandade, morticínio.
CAR.NAL, *adj.*, carnal, sensual, lascivo.
CAR.NAL.I.TY, *s.*, carnalidade, sensualismo.
CAR.NI.VAL, *s.*, carnaval, entrudo.
CAR.NIV.O.ROUS, *adj.*, carnívoro.
CA.ROT.ID, *s.*, carótida.
CARP, *s.*, carpa.
CAR.PEN.TER, *s.*, carpinteiro.
CAR.PEN.TRY, *s.*, carpintaria.
CAR.PER, *s.*, crítico, maldizente, praguejador.
CAR.PET, *s.*, carpete, tapete; *v.*, acarpetar, atapetar.
CAR.RIAGE, *s.*, carruagem; vagão.
CAR.RI.ER, *s.*, transportador; empresa de transportes.
CAR.ROT, *s.*, cenoura.
CAR.ROTY, *adj.*, cor de cenoura.
CAR.RY, *v.*, transportar, carregar, levar.
CAR.RY.ING, *s.*, transporte.
CAR.TER, *s.*, carreteiro.
CAR.TI.LAGE, *s.*, cartilagem.
CAR.TOG.RA.PHY, *s.*, cartografia.
CAR.TOON, *s.*, cartão, papelão, cartaz.
CAR.TOON.IST, *s.*, cartunista, caricaturista.
CARVE, *v.*, trinchar carne, cortar carne.
CAR.VEL, *s.*, caravela.
CARV.ING, *s.*, escultura, entalhe.
CAS.CADE, *s.*, cascata, queda-d'água; *v.*, cair, cair em cascata.
CASE, *s.*, estojo, caixa, cápsula; caso, desinência, acidente.
CASE.MENT, *s.*, caixilho, batente de janela.
CASH, *s.*, dinheiro vivo, caixa; *v.*, pagar com dinheiro.
CASH.BOOK, *s.*, livro-caixa.
CASH.IER, *s.*, caixeiro; *v.*, despedir, demitir.
CASH.IER.MENT, *s.*, demissão de alguém.
CASH.LESS, *adj.*, sem dinheiro.
CASK, *s.*, barril, tonel, pipa, invólucro; *v.*, engarrafar, envasilhar.
CAS.KET, *s.*, guarda-joias, cofrezinho; *v.*, colocar no cofre.
CAS.SE.ROLE, *s.*, caçarola, panela.
CAS.SETTE, *s.*, cassete.
CAST, *s.*, elenco; lance, arremesso, distância, trajeto.
CAST ASIDE, *v.*, exilar, expatriar.
CAST.AWAY, *s.*, náufrago; *adj.*, abandonado.
CASTE, *s.*, casta.

CAS.TI.GATE, *v.*, castigar, corrigir, punir.
CAS.TI.GA.TION, *s.*, castigo, punição.
CAST.ING, *s.*, fundição.
CAS.TLE, *s.*, castelo, fortaleza, torre.
CAS.TOR, *s.*, castor.
CAS.TRATE, *v.*, castrar, capar.
CAS.TRA.TION, *s.*, castração, castramento.
CA.SU.AL, *adj.*, casual, fortuito, acidental; *s.*, trabalhador avulso; chapa.
CA.SU.IST, *s.*, casuísta.
CA.SU.IS.TIC, *adj.*, casuístico.
CAT, *s.*, gato.
CAT.A.CLYSM, *s.*, cataclismo, desgraça, calamidade.
CAT.A.COMB, *s.*, catacumba.
CAT.A.LEP.SY, *s.*, catalepsia.
CAT.A.LEP.TIC, *adj.*, caléptico.
CAT.A.LOG, *s.*, catálogo.
CAT.A.LOGUE, *s.*, catálogo; *v.*, catalogar.
CAT.A.PLASM, *s.*, cataplasma.
CAT.A.RACT, *s.*, catarata; queda-d'água, cachoeira.
CA.TARRH, *s.*, catarro.
CA.TAS.TRO.PHE, *s.*, catástrofe, cataclismo.
CATCH, *v.*, pagar, apanhar, prender, reter, deter, surpreender, atrair.
CATCH.ER, *s.*, pegador, apanhador; quem pega a bola no basebol.
CATCH.UP, *s.*, molho de tomates, catchup.
CATCHY, *adj.*, cativante, fascinante.
CAT.E.CHET.IC, *adj.*, catequético.
CAT.E.CHISM, *s.*, catecismo.
CAT.E.GOR.I.CAL, *adj.*, categórico.
CAT.E.GO.RY, *s.*, categoria.
CAT.E.NATE, *v.*, concatenar, reunir, ligar.
CA.TER, *v.*, aprovisionar, prover, suprir.
CA.THAR.SIS, *s.*, catarse.
CA.THE.DRAL, *s.*, catedral.
CATH.ODE, *s.*, cátodo.
CATH.O.LIC, *adj.*, universal; *adj.*, *s.*, católico.
CA.THOL.I.CISM, *s.*, catolicismo.
CA.THOL.I.CIZE, *v.*, catolicizar, converter ao catolicismo.
CAT.LIKE, *adj.*, semelhante a gato, felídeo.

CAT.TLE, *s.*, gato.
CAT.TY, *adj.*, malicioso.
CAUL.DRON, *s.*, caldeirão.
CAU.LI.FLOW.ER, *s.*, couve-flor.
CAULK, *v.*, calafetar.
CAUS.AL, *adj.*, causal.
CAU.SAL.I.TY, *s.*, causalidade.
CAUSE, *s.*, causa, motivo, porquê; *v.*, provocar, causar.
CAUSE.LESS, *adj.*, sem causa, sem motivo.
CAUS.TIC, *adj.*, cáustico; irônico.
CAU.TER.IZA.TION, *s.*, cauterização.
CAU.TE.RIZE, *v.*, cauterizar.
CAU.TION, *s.*, cautela, cuidado, prudência.
CAU.TIOUS, *adj.*, cauteloso, cuidadoso.
CAU.TIOUS.NESS, *s.*, cautela, cuidado, prudência.
CAV.A.LIER, *s.*, cavaleiro.
CAV.AL.RY, *s.*, cavalaria.
CAVE, *s.*, caverna, gruta, subterrâneo.
CAV.ERN, *s.*, caverna.
CAV.I.AR, *s.*, caviar.
CAV.I.TY, *s.*, cavidade, buraco, cárie.
CAW, *v.*, crocitar, voz do corvo, grasnar.
CAY.ENNE, *s.*, malagueta, pimenta malagueta.
CEASE, *v.*, cessar, terminar, acabar.
CEASE.FIRE, *s.*, cessar-fogo.
CEAS.ING, *s.*, cessação.
CEDE, *v.*, ceder, deixar, renunciar.
CEL.E.BRANT, *s.*, celebrante; sacerdote.
CEL.E.BRA.TION, *s.*, celebração, solenidade, festa.
CE.LEB.RI.TY, *s.*, celebridade, fama.
CE.LER.I.TY, *s.*, celeridade, rapidez.
CEL.ERY, *s.*, aipo.
CE.LES.TIAL, *adj.*, celestial.
CEL.I.BA.CY, *s.*, celibato.
CEL.I.BATE, *adj.*, *s.*, solteiro, celibatário.
CELL, *s.*, cela, cubículo; pilha, célula.
CEL.LAR, *s.*, celeiro, porão, adega.
CEL.LO, *s.*, violoncelo.
CEL.LO.PHANE, *s.*, celofane.
CEL.LU.LAR, *adj.*, celular.
CEL.LULE, *s.*, célula.
CEL.LU.LOID, *s.*, celuloide, película.

CEL.LU.LOSE, *s.*, celulose.
CELT, *adj., s.*, celta.
CE.MENT, *s.*, cimento; *v.*, cimentar, ligar com cimento.
CEM.E.TERY, *s.*, cemitério, campo-santo.
CENSE, *v.*, incensar.
CEN.SOR, *s.*, censor; *v.*, censurar.
CEN.SOR.SHIP, *s.*, censura.
CEN.SUR.ABLE, *adj.*, censurável.
CEN.SURE, *v.*, censurar, criticar.
CEN.SUS, *s.*, censo.
CENT, *s.*, cêntimo.
CENT.AGE, *s.*, percentagem, porcentagem.
CEN.TE.NAR.I.AN, *adj., s.*, centenário.
CEN.TE.NA.RY, *adj., s.*, centenário.
CEN.TI.GRADE, *s.*, centígrado.
CEN.TI.ME.TER, *s.*, centímetro.
CEN.TI.PEDE, *s.*, centopeia.
CEN.TRAL, *adj.*, central.
CEN.TRAL.I.TY, *s.*, centralidade, centralização.
CEN.TRAL.IZE, *v.*, centralizar.
CEN.TRE, *v.*, centro; *v.*, centrar, centralizar.
CEN.TRIC, *adj.*, central.
CEN.TUPLE, *s.*, cêntuplo.
CEN.TU.RI.ON, *s.*, centurião.
CEN.TU.RY, *s.*, século.
CE.PHAL.IC, *adj.*, cefálico.
CE.RAM.IC, *s.*, cerâmica.
CE.RE.AL, *s.*, cereal.
CER.E.BEL.LUM, *s.*, cerebelo.
CE.RE.BRAL, *adj.*, cerebral.
CE.RE.BRUM, *s.*, cérebro.
CER.E.MO.NI.AL, *s.*, cerimonial.
CER.E.MO.NI.OUS, *adj.*, cerimonioso, formal.
CER.E.MO.NI.OUS.NESS, *s.*, cerimônia.
CER.E.MO.NY, *s.*, cerimônia, rito, ritual.
CE.RE.OUS, *adj.*, de cera.
CER.TAIN, *adj.*, certo, seguro.
CER.TAIN.LY, *adv.*, certamente, seguramente.
CER.TAIN.TY, *s.*, certeza, firmeza.
CER.TIF.I.CATE, *s.*, certidão, certificado; *v.*, certificar, atestar.
CER.TI.FY, *v.*, certificar, atestar.
CER.VI.CAL, *adj.*, cervical.

CES.SA.TION, *s.*, cessação, suspensão, pausa.
CES.SION, *s.*, cessão, cedimento, ação de ceder.
CESS.PIT, *s.*, fossa, cloaca, esgoto.
CE.TA.CEAN, *s.*, cetáceo.
CHAFE, *v.*, roçar.
CHA.FER, *s.*, besouro.
CHAF.FER, *v.*, pechinchar, regatear.
CHA.GRIN, *s.*, tristeza, desgosto; *v.*, desgostar, entristecer.
CHAIN, *s.*, cadeia, corrente, grupo, cadeia de montanhas; *v.*, acorrentar.
CHAIN.ING, *s.*, encadeamento, ligação.
CHAIR, *s.*, cadeira, poltrona.
CHAIR.LIFT, *s.*, teleférico.
CHAIR.MAN, *s.*, presidente.
CHAIR.MAN.SHIP, *s.*, presidência.
CHAL.ICE, *s.*, cálice.
CHALK, *s.*, giz.
CHAL.LENGE, *s.*, desafio; *v.*, desafiar, provocar.
CHAL.LENG.ING, *adj.*, desafiante, provocador.
CHAM.BER, *s.*, câmara, sala de audiências.
CHAM.BER.LAIN, *s.*, camareiro, camarista.
CHAM.BER.MAID, *s.*, criada de quarto, camareira.
CHA.ME.LEON, *s.*, camaleão.
CHAM.OIS, *s.*, camurça.
CHAM.O.MILE, *s.*, camomila.
CHAMP, *v.*, mastigar, morder.
CHAM.PAGNE, *s.*, champanhe, champanha.
CHAM.PAIGN, *s.*, campina, planície, várzea.
CHAM.PI.ON, *s.*, campeão.
CHANCE, *s.*, chance, oportunidade, momento; *v.*, arriscar, aproveitar.
CHAN.CEL.LERY, *s.*, chancelaria.
CHANCY, *adj.*, duvidoso, incerto, arriscado.
CHAN.DE.LIER, *s.*, lustre.
CHANGE, *v.*, cambiar, trocar, mudar.
CHANGE.LESS, *adj.*, inconstante, passageiro.
CHANG.ER, *s.*, mudador, o que muda.
CHAN.NEL, *s.*, canal, ranhura, leito de rio; *v.*, canalizar.
CHANT, *s.*, canto; *v.*, cantar, entoar.
CHA.OS, *s.*, caos.
CHA.OT.IC, *adj.*, caótico.
CHAP.EL, *s.*, capela.

CHAPLET   **CHIROGRAPHY**

CHAP.LET, s., terço, grinalda.
CHAP.TER, s., capítulo.
CHAR, v., tostar, queimar.
CHAR.AC.TER, s., caráter, índole.
CHAR.AC.TER.IS.TIC, adj., característico.
CHAR.AC.TER.IZE, v., caracterizar.
CHAR.ADE s., charada.
CHARGE, s., acusação, encargo, preço, custo; v., carregar, cobrar, atacar.
CHAR.I.NESS, s., cuidado, cautela.
CHA.RIS.MA, s., carisma.
CHAR.I.TA.BLE.NESS, s., caridade.
CHAR.I.TY, s., caridade, donativo, amor puro.
CHAR.LA.TAN, s., charlatão.
CHARM, s., charme, encanto, fascínio; v., encantar, fascinar, seduzir.
CHARM.ER, s., encantador.
CHART, s., gráfico, lista; v., traçar.
CHAR.TER, v., fretar, alugar; s., frete, voo fretado, alvará.
CHAR.TER.ER, s., fretador.
CHARY, adj., cuidadoso, cauteloso, prudente, solícito.
CHASE, v., perseguir, afugentar.
CHAS.ING, s., perseguição.
CHAS.SIS, s., chassis.
CHASTE, s., casto, puro, cândido.
CHASTE.NESS, s., castidade, pureza.
CHAS.TISE, v., castigar, punir, açoitar.
CHAS.TI.TY, s., castidade.
CHAT, v., palestra, tagarelice, colóquio; v., tagarelar, conversar.
CHAUF.FEUR, s., chofer, motorista.
CHAU.VIN.ISM, s., chauvinismo.
CHEAP, adj., barato, sem valor, ordinário, comum.
CHEAP.EN, v., degradar, depreciar.
CHEAT, v., trapacear, enganar, lograr.
CHECK, s., controle, inspeção, conta, cheque; v., controlar, verificar.
CHECK.ER, s., controlador.
CHECK.OUT, s., caixa de mercado.
CHECK.UP, s., consulta, verificação total da saúde.
CHEEKY, adj., atrevido, petulante, descarado.

CHEER.FUL, adj., alegre, satisfeito.
CHEER.I.NESS, s., alegria.
CHEESE, s., queijo.
CHEESE.CAKE, s., bolo de queijo.
CHEF, s., cozinheiro-chefe.
CHEM.IC, adj., químico.
CHEM.IST, s., químico, farmacêutico.
CHEM.IS.TRY, s., química.
CHEQUE, s., cheque.
CHEQUE.BOOK, s., talão de cheques, talonário.
CHER.ISH, v., acarinhar, tratar com carinho.
CHER.RY, s., cereja.
CHER.UB, s., querubim.
CHE.RU.BIC, adj., próprio de querubim.
CHESS, s., jogo de xadrez.
CHESS.BOARD, s., tabuleiro de xadrez.
CHEST, s., peito, caixa, cofre.
CHEST.NUT, s., castanha.
CHEW, v., mastigar.
CHEW.ING, s., mastigação.
CHIC, adj., chique, elegante.
CHICK, s., pinto.
CHICK.EN, s., galinha, frango.
CHIC.O.RY, s., chicória.
CHIF.FON, s., gaze.
CHILD, s., criança, filho.
CHILD.BIRTH, s., parto.
CHILD.HOOD, s., infância.
CHILD.ISH, adj., infantil.
CHILD.LIKE, adj., infantil, pueril, inocente.
CHIL.DREN, s., prole, filhos.
CHILE.AN, adj., s., chileno.
CHILL, s., frio, friagem.
CHILLI, s., pimentão forte.
CHILLY, adj., frio, friorento.
CHI.ME.RA, s., quimera.
CHIM.NEY, s., chaminé.
CHIM.PAN.ZEE, s., chimpanzé.
CHIN, s., queixo.
CHI.NESE, adj., s., chinês.
CHIP, s., batata frita, lasca, caco de qualquer coisa, circuito; v., lascar.
CHIP.PING, s., estilhaço, lasca, caco.
CHI.ROG.RA.PHY, s., quirografia.

CHI.ROP.O.DY, s., tratamento dos pés, serviço de pedicuro.
CHIT, s., talão.
CHIT.CHAT, s. conversa mole, conversa fiada.
CHLO.RATE, s., clorato.
CHLO.RIDE, s., cloreto.
CHLO.RINE, s., cloro.
CHLO.RO.FORM; s., clorofórmio; v., cloroformizar.
CHLO.RO.PHYL, s., clorofila.
CHOC.O.LATE, s., chocolate.
CHOICE, s., escolha, seleção; adj., seleto, escolhido, preferido.
CHOIR, s., coro.
CHOKE, s., sufocar, engasgar, obstruir.
CHOK.ING, s., sufocação.
CHOKY, adj., sufocado, abafado, engasgado.
CHOL.ERA, s., cólera.
CHO.LER.IC, adj., irado, raivoso, colérico.
CHO.LES.TER.OL, s., colesterol.
CHOOS.ER, s., escolhedor, selecionador.
CHOOS.ING, s., escolha, seleção.
CHOP, v., cortar, talhar.
CHOP.PER, s., cutelo, faca.
CHO.RAL, s., coral.
CHO.RIS.TER, s., corista.
CHO.ROG.RA.PHY, s., coreografia.
CHRISM, s., crisma.
CHRISM.AL, adj., crismal.
CHRIST, s., Cristo.
CHRIS.TIAN, adj., s., cristão.
CHRIS.TIAN.ISM, s, cristianismo.
CHRIS.TIAN.I.TY, s., cristandade.
CHRIS.TIAN.IZE, v., cristianizar.
CHRIST.MAS, s., Natal; **HAP.PY CHRIST.MAS** – Feliz Natal.
CHRO.MAT.IC, adj., cromático.
CHRO.MO.SOME, s., cromossoma.
CHRON.IC, adj., crônico.
CHRON.I.CLE, s., crônica; v., escrever crônica.
CHON.I.CLER, s., cronista.
CHRO.NO.GRAM, s., cronograma.
CHRO.NOL.O.GY, s., cronologia.
CHRO.NOM.E.TER, s., cronômetro.

CHRYS.A.LIS, s., crisálida.
CHUB.BI.NESS, s., gordura, adiposidade.
CHUB.BY, adj., gordo.
CHUCK, v., atirar, jogar, sair, deixar.
CHUCK IN, v., despedir-se.
CHUCK.LE, v., rir à socapa.
CHUM, s., companheiro, amigo.
CHURCH, s., igreja, templo cristão, serviço religioso.
CHURCH.GO.ER, s. devoto, fiel, carola.
CHURCH.MAN, s., membro da igreja, clérigo, pastor.
CHURCH.SERVICE, s., serviço religioso.
CHURL, s., camponês, tipo rude.
CHURL.ISH, adj., rude, rústico, grosseiro.
CI.CA.DA, s., cigarra.
CI.CA.TRI.CE, s., cicatriz.
CI.CA.TRI.ZA.TION, s., cicatrização.
CIC.A.TRIZE, s., cicatrizar.
CI.DER, s., sidra, vinho de maçã.
CI.GAR, s., charuto.
CIG.A.RETTE, s., cigarro.
CINC.TURE, s., cinta, cinto, cinturão.
CIN.E.MA, s., cinema.
CIN.E.MAT.O.GRAPH, s., projetor de filmes.
CIN.E.RA.TION, s., incineração, cremação.
CI.PHER, s., cifra, algarismo arábico, zero: v., cifrar, calcular.
CIR.CLE, s., círculo, balcão; v., rodear, dar voltas.
CIR.CUIT, s., circuito, volta.
CIR.CU.I.TOUS.NESS, s., rodeio, circuito.
CIR.CU.LAR, adj., s., circular.
CIR.CU.LAR LET.TER, s., carta-circular.
CIR.CU.LATE, v., circular.
CIR.CU.LA.TION, s., circulação, tiragem de jornais e revistas.
CIR.CUM.CISE, v., circuncidar.
CIR.CUM.FER.ENCE, s., circunferência, periferia.
CIR.CUM.FLEX, s., acento circunflexo.
CIR.CUM.SCRIBE, v., circunscrever.
CIR.CUM.SCRIP.TION, s., circunscrição.
CIR.CUM.SPECT, adj., circunspecto, grave, sério.
CIR.CUM.STANCE, s., circunstância, situação;

v., circunstanciar.
CIR.CUM.STANCED, *adj.*, circunstanciado, detalhado.
CIR.CUM.STAN.TI.ATE, *v.*, circunstanciar, detalhar, pormenorizar.
CIR.CUM.VENT, *v.*, driblar, enganar, lograr.
CIR.CUM.VEN.TION, *s.*, engano, logro.
CIR.CUS, *s.*, circo, anfiteatro.
CIR.ROSE, *adj.*, cirroso.
CIS.AL.PINE, *adj.*, cisalpino.
CIS.TERN, *s.*, cisterna, poço, reserva de água.
CI.TA.TION, *s.*, citação, intimação, apelo, menção.
CITE, *v.*, citar, mencionar, referir, chamar, intimar.
CIT.I.ZEN, *s.*, cidadão; pessoa civil; habitante.
CIT.I.ZEN.SHIP, *s.*, cidadania.
CIT.RIC, *adj.*, cítrico.
CIT.RON, *s.*, cidra, lima.
CITY, *s.*, cidade, metrópole, centro urbano.
CITY FATHER, *s.*, vereador, edil.
CITY HALL, *s.*, prefeitura.
CIV.IC, *adj.*, cívico, urbano.
CIV.IL, *adj.*, civil, cívico, próprio do governo; cortês, delicado, polido.
CIV.IL EN.GI.NEER, *s.*, engenheiro civil.
CI.VIL.IAN, *s.*, cidadão civil, paisano; não militar.
CI.VIL.I.TY, *s.*, civilidade, polidez, cortesia.
CIV.I.LI.ZA.TION, *s.*, civilização, desenvolvimento, educação.
CIV.I.LIZE, *v.*, civilizar, desenvolver, educar.
CIV.I.LIZED, *adj., part.*, civilizado, educado.
CIVIL LAW, *s.*, direito civil.
CIV.ISM, *s.*, civismo.
CLAIM, *s.*, reivindicação, exigência, pretensão; *v.*, exigir, postular.
CLAIM.ANT, *s.*, pretendente, candidato, reclamante.
CLAIR.VOY.ANCE, *s.*, clarividência, esperteza, argúcia.
CLAIR.VOY.ANT, *s.*, clarividente, vidente.
CLAM.BER, *s.*, subida, ladeira, escalada íngreme; *v.*, subir, escalar.
CLAM.MY, *adj.*, viscoso, pegajoso.
CLAM.OR.OUS, *adj.*, clamoroso, barulhento, evidente.
CLAM.OR.OUS.NESS, *s.*, clamor, clamorosidade.
CLAM.OUR, *v.*, clamar, berrar, pedir.
CLAMP, *v.*, grampear, fixar, prender; *s.*, braçadeira, fita.
CLAN, *s.*, clã, tribo.
CLAN.DES.TINE, *adj.*, clandestino, secreto, oculto.
CLAN.DES.TINE.NESS, *s.*, clandestinidade.
CLAN.GOUR, *s.*, clangor, ruído, estrondo, estrépito.
CLANK, *s.*, ruído, barulho; *v.*, provocar ruído.
CLAP, *v.*, aplaudir, ovacionar, bater palmas.
CLAP.PER, *s.*, quem bate palmas, ovacionador.
CLAP.PING, *s.*, palmas, aplausos, ovações.
CLAR.I.FIED, *adj.*, clarificado, esclarecido.
CLAR.I.FY, *v.*, clarificar, esclarecer.
CLAR.I.NET, *s.*, clarineta.
CLAR.I.TY, *s.*, clareza.
CLASH, *s.*, estrondo, divergência; *v.*, chorar, entrar em confronto.
CLAS.SIC, *s.*, obra clássica, clássico, literatura clássica; *adj.*, clássico.
CLAS.SI.CISM, *s.*, classicismo.
CLAS.SI.FI.CA.TION, *s.*, classificação, ordenamento.
CLAS.SI.FY, *v.*, classificar.
CLASS.MATE, *s.*, colega de classe.
CLASS.ROOM, *s.*, sala de aula.
CLAT.TER, *s.*, barulho, ruído; *v.*, fazer barulho.
CLAUSE, *s.*, cláusula, regra; frase, oração.
CLAUS.TRAL, *adj.*, claustral.
CLAUS.TRO.PHO.BIA, *s.*, claustrofobia.
CLAV.I.CLE, *s.*, clavícula.
CLAW, *s.*, garra, pata; unha afiada.
CLAY, *s.*, barro, argila, terra; *v.*, cobrir com argila.
CLAY.EY, *adj.*, argiloso, de barro, terroso.
CLEAN, *adj.*, limpo, puro, inocente; *v.*, limpar, purificar, assear.
CLEAN.ER, *s.*, limpador, faxineiro; produto de limpeza.
CLEAN.ING, *s.*, limpeza.
CLEAN.LI.NESS, *s.*, limpeza, asseio.
CLEANSE, *v.*, limpar, purificar, assear.
CLEANS.ER, *s.*, creme de limpeza.

CLEAN.SHAV.EN, *adj.*, imberbe, sem barba.
CLEAR, *adj.*, claro, nítido, diáfano, limpo, evidente; *v.*, abrir, absolver.
CLEAR.ER, *s.*, limpador.
CLEAR.ING, *s.*, clareira.
CLEAR.LY, *adv.*, claramente, nitidamente.
CLEAR.NESS, *s.*, clareza, evidência.
CLEAR UP, *v.*, limpar, solucionar, esclarecer.
CLEAV.AGE, *s.*, ato de fender, rachadura.
CLEF, *s.*, chave de música.
CLEM.EN.CY, *s.*, clemência.
CLEM.ENT, *adj.*, clemente.
CLER.GY, *s.*, clero.
CLER.GY.MAN, *s.*, clérigo, padre, religioso, sacerdote, pastor.
CLER.IC, *s.*, clérigo.
CLERK, *s.*, balconista, escriturário, escrevente.
CLEV.ER, *adj.*, perspicaz, inteligente, engenhoso, hábil.
CLEV.ER.NESS, *s.*, habilidade.
CLI.CHÉ, *s.*, clichê, nariz de cera, coisa pronta, chavão.
CLIK, *s.*, tique-taque, ruído; lingueta; *v.*, estalar, fazer estalidos.
CLI.ENT, *s.*, cliente, freguês.
CLI.EN.TELE, *s.*, clientela, freguesia.
CLI.MATE, *s.*, clima.
CLI.MAT.IC, *adj.*, climático.
CLI.MA.TOL.O.GIST, *s.*, climatologista.
CLI.MAX, *s.*, clímax, auge, ápice.
CLIMB, *v.*, trepar, subir, ascender; *s.*, subida, escarpa, escalada.
CLIMB.ER, *s.*, alpinista; trepadeira.
CLIMB.ING, *s.*, alpinismo, montanhismo.
CLINGY, *adj.*, adesivo.
CLIN.IC, *s.*, clínica.
CLIN.I.CAL, *adj.*, clínico.
CLINK, *v.*, tinir, soar.
CLIP, *s.*, gancho para cabelos, clipe, grampo; *v.*, grampear cabelos.
CLIP.PING, *s.*, recorte, apara.
CLIQUE, *s.*, grupo fechado; panelinha, roda, facção.
CLIQU.ISH, *adj.*, sequaz, faccioso.

CLO.A.CA, *s.*, cloaca, esgoto.
CLOAK, *s.*, capa, capote, vestes; *v.*, vestir, encobrir.
CLOAK.ROOM, *s.*, vestiário.
CLOCK, *s.*, relógio.
CLOCK.CASE, *s.*, caixa de relógio.
CLOCK.HAND, *s.*, ponteiro de relógio.
CLOCK.MAK.ER, *s.*, relojoeiro.
CLOD, *s.*, torrão, terra, solo, barro.
CLOG, *s.*, tamanco, sapatão; obstáculo, impedimento, obstrução.
CLOIS.TER, *s.*, claustro; *v.*, enclausurar, ir para o convento.
CLONE, *s.*, clone.
CLOSE, *s.*, fim, conclusão, luta; *v.*, encerrar, confinar; *adj.*, próximo.
CLOSED, *adj., part.*, fechado.
CLOSE DOWN, *v.*, fechar em definitivo.
CLOSE.LY, *adv.*, intimamente.
CLOS.ET, *s.*, cubículo, quarto, despensa; gabinete; *v.*, fechar em quarto.
CLOT, *s.*, coágulo; *v.*, coagular.
CLOTH, *s.*, pano, tecido, fazenda.
CLOTHE, *v.*, vestir.
CLOTHES, *s., pl.*, roupa, vestuário.
CLOUD, *s.* nuvem; *v.*, escurecer, nublar.
CLOUD.BURST, *s.*, aguaceiro, toró.
CLOUD.I.NESS, *s.*, escuridão.
CLOUDY, *adj.*, nublado, escuro, sombrio, triste.
CLOVE, *s.*, cravo-da-índia.
CLOWN, *s.*, palhaço; *v.*, fazer palhaçadas.
CLOWN.ISH, *adj.*, como palhaço, igual a palhaço.
CLOY, *v.*, saciar, fartar, enjoar.
CLUB, *s.*, clube, sociedade recreativa; taco.
CLUB.BA.BLE, *adj.*, sociável.
CLUB TO.GETH.ER, *v.*, quotizar-se.
CLUE, *s.*, pista, indício, solução.
CLUMP, *s.*, moita, arvoredo, cepo; *v.*, plantar árvores, andar forte.
CLUM.SY, *adj.*, desajeitado, desgracioso, malfeito.
CLUS.TER, *s.*, cacho, grupo, bando, quantidade; *v.*, crescer em cachos.

CLUTCH, s., aperto, garra; embreagem, alavanca; v., embrear, arrebatar.
CLUTCH PEDAL, s., pedal de embreagem.
COACH, s., carruagem, vagão, ônibus; v., ensinar, treinar, viajar.
COACH.ING, s., treino, preparo, ensino.
CO.AC.TION, s., cooperação, coação.
CO.AG.U.LATE, v., coagular, coalhar.
CO.AG.U.LA.TION, s., coagulação.
COAL, s., carvão de pedra, brasa, tição; v., abastecer, fornecer carvão.
COAL.BOX, s., caixa para o carvão.
COAL.MAN, s., carvoreiro.
COAL.MINE, s., mina de carvão.
COARSE, adj., áspero, grosseiro, grosso.
COARSE.BREAD, s., pão integral.
COARSEN, v., embrutecer, tornar grosseiro.
COAST, s., costa, litoral, beira-mar, praia.
COAST.AL, adj., costeiro.
COAST GUARD, s., guarda costeira.
COAST.LINE, s., litoral.
COAT, s., paletó, casaco, pintura, demão; cobrir com tinta, revestir.
COAT.ING, s., revestimento, pintura, camada.
COAX, v., persuadir, influenciar, lisonjear, convencer.
COAXER, s., lisonjeador, bajulador; pop., puxa-saco.
CO.BALT, s., cobalto.
COB.BLE, s. pedra redonda; v., pavimentar com pedras; consertar sapatos.
COB.BLER, s., sapateiro.
COB.WEB, s., teia de aranha.
CO.CA, s., coca.
CO.CAINE, s., cocaína.
COCK, s., galo, frango, macho de ave; v., engatilhar uma arma.
COCK.ER.EL, s., frango, galo novo.
COCK.I.NESS, s., afetação, insolência, petulância.
COCK.NEY, s., habitantes dos bairros de Londres.
COCK.PIT, s., cabina de pilotagem no avião.
COCK.ROACH, s., barata.
COCK.SPUR, s., espora de galo.
COCK.TAIL, s., coquetel, mistura de bebidas, salada mista.
COCKY, adj., vaidoso, afetado.
CO.COA, s., cacau, chocolate.
CO.CO.NUT, s., coco.
CO.COON, s., casulo.
COD, s., bacalhau.
COD.DLE v., afagar, acariciar, acariciar; cozer em fogo lento.
CODE, s., cifra, código; folheto.
COD.I.CIL, s., codicilo.
COD.I.FY, v., codificar.
CO.ED.U.CA.TION, s., coeducação, cocapacitação.
CO.EF.FI.CIENT, s., coeficiente.
CO.EQUAL.I.TY, s., igualdade.
CO.ERCE, v., coagir, obrigar, reprimir, refrear.
CO.ERC.IBLE, adj., coercível.
CO.E.VAL, adj., coevo, contemporâneo.
CO.EX.IST, v., coexistir.
CO.EX.IS.TENCE, s., coexistência.
CO.EX.IS.TENT, s., coexistente.
COF.FEE, s., café, bebida, grão, local onde se toma café.
COF.FEE.POT, s., cafeteira.
COF.FEE.CUP, s., xícara para café.
COF.FEE.TREE, s., cafezeiro, cafeeiro.
COF.FER, s., cofre, arca, baú; v., colocar no cofre.
COG, s., dente de roda dentada, roda dentada; v., enganar, lograr.
CO.GENT, adj., convincente, persuasivo.
COG.I.TATE, v., cogitar, pensar, refletir, meditar.
COG.I.TA.TION, s., cogitação, meditação, pensamento.
COG.NATE, adj., s., cognato, análogo, idêntico.
COG.NI.TION, s., cognição, conhecimento.
COG.NI.ZANCE, s., conhecimento, reconhecimento, percepção.
COG.NI.ZANT, adj., conhecedor, informado.
COG.NO.MEN, s., cognome.
COG.WHEEL, s., roda dentada.
CO.HAB.IT, v., coabitar, viver junto.
CO.HAB.I.TA.TION, s., coabitação.
CO.HEIR, s., coerdeiro.

COHERENCE — COME ABOUT

CO.HER.ENCE, *s.*, coerência.
CO.HER.ENT, *adj.*, *s.*, coerente.
CO.HE.SION, *s.*, coesão.
COIF, *s.*, coifa, touca.
COIF.FEUR, *s.*, cabeleireiro.
COIL, *s.*, rolo, bobina, espiral; *v.*, enrolar, bobinar.
COIN, *s.*, moeda, esquina; *v.*, cunhar moedas, inventar.
COIN.AGE, *s.*, cunhagem de moedas; moedas, sistema monetário.
CO.IN.CIDE, *v.*, coincidir.
CO.IN.CI.DENCE, *s.*, coincidência.
COKE, *s.*, abrev., cocaína.
COLD, *adj.*, *s.*, frio; *s.*, resfriado, constipação.
COLD-BLOOD.ED, *adj.*, desumano, cruel, perverso.
COLD-BLOODEDNESS, *s.* desumanidade, crueldade, sangue frio.
COLD.NESS, *s.*, friagem, frialdade; indiferença, frieza.
COLE, *s.*, couve.
COLE.SLAW, *s.*, salada de repolho cru.
COLIC, *s.*, cólica.
COL.LAB.O.RATE, *v.*, colaborar.
COL.LAB.O.RA.TION, *s.*, colaboração.
COL.LAB.O.RA.TOR, *s.*, colaborador.
COL.LAPSE, *s.*, colapso, tombamento, queda; *v.*, cair, tombar, sucumbir.
COL.LAR, *s.*, colarinho, gola; *v.*, pôr o colarinho.
COL.LA.TION, *s.*, colação, desjejum, exame, verificação.
COL.LEAGUE, *s.*, colega; *v.*, tornar-se colega, aliar-se.
COL.LECT, *v.*, colecionar, recolher, cobrar, reunir.
COL.LECT.ED, *adj.*, *part.*, reunido, agrupado, calmo, sereno.
COL.LECT.ED.NESS, *s.*, calma, paz, tranquilidade.
COL.LECT.ING, *s.*, reunião, encontro.
COL.LEC.TION, *s.*, coleção.
COL.LEGE, *s.*, colégio superior, faculdade.
COL.LE.GIAN, *s.*, colegial, membro de um colégio.
COL.LIDE, *v.*, colidir.

COL.LI.MATE, *s.*, colimar, objetivar.
COL.LI.SION, *s.*, colisão, choque, batida.
COL.LO.CATE, *v.*, colocar, pôr, dispor.
COL.LO.CA.TION, *s.*, colocação, disposição.
COL.LO.QUI.AL, *adj.*, coloquial.
COL.LO.QUY, *s.*, cólóquio, fala.
COL.LUDE, *v.*, conspirar, tramar, conluiar.
COL.LUD.ER, *s.*, conspirador.
COL.LU.SION, *s.*, conspiração, tramoia, conluio.
CO.LOM.BI.AN, *adj.*, *s.*, colombiano.
COLONEL, *s.*, coronel.
CO.LO.NIAL, *adj.*, colonial.
CO.LO.NIAL.ISM, *s.*, colonialismo.
COL.O.NIST, *s.*, colono, agricultor.
COL.O.NI.ZA.TION, *s.*, colonização, desbravamento.
COL.O.NIZE, *v.*, colonizar.
COL.O.NY, *s.*, colônia.
COL.OR.A.TION, *s.*, coloração.
CO.LOS.SAL, *adj.*, colossal, imenso.
COL.OUR, *s.*, cor, coloração.
COL.OUR-BLIND, *adj.*, *s.*, daltônico.
COL.OUR.FUL, *adj.*, colorido, animado, vivaz.
COL.OUR.ING, *s.*, cor, colorido, tez, matiz.
COL.OUR.LESS, *adj.*, descolorido, sem cores.
COLT, *s.*, potro; tipo sem experiência.
COL.UMN, *s.*, fila, fileira, coluna, pilar.
COL.UMN.IST, *s.*, colunista de jornal, colaborador, cronista.
COMB, *s.*, pente, rastelo, crista; *v.*, pentear, alisar, rastelar.
COM.BAT, *s.*, combate, luta; *v.*, combater, lutar.
COM.BAT.ANT, *s.*, combatente, lutador.
COMB.ED, *adj.*, *part.*, penteado, alisado.
COM.BIN.ABLE, *adj.*, combinável.
COM.BI.NA.TION, *s.*, combinação.
COM.BINE, *v.*, combinar, acertar, reunir; *s.*, associação.
COM.BUST, *adj.*, queimado.
COM.BUS.TI.BIL.I.TY, *s.*, combustibilidade.
COM.BUS.TI.BLE, *s.*, combustível.
COME, *v.*, vir, chegar, aproximar-se, resultar, suceder, tornar-se.
COME ABOUT, *v.*, acontecer, suceder.

COME AFTER — COMPASSION

COME AF.TER, v., suceder, vir após.
COME AWAY, v., ir embora, despedir-se.
COME BACK, v., voltar, regressar; recordar, vir à memória.
CO.ME.DI.AN, s., comediante, cômico, humorista.
COM.E.DY, s., comédia, humor.
COME IN, v., entrar, adentrar, participar de.
COME.LI.NESS, s., elegância.
COME.LY, adj., elegante, sedutor.
COME ROUND, v., voltar a si.
CO.MES.TI.BLE, s., comestível, alimento.
COM.ET, s., cometa.
COM.FORT, s., conforto, bem-estar.
COM.FORT.ABLE, adj., confortável.
COM.FORT.LESS, adj., sem conforto.
COM.IC, adj., cômico; s., cômico, humorista.
COM.ING, s., chegada, vinda.
COM.MA, s., vírgula.
COM.MAND, s., mando, ordem, comando.
COM.MAN.DANT, s., comandante, chefe, dirigente.
COM.MAND.ER, s., comandante, capitão de navio, chefe.
COM.MAND.ER.SHIP, s., comando.
COM.MAND.MENT, s., mandamento.
COM.MEM.O.RATE, v., comemorar, celebrar, festejar.
COM.MEM.O.RA.TION, s., comemoração.
COM.MEM.O.RA.TIVE, adj., comemorativo.
COM.MENCE, v., começar, iniciar, principiar.
COM.MENCE.MENT, s., começo, princípio, início.
COM.MEND, v., elogiar, louvar, recomendar.
COM.MENT, s., comentário; v., comentar.
COM.MEN.TARY, s., comentário, referência.
COM.MEN.TA.TOR, s., comentador, comentarista.
COM.MERCE, s., comércio.
COM.MER.CIAL, adj., comercial; s., anúncio, propaganda.
COM.MIN.ATE, v., cominar, reunir; anatemizar.
COM.MIS.ER.A.TION, s., comiseração, pena.
COM.MIS.SAR.I.AT, s., comissariado.
COM.MIS.SARY, s., comissário.
COM.MIS.SION, s., comissão, empreitada; v., encomendar.
COM.MIS.SION.AIRE, s., porteiro.
COM.MIT, v., cometer, praticar, depositar, entregar.
COM.MIT.MENT, s., compromisso, engajamento.
COM.MODE, s., cômoda, pia, lavatório.
COM.MOD.I.TY, s., mercadoria.
COM.MON, adj., comum, ordinário, vulgar; s., área pública.
COM.MON.AL.I.TY, s., povo, população, vulgo, plebe.
COM.MON.ER, s., plebeu.
COM.MON.WEALTH, s., população de um Estado; comunidade de língua inglesa.
COM.MU.NAL, adj., comum, comunal.
COM.MU.NI.CA.BIL.I.TY, s., comunicabilidade.
COM.MU.NI.CA.BLE, adj., comunicável.
COM.MU.NI.CATE, v., comunicar.
COM.MU.NI.CA.TION, s., comunicação.
COM.MU.NION, s., comunhão, eucaristia.
COM.MU.NISM, s., comunismo.
COM.MU.NIST, s., comunista.
COM.MU.NI.TY, s., comunidade.
COM.MU.TA.TION, s., comutação, redução de pena, permuta.
COM.MUTE, v., viajar habitualmente.
COM.PACT, s., estojo, acordo; adj., compacto.
COM.PAN.ION, s., companheiro.
COM.PAN.ION.SHIP, s., companhia, companheirismo.
COM.PA.NY, s., companhia, sociedade; v., associar-se.
COM.PA.RA.BLE, adj., comparável.
COM.PARE, v., comparar.
COM.PAR.I.SON, s., comparação.
COM.PART.MENT, s., compartimento, divisão, seção.
COM.PASS, s., bússola, compasso, limite; v., circular, compreender.
COM.PAS.SION, s., compaixão.

COM.PAT.IBLE, *adj.*, compatível.
COM.PEL, *v.*, compelir, obrigar, forçar.
COM.PEN.SATE, *v.*, compensar, contrabalançar, estabilizar.
COM.PEN.SA.TION, *s.*, compensação, recompensa.
COM.PETE, *v.*, competir, concorrer, rivalizar, emular.
COM.PE.TENCE, *s.*, competência, habilidade, capacidade.
COM.PE.TI.TION, *s.*, concurso, competição.
COM.PET.I.TIVE, *adj.*, competitivo.
COM.PI.LA.TION, *s.*, compilação.
COM.PILE, *v.*, compilar, compor.
COM.PLA.CEN.CY, *s.*, complacência, satisfação pessoal.
COM.PLAIN, *v.*, queixar-se.
COM.PLAIN.ER, *s.*, queixoso.
COM.PLE.MENT, *s.*, complemento; tripulação; *v.*, complementar.
COM.PLE.MEN.TA.RY, *adj.*, complementar.
COM.PLETE, *adj.* completo, inteiro; *v.*, completar, encher.
COM.PLETE.NESS, *s.*, perfeição.
COM.PLE.TION, *s.*, conclusão, término.
COM.PLEX, *adj., s.*, complexo; complexo de edifícios.
COM.PLEX.I.TY, *s.*, complexidade.
COM.PLI.CATE, *v.*, complicar.
COM.PLI.CA.TION, *s.*, complicação, problema.
COM.PLIC.I.TY, *s.*, cumplicidade.
COM.PO, *s.*, estuque, argamassa.
COM.PO.NENT, *adj.*, componente, acessório; *s.*, peça acessória.
COM.PORT, *v.*, comportar-se.
COM.PORT.MENT, *s.*, conduta, comportamento, atitude.
COM.POSE, *v.*, compor.
COM.POS.ER, *s.*, compositor.
COM.PO.SI.TION, *s.*, composição.
COM.POS.I.TOR, *s.*, compositor.
COM.POST, *s.*, adubo.
COM.POTE, *s.*, compota.
COM.PRE.HEND, *v.*, compreender, entender, perceber.
COM.PRE.HEN.SION, *s.*, compreensão.
COM.PRESS, *v.*, comprimir, reduzir.
COM.PRESS.IBIL.I.TY, *s.*, compressibilidade.
COM.PRES.SION, *s.*, compressão.
COM.PRES.SIVE, *adj.*, compressivo.
COM.PRES.SOR, *s.*, compressor.
COM.PRISE, *v.*, compreender, constituir, ser parte, incluir.
COM.PRO.MISE, *s.*, compromisso, ajuste; *v.*, ajustar, acordar.
COM.PUL.SION, *s.*, compulsão, coação.
COM.PUL.SIVE, *adj.*, compulsório, obrigatório.
COM.PUL.SO.RY, *adj.*, compulsório, coercivo.
COM.PUT.ABLE, *adj.*, computável.
COM.PU.TA.TION, *s.*, computação, cômputo.
COM.PUTE, *v.*, computar, calcular, avaliar.
COM.PUT.ER, *s.*, computador.
COM.PUT.ING, *s.*, computação, informática.
COM.RADE, *s.*, camarada.
CON, *s.*, trapaça, vigarice; *v.*, enganar, trapacear; estudar, decorar.
CON.CAT.E.NATE, *v.*, concatenar, encadear, unir.
CON.CAT.E.NA.TION, *s.*, concatenação, ligação.
CON.CAVE, *s.*, côncavo, concavidade; *adj.*, côncavo, cavado.
CON.CAV.I.TY, *s.*, concavidade.
CON.CEAL, *v.*, ocultar, esconder, guardar segredo.
CON.CEAL.ED, *adj.*, oculto, escondido, secreto.
CON.CEAL.MENT, *s.*, ocultamento, segredo, esconderijo.
CON.CEDE, *v.*, conceder, admitir, reconhecer.
CON.CEIT, *s.*, presunção, vaidade; dito chistoso.
CON.CEIT.ED, *adj.*, vaidoso, presunçoso.
CON.CEIVE, *v.*, conceber, imaginar; engravidar, compreender.
CON.CEIV.ING, *s.*, concepção.
CON.CEN.TER, *v.*, concentrar, convergir.
CON.CEN.TRATE, *v.*, concentrar.
CON.CEPT, *s.*, conceito.
CON.CEP.TION, *s.*, concepção, ideia, pensamento.

CON.CERN, *s.*, concernência, negócio, inquietação; *v.*, concernir.
CON.CERN.ING, *prep.*, referente, a respeito de, concernente.
CON.CERT, *s.*, concerto; *v.*, concertar, ajustar.
CON.CES.SION, *s.*, concessão.
CON.CES.SION.ARY, *s.*, concessionário.
CON.CIL.I.ATE, *v.*, conciliar, reconciliar, harmonizar.
CON.CIL.I.A.TION, *s.*, conciliação, harmonização, acordo.
CON.CIL.I.A.TOR, *s.*, conciliador.
CON.CISE, *adj.*, conciso.
CON.CI.SION, *s.*, concisão.
CON.CLUDE, *v.*, concluir, acabar, acordar.
CON.CLU.SION, *s.*, conclusão.
CON.CLU.SIVE, *adj.*, conclusivo.
CON.COCT, *v.*, fabricar, preparar, planejar.
CON.CORD, *s.*, concórdia, paz.
CON.COR.DANCE, *s.*, concordância.
CON.CRETE, *s.*, concreto, massa de cimento; *v.*, fazer com concreto.
CON.CRETE MIX.ER, *s.*, betoneira.
CON.CRET.IZE, *v.*, concretizar.
CON.CU.BI.NAGE, *s.*, concubinato.
CON.CU.BINE, *s.*, concubina.
CON.CUR,*v.*,estar de acordo,acordar, concordar.
CON.CUR.RENCE, *s.*, concordância, cooperação.
CON.CUR.RENT, *adj.*, coincidente, simultâneo.
CON.DEMN, *v.*, denunciar, condenar, censurar.
CON.DEM.NA.TION, *s.*, condenação, censura, reprovação.
CON.DENS.ABLE, *adj.*, condensável.
CON.DEN.SA.TION, *s.*, condensação.
CON.DENSE, *v.*, condensar.
CON.DIGN, *adj.*, justo, certo, merecido.
CON.DI.MENT, *s.*, condimento, tempero; *v.*, temperar.
CON.DI.TION, *s.*, condição, situação, estado, circunstância.
CON.DI.TION.AL, *adj.*, condicional.
CON.DOLE, *v.*, condoer-se.
CON.DO.LENCES, s, condolências, pêsames.
CON.DOM, *s.*, preservativo.
CON.DONE, *v.*, perdoar, aceitar, reconhecer.
CON.DOR, *s.*, condor.
CON.DUCE, *v.*, levar a, conduzir.
CON.DUCE.MENT, *s.*, tendência.
CON.DUCT, *s.*, conduta, comportamento; *v.*, conduzir, dirigir.
CON.DUC.TION, *s.*, condução.
CON.DUC.TIV.I.TY, *s.*, condutividade.
CON.DUIT, *s.*, canal, conduto, cano, tubo.
CONE, *s.*, cone, peça com forma de cone.
CON.FAB.U.LA.TION, *s.*, colóquio, conversa familiar.
CON.FEC.TION, *s.*, confecção, preparação; *v.*, confeccionar, fazer.
CON.FEC.TION.ERY, *s.*, doces, confeitos.
CON.FED.ER.A.CY, *s.*, confederação, aliança, união.
CON.FED.ER.ATE, *adj., s.*, confederado, aliado, unido.
CON.FED.ER.A.TION, *s.*, confederação.
CON.FER, *v.*, conferir, avaliar, conceder, dar.
CON.FER.ENCE, *s.*, conferência, congresso, reunião.
CON.FESS, *v.*, admitir, confessar, contar, dizer.
CON.FES.SION, *s.*, confissão, reconhecimento, admissão.
CON.FES.SOR, *s.*, confessor.
CON.FIDE, *v.*, confiar, fiar-se em.
CON.FI.DENCE, *s.*, confiança, fé.
CON.FI.DENT, *adj.*, confiante, convicto.
CON.FIG.U.RA.TION, *s.*, configuração.
CON.FINE, *v.*, confinar, prender, encarcerar.
CON.FINE.MENT, *s.*, aprisionamento.
CON.FIRM, *v.*, confirmar.
CON.FIR.MA.TION, *s.*, confirmação; crisma.
CON.FIRM.ER, *s.*, corroborador.
CON.FIS.CATE, *v.*, confiscar.
CON.FIS.CA.TOR, *s.*, confiscador.
CON.FLICT, *s.*, conflito, divergência, embate; *v.*, divergir, conflitar.
CON.FLU.ENCE, *s.*, confluência.
CON.FLU.ENT, *adj.*, confluente; *s.*, afluente, caudatário.

CON.FORM, *v.*, conformar; acomodar-se.
CON.FORM.ABIL.I.TY, *s.*, conformabilidade.
CON.FOR.MA.TION, *s.*, conformação.
CON.FOR.MI.TY, *s.*, conformidade.
CON.FRA.TER.NI.TY, *s.*, confraria, fraternidade.
CON.FRONT, *v.*, enfrentar, defrontar.
CON.FRON.TA.TION, *s.*, confrontação, enfrentamento.
CON.FUSE, *v.*, confundir, desordenar, desconcertar.
CON.FUS.ING, *adj.*, confuso, atrapalhado.
CON.FU.SION, *s.*, confusão, mal-entendido.
CON.GEAL, *v.*, coagular.
CON.GEAL.MENT, *s.*, coagulação.
CON.GE.LA.TION, *s.*, congelamento, solidificação.
CON.GE.NER, *adj.*, congênere.
CON.GE.NIAL.I.TY, *s.*, simpatia.
CON.GEN.I.TAL, *adj.*, congênito, inato.
CON.GEST, *v.*, congestionar, acumular.
CON.GES.TION, *s.*, congestão, congestionamento.
CON.GLOM.ER.A.TION, *s.*, conglomeração, aglomeração.
CON.GRAT.U.LATE, *v.*, congratular, dar parabéns, cumprimentar.
CON.GRAT.U.LA.TIONS, *s.*, congratulações, cumprimentos.
CON.GRE.GATE, *v.*, congregar, reunir, ajuntar.
CON.GRE.GA.TION, *s.*, congregação, grupo de pessoas.
CON.GRESS, *s.*, congresso, assembleia; câmara e senado.
CON.GRESS.MAN, *s.* congressista, homem do congresso.
CON.IC, *adj.*, cônico.
CON.I.CAL.NESS, *s.*, conicidade.
CO.NI.FER, *s.*, conífera.
CON.JEC.TU.RAL, *adj.*, conjetural.
CON.JEC.TURE, *s.*, conjetura, ideia; *v.*, conjeturar, imaginar, achar.
CON.JOIN, *v.*, reunir, unir, ligar, conectar.
CON.JOINT, *adj.*, unido, ligado, conectado, reunido.

CON.JU.GAL, *adj.*, conjugal.
CON.JU.GATE, *v.*, conjugar, unir; *adj.*, conjugado, ligado.
CON.JU.GA.TION, *s.*, conjugação, ligamento, união.
CON.JUNC.TION, *s.*, conjunção; coincidência; ligação.
CON.JUNC.TI.VI.TIS, *s.*, conjuntivite.
CON.JUNC.TURE, *s.*, conjuntura, momento, situação.
CON.JU.RA.TION, *s.*, conjuração, trama, sedição.
CON.NATE, *adj.*, congênito, inato.
CON.NECT, *v.*, conectar, ligar, unir.
CON.NEC.TION, *s.*, conexão, ligação, união.
CON.NIV.ANCE, *s.*, conivência, cumplicidade.
CON.NIVE, *v.*, ser conivente, ser cúmplice.
CON.NO.TA.TION, *s.*, conotação, palavra figurada.
CON.NOTE, *v.*, conotar, indicar.
CON.NU.BI.AL, *s.*, conjugal.
CON.QUER, *v.*, conquistar, apoderar-se de.
CON.QUER.OR, *s.*, conquistador.
CON.QUEST, *s.*, conquista.
CON.SAN.GUIN.I.TY, *s.*, consanguinidade.
CON.SCIENCE, *s.*, consciência.
CON.SCIENCE.LESS, *adj.*, sem consciência, inescrupuloso.
CON.SCI.EN.TIOUS, *adj.*, consciencioso.
CON.SCRIPT, *s.*, recruta, alistado no exército; *v.*, recrutar, alistar.
CON.SE.CRA.TION, *s.*, consagração, sagração.
CON.SEC.U.TIVE, *adj.*, consecutivo.
CON.SEN.SUS, *v.*, consenso.
CON.SENT, *s.*, consentimento; *v.*, consentir.
CON.SE.QUENCE, *s.*, consequência.
CON.SE.QUENT, *adj.*, consequente.
CON.SERV.ABLE, *adj.*, conservável.
CON.SER.VA.TION, *s.*, conservação, preservação.
CON.SER.VA.TOR, *s.*, protetor.
CON.SERVE, *v.*, conservar, preservar.
CON.SID.ER, *v.*, considerar, respeitar, ter em consideração.
CON.SID.ER.ABLE, *adj.*, considerável.

CON.SID.ER.ATE, *adj.*, atencioso, respeitoso.
CON.SID.ER.ATION, *s.*, consideração, exame, deliberação, estima.
CON.SID.ER.ING, *prep.*, referente a, em consideração de.
CON.SIST, *v.*, consistir.
CON.SIS.TEN.CY, *s.*, consistência, coerência.
CON.SO.LA.TION, *s.*, consolo, consolação, conforto.
CON.SOLE, *v.*, consolar, confortar, aliviar; *s.*, consolo.
CON.SOL.I.DATE, *s.*, consolidar, firmar.
CON.SOL.I.DA.TION, *s.*, consolidação, afirmação, unificação.
CON.SO.NANCE, *s.*, consonância.
CON.SORT, *v.*, acompanhar, associar-se, ligar-se.
CON.SOR.TIUM, *s.*, consórcio.
CON.SPIRE, *v.*, conspirar, tramar.
CON.STAN.CY, *s.*, constância, persistência, lealdade.
CON.STANT, *adj.*, constante.
CON.STANT.LY, *adv.*, constantemente.
CON.STEL.LA.TION, *s.*, constelação.
CON.STER.NATE, *v.*, consternar, entristecer.
CON.STI.PA.TION, *s.*, constipação, prisão de ventre.
CON.STIT.U.ENT, *s.*, eleitor.
CON.STI.TUTE, *v.*, constituir, representar.
CON.STI.TU.TION, *s.*, constituição; forma, compleição.
CON.STI.TU.TION.AL, *adj.*, constitucional.
CON.STI.TU.TION.AL.ISM, *s.*, constitucionalismo.
CON.STRAIN, *v.*, constranger, reprimir, forçar.
CON.STRAINT, *s.*, pressão, coação, repressão.
CON.STRICT, *v.*, constringir.
CON.STRUCT, *v.*, construir.
CON.STRUC.TION, *s.*, construção, edificação.
CON.STRUCT.OR, *s.*, construtor.
CON.SUL, *s.*, cônsul.
CON.SUL.ATE, *s.*, consulado.
CON.SULT, *v.*, consultar; *s.*, consultório médico.
CON.SUL.TA.TION, *s.*, consulta; discussão, disputa.
CON.SUME, *v.*, consumir, alimentar-se.
CON.SUM.ER, *s.*, consumidor.
CON.SUM.ER.ISM, *s.*, consumismo, consumo exagerado.
CON.TACT, *s.* contato; *v.*, contatar.
CON.TA.GION, *s.*, contágio.
CON.TA.GIOUS, *adj.*, contagioso.
CON.TAIN, *v.*, conter, reter.
CON.TAIN.ER, *s.*, recipiente, contêiner.
CON.TAM.I.NATE, *v.*, contaminar, afetar.
CON.TAM.I.NA.TION, *s.*, contaminação.
CON.TEM.PLATE, *v.*, contemplar, olhar, considerar.
CON.TEM.PLA.TION, *s.*, contemplação; reflexão.
CON.TEM.PO.RA.NE.I.TY, *s.*, contemporaneidade.
CON.TEM.PO.RA.NE.OUS, *adj.*, contemporâneo.
CON.TEMPT, *s.*, desprezo.
CON.TEND, *v.*, contender, enfrentar.
CON.TEND.ER, *s.*, contendor, lutador, rival.
CON.TENT, *v.*, contentar; *adj.*, contente, satisfeito; *s.*, conteúdo, teor.
CON.TEN.TION, *s.*, disputa, contenda, altercação.
CON.TEN.TIOUS, *adj.*, contencioso, disputado.
CON.TENT.MENT, *s.*, contentamento, satisfação.
CON.TEST, *v.*, contestar, opor; *s.*, contenda, disputa, competição.
CON.TES.TA.TION, *s.*, contestação, contenda.
CON.TEXT, *s.*, contexto, momento, situação.
CON.TI.NENT, *s.*, continente; *adj.*, continente, controlado.
CON.TI.NEN.TAL, *adj.*, continental.
CON.TIN.GEN.CY, *s.*, contingência.
CON.TIN.U.AL, *adj.*, contínuo.
CON.TIN.U.ANCE, *s.*, duração, durabilidade, permanência.
CON.TIN.U.A.TION, *s.*, continuação, prolongamento.
CON.TIN.UE, *v.*, continuar, retomar.
CON.TI.NU.I.TY, *s.*, continuidade.
CON.TIN.U.OS, *adj.*, contínuo.
CON.TOUR, *s.*, contorno.

CON.TRA.BAND, *s.*, contrabando.
CON.TRA.BAND.IST, *s.*, contrabandista.
CON.TRA.CEP.TIVE, *adj.*, anticonceptivo, anticoncepcional.
CON.TRACT, *s.*, contrato; *v.*, contrair, encolher.
CON.TRAC.TION, *s.*, contração.
CON.TRAC.TOR, *s.*, contratante.
CON.TRAC.TU.AL, *adj.*, contratual.
CON.TRA.DICT, *v.*, contradizer, desmentir, negar.
CON.TRA.DIC.TION, *s.*, contradição.
CON.TRA.DIC.TO.RY, *adj.*, contraditório.
CON.TRA.PO.SI.TION, *s.*, contraposição.
CON.TRARI.NESS, *s.*, oposição.
CON.TRARY, *adj.*, contrário.
CON.TRAST, *s.*, contraste; *v.*, comparar.
CON.TRA.VENE, *v.*, transgredir, infringir, desrespeitar.
CON.TRA.VEN.TION, *s.*, contravenção, infração.
CON.TRIB.UTE, *v.*, contribuir, participar.
CON.TRI.BU.TION, *s.*, contribuição, doação, participação.
CON.TRIB.U.TIVE, *adj.*, contributivo.
CON.TRIB.U.TOR, *s.*, contribuinte, colaborador de órgão de imprensa.
CON.TRIVE, *v.*, inventar, idear, imaginar.
CON.TRIV.ER, *s.*, inventor.
CON.TROL, *s.*, controle, direção: *v.*, controlar, dirigir, guiar.
CON.TROL.LA.BLE, *adj.*, controlável.
CON.TROL.LER, *s.*, controlador, diretor, executivo, contrôler.
CON.TROL.LING, *s.*, verificação.
CON.TRO.VER.SY, *s.*, controvérsia.
CON.TRO.VERT, *v.*, discutir, polemizar.
CON.TU.MA.CY, *s.*, contumácia.
CON.TUSE, *v.*, contundir, machucar, magoar.
CON.TU.SION, *s.*, contusão, machucadura.
CON.VA.LESCE, *v.*, convalescer.
CON.VA.LES.CENCE, *s.*, convalescença.
CON.VE.NIENCE, *s.*, conveniência, facilidade.
CON.VE.NIENT, *adj.*, conveniente.
CON.VENT, *s.*, convento.
CON.VEN.TION.AL, *adj.*, convencional.
CON.VEN.TION.AL.ISM, *s.*, convencionalismo.
CON.VEN.TION.AL.IZE, *v.*, convencionalizar.
CON.VERGE, *v.*, convergir, ir para, dirigir-se para.
CON.VER.GENCE, *s.*, convergência.
CON.VER.SA.TION, *s.*, conversação, colóquio.
CON.VERSE, *s.*, contrário, inverso.
CON.VER.SION, *s.*, conversão, mudança.
CON.VERT *v.*, converter; *s.*, convertido.
CON.VEX, *adj.*, convexo.
CON.VEY, *v.*, transportar, levar, carregar.
CON.VEY.ANCE, *s.*, transporte, transmissão, transferência.
CON.VEY.OR, *s.*, transportador, carregador.
CON.VICT, *v.*, condenar; *s.*, condenado, presidiário, preso.
CON.VINCE, *v.*, convencer, garantir, assegurar.
CON.VINC.ING, *adj.*, convincente.
CON.VIV.IAL, *adj.*, sociável, festivo, alegre.
CON.VIV.I.AL.I.TY, *s.*, sociabilidade, convívio, convivência.
CON.VO.CA.TION, *s.*, convocação, reunião, assembleia.
CON.VOY, *v.*, escoltar; *s.*, escolta.
CON.VULSE, *v.*, convulsionar, agitar, sacudir.
CON.VUL.SION, *s.*, convulsão.
CONY, *s.*, coelho.
COO, *s.*, arrulho, fala suave; *v.*, arrulhar, namorar, falar com doçura.
COOK, *v.*, cozinhar, preparar a comida; *s.*, cozinheiro.
COOK.ER, *s.*, fogão, fogareiro.
COOK.ERY, *s.*, arte culinária; culinária.
COOK.IE, *s.*, biscoito, bolacha.
COOK.ING, *s.*, cozinha, arte culinária.
COOL, *v.*, esfriar, refrescar; *adj.*, fresco, frio; *s.*, frescor, frescura.
COOL.ER, *s.*, geladeira.
COOP, *s.*, galinheiro, gaiola; coelheira.
CO.OP.ER.ATE, *v.*, cooperar, colaborar, ajudar.
CO.OP.ER.A.TION, *s.*, cooperação, colaboração.
CO.OP.ER.A.TIVE, *s.*, cooperativa; *adj.*, cooperativo.

CO.OR.DI.NA.TION, *s.*, coordenação, direção.
COO.TIE, *s.*, piolho.
COP, *s.*, polícia, guarda policial; *v.*, prender.
CO-PART.NER, *s.*, sócio.
COPI.ER, *s.*, copista.
CO.PI.OUS, *adj.*, copioso, abundante, farto.
CO.PI.OUS.NESS, *s.*, abundância, fartura, copiosidade.
COP.PER, *s.*, cobre.
COP.U.LA, *s.*, cópula.
COP.U.LATE, *v.*, copular.
COPY, *s.*, cópia, reprodução; *v.*, reproduzir, copiar.
COPY.ING, *s.*, ato de copiar; reprodução, cópia.
COPY.RIGHT, *s.*, direitos do autor.
CO.QUE.TRY, *s.*, galanteio, coqueteria.
COR.AL, *s.*, coral, recife de coral.
CORD, *s.*, corda, cabo, fio, linha.
COR.DIAL, *adj.*, cordial.
COR.DIAL.I.TY, *s.*, cordialidade, sinceridade, afeição.
CORE, *s.*, caroço, centro, âmago.
CO.RE.LI.GION.IST, *s.*, correligionário, partidário.
CO.RI.AN.DER, *s.*, coentro.
CORK, *s.*, cortiça, rolha; *v.*, colocar rolha.
CORK.SCREW, *s.*, saca-rolhas.
CORN, *s.*, cereal, trigo, milho, aveia.
COR.NEA, *s.*, córnea.
COR.NER, *s.*, esquina, ângulo, canto, escanteio; *v.*, encurralar, encurvar.
CORN.FLAKES, *s.*, flocos de milho.
CO.ROL.LA, *s.*, corola.
COR.OL.LARY, *s.*, corolário.
COR.O.NER, *s.*, médico legista.
COR.PO.RA.TION, *s.*, município, junta; sociedade, corporação.
COR.PO.RE.AL, *adj.*, corpóreo.
CORPS, *s.*, unidade, corpo.
CORPSE, *s.*, cadáver, defunto.
COR.PU.LENT, *adj.*, corpulento.
COR.RAL, *s.*, curral.
COR.RECT, *adj.*, correto, exato.
COR.REC.TION, *s.*, correção.
COR.REC.TIVE, *adj.*, *s.*, corretivo.
COR.RE.LATE, *v.*, correlacionar.
COR.RE.LA.TION, *s.*, correlação.
COR.RE.SPOND, *v.*, corresponder.
COR.RE.SPON.DENCE, *s.*, correspondência.
COR.RE.SPON.DENT, *s.*, correspondente.
COR.RI.DOR, *s.*, corredor.
COR.ROB.O.RATE, *v.*, corroborar.
COR.ROB.O.RA.TION, *s.*, corroboração.
COR.RODE, *v.*, corroer.
COR.RO.SION, *s.*, corrosão.
COR.RO.SIVE, *adj.*, corrosivo.
COR.RU.GATE, *v.*, enrugar, franzir.
COR.RUPT, *adj.*, corrupto; *v.*, corromper.
COR.RUPT.ER, *s.*, corruptor, sedutor.
COR.RUP.TION, *s.*, corrupção.
COR.SAIR, *s.*, corsário, pirata.
COS.I.NESS, *s.*, comodidade.
COS.MET.IC, *s.*, cosmético.
COS.MIC, *adj.*, cósmico.
COS.MOG.RA.PHY, *s.*, cosmografia.
COS.MOL.O.GY, *s.*, cosmologia.
COS.MO.NAUT, *s.*, cosmonauta.
COS.MOP.O.LITE, *s.*, cosmopolita.
COS.MOS, *s.*, cosmos, universo.
COST, *s.*, custo, preço, custas; *v.*, custar.
COST.ING, *s.*, custo.
COS.TIVE.NESS, *s.*, prisão de ventre.
COS.TUME, *s.*, traje, vestimenta; short para banho.
CO.SY, *adj.*, aconchegante, confortável.
COT.TAGE, *s.*, casa de campo.
COT.TON, *s.*, algodão.
COUCH, *v.*, deitar, recostar, estirar-se.
COUGH, *v.*, tossir; *s.*, tosse.
COUGH.ING, *s.*, tossidela, tossido; *adj.*, que tosse.
COUN.CIL, *s.*, conselho.
COUN.CIL.LOR, *s.*, vereador.
COUNT, *v.*, contar; *s.*, contagem; conde.
COUNT.ER, *s.*, balcão, guichê, ficha; *v.*, contrair.
COUN.TER.ACT, *v.*, neutralizar, anular.
COUN.TER.CHARGE, *s.*, contestação, recriminação.

COUN.TER.FEIT, *s.*, falsificação; *v.*, falsificar.
COUN.TER.FOIL, *s.*, talão.
COUN.TER.PANE, *s.*, coberta para dormir, colcha.
COUN.TER.SIGN, *v.*, autenticar.
COUNT.ESS, *s.*, condessa.
COUNT.LESS, *adj.*, inumerável.
COUN.TRY, *s.*, país, terra, nação, região, localidade.
COUN.TRY.MAN, *s.*, camponês, caipira.
COUN.TRY.SIDE, *s.*, campo, sítio, interior, sertão.
COUN.TY, *s.*, condado.
COUP, *s.*, golpe de mestre.
COU.PLE, *s.*, casal, par, parelha; *v.*, emparelhar, juntar dois.
COU.PLING, *s.*, ligação, união.
COU.PON, *s.*, cupão, vale.
COUR.AGE, *s.*, coragem, valentia.
COU.RA.GEOUS, *adj.*, corajoso.
COU.RA.GEOUS.NESS, *s.*, coragem, valentia, intrepidez.
COU.RI.ER, *s.*, correio, mensageiro, guia turístico.
COURSE, *s.*, curso, progresso, direção, processo; *v.*, rumar, acossar.
COURT, *s.*, corte, tribunal; *v.*, cortejar, namorar.
COUR.TE.OUS, *adj.*, cortês, polido, educado.
COUR.TE.OUS.NESS, *s.*, cortesia, polidez.
COUR.TE.SY, *s.*, cortesia.
COURT.HOUSE, *s.*, palácio da justiça.
COURT.YARD, *s.*, pátio.
COUS.IN, *s.*, primo, prima.
COVE, *s.*, enseada, angra, refúgio; *v.*, arquear, fazer uma abóbada.
COV.ER, *v.*, cobrir ou fazer reportagem, percorrer, revestir; *s.*, tampa.
COV.ER.AGE, *s.*, cobertura, informe.
COV.ER OVER, *v.*, cobrir.
COV.ET, *v.*, cobiçar.
COV.E.TOUS, *adj.*, ambicioso, ganancioso.
COW, *s.*, vaca; fêmea de animal.
COW.ARD, *adj.*, covarde, cobarde.
COW.ARD.ICE, *s.*, covardia.
COW.BOY, *s.*, vaqueiro, peão, boiadeiro.
COW.HERD, *s.*, vaqueiro.
COW.HIDE, *s.*, couro bovino, relho.
COY, *adj.*, tímido, envergonhado; *v.*, envergonhar-se.
COY.NESS, *s.*, timidez, modéstia.
COY.OTE, *s.*, coiote.
CRAB, *s.*, caranguejo, siri; *v.*, criticar, rebaixar, arranhar, ferir.
CRACK, *s.*, rachadura, brecha; *v.*, quebrar, rachar, partir.
CRACK.ER, *s.*, biscoito.
CRACK.ING, *s.*, estalo, ruído de rachadura.
CRACK.LE, *v.*, estalar, crepitar.
CRACK.LING, *s.*, crepitação.
CRA.DLE, *s.*, berço; *v.*, pôr no berço.
CRAFT, *s.*, arte, ofício.
CRAFTS.MAN, *s.*, artesão, artífice.
CRAFTY, *adj.*, astuto, esperto, sagaz, vivo.
CRAGS.MAN, *s.*, montanhista, alpinista.
CRAMP, *s.*, cãibra.
CRANE, *s.*, guindaste; *v.*, alçar com guindaste.
CRA.NI.UM, *s.*, crânio.
CRANK, *s.*, manivela.
CRANKY, *adj.*, excêntrico, débil.
CRAPE, *s.*, crepe.
CRA.PUL.ENCE, *s.*, crapulice, embriaguez.
CRASH, *s.*, choque, batida de carros; estrondo, desastre, falência.
CRASIS, *s.*, crase.
CRASS, *adj.*, grosseiro.
CRASS.NESS, *s.*, grosseria, estupidez.
CRA.TER, *s.*, cratera.
CRA.VAT, *s.*, gravata.
CRAV.ER, *s.*, suplicante, requerente.
CRAV.ING, *s.*, desejo ardente, súplica.
CRAW, *s.*, papo de aves.
CRAWL, *v.*, arrastar-se, engatinhar como nenê, andar muito devagar.
CRAY.ON, *s.*, lápis de cera; *v.*, desenhar com lápis de cera.
CRA.ZI.NESS, *s.*, loucura, demência, desvario.
CRA.ZY, *adj.*, louco, doido, maluco, desvairado.
CREAM, *s.*, creme, nata; *v.*, desnatar, transformar

alimentos em purê.
CREAMY, *adj.*, cremoso, cor de creme.
CRE.ATE, *v.*, criar, produzir.
CRE.A.TION, *s.*, criação.
CRE.A.TIVE, *adj.*, criativo.
CRE.A.TOR, *s.*, criador, inventor.
CREA.TURE, *s.*, criatura, ser, vivente, ente, animal.
CRE.DENCE, *s.*, crédito, fé.
CRE.DEN.TIALS, *s., pl.*, credenciais.
CRED.I.BIL.I.TY, *s.*, credibilidade.
CRED.IT, *s.*, crédito, mérito; acreditar, crer.
CRED.I.TOR, *s.*, credor.
CRE.DU.LI.TY, *s.*, credulidade.
CREED, *s.*, credo.
CREEP, *v.*, deslizar.
CREEP.ER, *s.*, trepadeira.
CRE.MATE, *v.*, cremar.
CRE.MA.TION, *s.*, cremação.
CRE.MA.TO.RY, *adj., s.*, crematório.
CRE.PUS.CU.LAR, *adj.*, crepuscular.
CRE.PUS.CULE, *s.*, crepúsculo.
CRES.CENT, *s.* crescente, meia-lua.
CRESS, *s.*, agrião.
CRE.TIN, *adj., s.*, cretino, idiota.
CRE.TIN.ISM, *s.*, cretinismo, idiotismo.
CRIB, *s.*, berço, manjedoura; *v.*, copiar, plagiar, furtar.
CRIB.BER, *s.*, plagiador.
CRICK, *s.*, cãibra.
CRICK.ET, *s.*, grilo, críquete, banquinho de madeira.
CRIME, *s.*, crime, delito.
CRIM.I.NAL, *s.*, criminoso; *adj.*, criminal.
CRIM.I.NAL.I.TY, *s.*, criminalidade.
CRIM.I.NATE, *v.*, incriminar, acusar.
CRINGE, *s.*, bajulação, servilismo; *v.*, encolher-se, rebaixar-se, bajular.
CRING.ER, *s.*, bajulador, servil.
CRIP.PLE, *s.*, aleijado; *v.*, aleijar.
CRI.SIS, *s.*, crise.
CRI.TE.RI.ON, *s.*, critério.
CRIT.IC, *adj.*, crítico.
CRIT.I.CISM, *s.*, crítica.
CRIT.I.CIZE, *v.*, criticar.
CROAK, *v.*, coaxar.
CROC.O.DILE, *s.*, crocodilo.
CROOK, *s.*, gancho, curva, curvatura; vigarista; *v.*, curvar, perverter.
CROP, *s.*, colheita, safra; *v.*, plantar, semear, colher.
CRO.QUETTE, *s.*, croquete.
CROSS, *s.*, cruz, cruzamento; *v.*, cruzar, atravessar.
CROSS-CHECK, *v.*, conferir com cruzamento de dados.
CROSS-EYED, *s.*, estrabismo.
CROSS FIRE, *s.*, fogo cruzado.
CROSS.NESS, *s.*, mau humor.
CROSS.ROADS, *s.*, cruzamento, trevo.
CROSS.WORD, *s.*, palavras cruzadas.
CROTCH.ETY, *adj.*, rabugento.
CROW, *s.*, corvo.
CROW.BAR, *s.*, pé de cabra.
CROWN, *s.*, coroa, topo, cimo.
CRU.CIAL, *adj.*, crucial, vital.
CRU.CI.FIX, *s.*, crucifixo.
CRU.CI.FY, *v.*, crucificar, afligir, atormentar.
CRUDE, *adj.*, bruto, duro; grosseiro.
CRU.DI.TY, *s.*, crueza.
CRU.EL, *adj.*, cruel.
CRU.EL.TY, *s.*, crueldade.
CRUISE, *s.*, cruzeiro; *v.*, fazer um cruzeiro.
CRUIS.ING, *s.*, cruzeiro.
CRUM.PLE, *v.*, amassar, amarrotar.
CRUNCH, *v.*, mastigar, morder, esmagar.
CRUNCHY, *adj.*, crocante.
CRUSH, *s.*, esmagamento, compressão; *v.*, esmagar, espremer.
CRUSH.ER, *s.*, esmagador, compressor.
CRUST, *s.*, crosta, côdea.
CRUS.TA.CEA, *s.*, crustáceos.
CRUSTY, *adj.*, coberto de crosta.
CRUTCH, *s.*, muleta.
CRY, *s.*, grito, *v.*, gritar.
CRY.ING, *s.*, grito, berro, choro.
CRY OUT, *v.*, gritar.
CRYPT, *s.*, cripta.
CRYP.TO.GRAM, *s.*, criptograma.

CRYSTAL / CZECHOSLOVAK

CRYS.TAL, *s.*, cristal.
CRYS.TAL.LINE, *adj.*, cristalino.
CRYS.TAL.LIZE, *v.*, cristalizar.
CUB, *s.*, filhote, cria; *v.*, dar à luz, parir.
CUB.BISH, *adj.*, desajeitado.
CUBE, *s.*, cubo.
CU.BIC, *adj.*, cúbico.
CU.BI.CLE, *s.*, cubículo.
CUCK.OO, *s.*, cuco.
CU.CUM.BER, *s.*, pepino.
CUD.GEL, *s.*, cacete, bastão; *v.*, bater com cacete, bastonar.
CUFF, *s.*, punho.
CUI.SINE, *s.*, culinária, arte de cozer.
CU.LI.NARY, *adj.*, culinário.
CUL.LEN.DER, *s.*, coador, peneira.
CUL.MI.NA.TION, *s.*, culminação, auge, conclusão, término.
CUL.PA.BIL.I.TY, *s.*, culpabilidade.
CUL.PA.BLE, *adj.*, culpável.
CULT, *s.*, culto.
CUL.TI.VA.BLE, *adj.*, cultivável.
CUL.TI.VATE, *v.*, cultivar.
CUL.TI.VA.TION, *s.*, cultivo.
CUL.TUR.AL, *adj.*, cultural.
CUL.TURE, *s.*, cultura.
CUM.BER, *v.*, obstruir, impedir; *s.*, impedimento, obstáculo.
CUM.IN, *s.*, cominho.
CU.MU.LATE, *v.*, acumular, amontoar; *adj.*, acumulado, amontoado.
CU.MU.LA.TION, *s.*, acumulação.
CUN.NING, *s.*, esperteza, astúcia; *adj.*, esperto, malandro.
CUP, *s.*, chávena, taça.
CUP.BOARD, *s.*, armário, guarda-louças.
CU.PID.I.TY, *s.*, cupidez, cobiça, ganância.
CUR.ABIL.I.TY, *s.*, curabilidade.
CUR.ABLE, *adj.*, curável.
CU.RA.TIVE, *adj., s.*, curativo.
CURD, *s.*, coalhada, ricota, requeijão; *v.*, coalhar.
CURE, *s.*, cura, tratamento; *v.*, curar.
CU.RI.OS.I.TY, *s.*, curiosidade.
CU.RI.OUS, *adj.*, curioso, intrometido.
CUR.RENT, *s.*, corrente, torrente; *adj.*, atual, corrente, conhecido.
CUR.RENT.LY, *adj.*, atualmente, correntemente.
CUR.RIC.U.LUM *s.*, curriculum vitae; programa, roteiro.
CUR.RISH.NESS, *s.*, grosseria, brutalidade, rudeza, estupidez.
CUR.SIVE, *adj.*, cursivo.
CUR.SOR, *s.*, cursor.
CURT, *adj.*, seco, brusco, ríspido; breve.
CUR.TAIN, *s.*, cortina; *v.*, cobrir com cortina.
CURT.SY, *s.*, reverência; *v.*, reverenciar, respeitar.
CUR.VA.TURE, *s.*, curvatura.
CURVE, *v.*, curvar, encurvar; *s.*, curva.
CUSS, *s.*, maldição.
CUSS.ED, *adj.*, amaldiçoado, desgraçado.
CUS.TARD, *s.*, nata, creme.
CUS.TOM, *s.*, costume, tradição, hábito.
CUS.TOM.ARY, *adj.*, costumeiro.
CUS.TOM.ER, *s.*, cliente.
CUS.TOM-MADE, *adj.*, feito sob encomenda.
CUS.TOMS, *s.*, alfândega.
CUT, *s.*, corte, redução; *v.*, cortar, reduzir.
CU.TA.NE.OUS, *adj.*, cutâneo.
CU.TI.CLE, *s.*, cutícula.
CU.TIS, *s.*, cútis, epiderme.
CUT.LASS, *s.*, alfanje.
CUT.LER, *s.*, cuteleiro.
CUT-PRICE, *s.*, preço reduzido.
CY.CLE, *s.*, ciclo, bicicleta; *v.*, andar de bicicleta.
CY.CLIC, *adj.*, cíclico.
CY.CLING, *s.*, ciclismo.
CY.CLIST, *s.*, ciclista.
CYL.IN.DER, *s.*, cilindro.
CY.MA, *s.*, cimalha.
CYN.IC, *adj.*, cínico.
CYN.I.CISM, *s.*, cinismo.
CYST, *s.*, cisto.
CZAR, *s.*, czar.
CZECH.O.SLO.VAK, *s.*, checoslovaco.

D

D, *s.*, quarta letra do alfabeto inglês; algarismo romano 500 (D).
DAB, *s.*, toque leve, palmadinha; *v.*, tocar de leve.
DAB.STER, *s.*, esperto, finório, esperto.
DAD, *s.*, papai, papá.
DAD.DY, *s.*, papai.
DAFT, *adj.*, imbecil, tolo, idiota, cretino.
DAFT.NESS, *s.*, tolice, imbecilidade, cretinice.
DAG.GER, *s.*, punhal, adaga, arma branca.
DAHL.IA, *s.*, dália.
DAI.LY, *adj.*, diário, cotidiano; *s.*, jornal, diário; *adv.*, diariamente.
DAI.LY RATE, *s.*, diária de hotel.
DAIN.TI.NESS, *s.*, delicadeza, finura, polidez; iguaria.
DAIN.TY, *s.*, iguaria, gulodice.
DAIRY, *s.*, fábrica de laticínios, leiteria.
DA.IS, *s.*, estrado.
DAI.SY, *s.*, margarida, bonina.
DAL.LI.ER, *s.*, brincalhão, galhofeiro.
DAM, *s.*, dique, represa, barragem; *v.*, represar, impedir, segurar.
DAM.AGE, *s.*, dano, prejuízo, perda; *v.*, prejudicar, danificar, estragar.
DAM.AGED, *s.*, prejudicado, danificado, avariado.
DAME, *s.*, senhora, dama, dona de casa.
DAM.NA.BLE, *adj.*, danável, condenável.
DAM.NA.TION, *s.*, maldição, condenação, danação.
DAM.NI.FY, *v.*, prejudicar, danificar, avariar.
DAMP, *s.*, umidade, abatimento; *v.*, umedecer, desanimar.
DAMP.EN, *v.*, umedecer, molhar.
DAMP.ER, *s.*, abafador, amortecedor.
DAMP.NESS, *s.*, umidade.
DAM.SEL, *s.*, moça, garota, donzela.
DANCE, *s.*, dança, baile; *v.*, dançar.
DANC.ER, *s.*, bailarino, dançarino.
DAN.DLE, *v.*, embalar, acariciar, acarinhar.
DAN.DRUFF, *s.*, caspa.
DAN.DY, *s.*, dândi, janota.
DANE, *adj.*, *s.*, dinamarquês.
DAN.GER, *s.*, perigo.
DAN.GER.OUS, *adj.*, perigoso.
DAN.ISH, *adj.*, *s.*, dinamarquês.
DANK, *s.*, lugar úmido, umidade; *adj.*, úmido, molhado.
DARE, *v.*, provocar, desafiar, ousar.
DAR.ING, *adj.*, audacioso, corajoso; *s.*, audácia, coragem, valentia.
DARK, *s.*, escuridão, noite, trevas; *adj.*, escuro, moreno; *v.*, escurecer.
DARK.EN, *v.*, escurecer, tornar escuro.
DARK.ROOM, *s.*, câmara escura.
DARKY, *s.*, negro, preto, mulato.
DAR.LING, *adj.*, *s.*, querido, querida.
DAR.NEL, *s.*, joio.
DASH, *s.*, hífen, travessão, arremesso, choque; *v.*, arremessar, bater.
DASH.BOARD, *s.*, painel, quadro de instrumentos.
DA.TA, *s.*, dados, informes, detalhes.
DATE, *s.*, data, época, prazo; tâmara; *v.*, datar, marcar data, namorar.
DATE BACK, *v.*, ser datado em.
DA.TIVE, *adj.*, dativo.
DAUGH.TER, *s.*, filha.
DAUGH.TER-IN-LAW, *s.*, nora.
DAUNT, *v.*, assustar, atemorizar.
DAV.EN.PORT, *s.*, escrivaninha.
DAW, *s.*, gralha; tipo imbecil.
DAW.DLE, *s.*, vadio, malandro; *v.*, vadiar, não fazer nada.
DAWN, *s.*, madrugada, alvorada, aurora; *v.*, amanhecer, raiar o dia.
DAWN.ING, *s.*, alvorada, amanhecer.

DAY, *s.*, dia, jornada.
DAY.BOOK, *s.*, diário.
DAY.BREAK, *s.*, amanhecer.
DAY.LIGHT, *s.*, luz do dia.
DAZ.ZLE, *s.*, deslumbramento; *v.*, ofuscar, deslumbrar.
DEA.CON, *s.*, diácono.
DEA.CON.ESS, *s.*, diaconisa.
DEAD, *adj., s.*, morto, defunto, falecido.
DEAD HOUSE, *s.*, necrotério.
DEAD.LINE, *s.*, prazo final.
DEAD.LOCK, *s.*, impasse, paralisação, beco; *v.*, chegar a nada.
DEAD.LY, *adj.*, mortal, fatal, mortífero.
DEAD LOSS, *s.*, prejuízo total.
DEAF, *adj.*, surdo.
DEAF-MUTE, *s.*, surdo-mudo.
DEAF.EN, *v.*, ensurdecer.
DEAF.NESS, *s.*, surdez.
DEAL, *s.*, acordo, quantidade, porção; *v.*, negociar, fazer um acordo, jogar.
DEAL.ER, *s.*, negociante, comerciante; jogador que distribui as cartas.
DEAN, *s.*, reitor de universidade, deão, decano.
DEAR, *adj.*, querido, querida, caro; custoso, caro, dispendioso.
DEARTH, *s.*, carência, penúria, carestia, fome, escassez.
DEATH, *s.*, morte, óbito, falecimento.
DEATH.LESS, *adj.*, imortal.
DE.BARK, *v.*, desembarcar.
DE.BAR.KA.TION, *s.*, desembarque.
DE.BASE.MENT, *s.*, degradação.
DE.BATE, *s.*, debate, contenda; *v.*, debater.
DE.BAUCH, *s.*, deboche, escárnio; *v.*, debochar, escarnecer.
DE.BAUCH.ERY, *s.*, deboche, depravação.
DE.BEN.TURE, *s.*, debênture, título de dívida.
DE.BIL.I.TATE, *v.*, debilitar, enfraquecer.
DE.BIL.I.TA.TION, *s.*, debilitação.
DEB.IT, *s.*, débito, dívida; *v.*, debitar, lançar em dívida.
DE.BOUCH, *v.*, desembocar; desfilar.
DE.BRIS, *s.*, ruínas, restos, escombros.

DEBT, *s.*, dívida, endividamento.
DÉ.BUT, *s.*, estreia.
DE.CADE, *s.*, década.
DEC.A.DENCE, *s.*, decadência.
DEC.A.DENT, *adj., s.*, decadente.
DECA.GRAM, *s.*, decagrama.
DECA.LI.TRE, *s.*, decalitro.
DECA.LOGUE, *s.*, decálogo.
DE.CAP.I.TATE, *v.*, decapitar, degolar.
DE.CAP.I.TA.TION, *s.*, decapitação.
DECA.SYL.LAB.IC, *adj.*, decassílabo.
DE.CAY, *s.* ruína, decadência, declínio; *v.*, decair, apodrecer, arruinar.
DE.CEASE, *s.*, desenlace, morte, óbito, falecimento; *v.*, morrer, falecer.
DE.CEIVE, *v.*, enganar, lograr, ludibriar.
DE.CEM.BER, *s.*, dezembro.
DE.CEN.CY, *s.*, decência, honradez, decoro.
DE.CEN.NI.AL, *adj.*, decenal.
DE.CENT, *adj.*, decente, digno, honrado.
DE.CEN.TRAL.IZA.TION, *s.*, descentralização.
DE.CEN.TRAL.IZE, *v.*, descentralizar.
DE.CEP.TION, *s.*, decepção, fraude, engano.
DE.CIDE, *v.*, decidir, resolver, solucionar; sentenciar, julgar.
DECI.GRAM, *s.*, decigrama.
DECI.MAL, *adj., s.*, decimal.
DEC.I.MATE, *v.*, dizimar, liquidar.
DE.CI.PHER, *v.*, decifrar, entender, explicar.
DE.CI.SION, *s.*, decisão, resolução, sentença.
DE.CI.SIVE, *adj.*, decisivo, resolutivo.
DECK, *s.*, convés, coberta de navio, tombadilho; baralho de cartas.
DE.CLAIM, *v.*, recitar, declamar.
DEC.LA.RA.TION, *s.*, declaração, dito, afirmação.
DE.CLARE, *v.*, declarar, revelar, proclamar, afirmar, depor.
DEC.LI.NA.TION, *s.*, declinação, inclinação, descida, decadência.
DE.CLINE, *s.*, declínio, diminuição; *v.*, diminuir, recusar.
DE.CLIV.I.TY, *s.*, declive, inclinação, ladeira, descida.

DECOMPOSE   332   **DELICATE**

DE.COM.POSE, *v.*, decompor.
DEC.O.RATE, *v.*, decorar, ornar, enfeitar.
DEC.O.ROUS, *adj.*, decoroso, honesto, sério.
DE.CRY, *v.*, censurar, advertir, admoestar.
DEC.U.PLE, *adj., s.*, décuplo.
DED.I.CATE, *v.*, dedicar, oferecer.
DED.I.CA.TION, *s.*, dedicação, oferenda, dedicatória.
DE.DUCE, *v.*, deduzir, conjeturar, inferir.
DE.DUCT, *v.*, deduzir, subtrair, diminuir.
DE.DUC.TION, *s.*, dedução, subtração, diminuição.
DEEM, *v.*, julgar, avaliar, estimar.
DEEM.STER, *s.*, juiz.
DEEP, *adj.*, fundo, profundo, baixo; *s.*, profundidade; abismo.
DEEP.EN, *v.*, afundar, aprofundar.
DEER, *s.*, veado, cervo, gamo.
DE.FACE, *v.*, desfigurar, deformar.
DE.FAL.CA.TION, *s.*, desfalque.
DEF.A.MA.TION, *s.*, difamação, calúnia.
DE.FAME, *v.*, difamar, caluniar, desonrar.
DE.FAULT, *s.*, falta, descuido, negligência; *v.*, negligenciar, estar ausente.
DE.FEAT, *s.*, derrota, revés, frustração; *v.*, derrotar, desbaratar.
DE.FECT, *s.*, defeito, deficiência, falha, vício.
DE.FEC.TION, *s.*, defecção, deserção.
DE.FENCE, *s.*, defesa.
DE.FEND, *v.*, defender, preservar, amparar.
DE.FEN.DER, *s.*, defensor.
DE.FEN.SI.BLE, *adj.*, defensível.
DE.FER, *v.*, adiar, diferir, protelar.
DEF.ER.ENCE, *s.*, deferência.
DE.FI.ANCE, *s.*, desafio, provocação, rebeldia.
DE.FI.CIEN.CY, *s.*, deficiência, insuficiência, falta.
DEF.I.CIT, *s.*, déficit, deficiência, o que falta.
DE.FILE, *s.*, desfiladeiro, garganta; *v.*, desonrar, corromper, manchar.
DE.FINE, *v.*, definir.
DEF.I.NITE, *adj.*, definitivo, evidente, claro, determinado.
DEF.I.NITE.LY, *adv.*, definitivamente.
DEF.I.NI.TION, *s.*, definição.
DE.FIN.I.TIVE, *adj.*, definitivo, conclusivo, terminativo.
DE.FLECT, *v.*, desviar.
DE.FLO.RA.TION, *s.*, defloração, violação, estupro.
DE.FORM, *v.*, deformar, distorcer.
DE.FOR.MA.TION, *s.*, deformação, distorção.
DE.FOR.MI.TY, *s.*, deformidade.
DE.FROST, *v.*, descongelar.
DEFT, *adj.*, destro, hábil, habilidoso, perito.
DEFT.NESS, *s.*, destreza, habilidade.
DE.FUNCT, *adj.*, defunto, morto, extinto, falecido.
DE.FY, *v.*, desafiar, provocar.
DE.GEN.ER.ATE, *v.*, degenerar; *adj.*, degenerado.
DE.GEN.E.RA.TION, *s.*, degeneração.
DEG.RA.DATION, *s.*, degradação.
DE.GRADE, *v.*, degradar, aviltar, rebaixar, humilhar.
DE.GREE, *s.*, título, diploma, degrau, grau.
DE.HU.MAN.IZE, *v.*, desumanizar, bestializar.
DE.HY.DRATE, *v.*, desidratar.
DE.ICE, *v.*, descongelar.
DEIC.TIC, *adj.*, demonstrativo, direto.
DE.I.TY, *s.*, divindade.
DE.JECT, *v.*, desanimar, deprimir, abater.
DE.JEC.TION, *s.*, depressão, abatimento, desânimo.
DE.LAY, *v.*, retardar, demorar, atrasar; *s.*, demora, atraso.
DE.LEC.TA.BLE, *adj.*, gostoso, deleitoso.
DE.LEC.TA.BLE.NESS, *s.*, deleite, prazer, gosto.
DEL.E.GA.CY, *s.*, delegacia, delegação, representação.
DEL.E.GATE, *s.*, delegado; *v.*, delegar, autorizar.
DEL.E.GA.TION, *s.*, delegação, autorização, permissão.
DE.LETE, *v.*, deletar, apagar, extinguir, eliminar.
DE.LIB.ER.ATE, *v.*, deliberar, considerar; *adj.*, intencional, ponderado.
DE.LIB.ER.A.TION, *s.*, deliberação, consideração, decisão.
DEL.I.CA.CY, *s.*, delicadeza, gentileza, sensibilidade; guloseima.
DEL.I.CATE, *adj.*, delicado, cortês, gentil,

sensível.
DE.LI.CIOUS, *adj.*, delicioso, gostoso, saboroso.
DE.LI.CIOUS.NESS, *s.*, delícia, prazer, deleite, gostosura.
DEL.ICT, *s.*, delito, crime, culpa.
DE.LIGHT, *s.*, prazer, deleite, maravilha, delícia; *v.*, deleitar, aprazer.
DE.LIM.IT, *v.*, delimitar, limitar, confinar.
DE.LIN.QUEN.CY, *s.*, delinquência, criminalidade.
DE.LIN.QUENT, *adj., s.*, delinquente.
DE.LIV.ER, *v.*, libertar, resgatar, soltar, liberar.
DE.LIV.ER.ANCE, *s.*, libertação, livramento, redenção, sentença; parto.
DE.LIV.ERY, *s.*, liberdade, libertação, resgate, soltura, rendição.
DE.LUDE, *v.*, iludir, enganar, fraudar.
DEL.UGE, *s.*, dilúvio; enxurrada; *v.*, inundar, alagar.
DE.LU.SION, *s.*, desilusão, ilusão.
DE.LU.SO.RY, *adj.*, ilusório, enganador.
DEM.A.GOG.IC, *adj.*, demagógico.
DEM.A.GOGUE, *s.*, demagogo.
DEM.A.GOGY, *s.*, demagogia.
DE.MAND, *v.*, postular, exigir, demandar, reivindicar; *s.*, exigência.
DE.MAR.CATE, *v.*, demarcar, limitar.
DE.MAR.CA.TION, *s.*, demarcação.
DE.MENT, *v.*, enlouquecer, tornar-se demente.
DE.MEN.TIA, *s.*, demência, loucura, desvario.
DE.MER.IT, *s.*, demérito.
DE.MISE, *s.*, falecimento, óbito.
DE.MIS.SION, *s.*, demissão.
DE.MO.BI.LIZE, *v.*, desmobilizar.
DE.MOC.RA.CY, *s.*, democracia.
DEM.O.CRAT, *s.*, democrata.
DE.MOC.RA.TIZE, *v.*, democratizar.
DE.MOG.RA.PHY, *s.*, demografia.
DE.MOL.ISH, *v.*, demolir.
DE.MON, *s.*, demônio, satã, satanás, diabo.
DE.MO.NI.AC, *adj.*, demoníaco.
DEM.ON.STRATE, *v.*, demonstrar, manifestar, expor.
DEM.ON.STRA.TION, *s.*, demonstração.

DE.MOR.AL.IZE, *v.*, desmoralizar.
DEN, *s.*, covil, antro, espelunca; aposento; *v.*, viver em caverna.
DENE, *s.*, duna, monte de areia.
DEN.GUE, *s.*, dengue.
DE.NI.AL, *s.*, negação, refutação, negativa.
DEN.I.ZEN, *s.*, estrangeiro naturalizado.
DE.NOM.I.NATE, *v.*, denominar, nomear, indicar.
DE.NOM.I.NA.TION, *s.*, denominação, indicação.
DE.NO.TA.TION, *s.*, denotação, designação, indicação.
DE.NOTE, *v.*, denotar, indicar, mostrar.
DE.NOUNCE, *v.*, denunciar.
DENSE, *adj.*, denso, espesso, fechado, compacto.
DEN.SI.TY, *s.*, densidade.
DEN.TAL, *adj.*, dental, dentário.
DEN.TATE, *adj.*, dentado.
DEN.TIST, *s.*, dentista, odontólogo.
DEN.TIST.RY, *s.*, odontologia.
DEN.TURES, *s., pl.*, dentadura.
DE.NUDE, *v.*, desnudar, despir.
DE.NUN.CI.ATE, *v.*, denunciar, delatar.
DE.NUN.CI.A.TION, *s.*, denúncia.
DE.NY, *v.*, negar, recusar.
DE.ODOR.IZE, *v.*, desodorizar.
DE.PART, *v.*, ir, partir, andar, sair.
DE.PART.MENT, *s.*, departamento, seção, repartição.
DE.PAR.TURE, *s.*, partida, saída, ida.
DE.PEND, *v.*, depender, sujeitar-se.
DE.PEND.ANT, *s.*, dependente.
DE.PEN.DENCE, *s.*, dependência.
DEP.I.LATE, *v.*, depilar.
DE.PLOR.ABLE, *adj.*, deplorável.
DE.PLORE, *v.*, deplorar.
DE.PLOY, *v.*, dispor.
DE.PLUME, *v.*, depenar.
DE.PO.NENT, *s.*, deponente, depoente, declarante.
DE.POP.U.LATE, *v.*, despovoar.
DE.PORT, *v.*, deportar.
DE.POR.TA.TION, *s.*, deportação.
DE.POSE, *v.*, depor.

DE.POS.I.TOR, *s.,* depositante.
DE.POT, *s.,* depósito, armazém.
DE.PRAVE, *v.,* depravar, viciar, corromper, estragar.
DE.PRE.CI.ATE, *v.,* depreciar, desvalorizar.
DEP.RE.DATE, *v.,* depredar, destruir, saquear.
DE.PRESS, *v.,* deprimir, reduzir.
DE.PRESS.ING, *adj.,* deprimente.
DE.PRES.SION, *s.,* depressão.
DE.PRIVE, *v.,* privar de.
DE.PUTE, *v.,* delegar.
DE.RAIL.MENT, *s.,* descarrilamento.
DE.RIDE, *v.,* ridicularizar, zombar, escarnecer.
DE.RID.ING, *s.,* zombaria, desprezo, escárnio.
DER.I.VA.TION, *s.,* derivação.
DE.RIVE, *v.,* derivar, provir, proceder de.
DERM, *s.,* derme.
DER.MA.TOL.O.GIST, *s.,* dermatologista.
DER.MA.TOL.O.GY, *s.,* dermatologia.
DER.RIK, *s.,* grua, guindaste.
DE.SCEND, *v.,* descer, baixar, descender.
DE.SCENT, *s.,* descida, descendência.
DE.SCRIBE, *v.,* descrever.
DE.SCRIP.TION, *s.,* descrição.
DES.E.CRAT, *v.,* profanar.
DES.ERT, *s.,* deserto; *v.,* desertar, tornar deserto, abandonar.
DE.SERT.ER, *s.,* desertor.
DE.SID.ER.ATE, *v.,* desejar, querer, pretender.
DE.SIGN, *s.,* desenho, esboço, projeto, propósito; *v.,* projetar.
DES.IG.NATE, *v.,* designar, indicar, nomear; *adj.,* designado, indicado.
DE.SIRE, *s.,* desejo, anseio; *v.,* querer, desejar, ansiar por.
DE.SIST, *v.,* desistir, renunciar.
DE.SIS.TANCE, *s.,* renúncia, desistência.
DESK, *s.,* carteira escolar, escrivaninha, secretária; balcão de aeroporto.
DES.O.LATE, *v.,* desolar, despovoar; *adj.,* despovoado, deserto.
DES.O.LA.TION *s.,* aflição, desolação, sofrimento.
DE.SPAIR, *v.,* desesperar, perder a esperança; *s.,* desespero.
DES.PER.ATE, *adj.,* desesperado, desesperador.
DE.SPISE, *v.,* desprezar.
DE.SPOIL, *v.,* despojar, espoliar, furtar.
DES.POT, *s.,* déspota, tirano.
DES.POT.IC, *adj.,* despótico.
DES.SERT, *s.,* sobremesa.
DES.TINE, *v.,* destinar, remeter, designar.
DES.TI.NY, *s.,* destino.
DES.TI.TU.TION, *s.,* privação, pobreza, carência.
DE.STROY, *v.,* destruir.
DE.STRUC.TION, *s.,* destruição.
DE.STRUC.TOR, *s.,* destruidor, exterminador.
DE.TACH, *v.,* destacar, separar, desprender.
DE.TAIL, *s.,* detalhe, ninharia; *v.,* detalhar, pormenorizar.
DE.TAIN, *v.,* deter, prender.
DE.TAIN.ER, *s.,* detenção.
DE.TECT, *v.,* detectar, perceber, notar.
DE.TEC.TIVE, *s.,* detetive.
DE.TEN.TION, *s.,* detenção.
DE.TER, *v.,* desanimar, desalentar-se.
DE.TER.GENT, *s.,* detergente.
DE.TER.MI.NATE, *adj.,* determinado.
DE.TER.MI.NA.TION, *s.,* determinação, resolução.
DE.TER.MINE, *v.,* demarcar, determinar, decidir.
DE.TEST, *v.,* detestar.
DE.TEST.ABLE, *adj.,* detestável.
DET.O.NATE, *v.,* detonar, explodir.
DET.O.NA.TION, *s.,* detonação.
DE.TOUR, *s.,* desvio.
DE.TRACT, *v.,* destratar, difamar, caluniar.
DET.RI.MENT, *s.,* detrimento, dano, prejuízo.
DE.VAL.U.ATE, *v.,* desvalorizar.
DE.VAL.UE, *v.,* desvalorizar.
DEV.AS.TATE, *v.,* devastar, arrasar.
DE.VEL.OP, *v.,* desenvolver, revelar, progredir, avançar, evoluir.
DE.VEL.OP.MENT, *s.,* desenvolvimento, progresso, evolução.
DE.VI.A.TION, *s.,* desvio.
DEV.IL, *s.,* diabo, demônio.
DEV.IL.ISH, *adj.,* diabólico.

DEVISE   **DIOCESE**

DE.VISE, *v.*, inventar, imaginar; deixar por testamento.
DE.VI.TAL.IZE, *v.*, desvitalizar.
DE.VO.LU.TION, *s.*, devolução, entrega.
DE.VOLVE, *v.*, devolver, entregar, transferir, transmitir.
DE.VOUR, *v.*, devorar.
DE.VOUT, *adj., s.*, devoto.
DEW, *s.*, orvalho.
DEX.TER.I.TY, *s.*, destreza, habilidade, capacidade.
DI.A.BE.TES, *s.*, diabetes.
DI.A.BOL.IC, *adj.*, diabólico.
DI.AC.O.NATE, *s.*, diaconato.
DI.A.DEM, *s.*, diadema.
DI.AG.NOSE, *v.*, diagnosticar.
DI.AG.NO.SIS, *s.*, diagnóstico.
DI.A.GRAM, *s.*, diagrama.
DI.A.LECT, *s.*, dialeto.
DI.A.LEC.TIC, *s.*, dialética; *adj.*, dialético.
DI.A.LEC.TICS, *s.*, dialética.
DI.A.LOGUE, *s.*, diálogo, colóquio.
DI.AM.E.TER, *s.*, diâmetro.
DI.A.MOND, *s.*, diamante, losango.
DI.A.PER, *s.*, fralda, pano de linho, guardanapo.
DI.APH.A.NOUS, *adj.*, diáfano, transparente, lúcido.
DI.A.PHRAGM, *s.*, diafragma.
DI.AR.RHOEA, *s.*, diarreia.
DI.A.RY, *s.*, diário.
DIB, *v.*, mergulhar.
DI.CHOT.O.MY, *s.*, dicotomia.
DIC.TATE, *v.*, ditar; *s.*, ditado.
DIC.TA.TION, *s.*, ditado, ordem.
DIC.TA.TOR, *s.*, ditador.
DIC.TION, *s.*, dicção.
DIC.TIO.NARY, *s.*, dicionário.
DI.DAC.TIC, *adj.*, didático.
DI.DAC.TI.CISM, *s.*, didática.
DIE, *v.*, morrer, falecer.
DIE.SEL, *s.*, diesel.
DIET, *s.*, dieta, regime; *v.*, fazer dieta.
DI.E.TET.IC, *adj.*, dietético.
DIF.FER, *v.*, diferir, ser diferente, discordar, divergir.
DIF.FER.ENCE, *s.*, diferença, diversidade, divergência.
DIF.FER.ENT, *adj.*, diferente.
DIF.FI.CULT, *adj.*, difícil, complicado.
DIF.FI.CUL.TY, *s.*, dificuldade, complicação.
DIF.FI.DENCE, *s.*, difidência, desconfiança, timidez.
DIF.FUSE, *v.*, difundir, espalhar; *adj.*, difuso, espalhado, esparramado.
DIF.FU.SION, *s.*, difusão.
DIG, *s.*, escavação; *v.*, cavar, escavar, revolver terra.
DI.GEST, *v.*, digerir, assimilar, aprender; *s.*, resumo, compêndio.
DI.GES.TION, *s.*, digestão.
DIG.GER, *s.*, escavador, cavador.
DIG.IT, *s.*, dígito, dedo; medida.
DIG.I.TAL, *adj.*, digital.
DIG.NI.FIED, *adj.*, digno, dignificado.
DIG.NI.FY, *v.*, dignificar, honrar, prestigiar.
DIG.NI.TY, *s.*, dignidade, honra.
DIGS, *s., pl.*, pensão.
DIKE, *s.*, dique, represa, açude.
DI.LA.TA.TION, *s.*, dilatação, aumento.
DI.LATE, *v.*, dilatar.
DI.LEM.MA, *s.*, dilema.
DIL.ET.TANTE, *s.*, diletante.
DIL.I.GENCE, *s.*, diligência, demanda; aplicação, cuidado.
DI.LUTE, *v.*, diluir.
DI.LU.VI.AL, *adj.*, diluviano.
DI.LU.VI.UM, *s.*, dilúvio.
DIM, *v.*, ofuscar, escurecer; *adj.*, escuro, ofuscado, sombrio, baço.
DIME, *s.*, moeda americana de prata de dez cents.
DI.MEN.SION, *s.*, dimensão, tamanho, grandeza.
DI.MIN.ISH, *v.*, diminuir, apequenar.
DIM.I.NU.TION, *s.*, diminuição.
DINE, *v.*, jantar, comer à noite.
DINE OUT, *v.*, jantar fora de casa.
DIN.ER, *s.*, quem janta; pequeno restaurante.
DIN.ING, *s.*, vagão restaurante nos trens.
DIN.NER, *s.*, jantar, ceia.
DI.NO.SAUR, *s.*, dinossauro.
DI.OC.ESE, *s.*, diocese.

DIP — **DISGRACE**

DIP, *s.*, mergulho, banho de mar, inclinação; *v.*, mergulhar, molhar-se.
DIPH.THE.RIA, *s.*, difteria.
DIPH.THONG, *s.*, ditongo.
DI.PLO.MA, *s.*, diploma.
DI.PLO.MA.CY, *s.*, diplomacia.
DIP.LO.MAT, *s.*, diplomata.
DIRE, *adj.*, terrível.
DI.RECT, *v.*, dirigir, conduzir, administrar; *adj.*, direito, reto.
DI.REC.TION, *s.*, direção, indicação, condução.
DI.RECT.LY, *adv.*, diretamente.
DI.REC.TOR, *s.*, diretor.
DI.REC.TO.RY, *s.*, comissão diretora; lista telefônica, lista de endereços.
DIRE.NESS, *s.*, pavor, medo, terror.
DIRT, *s.*, sujeira, lodo, imundície, sujidade.
DIRTY, *adj.*, sujo, imundo, sórdido.
DIS.ABIL.I.TY, *s.*, inabilidade, incapacidade.
DIS.AC.CUS.TOM, *v.*, desacostumar, perder o hábito.
DIS.AD.VAN.TAGE, *s.*, desvantagem, desfavor.
DIS.AF.FECT, *adj.*, desafeto, desleal, infiel.
DIS.AGREED, *adj.*, discordante, contrário, oposto.
DIS.AP.PEAR, *v.*, desaparecer.
DIS.AP.POINT, *v.*, desapontar, decepcionar.
DIS.AP.PRO.BA.TION, *s.*, desaprovação, negativa.
DIS.AP.PROVE, *v.*, desaprovar, não aceitar.
DIS.ARM, *v.*, desarmar.
DIS.AR.MA.MENT, *s.*, desarmamento.
DIS.AR.RAY, *v.*, desorganizar, desordenar; *s.*, desordem, confusão.
DI.SAS.TER, *s.*, desastre, calamidade.
DI.SAS.TROUS, *adj.*, desastroso, calamitoso.
DIS.BE.LIEVE, *v.*, descrer, desconfiar.
DIS.BURSE, *v.*, desembolsar, gastar.
DISC, *s.*, disco.
DIS.CARD, *s.*, descarte; *v.*, descartar, jogar fora.
DIS.CERN, *v.*, discernir, perceber.
DIS.CERN.IBLE.NESS, *s.*, discernimento, perceptibilidade.
DIS.CHARGE, *s.*, descarga, demissão, soltura; *v.*, descarregar, desempenhar.
DIS.CHARG.ER, *s.*, descarregador.
DIS.CI.PLE, *s.*, discípulo, aprendiz.
DIS.CI.PLI.NAR.IAN, *s.*, disciplinador.
DIS.CI.PLINE, *s.*, disciplina; *v.*, disciplinar, educar.
DIS.CLAIM, *v.*, negar.
DIS.CLOSE, *v.*, revelar, abrir.
DIS.CO, *s.*, discoteca.
DIS.COL.OUR, *v.*, descolorar, descolorir.
DIS.COM.FORT, *s.*, desconforto, inquietação.
DIS.CON.CERT, *v.*, desconcertar, desordenar.
DIS.CON.NECT, *v.*, desconectar, desligar.
DIS.CON.NEC.TION, *s.*, desconexão, separação.
DIS.CON.TENT, *s.*, descontentamento; *v.*, descontentar.
DIS.CON.TIN.UE, *s.*, descontinuar, interromper.
DIS.CON.TIN.U.OUS, *adj.*, descontínuo, interrompido.
DIS.CORD, *s.*, discórdia; *v.*, discordar.
DIS.CO.THEQUE, *s.*, discoteca.
DIS.COUNT, *s.*, desconto; *v.*, descontar.
DIS.COU.RAGE, *v.*, desanimar, desencorajar, intimidar.
DIS.COUR.AGE.MENT, *s.*, desânimo, desencorajamento.
DIS.COURSE, *s.*, discurso, oração; *v.*, discursar, falar.
DIS.COURS.ER, *s.*, orador.
DIS.COV.ER, *v.*, descobrir, achar, encontrar, inventar.
DIS.COV.ER.ER, *s.*, descobridor, explorador.
DIS.COV.ERY, *s.*, descoberta, descobrimento.
DIS.CRED.IT, *v.*, descrer, desacreditar, desconfiar.
DIS.CRE.TION, *s.*, discrição.
DIS.CRIM.I.NATE, *v.*, discriminar.
DIS.CUSS, *v.*, discutir, analisar.
DIS.CUS.SION, *s.*, discussão.
DIS.DAIN, *s.*, desdém, desprezo; *v.*, desdenhar.
DIS.EASE, *s.*, doença.
DIS.EM.BARK, *v.*, desembarcar.
DIS.EM.BAR.KA.TION, *s.*, desembarque.
DIS.EN.CHANT, *v.*, desencantar.
DIS.EN.TAIL, *v.*, desvincular.
DIS.FA.VOUR, *s.*, desfavor.
DIS.FIG.URE, *v.*, desfigurar.
DIS.GORGE, *v.*, vomitar.
DIS.GRACE, *s.*, desgraça, desonra; *v.*, desgraçar,

desonrar.
DIS.GRACE.FUL, *adj.*, desgraçado, vergonhoso.
DIS.GUST, *s.*, desgosto, repugnância; *v.*, repugnar, desgostar, enojar.
DISH, *s.*, prato, travessa.
DISH.CLOTH, *s.*, pano de louça.
DISH.FUL, *s.*, prato cheio de comida.
DIS.HON.EST, *adj.*, desonesto.
DIS.HON.ES.TY, *s.*, desonestidade.
DIS.HON.OR, *s.*, desonra; *v.*, desonrar.
DISH OUT, *v.*, repartir.
DISH.WASH.ER, *s.*, máquina de lavar louça.
DIS.IL.LU.SION, *s.*, desilusão; *v.*, desiludir.
DIS.IN.FECT, *v.*, desinfetar.
DIS.IN.FEC.TANT, *s.*, desinfetante.
DIS.IN.HER.IT, *v.*, deserdar.
DIS.JOIN, *v.*, separar, desconectar.
DIS.JOINT, *v.*, desconjuntar, separar.
DIS.JUNCT, *adj.*, separado, desunido.
DIS.JUNC.TION, *s.*, disjunção, separação.
DISK, *s.*, disco; disquete.
DIS.KETTE, *s.*, disquete.
DIS.LO.CATE, *v.*, deslocar, distanciar.
DIS.LOY.AL, *adj.*, desleal.
DIS.LOY.AL.TY, *s.*, deslealdade, perversidade.
DIS.MAY, *s.*, consternação, tristeza; *v.*, entristecer, consternar.
DIS.MISS, *v.*, despedir, demitir.
DIS.OBE.DI.ENCE, *s.*, desobediência.
DIS.OBEY, *v.*, desobedecer.
DIS.OR.DER, *s.*, desordem, balbúrdia, confusão; *v.*, desordenar.
DIS.OR.GA.NIZE, *v.*, desorganizar, desordenar, badernar.
DIS.OWN, *v.*, rejeitar, refutar, renegar, repudiar.
DIS.PAR.I.TY, *s.*, disparidade, desigualdade.
DIS.PATCH, *s.*, remessa, despacho, urgência; *v.*, despachar, mandar.
DIS.PATCH.ER, *s.*, expedidor.
DIS.PERSE, *v.*, dispersar, espalhar.
DIS.PLACE, *v.*, deslocar.
DIS.PLEASE, *v.*, ofender, incomodar, aborrecer.
DIS.PLEA.SURE, *s.*, desprazer, desgosto.
DIS.POSE, *v.*, dispor, ajustar, colocar.

DIS.PO.SI.TION, *s.*, disposição, ordenamento.
DIS.PROVE, *v.*, refutar.
DIS.PUTE, *v.*, disputar, contender; *s.*, disputa, contenda, luta.
DIS.QUAL.I.FY, *v.*, desqualificar.
DIS.RE.GARD, *v.*, ignorar, não ver.
DIS.RE.SPECT, *v.*, desrespeitar; *s.*, desrespeito.
DIS.ROBE, *v.*, despir, desnudar.
DIS.RUPT, *v.*, destacar, perturbar.
DIS.SECT, *v.*, dissecar.
DIS.SEC.TION, *s.*, dissecação.
DIS.SEM.I.NATE, *v.*, disseminar.
DIS.SEM.I.NA.TION, *s.*, disseminação.
DIS.SENT.ER, *s.*, dissidente.
DIS.SERT, *v.*, dissertar, discorrer.
DIS.SER.TA.TION, *s.*, dissertação, redação.
DIS.SI.DENCE, *s.*, dissidência.
DIS.SI.DENT, *s.*, dissidente.
DIS.SIM.U.LATE, *s.*, dissimular, disfarçar.
DIS.SI.PATE, *v.*, dissipar, gastar.
DIS.SO.LUTE, *adj.*, dissoluto, devasso.
DIS.SO.LU.TION, *s.*, dissolução.
DIS.SOLVE, *v.*, dissolver, desmanchar.
DIS.TANCE, *s.*, distância, lonjura; *v.*, distanciar, estar distante.
DIS.TANT, *adj.*, distante, afastado, longe.
DIS.TIL, *v.*, distilar.
DIS.TINCT, *adj.*, distinto, claro, evidente.
DIS.TINC.TION, *s.*, distinção.
DIS.TIN.GUISH, *v.*, distinguir, diferenciar.
DIS.TORT, *v.*, distorcer.
DIS.TOR.TION, *s.*, distorção.
DIS.TRESS, *s.*, angústia; *v.*, angustiar, afligir.
DIS.TRESS.FUL, *adj.*, angustiado, aflito, consternado.
DIS.TRIB.UTE, *v.*, distribuir, dividir.
DIS.TRICT, *s.*, distrito, região, zona.
DIS.TRUST, *v.*, desconfiar, descrer; *s.*, desconfiança.
DIS.TURB, *v.*, perturbar, atrapalhar, transtornar.
DI.SYL.LA.BLE, *s.*, dissílabo.
DI.UR.NAL, *adj.*, diurno, diário, quotidiano.
DI.VA.GATE, *v.*, divagar.
DI.VAN, *s.*, divã.

DIVE, *v.*, mergulhar; *s.*, mergulho.
DIV.ER, *s.*, mergulhador.
DI.VERGE, *v.*, divergir.
DI.VER.GENCE, *s.*, divergência.
DI.VERSE, *adj.*, diverso.
DI.VER.SI.FY, *v.*, diversificar.
DI.VER.SI.TY, *s.*, diversidade.
DI.VIDE, *v.*, dividir, repartir, bifurcar.
DIV.I.DEND, *s.*, dividendo.
DI.VINE, *adj.*, divino, sagrado; *v.*, adivinhar.
DI.VIN.I.TY, *s.*, divindade.
DI.VI.SION, *s.*, divisão, repartição.
DI.VI.SOR, *s.*, divisor.
DI.VORCE, *s.*, divórcio; *v.*, divorciar.
DI.VULGE, *v.*, divulgar, publicar.
DIZ.ZI.NESS, *s.*, tontura.
DIZ.ZY, *adj.*, tonto.
DO, *v. aux.*, fazer.
DOC.ILE, *adj.*, dócil, afável, manso.
DO.CIL.I.TY, *s.*, docilidade.
DOC.TOR, *s.*, doutor, médico.
DOC.TRINE, *s.*, doutrina.
DOC.U.MENT, *s.*, documento; *v.*, documentar.
DOC.U.MEN.TA.TION, *s.*, documentação.
DOER, *s.*, agente, autor, fazedor.
DOG, *s.*, cachorro, cão; *v.*, seguir, perseguir.
DOG.GISH, *adj.*, relativo aos cães, canino.
DOG.MA, *s.*, dogma.
DOG.MA.TIZE, *v.*, dogmatizar.
DO.INGS, *s., pl.*, afazeres, atividades.
DOLL, *s.*, boneca.
DOL.LAR, *s.*, dólar.
DOL.LY, *s.*, boneca.
DO.LOR.OUS, *adj.*, doloroso, aflitivo.
DO.LOUR, *s.*, angústia, aflição.
DOL.PHIN, *s.*, golfinho.
DOLT, *s.*, imbecil, idiota, bobo.
DO.MAIN, *s.*, domínio.
DO.MES.TIC, *adj.*, doméstico, da casa.
DO.MES.TI.CATE, *v.*, domesticar, domar, amansar, civilizar.
DO.MI.CILE, *s.*, domicílio, casa, residência.
DO.MI.CIL.I.ARY, *adj.*, domiciliar.
DOM.I.NATE, *v.*, dominar.

DO.NATE, *v.*, doar.
DO.NA.TION, *s.*, doação.
DON.KEY, *s.*, burro, asno, jumento.
DO.NOR, *s.*, doador.
DOOR, *s.*, porta.
DOORBELL, *s.*, campainha.
DOOR.MAN, *s.*, porteiro.
DOR.MI.TO.RY, *s.*, dormitório.
DOR.SAL, *adj.*, dorsal.
DOSE, *s.*, dose; *v.*, dosar.
DOT.TY, *adj.*, estúpido, louco.
DOU.BLE, *adj., s.*, duplo; *v.*, dobrar, duplicar.
DOU.BLE.NESS, *s.*, duplicidade.
DOUBT, *s.*, dúvida, incerteza; *v.*, duvidar.
DOUBT.FUL, *adj.*, duvidoso.
DOVE, *s.*, pomba.
DOWN, *adv.*, para baixo; *prep.*, embaixo de, sob; *s.*, penugem.
DOWN.FALL, *s.*, queda, ruína.
DOW.RY, *s.*, dote.
DOZ, *s.*, dúzia.
DOZE, *v.*, dormitar.
DOZEN, *s.*, dúzia.
DRAFT, *s.*, rascunho, projeto de lei.
DRAG, *v.*, dragar, arrastar.
DRAG.ON, *s.*, dragão.
DRAIN, *s.*, dreno, bueiro; *v.*, drenar, esvaziar.
DRAIN.AGE, *s.*, drenagem, esgoto.
DRA.MA, *s.*, drama, teatro.
DRA.MAT.IC, *adj.*, dramático.
DRA.MA.TIZE, *v.*, dramatizar.
DRAW, *s.*, ato de puxar, atrativo, sorte; *v.*, desenhar, puxar, fechar.
DRAW.BRIDGE, *s.*, ponte levadiça.
DRAW.ERS, *s., pl.*, ceroulas.
DRAW.ING, *s.*, desenho.
DREAD, *s.*, medo, pavor, terror; *v.*, temer.
DREAD.FUL, *adj.*, terrível, pavoroso.
DREAM, *s.*, sonho; *v.*, sonhar.
DREAM.ER, *s.*, sonhador.
DREAM.I.NESS, *s.*, fantasia, utopia.
DREAMY, *adj.*, sonhador, fantasioso, distraído.
DREA.RY, *adj.*, monótono, aborrecido.
DRENCH, *v.*, encharcar.

DRESS, s., vestido, traje, roupa; v., vestir.
DRESS.MAK.ER, s. costureiro, costureira.
DRESSY, adj., elegante.
DRIED, v. imp. e p.p. de **TO DRY**, seco.
DRINK, s., bebida, trago, gole; v., beber, servir-se de bebida.
DRINK.ABLE, adj., potável.
DRIP, s., gota, goteira.
DRIVE, s., passeio de carro, trajeto; energia, vigor; v., guiar, dirigir.
DRIVE OFF, v., expulsar, mandar embora.
DRIV.ER, s., motorista, dirigente de carro ou trem.
DRIZZLE, s., chuvisco, garoa; v., garoar, chuviscar.
DROLL, adj., engraçado, cômico, alegre.
DROM.E.DARY, s., dromedário.
DROP, s., gota, pingo, pingente; v., deixar cair, baixar, descer.
DROP.PER, s., conta-gotas.
DROP.SY, s., hidropisia.
DROSS, s., escória, restos, sobras.
DROUGHT, s., seca.
DROWN, v., afogar, diminuir o som.
DROWSE, v., dormitar, dormir de leve.
DRUB, v., espancar, bater, surrar, dar uma tunda.
DRUG, s., remédio, medicamento, droga.
DRUG.GIST, s., farmacêutico.
DRUG.STORE, s., drogaria.
DRUM, s., tambor.
DRUNK.ARD, s., beberrão, bêbado.
DRUNK.EN.NESS, s., bebedeira, embriaguez.
DRY, adj., seco, sem chuva; v., secar, enxugar.
DRY.ER, s., secador.
DU.AL, adj., dual, duplo.
DU.AL.I.TY, s., dualidade.
DU.BI.ETY, s., dubiedade, dúvida.
DU.BI.OUS, adj., duvidoso, incerto.
DU.BI.TA.TION, s., dúvida.
DUCH.ESS, s., duquesa.
DUCK, s., pato.
DUCK.LING, s., patinho.
DUE, adj., devido, aguardado.
DU.EL, s., duelo, luta, contenda.
DUKE, s., duque.

DUL.CET, adj., doce, suave, afável, meigo.
DUL.CI.FY, v., dulcificar, adoçar, suavizar.
DUMB, adj., mudo.
DUMB.NESS, s., surdez.
DUMP, s., depósito de lixo, lixeira; v., depositar, jogar fora.
DUMPS, s., pl., depressão.
DUNE, s., duna.
DUNG, s., estrume.
DUO, s., duo, dupla.
DU.O.DE.NUM, s., duodeno.
DUPE, s., tolo, otário; v., enganar, lograr.
DU.PLI.CATE, s., duplicação, cópia; v., duplicar, copiar, fotocopiar.
DU.PLI.CA.TION, s., duplicação.
DU.PLIC.I.TY, s., duplicidade, ambiguidade, falsidade.
DU.RA.BIL.I.TY, s., durabilidade, duração.
DUR.ING, prep., durante.
DUSK, s., crepúsculo, lusco-fusco, anoitecer; v., anoitecer.
DUSKY, adj., escuro, escurecido.
DUST, s., pó, poeira.
DUST.ER, s., pano para pó.
DUTCH, adj., s., holandês, batavo.
DU.TI.FUL, adj., cumpridor, que executa.
DU.TI.FUL.NESS, s., cumprimento do dever.
DU.TY, s., dever; taxa, imposto.
DUTY.FREE, adj., livre de impostos; s., loja de aeroporto.
DU.VET, s., edredão.
DWELL, v., morar, habitar.
DWELL.ER, s., morador, habitante.
DWELL.ING, s., habitação, moradia.
DYE, s., tinta, tintura; v., tingir.
DY.ER, s., tintureiro.
DYKE, s., dique, represa.
DY.NAM.IC, adj., dinâmico.
DY.NAM.ICS, s., dinâmica.
DY.NA.MITE, s., dinamite; v., dinamitar.
DY.NA.MO, s., dínamo.
DY.NAS.TY, s., dinastia.
DYS.EN.TERY, s., disenteria.

E

E, *s.*, quinta-letra do alfabeto inglês.
EACH, *adj.*, cada; *pron.*, cada, cada um, cada qual.
EA.GER, *adj.*, ansioso, zeloso, ávido.
EA.GER.NESS, *s.*, ânsia, avidez, zelo, impaciência.
EA.GLE, *s.*, águia.
EA.GLET, *s.*, filhote de águia.
EAR, *s.*, ouvido, orelha, audição; *v.*, espigar.
EAR.DROPS, *s.*, pl., brincos.
EARL, *s.*, conde.
EAR.LY, *adj.*, cedo, matinal, precoce; *adv.*, de madrugada, em breve.
EARN, *v.*, ganhar, lucrar.
EAR.NEST, *s.*, seriedade, determinação; *adj.*, sério, honesto, determinado.
EARN.INGS, *s.*, salário, vencimento, ordenado.
EAR.RING, *s.*, brinco.
EARTH, *s.*, terra, globo terrestre, mundo, chão; *v.*, enterrar, ligar à terra.
EARTH.LY, *adj.*, terrestre, térreo, mundano, profano.
EARTH.QUAKE, *s.*, terremoto, sismo.
EARTH.WORM, *s.*, minhoca.
EASE, *s.*, tranquilidade, sossego, conforto, bem-estar; *v.*, aliviar, atenuar.
EASE.FUL, *adj.*, tranquilo, sossegado, confortável.
EASE.MENT, *s.*, facilidade, conforto, vantagem.
EAS.I.LY, *adv.*, facilmente.
EASI.NESS, *s.*, facilidade, conforto, docilidade.
EAST, *s.*, leste, este, oriente.
EAS.TER, *s.*, Páscoa.
EASTE.RN, *adj.*, oriental, do leste, levantino.
EAST.WARDS, *s.*, leste; *adv.*, para o leste.
EASY, *adj.*, fácil, leve, cômodo, confortável; *adv.*, facilmente.
EAT, *v.*, comer.
EAT.ABLE, *s.*, *pl.*, víveres, alimentos.
EATER, *s.*, comedor.
EAT IN, *v.*, comer em casa.
EAT.ING-HOUSE, *s.*, restaurante, lanchonete.
EAVES, *s.*, beirada, beiral.
EBB, *s.*, maré baixa, vazante, refluxo; *v.*, diminuir, baixar, refluir.
EBB TIDE, *s.*, maré baixa, baixa mar, vazante.
EB.O.NY, *s.*, ébano, cor escura; *adj.*, escuro, negro, feito de ébano.
EBUL.IENCE, *s.*, ebulição, fervura.
EBUL.IENT, *adj.*, ebuliente, fervente.
EB.UL.LI.ION, *s.*, ebulição, fervura; entusiasmo.
EC.CEN.TRIC, *adj.*, excêntrico, exótico, estranho.
EC.CEN.TRIC.I.TY, *s.*, excentricidade.
EC.CLE.SI.AS.TIC, *adj.*, *s.*, eclesiástico.
ECHO, *s.*, eco; repetição; *v.*, ecoar, ressoar.
ECLEC.TIC, *adj.*, eclético.
ECLIPSE, *s.*, eclipse, escurecimento; *v.*, eclipsar-se, sumir.
ECO.LOG.IC, *adj.*, ecológico.
ECO.LOG.IST, *s.*, ecologista.
ECOL.O.GY, *s.*, ecologia.
ECO.NOM.IC, *adj.*, econômico, produtivo, lucrativo.
ECO.NOM.ICS, *s.*, economia.
ECON.O.MIST, *s.*, economista.
ECON.O.MIZE, *v.*, economizar.
ECON.O.MY, *s.*, economia.
EC.STA.SY, *s.*, êxtase.
EC.UA.DOR, *s.*, Equador.
EC.UA.DOR.IAN, *adj.*, *s.*, equatoriano.
EC.U.MEN.IC, *adj.*, ecumênico, universal.
ED.DY, *s.*, redemoinho; *v.*, redemoinhar.
EDEN, *s.*, éden, paraíso.
EDEN.TATE, *adj.*, desdentado.
EDGE, *s.*, canto, beira, bainha, margem; *v.*,

EDGEWAYS — ELECTROMAGNETISM

embainhar, margear.
EDGE.WAYS, *adv.*, lateralmente, pelo lado.
EDGY, *adj.*, nervoso, inquieto, preocupado.
ED.I.BIL.I.TY, *s.*, comestibilidade.
ED.I.BLE, *adj.*, comestível, digerível.
ED.I.FI.CA.TION, *s.*, edificação.
ED.I.FI.CA.TO.RY, *adj.*, edificante, santificante.
ED.I.FICE, *s.*, edifício.
ED.I.FY, *v.*, edificar, instruir, ensinar.
ED.IT, *v.*, editar, publicar, editorar.
EDI.TION, *s.*, edição, publicação, impressão.
ED.I.TOR, *s.*, editor, redator, jornalista.
ED.I.TO.RI.AL, *adj., s.*, editorial.
ED.I.TRESS, *s.*, editora.
ED.U.CATE, *v.*, educar, instruir, preparar.
ED.U.CA.TION, *s.*, educação, ensino.
ED.U.CA.TIVE, *adj.*, educativo, instrutivo.
ED.U.CA.TOR, *s.*, educador, pedagogo.
EDUCE, *v.*, deduzir, eduzir.
EDUC.TION, *s.*, dedução.
EEL, *s.*, enguia.
EF.FACE, *v.*, obscurecer, apagar, extinguir.
EF.FECT, *s.*, efeito, resultado, eficiência; *v.*, efetuar, fazer, realizar.
EF.FEC.TIVE, *adj.*, efetivo, eficaz.
EF.FEC.TIVE.NESS, *s.*, eficácia, eficiência, efetividade.
EF.FEC.TU.ATE, *v.*, efetuar, executar, concretizar.
EF.FE.MI.NATE, *adj.*, efeminado, afeminado; mulherengo; fraco.
EF.FE.MI.NA.TION, *s.*, efeminação.
EF.FER.VESCE, *v.*, efervescer, ferver.
EF.FETE, *adj.*, cansado, fraco, gasto.
EF.FI.CA.CIOUS, *adj.*, eficaz, eficiente.
EF.FI.CA.CY, *s.*, eficácia.
EF.FI.CIENT, *adj.*, eficiente, competente.
EF.FI.GY, *s.*, efígie, imagem, figura.
EF.FLO.RESCE, *v.*, eflorescer.
EF.FLO.RES.CENCE, *s.*, eflorescência.
EF.FORT, *s.*, esforço, empenho, tentativa.
EF.FRON.TERY, *s.*, descaramento.
EF.FUSE, *v.*, efundir, derramar, espalhar.
EF.FU.SION, *s.*, efusão, chá, eflúvio.
EF.FU.SIVE, *adj.*, efusivo.

EGG, *s.*, ovo; óvulo, germe.
EGG.BEAT.ER, *s.*, batedeira de ovos.
EGG.ING, *s.*, postura de ovos.
EGG.SHELL, *s.*, casca de ovos.
EGO, *s.*, ego, eu.
EGO.ISM, *s.*, egoísmo.
EGO.IST, *s.*, egoísta.
EGRESS, *s.*, saída, egresso.
EGYP.TIAN, *adj., s.*, egípcio.
EI.DER.DOWN, *s.*, edredão.
EIGHT, *num.*, oito.
EIGH.TEEN, *num.*, dezoito.
EIGHTH, *num.*, oitavo.
EIGTY, *num.*, oitenta.
EIRE, *s.* República da Irlanda.
EI.THER, *pron.*, cada um, um ou outro, ambos.
EJAC.U.LATE, *v.*, ejacular.
EJAC.U.LA.TION, *s.*, ejaculação.
EJECT, *v.*, lançar, jogar, ejetar, expelir.
EJEC.TION, *s.*, ejeção, lançamento.
ELAB.O.RATE, *v.*, aperfeiçoar, elaborar; *adj.*, elaborado, aperfeiçoado.
ELAB.O.RA.TION, *s.*, elaboração.
ELAST.IC, *adj.*, elástico, flexível.
ELAS.TIC.I.TY, *s.*, elasticidade.
EL.BOW, *s.*, cotovelo; *v.*, acotovelar.
EL.DER, *adj.*, mais velho, o mais velho; *s.*, pessoa idosa, ancião.
EL.DER.LY, *adj.*, de idade mais avançada.
EL.DEST, *adj.*, mais velho, o mais velho.
ELECT, *s.*, os eleitos, os escolhidos; *v.*, eleger, escolher, selecionar.
ELEC.TION, *s.*, eleição, escolha.
ELEC.TOR, *s.*, eleitor, votante.
ELEC.TOR.ATE, *s.*, eleitorado.
ELEC.TRIC, *adj.*, elétrico.
ELEC.TRI.CIAN, *s.*, eletricista.
ELEC.TRI.CI.TY, *s.*, eletricidade.
ELEC.TRI.FI.CA.TION, *s.*, eletrificação.
ELEC.TRI.FY, *v.*, eletrificar; eletrizar.
ELEC.TRO.CUTE, *v.*, eletrocutar.
ELEC.TRO.MAG.NET.IC, *adj.*, eletromagnético.
ELEC.TRO.MAG.NE.TISM, *s.*, eletromagnetismo.

ELEC.TRON.IC, *adj.*, eletrônico.
ELEC.TRON.ICS, *s.*, eletrônica.
EL.E.GANCE, *s.*, elegância.
EL.E.GANT, *adj.*, elegante, garboso.
EL.E.GY, *s.*, elegia.
EL.E.MENT, *s.*, elemento, componente, fundamento.
EL.E.MEN.TAL, *adj.*, elementar, básico.
EL.E.PHANT, *s.*, elefante.
EL.E.VATE, *v.*, elevar, levantar, alçar.
EL.E.VA.TION, *s.*, elevação, altura, altitude.
EL.E.VA.TOR, *s.*, elevador, ascensor.
ELEV.EN, *num.*, onze.
ELEV.ENTH, *num.*, undécimo, décimo primeiro.
ELF, *s.*, elfo, duende.
ELIDE, *v.*, elidir, suprimir.
EL.I.GI.BIL.I.TY, *s.*, elegibilidade.
EL.I.GI.BLE, *adj.*, elegível.
ELIM.I.NATE, *v.*, eliminar, erradicar, tirar tudo.
ELIM.I.NA.TION, *s.*, eliminação.
ELI.SION, *s.*, elisão.
ELIX.IR, *s.*, elixir.
EL.LIPSE, *s.*, elipse.
EL.LIP.TIC, *adj.*, elíptico.
EL.O.CU.TION, *s.*, elocução.
ELON.GATE, *v.*, alongar, esticar.
ELOPE, *v.*, fugir.
EL.O.QUENCE, *s.*, eloquência.
EL.O.QUENT, *adj.*, eloquente.
ELSE, *adj.*, outro, diverso; *adv.*, em vez de; *conj.*, senão.
ELU.CI.DATE, *v.*, elucidar, explicar, explanar.
ELU.CI.DA.TIVE, *adj.*, elucidativo.
ELUDE, *v.*, iludir, fugir, esquivar-se.
ELU.SIVE, *adj.*, enganoso, ilusório.
EMA.CI.ATE, *v.*, emaciar, definhar, emagrecer.
EM.A.NATE, *v.*, emanar, proceder, vir de.
EMAN.CI.PATE, *v.*, emancipar, livrar.
EM.BALM, *v.*, embalsamar.
EM.BANK, *v.*, colocar dique; represar, terraplanar.
EM.BANK.MENT, *s.*, dique, represa, aterro.
EM.BAR.GO, *s.*, proibição, embargo, veto.
EM.BARK, *v.*, embarcar.
EM.BAR.KA.TION, *s.*, embarque.

EM.BAS.SY, *s.*, embaixada.
EM.BEL.LISH, *v.*, embelezar, ornamentar.
EM.BEL.LISH.MENT, *s.*, embelezamento.
EMB.ER, *s.*, tição, brasa, borralho.
EM.BIT.TER, *v.*, azedar, amargar, angustiar.
EM.BLEM, *s.*, emblema.
EM.BLEM.AT.IC, *adj.*, emblemático.
EM.BOD.I.MENT, *s.*, encarnação, personificação.
EM.BODY, *v.*, incorporar, personificar.
EM.BOSS.MENT, *s.*, relevo, gravura em relevo.
EM.BRACE, *v.*, abraçar, dar um abraço.
EM.BRACE.MENT, *s.*, abraço.
EM.BROI.DER, *v.*, bordar.
EM.BROI.DERY, *s.*, bordado.
EM.BROIL, *v.*, embrulhar, complicar.
EM.BRYO, *s.*, embrião.
EM.BRY.OL.O.GY, *s.*, embriologia.
EMEND, *v.*, corrigir, emendar.
EMEND.ATE, *v.*, emendar, corrigir.
EMEN.DA.TION, *s.*, correção, emenda.
EM.ER.ALD, *s.*, esmeralda.
EMERGE, *v.*, emergir, sair, vir para fora.
EMER.GENCE, *s.*, emergência.
EMER.GEN.CY, *s.*, emergência.
EMER.I.TUS, *adj., s.*, jubilado; aposentado.
EMIC.TION, *s.*, urina.
EM.I.GRANT, *s.*, emigrante.
EM.I.GRATE, *v.*, emigrar.
EM.I.GRA.TION, *s.*, emigração.
EM.I.GRA.TOR, *s.*, emigrante.
EM.IS.SARY, *s.*, emissário, mensageiro.
EMIS.SION, *s.*, emissão.
EMOL.U.MENT, *s.*, emolumento, pagamento.
EMO.TION, *s.*, emoção.
EMO.TIVE, *adj.*, emotivo, sensível.
EM.PER.OR, *s.*, imperador.
EM.PHA.SIS, *s.*, ênfase.
EM.PHA.SIZE, *v.*, enfatizar, destacar, salientar.
EM.PHAT.IC, *adj.*, enfático, saliente.
EM.PHY.SE.MA, *s.*, enfizema.
EM.PIRE, *s.*, império.
EM.PIR.I.CISM, *s.*, empirismo.
EM.PLOY, *v.*, empregar, usar, utilizar.

EM.PLOY.EE, *s.*, empregado.
EM.PLOY.ER, *s.*, empregador, patrão.
EM.PLOY.MENT, *s.*, emprego, trabalho, ocupação.
EM.PRESS, *s.*, imperatriz.
EMP.TY, *v.*, esvaziar, evacuar, desocupar; *adj.*, vazio, desocupado.
EMP.TY.HAND.ED, *adv.*, de mãos vazias.
EMU, *s.*, ema.
EM.UL.ATE, *v.*, emular, rivalizar, competir.
EM.U.LA.TION, *s.*, emulação, rivalidade.
EMUL.SION, *s.*, emulsão.
EN.ABLE, *v.*, habilitar, capacitar, permitir.
EN.ACT, *v.*, ordenar, decretar, promulgar, legalizar.
EN.ACT.MENT, *s.*, lei, decreto, promulgação.
EN.AC.TOR, *s.*, legislador, executivo da lei.
ENAM.EL, *s.*, esmalte; *v.*, esmaltar.
EN.AM.OUR, *v.*, enamorar.
EN.AM.OUR.ED, *adj.*, apaixonado, enamorado, cativo.
EN.CAGE, *v.*, engaiolar, prender, encarcerar.
EN.CAMP.MENT, *s.*, acampamento.
EN.CASE, *v.*, encaixotar, colocar dentro, encerrar.
EN.CHAIN, *v.*, prender com corrente, acorrentar, prender.
EN.CHANT, *v.*, encantar, enfeitiçar.
EN.CHANT.ER, *s.*, encantador, mágico, feiticeiro.
EN.CHANT.MENT, *s.*, encantamento, sedução.
EN.CIR.CLE, *v.*, cercar, circundar, circular.
EN.CLIT.IC, enclítica; *adj.*, enclítico.
EN.CLOSE, *v.*, fechar, encerrar, cercar; incluir, anexar.
EN.CLO.SURE, *s.*, cerca, cercado.
EN.COUN.TER, *s.*, encontro; *v.*, encontrar, achar, topar com.
EN.COUR.AGE, *v.*, encorajar, animar, entusiasmar, estimular.
EN.COUR.AGE.MENT, *s.*, estímulo, encorajamento.
EN.CRUST, *v.*, incrustar, embutir.
EN.CYC.LI.CAL, *s.*, encíclica, *adj.*, encíclico.
EN.CY.CLO.PE.DIA, *s.*, enciclopédia.
EN.CY.CLO.PE.DIST, *s.*, enciclopedista.
END, *s.*, fim, ponta, final, término; *v.*, acabar, pôr fim, terminar.
EN.DAN.GER, *v.*, pôr em perigo, arriscar, expor.
EN.DEAR, *v.*, encarecer, levantar o preço; ser amável, agradar.
EN.DEAR.MENT, *s.*, carinho, apreço, amor, ternura.
EN.DEAV.OUR, *s.*, empenho, esforço; *v.*, esforçar-se, empenhar-se.
EN.DEM.IC, *adj.*, endêmico; *s.*, doença endêmica; endemia.
END.ING, *s.*, fim, término, final, conclusão.
EN.DIVE, *s.*, endívia, chicória.
END.LESS.NESS, *s.*, eternidade, perpetuidade.
END.MOST, *adj.*, o mais distante, o mais longe.
EN.DORSE, *v.*, endossar cheque; endossar documento.
EN.DOW, *v.*, doar, dar, proporcionar, dotar.
EN.DOW.ER, *s.*, doador, dotador.
EN.DUR.ANCE, *s.*, resistência, paciência, duração, persistência.
EN.DURE, *v.*, aguentar, suportar, tolerar.
EN.DUR.ER, *s.*, tolerante, quem suporta.
EN.DUR.ING, *adj.*, sofredor, paciente, tolerante.
EN.E.MY, *s.*, inimigo, adversário.
EN.ER.GET.IC, *adj.*, energético.
EN.ER.GET.ICS, *s.*, energética.
EN.ER.GY, *s.*, energia.
EN.ER.VA.TION, *s.*, enfraquecimento, enervamento.
EN.FEE.BLE, *v.*, enfraquecer, debilitar.
EN.FEE.BLE.MENT, *s.*, enfraquecimento, debilitação.
EN.FORCE, *v.*, obrigar, forçar, fazer cumprir, coagir, constranger.
EN.FORCE.MENT, *s.*, coação, obrigação, constrangimento.
EN.FRAN.CHISE, *v.*, emancipar, liberar, conceder direitos civis.
EN.GAGE, *v.*, empenhar, comprometer, dedicar-se, engajar-se.
EN.GAGE.MENT, *s.*, compromisso, engajamento, noivado.
EN.GAGE.MENT RING, *s.*, anel de noivado, aliança de noivado.

EN.GEN.DER, v., engendrar, plasmar, gerar, criar.
EN.GINE, s., motor, engenho, locomotiva.
EN.GI.NEER, s., engenheiro, técnico, maquinista de locomotiva.
EN.GI.NEER.ING, s., engenharia.
EN.GINE.RY, s., maquinaria.
ENG.LAND, s., Inglaterra.
ENG.LISH, adj., s., inglês.
EN.GRAFT, v., enxertar, implantar, colocar dentro.
EN.GROSS, v., passar a limpo, absorver, apoderar-se.
EN.GROSS.ER, s., copista.
EN.GULF, v., engolir, tragar.
EN.HANCE, v., enfatizar, salientar, aumentar.
ENIG.MA, s., enigma.
ENIG.MAT.IC, adj., enigmático.
EN.JOIN, v., mandar, impor, ordenar, prescrever.
EN.JOY, v., usufruir, desfrutar, gostar de.
EN.JOY.MENT, s., prazer.
EN.LACE, v., enlaçar, envolver.
EN.LARGE, v., alargar, aumentar, dilatar.
EN.LARGE.MENT, s., ampliação, aumento, dilatação.
EN.LIV.EN, v., avivar, animar, divertir.
EN.MESH, v., enredar, embaralhar, emaranhar.
EN.MI.TY, s., inimizade.
EN.NO.BLE, v., enobrecer, engrandecer, honorificar.
EN.NO.BLE.MENT, s., enobrecimento.
ENOR.MI.TY, s., enormidade, amplidão.
ENOUGH, adj., suficiente, bastante.
ENOUNCE, v., enunciar.
EN.RICH, v., enriquecer.
EN.SEM.BLE, s., conjunto, união.
EN.SLAVE, v., escravizar, dominar, subjugar.
EN.SLAVE.MENT, s., escravidão.
EN.SLAV.ER, s., escravizador, escravizante.
EN.SUE, v., seguir, suceder, vir depois.
EN.SU.ING, adj., seguinte.
EN.SURE, v., assegurar.
EN.TER, v., entrar em, associar-se, inscrever-se.
EN.TER.ING, adj., entrante.
EN.TER.PRISE, s., empresa, empreendimento.
EN.TER.PRIS.ER, s., empreendedor.
EN.TER.TAIN, v., entreter, divertir, receber.
EN.TER.TAIN.ER, s., artista.
EN.TER.TAIN.MENT, s., divertimento, diversão.
EN.THRONE, v., entronizar.
EN.THUSE, v., entusiasmar, animar, estimular.
EN.THU.SI.ASM, s., entusiasmo.
EN.THU.SI.AS.TIC, adj., entusiástico, animador.
EN.TIRE, adj., inteiro.
EN.TIRE.NESS, s., totalidade.
EN.TI.TY, s., ente.
EN.TOMB, v., enterrar, sepultar.
EN.TOMB.MENT, s., sepultamento, enterro.
EN.TRAILS, s., pl., entranhas.
EN.TRANCE, s., chegada, entrada, ingresso, porta, acesso.
EN.TRAP, v., prender, pegar em armadilha.
EN.TRAP.MENT, s., armadilha.
EN.TREAT, v., suplicar, pedir, solicitar.
EN.TREATY, s., súplica.
EN.TRE.PRE.NEUR, s., empresário.
EN.TRUST, v., confiar.
EN.TRY, s., entrada, ingresso, saguão, anotação, apontamento.
EN.TWINE, v., enlaçar, entrelaçar.
ENU.MER.ATE, v., enumerar.
ENU.MER.A.TION, s., enumeração.
ENUN.CI.ATE, v., enunciar, pronunciar, prolatar.
ENUN.CI.A.TION, s., enunciação.
EN.VEL.OP, v., envolver.
EN.VE.LOPE, s., envelope.
EN.VEN.OM, v., envenenar, irritar.
EN.VI.OUS, adj., invejoso.
EN.VI.OUS.NESS, s., inveja.
EN.VI.RON, v., rodear, cercar, estar em torno.
EN.VI.RON.MENT, s., meio ambiente, arredores, cercanias.
EN.VIS.AGE, v., prever.
EN.VY, s., inveja; v., invejar.
EN.ZYME, s., enzima.
EPHEM.ERA, s., efemeridade; coisa efêmera.
EPHEM.EROUS, adj., efêmero.
EP.IC, s., epopeia; adj., épico.
EP.I.CUR.ISM, s., epicurismo.

EP.I.DEM.IC, *adj.*, epidêmico; *s.*, epidemia.
EPI.DER.MIS, *s.*, epiderme.
EP.I.GRAM, *s.*, epigrama.
EP.I.GRAPH, *s.*, epígrafe.
EP.I.LEP.SY, *s.*, epilepsia.
EP.I.LEP.TIC, *adj.*, epiléptico.
EP.I.LOGUE, *s.*, epílogo.
EPIPH.A.NY, *s.*, epifania.
EPIS.CO.PAL, *adj.*, episcopal.
EP.I.SODE, *s.*, episódio, fato, momento.
EP.I.SOD.IC, *adj.*, episódico.
EPIS.TLE, *s.*, epístola, carta.
EP.I.TAPH, *s.*, epitáfio.
EP.I.THET, *s.*, epíteto.
EP.OCH, *s.*, época.
EP.O.PEE, *s.*, epopeia.
EQUA.BIL.I.TY, *s.*, uniformidade, igualdade.
EQUA.BLE, *adj.*, plácido, sereno, uniforme.
EQUAL, *s.*, igual, equitativo.
EQUAL.I.TY, *s.*, igualdade.
EQUAL.IZE, *v.*, igualar.
EQUA.NIM.I.TY, *s.*, equanimidade.
EQUA.NIM.OUS, *adj.*, equânime, justo, imparcial.
EQUA.TION, *s.*, equação.
EQUA.TOR, *s.*, equador, paralelo.
EQUA.TO.RI.AL, *adj.*, equatorial.
EQUES.TRI.AN, *adj.*, equestre.
EQUI.DIS.TANT, *adj.*, equidistante.
EQUIL.I.BRATE, *v.*, equilibrar.
EQUIL.I.BRA.TION, *s.*, equilíbrio, equilibramento.
EQUIL.I.BRIST, *s.*, equilibrista.
EQUI.LIB.RI.UM, *s.*, equilíbrio.
EQUINE, *adj.*, equino.
EQUI.NOX, *s.*, equinócio.
EQUIP, *v.*, equipar, munir, fornecer.
EQ.UI.PAGE, *s.*, equipamento, equipagem.
EQ.UI.TA.BLE, *adj.*, equitativo.
EQ.UI.TA.TION, *s.*, equitação.
EQ.UI.TY, *s.*, equidade, justiça, paridade.
EQUIV.A.LENCE, *s.*, equivalência, igualdade.
EQUIV.O.CAL.NESS, *s.*, equívoco.
EQUIV.O.CATE, *v.*, equivocar, equivocar-se, usar de ambiguidades.
EQUIV.O.CA.TION, *s.*, equívoco, erro, engano.
ERA, *s.*, era, época.
ERAD.I.CATE, *v.*, erradicar, eliminar, arrancar.
ERAD.I.CA.TION, *s.*, erradicação, eliminação.
ERAS.ABLE, *adj.*, apagável, desmanchável.
ERASE, *v.*, apagar, desmanchar, desgraçar.
ERAS.ER, *s.* apagador, objeto para apagar.
ERE, *conj.*, antes de, antes que.
ERECT, *v.*, erigir, levantar, alçar; *adj.*, levantado, ereto, alçado.
EREC.TION, *s.*, ereção, construção, montagem.
ERODE, *v.*, corroer, provocar erosão.
ERO.SION, *s.*, erosão.
EROT.IC, *adj.*, erótico.
ER.O.TISM, *s.*, erotismo.
ERR, *v.*, errar, falhar, enganar, enganar-se.
ER.RAND, *s.*, mensagem, missão, recado.
ER.RANT, *s.*, errante, vagabundo.
ER.RA.TUM, *s.*, errata.
ER.RO.NE.OUS, *adj.*, errôneo.
ER.ROR, *s.*, erro.
ERST.WHILE, *adj.*, antigo.
ERUCT.ATE, *v.*, arrotar.
ERUC.TA.TION, *s.*, arroto.
ER.U.DITE, *adj.*, erudito.
ER.U.DITE.NESS, *s.*, erudição.
ERUPT, *v.*, entrar em erupção.
ERUP.TION, *s.*, erupção.
ES.CA.LADE, *v.*, escalar, subir, ascender; *s.*, escalada.
ES.CA.LA.TOR, *s.*, escada rolante.
ES.CAPE, *s.*, fuga, escapada; *v.*, escapar, fugir, evadir-se.
ES.CORT, *s.*, escolta, acompanhante; *v.*, acompanhar.
ES.KI.MO, *s.*, esquimó.
ESOPH.A.GUS, *s.*, esôfago.
ES.O.TER.IC, *adj.*, esotérico.
ES.PE.CIAL, *adj.*, especial, particular, único.
ES.PE.CIAL.LY, *adv.*, especialmente, sobretudo, preferentemente.
ES.PI.O.NAGE, *s.*, espionagem.
ES.POUSE, *v.*, esposar, abraçar, abarcar.

ES.PY, v., avistar, divisar, ver.
ES.SAY, s., ensaio; v., tentar, pretender, ensaiar.
ES.SAY.ST, s., ensaísta.
ES.SENCE, s., essência.
ES.SEN.TIAL, adj., essencial.
ES.SEN.TI.AL.I.TY, s., essencialidade.
ES.TAB.LISH, v., estabelecer, instituir, firmar, assentar.
ES.TAB.LISH.MENT, s., estabelecimento, instituição.
ES.TATE, s., fazenda, bens, patrimônio, estado.
ES.TEEM, s., estima, consideração; v., estimar, prezar, amar.
ES.TI.MA.BLE, adj., estimável.
ES.TI.MA.BLE.NESS, s., apreço, estima, respeito.
ES.TI.MATE, v., calcular, estimar, avaliar; s., cálculo, orçamento.
ES.TI.MA.TION, s., cálculo, avaliação.
ES.TOP, v., impedir, obstruir.
ES.TRADE, s., palco, estrado, plataforma.
ES.TU.ARY, s., estuário.
ESU.RI.ENCE, s., miséria, fome, indigência.
ESU.RI.ENT, adj., faminto, miserável, indigente.
ETER.NAL, adj., eterno, perene, perpétuo.
ETH.IC, adj., ético.
ETHI.CS, s., ética.
ETH.NIC, adj., étnico, racial.
ETH.NOG.RA.PHY, s., etnografia.
ETHOL.O.GY, s., etologia.
ET.I.QUETTE, s., etiqueta, boas maneiras sociais.
ET.Y.MO.LOG.IC, adj., etimológico.
ET.Y.MOL.O.GIST, s., etimologista.
ET.Y.MOL.O.GY, s., etimologia.
EU.CA.LYP.TUS, s., eucalipto.
EU.CHA.RIST, s., eucaristia.
EU.CHA.RIS.TIC, adj., eucarístico.
EU.GEN.IC, adj., eugênico.
EU.GEN.ICS, s., eugenia.
EU.LO.GIS.TIC, adj., elogioso, louvador.
EU.LO.GIZE, v., elogiar, louvar, enaltecer.
EU.LO.GY, s., elogio, louvor.
EU.NUCH, adj., s., eunuco.
EU.PHE.MISM, s., eufemismo.
EU.PHE.MIS.TIC, adj., eufemístico.
EU.PHE.MIZE, v., eufemizar.
EU.PHON.IC, adj., eufônico, suave, brando.
EU.PHO.NY, s., eufonia, harmonia.
EU.PHO.RIA, s., euforia.
EU.RO.PE, s., Europa.
EU.RO.PEAN, adj., europeu.
EU.THA.NA.SIA, s., eutanásia.
EVAC.U.ATE, v., evacuar, esvaziar.
EVAC.U.A.TION, s., evacuação.
EVAL.U.ATE, v., avaliar, estimar, calcular.
EVAL.U.A.TION, s., avaliação, cálculo, estimativa.
EVAN.GEL, s., evangelho.
EVAN.GEL.I.CAL, adj., evangélico; protestante.
EVAN.GE.LIST, s., evangelista.
EVAN.GE.LI.ZA.TION, s., evangelização.
EVAN.GE.LIZE, v., evangelizar.
EVAP.OR.ABLE, adj., evaporável.
EVAP.O.RATE, v., evaporar, evaporar-se.
EVAP.O.RA.TION, s., evaporação.
EVA.SION, s., evasão.
EVE, s., véspera, vigília, anoitecer.
EVEN, v., entardecer, equilibrar, emparelhar; adj., plano, liso, calmo.
EVEN.ING, s., tarde, noite.
EVENT, s., evento, fato, acontecimento.
EVENT.FUL, adj., emocionante, agitado, movimentado, corrido.
EVEN.TU.AL, adj., eventual, possível, final.
EVEN.TU.AL.I.TY, s., eventualidade.
EVEN.TU.ATE, v., acontecer, suceder.
EV.ER, adv., sempre, toda hora, conj., depois que.
EV.ER.LAST.ING, adj., eterno, perene.
EV.ER.MORE, adj., eternamente, para sempre.
EV.ERY, adj., cada, todo.
EV.ERY.BODY, pron., todos, todo mundo.
EV.ERY.DAY, adj., diário, comum, cotidiano.
EV.ERY.ONE, pron., todos, todo mundo.
EV.ERY.THING, pron., tudo.
EV.ERY.WAY, adv., de todas as maneiras, de todos os modos.
EV.ERY.WHERE, adv., em toda parte, em todo

lugar.
EVICT, *v.*, despejar.
EVIC.TION, *s.*, despejo.
EV.I.DENCE, *s.*, evidência, prova, testemunho; *v.*, evidenciar, provar.
EV.I.DENT, *adj.*, evidente, claro, provado.
EVIL, *s.*, mal, maldade, ruindade; *adj.*, mau, maldoso.
EVIL.NESS, *s.*, maldade, ruindade.
EVIS.CER.ATE, *v.*, eviscerar, estripar.
EVO.CA.TION, *s.*, evocação.
EVOKE, *v.*, evocar, lembrar.
EVOLV.ABLE, *adj.*, progressista, desenvolvível.
EVOLVE, *v.*, desenvolver.
EWE, *s.*, ovelha.
EX.AC.ER.BATE, *v.*, exacerbar, agravar.
EX.AC.ER.BA.TION, *s.*, exacerbação.
EX.ACT, *adj.*, exato, justo, meticuloso.
EX.AC.TI.TUDE, *s.*, exatidão, precisão.
EX.ACT.LY, *adv.*, exatamente.
EX.ACT.NESS, *s.*, exatidão.
EX.AG.GER.ATE, *v.*, exagerar.
EX.AG.GER.A.TION, *s.*, exagero.
EX.ALT, *v.*, exaltar, enaltecer, engrandecer.
EX.AL.TA.TION, *s.*, exaltação.
EX.AM.I.NA.TION, *s.*, exame, verificação, investigação.
EX.AM.INE, *v.*, examinar, verificar, investigar.
EX.AM.IN.ER, *s.*, examinador, investigador.
EX.AM.PLE, *s.*, exemplo, modelo; *v.*, exemplificar.
EX.AS.PER.ATE, *v.*, exasperar, incomodar, irritar.
EX.AS.PER.A.TION, *s.*, exasperação, incômodo.
EX.CEED, *v.*, exceder, ser a mais, suplantar, ultrapassar.
EX.CEED.ING, *adj.*, excessivo.
EX.CEL.LENCE, *s.*, excelência.
EX.CEL.LENT, *adj.*, excelente.
EX.CEPT, *prep.*, exceto; *v.*, excluir.
EX.CEPT.ING, *prep.*, com exceção de.
EX.CEP.TION, *s.*, exceção.
EX.CEP.TION.AL, *adj.*, excepcional.
EX.CESS, *s.*, excesso.

EX.CES.SIVE, *adj.*, excessivo.
EX.CES.SIVE.NESS, *s.*, excesso.
EX.CHANGE, *s.*, troca, câmbio, permuta.
EX.CHANG.ER, *s.*, cambista, permutador.
EX.CI.SION, *s.*, amputação, corte.
EX.CIT.ABIL.I.TY, *s.*, excitabilidade.
EX.CI.TANT, *adj.*, excitante.
EX.CI.TA.TION, *s.*, excitação.
EX.CITE, *v.*, excitar, provocar.
EX.CITE.MENT, *s.*, excitação, excitamento, emoção.
EX.CLAIM, *v.*, exclamar.
EX.CLA.MA.TION, *s.*, exclamação.
EX.CLUDE, *v.*, excluir.
EX.CLU.SION, *s.*, exclusão.
EX.COM.MU.NI.CATE, *v.*, excomungar.
EX.CRE.MENT, *s.*, excremento.
EX.CRE.TION, *s.*, excreção.
EX.CUL.PATE, *v.*, desculpar.
EX.CUL.PA.TION, *s.*, desculpa.
EX.CUR.SION, *s.*, excursão.
EX.CUR.SION.IST, *s.*, excursionista.
EX.CUSE, *v.*, desculpar, escusar.
EX.E.CRA.BLE, *adj.*, execrável.
EX.E.CUTE, *v.*, executar, cumprir, desempenhar, realizar.
EX.E.CU.TION, *s.*, execução.
EX.E.GE.SIS, *s.*, exegese.
EX.E.GET.IC, *adj.*, exegético.
EX.EM.PLAR, *s.*, exemplar, modelo.
EX.EM.PLA.RY, *adj.*, exemplar, modelar.
EX.EM.PLI.FY, *v.*, exemplificar, dar como modelo.
EX.ER.CISE, *s.*, exercício; *v.*, exercer, agir, trabalhar.
EX.ER.TION, *s.*, esforço, empenho.
EX.HA.LA.TION, *s.*, exalação.
EX.HALE, *v.*, exalar, expirar.
EX.HAUST.ING, *adj.*, exaustivo, fatigante.
EX.HAUS.TION, *s.*, exaustão.
EX.HIB.IT, *v.*, mostrar, exibir; *s.*, obra exposta.
EX.HI.BI.TION, *s.*, exibição, mostra.
EX.HORT, *v.*, exortar.
EX.HOR.TA.TION, *s.*, exortação, moção, recomendação.

EX.HU.MA.TION, s., exumação.
EX.HUME, v., exumar, desenterrar.
EX.I.GEN.CY, s., exigência.
EX.I.GENT, adj., exigente.
EX.I.GU.ITY, s. exiguidade.
EX.IG.U.OUS, adj., exíguo, parco, reduzido.
EX.ILE, s., exílio, exilado, v., exilar.
EX.IST, v., existir, ser, viver.
EX.IS.TENCE, s., existência, vida.
EX.IT, s., saída; v., sair.
EX.O.DUS, s., êxodo.
EX.ON.ER.ATE, v., exonerar, desobrigar.
EX.ON.ER.A.TION, s., exoneração, desculpa, desobrigação.
EX.OR.BI.TANCE, s., exorbitância, exagero, excesso.
EX.OR.BI.TANT, adj., exorbitante.
EX.OR.CIST, s., exorcista.
EX.OR.CIZE, v., exorcizar, expulsar os demônios.
EX.O.TER.IC, adj., exotérico.
EX.OT.IC, adj., exótico.
EX.PAND, v., expandir, aumentar, dilatar.
EX.PANSE, s., extensão.
EX.PAN.SION, s., expansão, desenvolvimento, propagação.
EX.PA.TRI.ATE, v., expatriar, desterrar.
EX.PECT, v., esperar, aguardar, supor.
EX.PEC.TAN.CY, s., expectativa.
EX.PEC.TO.RATE, s., expectorar.
EX.PE.DITE, v., expedir, apressar.
EX.PE.DI.TION, s., expedição.
EX.PEL, v., expelir, expulsar, retirar de.
EX.PEND, v., gastar.
EX.PENSE, s., gasto, despesa.
EX.PEN.SIVE, adj., caro, de preço alto.
EX.PE.RI.ENCE, s., experiência; v., experimentar, conhecer.
EX.PER.I.MENT, s., experiência, experimentação; v., experimentar.
EX.PER.I.MEN.TAL.IZE, v., experimentar.
EX.PER.I.MEN.TA.TION, s., experimentação.
EX.PERT, adj., hábil, esperto, perito; s., experto, especialista.
EX.PER.TISE, s., perícia.

EX.PI.ATE, v., expiar, pagar as penas.
EX.PI.A.TION, s., expiação, pagamento de penas.
EX.PIRE, v., expirar, expelir, morrer.
EX.PLAIN, v., explanar, explicar, esclarecer.
EX.PLA.NA.TION, s., explanação, explicação.
EX.PLI.CATE, v., explicar, esclarecer, explanar.
EX.PLI.CA.TION, s., explicação.
EX.PLIC.IT, adj., explícito.
EX.PLODE, v., explodir.
EX.PLOIT, v., explorar, utilizar-se, aproveitar-se; s., façanha, bravura.
EX.PLO.RA.TION, s., exploração.
EX.PLORE, v., explorar, pesquisar, examinar.
EX.PLOR.ER, s., explorador, investigador.
EX.PLO.SION, s., explosão, estouro.
EX.PORT, v., exportar; s., exportação.
EX.PORT.ABLE, adj., exportável.
EX.POR.TA.TION, s., exportação.
EX.PORT.ER, s., exportador.
EX.POSE, v., expor, apresentar, exibir, desmascarar.
EX.POS.ER, s., expositor.
EX.PO.SURE, s., exposição, exibição, revelação, publicidade.
EX.POUND, v., expor, explicar, apresentar.
EX.PRESS, v., expressar, despachar; adj., expresso, claro; s. rápido.
EX.PRES.SION, s., expressão.
EX.PRESS.NESS, s., clareza.
EX.PRESS.WAY, s., autoestrada, rodovia.
EX.QUI.SITE.NESS, s., maravilha, requinte.
EX.SCIND, v., cortar.
EX.SERT, v., amputar, cortar, retirar.
EX.TANT, adj., existente, sobrevivente.
EX.TEM.PO.RARY, adj., extemporâneo.
EX.TEM.PO.RI.ZA.TION, s., extemporização, improvisamento.
EX.TEM.PO.RIZE, v., improvisar, extemporizar.
EX.TEND, v., dilatar, estender, aumentar.
EX.TEN.SION, s., extensão, acréscimo, expansão, aumento.
EX.TEN.SIVE, adj., extensivo, amplo, vasto, considerado.
EX.TENT, s., extensão, alcance, tamanho.

EX.TEN.U.ATE, *v.*, diminuir, atenuar, suavizar.
EX.TEN.U.A.TION, *s.*, atenuação, suavização.
EX.TE.RI.OR, *adj.*, externo, exterior; *s.*, exterior.
EX.TE.RI.OR.I.TY, *s.*, exterioridade.
EX.TER.MI.NATE, *v.*, exterminar, liquidar, acabar.
EX.TER.MI.NA.TION, *s.*, extermínio.
EX.TER.NAL, *adj.*, externo.
EX.TINCT, *adj.*, extinto, terminado, acabado.
EX.TINC.TION, *s.*, extinção.
EX.TIN.GUISH, *v.*, extinguir, liquidar, acabar.
EX.TIN.GUISH.MENT, *s.*, extinção.
EX.TIR.PATE, *v.*, extirpar, erradicar.
EX.TORT, *v.*, extorquir.
EX.TOR.TION, *s.*, extorsão.
EX.TRA, *adj.*, extra, extraordinário, adicional; *s.*, extra, extraordinário.
EX.TRACT, *s.*, extrato; *v.*, extrair, arrancar, tirar de, extorquir.
EX.TRAC.TION, *s.*, extração.
EX.TRA.CUR.RIC.U.LAR, *adj.*, extracurricular.
EX.TRA.DITE, *v.*, extraditar, expulsar.
EX.TRA.JU.DI.CIAL, *adj.*, extrajudicial.
EX.TRAOR.DI.NARY, *adj.*, extraordinário.
EX.TRAV.A.GANCE, *s.*, extravagância.
EX.TREME, *adj.*, *s.*, extremo.
EX.TREM.ISM, *s.*, extremismo, radicalismo.
EX.TREM.IST, *s.*, extremista.
EX.TRIN.SIC, *adj.*, extrínseco, externo, exterior.
EX.TRUDE, *v.*, expulsar, retirar.
EX.U.BER.ANCE, *s.*, exuberância.
EX.U.BER.ANT, *adj.*, exuberante.
EX.U.BER.ATE, *v.*, exuberar, tornar-se exuberante.
EX.UDE, *v.*, suar, exsudar.
EX.ULT, *v.*, exultar, regozijar.
EX.UL.TANCE, *s.*, exultação, alegria, regozijo.
EYE, *s.*, olho, buraco de agulha; *v.*, olhar, observar, fixar.
EYE.BALL, *s.*, globo ocular.
EYE.BROW, *s.*, sobrancelha.
EYE.LASH, *s.*, pestana.
EYE.LID, *s.*, pálpebra.
EYE.SIGHT, *s.*, vista, visão, olhar.
EYE.WIT.NESS, *s.*, testemunha ocular.

F, s., sexta letra do alfabeto inglês; fá ; **F**, abrev. de fahrenheit.
FA, s., fá.
FA.BLE, s., fábula, história, narração, alegoria.
FAB.RIC, s., tecido, pano, fazenda, ficção; v., fingir, inventar.
FAB.RI.CATE, v., fabricar, confeccionar, manufaturar.
FAB.RI.CA.TION, s., fabricação, construção.
FAB.U.LOUS, adj., fabuloso, extraordinário, lendário.
FA.ÇADE, s., fachada, frontispício.
FACE, s., face, rosto, cara, fisionomia; superfície; v., enfrentar.
FA.CIAL, adj., facial.
FAC.ILE, adj., fácil, simples, afável, dócil, superficial.
FA.CIL.I.TATE, v., facilitar.
FA.CIL.I.TA.TION, s., facilitação.
FA.CIL.I.TY, s., facilidade, habilidade.
FACT, s., fato, acontecimento, caso, ocorrência.
FAC.TION, s., facção, partido, seita.
FAC.TIOUS, adj., faccioso, partidário, sectário.
FAC.TOR, s., fator.
FAC.TO.RY, s., fábrica, usina, estabelecimento.
FAC.UL.TY, s., faculdade; direito, capacidade, habilidade.
FAD, s., moda passageira, modismo, mania.
FAD.DISH, adj., maníaco, caprichoso.
FAD.DY, adj., caprichoso.
FADE, v., murchar, desbotar, enfraquecer, apagar-se.
FAD.ING, adj., murcho, pálido, que definha, que desbota.
FAG.GING, adj., cansativo, fatigante.
FAG.GOT, s., feixe, molho de lenha, trouxa; v., enfeixar.
FAIL.URE, s., falta, falha, fracasso, deficiência, omissão.
FAINT, s., desmaio, desfalecimento; adj., débil, fraco; v., desmaiar.
FAINT.ISH, adj., fraco, débil.
FAINT.NESS, s., debilidade, fraqueza.
FAIR, adj., belo, claro, louro, íntegro; s., beleza, namorada.
FAIR.NESS, s., alvura, beleza, formosura.
FAIR.PLAY, s., jogo limpo, honestidade.
FAIRY, s., fada, duende.
FAITH, s., fé, crença, credulidade, convicção, religião; verdade.
FAITH.FUL, adj., fiel, correto.
FAITH.FUL.NESS, s., fidelidade, lealdade, retidão.
FAITH.LESS, adj., incrédulo, sem fé.
FAITH.LESS.NESS, s., incredulidade, falta de fé.
FAKE, s., truque, fraude; adj., falso; v., falsear, enganar, fraudar, fingir.
FAK.ER, s., falsificador.
FA.KIR, s., faquir.
FAL.CON, s., falcão.
FAL.DE.RAL, s., ninharia, bagatela, frivolidade.
FALL, s., queda, tombo, baixa, diminuição; v., cair, baixar, cair de cara.
FALL-BACK, v., retroceder; s., retirada.
FAL.LI.BIL.I.TY, s., falibilidade.
FALL.ING, s., queda, rebaixamento.
FALSE, adj., falso, inverídico, desonesto, infiel, adulterado.
FALSE.HOOD, s., falsidade, engano, desonestidade.
FAL.SI.FI.CA.TION, s., falsificação.
FAL.SI.FY, v., falsificar, adulterar, corromper.
FAL.TER, s., vacilação, hesitação; v., gaguejar, hesitar, vacilar.
FAL.TER.ING, s., hesitação, vacilação.

FAME, *s.*, fama, notoriedade, celebridade; *v.*, celebrar, notabilizar.
FA.MIL.IAR, *adj.*, familiar, conhecido.
FA.MIL.IAR.I.TY, *s.*, familiaridade, conhecimento.
FA.MIL.IAR.IZE, *v.*, familiarizar.
FAM.I.LY, *s.*, família, descendência, linhagem.
FAM.INE, *s.*, carência, carestia, penúria, fome.
FAM.OUS, *adj.*, famoso, conhecido, célebre.
FA.MOUS.NESS, *s.*, fama, celebridade, notoriedade.
FAN, *s.*, leque, ventilador; *v.*, abanar.
FA.NAT.IC, *s.*, fanático, fã.
FA.NAT.I.CISM, *s.*, fanatismo.
FA.NAT.I.CIZE, *v.*, fanatizar.
FAN.CY, *s.*, fantasia, imaginação, capricho; *v.*, imaginar, fantasiar, julgar.
FAN.FARE, *s.*, fanfarra.
FAN.NER, *s.*, ventilador, abanador.
FAN.TAS.TIC, *adj.*, fantástico, extraordinário, fantasioso; *s.*, fantasista.
FAN.TA.SY, *s.*, fantasia, imaginação, utopia, ideal.
FAR, *s.*, o distante; *adj.*, distante, longínquo.
FARE, *s.*, custo de uma passagem; bandeirada/táxi; *v.*, passar bem ou mal.
FAR.I.NA.CEOUS, *adj.*, farináceo, farinhoso.
FARM, *s.*, fazenda, chácara, sítio; *v.*, cultivar, plantar, criar gado.
FARM.ER, *s.*, fazendeiro, granjeiro, agricultor.
FARM.ING, *s.*, agricultura, cultura.
FAR-OFF, *adj.*, distante, afastado, longínquo.
FAR.THER, *adv.*, mais longe; *adj.*, mais afastado, mais distante.
FAR.THEST *adj.*, longíssimo, o mais distante.
FAS.CI.CLE, *s.*, fascículo.
FAS.CI.NATE, *v.*, fascinar, encantar.
FAS.CI.NA.TION, *s.*, fascinação, encanto.
FASH.ION, *s.*, maneira, moda, talhe, costume; *v.*, moldar, dar fórma.
FASH.ION.ABLE, *adj.*, próprio da moda, elegante.
FASH.ION.ER, *s.*, costureiro, modista, estilista.
FAST, *adj.*, rápido, permanente, firme; *s.*, jejum, abstinência; *v.*, jejuar.

FAST-FOOD, *s.*, comida pronta, comida pronta na hora.
FAS.TEN, *v.*, fixar, firmar, prender.
FAS.TEN.ER, *s.*, presilha, fecho, prendedor.
FAS.TID.I.OUS, *adj.*, fastidioso, enjoativo.
FAT, *adj.*, gordo, grande, grosso; *s.*, gordura, banha; *v.*, engordar.
FA.TAL, *adj.*, fatal, mortal, letal.
FA.TAL.ISM, *s.*, fatalismo.
FA.TAL.I.TY, *s.*, fatalidade, sorte, destino, desgraça, acidente fatal.
FATE, *s.*, sorte, destino, fado.
FAT.HEAD, *adj.*, tolo, bobo, imbecil.
FA.THER, *s.*, pai; *v.*, procriar.
FA.THER.HOOD, *s.*, paternidade.
FA.THER-IN-LAW, *s.*, sogro.
FA.THER.LAND, *s.*, pátria, terra de nascimento.
FA.THER.LESS, *s.*, órfão, órfão de pai.
FA.THER.LY, *adj.*, paternal, paterno.
FA.TID.IC, *adj.*, fatídico.
FA.TIGUE, *s.*, fadiga, cansaço, afã, trabalho.
FAT.NESS, *s.*, gordura, corpulência.
FAU.CET, *s.*, torneira.
FAULT, *s.*, culpa, defeito; *adj.*, culpado, defeituoso, errado, errôneo.
FAULT.I.NESS, *s.*, imperfeição, defeito.
FAULTY, *adj.*, defeituoso.
FAU.NA, *s.*, fauna.
FA.VOUR, *s.*, favor; *v.*, favorecer, auxiliar.
FA.VOUR.ABLE, *adj.*, favorável.
FA.VOUR.ITE, *s.*, favorito, predileto; *adj.*, predileto.
FA.VOUR.LESS, *adj.*, desprestigiado, desfavorecido.
FAWN.ER, *s.*, adulador, bajulador; puxa-saco.
FAWN.ING, *s.*, lisonja, adulação; *adj.*, adulador.
FAX, *s.*, fax, fac-símile; *v.*, remeter um fax.
FAY, *s.*, fada.
FEAR, *s.*, medo; *v.*, temer, ter medo.
FEAR.ING, *adj.*, receoso, temeroso; *s.*, receio, temor.
FEAR.LESS, *adj.*, sem medo, destemido.
FEA.SI.BIL.I.TY, *s.*, viabilidade.
FEA.SI.BLE, *adj.*, viável.

FEAST, s., festa, banquete, ágape; v., festejar, banquetear-se.
FEATH.ER, s., pena, pluma.
FEATH.ER.ING, s., plumagem.
FEA.TURE, s., feição, fisionomia, rosto, reportagem; v., caracterizar.
FEB.RI.FUGE, s., febrífugo, remédio para baixar a febre.
FE.BRILE, adj., febril.
FEB.RU.ARY, s., fevereiro.
FE.CAL, adj., fecal.
FE.CUND, adj., fecundo, fértil, produtivo.
FE.CUN.DATE, v., fecundar, fertilizar.
FE.CUN.DA.TION, s., fecundação, fertilização.
FED.ER.AL, adj., federal.
FED.ER.AL.ISM, s., federalismo.
FED.ER.A.TION, s., federação, confederação.
FEE, s., propriedade, honorários, propina, taxa; v., pagar, gratificar.
FEE.BLE, adj., fraco, débil, ineficaz.
FEE.BLE.NESS, s., fraqueza, debilidade.
FEED, s., alimento, alimentação, comida, refeição, v., alimentar.
FEED.BACK, s., realimentação, regeneração.
FEED.ING-BOT.TLE, s., mamadeira.
FEEL, s., tato, sensação, percepção; v., sentir, perceber, notar.
FEEL.ER, s., quem sente; antena de bicho.
FEEL.ING, s., sensação, sentimento, percepção.
FEET, s., pl., pés.
FEIGN, v., fingir.
FEIGN.ED.NESS, s., fingimento.
FEINT, s., finta, simulação.
FE.LIC.I.TATE, v., felicitar, dar parabéns.
FE.LIC.I.TA.TION, s., felicitação, parabéns, congratulação.
FE.LIC.I.TY, s., felicidade, ventura, contentamento.
FE.LINE, adj., s., felino.
FEL.LOW, s., companheiro, camarada, colega.
FEL.LOW-CIT.I.ZEN, s., concidadão.
FEL.LOW.SHIP, s., amizade, coleguismo, companheirismo.
FEL.ON, s., réu, criminoso, delinquente; adj., cruel, malvado.
FEL.O.NY, s., felonia, crime, delito.
FE.MALE, s., fêmea, mulher; adj., feminino, feminil.
FEM.I.NAL.I.TY, s., feminilidade.
FEM.I.NINE, adj., feminino.
FEM.I.NISM, s., feminismo.
FE.MUR, s., fêmur.
FEN, s., pântano, paul, charco, brejo.
FENCE, s., cerca, cercado, grade; v., cercar.
FENC.ING, s., esgrima.
FEN.NEL, s., funcho, erva-doce.
FEN.NY, adj., pantanoso.
FE.RAL, adj., feral, feroz, selvagem.
FE.RINE, adj., ferino, feroz, selvagem.
FER.MENT, s., fermento; v., fermentar.
FER.MEN.TA.TION, s., fermentação.
FERN, s., feto, samambaia.
FE.RO.CIOUS, adj., feroz.
FE.ROC.I.TY, s., ferocidade.
FER.RU.GI.NOUS, adj., ferruginoso.
FER.RY, s., balsa, ferribot, barco para travessias; v., transportar por barco.
FER.TILE, adj., fértil, fecundo, produtivo.
FER.TIL.I.TY, s., fertilidade.
FER.TIL.IZE, v., fertilizar.
FER.TIL.IZ.ER, s., adubo, fertilizante.
FER.VOUR, s., fervor.
FES.TAL, adj., festivo.
FES.TER, v., inflamar-se.
FES.TI.VAL, s., festival, festa.
FES.TIV.I.TY, s., festa, festividade.
FET.ID, adj., fétido, fedido.
FE.TISH, s., feitiço, fetiche.
FET.TER, s., ferros, grilhões, algemas; v., prender, algemar.
FEUD, s., disputa, contenda, rixa.
FEU.DAL.ISM, s., feudalismo.
FE.VER, s., febre; v., ter febre, causar febre.
FEW, adj., pron., poucos, poucas.
FEW.ER, adj., menos.
FEW.EST, adj., mínimo, a menor quantidade.
FI.AN.CÉ, s., noivo.
FI.AN.CÉE, s., noiva.
FI.AS.CO, s., fiasco.

FIB   353   **FISHERMAN**

FIB, *s.*, mentira, lorota, peta; *v.*, mentir.
FIB.BER, *s.*, mentiroso.
FI.BRE, *s.*, fibra.
FI.BRE.GLASS, *s.*, fibra de vidro.
FI.BROUS, *adj.*, fibroso.
FIC.TION, *s.*, ficção.
FIC.TION.AL, *adj.*, fictício.
FIC.TION.IST, *s.*, ficcionista.
FI.DEL.I.TY, *s.*, fidelidade.
FI.DU.CIAL, *adj.*, fiducial, confiado.
FIELD, *s.*, campo; área, especialidade.
FIELD.WORK, *s.*, trabalho de campo, lavoura.
FIEND, *s.*, demônio.
FIEND.ISH, *s.*, diabólico, demoníaco.
FIERCE, *adj.*, feroz, violento.
FIERCE.NESS, *s.*, ferocidade, crueldade, maldade, violência.
FIF.TEEN, *num.*, quinze.
FIF.TEENTH, *s.*, décimo quinto.
FIFTH, *num.*, quinto.
FIF.TY, *num.*, cinquenta.
FIG, *s.*, figo.
FIGHT, *s.*, batalha, luta, briga.
FIGHT.ER, *s.*, combatente.
FIGHT.ING, *s.*, luta, combate.
FIG.TREE, *s.*, figueira, planta que produz figo.
FIG.UR.ABLE, *adj.*, figurável.
FIG.U.RA.TION, *s.*, figuração.
FIG.URE, *s.*, figura, desenho, silhueta, forma.
FILCH, *v.*, surrupiar, furtar.
FILCH.ING, *s.*, furto, roubo.
FILE, *s.*, lixa, fio, arame, espeto; *v.*, lixar, arquivar, fichar.
FIL.ER, *s.*, limador.
FIL.IAL, *adj.*, filial.
FIL.I.GREE, *s.*, filigrana.
FILL, *s.*, suficiência, abastecimento; *v.*, encher, acumular, fartar.
FILL.ING, *s.*, recheio.
FILM, *s.*, filme, película, fita de cinema, véu; *v.*, filmar, velar.
FILMY, *adj.*, transparente.
FIL.TER, *s.*, filtro; *v.*, filtrar.
FIL.TER.ING, *s.*, filtragem.

FILTH, *s.*, sujidade, sujeira, imundície.
FILTH.I.NESS, *s.*, sujeira, imundície.
FILTHY, *adj.*, sujo, imundo.
FIL.TRATE, *v.*, filtrar; *s.*, líquido filtrado.
FIN, *s.*, nadadeira, barbatana, asa; *v.*, nadar com barbatana, mover as asas.
FI.NAL, *adj.*, final, último, definitivo.
FI.NAL.I.TY, *s.*, finalidade.
FI.NAL.IZE, *v.*, finalizar, completar, concluir.
FI.NANCE, *s.*, finanças, fundos; *v.*, financiar.
FI.NAN.CIAL, *adj.*, financeiro.
FIND, *v.*, encontrar, achar, descobrir.
FINE, *adj.*, fino, excelente, ótimo; *adv.*, muito bem.
FINE-LOOK.ING, *adj.*, atraente, fascinante, elegante.
FINE.NESS, *s.*, fineza, primor, maravilha.
FIN.GER, *s.*, dedo; *v.*, manusear, apalpar, tocar com os dedos.
FIN.GER.NAIL, *s.*, unha.
FI.NIS, *s.*, fim, termo.
FIN.ISH, *s.*, fim; *v.*, terminar, acabar, finalizar.
FIN.ISH.ING, *s.*, acabamento, conclusão.
FI.NITE, *adj.*, finito.
FIN.LAND, *s.*, Finlândia.
FINN, *s.*, finlandês.
FIORD, *s.*, fiorde.
FIRE, *s.*, fogo, incêndio; *v.*, disparar, atirar, estimular.
FIRE.MAN, *s.*, bombeiro.
FIRE.PLACE, *s.*, lareira.
FIRE.WOOD, *s.*, lenha.
FIRE.WORKS, *s.*, fogos de artifício.
FIRM, *s.*, firma, empresa; *adj.*, firme; *v.*, firmar.
FIR.MA.MENT, *s.*, firmamento, céu.
FIRM.NESS, *s.*, firmeza.
FIRST, *adj.*, primeiro; *adv.*, primeiramente; *s.*, primeira marcha de carro.
FIRST-CLASS, *adj.*, de primeira classe.
FIRST-HAND, *adv.*, em primeira mão.
FIS.CAL, *adj.*, fiscal.
FISH, *s.*, peixe; *v.*, pescar.
FISH.ER, *s.*, pescador.
FISH.ER.MAN, *s.*, pescador.

FISHERY 354 **FLINTSTONE**

FISH.ERY, s., indústria de pesca.
FISH.ING, s., pesca.
FIS.SURE, s., fissura, fenda.
FIST, s., punho.
FIS.TU.LA, s., fístula.
FIT, s., ajuste, ajustamento; adj., bom, próprio, apto; v., assentar, ajustar.
FIT.MENT, s., móvel.
FIT.NESS, s., boa saúde, boa forma.
FIVE, num., cinco.
FIVE.FOLD, adj., quíntuplo.
FIX, v., fixar, pregar, grudar, preparar.
FIX.ABLE, adj., fixável.
FIX.A.TION, s., fixação.
FIX.ER, s., fixador.
FIX.I.TY, s., fixidez, estabilidade.
FIZZ, v., assobiar, zunir.
FIZZ.ER, s., assobiador.
FIZ.ZLE, s., efervescência, assobio, crepitação; v., sibilar, assobiar.
FIZZY, adj., gasoso, com gás.
FLAB.BY, adj., flácido.
FLAC.CID.I.TY, s., flacidez, moleza.
FLAG.EL.LATE, v., flagelar, açoitar, surrar.
FLAG.EL.LA.TION, s., flagelação, flagelo, açoitamento.
FLA.GI.TIOUS, adj., mau, perverso, ruim, malvado.
FLA.GI.TIOUS.NESS, s., perversidade, maldade.
FLA.GRAN.CY, s., flagrante, imprevisto.
FLA.GRANT, adj., flagrante, evidente, claro.
FLAIR, s., talento, capacidade, tirocínio, habilidade.
FLAM, s., mentira, engano, logro.
FLAME, s., chama; v., inflamar, arder.
FLAM.ING, adj., inflamado, cheio de chamas.
FLAN, s., torta, bolo.
FLANK, s., flanco; v., flanquear, ladear.
FLAN.NEL, s., toalha de rosto, flanela.
FLAP, s., aba, dobra; v., oscilar, bater, ondular.
FLAR.ING, adj., brilhante.
FLASH, s., brilho, clarão, furo de reportagem; v., brilhar, cintilar.
FLASH.BACK, s., recuo no tempo, volta, retorno.

FLASH.LIGHT, s., lanterna de bolso.
FLAT, s., superfície plana, planície, pântano; adj., plano, vazio, liso.
FLAT.NESS, s., lisura, planura.
FLAT.TEN, v., aplainar, arrasar, alisar.
FLAT.TER, v., lisonjear.
FLAT.TER.ER, s., lisonjeiro, bajulador.
FLAT.TER.ING, adj., lisonjeiro, favorável, favorecedor.
FLAT.TERY, s., bajulação, adulação.
FLAUNT, v., ostentar, mostrar.
FLA.VOR.OUS, adj., saboroso.
FLA.VOUR, s., sabor; v., condimentar, temperar.
FLA.VOUR.ING, s., tempero, condimento.
FLA.VOUR.LESS, adj., insípido, sem sabor.
FLAW, s., defeito, falha; v., quebrar, inutilizar, fender.
FLAWY, adj., imperfeito, defeituoso, manchado.
FLAX, s., linho.
FLAY, v., esfolar, tirar a pele, despir.
FLEA, s., pulga.
FLEE, v., fugir, escapar.
FLEECE, s., velo, tosão, lã; v., tosquiar, tosar, espoliar.
FLEER.ING, s., zombaria, escárnio; v., escarnecer, zombar.
FLEET, s., frota, esquadra.
FLEET.ING, adj., passageiro, transitório.
FLEM.ING, s., flamingo.
FLESH, s., carne, gordura, robustez; v., descarnar, alimentar com carne.
FLESH.I.NESS, s., gordura, corpulência.
FLEX.I.BIL.I.TY, s., flexibilidade.
FLEX.I.BLE, adj., flexível.
FLEX.ION, s., flexão.
FLICK, s., pancada leve, chicotada, piparote.
FLICK.ER, v., tremular, vacilar, bruxulear; s., vacilação, centelha.
FLI.ER, s., aviador.
FLIGHT, s., voo, fuga, lance de escada.
FLINCH.ING, s., vacilante, hesitante, trêmulo.
FLIN.DERS, s., fragmentos.
FLINT.I.NESS, s., dureza, insensibilidade.
FLINT.STONE, s., pederneira.

FLIP, *s.*, sacudida, estalido; *v.*, sacudir, mover bruscamente.
FLIP.PER, *s.*, barbatana.
FLIRT, *v.*, namorar, namoricar, flertar; *s.*, namoradinho.
FLIR.TA.TION, *s.*, namoro, namorisco.
FLIT, *v.*, esvoaçar.
FLIT.TER, *v.*, esvoaçar, voejar, voar.
FLIT.TING, *s.*, voo rápido.
FLOAT, *s.*, boia, caixa; *v.*, flutuar, boiar.
FLOAT.AGE, *s.*, flutuação.
FLOAT.ING, *adj.*, flutuante, móvel.
FLOCK, *s.*, rebanho, bando.
FLOG, *v.*, açoitar.
FLOOD, *s.*, enchente, inundação, enxurrada; *v.*, inundar, alagar.
FLOOD.ING, *s.*, inundação, alagamento.
FLOOR, *s.*, chão, piso, andar, assoalho; *v.*, assoalhar, pavimentar.
FLOOR.ER, *s.*, muro.
FLOOR.ING, *s.*, chão, assoalho.
FLOP, *s.*, fracasso; *v.*, fracassar.
FLO.RA, *s.*, flora.
FLO.RES.CENCE, *s.*, florescência.
FLO.RES.CENT, *adj.*, florescente.
FLO.RI.CUL.TURE, *s.*, floricultura.
FLOR.ID, *adj.*, florido.
FLOR.IST, *s.*, florista.
FLOUR, *s.*, farinha; *v.*, enfarinhar, moer.
FLOUR.ISH, *v.*, florescer; menear.
FLOURY, *adj.*, farinhento, farinhoso.
FLOW, *s.*, fluxo, circulação; *v.*, circular, correr, ondular.
FLOW.ER, *s.*, flor, escol, elite, *v.*, florescer, florir.
FLOW.ER.LESS, *adj.*, sem flores.
FLOW.ER.POT, *s.*, vaso.
FLU, *s.*, gripe.
FLUC.TU.ATE, *v.*, flutuar.
FLUC.TU.A.TION, *s.*, flutuação, vacilação.
FLU.EN.CY, *s.*, fluência.
FLU.ENT, *adj.*, fluente, eloquente.
FLUFFY, *adj.*, macio, fofo.
FLU.ID, *adj.*, *s.*, fluido.
FLU.ID.I.TY, *s.*, fluidez.

FLUMP, *v.*, jogar-se ao chão, arremessar; *s.*, estrondo.
FLUN.KEY, *s.*, lacaio, serviçal.
FLU.OR, *s.*, flúor.
FLUR.RY, *s.*, lufada; atividade, animação.
FLUSH, *s.*, rubor, brilho; *v.*, ruborizar-se.
FLUSH.ING, *s.*, rubor.
FLUT.TER, *s.*, agitação, o bater de asas; *v.*, esvoaçar, voejar.
FLU.VI.AL, *adj.*, fluvial.
FLUX, *s.*, fluxo.
FLY, *s.*, mosca; *v.*, pilotar avião, levar no avião, viajar de avião, voar.
FLY IN, *v.*, chegar ou vir de avião.
FLY.ING, *s.*, aviação.
FO.CAL, *adj.*, focal.
FO.CAL.ISE, *v.*, focar, enfocar, focalizar.
FOD.DER, *s.*, forragem; *v.*, alimentar o gado com forragem.
FOE, *s.*, inimigo.
FOE.TAL, *adj.*, fetal.
FOE.TID, *adj.*, fétido.
FOE.TUS, *s.*, feto.
FOG, *s.*, nevoeiro, cerração; *v.*, enevoar-se.
FOG.GI.NESS, *s.*, nebulosidade.
FOG.GY, *adj.*, enevoado.
FOI.BLE, *adj.*, fraco, frágil.
FOIL, *v.*, frustrar.
FOIST, *v.*, impingir.
FOLD, *s.*, dobra, prega, ruga; curral; *v.*, dobrar, enrugar, vincar.
FOLD.ER, *s.* pasta para papéis.
FOLD.ING, *adj.*, dobrável.
FO.LIAGE, *s.*, folhagem.
FO.LI.ATE, *adj.*, próprio de folhagem; *v.*, enfeitar com folhagens.
FOLK, *s.*, gente, povo; *adj.*, popular; familiares, parentes, pais.
FOLK.LORE, *s.*, folclore.
FOL.LOW, *v.*, seguir, acompanhar.
FOL.LOW.ER, *s.*, seguidor, sequaz.
FOL.LOW.ING, *adj.*, *s.*, seguinte, adepto, seguidor.
FOL.LY, *s.*, loucura, desvario.
FON.DLE, *v.*, acariciar, afagar.

FON.DLING, *s.*, carinho, afago.
FOND.NESS, *s.*, carinho, afago, ternura, carícia.
FOOD, *s.*, comida, alimento.
FOOD.STUFFS, *s.*, gêneros alimentícios, comida.
FOOL, *adj.*, tolo, imbecil; *v.*, enganar, lograr.
FOOL.ERY, *s.*, loucura, imbecilidade, tolice, desvario.
FOOL.ISH, *adj.*, tolo, bobo, imbecil.
FOOL.ISH.NESS, *s.*, tolice, loucura.
FOOT, *s.*, pé, pata, medida de 304mm.
FOOT.BALL, *s.*, futebol.
FOOT.BRIDGE, *s.*, passarela.
FOOT.GEAR, *s.*, calçado.
FOOT.ING, *s.*, posição; giro, andada.
FOOT.MAN, *s.*, lacaio, serviçal.
FOOT.PATH, *s.*, caminho, atalho, desvio.
FOOT.PRINT, *s.*, pegada, indício.
FOP.PISH, *adj.*, afetado, ridículo.
FOR, *prep.*, para, por, por causa de, apesar de.
FOR.AGE, *s.*, forragem.
FOR.AY, *s.*, incursão, pilhagem; *v.*, saquear, pilhar.
FOR.BEAR, *v.*, não querer, reprimir, abster-se.
FOR.BEAR.ING, *adj.*, controlado, paciente.
FORCE, *s.*, força; *v.*, forçar.
FORCED, *adj.*, forçado.
FORCED.NESS, *s.*, constrangimento, coação.
FORCE.FUL, *adj.*, rigoroso, enérgico, forte.
FOR.CEPS, *s.*, fórceps.
FORC.IBLE.NESS, *s.*, força.
FORD, *s.*, vau; *v.*, passar a vau, atravessar um rio a pé.
FORE.ARM, *s.*, antebraço.
FORE.BODE, *v.*, pressagiar, prognosticar, vaticinar.
FORE.BOD.ING, *s.*, mau presságio.
FORE.CAST, *s.*, prenúncio de chuva, previsão meteorológica.
FORE.COURT, *s.*, estacionamento, área de estacionamento.
FORE.DATE, *v.*, antedatar.
FORE.FATHERS, *s.*, antepassados, ascendentes.
FORE.FIN.GER, *s.*, dedo indicador.
FORE.FOOT, *s.*, pata dianteira de um quadrúpede.
FORE.GROUND, *s.*, primeiro plano.
FORE.HEAD, *s.*, testa.
FOR.EIGN, *adj.*, estrangeiro, exterior, estranho.
FOR.EIGN.ER, *s.*, estrangeiro, forasteiro.
FORE.JUDGE, *v.*, prejulgar, julgar antecipadamente.
FORE.KNOWL.EDGE, *s.*, previsão.
FORE.LAND, *s.*, cabo, promontório.
FORE.MAN, *s.*, capataz, mestre, chefe.
FORE.NOON, *s.*, manhã.
FORE.PART, *s.*, parte dianteira.
FORE.SAID, *adj.*, supra referido.
FORE.SEE.ABLE, *adj.*, previsível.
FORE.SHAD.OW, *v.*, prenunciar.
FORE.SIGHT, *s.*, previdência.
FORE.SKIN, *s.*, prepúcio.
FOR.EST, *s.*, floresta; *v.*, arborizar.
FOR.EST.ER, *s.*, guarda-florestal.
FORE.TELL.ER, *s.*, profeta.
FORE.TO.KEN, *s.*, prenúncio; *v.*, prenunciar.
FOR.EV.ER, *adj.*, para sempre.
FORE.WARN, *v.*, prevenir, acautelar.
FORE.WARD, *s.*, prefácio.
FOR.FEIT, *s.*, falta, omissão, crime; *v.*, perder, ser confiscado de.
FOR.FEIT.ABLE, *adj.*, confiscável.
FOR.FEI.TURE, *s.*, multa, confisco.
FOR.GATH.ER, *v.*, reunir-se, juntar-se, associar-se.
FORGE, *s.*, forja; *v.*, falsificar, adulterar.
FORG.ER, *s.*, falsificador.
FOR.GET, *v.*, esquecer, olvidar.
FOR.GET.FUL, *adj.*, esquecido.
FOR.GET.FUL.NESS, *s.*, esquecimento.
FOR.GIVE, *v.*, perdoar, escusar, desculpar.
FOR.GIVE.NESS, *s.*, desculpa, perdão.
FOR.GIV.ING, *adj.*, indulgente, bondoso, generoso.
FORK, *s.*, garfo, bifurcação; *v.*, bifurcar-se.
FORK.ED.NESS, *s.*, bifurcação, encruzilhada.
FORKY, *adj.*, bifurcado.
FORM, *s.*, forma, tipo, formulário; *v.*, formar, criar, formular.

FORMAL / **FRATERNAL**

FOR.MAL, *adj.*, formal, oficial, cerimonioso.
FOR.MAL.ISM, *s.*, formalismo.
FOR.MAL.I.TIES, *s.*, formalidades.
FOR.MAL.I.TY, *s.*, formalidade, formalismo.
FOR.MAL.IZE, *v.*, formalizar.
FOR.MAT, *s.*, formato; *v.*, formatar.
FOR.MA.TION, *s.*, formação.
FOR.MENT, *v.*, fomentar, promover, estimular.
FOR.MENT.A.TION, *s.*, fomento, estímulo, incentivo.
FOR.MENT.ER, *s.*, fomentador, incentivador.
FOR.MER, *adj.*, antigo, velho, anterior; *s.*, formador, autor, criador.
FOR.MIC.ANT, *adj.*, formigante.
FOR.MI.DA.BLE, *adj.*, terrível, atemorizante.
FOR.MU.LARY, *s.*, formulário; *adj.*, próprio de fórmula.
FOR.MU.LATE, *v.*, formular.
FOR.NI.CATE, *v.*, fornicar.
FOR.NI.CA.TION, *s.*, fornicação.
FOR.SAKE, *v.*, abandonar.
FOR.SAK.EN, *s.*, abandonado, desamparado.
FOR.SWEAR, *v.*, abjurar, repudiar, negar, renegar.
FORT, *s.*, forte.
FORTH.COM.ING, *adj.*, próximo, vizinho, disponível.
FORTH.RIGHT, *adj.*, franco.
FORTH.WITH, *adv.*, em seguida, a seguir.
FOR.TI.FI.CA.TION, *s.*, fortificação.
FOR.TI.FY, *v.*, fortificar, fortalecer.
FOR.TI.TUDE, *s.*, fortaleza, força.
FORT.NIGHT, *s.*, quinzena, 15 dias.
FOR.TRESS, *s.*, fortaleza.
FOR.TU.ITOUS, *adj.*, fortuito, casual, imprevisto.
FOR.TU.ITY, *s.*, casualidade.
FOR.TU.NATE, *adj.*, afortunado, feliz, com sorte.
FOR.TU.NATE.NESS, *s.*, felicidade, bom êxito.
FOR.TUNE, *s.*, fortuna, sorte, ventura.
FOR.TY, *num.*, quarenta.
FOR.WARD, *adj.*, para a frente, adiantado, futuro; atacante no jogo; *v.*, expedir, remeter.
FOR.WARD.ER, *s.*, expedidor.
FOR.WARD.ING, *s.*, expedição, remessa, despacho.
FOSS, *s.*, fosso.
FOS.SIL, *s.*, fóssil.
FOS.SIL.IZE, *v.*, fossilizar.
FOS.TER.ING, *adj.*, benéfico; *s.*, amparo, benefício.
FOUL, *adj.*, horrível, obsceno; *s.*, falta; *v.*, sujar, emporcalhar.
FOUND, *v.*, fundar, fundir.
FOUN.DA.TION, *s.*, fundação, base.
FOUN.DER, *s.*, fundador; *v.*, naufragar.
FOUND.ING, *s.*, fundição.
FOUND.RY, *s.*, fundição.
FOUN.TAIN, *s.*, chafariz, fonte.
FOUR, *num.*, quatro.
FOUR.FOLD, *adj.*, quádruplo.
FOUR.TEEN, *num.*, quatorze, catorze.
FOUR.TEENTH, *num.*, décimo quarto.
FOURTH, *num., adj.*, quarto.
FOWL, *s.*, ave de criação; *v.*, caçar aves selvagens.
FOWL.ER, *s.*, criador de aves.
FOX, *s.*, raposa.
FOX.I.NESS, *s.*, astúcia, esperteza.
FOXY, *adj.*, astuto, esperto.
FRAC.TION, *s.*, fração, fragmento, parte.
FRAC.TION.AL, *adj.*, fracionário.
FRAC.TURE, *s.*, fratura.
FRAG.ILE, *adj.*, frágil.
FRAG.ILE.NESS, *s.*, fragilidade.
FRA.GIL.I.TY, *s.*, fragilidade.
FRAG.MENT, *s.*, fragmento.
FRA.GRANCE, *s.*, fragrância, aroma, perfume.
FRA.GRANT, *adj.*, fragrante, perfumado, aromatizado.
FRANCE, *s.*, França.
FRAN.CHISE, *s.*, franquia, concessão; direito de voto.
FRAN.CHISE.MENT, *s.*, isenção, concessão, privilégio.
FRAN.CIS.CAN, *adj., s.*, franciscano.
FRANK, *adj.*, franco; *v.*, franquear.
FRANK.LY, *adv.*, francamente, abertamente.
FRANK.NESS, *s.*, franqueza, sinceridade.
FRA.TER.NAL, *adj.*, fraternal, fraterno.

FRA.TER.NI.TY, *s.*, fraternidade, irmandade.
FRAT.ER.NIZE, *v.*, fraternizar, confraternizar.
FRAT.RI.CIDE, *s.*, fratricídio.
FRAUD, *s.*, fraude, engano; impostor.
FRAUD.U.LENT, *adj.*, fraudulento.
FRAY, *s.*, guerra.
FREAK.ISH, *adj.*, excêntrico, exótico.
FRECK.LY, *adj.*, sardento.
FREE, *adj.*, livre, desocupado, grátis, gratuito; *v.*, libertar, soltar.
FREE.BOO.TER, *s.*, pirata.
FREE.BOOT.ING, *s.*, saque, pilhagem.
FREE.DOM, *s.*, liberdade.
FREE.GIFT, *s.*, brinde.
FREE.LANCE, *adj.*, autônomo.
FREE.MAN, *s.*, liberto, cidadão.
FREE.THINK.ER, *s.*, livre-pensador.
FREEZE, *v.*, gelar, congelar; *s.*, geada, congelamento.
FREEZ.ER, *s.*, congelador, frizer.
FREEZ.ING, *adj.*, glacial, gelado.
FREIGHT, *s.*, carga, frete.
FREIGHT.AGE, *s.*, frete, fretagem.
FRENCH, *adj., s.*, francês, franco, gaulês.
FRENCH.IFY, *v.*, afrancesar.
FRE.NET.IC, *adj.*, frenético.
FREN.ZY, *s.*, frenesi, furor.
FRE.QUENCE, *s.*, frequência.
FRE.QUENT, *adj.*, frequente.
FRE.QUENT.ER, *s.*, frequentador.
FRESH, *adj.*, fresco, novo, recente.
FRESH.ET, *s.*, inundação, alagamento, cheia.
FRESH.MAN, *s.*, calouro, novato.
FRET, *v.*, afligir, afligir-se, irritar; *s.*, irritação, raiva.
FRET.FUL, *adj.*, irritado, aborrecido, incomodado.
FRIAR, *s.*, frade, frei.
FRI.ARY, *s.*, convento de frades.
FRIC.AS.SEE, *s.*, fricassê; *v.*, preparar um fricassê.
FRIC.TION, *s.*, fricção, atrito.
FRI.DAY, *s.*, sexta-feira.
FRIDGE, *s.*, abr. de **REFRIGERATOR**.
FRIEND, *s.*, amigo.
FRIEND.LI.NESS, *s.*, amizade.
FRIEND.LY, *adj.*, simpático, amistoso, amigável.
FRIEND.SHIP, *s.*, amizade.
FRIEZE, *s.*, friso.
FRIGHT, *s.*, temor, pavor, terror; *v.*, assustar, apavorar.
FRIGHT.EN, *v.*, assustar.
FRIGHT.FUL, *adj.*, terrível, pavoroso, horrível.
FRIG.ID, *adj.*, frígido, frio.
FRI.GID.I.TY, *s.*, frigidez.
FRINGE, *s.*, franja, orla, borda, margem; *v.*, franjar, orlar.
FRISK, *s.*, salto, pulo, brincadeira, cambalhota; *v.*, brincar, saltar, dançar.
FRISK.I.NESS, *s.*, alegria, vivacidade, contentamento.
FRISKY, *adj.*, alegre, animado.
FRIT.TER, *s.*, pedaço, fragmento, bolinho de carne; *v.*, fragmentar, gastar.
FRI.VOL.I.TY, *s.*, frivolidade, bagatela.
FRIV.O.LOUS, *adj.*, frívolo, fútil.
FRIZZY, *adj.*, crespo, frisado, encrespado.
FRO, *adv.*, de, atrás, para trás.
FROCK, *s.*, vestido, saia, roupa.
FROG, *s.*, rã.
FROG.MAN, *s.*, homem-rã.
FROL.IC, *v.*, brincar, folgar, gracejar; *s.*, brincadeira, alegria, travessura.
FROM, *prep.*, de, da parte, a partir de, desde, da parte de.
FROND, *s.*, fronde, copa de árvore.
FRONT, *s.*, fronte, dianteira, fachada, frente; *v.*, olhar de frente.
FRONT.AL, *adj.*, frontal, fronteiro.
FRON.TIS.PIECE, *s.*, frontispício, fachada, frente.
FROST, *s.*, gelo, geada; *v.*, gelar, congelar.
FROST.I.NESS, *s.*, frio excessivo.
FROSTY, *adj.*, coberto de gelo, gelado, glacial.
FROTH, *s.*, espuma; *v.*, espumar.
FRO.WARD, *adj.*, insubmisso, teimoso.
FROWST, *s.*, cheiro de mofo.
FROWS.TY, *adj.*, mofento.
FRUC.TIF.ER.OUS, *adj.*, frutífero.

FRUC.TI.FI.CA.TION, s., frutificação.
FRUC.TI.FY, v., frutificar.
FRU.GAL, adj., frugal.
FRU.GAL.I.TY, s., frugalidade.
FRUIT, s., fruta, fruto; v., frutificar.
FRUIT.FUL, adj., frutuoso, fértil, proveitoso.
FRUIT.FUL.NESS, s., fertilidade, fecundidade.
FRUMP.ISH, adj., desleixado.
FRUS.TRATE, v., frustrar.
FRUS.TRA.TION, s., frustração.
FRY, v., fritar; s., fritada.
FU.EL, s., combustível; v., fornecer combustível.
FUG, s., mofo, cheiro de mofo.
FU.GA.CIOUS, adj., fugaz, transitório, efêmero.
FU.GAC.I.TY, s., fugacidade.
FU.GI.TIVE, s., fugitivo.
FUL.CRUM, s., apoio, fulcro, base, sustentáculo.
FUL.FIL, v., cumprir, realizar, satisfazer, completar.
FUL.FILL.MENT, s., realização, satisfação.
FUL.GU.RATE, v., fulgurar, brilhar, resplandecer.
FULL, adj., cheio, completo, folgado; v., complementar, totalizar.
FULL-TIME, adj., de tempo integral.
FUL.MI.NANT, adj., fulminante.
FUL.NESS, s., plenitude, força.
FUL.VOUS, adj., s., fulvo, louro.
FUME, v., fumegar.
FU.MI.GATE, v., defumar.
FUMY, adj., cheio de fumaça, fumegante.
FUN, s., brincadeira, graça, gracejo; v., brincar, divertir-se, gracejar.
FUNC.TION, s., função, exercício, uso; v., funcionar, trabalhar.
FUNC.TION.AL, adj., funcional, prático.
FUNC.TION.ARY, s., funcionário.
FUND, s., fundo, fonte; pl., fundos.
FUND.ED, adj., consolidado, fundado, baseado.
FU.NER.AL, s., funeral, sepultamento.
FUN.FAIR, s., parque de diversões.
FUN.GOUS, adj., fungoso.

FUN.GUS, s., fungo; bolor, mofo.
FUNK, s., medo, embaraço, temor; tipo de música; v., fugir, intimidar.
FUNK.I.NESS, s., medo, pavor, timidez.
FUN.NY, adj., engraçado, divertido, estranho, diferente.
FUR, s., pele de animal, crosta; v., forrar com peles, formar crosta.
FUR.BISH, v., polir, limpar.
FUR.CATE, v., bifurcar; adj., bifurcado.
FU.RI.OUS, adj., furioso.
FU.RI.OUS.NESS, s., fúria, raiva, ira, furor.
FUR.LOUGH, s., licença.
FUR.NACE, s., forno, fornalha.
FUR.NISH, v., fornecer, prover, sortir, equipar, aparelhar.
FUR.NI.TURE, s., mobília, móveis, acessórios.
FUR.RY, adj., peludo.
FUR.THER, adj., novo, adicional; adv., mais longe, mais; v., promover.
FUR.THER.ANCE, s., adiantamento.
FUR.THEST, adj., adv., o mais distante.
FUR.TIVE, adj., furtivo.
FU.RUN.CLE, s., furúnculo.
FU.RY, s., fúria, ira.
FUSE, s., fusível, espoleta; v., fundir, fundir-se.
FU.SE.LAGE, s., fuselagem.
FUS.IBLE, adj., fusível.
FU.SIL.IER, s., fuzileiro.
FU.SION, s., fusão.
FUSS, s., barulho, escândalo.
FUSSY, adj., exigente, complicado.
FUS.TI.GATE, v., fustigar, açoitar.
FUS.TI.GA.TION, s., fustigação.
FUS.TY, adj., bolorento, mofado.
FU.TILE, adj., fútil, inútil.
FU.TILE.NESS, s., futilidade.
FU.TIL.I.TY, s., futilidade.
FU.TURE, adj., s., futuro.
FU.TU.RI.TY, s., futuro, futuridade.
FUZZ, s., flocos, partículas finas; penugem.

G

G, *s.*, sétima letra do alfabeto inglês; sol *(mús.)*; grama.
GAB, *s.*, conversa, colóquio; *v.*, palrar, conversar, tagarelar.
GAB.AR.DINE, *s.*, gabardina.
GAB.BLE, *s.*, conversa, tagarelice, palavrório; *v.*, tagarelar, falar.
GA.BY, *s.*, simplório, tolo, ingênuo.
GAD, *s.*, talhadeira, estilete; *v.*, vaguear.
GAD.ABOUT, *s.*, vagabundo.
GAD.GET, *s.*, coisa, aparelho, engenhoca, insignificância.
GAG, *s.*, mordaça, impedimento, brincadeira; amordaçar, silenciar.
GAGE, *s.*, penhor, fiança, desafio; *v.*, caucionar, dar em penhor.
GAIN, *s.*, ganho, lucro, benefício, salário, vantagem; *v.*, ganhar, lucrar.
GAIN.ABLE, *adj.*, ganhável, lucrável.
GAIN.ER, *s.*, beneficiário, ganhador.
GAIN.ING, *s.*, lucro.
GAIN.SAY, *v.*, contradizer, negar.
GAIT, *s.*, modo de andar.
GA.LA, *s.*, festa, gala.
GA.LAC.TIC, *adj.*, galáctico.
GALE, *s.*, ventania, vento.
GAL.I.LE.AN, *adj., s.*, galileu.
GALL, *s.*, fel, bilis, amargor; ódio; *v.*, mortificar.
GAL.LANT, *adj., s.*, galante, cortês, namorador; *v.*, namorar, galantear.
GAL.LERY, *s.*, galeria; galeria de artes.
GAL.LIC, *adj., s.*, gaulês.
GAL.LI.CISM, *s.*, galicismo.
GAL.LI.NA.CEOUS, *adj.*, galináceo.
GAL.LON, *s.*, galão.
GAL.LOP, *s.*, galope; *v.*, galopar.
GAL.LOWS, *s.*, forca.
GA.LOSH, *s.*, galocha.
GAL.VAN.IC, *adj.*, galvânico.
GAL.VA.NIZE, *v.*, galvanizar.
GAN.GRENE, *v.*, gangrenar; *s.*, gangrena.
GANG.STER, *s.*, gângster, bandido, criminoso.
GANG.WAY, *s.*, corredor em cinema e ônibus.
GAP, *s.*, fenda, racha, buraco, hiato; *v.*, fender, abrir.
GAPE, *v.*, ficar boquiaberto, ficar de boca aberta.
GA.RAGE, *s.*, garagem, oficina de carros.
GARB, *s.*, garbo, elegância, vestuário; *v.*, vestir.
GAR.BAGE, *s.*, lixo.
GAR.BOIL, *s.*, desordem, tumulto.
GAR.DEN, *s.*, jardim, jardim público, parque urbano.
GAR.DEN.ER, *s.*, jardineiro.
GAR.DEN.ING, *s.*, jardinagem.
GAR.GLE, *v.*, gargarejar; *s.*, gargarejo.
GAR.GLING, *s.*, gargarejo.
GAR.ISH, *adj.*, de cor forte, vivo, luminoso.
GAR.LAND, *s.*, coroa, grinalda; *v.*, engrinaldar.
GAR.LIC, *s.*, alho.
GAR.LICHY, *adj.*, com alho, com cheiro de alho.
GAR.NER, *s.*, celeiro, paiol; *v.*, enceleirar, colocar em celeiro.
GAR.NI.TURE, *s.*, guarnição, enfeite.
GAR.RET, *s.*, sótão.
GAR.RU.LOUS, *s.*, palrador, tagarela.
GAR.TER, *s.*, liga; *v.*, prender com liga.
GARTH, *s.*, pátio interno, jardim.
GAS, *s.*, gás, gasolina; *v.*, sufocar com gás.
GAS.ELIER, *s.*, lampião a gás, fogareiro a gás.
GAS.EOUS, *adj.*, gasoso.
GASH, *s.*, talha, corte, facada; *v.*, cortar, talhar.
GAS.I.FI.CA.TION, *s.*, gaseificação.
GAS.I.FY, *s.*, gaseificar.
GAS.O.GENE, *s.*, gasogênio.
GAS.O.LINE, *s.*, gasolina.

GAS.OM.E.TER, *s.*, gasômetro.
GAS.SI.NESS, *s.*, vaidade, presunção, loquacidade.
GAS.SY, *adj.*, gasoso, cheio de gás.
GAS.TRIC, *adj.*, gástrico.
GAS.TRI.TIS, *s.*, gastrite.
GAS.TRO.NOM.IC, *adj.*, gastronômico.
GAS.TRON.O.MY, *s.*, gastronomia.
GAS.WORKS, *s.*, refinaria de gás.
GATE, *s.*, portão; *v.*, fechar o portão.
GATE.WAY, *s.*, passagem, passadiço, portão.
GATH.ER, *v.*, colher flores, apanhar flores.
GATH.ER.ER, *s.*, coletor, cobrador.
GATH.ER.ING, *s.*, reunião, encontro, assembleia.
GAUCHE, *adj.*, inábil, desajeitado, canhestro.
GAU.DY, *adj.*, apelativo, chamativo.
GAUG.ER, *s.*, medidor, aferidor.
GAUG.ING, *s.*, medida.
GAUL.ISH, *adj.*, *s.*, gaulês, francês.
GAUZE, *s.*, gaze.
GAUZY, *adj.*, próprio de gaze, referente a gaze.
GAV.EL, *s.*, martelo; *v.*, dividir.
GAWKY, *adj.*, tolo, bobo, inábil.
GAY, *adj.*, homossexual, aparatoso.
GAY.NESS, *s.*, jovialidade; homossexualidade.
GAZE, *v.*, olhar fixamente, fixar, mirar, observar.
GA.ZE.BO, *s.*, varanda, terraço, belvedere.
GA.ZELLE, *s.*, gazela.
GAZ.ET.TEER, *s.*, dicionário geográfico.
GEAR, *s.*, equipamento, engrenagem, marcha de carro.
GEAR.BOX, *s.*, caixa de marcha.
GEAR.ING, *s.*, engrenagem, encaixe.
GEE, *interj.*, credo!, ora bolas!
GEESE, *s.*, *pl.*, gansos.
GEI.SHA, *s.*, gueixa.
GEL.A.TINE, *s.*, gelatina.
GE.LAT.I.NOUS, *adj.*, gelatinoso.
GELD, *v.*, castrar, capar; *adj.*, castrado, eunuco, mutilado.
GELD.ING, *s.*, animal capado; castração.
GEL.ID, *adj.*, gélido, gelado.
GE.LID.NESS, *s.*, friagem, frialdade, frio.
GEM, *s.*, gema, joia; *v.*, cobrir com joias, enfeitar com joias.
GEM.I.NATE, *adj.*, geminado, duplo, unido; *v.*, geminar.
GEM.I.NA.TION, *s.*, geminação.
GEN.DER, *s.*, gênero; *v.*, gerar, engendrar.
GENE, *s.*, gene.
GEN.ER.AL, *s.*, general; *adj.*, geral.
GEN.ER.AL.I.TY, *s.*, generalidade.
GEN.ER.AL.IZ.ABLE, *adj.*, generalizável.
GEN.ER.AL.IZE, *v.*, generalizar.
GEN.ER.AL.SHIP, *s.*, generalato.
GEN.ER.ATE, *v.*, gerar, produzir, procriar, engendrar.
GEN.ER.A.TION, *s.*, geração.
GEN.ER.A.TOR, *s.*, gerador.
GE.NER.IC, *adj.*, genérico.
GEN.ER.OS.I.TY, *s.*, generosidade.
GEN.ER.OUS, *adj.*, generoso, magnânimo.
GEN.ER.OUS.NESS, *s.*, generosidade.
GEN.E.SIS, *s.*, gênese, origem, gênesis, começo, alfa.
GE.NET.IC, *adj.*, genético.
GE.NET.ICS, *s.*, genética.
GE.NIAL, *adj.*, simpático, cordial, alegre, comunicativo.
GE.NIAL.I.TY, *s.*, cordialidade, alegria, simpatia, comunicabilidade.
GE.NIE, *s.*, gênio, espírito, fantasma.
GEN.I.TAL, *adj.*, genital, sexual.
GE.NIUS, *s.*, gênio.
GENO.CIDE, *s.*, genocídio.
GEN.TILE, *adj.*, *s.*, gentio, pagão.
GEN.TLE, *s.*, pessoa de boa família; *adj.*, educado, gentil, suave.
GEN.TLE.MAN, *s.*, senhor, cavalheiro, nobre, pessoa educada.
GEN.TLE.NESS, *s.*, doçura, suavidade, gentileza.
GEN.TLE.WOM.AN, *s.*, senhora, dama.
GEN.U.FLECT, *v.*, ajoelhar, genuflectir.
GEN.U.FLEC.TION, *s.*, genuflexão.
GEN.U.INE, *adj.*, genuíno, legítimo, autêntico.
GEN.U.INE.NESS, *s.*, genuinidade, legitimidade.
GE.NUS, *s.*, gênero.
GE.OD.E.SY, *s.*, geodesia.

GE.OG.RA.PHER, s. geógrafo.
GEO.GRAPH.IC, adj., geográfico.
GE.OG.RA.PHY, s., geografia.
GEO.LOG.IC, adj., geológico.
GE.OL.O.GIST, s., geólogo.
GE.OL.O.GY, s., geologia.
GE.OM.E.TRY, s., geometria.
GE.RA.NI.UM, s., gerânio.
GE.RI.AT.RIC, adj., geriátrico.
GERM, s., germe, micróbio, vírus.
GER.MAN, adj., s., alemão.
GER.MAN.IC, adj., germânico.
GER.MAN.IZE, v., germanizar, tornar alemão.
GER.MA.NY, s., Alemanha.
GER.MI.CIDE, s., germicida.
GER.MI.NAL, adj., germinal.
GER.MI.NATE, v., germinar, surgir, brotar, nascer.
GER.MI.NA.TION, s., germinação, nascença.
GER.UND, s., gerúndio.
GES.TA.TION, s., gestação, gravidez.
GES.TIC.U.LATE, v., gesticular, fazer gestos.
GES.TIC.U.LA.TION, s., gesticulação.
GES.TURE, s., gesto.
GET, v., ficar, obter, receber, ganhar, aprender, suceder, causar, pegar.
GET ABOUT, v., espalhar-se.
GET AFTER, v., perseguir.
GET AT, v., alcançar, atacar, agredir.
GET AWAY, v., ir, partir, sair.
GET-AWAY, s., fuga, escapada.
GET BACK, v., regressar, retornar, voltar.
GET BEHIND, v., atrasar-se, demorar-se.
GET BEYOND, v., ultrapassar, passar além.
GET IN, v., entrar, adentrar.
GET OFF, v., descer do ônibus, sair de um carro, trem.
GET OUT, v., retirar-se, sair.
GET.TER, s., adquirente.
GET.TING, s., compra, aquisição, lucro.
GET-TO.GETH.ER, v., reunir-se, agrupar-se, ajuntar-se.
GEY.SER, s., gêiser, fonte de água quente.
GHER.KIN, s., pepino em conserva.

GHET.TO, s., gueto.
GHOST, s., espírito, fantasma.
GHOST.LI.NESS, s., espiritualidade.
GHOUL, s., vampiro.
GI.ANT, s., gigante; adj., gigantesco.
GIB.BET, s., forca, patíbulo; v., enforcar.
GIB.BOS.I.TY, s., corcunda, corcova.
GIB.BOUS, adj., corcunda.
GIBE, s., deboche, escárnio; v., escarnecer, debochar.
GIB.ING, s., zombaria, deboche, escárnio.
GIFT, s., presente, dádiva, talento.
GIFT.ED, adj., dotado, talentoso.
GI.GAN.TIC, adj., gigantesco.
GIG.GLE, v., dar risadinhas, ridicularizar, zombar.
GIG.GLER, s., escarnecedor, zombeteiro.
GILD, v., enfeitar, embelezar, dourar.
GILD.ER, s., dourador.
GIL.LIE, s., jovem, moço, criado.
GILLS, s., guelras, brânquias.
GIM.LET, s., verruma, furador.
GIN, s., gim, bebida alcoólica.
GIN.GER, s., gengibre.
GIN.GI.VAL, adj., próprio das gengivas.
GIP.SY, s., cigano.
GI.RAFFE, s., girafa.
GIR.A.SOL, s., girassol, tipo de opala.
GIR.DLE, s., cinta.
GIRL, s., moça, jovem, garota.
GIRL.FRIEND, s. amiga, namorada, garota.
GIRL.HOOD, s., mocidade, juventude, adolescência.
GIRL.ISH, adj., juvenil, próprio de moça.
GIST, s., essencial.
GIVE, v., dar, entregar, conceder, dedicar.
GIVE BACK, v., devolver.
GIV.EN, s., doador.
GIV.IN, s., dádiva, presente, oferta.
GLA.CIAL, adj., glacial.
GLA.CIER, s., geleira.
GLAD, adj., satisfeito, contente; contentar, satisfazer.
GLAD.DEN, v., contentar, alegrar, satisfazer.
GLADE, s., clareira, picada em floresta.

GLADIATOR   363   **GLUTTONY**

GLAD.I.A.TOR, *s.*, gladiador.
GLAD.NESS, *s.*, alegria, felicidade, satisfação.
GLAIR, *s.*, clara de ovo.
GLAM.OR.OUS, *adj.*, glamuroso, encantador.
GLAM.OUR, *s.*, glamur, encanto, brilho, majestade.
GLAND, *s.*, glândula.
GLAN.DU.LAR, *adj.*, glandular.
GLAN.DULE, *s.*, glândula.
GLAN.DUL.OUS, *adj.*, glandular.
GLASS, *s.*, vidro, cristal, copo; *pl.*, **GLASSES** – óculos; *v.*, vidrar, refletir.
GLASS.FUL, *adj.*, copo cheio.
GLASS.HOUSE, *s.*, estufa.
GLASSY, *adj.*, vítreo, cristalino.
GLAU.CO.MA, *s.*, glaucoma.
GLAU.COUS, *adj.*, glauco, verde-mar, verde-azulado.
GLAZE, *v.*, envidraçar, vitrificar.
GLAZER, *s.*, vidreiro.
GLA.ZIER, *s.*, vidraceiro, vidreiro.
GLEAMY, *adj.*, luminoso, brilhante, esplendente.
GLEAN, *v.*, colher informações, pesquisar.
GLEBE, *s.*, terra, torrão, gleba.
GLEBE-HOUSE, *s.*, casa paroquial.
GLEE, *s.*, alegria, felicidade, satisfação, contentamento.
GLEE-CLUB, *s.*, sociedade de canto; grupo de cantores.
GLEE.FUL, *adj.*, jovial, alegre, satisfeito, contente.
GLEET, *s.*, gonorreia.
GLEN, *s.*, vale.
GLIB, *adj.*, lisonjeiro, adulador, conversador.
GLIDE, *s.*, deslize, deslizamento; *v.*, deslizar, escorregar.
GLID.ING, *s.*, voo de planador.
GLIM.MER, *s.*, luz fraca, ideia vaga; *v.*, vislumbrar, luzir pouco.
GLIMPSE, *s.*, olhada rápida, vislumbre; *v.*, ver de relance.
GLINT, *s.*, resplendor, raio de luz; *v.*, reluzir, brilhar.
GLIT.TER, *s.*, brilho, resplendor; *v.*, brilhar, resplandecer.
GLOB.AL, *adj.*, global, mundial.
GLOBE, *s.*, globo, esfera; *v.*, arredondar, dar forma de esfera.
GLOB.U.LAR, *adj.*, globular, esférico.
GLOB.ULE, *s.*, glóbulo.
GLOOM, *s.*, escuridão, tristeza, melancolia; *v.*, escurecer, ficar triste.
GLOOM.I.NESS, *s.*, obscuridade, escuridão, tristeza, melancolia.
GLOOMY, *adj.*, escuro, triste, melancólico.
GLO.RIA, *s.*, auréola, brilho.
GLO.RI.FI.CA.TION, *s.*, glorificação, celebração, clímax.
GLO.RI.FY, *v.*, glorificar, celebrar, enaltecer.
GLO.RI.OUS, *adj.*, glorioso, magnífico, extraordinário.
GLO.RI.OUS.NESS, *s.*, glória, triunfo, apoteose, brilho.
GLO.RY, *s.*, glória; *v.*, gloriar, exaltar, enaltecer.
GLOS.SA.RIST, *s.*, dicionarista, compilador de um glossário.
GLOS.SA.RY, *s.*, glossário, dicionário.
GLOS.SO.LO.GY, *s.*, glossologia.
GLOSS OVER, *v.*, encobrir, esconder.
GLOSSY, *adj.*, lustroso.
GLOT.TIS, *s.*, glote.
GLOT.TOL.O.GY, *s.*, glotologia.
GLOVE, *s.*, luva; *v.*, enluvar, calçar luvas.
GLOW, *v.*, brilhar, arder; *s.*, brilho, esplendor.
GLOW.ING, *adj.*, resplandecente, brilhante.
GLOZE, *v.*, iludir, enganar, lisonjear, glosar.
GLU.COSE, *s.*, glicose.
GLUE, *s.*, cola; *v.*, colar.
GLU.EY, *adj.*, viscoso, pegajoso, colante.
GLU.EY.NESS, *s.*, viscosidade.
GLUM.NESS, *s.*, mau humor.
GLUT, *s.*, abundância, fartura, copiosidade; *v.*, fartar, saturar, encher.
GLUT.TON, *s.*, glutão.
GLUT.TON.IZE, *v.*, comer muito, exceder-se no comer.
GLUT.TON.OUS, *adj.*, voraz, comilão.
GLUT.TONY, *s.*, gula.

GNAR, *v.*, grunhir, rosnar.
GNASH, *v.*, ranger os dentes.
GNAT, *s.*, mosquito.
GNAW, *v.*, roer, corroer, morder.
GNAW.ER, *s.*, roedor.
GNEISS, *s.*, gnaisse.
GNOME, *s.*, gnomo.
GNU, *s.*, gnu.
GO, *v.*, ir, partir, sair, viajar, andar, funcionar, ser, passar, caminhar.
GO AFTER, *v.*, ir atrás de, perseguir.
GOAL, *s.*, gol, meta, objetivo, mira.
GOAL.KEEP.ER, *s.*, goleiro.
GOAL.POST, *s.*, travessão da trave.
GO AT, *v.*, atirar-se a, jogar-se a.
GOAT, *s.*, cabra.
GOAT.ISH, *adj.*, caprino, sensual, erótico, lascivo.
GOAT.LING, *s.*, cabrito.
GO AWAY, *v.*, ir-se, ir embora, partir, sumir.
GOB, *s.*, pedaço, parte, partícula.
GO BACK, *v.*, voltar, retornar.
GOB.BET, *s.*, pedaço, parte, bocado.
GOB.BLE, *v.*, engolir rapidamente.
GO-BE.TWEEN, *s.*, intermediário.
GOB.LET, *s.*, copo, taça.
GOD, *s.*, deus; **GOD**, Deus.
GOD.CHILD, *s.*, afilhado.
GOD.DAUGHT.ER, *s.*, afilhada.
GOD.DESS, *s.*, deusa.
GOD.FA.THER, *s.*, padrinho.
GOD.LESS, *adj., s.*, ateu, incrédulo, ímpio.
GOD.LIKE, *adj.*, divino, sacro, santo.
GOD.LI.NESS, *s.*, devoção, religiosidade.
GOD.MOTH.ER, *s.*, madrinha.
GOD.SON, *s.*, afilhado.
GOG.GLE, *s.*, óculos; *v.*, arregalar os olhos.
GO IN, *v.*, entrar.
GO.ING, *s.*, andamento, andada, partida, ida.
GOLD, *s.*, ouro; *adj.*, dourado, de ouro.
GOLD.EN, *adj.*, dourado, de ouro.
GOLD MINE, *s.*, mina de ouro.
GOLD.SMITH *s.*, ourives.
GOLF, *s.*, golfe.
GOLF.ER, *s.*, jogador de golfe.
GOL.GO.THA, *s.*, Gólgota, calvário.
GON.DO.LA, *s.*, gôndola.
GONG, *s.*, gongo.
GOOD, *adj.*, bom, bondoso, educado, polido; *s.*, bem.
GOOD-BYE, *interj.*, adeus.
GOOD.NESS, *s.*, bondade, benevolência.
GOODS, *s.*, bens, posses, mercadoria.
GOOD.WILL, *s.*, benevolência, boa vontade.
GOODY, *adj.*, bonachão, ingênuo.
GOOSE, *s.*, ganso; **GEESE**, *s.*, gansos.
GOOSE.BER.RY, *s.*, groselha.
GO.PHER, *s.*, esquilo.
GORGE, *s.*, desfiladeiro, garganta.
GO.RIL.LA, *s.*, gorila.
GO ROUND, *v.*, circular, rodear.
GORY, *adj.*, sangrento.
GOS.PEL, *s.*, evangelho.
GOS.SIP, *s.*, mexericos, fofoca; *v.*, mexericar.
GOS.SIPY, *adj.*, metido, bisbilhoteiro.
GOTH.IC, *adj., s.*, gótico.
GOURD, *s.*, abóbora.
GOUT, *s.*, gota.
GOUTI.NESS, *s.*, gota, artritismo.
GOV.ERN, *v.*, governar, dirigir.
GOV.ERN.ABLE, *adj.*, governável, obediente.
GOV.ER.NANCE, *s.*, governo, autoridade.
GOV.ER.NESS, *s.*, governanta.
GOV.ERN.MENT, *s.*, governo.
GOV.ER.NOR, *s.*, governador, diretor.
GRAB, *v.*, agarrar.
GRACE, *s.*, graça, favor, elegância; *v.*, honrar, enfeitar.
GRACE.FUL, *adj.*, elegante, gracioso.
GRACE.LESS, *adj.*, sem graça, canhestro.
GRA.CIOUS, *adj.*, gracioso, elegante, afável.
GRA.CIOUS.NESS, *s.*, afabilidade, graça, benignidade.
GRA.DA.TION, *s.*, gradação.
GRADE, *s.*, grau, classe; *v.*, classificar.
GRA.DI.ENT, *s.*, declive, encosta.
GRAD.U.AL, *adj.*, gradual, gradativo.
GRAD.U.ATE, *s.*, graduado, licenciado; *v.*, licenciar-se.

GRADUATION — GRENADE

GRAD.U.A.TION, *s.*, graduação, formatura.
GRAIN, *s.*, grão, cereal; fibra; *v.*, granular.
GRAINY, *adj.*, granuloso.
GRAM, *s.*, grama.
GRAMA, *s.*, grama, erva, capim.
GRA.MI.NA.CE.OUS, *adj.*, gramíneo.
GRAM.MAR, *s.*, gramática.
GRAM.MAR.I.AN, *s.*, gramático.
GRAM.MAT.IC, *adj.*, gramatical.
GRAMME, *s.*, grama.
GRA.NA.RY, *s.*, celeiro.
GRAND.CHILD, *s.*, neto, neta.
GRAND.CHIL.DREN, *s.*, netos.
GRAND.DAD, *s.*, vovô.
GRAND.DAUGHT.ER, *s.*, neta.
GRAN.DEUR, *s.*, grandeza, maravilha.
GRAND.FA.THER, *s.*, avô.
GRAN.DI.OSE, *adj.*, grandioso, maravilhoso, imponente.
GRAN.DI.OS.I.TY, *s.*, grandiosidade.
GRAND.MOTH.ER, *s.*, avó.
GRAND.SON, *s.*, neto.
GRANGE, *s.*, granja, chácara.
GRANG.ER, *s.*, granjeiro, chacareiro.
GRAN.ITE, *s.*, granito.
GRA.NIT.IC, *adj.*, granítico.
GRAN.NY, *s.*, vovó.
GRANT, *v.*, conceder, deferir, anuir; *s.*, bolsa de estudo, subsídio.
GRANT.OR, *s.*, outorgante.
GRAN.U.LAR, *adj.*, granular.
GRAN.ULE, *s.*, grânulo.
GRAN.U.LOUS, *adj.*, granuloso.
GRAPE, *s.*, uva.
GRAPH, *s.*, gráfico.
GRAPH.IC, *adj.*, gráfico.
GRAPH.ICS, *s.*, artes gráficas.
GRAPH.ITE, *s.*, grafite.
GRA.PHOL.O.GY, *s.*, grafologia.
GRAPY, *adj.*, feito com uva.
GRASP, *v.*, pegar, agarrar, segurar, compreender.
GRASP.ING, *adj.*, avaro, avarento.
GRASS, *s.*, relva, gramado, grama, relvado.
GRASS.HOP.PER, *s.*, gafanhoto.

GRATE, *s.*, lareira; *v.*, ranger, ralar.
GRATE.FUL, *adj.*, grato, agradecido.
GRATE.FUL.NESS, *s.*, agradecimento, gratidão.
GRAT.ER, *s.*, ralador.
GRAT.I.FI.CA.TION, *s.*, gratificação, satisfação.
GRAT.I.FY, *v.*, satisfazer, contentar, agradar.
GRAT.I.FY.ING, *adj.*, gratificante.
GRATIS, *adv.*, grátis.
GRA.TU.ITOUS, *adj.*, gratuito, grátis.
GRA.TU.ITY, *s.*, gratuidade, gratificação, gorjeta.
GRAVE, *s.*, sepultura, cova.
GRAVE.NESS, *s.*, gravidade, seriedade, respeito.
GRAVE.YARD, *s.*, cemitério.
GRAV.ID, *adj.*, grávida.
GRAV.I.TATE, *s.*, gravitar.
GRAV.I.TA.TION, *s.*, gravitação.
GRAV.I.TY, *s.*, gravidade, seriedade.
GRA.ZIER, *s.*, negociante de gado.
GREAT, *adj.*, grande, genial, forte.
GREAT-AUNT, *s.*, tia-avó.
GREAT-GRAND.CHIL.DREN, *s.*, bisnetos.
GREAT-GRAND.DAUGHT.ER, *s.*, bisneta.
GREAT-GRAND.FA.THER, *s.*, bisavô.
GREAT-GRAND.MOTH.ER, *s.*, bisavó.
GREAT-GRAND.SON, *s.*, bisneto.
GREAT.NESS, *s.*, grandeza, magnitude.
GRE.CIAN, *adj.*, *s.*, grego.
GREECE, *s.*, Grécia.
GREED, *s.*, cobiça, ganância, avidez.
GREEK, *adj.*, *s.*, grego.
GREEN, *adj.*, verde, inexperiente, simplório; *s.*, verde, verdor.
GREEN.ERY, *s.*, verdura.
GREEN.HOUSE, *s.*, estufa.
GREEN.NESS, *s.*, verdura.
GREEN.SWARD, *s.*, relva, relvado, gramado.
GREEN.WOOD, *s.*, floresta verde.
GREENY, *s.*, ingênuo, simplório, tolo.
GREET, *v.*, cumprimentar, saudar, acolher, receber, dirigir-se.
GREET.ING, *s.*, cumprimento, saudação.
GRE.GAR.I.OUS, *adj.*, gregário.
GRE.GO.RI.AN, *adj.*, *s.*, gregoriano.
GRE.NADE, *s.*, granada.

GREY, *s.*, cor cinza; *v.*, ter cor cinza, acinzentar; *adj.*, cinzento, gris.
GREY-HEAD, *s.*, cabeça grisalha, cãs.
GRID, *s.*, grade, grelha.
GRIEF, *s.*, aflição, tristeza.
GRIEV.ANCE, *s.*, queixa, mágoa, injustiça.
GRIEVE, *v.*, afligir, molestar, ofender.
GRIEV.OUS, *adj.*, doloroso, penoso, atroz, repugnante.
GRILL, *s.*, grelha, comida grelhada; *v.*, grelhar, assar em grelha.
GRIM, *adj.*, severo, rígido, repugnante.
GRI.MACE, *s.*, trejeito, careta.
GRIM, *s.*, sujeira, sujidade, fuligem; *v.*, sujar, encardir.
GRIMY, *adj.*, sujo, encardido.
GRIND, *s.*, moedura, trituramento; *v.*, moer, triturar, picar.
GRIND.ER, *s.*, moleiro, pedra de amolar, mó.
GRIND-STONE, *s.*, pedra de amolar.
GRIP, *s.*, aperto de mão, força da mão; *v.*, agarrar, segurar, apertar.
GRIPE, *s.*, ato de agarrar, pressão, controle.
GRIS.KIN, *s.*, lombo de porco.
GRIT, *s.*, grão, pedregulho, grão de areia; *v.*, friccionar, roer.
GRIZ.ZLE, *adj.*, cinzento, cor cinza.
GRIZ.ZLY, *s.*, urso-pardo; *adj.*, cor cinza, cinzento.
GROAN, *s.*, gemido, suspiro; *v.*, gemer, suspirar, sofrer.
GROAN.ING, *s.*, gemido, suspiro.
GRO.CER, *s.*, merceeiro, vendedor.
GRO.CER.IES, *s.*, mantimentos, víveres.
GRO.CERY, *s.*, armazém, empório, mercearia.
GROG, *s.*, grogue, embriagado.
GROG.GI.NESS, *s.*, embriaguez, bebedeira.
GROG.GY, *adj.*, grogue, embriagado, bêbado.
GROIN, *s.*, virilha.
GROOVE, *s.*, ranhura, encaixe, entalhe; *v.*, entalhar, escavar, sulcar.
GROSS, *adj.*, grosseiro, ordinário, bruto; *s.*, massa, parte principal.
GROSS.NESS, *s.*, grosseria, rudeza.

GRO.TESQUE, *adj.*, grotesco.
GROT.TO, *s.*, gruta, caverna.
GROUND, *s.*, terra, solo, chão, soalho; *v.*, pôr no chão, depor.
GROUND FLOOR, *s.*, andar térreo.
GROUND.WORK, *s.*, base, preparação.
GROUP, *s.*, grupo, conjunto, classe; *v.*, agrupar, reunir.
GROUP.ING, *s.*, agrupamento, série, classe.
GROVE, *s.*, bosque, arvoredo.
GROW, *v.*, crescer, germinar, brotar, arraigar-se, criar raízes.
GROWL, *s.*, resmungo, rosnadura, trovoada; *v.*, rosnar, rugir, troar.
GROWN, *adj.*, crescido, avolumado, desenvolvido.
GROWTH, *s.*, crescimento, aumento, desenvolvimento.
GRUB, *s.*, larva, lagarta.
GRUB.BY, *adj.*, encardido, sujo.
GRUDGE, *s.*, rancor, ódio, aversão; *v.*, invejar, fazer de má vontade.
GRUDG.ING, *s.*, inveja, ódio, mesquinhez.
GRU.EL.LING, *adj.*, duro, difícil, árduo, penoso.
GRUFF, *s.*, brusco, repentino, rouco.
GRUM.BLE, *v.*, resmungar, bufar, reclamar.
GRUM.BLER, *s.*, resmungão, reclamador, neurótico.
GRUMP.I.NESS, *s.*, rabugice.
GRUMPY, *adj.*, rabugento, aborrecido, áspero.
GUAR.AN.TEE, *s.*, garantia, fiança, caução; *v.*, garantir, afiançar, abonar.
GUAR.AN.TOR, *s.*, fiador.
GUAR.AN.TY, *s.*, garantia, fiança, caução.
GUARD, *s.*, guarda, vigia, sentinela, vigilante; *v.*, viajar, defender.
GUARD.IAN, *s.*, protetor, guardião, tutor.
GUARD.IAN.SHIP, *s.*, tutela, tutoria, proteção.
GUA.VA, *s.*, goiaba.
GUER.RIL.LA, *s.*, guerrilha, guerrilheiro.
GUESS, *s.*, suposição, hipótese; *v.*, conjeturar, adivinhar, imaginar.
GUEST, *s.*, hóspede, convidado.
GUEST-HOUSE, *s.*, cadeia, prisão.

GUIDE, *s.*, guia, sinal, vestígio, roteiro; *v.*, guiar, conduzir, levar.
GUIDE.BOOK, *s.*, guia de viagem.
GUILD, GILD, *s.*, grêmio, associação, sociedade.
GUILE, *s.*, fraude, malícia, astúcia.
GUILE.FUL, *adj.*, malicioso, astucioso, astuto.
GUIL.LO.TINE, *s.*, guilhotina, máquina para cortar papel; *v.*, guilhotinar.
GUILT, *s.*, culpa, criminalidade.
GUILTY, *adj.*, culpado, criminoso, condenável.
GUI.TAR, *s.*, guitarra, violão, viola.
GULF, *s.*, golfo, abismo, baía, braço de mar.
GULF.STREAM, *s.*, Corrente do Golfo do México.
GULL, *s.*, gaivota; tolo, bobo; *v.*, enganar, lograr, seduzir.
GUL.LERY, *s.*, fraude, logro, engano.
GUL.LET, *s.*, esôfago.
GUL.LY, *s.*, bueiro, barranco, sarjeta, fossa.
GULP, *v.*, engolir, tragar, devorar; *s.*, gole, trago.
GUM, *s.*, gengiva; cola, goma.
GUN, *s.*, canhão, espingarda, arma de fogo, revólver; *v.*, atirar com arma.
GUN.FIRE, *s.*, tiroteio.
GUN.MAN, *s.*, pistoleiro.
GUN.NER, *s.*, artilheiro.
GUN.NING, *s.*, caça, tiro.
GUN.POW.DER, *s.*, pólvora.
GUN.SHOT, *s.*, tiro com arma de fogo.
GUSH, *s.*, erupção, torrente, jato, arroubo; *v.*, jorrar, transbordar.
GUST, *s.*, lufada de vento, toró, pé de vento, trovoada.
GUS.TA.TION, *s.*, gustação, experimentação, ato de provar.
GUSTY, *adj.*, tempestuoso, borrascoso, violento.
GUT, *s.*, intestino, tripa, entranhas; *v.*, estripar.
GUT.TER, *s.*, sarjeta, calha; *v.*, escavar, colocar calhas.
GUT.TER.MAN, *s.*, camelô, comerciante informal.
GUT.TER.SNIPE, *s.*, menino de rua, moleque.
GUT.TUR.AL, *adj.*, gutural.
GUY, *s.*, corda, cabo; *v.*, firmar, aguentar, segurar.
GUY.ANA, *s.* Guiana.
GUY.A.NESE, *s.*, guianense.
GUY.ROPE, *s.*, corda.
GUZ.ZLE, *v.*, engolir com gula, empanturrar-se, comer muito, esbanjar.
GUZ.ZLER, *s.*, glutão, comilão.
GYM, *s.*, ginásio, ginástica.
GYM.KHA.NA, *s.*, gincana; competição entre grupos.
GYM.NA.SI.UM, *s.*, ginásio.
GYM.NAST, *s.*, ginasta.
GYM.NAST.IC, *adj.*, ginástico.
GYM.NAST.ICS, *s.*, ginástica.
GY.NE.CO.LOG.I.CAL, *adj.*, ginecológico.
GY.NE.COL.O.GIST, *s.*, ginecologista.
GY.RATE, *v.*, girar, rodar.
GY.RO.SCOPE, *s.*, giroscópio.
GYVE, *s.*, algemas, grilhões; *v.*, algemar.

H

H, *s.*, oitava letra do alfabeto inglês; hora.
HA.BE.AS COR.PUS, *s.*, habeas corpus.
HA.BIL.I.TATE, *v.*, habilitar.
HAB.IT, *s.*, hábito, costume, usança; traje, hábito; *v.*, habitar, acostumar.
HA.BI.TANT, *s.*, habitante, morador.
HA.BIT.U.AL, *adj.*, habitual, costumeiro, tradicional.
HA.BIT.U.ATE, *v.*, habituar, acostumar, habitualizar.
HAB.I.TUDE, *s.*, hábito, costume, uso, usança.
HA.CI.EN.DA, *s.*, fazenda, estância.
HACK, *v.*, cortar, talhar, entalhar: *s.*, corte, fenda, carro de aluguel, táxi.
HACKER, *s.*, pirata de computador.
HACK.ING, *s.*, pirataria em computador, acesso ilegal.
HAD, *part.*, *adj.*, tido, havido.
HAE.MO.PHIL.IA, *s.*, hemofilia.
HAEM.OR.RHAGE, *s.*, hemorragia.
HAEM.OR.RHOIDS, *s.*, hemorroidas.
HAG, *s.*, bruxa, feiticeira, megera.
HAG.GISH, *adj.*, feio, velho, horrendo, abominável, nojento.
HAG.GLE, *s.*, regateio, pechincha; *v.*, regatear, pechinchar.
HAG.GLING, *s.*, pechincha, regateio, ato de pechinchar.
HAIL, *s.*, granizo, saraiva; *v.*, chover pedras, cair granizo, cumprimentar.
HAIR, *s.*, cabelo, pelo.
HAIR.BRUSH, *s.*, escova de cabelos.
HAIR.DRESS.ER, *s.*, cabeleireiro.
HAIRED, *adj.*, cabeludo, peludo.
HAIR.LESS, *adj.*, calvo, sem cabelos.
HAIR.PIN, *s.*, grampo de cabelos.
HAIRY, *adj.*, cabeludo, peludo.
HA.LA.TION, *s.*, halo, auréola.
HALE, *adj.*, forte, vigoroso, robusto; *v.*, puxar.
HALF, *s.*, metade, meio bilhete; *adj.*, meio; *adv.*, pelo meio, pela metade.
HALF BROTHER, *s.*, meio irmão.
HALF HOUR, *s.*, meia hora.
HALF SISTER, *s.*, meia irmã.
HALF-TIME, *s.*, meio tempo.
HALL, *s.*, entrada, saguão, átrio.
HALL.MARK, *s.*, marca.
HAL.LOW.EEN, *s.*, dia 31 de outubro, Dia das Bruxas.
HAL.LOW.MAS, *s.*, Dia de Todos os Santos.
HAL.LU.CI.NATE, *s.*, alucinar, desvairar.
HAL.LU.CI.NA.TION, *s.*, alucinação.
HALL.WAY, *s.*, sala de entrada, corredor.
HAL.TER, *s.*, cabresto, corda, laço, forca; *v.*, encabrestar, amarrar.
HALVE, *v.*, dividir ao meio, cortar pela metade.
HAM, *s.*, presunto, fiambre.
HAM.BURG.ER, *s.*, hambúrguer.
HAM.LET, *s.*, aldeia, localidade, aldeola, vila.
HAM.MER, *s.*, martelo; *v.*, martelar, bater com força.
HAM.MOCK, *s.*, rede para descansar.
HAM.STER, *s.*, hâmster.
HAND, *s.*, mão, ponteiro; letra, cartada.
HAND BACK, *v.*, devolver.
HAND.BAG, *s.*, valise, maleta de mão, sacola.
HAND.BOOK, *s.*, manual, guia de mão.
HAND.I.CAP, *s.*, vantagem, desvantagem, obstáculo, dificuldade.
HAND.I.NESS, *s.*, destreza, perícia.
HAND.KER.CHIEF, *s.*, lenço.
HAND.RAIL, *s.*, corrimão.
HAND.SHAKE, *s.*, aperto de mão.
HAND.SOME, *adj.*, belo, bonito, elegante.
HAND.WRIT.ING, *s.*, caligrafia, letra.
HANG, *v.*, pendurar, enforcar.

HAN.GAR, *s.*, hangar.
HANG.ER, *s.*, cabide.
HANG.ER-ON, *s.*, parasita.
HANG.OVER, *s.*, restos; ressaca de bebedeira.
HAN.KER, *s.*, desejar, querer muito, ansiar por.
HAN.KER.ING, *s.*, desejo ardente, anelo fortíssimo.
HAP.LESS, *adj.*, infeliz, desgraçado, infausto.
HAP.LESS.NESS, *s.*, infelicidade, desgraça.
HAP.PEN, *v.*, acontecer, suceder, ocorrer.
HAP.PI.LY, *adj.*, felizmente.
HAP.PI.NESS, *s.*, felicidade.
HAP.PY, *adj.*, feliz, contente, satisfeito.
HA.RASS, *v.*, importunar, aborrecer, perturbar.
HAR.BOUR, *s.*, porto; *v.*, abrigar, acolher, proteger.
HARD, *adj.*, duro, difícil, complicado, árduo, severo, rígido.
HARD.BACK, *s.*, livro encadernado, livro de capa dura.
HARD.EN, *v.*, endurecer, insensibilizar.
HARD.EN.ING, *s.*, endurecimento, firmeza, dureza.
HAR.DI.HOOD, *s.*, coragem, valentia, intrepidez.
HAR.DI.NESS, *s.*, coragem, valentia, denodo.
HARD.LY, *adv.*, apenas, somente, mal, logo que.
HARD.WARE, *s.*, ferragens, material componente de um computador.
HARE, *s.*, lebre.
HARE.LIP, *s.*, lábio leporino.
HAR.EM, *s.*, harém.
HARK, *v.*, ouvir com atenção.
HAR.LOT, *s.*, meretriz, prostituta, rameira, vagabunda, puta.
HARM, *s.*, mal, dano; *v.*, prejudicar, fazer mal a.
HARM.FUL, *adj.*, prejudicial, nocivo, danoso.
HARM.FUL.NESS, *s.*, maldade, prejuízo, dano.
HAR.MON.I.CA, *s.*, harmônica, gaita.
HAR.MO.NI.OUS, *adj.*, harmonioso.
HAR.MO.NI.OUS.NESS, *s.*, harmonia, musicalidade.
HAR.MO.NIZE, *v.*, harmonizar.
HARP, *s.*, harpa; *v.*, tocar harpa.
HAR.POON, *s.*, arpão; *v.*, arpoar, pegar com o arpão.
HAR.PY, *s.*, harpia.
HAR.RY, *v.*, maltratar, assolar, destruir.
HARTS.HORN, *s.*, amoníaco.
HAR.VEST, *s.*, colheita; *v.*, colher.
HASH.ISH, *s.*, haxixe.
HASTE, *s.*, pressa.
HAS.TEN, *v.*, apressar-se, acelerar, ter pressa.
HAT, *s.*, chapéu; *v.*, colocar chapéu, cobrir com chapéu.
HATE, *s.*, ódio, aversão; *v.*, odiar, detestar.
HATE.FUL, *adj.*, odioso, odiento.
HAT.ING, *s.*, ódio, rancor.
HAUL, *v.*, puxar; *s.*, pilhagem.
HAUL.AGE, *s.*, transporte, frete.
HAUL.ING, *s.*, reboque, transporte.
HAUNCH, *s.*, quadril, anca, quarto traseiro vacum.
HAU.TEUR, *s.*, arrogância, soberba, vaidade.
HAVE, *v.*, *aux.*, ter, haver, possuir, deter, conseguir.
HA.VEN, *s.*, porto; refúgio, abrigo.
HAV.ER.SACK, *s.*, mochila.
HAV.ING, *s.*, *pl.*, bens, haveres.
HAV.OC, *s.*, destruição.
HAWK, *s.*, falcão; *v.*, caçar com falcão.
HAY, *s.*, feno; *v.*, arrumar ou preparar o feno.
HAY.STACK, *s.*, palheiro, paiol.
HAZ.ARD, *s.*, risco, perigo; *v.*, aventurar-se, arriscar-se.
HAZ.ARD.OUS, *s.*, perigoso, arriscado.
HAZ.ARD.OUS.NESS, *s.*, perigo, periculosidade.
HAZE, *s.*, névoa, cerração; *v.*, enevoar, nublar.
HAZ.I.NESS, *s.*, cerração, névoa.
HAZY, *adj.*, nublado, escuro, enevoado.
HEAD, *s.*, cabeça, ponta, frente, chefe, diretor.
HEAD.ACHE, *s.*, dor de cabeça.
HEAD.I.NESS, *s.*, teimosia, obstinação, cabeça dura.
HEAD.ING, *s.*, cabeçalho.
HEAD.LESS, *adj.*, decapitado, sem cabeça.
HEAD.LIGHT, *s.*, farol de carro.
HEAD.MAN, *s.*, chefe, dirigente, diretor.
HEAD.MAS.TER, *s.*, diretor de escola.
HEAD.QUAR.TERS, *s.*, sede de empresa, quartel-general.

HEAD.SHIP, *s.*, direção, domínio, chefia.
HEADS.MAN, *s.*, carrasco, verdugo.
HEAL, *v.*, curar, sarar.
HEAL.ING, *s.*, cura.
HEAL OVER, *v.*, curar, sarar.
HEALTH, *s.*, saúde.
HEALTH.FUL, *adj.*, saudável, sanado, são, curado.
HEALTH.FUL.NESS, *s.*, saúde.
HEAR, *v.*, ouvir, escutar, sentir, perceber.
HEAR.ER, *s.*, ouvinte, auditor, quem ouve.
HEAR FROM, *v.*, receber notícias, ser informado.
HEAR.ING, *s.*, audição.
HEAR.SAY, *s.*, boato, história.
HEART, *s.*, coração, centro, local central, copas.
HEART.BEAT, *s.*, batida do coração, pulsação do coração.
HEART.BURN, *s.*, azia.
HEARTH, *s.*, lar, morada, lareira, forno.
HEART.I.NESS, *s.*, cordialidade, amizade, sinceridade.
HEARTY, *adj.*, animado, enérgico, sincero, genuíno, substancioso.
HEAT, *s.*, calor, ardor, excitação, entusiasmo; *v.*, aquecer.
HEAT.ER, *s.*, aquecedor.
HEA.THEN, *adj., s.*, pagão, não batizado.
HEAT.ING, *s.*, aquecimento.
HEAT WAVE, *s.*, onda de calor.
HEAVE, *v.*, puxar, empurrar, levantar, alçar; *s.*, hasteamento.
HEAV.EN, *s.*, céu, paraíso, éden.
HEAV.EN.LY, *adj.*, celeste, celestial, divino.
HEAVI.NESS, *s.*, peso.
HEAVY, *adj.*, pesado, duro, resistente.
HE.BRA.IC, *adj.*, hebraico.
HE.BREW, *adj., s.*, hebraico, hebreu.
HEC.A.TOMB, *s.*, hecatombe, matança, destruição.
HECK, *s.*, vara para pescar.
HECK.LE, *v.*, importunar, incomodar, interromper.
HECT.ARE, *s.*, hectare.
HEC.TOR, *s.*, valentão, metido; *v.*, maltratar, machucar.

HE.DERA, *s.*, era, erva trepadeira.
HEDGE.ROW, *s.*, sebe, cerca viva.
HEED, *s.*, atenção, cuidado; *v.*, dar atenção, ter cuidado.
HEED.FUL, *adj.*, cuidadoso, cauteloso.
HEED.FUL.NESS, *s.*, cuidado, atenção, cautela.
HEEL, *s.*, salto com o sapato; calcanhar; *v.*, pregar salto em.
HE.GE.MO.NY, *s.*, hegemonia, supremacia, domínio.
HEIF.ER, *s.*, novilha, bezerra.
HEIGHT, *s.*, tamanho, altura, estatura.
HEIGHT.EN, *v.*, elevar, aumentar.
HEI.NOUS, *adj.*, odioso, nefando, asqueroso, perverso, cruel.
HEI.NOUS.NESS, *s.*, atrocidade, perversidade.
HEIR, *s.*, herdeiro.
HEIR.DOM, *s.*, herança, direito a herdar.
HEIR.ESS, *s.*, herdeira.
HE.LI.COP.TER, *s.*, helicóptero.
HE.LIO.GRAPHY, *s.*, heliografia.
HE.LI.PORT, *s.*, heliporto.
HE.LI.UM, *s.*, hélio.
HELL, *s.*, inferno.
HEL.LEN.IC, *adj.*, helênico.
HEL.LE.NISM, *s.*, helenismo.
HELL.ISH, *adj.*, infernal.
HELLO!, *interj.*, oi!, olá! Salve!
HELP, *s.*, ajuda, auxílio; *v.*, ajudar, socorrer, auxiliar.
HELP.ER, *s.*, ajudante, auxiliar.
HELP.FUL, *adj.*, prestativo, prestimoso, solícito.
HELP.MATE, *s.*, colega, companheiro, ajudante.
HEL.VE.TIAN, *adj., s.*, helvético, suíço.
HEL.VET.IC, *adj.*, helvético, suíço.
HEM, *s.*, bainha; *v.*, embainhar, colocar na bainha.
HE.MA.TITE, *s.*, hematite.
HEMI.SPHERE, *s.*, hemisfério.
HE.MO.GLO.BIN, *s.*, hemoglobina.
HEN, *s.*, galinha, fêmea de qualquer ave.
HENCE, *adv.*, daqui a, por isso, por esse motivo; *v.*, afastar-se.
HENCE.FORTH, *adv.*, daqui em diante, doravante.

HEN.NERY, *s.*, galinheiro.
HEN.PECK, *v.*, dominar o marido.
HE.PAT.IC, *adj.*, hepático.
HEP.A.TI.TIS, *s.*, hepatite.
HER, *pron.*, a, lhe, seu, sua.
HERB, *s.*, erva; ervas aromáticas.
HER.BA.CEOUS, , *adj.*, herbáceo.
HERB.AGE, *s.*, pasto, pastagem.
HERD, *s.*, rebanho; *v.*, compor um rebanho, arrebanhar, associar, reunir.
HERE, *adv.*, aqui, neste local.
HERE.ABOUT, *adv.*, por aqui, nas vizinhanças.
HERE.AF.TER, *adv.*, daqui por diante.
HERE.E.DIT.A.MENT, *s.*, herança, propriedades.
HERE.IN, *adv.*, aqui dentro, incluso, incluído.
HER.E.SY, *s.*, heresia.
HER.E.TIC, *s.*, herege.
HERE.WITH, *adv.*, com isto.
HER.I.TA.BLE, *adj.*, herdável, que se pode herdar.
HER.MAPH.RO.DITE, *s.*, hermafrodita.
HER.MET.IC, *adj.*, hermético, fechado.
HER.MIT, *s.*, ermitão, eremita.
HER.NIA, *s.*, hérnia.
HE.RO, *s.*, herói, protagonista de uma cena.
HE.RO.IC, *adj.*, heroico.
HER.O.IN, *s.*, heroína, droga, tóxico.
HER.ON, *s.*, garça.
HER.PES, *s.*, herpes.
HER.RING, *s.*, arenque.
HERS, *pron.*, o, lhe, seu, sua.
HER.SELF, *pron.*, si, se, ela mesma, ele mesmo.
HES.I.TAN.CY, *s.*, hesitação, titubeamento, vacilação.
HES.I.TANT, *adj.*, hesitante, vacilante.
HES.I.TATE, *v.*, hesitar, vacilar.
HES.I.TA.TION, *s.*, hesitação, vacilação.
HET.ERO.DOX, *adj.*, heterodoxo.
HET.ERO.GE.NEOUS, *adj.*, heterogêneo.
HET.ERO.NY.MOUS, *s.*, heterônimo.
HET.ERO.SEX.U.AL, *adj.*, heterossexual.
HEW, *v.*, cortar, cortar com machado.
HEXA.GON, *s.*, hexágono.
HI, *interj.*, oi!, olá!

HI.A.TUS, *s.*, hiato.
HI.BER.NAL, *adj.*, invernal, hibernal.
HI.BER.NATE, *v.*, hibernar.
HIC.COUGH, *v.*, soluçar; *s.*, soluço.
HIDE, *s.*, couro, pele; *v.*, esconder, ocultar.
HIDE.AWAY, *s.*, esconderijo.
HID.EOUS, *adj.*, horrível, medonho, horrendo.
HID.EOUS.NESS, *s.*, horror, feiura, pavor.
HI.ER.AR.CHIC, *adj.*, hierárquico.
HI.ER.AR.CHY, *s.*, hierarquia.
HIGH, *adj.*, alto, forte, elevado, grande, superior.
HIGH.BROW, *adj.*, intelectual, erudito, instruído.
HIGH.LAND.ER, *s.*, montanhês, escocês.
HIGH.WAY, *s.*, autoestrada, rodovia.
HI.JACK, *v.*, sequestrar.
HIKE, *s.*, marcha, caminhada; marchar, caminhar, andar, ir.
HIK.ER, *s.*, caminhante, pedestre.
HILL, *s.*, colina, cômoro, elevação; *v.*, amontoar.
HILLY, *adj.*, montanhoso.
HIM, *pron.*, o, lhe.
HIM.SELF, *pron.*, ele mesmo, ela mesma, si, se, o, lhe.
HIND.MOST, *adv.*, mais atrasado.
HIN.DU, *adj.*, *s.*, hindu, indiano.
HINGE, *s.*, dobradiça; *v.*, colocar dobradiças.
HINT, *s.*, insinuação, ideia, palpite; *v.*, insinuar.
HIP, *s.*, quadril, anca.
HIP.PO.DROME, *s.*, hipódromo.
HIP.PO.POT.A.MUS, *s.*, hipopótamo.
HIRE, *v.*, alugar carro; *s.*, aluguel.
HIR.ER, *s.*, alugador, locatário.
HIR.PLE, *v.*, coxear.
HIS, *pron.*, o, seu, seus, sua, suas, os.
HISS, *v.*, assobiar, vaiar, assuar; *s.*, assobio, vaia.
HIS.TOL.O.GY, *s.*, histologia.
HIS.TO.RI.AN, *s.*, historiador.
HIS.TOR.IC, *adj.*, histórico.
HIS.TO.RY, *s.*, história.
HITCH, *v.*, atar, amarrar, prender.
HI.TECH, *s.*, alta tecnologia, tecnologia de ponta.
HITH.ER, *adv.*, para cá.
HIVE, *s.*, colmeia, cortiço, enxame.
HOARD, *s.*, provisão, acúmulo; *v.*, provisionar,

acumular.
HOARD.ING, *s.*, tapume, dique.
HOB.BLE, *v.*, coxear, mancar.
HOB.BLER, *s.*, manco, coxo.
HOBBY, *s.*, passatempo, diversão, lazer.
HOB.NOB, *v.*, conversar.
HOCK.EY, *s.*, hóquei.
HOG, *s.*, porco capado, tipo porcalhão; *v.*, monopolizar, comer muito.
HOG.GERY, *s.*, porcaria, sujeira, imundície; grosseria.
HOIST, *v.*, alçar, içar.
HOLD, *v.*, conter, segurar, ter, realizar; resistir.
HOLD.ER, *s.*, proprietário, dono, recipiente, detentor de títulos.
HOLD WITH, *v.*, concordar com.
HOLE, *v.*, cavar, esburacar; *s.*, buraco, furo.
HOL.I.DAY, *s.*, férias, dia de folga, feriado.
HO.LI.NESS, *s.*, santidade.
HOL.LAND, *s.*, Holanda.
HOL.LAND.ER, *adj.*, *s.*, holandês.
HOL.LOW, *s.*, cavidade; *adj.*, oco, vazio, côncavo, falso.
HO.LO.CAUST, *s.*, holocausto.
HO.LO.GRAM, *s.*, holograma.
HO.LY, *adj.*, sagrado, santo, puro, santificado.
HOM.AGE, *s.*, homenagem; *v.*, homenagear.
HOME, *s.*, lar, casa, morada; pátria, país.
HOME.LAND, *s.*, terra pátria, terra natal.
HOME.LESS, *adj.*, sem casa, sem teto.
HOME.MADE, *s.*, caseiro, chacareiro.
HO.MEO.PATH, *s.*, homeopata.
HO.ME.OP.A.THY, *s.*, homeopatia.
HOME.WORK, *s.*, trabalho de casa, tarefa.
HO.MI.CIDE, *s.*, homicida; homicídio.
HOM.I.LLY, *s.*, homilia, sermão, prédica.
HO.MO.GE.NE.I.TY, *s.*, homogeneidade.
HO.MOG.E.NEOUS, *adj.*, homogêneo.
HO.MOL.O.GOUS, *adj.*, homólogo.
HO.MOL.O.GY, *s.*, homologia.
HO.MO.PHONE, *s.*, homófono.
HO.MO.SEX.U.AL, *adj.*, homossexual.
HON.EST, *adj.*, honesto, correto, franco, sincero.
HON.ES.TY, *s.*, honestidade, honradez, sinceridade.
HON.EY, *s.*, mel.
HON.EY.COMB, *s.*, favo de mel.
HON.EY.MOON, *s.*, lua de mel.
HONK, *v.*, buzinar.
HON.OR.ARY, *adj.*, honorário, grátis, não remunerado.
HON.OUR, *v.*, honrar, prestigiar; *s.*, honra, prestígio.
HOOD, *s.*, capuz, capota de carro, tampa de panela.
HOOD.WINK, *v.*, enganar, lograr.
HOOF, *s.*, unha, casco, pata.
HOOK, *s.*, gancho, anzol, armadilha, laço; *v.*, fisgar, pescar com anzol.
HOO.LI.GAN, *s.*, desordeiro, baderneiro.
HOOP, *s.*, arco; *v.*, arcar, pôr arcos em.
HOOT, *v.*, buzinar tocar, piar, chiar.
HOOT.ER, *s.*, buzina, sirene.
HOO.VER, *s.*, aspirador; *v.*, aspirar.
HOPE, *s.*, esperança, fé, espera; *v.*, esperar, ter esperança.
HOPE.FUL, *adj.*, esperançoso, crédulo, otimista.
HOPE.LESS, *adj.*, desesperado, angustiado, sem fé.
HORDE, *s.*, horda, multidão, bando, leva.
HO.RI.ZON, *s.*, horizonte.
HORN, *s.*, chifre, corno, galho; buzina de carro.
HORNED, *adj.*, chifrudo, cornudo, galhudo.
HORO.GRAPHY, *s.*, horografia.
HOR.O.LOGE, *s.*, relógio.
HOR.O.LOG.ER, *s.*, fabricante de relógios, relojoeiro.
HORO.SCOPE, *s.*, horóscopo.
HOR.REN.DOUS, *adj.*, horrendo, horrível, nefando.
HOR.RI.BLE, *adj.*, horrível, terrível, pavoroso, medonho.
HOR.RID, *adj.*, horrível, hórrido.
HOR.RID.NESS, *s.*, horror, pavor.
HOR.RI.FY, *v.*, horrorizar.
HORSE, *s.*, cavalo.
HORSE.MAN, *s.*, cavaleiro.
HORSE.MAN.SHIP, *s.*, equitação, cavalaria.
HORSE.POW.ER, *s.*, cavalo-vapor.

HORSE.SHOE, *s.,* ferradura.
HORSY, *adj.,* equino, referente a cavalos.
HOR.TI.CUL.TURE, *s.,* horticultura.
HOR.TI.CUL.TUR.IST, *s.,* horticultor.
HO.SAN.NA, *interj.,* hosana.
HOSE, *s.,* mangueira, meias, tubo de mangueira.
HOSE.PIPE, *s.,* mangueira.
HO.SIERY, *s.,* meias, roupas íntimas.
HOS.PICE, *s.,* asilo, hospício, abrigo.
HOS.PI.TA.BLE.NESS, *s.,* hospitalidade.
HOS.PI.TAL, *s.,* hospital.
HOS.PI.TAL.I.TY, *s.,* hospitalidade.
HOST, *s.,* anfitrião; apresentador de TV ou rádio; hóstia.
HOS.TAGE, *s.,* refém.
HOSTESS, *s.,* anfitriã, hospedeira, apresentadora de rádio ou TV.
HOS.TIL.I.TY, *s.,* hostilidade.
HOT, *adj.,* quente, quentíssimo, picante.
HO.TEL, *s.,* hotel.
HO.TE.LIER, *s.,* hoteleiro, gerente de hotel.
HOT.HOUSE, *s.,* estufa.
HOT.NESS, *s.,* calor, ardor, furor, ardência.
HOUND, *v.,* perseguir, ir atrás, acossar.
HOUR, *s.,* hora.
HOUR.LY, *adv.,* de hora em hora.
HOUSE, *s.,* casa, residência, moradia; câmara; assembleia; *v.,* alojar.
HOUSE.BREAK.ING, *s.,* arrombamento de casa.
HOUSE.COAT, *s.,* roupão.
HOUSE.HOLD, *s.,* casa, família, lar, residência.
HOUSE.HOLD.ER, *s.,* chefe de família, patrão.
HOUSE.KEEP.ER, *s.,* governante, aia.
HOUSE.WIFE, *s.,* dona de casa, proprietária.
HOUSE.WORK, *s.,* afazeres domésticos, serviços caseiros.
HOV.EL, *s.,* casebre, cabana, choça.
HOV.ER, *v.,* pairar, voejar, flutuar no ar.
HOV.ER.CRAFT, *s.,* veículo que se desloca sobre colchões de ar.
HOW, *adv.,* como, quanto.
HOW.EVER, *adv.* e *conj.,* todavia, contudo, não obstante.

HOWL, *s.,* uivo, bramido, berro; *v.,* uivar, berrar, urrar.
HUB, *s.,* cubo de roda, centro.
HUB.BUB, *s.,* algazarra, balbúrdia, confusão, bagunça.
HUB.CAP, *s.,* calota de roda de carro.
HUCK.LE, *s.,* anca.
HUE, *s.,* cor, colorido, matiz.
HUFF.I.NESS, *s.,* arrogância, soberba, vaidade.
HUFFY, *adj.,* arrogante, soberbo, vaidoso, petulante, atrevido.
HUG, *s.,* abraço, estreitamento; *v.,* abraçar, apertar.
HUGE, *adj.,* imenso, grande, enorme.
HUGE.NESS, *s.,* vastidão, amplidão.
HULL, *s.,* casco de navio, fuselagem.
HUM, *v.,* zumbir, zunir, cantarolar.
HU.MAN, *adj.,* humano.
HU.MANE, *adj.,* humano.
HU.MAN.ISM, *s.,* humanismo.
HU.MAN.IST, *s.,* humanista.
HU.MAN.I.TIES, *s.,* humanidades, cultura clássica.
HU.MAN.I.TY, *s.,* humanidade.
HU.MAN.IZE, *v.,* humanizar.
HUM.BLE, *adj.,* humilde, respeitoso; *v.,* humilhar.
HUM.DRUM, *adj.,* monótono, aborrecido, enfadonho.
HU.MER.US, *s.,* úmero.
HU.MID, *adj.,* úmido.
HU.MID.I.TY, *s.,* umidade.
HU.MIL.I.ATE, *v.,* humilhar, rebaixar.
HU.MIL.I.A.TION, *s.,* humilhação, degradação.
HU.MIL.I.TY, *s.,* humildade.
HUM.MING.BIRD, *s.,* beija-flor, colibri.
HU.MOR.IST, *s.,* humorista.
HU.MOR.OUS, *adj.,* humorístico, cômico, engraçado.
HU.MOUR, *s.,* humorismo, humor, comicidade.
HUMP, *s.,* corcunda, pequeno monte; *v.,* corcovar, dobrar.
HUMP.BACK, *s.,* corcunda, corcova.
HU.MUS, *s.,* húmus.
HUNCH, *s.,* corcova; intuição, pressentimento; *v.,* curvar-se.

HUNCH.BACK, *s.*, corcunda, corcova.
HUN.DRED, *num.*, cem, cento, centena.
HUN.DRED.FOLD, *adj.*, cêntuplo.
HUN.DRETH, *num.*, centésimo.
HUN.GAR.I.AN, *adj.*, *s.*, húngaro.
HUN.GA.RY, *s.*, Hungria.
HUN.GER, *s.*, fome; *v.*, estar com fome, estar desejoso.
HUN.GER.STRIK.ER, *s.*, greve de fome.
HUN.GER.STRUK, *s.*, faminto, esfomeado.
HUN.GRY, *adj.*, faminto, esfomeado.
HUNT, *v.*, caçar, perseguir; *s.*, caça, caçada.
HUNT DOWN, *v.*, caçar algo, alguém.
HUNT.ER, *s.*, caçador.
HUNT.ING, *s.*, caça.
HURL, *v.*, arremessar, atirar, lançar, jogar, gritar, berrar.
HUR.RAH!, *interj.*, hurra!, viva!; *v.*, saudar, dar vivas.
HUR.RI.CANE, *s.*, furacão, tormenta.
HUR.RIED, *s.*, apressado.
HUR.RY, *s.*, pressa, afobamento; *v.*, apressar-se, ter pressa.
HURT, *v.*, magoar, ferir, machucar.
HURT.ING, *s.*, ofensa, mágoa, sofrimento.
HUS.BAND, *s.*, marido, esposo; *v.*, poupar.
HUSH, *s.*, silêncio, quietude, calma; *v.*, silenciar, aquietar, acalmar.
HUS.KI.NESS, *s.*, rouquidão, voz áspera.
HUS.SY, *s.*, moça, jovem esperta.
HUT, *s.*, choupana, choça, cabana; *v.*, viver em barraca.
HUTCH, *s.*, coelheira.
HY.A.CINTH, *s.*, jacinto.

HY.AE.NA, *s.*, hiena.
HY.BRID, *s.*, híbrido.
HY.BRID.ISM, *s.*, hibridismo.
HY.DRAU.LIC, *adj.*, hidráulico.
HY.DRAU.LICS, *s.*, hidráulica.
HY.DRO.GEN, *s.*, hidrogênio.
HY.DROM.E.TER, *s.*, hidrômetro.
HY.DRO.PHO.BIA, *s.*, hidrofobia.
HY.E.NA, *s.*, hiena.
HY.GIENE, *s.*, higiene.
HY.GIEN.IC, *adj.*, higiênico.
HY.GROM.E.TER, *s.*, higrômetro.
HY.MEN, *s.*, hímen.
HYMN, *s.*, hino, canto; *v.*, celebrar, cantar um hino.
HYM.NAL, *s.*, hinário, conjunto de hinos.
HY.PER.BO.LA, *s.*, hiperboloide.
HY.PER.BO.LE, *s.*, hipérbole, exagero retórico.
HY.PER.CRIT.I.CIZE, *v.*, criticar exageradamente.
HY.PER.MAR.KET, *s.*, hipermercado.
HY.PER.TRO.PHY, *s.*, hipertrofia.
HY.PHEN *s.*, hífen.
HYP.NO.SIS, *s.*, hipnose.
HYP.NO.TIZE, *v.*, hipnotizar.
HY.PO.CHON.DRIA, *s.*, hipocondria.
HY.POC.RI.SY, *s.*, hipocrisia.
HYP.O.CRITE, *s.*, hipócrita.
HY.PO.DERM, *s.*, hipoderme.
HY.POT.E.NUSE, *s.*, hipotenusa.
HY.POTH.E.CATE, *v.*, hipotecar.
HY.POTH.E.SIS, *s.*, hipótese.
HYS.TE.RIA, *s.*, histeria.
HYS.TER.IC, *adj.*, histérico.

I

I, *s.*, nona letra do alfabeto inglês.
I, *pron.*, eu; núm. romano 1.
IAMB, *s.*, jambo.
IBE.RI.AN, *adj.*, *s.*, ibero, ibérico.
ICE, *s.*, gelo, sorvete; *v.*, gelar, congelar, esfriar.
ICE.BERG, *s.*, icebergue.
ICE.BOAT, *s.*, navio quebra-gelo.
ICE.BOX, *s.*, geladeira.
ICE.CREAM, *s.*, sorvete.
ICE.RINK, *s.*, pista para patinação.
ICI.NESS, *s.*, congelamento, frio intenso.
ICING, *s.*, glacê.
ICON, *s.*, ícone.
IC.TUS, *s.*, ataque.
ICY, *adj.*, gelado, congelado.
IDEA, *s.*, ideia, pensamento.
IDE.AL, *adj.*, *s.*, ideal.
IDE.AL.ISM, *s.*, idealismo.
IDE.AL.I.ZA.TION, *s.*, idealização.
IDE.AL.IZE, *v.*, idealizar.
IDEN.TI.CAL, *adj.*, idêntico.
IDEN.TI.CAL.NESS, *s.*, identidade.
IDEN.TI.FI.CA.TION, *s.*, identificação.
IDEN.TI.FI.ER, *s.*, identificador.
IDEN.TI.FY, *v.*, identificar.
IDEN.TI.TY, *s.*, identidade.
IDE.OL.O.GY, *s.*, ideologia.
ID.I.O.CY, *s.*, idiotismo, imbecilidade, burrice.
ID.I.OM, *s.*, idioma, língua; linguagem; idiomatismo.
ID.I.O.SYN.CRA.SY, *s.*, idiossincrasia.
ID.I.OT, *s.*, idiota, imbecil.
ID.I.OT.IZE, *v.*, idiotizar, tornar idiota.
IDLE, *v.*, ficar à toa, não fazer nada; *s.*, indolente; *adj.*, inativo, ocioso.
IDOL, *s.*, ídolo.
IDOL.A.TRY, *s.*, idolatria.
IDOL.IST, *s.*, idólatra.
IDOL.IZE, *v.*, idolatrar.
IF, *conj.*, se, caso, mesmo que, ainda que.
IG.LOO, *s.*, iglu.
IG.NIT.ABLE, *adj.*, inflamável.
IG.NITE, *v.*, incendiar, inflamar, acender, colocar fogo.
IG.NI.TION, *s.*, ignição.
IG.NO.BLE, *adj.*, ignóbil, vil, desprezível.
IG.NO.MI.NY, *s.*, ignomínia, vileza, infâmia.
IG.NO.RANCE, *s.*, ignorância.
IG.NORE, *v.*, ignorar, desconhecer, fazer pouco caso.
IGUA.NA, *s.*, iguana.
IL.I.AC, *adj.*, ilíaco.
ILL, *adj.*, doente, danoso, nocivo; *s.*, mal.
IL.LE.GAL, *adj.*, ilegal.
IL.LE.GAL.I.TY, *s.*, ilegalidade.
IL.LEG.I.BLE, *adj.*, ilegível.
IL.LE.GIT.I.MA.CY, *s.*, ilegitimidade.
IL.LE.GIT.I.MATE, *adj.*, ilegítimo.
IL.LIC.IT, *adj.*, ilícito.
IL.LIC.IT.NESS, *s.*, ilegalidade, ilicitude.
IL.LIT.ER.A.CY, *s.*, ignorância, analfabetismo.
IL.LIT.ER.ATE, *adj.*, iletrado, analfabeto.
ILL.NESS, *s.*, doença.
IL.LOG.I.CAL, *adj.*, ilógico.
IL.LU.MI.NATE, *v.*, iluminar, esclarecer, aclarar.
IL.LU.MI.NA.TION, *s.*, iluminação.
IL.LU.MINE, *v.*, iluminar, aclarar.
IL.LU.SION, *s.*, ilusão.
IL.LU.SION.ISM, *s.*, ilusionismo.
IL.LU.SO.RY, *adj.*, ilusório.
IL.LUS.TRATE, *v.*, ilustrar, exemplificar.
IL.LUS.TRA.TION, *s.*, ilustração, exemplo.
IL.LUS.TRI.OUS, *adj.*, ilustre.
IM.AGE, *s.*, imagem.
IMAG.IN.ABLE, *adj.*, imaginável.
IMAG.I.NARY, *adj.*, imaginário.

IMAG.I.NA.TION, *s.*, imaginação.
IMAG.I.NA.TIVE, *adj.*, imaginativo.
IMAG.INE, *v.*, imaginar, achar.
IM.BAL.ANCE, *s.*, desigualdade.
IM.BE.CILE, *s.*, imbecil, idiota, tolo.
IM.BE.CIL.I.TY, *s.*, imbecilidade.
IM.BUE, *v.*, imbuir, inocular.
IM.I.TATE, *v.*, imitar.
IM.I.TA.TION, *s.*, imitação.
IM.I.TA.TOR, *s.*, imitador.
IM.MAC.U.LATE, *adj.*, imaculado, sem mancha, puro.
IM.MA.TE.RI.AL, *adj.*, imaterial, incorpóreo.
IM.MA.TE.RI.AL.I.TY, *s.*, imaterialidade.
IM.MA.TURE, *adj.*, imaturo, precoce, verde.
IM.MA.TURE.NESS, *s.*, imaturidade, prematuridade.
IM.MA.TU.RI.TY, *s.*, imaturidade.
IM.ME.DI.ATE, *adj.*, imediato, súbito, urgente, próximo.
IM.MENSE, *adj.*, imenso, enorme, vasto, amplo.
IM.MENSE.NESS, *s.*, imensidão, enormidade, vastidão.
IM.MERSE, *v.*, imergir, submergir.
IM.MER.SION, *s.*, imersão, submersão.
IM.MI.GRANT, *adj., s.*, imigrante.
IM.MI.GRA.TION, *s.*, imigração.
IM.MI.NENCE, *s.*, iminência, proximidade, urgência.
IM.MI.NENT, *adj.*, iminente, próximo.
IM.MO.BILE, *adj.*, imóvel.
IM.MO.BIL.I.TY, *s.*, imobilidade.
IM.MO.BI.LIZE, *v.*, imobilizar.
IM.MOD.ER.ATE, *adj.*, imoderado, excessivo, demasiado.
IM.MOD.ER.A.TION, *s.*, imoderação, desmando.
IM.MO.LA.TION, *s.*, imolação, sacrifício, dificuldade.
IM.MOR.AL, *adj.*, imoral.
IM.MO.RAL.I.TY, *s.*, imoralidade.
IM.MOR.TAL, *adj.*, imortal.
IM.MOR.TAL.I.TY, *s.*, imortalidade.
IM.MOR.TAL.IZE, *v.*, imortalizar.
IM.MUNE, *adj.*, imune.
IM.MU.NI.TY, *s.*, imunidade.
IM.MU.NIZE, *v.*, imunizar.
IM.MU.TA.BIL.I.TY, *s.*, imutabilidade.
IM.MU.TA.BLE, *adj.*, imutável.
IMP, *s.*, criança travessa, diabinho, moleque.
IM.PACT, *s.*, colisão, impacto; *v.*, colidir, imprensar.
IM.PAIR, *v.*, prejudicar, enfraquecer.
IM.PAIR.MENT, *s.*, prejuízo, depreciação.
IM.PART, *v.*, dar, conceder, comunicar.
IM.PAR.TIAL, *adj.*, imparcial, justo.
IM.PAR.TIAL.I.TY, *s.*, imparcialidade.
IM.PASSE, *s.*, impasse.
IM.PAS.SIONED, *adj.*, apaixonado.
IM.PA.TIENCE, *s.*, impaciência.
IM.PA.TIENT, *adj.*, impaciente.
IM.PAY.ABLE, *adj.*, impagável.
IM.PEACH, *v.*, acusar, contestar, pôr em dúvida, denunciar.
IM.PEACH.ER, *s.*, acusador.
IM.PEACH.MENT, *s.*, acusação, contestação.
IM.PEC.CA.BLE, *adj.*, impecável.
IM.PEDE, *v.*, impedir, perturbar, incomodar.
IM.PED.I.MENT, *s.*, impedimento, empecilho, obstáculo.
IM.PEL, *v.*, impelir, empurrar.
IM.PEND, *v.*, pender, pairar; ser iminente, urgir, ameaçar.
IM.PEND.ING, *adj.*, iminente, próximo.
IM.PEN.E.TRA.BLE, *adj.*, impenetrável.
IM.PER.A.TIVE, *adj.*, imperioso, imperativo, obrigado, vital.
IM.PER.CEP.TI.BLE, *adj.*, imperceptível.
IM.PER.FECT, *adj.*, imperfeito, falho, defeituoso.
IM.PER.FEC.TION, *s.*, imperfeição, prejuízo, defeito.
IM.PE.RI.AL, *adj.*, imperial.
IM.PE.RI.AL.ISM, *s.*, imperialismo.
IM.PER.ME.ABLE, *adj.*, impermeável.
IM.PER.ME.ABLE.NESS, *s.*, impermeabilidade.
IM.PER.SON.AL, *adj.*, impessoal.
IM.PER.SON.AL.I.TY, *s.*, impersonalidade, impessoalidade.
IM.PER.TI.NENCE, *s.*, impertinência, teimosia.
IM.PER.TI.NENT, *adj.*, impertinente.
IM.PER.TURB.ABLE, *adj.*, imperturbável.

IM.PER.VI.OUS, *adj.*, impermeável, inacessível.
IM.PET.U.OS.I.TY, *s.*, impetuosidade, afobamento, pressa.
IM.PET.U.OUS, *adj.*, impetuoso, arrojado, precipitado.
IM.PE.TUS, *s.*, ímpeto, impulso, arrojo, salto.
IM.PINGE, *v.*, chocar, colidir, ir de encontro.
IM.PINGE.MENT, *s.*, colisão, choque, embate.
IM.PI.OUS, *adj.*, ímpio, incrédulo, descrente.
IM.PLA.CA.BIL.I.TY, *s.*, implacabilidade.
IM.PLA.CA.BLE, *adj.*, implacável, inexorável.
IM.PLANT, *v.*, implantar, fixar, firmar, estabelecer.
IM.PLAN.TA.TION, *s.*, implantação.
IM.PLANT.ER, *s.*, implantador, colocador.
IM.PLE.MENT, *s.*, implemento, utensílio, instrumento; *v.*, efetivar.
IM.PLI.CATE, *v.*, implicar, comprometer.
IM.PLI.CA.TION, *s.*, implicação, complicação, envolvimento.
IM.PLIC.IT, *adj.*, implícito, subentendido, irrestrito.
IM.PLORE, *v.*, implorar, suplicar, pedir, solicitar.
IM.PLOR.ER, *s.*, suplicante, implorador, pedinte.
IM.PLY, *v.*, conter, encerrar, significar, deduzir.
IM.PON.DER.A.BLE, *adj.*, imponderável.
IM.PORT, *s.*, importação, importância, valor; *v.*, importar, significar.
IM.POR.TANCE, *s.*, importância, presunção, consideração.
IM.POR.TANT, *adj.*, importante, influente, significativo.
IM.PORT.ER, *s.*, importador.
IM.PORTS, *s.*, produtos importados.
IM.POR.TU.NATE, *adj.*, inoportuno, desfavorável.
IM.POR.TUNE, *v.*, importunar.
IM.POSE, *v.*, impor, obrigar a.
IM.PO.SI.TION, *s.*, imposição.
IM.POS.SI.BIL.I.TY, *s.*, impossibilidade.
IM.POS.SI.BLE, *adj.*, impossível.
IM.POST, *s.*, imposto, tributo, taxa.
IM.POS.TOR, *s.*, impostor, charlatão, falso, enganador.
IM.PO.TENCE, *s.*, impotência.
IM.PO.TENT, *adj.*, impotente.
IM.POV.ER.ISH, *v.*, empobrecer, tornar-se pobre.
IM.POV.ER.ISH.MENT, *s.*, empobrecimento.
IM.PRAC.TI.CA.BLE, *adj.*, impraticável.
IM.PRE.CATE, *s.*, imprecar, amaldiçoar, maldizer.
IM.PRE.CA.TION, *s.*, imprecação, maldição.
IM.PRE.CISE, *adj.*, impreciso, inexato.
IM.PREG.NA.TION, *s.*, impregnação.
IM.PRE.SA.RIO, *s.*, empresário.
IM.PRESS, *s.*, impressão, carimbo, marca; *v.*, impressionar, imprimir.
IM.PRES.SION, *s.*, impressão, estampa, sinal, caricatura.
IM.PRES.SION.ABLE, *adj.*, impressionável.
IM.PREST, *s.*, empréstimo.
IM.PRINT, *v.*, imprimir; *s.*, impressão, ficha catalográfica do livro.
IM.PRIS.ON, *v.*, encarcerar, aprisionar, pôr na cadeia.
IM.PRIS.ON.MENT, *s.*, cadeia, prisão, encarceramento.
IM.PROB.A.BIL.I.TY, *s.*, improbabilidade.
IM.PROB.A.BLE, *adj.*, improvável, duvidoso.
IM.PROB.I.TY, *s.*, improbidade, desonestidade, safadeza.
IM.PROP.ER, *adj.*, impróprio.
IM.PRO.PRI.E.TY, *s.*, impropriedade.
IM.PROVE, *v.*, melhorar, aperfeiçoar, cultivar.
IM.PROVE.MENT, *s.*, melhoria, aperfeiçoamento; progresso.
IM.PROV.I.DENCE, *s.*, imprevidência.
IM.PROV.I.DENT, *adj.*, imprevidente, descurado, descuidado.
IM.PRO.VI.SA.TION, *s.*, improvisação.
IM.PRO.VISE, *v.*, improvisar, inventar.
IM.PRO.VIS.ER, *s.*, improvisador.
IM.PRU.DENCE, *s.*, imprudência.
IM.PRU.DENT, *adj.*, imprudente.
IM.PUGN, *v.*, impugnar, opor-se, refutar, recusar.
IM.PULSE, *s.*, impulso, ímpeto; *v.*, agir por impulso.
IM.PUL.SION, *s.*, impulsão, impulso.
IM.PUL.SIVE, *adj.*, impulsivo, desenfreado.
IM.PURE, *adj.*, impuro, manchado.

IM.PU.TA.TION, *s.*, imputação.
IM.PUTE, *v.*, imputar, atribuir, ligar com.
IN, *prep.*, em, dentro, de, por, a, com, durante; *s.* abrev. de polegada.
IN.ABIL.I.TY, *s.*, inabilidade, incapacidade.
IN.AC.CES.SI.BIL.I.TY, *s.*, inacessibilidade.
IN.AC.CES.SI.BLE, *adj.*, inacessível.
IN.AC.TION, *s.*, inação, inércia.
IN.AC.TIVE, *adj.*, inativo, parado.
IN.AC.TIV.I.TY, *s.*, inatividade.
IN.AD.E.QUA.CY, *s.*, incapacidade, insuficiência.
IN.AD.E.QUATE, *adj.*, inadequado, insuficiente.
IN.AD.MIS.SI.BLE, *adj.*, inadmissível.
IN.ALIEN.ABLE, *adj.*, inalienável.
IN.ALIEN.ABLE.NESS, *s.*, inalienabilidade.
INANE, *adj.*, vazio, oco, inane, fútil, inútil.
IN.AN.I.MATE, *adj.*, inanimado, inerte, parado.
IN.A.NI.TION, *s.*, inanição, debilidade, fraqueza.
INAN.I.TY, *s.*, inanidade, inércia, nulidade, imobilidade.
IN.AP.PEAS.ABLE, *adj.*, inexorável, implacável, definitivo.
IN.AP.PLI.CA.BLE, *adj.*, inaplicável, inadequado.
IN.AP.PROACH.ABLE, *adj.*, inacessível, inaproximável.
IN.AP.PRO.PRI.ATE, *adj.*, inadequado, impróprio, inservível.
IN.APT, *adj.*, inapto, inábil, incapaz.
IN.AP.TI.TUDE, *s.*, inaptidão, incapacidade, inabilidade.
IN.AT.TEN.TION, *s.*, desatenção, incúria, negligência.
IN.AT.TEN.TIVE, *adj.*, desatento, descuidado, desleixado.
IN.AU.DI.BLE, *adj.*, inaudível.
IN.AU.GU.RAL, *adj.*, inaugural, inicial.
IN.AU.GU.RATE, *v.*, inaugurar, iniciar.
IN.AU.GU.RA.TION, *s.*, inauguração, início, abertura.
IN-BE.TWEEN, *s.*, intermediário.
IN.BORN, *adj.*, inato, congênito.
IN.BRED, *adj.*, inato, congênito, consanguíneo.
IN.BREED, *v.*, procriar, criar na família.

IN.CAL.CU.LA.BLE, *adj.*, incalculável.
IN.CAN.DES.CENCE, *s.*, incandescência.
IN.CAN.DES.CENT, *adj.*, incandescente.
IN.CA.PA.BIL.I.TY, *s.*, incapacidade, inabilidade.
IN.CA.PA.BLE, *adj.*, incapaz, inábil.
IN.CA.PAC.I.TY, *s.*, incapacidade, inabilidade.
IN.CAR.CER.ATE, *v.*, encarcerar, aprisionar, colocar na cadeia.
IN.CAR.CER.A.TION, *s.*, encarceramento, aprisionamento.
IN.CAR.NATE, *adj.*, encarnado, avermelhado; *v.*, encarnar.
IN.CAR.NA.TION, *s.*, encarnação.
IN.CAU.TION, *s.*, descuido, falta de cautela, negligência.
IN.CAU.TIOUS, *adj.*, incauto, imprudente, negligente.
IN.CEN.DI.ARY, *adj.*, incendiário.
IN.CENSE, *s.*, incenso; *v.*, irritar, incomodar.
IN.CEN.TIVE, *s.*, incentivo, estímulo.
IN.CEPT, *v.*, ingerir, deglutir, comer.
IN.CES.SANT, *adj.*, incessante, ininterrupto.
IN.CEST, *s.*, incesto.
IN.CES.TU.OUS, *adj.*, incestuoso.
INCH, *s.*, polegada; *abrev.*, in.
IN.CHO.ATE, *adj.*, começado, iniciado, incipiente; *v.*, começar, iniciar.
IN.CHO.A.TION, *s.*, princípio, início, começo.
IN.CI.DENCE, *s.*, incidência.
IN.CI.DENT, *s.*, incidente, evento, fato, acontecimento.
IN.CIN.ER.ATE, *v.*, incinerar, queimar, reduzir a cinzas.
IN.CIN.ER.A.TION, *s.*, incineração.
IN.CIP.I.ENT, *adj.*, incipiente, iniciante.
IN.CISE, *v.*, fazer uma incisão, cortar, talhar.
IN.CI.SION, *s.*, incisão, corte, talho.
IN.CI.TA.TION, *s.*, incitação, incitamento, estímulo.
IN.CITE, *v.*, incitar, estimular, provocar.
IN.CITE.MENT, *s.*, incitamento, estímulo.
IN.CIT.ING, *adj.*, incitante, estimulante, que provoca.
IN.CLEM.ENT, *adj.*, inclemente, duro, ríspido.

IN.CLIN.ABLE, *adj.*, inclinável, inclinado, pendente.
IN.CLI.NA.TION, *s.*, inclinação, tendência, pendor, vocação.
IN.CLINE, *s.*, inclinação, tendência; *v.*, inclinar, tender para, curvar.
IN.CLOSE, *v.*, incluir, conter, reter, cercar, rodear.
IN.CLOSURE, *s.*, cerca, cercado.
IN.CLUDE, *v.*, incluir, colocar dentro.
IN.CLUD.ING, *prep.*, inclusive.
IN.CLU.SION, *s.*, inclusão.
IN.CLU.SIVE, *adj.*, incluso, incluído.
IN.CO.HER.ENCE, *s.*, incoerência, incongruência.
IN.COMER, *s.*, recém-chegado, recém-vindo.
IN.COM.MEN.SU.RA.BLE, *adj.*, incomensurável.
IN.COM.MODE, *v.*, incomodar, perturbar.
IN.COM.MO.DI.OUS, *adj.*, incômodo.
IN.COM.MU.NI.CA.BLE, *adj.*, incomunicável.
IN.COM.MU.NI.CA.BLE.NESS, *s.*, incomunicabilidade.
IN.COM.PA.RA.BIL.I.TY, *s.*, incomparabilidade.
IN.COM.PA.RA.BLE, *adj.*, incomparável.
IN.COM.PE.TENCE, *s.*, incompetência.
IN.COM.PE.TENT, *adj.*, incompetente.
IN.COM.PLETE, *adj.*, incompleto, não terminado.
IN.COM.PRE.HEN.SI.BLE, *adj.*, incompreensível.
IN.CON.CEIV.A.BLE, *adj.*, inconcebível.
IN.CON.SE.QUENT, *adj.*, inconsequente, desmiolado.
IN.CON.SIS.TEN.CY, *s.*, inconsistência.
IN.CON.SOL.ABLE, *adj.*, inconsolável.
IN.CON.STAN.CY, *s.*, inconstância, mutabilidade.
IN.CON.STANT, *adj.*, inconstante, volúvel.
IN.CON.TI.NENCE, *s.*, incontinência.
IN.CON.TROL.LA.BLE, *adj.*, incontrolável.
IN.CON.VE.NIENCE, *s.*, inconveniência, despudor; *v.*, incomodar.
IN.COR.PO.RATE, *v.*, incorporar, conter; *adj.*, incorporado, unido.
IN.COR.PO.RA.TION, *s.*, incorporação, ligação, associação.
IN.COR.RECT, *adj.*, incorreto.
IN.COR.RI.GI.BLE, *adj.*, incorrigível.

IN.CREASE, *s.*, aumento; *v.*, aumentar, crescer.
IN.CREAS.ING, *adj.*, crescente, que aumenta.
IN.CRED.I.BIL.I.TY, *s.*, incredibilidade.
IN.CRED.I.BLE, *adj.*, incrível, inacreditável.
IN.CRE.DU.LI.TY, *s.*, incredulidade, descrença.
IN.CRED.U.LOUS, *adj.*, incrédulo, descrente.
IN.CRIM.I.NATE, *v.*, incriminar, acusar, culpar.
IN.CRUST, *v.*, incrustar, fixar.
IN.CU.BATE, *v.*, incubar, chocar.
IN.CUL.CATE, *v.*, inculcar, impingir.
IN.CUL.PATE, *v.*, culpar, incriminar, acusar.
IN.CUR, *v.*, incorrer em.
IN.CUR.A.BIL.I.TY, *s.*, incurabilidade.
IN.CUR.ABLE, *adj.*, incurável.
IN.CURVE, *v.*, curvar, dobrar.
IN.DA.GATE, *v.*, indagar.
IN.DE.CEN.CY, *s.*, indecência, indecoro, despudor.
IN.DE.CI.SION, *s.*, indecisão, incerteza.
IN.DE.CO.ROUS, *adj.*, indecoroso.
IN.DEF.I.NITE, *adj.*, indefinido, indeciso.
IN.DEL.I.BLE, *adj.*, indelével, inapagável.
IN.DEL.I.CA.CY, *s.*, indelicadeza, polidez, finura.
IN.DEL.I.CATE, *adj.*, indelicado, grosseiro, incivilizado, rude.
IN.DEM.NI.FI.CA.TION, *s.*, indenização, pagamento.
IN.DEM.NI.FY, *v.*, indenizar, ressarcir prejuízos.
IN.DE.PEN.DENCE, *s.*, independência.
IN.DE.PEN.DENT, *adj.*, independente, livre, justo.
IN.DE.TER.MIN.ABLE, *adj.*, indeterminável.
IN.DE.TER.MI.NATE, *adj.*, indeterminado.
IN.DIA, *s.*, Índia.
IN.DI.AN, *adj., s.*, indiano; índio.
IN.DI.CATE, *v.*, indicar, sugerir, apresentar.
IN.DI.CA.TION, *s.*, indicação, indício.
IN.DICT, *v.*, acusar, culpar, processar.
IN.DICT.ER, *s.*, acusador, processante.
IN.DIF.FER.ENCE, *s.*, indiferença.
IN.DI.GENCE, *s.*, indigência, miséria.
IN.DI.GENT, *adj., s.*, indigente, carente, necessitado.
IN.DI.GEST.ED, *adj.*, indigesto, indigerível.

IN.DIG.NA.TION, *s.*, indignação.
IN.DIG.NI.TY, *s.*, indignidade.
IN.DI.GO, *s.*, anil, cor azul.
IN.DI.RECT, *adj.*, indireto.
IN.DIS.CI.PLIN.ABLE, *adj.*, indisciplinável.
IN.DIS.CI.PLINE, *s.*, indisciplina.
IN.DIS.CREET, *adj.*, indiscreto.
IN.DIS.CRIM.I.NATE, *adj.*, indiscriminado.
IN.DIS.CRIM.I.NA.TION, *s.*, indiscriminação.
IN.DIS.POSE, *v.*, indispor, inimizar, provocar.
IN.DIS.PO.SI.TION, *s.*, indisposição, aversão, mal-estar.
IN.DIS.SOL.U.BLE, *adj.*, indissolúvel.
IN.DIS.TINCT, *adj.*, indistinto, confuso.
IN.DITE, *v.*, escrever, redigir, compor.
IN.DIT.ER, *adj.*, individual, pessoal; *s.*, indivíduo.
IN.DI.VID.U.AL.ISM, *s.*, individualismo.
IN.DI.VID.U.AL.IST, *s.*, individualista.
IN.DI.VID.U.AL.I.TY, *s.*, individualidade.
IN.DI.VID.U.AL.IZE, *v.*, individualizar.
IN.DI.VIS.I.BLE, *adj.*, indivisível.
IN.DOC.ILE, *adj.*, indócil, rebelde, revoltado.
IN.DO.CIL.I.TY, *s.*, indocilidade.
IN.DOC.TRI.NATE, *v.*, doutrinar, catequizar.
IN.DO.LENCE, *s.*, indolência, preguiça, ócio.
IN.DO.LENT, *adj.*, indolente.
IN.DOOR, *adj.*, interno, interior, de dentro de casa.
IN.DORSE, *v.*, endossar, aprovar, deferir.
IN.DUCE, *v.*, induzir, provocar, causar.
IN.DUCT, *v.*, estabelecer, instalar, ajeitar.
IN.DULGE, *v.*, favorecer, ser indulgente, satisfazer, tolerar.
IN.DUL.GENCE, *s.*, satisfação, indulgência.
IN.DUS.TRI.AL, *adj.*, industrial.
IN.DUS.TRI.AL.IST, *s.*, industrial.
IN.DUS.TRI.AL.IZE, *v.*, industrializar.
IN.DUS.TRY, *s.*, indústria, diligência, aplicação, trabalho.
IN.DWEL, *v.*, morar, residir, habitar, viver.
IN.DWELL.ER, *s.*, morador, habitante.
IN.DWELL.ING, *s.*, moradia, residência.
IN.EBRI.ATE, *v.*, inebriar, embriagar, embebedar.
IN.EBRI.ETY, *s.*, embriaguez, bebedeira.
IN.EF.FA.BLE, *adj.*, inefável, doce.

IN.EF.FEC.TIVE, *adj.*, ineficaz, inútil.
IN.EF.FI.CA.CY, *s.*, ineficácia.
IN.EF.FI.CIEN.CY, *s.*, ineficiência.
IN.EPT, *adj.*, inepto.
IN.EQUAL.I.TY, *s.*, desigualdade.
IN.ERT, *adj.*, inerte, parado, imóvel.
IN.ER.TIA, *s.*, inércia.
IN.ES.TI.MA.BLE, *adj.*, inestimável.
IN.EX.ACT, *adj.*, inexato.
IN.EX.AC.TI.TUDE, *s.*, inexatidão.
IN.EX.O.RA.BLE, *adj.*, inexorável.
IN.EX.PE.RI.ENCE, *s.*, inexperiência, despreparo.
IN.EX.PERT, *adj.*, inábil, despreparado.
IN.EX.PLI.CA.BLE, *adj.*, inexplicável.
IN.EX.PLOR.ABLE, *adj.*, inexplorável.
IN.FAL.LI.BIL.I.TY, *s.*, infalibilidade.
IN.FAL.LI.BLE, *adj.*, infalível.
IN.FA.MOUS, *adj.*, infame, abominável, detestável.
IN.FA.MY, *s.*, infâmia.
IN.FAN.CY, *s.*, infância.
IN.FANT, *s.*, bebê, nenê, criança, infante.
IN.FAN.TI.CIDE, *s.*, infanticídio.
IN.FAT.U.ATE, *v.*, apaixonar; *adj.*, apaixonado.
IN.FAT.U.A.TION, *s.*, paixão louca, paixão profunda.
IN.FECT, *v.*, infectar, contagiar, contaminar.
IN.FER, *v.*, inferir, deduzir, perceber.
IN.FER.ABLE, *adj.*, dedutivo.
IN.FE.RI.OR, *adj.*, inferior; *s.*, inferior, subordinado.
IN.FE.RI.OR.I.TY, *s.*, inferioridade.
IN.FER.NAL, *adj.*, infernal.
IN.FER.NO, *s.*, inferno.
IN.FER.TIL.I.TY, *s.*, infertilidade, infecundidade.
IN.FEST, *v.*, infestar.
IN.FI.DEL, *adj.*, *s.*, infiel.
IN.FIL.TRATE, *v.*, infiltrar, infiltrar-se, enfiar-se, penetrar.
IN.FI.NITE, *adj.*, infinito.
IN.FI.NITE.NESS, *s.*, infinidade.
IN.FIN.I.TIVE, *s.*, infinitivo.
IN.FIRM, *adj.*, fraco, débil, instável.

IN.FIR.MA.RY, s., enfermaria.
IN.FLAME, v., inflamar, arder.
IN.FLAM.MA.BLE, adj., inflamável.
IN.FLAM.MA.TION, s., inflamação.
IN.FLA.TION, s., inflação.
IN.FLEX.I.BLE, adj., inflexível.
IN.FLICT, v., infligir, impor, obrigar a.
IN.FLOW, s., influxo.
IN.FLU.ENCE, s., influência; v., influir, influenciar.
IN.FLU.ENT, adj., influente.
IN.FLU.EN.ZA, s., gripe.
IN.FORM, v., informar.
IN.FOR.MAL, adj., informal.
IN.FOR.MAL.I.TY, s., informalidade.
IN.FOR.MA.TION, s., informação, informe, conhecimento.
IN.FRACT, v., infringir, quebrar a lei, delinquir.
IN.FRAC.TION, s., infração, transgressão.
IN.FRAC.TOR, s., infrator, transgressor, delinquente.
IN.FRINGE, v., infringir, transgredir.
IN.FRINGE.MENT, s., transgressão, infração.
IN.FRING.ER, s., infrator, transgressor, delinquente.
IN.FU.SION, s., infusão.
IN.GE.NIOUS, adj., engenhoso, esperto, perito.
IN.GE.NU.I.TY, s., engenho, habilidade, esperteza, capacidade.
IN.GEN.U.OUS, adj., ingênuo.
IN.GOT, s., lingote.
IN.GRAIN, v., arraigar, enraizar.
IN.GRATE, adj., ingrato.
IN.GRAT.I.TUDE, s., ingratidão.
IN.GRE.DI.ENT, s., ingrediente.
IN.GRESS, s., ingresso, entrada, acesso.
IN.HAB.IT, v., habitar.
IN.HAB.IT.ABLE, adj., habitável.
IN.HAB.I.TANT, s., habitante.
IN.HAB.I.TA.TION, s., habitação.
IN.HERE, v., estar inerente, ligar-se.
IN.HER.ENCE, s., inerência, ligação, ligadura.
IN.HER.ENT, adj., inerente.
IN.HER.IT, v., herdar.
IN.HER.I.TANCE, s., herança.

IN.HIB.IT, v., inibir, impedir.
IN.HI.BI.TION, s., inibição.
IN.HU.MAN, adj., inumano, desumano.
IN.HU.MAN.I.TY, s., desumanidade.
IN.HU.MA.TION, s., inumação.
IN.HUME, v., inumar, sepultar, enterrar.
IN.IM.I.TA.BLE, adj., inimitável.
IN.IQ.UI.TY, s., iniquidade.
INI.TIAL, adj., s., inicial; v., colocar as iniciais em.
INI.TI.A.TION, s., iniciação, princípio, início.
INI.TIA.TIVE, s., iniciativa.
IN.JECT, v., injetar, inocular, dar injeção.
IN.JEC.TION, s., injeção.
IN.JURE, v., injuriar, ofender, prejudicar.
IN.JU.RI.OUS, adj., injurioso, ofensivo, prejudicial.
IN.JUS.TICE, s., injustiça.
INK, s., tinta; v., cobrir com tinta, borrar com tinta.
INK.STAND, s., tinteiro.
IN.LAND, s., interior, interland, sertão.
IN-LAWS, s., sogros.
IN.LET, s., baía, enseada, angra.
IN.MOST, adj., interior, íntimo, profundo.
INN, s., hospedaria, taberna, bar.
IN.NATE, adj., inato, congênito.
IN.NER, adj., interno, interior.
IN.NO.CENCE, s., inocência.
IN.NO.CEN.CY, s., inocência.
IN.NO.CENT, adj., inocente.
IN.NOC.U.OUS, adj., inócuo.
IN.NO.VATE, v., inovar.
IN.NO.VA.TION, s., inovação.
IN.NU.MER.ABLE, adj., incontável, inumerável.
IN.OC.U.LATE, v., inocular, injetar; vacinar.
IN.OC.U.LA.TION, s., inoculação.
IN.OF.FEN.SIVE, adj., inofensivo.
IN.OP.ER.A.TIVE, adj., ineficaz.
IN.OP.POR.TUNE, adj., inoportuno.
IN.OR.GAN.IC, adj., inorgânico.
IN.PUT, s., entrada, investimento, informação para o computador.
IN.QUI.ETUDE, s., inquietude.
IN.QUIRE, v., inquirir, buscar informações.
IN.QUIR.ING, s., interrogador.

IN.QUI.RY, s., pergunta, inquirição.
IN.QUI.SI.TION, s., inquisição, investigação.
IN.RUSH, s., invasão.
IN.SA.LU.BRI.OUS, adj., insalubre.
IN.SA.LU.BRI.TY, s., insalubridade.
IN.SANE, adj., insano, louco, doido, desvairado.
IN.SAN.I.TY, s., insanidade, loucura, desvario.
IN.SA.TIA.BLE, adj., insaciável.
IN.SCRIBE, v., inscrever.
IN.SCRIP.TION, s., inscrição.
IN.SECT, s., inseto.
IN.SE.CURE, adj., inseguro.
IN.SE.CU.RI.TY, s., insegurança.
IN.SEM.I.NA.TION, s., inseminação.
IN.SEN.SATE, adj., insensato.
IN.SEN.SI.BLE, adj., inconsciente, insensível.
IN.SEN.SI.TIVE, adj., insensível.
IN.SEP.A.RA.BLE, adj., inseparável.
IN.SERT, v., inserir, introduzir, colocar dentro; s., suplemento.
IN.SER.TION, s., inserção.
IN.SHORE, adj., costeiro, litorâneo: adv., perto da costa.
IN.SIDE, s., interior, parte interna, entranhas; prep., dentro de.
IN.SID.ER, s., o que está dentro.
IN.SID.I.OUS, adj., insidioso.
IN.SIGHT, s., introspecção, perspicácia, conhecimento.
IN.SIG.NIA, s., insígnia, emblema.
IN.SIG.NIF.I.CANT, adj., insignificante, sem valor.
IN.SIN.U.ATE, v., insinuar, sugerir, dar a entender.
IN.SIN.U.A.TION, s., insinuação, sugestão.
IN.SIP.ID, adj., insípido, sem gosto, sem sabor, enfadonho.
IN.SIST, v., insistir, persistir, sustentar.
IN.SIS.TENCE, s., insistência.
IN.SO.LENT, adj., insolente, atrevido, petulante.
IN.SOL.U.BLE, adj., insolúvel.
IN.SOM.NIA, s., insônia.
IN.SO.MUCH AS, adv., a tal ponto que, tanto que.
IN.SPECT, v., inspecionar, examinar, verificar.
IN.SPEC.TION, s., inspeção, vistoria, exame.

IN.SPEC.TOR, s., inspetor, fiscal.
IN.SPI.RA.TION, s., inspiração, influência, tendência.
IN.SPIRE, v., inspirar, incutir, insuflar, sugerir.
IN.SPIR.IT, v., estimular, entusiasmar, excitar, animar.
IN.STALL, v., instalar, colocar, nomear.
IN.STAL.LA.TION, s., instalação.
IN.STAL.MENT, s., prestação, parte, capítulo de TV.
IN.STANCE, s., exemplo, instância; v., exemplificar, dar como exemplo.
IN.STANT, s., instante, momento; adj., instantâneo, imediato, súbito.
IN.STEAD, adv., em vez disso, em lugar de.
IN.STI.GATE, v., instigar, fomentar, suscitar.
IN.STI.GA.TION, s., instigamento, instigação.
IN.STIL, v., instilar, inocular, infundir, injetar.
IN.STINCT, s., instinto; adj., instintivo, excitado, entusiasmado.
IN.STI.TUTE, s., instituto, instituição, sociedade; v., instituir, nomear.
IN.STI.TU.TION, s., instituição, instituto, costume, praxe.
IN.STI.TU.TOR, s., instituidor, fundador.
IN.STRUCT, v., instruir, doutrinar, catequizar.
IN.STRUC.TION, s., instrução.
IN.STRUC.TIVE, adj., instrutivo.
IN.STRUC.TOR, s., instrutor.
IN.STRU.MENT, s., instrumento.
IN.STRU.MEN.TA.TION, s., instrumentação.
IN.SUB.OR.DI.NATE, adj., insubordinado, indisciplinado, rebelde.
IN.SUB.OR.DI.NA.TION, s., insubordinação.
IN.SUF.FI.CIEN.CY, s., insuficiência.
IN.SUF.FI.CIENT, adj., insuficiente.
IN.SU.LATE, v., isolar, segregar, separar.
IN.SU.LA.TION, s., isolamento, solidão.
IN.SU.LIN, s., insulina.
IN.SULT, s., insulto; v., insultar, ofender.
IN.SULT.ING, adj., insultante, ofensivo.
IN.SU.PER.A.BLE, adj., insuperável.
IN.SUR.ABLE, adj., segurável.
IN.SUR.ANCE, s., seguro; segurança.

IN.SURE, v., segurar.
IN.SUR.GENT, adj., s., rebelde, revoltado, insubordinado.
IN.SUR.REC.TION, s., insurreição, revolta.
IN.TACT, adj., intacto, íntegro, ileso, indene.
IN.TACT.NESS, s., integridade, inteireza, totalidade.
IN.TE.GRAL, adj., integrante, essencial, integral.
IN.TE.GRATE, v., integrar, completar, integrar-se.
IN.TE.GRA.TION, s., integração.
IN.TEG.RI.TY, s., integridade, retidão.
IN.TEL.LECT, s., intelecto.
IN.TEL.LEC.TU.AL, adj., s., intelectual.
IN.TEL.LEC.TU.AL.I.TY, s., intelectualidade.
IN.TEL.LEC.TU.AL.IZE, v., intelectualizar.
IN.TEL.LI.GENCE, s., inteligência; informações confidenciais.
IN.TEL.LI.GENT, adj., s., inteligente.
IN.TEN.DANCE, s., intendência.
IN.TEN.DANT, s., intendente.
IN.TENSE, adj., intenso, emocional, sensitivo.
IN.TENSE.NESS, s., intensidade, força, arrojo.
IN.TEN.SI.FI.CA.TION, s., intensificação.
IN.TEN.SI.FI.ER, s., intensificador, ampliador.
IN.TEN.SI.FY, v., intensificar.
IN.TENT, s., intenção; adj., atento, concentrado em.
IN.TEN.TION, s., intenção, propósito, desejo.
IN.TEN.TION.AL, adj., intencional.
IN.TER, v., enterrar, sepultar.
IN.TER.ACT, v., interagir.
IN.TER.AC.TION, s., interação.
IN.TER.CA.LATE, v., intercalar, interpor.
IN.TER.CEDE, v., interceder, pedir, suplicar.
IN.TER.CED.ER, s., intercessor.
IN.TER.CEPT, v., interceptar, deter, segurar.
IN.TER.CES.SION, s., intercessão, pedido.
IN.TER.CHANGE, s., câmbio, intercâmbio, permuta; trocar, cambiar.
IN.TER.COM, s., intercomunicador.
IN.TER.COM.MU.NI.CATE, v., intercomunicar.
IN.TER.COM.MU.NI.CA.TION, s., intercomunicação.
IN.TER.COURSE, s., intercâmbio.

IN.TER.DE.PEND.ENCE, s., interdependência, dependência.
IN.TER.DICT, s., interdito; v., interdizer, vetar, proibir.
IN.TER.DIC.TION, s., interdição, proibição, veto.
IN.TER.EST, s., interesse; juros; v., interessar.
IN.TER.EST.ING, adj., interessante.
IN.TER.FACE, s., interface.
IN.TER.FERE, v., interferir, intervir.
IN.TER.FER.ENCE, s., interferência, intromissão.
IN.TER.IM, adj., interino, momentâneo; s., ínterim, meio tempo.
IN.TE.RI.OR, adj., interior, interno; s., interior.
IN.TER.JECT, v., interpor, intercalar, injetar.
IN.TER.JEC.TION, s., interjeição; parada, interrupção.
IN.TER.LACE, v., entrelaçar.
IN.TER.LACE.MENT, s., entrelaçamento.
IN.TER.LINE, v., pôr nas entrelinhas.
IN.TER.LINK, v., ligar, encadear, concatenar.
IN.TER.LOC.U.TION, s., interlocução.
IN.TER.LOC.U.TOR, s., interlocutor.
IN.TER.LOP.ER, s., intruso.
IN.TER.ME.DI.ARY, s., intermediário.
IN.TER.MENT, s., enterro, sepultamento, funeral.
IN.TER.MI.NA.BLE, adj., interminável.
IN.TER.MIN.GLE, v., misturar, misturar-se.
IN.TER.MIS.SION, s., intervalo, interrupção.
IN.TER.MIT, v., interromper.
IN.TER.MIX, v., misturar.
IN.TERN, v., internar.
IN.TER.NAL, adj., interno.
IN.TER.NA.TION.AL, adj., internacional.
IN.TER.NA.TION.AL.ISM, s., internacionalismo.
IN.TER.NE.CINE, adj., mortal, letal.
IN.TERN.MENT, s., internamento.
IN.TER.POSAL, s., interposição.
IN.TER.POSE, v., interpor.
IN.TER.PO.SI.TION, s., interposição.
IN.TER.PRET, v., interpretar, traduzir, verter.
IN.TER.PRE.TA.TION, s., interpretação, tradução.
IN.TER.PRET.ER, s., intérprete, tradutor.

INTERRACIAL / **INWARD**

IN.TER.RA.CIAL, *adj.*, inter-racial.
IN.TER.RO.GATE, *v.*, interrogar, questionar.
IN.TER.RO.GA.TION, *s.*, interrogação.
IN.TER.RO.GA.TO.RY, *s.*, interrogatório.
IN.TER.RUPT, *v.*, interromper, parar, seccionar.
IN.TER.RUPT.ER, *s.*, interruptor.
IN.TER.RUP.TION, *s.*, interrupção.
IN.TER.SECT, *v.*, cruzar, ocorrer um trevo, cruzar-se, entroncar-se.
IN.TER.VAL, *s.*, intervalo.
IN.TER.VENE, *v.*, intervir, ocorrer, acontecer.
IN.TER.VEN.TION, *s.*, intervenção.
IN.TER.VIEW, *s.*, entrevista; *v.*, entrevistar.
IN.TER.VIW.ER, *s.*, entrevistador.
IN.TES.TI.NAL, *adj.*, intestinal.
IN.TES.TINE, *s.*, intestino, vísceras, tripas.
IN.TI.MA.CY, *s.*, intimidade.
IN.TI.MATE, *adj.*, íntimo, imo; *v.*, insinuar, propor.
IN.TIM.I.DATE, *v.*, intimidar.
IN.TO, *prep.*, em, para, dentro de, para.
IN.TOL.ER.A.BLE, *adj.*, intolerável.
IN.TOL.ER.ANCE, *s.*, intolerância.
IN.TO.NATE, *v.*, entoar.
IN.TOX.I.CANT, *adj.*, intoxicante, inebriante.
IN.TOX.I.CATE, *v.*, intoxicar, embriagar.
IN.TOX.I.CA.TION, *s.*, intoxicação.
IN.TRA.VE.NOUS, *adj.*, intravenoso.
IN-TRAY, *s.*, caixa ou receptáculo para correspondência.
IN.TREP.ID, *adj.*, intrépido, valente, denodado.
IN.TRIGUE, *s.*, intriga; *v.*, intrigar.
IN.TRIN.SIC, *adj.*, intrínseco.
IN.TRO.DUCE, *v.*, introduzir.
IN.TRO.DUC.TION, *s.*, introdução.
IN.TRO.DUC.TIVE, *adj.*, introdutivo.
IN.TRO.SPEC.TION, *s.*, introspecção.
IN.TRO.VERT, *adj.*, *s.*, introvertido.
IN.TRUDE, *v.*, intrometer-se.
IN.TRUD.ER, *s.*, intruso.
IN.TRU.SION, *s.*, intromissão.
IN.TU.I.TION, *s.*, intuição.
IN.TU.I.TIVE, *adj.*, intuitivo.
IN.UN.DATE, *v.*, inundar.
IN.UN.DA.TION, *s.*, inundação.
IN.URE, *v.*, acostumar, habituar.
IN.URE.MENT, *s.*, costume, hábito.
IN.UTIL.I.TY, *s.*, inutilidade.
IN.VADE, *v.*, invadir.
IN.VAD.ER, *s.*, invasor.
IN.VAL.ID, *adj.*, inválido, nulo, sem valor.
IN.VAL.I.DATE, *v.*, invalidar, anular, desfazer.
IN.VAL.ID.I.TY, *s.*, invalidade.
IN.VALU.ABLE, *adj.*, valioso.
IN.VARI.ABLE, *adj.*, invariável.
IN.VA.SION, *s.*, invasão.
IN.VEIGH, *v.*, invectivar, ofender, injuriar, destratar, xingar.
IN.VENT, *v.*, inventar.
IN.VENT.ER, *s.*, inventor.
IN.VEN.TION, *s.*, invenção, invento; ficção.
IN.VENT.OR, *s.*, inventor.
IN.VERSE, *adj.*, *s.*, inverso.
IN.VER.SION, *s.*, inversão.
IN.VERT, *v.*, inverter.
IN.VER.TE.BRATE, *adj.*, *s.*, invertebrado.
IN.VEST, *v.*, investir.
IN.VES.TI.GATE, *v.*, investigar.
IN.VEST.MENT, *s.*, investimento.
IN.VID.I.OUS, *adj.*, invejoso, injusto.
IN.VIG.O.RATE, *v.*, revigorar, fortificar, fortalecer.
IN.VIN.CI.BLE, *adj.*, invencível.
IN.VI.O.LA.BLE, *adj.*, inviolável.
IN.VIS.I.BIL.I.TY, *s.*, invisibilidade.
IN.VIS.I.BLE, *adj.*, invisível.
IN.VI.TA.TION, *s.*, convite.
IN.VITE, *v.*, convidar.
IN.VIT.ER, *s.*, convidante.
IN.VOICE, *s.*, fatura, documento de cobrança; *v.*, faturar.
IN.VOKE, *v.*, invocar.
IN.VO.LU.CRE, *s.*, invólucro.
IN.VOL.UN.TARY, *adj.*, involuntário.
IN.VO.LU.TION, *s.*, envolvimento.
IN.VOLVE, *v.*, envolver, implicar.
IN.VOLVE.MENT, *s.*, envolvimento.
IN.WARD, *adj.*, interior, interno; íntimo, imo, profundo.

IO.DATE, *s.,* iodato.
IO.DINE, *s.,* iodo.
ION, *s.,* íon.
I.RAN, *s.,* Irã.
IRA.NI.AN, *adj., s.,* iraniano.
I.RAQ, *s.,* Iraque.
I.RA.QI, *s.,* iraquiano.
IRATE, *adj.,* irado, irritado, enfurecido, brabo.
IRE, *s.,* ira, raiva, cólera, brabeza.
IREFUL, *adj.,* raivoso, irado, irritado.
IRE.LAND, *s.,* Irlanda.
IRID.I.UM, *s.,* irídio.
IRIS, *s.,* íris.
IRISH, *adj., s.,* irlandês.
IRK, *v.,* aborrecer, enfadar, incomodar.
IRON, *s.,* ferro; ferro de passar roupa; *v.,* passar a ferro.
IRON.IC, *adj.,* irônico.
IRON.ING, *v.,* passar roupa a ferro.
IRON.MONG.ER, *s.,* ferreiro.
IRON.WORK, *s.,* armação de ferro.
IRO.NY, *s.,* ironia.
IR.RA.DI.ATE, *v.,* irradiar.
IR.RA.TIO.NAL, *adj.,* irracional.
IR.RA.TIO.NAL.I.TY, *s.,* irracionalidade.
IR.REC.ON.CIL.ABLE, *adj.,* irreconciliável.
IR.RE.DEEM.ABLE, *adj.,* irremediável.
IR.RE.DUC.IBLE, *adj.,* irredutível.
IR.REG.U.LAR, *adj.,* irregular.
IR.REG.U.LAR.I.TY, *s.,* irregularidade.
IR.REL.E.VANT, *adj.,* irrelevante.
IR.RE.ME.DI.A.BLE, *adj.,* irremediável.
IR.RE.PLACE.ABLE, *adj.,* insubstituível.
IR.RE.SIST.I.BIL.I.TY, *s.,* irresistibilidade.
IR.RES.O.LU.TE, *adj.,* irresoluto.
IR.REV.ER.ENCE, *s.,* irreverência.
IR.REV.ER.ENT, *adj.,* irreverente.
IR.REV.O.CA.BLE, *adj.,* irrevogável.
IR.RIG.ABLE, *adj.,* irrigável.
IR.RI.GATE, *v.,* irrigar.
IR.RI.GA.TION, *s.,* irrigação.

IR.RI.TA.BLE, *adj.,* irritável.
IR.RI.TATE, *v.,* irritar, enfurecer.
IR.RI.TAT.ING, *adj.,* irritante.
IR.RI.TA.TION, *s.,* irritação.
IR.RUP.TION, *s.,* irrupção.
ISH.MA.EL.ITE, *adj., s.,* ismaelita, descendente de Ismael.
IS.LAM, *s.,* islamismo.
IS.LAM.ISM, *s.,* islamismo.
IS.LAND, *s.,* ilha.
IS.LAND.ER, *s.,* ilhéu, ilhoa.
ISLE, *s.,* ilhota, ilha, ilhazinha.
ISO.LATE, *v.,* isolar.
ISO.LA.TION, *s.,* isolamento.
ISO.MET.RIC, *adj.,* isométrico.
ISO.THER.MAL, *adj.,* isotérmico.
IS.ERA.LI, *adj., s.,* israelita.
IS.SUE, *s.,* questão, tema, edição.
IS.SU.ER, *s.,* emissor.
ISTH.MUS, *s.,* istmo.
IT, *pron.,* ele, ela, o, a, lhe, isto, isso.
I.TAL.IAN, *adj., s.,* italiano.
I.TAL.IAN.ISM, *s.,* italianismo.
I.TAL.IAN.IZE, *v.,* italianizar.
IT.A.LY, *s.,* Itália.
ITCH, *s.,* comichão, coceira; *v.,* sentir coceira, sentir comichão.
ITCH.I.NESS, *s.,* comichão, coceira.
ITCHY, *adj.,* que provoca coceira.
ITEM, *s.,* item, assunto, tema, notícia.
ITEM.IZE, *v.,* pormenorizar, detalhar.
IT.ER.ATE, *s.,* reiterar, repetir, tornar a fazer.
IT.ER.A.TION, *s.,* reiteração.
ITIN.ER.ANT, *adj.,* itinerante.
ITIN.ER.ARY, *s.,* itinerário.
ITIN.ER.ATE, *v.,* andar, viajar de um lugar para o outro.
ITS, *pron.,* seu, sua.
IT.SELF, *pron.,* si mesmo.
IVO.RY, *s.,* marfim, cor de marfim.
IVY, *s.,* hera, trepadeira.

J

J, *s.*, décima letra do alfabeto inglês.
JAB, *s.*, golpe, facada, estocada; *v.*, picar, furar, esfaquear, apunhalar.
JAB.BER, *s.*, tagarelice, falatório; *v.*, tagarelar, palrar, falar muito.
JA.CINTH, *s.*, jacinto.
JACK, *s.*, popular, camarada, colega, macaco, guindaste, guincho.
JACK.AL *s.*, chacal.
JACK.ASS, *s.*, asno, burro, jumento; tolo, imbecil.
JACK.ET, *s.*, jaqueta, paletó, casaco; sobrecapa de livro.
JACK.POT, *s.*, sorte grande, fortuna.
JADE, *s.*, jade, pedra.
JAG, *s.*, corte, dente de serra; *v.*, dentear, pontear.
JAG.UAR, *s.*, jaguar, onça.
JAH.VEH, *s.*, Javé, Jeová, Deus.
JAIL, *s.*, cadeia, prisão, xilindró; *v.*, prender, pôr na cadeia, encarcerar.
JAIL.ER, *s.*, carcereiro.
JAM, *s.*, aperto, esmagamento, geleia; *v.*, esmagar, apertar, obstruir.
JA.MAI.CAN, *adj., s.*, jamaicano.
JAM.BO.REE, *s.*, reunião mundial de escoteiros.
JAN.GLE, *v.*, soar com estridência.
JAN.I.TOR, *s.*, bedel, zelador, porteiro.
JAN.U.ARY, *s.*, janeiro.
JA.PAN, *s.*, Japão.
JAP.A.NESE, *adj., s.*, japonês, nipônico, nipo.
JAR, *v.*, chiar, ranger, estridular; *s.*, estridor, ruído, dissonância.
JAR.GON, *s.*, jargão.
JAR.RING, *adj.*, que discorda.
JAS.MINE, *s.*, jasmim.
JAUN.DICE, *s.*, icterícia; inveja, ciúme; *v.*, causar icterícia, amarelar.
JAUNT, *s.*, excursão, passeio; *v.*, excursionar, passear.
JAUN.TY, *adj.*, alegre, jovial, animado, vivo.
JAW, *s.*, mandíbula, maxila, maxilar, tagarelice; *v.*, tagarelar, palrar.
JAZZ, *s.*, jazz.
JEAL.OUS, *adj.*, ciumento, cioso, desconfiado, invejoso.
JEAL.OU.SY, *s.*, ciúme, desconfiança, inveja, zelo.
JEAN, *s.*, tipo de tecido forte.
JEANS, *s.*, jeans, roupa confeccionada com tecido especial.
JEEP, *s.*, jipe.
JEER, *s.*, zombaria, escarnecimento; *v.*, zombar, escarnecer.
JE.HO.VAH, *s.*, Jeová.
JE.JUNE, *adj.*, ingênuo, ávido, faminto, magro.
JE.JUNE.NESS, *s.*, ingenuidade, magreza, fome.
JEL.LY, *s.*, gelatina, geleia; *v.*, tornar gelatinoso.
JEOP.AR.DY, *s.*, perigo, risco; *v.*, correr perigo, arriscar-se.
JERK, *s.*, empurrão, solavanco, puxão; *v.*, sacudir, empurrar, lançar.
JER.KIN, *s.*, jaqueta.
JER.SEY, *s.*, malha, suéter, camisola, tipo de tecido.
JES.SA.MINE, *s.*, jasmim.
JEST, *s.*, gracejo, troça, brincadeira, graça, zombaria; *v.*, gracejar, rir.
JEST.ER, *s.*, zombador, gracejador, bobo, palhaço.
JE.SU.IT, *s.*, jesuíta.
JE.SUS, *s.*, Jesus, Cristo.
JET, *s.*, jato, jorro, azeviche, esguicho; *v.*, jorrar, sair a jato.
JET-BLACK, *s.*, cor de azeviche, cor escura.
JET.TON, *s.*, ficha de jogo.
JEW, *s.*, judeu, israelita, hebreu, judia, hebreia.
JEW.EL, *s.*, joia, pedra preciosa; *v.*, enfeitar com joias.
JEW.EL.LER, *s.*, joalheiro.

JEWELLERY / JUDGESHIP

JEW.EL.LERY, *s.,* joias, pedrarias.
JIG, *s.,* jiga, dança; *v.,* dançar, sacudir-se, dançar uma jiga.
JIG.GLE, *s.,* sacudida, sacolejo; *v.,* gingar, balançar-se, sacudir-se.
JIG.SAW, *s.,* serrote, serra.
JILT, *s.,* namoradeira; *v.,* dar o fora em quem se ama, flertar.
JIN.GLE, *s.,* som, tinido, música de propaganda; *v.,* soar, tinir, retinir.
JIN.GO.IST, *s.,* chauvinista.
JINX, *s.,* objeto ou ser que traz azar, caipora, azar.
JOB, *s.,* obra, empreitada, tarefa, dever; *v.,* trabalhar, fazer biscates.
JOB.BER, *s.,* operário, trabalhador, empreiteiro; especulador.
JOB.BERY, *s.,* especulação, agiotagem, desonestidade em negócios.
JOB.LESS, *adj.* desempregado, desocupado.
JOCK.EY, *s.,* jóquei, velhaco; *v.,* montar um cavalo, enganar.
JO.COSE, *adj.,* jocoso, satisfeito, brincalhão.
JO.COSE.NESS, *s.,* jocosidade, brincadeira.
JOC.U.LAR.I.TY, *s.,* jovialidade, alegria, satisfação.
JOG, *s.,* sacudida, empurrão, cutucada; *v.,* sacudir, empurrar, mover.
JOG.GLE, *s.,* estremeção, solavanco; *v.,* estremecer, sacudir, saltar.
JOIN, *s.,* junção, união, encaixe; *v.,* juntar, atar, reunir, associar-se.
JOIN.ER, *s.,* marceneiro.
JOIN.ING, *s.,* junção.
JOINT, *s.,* junta, junção, laço, união; *v.,* ligar, unir; *adj.,* unido, ligado.
JOINT VEN.TURE, *s.,* "joint venture", projeto para duas empresas.
JOIST, *s.,* viga, barrote, travessa; *v.,* sustentar com barrote.
JOKE, *s.,* piada, chiste, brincadeira; *v.,* brincar, gracejar, zombar.
JOK.ER, *s.,* piadista, brincalhão, zombador, cláusula leonina.
JOK.ING, *s.,* gracejo, piada, brincadeira.
JOL.LI.TY, *s.,* jovialidade, regozijo, alegria, satisfação.
JOL.LY, *adj.,* alegre, festivo, divertido, feliz; *v.,* festejar, celebrar, alegrar.
JOLT, *s.,* sacudida, solavanco, choque; *v.,* sacudir.
JOLT.ING, *s.,* solavanco, sacudida.
JOS.TLE, *s.,* colisão, choque; *v.,* acotovelar, empurrar, colidir, abalroar.
JOT, *s.,* um jota, ninharia, insignificância; *v.,* tomar apontamentos.
JOT.TER, *s.,* bloco de notas.
JOT.TING, *s.,* nota, apontamento, anotação.
JOUR.NAL, *s.,* jornal, revista, periódico, diário, gazeta.
JOUR.NAL.ISM, *s.,* jornalismo.
JOUR.NAL.IST, *s.,* jornalista.
JOUR.NEY, *s.,* jornada, viagem, excursão; *v.,* viajar, excursionar.
JOUR.NEY-WORK, *s.,* dia de trabalho, jornada de trabalho, tarefa.
JO.VIAL, *adj.,* jovial, alegre, risonho, sorridente.
JO.VI.AL.I.TY, *s.,* jovialidade, satisfação, alegria.
JOWL, *s.,* rosto, cara, bochecha, mandíbula, maxilar.
JOY, *s.,* alegria, regozijo, júbilo; *v.,* alegrar-se, contentar-se, ficar feliz.
JOY.FUL, *adj.,* alegre, feliz, jovial.
JOY.LESS, *adj.,* triste, tristonho, infeliz.
JOY.STICK, *s.,* manche, alavanca de controle em jogos de micro, avião.
JU.BI.LATE, *v.,* regozijar-se, alegrar-se, jubilar, exultar.
JU.BI.LEE, *s.,* jubileu, aniversário, comemoração.
JU.DA.IC, *adj.,* judaico.
JU.DA.ISM, *s.,* judaísmo.
JU.DA.IZE, *v.,* judaizar.
JUDG.MENT, *s.,* julgamento, juízo, discernimento.
JUDG.MENT HALL, *s.,* sala de audiências.
JUDGE, *s.,* juiz, juíza, árbitro; *v.,* julgar, arbitrar, examinar, conhecer.
JUDGE.SHIP, *s.,* magistratura, juizado, cargo de juiz.

JU.DI.CA.BLE, *adj.*, julgável, ajuizável.
JU.DI.CIAL, *adj.*, judicial.
JU.DI.CIA.RY, *adj.*, judiciário; *s.*, o poder judiciário.
JU.DI.CIOUS, *adj.*, judicioso.
JU.DO, *s.*, judô.
JUG, *s.*, jarro; *v.*, estufar, rechear, cozer a fogo lento.
JUG.GLE, *s.*, prestidigitação, malabarismo; *v.*, fazer malabarismo.
JUG.GLER, *s.*, prestidigitador, malabarista.
JUG.U.LAR, *s.*, jugular, veia jugular; *adv.*, jugular.
JUICE, *s.*, suco, sumo.
JUICY, *adj.*, suculento, sumarento, cheio de sumo.
JU.LIAN, *adj., s.*, juliano.
JU.LY, *s.*, julho.
JUM.BLE, *s.*, desordem, confusão, mistura; *v.*, misturar, embaralhar.
JUM.BO, *s.*, colosso, algo grandioso; avião-jumbo; *adj.*, gigantesco.
JUMP, *s.*, salto, pulo, óbice; *v.*, saltar, pular, assustar, disparar.
JUMP.ER, *s.*, blusa, pulôver, colete, avental.
JUMP.ING, *s.*, salto, pulo; *s.*, saltador, pulador.
JUMPY, *adj.*, nervoso, irrequieto.
JUN., *abrev.* de **JUNE** e de **JUNIOR**; *s.*, júnior.
JUNC.TION, *s.*, junção, conexão, cruzamento, entroncamento, trevo.
JUNC.TURE, *s.*, conjuntura, momento, contexto, encontro, crise.
JUNE, *s.*, junho.
JUN.GLE, *s.*, mata, floresta, selva.
JU.NIOR, *s.*, júnior, jovem; *adj.*, júnior, mais novo, filho de.
JUNK, *s.*, junco; velharias, trastes; *v.*, jogar fora, descartar.
JU.RID.I.CAL, *adj.*, jurídico.
JU.RIS.CON.SULT, *s.*, jurisconsulto, advogado.
JU.RIS.DIC.TION, *s.*, jurisdição.
JU.RIS.PRU.DENCE, *s.*, jurisprudência.
JU.RIST, *s.*, jurista, advogado.
JU.ROR, *s.*, jurado.
JU.RY, *s.*, júri.
JUS, *s.*, direito, jus.
JUST, *adj.*, justo, imparcial, legal; *adv.*, apenas, justamente, somente.
JUS.TICE, *s.*, justiça, equidade; juiz, magistrado.
JUS.TI.CIA.RY, *s.*, juiz.
JUS.TI.FI.CA.TION, *s.*, justificação.
JUS.TI.FIED, *adj.*, justificado.
JUS.TI.FY, *v.*, justificar.
JUST.NESS, *s.*, precisão.
JUT, *s.*, saliência, ressalto; *v.*, sobressair, ressaltar, destacar.
JUTE, *s.*, juta.
JU.VE.NILE, *adj.*, juvenil, adolescente; *s.*, menor de idade.
JUX.TA.POSE, *v.*, justapor, colocar junto.
JUX.TA.PO.SI.TION, *s.*, justaposição.

K

K, *s.*, décima primeira letra do alfabeto inglês.
KAIL.YARD, *s.*, horta.
KA.LEI.DO.SCOPE, *s.*, caleidoscópio.
KA.LENDS, *s.*, calendas.
KAN.GA.ROO, *s.*, canguru.
KA.O.LIN, *s.*, caulim.
KA.RA.TE, *s.*, karatê, luta corporal.
KAY.AK, *s.*, caiaque.
KEEL, *s.*, quilha de navio, chata, barcaça; *v.*, mostrar a quilha, soçobrar.
KEEN, *adj.*, vivo, agudo, grande, mordaz, acirrado, vivaz, fogoso.
KEEP, *s.*, sustento, alimentação, prisão; *v.*, deter, ter, possuir, proteger.
KEEP.ER, *s.*, proprietário, dono, carcereiro, capataz, zelador, guardador.
KEEP.ING, *s.*, manutenção, alimentação, cuidado, guarda.
KEEP.SAKE, *s.*, recordação, lembrança, presente.
KEG, *s.*, barril, tonel.
KELT, *s.*, celta.
KEN, *s.*, círculo visual, alcance do conhecimento; *v.*, perceber.
KEN.NEL, *s.*, canil, casinha para cães; *v.*, abrigar cães.
KERB, *s.*, meio-fio, borda de calçada, passeio.
KER.CHIEF, *s.*, lenço de cabeça.
KER.MES, *s.*, quermesse, festa pública.
KER.O.SENE, *s.*, querosene.
KETCH, *s.*, caiaque, chalupa, canoa.
KETCH.UP, *s.*, "ketchup", molho picante de tomate.
KET.TLE, *s.*, chaleira.
KEY, *s.*, chave, chaveta, código, solução, decifração; *v.*, chavear, encaixar.
KEY.BOARD, *s.*, teclado.
KEY.HOLE, *s.*, buraco de fechadura.
KEY.RING, *s.*, chaveiro.

KEY.STONE, *s.*, pedra fundamental, pedra angular, pedra de toque.
KHA.LI.FA, *s.*, califa.
KIB.BUTZ, *s.*, kibutz, quibutz, *pl.* kibutsim, fazenda coletiva agrícola em Israel.
KICK, *s.*, pontapé, chute, coice; *v.*, chutar, dar um pontapé, escoicear.
KICK.ER, *s.*, chutador, escoiceador.
KICK.ING, *s.*, chute, patada, coice.
KID, *s.*, cabrito, pele; criança, garoto; *v.*, zombar, tratar como criança.
KID.NAP, *v.*, sequestrar, raptar.
KID.NAP.PER, *s.*, sequestrador, raptor.
KID.NEY, *s.*, rim.
KILL, *v.*, matar, assassinar, trucidar; *s.*, assassinato, matança.
KILL.ER, *s.*, assassino, matador, criminoso.
KILL.ING, *s.*, assassinato, matança, crime, homicídio.
KILN, *s.*, forno, estufa; *v.*, secar, ressecar.
KI.LO, *s.*, quilo, quilograma.
KI.LO.GRAM.ME, *s.*, quilograma, quilo.
KI.LO.ME.TER, *s.*, quilômetro.
KI.LO.ME.TRE, *s.*, quilômetro.
KILO.WATT, *s.*, quilowatt.
KILT, *s.*, saiote usado pelos escoceses.
KI.MO.NO, *s.*, quimono.
KIN, *s.*, família, parentes, afins, parentesco, parentela.
KIND, *s.*, tipo, espécie, gênero, raça; *adj.*, gentil, generoso, amável.
KIN.DER.GAR.DEN, *s.*, jardim de infância.
KIN.DLE, *v.*, acender, inflamar, pôr fogo; incitar, entusiasmar.
KIND.LY, *adj.*, amável, bondoso, suave, gentil; *adv.*, amavelmente.
KIND.NESS, *s.*, bondade, amabilidade, suavidade, gentileza.
KIN.DRED, *s.*, parentela, parentesco, afim; *adj.*,

KINETIC / KURDISH

aparentado, similar.
KI.NET.IC, *adj.*, cinético.
KI.NET.ICS, *s.*, dinâmica.
KING, *s.*, rei, soberano, monarca; líder.
KING.DOM, *s.*, monarquia, reinado, reino.
KING.HOOD, *s.*, soberania, realeza.
KING.LIKE, *adj.*, régio, real.
KIN.LESS, *adj.*, sem parentes.
KIN.SHIP, *s.*, parentesco, parentela.
KI.OSK, *s.*, quiosque.
KIR.MESS, *s.*, quermesse.
KISS, *s.*, beijo, ósculo, toque leve; *v.*, beijar, oscular.
KISS.ER, *s.*, beijador.
KISS.ING, *s.*, beijo, ato de beijar.
KIT, *s.*, kit, caixa de ferramentas, conjunto de ferramentas; *v.*, montar.
KITCH.EN, *s.*, cozinha.
KIT.TEN, *s.*, gatinho.
KIT.TEN.ISH, *adj.*, felino.
KIT.TLE, *adj.*, caprichoso, rabugento, melindroso, intratável.
KI.WI, *s.*, kiwi, tipo de fruta.
KLEP.TO.MA.NIA, *s.*, cleptomania.
KM, *abrev.* de **KILOMETER**, *s.*, km, quilômetro.
KNACK, *s.*, destreza, habilidade, competência.
KNAR, *s.*, nó de madeira.
KNAR.RY, *adj.*, nodoso.
KNAVE, *s.*, velhaco, cafajeste, tratante; valete no baralho.
KNAV.ERY, *s.*, velhacaria, cafajestice, safadeza.
KNEAD, *v.*, amassar.
KNEE, *s.*, joelho; cotovelo, joelheira; *v.*, ajoelhar-se, cair de joelhos.
KNEE.CAP, *s.*, rótula.
KNEEL, *v.*, ajoelhar-se, ficar de joelhos, genuflectir-se.
KNELL, *s.*, dobre fúnebre, toque de sinos para falecimento; *v.*, dobrar.
KNIFE, *s.*, faca, lâmina; *v.*, esfaquear, apunhalar, ferir com faca.
KNIGHT, *s.*, cavaleiro, fidalgo, cavalo no jogo de xadrez.
KNIT, *v.*, tricotar, fazer tricô, entretecer, tecer, entrelaçar.
KNIT.TER, *s.*, tecelão, quem tece malha.
KNIT.WEAR, *s.*, malha, roupa de malha.
KNIVES, *s.*, facas.
KNOB, *s.*, maçaneta de porta, punho, puxador, botão de rádio, TV.
KNOCK, *s.*, pancada, golpe, batida; *v.*, bater, surrar, dar pancadas.
KNOCK.ED, *adj.*, derrubado, batido.
KNOCK.ING, *s.*, ato de bater; pancada, pancadaria.
KNOCK OUT, *v.*, deixar inconsciente, derrotar, abater.
KNOCK-OUT, *s.*, nocaute, derrubada do adversário.
KNOLL, *s.*, colina, outeiro, cômoro; dobre de sinos; *v.*, tanger os sinos.
KNOP, *s.*, botão de flor, botão, saliência.
KNOT, *s.*, laço, nó, laçada, módulo; *v.*, laçar, amarrar.
KNOUT, *s.*, cnute, chicote, azorrague; *v.*, chicotear, surrar.
KNOW, *s.*, conhecimento; *v.*, conhecer, saber, reconhecer, identificar.
KNOW.ER, *s.*, conhecedor, sabedor.
KNOW-HOW, *s.*, conhecimento, experiência, domínio de uma técnica.
KNOW.ING.NESS, *s.*, esperteza, sagacidade, perspicácia.
KNOWL.EDGE, *s.*, conhecimento, saber.
KNOWN, *adj.*, conhecido, declarado, reconhecido.
KNOW-NOTH.ING, *s.*, ignorante, muito ignorante.
KNUCK.LE, *s.*, nó dos dedos; articulação, junta; *v.*, render-se, submeter.
KNURL, *s.*, saliência, nó, borda.
KO.RAN, *s.*, Corão.
KO.REA, *s.*, Coreia.
KOW.TOW, *s.*, ato de prostrar-se até tocar o chão, reverência.
KU-KLUX-KLAN, *s.*, sociedade secreta americana.
KUNG FU, *s.*, kung fu, tipo de luta chinesa.
KURD.ISH, *adj.*, *s.*, curdo, idioma curdo.

L

L, *s.*, décima segunda letra do alfabeto inglês; litro.
L, algarismo romano, que vale 50.
LA, *s.*, lá.
LA.BEL, *s.*, rótulo, etiqueta, letreiro, legenda; *v.,* etiquetar, rotular.
LA.BI.AL, *adj.*, labial.
LAB.O.RA.TO.RY, *s.*, laboratório.
LA.BO.RI.OUS, *adj.*, laborioso, trabalhador, diligente.
LA.BOUR, *s.*, trabalho, labor, mão de obra, fadiga; *v.,* trabalhar, labutar.
LA.BOUR.ER, *s.*, trabalhador, operário.
LA.BOUR.ING, *s.*, trabalho, esforço.
LAB.Y.RINTH, *s.*, labirinto.
LACE, *s.*, cordão, laço, cadarço; *v.,* atar, apertar.
LAC.ER.ATE, *v.*, machucar, lacerar, ferir.
LACH.RY.MAL, *adj.*, lacrimal.
LACH.RY.MOSE, *adj.*, lacrimoso.
LAC.ING, *s.*, ato de amarrar, atar; laço.
LACK, *s.*, falta, carência, necessidade; *v.,* faltar, carecer, necessitar.
LACK.EY, *s.*, lacaio, servente, criado.
LACK.ING, *adj.*, carente, necessitado.
LAC.QUER, *s.*, laca, verniz.
LAC.QUER.ING, *s.*, envernizamento.
LAC.TA.TION, *s.*, lactação.
LA.CU.NA, *s.*, omissão, lacuna, cavidade.
LAD, *s.*, rapaz, moço, garoto.
LAD.DER, *s.*, escada de mão.
LAD.DIE, *s.*, rapazinho, rapazelho.
LADE, *s.*, foz de rio; *v.,* carregar, despachar, empilhar.
LAD.ING, *s.*, carregamento, carga.
LA.DLE, *s.*, concha para sopa.
LA.DY, *s.*, senhora, dama; esposa, dona.
LA.DY.LIKE, *adj.*, elegante, fino, refinado, distinto.
LAG, *s.*, retardamento, atraso; *v.,* atrasar-se, retardar-se, encarcerar.
LA.GER, *s.*, cerveja leve e clara.
LAG.GARD, *adj.*, vagaroso, atrasado, tardio.
LAG.GING, *adj.*, demorado, vagaroso, lento.
LA.GOON, *s.*, lagoa, lago.
LA.IC, *adj.*, *s.*, laico, leigo.
LA.ICAL, *adj.*, laico, secular, mundano, profano.
LAIR, *s.*, covil, toca.
LAKE, *s.*, lago.
LAMB, *s.*, cordeiro, carne de cordeiro; *v.,* parir ovelha.
LAMB.KIN, *s.*, cordeirinho.
LAMB'S-WOOL, *s.*, lã de cordeiro.
LAME, *adj.*, coxo, manco, fraco; *v.,* estropiar, aleijar.
LA.MENT, *s.*, lamento, reclamação, queixa; *v.,* lamentar-se, queixar-se.
LA.MEN.TA.BLE, *adj.*, lamentável.
LAM.EN.TA.TION, *s.*, lamentação, lamento.
LAM.I.NA, *s.*, lâmina.
LAM.I.NATE, *v.*, laminar, reduzir a lâminas.
LAMP, *s.*, lâmpada, lanterna, lamparina.
LAMP-BLACK, *s.*, fuligem, negro de fumo, sujeira.
LAMP.ION, *s.*, lampião.
LAM.POON, *s.*, pasquim; *v.,* difamar, satirizar.
LAMP.POST, *s.*, poste de luz.
LAMP.SHADE, *s.*, abajur.
LANCE, *s.*, lança.
LAND, *s.*, terra, país, terras, propriedades; *v.,* desembarcar, aterrar.
LAND.FORCE, *s.*, exército de terra.
LAND.HOLD.ER, *s.*, proprietário de terras, sitiante, fazendeiro.
LAND.LA.DY, *s.*, dona, proprietária de bar ou pub.
LAND.LORD, *s.*, dono, proprietário de bar ou pub.
LAND.MARK, *s.*, marco, limite, local conhecido.
LAND.OWN.ER, *s.*, proprietário de terras, latifundiário.
LAND.SLIDE, *s.*, desabamento, desmoronamento, grande vitória.

LANDWORK — LAWFULNESS

LAND.WORK, *s.*, agricultor, lavrador.
LANE, *s.*, travessa, beco, viela, rota.
LAN.GUAGE, *s.*, linguagem, língua, estilo.
LAN.GUID, *adj.*, lânguido, frágil, debilitado.
LAN.GUISH, *v.*, definhar, enfraquecer-se.
LAN.GUISH.MENT, *s.*, desfalecimento, abatimento.
LAN.GUOR.OUS, *adj.*, langoroso.
LANK.I.NESS, *s.*, magreza.
LANKY, *adj.*, magro, esbelto, fino, delgado, magricela.
LAN.TERN, *s.*, lanterna.
LAP, *s.*, regaço, colo, descanso, disco rotativo, volta completa em uma pista; *v.*, lamber, embrulhar.
LA.PEL, *s.*, lapela.
LAP.I.DATE, *v.*, lapidar, apedrejar, matar a pedradas.
LAP.I.DA.TION, *s.*, lapidação, apedrejamento.
LAPSE, *s.*, lapso, espaço, período; negligência; *v.*, escoar, passar.
LAR.BOARD, *s.*, bombordo.
LAR.CE.NOUS, *adj.*, ladrão.
LAR.CE.NY, *s.*, furto, roubo.
LARD, *s.*, banha de porco; *v.*, engordar.
LARGE, *s.*, largo, amplo, grande.
LARGE.NESS, *s.*, grandeza, amplidão.
LAR.GESS, *s.*, donativo, dádiva, presente.
LAR.GESSE, *s.*, generosidade.
LARK.SPUR, *s.*, espora.
LARKY, *adj.*, brincalhão, traquinas, travesso.
LAR.VA, *s.*, larva.
LAR.YN.GI.TIS, *s.*, laringite.
LAR.YN.GOL.O.GY, *s.*, laringologia.
LAR.YNX, *s.*, laringe.
LAS.CIV.I.OUS, *adj.*, lascivo, devasso.
LAS.CIV.I.OUS.NESS, *s.*, lascívia, devassidão.
LA.SER, *s.*, lêiser, raio lêiser.
LASH, *s.*, chicotada, cílio; *v.*, chicotear, açoitar, surrar.
LASH.ER, *s.*, açoitador.
LASS, *s.*, moça, jovem, garota.
LASS.IE, *s.*, mocinha, garotinha.
LAS.SI.TUDE, *s.*, cansaço, fadiga, esgotamento.
LAS.SO, *s.*, laço; *v.*, laçar, pegar com o laço.
LAST, *adj.*, último, derradeiro; *adv.*, em último lugar; *v.*, durar.
LAST.ING, *adj.*, duradouro, permanente.
LATCH, *s.*, trinco, fecho, tranca; *v.*, fechar.
LATCH.KEY, *s.*, chave de trinco.
LATE, *adj.*, atrasado, tardio, lento; *adv.*, tarde.
LATE.COM.ER, *s.*, retardatário.
LATE.NESS, *s.*, demora, atraso.
LA.TENT, *adj.*, latente.
LAT.ER, *adj.*, posterior; *adv.*, mais tarde, depois.
LAT.ER.AL, *adj.*, lateral.
LAT.EST, *adj.*, último.
LATHE, *s.*, torno mecânico.
LAT.IN, *s.*, latim; *adj.*, latino.
LAT.IN-AMER.I.CAN, *s.*, latino-americano.
LAT.IN.ISM, *s.*, latinismo.
LA.TIN.I.TY, *s.*, latinidade.
LAT.IN.IZE, *v.*, latinizar.
LAT.ISH, *adv.*, um pouco tarde.
LAT.I.TUDE, *s.*, latitude, largura, clima.
LA.TRINE, *s.*, latrina, privada.
LAT.TER, *adj.*, último, posterior; recente, moderno.
LAUD, *s.*, louvor, elogio; *v.*, louvar, exaltar, enaltecer.
LAUD.ABLE, *adj.*, louvável.
LAUGH, *s.*, gargalhada, riso, risada; *v.*, rir, gargalhar, dar risada.
LAUGH.ABLE, *adj.*, ridículo, risível, absurdo.
LAUGH.ING, *s.*, riso, risada; *adj.*, risonho.
LAUGH.TER, *s.*, riso, risada.
LAUNCH, *s.*, lancha; lançamento.
LAUN.DRESS, *s.*, lavadeira.
LAUN.DRY, *s.*, lavanderia.
LA.VA, *s.*, lava.
LA.VA.BO, *s.*, lavabo.
LAVE, *v.*, lavar, banhar.
LAV.EN.DER, *s.*, lavanda, alfazema; *v.*, perfumar, aromatizar.
LAV.ISH, *adj.*, generoso, pródigo, excessivo; *v.*, dissipar, esbanjar.
LAW, *s.*, lei, norma, mandamento, foro, jurisprudência.
LAW.FUL, *adj.*, legal, legítimo.
LAW.FUL.NESS, *s.*, legalidade.

LAW.LESS, *adj.*, ilegal, ilegítimo.
LAWN, *s.*, relvado.
LAW.YER, *s.*, advogado, causídico, notário.
LAX.A.TIVE, *s.*, laxante; *adj.*, laxativo.
LAX.ITY, *s.*, lassidão, frouxidão.
LAY, *s.*, situação, postura; *adj.*, leigo; *v.*, colocar, pôr, derrubar, preparar.
LAY.ER, *s.*, camada, leito; *v.*, mergulhar.
LAY IN, *v.*, armazenar.
LAY.MAN, *s.*, leigo.
LAY.OUT, *s.*, desenho, disposição de móveis, ordem em um ambiente.
LAZE, *v.*, vadiar, vagabundear.
LA.ZI.NESS, *s.*, preguiça.
LAZ.ING, *adj.*, preguiçoso, vadio.
LA.ZY, *adj.*, preguiçoso.
LEA, *s.*, prado, pradaria, várzea, campina.
LEAD, *s.*, chumbo, sonda, conduta, guia, cabo, protagonista; *v.*, conduzir, dirigir, comandar, persuadir, jogar de mão.
LEAD.ER, *s.*, líder, comandante, chefe.
LEAD.ER.SHIP, *s.*, liderança, comando, condução.
LEAD.ING, *s.*, direção, liderança, comando; *adj.*, principal, primeiro.
LEAD LINE, *s.*, sonda.
LEAF, *s.*, folha, folhagem, pétala, chapa; *v.*, cobrir de folhas, folhear.
LEAF.LESS, *adj.*, sem folhas, desfolhado.
LEAF.LET, *s.*, folhinha, folheto.
LEAFY, *adj.*, frondoso, copado, cheio de folhas.
LEAGUE, *s.*, liga, aliança, confederação; *v.*, associar-se, unir-se, ligar-se.
LEAK, *s.*, fuga, vazamento, rombo; *v.*, escoar, vazar, derramar, gotejar.
LEAK.AGE, *s.*, escoamento, vazamento, derrame.
LEAK.ING, *s.*, derrame, vazamento, escoamento.
LEAN, *s.*, carne magra, inclinação; *adj.*, magro, pobre; *v.*, tender, inclinar-se.
LEAN.ING, *s.*, inclinação, propensão, *adj.*, inclinado, desviado.
LEAP, *s.*, salto, pulo; saltar, pular, arremessar-se.
LEAP DAY, *s.* o dia 29 de fevereiro.
LEAP YEAR, *s.*, ano bissexto.

LEAP.ING, *s.*, salto, pulo.
LEARN, *v.*, aprender, compreender, decorar, assimilar.
LEARN.ED.NESS, *s.*, erudição, aprendizagem.
LEARN.ER, *s.*, principiante, aprendiz.
LEARN.ING, *s.*, saber, aprendizagem.
LEASE.HOLD.ER, *s.*, arrendatário.
LEASH, *s.*, correia, trela; *v.*, controlar, atrelar.
LEAST, *s.*, o mínimo; *adj.*, menor, mínimo; *adv.*, o menos.
LEAST.WAYS, *adv.*, ao menos, pelo menos.
LEATH.ER, *s.*, couro; *v.*, cobrir com couro, revestir com couro.
LEATH.ERY, *adj.*, semelhante a couro.
LEAVE, *s.*, licença, partida; *v.*, partir, ir, viajar, abandonar, sobrar, falecer.
LEAV.EN, *s.*, fermento, levedura; *v.*, fermentar, levedar.
LEAV.ING, *s.*, partida, saída, ida.
LEB.A.NON, *s.*, Líbano.
LECH.ER, *adj.*, lascivo, devasso.
LEC.TION, *s.*, lição.
LEC.TURE, *s.*, preleção, conferência, palestra; *v.*, palestrar, lecionar.
LED.GER, *s.*, livro-razão na contabilidade.
LEECH, *s.*, sanguessuga.
LEEK, *s.*, alho-porro.
LEFT, *s.*, esquerda, lado esquerdo; *adv.*, à esquerda.
LEFT-HAND.ED, *s.*, canhoto.
LEFT.OVERS, *s.*, sobras, restos.
LEG, *s.*, perna, pata, pé, suporte, trecho de um trajeto.
LEG.A.CY, *s.*, legado, herança, doação.
LE.GAL, *adj.*, legal, legítimo, justo, lícito.
LE.GAL.ISM, *s.*, legalismo.
LE.GAL.I.TY, *s.*, legalidade.
LE.GAL.I.ZA.TION, *s.*, legalização.
LE.GAL.IZE, *v.*, legalizar.
LE.GATE, *s.*, legado, delegado; *v.*, legar.
LE.GA.TION, *s.*, legação, missão diplomática.
LEG.END, *s.*, lenda, legenda, mito, fábula.
LEG.I.BLE, *adj.*, legível, evidente, óbvio.
LEG.IS.LATE, *v.*, legislar.
LEG.IS.LA.TION, *s.*, legislação.

LEGISLATIVE / LIBRATE

LEG.IS.LA.TIVE, *adj.*, legislativo.
LEG.IS.LA.TOR, *s.*, legislador.
LEG.IS.LA.TURE, *s.*, legislatura.
LE.GIST, *s.*, legista.
LE.GIT.I.MATE, *v.*, legitimar, tornar legítimo; *adj.*, legítimo, lídimo.
LE.GIT.I.MI.ZA.TION, *s.*, legitimação.
LEG-ROOM, *s.*, espaço para pôr as pernas.
LE.GUME, *s.*, legume.
LE.GU.MI.NOUS, *adj.*, leguminoso.
LEI.SURE, *s.*, lazer, ócio, folga; *adj.*, desocupado, ocioso.
LEM.ON, *s.*, limão, limoeiro; *adj.*, cor de limão.
LEM.ON.ADE, *s.*, limonada.
LEM.ON-JUICE, *s.*, suco de limão.
LEND, *v.*, emprestar.
LEND.ING, *s.*, empréstimo.
LENGHT, *s.*, comprimento, extensão, duração.
LENGHT.EN, *v.*, alongar, encompridar.
LENGHTY, *adj.*, comprido, longo, alongado, esticado.
LE.NIENCE, *s.*, suavidade, brandura, clemência, indulgência.
LE.NIENT, *adj.*, brando, indulgente.
LEN.I.TIVE, *adj., s.*, lenitivo.
LENS, *s.*, lente, objetiva.
LEN.TIL, *s.*, lentilha.
LE.O.NINE, *adj.*, leonino.
LEOP.ARD, *s.*, leopardo.
LEP.ER, *s.*, leproso, hanseniano.
LEP.RO.SY, *s.*, lepra.
LEP.ROUS, *adj.*, leproso.
LES.BI.AN, *s.*, lésbica; *adj.*, lésbico.
LE.SION, *s.*, lesão, machucadura, contusão.
LESS, *s.*, menos; *adj.*, menor, inferior; *adv.*, menos.
LESS.EN, *v.*, diminuir, reduzir.
LESS.ER, *adj.*, menor, inferior.
LES.SON, *s.*, lição, aula; *v.*, repreender, recriminar.
LEST, *conj.*, a fim de que não.
LET, *v.*, deixar, permitir, concordar, aceitar, fazer com que.
LE.THAL, *adj.*, letal, mortal.
LE.THAR.GIC, *adj.*, letárgico.
LETH.AR.GY, *s.*, letargia.

LET INTO, *v.*, deixar entrar, entrar.
LET ON, *v.*, revelar.
LET.TER, *s.*, letra, carta, tipo; *v.*, rotular, marcar com letras.
LET.TER.BOX, *s.*, caixa postal.
LET.TERED, *adj.*, letrado, erudito.
LET.TER.HEAD, *s.*, cabeçalho.
LET.TUCE, *s.*, alface.
LEU.CO.CYTE, *s.*, leucócito.
LEU.KAE.MIA, *s.*, leucemia.
LE.VEE, *s.*, dique, represa.
LEV.EL, *s.*, nível, plano horizontal, altura, estrato; *v.*, nivelar, aplainar.
LEV.EL.LER, *s.*, nivelador.
LEV.EL.LING, *s.*, nivelamento.
LEV.EL UP, *v.*, nivelar.
LE.VER, *s.*, alavanca.
LEV.I.GATE, *v.*, pulverizar, moer, triturar.
LEV.I.TATE, *v.*, levitar.
LEV.I.TA.TION, *s.*, levitação.
LEV.I.TY, *s.*, leviandade, futilidade.
LEVY, *s.*, tributo, imposto, arrecadação; *v.*, arrecadar, cobrar impostos.
LEWD, *adj.*, devasso, obsceno, lascivo, carnal.
LEX.I.CON, *s.*, léxico, dicionário, glossário.
LI.ABIL.I.TY, *s.*, responsabilidade, dívida, dependência.
LI.AI.SON, *s.*, ligação, liame.
LI.AR, *s.*, mentiroso.
LI.BA.TION, *s.*, libação.
LI.BEL, *s.*, libelo, ataque, difamação; *v.*, caluniar, difamar.
LI.BEL.LING, *s.*, difamação.
LIB.ER.AL, *adj.*, liberal, dadivoso, generoso.
LIB.ER.AL.ISM, *s.*, liberalismo.
LIB.ER.AL.I.TY, *s.*, liberalidade.
LIB.ER.AL.IZE, *v.*, liberalizar.
LIB.ER.ATE, *v.*, liberar, libertar.
LIB.ER.A.TION, *s.*, liberação, libertação.
LIB.ER.TY, *s.*, liberdade.
LI.BID.I.NOUS, *adj.*, libidinoso, devasso, lascivo.
LI.BRA.R.IAN, *s.*, bibliotecário.
LI.BRARY, *s.*, biblioteca.
LI.BRATE, *v.*, equilibrar, librar.

LIB.YA, *s.*, Líbia.
LIB.YAN, *adj.*, *s.*, líbio.
LICE, *s.*, piolhos.
LI.CENCE, *s.*, licença; carteira de motorista.
LI.CEN.TI.ATE, *adj.*, licenciado.
LI.CHEN, *s.*, líquen.
LIC.IT, *adj.*, lícito, permitido.
LICK, *s.*, lambida, golpe, pancada; *v.*, lamber, bater, dar pancada.
LICK.ER.ISH, *adj.*, saboroso, delicado.
LID, *s.*, tampa; pálpebra.
LIE, *s.*, mentira; antro; *v.*, deitar-se, estar deitado, encontrar-se; mentir.
LIE-DOWN, *v.*, descansar.
LIEF, *adv.*, de bom grado, agradavelmente.
LIEN, *s.*, hipoteca.
LIEU.TEN.ANT, *s.*, tenente.
LIFE, *s.*, vida, existência, duração, conduta, animação, biografia.
LIFE BELT, *s.*, cinto salva-vidas.
LIFE.GUARD, *s.*, salva-vidas.
LIFE.LESS, *adj.*, inerte, sem vida, morto.
LIFE.LIKE, *adj.*, natural, próprio, realista.
LIFE.LONG, *adj.*, vitalício, eterno, perene.
LIFT, *s.*, levantamento, ascensor, carga; *v.*, levantar, erguer, alçar.
LIFT-OFF, *s.*, decolagem de avião; *v.*, decolar, alçar voo.
LIG.A.MENT, *s.*, ligamento, ligação.
LI.GA.TION, *s.*, ligação, liame.
LIGHT, *s.*, luz, farol de carro, semáforo, vela, brilho; *v.*, acender, iluminar.
LIGHT.ER, *s.*, isqueiro, acendedor; barca, barcaça.
LIGHT.HOUSE, *s.*, farol.
LIGHT.ING, *s.*, iluminação.
LIGHT.LESS, *adj.*, sem luz, escuro, apagado.
LIGHT.NESS, *s.*, leveza, destreza, rapidez.
LIGHT.NING, *s.*, relâmpago, brilho, raio.
LIGHT.SOME, *adj.*, claro, brilhante.
LIGHT.SOME.NESS, *s.*, alegria, regozijo, luminosidade.
LIKE, *s.*, gosto, preferência, amor, semelhante; *v.*, gostar, amar, semelhar, parecer, querer, desejar, agradar.
LIKE.ABLE, *adj.*, simpático, agradável, afável.
LIKE.LI.NESS, *s.*, semelhança, igualdade, verossimilhança.
LIKE.LY, *adj.*, provável, possível.
LIK.EN, *v.*, assemelhar, parecer, comparar.
LIK.ING, *s.*, simpatia, afeição.
LI.LAC, *adj.*, lilás.
LILT, *s.*, canção alegre, cadência; *v.*,
LILY, *s.*, lírio, açucena, flor de lis; *adj.*, branco, alvo, claro, cândido.
LIMB, *s.*, membro, borda, orla.
LIMBED, *adj.*, com membros.
LIMB.LESS, *adj.*, sem membros.
LIM.BO, *s.*, limbo, prisão; exílio, ostracismo.
LIME.STONE, *s.*, pedra calcária.
LIM.IT, *s.*, limite, marco; *v.*, limitar, demarcar, restringir.
LIM.I.TARY, *adj.*, limítrofe.
LIM.I.TA.TION, *s.*, limitação.
LIM.IT.ED, *adj.*, limitado.
LIM.OU.SINE, *s.*, limusina.
LIMP, *s.*, ato de coxear; *v.*, coxear, mancar; *adj.*, flexível, mole.
LIMP.ER, *s.*, coxo, manco.
LIM.PID, *adj.*, límpido, claro, puro, calmo.
LIM.PID.I.TY, *s.*, limpidez, clareza, claridade.
LIMY, *adj.*, calcário, lodoso, viscoso.
LINE, *s.*, linha, corda, fio, fila, ruga; *v.*, enfileirar, alinhar, riscar.
LIN.E.AGE, *s.*, linhagem, estirpe, descendência.
LIN.E.AR, *adj.*, linear.
LIN.E.A.TION, *s.*, esboço, lineamento.
LIN.EN, *s.*, linho, roupas de cama, roupa branca; *adj.*, feito de linho.
LIN.GUIST, *s.*, linguista.
LIN.GUIS.TIC, *adj.*, linguístico.
LIN.GUIS.TICS, *s.*, linguística.
LIN.I.MENT, *s.*, linimento, loção, unguento.
LIN.ING, *s.*, forro, parede.
LINK, *s.*, elo, aro, ligação, conexão, vínculo; *v.*, vincular, conectar, ligar.
LINK.ING, *s.*, ligação, conexão, união.
LINN, *s.*, cachoeira, catarata, queda-d'água.

LI.ON, s., leão.
LI.ON.ESS, s., leoa.
LIP, s., lábio, beiço; v., tocar com os lábios, murmurar, beijar.
LIPPED, adj., que tem lábios.
LIP.STICK, s., batom.
LIQ.UE.FAC.TION, s., liquefação.
LIQ.UE.FY, v., liquefazer, derreter, desmanchar.
LI.QUEUR, s., licor.
LIQ.UID, adj., s., líquido.
LIQ.UI.DATE, v., liquidar.
LIQ.UI.DA.TION, s., liquidação.
LIQ.UID.IZER, s., liquidificador.
LIQ.UID.NESS, s., liquidez.
LI.QUOR, s., licor.
LIS.BON, s., Lisboa.
LIST, s., lista, rol, relação, v., listar, fazer uma lista.
LIST.EN, v., escutar, ouvir, perceber.
LIS.TEN.ER, s., ouvinte.
LIST.EN IN, v., ouvir conversa alheia.
LIS.TEN.ING, s., ato de ouvir, audição.
LIST.LESS adj., apático, indiferente, murcho.
LIST.LESS.NESS, s., indiferença, apatia.
LIT.ER.AL, adj., literal, ao pé da letra.
LIT.ER.AL.I.TY, s., literalidade, sentido literal.
LIT.ER.ARY, adj., literário.
LIT.ER.ATE, adj., alfabetizado, letrado, instruído.
LIT.ER.A.TURE, s., literatura.
LITHE, adj., ágil, rápido, destro.
LITHE.NESS, s., agilidade, rapidez, destreza.
LITHER, adj., flexível, plasmável, plástico.
LITH.O.GRAPH, s., litografia; v., litografar.
LI.THOG.RA.PHY, s., litografia.
LIT.I.GANT, adj., s., litigante.
LIT.I.GATE, v., litigar, contender.
LIT.I.GA.TION, s., litígio, contenda, disputa.
LI.TI.GIOUS, adj., litigioso, contencioso.
LI.TRE, s., litro.
LIT.TER, s., liteira, maca, padiola, desordem; v., espalhar feno, dar à luz uma ninhada.
LIT.TLE, adj., pequeno, pouco, breve, fraco; adv., pouco; s., pouca coisa.
LIT.TLE.NESS, s., ninharia, bagatela, pequena quantidade, pequenez.

LIT.TO.RAL, adj., s., litoral.
LI.TUR.GIC, adj., litúrgico.
LIT.UR.GY, s., liturgia.
LIV.ABLE, adj., habitável, suportável.
LIVE, v., viver, existir, subsistir, estar, ser, morar.
LIVED, adj., com vida, existente, vivente.
LIVE.LI.HOOD, s., subsistência, meio de vida.
LIVE.LI.NESS, s., vida, vigor, vivência, vivacidade.
LIVE.LY, adj., vivo.
LIV.ER, s., fígado.
LIVE.STOCK, s., gado, rebanho.
LIV.ID, adj., lívido, pálido; furioso.
LI.VID.I.TY, s., lividez, palidez.
LIV.ING, adj., vivo.
LIV.ING-ROOM, s., sala de estar.
LIZ.ARD, s., lagarto.
LOAD, s., carga, peso, carregamento; v., carregar, pesar, oprimir.
LOAD.ER, s., carregador.
LOAD.STONE, s., pedra-ímã.
LOAF, s., pão de forma.
LOAN, s., empréstimo; v., emprestar.
LOATHE, v., detestar, odiar, ter aversão.
LOATH.ING, s., asco, repugnância, nojo, ódio.
LOB.BY, s., saguão, entrada; lóbi, grupo de pressão política; v., pressionar.
LOB.STER, s., lagosta, lagostim.
LOB.ULE, s., lóbulo.
LO.CAL, adj., local; s., trem local.
LO.CAL.I.TY, s., localidade.
LO.CAL.I.ZA.TION, s., localização.
LO.CAL.IZE, v., localizar.
LO.CATE, v., localizar, situar.
LO.CAT.ED, adj., localizado, sito, situado.
LO.CA.TION, s., local, situação, posição.
LOCH, s., lago.
LOCK, s., fechadura; eclusa, comporta; v., chavear, fechar, travar.
LOCK.ET, s., medalhão.
LOCK.OUT, s., locaute, greve de patrões.
LOCK.RAM, s., estopa.
LOCK.SMITH, s., serralheiro, chaveiro.
LOCK.UP, s., prisão, cadeia.

LO.CO.MO.TION, s., locomoção.
LO.CO.MO.TIVE, s., locomotiva.
LO.CUST, s., gafanhoto.
LO.CU.TION, s., locução, frase, expressão verbal.
LO.CU.TO.RY, s., locutório.
LODGE.MENT, s., alojamento.
LODG.ER, s., inquilino, hóspede.
LODG.ING, s., alojamento, casa, moradia, habitação.
LOFT, s., sótão.
LOFTY, adj., soberbo, arrogante, orgulhoso.
LOG, s., tora, tronco, cepo, lenho; v., cortar, derrubar árvores.
LOG.A.RITHM s., logaritmo.
LOG.GER, s., madeireiro.
LOG.IC, s., lógica.
LOG.I.CAL, adj., lógico, racional, metódico.
LOG.MAN, s., lenhador.
LOIN, s., quadril, lombo, carne de lombo assada.
LOIN.CLOTH, s., tanga.
LOI.TER, v., demorar, vadiar, atrasar-se, perder tempo.
LON.DON, s., Londres.
LONE, adj., solitário, só, retirado; solteira, viúva.
LONE.LI.NESS, s., solidão, isolamento.
LONE.LY, adj., solitário, só.
LONG, adj., longo, comprido, extenso; adv., durante, longamente.
LONG.BOAT, s., chalupa; lancha.
LON.GEV.I.TY, s., longevidade.
LONG.ING, s., desejo, anseio, desejo ardente; adj., ansioso, ardente.
LON.GI.TUDE, s., longitude.
LONG-LOST, adj., perdido há muito tempo.
LONG-TERM, adj., a longo prazo.
LOO, s., casa de banho.
LOO.BY, adj., tolo, bobo.
LOOK, v., olhar, parecer, fixar-se em; s., olhar, olhadela, vista.
LOOK AFTER, v., cuidar de, tratar com.
LOOK BACK, v., lembrar, recordar, relembrar.
LOOK.ING, s., olhar, olhada.
LOOK.OUT, s., posto de observação, vigia, vigilância.
LOOK OVER, v., examinar, verificar.

LOOM, s., tear, cabo de remo; v., aparecer, agigantar-se, surgir um vulto.
LOOM.ING, s., miragem, ilusão, visão; adj., indefinido.
LOON, s., pateta, bobo.
LOO.NY, adj., adoidado, meio doido; s., tolo, pateta, bobo, imbecil.
LOOP.HOLE, s., saída, buraco, abertura.
LOOSE, adj., solto, livre, frouxo.
LOOS.EN, v., soltar, desatar, afrouxar, desprender.
LOOSE.NESS, s., frouxidão; diarreia.
LOOT, s., pilhagem, saque, despojos; v., saquear, pilhar.
LOOT.ER, s., saqueador.
LOP, v., podar, desbastar; s., ramos cortados, ramos podados.
LOP.PER, s., podador.
LOP.PING, s., poda, desbaste.
LORD, s., senhor, amo, patrão; v., dominar, elevar, governar.
LORN, adj., sem parentes, sem amigos.
LOR.RY, s., caminhão, carro; **LORRY DRIVER**, s., caminhoneiro.
LOSE, v., perder.
LOS.ER, s., perdedor, derrotado.
LOSS, s., perda.
LOST, adj., perdido.
LOT, s., lote, porção, quantidade; v., lotear, dividir em lotes.
LO.TION, s., loção.
LOT.TERY, s., loteria.
LO.TUS, s., loto, lótus.
LOUD, adj., forte, alto, rumoroso, estrepitoso.
LOUD-HAIL.ER, s., megafone.
LOUD.NESS, s., ruído, rumor, barulho.
LOUD.SPEAK.ER, s., alto-falante.
LOUGH, s., lago.
LOUR, s., rosto carrancudo, face carregada; v., mostrar-se severo.
LOUSE, s., piolho.
LOUSY, adj., ruim, péssimo.
LOUT, s., rústico.
LOV.ABLE, adj., louvável, adorável, simpático.
LOV.ABLE.NESS, s., amabilidade, simpatia.

LOVE, s., amor; v., amar, gostar, preferir.
LOVE.LESS, adj., sem amor.
LOVE.LI.NESS, s., amabilidade, beleza, graciosidade.
LOVE.LY, adj., encantador, fascinante, apaixonante, belo.
LOV.ER, s., amante.
LOV.ING, adj., carinhoso, encantador.
LOW, adj., baixo, doente, pessimista; v., balir, mugir.
LOW-CUT, adj., decotado.
LOW.ER, adj., mais baixo, inferior; v., rebaixar, abaixar, reduzir.
LOW.ER.MOST, adj., o mais baixo, ínfimo.
LOW.LANDS, s., pl., planície.
LOW.LI.NESS, s., humildade, vileza, torpeza.
LOW.LY, adj., humilde.
LOY.AL, adj., leal.
LOY.AL.TY, s., lealdade.
LU.BRI.CANT, adj., s., lubrificante; adj., untado.
LU.BRI.CA.TION, s., lubrificação.
LU.CEN.CY, s., brilho, fulgor, resplendor.
LU.CENT, adj., luzente, brilhante, luminoso.
LU.CERNE, s., luzerna.
LU.CID.I.TY, s., lucidez, brilho, luminosidade, clareza.
LUCK, s., acaso, sorte, felicidade.
LUCKY, adj., afortunado, ditoso, sortudo.
LU.CRA.TIVE, adj., lucrativo.
LU.CRE, s., lucro, proveito.
LU.DI.CROUS, adj., ridículo.
LUG, s., puxão, arrasto; v., arrastar, puxar.
LUG.GAGE, s., bagagem.
LUKE.WARM, adj., tépido, morno.
LUKE.WARM.NESS, s., tibieza, tepidez, mornidade.
LULL, s., calmaria, pausa; v., acalmar, aquietar; embalar alguém.
LUM.BAR, adj., lombar.
LUM.BER, s., trastes, restos, madeira serrada, tábua.
LUM.BER.JACK, s., madeireiro, lenhador.
LU.MI.NOS.I.TY, s., luminosidade.
LU.MI.NOUS, adj., luminoso.

LUMP.ER, s., estivador.
LUMP.ISH, adj., pesado, grosseiro.
LUMPY, adj., encaroçado.
LU.NAR, adj., lunar.
LU.NA.TIC, adj., lunático.
LUNCH, s., lanche, almoço, merenda; v., lanchar, comer, alimentar-se.
LUN.CHEON.ETTE, s., lanchonete.
LUNCH.TIME, s., hora de almoço.
LU.NETTE, s., luneta.
LUNG, s., pulmão.
LURCH, s., desamparo, abandono, solavanco; v., balançar.
LURCH.ING, s., solavanco.
LURE, s., isca, engodo, engano; v., engodar, enganar, seduzir.
LU.RID, adj., lúrido, pálido, lívido, branco, esbranquiçado.
LUSH, adj., exuberante, luxuriante, viçoso, suculento.
LUSH.NESS, s., viço, exuberância, sumo.
LUST, s., luxo, luxúria, concupiscência.
LUST.FUL, adj., sensual, luxurioso.
LUS.TRA.TION, s., lustração, polimento.
LUSTRE, s., lustre, brilho.
LUS.TROUS, adj., lustroso, brilhante, reluzente.
LUSTY, adj., robusto, forte.
LU.THER.AN, adj., s., luterano.
LUX, s, lux.
LUX.ATE, v., luxar, provocar uma luxação.
LUX.A.TION, s., luxação.
LUXE, s., luxo.
LUX.U.RI.ANT, adj., luxuriante, viçoso.
LUX.U.RY, s., luxo, fausto, delícia.
LY.CE.UM, s., liceu.
LYMPH, s., linfa.
LYNCH, v., linchar.
LYNX, s., lince.
LYRE, s., lira.
LYR.IC, adj., lírico; s., lírica.
LYR.I.CAL, adj., lírico.
LYRICISM, s., lirismo.

M

M, *s.*, décima terceira letra do alfabeto inglês.
M, algarismo romano – 1.000.
MA, *s.*, *abrev.* de mamãe.
MA.CA.BRE, *adj.*, macabro.
MAC.AD.AM.I.ZA.TION, *s.*, macadamização, macadame.
MAC.AD.AM.IZE, *v.*, macadamizar.
MAC.A.RO.NI, *s.*, macarrão.
MACE, *s.*, maça, clava, bastão.
MAC.ER.ATE, *v.*, macerar.
MACH.I.NATE, *v.*, maquinar, tramar, engendrar, conspirar.
MACH.I.NA.TION, *s.*, maquinação, conspiração, trama.
MA.CHINE, *s.*, máquina, mecanismo, carro, autômato.
MA.CHIN.ERY, *s.*, maquinaria, mecanismo.
MA.CHIN.IST, *s.*, maquinista, engenheiro, mecânico.
MACK.IN.TOSH, *s.*, capa impermeável.
MAC.U.LATE, *v.*, macular, manchar, sujar; *adj.*, maculado, manchado.
MAD, *adj.*, louco, desvairado, tolo, furioso, brabo, enfurecido.
MAD.AM, *s.*, senhora.
MAD.CAP, *s.*, louco, maluco; *adj.*, descontrolado, excêntrico.
MAD.DEN, *v.*, enlouquecer, enfurecer, enraivécer.
MADE, *adj.*, *part.*, feito, fabricado, terminado.
MADE-CIR.CUIT, *s.*, circuito fechado.
MAD.HOUSE, *s.*, hospício, manicômio.
MAD.MAN, *s.*, louco, doido, alienado, desvairado.
MAD.NESS, *s.*, loucura, demência, raiva.
MA.DON.NA, *s.*, Nossa Senhora, estátua de Nossa Senhora.
MAG.A.ZINE, *s.*, magazine, revista, programa de TV; *s.*, armazém.
MAG.IC, *adj.*, mágico; *s.*, magia.

MAG.I.CAL, *adj.*, mágico.
MA.GI.CIAN, *s.*, mágico, prestidigitador, bruxo.
MAG.IS.TRA.CY, *s.*, magistratura.
MAG.IS.TRATE, *s.*, magistrado, juiz.
MAG.NATE, *s.*, magnata, pessoa muito rica.
MAG.NE.SIA, *s.*, magnésia.
MAG.NET.IC, *adj.*, magnético, imantizado.
MAG.NE.TISM, *s.*, magnetismo, imã.
MAG.NE.TIZE, *v.*, magnetizar, imantizar.
MAG.NI.FI.ER, *s.*, ampliador, lente de aumento.
MAG.NI.FY, *v.*, magnificar, engrandecer, aumentar.
MAG.YAR *adj.*, húngaro.
MA.HA.RA.JAH, *s.*, marajá.
MA.HOM.ET, *s.*, Maomé.
MAID, *s.*, donzela, solteira, senhorita; criada, empregada.
MAID.EN, *s.*, donzela, senhorita, solteirona; *adj.*, solteira.
MAIDEN.HOOD, *s.*, virgindade, estado de solteira.
MAIL, *s.*, correio, correspondência; *v.*, remeter cartas pelo correio.
MAIL.ABLE, *adj.*, que se pode remeter por correio.
MAIL.BOX, *s.*, caixa de correio, caixa de correspondência.
MAIM, *s.*, mutilação, aleijamento, defeito físico; *v.*, mutilar, aleijar.
MAIN, *adj.*, fundamental, principal; *s.*, cano, esgoto, oceano, mar alto.
MAIN.LAND, *s.*, continente.
MAIN.TAIN, *v.*, manter, conservar, afirmar.
MAIN.TAIN.ABLE, *adj.*, suportável.
MAIN.TAIN.ER, *s.*, mantenedor.
MAIN.TE.NANCE, *s.*, manutenção, sustento, alimentação.
MAIZE, *s.*, milho.

MA.JES.TIC, *adj.*, majestoso, grandioso.
MAJ.ES.TY, *s.*, majestade.
MA.JOR, *s.*, major; *adj.*, maior, principal.
MA.JOR.I.TY, *s.*, maioria.
MA.JUS.CULE, *s.*, maiúscula; *adj.*, maiúsculo.
MAKE, *v.*, fazer, fabricar, produzir; *s.*, marca, feitura, feitio, forma.
MAKE-BE.LIEVE, *v.*, fingir, fazer de conta.
MAKE FOR, *v.*, dirigir-se, rumar.
MAK.ER, *s.*, fabricante, criador, inventor.
MAL.A.DY, *s.*, doença, enfermidade.
MAL.AISE, *s.*, mal-estar, indisposição.
MAL.AP.RO.POS, *adj.*, inconveniente, que fala palavrões.
MA.LAR.IA, *s.*, malária.
MA.LAY, *adj.*, malaio.
MA.LAY.SIA, *s.*, Malásia.
MAL.CON.TENT, *adj., s.*, descontente, infeliz.
MALE, *s.*, macho, varão, sexo masculino: *adj.*, masculino, viril.
MAL.E.DIC.TION, *s.*, maldição.
MAL.E.FAC.TOR, *s.*, malfeitor.
MA.LEF.I.CENT, *adj.*, maléfico, maldoso.
MAL.FEA.SANCE, *s.*, prevaricação.
MA.LIC, *adj.*, próprio da maçã.
MAL.ICE, *s.*, malícia, despudor.
MA.LI.CIOUS, *adj.*, malicioso, maldoso, malevolente.
MA.LIGN, *adj.*, maligno, pernicioso, maldoso; *v.*, difamar, caluniar.
MA.LIG.NANT, *adj.*, maligno, diabólico.
MA.LIG.NI.TY, *s.*, malignidade, maldade.
MALL, *s.*, centro comercial; **SHOPPING MALL**, *s.*, shopping center.
MAL.LEA.BIL.I.TY, *s.*, maleabilidade.
MAL.LEA.BLE, *adj.*, maleável.
MAL.LOW, *s.*, malva.
MAL.NU.TRI.TION, *s.*, má nutrição, má alimentação.
MAL.ODOR.OUS, *adj.*, malcheiroso, fétido.
MALT, *s.*, malte; *v.*, preparar o malte para cerveja.
MAL.TREAT, *v.*, maltratar, atormentar.
MAL.TREAT.MENT, *s.*, mau trato, tormento.
MAM.MA, *s.*, mama, mamãe.
MAM.MAL, *s.*, mamífero.
MAM.MA.LIA, *s.*, mamíferos.
MAM.MOTH, *s.*, mamute.
MAM.MY, *s.*, mamãe; ama de leite preta.
MAN, *s.*, homem, varão, ser humano, pessoa, indivíduo; *v.*, colocar soldados, tripular, equipar.
MAN.A.CLE, *s.*, algemas, grilhetas; *v.*, algemar, prender, manietar.
MAN.AGE, *v.*, arranjar-se, dirigir, administrar, manejar.
MAN.AGE.MENT, *s.*, administração, direção, governo.
MAN.AG.ER, *s.*, gerente, administrador.
MAN.AG.ER.ESS, *s.*, gerente.
MAN.A.TEE, *s.*, peixe-boi.
MAN.DA.RIN, *s.*, mandarim; tangerina; cor amarelo-alaranjada.
MAN.DATE, *s.*, mandato, delegação.
MAN.DA.TO.RY, *s.*, mandatário.
MAN.DI.BLE, *s.*, mandíbula, maxilar inferior.
MANE, *s.*, juba, crina.
MA.NEU.VER, *s.*, manobra, evolução; *v.*, manobrar, dirigir.
MAN.FUL, *adj.*, másculo, varonil, viril, corajoso.
MAN.GA.NESE, *s.*, manganês.
MAN.GER, *s.*, manjedoura.
MAN.GO, *s.*, manga, mangueira.
MANGY, *adj.*, sarnento, chaguento.
MAN.HOLE, *s.*, bueiro, boca de lobo.
MAN.HOOD, *s.*, idade adulta, varonilidade, masculinidade.
MA.NIA, *s.*, mania.
MA.NI.AC, *adj.*, maníaco.
MAN.IC-DE.PRES.SIVE, *adj., s.*, maníaco-depressivo.
MAN.I.CURE, *s.*, manicure; *v.*, tratar das unhas das mãos e pés.
MAN.I.FEST, *s.*, manifesto, ; *v.*, manifestar, declarar; *adj.* manifesto.
MAN.I.FES.TA.TION, *s.*, manifestação, declaração.
MAN.I.FES.TO, *s.*, manifesto, declaração, proclamação.
MANIFOLD, *s.*, cópia; *v.*, mimeografar,

reproduzir; *adj.*, muitos.
MAN.I.FOLD, *s.*, mimeógrafo, fotocopiadora, xérox.
MAN.I.KIN, *s.*, manequim, boneco.
MAN.I.OC, *s.*, mandioca, aipim, macaxeira.
MA.NIP.U.LATE, *v.*, manipular.
MA.NIP.U.LA.TION, *s.*, manipulação.
MAN.KIND, *s.*, humanidade, gênero humano, espécie humana.
MAN.LIKE, *adj.*, característico do homem, viril, varonil.
MAN.LY, *adj.*, másculo, varonil, viril.
MAN.NA, *s.*, maná.
MAN.NER, *s.*, modo, maneira, comportamento, procedimento.
MAN.NERED, *adj.*, educado, cortês, polido, gentil.
MAN.NISH, *adj.*, másculo, varonil, viril.
MA.NOM.E.TER, *s.*, manômetro.
MAN.POW.ER, *s.*, potencial humano, mão de obra, capacidade.
MAN.SION, *s.*, mansão, palácio, palacete.
MAN.SLAUGH.TER, *s.*, matança, assassinato involuntário.
MAN-SLAY.ER, *s.*, homicida.
MAN.TLE, *s.*, manto, capa; *v.*, cobrir, tampar.
MAN.U.AL, *s.*, manual, compêndio: *adj.*, manual, feito à mão.
MAN.U.FAC.TO.RY, *s.*, fábrica, oficina.
MAN.U.FAC.TURE, *s.*, manufatura, fabricação; *v.*, manufaturar.
MAN.U.FAC.TUR.ER, *s.*, fabricante, manufaturador.
MA.NURE, *s.*, estrume, adubo; *v.*, adubar, estrumar, fertilizar.
MA.NUR.ING, *s.*, fertilização, adubação.
MAN.U.SCRIPT, *s.*, manuscrito.
MANY, *adj.*, *pron.*, muitos, muitas.
MAP, *s.*, mapa; *v.*, mapear, desenhar mapas.
MAR, *v.*, estragar, frustrar, arruinar.
MAR.A.THON, *s.*, maratona.
MAR.BLE, *s.*, mármore.
MARCH, *s.*, março; **MARCH**, marcha, passeata; *v.*, marchar, fazer passeata.
MARCH.ER, *s.*, marchador, indivíduo que marcha.
MARCH.ING, *s.*, marcha.
MAR.CHIO.NESS, *s.*, marquesa.
MARE, *s.*, égua.
MAR.GA.RINE, *s.*, margarina.
MAR.GIN, *s.*, margem, orla, borda; *v.*, margear, orlar, marginar.
MAR.I.AN, *adj.*, mariano, referente a Nossa Senhora.
MARI.GOLD, *s.*, malmequer.
MAR.I.JUA.NA, *s.*, maconha, marijuana.
MA.RI.NA, *s.*, marina.
MAR.I.NADE, *s.*, marinada.
MAR.I.NATE, *v.*, marinar, pôr em vinha d'alhos.
MA.RINE, *s.*, fuzileiro naval americano; *adj.*, marinho.
MAR.I.NER, *s.*, marinheiro.
MAR.I.TAL, *adj.*, marital, matrimonial.
MAR.I.TIME, *adj.*, marítimo.
MAR.JO.RAM, *s.*, mánjerona.
MARK, *s.*, marca, sinal, impressão, símbolo, alvo; *v.*, marcar, assinalar, distinguir, indicar, escolher, designar.
MARK AS, *v.*, marcar, rotular, etiquetar.
MARK.ER, *s.*, marcador, rotulador.
MAR.KET, *s.*, mercado, supermercado; *v.*, comerciar, comercializar.
MAR.KET.ING, *s.*, marketing, marquetim, propaganda para vendas.
MAR.KET.PLACE, *s.*, mercado, praça de vendas.
MAR.MA.LADE, *s.*, marmelada, doce, geleia.
MAR.MOT, *s.*, marmota.
MAR.RIAGE, *s.*, casamento, matrimônio, núpcias.
MAR.RIED, *adj.*, casado, esposado, matrimonial.
MAR.RON, *adj.*, cor castanha, castanho.
MAR.ROW, *s.*, medula, tutano; essência.
MAR.RY, *v.*, casar, desposar, unir em matrimônio.
MARS, *s.*, marte.
MARSHAL, *s.*, marechal, chefe de polícia; ordenar, dispor, dirigir.
MARSHY, *adj.*, pantanoso.
MAR.SU.PI.AL, *adj.*, *s.*, marsupial.
MART, *s.*, mercado, feira.

MARTIAL   402   **MAWKISH**

MAR.TIAL, *adj.*, marcial, guerreiro, lutador.
MAR.TYR, *s.*, mártir; *v.*, martirizar, torturar, atormentar.
MAR.TYR.DOM, *s.*, martírio, tortura.
MAR.VEL, *s.*, maravilha, prodígio, magia; *v.*, maravilhar-se, admirar.
MAR.VEL.OUS, *adj.*, maravilhoso, mágico, extraordinário.
MARX.ISM, *s.*, marxismo.
MAR.ZI.PAN, *s.*, maçapão.
MAS.COT, *s.*, mascote.
MAS.CU.LINE, *s.*, masculino; *adj.*, masculino, viril, forte.
MASH, *s.*, mistura, pasta, mingau, purê; *v.*, misturar, triturar.
MASK, *s.*, máscara; *v.*, mascarar, esconder o rosto com máscara.
MASK.ER, *s.*, mascarado.
MAS.OCH.IST, *s.*, masoquista.
MA.SON, *s.*, mação, pedreiro.
MA.SON.RY, *s.*, alvenaria, maçonaria.
MASS, *s.*, missa; massa, montão; *v.*, reunir-se, concentrar-se.
MAS.SA.CRE, *s.*, massacre, carnificina; *v.*, massacrar.
MAS.SAGE, *s.*, massagem; *v.*, massagear, fazer massagens.
MAS.SIVE, *adj.*, maciço, compacto, enorme.
MAST, *s.*, mastro, poste.
MAS.TER, *s.*, mestre, senhor, patrão, professor; *v.*, dominar, controlar.
MAS.TER.FUL, *adj.*, autoritário, dominador, magistral, destro.
MAS.TER-KEY, *s.*, chave-mestra.
MAS.TER.LESS, *adj.*, sem dono, sem mestre.
MAS.TER.LI.NESS, *s.*, mestria, habilidade.
MAS.TER.PIECE, *s.*, obra-prima.
MAS.TI.CATE, *v.*, mastigar, morder.
MAS.TI.CA.TION, *s.*, mastigação.
MAS.TIFF, *s.*, mastim, cão.
MAS.TO.DON, *s.*, mastodonte.
MAS.TUR.BATE, *s.*, masturbar-se, masturbar.
MAS.TUR.BA.TION, *s.*, masturbação.
MAT, *s.*, esteira, capacho, tapete; *v.*, esteirar, entrançar.
MATCH, *s.*, fósforo, jogo, luta, partida; *v.*, emparelhar, casar, competir.
MATCH.BOX, *s.*, caixa de fósforos.
MATE, *s.*, colega, camarada, cônjuge, macho/fêmea; *v.*, casar, unir.
MA.TE.RI.AL, *s.*, material, matéria, ingrediente, tecido, anotações.
MA.TE.RI.AL.ISM, *s.*, materialismo.
MA.TE.RI.AL.IST, *s.*, materialista.
MA.TE.RI.AL.IZE, *v.*, materializar.
MA.TER.NAL, *adj.*, maternal.
MA.TER.NI.TY, *s.*, maternidade.
MATH.E.MA.TI.CIAN, *s.*, matemático.
MATH.E.MAT.ICS, *s.*, matemática.
MAT.I.NÉE, *s.*, matinê.
MA.TRI.CIDE, *s.*, matricídio; matricida.
MA.TRIC.U.LATE, *v.*, matricular, matricular-se.
MA.TRIC.U.LA.TION, *s.*, matrícula.
MAT.RI.MO.NIAL, *adj.*, matrimonial.
MAT.RI.MO.NY, *s.*, matrimônio, casamento.
MA.TRIX, *s.*, matriz, madre.
MA.TRON, *s.*, enfermeira-chefe; matrona.
MATT, *adj.*, fusco, opaco, sem brilho.
MAT.TER, *s.*, assunto, tema, questão, matéria, substância.
MAT.TING, *s.*, esteira, capacho, tapete.
MAT.TOCK, *s.*, enxadão.
MAT.TRESS, *s.*, colchão.
MAT.U.RATE, *v.*, maturar, amadurecer, fazer amadurecer.
MAT.U.RA.TION, *s.*, maturação.
MA.TURE, *adj.*, maduro, amadurecido; *v.*, amadurecer.
MA.TU.RI.TY, *s.*, maturidade.
MA.TU.TI.NAL, *adj.*, matutinal, matutino.
MAUD.LIN, *s.*, sentimentalismo; *adj.*, sentimental, embriagado.
MAUL, *s.*, marreta, malho; *v.*, malhar, espancar.
MAUN.DER, *v.*, murmurar, divagar, rosnar, dizer bobagens.
MAU.SO.LE.UM, *s.*, mausoléu.
MAWK.ISH, *adj.*, enjoativo, repugnante, lamuriento.

MAX.IL.LA, *s.*, osso maxilar.
MAX.IL.LARY, *adj.*, maxilar.
MAX.IM, *s.*, máxima.
MAX.I.MUM, *s.*, máximo.
MAY, *s.*, maio; **MAY DAY** – 1.° de maio.
MAY.BE, *adv.*, talvez, quiçá.
MAY.HEM, *s.*, caos.
MAY.ON.NAISE, *s.*, maionese.
MAY.OR, *s.*, prefeito.
MAZE, *s.*, labirinto, confusão; *v.*, confundir, embaraçar.
ME, *pron.*, me, mim, eu.
MEAD.OW, *s.*, prado, campina.
MEA.GRE, *adj.*, escasso, magro, estéril.
MEAL, *s.*, refeição, farinha; *v.*, comer, alimentar-se.
MEAL.TIME, *s.*, hora da refeição.
MEAN, *s.*, meio, meio-termo, média; *adj.*, sovina, mesquinho, médio.
MEAN.ING, *s.*, sentido, significado.
MEAN.NESS, *s.*, baixeza, vileza, pobreza, maldade.
MEAN.TIME, *adv.*, entrementes; *conj.*, entretanto.
MEA.SLES, *s.*, sarampo.
MEA.SLY, *adj.*, miserável.
MEA.SUR.ABLE, *adj.*, mensurável.
MEA.SURE, *s.*, medida, extensão, proporção, fita métrica, métrica.
MEA.SURE.MENT, *s.*, medida, medição.
MEA.SUR.ER, *s.*, medidor.
MEA.SUR.ING, *s.*, medição.
MEAT, *s.*, carne, alimento, comida, refeição.
MEAT.BALL, *s.*, almôndega.
ME.A.TUS, *s.*, meato.
MEATY, *adj.*, carnudo.
ME.CHAN.IC, *s.*, mecânico.
ME.CHAN.I.CAL, *adj.*, mecânico.
ME.CHAN.ICS, *s.*, mecânica.
MED.AL, *s.*, medalha.
ME.DAL.LION, *s.*, medalhão.
MED.DLE, *v.*, interferir, intrometer-se, meter-se.
MED.LER, *s.*, intruso, intrometido.
MED.DLING, *s.*, intromissão, ingerência.

ME.DIA, *s., pl.*, **MÍDIA**, meios de comunicação.
ME.DI.ATE, *v.*, mediar.
ME.DI.ATE.NESS, *s.*, mediação, intervenção.
ME.DI.A.TION, *s.*, mediação.
ME.DI.CA.MENT, *s.*, medicamento, remédio.
MED.I.CATE, *v.*, medicar, tratar.
MED.I.CA.TION, *s.*, medicação.
ME.DIC.I.NAL, *adj.*, medicinal.
MED.I.CINE, *s.*, medicina, remédio.
MED.I.CO, *s.*, médico, acadêmico de medicina.
ME.DI.E.VAL, *adj.*, medieval.
ME.DI.O.CRE, *adj., s.*, mediocre.
ME.DI.OC.RI.TY, *s.*, mediocridade.
MED.I.TATE, *v.*, meditar, refletir, pensar.
MED.I.TA.TION, *s.*, meditação.
MED.I.TER.RA.NEAN, *s.*, Mediterrâneo.
ME.DI.UM, *s.*, médio, meio-termo, médium; *adj.*, médio, mediano.
ME.DUL.LA, *s.*, medula.
MEED, *s.*, prêmio, presente.
MEEK, *adj.*, manso.
MEET, *s.*, reunião, encontro; *v.*, encontrar, reunir, conhecer, ajuntar-se.
MEET.ING, *s.*, reunião, encontro, assembleia.
MEET.NESS, *s.*, propriedade, conveniência.
MEG.A.LO.MA.NIA, *s.*, megalomania.
MEGA.PHONE, *s.*, megafone.
MEL.AN.CHO.LIA, *s.*, melancolia, alienação, doença mental.
MEL.AN.CHOL.IC, *adj.*, melancólico.
ME.LIO.RATE, *v.*, melhorar.
MEL.LOW, *adj.*, melodioso, suave.
ME.LO.DI.OUS, *adj.*, melodioso, harmonioso, musical.
ME.LO.DI.OUS.NESS, *s.*, melodia.
MEL.O.DY, *s.*, melodia.
ME.LON, *s.*, melão.
MELT, *s.*, fundição, metal fundido; *v.*, fundir, derreter, dissolver.
MELT.DOWN, *s.*, fusão.
MELT.ER, *s.*, fundidor, cadinho.
MEM.BER, *s.*, membro; sócio, associado.
MEM.BRANE, *s.*, membrana.
ME.MEN.TO, *s.*, memento, memorial.

MEMO, s., memorando, nota, bilhete.
MEM.OIR, s., memória, autobiografia.
MEM.O.RAN.DUM, s., memorando.
ME.MO.RI.AL, s., memorial, monumento de memórias.
MEM.O.RIZE, v., decorar, memorizar.
MEM.O.RY, s., memória, recordação, lembrança.
MEN, s., pl., homens.
MEN.ACE, v., ameaçar; s., ameaça.
MEND, v., consertar, remendar.
MEN.DA.CIOUS, adj., mentiroso, falso.
MEN.DAC.I.TY, s., mentira, mendacidade, falsidade.
MEN.DI.CANT, adj., s., mendicante, mendigo, pedinte.
MEN.IN.GI.TIS, s., meningite.
MEN.O.PAUSE, s., menopausa.
MEN.STRU.AL, adj., menstrual.
MEN.STRU.A.TION, s., menstruação.
MEN.SU.RA.TION, s., medição, medida.
MEN.TAL, adj., mental.
MEN.TAL.I.TY, s., mentalidade.
MEN.TION, s., menção, lembrança; v., mencionar, referir.
MEN.TION.ABLE, s., referível, citável.
MEN.TOR, s., mentor.
MENU, s., menu, cardápio.
MER.CAN.TILE, adj., mercantil.
MER.CE.NARY, adj., s., mercenário.
MER.CHAN.DISE, s., mercadoria; v., negociar, mercantilizar.
MER.CHANT, s., comerciante, negociante.
MER.CHANT.SHIP, s., navio mercante.
MER.CI.FUL, adj., misericordioso, piedoso, bondoso.
MER.CI.FUL.NESS, s., misericórdia, bondade.
MER.CI.LESS, adj., desumano, cruel, perverso.
MER.CU.RY, s., mercúrio; v., limpar com solução de mercúrio.
MER.CU.RY, s., Mercúrio.
MER.CY, s., piedade, compaixão, misericórdia.
MERE, adj., mero, simples.
MER.E.TRI.CIOUS.NESS, s., vida ou conduta de meretriz.

ME.RID.IAN, adj., s., meridiano; s., zênite.
ME.RID.I.O.NAL, adj., meridional.
ME.RINGUE, s., merengue, suspiro.
MER.IT, s., mérito, merecimento, vantagem; v., merecer.
MER.I.TO.RI.OUS, adj., meritório, merecedor.
MER.MAID, s., sereia.
MER.RI.MENT, s., alegria, contentamento, felicidade.
MER.RI.NESS, adj., alegre, jovial, feliz, satisfeito.
MER.RY, adj., feliz; Merry Christmas!, Feliz Natal.
MER.RY-GO-ROUND, s., carrossel.
MESH, s., malha; v., prender com rede; enredar, enredar-se.
MES.MER.IZE, s., hipnotizar, mesmerizar, magnetizar.
MESS, s., confusão, baderna; rancho.
MES.SEN.GER, s., mensageiro.
MES.SI.AH, s., Messias, Cristo.
MES.SI.NESS, s., desordem.
MES.SING, s., rancho, ato de arranchar, agrupamento.
MESS.MATE, s., comensal, conviva, companheiro de mesa.
MESSY, adj., desorganizado, confuso, sujo.
ME.TAB.O.LISM, s., metabolismo.
MET.AL, s., metal; v., cobrir com metal.
ME.TAL.LIC, adj., metálico.
MET.AL.LIZE, v., metalizar.
MET.AL.LUR.GIST, s., metalurgista, metalúrgico.
MET.AL.LUR.GY, s., metalurgia.
META.MOR.PHOSE, s., metamorfose; v., metamorfosear.
MET.A.PHOR, s., metáfora.
META.PHYS.I.CAL, adj., metafísico.
METE, v., medir, repartir.
ME.TE.OR, s., meteoro.
ME.TE.OR.ITE, s., meteorito.
ME.TE.O.RO.LOG.IC, adj., meteorológico.
ME.TE.O.ROL.O.GIST, s., meteorologista.
ME.TE.O.ROL.O.GY, s., meteorologia.
ME.TER, s., medidor, parquímetro.

METH.OD, s., método.
ME.THOD.I.CAL, adj., metódico.
METH.OD.IZE, v., metodizar, organizar.
METH.OD.OL.O.GY, s., metodologia.
ME.TIC.U.LOUS, adj., meticuloso.
ME.TON.Y.MY, s., metonímia.
METRE, s., metro.
MET.RIC, adj., métrico.
ME.TROP.O.LIS, s., metrópole, cidade, capital.
MET.RO.POL.I.TAN, adj., metropolitano.
MET.TLE, s., brio, coragem, valor, denodo, ânimo.
MEW, v., miar.
MEW.ING, s., miado.
MEWL, v., choramingar, chorar, lamentar.
MEX.I.CAN, adj., s., mexicano.
MEX.I.CO, s., México.
MEZ.ZA.NINE, s., mezanino, sobreloja.
MI, s., mi.
MIAOW, s., miar.
MI.CA, s., mica.
MI.CROBE, s., micróbio.
MI.CRO.CHIP, s., "microchip", circuito gravado.
MI.CRO.COM.PUT.ER, s., microcomputador, computador.
MI.CRO.COSM, s., microcosmo.
MI.CRO.FILM, s., microfilme.
MI.CROM.E.TER, s., micrômetro.
MI.CRO.PHONE, s., microfone.
MI.CRO.PRO.CES.SOR, s., microprocessador.
MI.CRO.SCOPE, s., microscópio.
MI.CROS.CO.PY, s., microscopia.
MI.CRO.WAVE, s., micro-ondas.
MID, adj., meio, médio, semi, hemi.
MID.DAY, s., meio-dia.
MID.DLE, s., meio, cintura; adj., meio, médio.
MID.DLE-AGED, s., meia-idade.
MID.DLE-CLASS, s., classe média.
MID.DLING, adj., médio, mediano.
MIDGE, s., mosquito.
MIDG.ET, s., anão.
MID.LANG, s., parte central de um país, região interiorana.
MID.NIGHT, s., meia-noite.

MID.RIFF, s., barriga.
MID.WAY, adv., a meio caminho.
MID.WEEK, adv., no meio da semana.
MID.WINTER, adv., no meio do inverno, em pleno inverno.
MIEN, s., ar, aparência, semblante, feição.
MIGHT, s., poder, força; v. imp. de **MAY**.
MIGHTY, adj., poderoso, forte.
MI.GRAINE, s., enxaqueca.
MI.GRANT, adj., migrante.
MI.GRATE, v., migrar.
MI.GRA.TION, s., migração.
MILCH, adj., lácteo, referente a leite.
MILD, adj., suave, brando, afável, tenro, lenitivo, compassivo.
MILD.EN, v., suavizar, abrandar.
MILD.NESS, s., suavidade, ternura, pena, compaixão.
MILE, s., milha.
MILE.AGE, s., milhagem.
MIL.I.TAN.CY, s., militância, luta, confiança.
MIL.I.TANT, s., militante, adepto.
MIL.I.TA.RISM, s., militarismo.
MIL.I.TA.RIST, s., militarista.
MIL.I.TATE, v., militar, lutar, combater.
MILK, s., leite; v., ordenhar, mungir, chupar.
MILK.ER, s., ordenhador; quem tira leite.
MILK.MAID, s., leiteira.
MILK.MAN, s., leiteiro.
MILK.TOOTH, s., dente de leite.
MILKY, adj., leitoso.
MILL, s., moinho, moedor de café, engenho; v., redemoinhar.
MILLED, adj., moído, triturado.
MIL.LE.NA.RY, adj., s., milenário, milênio.
MIL.LE.NI.UM, s., milênio, mil anos, milenário.
MIL.LE.PEDE, s., centopeia.
MILL.ER, s., moleiro.
MIL.LI.GRAM.ME, s., miligrama.
MIL.LI.ME.TRE, s., milímetro.
MIL.LION, s., milhão.
MIL.LION.AIRE, s., milionário.
MILT, s., ova de peixes.
MIM.EO.GRAPH, s., mimeógrafo.

MIM.IC, *adj.*, mímico; *v.*, imitar.
MIM.IC.RY, *s.*, mímica, imitação.
MI.NA.TO.RY, *adj.*, ameaçador.
MINCE, *s.*, carne moída, recheio; *v.*, moer, triturar.
MIND, *s.*, mente, intelecto; *v.*, cuidar, tomar conta de, preocupar-se.
MIND.ER, *s.*, quem cuida de crianças; guarda-costas.
MIND.FUL.NESS, *s.*, cuidado, atenção, preocupação.
MINE, *pron.*, meu, minha; *s.*, mina.
MINE.FIELD, *s.*, campo minado.
MIN.ER, *s.*, mineiro.
MIN.ER.AL, *v.*, mineralizar.
MIN.ER.AL.O.GY, *s.*, mineralogia.
MIN.GLING, *s.*, mistura.
MINI.BUS, *s.*, micro-ônibus.
MIN.I.KIN, *adj.*, pequeno, diminuto, reduzido, ínfimo.
MIN.I.MAL, *adj.*, mínimo.
MIN.I.MIZE, *v.*, reduzir, minimizar.
MIN.ISH, *v.*, diminuir, reduzir, apequenar.
MINI.SKIRT, *s.*, minissaia.
MIN.IS.TER, *s.*, ministro, pastor.
MIN.IS.TE.RI.AL, *adj.*, ministerial.
MIN.IS.TRA.TION, *s.*, administração, governo, agência, sacerdócio.
MIN.IS.TRY, *s.*, ministério.
MI.NOR, *adj.*, menor, sem importância, menor de idade.
MI.NOR.I.TY, *s.*, minoria; menoridade.
MIN.STER, *s.*, mosteiro, catedral.
MINT, *s.*, hortelã; *v.*, cunhar moeda; *s.* casa da moeda.
MINT.AGE, *s.*, moeda cunhada.
MINT.ER, *s.*, moedeiro.
MI.NUS.CULE, *s.*, letra minúscula, *adj.*, minúsculo.
MIN.UTE, *adj.*, miúdo, minúsculo, pequeno; preciso.
MI.NUTE.NESS, *s.*, minuciosidade.
MIR.A.CLE, *s.*, milagre.
MI.RAC.U.LOUS, *adj.*, miraculoso, milagroso.
MI.RAGE, *s.*, ilusão, miragem.
MIRE, *s.*, lodo, lama, lodaçal; *v.*, enlamear, atolar.
MIR.ROR, *s.*, espelho, retrovisor; modelo; *v.*, espelhar, refletir.
MIRTH, *s.*, risada, jovialidade, alegria.
MIRTH.FUL, *adj.*, alegre, jovial, satisfeito, risonho.
MIRTH.LESS, *adj.*, tristonho, triste.
MIRY, *adj.*, lamacento.
MIS.AD.VEN.TURE, *s.*, desgraça, infelicidade, infortúnio.
MIS.AN.THROPE, *s.*, misantropo.
MIS.AN.THRO.PY, *s.*, misantropia.
MIS.AP.PLY, *v.*, dar má aplicação, fazer mau uso.
MIS.AP.PRE.HEND, *v.*, entender mal.
MIS.AP.PRO.PRI.A.TION, *s.*, desvio, apropriação indevida.
MIS.BE.HAVE, *v.*, comportar-se mal, agir de modo errado.
MIS.BE.LIEVE, *v.*, descrer, acreditar em algo errado, estar errado.
MIS.CAL.CU.LATE, *v.*, calcular mal, calcular errado.
MIS.CALL, *v.*, dar nome errado.
MIS.CEL.LA.NEOUS, *adj.*, diverso, vário, variado, misturado.
MIS.CEL.LA.NY, *s.*, miscelânea.
MIS.CHANCE, *s.*, infelicidade, desgraça.
MIS.CHIEF, *s.*, dano; prejuízo; travessura, diabrura.
MIS.CHIE.VOUS, *adj.*, travesso, brincalhão, peralta, moleque.
MIS.COUNT, *v.*, contar mal, errar a conta, enganar-se nas contas.
MIS.CRE.ANT, *adj.*, vil, desprezível, miserável.
MIS.DEED, *s.*, delito, crime, culpa.
MIS.DE.MEAN, *v.*, comportar-se mal.
MIS.DI.RECT, *v.*, dirigir mal, guiar mal, administrar mal.
MIS.DOING, *s.*, delito, culpa, falta, erro.
MI.SER, *s.*, sovina, avarento, avaro, unha de fome.
MIS.ER.ABLE, *adj.*, miserável, triste, deprimido.
MIS.ERY, *s.*, tristeza, miséria, depressão.

MIS.FAITH, *s.*, descrença.
MIS.FOR.TUNE, *s.*, desgraça, infelicidade.
MIS.GOV.ERN, *v.*, governar mal, desgovernar.
MIS.GUIDE, *v.*, extraviar, perder o rumo, desviar, desencaminhar.
MIS.HAP, *s.*, infortúnio, desgraça, desastre.
MIS.IN.FORM, *v.*, informar mal, dar informações erradas.
MIS.IN.TER.PRET, *v.*, interpretar mal, traduzir de modo errado.
MIS.JUDGE, *v.*, julgar mal, fazer juízo errado.
MIS.LAY, *v.*, extraviar, perder, desviar.
MIS.PLACE, *v.*, extraviar, perder o rumo, desviar.
MIS.PRI.SION, *s.*, menosprezo, desprezo, relaxamento.
MIS.PRO.NOUNCE, *v.*, pronunciar mal.
MIS.QUOTE, *v.*, citar erradamente, dizer de modo errado.
MIS.RE.PORT, *s.*, informação errônea, informe errado.
MIS.RULE, *s.*, desgoverno, confusão.
MISS, *s.*, senhorita, jovem, moça.
MISS.HAP.EN, *adj.*, disforme, desengonçado.
MIS.SILE, *s.*, míssil, projétil, foguete, bomba.
MIS.SION, *s.*, missão, expedição.
MIS.SION.ARY, *s.*, missionário.
MIS.SIVE, *s.*, missiva, carta.
MIS.SPEND, *v.*, dissipar, desperdiçar, estragar.
MISSY, *s.*, senhorita, jovem.
MIST, *s.*, neblina, névoa, bruma, cerração; *v.*, enevoar, cobrir de bruma.
MIS.TAKE, *s.*, engano, erro, falha; *v.*, falhar, entender mal.
MIS.TER, *s.*, senhor; *abrev.*, Mr.
MIST.I.NESS, *s.*, tempo enevoado, tempo coberto de nuvens.
MIS.TRANS.LATE, *v.*, traduzir erradamente, verter de modo errado.
MIS.TRESS, *s.*, professora, mestra; amante, amásia.
MIS.TRUST, *v.*, desconfiar de, desacreditar, temer.
MIS.UN.DER.STAND, *v.*, entender mal, interpretar de modo errado.

MIS.USE, *s.*, abuso, desvio, uso errado; *v.*, abusar, desviar.
MIT.I.GANT, *adj.*, mitigante, suavizante.
MIT.I.GATE, *v.*, mitigar, suavizar, atenuar, abrandar.
MIT.I.GA.TION, *s.*, mitigação.
MIT.TI.MUS, *s.*, mandado de prisão.
MIX, *v.*, misturar; *s.*, mistura, combinação.
MIX.ER, *s.*, batedeira, misturador.
MIX.TURE, *s.*, mistura, mescla.
MIZ.ZLE, *s.*, garoa, chuvinha, chuva miúda; *v.*, garoar, chuviscar.
MOAN, *s.*, gemido, queixume; *v.*, lamentar-se, queixar-se, resmungar.
MOAN.FUL, *adj.*, queixoso, lastimoso.
MOB, *s.*, plebe, ralé, raia miúda, gentalha; *v.*, tumultuar, badernar.
MO.BILE, *adj.*, móvel, inconstante, fútil, volátil, volúvel.
MO.BIL.I.TY, *s.*, mobilidade.
MO.BI.LIZE, *v.*, mobilizar.
MOCK, *s.*, zombaria, escárnio; *v.*, escarnecer, ridicularizar; *adj.*, falso.
MOCK.ERY, *s.*, escárnio, zombaria, ridicularização.
MODE, *s.*, modo, meio.
MOD.EL, *s.*, molde, modelo, maquete, exemplo; *v.*, modelar, moldar.
MO.DEM, *s.*, modem.
MOD.ER.ATE, *v.*, moderar, aquietar, restringir; *adj.*, moderado.
MOD.ER.A.TION, *s.*, moderação.
MOD.ERN, *adj.*, moderno.
MOD.ERN.ISM, *s.*, modernismo.
MOD.ERN.IST, *s.*, modernista.
MO.DER.NI.TY, *s.*, modernidade.
MOD.ERN.IZE, *v.*, modernizar.
MOD.EST, *adj.*, modesto.
MOD.ES.TY, *s.*, modéstia.
MOD.I.FI.CA.TION, *s.*, modificação.
MOD.I.FY, *v.*, modificar.
MOD.ISH, *adj.*, da moda, que está na moda.
MOD.U.LAR, *v.*, modular o tom, modular um conjunto.

MOD.ULE, *s.*, módulo.
MO.HAM.MED.AN, *adj.*, *s.*, maometano.
MOI.E.TY, *s.*, metade.
MOIL, *s.*, trabalho difícil, labuta; *v.*, cansar, estafar, labutar.
MOIST, *adj.*, úmido, molhado, chuvoso.
MOIST.EN, *v.*, umedecer, molhar.
MOKE, *s.*, jumento, burro, asno, jegue.
MO.LAR, *s.*, molar, dente molar; *adj.*, próprio para moer.
MO.LAS.SES, *s.*, melado.
MOLE, *s.*, toupeira; dique, cais, porto; *v.*, cavar, escavar.
MO.LEC.U.LAR, *adj.*, molecular.
MOL.E.CULE, *s.*, molécula.
MO.LEST, *v.*, molestar, perturbar, assediar.
MO.LES.TA.TION, *s.*, molestação.
MOL.LI.FY, *v.*, abrandar, suavizar, atenuar.
MOL.LUSC, *s.*, molusco.
MOL.LY, *s.*, indivíduo do sexo masculino, mas efeminado.
MOL.TEN, *adj.*, fundido, derretido, liquefeito.
MO.MENT, *s.*, momento.
MO.MEN.TARY, *adj.*, momentâneo, instantâneo.
MO.MEN.TUM, *s.*, momento.
MON.ARCH, *s.*, monarca, soberano.
MO.NAR.CHIC, *adj.*, monárquico.
MON.AR.CHIST, *s.*, monarquista.
MON.AR.CHY, *s.*, monarquia.
MON.AS.TERY, *s.*, monastério, mosteiro.
MO.NAS.TIC, *adj.*, monástico.
MON.DAY, *s.*, segunda-feira.
MON.E.TARY, *adj.*, monetário.
MON.EY, *s.*, dinheiro, moeda.
MON.EY.LESS, *adj.*, sem dinheiro, pobre.
MON.GOL, *s.*, mongoloide.
MON.GO.LIAN, *adj.*, *s.*, mongol.
MON.GREL, *s.*, cão, vira-lata.
MO.NI.TION, *s.*, advertência, admoestação, aviso.
MON.I.TOR, *s.*, monitor, instrutor, monitor de TV; *v.*, monitorar.
MON.I.TO.RY, *adj.*, admonitório.
MONK, *s.*, monge.

MON.KEY, *s.*, macaco.
MONO, *adj.*, mono.
MONO.CHROME, *adj.*, monocromo, de uma única cor.
MO.NOG.A.MIST, *s.*, monógamo.
MO.NOG.A.MY, *s.*, monogamia.
MONO.GRAM, *s.*, monograma.
MONO.LOGUE, *s.*, monólogo.
MO.NOP.O.LIST, *s.*, monopolista.
MO.NOP.O.LIZE, *v.*, monopolizar.
MO.NOP.O.LY, *s.*, monopólio.
MONO.SYL.LAB.IC, *adj.*, monossilábico.
MONO.SYL.LA.BLE, *s.*, monossílabo.
MONO.THE.ISM, *s.*, monoteísmo.
MO.NOT.O.NOUS, *adj.*, monótono.
MO.NOT.O.NY, *s.*, monotonia.
MON.OX.IDE, *s.*, monóxido.
MON.STER, *s.*, monstro.
MON.STROS.I.TY, *s.*, monstruosidade.
MON.STROUS, *adj.*, monstruoso.
MONTH, *s.*, mês.
MONTH.LY, *adj.*, mensal; *adv.*, mensalmente.
MON.U.MENT, *s.*, monumento.
MOO, *v.*, mugir, berrar; *s.*, mugido.
MOOD, *s.*, humor, atmosfera.
MOOD.I.NESS, *s.*, capricho, rabugem, teimosia.
MOODY, *adj.*, caprichoso, teimoso, rabugento.
MOON, *s.*, lua; *v.*, andar à toa.
MOON.LIGHT, *s.*, luar; *v.*, fazer um biscate.
MOON.STRUCK, *adj.*, lunático, doido, desvairado.
MOONY, *adj.*, sonhador, sentimental, do mundo da lua.
MOOR, *s.*, mouro.
MOOR.ISH, *adj.*, pantanoso, lodoso.
MOOR.LAND, *s.*, terra pantanosa, banhado.
MOOT, *v.*, debater, discutir; *s.*, discussão, debate.
MOP, *s.*, esfregão; *v.*, esfregar.
MOP-BOARD, *s.*, rodapé.
MOP.ISH, *adj.*, triste, aborrecido.
MOR.AL, *adj.*, *s.*, moral; moralidade, costumes.
MOR.AL.ISM, *s.*, moralismo.
MOR.AL.IST, *s.*, moralista.
MO.RAL.I.TY, *s.*, moralidade.

MORALIZATION — MOW DOWN

MOR.AL.I.ZA.TION, *s.*, moralização.
MOR.AL.IZE, *v.*, moralizar.
MOR.A.TO.RI.UM, *s.*, moratória.
MOR.BID, *adj.*, mórbido, doentio, doente.
MOR.BID.I.TY, *s.*, morbidez, doença.
MORE, *adv.*, mais.
MO.REL, *s.*, cogumelo.
MORE.OVER, *adv.*, além disso, além do mais.
MORGUE, *s.*, morgue, necrotério.
MOR.I.BUND, *adj.*, moribundo, agonizante, morrente.
MOR.MON, *s.*, mórmon.
MORN.ING, *s.*, manhã, madrugada.
MO.ROC.CAN, *adj., s.*, marroquino.
MO.ROC.CO, *s.*, Marrocos.
MOR.PHIA, *s.*, morfina.
MOR.PHO.LOG.IC, *adj.*, morfológico.
MOR.PHOL.O.GY, *s.*, morfologia.
MORSE CODE, *s.*, código morse.
MORSE, *s.*, morsa.
MOR.TAL, *adj.*, mortal.
MOR.TAL.I.TY, *s.*, mortalidade.
MORT.GAGE, *s.*, hipoteca; *v.*, hipotecar.
MORT.I.FER.OUS, *adj.*, mortífero, mortal, letal.
MOR.TI.FY, *v.*, mortificar, sacrificar.
MOR.TU.ARY, *s.*, necrotério.
MO.SA.IC, *s.*, mosaico.
MOS.COW, *s.*, Moscou.
MOSQUE, *s.*, mesquita.
MOS.QUI.TO, *s.*, mosquito.
MOSS, *s.*, musgo; *v.*, cobrir com musgo.
MOSSY, *adj.*, musgoso, cheio de musgo.
MOST, *s.*, a maior parte, o maior número; *adj.*, o mais; *adv.*, o mais.
MOTE, *s.*, partícula.
MO.TEL, *s.*, motel.
MOTH, *s.*, mariposa, traça.
MOTH.BALL, *s.*, naftalina, bola de naftalina.
MOTH.ER, *s.*, mãe; *v.*, cuidar de criança como mãe.
MOTH.ER.HOOD, *s.*, maternidade.
MOTH.ER-IN-LAW, *s.*, sogra.
MOTH.ER.LESS, *s.* órfão de mãe.
MOTH.ER.LY, *adj.*, maternal.

MO.TIF, *s.*, motivo, razão.
MO.TION, *s.*, movimento, gesto.
MO.TI.VA.TION, *s.*, motivação.
MO.TIVE, *s.*, motivo.
MO.TIV.I.TY, *s.*, potência do motor.
MO.TOR, *s.*, motor, carro.
MO.TOR.BIKE, *s.*, moto, motocicleta.
MO.TOR.BOAT, *s.*, barco a motor.
MO.TOR.BUS, *s.*, ônibus.
MO.TOR.IST, *s.*, motorista.
MO.TOR.WAY, *s.*, rodovia, autoestrada.
MOT.TLE, *v.*, matizar, colorir com várias cores.
MOULD, *s.*, molde, mofo, bolor.
MOULD.ER, *s.*, moldador, carpinteiro; *v.*, pulverizar, reduzir a pó.
MOULD.I.NESS, *s.*, mofo, bolor.
MOULD.ING, *s.*, moldura, modelação.
MOUND, *s.*, pilha, monte; *v.*, amontoar.
MOUNT, *s.*, monte; *v.*, montar, trepar, subir, ascender.
MOUN.TAIN, *s.*, montanha.
MOUN.TAIN.EER, *s.*, montanhista, alpinista.
MOUN.TAIN.OUS, *adj.*, montanhoso.
MOURN, *v.*, chorar, lamentar.
MOURN.FUL, *adj.*, desolado, triste.
MOUSE, *s.*, camundongo, rato; *v.*, caçar ratos.
MOUSE.TRAP, *s.*, ratoeira.
MOUSSE, *s.*, musse, doce, sobremesa.
MOUS.TACHE, *s.*, bigode.
MOUTH, *s.*, boca, entrada, foz; *v.*, comer, mastigar, abocanhar, morder.
MOUTH.FUL, *s.*, bocado.
MOUTH.LESS, *adj.*, sem boca.
MOV.ABLE, *adj.*, móvel.
MOV.ABLE.NESS, *s.*, mobilidade.
MOVE, *s.*, movimento, lance, jogada; mudança; *v.*, mover-se, mexer-se.
MOVE BACK, *v.*, voltar.
MOVE.MENT, *s.*, movimento, gesto, mudança.
MOV.ER, *s.*, motor.
MOV.IE, *s.*, filme, cinema.
MOV.ING, *adj.*, comovente.
MOW, *v.*, colher, cortar.
MOW DOWN, *v.*, chacinar, liquidar, matar.

MOW.ER, *s.*, colhedor, cortador.
MO.ZAM.BIQUE, *s.*, Moçambique.
MUCH, *pron.*, muito, *adj.*, muito.
MUCH.NESS, *s.*, quantidade, totalidade.
MUCK, *s.*, sujeira, sujidade; *v.*, sujar.
MUCK.I.NESS, *s.*, imundície, sujeira.
MUCKY, *adj.*, sujo, imundo, emporcalhado.
MU.CUS, *s.*, muco.
MUD, *s.*, lama, lodo; *v.*, enlamear.
MUD.DLE, *s.*, confusão, trapalhada; *v.*, confundir, atrapalhar.
MUD.DY, *adj.*, lamacento, lodoso.
MUD.GUARD, *s.*, para-lamas.
MUF.FLE, *v.*, abafar o som; agasalhar, abrigar.
MUG, *s.*, caneca, caneco; *v.*, assaltar.
MUG.GER, *s.*, crocodilo.
MUG.GING, *s.*, assalto.
MUG.GY, *adj.*, úmido, molhado, abafado.
MU.LAT.TO, *s.*, mulato.
MUL.BER.RY, *s.*, amora.
MULCT, *v.*, enganar, defraudar.
MULE, *s.*, mula, burra.
MUL.ISH, *adj.*, teimoso.
MUL.ISH.NESS, *s.*, teimosia, obstinação.
MUL.TI.COL.ORED, *adj.*, multicolor.
MUL.TI.FORM, *adj.*, multiforme.
MUL.TI.NA.TION.AL, *adj.*, multinacional.
MUL.TI.PLE, *adj., s.*, múltiplo.
MUL.TI.PLI.CA.TION, *s.*, multiplicação.
MUL.TI.PLIC.I.TY, *s.*, multiplicidade.
MUL.TI.PLI.ER, *s.*, multiplicador.
MUL.TI.PLY, *v.*, multiplicar.
MUL.TI.TUDE, *s.*, multidão.
MUL.TI.TU.DI.NOUS, *adj.*, múltiplo, numeroso, diverso.
MUM.BLE, *v.*, resmungar, murmurar, reclamar.
MUM.BLER, *s.*, resmungão, murmurador.
MUM.BLING, *s.*, murmuração.
MUM.MI.FI.CA.TION, *s.*, mumificação.
MUM.MI.FY, *v.*, mumificar.
MUMPS, *s.*, papeira.
MUN.DANE, *adj.*, mundano, trivial, profano.
MU.NIC.I.PAL, *adj.*, municipal.
MU.NIC.I.PAL.I.TY, *s.*, municipalidade.

MU.NI.TIONS, *s.*, munições.
MU.RAL, *s.*, mural, quadro pintado na parede.
MUR.DER, *s.*, assassinato, homicídio; *v.*, assassinar, matar.
MUR.DER.ER, *s.*, assassino.
MUR.DER.ESS, *s.*, assassina.
MUR.DER.ING, *s.*, assassinato, homicídio.
MURE, *v.*, murar, emparedar, encarcerar.
MURK.I.NESS, *s.*, escuridão, trevas, noite.
MURKY, *adj.*, escuro, negro, turvo, enegrecido.
MUR.MUR, *s.*, murmúrio, sussurro; *v.*, murmurar.
MUR.PHY, *s.*, batata.
MUS.CLE, *s.*, músculo; força, energia.
MUS.CO.VITE, *adj., s.*, moscovita.
MUS.CU.LAR, *adj.*, muscular.
MUSE, *s.*, musa; *v.*, pensar, meditar.
MU.SE.UM, *s.*, museu.
MU.SIC, *s.*, música.
MU.SI.CAL, *adj.*, musical, melodioso, harmonioso.
MU.SI.CAL.NESS, *s.*, musicalidade, harmonia, melodia.
MU.SI.CIAN, *s.*, músico.
MUSK.ET, *s.*, mosquete, arma de fogo antiga.
MUSK.ET.EER, *s.*, mosqueteiro.
MUSKY, *adj.*, almiscarado.
MUS.LIN, *s.*, musselina.
MUSS, *s.*, desordem, balbúrdia, confusão; *v.*, desordenar, badernar.
MUS.SEL, *s.*, mexilhão.
MUST, *v.*, ter de, dever, ser forçado a.
MUS.TARD, *s.*, mostarda.
MU.TA.BIL.I.TY, *s.*, mutabilidade.
MU.TA.BLE, *adj.*, mutável, volúvel, transitório, efêmero.
MU.TATE, *v.*, mudar, alterar, transformar.
MU.TA.TION, *s.*, mutação, transformação.
MUTE, *adj.*, mudo.
MU.TI.LATE, *v.*, mutilar, deformar.
MU.TI.LA.TION, *s.*, mutilação.
MU.TI.NOUS, *adj.*, amotinado, revoltado, rebelde.
MU.TI.NOUS.NESS, *s.*, revolta, rebeldia, tumulto, revolução.

MU.TI.NY, *s.*, motim; *v.*, amotinar-se.
MUT.ISM, *s.*, mutismo, silêncio, mudez.
MUT.TON, *s.*, carne de carneiro.
MU.TU.AL, *adj.*, mútuo, recíproco.
MU.TU.AL.I.TY, *s.*, mutualidade, reciprocidade.
MUZ.ZLE, *s.*, focinho, mordaça, boca de arma de fogo; *v.*, amordaçar.
MUZ.ZY, *adj.*, absorto, distraído.
MY, *pron.*, meu, minha, meus, minhas.
MY.OPE, *s.*, míope.
MY.O.PIA, *s.*, miopia.
MY.O.PIC, *adj.*, míope.
MYO.SO.TIS, *s.*, miosótis.

MYR.I.AD, *s.*, miríade.
MYRRH, *s.*, mirra.
MY.SELF, *pron.*, eu mesmo, a mim mesmo.
MYS.TE.RI.OUS, *adj.*, misterioso.
MYS.TERY, *s.*, mistério.
MYS.TIC, *adj., s.*, místico.
MYS.TI.CISM, *s.*, misticismo.
MYS.TI.FY, *v.*, mistificar.
MYS.TIQUE, *s.*, mística.
MYTH, *s.*, mito.
MYTH.IC, *adj.*, mítico.
MYTH.O.LOG.IC, *adj.*, mitológico.
MY.THOL.O.GY, *s.*, mitologia.

N

N, *s.*, décima quarta letra do alfabeto inglês.
NAB, *v.*, arrebatar subitamente, pegar, pegar em flagrante.
NA-BOB, *s.*, nababo, ricaço, milionário.
NA-CRE, *s.*, madrepérola, nácar.
NAG, *s.*, cavalo ruim, pangaré, matungo; *v.*, resmungar, incomodar.
NAIL, *s.*, neil, *s.*, prego, unha, garra; *v.*, pregar, fixar, agarrar.
NAIL-BRUSH, *s.*, escova para unhas.
NA-ÏVE, *adj.*, ingênuo, tolo, inocente, simplório.
NA-KED, *adj.*, despido, nu, exposto, desprotegido.
NA-KED-NESS, *s.*, nudez, exposição, falta de proteção.
NAME, *s.*, nome, sobrenome, título, autoridade, renome; *v.*, nomear, chamar, citar, dar nome.
NAME.LESS, *adj.*, sem nome, anônimo, inominado.
NAME.LY, *adv.*, isto é, a saber.
NAME.SAKE, *s.*, homônimo, xará, quem tem o mesmo nome.
NAN.NY, *s.*, ama, aia.
NAP, *s.*, soneca, sesta, cochilo; *s.*, cochilar, dormitar, ficar desprevenido.
NAPE, *s.*, nuca.
NAPH.THA, *s.*, nafta.
NAPH.THA.LENE, *s.*, naftalina.
NAP.KIN, *s.*, guardanapo.
NAP.PER, *adj.*, dorminhoco.
NAP.PING, *s.*, sesta, dormida, dormidela.
NAR.CIS.SISM, *s.*, narcisismo.
NAR.COT.IC, *adj.*, *s.*, narcótico.
NAR.CO.TIZE, *v.*, narcotizar.
NAR.RATE, *v.*, narrar, contar, referir, relatar.
NAR.RA.TION, *s.*, narração, conto, narrativa, história.
NAR.RA.TIVE, *s.*, narrativa.
NAR.RA.TOR, *s.*, narrador, cronista, historiador.
NAR.ROW, *s.*, desfiladeiro, estreito, braço de mar; *v.*, estreitar, apertar; *adj.*, estreito, apertado, restrito.
NAR.ROW.ING, *s.*, aperto, restrição.
NAR.ROW.NESS, *s.*, estreiteza, pequenez, restrição.
NA.SAL, *adj.*, nasal.
NA.SAL.A.TION, *s.*, nasalização.
NA.SAL.IZE, *v.*, nasalar, nasalizar.
NAS.CENT, *adj.*, nascente.
NAS.TI.NESS, *s.*, torpeza, maldade.
NAS.TY, *adj.*, sórdido, mau, maldoso, repugnante, vexatório.
NA.TAL, *adj.*, natal.
NA.TAL.I.TY, *s.*, natalidade.
NA.TA.TION, *s.*, natação.
NA.TION, *s.*, nação, país, povo.
NA.TION.AL, *adj.*, *s.*, nacional.
NA.TION.AL.ISM, *s.*, nacionalismo.
NA.TION.AL.I.TY, *s.*, nacionalidade.
NA.TION.AL.IZE, *v.*, nacionalizar.
NA.TION.WIDE, *s.*, âmbito nacional, contexto nacional.
NA.TIVE, *adj.*, nativo, natural, genuíno, inato, puro.
NA.TIV.I.TY, *s.*, natividade; Natividade de Jesus Cristo.
NA.TRON, *s.*, sódio.
NAT.U.RAL, *adj.*, natural, ingênuo, oriundo, nativo, inato.
NAT.U.RAL.ISM, *s.*, naturalismo.
NAT.U.RAL.I.ZA.TION, *s.*, naturalização.
NAT.U.RAL.IZE, *v.*, naturalizar.
NA.TURE, *s.*, natureza, índole.
NAUGH.TY, *adj.*, desobediente, travesso, malcriado, mau.
NAU.SEA, *s.*, náusea, repugnância, enjoo.
NAU.SE.ANT, *adj.*, nauseante, enjoativo,

repugnante.
NAU.SE.ATE, *v.*, nausear, enjoar, provocar nojo.
NAU.SEOUS, *adj.*, nauseabundo, repugnante, enjoativo, nojento.
NA.VAL, *adj.*, naval, marítimo, próprio do mar.
NAVE, *s.*, nave de igreja.
NA.VEL, *s.*, umbigo, centro, meio.
NAV.I.GA.BIL.I.TY, *s.*, navegabilidade.
NAV.I.GA.BLE, *adj.*, navegável.
NAV.I.GATE, *v.*, navegar, pilotar uma nave.
NAV.I.GA.TION, *s.*, navegação.
NAV.I.GA.TOR, *s.*, navegador.
NA.VY, *s.*, esquadra, conjunto das forças marítimas, armada.
NAZ.A.RENE, *adj.*, *s.*, nazareno.
NAZE, *s.*, cabo, promontório.
NA.ZI, *adj.*, *s.*, nazista, nazi.
NA.ZISM, *s.*, nazismo.
NEAR, *adj.*, vizinho, próximo; *adv.*, perto; *prep.*, perto de; *v.*, aproximar.
NEAR.LY, *adv.*, quase.
NEAR.NESS, *s.*, proximidade, cercanias, vizinhança; intimidade.
NEAR.SIGHT.ED, *s.*, míope.
NEAT, *adj.*, ajeitado, arrumado, organizado, limpo, asseado.
NEAT.NESS, *s.*, capricho, asseio, ordem.
NEB, *s.*, bico, ponta, pena de escrever.
NEB.U.LA, *s.*, nebulosa, galáxia.
NEB.U.LOS.I.TY, *s.*, nebulosidade, cerração, enevoamento.
NEB.U.LOUS, *adj.*, nebuloso, enevoado.
NEC.ES.SAR.I.LY, *adv.*, necessariamente, obrigatoriamente.
NEC.ES.SARY, *adj.*, necessário, preciso, obrigatório.
NE.CES.SI.TATE, *v.*, necessitar, obrigar, exigir, tornar necessário.
NE.CES.SI.TY, *s.*, necessidade, exigência, requisito; carência, pobreza.
NECK, *s.*, pescoço, gola, gargalo, estreito, istmo.
NECK-BAND, *s.*, colarinho, gola de camisa.
NECK.ER.CHIEF, *s.*, lenço para pescoço.
NECK.TIE, *s.*, gravata.

NE.CROL.O.GIC, *adj.*, necrológico.
NE.CROL.O.GY, *s.*, necrologia.
NE.CROP.O.LIS, *s.*, necrópole, cemitério.
NEC.ROP.SY, *s.*, necropsia, autópsia.
NE.CRO.SIS, *s.*, necrose.
NEC.TAR, *s.*, néctar.
NEC.TAR.INE, *s.*, nectarina.
NEED, *s.*, necessidade, carência, falta, dificuldade; *v.*, necessitar, precisar.
NEED.FUL, *adj.*, necessário, preciso, indispensável.
NEED.NESS, *s.*, pobreza, indigência, carência.
NEE.DLE, *s.*, agulha, bússola; *v.*, alfinetar, costurar, usar a agulha.
NEE.DLER, *s.*, fabricante de agulhas.
NEED.LESS, *adj.*, inútil, desnecessário.
NEED.LESS.NESS, *s.*, inutilidade.
NEE.DLE.WO.MAN, *s.*, costureira.
NEEDY, *adj.*, necessitado, carente.
NE.FAR.I.OUS, *adj.*, nefando, abominável, nojento.
NE.GATE, *v.*, negar, desmentir.
NE.GA.TION, *s.*, negação, negativa.
NEG.A.TIVE, *s.*, negativo, negativo de foto, negação, veto; *v.*, negar.
NEG.A.TIV.ISM, *s.*, negativismo, pessimismo, nulidade.
NE.GLECT, *s.*, negligência, relaxamento; *v.*, negligenciar, descuidar.
NE.GLECT.ER, *s.*, negligente, descuidado.
NE.GLECT.FUL.NESS, *s.*, negligência, relaxamento.
NEG.LI.GENCE, *s.*, negligência, relaxamento, descuido.
NEG.LI.GENT, *adj.*, *s.*, negligente.
NE.GO.TIA.BIL.I.TY, *s.*, negociabilidade, a arte de negociar.
NE.GO.TIA.BLE, *adj.*, negociável.
NE.GO.TI.ATE, *v.*, negociar, intermediar, resolver conflitos.
NE.GO.TI.A.TION, *s.*, negociação, negócio.
NE.GRO, *adj.*, *s.*, negro, preto.
NEIGH, *v.*, relinchar, rinchar.
NEIGH.BOUR, *s.*, vizinho.

NEIGH.BOUR.HOOD, s., vizinhança, cercanias.
NEI.THER, pron., nenhum, nem um nem outro.
NEO.LITH.IC, adj., neolítico.
NE.OL.O.GISM, s., neologismo.
NEON, s., néon, neônio.
NEO.PHYTE, s., neófito, principiante, noviço.
NEPH.EW, s., sobrinho.
NE.PHRI.TIS s., nefrite.
NEP.TUNE, s., Netuno.
NERVE, s., nervo; coragem, afoiteza, vigor, descaramento; v., animar.
NERVED, adj., vigoroso, forte, robusto.
NER.VOUS, adj., nervoso, agitado, apreensivo.
NER.VURE, s., nervura de folha de planta.
NEST, s., ninho, toca, covil; v., aninhar-se, colocar-se em ninho.
NES.TLE, v., abrigar, aninhar, proteger, abraçar.
NEST.LING, s., passarinho, filhote de pássaro.
NET, s., rede, malha, armadilha; v., lançar a rede, pegar com a rede.
NETH.ER, adj., inferior, mais baixo.
NETH.ER.LAND.ER, adj., s., holandês, batavo, flamengo.
NETH.ER.LANDS, s., Holanda, Países-Baixos.
NETH.ER.MOST, adj., o mais baixo, o ínfimo.
NET.TLE, s., urtiga; v., irritar, incomodar, perturbar, exacerbar.
NET.TLING, s.,irritação,exasperação, incômodo.
NET.WORK, s., rede.
NEU.RAL.GIA, s., neuralgia, nevralgia.
NEU.RAL.GIC, adj., nevrálgico.
NEUR.AS.THE.NIA, s., neurastenia.
NEU.ROL.O.GIST, s., neurologista.
NEU.ROL.O.GY, s., neurologia.
NEU.RO.SIS, s., neurose.
NEU.ROT.IC, adj., s., neurótico.
NEU.TER, s., neutro, gênero neutro, ponto morto; adj., assexuado, neutro.
NEU.TRAL, adj., neutro, imparcial; s., ponto morto/carro, nação neutra.
NEU.TRAL.ISM, s., neutralismo, neutralidade.
NEU.TRAL.I.TY, s., neutralidade.
NEU.TRAL.IZE, v., neutralizar, anular.
NEV.ER, adv., nunca; nunca mais, jamais.
NEV.ER.MORE, adv., nunca, jamais, nunca mais.
NEV.ER.THE.LESS, conj., todavia, não obstante, contudo.
NEW, adj., novo, recente, moderno, fresco, complementar, atual.
NEW.BORN, s., recém-nascido.
NEW.COMER, s., recém-vindo, recém-chegado.
NEW.ISH, adj., quase novo.
NEW.LY, adv., novamente.
NEW.NESS, s., novidade.
NEWS, s., notícias, novidades, noticiário.
NEWS-BOY, s., rapaz que vende jornais, jornaleiro.
NEWS.CAST.ER, s., locutor, noticiarista, repórter.
NEWS.MAN, s., jornalista, repórter.
NEWS.PA.PER, s., jornal, diário, gazeta.
NEWS.STAND, s., banca de jornais.
NEWSY, adj., noticioso.
NEW YEAR, s., Ano Novo.
NEW ZEA.LAND.ER, adj., s., neozelandês.
NEXT, adj., s., próximo, vizinho, seguinte; adv., depois, logo.
NEX.US, s., nexo, vínculo, ligação.
NIB, s., ponta, bico de pena; v., apontar, fazer a ponta.
NIB.BLE, v., mordiscar, beliscar, morder.
NIC.A.RA.GUA, s., Nicarágua.
NIC.A.RA.GUAN, adj., s., nicaraguense.
NICE, adj., simpático, amável, atencioso, agradável, belo.
NICE.NESS, s., simpatia, agradabilidade, gentileza, delicadeza.
NICHE, s., nicho.
NICK, s., corte, entalhe, incisão, momento; v., entalhar, cortar, inserir.
NICK.EL, s., níquel; v., niquelar, cobrir com níquel.
NICK.NAME, s., apelido, alcunha; v., apelidar, alcunhar.
NIC.O.TINE, s., nicotina.
NIECE, s., sobrinha.
NI.GE.RIA, s., Nigéria.
NI.GE.RI.AN, adj., s., nigeriano.

NIGH, *adv.*, *prep.*, perto de, próximo.
NIGHT, *s.*, noite.
NIGHT.CLUB, *s.*, clube noturno.
NIGHT.FALL, *s.*, anoitecer, crepúsculo.
NIGHT.IN.GALE, *s.*, rouxinol.
NIGHT.LIFE, *s.*, vida noturna.
NIGHTY, *adj.*, noturno; *adv.*, a cada noite.
NIGHT-SHIRT, *s.*, camisola.
NIGHT-TIME, *s.*, noite.
NI.HIL.IST, *s.*, niilista.
NIL, *s.* nada, zero.
NIM.BLE, *adj.*, ágil, rápido, ligeiro, vivo.
NIM.BLE.NESS, *s.*, agilidade, rapidez.
NINE, *num.*, nove.
NINE.TEEN, *num.*, dezenove.
NINE.TY, *num.*, noventa.
NIN.NY, *s.*, tolo, simplório, parvo, bobo.
NINTH, *num.*, nono.
NIP, *v.*, beliscar, mordiscar; *s.*, beliscão, picada, mordida.
NIP.PLE, *s.*, mamilo, bico de seio.
NIP.PON, *s.*, Japão.
NIP.PON.ESE, *adj.*, *s.*, japonês, nipônico.
NI.TRO.GEN, *s.*, nitrogênio.
NI.TRO.GLYC.ER.IN, *s.*, nitroglicerina.
NI.TROUS, *adj.*, nitroso.
NIX, *s.*, nada, ninguém.
NO, *adv.*, não.
NO.BIL.I.TY, *s.*, nobreza, aristocracia.
NO.BLE, *adj.*, nobre, relativo à nobreza.
NO.BLE.NESS, *s.*, nobreza, grandeza, magnificência.
NO.BODY, *pron.*, ninguém, nenhuma pessoa.
NOC.TUR.NAL, *adj.*, noturno.
NOD, *s.*, aceno de cabeça, aquiescência; ordem; *v.*, acenar com a cabeça.
NOD.U.LAR, *adj.*, nodoso.
NOD.ULE, *s.*, nódulo.
NOD.UL.OUS, *adj.*, nodoso.
NO.EL, *s.*, noel, Natal, canção de natal.
NO.HOW, *adv.*, de modo algum.
NOISE, *s.*, barulho, ruído, estrépito, clamor; *v.*, estrepitar, fazer barulho, falar demais.
NOISE.LESS, *adj.*, silencioso, silente, sem barulho.
NOISY, *adj.*, barulhento, ruidoso, estrepitoso, rumoroso.
NO.MAD, *adj.*, *s.*, nômade.
NO.MEN.CLA.TURE, *s.*, nomenclatura.
NOM.I.NAL, *adj.*, nominal.
NOM.I.NATE, *v.*, nomear, referir, mencionar.
NOM.I.NA.TION, *s.*, nomeação.
NON.AGE, *s.*, menoridade.
NO.NA.GE.NAR.I.AN, *adj.*, *s.*, nonagenário.
NON-AL.CO.HOL.IC, *adj.*, não alcoólico, sem álcool.
NONE, *pron.*, ninguém, nenhum, nada.
NON-EX.IS.TENT, *adj.*, não existente, inexistente.
NON-HE.RO, *s.*, anti-herói.
NON.PLUS, *s.*, confusão, balbúrdia, perplexidade; *v.*, confundir, embaraçar.
NON.SENSE, *s.*, absurdo, disparate, contrassenso.
NON-SMOK.ER, *s.*, não fumante.
NON-STOP, *adj.*, contínuo, ininterrupto.
NON-SUIT, *s.*, processo anulado por falta de provas; *v.*, anular processo.
NOO.DLE, *s.*, talharim; tolo, bobo, imbecil.
NOOK, *s.*, canto, recanto, local ermo, retiro.
NOON, *s.*, meio-dia, apogeu.
NOON.DAY, *s.*, meio-dia; *adj.*, meridional.
NOOSE, *s.*, laço, nó corrediço; *v.*, fazer um nó; preparar uma armadilha.
NOR, *conj.*, nem, também não.
NOR.DIC, *adj.*, *s.*, nórdico.
NORM, *s.*, norma, regra, mandamento, padrão.
NOR.MAL, *adj.*, normal, regular.
NOR.MAL.I.TY, *s.*, normalidade.
NOR.MAL.I.ZA.TION, *s.*, normalização.
NOR.MAL.IZE, *v.*, normalizar.
NOR.MAN, *adj.*, *s.*, normando.
NORSE, *adj.*, *s.*, escandinavo.
NORTH, *s.*, norte, setentrião; *adj.*, nórdico, setentrional; *v.*, ir para o norte.
NORTH AMER.I.CAN, *adj.*, *s.*, norte-americano.
NORTH-EAST, *s.*, nordeste.
NORTHERN, *adj.*, do norte, nórdico, setentrional.
NORTHERNER, *s.*, habitante do norte.

NORTH-WEST, s., noroeste.
NOR.WAY, s., Noruega.
NOR.WE.GIAN, adj., s., norueguês.
NOSE, s., nariz, focinho, olfato, faro, bico; v., cheirar, focinhar, procurar.
NOSE.BAND, s., focinheira.
NOSE.BLEED, s., hemorragia pelo nariz.
NOSE.GAY, s., buquê, ramalhete, maço de flores.
NOS.TAL.GIA, s., nostalgia, saudade.
NOSY, adj., metido, abelhudo, bisbilhoteiro.
NOT, adv., não.
NO.TA.BLE, s., pessoa notável; adj., notável, famoso, célebre.
NO.TA.BLE.NESS, s., celebridade, fama.
NO.TA.RY, s., notário, tabelião.
NO.TA.TION, s., anotação, nota, notação.
NOTE, s., nota, bilhete, aviso, anotação, nota musical; v., anotar, tomar nota, observar.
NOTE.BOOK, s., caderno; microcomputador portátil, agenda, agenda eletrônica.
NOT.ED, adj., conhecido, renomado, famoso.
NOTE.LESS, adj., desconhecido, obscuro.
NOTH.ING, s., nada, zero, coisa nenhuma, nulidade.
NO.TICE, s., aviso, notícia, anúncio, aviso prévio, prazo, notificação, informação.
NO.TI.FI.CA.TION, s., notificação, aviso, informação.
NO.TI.FY, v., notificar, avisar, intimar.
NO.TION, s., noção, conhecimento elementar, ideia, opinião.
NO.TO.RI.E.TY, s., notoriedade, fama.
NOT.WITH.STAND.ING, conj., no entanto, não obstante.
NOUGHT, s., zero.
NOUN, s. substantivo, nome.
NOUR.ISH, v., alimentar, nutrir, sustentar.
NOUR.ISH.ABLE, adj., nutrível, alimentável.
NOUR.ISH.ING adj., nutritivo, alimentício.
NOUR.ISH.MENT, s., alimento, nutrimento, comida.
NOV.EL, s., novela, romance; adj., novo, novel, recente.
NOV.EL.IST, s., novelista.
NOV.EL.TY, s., novidade.
NO.VEM.BER, s., novembro.
NOV.ICE, s., noviço, neófito, iniciante, principiante, novato.
NOW, adv., agora, hoje, atualmente, neste momento.
NOW.A.DAYS, adv., atualmente, hoje em dia.
NO.WHERE, adj., a lugar nenhum, em nenhum lugar.
NO.WISE, adv., de modo algum.
NOX.IOUS, adj., nocivo, prejudicial, danoso.
NOZ.ZLE, s., boca, bico.
NU.ANCE, s., nuança, matiz, meio tom.
NU.CLE.AR, adj., nuclear.
NU.CLE.US, s., núcleo.
NUDE, adj., nu, despido, sem roupas, descoberto, liso.
NUDGE, v., acotovelar, cutucar.
NUD.IST, s., nudista.
NU.DI.TY, s., nudez.
NUI.SANCE, s., incômodo, aborrecimento, tipo desagradável; praga.
NULL, adj., nulo, sem validade; v., anular, invalidar.
NUL.LI.FI.CA.TION, s., anulação, invalidade.
NUL.LI.FY, v., anular, invalidar, nulificar.
NUL.LI.TY, s., nulidade.
NUMB, adj., entorpecido, paralisado, dormente; v., paralisar, entorpecer.
NUMB.ER, s., número, algarismo, soma; v., numerar, quantificar.
NUM.BER.ER, s., numerador.
NU.MER.A.BLE, adj., numerável.
NU.MER.AL, s., numeral.
NU.MER.ATE, v., numerar, enumerar.
NU.MER.IC, adj., numérico.
NU.MER.OUS, adj., numeroso, abundante.
NU.MIS.MAT.ICS, s., numismática.
NUM.SKULL, adj., tolo, néscio, bobo, imbecil.
NUN, s., freira.
NUN.CIO, s., núncio.
NUN.NERY, s., convento de freiras.
NUP.TIAL, adj., nupcial, matrimonial.
NURSE, s., enfermeira, ama-seca, governanta,

aia; *v.*, trabalhar como enfermeira, criar.
NURS.ERY, *s.*, creche, berçário, quarto de crianças, viveiro.
NURS.ING, *s.*, enfermagem, cuidados.
NUR.TURE, *v.*, nutrir, alimentar; *s.*, criação, educação, alimentação.
NUT, *s.*, noz; porca de parafuso.
NUT-BROWN, *adj.*, cor de castanha, acastanhado.
NUT.CRACK.ER, *s.*, quebra-nozes.
NUT.HATCH, *s.*, pica-pau.
NUT.MEG, *s.*, noz-moscada.
NU.TRI.ENT, *adj.*, *s.*, nutriente.
NU.TRI.MENT, *s.*, nutrimento, alimentação, sustento.
NU.TRI.TION, *s.*, nutrição, alimentação.
NU.TRI.TIVE, *adj.*, nutritivo.
NUT.TY, *adj.*, com sabor de noz.
NY.LON, *s.*, náilon, fibra sintética.
NYMPH, *s.*, ninfa.
NYM.PHO.MA.NIA, *s.*, ninfomania.

O

O, décima quinta letra do alfabeto inglês; zero.
OAF, *s.*, imbecil, tolo, idiota, simplório, parvo.
OAK, *s.*, carvalho; *adj.*, próprio do carvalho.
OA.KUM, *s.*, estopa, estopa para calafetar.
OAR, *s.*, remo, remador; *v.*, remar.
OARS.MAN, *s.*, remador.
OA.SIS, *s.*, oásis.
OAT, *s.*, aveia, flauta de pastor.
OAT.CAKE, *s.*, bolo feito de aveia.
OATH, *s.*, juramento; praga, palavrão.
OATH.BREAK.ER, *s.*, perjuro, juramento falso.
OAT.MEAL, *s.*, farinha de aveia.
OB.DU.RATE, *adj.*, teimoso, obstinado, duro.
OB.DU.RA.TION, *s.*, teimosia, insistência.
OBE.DI.ENCE, *s.*, obediência, atendimento.
OBE.DI.ENT, *adj.*, obediente, atencioso.
OBEI.SANCE, *s.*, reverência, mesura, deferência, respeito.
OBE.LISK, *s.*, obelisco.
OBESE, *adj.*, obeso, gordo, barrigudo.
OBESE.NESS, *s.*, obesidade, gordura excessiva.
OBE.SI.TY, *s.*, obesidade.
OBEY, *v.*, obedecer, acatar, respeitar.
OB.FUS.CA.TION, *s.*, ofuscação, deslumbramento, brilho intenso.
OBIT, *s.*, óbito, falecimento, obituário, morte.
OBIT.U.ARY, *s.*, obituário, necrologia.
OB.JECT, *s.*, objeto, coisa, objetivo, propósito; *v.*, objetar, alegar, contrapor-se.
OB.JEC.TI.FY, *v.*, objetivar, pretender, colimar.
OB.JEC.TION, *s.*, objeção, oposição, contraposição.
OB.JEC.TIVE, *adj.*, *s.*, objetivo.
OB.JEC.TIVE.NESS, *s.*, objetividade.
OB.JEC.TIV.I.TY, *s.*, objetividade, imparcialidade.
OB.JUR.GATE, *v.*, censurar, admoestar, advertir.
OB.JUR.GA.TION, *s.*, censura, advertência, admoestação.
OB.LI.GATE, *v.*, obrigar, constranger, forçar a.
OB.LI.GA.TION, *s.*, obrigação, constrangimento, compromisso, dever.
OBLIG.A.TOR, *s.*, devedor.
OBLIG.A.TO.RY, *adj.*, obrigatório, forçado.
OBLIGE, *v.*, favorecer, obrigar, forçar.
OBLIG.ING, *adj.*, amável, obsequiador, gentil, cortês.
OB.LI.GOR, *s.*, devedor.
OBLIQUE, *adj.*, oblíquo, indeciso, indeterminado.
OBLIQUE.NESS, *s.*, obliquidade, indecisão.
OBLIT.ER.ATE, *v.*, obliterar, apagar, retirar, esquecer.
OBLIT.ER.A.TION, *s.*, obliteração, esquecimento.
OBLIV.I.ON, *s.*, esquecimento.
OB.LONG, *adj.*, oblongo, retangular; *s.*, retângulo, figura oblonga.
OB.NOX.IOUS, *adj.*, odioso, detestável, nojento, intragável.
OB.SCENE, *adj.*, obsceno, devasso.
OB.SCEN.I.TY, *s.*, obscenidade, devassidão.
OB.SCU.RA.TION, *s.*, obscurecimento.
OB.SCURE, *adj.*, obscuro, ignorado, ambíguo; *v.*, ocultar, escurecer; *s.*, obscuridade.
OB.SCU.RI.TY, *s.*, obscuridade, escuridão, ambiguidade, incerteza.
OB.SE.QUI.OUS, *adj.*, obsequioso, atencioso, cortês.
OB.SERV.ABLE, *adj.*, observável, que se percebe, notável.
OB.SER.VANCE, *s.*, observação, acompanhamento, hábito.
OB.SER.VANT, *adj.*, observador, observante.
OB.SER.VA.TION, *s.*, observação, exame, verificação.
OB.SER.VA.TO.RY, *s.*, observatório.
OB.SERVE, *v.*, observar, cumprir, respeitar.

OB.SES.SION, *s.*, obsessão, ideia fixa, mania.
OB.SES.SIVE, *adj.*, obsessivo.
OB.SO.LES.CENSE, *s.*, obsolescência, velhice, desuso.
OB.SO.LETE, *adj.*, obsoleto.
OB.STA.CLE, *s.*, obstáculo, empecilho, óbice, impedimento.
OB.STET.RIC, *adj.*, obstétrico.
OB.STE.TRI.CIAN, *s.*, obstetra, médico parteiro, parteiro, parteira.
OB.STI.NA.CY, *s.*, obstinação, teimosia.
OB.STI.NATE, *adj.*, obstinado, teimoso.
OB.STREP.ER.OUS, *adj.*, ruidoso, estrepitoso, barulhento.
OB.STREP.ER.OUS.NESS, *s.*, ruído, barulho, rumor, estrépito.
OB.STRUCT, *v.* estorvar, incomodar, perturbar, obstruir.
OB.STRUCT.ED, *adj.*, *part.*, obstruído, impedido, incomodado.
OB.STRUC.TION, *s.*, obstrução, obstáculo, óbice.
OB.TAIN, *v.*, obter, conseguir, lograr.
OB.TAIN.ABLE, *adj.*, obtenível, disponível.
OB.TRUDE, *v.*, impor com violência, impor.
OB.TU.RATE, *v.*, obturar, fechar, tapar.
OB.TU.RA.TION, *s.*, obturação.
OB.TUSE, *adj.*, obtuso.
OB.VERT, *v.*, voltar, dirigir para, reverter, pôr do avesso.
OB.VERT.ING, *adj.*, revertido, do avesso.
OB.VI.ATE, *v.*, obviar, prevenir.
OB.VI.OUS, *adj.*, óbvio, evidente, claro.
OB.VI.OUS.NESS, *s.*, obviedade, evidência.
OC.CA.SION, *s.*, ocasião, fato, acontecimento, momento.
OC.CA.SION.AL, *adj.*, ocasional, momentâneo, acidental.
OC.CA.SION.AL.LY, *adv.*, ocasionalmente, vez por outra.
OC.CIDENT, *s.*, ocidente, poente.
OC.CI.DEN.TAL, *adj.*, ocidental.
OC.CIP.I.TAL, *s.*, occipital.
OC.CLUDE, *v.*, fechar, tapar.

OC.CLU.SION, *s.*, oclusão, fechamento.
OC.CULT, *v.*, ocultar, esconder, dissimular; *adj.*, oculto, secreto, dissimulado.
OC.CUL.TA.TION, *s.*, ocultação, ocultamento.
OC.CULT.ISM, *s.*, ocultismo.
OC.CULT.NESS, *s.*, ocultação, confidência, segredo.
OC.CU.PA.TION, *s.*, ocupação, profissão, trabalho.
OC.CU.PI.ED, *adj.*, ocupado, aplicado, atarefado, diligente.
OC.CU.PY, *v.*, ocupar, acomodar-se, morar.
OC.CUR, *v.*, ocorrer, acontecer, suceder.
OC.CUR.RENCE, *s.*, ocorrência, fato, acontecimento, evento, sucesso.
OCEAN, *s.*, oceano.
OCEAN.I.AN, *adj.*, oceânico.
OCEAN.OG.RA.PHER, *s.*, oceanógrafo.
OCHRE, *s.*, ocre; *adj.*, cor de ocre.
OC.TA.GON, *s.*, octógono.
OC.TA.HE.DRON, *s.*, octaedro.
OC.TA.VO, *adj.*, oitavo.
OC.TO.BER, *s.*, outubro.
OC.TO.GE.NAR.I.AN, *adj.*, *s.*, octogenário.
OC.TO.PUS, *s.*, polvo.
OC.TUPLE, *adj.*, *num.*, óctuplo.
OC.U.LAR, *adj.*, ocular, visual.
OC.U.LIST, *s.*, oculista, oftalmologista.
ODA.LISQUE, *s.*, odalisca.
ODD, *adj.*, excelente, ótimo, ocasional, casual, esquisito, excêntrico, estranho.
ODD.I.TY, *s.*, esquisitice, excentricidade, extravagância, coisa estranha.
ODD.NESS, *s.*, desigualdade, excentricidade, esquisitice.
ODI.OUS, *adj.*, odioso, nojento.
ODI.OUS.NESS, *s.*, ódio, odiosidade, aversão, repugnância.
ODOM.E.TER, *s.*, odômetro.
ODON.TOL.O.GIST, *s.*, odontologista, dentista, odontólogo.
ODON.TOL.O.GY, *s.*, odontologia.
ODOR.IF.ER.OUS, *adj.*, odorífero, aromatizado, perfumado.

ODOROUS — ONENESS

ODOR.OUS, *adj.*, perfumado, aromático.
ODOUR, *s.*, odor, perfume; cheiro, fedor.
OE.CU.MEN.IC, *adj.*, ecumênico.
OE.DE.MA, *s.*, edema, tumor.
OE.SOPH.A.GUS, *s.*, esôfago.
OF, *prep.*, de, por, devido, entre.
OFF, *adj.*, cancelado, desligado, ausente; *prep.* fora de, fora.
OFF LINE, *adj.*, fora de linha.
OF.FAL, *s.*, restos de comida, sobras.
OF.FENCE, *s.*, delito, crime, ofensa, injúria, ataque, desgosto.
OF.FEND, *v.*, ofender, injuriar, magoar, desgostar, escandalizar.
OF.FEND.ER, *s.*, ofensor, transgressor, delinquente.
OF.FEN.SIVE, *adj.*, ofensivo.
OF.FER, *s.*, oferta, oferenda, dádiva, oferecimento; *v.*, oferecer, ofertar, doar.
OF.FER.ER, *s.*, oferente, ofertador.
OF.FER.ING, *s.*, oferta, dádiva, oferenda.
OF.FER.TO.RY, *s.*, ofertório, oferecimento.
OF.FICE, *s.*, escritório, gabinete, cargo, função, posto, seção, préstimos.
OF.FICE-BOY, *s.*, estafeta, mensageiro, office-boy.
OF.FIC.ER, *s.*, oficial, diretor, agente, administrador, ministro, dirigente.
OF.FI.CIAL, *adj.*, *s.*, oficial; servidor público.
OF.FI.CIAL.DOM, *s.*, burocracia, administração pública.
OF.FI.CI.ATE, *v.*, oficiar, empreender algo oficial.
OF.FI.CIOUS, *adj.*, oficioso, metido, intrometido.
OFF.SET, *s.*, offset, processo de impressão; *v.*, compensar, equiparar.
OFF.SHORE, *adj.*, costeiro, litorâneo.
OFF.SIDE, *s.*, impedimento, fora de jogo; *adj.*, na lateral, do lado errado.
OFF.SPRING, *s.*, descendência, filhos, prole.
OF.TEN, *adv.*, muitas vezes, frequentemente, amiúde.
OGI.VAL, *adj.*, ogival.
OGIVE, *s.*, ogiva.
OGRE, *s.*, ogro, bicho papão.
OIL, *s.*, óleo, petróleo; azeite; *v.*, lubrificar, azeitar, passar óleo, untar.
OIL FIELD, *s.*, campo petrolífero, bacia petrolífera.
OIL.SKIN, *s.*, oleado, capa.
OILY, *adj.*, oleoso, gorduroso, banhoso.
OINT.MENT, *s.*, unguento, pomada.
O. K., *abrev.* de "okay", *adj.* e *adv.*, tudo bem, ótimo, certo, aprovado.
OKRA, *s.*, quiabo.
OLD, *adj.*, velho, antigo, anterior.
OLD.EN, *adj.*, velho, antigo.
OLD-FASH.IONED, *adj.*, fora de moda, obsoleto, velho.
OLD.NESS, *s.*, velhice, antiguidade.
OLE.AG.I.NOUS.NESS, *s.*, oleosidade.
OLEO.MAR.GA.RINE, *s.*, margarina.
OL.I.GARCH, *s.*, oligarca.
OL.I.GAR.CHIC, *adj.*, oligárquico.
OL.I.GAR.CHY, *s.*, oligarquia.
OLIO, *s.*, mistura, miscelânea.
OL.IVE, *s.*, azeitona, oliveira.
OLIVE GREEN, *adj.*, verde-oliva.
OLYM.PI.AD, *s.*, olimpíada.
OLYM.PIC, *adj.*, olímpico.
OLYM.PUS, *s.*, Olimpo.
OM.E.LET, *s.*, omelete.
OMEN, *s.*, agouro, presságio; *v.*, augurar, pressagiar.
OMENED, *adj.*, fatal, fatídico.
OMIS.SION, *s.*, omissão, lacuna, falta.
OMIT, *v.*, omitir, deixar fora, excluir.
OM.NI.BUS, *s.*, ônibus.
OM.NIP.O.TENCE, *s.*, onipotência.
OM.NI.PRES.ENCE, *s.*, onipresença, ubiquidade.
OM.NI.SCIENCE, *s.*, onisciência.
OM.NIV.O.ROUS, *adj.*, *s.*, onívoro.
ON, *prep.*, sobre, em, em cima de.
ONCE, *adv.*, uma vez, outrora, antigamente; *prep.*, depois que.
ONE, *num.*, um; *adj.*, único, típico.
ONE-EYED, *adj.*, caolho, cego somente de um olho.
ONE-LEG.GED, *adj.*, coxo, manco; *s.*, perneta.
ONE.NESS, *s.*, unidade, identidade.

ONER.OUS, *adj.*, oneroso, pesado.
ONE.SELF, *pron.*, se, si; si mesmo, si próprio.
ONE-SID.ED, *adj.*, parcial, injusto, desigual.
ONE-SID.ED.NESS, *s.*, imparcialidade.
ONE-WAY,*adj.*,de sentido único,de mão única.
ON.ION, *s.*, cebola.
ON.IONY, *adj.*, acebolado, igual a cebola.
ON-LOOK.ER, *s.*, espectador.
ONLY, *adv.*, somente, apenas; *adj.*, único, só; *conj.*, exceto, porém.
ON.O.MATO.POE.IA, *s.*, onomatopeia.
ON.RUSH, *s.*, carga, arremetida.
ON.SET, *s.*, início, começo; assalto, ataque.
ON.TOL.O.GY, *s.*, ontologia.
ONUS, *s.*, ônus, carga, peso, obrigação, responsabilidade.
ON.WARD, *adv.*, para frente, adiante; *adj.*, avançado, adiantado.
OOZE, *s.*, limo, lodo; infusão; *v.*, correr líquidos; escoar líquidos, pingar, gotejar.
OPAL, *s.*, opala.
OPAQUE, *adj.*, opaco, fusco, embaçado.
OPAQUE.NESS, *s.*, opacidade.
OPEN, *s.*, campo raso, clareira, abertura; *adj.*, aberto, descoberto, livre, franco, irrestrito; *v.*, abrir, descerrar, franquear, liberar.
OPEN-MAR.KET, *s.*, mercado livre.
OPEN.ER, *s.*, abridor.
OP.ER.ANT, *adj.*, operante.
OP.ER.ATE, *v.*, fazer funcionar, colocar em funcionamento, funcionar.
OP.ER.AT.ING, *s.*, funcionamento; *adj.*, operante, operador.
OP.ER.A.TION, *s.*, operação, funcionamento; cirurgia.
OP.ER.A.TION.AL, *adj.*, operacional.
OP.ER.A.TOR, *s.*, operador, operante, manipulador.
OPHID.I.A, *s.*, *pl.*, ofídios.
OPH.THAL.MIA, *s.*, oftalmologia.
OPINE, *v.*, opinar, julgar, dar sugestão.
OPIN.ION, *s.*, opinião, parecer, julgamento.
OPI.UM, *s.*, ópio.
OP.PO.NENT, *s.*, oponente, adversário.

OP.POR.TUNE, *adj.*, oportuno.
OP.POR.TUNE.NESS, *s.*, oportunidade.
OP.POR.TU.NI.TY, *s.*, oportunidade.
OP.POSE, *v.*, opor-se, estar contra.
OP.POSED, *adj.*, oposto, contrário.
OP.POS.ER, *s.*, opositor, adversário, antagonista.
OP.PO.SITE, *s.*, oposto, contrário, adversário; *adj.*, oposto, contrário, oponente.
OP.PO.SI.TION, *s.*, oposição.
OP.PRESS, *v.*, oprimir.
OP.PRES.SION, *s.*, opressão.
OP.PRES.SOR, *s.*, opressor, carrasco, ditador, tirano.
OP.PRO.BRI.OUS, *adj.*, infamante, humilhante.
OP.PRO.BRI.OUS.NESS, *s.*, opróbrio, vergonha, humilhação.
OP.PRO.BRI.UM *s.*, opróbrio, vergonha.
OP.PUGN.ANCY, *s.*, oposição, confronto.
OPT, *v.*, optar, escolher.
OP.TIC, *adj.*, óptico.
OP.TI.CIAN, *s.*, oculista.
OP.TICS, *s.*, óptica.
OP.TI.MISM, *s.*, otimismo.
OP.TI.MUM, *adj.*, ótimo.
OPTION, *s.*, opção, direito de optar em um negócio, escolha.
OP.TION.AL, *adj.*, opcional, facultativo.
OP.U.LENCE, *s.*, opulência, riqueza, abundância.
OPUS.CULE, *s.*, opúsculo.
OR, *conj.*, ou, ou ... ou.
OR.A.CLE, *s.*, oráculo.
ORAL, *adj.*, oral, falado.
ORANG, *s.*, *abrev.*, orangotango.
OR.ANGE, *s.*, laranja; *adj.*, cor de laranja, alaranjado.
OR.ANGE.ADE, *s.*, laranjada.
OR.ANGE.RY, *s.*, laranjal.
ORANG.U.TAN, *s.*, orangotango.
ORA.TION, *s.*, oração, discurso, alocução.
OR.A.TOR, *s.*, orador.
OR.A.TO.RY, *s.*, oratório.
ORB, *s.*, esfera, globo; *v.*, tornar esférico.
OR.BIC.U.LAR, *adj.*, orbicular.
OR.BIT, *s.*, órbita; *v.*, orbitar.

OR.CHARD, *s.*, pomar, vergel.
OR.CHES.TRA, *s.*, orquestra.
OR.CHES.TRATE, *v.*, orquestrar.
OR.CHES.TRA.TION, *s.*, orquestração, conjunto de instrumentos.
OR.CHID, *s.*, orquídea.
OR.CHIS, *s.*, orquídea.
OR.DAIN, *v.*, ordenar, comandar, decidir, decretar.
OR.DAIN.ER, *s.*, ordenador, quem decreta.
OR.DER, *s.*, ordem, encomenda, pedido; *v.*, ordenar, pôr em ordem, arrumar, pedir.
OR.DER.ING, *s.*, disposição.
OR.DER.LESS, *adj.*, desorganizado, confuso, embaralhado, desajustado.
OR.DER.LY, *s.*, ordenança, assistente hospitalar; *adj.*, organizado, ordenado.
OR.DI.NAL, *adj.*, ordinal; número ordinal.
OR.DI.NARY, *adj.*, ordinário, comum, usual; ordinário, vulgar.
ORE, *s.*, minério.
OR.GAN, *s.*, órgão.
OR.GAN.IC, *adj.*, orgânico.
OR.GAN.ISM, *s.*, organismo.
OR.GAN.IST, *s.*, organista.
OR.GA.NI.ZA.TION, *s.*, organização.
OR.GA.NIZE, *v.*, organizar.
OR.GASM, *s.*, orgasmo.
OR.GY, *s.*, orgia, bacanal.
ORI.ENT, *s.*, Oriente, Nascente, Levante.
ORI.EN.TAL, *v.*, orientar, orientar-se; colocar no rumo, rumar.
ORI.EN.TA.TION, *s.*, orientação.
OR.I.FICE, *s.*, buraco, orifício.
OR.I.GIN, *s.*, origem.
ORIG.I.NAL, *adj.*, original, genuíno.
ORIG.I.NAL.I.TY, *s.*, originalidade.
ORIG.I.NATE, *v.*, originar-se, surgir, começar, iniciar.
ORIG.I.NA.TION, *s.*, origem, causa, princípio.
ORIG.I.NA.TOR, *s.*, originador, causador, autor, criador.
OR.I.SON, *s.*, oração, reza.
OR.NA.MENT, *s.*, ornato, ornamento, enfeite.
OR.NA.MEN.TAL, *adj.*, ornamental, que enfeita.
OR.NA.MEN.TA.TION, *s.*, ornamentação, enfeite.
OR.NI.THOL.O.GIST, *s.*, ornitólogo, ornitologista.
OR.NI.THOL.O.GY, *s.*, ornitologia.
OROG.RA.PHY, *s.*, orografia.
OR.PHAN, *s.*, órfão.
OR.PHAN.AGE, *s.*, orfanato.
OR.RERY, *s.*, planetário.
OR.THO.DOX, *adj.*, *s.*, ortodoxo.
OR.THO.DOXY, *s.*, ortodoxia.
OR.THO.EPY, *s.*, ortoépia.
OR.THO.GRAPH.IC, *adj.*, ortográfico.
OR.THOG.RA.PHY, *s.*, ortografia.
OR.THO.PAE.DIC, *adj.*, ortopédico.
OR.THO.PAE.DICS, *s.*, ortopedia.
OS.CIL.LATE, *v.*, oscilar, vacilar, titubear.
OS.CIL.LAT.ING, *adj.*, oscilante, vacilante.
OS.CIL.LA.TION, *s.*, oscilação, vacilação, hesitação.
OS.CIL.LA.TOR, *s.*, oscilador.
OS.CU.LATE, *v.*, oscular, beijar.
OS.CU.LA.TION, *s.*, beijo, osculação.
OS.SE.OUS, *adj.*, ósseo.
OS.SI.FIED, *adj.*, ossificado.
OS.SI.FY, *v.*, ossificar.
OS.SU.ARY, *s.*, ossário.
OS.TEN.SIB.IL.I.TY, *s.*, ostensibilidade.
OS.TEN.SIVE, *adj.*, ostensivo.
OS.TEN.TA.TION, *s.*, ostentação, exibição, barulho.
OS.TE.OL.O.GIST, *s.*, osteologista.
OS.TE.OL.O.GY, *s.*, osteologia.
OS.TE.OP.A.THY, *s.*, osteopatia.
OS.TI.ARY, *s.*, hostiário, local para guardar as hóstias na igreja.
OS.TRA.CISM, *s.*, ostracismo, exílio.
OS.TRA.CIZE, *v.*, exilar, desterrar, condenar ao ostracismo.
OS.TRICH, *s.*, avestruz.
OTH.ER, *adj.*, *pron.*, outro, outra; outros, outras.
OTH.ER.WISE, *adj.*, diferente; *adv.*, de outra maneira, por outro lado.
OTI.OSE, *adj.*, ocioso, vadio, malandro.

OTI.OS.I.TY, *s.*, ociosidade.
OT.TER, *s.*, lontra.
OUNCE, *s.*, onça – medida de peso
OUR, *pron.*, nosso.
OURS, *pron.*, nosso, nossa, nossos, nossas.
OUR.SELVES, *pron., pl.*, nós, nós mesmos, nós mesmas.
OUST, *v.*, expulsar.
OUST.ER, *s.* desapropriação.
OUT, *s.*, espaço aberto, local fora; *v.*, expulsar, desligar; *adv.*, fora, para fora.
OUT.BORN, *adj.*, *s.*, nascido no estrangeiro, estrangeiro.
OUT.BREAK, *s.*, deflagração, surto, erupção, eclosão; *v.*, eclodir, irromper.
OUT.BUILD.ING, *s.*, pavilhão, anexo, dependência do prédio principal.
OUT.BURST, *s.*, explosão.
OUT.CAST, *s.*, pária, proscrito, exilado; *adj.*, exilado, desterrado, abandonado.
OUT.COME, *s.*, resultado, consequência, efeito.
OUT.CRY, *s.*, grito, berro, clamor, tumulto; *v.*, berrar, gritar, exclamar.
OUT.DO, *v.*, ultrapassar, exceder, ir além.
OUT.DOOR, *s.*, cartaz publicitário, "outdor"; *adj.*, exposto, colocado ao ar livre.
OUT.ER, *adj.*, exterior, externo, fora, ao ar livre.
OUT.ER.MOST, *adj.*, o mais afastado, o mais longe.
OUT.GO.ING, *s.*, partida, saída, eflúvio, despesas.
OUT.GROW, *v.*, crescer em excesso, crescer demais.
OUT.GUARD, *s.*, sentinela, vigilância, guarda avançada.
OUT.HOUSE, *s.*, varanda, anexo externo, alpendre.
OUT.ING, *s.*, passeio, excursão, caminhada.
OUT.LAND, *s.*, estrangeiro, terras estrangeiras, exterior.
OUT.LAST, *v.*, exceder no tempo, ir além do tempo previsto.
OUT.LAW, *s.*, fora da lei, proscrito, criminoso; *v.*, proscrever, declarar fora da lei.
OUT.LET, *s.*, saída, escoamento, posto de vendas; tomada elétrica; *v.*, escoar.
OUT.LINE, *s.*, contorno, esboço, silhueta, sumário; *v.*, esboçar, delinear.
OUT.LIVE, *v.*, sobreviver, subsistir.
OUT.LOOK, *s.*, perspectiva, panorama, ponto de vista, previsão.
OUT.MOD.ED, *adj.*, afastado, antiquado, obsoleto, arcaico.
OUT-OF-DATE, *adj.*, sem validade de data, obsoleto.
OUT-OF-DOORS, *adj.*, ao ar livre, fora, fora de casa.
OUT.PACE, *v.*, sobrepujar, passar de alguém, ultrapassar.
OUT.PASS, *v.*, ultrapassar, exceder.
OUT.POST, *s.*, posto avançado, guarita.
OUT.PUT, *s.*, produção, rendimento; saída.
OUTRAGE, *s.*, ultraje, injúria, escândalo, abuso; *v.*, injuriar, ultrapassar, abusar.
OUT.RA.GEOUS, *adj.*, ultrajante, injurioso, escandaloso, abusivo.
OUT.REACH, *v.*, alcançar, conseguir, passar.
OUT.RIGHT, *adj.*, sincero, franco; *adv.*, completamente, imediatamente.
OUT.ROOT, *v.*, extirpar, erradicar, arrancar.
OUT.SELL, *v.*, vender mais, vender mais caro.
OUT.SET, *s.*, início, começo, princípio.
OUT.SHINE, *v.*, exceder em brilho, brilhar muito.
OUT.SIDE, *s.*, exterior, aparência; *adj.*, externo, exterior; *adv.*, para fora, sem.
OUT.SID.ER, *s.*, estranho, forasteiro, intruso.
OUT.SKIRT, *s.*, limite, margem, borda; **OUT.SKIRTS** - bairros, subúrbios.
OUT.SPO.KEN, *adj.*, franco, sincero.
OUT.STAND, *v.*, demorar-se, parar.
OUT.STA.TION, *s.*, posto avançado, posto fronteiriço.
OUT.TOP, *v.*, exceder, ir além de, ultrapassar.
OUT.WARD, *adj.*, externo, de aparência externa, aparente; *adv.*, do lado de fora.
OUT.WARD.NESS, *s.*, exterioridade.
OUT.WIT, *v.*, exceder, ser mais esperto, exceder em esperteza.
OUT.WORK, *s.*, fortificação, fortaleza exterior,

trabalho externo.
OVAL, *adj.*, oval.
OVA.RY, *s.*, ovário.
OVATE, *adj.*, ovalado, com formato de ovo, oval.
OVA.TION, *s.*, ovação.
OV.EN, *s.*, forno; *v.*, assar no forno.
OV.EN.BIRD, *s.*, joão-de-barro.
OV.EN.PROOF, *adj.*, refratário, resistente a temperaturas variadas.
OVER, *s.*, excesso, demasia; *adj.*, excedente; *adv.*, por cima, em cima, demais.
OVER.ALL, *s.*, *adj.*, total, global; *adv.*, completamente, em toda parte, especialmente.
OVER.AWE, *v.*, intimidar, atemorizar, assustar.
OVER.BEAR, *v.*, sobrepujar, oprimir, vencer.
OVER.BEAR.ING, *adj.*, autoritário, mandão, dominador, categórico.
OVER.BOIL, *v.*, ferver demais, cozinhar muito, exceder no cozimento.
OVER.BRIM, *v.*, transbordar, vazar.
OVER.BUSY, *adj.*, demasiadamente ocupado, muito ocupado.
OVER.CARE, *s.*, solicitude, cuidado.
OVER.CARE.FUL, *adj.*, cuidadoso, solícito, cuidadoso em excesso.
OVER.CAST, *v.*, obscurecer, toldar, entristecer; *adj.*, nublado, toldado.
OVER.CHARGE, *s.*, sobrecarga, preço alto; *v.*, sobrecarregar, cobrar demais.
OVER.COAT, *s.*, sobretudo.
OVER.COME, *v.*, superar, sobrepujar, dominar.
OVER.COOK.ED, *adj.*, cozido em demasia.
OVER.DOSE, *s.*, overdose, dose excessiva.
OVER.DRAFT, *s.*, saldo bancário negativo.
OVER.DUE, *adj.*, atrasado, tardio, demorado.
OVER.EAT, *v.*, comer em excesso, comer demais.
OVER.ES.TI.MATE, *v.*, estimar em demasia, preferir a tudo.
OVER.FALL, *s.*, queda-d'água, cachoeira.
OVER.FEED, *v.*, saciar, saturar, encher.
OVER.FLOW, *s.*, inundação, transbordamento; *v.*, transbordar, inundar.
OVER.FLY, *v.*, voar sobre, voar por cima.
OVER.GROW, *v.*, cobrir com vegetação, crescer muito.
OVER.GROWTH, *s.*, vegetação viçosa.
OVER.HAND, *s.*, superioridade, supremacia.
OVER.HANG, *s.*, projeção, saliência; *v.*, pender, projetar-se, estender-se sobre.
OVER.HAUL, *s.*, revisão, vistoria; *v.*, inspecionar, vistoriar, revisar.
OVER.HEAD, *s.*, despesas; *adj.*, na parte de cima, aéreo; *adv.*, por cima, em cima.
OVER.HEAR, *v.*, ouvir por acaso, escutar, entreouvir.
OVER.HEAT, *v.*, aquecer demais, esquentar em excesso.
OVER.HOUR, *s.*, hora extra no trabalho.
OVER.JOY, *s.*, arrebatamento, grande alegria; *v.*, dar uma grande alegria.
OVER.LADE, *v.*, sobrecarregar.
OVER.LAND, *adj.*, *adv.*, por terra, por via terrestre.
OVER.LAY, *s.*, revestimento, capa, cobertura, colcha; *v.*, cobrir, revestir.
OVER.LAY.ING, *s.*, cobertura, revestimento, camada.
OVER.LEAF, *adv.*, no verso, atrás.
OVER.LEAP, *v.*, saltar por cima, omitir, deixar de lado.
OVER.LOOK, *s.*, ato de olhar; omissão; *v.*, contemplar, admirar, olhar.
OVER.MAN, *s.*, inspetor.
OVER.MAS.TER, *v.*, dominar, subjugar, conter.
OVER.MUCH, *adj.*, demasiado; *adv.*, demasiadamente.
OVER.NIGHT, *s.*, a tarde do dia anterior, uma noite; *adj.*, noturno, que dura uma noite; *adv.*, durante a noite, de um dia para o outro.
OVER.PASS, *s.*, viaduto, passagem elevada; *v.*, transpor, passar por cima, vencer.
OVER.PAST, *adj.*, passado, superado, transposto.
OVER.PAY, *v.*, pagar em excesso, pagar a mais.
OVER.PLUS, *s.*, excedente, sobra, demasia, excesso.
OVER.POW.ER, *s.*, excesso de força, domínio; *v.*, dominar, subjugar, vencer.
OVER.PRESS, *v.*, oprimir, perseguir, castigar.
OVER.PRO.DUC.TION, *s.*, superprodução,

produção excessiva.
OVER.RATE, *v.*, superestimar, estimar em demasia.
OVER.RUN.NING, *s.*, invasão.
OVER.SEA, *adj.*, ultramarino, além-mar, transatlântico.
OVER.SEE, *v.*, inspecionar, vistoriar, vigiar, rever.
OVER.SEER, *s.*, inspetor, vistoriador.
OVER.SHADE, *v.*, escurecer, nublar, sombrear.
OVER.SHAD.OW, *v.*, escurecer, sombrear, ofuscar.
OVER.SKIRT, *s.*, sobressaia.
OVER.SLEEP, *v.*, dormir em excesso, dormir demais, dormir além da hora.
OVER.SNOW, *v.*, cobrir com neve, nevar muito.
OVER.SPREAD, *v.*, espalhar, espargir, estender.
OVER.STATE, *v.*, exagerar, sair dos limites.
OVER.STOCK, *s.*, estoque excessivo; *v.*, abarrotar, acumular, encher demais.
OVER.SUP.PLY, *s.*, abundância, copiosidade.
OVERT, *adj.*, aberto, público, manifesto.
OVER.TAKE, *v.*, ultrapassar, passar além de.
OVER.TAX, *v.*, exagerar nos impostos, sobrecarregar nos impostos.
OVER.TIME, *s.*, horas extras, serão; *v.*, passar do tempo.
OVER.TOP, *v.*, exceder, dominar, subjugar.
OVER.TURE, *s.*, abertura de uma música.
OVER.TURN, *s.*, transtorno, reviravolta; *v.*, virar, derrubar, anular, aniquilar.
OVER.VAL.UE, *v.*, encarecer, exagerar o preço, cobrar valor exagerado.
OVER.WEIGHT, *s.*, sobrepeso, peso excessivo; *v.*, pesar em excesso, pesar muito.
OVER.WHELM, *v.*, esmagar, oprimir, subjugar; inundar.
OVER.WORK, *s.*, trabalho extra; *v.*, trabalhar em excesso, exagerar no trabalho.
OVER.WORN, *adj.*, gasto pelo trabalho.
OVI.FORM, *adj.*, oviforme, oval.
OVINE, *adj.*, ovino.
OVIP.A.ROUS, *adj.*, ovíparo.
OVULE, *s.*, óvulo.
OWE, *v.*, dever a alguém, ter dívidas.
OW.ING, *adj.*, devido; **OWING TO**, *prep.*, devido a.
OWL, *s.*, coruja, mocho.
OWN, *v.*, ter, possuir, reconhecer, confessar.
OWN.ER, *s.*, dono, possuidor, proprietário.
OWN.ER.SHIP, *s.*, posse, propriedade.
OX, *s.*, boi.
OX.CART, *s.*, carro de boi.
OX.EN, *s.*, bois.
OX.EYE, *s.*, olho de boi.
OX.I.DA.TION, *s.*, oxidação.
OX.IDE, *s.*, óxido.
OX.I.DIZE, *v.*, oxidar.
OX.MAN, *s.*, boiadeiro, vaqueiro.
OX.Y.GEN, *s.*, oxigênio.
OX.Y.GEN.ATE, *v.*, oxigenar.
OX.Y.GEN.A.TION, *s.*, oxigenação.
OX.Y.GEN.AT.ED-WA.TER, *s.*, água oxigenada.
OXY.TONE, *s.*, oxítono.
OY.ER, *s.*, audiência.
OYS.TER, *s.*, ostra.
OZONE, *s.*, ozônio.

P, décima sexta letra do alfabeto inglês; *abrev.* de penny, pence.
PA, *s.*, papá, papai.
PAB.U.LUM, *s.*, sustento, pasto, alimento.
PACE, *s.*, passo, passada, medida, movimento, velocidade; *v.*, andar a passo.
PA.CIF.IC, *adj.*, pacífico, calmo, tranquilo, sossegado.
PAC.I.FI.CA.TION, *s.*, pacificação.
PAC.I.FI.ER, *s.*, pacificador.
PAC.I.FIST, *s.*, pacifista.
PAC.I.FY, *v.*, pacificar, acalmar.
PACK, *s.*, bando, matilha; pacote, carga, fardo, mochila; encher, arrumar a mala.
PACK.AGE, *s.*, pacote, embrulho, fardo; *v.*, acondicionar, empacotar, enfardar.
PACK.ER, *s.*, enfardador, empacotador.
PACK.ET, *s.*, pacote, maço de cigarros.
PACK.ING, *s.*, embalagem, empacotamento, acondicionamento.
PACT, *s.*, pacto, tratado, ajuste, aliança, convenção.
PAD, *s.*, almofada, enchimento, bloco para notas; *v.*, acolchoar, encher.
PAD.DLER, *s.*, remador.
PAD.DOCK, *s.*, recinto fechado nos hipódromos, cercado.
PAD.LOCK, *s.*, cadeado.
PAE.DI.AT.RICS, *s.*, pediatria.
PA.GAN, *adj.*, *s.*, pagão.
PA.GAN.ISM, *s.*, paganismo.
PA.GAN.IZE, *v.*, paganizar.
PAGE, *s.*, página, trecho, passagem; *v.*, paginar, mandar chamar.
PAG.I.NATE, *v.*, paginar, folhear.
PAG.I.NA.TION, *s.*, paginação.
PAG.ING, *s.*, paginação.
PAID, *adj.*, remunerado, pago.
PAIL, *s.*, balde.

PAIN, *s.*, dor, sofrimento, tormento; *v.*, atormentar, afligir, magoar, causar dor.
PAIN.FUL, *adj.*, doloroso, aflitivo, magoado.
PAIN.LESS, *adj.*, indolor, sem dor.
PAINT, *s.*, pintura, tinta; *v.*, pintar.
PAIN.TER, *s.*, pintor, pintor de paredes.
PAINT.ING, *s.*, pintura, tela, quadro.
PAINTY, *adj.*, sujo de tinta, manchado de tinta.
PAIR, *s.*, par, dupla, parelha, casal; *v.*, emparelhar, juntar, unir.
PA.JA.MAS, *s.*, pijama.
PA.KI.STAN, *s.*, Paquistão.
PA.KI.STANI, *adj.*, *s.*, paquistanês.
PAL, *s.*, colega, camarada, companheiro.
PAL.ACE, *s.*, palácio.
PAL.LAE.OG.RA.PHY, *s.*, paleografia.
PAL.AT.ABLE, *adj.*, palatável, saboroso, gostoso.
PAL.A.TAL, *adj.*, *s.*, palatal.
PAL.ATE, *s.*, palato.
PA.LAV.ER, *s.*, palavreado, balbúrdia; *v.*, palavrear.
PALE, *adj.*, pálido, fraco, claro; *v.*, empalidecer.
PALE.NESS, *s.*, palidez.
PA.LE.OG.RA.PHY, *s.*, paleografia.
PA.LE.ON.TOL.O.GY, *s.*, paleontologia.
PAL.ES.TINE, *s.*, Palestina.
PAL.ES.TIN.IAN, *adj.*, *s.*, palestino.
PAL.ING, *s.*, paliçada.
PAL.LI.A.TIVE, *adj.*, *s.*, paliativo.
PAL.LID, *adj.*, pálido, descorado, empalidecido.
PAL.LOR, *s.*, palidez, palor.
PALM, *s.*, palma, palma da mão, palmeira; *v.*, empalmar; trapacear, fraudar.
PAL.MATE, *adj.*, espalmado.
PALM.IST.RY, *s.*, quiromancia.
PALMY, *adj.*, palmífero, florescente, próspero.
PALP, *v.*, apalpar.
PAL.PATE, *v.*, apalpar.

PAL.PI.TATE, *v.*, palpitar.
PAL.PI.TA.TION, *s.*, palpitação.
PAL.SY, *s.*, paralisia; entorpecimento, marasmo.
PAL.TER, *v.*, simular, enganar, barganhar, lograr.
PAL.TRY, *adj.*, irrisório, ridículo.
PAM.PER, *v.*, mimar, acarinhar.
PAM.PHLET, *s.*, panfleto.
PAN, *s.*, frigideira, caçarola, prato, tacho, tina; *v.*, garimpar, fritar, criticar.
PAN.A.CEA, *s.*, panaceia.
PAN.CAKE, *s.*, panqueca.
PAN.CRE.AS, *s.*, pâncreas.
PAN.DA, *s.*, panda, urso panda.
PAN.DECT, *s.*, tratado, acordo, ajuste, acerto.
PAN.DE.MO.NI.UM, *s.*, pandemônio.
PAN.DER, *s.*, alcoviteiro.
PANE, *s.*, vidraça, vidro, chapa, almofada; *v.*, envidraçar, forrar com madeira.
PAN.EL, *s.*, painel, almofada, barra.
PAN.FUL, *s.*, panelada, panela cheia.
PAN.IC, *s.*, pânico, temor; *v.*, temer, entrar em pânico.
PAN.NI.KIN, *s.*, panelinha, copo de metal.
PAN.O.RAMA, *s.*, panorama.
PAN.O.RA.MIC, *adj.*, panorâmico.
PA.NSY, *s.*, amor-perfeito.
PANT, *s.*, arquejo, palpitação; *v.*, arquejar, palpitar, latejar, almejar.
PAN.THE.ISM, *s.*, panteísmo.
PAN.THE.IST, *s.*, panteísta.
PAN.THER, *s.*, pantera.
PANT.IES, *s.*, *pl.*, cuecas, calcinhas.
PAN.TO.GRAPH, *s.*, pantógrafo.
PAN.TRY, *s.*, despensa, copa.
PANTS, *s.*, cuecas, ceroulas.
PANTY, *s.*, cueca, calcinha.
PAP, *s.*, papa, mingau.
PA.PA, *s.*, papai.
PA.PAL, *adj.*, papal.
PA.PER, *s.*, papel, jornal, pedaço de papel; artigo; *v.*, revestir com papel.
PA.PER.BACK, *s.*, brochura, livro não encadernado.
PA.PER.BOARD, *s.*, papelão, papel grosso.

PA.PER CUT.TER, *s.*, guilhotina, máquina para cortar papel.
PA.PER-MON.EY, *s.*, papel-moeda.
PA.PRI.KA, *s.*, páprica, pimentão doce.
PAR, *s.*, paridade, igualdade; *v.*, colocar a par.
PAR.A.BLE, *s.*, parábola, alegoria.
PA.RAB.O.LA, *s.*, parábola, figura matemática.
PAR.A.BOL.IC, *adj.*, parabólico.
PARA.CHUTE, *s.*, paraquedas.
PARA.CHUT.IST, *s.*, paraquedista.
PA.RADE, *s.*, parada, desfile, ostentação, passeata; *v.*, ostentar, desfilar, mostrar.
PAR.A.DIGM, *s.*, paradigma, modelo, padrão, exemplar.
PAR.A.DISE, *s.*, paraíso, éden, local agradável; felicidade.
PAR.A.DIS.IC, *adj.*, paradisíaco.
PAR.A.DOX, *s.*, paradoxo; *v.*, exprimir-se por paradoxos.
PAR.AF.FIN, *s.*, parafina.
PAR.AF.FIN OIL, *s.*, querosene.
PAR.A.GON, *s.*, modelo, padrão, protótipo; *v.*, comparar.
PAR.A.GRAPH, *s.*, parágrafo.
PAR.A.GUAY, *s.*, Paraguai.
PAR.A.KEET, *s.*, periquito.
PAR.AL.LEL, *s.*, paralelo, linha paralela, analogia, correspondência; *v.*, comparar.
PAR.AL.LEL.E.PI.PED, *s.*, paralelepípedo.
PAR.A.LYSE, *v.*, paralisar, entorpecer, parar.
PA.RAL.Y.SIS, *s.*, paralisia.
PAR.A.LYT.IC, *adj.*, *s.*, paralítico.
PA.RAM.E.TER, *s.*, parâmetro.
PARA.NOIA, *s.*, paranoia.
PARA.NYMPH, *s.*, paraninfo, padrinho.
PAR.A.PET, *s.*, parapeito.
PAR.A.PHER.NA.LIA, *s.*, parafernália.
PARA.PHRASE, *s.*, paráfrase; *v.*, parafrasear.
PARA.PLE.GIA, *s.*, paraplegia.
PARA.PLE.GIC, *s.*, paraplégico.
PARA.PSY.CHOL.O.GY, *s.*, parapsicologia.
PAR.A.SITE, *s.*, parasita.
PAR.A.SOL, *s.*, guarda-sol, guarda-chuva, sombrinha.

PARA.TROOP.ER, *s.*, paraquedista.
PAR.BOIL, *v.*, cozer de leve, cozinhar um pouco.
PAR.CEL, *s.*, parcela, quantia, pacote, embrulho; pedaço; *v.*, embrulhar, lotear.
PAR.CE.NARY, *s.*, herança.
PARCH, *v.*, tostar, secar, ressecar.
PARCH.ING, *adj.*, abrasador.
PARD, *s.*, leopardo.
PAR.DON, *s.*, perdão, indulto, indulgência; *v.*, perdoar, desculpar, absolver.
PAR.DON.ABLE, *adj.*, perdoável.
PAR.DON.ING, *adj.*, indulgente, generoso.
PARE, *v.*, aparar, desbastar, cortar, podar.
PAR.ENT, *s.*, parente, pai ou mãe; **PARENTS**, pais.
PAR.ENT.AGE, *s.*, parentesco, parentela, família.
PA.REN.THE.SIS, *s.*, parêntese.
PAR.ENT.HOOD, *s.*, paternidade, maternidade.
PAR.ENT.LESS, *adj.*, órfão, que perdeu os pais.
PA.RI.AH, *s.*, pária.
PA.RI.E.TAL, *s.*, parietal.
PAR.ISH, *s.*, paróquia; *adj.*, paroquial.
PA.RISH.ION.ER, *s.*, paroquiano.
PA.RI.SIAN, *adj.*, parisiense.
PAR.I.TY, *s.*, paridade, igualdade.
PARK, *s.*, parque; estacionamento; *v.*, estacionar, transformar em parque.
PARK.ING, *s.*, estacionamento, local para estacionamento.
PAR.LEY, *s.*, parlamentação, discussão; *v.*, parlamentar, conferenciar, discutir.
PAR.LIA.MENT, *s.*, parlamento.
PARL.ING, *s.*, conferência, debate, discussão.
PAR.LOUR, *s.*, locutório; sala de visitas, saleta.
PAR.NAS.SI.AN, *adj., s.*, parnasiano.
PA.RO.CHI.AL, *adj.*, interiorano, provincial; paroquial.
PAR.O.DY, *s.*, paródia; *v.*, parodiar.
PA.ROLE, *s.*, palavra, promessa oral, senha; juramento; liberar mediante palavra.
PAR.OX.YSM, *s.*, paroxismo.
PAR.OX.Y.TONE, *s.*, paroxítono.
PAR.QUET, *s.*, parquê, assoalho de tacos, taco; *v.*, revestir com tacos.

PAR.RI.CIDE, *s.*, parricida; parricídio.
PAR.ROT, *s.*, papagaio.
PARSE, *v.*, analisar gramaticalmente, analisar.
PAR.SI.MO.NI.OUS, *adj.*, parcimonioso, simples, frugal, avarento, avaro.
PAR.SI.MO.NY, *s.*, parcimônia, poupança, economia.
PARS.ING, *s.*, análise gramatical.
PARS.LEY, *s.*, salsa.
PAR.SON, *s.*, pároco, padre, clérigo, pastor, vigário.
PART, *s.*, parte, parcela, porção, cena, capítulo, divisão; *v.*, dividir, partir, separar.
PART.AGE, *s.*, partilha, divisão.
PAR.TAKE, *v.*, partilhar, participar, compartilhar.
PAR.TAK.ER, *s.*, participante, apaniguado, cúmplice.
PAR.TAK.ING, *s.*, participação.
PAR.TIAL, *adj.*, parcial, faccioso, fracionário.
PAR.TIAL.I.TY, *s.*, parcialidade.
PAR.TIC.I.PANT, *s.*, participante.
PAR.TIC.I.PATE, *v.*, participar de.
PAR.TIC.I.PA.TION, *s.*, participação.
PAR.TI.CI.PLE, *s.*, particípio.
PAR.TI.CLE, *s.*, partícula, parcela, parte.
PAR.TIC.U.LAR, *s.*, particular, qualquer indivíduo; *adj.*, particular, específico, único.
PAR.TIC.U.LAR.I.TY, *s.*, particularidade, especialidade, minuciosidade, pormenor.
PAR.TIC.U.LAR.IZE, *v.*, particularizar.
PAR.TI.TION, *s.*, partição, divisão, divisória, seção; *v.*, dividir, repartir.
PART.LY, *adv.*, em parte, parcialmente.
PART.NER, *s.*, sócio, parceiro; par, cônjuge, consorte.
PAR.TRIDGE, *s.*, perdiz.
PAR.TU.RI.TION, *s.*, parturição, parto.
PAR.TY, *s.*, partido, festa; parte interessada, litigante, processante.
PAS.QUIM, *s.*, pasquim, jornal satírico.
PASS, *s.*, passagem, passo, desfiladeiro, estreito, vão; *v.*, passar, transpor, atravessar.
PAS.SAGE, *s.*, passagem, corredor, trânsito, caminho, travessia, trecho de livro.

PASS AWAY, v., falecer.
PASS.BOOK, s., caderneta.
PAS.SEN.GER, s., passageiro.
PAS.SER, s., passante, caminhante.
PAS.SER-BY, s., transeunte, passante.
PAS.SIB.I.LI.TY, s., passibilidade.
PAS.SING, adj., passageiro, transitório, efêmero.
PAS.SION, s., paixão.
PAS.SION.ATE, adj., apaixonado.
PAS.SIVE, adj., passivo.
PAS.SIV.I.TY, s., paciência, passividade, inércia.
PASS.PORT, s., passaporte.
PASS TO, v., passar para.
PASS.WORD, s., senha, contrassenha.
PAST, s., passado, tempo passado; adj., passado, findo; prep., por, adiante de.
PAST.TA, s., massa, massas de culinária.
PAS.TEL, s., pastel.
PAS.TEUR.I.ZA.TION, s., pasteurização.
PAS.TEUR.IZE, v., pasteurizar.
PAS.TIL, s., pastilha.
PAS.TIME, s., passatempo.
PAS.TRY, s., massa, bolo.
PAS.TRY.COOK, s., pasteleiro.
PAS.TUR.AGE, s., pastagem, pasto, comida.
PAS.TURE, s., pasto, comida, refeição.
PAT, s., pancadinha, tapinha; v., bater de leve, dar tapinhas.
PATCH, s., retalho, pedaço de fazenda, sinal, remendo; v., remendar, consertar.
PATCH.ABLE, adj., remendável.
PATCH.ING, s., remendo, remendagem.
PATCH.WORK, s., colcha de retalhos.
PATE, s., cabeça.
PA.TEL.LA, s., patela, rótula, rótula do joelho.
PAT.ENT, s., patente; v., patentear, registrar.
PA.TER, s., pai.
PA.TER.NAL, adj., paternal, paterno.
PA.TER.NI.TY, s., paternidade.
PATH, s., caminho, vereda, senda, trajeto, trajetória.
PA.THET.IC, adj., patético, lastimável.
PATH.FIND.ER, s., explorador, batedor, guia.
PATH.LESS, adj., intransitável.
PATH.O.LOG.IC, adj., patológico.

PA.THOL.O.GIST, s., patologista.
PA.THOL.O.GY, s., patologia.
PATH.WAY, s., caminho, estrada, trilha, senda.
PA.TIENCE, s., paciência.
PA.TIENT, adj., s., paciente.
PA.TIO, s., pátio.
PA.TOIS, s., patoá, dialeto, regionalismo.
PA.TRI.ARCH, s., patriarca.
PAT.RI.MO.NI.AL, adj., patrimonial.
PAT.RI.MO.NY, s., patrimônio.
PA.TRI.OT, s., patriota.
PA.TRI.OT.ISM, s., patriotismo.
PA.TROL, s., patrulha; v., patrulhar.
PA.TRON, s., cliente, freguês.
PA.TRON.AGE, s., patrocínio.
PA.TRON.ESS, s., defensora.
PA.TRON.IZER, s., protetor.
PAT.RO.NYM.IC, adj., patronímico.
PAT.TEN, s., tamanco, soco.
PAT.TERN, s., exemplo, amostra, padrão, molde; v., copiar, imitar.
PAT.TY, s., pequeno pastel, torta, empada.
PAU.CI.TY, s., escassez, insuficiência, falta.
PAUNCH, s., pança, barriga.
PAUNCHY, adj., pançudo, barrigudo.
PAU.PER.DOM, s., pobreza.
PAU.PER, s., pobre.
PAU.PER.ISM, s., pobreza, miséria, indigência.
PAU.PER.IZE, s., empobrecer.
PAUSE, s., pausa, intervalo; v., fazer uma pausa.
PAUS.ING, s., pausa.
PAVE, v., pavimentar, calçar, calcetar.
PAVE.MENT, s., pavimento, pavimentação, calçamento.
PA.VIL.ION, s., pavilhão, barraca, anexo.
PAV.ING, s., calçamento, pavimento.
PAW, s., pata, garra; v., escavar.
PAW.KY, adj., astuto, velhaco.
PAWN.SHOP, s., loja de penhores.
PAX, s., pax, paz.
PAY, s., paga, pagamento, salário; v., pagar, saldar, liquidar.
PAY.EE, s., beneficiário.
PAY.ER, s., pagador.

PAYMENT | **PENITENCE**

PAY.MENT, s., pagamento, remuneração.
PAY.NIM, s., pagão.
PAY OFF, v., pagar, saldar.
PAY.ROLL, s., folha de pagamento, importância.
PEA, s., ervilha.
PEACE, s., paz, tranquilidade, ordem, harmonia, sossego, trabalho.
PEACE.FUL, adj., quieto, calmo, sereno, pacífico.
PEACH, s., pêssego; adj., cor de pêssego.
PEA.COCK, s., pavão.
PEA.COCK.ISH, adj., vaidoso, fútil, volúvel.
PEAK, s., cume, pico, cimo, ponta, auge, apogeu; v., definhar, emagrecer.
PEAL, s., repique de sinos, bimbalhar; v., repicar, badalar.
PEA.NUT, s., amendoim.
PEAR, s., pera.
PEARL, s., pérola.
PEAS.ANT, s., camponês.
PEB.BLE, s., calhau, seixo; v., apedrejar, pavimentar com pedras.
PEC.CAN.CY, s., pecado, vício, defeito.
PECK, s., bicada; v., bicar, dar bicadas.
PECK.ING, s., picada.
PEC.U.LATE, v., fraudar, furtar, defraudar.
PEC.U.LA.TION, s., concussão, fraude, peculato.
PE.CU.LIAR, adj., peculiar, estranho.
PE.CU.LIAR.I.TY, s., peculiaridade, genuinidade, particularidade.
PE.CU.LI.UM, s., pecúlio.
PE.CU.NI.ARY, adj., pecuniário.
PED.A.GOG.IC, adj., pedagógico.
PED.A.GOG.ICS, s., pedagogia.
PED.A.GOGUE, s., pedagogo.
PED.A.GO.GY, s., pedagogia.
PED.AL, s., pedal; v., pedalar.
PED.ANT, s., pedante.
PED.ANT.RY, s., pedantismo.
PED.ES.TAL, s., pedestal.
PE.DES.TRI.AN, s., pedestre, transeunte.
PED.I.CURE, s., pedicuro.
PED.I.GREE, s., "pedigree", raça, genealogia.
PE.DOM.E.TER, s., pedômetro.
PEEL, s., casca; v., descascar.

PEEP, s., espiada, olhadela, aurora; v., espreitar, espiar, raiar, romper.
PEEP.HOLE, s., vigia, olho mágico, orifício para espreitar.
PEER, v., observar, mirar, olhar com atenção.
PEEVE, v., irritar, provocar, exacerbar.
PEE.VISH, adj., rabugento, obstinado, teimoso.
PEG, s., cabide, grampo, cavilha, pé; pregar, confinar, restringir.
PE.JO.RA.TIVE, adj., pejorativo, depreciativo, humilhante.
PE.KIN, s., Pequim.
PELF, s., produto de saque; bens, riquezas adquiridas ilicitamente.
PEL.I.CAN, s., pelicano.
PEL.LI.CLE, s., película.
PEL.LU.CID, adj., claro, diáfano, transparente.
PEL.LU.CID.I.TY, s., transparência.
PEL.VIS, s., pélvis, bacia.
PEN, s., pena, caneta, estilo literário, expressão própria; redil, cercado, curral.
PE.NAL, adj., penal, punível, castigável.
PE.NAL.IZE, v., penalizar, infligir penas, castigar, punir.
PEN.AL.TY, s., penalidade, castigo, pena, punição.
PEN.ANCE, s., penitência, arrependimento, sofrimento.
PEN.CIL, s., lápis, pincel fino; v., escrever com lápis, desenhar.
PEN.DANT, s., pingente.
PEN.DEN.CY, s., pendência.
PEN.DU.LOUS, adj., pendente, suspenso, pendular.
PEN.DU.LUM, s., pêndulo.
PEN.E.TRA.BIL.I.TY, s., penetrabilidade.
PEN.E.TRATE, s., penetrar, entrar, adentrar.
PEN.E.TRAT.ING, adj., penetrante.
PEN.E.TRA.TION, s., penetração.
PEN.GUIN, s., pinguim.
PEN.I.CIL.LIN, s., penicilina.
PEN.IN.SU.LA, s., península.
PE.NIS, s., pênis.
PEN.I.TENCE, s., penitência.

PEN.I.TENT, *s.*, penitente, arrependido; *s.*, penitente.
PEN.I.TEN.TIA.RY, *s.*, penitenciária.
PEN.KNIFE, *s.*, canivete.
PEN.MAN.SHIP, *s.*, caligrafia.
PEN.SION, *s.*, pensão, aposentadoria; *v.*, aposentar, dar uma pensão.
PEN.SION.ER, *s.*, aposentado, pensionista.
PEN.SIVE, *adj.*, pensativo.
PEN.STOCK, *s.*, comporta, açude, dique, represa.
PEN.TA.GON, *s.*, pentágono.
PENT.HOUSE, *s.*, alpendre, varanda, telheiro, cobertura.
PEN.UL.TI.MATE, *adj.*, penúltimo.
PEN.UM.BRA, *s.*, penumbra.
PE.NU.RI.OUS, *adj.*, miserável, avaro, sovina.
PEN.U.RY, *s.*, penúria, miséria.
PEO.PLE, *s.*, *pl.*, gente, pessoas, povo, pessoas de modo geral.
PEP, *s.*, energia, dinamismo, vigor, disposição.
PEP.PER, *s.*, pimenta; *v.*, apimentar.
PEP.PER.ING, *adj.*, picante, ardente.
PEP.PERY, *adj.*, apimentado, picante.
PEP.TIC, *adj.*, digestivo.
PER, *prep.*, por, mediante.
PER.AM.BU.LATE, *v.*, perambular, andar, percorrer, inspecionar.
PER.CEIV.ABLE, *adj.*, perceptível.
PER.CEIVE, *v.*, perceber, notar, compreender, entender, captar, ouvir.
PER.CENT.AGE, *s.*, percentagem.
PER.CEP.TION, *s.*, percepção.
PER.CEP.TIVE, *adj.*, perceptivo.
PER.CIP.I.ENCE, *s.*, percepção.
PER.CO.LATE, *v.*, coar, filtrar.
PER.CUSS, *v.*, percutir, ferir.
PER.CUS.SION, *s.*, percussão, choque.
PER.DI.TION, *s.*, perdição, ruína, desgraça.
PER.DU.RA.BLE, *adj.*, perdurável.
PER.DUR.ING, *adj.*, duradouro, durável.
PER.E.GRI.NATE, *v.*, peregrinar, andar, viajar.
PER.E.GRI.NA.TION, *s.*, peregrinação, romaria, viagem.
PE.REN.NI.AL, *adj.*, perene, eterno.

PER.FECT, *adj.*, perfeito, completo; *s.*, perfeito; *v.*, aperfeiçoar, aprimorar.
PER.FEC.TION, *s.*, perfeição.
PER.FEC.TION.IST, *s.*, perfeccionista.
PER.FID.I.OUS, *adj.*, pérfido, falso, traiçoeiro.
PER.FI.DY, *s.*, perfídia, traição, falsidade.
PER.FO.RATE, *v.*, perfurar.
PER.FO.RA.TION, *s.*, perfuração.
PER.FORM, *v.*, realizar, fazer, concretizar.
PER.FOR.MANCE, *s.*, performance, desempenho.
PER.FORM.ER, *s.*, ator, atriz, executor.
PER.FUME, *s.*, perfume; *v.*, perfumar, aromatizar.
PER.HAPS, *adv.*, talvez.
PER.IL, *s.*, perigo, risco, problema.
PER.IL.OUS, *adj.*, perigoso.
PE.RIM.E.TER, *s.*, perímetro.
PE.RI.OD, *s.*, período, lapso de tempo, divisão, espaço; menstruação.
PE.RI.OD.IC, *adj.*, periódico.
PE.RI.OD.IC.I.TY, *s.*, periodicidade.
PE.RIPH.ERY, *s.*, periferia.
PE.RIPH.RA.SIS, *s.*, perífrase.
PER.ISH, *v.*, perecer, sucumbir, deteriorar-se.
PER.ISH.ABLE, *adj.*, perecível, deteriorável.
PERI.WIG, *s.*, peruca, cabeleira postiça.
PER.JURE, *v.*, perjurar, jurar falsamente.
PER.JUR.ER, *s.*, perjuro.
PER.JU.RY, *s.*, perjúrio, juramento falso.
PERKY, *adj.*, animado, alegre, feliz, satisfeito.
PER.MA.NENCE, *s.*, permanência, perseverança, continuidade.
PER.MA.NENT, *adj.*, permanente.
PER.ME.ABIL.I.TY, *s.*, permeabilidade.
PER.ME.ATE, *v.*, permear, penetrar, difundir.
PER.MIS.SION, *s.*, permissão, concessão, licença.
PER.MIS.SIVE, *adj.*, permissivo.
PER.MIT, *s.*, licença; *v.*, permitir, deixar, deferir.
PER.MU.TA.TION, *s.*, permuta, câmbio, troca, permutação.
PER.MUTE, *v.*, permutar, trocar, cambiar.
PER.NI.CIOUS, *adj.*, pernicioso, nocivo, danoso.
PER.PEND, *v.*, ponderar, arrazoar, pensar, avaliar.
PER.PEN.DIC.U.LAR, *adj.*, perpendicular.

PER.PE.TRATE, *v.*, perpetrar, executar, realizar, cometer.
PER.PET.U.AL, *adj.*, perpétuo, perene, eterno.
PER.PET.U.ATE, *v.*, perpetuar, perenizar, eternizar.
PER.PE.TU.I.TY, *s.*, perpetuidade, perenidade, eternidade.
PER.PLEX.ING, *adj.*, perplexo, complicado.
PER.SE.CUTE, *v.*, perseguir, incomodar, perturbar.
PER.SE.CU.TION, *s.*, perseguição.
PER.SE.VER.ANCE, *s.*, perseverança.
PER.SE.VERE, *v.*, perseverar, continuar, persistir.
PER.SIAN, *adj., s.*, persa.
PER.SIS.TENCE, *s.*, persistência.
PER.SIS.TENT, *adj.*, persistente.
PER.SON, *s.*, pessoa.
PER.SON.AGE, *s.*, personagem, personalidade.
PER.SON.AL, *adj.*, pessoal, individual, próprio.
PER.SON.AL.I.TY, *s.*, personalidade.
PER.SON.I.FI.CA.TION, *s.*, personificação.
PER.SON.I.FY, *v.*, personificar.
PER.SPEC.TIVE, *s.*, perspectiva.
PER.SPI.CA.CIOUS, *adj.*, perspicaz, sagaz, inteligente.
PER.SPI.CAC.I.TY, *s.*, perspicácia.
PER.SPIRE, *v.*, suar, exsudar, transpirar.
PER.SUADE, *v.*, persuadir, convencer, levar a.
PER.SUA.SION, *s.*, persuasão, convencimento, convicção.
PER.SUA.SIVE, *adj.*, persuasivo.
PERT, *adj.*, atrevido, ousado, descarado, insolente.
PER.TAIN, *v.*, pertencer, ser propriedade, concernir, referir-se.
PER.TI.NA.CIOUS, *adj.*, pertinaz, teimoso, obstinado.
PER.TI.NAC.I.TY, *s.*, pertinácia, teimosia.
PER.TI.NENT, *adj.*, pertinente, referente, concernente.
PERT.NESS, *s.*, audácia, ousadia, atrevimento.
PER.TURB, *v.*, perturbar, incomodar, aborrecer.
PER.TUR.BA.TION, *s.*, perturbação, incômodo.
PE.RUKE, *s.*, peruca, cabeleira.
PE.RU.VI.AN, *adj., s.*, peruano, habitante do Peru.
PER.VERSE, *adj.*, perverso, maldoso, cruel.
PER.VER.SION, *s.*, perversão, corrupção, maldade.
PER.VER.SI.TY, *s.*, perversidade.
PER.VERT, *v.*, perverter, corromper; *adj.*, pervertido.
PES.SI.MISM, *s.*, pessimismo.
PES.SI.MIST, *s.*, pessimista.
PEST, *s.*, peste, pestilência, epidemia.
PEST.ER, *v.*, incomodar, perturbar.
PES.TER.ING, *adj.*, inoportuno, perturbador, abusivo.
PES.TI.CIDE, *s.*, pesticida.
PES.TI.LENCE, *s.*, pestilência, peste.
PES.TI.LENT, *adj.*, pestilento.
PET, *s.*, animal de estimação; *v.*, acariciar, acarinhar.
PET.AL, *s.*, pétala.
PE.TARD, *s.*, petardo, bomba.
PE.TER, *v.*, diminuir gradualmente, esgotar-se, ficar exausto.
PE.TI.TION, *s.*, petição, pedido, requerimento; *v.*, peticionar, pedir, requerer.
PE.TI.TION.ER, *s.*, suplicante, peticionante, requerente.
PET.RI.FY, *v.*, petrificar.
PET.ROL, *s.*, gasolina; *v.*, abastecer com gasolina.
PE.TRO.LEUM, *s.*, petróleo.
PET.TI.NESS, *s.*, insignificância, ninharia, bagatela.
PET.TISH, *adj.*, rabugento, desagradável, aborrecido, ranzinza.
PET.TISH.NESS, *s.*, rabugice.
PET.TY, *adj.*, mesquinho, ridículo, insignificante.
PET.U.LANCE, *s.*, petulância, atrevimento.
PE.TU.NIA, *s.*, petúnia.
PEW, *s.*, banco de igreja.
PHA.LANGE, *s.*, falange.
PHAL.LIC, *adj.*, fálico.
PHAN.TASM, *s.*, fantasma.
PHAN.TAS.MA.GO.RIA, *s.*, fantasmagoria.
PHAN.TOM, *s.*, fantasma.
PHA.RAOH, *s.*, faraó.

PHAR.I.SA.IC, *adj.*, farisaico.
PHAR.I.SEE, *s.*, fariseu; hipócrita.
PHAR.MA.CEU.TIC, *adj.*, farmacêutico.
PHAR.MA.CEU.TICS, *s.*, farmácia, ciência farmacêutica.
PHAR.MA.CIST, *s.*, farmacêutico, oficial de farmácia.
PHAR.MA.CY, *s.*, farmácia.
PHA.ROS, *s.*, farol.
PHAR.YN.GI.TIS, *s.*, faringite.
PHAR.YNX, *s.*, faringe.
PHASE, *s.*, fase.
PHEAS.ANT, *s.*, faisão.
PHE.NOM.E.NA, *s.*, *pl.*, fenômenos.
PHE.NOM.E.NON, *s.*, fenômeno.
PHI.LAN.THROPE, *s.*, filantropo.
PHI.LAN.THRO.PY, *s.*, filantropia.
PHI.LAT.E.LY, *s.*, filatelia.
PHIL.IP.PINE, *adj.*, *s.*, filipino.
PHI.LOL.O.GY, *s.*, filologia.
PHI.LOS.O.PHER, *s.*, filósofo.
PHIL.O.SOPH.IC, *adj.*, filosófico.
PHI.LOS.O.PHIZE, *v.*, filosofar.
PHI.LOS.O.PHY, *s.*, filosofia.
PHLEGM, *s.* fleuma.
PHLEG.MAT.IC, *adj.*, fleumático.
PHO.BIA, *s.*, fobia.
PHOE.NI.CIAN, *adj.*, *s.*, fenício.
PHOE.NIX, *s.*, fênix.
PHONE, *s.*, fonema; *abrev.* de **TELEPHONE**; *v.*, telefonar.
PHONE-BOOTH, *s.*, cabina de telefone.
PHO.NET.IC, *adj.*, fonético.
PHO.NET.ICS, *s.*, fonética.
PHO.NIC, *adj.*, fônico; acústico.
PHO.NOL.O.GY, *s.*, fonologia.
PHO.NOM.E.TER, *s.*, fonômetro.
PHOS.PHATE, *s.*, fosfato.
PHOS.PHO.RES.CENCE, *s.*, fosforescência.
PHOS.PHO.RIC, *adj.*, fosfórico, fosforescente.
PHOS.PHO.RUS, *s.*, fósforo.
PHO.TO, *s.*, foto.
PHO.TO.COPI.ER, *s.*, fotocopiadora.
PHO.TO.COPY, *s.*, fotocópia; *v.*, fotocopiar.

PHO.TO.GE.NIC, *adj.*, fotogênico.
PHO.TO.GRAPH, *s.*, fotografia, foto; *v.*, fotografar.
PHO.TOG.RA.PHER, *s.*, fotógrafo.
PHO.TOG.RA.PHY, *s.*, fotografia.
PHO.TOM.E.TER, *s.*, fotômetro.
PHRASE, *s.*, frase; *v.*, traduzir por frase.
PHRA.SE.OL.O.GIC, *adj.*, fraseológico.
PHRAS.ING, *s.*, fraseologia.
PHRE.NET.IC, *adj.*, frenético.
PHRE.NI.TIS, *s.*, frenesi, delírio.
PHTHI.SIS, *s.*, tísica, tuberculose.
PHYS.IC, *s.*, remédio, purgante; *v.*, purgar, dar remédio.
PHYS.I.CAL, *adj.*, físico.
PHY.SI.CIAN, *s.*, médico.
PHYS.I.CIST, *s.*, físico.
PHYS.ICS, *s.*, física.
PHYS.I.OG.NOM.IC, *adj.*, fisionômico.
PHYS.I.OG.NO.MY, *s.*, fisionomia.
PHYS.I.OL.O.GIST, *s.*, fisiologista.
PHYS.I.OL.O.GY, *s.*, fisiologia.
PHYS.IO.THER.A.PY, *s.*, fisioterapia.
PHY.SIQUE, *s.*, físico, estrutura física.
PI, *s.*, símbolo matemático.
PI.A.NIST, *s.*, pianista.
PI.ANO, *s.*, piano.
PIC.A.ROON, *s.*, pirata, corsário, assaltante, safado.
PICK, *s.*, picareta, enxadão; picada; *v.*, picar, cavar, colher, apanhar, provocar.
PICK.ER, *s.*, colhedor, apanhador, cavador, batedor.
PICK.ET, *s.*, piquete, estaca, marco; *v.*, cercar, limitar, piquetar, marcar.
PICK.ING, *s.*, escolha, colheita.
PICK.LE, *s.*, picles, conservas; *v.*, conservar no tempero.
PICK.UP, *s.*, picape, camioneta.
PIC.NIC, *s.*, piquenique, passeio; *v.*, passear, fazer um piquenique.
PIC.TURE, *s.*, pintura, desenho, quadro, tela, filme; *v.*, pintar, retratar, descrever.
PIC.TUR.ESQUE, *adj.*, pitoresco.

PIECE, *s.*, peça, pedaço, fatia, parte, coleção, amostra, obra.
PIECE.MEAL, *adj.*, pouco a pouco, aos poucos, a pouco e pouco.
PIECE.WORK, *s.*, trabalho por empreitada.
PIED, *adj.*, vário, variado.
PIER, *s.*, cais, molhe.
PIERCE, *v.*, furar, penetrar, trespassar, perfurar.
PIERC.ING, *adj.*, penetrante, cortante.
PI.E.TISM, *s.*, carolice, pieguice, beatice.
PI.E.TY, *s.*, piedade, fervor, respeito.
PIF.FLE, *s.*, tolice, disparate, bagatela; *v.*, dizer bobagens.
PIG, *s.*, porco, suíno.
PI.GEON, *s.*, pombo, pomba.
PIG.GERY, *s.*, chiqueiro, sujeira, porcaria, pocilga.
PIG.GY, *s.*, porquinho, leitão, bácaro.
PIG.MENT, *s.*, pigmento.
PIG.MY, *s.*, pigmeu.
PIG.STY, *s.*, pocilga, chiqueiro.
PIKE, *s.*, pico, cume, montanha, barreira; pedágio rodoviário.
PIL.CHARD, *s.*, sardinha.
PILE, *s.*, pelo, pilha, monte, pira funerária.
PIL.FER, *v.*, furtar, desviar, roubar, enganar.
PIL.FER.AGE, *s.*, roubo, furto.
PIL.FER.ER, *s.*, ladrão, gatuno.
PIL.FER.ING, *s.*, roubo, furto.
PIL.GRIM, *s.*, peregrino, romeiro.
PIL.GRIM.AGE, *s.*, peregrinação, romaria.
PILL, *s.*, pílula, comprimido.
PIL.LAGE, *s.*, pilhagem, saque, botim; *v.*, pilhar, saquear.
PIL.LAR, *s.*, pilar; *v.*, suportar com pilares, firmar com pilares.
PIL.LOW, *s.*, almofada.
PIL.LOW.CASE, *s.*, fronha.
PIL.LOWY, *adj.*, macio, delicado, mole, suave.
PI.LOT, *s.*, piloto; pilotar.
PI.LOT.AGE, *s.*, pilotagem.
PIMP, *s.*, chulo, calão.
PIN, *s.*, alfinete, pino; *v.*, alfinetar, espetar.
PIN.BALL, *s.*, pimbol.
PIN.CERS, *s.*, torquês, pinça.

PINCH, *s.*, beliscão, aperto, adversidade; *v.*, beliscar, arrancar, extorquir.
PINCH.ING, *s.*, beliscada, beliscão.
PINE, *s.*, pinheiro, pinho, madeira de pinheiro.
PINE.AP.PLE, *s.*, ananás, abacaxi.
PIN.ERY, *s.*, abacaxizal.
PING, *s.*, assobio, silvo, sibilo; *v.*, assobiar, silvar, sibilar.
PING-PONG, *s.*, pingue-pongue, tênis de mesa.
PIN.GUID, *adj.*, pingue, gordo, obeso.
PINK, *adj.*, cor-de-rosa, rosado; *s.*, cravo, cravina.
PINK.ISH, *adj.*, rosado.
PINKY, *adj.*, rosado.
PIN.NA.CLE, *s.*, pináculo, cume, auge, clímax.
PI.O.NEER, *s.*, pioneiro.
PI.OUS, *adj.*, pio, devoto, religioso.
PI.OUS.NESS, *s.*, piedade, devoção.
PIP, *s.*, semente, caroço.
PIPE, *s.*, cachimbo; gaita de foles; cano, tubo; *v.*, tocar flauta, assobiar; cachimbar.
PIPE.LINE, *s.*, gasoduto, oleoduto.
PIP.KIN, *s.*, panela de barro, escudela, bacia.
PI.QUAN.CY, *s.*, picância, sabor picante, amargura, aspereza.
PIQUE, *s.*, ressentimento, amuo; *v.*, melindrar, amuar, ressentir.
PI.QUET, *s.*, piquete, estaca, marco.
PI.RA.CY, *s.*, pirataria.
PI.RATE, *s.*, pirata, corsário; *v.*, piratear.
PIR.OU.ETTE, *s.*, pirueta.
PIS.CA.TO.RY, *adj.*, piscoso, piscatório.
PI.SCES, *s.*, Peixes.
PI.SCI.CUL.TURE, *s.*, piscicultura.
PIS.MIRE, *s.*, formiga.
PIS.TOL, *s.*, pistola; *v.*, atirar com pistola.
PIT, *s.*, fosso, cova, fossa; *v.*, enterrar, colocar em cova, opor, escavar.
PITCH, *s.*, piche, pez, lançamento, lote de coisas; tom musical; montar, lançar.
PITCH.I.NESS, *s.*, escuridão, negrume, trevas.
PIT.E.OUS, *adj.*, comovente, lamentável, doloroso.
PIT.FALL, *s.*, queda, alçapão, armadilha, perigo.
PITH.I.NESS, *s.*, vigor, energia, força, robustez.

PITIFUL   **PLAY OFF**

PITI.FUL, *adj.*, comovente, tocante.
PITI.FUL.NESS, *s.*, misericórdia, piedade, compaixão.
PIT.TED, *adj.*, corroído, picado, roído.
PIT.TING, *s.*, corrosão.
PIV.OT, *s.*, pivô, eixo; *v.*, girar.
PIX.IE, *s.*, fada.
PIZ.ZA, *s.*, pizza.
PLA.CA.BLE, *adj.*, placável, brando.
PLAC.ARD, *s.*, placar, quadro de avisos.
PLA.CATE, *v.*, aplacar, apaziguar, acalmar.
PLACE, *s.*, lugar, posto, situação; *v.*, pôr, colocar, situar, alocar.
PLA.CEN.TA, *s.*, placenta.
PLAC.ET, *s.*, permissão.
PLAC.ID, *adj.*, plácido, sereno, calmo, tranquilo.
PLA.CID.I.TY, *s.*, placidez, serenidade, tranquilidade, calma.
PLA.GIA.RISM, *s.*, plágio.
PLA.GIA.RIZE, *v.*, plagiar.
PLAGUE, *s.*, peste, praga, endemia; *v.*, atormentar, incomodar, perturbar.
PLAGUY, *adj.*, inoportuno, maldoso, ruim.
PLAIN, *s.*, planície, planura, várzea; *adj.*, plano, liso, manifesto, evidente, natural.
PLAIN.NESS, *s.*, franqueza, clareza, lisura.
PLAINT, *s.*, queixa, reclamação.
PLAIN.TIFF, *adj.*, queixoso, reclamante.
PLAIN.TIVE, *adj.*, queixoso.
PLAN, *s.*, plano, proposta, projeto, programa; *v.*, planejar, fazer planos.
PLAN.CHETTE, *s.*, prancheta, mesa para desenho.
PLANE, *s.*, plano, nível, avião, plaina; *v.*, voar de avião, planar.
PLAN.ET, *s.*, planeta.
PLAN.E.TAR.I.UM, *s.*, planetário.
PLANK, *s.*, prancha, tábua, suporte; *v.*, assoalhar, colocar tábuas.
PLAN.LESS, *adj.*, desorganizado, sem plano.
PLAN.NER, *s.*, planejador, projetista, idealizador.
PLANT, *s.*, planta, vegetal, máquina, fábrica, plantação; *v.*, plantar, semear, fundar.
PLAN.TA.TION, *s.*, plantação, vegetação, cobertura vegetal.
PLANT.ER, *s.*, plantador.
PLANT.ING, *s.*, plantação.
PLAQUE, *s.*, placa, broche, insígnia.
PLASH, *s.*, charco, poço; *v.*, enlamear, borrifar.
PLASHY, *adj.*, pantanoso, lamacento.
PLASM, *s.*, plasma, protoplasma.
PLAS.MA, *s.*, plasma.
PLAS.TER, *s.*, reboco, gesso, emplastro; *v.*, rebocar, remendar, emplastar.
PLAS.TER.STONE, *s.*, gesso.
PLAS.TIC, *s.*, plástico, plástica, material de plástico; *adj.*, plástico, moldável.
PLAS.TIC BAG, *s.*, saco de plástico.
PLATE, *s.*, prato, chapa, gravura, lâmina, folha, baixela; *v.*, chapear, blindar.
PLA.TEAU, *s.*, platô, planalto, altiplano.
PLATE.FUL, *s.*, pratada, prato cheio.
PLAT.EN, *s.*, platina.
PLAT.FORM, *s.*, plataforma, cais, palanque, programa partidário.
PLAT.I.NUM, *s.*, platina.
PLAT.I.TUDE, *s.*, lugar comum, chavão, trivialidade, nariz de cera.
PLAT.I.TU.DI.NOUS, *adj.*, comum, trivial, ordinário, vulgar.
PLA.TON.IC, *adj.*, platônico.
PLA.TO.NISM, *s.*, platonismo.
PLA.TOON, *s.*, pelotão, grupo de soldados.
PLAT.TER, *s.*, travessa.
PLAU.SI.BLE, *adj.*, plausível, razoável, aceitável.
PLAY, *s.*, jogo, peça, diversão, filme, brincadeira; *v.*, jogar, brincar, tocar instrumento.
PLAY.BOY, *s.*, playboy, pessoa de festas, farrista.
PLAY.ER, *s.*, jogador, músico, tocador de instrumento musical.
PLAY.FUL, *adj.*, brincalhão.
PLAY.GROUND, *s.*, pátio para recreio; local para jogos.
PLAY.HOUSE, *s.*, cinema, teatro, casa de espetáculos.
PLAY.MATE, *s.*, colega, companheiro, camarada.
PLAY OFF, *s.*, jogo decisivo, jogo final, jogo de decisão; *v.*, desempatar.

PLAY.TIME, s., recreio, folguedo.
PLEA, s., apelo, apelação, pretexto, disputa, litígio.
PLEACH, v., entretecer, encurvar ramos.
PLEAD.ER, s., defensor, advogado.
PLEAD.ING, s., alegação, defesa.
PLEAS.ANT, adj., agradável, brincalhão, simpático.
PLEAS.ANT.RY, s., gracejo, graça, jovialidade.
PLEASE, interj., por favor!; v., agradar, dar prazer, satisfazer, deleitar.
PLEASED, adj., satisfeito, contente, agradado.
PLEAS.ING, adj., agradável, aprazível.
PLEA.SURE, s., prazer, agrado, satisfação.
PLEAT, s., dobra, prega, ruga; v., dobrar.
PLE.BE.IAN, adj., s., plebeu.
PLEBS, s., plebe, ralé, raia miúda, gentalha, populaça.
PLEDGE, s., penhor, fiança, garantia, brinde, promessa; v., empenhar, caucionar.
PLE.NA.RY, adj., plenário, pleno, completo.
PLEN.I.TUDE, s., plenitude, totalidade.
PLEN.TI.FUL, adj., abundante, copioso, variado.
PLEN.TY, s., abundância, copiosidade.
PLE.O.NASM, s., pleonasmo.
PLEU.RA, s., pleura.
PLEX.US, s., plexo, amplexo, ligação.
PLI.ABIL.I.TY, s., flexibilidade, docilidade, afabilidade.
PLI.AN.CY, s., flexibilidade, brandura.
PLI.ERS, s., pl., alicates.
PLIGHT, s., condição, situação, compromisso; v., comprometer, empenhar.
PLOD, v., caminhar com dificuldade, caminhar pesadamente, labutar.
PLOD.DING, s., trabalho pesado, faina, labuta.
PLOT, s., conspiração, enredo, pedaço de terra, lote, conluio; v., delinear, marcar.
PLOT.TER, s., agrimensor, cartógrafo, maquinador.
PLOUGH, s., arado, máquina para arar, terra arada; v., arar, lavrar, sulcar.
PLOUGH.ABLE, adj., arável, lavrável, cultivável.
PLOUGH.ER, s., arador, lavrador, agricultor.

PLUCK, s., arrancada, puxão, determinação; v., arrancar, puxar, apanhar, reprovar.
PLUCK.I.NESS, s., valentia, bravura, coragem.
PLUG, s., plugue, tomada elétrica, tampa para lavabo; v., tapar, fechar, arrolhar.
PLUM, s., ameixa, ameixeira, uva passa.
PLUM.AGE, s., plumagem.
PLUMB, s., prumo, nível; adj., aprumado, perpendicular; v., aprumar.
PLUMB.ER, s., encanador, bombeiro.
PLUME, s., pluma, pena, plumagem, prêmio; v., emplumar, alisar as penas.
PLUMP, s., toró, aguaceiro, baque; v., cair, baquear, arremessar.
PLUMP.NESS, s., gordura, atrevimento.
PLUMPY, adj., gordo, cheio.
PLUMY, adj., emplumado, plumoso, cheio de penas.
PLUN.DER, s., saque, pilhagem; saquear, pilhar, rapinar.
PLUN.DER.ER, s., saqueador, assaltante, ladrão.
PLUNGE, s., mergulho, imersão, queda, salto; mergulhar, submergir, cravar.
PLUNG.ER, s., mergulhador; desentupidor.
PLU.PER.FECT, s., mais-que-perfeito.
PLU.RAL, adj., s., plural.
PLU.RAL.I.TY, s., pluralidade.
PLUS, s., sinal de adição; adv., mais; adj., aditivo, positivo.
PLUSHY, adj., felpudo.
PLU.TOC.RA.CY, s., plutocracia.
PLU.TO.CRAT, s., plutocrata.
PLU.TO.NI.UM, s., plutônio.
PLU.VI.AL, adj., pluvial, chuvoso, próprio da chuva.
PLU.VI.O.ME.TER, s., pluviômetro.
PLU.VI.OUS, adj., chuvoso.
PLY, s., dobra, prega; v., manipular, importunar, aplicar-se, diligenciar.
PNEU.MAT.IC, adj., pneumático.
PNEU.MAT.ICS, s., pneumática.
PNEU.MO.NIA, s., pneumonia.
PNEU.MON.IC, adj., pulmonar.
POACH, v., pisar, pisotear, umedecer, reduzir,

caçar às escondidas.
P.O BOX, *s.*, caixa postal
POCK.ET, *s.*, bolso, algibeira, bolsa; colocar no bolso, embolsar, reprimir-se.
POD, *s.*, vagem.
PODG.I.NESS, *s.*, gordura.
PODGY, *adj.*, gordo, rechonchudo, obeso.
PO.EM, *s.*, poema.
PO.E.SY, *s.*, poesia, arte poética.
PO.ET, *s.*, poeta, poetisa, vate.
PO.ET.AS.TER, *s.*, poetastro.
PO.ET.ESS, *s.*, poetisa.
PO.ET.IC, *s.*, poético.
PO.ET.ICS, *s.*, poética, arte poética.
PO.ET.RY, *s.*, poesia.
POINT, *s.*, ponto, fim, ponto essencial, sinal, mancha; *v.*, apontar, indicar, referir.
POINT.ED, *adj.*, pontudo, irônico.
POINT.ER, *s.*, ponteiro, indicador.
POINT.LESS, *adj.*, sem ponta, inútil, desnecessário.
POISE, *s.*, equilíbrio, elegância, garbo, pausa; *v.*, equilibrar, balançar.
POI.SON, *s.*, veneno, tóxico; *v.*, envenenar, intoxicar.
POI.SON.ING, *s.*, envenenamento.
POI.SON.OUS, *adj.*, venenoso, tóxico, danoso, nocivo.
POKE, *s.*, empurrão, cutucada, canga para boi; *v.*, empurrar, ressaltar, sobressair.
POK.ER, *s.*, atiçador, intrometido; pôquer.
PO.LAND, *s.*, Polônia.
PO.LAR, *adj.*, polar.
PO.LAR.I.TY, *s.*, polaridade.
PO.LAR.I.ZA.TION, *s.*, polarização.
PO.LAR.IZE, *v.*, polarizar.
POLE, *adj.*, *s.*, polaco.
POLE, *s.*, polo, vara, poste, mastro; *v.*, suportar, impelir, empurrar com vara.
PO.LEM.IC, *adj.*, polêmico, contundente.
PO.LEM.ICS, *s.*, polêmica.
POL.E.MIZE, *v.*, polemizar.
PO.LICE, *s.*, polícia; *v.*, policiar, legalizar, regulamentar.
PO.LICE.MAN, *s.*, policial, agente de polícia.
POL.I.CY, *s.*, diplomacia, habilidade política; apólice de seguro.
PO.LIO.MY.ELI.TIS, *s.*, poliomielite.
POL.ISH, *adj.*, polaco, polonês.
POL.ISH, *s.*, graxa, lustro, polimento, cultura; *v.*, lustrar, polir, engraxar.
POL.ISH.ING, *s.*, polimento, lustro.
PO.LITE, *adj.*, polido, cortês, educado, fino.
PO.LITE.NESS, *s.*, delicadeza, polidez, cortesia, educação, fineza.
POL.I.TIC, *adj.*, político, esperto, sagaz.
POL.I.TI.CIAN, *s.*, político.
PO.LIT.I.CIZE, *v.*, politicar.
POL.I.TICS, *s.*, política.
POL.KA, *s.*, polca.
POLL, *s.*, votação, pesquisa, apuração; *v.*, colher votos, votar, apurar votos.
POL.LEN, *s.*, pólen; *v.*, polinizar.
POL.LING, *s.*, votação.
POL.LUTE, *v.*, poluir, sujar, turvar.
POL.LU.TION, *s.*, poluição, sujeira, corrupção, depravação.
PO.LO, *s.*, polo.
POL.TER.GEIST, *s.*, fantasma, espírito perturbador.
POLY.ES.TER, *s.*, poliéster.
PO.LYG.A.MIST, *s.*, polígamo.
PO.LYG.A.MY, *s.*, poligamia.
POLY.GLOT, *adj.*, *s.*, poliglota.
POLY.GRAPH, *s.*, polígrafo.
POLY.NO.MI.AL, *s.*, polinômio.
POLY.SYL.LA.BLE, *s.*, polissílabo.
POLY.TECH.NIC, *s.*, politécnica, escola politécnica.
POLY.THE.ISM, *s.*, politeísmo.
POLY.VA.LENT, *adj.*, *s.*, polivalente.
PO.MADE, *s.*, pomada.
POME.GRAN.ATE, *s.*, romã.
POM.POS.I.TY, *s.*, pomposidade, ostentação, exibição.
POMP.OUS, *adj.*, pomposo, luxuoso.
POND, *s.*, lago pequeno, lagoa, tanque; *v.*, represar águas.

PON.DER, *v.*, meditar, raciocinar, refletir.
PON.DER.A.BIL.I.TY, *s.*, ponderabilidade.
PON.DER.ING, *adj.*, ponderado.
PONE, *s.*, broa, pão de milho.
PON.IARD, *s.*, punhal, adaga; *v.*, apunhalar, esfaquear.
PON.TIFF, *s.*, pontífice, papa.
PON.TIF.I.CATE, *s.*, pontificado, papado.
PO.NY, *s.*, pônei, cavalo pequeno.
POOL, *s.*, poça, quantia apostada, bolo; associação de empresas.
POOR, *adj.*, pobre, inferior, ruim, deselegante, mirrado; *s.*, *pl.*, os pobres.
POOR.HOUSE, *s.*, asilo, hospedaria para pobres.
POP, *s.*, estouro, estrépito, detonação de arma de fogo; *v.*, estourar, estalar.
POP.CORN, *s.*, milho para pipocas.
POPE, *s.*, papa.
POP.LAR, *s.*, álamo.
POP.PLE, *s.*, borbulho; *v.*, borbulhar, deslizar, rolar.
POP.PY, *s.*, papoula.
POP.U.LACE, *s.*, povo, população.
POP.U.LAR, *adj.*, popular, conhecido.
POP.U.LAR.I.TY, *s.*, popularidade.
POP.U.LAR.IZE, *v.*, popularizar.
POP.U.LATE, *v.*, povoar, habitar, divulgar.
POP.U.LA.TION, *s.*, população, povo.
POP.U.LOUS, *adj.*, populoso.
POR.CE.LAIN, *s.*, porcelana.
POR.CU.PINE, *s.*, porco-espinho.
PORK, *s.*, carne de porco.
PORK.ER, *s.*, porco cevado.
PORK.ING, *s.*, porco, leitão, suíno.
POR.KY, *adj.*, gordo, obeso.
POR.NOG.RA.PHY, *s.*, pornografia.
PO.ROS.I.TY, *s.*, porosidade.
PO.ROUS, *adj.*, poroso.
POR.POISE, *s.*, golfinho, boto.
PORT, *s.*, porto, ancoradouro, canal; portão, entrada, bombordo.
POR.TA.BIL.I.TY, *s.*, portabilidade, ação de portar.
POR.TAGE, *s.*, transporte, carreto, frete, despesas.
POR.TAL, *s.*, portal.
POR.TEND, *v.*, pressagiar, prever, agourar, vaticinar.
POR.TENT, *s.*, prognóstico, presságio, agouro, vaticínio.
POR.TEN.TOUS, *adj.*, prodigioso, extraordinário, fantástico.
POR.TER, *s.*, porteiro, portador, carregador.
PORT.FO.LIO, *s.*, pasta, carteira, valise.
POR.TION, *s.*, porção, quantia, parte, fração; *v.*, repartir, dividir.
POR.TRAIT, *s.*, retrato, imagem, foto, fotografia.
POR.TRAY, *v.*, fotografar, retratar, reproduzir a imagem, pintar.
POR.TU.GUESE, *adj.*, *s.*, português, língua portuguesa, habitante de Portugal.
POSE, *s.*, pose, postura, conduta, atitude; *v.*, posar, colocar-se, propor.
PO.SI.TION, *s.*, posição, situação, cargo, função, ocupação, ponto de vista.
POS.I.TIVE, *adj.*, positivo, certo, real, concreto, definido.
POS.I.TIV.ISM, *s.*, positivismo.
POS.SESS, *v.*, possuir, ter, deter, reter; copular.
POS.SESSED, *adj.*, possuído, possesso.
POS.SES.SION, *s.*, posse, possessão; objetos pessoais.
POS.SES.SIVE, *adj.*, possessivo, dominador.
POS.SES.SO.RY, *s.*, possuidor.
POS.SI.BIL.I.TY, *s.*, possibilidade, circunstância, oportunidade.
POS.SI.BLE, *adj.*, possível.
POS.SI.BLY, *adv.*, possivelmente, talvez, quiçá.
POST, *s.*, correio, cargo, posto, poste, estação; *v.*, fixar em poste, pendurar.
POST.AGE, *s.*, postagem, porte, franquia.
POST.AL, *adj.*, postal.
POST.BOX, *s.*, caixa postal.
POST.CARD, *s.*, cartão postal, cartão, postal.
POST.CODE, *s.*, código postal, código de endereçamento postal, CEP.
POST.ER, *s.*, cartaz, *v.*, afixar cartazes.
POS.TE.RI.OR, *adj.*, posterior.
POS.TE.RI.OR.I.TY, *s.*, posterioridade.
POS.TER.I.TY, *s.*, posteridade.

POST.GRAD.U.ATE, *adj.*, *s.*, pós-graduado.
POST.HU.MOUS, *adj.*, póstumo, depois de falecido.
POS.TIL, *s.*, apostila, nota.
POST.MAN, *s.*, carteiro.
POST.MARK, *s.*, carimbo postal; *v.*, carimbar.
POST.MAST.ER, *s.*, chefe do correio, gerente do correio.
POST.PONE, *v.*, adiar, pospor, transferir.
POST.PONE.MENT, *s.*, adiamento.
POST.SCRIPT, *s.*, pós-escrito, P.S.
POS.TU.LATE, *s.*, postulado; *v.*, postular, peticionar.
POS.TU.LA.TION, *s.*, postulação, petição, exigência.
POS.TURE, *s.*, postura, atitude, conduta.
POST.WAR, *adj.*, do pós-guerra.
POT, *s.*, pote, panela, vaso, vasilhame, caneca, urinol; *v.*, pôr em conserva.
PO.TA.BLE, *adj.*, potável.
POT.ASH, *s.*, potassa.
PO.TAS.SI.UM, *s.*, potássio.
PO.TA.TION, *s.*, bebida, libação, trago, gole.
PO.TA.TO, *s.*, batata, batata-doce, batata frita.
PO.TEN.CY, *s.*, potência, força, vigor, energia, poder.
PO.TENT, *adj.*, poderoso, potente, forte, vigoroso, enérgico.
PO.TEN.TIAL, *s.*, potencial, potencialidade; potencial.
PO.TEN.TI.AL.I.TY, *s.*, potencialidade.
POT.HERB, *s.*, hortaliça.
POT.TAGE, *s.*, sopa, caldo.
POT.TER, *s.*, oleiro.
POT.TERY, *s.*, olaria, cerâmica, louça de barro.
POT.WARE, *s.*, cerâmica.
POUCH, *s.*, bolso, algibeira, tabaqueira.
POULT, *s.*, frango, pinto.
POUL.TER.ER, *s.*, galinheiro, vendedor de aves.
POUND, *s.*, curral para gado; libra, medida com 453,59g; *v.*, socar, bater, esmurrar.
POUND.AGE, *s.*, comissão, porcentagem, pagamento.
POUR, *s.*, aguaceiro, toró; *v.*, despejar, vazar, soltar, brotar, chover, fluir.
POUR.ER, *s.*, funil.
POUR.ING, *adj.*, torrencial, copioso, abundante.
POV.ER.TY, *s.*, pobreza, indigência, miséria.
POW.DER, *s.*, pó, pó de arroz, polvilho, pólvora; *v.*, polvilhar, empoar, salgar.
POW.ER, *s.*, poder, força, autoridade, comando, energia, aparelho-motor, potência.
POW.ER.BOAT, *s.*, barco a motor.
POW.ER.FUL, *adj.*, forte, poderoso, dominador, enérgico.
POW.ER.HOUSE, *s.*, casa de máquinas.
POX, *s.*, pústula, varíola.
PRAC.TI.CA.BLE, *adj.*, praticável.
PRAC.TICE, *s.*, prática, uso, costume, experiência, exercício; *v.*, praticar, exercitar.
PRAC.TIC.ER, *s.*, prático.
PRAG.MAT.IC, *s.*, pragmática; *adj.*, pragmático.
PRAG.MA.TISM, *s.*, pragmatismo.
PRAI.RIE, *s.*, pradaria, prado, campo, campina.
PRAISE, *s.*, louvor, aplauso, exaltação; *v.*, louvar, aplaudir, elogiar.
PRAM, *s.*, carrinho de bebê.
PRANK, *s.*, logro, travessura, brincadeira; *v.*, brincar, fazer travessuras; adornar.
PRANK.ING, *s.*, enfeite, adorno.
PRANK.ISH, *adj.*, travesso, traquinas, brincalhão, peralta.
PRATE, *s.*, tagarelice; *v.*, tagarelar, falar pelos cotovelos.
PRA.TIQUE, *s.*, prático de porto, piloto de navio em porto.
PRAWN, *s.*, camarão, lagostim.
PRAX.IS, *s.*, práxis, praxe, prática.
PRAY, *v.*, rezar, orar.
PRAY.ER, *s.*, oração, súplica, pedido, prece.
PRAYER.FUL, *adj.*, piedoso, devoto.
PREACH, *s.*, prédica, sermão; *v.*, pregar, predicar, aconselhar, catequizar.
PRE.AM.BLE, *s.*, preâmbulo, prefácio, abertura, exórdio.
PRE.AR.RANGE, *v.*, arranjar antes, predispor.
PRE.CAR.I.OUS, *adj.*, precário.
PRE.CAU.TION, *s.*, precaução.

PRE.CEDE, v., preceder, anteceder.
PRE.CE.DENCE, s., precedência, prioridade, antecedência.
PRE.CE.DENT, s., precedente.
PRE.CEPT, s., preceito, norma, determinação.
PRE.CEP.TOR, s., preceptor, mestre, guia.
PRE.CINCT, s., distrito policial; vizinhanças, arredores, cercanias.
PRE.CI.OS.I.TY, s., preciosidade.
PRE.CIOUS, adj., precioso.
PREC.I.PICE, s., precipício.
PRE.CIP.I.TAN.CY, s., precipitação, afobamento.
PRE.CIP.I.TATE, v., precipitar, afobar, acelerar.
PRE.CIP.I.TA.TION, s., precipitação, afobamento.
PRE.CISE, adj., preciso, exato, detalhado.
PRE.CISE.NESS, s., precisão, exatidão.
PRE.CLUDE, v., precludir, excluir.
PRE.CO.CIOUS, adj., precoce.
PRE.CO.CIOUS.NESS, s., precocidade.
PRE.CON.DI.TION, s., pré-condição, condição prévia.
PRE.CUR.SOR, s., precursor.
PRE.DATE, v., predatar, antedatar.
PRE.DA.TION, s., predação, destruição.
PRED.A.TOR, s., predador.
PRED.A.TO.RY, adj., predador, voraz, destruidor.
PRE.DE.CES.SOR, s., predecessor, antecessor, antepassado.
PRE.DES.TI.NATE, v., predestinar.
PRE.DES.TI.NA.TION, s., predestinação, sina, destino.
PRE.DE.TER.MINE, v., predeterminar, prefixar, preestabelecer.
PRED.I.CATE, s., predicado, qualidade, atributo; v., afirmar, confirmar.
PRED.I.CA.TION, s., predicação.
PRED.I.CA.TIVE, adj., s., predicativo.
PRE.DIC.TOR, s., profeta.
PRE.DI.LEC.TION, s., predileção, preferência.
PRE.DIS.POSE, v., predispor.
PRE.DIS.PO.SI.TION, s., predisposição, inclinação, rumo, tendência.
PRE.DOM.I.NANCE, s., predominância, predomínio.
PRE.DOM.I.NATE, v., predominar, dominar.
PRE.DOM.I.NA.TION, s., predominação, dominação.
PRE.EM.I.NENCE, s., preeminência, primazia.
PRE-EX.IST, v., preexistir.
PRE-EX.IS.TENCE, s., preexistência.
PRE.FAB, s., casa pré-fabricada.
PREF.ACE, s., prefácio, preâmbulo; v., prefaciar.
PRE.FECT, s., prefeito, dirigente, monitor.
PRE.FEC.TURE, s., prefeitura, governo.
PRE.FER, v., preferir, escolher, dar preferência.
PREF.ER.ABLE, adj., preferível.
PREF.ER.ENCE, s., preferência, antecedência.
PREF.ER.EN.TIAL, adj., preferencial.
PRE.FIX, s., prefixo.
PREG.NAN.CY, s., gravidez, fertilidade.
PRE.HIS.TOR.IC, adj., pré-histórico.
PRE.JUDGE, v., prejulgar, julgar antes.
PRE.JUDG.MENT, s., prejulgamento.
PREJ.U.DICE, s., preconceito.
PREJ.U.DI.CIAL, adj., prejudicial.
PREL.A.CY, s., prelazia, episcopado.
PRE.LIM.I.NARY, s., preliminar, abertura.
PRE.LUDE, s., prelúdio, abertura, prólogo; v., preludiar.
PRE.MA.TURE, adj., prematuro.
PRE.MED.I.TATE, v., premeditar, pensar antes.
PRE.MED.I.TA.TION, s., premeditação.
PRE.MIER, s., primeiro ministro.
PREM.ISE, s., premissa.
PRE.MI.UM, s., prêmio.
PRE.MO.NI.TION, s., premonição, pressentimento.
PRE.OC.CU.PA.TION, s., preocupação.
PRE.OC.CU.PY, v., preocupar.
PREP.A.RA.TION, s., preparação, arrumação; s., preparativos.
PRE.PARE, v., preparar, aprontar, elaborar.
PRE.PARED, adj., preparado, pronto.
PRE.PAY, v., pagar antecipadamente.
PRE.PON.DER.ANCE, s., preponderância, hegemonia, comando.
PRE.PON.DER.ATE, v., preponderar.

PREP.O.SI.TION, s., preposição.
PRE.REQ.UI.SITE, s., pré-requisito.
PRE.ROG.A.TIVE, s., prerrogativa.
PRES.AGE, s., presságio, auspício, vaticínio; v., pressagiar.
PRES.BY.O.PIA, s., presbiopia.
PRES.BY.TER, s., presbítero.
PRES.BY.TE.RI.AN, adj., s., presbiteriano.
PRE.SCHOOL, adj., pré-escolar.
PRE.SCRIBE, v., prescrever, receitar, indicar.
PRE.SCRIPT, s., preceito, norma, regra; adj., prescrito.
PRE.SCRIP.TION, s., prescrição, receita.
PRES.ENCE, s., presença.
PRE.SENT, s., presente; adj., presente, atual, momentâneo; v., apresentar, ofertar.
PRE.SEN.TA.TION, s., apresentação, demonstração, exposição.
PRE.SENT.ER, s., apresentador.
PRE.SEN.TI.MENT, s., pressentimento, impressão.
PRES.ENT.LY, adv., presentemente, atualmente, em breve.
PRES.ER.VA.TION, s., preservação, conservação.
PRE.SER.VA.TIVE, s., conservante.
PRE.SERVE, v., conservar, preservar, manter; manter em conserva.
PRE.SIDE, v., presidir, dirigir, comandar como presidente.
PRES.I.DEN.CY, s., presidência, comando, direção.
PRES.I.DENT, s., presidente.
PRESS, s., pressão, multidão; prelo, prensa, impressora; v., apertar, oprimir, forçar.
PRESS.ING, adj., urgente, apressado.
PRESS.MAN, s., jornalista; impressor, tipógrafo.
PRES.SURE, s., pressão, aperto, compressão, força, coação, pressão atmosférica.
PRES.SUR.IZED, adj., pressurizado.
PRES.TIGE, s., prestígio.
PRES.TI.GIOUS, adj., prestigioso.
PRE.SUME, v., presumir, supor, achar, pensar.
PRE.SUMP.TION, s., presunção, suposição, hipótese.
PRE.SUP.POSE, v., pressupor, imaginar, achar.
PRE.SUP.PO.SI.TION, s., pressuposição, hipótese, suposição.
PRE.TEN.SION, s., pretensão.
PRE.TEN.TIOUS, adj., pretensioso.
PRET.ER.IT, s., pretérito.
PRE.TER.MIT, v., preterir, deixar fora, omitir.
PRE.TEXT, s., pretexto.
PRET.TI.NESS, s., beleza, formosura, elegância.
PRET.TY, adj., belo, formoso, elegante, bonito.
PRET.TY.ISH, adj., abonitado, mais ou menos belo.
PRE.VAIL, v., vencer, triunfar.
PREV.A.LENCE, s., prevalência, domínio, predomínio.
PRE.VENT, v., prevenir, impedir, obstar.
PRE.VEN.TION, s., prevenção, cuidado.
PRE.VEN.TIVE, adj., preventivo.
PRE.VI.OUS, adj., prévio, anterior.
PRE.VI.OUS.NESS, s., anterioridade, precedência.
PRE.VISE, v., prever, vaticinar.
PRE.VI.SION, v., previsão.
PREY, s., rapina, saque, pilhagem; v., saquear, pilhar, rapinar.
PRICE, s., preço, valor, custo, recompensa; v., colocar preço, avaliar.
PRICE.LESS, adj., sem preço, impossível de ser pago.
PRICK, s., punctura, picada, ferroada, remorso; v., picar, pungir, afligir, ferroar.
PRICK.LY, adj., espinhoso, espinhento, pontudo.
PRIDE, s., orgulho, soberba, vaidade, exibição; v., orgulhar-se, envaidecer-se.
PRIEST, s., sacerdote, padre.
PRIEST.HOOD, s., sacerdócio.
PRIEST.LIKE, adj., sacerdotal, referente a sacerdote.
PRIG, s., ladrão, pedante, presunçoso; v., roubar, furtar.
PRI.MA.CY, s., primazia, antecedência, superioridade.
PRI.MAL, adj., primitivo, primeiro.

PRI.MA.RY, s., tema principal; eleição primária; adj., primário, primitivo, essencial.
PRIME, s., início, aurora, juventude, número primo; adj., primitivo, primeiro.
PRIME MIN.IS.TER, s., primeiro ministro.
PRIM.ER, s., cartilha, livro de ensino elementar.
PRIM.I.TIVE, adj., primitivo, elementar, rudimentar.
PRIM.NESS, s., afetação, pedantismo, petulância.
PRI.MO.GEN.I.TURE, s., primogenitura.
PRI.MOR.DI.AL, adj., primitivo, primário, primordial.
PRINCE, s., príncipe.
PRINCE.DOM, s., principado.
PRINCE.LIKE, adj., principesco.
PRIN.CESS, s., princesa.
PRIN.CI.PAL, adj., principal, fundamental; s., diretor.
PRIN.CI.PATE, s., principado.
PRIN.CI.PLE, s., princípio, início, começo.
PRINT, s., impressão, letra de forma, marca, vestígio, ato de imprimir; v., gravar, imprimir, marcar, colocar sinais, copiar, fazer cópias.
PRINT.ER, s., impressor.
PRINT.ERY, s., oficina gráfica, gráfica, impressora.
PRINT.ING, s., impressão, estampagem, tiragem, cópias.
PRI.OR.I.TY, s., prioridade, precedência.
PRISM, s., prisma.
PRIS.ON, s., prisão, cárcere, cadeia.
PRIS.ON.ER, s., preso, prisioneiro, encarcerado.
PRI.VA.CY, s., privacidade, solidão, segredo, confidência.
PRI.VATE, s., soldado raso; adj., privado, particular, reservado, individual, secreto.
PRI.VA.TION, s., privação, falta, carência, ausência.
PRIV.A.TIVE, adj., privativo, reservado.
PRI.VAT.IZE, v., privatizar, particularizar.
PRIV.I.LEGE, s., privilégio, regalia, prerrogativa; v., privilegiar, favorecer.
PRIVY, s., latrina, privada; adj., particular, pessoal, individual.

PRIZE, s., prêmio, presente, recompensa, privilégio; v., avaliar, estimar, elogiar.
PRO, s., pró, vantagem; adv., em favor.
PROB.A.BIL.I.TY, s., probabilidade, possibilidade.
PROB.A.BLE, adj., provável.
PRO.BATE, s., aprovação de um testamento, cópia legítima.
PRO.BA.TION, s., provação, experimento, experiência, noviciado.
PROBE, s., sonda, sindicância, investigação; v., investigar, fazer sindicância.
PROB.LEM, s., problema, questão, dificuldade, charada, enigma.
PROB.LEM.AT.IC, adj., problemático.
PRO.CE.DURE, s., conduta, procedimento, comportamento, método.
PRO.CEED, v., proceder, prosseguir, derivar, provir, continuar.
PRO.CEED.ING, s., procedimento, prosseguimento, continuação.
PRO.CESS, s., processo, progresso, curso, decurso; citação, intimação; v., processar.
PRO.CES.SION, s., procissão, séquito, cortejo, marcha; v., desfilar, andar.
PRO.CLAIM, v., proclamar, apregoar, pregar, decretar, publicar.
PROC.LA.MA.TION, s., proclamação, apregoamento.
PRO.CRE.ATE, v., procriar, gerar.
PRO.CRE.ATION, s., procriação, geração, reprodução.
PRO.CRE.ATOR, s., procriador.
PROC.TOR.IZE, v., disciplinar, ordenar, organizar.
PROC.U.RA.CY, s., procuradoria.
PROC.U.RA.TION, s., procuração.
PROC.U.RA.TOR, s., procurador.
PRO.CURE, v., obter, conseguir, alcançar, somar; agir como procurador.
PROD, s., alfinetada, picada, cutucada, estímulo; v., picar, cutucar, incitar.
PROD.I.GAL.I.TY, s., prodigalidade.
PRO.DI.GIOUS, adj., prodigioso, maravilhoso,

estupendo, incomum.
PROD.I.GY, *s.*, maravilha, milagre, prodígio.
PRO.DUCE, *s.*, produto, artigo manufaturado, lucro; *v.*, produzir, exibir, gerar.
PRO.DUC.ER, *s.*, produtor.
PROD.UCT, *s.*, produto, fruto, artigo, resultado, consequência.
PRO.DUC.TION, *s.*, produção, manufatura, exibição, obra, criação.
PRO.DUC.TIVE, *adj.*, produtivo.
PRO.EM, *s.*, prefácio.
PROF.A.NA.TION, *s.*, profanação.
PRO.FANE, *adj.*, profano, laico, secular, impuro; *v.*, profanar, manchar, desrespeitar.
PRO.FESS, *v.*, professar, fazer votos, prometer, confessar, reconhecer.
PRO.FES.SION, *s.*, profissão, declaração, confissão; fé, crença.
PRO.FES.SION.AL, *adj.*, *s.*, profissional.
PRO.FES.SOR, *s.*, professor, mestre.
PROF.FER, *s.*, oferenda, oferta; *v.*, ofertar, oferecer.
PRO.FILE, *s.*, perfil, contorno, corte, talhe; *v.*, perfilar, moldar, modelar.
PROF.IT, *s.*, proveito, lucro, rendimento, benefício; *v.*, aproveitar, obter proveito.
PROF.IT.ABIL.I.TY, *s.*, lucro, rentabilidade.
PRO.FOUND, *adj.*, profundo.
PRO.FOUND.NESS, *s.*, profundidade.
PRO.FUN.DI.TY, *s.*, profundidade.
PRO.FU.SION, *s.*, profusão, copiosidade, abundância.
PRO.GEN.I.TOR, *s.*, progenitor.
PROG.E.NY, *s.*, progênie, prole.
PROG.NO.SIS, *s.*, prognóstico.
PROG.NOS.TI.CATE, *v.*, prognosticar, vaticinar, prever.
PRO.GRAM.ME, *s.*, programa, roteiro; *v.*, programar.
PRO.GRAM.MER, *s.*, programador.
PRO.GRAM.MING, *s.*, programação.
PROG.RESS, *s.*, progresso; *v.*, progredir, desenvolver.
PRO.GRES.SION, *s.*, progressão, avanço.
PRO.GRES.SIVE, *adj.*, progressivo.
PRO.HIB.IT, *v.*, proibir, vetar.
PRO.HI.BI.TION, *s.*, proibição, veto, negativa.
PRO.HIB.I.TIVE, *adj.*, proibitivo.
PROJ.ECT, *s.*, projeto, plano, pesquisa, intento; *v.*, projetar, estimar, tentar.
PRO.JEC.TILE, *s.*, projétil.
PRO.JEC.TION, *s.*, projeção, destaque, ênfase.
PRO.JEC.TOR, *s.*, projetor.
PRO.LE.TAR.I.AN, *adj.*, proletário.
PRO.LE.TAR.I.AT, *s.*, proletariado.
PRO.LIF.ER.ATE, *v.*, proliferar, espalhar, difundir.
PRO.LIX, *adj.*, prolixo, longo, difuso, complexo.
PRO.LIX.I.TY, *s.*, prolixidade.
PRO.LOGUE, *s.*, prólogo, prefácio, início.
PRO.LONG, *v.*, prolongar.
PRO.LON.GA.TION, *s.*, prolongamento, prolongação.
PROM.E.NADE, *s.*, passeio, giro, convescote, piquenique.
PROM.I.NENCE, *s.*, proeminência, eminência, valor, importância.
PRO.MIS.CU.I.TY, *s.*, promiscuidade.
PRO.MIS.CU.OUS, *adj.*, promíscuo.
PROM.ISE, *s.*, promessa, espera, esperança, compromisso, palavra.
PROM.IS.ER, *s.*, prometedor.
PROM.IS.ING, *adj.*, promissor.
PRO.MOTE, *v.*, promover, divulgar.
PRO.MOT.ER, *s.*, patrocinador, divulgador.
PRO.MO.TION, *s.*, promoção.
PROMPT, *v.*, iniciar, impelir, recordar, sugerir; *adj.*, pronto, alerta, rápido.
PROMP.TI.TUDE, *s.*, prontidão, presteza.
PROMPT.LY, *adv.*, prontamente, imediatamente.
PRO.MUL.GATE, *v.*, promulgar, divulgar.
PRO.MUL.GA.TION, *s.*, promulgação, divulgação.
PRONE, *adj.*, inclinado, propenso, de borco, de bruços.
PRONG, *adj.*, forcado, dente de garfo; *v.*, forcar.
PRO.NOM.I.NAL, *adj.*, pronominal.
PRO.NOUN, *s.*, pronome.

PRO.NOUNCE, v., pronunciar, articular, declarar, afirmar.
PRO.NOUNCE.MENT, s., pronunciamento, declaração.
PRO.NOUNC.ING, s., pronúncia.
PRO.NUN.CI.A.TION, s., pronúncia, pronunciação.
PROOF, s., prova, demonstração, exame, experiência, comprovante.
PROP, s., estaca, escora, estepe.
PRO.PA.GAN.DA, s., propaganda.
PRO.PA.GAN.DIST, s., propagandista.
PROP.A.GATE, v., propagar, difundir, divulgar.
PROP.A.GA.TION, s., propagação, divulgação.
PRO.PAR.OX.Y.TONE, s., proparoxítono.
PRO.PEL, v., propelir, impelir.
PRO.PEL.LER, s., propulsor, hélice.
PROP.ER, adj., próprio, particular, genuíno, característico, privativo, inerente.
PROP.ER.TY, s., propriedade, característica, caráter; propriedade de bens de raiz.
PROPH.E.CY, s., profecia, vaticínio.
PROPH.E.SY, v., profetizar, vaticinar.
PROPH.ET, s., profeta.
PRO.PHET.IC, adj., profético.
PRO.PI.TI.ATE, v., propiciar, favorecer, ajudar.
PRO.PI.TIOUS, adj., propício, favorável.
PRO.POR.TION, s., proporção.
PRO.POR.TION.AL, adj., proporcional.
PRO.POR.TION.AL.I.TY, s., proporcionalidade.
PRO.POR.TION.ATE, v., proporcionar, conceder; adj., proporcional.
PRO.POS.AL, s., proposta, solicitação, pedido.
PRO.POSE, v., propor, expor, oferecer, indicar.
PROP.O.SI.TION, s., proposição, proposta.
PRO.POUND, v., propor, oferecer, indicar.
PRO.PRI.E.TARY, s., dono, proprietário, propriedade; adj., proprietário.
PRO.PUL.SION, s., propulsão, impulsão, impulso.
PRO.RO.GA.TION, s., prorrogação, adiamento.
PRO.ROGUE, v., prorrogar, adiar.
PRO.SA.IC, adj., prosaico.
PRO.SCRIBE, s., proscrever, desterrar, condenar ao exílio, condenar.

PRO.SCRIP.TION, s., proscrição.
PROSE, s., prosa; v., escrever em prosa, usar de prosa.
PROS.E.CUTE, v., processar.
PROS.E.LYTE, s., prosélito, sequaz, seguidor, sectário.
PROS.E.LY.TISM, s., proselitismo.
PROS.ER, s., prosador, escritor, narrador, cronista.
PROS.O.DY, s., prosódia.
PROS.PECT, s., prospecto, vista, perspectiva; v., pesquisar, investigar, explorar.
PROS.PECT.ING, s., prospecção.
PRO.SPECT.IVE.NESS, s., prospeção, perspectiva, possibilidade.
PROSP.ER, v., prosperar, melhorar.
PROS.PER.I.TY, s., prosperidade, melhoria.
PROS.PER.OUS, adj., próspero, progressivo.
PROS.TATE, s., próstata.
PROS.TI.TUTE, s., prostituta, meretriz; v., dedicar-se à prostituição, prostituir-se.
PROS.TI.TU.TION, s., prostituição, meretrício.
PRO.TAG.O.NIST, s., protagonista, personagem principal, líder, guia.
PROT.A.SIS, s., prótese.
PRO.TECT, v., proteger, resguardar.
PRO.TECT.ING, adj., protetor.
PRO.TEC.TION, s., proteção.
PRO.TEC.TION.ISM, s., protecionismo.
PRO.TEC.TION.IST, s., protecionista.
PRO.TEC.TOR, s., protetor, tutor.
PRO.TEIN, s., proteína.
PRO.TEST, s., protesto, reclamação, queixa; v., protestar, reclamar, queixar-se.
PROT.ES.TANT, adj., s., protestante.
PROT.ES.TANT.ISM, s., protestantismo.
PRO.TES.TA.TION, s., protesto, reclamação.
PROTH.E.SIS, s., prótese.
PRO.TO.COL, s., protocolo, cerimonial, etiqueta.
PRO.TO.TYPE, s., protótipo.
PRO.TO.ZO.AN, adj., protozoário.
PRO.TO.ZO.ON, s., protozoário.
PRO.TRACT, v., protrair, adiar, prolongar.
PRO.TRAC.TOR, s., transferidor.
PRO.TU.BER.ANCE, s., protuberância, saliência,

bossa.
PRO.TU.BER.ANT, *adj.*, protuberante, saliente, destacado.
PROV.ABLE, *adj.*, provável, possível.
PROVE, *v.*, provar, experimentar, tentar, comprovar, patentear, evidenciar.
PROV.E.NANCE, *s.*, proveniência, origem, procedência.
PROV.EN.DER, *s.*, forragem seca, ração animal, alimento para animais.
PROV.ER, *s.*, provador, experimentador, degustador.
PROV.ERB, *s.*, provérbio, máxima, dito, adágio.
PRO.VIDE, *v.*, prover, fornecer, abastecer, suprir, providenciar.
PRO.VID.ED, *adj.*, provido, fornecido, abastecido, suprido.
PROV.I.DENT, *adj.*, previdente, prudente, avisado.
PROV.INCE, *s.*, província, região, estado.
PRO.VIN.CIAL, *adj.*, provinciano, provincial, caipira, interiorano.
PROV.ING, *s.*, prova.
PRO.VI.SION, *s.*, provisão, abastecimento, suprimento.
PRO.VI.SO.RY, *adj.*, provisório, condicional.
PROV.O.CA.TION, *s.*, provocação.
PRO.VOKE, *v.*, provocar, instigar, causar.
PRO.VOK.ER, *s.*, provocador, instigador.
PROW, *s.*, proa.
PROW.ESS, *s.*, habilidade, destreza, rapidez.
PROWL, *v.*, ronda, vigilância, sentinela; *v.*, rondar, vigiar, andar a esmo.
PROX.I.MATE, *adj.*, próximo, vizinho, achegado, imediato.
PROX.IM.I.TY, *s.*, proximidade, vizinhança, adjacência.
PROXY, *s.*, procuração, procurador, representante; *v.*, agir como procurador.
PRUDE, *adj.*, pudico, melindroso.
PRU.DENCE, *s.*, prudência, cuidado, cautela.
PRU.DENT, *adj.*, prudente, cauteloso, cuidadoso.
PRUD.ERY, *s.*, afetação, melindre.
PRUD.ISH, *s.*, afetado, melindroso, prudente.

PRUNE, *s.*, ameixa seca.
PRUN.ING, *s.*, poda, podadura.
PRUS.SIAN, *adj.*, *s.*, prussiano.
PRY, *v.*, meter-se, intrometer-se, investigar.
PSALM, *s.*, salmo.
PSALM.IST, *s.*, salmista.
PSEUDO, *adj.*, pseudo, falso.
PSEU.DO.NYM, *s.*, pseudônimo.
PSYCHE, *s.*, psique.
PSY.CHI.AT.RIC, *adj.*, psiquiátrico.
PSY.CHI.A.TRIST, *s.*, psiquiatra.
PSY.CHI.A.TRY, *s.*, psiquiatria.
PSY.CHIC, *adj.*, psíquico.
PSY.CHO.AN.A.LYSE, *s.*, psicanalizar.
PSY.CHO.ANAL.Y.SIS, *s.*, psicanálise.
PSY.CHO.AN.A.LYST, *s.*, psicanalista.
PSY.CHOL.O.GIST, *s.*, psicólogo.
PSY.CHOL.O.GY, *s.*, psicologia.
PSY.CHO.PATH, *s.*, psicopata.
PUB, *s.*, bar, pub.
PU.BER.TY, *s.*, puberdade.
PU.BES, *s.*, púbis.
PU.BES.CENCE, *s.*, puberdade, pubescência.
PUB.LIC, *s.*, público, povo, assistência; taberna, bar; *adj.*, público, comum.
PUB.LI.CA.TION, *s.*, publicação, proclamação, editoração.
PUB.LI.CIST, *s.*, publicista, publicitário.
PUB.LIC.I.TY, *s.*, publicidade, propaganda.
PUB.LI.CIZE, *v.*, publicar, divulgar, propagar.
PUB.LISH, *v.*, publicar, divulgar.
PUB.LISH.ER, *s.*, publicador, editor, divulgador.
PUCK, *s.*, duende, fantasma.
PUCK.ER, *s.*, ruga, prega, dobra; *v.*, amarrotar, enrugar, franzir.
PUD.DING, *s.*, pudim, sobremesa.
PUD.DLE, *s.*, poça, atoleiro, lamaçal; *v.*, embaciar, ofuscar, turvar.
PU.ER.ILE, *adj.*, pueril, infantil.
PU.ER.IL.I.TY, *s.*, puerilidade, infantilidade.
PUFF, *s.*, sopro, baforada, lufada, bomba, protuberância; *v.*, soprar, bufar, ofegar.
PUF.FY, *adj.*, inchado.
PU.GI.LISM, *s.*, pugilismo, luta.

PU.GI.LIST, s., pugilista.
PUG.NAC.I.TY, s., belicosidade, pugnacidade.
PUIS.SANCE, s., força, vigor, domínio.
PUKE, s., vômito; v., vomitar, lançar.
PULE, s., choro, gemido.
PULL, s., puxão, arranco, arrancada, força, gole; v., puxar, arrastar, colher, remover.
PULL.OVER, s., pulôver, agasalho.
PUL.MO.NARY, adj., pulmonar.
PULP, s., polpa de frutas.
PUL.PIT, s., púlpito.
PULPY, adj., polposo, carnudo.
PUL.SATE, v., pulsar, latejar, arquejar.
PUL.SA.TION, s., pulsação, latejamento.
PULSE, s., pulso, cadência, compasso; legume.
PUL.VER.I.ZA.TION, s., pulverização.
PUL.VER.IZE, v., pulverizar.
PU.MA, s., puma.
PUMP, s., bomba, sondagem; v., bombear, arrojar, esgotar.
PUMP.KIN s., abóbora.
PUN, s., trocadilho, jogo de palavras.
PUNCH, s., soco, murro, pancada, ímpeto, ponche; v., picar, socar, furar.
PUNCH.ER, s., furador.
PUNC.TIL.I.OUS, adj., escrupuloso, preocupado.
PUNC.TIL.I.OUS.NESS, s., meticulosidade, detalhe.
PUNC.TU.AL, adj., pontual.
PUNC.TU.AL.I.TY, s., pontualidade, exatidão, assiduidade.
PUNC.TU.ATE, v., pontuar, enfatizar, destacar, realçar.
PUNC.TU.A.TION, s., pontuação, ênfase.
PUN.GEN.CY, s., pungência, acidez, agrura.
PUN.ISH, v., punir, castigar.
PUN.ISH.ABLE, adj., punível, castigável.
PUN.ISH.MENT, s., castigo, punição, pena.
PUNK, s., rufião, punk.
PU.NY, adj., fraco, débil.
PU.PIL, s., pupila, pupilo, aluno, discípulo.
PUP.PY, s., cachorrinho, filhote de cachorro.
PUR.BLIND.NESS, s., cegueira relativa.
PUR.CHASE, s., compra, aquisição.
PUR.CHAS.ER, s., comprador.
PURE, adj., puro.
PU.RÉE, s., purê.
PURE.NESS, s., pureza.
PUR.GA.TION, s., purgação, limpeza.
PUR.GA.TIVE, s., purgante; adj., purificador, purgador.
PUR.GA.TO.RY, s., purgatório.
PURGE, s., purgação, purgante; v., purgar, purificar, limpar, sanar.
PU.RI.FI.CA.TION, s., purificação, purgação.
PU.RI.FY, v., purificar, purgar, limpar.
PU.RI.FY.ING, s., purificação.
PU.RI.TAN, s., puritano.
PU.RI.TAN.ISM, s., puritanismo.
PU.RI.TY, s., pureza.
PUR.LOIN, v., furtar, plagiar, roubar.
PUR.LOIN.ER, s., ladrão, gatuno.
PUR.PLE, adj., purpúreo, roxo.
PUR.POSE, s., propósito, objetivo, intenção.
PUR.POSE.FUL, adj., decidido, resoluto, incisivo.
PURR, s., ronrom; v., ronronar.
PURSE, s., bolsa, carteira, erário, dinheiro, caixa; v., enrugar, franzir.
PUR.SU.ANCE, s., prosseguimento, seguimento, continuação.
PUR.SUE, v., perseguir, procurar, seguir, adotar.
PUR.SU.ER, s., perseguidor.
PU.RU.LENCE, s., purulência.
PU.RU.LENT, adj., purulento.
PUR.VEY, v., prover, abastecer, suprir.
PUR.VEY.ANCE, s., abastecimento.
PUR.VEY.OR, s., fornecedor.
PUSH, s., empurrão, tentativa, emergência, impulso; v., empurrar, impulsionar.
PUSHY, adj., intrometido, metido.
PU.SIL.LA.NIM.I.TY, s., pusilanimidade.
PU.SIL.LAN.I.MOUS, adj., pusilânime.
PUS.TU.LATE, v., criar pústulas; adj., pustulento.
PUS.TU.LA.TION, s., pustulação.
PUT, s., lance, arremesso; v., pôr, colocar, meter, atribuir, guardar, expor, calcular.
PUT ABOVE, v., colocar acima de, pôr em

cima de.
PU.TA.TIVE, *adj.*, putativo.
PU.TRE.FAC.TION, *s.*, putrefação.
PU.TRE.FY, *v.*, apodrecer, putrefazer.
PU.TRID, *adj.*, pútrido, fedido, fedorento.
PU.TRID.I.TY, *s.*, podridão.
PUT UPON, *v.*, pôr por cima.
PUZ.ZLE, *s.*, charada, quebra-cabeças, palavras cruzadas; *v.*, confundir, embaraçar.
PUZ.ZLED, *adj.*, embaraçado, complicado, confuso.
PUZ.ZLER, *s.*, embaraçador.
PYG.MAE.AN, *adj.*, pigmeu.

PYG.MY, *s.*, pigmeu.
PY.JA.MAS, *s.*, pijama.
PY.LON, *s.*, pilão, poste, torre.
PYR.A.MID, *s.*, pirâmide.
PYRE, *s.*, pira, fogueira, pira funerária.
PY.REX, *s.*, pirex.
PY.ROG.RA.PHY, *s.*, pirografia.
PY.ROM.E.TER, *s.*, pirômetro.
PY.ROM.E.TRY, *s.*, pirometria.
PY.RO.TECH.NIC, *adj.*, pirotécnico.
PY.THAG.O.RE.AN, *adj.*, pitagórico.
PY.THON, *s.*, pitão, serpente.
PYX, *s.*, cibório, cálice, píxide.

Q

Q, *s.*, décima sétima letra do alfabeto inglês.
QUACK, *s.*, grasnido de pato; *v.*, grasnar; *adj.*, charlatão.
QUACK.ERY, *s.*, charlatanismo, curandeirismo.
QUAD.RAN.GLE, *s.*, quadrângulo; *adj.*, quadrangular.
QUA.DRAN.GU.LAR, *adj.*, quadrangular.
QUAD.RANT, *s.*, quadrante.
QUAD.RATE, *s.*, quadrado, quadrilátero; *v.*, quadrar; *adj.*, quadrado.
QUAD.RA.TURE, *s.*, quadratura.
QUAD.RI.LAT.ER.AL, *adj.*, *s.*, quadrilátero.
QUA.DRILLE, *s.*, quadrilha.
QUA.DROON, *s.*, quarteirão.
QUAD.RU.PED, *adj.*, *s.*, quadrúpede.
QUA.DRU.PLE, *v.*, quadruplicar.
QUA.DRU.PLEX, *adj.*, *s.*, quádruplo.
QUA.DRU.PLI.CATE, *v.*, quadruplicar; quadruplicado.
QUAG, *s.*, pântano, charco, brejo, paul.
QUAG.MIRE, *s.*, pântano, brejo.
QUAIL, *s.*, codorniz; *v.*, ceder, amedrontar-se.
QUAINT, *adj.*, curioso, estranho, esquisito.
QUAKE, *s.*, tremor, abalo sísmico; *v.*, tremer, estremecer.
QUAK.ING, *s.*, tremor; *adj.*, trêmulo, tremente, medroso.
QUAL.I.FI.CA.TION, *s.*, qualificação, requisito, modificação, título.
QUAL.I.FIED, *adj.*, qualificado, capacitado, habilitado.
QUAL.I.FY, *v.*, qualificar, capacitar, habilitar, educar, modificar.
QUAL.I.TA.TIVE, *adj.*, qualitativo.
QUAL.I.TY, *s.*, qualidade, predicado.
QUALM, *s.*, desânimo, desmaio, desfalecimento, náusea, dúvida.
QUANT.IC, *s.*, quântico.
QUAN.TI.TY, *s.*, quantidade, valor, soma.
QUAR.AN.TINE, *s.*, quarentena.
QUAR.REL, *s.*, disputa, contenda, rixa, discussão; *v.*, discutir, disputar, querelar.
QUAR.REL.LER, *s.*, altercador, polemista, querelante.
QUAR.REL.SOM, *adj.*, briguento, brigão, queteloso.
QUAR.RY, *s.*, pedreira, caça, presa; *v.*, tirar macadame, extrair pedras.
QUART, *s.*, quarto, medida para líquidos com 1.136 litros.
QUART.ER, *s.*, quarto, quarta parte, trimestre, quarteirão; *v.*, esquartejar.
QUAR.TER.ING, *s.*, esquartejamento, aquartelamento.
QUAR.TET, *s.*, quarteto.
QUARTZ, *s.*, quartzo.
QUASH, *v.*, anular, destruir, suprimir.
QUA.TER.NA.RY, *adj.*, quaternário.
QUA.TRAIN, *s.*, quarteto, estrofe com quatro versos, quadra.
QUA.VER.ING, *adj.*, trêmulo.
QUAY, *s.*, cais, ancoradouro.
QUAY.SIDE, *s.*, cais.
QUEA.SI.NESS, *s.*, enjoo, náusea.
QUEA.SY, *adj.*, enjoado.
QUEEN, *s.*, rainha, dama, carta de baralho e peça no xadrez; *v.*, coroar alguém rainha.
QUEEN.LY, *adj.*, régio, próprio de rainha.
QUEER, *adj.*, esquisito, estranho, adoentado; *v.*, arruinar, embaraçar.
QUER.IST, *s.*, interrogador, curioso.
QUER.U.LOUS, *adj.*, queixoso, choroso, queteloso.
QUE.RY, *s.*, pergunta, questão, ponto de interrogação; *v.*, perguntar, indagar.
QUEST, *s.*, indagação, busca, pergunta; *v.*, indagar, buscar, procurar.

QUES.TION, *s.*, questão, pergunta, exame, disputa; *v.*, examinar, perguntar, duvidar.
QUES.TION.ABLE, *adj.*, questionável, duvidoso.
QUES.TION.ARY, *s.*, questionário.
QUEUE, *s.*, fila; *v.*, fazer fila, enfileirar.
QUICK, *s.*, ser vivo, carne viva; *adj.*, rápido, vivo, ativo, intenso, esperto.
QUICK.EN, *v.*, apressar, acelerar, estimular.
QUICK.LY, *adv.*, rapidamente, subitamente, de súbito.
QUICK.NESS, *s.*, rapidez, celeridade, pressa.
QUICK.SAND, *s.*, areia movediça.
QUICK.SIL.VER, *s.*, mercúrio.
QUI.ESCE, *v.*, emudecer, calar-se, ficar em silêncio.
QUI.ES.CENCE, *s.*, quietude, tranquilidade, paz, sossego.
QUI.ET, *s.*, sossego, paz, quietude; *adj.*, calmo, tranquilo; *v.*, aquietar, acalmar.
QUI.ET.NESS, *s.*, tranquilidade, quietude, sossego, calma, paz.
QUILL, *s.*, pluma, pena para escrever; *v.*, enrolar, dobrar.
QUILT, *s.*, colcha, acolchoado; *v.*, acolchoar, forrar.
QUINCE, *s.*, marmelo.
QUINIA, *s.*, quina, quinina.
QUIN.QUAG.E.NA.RI.AN, *adj.*, *s.*, quinquagenário.
QUIN.TU.PLE, *adj.*, *s.*, quíntuplo; *v.*, quintuplicar.
QUIP, *s.*, escárnio, zombaria, sátira; *v.*, zombar, mofar, rir de.
QUIRK, *s.*, truque, subterfúgio, artimanha.
QUIT, *v.*, renunciar, abandonar, partir, quitar; *adj.*, quite, livre.
QUITE, *adv.*, completamente, totalmente.
QUIT.TANCE, *s.*, quitação, recibo.
QUIV.ER, *s.*, aljava; *v.*, tremer, estremecer.
QUIX.OT.IC, *adj.*, quixotesco.
QUIZ, *s.*, problema, enigma; *v.*, embaraçar, dificultar.
QUIS.ZI.CAL, *adj.*, zombeteiro, excêntrico, estranho.
QUOD, *s.*, prisão, cadeia, xadrez; *v.*, prender, encarcerar.
QUOIN, *s.*, ângulo, pedra angular, esquina; *v.*, firmar com pedra.
QUOTA, *s.*, quota, cota.
QUOT.ABLE, *adj.*, quotável.
QUO.TA.TION, *s.*, quotação, citação.
QUOTE, *s.*, citação; *v.*, citar, orçar, cotar.
QUO.TID.IAN, *adj.*, quotidiano, cotidiano, diário.
QUO.TIENT, *s.*, quociente, cociente.

R, décima oitava letra do alfabeto inglês.
RAB.BET, s., entalhe, encaixe; v., encaixar, entalhar.
RAB.BI, s., rabino, mestre.
RAB.BIT, s., coelho.
RAB.BLE, s., poviléu, plebe, ralé, povinho, populaça, gentalha; v., arruaçar, badernar.
RA.BID, adj., furioso, violento, raivento, hidrófobo.
RACE, s., corrida, competição, raça, raça humana, povo, canal; v., competir, correr.
RACE.COURSE, s., pista de corridas, hipódromo.
RACE.HORSE, s., corrida de cavalos.
RA.CHI.TIS, s., raquitismo.
RA.CIAL, adj., racial.
RA.CI.NESS, s., força, vigor, robustez, fortaleza.
RAC.ING, s., corrida.
RAC.ISM, s., racismo.
RAC.IST, s., racista.
RACK, s., prateleira, cavalete, cabide, porta-bagagem; ruína, destroços.
RACK.ET s., raquete, barulho, estrépito, negociata, negócio ilegal, fraude, safadeza.
RACY, adj., corajoso, ousado, picante, mordaz.
RA.DAR, s., radar.
RA.DI.ANCE, s., radiação, brilho, esplendor.
RA.DI.ANT, adj., radiante, brilhante, luminoso.
RA.DI.A.TION, s., radiação.
RA.DI.A.TOR, s., radiador.
RAD.I.CAL, adj., radical.
RAD.I.CAL.ISM, s., radicalismo.
RA.DIO, s., rádio, radiotransmissão, aparelho de rádio.
RA.DIO.AC.TIVE, adj., radioativo.
RA.DIO.AC.TIV.I.TY, s., radioatividade.
RA.DIO.BROAD.CAST.ING, s., radiotransmissão.
RA.DIO.GRAPH, s., radiografia, raios X, cópia.
RA.DIO.SCOPY, s., radioscopia.
RAD.ISH, s., rabanete.
RA.DI.UM s., rádio.
RAFT, s., balsa, jangada.
RAF.TER, s., viga, esteio, coluna.
RAG, s., trapo, farrapo, repreensão; jornaleco.
RAG.A.MUF.FIN, adj., s., vagabundo, esfarrapado.
RAGE, s., raiva, ira, ódio, furor, violência; v., enfurecer-se, irritar-se.
RAGE.FUL, adj., raivoso, furioso, irado, irritado.
RAGING, adj., furioso, raivoso.
RAG.MAN, s., negociante de coisas velhas.
RAID, s., incursão, assalto, ataque, reide; v., atacar repentinamente, invadir.
RAIL, s., corrimão, parapeito, grade, trilho de ferrovia; v., xingar, insultar, cercar.
RAIL.ING, s., grade.
RAIL.ROAD, s., ferrovia, estrada de ferro.
RAIL.WAY, s., estrada de ferro.
RAIN, s., chuva; v., chover, gotejar, garoar.
RAIN.BOW, s., arco-íris.
RAIN.COAT, s., impermeável, capa de chuva.
RAIN.DROP, s., gota de chuva, pingo de chuva.
RAIN.FALL s., chuva, aguaceiro.
RAINY, adj., chuvoso.
RAISE, s., aumento, elevação; v., elevar, levantar, engrandecer, ajuntar, criar, educar.
RAI.SIN, s., uva seca, passa.
RAKE, s., ancinho, rodo, tipo dissoluto; v., limpar, ajuntar, farrear, revolver, remexer.
RAK.ER, s., ancinho, raspador.
RAK.ISH, adj., dissoluto, devasso, lascivo.
RAL.LY, s., reunião, reagrupamento; v., reunir, agrupar, ajuntar, organizar, reanimar.
RAM, s., carneiro; v., bater, golpear, forçar.
RAM.BLE, s. ato de vaguear; v., vaguear, vagabundear.

RAMB.LER, *s.*, vagabundo, errante, vadio.
RAM.I.FI.CA.TION, *s.*, ramificação.
RAM.I.FY, *v.*, ramificar.
RAMP, *s.*, rampa, declive, inclinação, fraude, embuste; *v.*, pular, saltar.
RAM.PA.GEOUS, *adj.*, violento, furioso.
RAM.SHACK.LE, *adj.*, periclitante; v, desmoronar, cair aos pedaços.
RANCH, *s.*, rancho, fazenda, estância, sítio.
RANCH.ER, *s.*, fazendeiro, rancheiro.
RAN.CID.I.TY, *s.*, ranço, rançosidade.
RAN.COR, RAN.COUR, *s.*, rancor, ódio, aversão.
RAN.DOM, *s.*, acaso; *adj.*, fortuito; *adv.*, por acaso, fortuitamente.
RANGE, *s.*, cadeia, cordilheira, extensão, calibre; *v.*, colocar, arrumar, percorrer.
RANG.ER, *s.*, guarda-florestal.
RANK, *s.*, fila, fileira, posto, categoria, nível, graduação; *v.*, enfileirar, organizar.
RAN.SACK, *v.*, revistar, explorar, saquear, pilhar.
RAN.SOM, *s.*, resgate, redenção, refém; *v.*, resgatar, remir.
RAN.SOM.ER, *s.*, resgatador, libertador.
RAP, *s.*, pancada, batida na porta; *v.*, bater, dar uma pancada, berrar.
RA.PA.CIOUS, *adj.*, rapace, voraz, ávido.
RAPE, *s.*, roubo, estupro, violação; *v.*, arrebentar, violentar, raptar.
RAP.ID, *adj.*, rápido; *s.*, torrente.
RA.PID.I.TY, *s.*, rapidez, celeridade, presteza.
RAP.TURE, *s.*, êxtase, enlevo, arrebatamento.
RARE, *adj.*, raro, rarefeito, bom, extraordinário.
RAR.E.FY, *v.*, rarefazer, rarear.
RARE.NESS, *s.*, raridade.
RAR.I.TY, *s.*, raridade.
RASE, *v.*, arrasar, destruir, demolir.
RASH, *adj.*, apressado, impetuoso; *v.*, arrebatar, tirar, arrancar.
RASP, *s.*, grosa, lima.
RASP.BER.RY, *s.*, framboesa.
RAT, *s.*, rato, ratazana; *v.*, caçar ratos, furar greves, comportar-se de maneira vil.
RATE, *s.*, razão, taxa, preço, medida, padrão, imposto predial; *v.*, taxar, cobrar imposto.
RATE.PAY.ER, *s.*, contribuinte de imposto predial.
RAT.ER, *s.*, avaliador.
RAT.I.FI.CA.TION, *s.*, ratificação.
RAT.I.FY, *v.*, ratificar, confirmar.
RAT.ING, *s.*, avaliação; censura.
RA.TIO, *s.*, razão, proporção.
RA.TI.O.CI.NA.TION, *s.*, raciocínio, tirocínio.
RA.TION, *s.*, ração; *pl.*, mantimentos, víveres; *v.*, racionar.
RA.TIO.NAL, *adj.*, racional, razoável, justo.
RA.TIO.NAL.ISM, *s.*, racionalismo.
RA.TIO.NAL.IZE, *v.*, racionalizar, raciocinar, medir, ponderar, avaliar.
RAT.TLE, *s.*, matraca, chocalho, tagarelice; *v.*, provocar ruído de matraca, chocalhar.
RAT.TLER, *s.*, falador, tagarela.
RAT.TLE.SNAKE, *s.*, cascavel.
RAU.CITY, *s.*, rouquidão.
RAU.COUS, *adj.*, rouco, rouquenho; espalhafatoso.
RAV.AGE, *s.*, devastação, destruição; *v.*, devastar, destruir, arruinar, roubar.
RAV.AG.ING, *s.*, saque; *adj.*, devastador, assolador.
RAVE, *s.*, delírio, fúria, raiva; *v.*, delirar, tornar-se furioso, desvairar.
RA.VEN, *s.*, corvo; pilhagem; *v.*, pilhar, saquear; *adj.*, de cor preta.
RAV.E.NOUS, *adj.*, famélico, esfomeado.
RA.VINE, *s.*, ravina, desfiladeiro, garganta.
RAV.ISH, *v.*, arrebatar, encantar, cativar; *v.*, raptar, violar.
RAV.ISH.MENT, *s.*, encanto, arrebatamento, sedução.
RAW, *s.*, ferida, inflamação; *adj.*, cru, insípido, bruto, novato, rude.
RAW.NESS, *s.*, crueza, dureza, aspereza.
RAY, *s.*, raio de luz, linha, corrente elétrica, traço; raia.
RAZE, *v.*, arrasar, destruir, aniquilar, extirpar, demolir.
RA.ZOR, *s.*, navalha, gilete, aparelho para fazer a barba.

RE, s., ré.
REACH, s., alcance, extensão, limite, objetivo; v., alcançar, atingir, obter, esticar.
REACT, v., reagir, retornar ao nível inicial.
RE.AC.TION, s., reação, reflexo; reflexos.
RE.AC.TION.ARY, adj., s., reacionário, revolucionário.
RE.AC.TOR, s., reator, reator nuclear.
READ, v., ler, entender, compreender.
READ.ABLE, adj., legível, compreensível, inteligível.
READ BACK, v., reler, tornar a ler.
READ.ER, s., leitor, declamador, quem faz leituras nas reuniões.
READ.I.NESS, s., prontidão, presteza, boa vontade, disposição.
READ.ING, s., leitura, revisão, correção, registro, interpretação.
RE.AD.JUST, v., reajustar, consertar, refazer.
RE.AD.JUST.ABLE, adj., reajustável, reformável.
RE.AD.MIS.SION, s., readmissão.
RE.AD.MIT, v., readmitir, tornar a aceitar.
READY, adj., pronto, preparado, disponível, fácil, acabado; adv., logo, imediatamente.
RE.AF.FIRM, v., reafirmar, confirmar.
RE.AGENT, s., reagente.
RE.AL, s., realidade, Real; adj., real, verdadeiro, verídico, legítimo, autêntico.
RE.AL.ISM, s., realismo.
RE.AL.IST, s., realista.
RE.AL.I.TY, s., realidade, verdade.
RE.AL.I.ZA.TION, s., realização.
RE.AL.IZE, v., realizar, efetuar, concretizar, cumprir, conceber.
REALM, s., reino, domínio, estado.
RE.AL.TY, s., bens de raiz.
REAM, s., resma.
RE.AN.I.MATE, v., reanimar, fazer reviver; adj., reanimado.
RE.AP.PEAR, v., reaparecer, ressurgir.
RE.AP.PEAR.ANCE, s., reaparição, reaparecimento.
REAR, s., parte traseira, traseiro, traseira, retaguarda; v., criar, educar, erguer, empinar.
REAR.GUARD, s., retaguarda.
REA.SON, s., razão, raciocínio, bom-senso; v., raciocinar, pensar, meditar.
REA.SON.ABLE, adj., razoável.
REA.SONED, adj., raciocinado, fundamentado.
REA.SON.ING, s., raciocínio.
RE.AS.SEM.BLE, v., reunir, reagrupar.
RE.AS.SERT, v., reafirmar, afirmar de novo.
RE.AS.SUR.ANCE, s., garantia, penhor.
RE.AS.SURE, v., tranquilizar, restaurar a confiança.
REB.EL, s., rebelde, revolucionário; v., rebelar-se, revoltar-se.
RE.BEL.LION, s., rebelião, revolta.
RE.BEL.LIOUS, s., rebelde, revolucionário, revoltado.
RE.BIRTH, s., renascimento.
RE.BOUND, s., ressalto, repercussão, ricochete; v., ressaltar.
RE.BUFF, s., repulsa, negativa, recusa.
RE.BUILD, v., reconstruir, refazer, remontar.
RE.BUT, v., refutar, retorquir, contradizer.
RE.BUT.TAL, s., refutação.
RE.CAL.CI.TRANT, adj., recalcitrante, obstinado, teimoso.
RE.CALL, s., revogação, chamada de volta; v., chamar de volta, revocar.
RE.CANT, v., retratar-se.
RE.CAP, s., pneu recapado; v., recauchutar um pneu, revestir, recapar.
RE.CA.PIT.U.LATE, v., recapitular, rever.
RE.CEDE, v., recuar, retornar, regredir; baixar a maré, escassear.
RE.CEIPT, s., recibo, recepção, recebimento; v., quitar, dar recibo.
RE.CEIVE, v., receber, aceitar, receptar, hospedar; sofrer, tolerar.
RE.CENT, adj., recente, novo, novel.
RE.CEP.TA.CLE, s., receptáculo, recipiente.
RE.CEP.TION, s., recepção, acolhida, recebimento, audiência.
RE.CESS, s., recesso, intervalo, pausa, segredo; v., fazer uma pausa, descansar.
RE.CES.SION, s., recessão.

REC.I.PE, *s.*, receita.
RE.CIP.I.ENT, *s.*, recipiente, recebedor.
RE.CIP.RO.CAL, *adj.*, recíproco, mútuo.
RE.CIP.RO.CAL.NESS, *s.*, reciprocidade.
REC.I.PROC.I.TY, *s.*, reciprocidade.
REC.I.TA.TION, *s.*, recitação, declamação.
RE.CITE, *v.*, recitar.
RE.CIT.ER, *s.*, recitador, declamador.
RECK.LESS, *adj.*, descuidado, imprudente, temerário.
RECK.ON, *v.*, contar, calcular, avaliar, pensar, supor.
RECK.ON.ER, *s.*, contador, calculista.
RECK.ON.ING, *s.*, cálculo, avaliação.
RE.CLAIM, *s.*, reclamação, reivindicação; *v.*, reclamar, reivindicar, aplainar.
RE.CLAIM.ING, *s.*, reivindicação.
RE.CLINE, *v.*, inclinar, inclinar-se, pender.
RE.CLUSE, *s.*, recluso, eremita.
RE.CLU.SION, *s.*, reclusão, detenção.
REC.OG.NI.TION, *s.*, reconhecimento, identificação.
REC.OG.NIZE, *v.*, reconhecer, identificar, confessar, saudar.
REC.OL.LECT, *v.*, lembrar, recordar.
REC.OL.LEC.TION, *s.*, recordação, lembrança.
REC.OM.MEND, *v.*, recomendar, insinuar.
REC.OM.MEN.DA.TION, *s.*, recomendação, aconselhamento.
REC.OM.PENSE, *s.*, recompensa, pagamento, indenização; *v.*, recompensar.
RE.COM.POSE, *v.*, recompor, refazer, reconstruir.
REC.ON.CILE, *v.*, reconciliar, harmonizar, ajustar, conciliar.
REC.ON.CIL.I.A.TION, *s.*, reconciliação, harmonização.
RE.CON.DUCT, *v.*, reconduzir.
RE.CON.NAIS.SANCE, *s.*, reconhecimento.
RE.CON.QUER, *v.*, reconquistar.
RE.CON.QUEST, *s.*, reconquista.
RE.CON.SID.ER, *v.*, reconsiderar.
RE.CON.SID.E.RA.TION, *s.*, reconsideração.
RE.CON.STI.TUTE, *v.*, reconstituir, refazer, recompor.
RE.CON.STI.TU.TION, *s.*, reconstituição.
RE.CON.STRUCT, *v.*, reconstruir, refazer.
RE.CON.STRUC.TION, *s.*, reconstrução, restauração.
RE.CORD, *s.*, registro, inscrição, protocolo, documento, arquivo; *v.*, registrar, anotar.
RE.CORD.ING, *s.*, gravação musical.
RE.COUNT, *v.*, relatar.
RE.COUP.MENT, *s.*, indenização, pagamento de danos; desquite.
RE.COURSE, *s.*, recurso, ajuda, auxílio.
RE.COV.ER, *v.*, recuperar, refazer.
RE.COV.ERY, *s.*, recuperação, melhora.
REC.RE.ATE, *v.*, recrear.
REC.RE.A.TION, *s.*, recreio, recreação.
REC.RE.A.TIVE, *adj.*, recreativo, divertido, alegre.
RE.CRIM.I.NATE, *v.*, censurar, recriminar, advertir.
RE.CROSS, *v.*, atravessar de novo, tornar a atravessar.
RE.CRUIT, *s.*, recruta, iniciante, novato; *v.*, recrutar.
RE.CRUIT.MENT, *s.*, recrutamento, alistamento.
RECT.AN.GLE, *s.*, retângulo.
REC.TI.FI.CA.TION, *s.*, retificação, acerto.
REC.TI.FY, *v.*, retificar.
REC.TI.LIN.E.AR, *adj.*, retilíneo.
REC.TI.TUDE, *s.*, retidão, retitude, equidade.
REC.TOR.ATE, *s.*, reitoria, reitorado.
REC.TUM, *s.*, reto, intestino reto.
RE.CUM.BENT, *adj.*, deitado, recostado.
RE.CU.PER.ATE, *v.*, recuperar, recuperar-se, recompor.
RE.CU.PER.A.TION, *s.*, recuperação.
RE.CUR.RENT, *adj.*, que se repete, periódico.
RED, *s.*, cor vermelha, rubor, vermelho; *adj.*, vermelho, ruivo, tinto; *v.*, avermelhar.
RE.DACT, *v.*, redigir, editar, escrever.
RE.DAC.TION, *s.*, redação, composição, escrito.
RE.DAC.TOR, *s.*, redator.
RED.DEN, *v.*, avermelhar, tornar vermelho, ruborizar.
RED.DISH, *adj.*, avermelhado, ruborizado.
RED.DISH.NESS, *s.*, vermelhidão, ruborização.

RE.DE.LIV.ER, *v.*, restituir, devolver.
RE.DE.LIV.ERY, *s.*, restituição, devolução.
RE.DEMP.TION, *s.*, redenção, libertação, liberação.
RED-HAIRED, *adj.*, com cabelo ruivo, ruivo.
RED.IN.TE.GRATE, *v.*, reintegrar, renovar, restaurar; *adj.*, renovado, refeito.
RED.IN.TE.GRA.TION, *s.*, reintegração, restauração.
RE.DO, *v.*, refazer, recompor.
RED.O.LENCE, *s.* perfume, aroma, odor.
RE.DOU.BLE, *v.*, redobrar, repetir.
RE.DOUND, *v.*, redundar, contribuir.
RE.DRAFT, *s.*, novo projeto.
RE.DRESS, *s.*, emenda, retificação, socorro; *v.*, emendar, retificar.
RED.SKIN, *s.*, pele-vermelha, índio.
RE.DUCE, *v.*, reduzir, rebaixar, diminuir, dar outra forma.
RE.DUC.ER, *s.*, redutor.
RE.DUC.TION, *s.*, redução, abatimento.
RE.DUN.DAN.CY, *s.*, demissão, exoneração, desemprego.
RE.DU.PLI.CATE, *v.*, reduplicar, duplicar, dobrar.
RE.DU.PLI.CA.TION, *s.*, duplicação, reduplicação.
REEF, *s.*, recife, escolho.
REEK, *s.*, fumo, vapor, fumaça; *v.*, esfumaçar, vaporizar, fumar.
REEL, *s.*, carretel, bobina, rolo, filme, molinete; *v.*, oscilar, bobinar, enrolar.
RE-ELECT, *v.*, reeleger.
RE-ELEC.TION, , *s.*, reeleição.
RE-EN.FORCE, *v.*, reforçar, fortificar; *s.*, reforço, fortalecimento.
RE-ES.TAB.LISH, *v.*, restabelecer, recompor.
RE-ES.TAB.LISH.MENT, *s.*, restabelecimento, restauração, reconstrução.
RE-EX.AM.INE, *v.*, reexaminar, rever.
RE.FEC.TION, *s.*, refeição, refeição frugal.
RE.FEC.TORY, *s.*, refeitório.
RE.FER, *v.*, referir, contar, dirigir, recorrer.
REF.ER.ENCE, *s.*, referência, menção, atenção.
REF.ER.EN.DUM, *s.*, referendum, referendo, plebiscito.
RE.FILL, *s.*, refil, carga nova; *v.*, reabastecer, recarregar.
RE.FINE, *v.*, refinar.
RE.FINE.MENT, *s.*, refinamento, requinte.
RE.FIN.ERY, *s.*, refinaria, usina de refino.
RE.FIT, *v.*, compor, consertar, refazer, fazer.
RE.FLECT, *v.*, refletir, meditar, pensar, raciocinar.
RE.FLEC.TION, *s.*, reflexão.
RE.FLEC.TOR, *s.*, refletor.
RE.FLEX, *adj.*, *s.*, reflexo.
RE.FLEX.IVE, *adj.*, reflexivo.
RE.FLOW, *s.*, refluxo.
RE.FORM, *s.*, reforma; *v.*, reformar.
REF.OR.MA.TION, *s.*, reforma, reestruturação, restabelecimento.
RE.FOR.MA.TO.RY, *s.*, reformatório.
RE.FRAC.TION, *s.*, refração.
RE.FRAIN, *v.*, abster-se de, deixar de.
RE.FRESH, *v.*, refrescar, reanimar, reabastecer, refrigerar.
RE.FRESH.ING, *adj.*, refrescante, calmante, repousante.
RE.FRESH.MENT, *s.*, refresco, descanso; lanche.
RE.FRIG.ER.ATE, *v.*, refrigerar, refrescar.
RE.FRIG.ER.A.TION, *s.*, refrigeração, refrescamento.
RE.FRIG.ER.A.TOR, *s.*, refrigerador, geladeira.
REF.UGE, *s.*, refúgio, esconderijo; *v.*, refugiar-se, retirar-se.
RE.FUND, *s.*, reembolso; *v.*, devolver, reembolsar.
RE.FUR.BISH, *v.*, renovar.
RE.FUS.AL, *s.*, recusa, negação, negativa.
RE.FUSE, *s.*, refugo, lixo, sucata; *v.*, recusar, recusar-se, negar.
RE.FUT.ABLE, *adj.*, refutável.
REF.U.TA.TION, *s.*, refutação, desmentido.
RE.FUTE, *v.*, refutar, contradizer, desmentir.
RE.GAIN, *v.*, recuperar, reaver.
RE.GAL, *adj.*, real, régio, próprio de um rei.
RE.GARD, *s.*, olhar, atenção, estima; *v.*, olhar fixamente, considerar, mirar.
RE.GARD.ING, *prep.*, com referência a, com respeito a.

RE.GAT.TA, *s.*, regata.
RE.GEN.CY, *s.*, regência.
RE.GEN.E.RA.TION, *s.*, regeneração.
RE.GENT, *s.*, regente.
REG.I.CIDE, *s.*, regicídio; regicida.
RE.GIME, *s.*, regime, sistema de governo.
REG.I.MENT, *s.*, regimento, grupo de soldados; *v.*, arregimentar, recrutar.
RE.GION, *s.*, região, zona, localidade.
RE.GION.AL, *adj.*, regional.
REG.IS.TER, *s.*, registro, inscrição, arquivo, torneira; *v.*, registrar, inscrever.
REG.IS.TRAR, *s.*, escrivão, registrador, oficial.
REG.IS.TRA.TION, *s.*, registro, matrícula, inscrição.
REG.IS.TRY, *s.*, registro, cartório.
RE.GORGE, *v.*, vomitar; engolir, sorver.
RE.GRESS, *s.*, regresso, volta, retorno; *v.*, regressar, tornar, voltar, retornar.
RE.GRES.SION, *s.*, regressão, regresso.
RE.GRET, *s.*, pesar, tristeza, arrependimento, desprazer; *v.*, lamentar, lastimar.
RE.GRET.FUL, *adj.*, pesaroso, lamentável, tristonho.
REG.U.LAR, *s.*, soldado regular, clérigo, partidário; *adj.*, regular, normal, ordeiro.
REG.U.LAR.I.TY, *s.*, regularidade, habitualidade, ordem.
REG.U.LAR.IZE, *v.*, regularizar, normalizar.
REG.U.LATE, *v.*, regular, regularizar, ajustar.
REG.U.LA.TION, *s.*, regulamento, norma, regra.
RE.HA.BIL.I.TA.TION, *s.*, reabilitação.
REIGN, *s.*, reino, reinado, domínio, poder; *v.*, dominar, reinar, governar.
RE.IM.BURSE, *v.*, reembolsar, pagar, quitar, saldar.
REIN, *s.*, rédea, refreamento, freio; *v.*, conduzir pelas rédeas, governar.
RE.IN.FORCE, *s.*, reforço; *v.*, reforçar.
RE.IN.FORCE.MENT, *s.*, reforço, apoio.
REIN.LESS, *adj.*, descontrolado, desgovernado.
RE.IN.SUR.ANCE, *s.*, resseguro.
RE.IN.TE.GRATE, *v.*, reintegrar, repor, recolocar.
RE.IN.TE.GRA.TION, *s.*, reintegração.

RE.IT.ER.ATE, *v.*, reiterar, refazer, repetir.
RE.JECT, *v.*, rejeitar, recusar, desprezar, negar.
RE.JEC.TION, *s.*, rejeição, desprezo, negativa.
RE.JOICE, *v.*, regozijar-se, alegrar-se, ficar satisfeito, alegrar-se.
RE.JOIN, *v.*, reunir, ajuntar, agrupar; responder, retrucar, retorquir.
RE.JU.VE.NATE, *v.*, rejuvenescer, remoçar, tornar-se jovem.
RE.JU.VE.NES.CENCE, *s.*, rejuvenescimento, remoçamento.
RE.LAPSE, *s.*, recaída, reincidência; *v.*, recair, reincidir.
RE.LATE, *v.*, relatar, contar, narrar, referir.
RE.LA.TION, *s.*, relação, narração, conto, alusão; parente.
REL.A.TIVE, *s.*, parente; o que é relativo; pronome, adjetivo ou advérbio relativos; *adj.*, relativo, referente.
RE.LAX, *v.*, relaxar, descontrair-se, pôr-se à vontade, descansar, repousar.
RE.LAX.A.TION, *s.*, relaxamento, repouso, lazer, ócio.
RE.LAX.ING, *adj.*, relaxante, repousante.
RE.LAY, *s.*, revezamento, estação de muda no correio antigo; *v.*, revezar, substituir.
RE.LEASE, *s.*, liberação, desobrigação, escape; *v.*, soltar, liberar, livrar.
REL.E.GATE, *v.*, relegar, exilar, banir, deportar, afastar.
REL.E.GA.TION, *s.*, desterro, exílio, expatriamento.
REL.E.VANT, *adj.*, relevante, destacado, relativo, pertinente.
RE.LI.ABIL.I.TY, *s.*, confiança, seriedade, fidelidade.
RE.LI.ABLE, *adj.*, confiável, seguro.
REL.IC, *s.*, relíquia, restos mortais.
REL.ICT, *s.*, viúva.
RE.LIEF, *s.*, alívio, socorro, assistência, apoio, remédio, relevo, saliência.
RE.LIEVE, *v.*, aliviar, assistir, ajudar, substituir, desobrigar.
RE.LI.GION, *s.*, religião, fé, crença, credo.

RE.LI.GION.LESS, *adj.*, sem religião, descrente.
RE.LI.GIOUS, *s.*, religioso, clérigo; *adj.*, religioso, devoto.
REL.ISH, *s.*, gosto, sabor, tempero, condimento, entusiasmo; *v.*, saborear, degustar.
RE.LIVE, *v.*, reviver.
RE.LUCT, *v.*, relutar, repugnar, resistir, opor-se.
RE.LUC.TANCE, *s.*, relutância, repugnância, oposição.
RE.LY, *v.*, confiar em, acreditar.
RE.MAIN, *s.*, sobra, resto, sobejo; *v.*, sobrar, restar, ficar, continuar.
RE.MAIN.DER, *s.*, resto, sobra, restante.
RE.MAKE, *v.*, refazer, recompor, reconstruir.
RE.MAR.RY, *v.*, recasar-se, casar de novo.
RE.ME.DI.AL, *adj.*, medicinal.
REM.E.DY, *s.*, remédio, curativo; *v.*, curar, remediar, corrigir.
RE.MEM.BER, *v.*, recordar, lembrar, relembrar, transmitir lembranças.
RE.MEM.BRANCE, *s.*, lembrança, recordação, memorial.
RE.MIND, *v.*, lembrar, recordar.
REM.I.NIS.CENCE, *s.*, reminiscência, lembrança, memória.
RE.MISS, *adj.*, negligente, desleixado, lento.
RE.MIS.SION, *s.*, remissão, perdão, absolvição.
RE.MIS.SIVE, *adj.*, remissivo.
RE.MIT, *v.*, remeter, enviar, mandar, adiar, absolver, desistir, reconduzir à cadeia.
RE.MIT.TEE, *s.*, destinatário.
RE.MIT.TER, *s.*, remetente.
RE.MOD.EL, *v.*, remodelar, refazer.
RE.MORSE, *s.*, remorso, escrúpulo, arrependimento.
RE.MORSE.FUL, *adj.*, arrependido, contrito.
RE.MOTE, *adj.*, remoto, antigo, distante, indireto, mediato, afastado.
RE.MOULD, *v.*, reformar, transformar, recriar.
RE.MOVE, *s.*, grau, degrau, distância, transferência, promoção; *v.*, remover, mudar.
RE.MU.NER.ATE, *v.*, remunerar, pagar, recompensar.

RE.MU.NER.A.TION, *s.*, remuneração.
RE.NAIS.SANCE, *s.*, Renascença, Renascimento.
RE.NAL, *adj.*, renal, próprio dos rins.
RE.NA.SCENCE, *s.*, renascença, renascimento.
REND, *v.*, rasgar, fender, despedaçar, rachar, lacerar.
REN.DER, *v.*, retribuir, devolver, dar, pagar, submeter, fazer, tomar.
REN.DER.ING, *s.*, interpretação.
REN.E.GADE, *s.*, renegado, traidor, desertor; *v.*, desertar, trair.
RE.NEW, *v.*, renovar, refazer, reanimar, reparar, recomeçar.
RE.NEW.AL, *s.*, renovação, renovamento, reforma.
RE.NOUNCE, *v.*, renunciar, desistir, abandonar, repudiar.
RE.NOUNCE.MENT, *s.*, renúncia, desistência.
REN.O.VATE, *v.*, renovar, reformar, refazer, recompor; *adj.*, renovado, refeito.
REN.O.VA.TION, *s.*, renovação.
REN.O.VA.TOR, *s.*, renovador.
RE.NOWN, *s.*, renome, fama.
RENT, *s.*, aluguel, renda, arrendamento; racha, fenda; *v.*, alugar, arrendar.
RENT.AL, *s.*, aluguel.
RENT-FREE, *adj.*, sem aluguel, livre de aluguel.
RE.NUN.CI.A.TION, *s.*, renúncia, desistência.
RE.OC.CU.PY, *v.*, reocupar.
RE.OPEN, *v.*, reabrir, tornar a abrir.
RE.OR.GA.NIZE, *v.*, reorganizar, recompor.
RE.PAIR, *s.*, reparo, conserto, reparação; *v.*, reparar, consertar, emendar.
REP.A.RA.TION, *s.*, reparação, restauração, indenização, satisfação.
RE.PAST, *s.*, refeição, ato de comer, comida.
RE.PAY, *v.*, reembolsar, retribuir.
RE.PEAL, *s.*, revogação, anulação; *v.*, revogar, anular, cassar.
RE.PEAT, *s.*, repetição, refrão; *v.*, repetir, reiterar, reproduzir.
RE.PEL, *v.*, repelir, rechaçar, repudiar, rejeitar.
RE.PEL.LENT, *s.*, repelente; *adj.*, repelente, que repele, repugnante.

RE.PENT, *v.*, arrepender-se.
RE.PEN.TANCE, *s.*, arrependimento, contrição.
RE.PER.CUS.SION, *s.*, repercussão.
REP.E.TI.TION, *s.*, repetição, recitação.
RE.PINE, *v.*, murmurar, lamentar-se.
RE.PLACE, *v.*, recolocar, tornar a pôr no mesmo lugar, repor, restituir.
RE.PLACE.MENT, *s.*, substituição, recolocação, reposição.
RE.PLAY, *s.*, partida decisiva; reprodução.
REP.LI.CA, *s.*, réplica, reprodução, resposta.
RE.PLY, *s.*, resposta, réplica; *v.*, responder, replicar, retorquir.
RE.PORT, *s.*, reportagem, relatório, informação, notícia; *v.*, relatar, referir, noticiar.
RE.PORT CARD, *s.*, boletim escolar.
RE.PORT.ER, *s.*, repórter, jornalista.
RE.PORT.ING, *s.*, reportagem, relatório de reportagem.
RE.POSE, *s.*, repouso, descanso, tranquilidade; *v.*, repousar, descansar.
RE.POSE.FUL, *adj.*, descansado, repousado, calmo, sossegado.
REP.RE.HEND, *v.*, repreender, censurar, advertir.
REP.RE.HEN.SION, *s.*, repreensão, advertência, censura.
REP.RE.SENT, *v.*, representar, constituir, revelar, simbolizar, encenar.
REP.RE.SEN.TA.TION, *s.*, representação, imagem, figura, espetáculo.
RE.PRESS, *v.*, reprimir, conter, subjugar, oprimir.
RE.PRES.SION, *s.*, repressão, opressão, subjugação.
RE.PRINT, *s.*, reedição, reimpressão; *v.*, reimprimir, reeditar.
RE.PRI.SAL, *s.*, represália, vingança, retaliação.
RE.PROACH, *s.*, repreensão, censura, vergonha; *v.*, repreender, advertir, difamar.
REP.RO.BATE, *s.*, réprobo; *v.*, reprovar, condenar; *adj.*, réprobo, condenado.
RE.PRO.DUCE, *v.*, reproduzir, reproduzir-se; multiplicar, propagar.
RE.PRO.DUC.TION, *s.*, reprodução, propagação, imitação.

RE.PROOF, *s.*, reprovação, repreensão, censura.
RE.PROV.ABLE, *adj.*, reprovável, censurável.
RE.PROV.AL, *s.*, censura, advertência, reprovação.
RE.PROVE, *v.*, reprovar, censurar, repreender.
REP.TILE, *s.*, réptil.
RE.PUB.LIC, *s.*, república.
RE.PUB.LI.CAN, *adj.*, *s.*, republicano.
RE.PUB.LI.CA.TION, *s.*, republicação, reedição, reimpressão.
RE.PUB.LISH, *v.*, republicar, reproduzir, reeditar, reimprimir.
RE.PU.DI.ATE, *v.*, repudiar, rejeitar, renegar, negar.
RE.PUG.NANCE, *s.*, repugnância, asco, aversão, nojo.
RE.PUG.NANT, *adj.*, repugnante, asqueroso, nojento.
RE.PULSE, *v.*, rejeitar, repudiar, repelir.
RE.PUL.SION, *s.*, aversão, repulsão, nojo.
REP.U.TA.BIL.I.TY, *s.*, respeitabilidade, respeito.
REP.U.TA.TION, *s.*, reputação, fama, honra.
RE.PUTE, *v.*, reputar, estimar.
RE.QUEST, *s.*, petição, requerimento, solicitação; *v.*, requerer, peticionar, solicitar.
RE.QUIRE, *v.*, requerer, pedir, solicitar, peticionar.
RE.QUIRE.MENT, *s.*, requerimento, exigência, necessidade, requisição.
REQ.UI.SITE, *s.*, requisito, pré-requisito.
REQ.UI.SI.TION, *s.*, requisição, requerimento, petição; *v.*, requisitar, confiscar.
RE.QUITE, *v.*, retribuir, recompensar, saldar, pagar.
RE.SALE, *s.*, revenda.
RES.CIND, *v.*, rescindir, revogar, quebrar, anular.
RE.SCIS.SION, *s.*, rescisão, anulação.
RES.CUE, *s.*, salvamento, liberação; *v.*, livrar, socorrer, ajudar.
RE.SEARCH, *s.*, pesquisa, investigação; *v.*, pesquisar, buscar, investigar.
RE.SEAT, *v.*, reassentar, colocar de novo.
RE.SECT, *v.*, ressecar, secar.
RE.SELL, *v.*, revender, tornar a vender.
RE.SELL.ER, *s.*, revendedor.
RE.SEM.BLANCE, *s.*, semelhança.

RE.SEM.BLE, v., assemelhar-se, parecer-se com, ser semelhante.
RE.SEM.BLING, adj., semelhante, parecido.
RE.SENT, v., ressentir-se com, magoar-se, ofender-se.
RE.SENT.MENT, s., ressentimento, rancor, ofensa.
RES.ER.VA.TION, s., reserva, restrição, limitação.
RE.SERVE, s., reserva, restrição, discrição; reservar, guardar, excluir.
RE.SERVED, adj., reservado, discreto, restrito.
RE.SERV.IST, s., reservista.
RE.SET, s., nova montagem, engaste; v., engastar, remontar.
RE.SIDE, v., morar, habitar, viver, residir.
RES.I.DENCE, s., residência, moradia, habitação.
RES.I.DENT, s., residente, habitante, morador; adj., residente.
RE.SID.U.AL, adj., residual, restante; s., saldo, resto.
RES.I.DUE, s., resíduo, resto, sucata.
RE.SIGN, v., renunciar, resignar-se, conformar-se, demitir-se.
RES.IG.NA.TION, s., resignação, demissão, exoneração, submissão.
RES.IN, s., resina.
RE.SIST, v., resistir, opor-se, repelir, impedir.
RE.SIS.TANCE, s., resistência, oposição.
RE.SIS.TANT, adj., s., resistente.
RE.SIST.I.BIL.I.TY, s., resistência, resistibilidade.
RE.SIST.LESS, adj., irresistível.
RES.O.LUTE, adj., resoluto, firme, determinado, consciente.
RES.O.LUTE.NESS, s., firmeza, determinação, resolução.
RE.SO.LU.TION, s., resolução, determinação, firmeza.
RE.SOLV.ABLE, adj., resolúvel.
RE.SOLVE, s., resolução, decisão; v., resolver, analisar, solucionar.
RES.O.NANCE, s., ressonância, repetição, eco.
RES.O.NATE, v., ressoar, ressonar, ecoar.
RE.SORT, s., estância turística, complexo para veraneio.
RE.SOUND, s., eco, ressonância; ressoar, ecoar.
RE.SOURCE, s., recurso, meio, fonte, riqueza.
RE.SOURCE.FUL, adj., habilidoso, hábil, desembaraçado.
RE.SPECT, s., respeito, preferência, deferência; respeitar, cumprimentar, acatar.
RE.SPECT.ABLE, adj., respeitável.
RE.SPECT.FUL, adj., respeitoso, atencioso.
RE.SPEC.TIVE, adj., respectivo, relativo, pertinente.
RES.PI.RA.TION, s., respiração.
RES.PI.RA.TOR, s., respirador, filtro, máscara de proteção.
RE.SPIRE, v., respirar.
RE.SPITE, s., repouso, pausa, intervalo, prorrogação.
RE.SPLEN.DENCE, s., resplendor, brilho.
RE.SPLEN.DENT, adj., resplandecente, brilhante.
RE.SPOND, v., responder, retrucar, reagir.
RE.SPON.DENT, adj., correspondente.
RE.SPONSE, s., resposta, réplica, responsório.
RE.SPON.SI.BIL.I.TY, s., responsabilidade.
REST, s., descanso, repouso, pausa, intervalo, resto, sobra; v., descansar, repousar.
RES.TAU.RANT, s., restaurante.
REST.DAY, s., dia de descanso, dia de repouso.
REST.FUL, adj., calmo, sossegado, tranquilo.
REST.ING, s., descanso, sossego, repouso.
RES.TI.TU.TION, s., restituição, indenização.
REST.LESS, adj., inquieto, irrequieto, impaciente, agitado.
RES.TO.RA.TION, s., restauração, restituição, restabelecimento, reparo.
RE.STORE, v., restaurar, restituir, restabelecer.
RE.STOR.ER, s., restaurador.
RE.STRAIN, v., reprimir, frear, refrear, dominar.
RE.STRICT, v., restringir, reprimir, limitar.
RE.STRIC.TION, s., restrição, limitação, repressão.
RE.SULT, s., resultado, consequência; v., resultar, originar, provir.
RE.SUME, v., recomeçar, retomar, reassumir, recuperar.

RÉ.SU.MÉ, s., resumo, sumário, compêndio.
RE.SURGE, v., ressurgir, ressuscitar, rugir.
RE.SUR.GENCE, s., ressurgimento.
RES.UR.REC.TION, s., ressurreição.
RE.SUS.CI.TATE, v., ressuscitar, ressurgir, reanimar.
RE.SUS.CI.TA.TION, s., ressuscitação, ressuscitamento.
RE.TAIL, s., retalho, varejo, venda a varejo; v., retalhar, vender a varejo.
RE.TAIN, v., reter, manter, conservar, guardar.
RE.TAKE, v., retomar.
RE.TAL.I.ATE, v., retaliar, vingar-se.
RE.TAL.I.A.TION, s., retaliação, vingança, desforra.
RE.TARD, s., retardamento, demora, atraso; v., retardar, demorar.
RETCH, v., ter ânsia de vômito, provocar vômito.
RE.TELL, v., repetir, tornar a dizer.
RE.TEN.TION, s., retenção, lembrança, memória.
RET.I.CENCE, s., reticência, reserva, discrição.
RET.I.CENT, adj., reticente, reservado, discreto.
RET.I.NA, s., retina.
RET.I.NUE, s., séquito, comitiva, acompanhamento, cortejo.
RE.TIRE, v., retirar-se, afastar-se, aposentar-se, recolher-se, deitar-se, ir dormir.
RE.TIRED.NESS, s., solidão, retiro.
RE.TIRE.MENT, s., retiro, afastamento, abandono, aposentadoria, intimidade.
RE.TIR.ING ROOM, s., privada, banheiro, lavabo, lavatório.
RE.TORT, s., réplica, resposta; v., responder, retrucar, replicar, retorquir, rebater.
RE.TOUCH, s., retoque; v., retocar, modificar, recompor.
RE.TRACE, v., volver pelo mesmo caminho; voltar, tornar, rememorar.
RE.TRACT, v., retrair, recolher.
RE.TRAIN, v., reciclar, retreinar.
RE.TRANS.FER, v., retransferir, transferir de novo.
RET.RI.BU.TION, s., retribuição, recompensa, castigo, pena, vingança.
RE.TRIEVE, v., reaver, recuperar, restaurar, corrigir, consertar.
RE.TRIM, v., arranjar de novo, rearranjar.
RET.RO.ACT, v., retroagir, reagir.
RET.RO.CEDE, v., retroceder, recuar, devolver.
RET.RO.CES.SION, s., retrocesso, recuo.
RET.RO.GRADE, adj., retrógrado, ultrapassado; v., regredir, retrogradar.
RET.RO.SPECT, s., retrospecto, rememorização; v., relembrar, rememorar.
RE.TRY, v., julgar novamente.
RE.TURN, s., regresso, retorno, volta, devolução, retribuição; v., voltar, regressar.
RE.TURN.ABLE, adj., retornável, restituível.
RE.UNION, s., reunião, encontro, assembleia.
RE.UNITE, v., reunir, unir, conciliar.
RE.VEAL, v., revelar, manifestar, mostrar, divulgar.
RE.VEAL.ER, s., revelador.
REV.E.LA.TION, s., revelação, anúncio.
REV.E.LA.TOR, s., revelador.
REV.EL.LER, s., pândego, festeiro, farrista, dissoluto.
REV.EL.RY, s., festança, orgia, folia.
RE.VENGE, s., vingança, desforra, represália, vendeta; v., vingar-se.
REV.E.NUE, s., renda, rendimento, proventos, taxas, impostos.
RE.VER.BER.ATE, v., reverberar, advertir, ecoar, repercutir.
REV.ER.ENCE, s., reverência, respeito, acatamento, deferência; v., reverenciar.
REV.ER.END, s., reverendo, clérigo, padre, pastor.
REV.ER.ENT, adj., reverente, respeitoso.
RE.VERSE, s., reverso, avesso, contrário, revés; v., inverter, transpor, abolir, anular.
RE.VERSE.LESS, adj., irreversível, imutável.
RE.VERS.ING, s., inversão.
RE.VERT, v., reverter, voltar, retroceder, retornar.
RE.VEST, v., revestir.
RE.VIEW, s., revista, inspeção de tropas, crítica literária, revisão; v., rever, recapitular.
RE.VIEW.AL, s., crítica, resenha.
RE.VIEW.ER, s., crítico, revisor.

RE.VILE, s., ultraje, injúria, ofensa; v., ofender, injuriar, ultrajar, insultar.
RE.VISE, s., revisão, conserto, emenda; v., revisar, corrigir, consertar, emendar.
RE.VI.SION, s., revisão, correção.
RE.VI.TAL.IZE, v., revitalizar, reforçar.
RE.VIVE, v., reviver, ressuscitar, surgir, renascer, animar.
RE.VIV.I.FY, v., revivificar, reviver, reanimar.
REV.O.CA.TION, s., revogação, derrogação, negação.
RE.VOLT, s., revolta, insurreição, sedição; v., revoltar-se, rebelar-se, rebelar.
RE.VOLT.ER, s., revoltoso, rebelde, revolucionário.
REV.O.LU.TION, s., revolução, levante, ciclo, revolução dos planetas.
REV.O.LU.TION.ARY, s., revolucionário, sedicioso.
REV.O.LU.TION.IZE, v., revolucionar.
RE.VOLVE, v., revolver, girar, ponderar.
RE.VOLV.ER, s., revólver, pistola.
RE.VUE, s., revista, teatro de revista.
RE.WARD, s., recompensa, gratificação; v., recompensar, gratificar.
RE.WRITE, v., reescrever, escrever de novo, tornar a escrever.
REY.NARD, s., raposa.
RHAP.SO.DY, s., rapsódia, elocução.
RHEA, s., ema, nandu, tipo de avestruz.
RHET.O.RIC, s., retórica, eloquência.
RHEU.MAT.IC, adj., reumático.
RHEU.MA.TISM, s., reumatismo.
RHI.NI.TIS, s., rinite.
RHI.NO, s., rinoceronte.
RHI.NOC.ER.OS, s., rinoceronte.
RHI.NOL.O.GIST, s., rinologista.
RHOMB, s., rombo.
RHOM.BOID, s., romboide.
RHUMBA, s., rumba.
RHYME, s., rima; v., rimar, versificar com rima.
RHYTHM, s., ritmo, cadência, compasso.
RHYTH.MIC, adj., rítmico, compassado.
RIB, s., costela, viga de uma ponta, filé, nervura; v., colocar vigas, zombar.
RIB.ALD, adj., velhaco, safado, cafajeste, grosseiro, depravado.
RIB.ALD.RY, s., velhacaria, safadeza, libertinagem.
RIB.BON, s., fita, tira, banda, fita de máquina de escrever; v., colocar fita.
RICE, s., arroz.
RICE.FIELD, s., arrozal; arrozeira.
RICE.POWD.ER, s., pó de arroz.
RICH, s., rico, ricos; adj., rico, valioso, forte, fértil, suculento, cheio, suave.
RICH.ES, s., riqueza, riquezas.
RICH.NESS, s., riqueza, opulência, abundância, fertilidade, excelência.
RICK.ETY,adj.,raquítico,fraco,débil, desnutrido.
RIC.O.CHET, v., ricochetear.
RID, v., libertar, livrar, liberar, desembaraçar.
RID.DANCE, s., libertação, liberação, desembaraço.
RID.DLE, s., enigma, charada, ambiguidade; v., decifrar, ler charada.
RIDE, s., passeio, passeio a cavalo, giro, percurso; v., cavalgar, passear, viajar, andar.
RID.ER, s., cavaleiro, amazona, viajante; ciclista, motociclista.
RIDGE, s., cume, cimo, pico; cumeeira, garupa; v., sulcar, arar.
RIDGY,adj.,sulcado,arado,trilhado pelo arado.
RID.I.CULE, s. ridículo, mofa, zombaria; adj., ridículo; v., ridicularizar, mofar, rir de.
RI.DIC.U.LOUS, adj., ridículo.
RID.ING, s., equitação, cavalgada.
RI.FLE, s., rifle, carabina, fuzil; v., saquear, roubar, pilhar.
RI.FLER, s., saqueador, salteador, bandido.
RIFT, s., fenda, greta, rombo; v., rachar, fender, abrir.
RIG, s., equipamento, torre para perfurar; fraude, brincadeira; v., equipar, fraudar.
RIG.GER, s., especulador.
RIGHT, s., direito, justiça, reivindicação, prerrogativa, a Direita; adj., direito, reto, justo, honesto, bom, sadio, normal; adv., corretamente,

com justiça.
RIGHT ANGLE, *s.*, ângulo reto.
RIGH.TEOUS, *adj.*, justo, reto, correto.
RIGHT.FUL, *adj.*, legítimo, justo.
RIGHT.LY, *adv.*, com razão, com justiça.
RIGHT.NESS, *s.*, retidão, justiça.
RIG.ID, *adj.*, rígido, duro, inflexível.
RI.GID.I.TY, *s.*, rigidez, inflexibilidade.
RIG.OR.OUS, *adj.*, rigoroso, severo, inflexível.
RIG.OUR, *s.*, rigor.
RILE, *v.*, irritar, aborrecer, incomodar.
RILL, *s.*, regato, riacho, arroio, ribeiro; *v.*, fluir, deslizar como água.
RIM, *s.*, borda, orla, aro, margem.
RING, *s.*, anel, aro, argola; ringue, picadeiro, arena; toque de campainha; *v.*, telefonar, soar campainha, bimbalhar de sino, badalar.
RING.ER, *s.*, sineiro.
RING.ING, *s.*, toque de sino, repicar, dobrar, bimbalhar.
RINK, *s.*, pista de patinação, rinque.
RINSE, *s.*, enxaguadura, lavagem; *v.*, lavar, bochechar.
RIOT, *s.*, distúrbio, motim, desordem, revolta; *v.*, amotinar, provocar distúrbios.
RI.OT.ER, *s.*, amotinador, sedicioso, revoltoso.
RIP, *s.*, rasgão, rasgo; *v.*, rasgar, dilacerar, romper; *adj.*, velhaco, patife, safado.
RIPE, *v.*, amadurecer, maturar; *adj.*, maduro, amadurecido, pronto, preparado.
RIP.EN, *v.*, amadurecer, maturar, desenvolver.
RIPE.NESS, *s.*, madureza, desenvolvimento, maturidade, desenvolvimento.
RIP.PING, *s.*, ato de rasgar, rasgamento.
RIP.PLE, *s.*, ondulação, onda; *v.*, ondular, encrespar.
RIP.SAW *s.*, serrote.
RISE, *s.*, ascensão, promoção, subida, lance de escada, cheia; *v.*, subir, levantar, aumentar, ressuscitar, crescer, vir à superfície.
RIS.ER, *s.*, degrau, levantador.
RIS.ING, *s.*, levante, ascensão, revolta, ressurreição, tumor.
RISK, *s.*, risco, perigo; *v.*, arriscar, pôr em risco, expor ao perigo.

RISK.FUL, *adj.*, perigoso, arriscado.
RISK.LESS, *adj.*, sem perigo, seguro.
RISKY, *adj.*, arriscado, perigoso, temerário.
RIS.SOLE, *s.*, rissole, pastelão, empada recheada com carne.
RITE, *s.*, rito, cerimonial, ritual, cerimônia.
RIT.U.AL, *s.*, ritual, cerimonial; *adj.*, ritual, cerimonial.
RIT.U.AL.ISM, *s.*, ritualismo.
RIT.U.AL.IS.TIC, *adj.*, ritualista.
RI.VAL, *s.*, rival, êmulo, adversário; *v.*, rivalizar, emular, competir; *adj.*, rival.
RI.VAL.RY, *s.*, rivalidade, emulação, competição.
RIV.ER, *s.*, rio.
RIV.ER.BANK, *s.*, margem de rio.
RIV.ER.BED, *s.*, leito do rio, álveo.
RIV.ET, *s.*, rebite; *v.*, arrebitar, rebitar.
RIV.U.LET, *s.*, ribeiro, riozinho, regato, arroio, córrego.
ROAD, *s.*, caminho, estrada, via, rodovia.
ROAD.BLOCK, *s.*, barreira em rodovia.
ROAD.HOUSE, *s.*, hospedaria à beira da estrada, estalagem.
ROAD.WAY, *s.*, estrada, rodovia, pista da estrada.
ROAM, *s.*, andança, passeio, caminhada ao léu; *v.*, vaguear, andar, girar, passear.
ROAM.ER, *s.*, errante, andarilho, caminhante.
ROAR, *s.*, rugido, urro, berro, bramido, barulho; *v.*, rugir, mugir, bramir, urrar, berrar.
ROAR.ING, *s.*, rugido, mugido, berro, bramido; *adj.*, estrondoso, estrepitoso.
ROAST, *s.*, assado, carne assada, assadura; *v.*, assar, tostar, assar muito.
ROAST.BEEF, *s.*, rosbife.
ROAST.ER, *s.*, assador, grelha.
ROB, *v.*, roubar, furtar, assaltar, pilhar.
ROB.BER, *s.*, ladrão, assaltante.
ROB.BERY, *s.*, ladroagem, roubalheira, furto, roubo, rapina.
ROBE, *s.*, toga, beca, vestimenta.
RO.BOT, *s.*, robô.
RO.BUST, *adj.*, robusto, forte, vigoroso, sadio, resoluto.
ROCK, *s.*, rocha, pedra, penedo, balanço; *v.*,

balançar, oscilar, embalar.
ROCK BREAK.ER, *s.*, britador.
ROCK.ER, *s.*, berço, cadeira de balanço; apreciador de música rock.
ROCK.ET, *s.*, foguete.
ROCK.LESS, *adj.*, sem rochas, sem pedras.
ROCKY, *adj.*, rochoso, instável, oscilante.
ROD, *s.*, vara, haste, bastão; **FISHING ROD** – vara de pescar.
RO.DENT, *adj.*, *s.*, roedor.
RO.DEO, *s.*, rodeio.
RO.GA.TION, *s.*, rogação, rogações, preces, pedidos.
ROGUE, *s.*, velhaco, safado, patife, cafajeste.
ROGU.ERY, *s.*, velhacaria, patifaria, safadeza.
ROGU.ISH, *adj.*, velhaco, safado, patife, maldoso.
ROIL, *v.*, turvar, perturbar, irritar.
ROIS.TER, *v.*, contar fanfarronices, alardear, vangloriar-se.
ROLE, *s.*, papel de artista, desempenho, função.
ROLL, *s.*, rolo, maço, cilindro, manobra, rol, lista; *v.*, rolar, enrolar, arregaçar, rufar.
ROLL.ER, *s.*, rolo, cilindro, roda, roldana, rolo compressor, laminador.
ROLL.ER COAST.ER, *s.*, montanha-russa.
ROLL.ING, *adj.*, ondulado.
RO.MAN, *adj.*, *s.*, romano.
RO.MANCE, *s.*, romance, aventura amorosa, romantismo.
RO.MAN.ESQUE, *adj.*, românico.
RO.MA.NIA, *s.*, Romênia.
RO.MA.NIAN, *adj.*, *s.*, romeno.
RO.MAN.ISM, *s.*, religião católica.
RO.MAN.I.ZA.TION, *s.*, romanização.
RO.MAN.IZE, *v.*, romanizar.
RO.MAN.TIC, *adj.*, romântico.
RO.MAN.TI.CISM, *s.*, romantismo.
ROME, *s.*, Roma.
ROM.ISH, *adj.*, católico romano.
ROMP, *s.*, brincadeira, travessura, traquinagem; *v.*, brincar ruidosamente.
ROMP.ISH, *adj.*, traquinas, moleque, travesso.
ROOF, *s.*, teto, telhado, cume, casa, abrigo; *v.*, cobrir com telhas, alojar, abrigar.

ROOK, *s.*, torre no jogo de xadrez; trapaceiro; *v.*, trapacear, fraudar, furtar.
ROOKY, *s.*, recruta, novato.
ROOM, *s.*, quarto, apartamento, cômodo, lugar, sala; morar em aposento.
ROOM.ER, *s.*, pensionista, sublocatário.
ROOMY, *adj.*, espaçoso, amplo, folgado.
ROOST, *s.*, poleiro, galinheiro, abrigo para aves; *v.*, alojar, empoleirar, pernoitar.
ROOST.ER, *s.*, galo.
ROOT, *s.*, raiz, causa, origem, começo, raiz matemática; *v.*, enraizar, arraigar, radicar.
ROOT.ED, *adj.*, enraizado, arraigado.
ROPE, *s.*, corda, cabo, baraço, fileira; *v.*, amarrar, atar com corda, laçar.
ROPE LAD.DER, *s.*, escada de cordas.
RO.SA.RY, *s.*, rosário.
ROSE, *s.*, rosa, roseira; *adj.*, cor-de-rosa.
RO.SE.ATE, *adj.*, rosado, cor-de-rosa.
ROSE.BUD, *s.*, botão de rosa.
ROSE.BUSH, *s.*, roseira.
ROSE.MARY, *s.*, alecrim.
RO.SETTE, *s.*, roseta.
ROS.IN, *s.*, resina, breu, pez.
ROS.TRUM, *s.*, tribuna, rostro; bico.
ROSY, *adj.*, rosado, rosáceo, cor-de-rosa, corado.
ROT, *s.*, podridão, putrefação; *v.*, apodrecer, putrefazer-se.
RO.TA.RY, *s.*, rotativa, máquina impressora; *adj.*, rotativo, giratório.
RO.TATE, *v.*, girar, rodar, revezar; *adj.*, em forma de roda.
RO.TA.TION, *s.*, rotação, revolução, movimento giratório, turno de revezamento.
ROTE, *s.*, rotina.
RO.TIS.SER.IE, *s.*, assadeira, churrasqueira, churrascaria.
ROT.TEN, *adj.*, podre, estragado, fedorento, corrupto.
RO.TUND, *adj.*, rechonchudo, redondo, roliço.
ROU.BLE, *s.*, rublo, moeda russa.
ROUGE, *s.*, ruge, carmim, batom; *v.*, passar batom.
ROUGH, *adj.*, tosco, áspero, rouco, violento, ríspido, mau; *v.*, domesticar, tornar áspero.

ROUGH.AGE, *s.*, fibras.
ROUGH.CAST, *s.*, reboco.
ROUGH.NESS, *s.*, aspereza, dureza, grosseria, rudeza.
ROU.LETTE, *s.*, roleta.
ROUND, *s.*, esfera, círculo, circunferência, anel, aro; *v.*, arredondar, arcar, circundar.
ROUND.ED, *adj.*, curvo, encurvado.
ROUND.ING, *s.*, arredondamento.
ROUND.NESS, *s.*, redondeza, esfericidade, clareza.
ROUND TA.BLE, *s.*, mesa redonda, conferência.
ROUSE, *s.*, alvorada, despertar; *v.*, acordar, despertar.
ROUT, *s.*, derrota.
ROUTE, *s.*, caminho, trajeto, via, rota, direção; determinar a rota.
ROU.TINE, *s.*, rotina, hábito; *adj.*, rotineiro, habitual, usual.
RO.VER, *s.*, errante, andarilho, caminhante; vagabundo, pirata.
ROW, *s.*, fila, fileira, travessa, motim; *v.*, enfileirar, remar, provocar desordem.
ROW.BOAT, *s.*, barco a remo.
ROW.DY, *s.*, desordeiro, baderneiro, arruaceiro; *adj.*, desordeiro.
ROW.ER, *s.*, remador.
ROY.AL, *adj.*, real, régio, majestoso.
ROY.AL.ISM, *s.*, realismo.
ROY.AL.IST, *s.*, realista.
ROY.AL.TY, *s.*, realeza, posição real.
RUB, *s.*, esfrega, fricção, atrito, obstáculo, crítica; *v.*, esfregar, atritar, roçar.
RUB.BER, *s.*, borracha, galocha, pneu, grosa, lima; *v.*, revestir com borracha.
RUB.BING, *s.*, fricção, atrito.
RUB.BISH, *s.*, sucata, lixo, detritos, refugo.
RUB.BISH.ING, *adj.*, inútil, insignificante, sem valor.
RU.BE.FY, *v.*, enrubescer, corar.
RU.BE.O.LA, *s.*, rubéola, sarampo.
RU.BI.OUS, *adj.*, vermelho, rubro.
RU.BRIC, *s.*, rubrica.
RU.BRI.CATE, *v.*, rubricar.

RU.BY, *s.*, rubi.
RUCK, *s.*, prega, dobra, ruga; *v.*, vincar, dobrar, enrugar.
RUCK.SACK, *s.*, mochila.
RUD.DER, *s.*, leme, timão.
RUD.DI.NESS, *s.*, rudeza, grosseria, aspereza.
RUD.DY, *adj.*, corado, avermelhado.
RUDE, *adj.*, rude, áspero, grosseiro, mal-educado, malcriado.
RUDE.NESS, má criação, má educação, incivilidade.
RU.DI.MENT, *s.*, rudimento, coisa elementar.
RUE, *s.*, pesar, compaixão, dó; *v.*, sentir pena, penalizar-se, condoer-se.
RUE.FUL, *adj.*, sentido, condoído, penalizado.
RUF.FI.AN, *s.*, rufião, desordeiro, malvado; *adj.*, brutal, perverso, malvado.
RUF.FLE, *s.*, folho, tufo, ondulação, irritação; *v.*, franzir, enrugar, irritar, amolar.
RUG, *s.*, tapete, capacho; *v.*, puxar, arrastar.
RUG.BY, *s.*, rúgbi, futebol americano.
RUG.GED, *adj.*, áspero, desigual, rugoso, austero, rigoroso, acidentado.
RU.GOSE, *adj.*, rugoso, enrugado, pregueado.
RU.IN, *s.*, ruína, destruição, queda, bancarrota; *v.*, arruinar, decair, falir, seduzir.
RU.IN.ATE, *v.*, arruinar, destruir, aniquilar.
RU.IN.OUS, *adj.*, ruinoso, desastroso.
RULE, *s.*, regra, norma, regulamento, domínio; régua; *v.*, determinar, regrar, decidir.
RULED, *adj.*, governado, dirigido, regrado.
RUL.ER, *s.*, governador, dirigente, regente.
RUM, *s.*, rum, aguardente.
RUM.BLE, *s.*, ruído surdo, assento traseiro, porta-bagagem; *v.*, fazer ruído.
RU.MI.NANT, *adj.*, *s.*, ruminante.
RU.MI.NATE, *v.*, ruminar, remoer; ponderar, considerar.
RU.MI.NA.TION, *s.*, ruminação.
RUM.MAGE, *s.*, busca minuciosa, desordem, confusão; *v.*, investigar, vistoriar.
RU.MOUR, *s.*, rumor, boato; *v.*, espalhar boatos.
RU.MOUR.ER, *s.*, boateiro.
RUMP, *s.*, anca, garupa, nádega, parte traseira.

RUM.PLE, *s.*, ruga, prega, dobra, vinco; *v.*, enrugar, amarrotar, preguear.
RUN, *s.*, corrida, passeio de carro, trajeto, percurso, pista, temporada; *v.*, correr, apressar, fugir, atingir, perseguir, pesquisar.
RUN.AWAY, *s.*, trânsfuga, desertor, vagabundo, fugitivo.
RUNG, *s.*, degrau, raio de roda.
RUN.NER, *s.*, corredor, mensageiro, espião, maquinista, corretor, anel.
RUN.NING, *s.*, corrida, direção, curso, contrabando; *adj.*, cursivo, corrente.
RUN.NING AC.COUNT, *s.*, conta-corrente.
RUN.NING WA.TER, *s.*, água corrente.
RUN.WAY, *s.*, pista de aterrissagem; canal, trilha.
RUP.TURE, *s.*, ruptura, hérnia; *v.*, romper, quebrar.
RU.RAL, *adj.*, rural, campestre, do sítio.
RU.RAL.IST, *s.*, camponês, colono.
RUSE, *s.*, ardil, artimanha, manha, armadilha.
RUSH, *s.*, pressa, ímpeto, movimento, fúria; *v.*, impelir, empurrar, apressar-se, atacar.
RUSH.ING, *s.*, carreira precipitada, ímpeto, arremetida; *adj.*, impetuoso.
RUSK, *s.*, rosca; biscoito.
RUS.SET, *s.*, cor avermelhada; *adj.*, avermelhado, ruivo.
RUS.SETY, *adj.*, moreno, trigueiro.
RUS.SIA, *s.*, Rússia.
RUS.SIAN, *adj.*, *s.*, russo.
RUST, *s.*, ferrugem, mofo, bolor; *v.*, enferrujar, mofar, criar bolor.
RUS.TIC, *s.*, pessoa rústica, camponês; *adj.*, rústico, agreste, rude, bruto.
RUS.TIC.I.TY, *s.*, rusticidade, vida rural, ignorância.
RUST.I.NESS, *s.*, estado de ferrugem.
RUS.TLE, *s.*, sussurro, murmúrio, ruído; *v.*, sussurrar, roçar, rugir.
RUST.LESS, *adj.*, sem ferrugem, desenferrujado.
RUST.PROOF, *adj.*, inoxidável.
RUS.TY, *adj.*, enferrujado, rançoso, bolorento.
RUT, *s.*, cio, excitação sexual de animais; sulco; *v.*, estar no cio.
RUTH, *s.*, pena, dó, compaixão.
RUTH.FUL, *adj.*, compassivo, penalizado, misericordioso.
RUTH.LESS, *adj.*, implacável, sem piedade, cruel.
RUT.TISH, *adj.*, lascivo, libidinoso.
RYE, *s.*, centeio.

S

S, *s.*, décima nona letra do alfabeto inglês.
SAB.BATH, *s.*, sábado para os judeus, domingo para os cristãos, dia de descanso.
SAB.BAT.IC, *adj.*, sabático.
SAB.O.TAGE, *s.*, sabotagem; *v.*, sabotar.
SA.BRE, *s.*, sabre.
SAC.CHA.RINE, *s.*, sacarina.
SA.CHET, *s.*, perfumador.
SACK, *s.*, saco, saca, despedida; *v.*, ensacar, exonerar, demitir.
SACK.ER, *s.*, saqueador.
SAC.RA.MENT, *s.*, sacramento.
SAC.RA.MEN.TAL, *adj.*, sacramental.
SA.CRED, *adj.*, sagrado, sacro.
SAC.RI.FICE, *s.*, sacrifício; *v.*, sacrificar.
SAC.RI.LEGE, *s.*, sacrilégio.
SAC.RI.LE.GIOUS, *adj.*, sacrílego, injurioso.
SACRING, *adj.*, sagrado, consagrado.
SAC.RIS.TAN, *s.*, sacristão.
SAC.RIS.TY, *s.*, sacristia.
SAD, *adj.*, triste, tristonho, deplorável, lamentável, escuro, sombrio.
SAD.DEN, *v.*, entristecer, tornar-se triste, deprimir.
SAD.DLE, *s.*, sela, selim, assento de bicicleta; *v.*, selar, pôr sela.
SAD.DLE.BAG, *s.*, alforje.
SAD.DLER, *s.*, seleiro.
SAD.IRON, *s.*, ferro de passar roupa, ferro de engomar.
SA.DISM, *s.*, sadismo, perversão.
SAD.NESS, *s.*, tristeza, melancolia.
SA.FA.RI, *s.*, safári.
SAFE, *s.*, cofre, caixa forte, guarda-comida; *adj.*, seguro, ileso, imune, cauteloso.
SAFE.NESS, *s.*, segurança, certeza.
SAFE.TY, *s.*, segurança, custódia.
SAFE.TY.BELT, *s.*, salva-vidas; cinto de segurança.
SAFE.TY-PIN, *s.*, pino de segurança.
SAF.FRON, *s.*, açafrão.
SAG, *s.*, queda, caída; *v.*, cair, afundar, desmanchar.
SA.GA, *s.*, saga.
SA.GA.CIOUS, *adj.*, sagaz, astuto, esperto, finório.
SA.GAC.I.TY, *s.*, sagacidade.
SAGE, *s.*, salva; sábio; *adj.*, sábio, instruído, letrado.
SAGE.NESS, *s.*, sabedoria, erudição, prudência.
SA.GO, *s.*, sagu.
SAID, *adj.*, *part.*, dito, referido, mencionado.
SAIL, *s.*, vela de navio, velame, veleiro; *v.*, velejar, viajar, navegar, singrar.
SAIL.BOAT, *s.*, veleiro.
SAIL.ING, *s.*, navegação a vela, partida.
SAIL.OR, *s.*, marinheiro, marujo, nauta.
SAINT, *s.*, santo, santa; *adj.*, santo; *v.*, santificar, canonizar.
SAINT.HOOD, *s.*, santidade.
SAINT.LIKE, *adj.*, santo, piedoso, devoto, pio.
SAKE, *s.*, causa, motivo, razão, fim, finalidade.
SAL.ABLE, *adj.*, vendável.
SAL.AD, *s.*, alface, prato de verduras, frios.
SA.LA.MI, *s.*, salame.
SAL.A.RIED, *adj.*, assalariado.
SAL.A.RY, *s.*, salário.
SALE, *s.*, venda, movimento de vendas, mercado.
SALE.ABLE, *adj.*, vendável.
SALE.ROOM, *s.*, sala de vendas.
SALES.MAN, *s.*, vendedor, caixeiro, balconista.
SA.LIENCE, *s.*, saliência, destaque.
SA.LIENT, *adj.*, saliente, destacado, evidente, óbvio, claro.
SA.LINE, *s.*, salina, solução de cloreto de sódio e água; *adj.*, salino.
SA.LI.VA, *s.*, saliva, cuspe.
SAL.I.VATE, *v.*, salivar, produzir saliva.

SAL.I.VA.TION, *s.*, salivação.
SAL.LOW, *adj.*, amarelado, pálido, esmaecido.
SAL.LOW.NESS, *s.*, palidez.
SALM.ON, *s.*, salmão.
SA.LON, *s.*, salão, sala, reunião; **BEAUTY SALON** – salão de beleza.
SA.LOON, *s.*, bar, salão, sala.
SALT.ERN, *s.*, salina, mina de sal.
SALT.ISH, *adj.*, um tanto salgado, salgado.
SALT.LESS, *adj.*, insosso, sem sal, insípido.
SALT.MINE, *s.*, salina, mina de sal.
SALT.PETRE, *s.*, salitre.
SALT.WA.TER, *s.*, água do mar; *adj.*, salgado, de água do mar.
SALTY, *adj.*, salgado.
SA.LU.BRI.OUS, *adj.*, salubre, saudável.
SA.LU.BRI.TY, *s.*, salubridade.
SAL.U.TARY, *adj.*, salutar.
SAL.U.TA.TION, *s.*, saudação.
SA.LUTE, *s.*, saudação, salva de tiros; continência; *v.*, saudar.
SAL.VAGE, *s.*, salvamento, recuperação; *v.*, salvar.
SALVE, *s.*, unguento, pomada, bálsamo, remédio; *v.*, untar, passar pomada.
SAL.VER, *s.*, bandeja, salva.
SAL.VIA, *s.*, salva, sálvia.
SA.MAR.I.TAN, *adj.*, *s.*, samaritano.
SAME, *pron., adj.*, mesmo, mesma, o mesmo, a mesma.
SAM.PLE, *s.*, amostra, prova; *v.*, examinar, provar, degustar.
SAN.ABLE, *adj.*, sanável, curável.
SAN.A.TO.RI.UM, *s.*, sanatório, hospital, casa de saúde.
SANC.TI.FI.CA.TION, *s.*, santificação.
SANC.TI.FY, *v.*, santificar.
SANC.TION, *s.*, sanção, autorização, confirmação; *v.*, sancionar, autorizar.
SANC.TI.TY, *s.*, santidade.
SANC.TU.ARY, *s.*, santuário, refúgio.
SAND, *s.*, areia, local de areia; *v.*, arear.
SAN.DAL, *s.*, sandália.
SAND.CASTLE, *s.*, castelo de areia.
SAND.GLASS, *s.*, ampulheta.
SAND.STONE, *s.*, arenito.
SAND.WICH, *s.*, sanduíche; *v.*, imprensar, colocar no meio de duas partes.
SANDY, *adj.*, arenoso, amarelado.
SANE, *adj.*, são, sadio, saudável, sensato, racional, ajuizado.
SAN.GUI.NARY, *adj.*, sanguinário.
SAN.GUINE, *adj.*, sanguíneo, vivo.
SAN.I.FY, *v.*, sanear, higienizar.
SAN.I.TARY, *adj.*, sanitário, higiênico, limpo.
SAN.I.TATE, *v.*, sanear.
SAN.I.TA.TION, *s.*, instalações sanitárias; serviço público de saúde.
SAN.I.TY, *s.*, sanidade mental, juízo, bom senso.
SAP, *s.*, seiva, humor; *v.*, esgotar, minar, sangrar.
SAP.FUL, *adj.*, cheio de seiva, viçoso, vigoroso.
SA.PID.I.TY, *s.*, gosto, sabor.
SA.PI.ENCE, *s.*, sapiência, sabedoria.
SAP.O.NA.CEOUS, *adj.*, saponáceo.
SAP.PHIRE, *s.*, safira.
SAR.A.CEN, *adj.*, *s.*, sarraceno.
SAR.CAS.TIC, *adj.*, sarcástico.
SAR.COPH.A.GUS, *s.*, sarcófago.
SAR.DINE, *s.*, sardinha.
SA.RI, *s.*, sari.
SA.TAN, *s.*, satã, satanás, diabo.
SA.TAN.IC, *adj.*, satânico.
SATE, *v.*, saciar, fartar, satisfazer.
SAT.EL.LITE, *s.*, satélite.
SA.TIA.BLE, *adj.*, saciável.
SA.TI.ATE, *v.*, saciar, fartar, satisfazer.
SA.TI.ETY, *s.*, saciedade, fartura.
SAT.IN, *s.*, cetim; *adj.*, acetinado; *v.*, acetinar, dar brilho de cetim.
SAT.IRE, *s.*, sátira, crítica, ironia.
SA.TIR.IC, *adj.*, satírico, irônico, crítico.
SAT.I.RIZE, *v.*, satirizar.
SAT.IS.FAC.TION, *s.*, satisfação, contentamento; indenização, pagamento.
SAT.IS.FIED, *adj.*, satisfeito, contente, farto, saciado.
SAT.IS.FY, *v.*, satisfazer, fartar, contentar, indenizar, agradar.

SAT.U.RATE, *v.*, saturar, fartar, satisfazer; *adj.*, saturado, farto, satisfeito.
SAT.U.RA.TION, *s.*, saturação, saciedade.
SAT.UR.DAY, *s.*, sábado.
SA.TYR, *s.*, sátiro.
SA.TY.RIC, *adj.*, satírico.
SAUCE, *s.*, molho, tempero, condimento; *v.*, temperar, condimentar.
SAUCE.PAN, *s.*, panela, caçarola.
SAUC.ER, *s.*, pires.
SAUCY, *adj.*, atrevido, descarado, petulante.
SAU.ER.KRAUT, *s.*, chucrute.
SAU.NA, *s.*, sauna.
SAUN.TER, *s.*, passeio, volta, giro; *v.*, andar ao léu, saracotear.
SAU.SAGE, *s.*, salsicha, linguiça.
SAV.AGE, *s.*, selvagem, bárbaro, pessoa bruta; *adj.*, bruto, rude, grosseiro, cruel.
SAV.AGE.RY, *s.*, selvajaria, barbaridade, grosseria.
SA.VANT, *s.*, sábio, cientista.
SAVE, *v.*, salvar, economizar, ganhar, defender, proteger, abrigar; *prep.*, exceto.
SAV.ER, *s.*, salvador, libertador.
SAV.ING, *s.*, economia; *pl.*, economias.
SA.VOUR, *s.*, sabor, gosto; *v.*, saborear, degustar, apreciar, provar.
SA.VOURY, *adj.*, saboroso, gostoso; salgado.
SAW, *s.*, serra, serrote; *v.*, serrar.
SAW.DUST, *s.*, serradura, serragem.
SAW.ER, *s.*, serrador.
SAW.YER, *s.*, serrador.
SAX.ON, *adj.*, *s.*, saxão; *adj.*, saxônico.
SAX.O.PHONE, *s.*, saxofone.
SAY, *s.*, palavra, fala, discurso; *v.*, dizer, falar, exprimir.
SAY.ING, *s.*, ditado, provérbio.
SCA.BIES, *s.*, sarna.
SCA.BI.OUS, *adj.*, sarnento.
SCA.BROUS, *adj.*, escabroso, áspero, rude.
SCAF.FOLD, *s.*, cadafalso, patíbulo, armação para enforcamento.
SCAF.FOLD.ING, *s.*, andaime.
SCALD, *s.*, escaldamento, queimadura; *v.*, escaldar, queimar, esterilizar.
SCALE, *s.*, escala; escama, caspa, crosta, cascão, graduação, balança; *v.*, escalar, subir, medir, ascender, pesar.
SCAL.ING, *s.*, escalada.
SCALP, *s.*, couro cabeludo do crânio; *v.*, escalpelar, tirar o couro da cabeça.
SCAL.PEL, *s.*, escalpelo, bisturi.
SCAMP, *s.*, velhaco, patife, cafajeste, safado.
SCAM.PI, *s.*, camarões fritos ao alho.
SCAN, *v.*, examinar, esquadrinhar, explorar, investigar, ajustar a *TV*.
SCAN.DAL, *s.*, escândalo, desonra, desgraça, difamação, calúnia.
SCAN.DAL.IZE, *v.*, escandalizar, desonrar, ofender, chocar.
SCAN.DAL.OUS, *adj.*, escandaloso, ofensivo, difamador, vergonhoso.
SCAN.DI.NA.VIAN, *adj.*, *s.*, escandinavo.
SCANT, *v.*, restringir, limitar, confinar; *adj.*, escasso, limitado, restrito.
SCANT.NESS, *s.*, insuficiência, escassez, limitação, carência.
SCAN.TLE, *v.*, cortar em pedaços, picar, fracionar.
SCANTY, *adj.*, escasso, insuficiente, limitado.
SCAPE.GOAT, *s.*, bode expiatório.
SCAR, *s.*, cicatriz, sinal; *v.*, cicatrizar, marcar.
SCARCE, *adj.*, escasso, raro, incomum.
SCARCE.NESS, *s.*, falta, carência, escassez, raridade.
SCAR.CITY, *s.*, escassez.
SCARE, *s.*, susto, espanto, assombro, pânico; *v.*, espantar, assustar.
SCARE.CROW, *s.*, espantalho.
SCARF, *s.*, cachecol, xale, lenço para a cabeça.
SCAR.LET, *adj.*, *s.*, vermelho.
SCARY, *adj.*, assustador, assustado, medroso.
SCAV.ENGE, *v.*, varrer, limpar.
SCE.NA, *s.*, cena.
SCE.NAR.IO, *s.*, cenário, panorama.
SCENE, *s.*, cenário, panorama, paisagem, escândalo, decoração teatral.
SCE.NIC, *adj.*, pitoresco, cênico.
SCENT, *s.*, cheiro, aroma, perfume, faro; pista,

pegada.
SCEP.TIC, *adj.*, *s.*, céptico.
SCEP.TI.CISM, *s.*, ceticismo.
SCEP.TRE, *s.*, cetro.
SCHED.ULE, *s.*, lista, programa, roteiro, tabela, horário; *v.*, tabelar, planejar, datar.
SCHE.MAT.IC, *adj.*, esquemático.
SCHEME, *s.*, esquema, maquinação, plano, sistema, método; *v.*, conspirar, maquinar.
SCHISM, *s.*, cisma, segregação, separação.
SCHIST, *s.*, xisto.
SCHO.LAR, *s.*, aluno, escolar, estudante; sábio, erudito, sabido.
SCHOL.AR.SHIP, *s.*, sabedoria, erudição; bolsa de estudos.
SCHOOL, *s.*, escola, colégio, universidade; aulas, corpo docente; *v.*, educar, ensinar.
SCHOOL.BOOK, *s.*, livro escolar.
SCHOOL.BOY, *s.*, aluno.
SCHOOL.GIRL, *s.*, aluna.
SCHOOL.ING, *s.*, educação, instrução, ensino, capacitação escolar.
SCHOOL.MAS.TER, *s.*, professor, mestre-escola.
SCHOOL.ROOM, *s.*, sala de aula.
SCHOO.NER, *s.*, escuna.
SCI.ENCE, *s.*, ciência, sabedoria, erudição.
SCI.EN.TIF.IC, *adj.*, científico.
SCI.EN.TIST, *s.*, cientista, sábio, pesquisador.
SCIN.TIL.LATE, *v.*, cintilar, brilhar.
SCIN.TIL.LA.TION, *s.*, cintilação, brilho, luminosidade.
SCIS.SION, *s.*, cisão, divisão, partição.
SCIS.SORS, *s.*, *pl.* tesouras.
SCLE.ROT.IC, *adj.*, esclerosado.
SCOFF, *s.*, zombaria, desprezo, escárnio; *v.*, zombar, escarnecer, mofar, ridicularizar.
SCOFF.ER, *s.*, zombador, escarnecedor, mofador.
SCONCE, *s.*, candeeiro, fortaleza; *v.*, fortificar.
SCOOP, *s.*, pá, concha, cavidade; espátula; furo jornalístico; *v.*, cavar, tirar com concha.
SCOOT, *s.*, corrida; *v.*, correr, fugir, andar apressadamente.
SCOPE, *s.*, escopo, objetivo, âmbito, abrangência, oportunidade, contexto.
SCORE, *s.*, escore, contagem, dívida, razão, motivo; *v.*, sulcar, arar, fazer pontos.
SCOR.ER, *s.*, marcador de pontos.
SCORN, *s.*, desprezo, escárnio, desdém; desprezar, desdenhar, escarnecer.
SCORN.FUL, *adj.*, desdenhoso, zombador, escarnecedor.
SCOR.PI.ON, *s.*, escorpião.
SCOTCH, *adj.*, *s.*, escocês, habitante da Escócia, dialeto escocês; uísque escocês.
SCOT.FREE, *adj.*, isento de impostos, livre de taxas.
SCOT.LAND, *s.*, Escócia.
SCOTS, *adj.*, escocês, escocesa.
SCOUN.DREL, *s.*, salafrário, patife, cafajeste; *adj.*, patife, safado, tratante.
SCOUR, *s.*, corrente, correnteza, lavação, *v.*, procurar, limpar, lavar, polir, perseguir.
SCOURGE, *s.*, flagelo, tormento, aflição, dor.
SCOUT, *s.*, batedor, explorador, escoteiro; *v.*, espiar, observar, examinar; **BOY SCOUT**, *s.*, escoteiro; **GIRL SCOUT**, *s.*, escoteira.
SCRAG.GY, *adj.*, magro, fino, esquelético.
SCRAM.BLE, *s.*, escalada íngreme, luta; *v.*, subir, ascender, lutar.
SCRAP, *s.*, pedaço, fragmento, resto, recorte; *v.*, despedaçar, fragmentar, esmagar.
SCRATCH, *s.*, arranhão, esfoladura, raspagem; *v.*, arranhar, riscar, marcar, labutar.
SCRATCH.ER, *s.*, raspador, raspadeira.
SCRAWL, *s.*, rabisco, garatuja, letra ilegível; *v.*, rabiscar, garatujar, escrever mal.
SCRAW.NY, *adj.*, magro, magricela, esquelético.
SCREAM, *s.*, grito, berro; *v.*, gritar, berrar, guinchar, rir alto.
SCREAM.ING, *s.*, gritaria; *adj.*, penetrante, agudo.
SCREECH, *s.*, guincho, grito forte, bramido, berro; *v.*, guinchar, berrar, bramir.
SCREEN, *s.*, biombo, divisória, tapume, para-brisa; *v.*, abrigar, esconder, examinar.
SCREEN.ING, *s.*, exame médico.
SCREW, *s.*, parafuso, porca, hélice; *v.*, parafusar,

atarraxar, montar, forçar, obrigar.
SCREW.DRIV.ER, *s.*, chave de fenda.
SCREW.NUT, *s.*, porca de parafuso.
SCRIBE, *s.*, escriba, copista, escrevente; *v.*, escrever, copiar.
SCRIM.MAGE, *s.*, escaramuça, contenda, disputa, luta.
SCRIPT, *s.*, argumento, roteiro, texto, escrita, caligrafia, enredo de um filme.
SCRIP.TURE, *s.*, Bíblia, Sagradas Escrituras.
SCRIV.EN.ER, *s.*, escriturário, secretário.
SCRO.TUM, *s.*, escroto.
SCROUNGE, *v.*, furtar, roubar, tirar de alguém.
SCRUB, *s.*, capoeira, mato, mata, moita; *v.*, esfregar, varrer, lavar, trabalhar.
SCRUBY, *adj.*, infeliz, inferior, miserável.
SCRUFF, *s.*, pescoço, nuca.
SCRU.PLE, *s.*, escrúpulo, hesitação, remorso; *v.*, hesitar, titubear, vacilar.
SCRU.PU.LOUS, *adj.*, escrupuloso, hesitante.
SCRU.TI.NEER, *s.*, escrutinador, conferente de votos em eleição.
SCRU.TI.NIZE, *v.*, escrutinar, examinar, conferir votos.
SCRU.TI.NY, *s.*, escrutínio, exame; apuração de votos.
SCUD, *s.*, fuga precipitada, vento forte, chuvisco; *v.*, chover, correr, fugir.
SCUF.FLE, *s.*, luta corporal, tumulto, pugilato, enxada; *v.*, lutar, brigar, arrastar os pés.
SCULP, *v.*, esculpir.
SCULP.TOR, *s.*, escultor.
SCUM, *s.*, espuma, escuma, ralé, escória; *v.*, escumar, formar espuma.
SCUM.MER, *v.*, escumadeira.
SCURF, *s.*, caspa.
SCUR.RY, *s.*, pressa, correria; *v.*, fugir, começar a correr.
SCUR.VI.NESS, *s.*, baixeza, vileza, baixaria.
SCUR.VY, *s.*, escorbuto.
SCUT.TLE, *s.*, cesto, balde; corrida, passeio; escotilha; *v.*, correr, afundar um navio.
SCYTHE, *s.*, segadeira, foice, alfanje; *v.*, ceifar, cortar, colher.

SEA, *s.*, mar, oceano, onda, movimento das ondas, dilúvio.
SEA.BOARD, *s.*, costa, litoral.
SEA.FAR.ER, *s.*, navegante, marinheiro.
SEA.FOOD, *s.*, marisco.
SEA.GULL, *s.*, gaivota.
SEA-HORSE, *s.*, cavalo-marinho.
SEAL, *s.*, foca; selo, brasão; *v.*, selar, fechar.
SEAM, *s.*, costura, sutura, ligação, cicatriz, sulco; *v.*, costurar, coser, fender.
SEA-MAID, *s.*, sereia.
SEA-MAN, *s.*, marinheiro, marujo.
SEAR, *s.*, marca, sinal de queimadura; *v.*, queimar, cauterizar, secar, murchar.
SEARCH, *s.*, busca, procura, pesquisa; *v.*, procurar, buscar, investigar.
SEARCH.ER, *s.*, pesquisador, investigador.
SEARCH-LIGHT, *s.*, farol, holofote.
SEA.SHORE, *s.*, costa, litoral, beira-mar, praia.
SEA.SICK, *adj.*, enjoado, enojado.
SEA.SICK.NESS, *s.*, enjoo do mar, nojo.
SEA.SON, *s.*, estação do ano, temporada; *v.*, temperar, condimentar, sazonar, madurar.
SEA.SON.AL, *adj.*, sazonal, próprio da estação.
SEA.SON.ING, *s.*, tempero, condimento.
SEAT, *s.*, assento, cadeira, poltrona, traseiro, nádegas, fundilho; *v.*, sentar-se, assentar-se, empossar, colocar, instituir.
SEAT.ING, *s.*, assento.
SE.BA.CEOUS, *adj.*, sebáceo, gorduroso.
SE.CEDE, *v.*, separar-se, retirar-se, abandonar.
SE.CES.SION, *s.*, secessão, separação, cisão.
SE.CLUDE, *v.*, excluir, segregar.
SE.CLU.SION, *s.*, segregação, exclusão.
SEC.OND, *s.*, segundo, segundo lugar; *adj.*, segundo; *adv.*, em segundo lugar.
SEC.OND.ARY, *adj.*, secundário.
SEC.OND.HAND, *adj.*, de segunda mão, usado.
SE.CRE.CY, *s.*, segredo, sigilo.
SE.CRET, *adj.*, secreto; *s.*, segredo.
SEC.RE.TAR.I.AT, *s.*, secretariado, secretaria.
SEC.RE.TARY, *s.*, secretária, secretário.
SEC.RE.TARY.SHIP, *s.*, secretariado.
SE.CRE.TION, *s.*, secreção.

SE.CRET.NESS, *s.*, segredo, sigilo.
SECT, *s.*, seita.
SEC.TAR.I.AN, *adj.*, sectário, sequaz.
SEC.TA.RY, *s.*, sectário, fanático.
SEC.TION, *s.*, seção, divisão, departamento.
SEC.TOR, *s.*, setor.
SEC.U.LAR, *adj.*, secular, leigo.
SEC.U.LAR.IZE, *v.*, secularizar.
SE.CURE, *adj.*, seguro, firme, rígido; *v.*, segurar, guardar, proteger, atar, ligar.
SE.CU.RI.TY, *s.*, segurança, fiança, garantia, apólice.
SE.DA.TION, *s.*, sedação.
SED.A.TIVE, *adj.*, sedativo, calmante.
SED.EN.TARY, *adj.*, sedentário.
SED.I.MENT, *s.*, sedimento, depósito, camada básica.
SE.DI.TION, *s.*, sedição, motim, revolta.
SE.DI.TIOUS, *adj.*, sedicioso, revoltoso, amotinado.
SE.DUCE, *v.*, seduzir, persuadir, convencer, corromper.
SE.DUC.ER, *s.*, sedutor.
SE.DUC.TION, *s.*, sedução.
SED.U.LOUS, *adj.*, diligente, assíduo, trabalhador, dinâmico.
SEE, *v.*, ver, perceber, olhar, observar, espiar, perceber, notar, descobrir, assistir.
SEED, *s.*, semente, grão, bulbo, broto, prole, esperma, muda; *v.*, semear, plantar.
SEED.ER, *s.*, semeador.
SEEK, *v.*, procurar, solicitar, tentar.
SEEK.ER, *s.*, investigador.
SEEK.ING, *s.*, procura, busca.
SEEM, *v.*, parecer, dar a impressão de.
SEEM.ING, *s.*, aparência, parecer, opinião.
SEEM.LI.NESS, *s.*, decoro.
SEEM.LY, *adj.*, decoroso, decente, pudico.
SEEP, *v.*, penetrar, infiltrar-se.
SEER, *s.*, vidente, profeta.
SEE.SAW, *s.*, gangorra, balanço, vaivém; *v.*, balançar, oscilar, brincar na gangorra.
SEG.MENT, *s.*, segmento, parte, divisão, seção; *v.*, segmentar.

SEG.RE.GATE, *v.*, segregar, afastar; *adj.*, segregado, afastado, separado.
SEG.RE.GA.TION, *s.*, segregação, afastamento.
SEIS.MO.GRAPH, *s.*, sismógrafo.
SEIS.MOL.O.GY, *s.*, sismologia.
SEIZE, *v.*, pegar, agarrar, pescar, entender, apreender, confiscar, capturar, ligar.
SEI.ZURE, *s.*, apreensão, confiscação, sequestro, embargo, ataque, derrame cerebral.
SEL.DOM, *adv.*, raramente.
SE.LECT, *v.*, selecionar, escolher; *adj.*, seleto, escolhido, fino, especial, exclusivo.
SE.LEC.TION, *s.*, seleção, escolha.
SELF, *pron.*, mesmo, mesma; próprio, própria.
SELF-CEN.TRED, *adj.*, egocêntrico, egoísta.
SELF-CON.FI.DENCE, *s.*, autoconfiança.
SELF-CON.SCIOUS, *adj.*, inibido, tímido, constrangido.
SELF-CON.TROL, *s.*, autodomínio.
SELF-DE.FENCE, *s.*, legítima defesa.
SELF-GOV.ERN.ING, *s.*, autônomo.
SELF-IN.TER.EST, *s.*, egoísmo.
SELF.ISH, *adj.*, egoísta.
SELF-POR.TRAIT, *s.*, autorretrato.
SELF-PRES.ER.VA.TION, *s.*, autodefesa.
SELF-RE.SPECT, *s.*, amor próprio.
SELF.SAME, *adj.*, mesmo, idêntico, igual.
SELF-SER.VICE, *s.*, self-service, serviço para si mesmo.
SELF-SUF.FI.CIENT, *adj.*, autossuficiente.
SELF-TAUGHT, *s.*, autodidata.
SELL, *v.*, vender; vender-se.
SELL.ER, *s.*, vendedor.
SELL.ING, *s.*, venda, ato de vender.
SEL.LO.TAPE, *s.*, fita adesiva.
SEL.VAGE, *s.*, borda, margem, borda; *v.*, orlar, margear.
SEM.A.PHORE, *s.*, semáforo.
SEM.BLANCE, *s.*, aparência, semelhança, imagem.
SE.MEN, *s.*, sêmen.
SE.MES.TER, *s.*, semestre.
SEMI.CIR.CLE, *s.*, semicírculo.
SEMI.CO.LON, *s.*, ponto e vírgula.

SEMI.CON.DUC.TOR, *s.*, semicondutor.
SEMI.FI.NAL, *s.*, semifinal.
SEM.I.NAR, *s.*, seminário, curso.
SEM.I.NARY, *s.*, seminário.
SEM.ITE, *s.*, semita.
SEMI.TROP.I.CAL, *adj.*, subtropical.
SEN.ATE, *s.*, senado.
SEN.A.TOR, *s.*, senador.
SEND, *v.*, enviar, mandar, remeter, expedir.
SEND.ER, *s.*, remetente.
SE.NILE, *adj.*, senil.
SE.NIL.I.TY, *s.*, senilidade, velhice.
SE.NIOR, *adj.*, sênior, mais velho, mais antigo.
SE.NIOR.I.TY, *s.*, antiguidade, senioridade.
SEN.SA.TION, *s.*, sensação, percepção, sentimento.
SENSE, *s.*, senso, sentido, sensação; *v.*, sentir, perceber.
SENSE.LESS, *adj.*, insensato, tolo, desajuizado.
SEN.SI.BIL.I.TY, *s.*, sensibilidade.
SEN.SI.BLE, *adj.*, sensível, sensato.
SEN.SI.TI.ZA.TION, *s.*, sensibilização.
SEN.SO.RI.AL, *adj.*, sensorial.
SEN.SU.AL, *adj.*, sensual.
SEN.SU.AL.ISM, *s.*, sensualismo.
SEN.SU.AL.I.TY, *s.*, sensualidade, libidinismo, lascívia.
SEN.TENCE, *s.*, frase, período, sentença; *v.*, sentenciar, condenar, absolver.
SEN.TEN.TIOUS, *adj.*, sentencioso.
SEN.TI.MENT, *s.*, sentimento, opinião, parecer.
SEN.TI.MEN.TAL.ISM, *s.*, sentimentalismo.
SEN.TRY, *s.*, sentinela.
SEP.A.RATE, *v.*, separar, apartar, desligar; *adj.*, separado, apartado.
SEP.A.RATE.NESS, *s.*, separação.
SEP.A.RA.TION, *s.*, separação.
SEP.TEM.BER, *s.*, setembro.
SEP.TIC, *adj.*, séptico.
SEP.TU.A.GE.NAR.I.AN, *adj., s.*, septuagenário.
SE.PUL.CHRAL, *adj.*, sepulcral.
SEP.UL.TURE, *s.*, sepultura, cova.
SE.QUEL, *s.*, resultado, consequência, continuação, sequência.
SE.QUENCE, *s.*, sequência, série, continuidade.
SE.QUES.TRATE, *v.*, sequestrar, raptar.
SER.APH, *s.*, serafim.
SERB, *adj., s.*, sérvio.
SER.E.NADE, *s.*, serenata; *v.*, fazer serenata, cantar serenatas.
SE.RENE, *adj.*, sereno, calmo, tranquilo.
SE.REN.I.TY, *s.*, serenidade, calmaria, calma.
SERF, *s.*, servo, serviçal, escravo.
SERF.DOM, *s.*, servidão, escravidão.
SER.GEANT, *s.*, sargento.
SE.RI.AL, *s.*, série, seriado, sequência de um filme durante dias.
SE.RIES, *s.*, série.
SE.RI.OUS, *adj.*, sério, severo, importante, grave.
SER.MON, *s.*, sermão.
SER.PENT, *s.*, serpente, cobra.
SE.RUM, *s.*, soro.
SER.VANT, *s.*, servo, empregado.
SERVE, *v.*, servir, atender, passar por, cumprir pena, trabalhar como criado.
SERV.ER, *s.*, servidor.
SER.VICE, *s.*, serviço, culto religioso, revisão de carro.
SER.VICE.MAN, *s.*, militar.
SER.VI.ETTE, *s.*, guardanapo.
SER.VIL.I.TY, *s.*, servilidade, servilismo, baixeza.
SER.VI.TOR, *s.*, servidor, criado, serviçal.
SER.VI.TUDE, *s.*, servidão, escravidão.
SES.SION, *s.*, sessão.
SET, *s.*, jogo, conjunto, aparelho elétrico, série, facção, forma, ajuste, desvio, cenário; *v.*, pôr, colocar, fixar, endurecer, solidificar.
SET.BACK, *s.*, revés, contratempo.
SET.TEE, *s.*, sofá.
SET.TING, *s.*, cenário, pôr do sol.
SET.TLE, *s.*, sofá, poltrona; *v.*, assentar, estabelecer, decidir, fixar, fixar residência.
SET.TLE.MENT, *s.*, liquidação, acordo, fixação, arranjo, pagamento, fundação.
SET.TLER, *s.*, colono, fazendeiro.
SEV.EN, *num.*, sete, número sete.
SEV.EN.FOLD, *adj.*, sétuplo; *adv.*, sete vezes.
SEV.EN.TEEN, *num.*, dezessete.

SEV.EN.TEENTH, *num.*, décimo sétimo.
SEV.ENTH, *num.*, sétimo.
SEV.EN.TY, *num.*, setenta.
SEV.ER, *v.*, cortar, partir, dividir, rachar.
SEV.ER.AL, *pron.*, vário, vários, vária, várias; algum, alguns.
SE.VERE, *adj.*, severo, austero, sério, violento, rígido.
SE.VER.I.TY, *s.*, severidade, rigor, austeridade.
SEW, *v.*, costurar.
SEW.AGE, *s.*, detritos, esgotos.
SEW.ING, *s.*, costura.
SEW UP, *v.*, coser, costurar.
SEX, *s.*, sexo; *adj.*, sexual, próprio do sexo.
SEX.A.GE.NAR.I.AN, *adj.*, *s.*, sexagenário.
SEX.LESS, *adj.*, assexuado, sem sexo.
SEX.TET, *s.*, sexteto.
SEX.U.AL, *adj.*, sexual.
SEX.U.AL.I.TY, *s.*, sexualidade.
SEXY, *adj.*, séxi, sensual, lascivo.
SHAB.BY, *adj.*, esfarrapado, maltrapilho, usado.
SHACK, *s.*, choupana, cabana, barraca.
SHADE, *s.*, sombra, abajur, tom, matiz; *v.*, sombrear, matizar.
SHADE.NESS, *s.*, escuridão, sombra, trevas.
SHAD.OW, *s.*, sombra; *v.*, acompanhar, seguir de perto sem ser visto, perseguir.
SHADY, *adj.*, sombreado, sombrio.
SHAH, *s.*, xá.
SHAKE, *s.*, abalo, agitação, vibração, terremoto, bebida batida; *v.*, agitar, derrubar.
SHAK.ING, *s.*, abalo, tremor, agitação; *adj.*, agitado, tremido.
SHALE, *s.*, xisto.
SHAL.LOW, *s.*, baixio, local raso; *v.*, tornar raso; *adj.*, raso, superficial.
SHAM, *s.*, fraude, fingimento, pretexto, logro; *v.*, pretender, fingir, fraudar.
SHAM.BLES, *s.*, matadouro, matança, confusão.
SHAME, *s.*, vergonha, humilhação, degradação, desgraça; *v.*, envergonhar, degradar.
SHAME.FUL, *adj.*, vergonhoso, degradado.
SHAME.FUL.NESS, *s.*, vergonha, humilhação.
SHAM.POO, *s.*, xampu, massagem; *v.*, lavar, massagear, lavar o cabelo.
SHAN.TY, *s.*, cabana, choça, choupana.
SHAPE, *s.*, forma, molde, formação, modelo; *v.*, moldar, formar, dar forma, adaptar.
SHAPE.LY, *adj.*, formoso, bem formado, simétrico.
SHARE, *s.*, parte, cota, ação, fração; *v.*, ter em comum, partilhar, dividir, ter interesse.
SHARK, *s.*, tubarão; tipo velhaco.
SHARP, *s.*, sustenido; *adj.*, afiado, pontiagudo, agudo, acre, desonesto, marcado.
SHARP.EN, *v.*, afiar, amolar, aguçar.
SHARP.EN.ER, *s.*, afiador, amolador; apontador de lápis.
SHARP.ER, *s.*, vigarista, trapaceiro, velhaco.
SHAT.TER, *v.*, despedaçar, fragmentar, rachar, perturbar, destruir, arrasar, assolar.
SHAVE, *s.*, barbeamento; navalha, gilete; *v.*, barbear, fazer a barba, raspar a barba.
SHAV.EN, *adj.*, barbeado, com a barba feita.
SHAV.ER, *s.*, barbeiro, aparelho para fazer a barba.
SHAWL, *s.*, xale, cachecol; *v.*, colocar xale.
SHE, *pron.*, ela.
SHEAR.ING, *s.*, tosquia.
SHEATH, *s.*, bainha, camisa de Vênus, preservativo, camisinha.
SHEEN, *s.*, brilho, resplendor, luminosidade.
SHEEP, *s.*, carneiro, ovelha.
SHEEP.DOG, *s.*, cão pastor.
SHEER, *adj.*, puro, diáfano, transparente, translúcido.
SHEET, *s.*, lençol, folha de papel, chapa, lâmina, camada.
SHELF, *s.*, estante, prateleira, banco de areia.
SHELL, *s.*, casca, concha, aparência; bomba, granada; *v.*, descascar, bombardear.
SHELL.FISH, *s.*, crustáceo, molusco, marisco; frutos do mar.
SHEL.TER, *s.*, defesa, coberta, refúgio, abrigo; *v.*, proteger, abrigar, esconder.
SHELVE, *v.*, descartar, pôr na prateleira; adiar.
SHEP.HERD, *s.*, pastor, zagal; *v.*, proteger, guiar, zelar.

SHEP.HERD.ESS, s., pastora.
SHER.IFF, s., xerife.
SHIELD, s., escudo, proteção, defesa; v., proteger, defender, cobrir, servir de escudo.
SHIFT, s., mudança, turno, troca, esquema, truque; v., mudar, variar, mudar de rumo.
SHIFT.ING, s., esperteza, astúcia, mudança.
SHIFTY, adj., esperto, sagaz, astuto, finório.
SHIL.LING, s., xelim.
SHIN, s., canela da perna.
SHINE, s., brilho, lustre, resplendor, luminosidade; v., brilhar, luzir, reluzir, ressaltar.
SHIN.GLE, s., seixos, cascalho, pedrinha, pedregulho.
SHINY, adj., lustroso, brilhante, luminoso.
SHIP, s., navio, embarcação, vapor; v., embarcar, colocar a bordo, enviar, mandar.
SHIP.MAS.TER, s., capitão de navio mercante.
SHIP.MENT, s., embarque, carregamento.
SHIP.PER, s., expedidor, exportador.
SHIP.WRECK, s., naufrágio, desastre, malogro.
SHIP.YARD, s., estaleiro.
SHIRT, s., camisa, blusa.
SHIV.ER, s., tremor, arrepio, pedaço; v., tremer, estremecer.
SHIV.ER.ING, s., arrepio, calafrio, tremor de frio.
SHOAL, s., cardume, bando, multidão, baixio.
SHOCK, s., choque, choque elétrico, susto, trauma; v., pregar um susto, escandalizar.
SHOCK.ING, adj., revoltante, chocante.
SHOE, s., sapato, ferradura; v., ferrar, colocar ferradura.
SHOE.BRUSH, s., escova de sapatos.
SHOE.LACE, s., cadarço, cordão de sapato.
SHOE.LESS, adj., descalço.
SHOE.MAK.ER, s., sapateiro.
SHOE.SHOP, s., loja que vende calçados; sapataria.
SHOOT, s., tiro, chute, caça, rebento, broto, filmagem; v., atirar, matar, dar tiro.
SHOOT.ER, s., atirador.
SHOOT.ING, s., caça, ação de atirar, tiroteio, fuzilamento.

SHOP, s., loja, oficina; v., fazer compras.
SHOP.KEEP.ER, s., lojista, comerciante.
SHOP.PER, s., comprador.
SHOP.PING, s., compras.
SHORE, s., costa, praia, litoral; v., escorar, estaquear, reforçar.
SHORT, s., short, calças curtas, som curto, curto-circuito; adj., curto, breve, baixo, pequeno, insuficiente, pouco, ab-rupto, rude.
SHORT.AGE, s., escassez, carência, falta.
SHORT.BREAD, s., biscoito.
SHORT.CUT, s., atalho.
SHORT.EN, v., encurtar, abreviar, resumir.
SHORT.FALL, s., déficit.
SHORT.NESS, s., brevidade, concisão.
SHOT, s., tiro, chumbo, injeção, projétil, descarga, fotografia.
SHOT.GUN, s., espingarda.
SHOUL.DER, s., ombro, costas, quarto dianteiro; v., pôr nos ombros, carregar.
SHOUL.DER-BLADE, s., omoplata.
SHOUT, s., grito, berro, gargalhada; v., berrar, gritar, rir alto, gargalhar.
SHOVE, s., empurrão; v., empurrar, impulsionar, atropelar.
SHOV.EL, s., escavadeira.
SHOW, s., show, espetáculo, apresentação, exposição; v., mostrar, exibir, expor.
SHOW.ER, s., aguaceiro, enxurrada; expositor, mostrador.
SHOW.ER.PROOF, adj., impermeável.
SHOW.ING, s., projeção, exibição.
SHOW.MAN, s., empresário, homem de espetáculos.
SHOW.ROOM, s., sala de exposições, mostruário.
SHRAP.NEL, s., estilhaços.
SHRED, s., tira, pedaço, fragmento; v., cortar em tiras, despedaçar.
SHREW, s., bruxa, mulher encrenqueira, megera; víbora.
SHREWD, adj., inteligente, astuto, sagaz, perspicaz.
SHREWD.NESS, s., astúcia, esperteza, sagacidade.

SHRIMP, s., camarão.
SHRINK, v., encolher, reduzir-se.
SHRINK.AGE, s., encolhimento, redução, apequenamento.
SHRINK.ING, s., contração, encolhimento.
SHROUD, s., mortalha, coberta; v., amortalhar, cobrir, envolver.
SHRUB, s., arbusto.
SHUCK, s., casca, vagem.
SHUD.DER, s., estremecimento, tremor, tremedeira; v., estremecer, tremer.
SHUF.FLER, s., trapaceiro, enganador.
SHUF.FLING, s., confusão, evasiva.
SHUT, v., fechar, tapar, tampar, cerrar.
SHUT.TER, s., veneziana, folha de janela.
SHUT.TLE, s., naveta, lançadeira, vaivém, máquina de costura.
SHY, s., sobressalto; adj., tímido, reservado, medroso; v., espantar-se, recuar.
SHY.NESS, s., timidez, acanhamento.
SI, s., nota musical si.
SI.BE.RI.AN, adj., s., siberiano.
SIB.I.LANT, s., consoante sibilante, sibilo; adj., sibilante.
SICK, pl., doentes; adj., doente, enfermo, enjoado, aflito; v., açular, instigar, atacar.
SICK BAY, s., enfermaria.
SICK.EN, v., ficar doente, adoentar-se.
SICK.LI.NESS, s., indisposição, náusea, mal-estar.
SICK.LY, adj., doente, enfermiço, adoentado, enfermo.
SICK.NESS, s., doença, enfermidade, náusea, enjoo, enfado.
SIDE, s., lado, flanco, margem, face, superfície, aspecto, declive, grupo; v., tomar partido, ser favorável a; adj., lateral, de lado.
SIDE.BOARD, s., guarda-louça.
SIDE.LIGHT, s., luz lateral do carro.
SIDE.SHOW, s., espetáculo colocado no intervalo de um grande espetáculo.
SIDE.TRACK, s., desvio, beco, rua sem saída.
SIDE.WALK, s., calçada, passeio.
SIDE.WAY, s., estrada secundária, rua lateral.

SIEVE, s., peneira; v., peneirar.
SIFT, v., peneirar, examinar, vistoriar.
SIGH, s., suspiro; v., suspirar, falar aos suspiros.
SIGHT, s., vista, visão, espetáculo, visibilidade, mira; v., ver, avistar, olhar, observar.
SIGHT.ING, s., pontaria.
SIGN, s., sinal, marca, gesto, letreiro, tabuleta; v., assinar, subscrever, contratar.
SIG.NAL, s., aviso, notícia, senha; v., sinalizar, dar sinais, fazer sinais.
SIG.NAL.IZE, v., assinalar, marcar, distinguir.
SIG.NAL.LING, s., sinalização.
SIG.NA.TURE, s., assinatura, sinal musical, abertura de programa radiofônico.
SIG.NIF.I.CANCE, s., importância, significação, significado.
SIG.NI.FI.CA.TION, s., significação, significado.
SIG.NI.FY, v., significar, representar, expressar, demonstrar, exibir.
SI.LENCE, s., silêncio, calma, sossego; v., silenciar, calar-se.
SI.LENT, adj., silencioso, calmo, quieto, calado, mudo.
SIL.HOU.ETTE, s., silhueta.
SILK, s., seda, tecido feito com seda; adj., sedoso, feito de seda.
SILK.WORM, s., bicho-da-seda.
SILKY, adj., sedoso, de seda, macio.
SILL, s., soleira de porta.
SILT, s., sedimento, limo, lodo; v., entupir, obstruir.
SILTY, adj., lodoso.
SIL.VER, s., prata, moedas de prata; prataria; adj., feito de prata, argênteo; v., pratear.
SIL.VER.IZE, v., pratear, cobrir com prata.
SIL.VERY, adj., prateado, argênteo, argentino.
SIM.I.LAR, adj., similar, semelhante, parecido.
SIM.I.LAR.I.TY, s., similaridade, semelhança.
SIM.I.LE, adj., símile, semelhante.
SIM.MER, s., cozimento em fogo lento; v., cozer em fogo lento, cozinhar devagar.
SIM.PER.ING, adj., idiota, imbecil.
SIM.PLE, adj., simples, ingênuo, simplório.
SIM.PLE.TON, s., idiota, imbecil, tolo.
SIM.PLIC.I.TY, s., simplicidade.

SIM.PLI.FI.CA.TION, *s.*, simplificação.
SIM.PLI.FY, *v.*, simplificar.
SIM.U.LATE, *v.*, simular, disfarçar.
SIM.U.LA.TION, *s.*, simulação.
SI.MUL.TA.NE.ITY, *s.*, simultaneidade.
SI.MUL.TA.NEOUS, *adj.*, simultâneo.
SIN, *s.*, pecado, ofensa, delito; *v.*, pecar.
SINCE, *adv.*, desde então, depois; *prep.*, desde; *conj.*, desde que.
SIN.CERE, *adj.*, sincero, franco.
SIN.CER.I.TY, *s.*, sinceridade.
SIN.EW, *s.*, tendão, nervo.
SIN.FUL, *adj.*, pecaminoso, pecador, cheio de pecados.
SING, *v.*, cantar.
SING.ER, *s.*, cantor.
SING.ING, *s.*, canto, canção.
SIN.GLE, *s.*, bilhete de ida, algo individual; *v.*, escolher; *adj.*, só, único, solteiro.
SIN.GLE-HAND.ED, *adj.*, sozinho, só.
SIN.GLE.NESS, *s.*, singeleza, simplicidade.
SIN.GU.LAR, *adj.*, singular, excepcional, único.
SIN.GU.LAR.I.TY, *s.*, singularidade.
SIN.IS.TER, *adj.*, sinistro.
SI.NIS.TRAL, *adj.*, esquerdo, sinistro.
SINK, *s.*, pia, lava-louça, esgoto, fossa; *v.*, afundar, descer, cair, deprimir-se, cavar.
SINK.AGE, *s.*, imersão, mergulho.
SIN.LESS, *adj.*, sem pecados.
SIN.NER, *s.*, pecador, pecadora.
SIN.U.OS.I.TY, *s.*, sinuosidade.
SIP, *s.*, gole, trago, gole pequeno; *v.*, beber aos goles pequenos, bebericar.
SI.PHON, *s.*, sifão, tubo.
SIR, *s.*, senhor, título de reverência.
SI.REN, *s.*, sirene; sereia, ninfa, mulher belíssima.
SI.SAL, *s.*, sisal.
SIS.SY, *s.*, maricas, pessoa afeminada.
SIST.ER, *s.*, irmã; enfermeira-chefe; freira, religiosa.
SIST.ER.HOOD, *s.*, congregação, irmandade.
SISTER-IN-LAW, *s.*, cunhada.
SIT, *v.*, sentar, sentar-se, assentar-se, acomodar, ter assento, ocupar cargo.

SIT DOWN, *v.*, sentar-se, assentar-se.
SITE, *s.*, saite, lugar, posição, página na Internet; terreno, sítio.
SIT.TER, *s.*, quem senta ou fica sentado.
SIT.U.ATE, *adj.*, situado, colocado, posto.
SIT.U.ATION, *s.*, situação, posição.
SIX, *num.*, seis.
SIX.FOLD, *adj.*, *num.*, sêxtuplo.
SIX.TEEN, *num.*, dezesseis.
SIX.TEENTH, *num.*, décimo sexto.
SIXTH, *num.*, sexto.
SIX.TI.ETH, *num.*, sexagésimo.
SIX.TY, *num.*, sessenta.
SIZE, *s.*, tamanho, extensão, medida, volume, quantidade, número de sapato.
SIZ.ZLE, *s.*, chiado, berro; *v.*, chiar.
SKATE, *s.*, patim, patinete; *v.*, patinar.
SKAT.ER, *s.*, patinador.
SKAT.ING, *s.*, patinagem, patinação.
SKEL.E.TON, *s.*, esqueleto, carcaça, armação, projeto.
SKEP, *s.*, cesto, colmeia.
SKETCH, *s.*, croqui, esboço, desenho, cena; *v.*, esboçar, desenhar.
SKETCH.BOOK, *s.*, rascunho, caderno para borrão.
SKEW, *adj.*, oblíquo, inclinado.
SKI, *s.*, esqui; *v.*, esquiar.
SKID, *s.*, escorregão, derrapada, deslizador; *v.*, deslizar, derrapar.
SKI.ER, *s.*, esquiador.
SKII.ING, *s.*, esqui.
SKIL.FUL, *adj.*, habilidoso, hábil.
SKILL, *s.*, habilidade, perícia, capacidade, destreza.
SKIM, *s.*, escuma, espuma; *v.*, escumar, espumar, desnatar, roçar.
SKIM.MER, *s.*, escumadeira.
SKIM.MILK, *adj.*, desnatado.
SKIN, *s.*, pele, casca, couro, crosta; *v.*, tirar a pele, pelar, esfolar, descascar.
SKIN-DEEP, *adj.*, superficial.
SKIN.NER, *s.*, esfolador.
SKIN.NY, *adj.*, magro, magriçela.

SKIP — **SLOPE**

SKIP, *s.*, salto, pulo, balde; *v.*, saltar, pular; omitir.
SKIP.PER *s.*, capitão de pequeno navio de pesca.
SKIRT, *s.*, saia, borda, bainha; *v.*, marginar, orlar, limitar, ladear.
SKIRT.ING, *s.*, rodapé.
SKIT.TLE *s.*, pau, pino.
SKULK, *s.*, medroso, covarde; *v.*, esconder-se.
SKULL, *s.*, caveira, crânio, cabeça.
SKY, *s.*, céu, firmamento, tempo, paraíso.
SKYDIVE, *v.*, saltar de paraquedas.
SKY.LIGHT, *s.*, claraboia.
SKY-LINE, *s.*, linha do horizonte, horizonte.
SKY.SCRAP.ER, *s.*, arranha-céu.
SLAB, *s.*, laje, bloco de pedra; *v.*, desbastar, cortar.
SLACK, *s.*, parte solta de algo; *adj.*, desmazelado, descuidado, frouxo.
SLAG, *s.*, escória, escombros.
SLAM, *s.*, batida forte de porta, estrondo, crítica dura; *v.*, fechar com estrondo, bater.
SLAND.ER, *s.*, difamação, calúnia; *v.*, difamar, caluniar.
SLAN.DER.OUS, *adj.*, caluniador, difamador.
SLANG, *s.*, gíria, calão, jargão; *v.*, usar de jargão.
SLANT, *s.*, declive, ladeira, inclinação; ponto de vista; *v.*, inclinar, inclinar-se.
SLAP, *s.*, tapa, bofetada, bofetão; *v.*, dar um tapa, esbofetear.
SLASH, *v.*, cortar, talhar, lascar, golpear.
SLAT, *s.*, sarrafo, ripa, tira.
SLATE, *s.*, ardósia, lousa; *v.*, cobrir com telhas de ardósia, criticar violentamente.
SLAUGHT.ER, *s.*, matança, carnificina, massacre; *v.*, abater, matar, massacrar.
SLAUGHT.ER-HOUSE, *s.*, matadouro.
SLAV, *adj.*, *s.*, eslavo.
SLAVE, *s.*, escravo, servo; *v.*, trabalhar como escravo, trabalhar muito.
SLA.VER, *s.*, escravocrata, dono de escravos.
SLAV.ERY, *v.*, escravidão.
SLAV.ISH, *adj.*, serviçal, servil, escravo.
SLAY, *v.*, matar, assassinar.
SLAY.ER, *s.*, matador, assassino.
SLEDGE, *s.*, trenó; marreta, malho.
SLEEP, *s.*, sono, soneca; *v.*, dormir, tirar uma soneca, descansar.
SLEEP.ER, *s.*, quem dorme, dorminhoco, dormente; vagão-dormitório.
SLEEP.I.NESS, *s.*, sonolência, torpor.
SLEEP.ING, *s.*, sono, dormida, descanso.
SLEEP.WALK.ER, *s.*, sonâmbulo.
SLEEPY, *adj.*, sonolento.
SLEET, *s.*, chuva com neve ou com granizo.
SLEEVE, *s.*, manga, luva, conexão, capa de disco; *v.*, colocar mangas.
SLEIGH, *s.*, trenó.
SLEND.ER, *adj.*, esbelto, delgado, fino, elegante, insuficiente.
SLICE, *s.*, fatia, rodela, espátula, faca, pedaço; *v.*, fatiar, cortar, talhar, dividir.
SLICK, *s.*, lugar liso; *v.*, alisar, lustrar; *adj.*, liso, escorregadio, jeitoso, hábil, esperto.
SLIDE, *s.*, eslaide, diapositivo, deslizamento, escorregão; *v.*, deslizar, escorregar.
SLID.ER, *s.*, cursor, corrediça.
SLIGHT, *s.*, desprezo, menoscabo; *v.*, desprezar, desconsiderar; *adj.*, franzino, fraco.
SLIGHT.ING, *adj.*, desprezivo, desdenhoso.
SLIM, *v.*, emagrecer, afinar; *adj.*, fino, delgado, esbelto.
SLIME, *s.*, lodo, lama, limo, muco.
SLING, *s.*, estilingue, funda, bodoque; lançamento; *v.*, atirar, arremessar, lançar.
SLIP, *s.*, escorregão, lapso, erro, coberta, fronha; *v.*, andar, mover-se, escapar, passar.
SLIP DOWN, *v.*, escorregar.
SLIP-ON, *s.*, pulôver.
SLIP.PER, *s.*, chinelo.
SLIP.PERY, *adj.*, escorregadio, liso, enganoso, obsceno.
SLIT, *s.*, fenda, greta, corte, racha; *v.*, fender, rachar.
SLITH.ER, *s.*, escorregadela; *v.*, escorregar, deslizar, derrapar.
SLI.VER, *s.*, lasca, pedaço, fatia; *v.*, lascar, fatiar.
SLO.GAN, *s.*, slogan, frase de efeito, dito, máxima, lema, grito de guerra.
SLOOP, *s.*, chalupa.
SLOPE, *s.*, declive, ladeira, rampa, encosta; *v.*,

inclinar-se, estar inclinado.
SLOP.ING, *adj.*, inclinado, declivado.
SLOP.PI.NESS, *s.*, umidade, lama, sujeira.
SLOP.PY, *adj.*, molhado, úmido, lamacento, descuidado.
SLOSH, *s.*, lama, limo, sujeira, neve.
SLOT, *s.*, ranhura, fenda; fazer uma fenda.
SLOTH, *s.*, preguiça, indolência, vadiagem.
SLOV.EN, *s.*, pessoa relaxada; *adj.*, sujo, relaxado, descuidado.
SLOW, *adj.*, lento, bronco, vagaroso, tardio; *adv.*, tardio, lentamente; *v.*, ir lento.
SLOW.LY, *adv.*, lentamente, devagar.
SLOW.NESS, *s.*, lentidão, vagareza, vagar.
SLUDGE, *s.*, lama, barro, lodo.
SLUG, *s.*, lesma.
SLUICE, *s.*, eclusa, comporta, dique, canal; *v.*, soltar a água; abrir comporta.
SLUM.BER, *s.*, sono leve, soneca.
SLUMP, *s.*, queda brusca na economia, baixa, colapso, depressão.
SLY, *adj.*, esperto, sagaz, astuto, malicioso, safado, velhaco.
SLY.NESS, *s.*, astúcia, esperteza.
SMACK, *s.*, sabor; palmada, estalo dos lábios, beijoca; *v.*, bater, cheirar, beijocar.
SMALL, *s.*, tipo pequeno, coisa pequena; *adj.*, pequeno, diminuto, trivial, baixo.
SMALL.POX, *s.*, varíola.
SMART, *s.*, dor aguda; *v.*, sofrer, sentir dor aguda; *adj.*, elegante, vivo, esperto, forte.
SMART.EN, *v.*, tornar bonito, embelezar.
SMASH, *s.*, colisão, choque, rompimento, estrondo, falência, desastre; *v.*, quebrar, esmagar, romper, arruinar, falir.
SMAT.TER, *s.*, conhecimento superficial; *v.*, falar sem conhecimento.
SMEAR, *s.*, mancha, nódoa; *v.*, manchar, sujar, enodoar, macular.
SMELL, *s.*, cheiro, olfato, aroma, odor, fedor; *v.*, cheirar, sentir cheiro, emitir cheiro.
SMILE, *s.*, sorriso; *v.*, sorrir, olhar com alegria.
SMIL.ING, *s.*, sorriso; *adj.*, sorridente, risonho.
SMITE, *s.*, soco, pancada; *v.*, bater, golpear, ferir, matar.
SMITH, *s.*, ferreiro; forjador.
SMITH.ERY, *s.*, ferraria, forja.
SMOCK, *s.*, guarda-pó, avental.
SMOG, *s.*, nevoeiro misturado com fumaça.
SMOKE, *s.*, fumo, fumaça, charuto, cigarro, cachimbo; *v.*, fumar, pitar, defumar.
SMOK.ER, *s.*, fumador; recinto próprio para fumantes.
SMOOTH, *s.*, polimento, alisamento; *v.*, polir, alisar; *adj.*, liso, plano, macio, calmo.
SMUDGE, *s.*, mancha, nódoa, marca; *v.*, sujar, manchar, enodoar, macular.
SMUG.GLER, *s.*, contrabandista.
SMUT, *s.*, fuligem, sujeira, mancha; obscenidade; *v.*, sujar, manchar, macular.
SMUT.TY, *adj.*, sujo, manchado, indecente, obsceno.
SNACK, *s.*, lanche, merenda.
SNACK BAR, *s.*, lanchonete.
SNAIL, *s.*, caracol.
SNAKE, *s.*, serpente, cobra, víbora.
SNAP, *s.*, estalo, estalido, ruptura, foto, cadeado; *v.*, estalar, quebrar, ceder, morder.
SNAP.SHOT, *s.*, foto instantânea.
SNARE, *s.*, armadilha, cilada, emboscada; *v.*, enredar, pegar com armadilha.
SNARL.ING, *adj.*, rabugento.
SNEAK, *v.*, andar furtivamente, mover-se às escondidas.
SNEAK.ERS, *s.*, tênis.
SNEEZE, *s.*, espirro; *v.*, espirrar.
SNIFF, *s.*, fungada, inalação, fungadela; *v.*, fungar, aspirar com ruído; assoar o nariz.
SNIP, *s.*, corte, incisão, tesourada, palpite; *v.*, cortar com tesoura, cortar em pedaços.
SNIP.ER, *s.*, franco-atirador.
SNOB, *s.*, esnobe, pretensioso, petulante, pernóstico.
SNOB.BERY, *s.*, esnobismo, pedantismo.
SNOOZE, *s.*, soneca, dormidela; *v.*, tirar uma soneca.
SNOUT, *s.*, focinho, tromba.
SNOW, *s.*, neve, nevada, nevasca; *v.*, nevar.

SNOW.FALL, *s.*, nevada, nevasca, caída de neve.
SNOW.FLAKE, *s.*, floco de neve.
SNOW.STORM, *s.*, nevasca, tempestade de neve.
SNOWY, *adj.*, nevado, nevoso, coberto de neve.
SNUB, *s.*, repulsa, repúdio; *v.*, desdenhar, desprezar, menosprezar.
SNUFF, *s.*, rapé, tabaco; pavio queimado; *v.*, cheirar, aspirar rapé, apagar vela.
SNUFF.BOX, *s.*, caixinha de rapé.
SNUG, *v.*, confortar, acomodar; *adj.*, confortável, acomodado, agasalhado.
SO, *adv.*, assim, deste modo, tão, de tal modo, muito, então, por isso.
SOAK, *s.*, pequena molhada; *v.*, embeber, molhar, ensopar.
SOAKY, *adj.*, molhado, ensopado, impregnado.
SOAP, *s.*, sabão; *v.*, ensaboar.
SOAPY, *adj.*, ensaboado, coberto de sabão.
SOB, *s.*, soluço; *v.*, soluçar.
SOC.CER, *s.*, futebol.
SO.CIA.BIL.I.TY, *s.*, sociabilidade.
SO.CIAL, *s.*, encontro social; *adj.*, social.
SO.CIAL.ISM, *s.*, socialismo.
SO.CIAL.IST, *s.*, socialista.
SO.CIAL.IZE, *v.*, socializar.
SO.CI.E.TY, *s.*, sociedade, associação.
SO.CI.OL.O.GIST, *s.*, sociólogo.
SO.CI.OL.O.GY, *s.*, sociologia.
SOCK, *s.*, meia, meia curta, soquete.
SOD, *s.*, relvado, gramado, grama, terreno com grama; *v.*, cobrir com grama, gramar.
SO.DA, *s.*, soda, barrilha, soda cáustica.
SO.DAL.I.TY, *s.*, congregação, confraria.
SO.DI.UM, *s.*, sódio.
SO.FA, *s.*, sofá.
SOFT, *adj.*, suave, leve, meigo, bom, fino, liso, macio, delicado.
SOFT.EN, *v.*, amolecer, amaciar, mitigar, acalmar, esmaecer.
SOFT.NESS, *s.*, maciez, moleza, delicadeza, generosidade.
SOFT.WARE, *s.*, programa de informática, software, conteúdo do programa.
SOIL, *s.*, solo, terra, terra para plantar, país; sujeira, esterco, brejo; *v.*, sujar, desonrar.
SO.JOURN, *s.*, estada, permanência rápida em; *v.*, permanecer por curto tempo.
SO.LACE, *s.*, consolo, conforto, alívio; *v.*, consolar, confortar, aliviar.
SO.LAR, *adj.*, solar, próprio do sol.
SOL.DER, *s.*, solda; soldar.
SOL.DIER, *s.*, soldado, militar; *v.*, servir o exército.
SOL.DIERY, *s.*, tropa, soldadesca, grupo de soldados.
SOLE, *s.*, sola dos pés, sola, sola de sapato; *adj.*, só, sozinho, solteiro; *v.*, pôr sola.
SOL.EMN, *adj.*, solene.
SO.LEM.NI.TY, *s.*, solenidade, festividade, cerimônia.
SOL.EM.NI.ZA.TION, *s.*, solenização.
SOL.EM.NIZE, *v.*, solenizar, ritualizar.
SO.LIC.IT, *v.*, solicitar, pedir, requerer, procurar, buscar.
SO.LIC.I.TA.TION, *s.*, solicitação.
SO.LIC.I.TOR, *s.*, requerente, solicitante; advogado.
SO.LIC.I.TUDE, *s.*, solicitude.
SOL.ID, *adj.*, sólido, robusto, forte, maciço; *s.*, corpo sólido, sólido.
SOL.I.DAR.I.TY, *s.*, solidariedade.
SO.LID.I.FY, *v.*, solidificar, tornar sólido.
SOL.I.TARY, *adj.*, solitário, só, isolado, retirado, único.
SOL.I.TUDE, *s.*, solidão, isolamento.
SOL.U.BLE, *adj.*, solúvel.
SO.LU.TION, *s.*, solução.
SOLVE, *v.*, resolver, solver, solucionar.
SOL.VEN.CY, *s.*, solvência, resolução.
SOL.VENT, *adj.*, *s.*, solvente.
SOM.BRE, *adj.*, sombrio, escuro, triste, lúgubre.
SOME, *adj.*, um, uma, um pouco, algum, alguma, alguém, cerca de, mais ou menos.
SOME.BODY, *pron.*, alguém.
SOME.HOW *adv.*, de qualquer maneira, por uma razão ou outra.
SOME.ONE, *pron.*, alguém.
SOME.THING, *pron.*, alguma coisa, algo.
SOME.TIME, *adv.*, algum dia, outra vez, em

alguma ocasião.
SOME.TIMES, *adv.*, por vezes, às vezes, de vez em quando.
SOME.WHAT, *adv.*, um tanto.
SOME.WHERE, *adv.*, em algum lugar, em alguma parte.
SOM.NAM.BU.LISM, *s.*, sonambulismo.
SON, *s.*, filho.
SONG, *s.*, canção, canto, som melodioso, melodia, poesia.
SON.IC, *adj.*, sônico.
SON-IN-LAW, *s.*, genro.
SON.NET, *s.*, soneto.
SON.NY, *s.*, meu filho, filhinho.
SON.SHIP, *s.*, filiação.
SOON, *adv.*, logo, brevemente, cedo, imediatamente.
SOON.ER, *adv.*, antes, mais cedo.
SOOTHE, *v.*, acalmar, sossegar, aquietar, aliviar.
SOOTH.SAY.ER, *s.*, vate, profeta, vaticinador, adivinho.
SO.PHIS.TI.CAT.ED, *adj.*, sofisticado.
SOP.O.RIF.IC, *adj.*, soporífico.
SOR.BET, *s.*, sorvete.
SOR.CER.ER, *s.*, feiticeiro, mágico, bruxo.
SOR.CERY, *s.* bruxaria, feitiçaria, magia.
SOR.DID, *adj.*, sórdido, imundo, sujo.
SOR.DID.NESS, *s.*, sordidez, imundície, sujeira.
SOR.ROW, *s.*, tristeza, mágoa, dor, pesar, aborrecimento.
SOR.ROW.FUL, *adj.*, triste, magoado, pesaroso, aborrecido.
SOR.RY, *adj.*, triste, magoado, pesaroso, arrependido, melancólico.
SORT, *s.*, tipo, espécie, caráter; *v.*, classificar, tipificar, selecionar, organizar.
SORT.ING, *s.*, escolha, distribuição, classificação.
SO-SO, *adv.*, mais ou menos, assim, assim; *adv.*, regularmente.
SOT, *s.*, beberrão, cachaceiro, ébrio; *v.*, embriagar-se.
SOUL, *s.*, alma, criatura, ser, espírito.
SOUL.FUL, *adj.*, emocionante, sentimental.
SOUND, *s.*, som, tom, ruído, canal, estreito, sonda; *adj.*, são, saudável, forte, sólido; *v.*, soar, fazer barulho, tocar, ressoar, sondar, pesquisar, mergulhar.
SOUP, *s.*, sopa.
SOUP.SPOON, *s.*, prato de sopa.
SOUR, *s.*, algo azedo; *adj.*, azedo, acre, ácido, amargo; *v.*, azedar, aborrecer.
SOURCE, *s.*, fonte, nascente.
SOUTH, *s.*, sul, direção sul, meridião; *adj.*, sul, meridional.
SOUTH-AMER.I.CAN, *adj.*, *s.*, sul-americano.
SOUTH-EAST, *s.*, sudeste.
SOUTH.ERN, *adj.*, direcionado para o sul, sulista; meridional.
SOUTH.WARD, *adv.*, para o sul, em direção ao sul.
SOUTH-WEST, *s.*, sudoeste.
SOU.VE.NIR, *s.*, suvenir, lembrança, recordação.
SOV.ER.EIGN, *s.*, soberano, governante.
SOV.ER.EIGN.TY, *s.*, soberania, soberania, poder, mando.
SO.VI.ET, *adj. s.*, soviético.
SOW, *s.*, porca, fêmea do porco; *v.*, semear.
SOW.ER, *s.*, semeador.
SOY, *s.*, soja.
SOYA, *s.*, soja.
SPA, *s.*, estância termal, balneário com água quente.
SPACE, *s.*, espaço, local, área, superfície, lapso de tempo; *v.*, espaçar, criar espaços.
SPACE.CRAFT, *s.*, nave espacial.
SPACE.MAN, *s.*, cosmonauta, astronauta.
SPA.CIOUS, *adj.*, espaçoso.
SPA.GHET.TI, *s.*, espaguete.
SPAIN, *s.*, Espanha.
SPAN.IARD, *adj.*, *s.*, espanhol.
SPAN.ISH, *adj.*, *s.*, espanhol.
SPANK, *s.*, golpe, palmada; *v.*, bater, golpear, chicotear.
SPAN.NER, *s.*, chave inglesa.
SPAR, *s.*, mastro, verga.
SPARE, *s.*, peça sobressalente, reserva; *v.*, economizar, dispor de; *adj.*, excedente.
SPARK, *s.*, chispa, faísca, brilho, luz; *v.*, reluzir,

faiscar, brilhar.
SPAR.ROW, *s.*, pardal.
SPARSE, *adj.*, esparso, ralo, disperso.
SPASM, *s.*, espasmo.
SPAS.MOD.IC, *adj.*, espasmódico.
SPAT.U.LA, *s.*, espátula.
SPAWN, *s.*, ovas, ova, cria, ovo; *v.*, criar, gerar.
SPEAK, *v.*, falar, dizer, discursar, conversar.
SPEAK.ER, *s.*, orador, falante, repórter, alto-falante.
SPE.CIAL, *adj.*, especial, extra.
SPE.CI.AL.I.TY, *s.*, especialidade.
SPE.CIAL.IZE, *v.*, especializar.
SPE.CIES, *s.*, espécies, ervas.
SPE.CIF.IC, *adj.*, específico, único, próprio.
SPEC.I.FI.CA.TION, *s.*, especificação.
SPEC.I.FY, *v.*, especificar.
SPEC.I.MEN, *s.*, espécime, amostra, exemplar.
SPECK, *s.*, mancha, pinta, salpico; *v.*, manchar, salpicar, colocar pinta.
SPECS, *s.*, óculos.
SPEC.TA.CLE, *s.*, espetáculo.
SPEC.TAC.U.LAR, *adj.*, espetacular.
SPEC.TA.TOR, *s.*, espectador, assistente.
SPEC.TRE, *s.*, espectro.
SPEC.U.LATE, *v.*, especular, verificar.
SPEC.U.LA.TION, *s.*, especulação, ideia, verificação.
SPEECH, *s.*, fala, discurso.
SPEED, *s.*, velocidade, rapidez, pressa; *v.*, acelerar, apressar, correr.
SPEED.BOAT, *s.*, lancha.
SPEED.ING, *s.*, excesso de velocidade.
SPEED.OM.E.TER, *s.*, velocímetro.
SPEEDY, *adj.*, veloz, rápido, imediato, célere.
SPELL, *s.*, palavra mágica, encanto, magia, fascinação; *v.*, pressagiar, soletrar.
SPELL.ING, *s.*, ortografia.
SPENSE, *s.*, despensa.
SPEND, *v.*, gastar, despender, consumir, passar.
SPENT, *adj.*, gasto, consumido; cansado, exausto.
SPERM, *s.*, esperma.
SPEW, *s.*, vômito; *v.*, vomitar.
SPHERE, *s.*, esfera.

SPHER.I.CAL, *adj.*, esférico, redondo, globular.
SPHINX, *s.*, esfinge.
SPICE, *s.*, condimento, tempero, sabor, especiaria; *v.*, condimentar, temperar.
SPIC.ERY, *s.*, especiaria.
SPICY, *adj.*, condimentado, temperado.
SPI.DER, *s.*, aranha.
SPIKE, *s.*, ponta, espigão, cume; espiga.
SPILL, *s.*, derramamento, aguaceiro, toró; *v.*, derramar, entornar, despejar.
SPIN, *s.*, parafuso, rotação, movimento rápido; *v.*, fiar, torcer, puxar, esticar.
SPIN.ACH, *s.*, espinafre.
SPINE, *s.*, espinha dorsal, espinha, suporte, espinho, ponta, saliência.
SPIN.NING, *s.*, fiação.
SPIN.STER, *s.*, solteira, solteirona.
SPI.RAL, *s.*, espiral, mola; *adj.*, espiralado; *v.*, formar espiral, elevar os preços.
SPIR.IT, *s.*, espírito, alma, fantasma, ânimo, coragem; *s., pl.*, bebidas alcoólicas.
SPIR.IT.ED, *adj.*, espirituoso, animado, entusiasmado.
SPIR.I.TU.AL, *adj.*, espiritual.
SPIR.I.TU.AL.I.TY, *s.*, espiritualidade.
SPIR.I.TU.OUS, *adj.*, espirituoso, alcoólico.
SPIT, *s.*, saliva, cuspida, cuspe, espeto para carne; *v.*, pôr no espeto, espetar; cuspir.
SPITE, *s.*, rancor, ressentimento, ódio; *v.*, ofender, injuriar, odiar.
SPLASH, *s.*, borrifo, esguicho, espirro; *v.*, chapinhar, espirrar, molhar.
SPLAY, *v.*, alargar, aumentar.
SPLEEN, *s.*, baço, mau humor, melancolia.
SPLEEN.FUL, *adj.*, rabugento, irritadiço, impertinente, insuportável.
SPLEN.DID, *adj.*, esplêndido, maravilhoso.
SPLEN.DOUR, *s.*, esplendor, brilho.
SPLIT, *s.*, fenda, brecha, greta, cisão, divisão; *v.*, cindir, rachar, fender, separar.
SPOIL, *s.*, despojos, saque, pilhagem; *v.*, arruinar, danificar, estragar, saquear.
SPOKES.MAN, *s.*, porta-voz.
SPONGE, *s.*, esponja; bolo, pão de ló; parasita;

v., lavar com esponja, esfregar.
SPONGY, *adj.*, esponjoso.
SPON.SOR, *s.*, patrocinador, quem patrocina esporte com fins de propaganda; *v.*, patrocinar, apadrinhar.
SPON.SOR.SHIP, *s.*, patrocínio, garantia.
SPON.TA.NE.I.TY, *s.*, espontaneidade.
SPON.TA.NE.OUS, *adj.*, espontâneo.
SPOOL, *s.*, carretel, bobina, rolo de filme; *v.*, enrolar, bobinar.
SPOON, *s.*, colher.
SPOON.FUL, *s.*, colherada.
SPO.RAD.IC, *adj.*, esporádico.
SPORT, *s.*, esporte, desporto, atletismo, divertimento; *v.*, brincar, jogar, divertir-se.
SPORT.FUL, *adj.*, alegre, brincalhão; zombador, irônico.
SPORTS.MAN, *s.*, esportista, desportista.
SPORTY, *adj.*, desportivo, esportivo.
SPOT, *s.*, marca, local, ponto, pinta, espaço publicitário; *v.*, notar, marcar, manchar.
SPOT.LIGHT, *s.*, luz, farol, holofote, refletor.
SPOT.TY, *adj.*, manchado, marcado, salpicado.
SPOUSE, *s.*, cônjuge, consorte.
SPRAY, *s.*, borrifo, vaporizador, spray; *v.*, borrifar, vaporizar, pulverizar.
SPREAD, *s.*, expansão, difusão, diferença entre preço de oferta e procura; *v.*, espalhar.
SPREAD.ING, *adj.*, extensivo, expansivo.
SPREE, *s.*, farra, folia; *v.*, fazer farra, farrear.
SPRING, *s.*, primavera, salto, pulo; *v.*, saltar, pular, nascer, brotar.
SPRING.BOARD, *s.*, trampolim.
SPRING.ER, *s.*, saltador, pulador.
SPRING.TIME, *s.*, primavera.
SPRIN.KLE, *s.*, chuvisco; *v.*, espalhar, pulverizar, polvilhar.
SPRIN.KLER, *s.*, regador, sistema de proteção contra incêndios por chuveirinho.
SPRINT.ER, *s.*, corredor.
SPRITE, *s.*, espírito, fantasma.
SPUNK, *s.*, isca.
SPUR, *s.*, espora, estímulo; *v.*, incitar, estimular.
SPU.RI.OUS, *adj.*, espúrio, falso, bastardo.

SPUT.TER, *s.*, saliva.
SPY, *s.*, espião, espia; *v.*, espiar, olhar, espionar, verificar.
SPY.ING, *s.*, espionagem.
SQUAD, *s.*, esquadra, pelotão, seleção, time.
SQUAD.RON, *s.*, esquadrão, pelotão.
SQUALL, *s.*, tempestade, lufada de vento, pé de vento.
SQUA.LOR, *s.*, sordidez.
SQUA.MOUS, *adj.*, escamoso, coberto de escamas.
SQUARE, *s.*, quadrado, praça, quadra, simetria; *v.*, esquadrar, dividir em quadras.
SQUASH, *s.*, squash, esporte; abóbora, polpa, baque; *v.*, espremer, amassar, apertar.
SQUASHY, *adj.*, amassado, espremido.
SQUEA.MISH, *adj.*, sensível, delicado.
SQUID, *s.*, lula.
SQUINT, *s.*, olhada, estrabismo; *v.*, piscar, olhar, olhar de soslaio, ser vesgo.
SQUIR.REL, *s.*, esquilo.
STAB, *s.*, facada, punhalada, pontada; *v.*, esfaquear, apunhalar, ferir com faca.
STA.BIL.I.TY, *s.*, estabilidade.
STA.BI.LIZE, *v.*, estabilizar.
STA.BLE, *adj.*, estável; firme, seguro; estábulo, estrebaria.
STA.DI.UM, *s.*, estádio.
STAFF, *s.*, pessoal, quadro de assessores, grupo; *v.*, assessorar com pessoas, ajudar.
STAG, *s.*, cervo, veado.
STAGE, *s.*, palco, teatro, ator, elenco, andaime; *v.*, encenar, representar no palco.
STAG.NAN.CY, *s.*, estagnação, parada.
STAG.NATE, *v.*, estagnar, parar.
STAIN, *s.*, mancha, tinta, nódoa; *v.*, manchar, macular, sujar.
STAIN.ER, *s.*, tintureiro.
STAIR, *s.*, escadaria, escada, degrau.
STAIR.CASE, *s.*, escadaria, escada.
STAKE, *s.*, estaca, poste, moirão, aposta; *v.*, fixar, estaquear, pôr piquetes, apostar.
STALK, *s.*, talo, caule, haste, tronco; caçar por emboscada, andar sem ruído.

STALL, *s.*, estábulo, baia; banca de frutas e verduras; *v.*, ter animal na baia.
STAL.LION, *s.*, garanhão.
STAMP, *s.*, selo, timbre, carimbo; *v.*, selar, carimbar carta, timbrar.
STAMP.ER, *s.*, estampador, impressor.
STAMP.ING, *s.*, estampagem.
STAND, *s.*, estante, postura, ponto de táxi, tribuna; *v.*, estar em pé, encontrar-se.
STAN.DARD, *s.*, standard, padrão, gabarito, critério; *adj.*, padronizado, regular.
STAN.DARD.IZE, *v.*, estandardizar, padronizar.
STAND-BY, *s.*, auxílio, apoio; *adj.*, preparado, a postos, pronto.
STAND-IN, *s.*, suplente.
STAND.POINT, *s.*, ponto de vista.
STAND.STILL, *s.*, parada, imobilização, paralisação.
STAN.ZA, *s.*, estância, estrofe.
STAR, *s.*, estrela; estrela de cinema, pessoa famosa; *v.*, ser a estrela de um evento.
STARCH, *s.*, amido, fécula.
STARE, *s.*, olhar fixo; *v.*, olhar fixamente, mirar, fixar, fitar.
STAR.FISH, *s.*, estrela-do-mar.
STARK-NAKED, *adj.*, nu, pelado, em pelo.
STAR.LIGHT, *s.*, luz das estrelas.
STAR.RY, *adj.*, estrelado.
START, *s.*, partida, começo, princípio, impulso, vantagem; *v.*, partir, começar, assustar.
START.ER, *s.*, autor, motor de arranque, arranque de carro; juiz; entradas.
START.ING, *s.*, começo, início, sobressalto.
STAR.VA.TION, *s.*, fome.
STARVE, *v.*, passar fome, morrer de fome.
STATE, *s.*, estado, situação, contexto, cargo, nação, país, governo; *v.*, declarar, exprimir, expor, referir, determinar; *adj.*, formal, cerimonial, próprio do governo.
STATES.MAN, *s.*, estadista, político renomado.
STAT.ICS, *s.*, estática.
STA.TION, *s.*, estação, estação emissora, ponto de parada; *v.*, parar, estacionar.
STA.TION.ARY, *adj.*, estacionário, fixo.

STAT.IST, *s.*, estadista.
STA.TIS.TIC, *s.*, estatística.
STA.TIS.TICS, *s.*, estatística.
STAT.UE, *s.*, estátua.
STAT.U.ETTE, *s.*, estatueta.
STAT.URE, *s.*, estatura, altura, dimensão, desenvolvimento.
STA.TUS, *s.*, status, posição, condição, estatuto.
STAT.UTE, *s.*, estatuto.
STAY, *s.*, estadia, estada, permanência, paralisação; *v.*, permanecer, ficar, hospedar-se.
STEAD, *s.*, sítio, lugar, lugarejo.
STEAD.FAST, *adj.*, firme, estável.
STEAK, *s.*, bife, pequeno filé, churrasquinho.
STEAL, *s.*, roubo, furto; *v.*, roubar, furtar.
STEAL.ER, *s.*, ladrão, gatuno, gato.
STEAL.ING, *s.*, furto, roubo.
STEAM, *s.*, vapor; *v.*, cozer a vapor, evaporar, fumegar.
STEAM.ER, *s.*, navio a vapor, vapor.
STEEL, *s.*, aço, *adj.*, de aço.
STEEP, *s.*, precipício, declive forte; *adj.*, íngreme, áspero, abrupto; infusão; *v.*, macerar, extrair, colocar para macerar.
STEE.PLE, *s.*, campanário, torre.
STEER, *s.*, boi, novilho; *v.*, dirigir, guiar carro, governar.
STEER.ING, *s.*, direção de veículo.
STEERS.MAN, *s.*, timoneiro, dirigente.
STEN.CIL, *s.*, estêncil, matriz para reproduzir figuras ou escritos.
STE.NOG.RA.PHY, *s.*, estenografia.
STEP, *s.*, passo, degrau, sinal, pulo, andar.
STEP BOARD, *s.*, estribo.
STEP.CHILD, *s.*, enteado, enteada.
STEP.DAUGH.TER, *s.*, enteada.
STEP.FA.THER, *s.*, padrasto.
STEP.MOTH.ER, *s.*, madrasta.
STEP.SON, *s.*, enteado.
STE.REO.PHON.IC, *adj.*, estereofônico.
STER.ILE, *adj.*, estéril, esterilizado.
STER.IL.IZE, *v.*, esterilizar.
STER.LING, *s.*, libra esterlina.
STETHO.SCOPE, *s.*, estetoscópio.

STEW, *s.*, guisado, carne cozida, ensopado; *v.*, cozinhar, ensopar.
STEW.ARD, *s.*, comissário de bordo.
STEW.ARD.ESS, *s.*, comissária de bordo, aeromoça.
STICK, *s.*, pau, cacete, bastão, galho, acha; *v.*, furar, matar, apunhalar, destruir.
STICK.ER, *s.*, autocolante.
STICK.ING, *adj.*, aderente.
STIFF, *s.*, caipira, matuto; *adj.*, rijo, duro, forte, teso, emperrado.
STIFF.NESS, *s.*, rigidez, dureza, tesão.
STIG.MA, *s.*, estigma.
STIG.MA.TIZE, *v.*, estigmatizar.
STILL, *adj.*, parado, fixo; *adv.*, ainda, contudo, entretanto, todavia.
STIM.U.LANT, *s.*, estimulante.
STIM.U.LATE, *v.*, estimular.
STING, *s.*, ferroada, picada, ferrão; picar, aguilhoar, ferroar.
STINK, *s.*, fedor, mau cheiro; *v.*, feder, cheirar mal; ter reputação duvidosa.
STINT, *s.*, limite, tarefa, economia; *v.*, restringir, limitar, poupar.
STIP.U.LATE, *v.*, estipular, determinar.
STIR.RING, *adj.*, excitante.
STOCK, *s.*, estoque, provisão, fornecimento, suprimento, reserva, gado, linhagem, estirpe, títulos; *v.*, fornecer, prover, abastecer, armazenar.
STOCK.BRO.KER, *s.*, corretor.
STOCK.HOLD.ER, *s.*, acionista.
STO.IC, *adj.*, estoico.
STO.I.CISM, *s.*, estoicismo.
STOK.ER, *s.*, foguista.
STOM.ACH, *s.*, estômago, barriga, ventre, pança.
STOM.ACH-ACHE, *s.*, dor de estômago.
STONE, *s.*, pedra, cálculo; rocha, caroço; *v.*, colocar pedras, apedrejar, descaroçar.
STONE-MA.SON, *s.*, pedreiro.
STONY, *adj.*, pedregoso.
STOP, *s.*, parada, pausa, interrupção, obstáculo; *v.*, parar, interromper, deter-se.
STOP.PAGE, *s.*, greve, obstrução, impedimento.
STOP.PER, *s.*, tampa, tampo, rolha.

STOP.WATCH, *s.*, cronômetro.
STOR.AGE, *s.*, armazenagem, armazenamento.
STORE, *s.*, provisão, armazenagem, fornecimento, mercado; *pl.*, víveres.
STOR.EY, *s.*, andar de um prédio.
STORK, *s.*, cegonha.
STORM, *s.*, tempestade, tormenta; *v.*, enfurecer, atormentar, assaltar.
STO.RY, *s.*, estória, lenda, fato folclórico, mentira.
STOVE, *s.*, fogão, estufa.
STOW.AWAY, *s.*, passageiro clandestino.
STOW.ER, *s.*, estivador.
STRAIN, *s.*, tensão, esforço; luxação, estirpe; forçar, distorcer, estirar.
STRAIN.ING, *s.*, esforço.
STRAIT, *s.*, estreito, garganta.
STRANGE, *s.*, estranho, estrangeiro, desconhecido.
STRANG.ER, *s.*, estrangeiro, forasteiro, estranho, desconhecido.
STRAN.GU.LATE, *v.*, estrangular, sufocar.
STRAP, *s.*, tira, correia, alça, cordão; *v.*, segurar, atar com tira.
STRAT.A.GEM, *s.*, estratagema.
STRA.TE.GIC, *adj.*, estratégico.
STRAT.E.GY, *s.*, estratégia.
STRAW, *s.*, palha, palhinha; ninharia, bagatela.
STRAW.BER.RY, *s.*, morango.
STRAY, *v.*, extraviar-se, perder-se, desviar-se; *adj.*, extraviado, perdido, desviado.
STREAM, *s.*, riacho, ribeiro, fluxo, torrente; *v.*, correr, fluir, deslizar.
STREET, *s.*, rua, via.
STRENGTH, *s.*, força, firmeza, resistência, robustez.
STRENGTH.EN, *v.*, fortificar, robustecer, tonificar.
STRESS, *s.*, estresse, pressão, tensão, cansaço; *v.*, destacar, realçar, enfatizar.
STREW, *s.*, espalhar, espargir, difundir.
STRICK.EN, *adj.*, ferido, machucado, atacado.
STRICT, *adj.*, rigoroso, austero, severo.
STRICT.NESS, *s.*, severidade, rigor, austeridade.
STRIDE, *s.*, passos largos, passadas longas; *v.*,

caminhar a passos largos, transpor.
STRIFE, *s.*, conflito, contenda, discussão.
STRIKE, *s.*, greve, ataque; *v.*, bater em, descobrir, estar em greve, atacar, destruir.
STRIK.ER, *s.*, grevista.
STRING, *s.*, cordão, fio, réstia, corda, instrumento de cordas, barbante, embira.
STRIP, *s.*, tira, faixa, risca; *v.*, despir, desnudar, despir-se, despojar-se.
STRIP.PER, *s.*, quem pratica o estriptise.
STRIP.TEASE, *s.*, estriptise, desnudamento artístico.
STRIVE, *v.*, esforçar-se, lutar por, empenhar-se.
STRIV.ING, *s.*, esforço, empenho.
STROKE, *s.*, golpe, soco, pancada, derrame cerebral; afago; *v.*, afagar, acariciar.
STROLL, *s.*, volta, passeio, giro; *v.*, passear, andar, girar, dar uma volta.
STRUC.TUR.AL, *adj.*, estrutural, próprio de estrutura.
STRUC.TURE, *s.*, estrutura, construção, edifício.
STRUG.GLE, *s.*, luta, combate, contenda; *v.*, lutar, batalhar, contender, porfiar.
STRUG.GLER, *s.*, lutador, combatente.
STRUT, *s.*, escora, suporte, apoio; *v.*, escorar, suportar.
STUB.BORN, *adj.*, teimoso, obstinado, cabeça-dura.
STUB.BORN.NESS, *s.*, teimosia, obstinação.
STU.DENT, *s.*, estudante, aluno.
STU.DIO, *s.*, estúdio, ateliê.
STU.DI.OUS, *adj.*, 1dioso, aplicado, diligente, assíduo.
STUDY, *s.*, estudo, sala de aula, aplicação; estudar.
STUFF, *s.*, matéria, material, matéria-prima, coisa; *v.*, rechear, encher, parar, estofar.
STUM.BLE, *s.*, falha, erro, lapso, deslize; *v.*, tropeçar, derrapar, cambalear.
STUN, *s.*, aturdimento, pasmaria; *v.*, aturdir, pasmar, espantar.
STUNT, *s.*, proeza, peripécia, façanha.
STU.PE.FY, *s.*, estupefazer, espantar, deixar estupefato.
STU.PID, *adj.*, idiota, imbecil, estúpido.

STU.PID.I.TY, *s.*, estupidez, imbecilidade, idiotice.
STU.POR, *s.*, estupor, espanto.
STY, *s.*, chiqueiro, curral, pocilga, antro; *v.*, viver em chiqueiro, viver em sujidade.
STYLE, *s.*, estilo, conduta, modo de vida, elegância.
STYL.IST, *s.*, estilista.
SUA.SION, *s.*, persuasão, convencimento.
SUAVE, *adj.*, suave, doce, melifluo.
SUB.CONS.CIOUS, *adj.*, subconsciente.
SUB.DI.VIDE, *v.*, subdividir.
SUB.DI.VI.SION, *s.*, subdivisão.
SUB.DUE, *v.*, subjugar, dominar, vencer.
SUB.JECT, *s.*, assunto, tema, objeto, tópico, súdito; sujeito; motivo; *v.*, subjugar, dominar, sujeitar, submeter.
SUB.JEC.TION, *s.*, sujeição, dominação, submissão.
SUB.JEC.TIVE, *adj.*, subjetivo, pessoal.
SUB.LIME, *adj.*, sublime, divino.
SUB.MA.RINE, *s.*, submarino.
SUB.MERGE, *v.*, submergir, imergir, afundar-se, mergulhar.
SUB.MIS.SION, *s.*, submissão, sujeição.
SUB.MIT, *v.*, submeter, subjugar, sujeitar, submeter-se.
SUB.OR.DI.NATE, *adj.*, subordinado, submisso.
SUB.ORN, *v.*, subornar, enganar, falsear.
SUB.OR.NA.TION, *s.*, suborno.
SUB.SCRIBE, *v.*, subscrever.
SUB.SCRIB.ER, *s.*, assinante de jornal, revista.
SUB.SID.I.ARY, *adj.*, secundário.
SUB.SI.DIZE, *v.*, subsidiar, auxiliar, ajudar.
SUB.SI.DY, *s.*, subsídio, auxílio, ajuda, apoio.
SUB.SIS.TENCE, *s.*, subsistência.
SUB.SOIL, *v.*, subsolo.
SUB.STANCE, *s.*, substância, matéria.
SUB.STAN.TIAL, *adj.*, substancial, material, sólido.
SUB.STAN.TIVE, *s.*, substantivo; *adj.*, real, certo.
SUB.STI.TUTE, *s.*, substituto.
SUB.TER.FUGE, *s.*, subterfúgio, desculpa, pretexto.

SUB.TER.RA.NEAN, *adj.*, *s.*, subterrâneo.
SUB.татотаL, *s.*, subtotal.
SUB.TRACT, *v.*, subtrair, deduzir, descontar.
SUB.URB, *s.*, subúrbio.
SUB.VEN.TION, *s.*, subvenção, ajuda.
SUB.VER.SION, *s.*, subversão, desordem, revolta.
SUB.WAY, *s.*, metrô, trem subterrâneo em cidades.
SUC.CEED, *v.*, suceder, ter êxito, obter sucesso, dar-se bem.
SUC.CESS, *s.*, sucesso, êxito.
SUC.CES.SION, *s.*, sucessão, série, descendência, sequência.
SUC.CINCT, *adj.*, resumido, breve, conciso, sucinto.
SUC.CU.LENT, *adj.*, suculento, saboroso.
SUC.CUMB, *v.*, sucumbir, falecer, perecer, morrer.
SUC.CUR.SAL, *s.*, sucursal.
SUCH, *adj.*, semelhante, igual; *adv.*, tanto, tão.
SUCK, *s.*, chupada, sucção; *v.*, chupar, sorver, mamar.
SUC.TION, *s.*, sucção.
SUD.DEN, *adj.*, subitâneo, repentino, inesperado.
SUE, *v.*, processar, peticionar contra outrem, mover um processo.
SUEDE, *s.*, camurça.
SUF.FER, *v.*, sofrer, aguentar, suportar, tolerar.
SUF.FER.ING, *s.*, sofrimento, dor, aflição.
SUF.FI.CIEN.CY, *s.*, suficiência.
SUF.FI.CIENT, *adj.*, suficiente, bastante.
SUF.FIX, *s.*, sufixo.
SUF.FO.CATE, *v.*, sufocar, asfixiar, matar por sufocação.
SUF.FRAGE, *s.*, sufrágio, voto, direito de voto.
SUG.AR, *s.*, açúcar; *v.*, açucarar, adoçar.
SUG.AR-BEET, *s.*, beterraba.
SUG.GEST, *v.*, sugerir, propor, lembrar, insinuar.
SUG.GES.TION, *s.*, sugestão, insinuação, proposição.
SUI.CIDE, *s.*, suicida; suicídio.
SUIT, *s.*, terno de roupa, processo, caso judicial, naipe, petição; *v.*, vestir, ajustar.
SUIT.ABIL.I.TY, *s.*, conveniência, necessidade.
SUITE, *s.*, conjunto de quartos, conjunto de salas em um hotel.

SUIT.OR, *s.*, pretendente.
SUL.LEN, *adj.*, rabujento, amuado, teimoso, melindroso.
SULPHUR, *s.*, enxofre.
SUL.TAN, *s.*, sultão.
SUL.TA.NA, *s.*, sultana.
SUM, *s.*, soma, total, cálculo.
SUM.MA.RIZE, *s.*, resumir, sumarizar, compendiar, sintetizar.
SUM.MA.RY, *s.*, sumário, resumo, compêndio, síntese.
SUM.MER, *s.*, verão.
SUMP.TU.OUS, *adj.*, suntuoso.
SUN, *s.*, sol.
SUN.BEAM, *s.*, raio de sol.
SUN.BURN, *s.*, queimadura de sol.
SUN.DAY, *s.*, domingo.
SUN.DOWN, *s.*, pôr do sol.
SUN.FLOW.ER, *s.*, girassol.
SUN.GLAS.SES, *s.*, óculos de sol.
SUN.LITHT, *s.*, luz do sol.
SUN.NY, *adj.*, ensolarado, cheio de sol.
SUN.RISE, *s.*, nascer do sol, nascente.
SUN.SET, *s.*, pôr do sol.
SUP.PER, *s.*, jantar.
SUP.PLANT, *v.*, suplantar, vencer.
SUP.PLE.MENT, *s.*, suplemento, complemento; *v.*, completar.
SUP.PLI.CANT, *s.*, suplicante, pedinte, requerente.
SUP.PLI.CA.TION, *s.*, súplica, pedido, petição.
SUP.PLI.ER, *s.*, fornecedor, abastecedor.
SUP.PLY, *s.*, suprimento, fornecimento, provisão; *v.*, fornecer, abastecer, suprir.
SUP.PORT, *s.*, suporte, apoio, auxílio; *v.*, apoiar, ajudar, manter.
SUP.POSE, *v.*, supor, imaginar, achar, fazer uma hipótese.
SUP.PRESS, *v.*, suprimir, tirar, contar, oprimir.
SUP.PRES.SION, *s.*, supressão.
SU.PREM.A.CY, *s.*, supremacia, domínio.
SU.PREME, *adj.*, supremo, máximo, o maior.
SUR.CHARGE, *s.*, sobrecarga, sobretaxa, sobrepeso.

SURE, *adj.*, certo, seguro, convencido, fiel.
SURE.TY, *s.*, garantia, segurança, fiança.
SURF, *s.*, surfe, rebentação das ondas, ressaca.
SUR.FACE, *s.*, superfície, face, lado; *v.*, revestir, vir à tona.
SURF.ING, *s.*, surfe.
SUR.GEON, *s.*, cirurgião, médico.
SUR.GERY, *s.*, cirurgia, sala de operação, consultório.
SUR.NAME, *s.*, apelido, sobrenome.
SUR.PASS, *s.*, ultrapassar, superar.
SUR.PRISE, *s.*, surpresa, espanto; *v.*, surpreender.
SUR.RE.AL.ISM, *s.*, surrealismo.
SUR.REP.TI.TIOUS, *adj.*, subrepticio, furtivo, oculto, tácito.
SUR.ROUND, *v.*, circundar, rodear, cercar.
SUR.TAX, *s.*, sobretaxa.
SUR.VEIL.LANCE, *s.*, vigilância, cuidado, atenção.
SUR.VEY, *s.*, visão, vistoria, inspeção, mapa, levantamento; *v.*, inspecionar, vistoriar.
SUR.VEY.OR, *s.*, agrimensor, inspetor, vistoriador.
SUR.VIVE, *v.*, sobreviver, perdurar, durar, continuar.
SUR.VI.VOR, *s.*, sobrevivente.
SUS.PECT, *adj.*, *s.*, suspeito; *v.*, suspeitar, desconfiar.
SUS.PEND, *v.*, suspender, interromper, cessar, remover.
SUS.PENSE, *s.*, incerteza, dúvida, ansiedade.
SUS.PI.CION, *s.*, suspeita, dúvida.
SUS.TAIN, *v.*, sustentar, manter, alimentar; sofrer, afligir-se.
SUS.TE.NANCE, *s.*, alimento, sustento, mantimento.
SWAL.LOW, *s.*, andorinha.
SWAMP, *s.*, brejo, pântano, charco; *v.*, atolar.
SWAN, *s.*, cisne.
SWAP, *s.*, troca, permuta, acordo para troca de pagamentos; *v.*, trocar, permutar.
SWARM, *s.*, enxame de abelhas, multidão, grande quantidade; *v.*, enxamear.
SWAT, *s.*, golpe, pancada; *v.*, esmagar, amassar, matar.
SWEAR, *v.*, jurar, prestar juramento; praguejar, blasfemar.
SWEAR.ING, *s.*, juramento; praga, blasfêmia, imprecação.
SWEAR.WORD, *s.*, palavrão.
SWEAT, *s.*, suor, transpiração; suar, transpirar.
SWEAT.ER, *s.*, camisola; suéter, pulôver.
SWEATY, *adj.*, suado.
SWEDE, *adj.*, *s.*, sueco.
SWE.DEN, *s.*, Suécia.
SWED.ISH, *s.*, língua sueca.
SWEEP AWAY, *v.*, varrer, limpar.
SWEEP.ER, *s.*, varredor.
SWEET, *s.*, coisa doce, doce, sobremesa; *adj.*, doce, açucarado, suave.
SWEET.EN, *s.*, adoçar, colocar açúcar em.
SWEET.EN.ING, *s.*, adoçante.
SWELL, *s.*, aumento, inchação, onda, vaga, vagalhão; *v.*, crescer, inchar, dilatar.
SWELL.ING, *s.*, inchação, intumescência, inchaço.
SWIFT, *s.*, andorinha; *adj.*, rápido, célere, rápido.
SWIG, *s.*, trago, gole.
SWIM, *s.*, ato de nadar, nado, natação; *v.*, nadar, flutuar, estar inundado.
SWIM.MER, *s.*, nadador.
SWIMMING, *s.*, natação.
SWIMMING.SUIT, *s.*, trajes para banho, roupa de banho.
SWIN.DLE, *s.*, fraude, logro; *v.*, fraudar, defraudar, enganar.
SWINE, *s.*, porco; velhaco, calhorda, cafajeste.
SWING, *s.*, balanço, oscilação, ritmo; *v.*, balançar, oscilar.
SWISH, *adj.*, *s.*, suíço.
SWITCH, *s.*, interruptor, interrupção; *v.*, mudar, interromper.
SWIT.ZER.LAND, *s.*, Suíça.
SWOON, *s.*, desmaio; *v.*, desmaiar, desfalecer, esmorecer.
SWORD, *s.*, espada.
SWORD.ISH, *s.*, peixe-espada.
SYL.LA.BLE, *s.*, sílaba.
SYM.BOL, *s.*, símbolo.

SYM.BOL.IC, *adj.*, simbólico.
SYM.BOL.ISM, *s.*, simbolismo.
SYM.MET.RIC, *adj.*, simétrico.
SYM.ME.TRY, *s.*, simetria.
SYM.PA.THET.IC, *adj.*, simpático, agradável.
SYM.PA.THIZE, *v.*, simpatizar com, entender.
SYM.PA.THY, *s.*, simpatia, compreensão, compaixão.
SYM.PHON.IC, *adj.*, sinfônico.
SYM.PHO.NY, *s.*, sinfonia.
SYM.PO.SIUM, *s.*, simpósio.
SYMP.TOM, *s.*, sintoma, indício, suspeita.
SYN.A.GOGUE, *s.*, sinagoga.
SYN.CHRO.NIZE, *v.*, sincronizar.
SYN.DROME, *s.*, síndrome.
SYN.O.NYN, *s.*, sinônimo.
SYN.OP.SIS, *s.*, sinopse, resumo, síntese.
SYN.TAX, *s.*, sintaxe.
SYN.THE.SIS, *s.*, síntese.
SYN.THET.IC, *adj.*, sintético.
SYPH.I.LIS, *s.*, sífilis.
SYR.IA, *s.*, Síria.
SY.RINGE, *s.*, seringa.
SYR.UP, *s.*, xarope.
SYS.TEM, *s.*, sistema, método, modo.
SYS.TEM.AT.IC, *adj.*, sistemático, metódico.
SYS.TEM.A.TIZE, *v.*, sistematizar.

T

T, vigésima letra do alfabeto inglês.
TAB, *s.*, tira, aba, lingueta, alça; etiqueta de roupa.
TAB.ER.NA.CLE, *s.*, tabernáculo.
TA.BLE, *s.*, mesa; refeição, comida; platô, tabela, lista; *v.*, colocar na mesa, listar.
TA.BLE.CLOTH, *s.*, toalha de mesa.
TA.BLE.LAND, *s.*, planalto.
TA.BLE.SPOON, *s.*, colher de sopa.
TAB.LET, *s.*, tabuleta, bloco de papel; comprimido.
TAB.LOID, *s.*, tabloide.
TA.BOO, *s.*, tabu.
TAB.U.LAR, *adj.*, tabular.
TAB.U.LATE, *v.*, tabular, dar forma de tabela.
TACHY.GRAPHY, *s.*, taquigrafia.
TAC.IT, *adj.*, tácito, implícito, oculto.
TAC.I.TURN, *adj.*, taciturno, tristonho.
TACK, *s.*, tacha, prego; *v.*, prender, fixar com tacha.
TACK.LE, *s.*, aparelho, equipamento, guincho; *v.*, manejar, tentar resolver, agarrar.
TACKY, *adj.*, pegajoso.
TACT, *s.*, tato, diplomacia, postura.
TAC.TIC, *adj.*, tático.
TACT.ICS, *s.*, tática.
TAC.TIL.I.TY, *s.*, tactilidade, perceptibilidade.
TAD.POLE, *s.*, girino.
TAE.NIA, *s.*, tênia.
TAF.FY, *s.*, caramelo.
TAG, *s.*, etiqueta.
TAG.RAG, *s.*, canalha, calhorda, safado, cafajeste.
TAIL, *s.*, rabo, cauda, cauda de avião, parte traseira; *v.*, pôr um rabo.
TAIL.GATE, *s.*, porta traseira.
TAIL.LESS, *adj.*, pitoco, sem cauda.
TAI.LOR, *s.*, alfaiate.
TAINT, *s.*, nódoa, mancha, mácula; *v.*, manchar, enodoar, macular.
TAKE, *v.*, tomar, requerer, fotografar, exigir, agendar, pegar, tolerar.
TAKE.OFF, *s.*, decolagem.
TAK.ER, *s.*, tomador, comprador.
TAK.ING, *s.*, tomada, apreensão, arresto.
TAK.ING.NESS, *s.*, sedução, fascinação, atração.
TALC, *s.*, talco.
TALE, *s.*, conto, enredo, narrativa.
TAL.ENT, *s.*, talento.
TAL.IS.MAN, *s.*, talismã.
TALK, *s.*, conversa, fala, conversação, discurso, conselho; *v.*, falar, conversar, dizer.
TALK.A.TIVE, *adj.*, loquaz, tagarela.
TALK.ER, *s.*, falador, falante, tagarela, palrador.
TALK.ING, *s.*, conversa, conversação, tagarelice.
TALK.SHOW, *s.*, programa de rádio ou *TV*, entrevistando pessoas.
TALL, *adj.*, alto, grande, elevado, exagerado.
TALL.NESS, *s.*, altura, estatura, dimensão.
TAL.LY, *s.*, conta, registro, cálculo, rótulo, marca; *v.*, marcar, designar, controlar.
TAL.MUD, *s.*, Talmude.
TAM.A.BIL.I.TY, *s.*, docilidade, afabilidade.
TAM.A.RIND, *s.*, tamarindo.
TAM.BOUR, *s.*, tambor.
TAM.BOU.RINE, *s.*, tamborim.
TAME, *v.*, amansar, domesticar, domar, submeter, dominar, sujeitar.
TAM.PON, *s.*, tampão.
TANG, *s.*, sabor forte.
TAN.GENT, *s.*, tangente.
TAN.GER.INE, *s.*, tangerina.
TAN.GI.BLE, *adj.*, tangível.
TANK, *s.*, tanque, depósito.
TANK.ER, *s.*, navio-tanque, caminhão-tanque.
TAN.NERY, *s.*, curtume, fábrica para curtir couros.
TAN.NIN, *s.*, tanino.

TAN.NING, *s.*, curtimento.
TAP, *s.*, torneira, pancadinha, batida leve; *v.*, bater de leve, remendar, destampar.
TA.PER, *s.*, vela, círio, diminuição; *v.*, diminuir, afilar.
TAPE.WORM, *s.*, tênia.
TA.PIR, *s.*, anta, tapir.
TAP.STER, *s.*, taberneiro, empregado de bar, dono de bar.
TAR, *s.*, piche, alcatrão; marujo, marinheiro; *v.*, pichar.
TA.RAN.TU.LA, *s.*, tarântula, aranha.
TAR.DI.NESS, *s.*, lentidão, demora.
TAR.DY, *adj.*, lento, moroso, vagaroso.
TAR.IFF, *s.*, tarifa.
TAR.SUS, *s.*, tarso.
TART, *s.*, torta.
TAR.TAR, *s.*, tártaro.
TART.NESS, *s.*, acidez, azedume, amargor.
TASK, *s.*, tarefa, dever.
TASK.ING, *s.*, empreitada, tarefa.
TAST.ABLE, *adj.*, degustável, saboroso.
TASTE, *s.*, gosto, sabor, paladar; *v.*, provar, experimentar, degustar, saborear.
TAST.ER, *s.*, degustador, provador.
TASTY, *adj.*, saboroso, gostoso, delicioso.
TAT.TER, *s.*, farrapo, andrajo, traste; *v.*, esfarrapar.
TAT.TOO, *s.*, tatuagem; *v.*, tatuar.
TAUNT, *s.*, zombaria, mofa, escárnio; *v.*, zombar, escarnecer.
TAV.ERN, *s.*, taverna, estalagem, bar.
TAW.NY, *adj.*, ruivo, fulvo, trigueiro.
TAX, *s.*, taxa, imposto; *v.*, tributar, taxar, sobrecarregar.
TAX.A.TION, *s.*, taxação, tributação.
TAX-FREE, *adj.*, livre de impostos.
TAXI, *s.*, táxi.
TAXI.ME.TER, *s.*, taxímetro.
TEA, *s.*, chá, refeição de final de tarde.
TEACH, *v.*, ensinar, instruir, educar, dar aula, lecionar.
TEACH.ER, *s.*, professor.
TEACH.ING, *s.*, ensino, magistério.
TEA.CUP, *s.*, chávena, chávena de chá.

TEAM, *s.*, time, esquadra.
TEAM.WORK, *s.*, equipe de trabalho, grupo de trabalho.
TEA.POT, *s.*, bule de chá.
TEAR, *s.*, lágrima; *v.*, rasgar.
TEAR.FUL, *adj.*, choroso, lacrimoso.
TEA.SPOON, *s.*, colher de chá.
TEAT, *s.*, teta.
TEA.TIME, *s.*, hora do chá.
TECH.NI.CAL, *adj.*, técnico.
TECH.NI.CIAN, *s.*, técnico.
TECH.NICS, *s.*, técnica, tecnologia.
TECH.NOL.O.GY, *s.*, tecnologia.
TE.DIOUS, *adj.*, tedioso, fastidioso, aborrecido.
TE.DI.UM, *s.*, tédio, aborrecimento.
TEEN.AG.ER, *s.*, adolescente, jovem.
TEETH, *s.*, *pl.*, dentes.
TEETH.ING, *s.*, dentição.
TEE.TO.TAL.ISM, *s.*, abstenção de bebidas alcoólicas.
TELE.COM.MU.NI.CA.TIONS, *s.*, telecomunicações.
TELE.GRAM, *s.*, telegrama.
TELE.GRAPH, *s.*, telégrafo.
TELE.GRAPH.IC, *adj.*, telegráfico.
TE.LEG.RA.PHIST, *s.*, telegrafista.
TE.LEG.RA.PHY, *s.*, telegrafia.
TE.LEP.A.THY, *s.*, telepatia.
TELE.PHONE, *s.*, telefone; *v.*, telefonar.
TELE.PHON.ER, *s.*, telefonista.
TE.LE.PHON.IST, *s.*, telefonista.
TE.LE.PHO.NY, *s.*, telefonia.
TELE.SCOPE, *s.*, telescópio.
TELE.VI.SION, *s.*, televisão.
TEL.EX, *s.*, telex; *v.*, remeter comunicação por telex.
TELL, *v.*, dizer, contar, narrar, falar, distinguir.
TEL.LY, *s.*, *abrev.* de televisão.
TE.MER.I.TY, *s.*, temeridade.
TEM.PER, *s.*, temperamento, humor, modo de ser; *v.*, moderar, controlar.
TEM.PERA, *s.*, têmpera.
TEM.PER.A.MENT, *s.*, temperamento.
TEM.PER.ANCE, *s.*, temperança, moderação.

TEM.PER.ATE, *adj.*, temperado, clima temperado.
TEM.PER.A.TURE, *s.*, temperatura.
TEM.PEST, *s.*, tempestade, furacão.
TEM.PLE, *s.*, templo.
TEM.PO.RAL, *adj.* temporal, mundano: *s.*, temporal, têmpora.
TEM.PO.RARY, *adj.*, passageiro, transitório, temporário, fugaz.
TEM.PO.RIZE, *s.*, temporizar, contemporizar.
TEMP.TA.TION, *s.*, tentação, sedução.
TEMPT.ER, *s.*, tentador, sedutor.
TEN, *num.*, dez.
TE.NA.CIOUS, *adj.*, tenaz, persistente, teimoso.
TE.NAC.I.TY, *s.*, tenacidade.
TENANCY, *s.*, aluguel, arrendamento.
TEN.ANT, *s.*, inquilino.
TEND, *v.*, cuidar, zelar, tomar conta, prestar atenção.
TEN.DEN.CY, *s.*, tendência, inclinação, pendor.
TEN.DER, *s.*, proposta, prova, carne macia; *adj.*, tenro, macio; *v.*, oferecer, provar.
TEN.DER.NESS, *s.*, ternura, suavidade; maciez.
TEN.DON, *s.*, tendão.
TEN.E.BROUS, *adj.*, tenebroso, terrível.
TEN.FOLD, *adj.*, décuplo.
TEN.NIS, *s.*, tênis.
TENSE, *adj.*, tenso, rígido, estressado.
TEN.SION, *s.*, tensão.
TEN.SI.TY, *s.*, tensidade, tensão, rigidez.
TENT, *s.*, tenda, barraca.
TEN.TA.CLE, *s.*, tentáculo.
TENTH, *num.*, décimo.
TE.NU.ITY, *s.*, tenuidade.
TEN.URE, *s.*, posse de uma propriedade; estabilidade no emprego.
TEP.ID, *adj.*, tépido, morno.
TE.PID.I.TY, *s.*, tepidez, mornidade.
TER.CEN.TE.NA.RY, *s.*, tricentenário.
TERM, *s.*, termo, palavra; expressão, período, trimestre escolar, cláusulas contratuais.
TER.MI.NATE, *v.*, terminar, concluir, finalizar.
TER.MI.NA.TION, *s.*, término, limitação.
TER.MI.NOL.O.GY, *s.*, terminologia.
TERM.LESS, *adj.*, ilimitado, sem limite.
TER.RA, *s.*, terra.
TER.RACE, *s.*, terraço, fila de casas, casas ladeadas.
TER.RAIN, *s.*, terreno.
TER.RI.BLE, *adj.*, terrível, pavoroso, horroroso.
TER.RI.FY, *v.*, apavorar, aterrorizar, amedrontar.
TER.RI.TO.RY, *s.*, território.
TER.ROR, *s.*, terror.
TERRORISM, *s.*, terrorismo.
TER.ROR.IST, *s.*, terrorista.
TER.ROR.IZE, *v.*, aterrorizar, apavorar, terrificar.
TEST, *s.*, teste, prova, exame; *v.*, testar, examinar, verificar.
TES.TA.MENT, *s.*, testamento; **THE OLD/NEW TESTAMENT,** O Velho/Novo Testamento.
TES.TER, *s.*, provador, degustador, experimentador.
TES.TI.CLE, *s.*, testículo.
TES.TI.FY, *s.*, testemunhar, depor, ser testemunha judicial.
TES.TI.MO.NY, *s.*, testemunho, depoimento.
TES.TI.NESS, *s.*, mau humor, rabugice, irascibilidade.
TEST.ING, *s.*, prova, experimentação, ensaio.
TES.TY, *adj.*, teimoso, obstinado, cabeça-dura, irascível.
TET.A.NUS, *s.*, tétano.
TEXT, *s.*, texto, livro, livro didático, leitura didática.
TEX.TILE, *adj.*, têxtil.
TEX.TU.AL, *adj.*, textual.
THAI.LAND, *s.*, Tailândia.
THAMES, *s.*, Tâmisa.
THAN, *conj.*, que, do que.
THANK, *v.*, agradecer; *s.*, agradecimento; *interj.*, obrigado/obrigada.
THANK.FUL, *adj.*, agradecido, grato.
THANK.LESS, *adj.*, ingrato.
THAT, *pron., adj.*, esse, essa; aquele, aquela; *pron.*, isso, aquilo, quem, qual; *adv.*, tão.
THAW, *s.*, degelo, descongelamento; *v.*, degelar, derreter; descongelar.
THE, *art.*, o, a, os, as.

THE.ATRE, *s.*, teatro.
THEIR, *pron.*, seu, sua, seus, suas, dele, dela, deles, delas.
THEIRS, *pron.*, o seu, a sua, os seus, as suas.
THE.ISM, *s.*, teísmo.
THEM, *pron.*, os, as, lhes, a eles, a elas.
THEME, *s.*, tema.
THEM.SELVES, *pron.*, elas mesmas, eles mesmos; a si próprios, a si próprias; a si mesmos, a si mesmas.
THEN, *adv.*, naquele tempo, logo, depois; *conj.*, então, portanto, nesse caso.
THENCE, *adv.*, dali, daquele lugar.
THENCE.FORTH, *adv.*, desde então.
THE.OC.RA.CY, *s.*, teocracia.
THEO.LO.GIAN, *s.*, teólogo.
THE.OL.O.GY, *s.*, teologia.
THE.O.REM, *s.*, teorema.
THE.O.RIZE, *v.*, teorizar, trabalhar com teorias.
THE.O.RY, *s.*, teoria, ideia.
THER.A.PEU.TICS, *s.*, terapêutica.
THER.A.PIST, *s.*, terapeuta.
THER.A.PY, *s.*, terapia.
THERE, *adv.*, ali, lá, acolá, além.
THERE.AF.TER, *adv.*, depois disso.
THERE.BY, *adv.*, assim, deste modo.
THERE.FORE, *conj.*, portanto.
THERE.IN, *adv.*, nisto, nisso, naquele lugar, lá.
THERE.OF, *adv.*, disto, disso, daquilo.
THERE.UP.ON, *adv.*, nisto, nisso, naquilo, por causa disso.
THERE.WITH, *adv.*, com isso, com aquilo.
THER.MAL, *adj.*, térmico.
THER.MIC, *adj.*, térmico.
THER.MOM.E.TER, *s.*, termômetro.
THER.MO.STAT, *s.*, termostato.
THE.SAU.RUS, *s.*, tesouro, dicionário de sinônimos.
THESE, *pron., pl.*, estes, estas.
THE.SIS, *s.*, tese.
THEY, *pron.*, eles, elas.
THICK, *adj.*, espesso, denso, grosso.
THICK.EN, *v.*, adensar-se, espessar-se; engrossar.
THICK.NESS, *s.*, espessura, grossura, densidade.

THIEF, *s.*, ladrão, gatuno.
THIEVE, *v.*, roubar, furtar, surrupiar.
THIGH, *s.*, coxa.
THIM.BLE, *s.*, dedal.
THIN, *v.*, afinar, adelgar, diminuir; *adj.*, fino, estreito, magro, delgado, franzino.
THINE, *pron.*, o teu, a tua, os teus, as tuas.
THING, *s.*, coisa, objeto, assunto, tema; *pl.*, pertences, objetos.
THINK, *v.*, pensar, achar, imaginar.
THINK.ER, *s.*, pensador, raciocinador.
THINK.ING, *s.*, pensamento, meditação, raciocínio, reflexão.
THIN.NESS, *s.*, magreza, tenuidade.
THIRD, *num.*, terceiro, terço.
THIRD.ING, *s.*, a terça parte.
THIRST, *s.*, sede.
THIRSTY, *adj.*, sedento.
THIR.TEEN, *num.*, treze.
THIR.TEENTH, *num.*, décimo terceiro.
THIR.TI.ETH, *num.*, trigésimo.
THIR.TY, *num.*, trinta.
THIS, *pron.*, este, esta, isto.
THO.RAC.IC, *adj.*, torácico.
THO.RAX, *s.*, tórax.
THORN, *s.*, espinho.
THOR.OUGH, *adj.*, minucioso, detalhado, metódico.
THOR.OUGH.FARE, *s.*, via, passagem, caminho.
THOSE, *pron., pl.*, esses, essas.
THOUGH, *conj.*, embora, se bem que, no entanto.
THOUGHT, *s.*, pensamento, ideia, reflexão, meditação.
THOUGHT.FUL, *adj.*, pensativo, meditativo.
THOU.SAND, *num.*, mil.
THOU.SANDTH, *num.*, milésimo.
THRASH, *s.*, sova, tunda, espancamento; *v.*, surrar, bater, espancar.
THREE, *s.*, três.
THREE.FOLD, *num.*, triplo.
THRICE, *adv.*, três vezes.
THRIFT, *s.*, economia, poupança.
THRIFT.NESS, *s.*, economia, parcimônia.

THRIL.LER, *s.*, filme ou romance de suspense.
THROAT, *s.*, garganta.
THROB, *s.*, batimento, pulso, pulsação, emoção; *v.*, pulsar, bater, palpitar.
THROM.BO.SIS, *s.*, trombose.
THRONE, *s.*, trono.
THROUGH, *prep.*, por, através de, durante, por meio de, devido a; *adj.*, direto.
THROW, *s.*, arremesso, tiro, lançamento; *v.*, jogar, atirar, lançar, arremessar.
THROW.AWAY, *adj.*, descartável.
THRUST, *s.*, empuxo, impulso, golpe; *v.*, empurrar, impulsionar.
THUG, *s.*, criminoso, facínora, bandido.
THUMB, *s.*, polegar.
THUMP, *s.*, murro, soco, golpe, baque; *v.*, esmurrar, golpear.
THUND.ER, *s.*, trovão; *v.*, trovejar.
THUN.DER.BOLT, *s.*, raio, corisco.
THUN.DER.OUS, *adj.*, fulminante, pavoroso, terrível.
THUN.DER.STORM, *s.*, temporal.
THURS.DAY, *s.*, quinta-feira.
THUS, *adv.*, assim, dessa maneira.
THYME, *s.*, tomilho.
THY.ROID, *s.*, tiroide.
TIB.IA, *s.*, tíbia.
TIC, *s.*, tique, cacoete.
TICK, *s.*, tique-taque, sinal, marca; carrapato; *v.*, marcar, produzir o som de tique-taque.
TICK.ET, *s.*, tíquete, bilhete, passagem, entrada para espetáculo, etiqueta.
TICK.LING, *s.*, cócegas.
TIDE, *s.*, maré, fluxo, tendência do tempo; *v.*, navegar com a maré.
TI.DI.NESS, *s.*, asseio, higiene.
TIE, *s.*, fita, corda, cordel; vínculo; *v.*, amarrar, ligar, atar.
TIFF, *s.*, trago, gole; *v.*, beber, tragar, engolir.
TI.GER, *s.*, tigre.
TI.GER.ISH, *adj.*, feroz, próprio do tigre.
TIGHT.EN, *v.*, esticar, apertar, estender.
TIGHT.NESS, *s.*, aperto.
TI.GRESS, *s.*, tigre fêmea.

TIL.DE, *s.*, til.
TILE, *s.*, telha, azulejo, ladrilho.
TILL, *s.*, caixa registradora; *conj.*, até que; *v.*, amanhar, cultivar a terra.
TILL.AGE, *s.*, lavoura, agricultura.
TIL.LER, *s.*, lavrador, agricultor, colono, sitiante.
TIME, *s.*, tempo, época, era, hora, momento; *v.*, medir o tempo, marcar o tempo.
TIME.KEEP.ER, *s.*, indivíduo pontual.
TIME.LESS, *adj.*, perene, eterno, perpétuo.
TIM.ID, *adj.*, tímido, timorato, acanhado.
TI.MID.I.TY, *s.*, timidez, acanhamento, vergonha.
TIM.O.ROUS, *adj.*, tímido, acanhado, envergonhado.
TIM.PA.NO, *s.*, tímpano.
TIN, *s.*, estanho, lata de estanho.
TINC.TURE, *s.*, tintura, tingimento; *v.*, tingir, colorir.
TIN.DER.BOX, *s.*, isqueiro.
TI.NI.NESS, *s.*, pequenez, finura.
TIN.KLE, *v.*, tinir, fazer tinir.
TIN.KLING, *s.*, tinido.
TIN.MAN, *s.*, funileiro.
TINT, *s.*, tinta para cabelo, matiz, cor.
TIP, *s.*, ponta, fim, gorjeta; *v.*, dar uma gorjeta.
TIP.PLE, *s.*, bebida alcoólica; *v.*, beber sempre bebida alcoólica.
TIP.PLER, *s.*, bebedor.
TIP.PLING, *s.*, bebedeira, embriaguez.
TI.RADE, *s.*, tirada, discurso, diatribe, crítica violenta.
TIRE, *s.*, pneu; *v.*, cansar-se, aborrecer, aborrecer-se.
TIRED.NESS, *s.*, cansaço, fadiga.
TI.SANE, *s.*, tisana, infusão.
TIS.SUE, *s.*, tecido, lenço de papel.
TITHE, *s.*, dízimo, décima parte.
TI.TLE, *s.*, título.
TIT.U.LAR, *adj.*, *s.*, titular.
TO, *prep.*, para, a, até, de; *adv.*, em direção a, para diante.
TOAD, *s.*, sapo.
TOADY, *adj.*, bajulador, servil, adulador.
TOAST, *s.*, torrada, pão torrado; *v.*, torrar.

TOAST.ER, *s.*, torradeira.
TO.BAC.CO, *s.*, tabaco.
TO.BA.CO.NIST, *s.*, vendedor de tabaco.
TO.BOG.GAN, *s.*, tobogã.
TOD, *s.*, raposa.
TO.DAY, *adv.*, hoje.
TOE, *s.*, dedo do pé, bico do sapato.
TOE.NAIL, *s.*, unha do pé.
TOF.FEE, *s.*, caramelo, bala.
TO.GA, *s.*, toga.
TO.GETH.ER, *adv.*, juntos.
TOIL, *s.*, afã, labuta, trabalho, faina; *v.*, trabalhar, labutar.
TOI.LET, *s.*, banheiro, privada; local para higiene pessoal.
TO.KEN, *s.*, prova, símbolo, sinal, ficha.
TOL.ER.A.BIL.I.TY, *s.*, tolerabilidade.
TOL.ER.ANCE, *s.*, tolerância.
TOL.ER.ANT, *adj.*, tolerante.
TOL.ER.A.TION, *s.*, tolerância.
TO.MA.TO, *s.*, tomate.
TOMB, *s.*, túmulo, sepultura, cova, tumba.
TOMB.STONE, *s.*, lápide, pedra do túmulo.
TOM.CAT, *s.*, gato.
TOME, *s.*, tomo, volume, exemplar.
TOM.MY, *s.*, soldado do exército inglês.
TO.MOR.ROW, *adv.*, amanhã.
TON, *s.*, tonelada.
TO.NAL.I.TY, *s.*, tonalidade, tom.
TONE, *s.*, tom, tonalidade; *v.*, entoar, dar o tom.
TONGUE, *s.*, língua.
TON.IC, *adj.*, tônico.
TO.NIGHT, *adv.*, esta noite, hoje, hoje à noite.
TON.NAGE, *s.*, tonelagem.
TON.SIL, *s.*, amígdala.
TON.SIL.LI.TIS, *s.*, amigdalite.
TOO, *adv.*, demais, muito, demasiadamente.
TOOL, *s.*, ferramenta, ferramental; **TOOL BOX**, *s.*, caixa de ferramentas.
TOOT, *s.*, buzinada; *v.*, buzinar.
TOOTH, *s.*, dente.
TOOTH.ACHE, *s.*, dor de dentes.
TOOTH.BRUSH, *s.*, escova de dentes.
TOOTH.PASTE, *s.*, pasta de dentes.
TOOTH.PICK, *s.*, palito para dentes.
TOP, *s.*, cume, cimo, pico; *adj.*, máximo, altíssimo; *v.*, exceder, estar alto.
TO.PAZ, *s.*, topázio.
TOP.IC, *s.*, tópico, tema, assunto.
TOP.LESS, *s.*, topless, falta da parte superior do biquíni ou maiô.
TOP-LEVEL, *adj.*, referente ao mais alto nível.
TOP.MOST, *adj.*, o mais alto, supremo.
TO.POG.RA.PHER, *s.*, topógrafo.
TO.POG.RA.PHY, *s.*, topografia.
TOP-SECRET, *adj.*, ultra secreto, secretíssimo.
TORCH, *s.*, tocha, archote.
TO.RE.A.DOR, *s.*, toureiro.
TOR.MENT, *s.*, tormento, aflição, suplício, dor; *v.*, atormentar, afligir.
TOR.NA.DO, *s.*, tornado, furacão.
TOR.PE.DO, *s.*, torpedo.
TOR.PID.I.TY, *s.*, torpor, entorpecimento, inanição.
TOR.RE.FAC.TION, *s.*, torrefação.
TOR.RE.FY, *s.*, torrar.
TOR.RENT, *s.*, torrente, caudal.
TOR.RID, *adj.*, tórrido, causticante.
TOR.SION, *s.*, torção.
TORT, *s.*, dano, prejuízo.
TORT.OISE, *s.*, tartaruga.
TOR.TU.OS.I.TY, *s.*, tortuosidade.
TOR.TURE, *s.*, tortura, suplício; *v.*, torturar, supliciar.
TOSS, *v.*, atirar, arremessar, lançar.
TO.TAL, *s.*, total, soma total; *adj.*, total; *v.*, somar, calcular, totalizar.
TO.TAL.I.TY, *s.*, totalidade, soma total.
TO.TAL.IZE, *v.*, totalizar.
TOUCH, *s.*, toque, tato, contato, apalpadela; *v.*, tocar, apalpar, contatar.
TOUCH.ABLE, *adj.*, palpável, contatável.
TOUCHED, *adj.*, comovido.
TOUCH.STONE, *s.*, pedra de toque, padrão, critério, medida.
TOUGH.EN, *v.*, endurecer, fortalecer, enrijecer.
TOUR, *s.*, viagem, excursão; *v.*, viajar, excursionar.
TOUR.ISM, *s.*, turismo.

TOUR.IST, *s.*, turista, viajante.
TOUR.NA.MENT, *s.*, torneio.
TOW.AGE, *s.*, reboque, reboque de carro.
TO.WARD, *prep.*, em direção a.
TOW.EL, *s.*, toalha.
TOW.ER, *s.*, torre, torreão, espigão.
TOWN, *s.*, cidade.
TOWN.ISH, *adj.*, urbano, citadino.
TOX.IC, *adj.*, tóxico.
TOX.I.CANT, *s.*, veneno, tóxico.
TOY, *s.*, brinquedo.
TOY.SHOP, *s.*, loja de brinquedos.
TRACE, *s.*, traço, vestígio, sinal; *v.*, traçar, verificar, seguir os vestígios.
TRACK, *s.*, sinal, marca, vestígio, caminho, trajetória; *v.*, seguir a pista.
TRACK.AGE, *s.*, reboque.
TRACK.ING, *s.*, reboque.
TRACT, *s.*, região, localidade, zona; panfleto.
TRAC.TA.BIL.I.TY, *s.*, afabilidade, delicadeza.
TRAC.TATE, *s.*, tratado, discurso.
TRAC.TION, *s.*, tração.
TRAC.TOR, *s.*, trator.
TRADE, *s.*, comércio, negócio; *v.*, comerciar, negociar.
TRAD.ER, *s.*, comerciante, negociante.
TRADES.MAN, *s.*, comerciante, negociante.
TRA.DI.TION, *s.*, tradição.
TRA.DI.TION.AL, *adj.*, tradicional.
TRAF.FIC, *s.*, tráfico, trânsito, tráfego.
TRAF.FICK.ER, *s.*, traficante.
TRAG.E.DY, *s.*, tragédia.
TRAG.IC, *adj.*, trágico.
TRAIL.ER, *s.*, reboque, treiler, amostra de trechos de um filme.
TRAIL.ING, *s.*, reboque, treiler.
TRAIN, *s.*, trem, sucessão de fatos; *v.*, treinar, capacitar, preparar.
TRAIN.EE, *s.*, aprendiz, estagiário.
TRAIN.ER, *s.*, treinador, instrutor.
TRAIT, *s.*, traço, sinal, caráter, característica, predicado.
TRAI.TOR, *s.*, traidor.
TRAI.TRESS, *s.*, traidora.

TRA.JECT, *s.*, trajeto, roteiro.
TRA.JEC.TO.RY, *s.*, trajetória.
TRAM, *s.*, bonde; **TRAM CAR**, bonde elétrico.
TRAMP, *s.*, vagabundo.
TRAM.PO.LINE, *s.*, trampolim.
TRANCE, *s.*, transe, torpor, êxtase.
TRAN.QUIL, *adj.*, tranquilo.
TRAN.QUIL.I.TY, *s.*, tranquilidade.
TRAN.QUIL.IZE, *v.*, tranquilizar.
TRANS.ACT, *v.*, negociar, comerciar.
TRANS.AC.TION, *s.*, transação, negócio.
TRAN.SCEND, *v.*, transcender, exceder, ir além.
TRAN.SCEN.DENCE, *s.*, transcendência.
TRAN.SCRIBE, *v.*, transcrever, reproduzir.
TRAN.SCRIPT, *s.*, transcrição, cópia, reprodução.
TRANS.FER, *v.*, transferir, mudar, deslocar.
TRANS.FER.ENCE, *s.*, transferência.
TRANS.FIG.U.RA.TION, *s.*, transfiguração.
TRANS.FIG.URE, *v.*, transfigurar.
TRANS.FIX, *v.*, trespassar.
TRANS.FORM, *v.*, transformar, mudar.
TRANS.FOR.MA.TION, *s.*, transformação, mudança.
TRANS.FORM.ER, *s.*, transformador.
TRANS.GRESS, *v.*, transgredir, violar, desrespeitar.
TRANS.GRES.SION, *s.*, transgressão, violação, desrespeito.
TRAN.SIT, *s.*, trânsito, tráfego, passagem.
TRAN.SI.TION, *s.*, transição, passagem, mudança.
TRAN.SI.TIVE, *adj.*, transitivo.
TRANS.LATE, *s.*, verter, traduzir.
TRANS.LA.TOR, *s.*, tradutor, intérprete.
TRANS.MI.GRA.TION, *s.*, transmigração.
TRANS.MIS.SION, *s.*, transmissão.
TRANS.MIT, *v.*, transmitir, enviar, remeter, mandar.
TRANS.MIT.TER, *s.*, transmissor.
TRAN.SOM, *s.*, trave, travessa.
TRANS.PAR.EN.CY, *s.*, transparência, diafaneidade.
TRAN.SPIRE, *v.*, transpirar, suar; tornar público.
TRANS.PLANT, *v.*, transplantar; *s.*, transplante.

TRANSPORT — **TRUCK**

TRANS.PORT, s., transporte; v., transportar.
TRANS.POR.TA.TION, s., transporte.
TRANS.POSE, v., transpor.
TRANS.VER.SAL, adj., transversal.
TRANS.VES.TITE, s., travesti.
TRA.PEZE, s., trapézio.
TRASH, s., lixo, rejeitos.
TRASHY, adj., desprezível, descartável.
TRAU.MA, s., trauma.
TRAU.MAT.IC, adj., traumático.
TRAV.EL, s., viagem; v., viajar, percorrer lugares.
TRAV.EL.LER, s., caixeiro viajante.
TRAV.EL.LING, s., viagem.
TRAV.ES.TY, s., paródia.
TRAY, s., bandeja, cesta, cesto.
TREACH.ERY, s., traição.
TREA.SURE, s., tesouro, joia; v., apreciar, admirar.
TREA.SUR.ER, s., tesoureiro.
TREAT, s., festim, prazer, satisfação.
TREATY, s., tratado, acordo, combinação.
TRE.BLE, adj., tríplice; v., triplicar.
TREE, s., árvore, planta.
TRE.FOIL, s., trevo, folha com três pontas.
TREK, s., jornada, viagem, caminhada.
TREL.LIS, s., latada, pérgola.
TREM.BLE, v., tremer.
TREM.OR, s., tremor, tremida.
TREM.U.LANT, adj., trêmulo, tremente.
TRENCH, s., trincheira.
TREND, s., tendência, pendor, inclinação.
TREP.I.DA.TION, s., trepidação, exaltação, alarme.
TRESS, s., trança, madeixa.
TREY, s., três, terno.
TRI.AN.GLE, s., triângulo.
TRIBE, s., tribo.
TRIB.U.LA.TION, s., tribulação, sofrimento, tormento.
TRI.BU.NAL, s., tribunal.
TRI.BUNE, s., tribuna; tribuno, orador.
TRIB.UTE, s., tributo, homenagem.
TRICK, s., truque, habilidade, peça, fraude, logro.

TRICK.ER, s., enganador, trapaceiro.
TRICK.STER, s., trapaceiro, velhaco, impostor.
TRICKSY, s., brincalhão.
TRI.CY.CLE, s., triciclo.
TRI.EN.NI.AL, adj., trienal; s., triênio.
TRIG.GER, s., gatilho.
TRIG.O.NOM.E.TRY, s., trigonometria.
TRILL, s., gorjeio; v., trilar, gorjear.
TRIL.O.GY, s., trilogia.
TRIM, s., decoração, ornamento; v., arranjar, ordenar, organizar, ajustar, equipar.
TRIM.MING, s., enfeite, ornato.
TRIM.NESS, s., asseio, higiene, elegância.
TRIN.I.TY, s., trindade.
TRI.NO.MI.AL, adj., s., trinômio.
TRIO, s., trio.
TRIP, s., viagem, excursão; v., andar, caminhar, viajar; tropeçar.
TRIPE, s., entranhas, tripas, vísceras, bucho.
TRIPH.THONG, s., tritongo.
TRI.PLE, s.m., adj., triplo, tríplice.
TRIP.LET, s., trigêmeo.
TRIP.LI.CATE, adj., triplicado.
TRI.POD, s., tripé.
TRI.SYL.LAB.IC, adj., trissilábico.
TRI.SYL.LA.BLE, s., trissílabo.
TRIT.NESS, s., banalidade, vulgaridade.
TRI.UMPH, s., triunfo, vitória; v., triunfar.
TRIV.I.AL, adj., trivial, comum, vulgar, ordinário.
TRIV.I.AL.I.TY, s., trivialidade, banalidade.
TROOP, s., tropa, grupo, bando.
TRO.PHY, s., troféu.
TROP.IC, s., trópico.
TROP.I.CAL, adj., tropical.
TROT.TING, s., trote.
TROU.BLE, s., problema, dificuldade, preocupação; v., incomodar, perturbar.
TROU.BLER, s., incomodador, perturbador.
TROU.BLE.SHOOT.ER, s., conciliador, árbitro.
TROUPE, s., trupe, companhia teatral.
TROUT, s., truta.
TROW, v., pensar, cogitar, refletir, crer.
TRUCE, s., armistício, trégua.
TRUCK, s., caminhão, vagão.

TRUCK.ER, *s.*, caminhoneiro.
TRU.CU.LENCE, *s.*, truculência, barbaridade.
TRUE, *adj.*, verdadeiro, correto, genuíno.
TRUE.NESS, *s.*, verdade, sinceridade, genuinidade.
TRUM.PET, *s.*, trombeta.
TRUN.CATE, *v.*, truncar, cortar, amputar.
TRUN.CHEON, *s.*, cacete, pau.
TRUNK, *s.*, tronco, tronco de pessoa, tromba de elefante.
TRUST, *s.*, confiança, fé; *v.*, confiar, acreditar, crer.
TRUST.ER, *s.*, quem confia, fiador.
TRUST.I.NESS, *s.*, fidelidade, confiança.
TRUSTY, *adj.*, fiel, confiável.
TRUTH, *s.*, verdade.
TRY, *s.*, tentativa; *v.*, julgar, examinar, provar, cansar, fatigar.
TSAR, *s.*, czar.
TUB, *s.*, tina, banheira.
TUB.BY, *adj.*, gorducho.
TUBE, *s.*, cano, tubo, câmara do pneu; metrô.
TU.BER.CLE, *s.*, tubérculo.
TU.BER.CU.LO.SIS, *s.*, tuberculose.
TU.BER.CU.LOUS, *adj.*, tuberculoso.
TUCK, *s.*, dobra, prega; *v.*, comprimir, enfiar, meter.
TUES.DAY, *s.*, terça-feira.
TUFT, *s.*, penacho, tufo.
TU.LIP, *s.*, tulipa.
TUM.BLE, *s.*, queda, caída; *v.*, cair, tombar.
TU.ME.FAC.TION, *s.*, tumefação, inchamento.
TU.ME.FY, *v.*, inchar, intumescer.
TU.MID, *adj.*, túmido, inchado.
TUM.MY, *s.*, barriga, estômago.
TU.MOUR, *s.*, tumor.
TU.MULT, *s.*, tumulto, confusão, baderna.
TUN, *s.*, tonel, barril, pipa.
TUNE, *s.*, melodia, tonalidade, canção; *v.*, afinar, sintonizar, cantar afinado.
TU.NIC, *s.*, túnica.
TUN.NEL, *s.*, túnel, galeria.
TUN.NY, *s.*, atum.
TUR.BINE, *s.*, turbina.
TUR.BU.LENCE, *s.*, turbulência.
TU.REEN, *s.*, terrina, sopeira.
TURK, *adj.*, *s.*, turco.
TUR.KEY, *s.*, peru.
TURN, *s.*, turno, volta, tendência, curva de estrada; *v.*, dar volta, virar, girar.
TURN BACK, *v.*, voltar, retornar.
TURN.ER, *s.*, torneiro.
TUR.NIP, *s.*, nabo.
TURN.KEY, *s.*, chaveiro, carcereiro.
TURN.OVER, *s.*, rotatividade de empregados; total de negócios.
TURN.PIKE, *s.*, posto de pedágio, estrada com pedágio.
TUR.QUOISE, *s.*, turquesa.
TUR.TLE, *s.*, tartaruga.
TU.TE.LAGE, *s.*, tutoria, tutela, guarda.
TU.TOR, *s.*, tutor, preceptor, professor universitário.
TWEED, *s.*, tecido de lã.
TWEE.ZERS, *s.*, pinça pequena.
TWELFTH, *num.*, décimo segundo, duodécimo.
TWUELVE, *num.*, doze.
TWEN.TI.ETH, *num.*, vigésimo.
TWEN.TY, *num.*, vinte.
TWICE, *adv.*, duas vezes.
TWI.LIGHT, *s.*, crepúsculo.
TWIN, *s.*, gêmeo idêntico, gêmeo.
TWIRL.ING, *s.*, volta, giro.
TWIST, *s.*, torção, giro, mudança imprevista, tipo de dança; *v.*, torcer, enrolar.
TWIT, *s.*, imbecil, idiota, pateta.
TWITCH, *s.*, puxão, contração, empurrão; *v.*, contrair-se.
TWIT.TER, *s.*, gorjeio, chilro; *v.*, gorjear.
TWO, *num.*, dois.
TWO.FOLD, *num.*, duplo, duplicado.
TWO.SOME, *s.*, casal, par, parelha.
TWO-WAY, *s.*, dois sentidos, caminho com dois sentidos.
TYM.PA.NUM, *s.*, tímpano.
TYPE, *s.*, tipo, espécie, padrão; *v.*, datilografar, digitar.
TYPE.FACE, *s.*, tipo de letra.
TYPE.WRITE, *v.*, datilografar.

TYPE.WRIT.ING, *s.*, datilografia.
TY.PHOID, *s.*, febre tifoide.
TY.PHOON, *s.*, tufão, furacão.
TY.PHUS, *s.*, tifo.
TYP.I.CAL, *adj.*, típico.
TYP.I.FY, *v.*, tipificar, simbolizar.
TYP.ING, *s.*, datilografia.
TYP.IST, *s.*, datilógrafo, datilógrafa.

TY.POG.RA.PHER, *s.*, tipógrafo.
TY.POG.RA.PHY, *s.*, tipografia.
TYR.AN.NIZE, *v.*, tiranizar, massacrar.
TYR.AN.NY, *s.*, tirania.
TY.RANT, *s.*, tirano, déspota.
TYRE, *s.*, pneu.
TY.RO.LESE, *adj.*, *s.*, tirolês.

U

U, *s.*, vigésima primeira letra do alfabeto inglês.
UBIQ.UI.TY, *s.*, ubiquidade.
UD.DER, *s.*, úbere.
UG.LI.FY, *v.*, enfear, tornar feio.
UG.LI.NESS, *s.*, feiura, fealdade.
UG.LY, *adj.*, feio, repulsivo, mau, desagradável.
UL.CER, *s.*, úlcera.
UL.CER.ATE, *v.*, ulcerar, provocar úlcera.
UL.CER.OUS, *adj.*, ulceroso.
UL.STER, *s.*, Irlanda do Norte.
UL.TE.RI.OR, *adj.*, ulterior, posterior.
UL.TI.MATE, *adj.*, último, final.
UL.TI.MA.TUM, *s.*, ultimato.
UL.TRA.MA.RINE, *adj.*, ultramarino.
UL.TRA.SOUND, *s.*, ultrassom.
UM.BER, *adj.*, sombreado; *v.*, sombrear, provocar sombra.
UM.BIL.I.CAL, *adj.*, umbilical.
UM.BRAGE, *s.*, sombra, suspeita, desconfiança.
UM.BREL.LA, *s.*, guarda-chuva.
UM.PIRE, *s.*, árbitro de jogo; *v.*, arbitrar, conduzir, apitar.
UMP.TEEN, *adj.*, inúmero, inúmeros.
UN.ABLE, *adj.*, incapaz, inábil, impotente, despreparado.
UN.AC.CEPT.ABLE, *adj.*, inaceitável.
UN.AC.COUNT.ABLE, *adj.*, inexplicável.
UN.AD.VISED, *adj.*, indiscreto.
UN.AF.FECT.ED, *adj.*, leal, sincero, discreto, franco, fiel.
UN.AL.LOW.ABLE, *adj.*, inadmissível.
UN.ALTER.ED, *adj.*, inalterado.
UNA.NIM.I.TY, *s.*, unanimidade.
UN.AP.PROVED, *adj.*, desaprovado, não aprovado.
UN.ARM, *v.*, desarmar, tornar desarmado.
UN.ASHAMED, *adj.*, descarado, desavergonhado.
UN.AT.TACHED, *adj.*, solto, liberado, livre.
UN.AU.THO.RIZED, *adj.*, não autorizado, desautorizado.
UN.AVAIL.ING, *adj.*, inútil.
UN.BAL.ANCE, *v.* desequilibrar.
UN.BE.COM.ING, *adj.*, indecente, indecoroso, despudorado.
UN.BE.LIEF, *s.*, descrença, descrédito, incredulidade.
UN.BE.LIEV.ER, *s.*, incrédulo, descrente, céptico, agnóstico.
UN.BEND.ING, *adj.*, intransigente, exigente, obstinado.
UN.BI.ASED, *adj.*, imparcial, justo.
UN.BID.DEN, *adj.*, espontâneo, natural.
UN.BOIL.ED, *adj.*, cru, não cozido.
UN.BORN, *adj.*, por nascer, nascituro, futuro.
UN.BOUND.ED, *adj.*, ilimitado, imenso, sem limites.
UN.BUR.DEN, *v.*, descarregar.
UN.CAN.NY, *adj.*, estranho, esquisito.
UN.CEAS.ING, *adj.*, contínuo, continuado.
UN.CER.TAIN, *adj.*, incerto, improvável, indeciso.
UN.CHAIN, *v.*, libertar, liberar.
UN.CHANGED, *adj.*, inalterado, imutável.
UN.CHAS.TI.TY, *s.*, despudor, impureza.
UN.CIV.IL, *adj.*, incivil, grosseiro, bruto.
UN.CLAIMED, *adj.*, não reclamado, não buscado.
UNCLE, *s.*, tio.
UN.CLEAN, *adj.*, sujo, imundo, porco, sórdido.
UN.CLEAN.NESS, *s.*, impureza, sujeira, sujidade, imundície.
UN.CLOSE, *v.*, abrir, desabotoar, desabrochar.
UN.CLOTHED, *adj.*, despido, nu, pelado.
UN.CO, *adj.*, raro, singular, único.
UN.COM.MON, *adj.*, incomum, raro, singular.
UN.CON.CERN, *s.*, indiferença.
UN.CON.CERNED, *adj.*, indiferente, insensível, despreocupado.
UN.CON.DI.TION.AL, *adj.*, incondicional.

UNCONNECTED — UNFASTEN

UN.CON.NECT.ED, *adj.*, desconectado, desligado, desatado.
UN.CON.STI.TU.TION.AL, *adj.*, inconstitucional.
UN.CON.TROL.LA.BLE, *adj.*, incontrolável.
UN.COOKED, *adj.*, cru, não cozido.
UN.COR.RECT.ED, *adj.*, incorreto, não correto.
UN.COR.RUPT, *adj.*, incorrupto, sério, puro.
UN.COUTH, *adj.*, rude, grosseiro, bruto, bárbaro.
UN.COV.ER, *v.*, destampar, destapar, descobrir.
UNC.TION, *s.*, unção, ungimento.
UN.CUL.TURED, *adj.*, inculto, não cultivado.
UN.CUT, *adj.*, inteiro, inteiriço, não cortado.
UN.DAT.ED, *adj.*, não datado.
UN.DE.CID.ED, *adj.*, indeciso, hesitante, vacilante.
UN.DE.CID.ED.NESS, *s.*, indecisão, hesitação.
UN.DE.FEND.ED, *adj.*, indefeso, sem defesa.
UN.DE.FINED, *adj.*, indefinido.
UN.DER, *prep.*, debaixo de, sob, segundo, de acordo com; *adv.*, debaixo.
UN.DER-AGE, *adj.*, menor, menor de idade, adolescente.
UN.DER.BUY, *v.*, comprar por preço menor, pagar menos do que vale.
UN.DER.COV.ER, *adj.*, secreto, sigiloso, clandestino, tácito.
UN.DER.ES.TI.MATE, *v.*, subestimar, não avaliar certo.
UN.DER.FEED, *adj.*, desnutrido.
UN.DER.GRAD.U.ATE, *s.*, universitário.
UN.DER.GROUND, *s.*, metrô, grupo clandestino; *adj.*, subterrâneo, clandestino.
UN.DER.LEASE, *s.*, sublocação; *v.*, sublocar.
UN.DER.LINE, *v.*, sublinhar, destacar.
UN.DER.LIN.EN, *s.*, roupa íntima.
UN.DER.LING, *s.*, subalterno.
UN.DER.MINE, *v.*, solapar, minar, colocar minas.
UN.DER.MOST, *adj.*, ínfimo, o mais baixo.
UN.DER.PAID, *adj.*, mal pago.
UN.DER.PRAISE, *v.*, desprezar, menosprezar, desdenhar.
UN.DER.SELL, *v.*, vender por preço inferior.
UN.DER.SET, *s.*, ressaca.
UN.DER.SIDE, *s.*, local inferior.
UN.DER.STAND, *v.*, entender, compreender.
UN.DER.STOOD, *adj.*, compreendido, entendido.
UN.DER.TAK.ER, *s.*, agente funerário; empresário.
UN.DER.VAL.UE, *v.*, subavaliar, subestimar.
UN.DER.WORLD, *s.*, submundo, baixo-mundo.
UN.DER.WRIT.ING, *s.*, seguro.
UN.DER.WRIT.TEN, *adj.*, abaixo-assinado.
UN.DE.SIR.ABLE, *adj.*, indesejável, impróprio.
UN.DE.TER.MI.NATE, *adj.*, indeterminado.
UN.DE.TERRED, *adj.*, valente, ousado, decidido.
UN.DIS.CI.PLINED, *adj.*, indisciplinado.
IN.DIS.COV.ERED, *adj.*, oculto, clandestino.
UN.DIS.PUT.ED, *adj.*, incontestável, irrefutável.
UN.DIS.TRACT.ED, *adj.*, atento, atencioso.
UN.DIS.TURBED, *adj.*, impassível, tranquilo.
UN.DI.VID.ED, *adj.*, inteiro, indiviso.
UN.DO, *v.*, desatar, desmanchar.
UN.DO.ING, *s.*, ruína, desgraça.
UN.DONE, *adj.*, incompleto, inacabado.
UN.DUE, *adj.*, impróprio, incorreto, inadequado.
UN.DY.ING, *adj.*, imortal, perene, eterno.
UN.EARNED, *adj.*, imerecido.
UN.EASY, *adj.*, preocupado, incômodo, desconfortável.
UN.ECO.NOM.IC, *adj.*, antieconômico.
UN.ED.U.CAT.ED, *adj.*, iletrado, analfabeto, não escolarizado.
UN.EM.PLOYED, *adj.*, desempregado.
UN.EQUAL, *adj.*, desigual, irregular.
UN.EQUIV.O.CAL, *adj.*, inequívoco, evidente, claro.
UN.ERR.ING, *adj.*, infalível.
UN.EVENT.FUL, *adj.*, calmo, tranquilo, sossegado.
UN.EX.CEP.TION.AL, *adj.*, usual, diário, corrente.
UN.EX.PE.RI.ENCED, *adj.*, inexperiente.
UN.EX.PECT.ED, *adj.*, inesperado.
UN.EX.PRES.SIVE, *adj.*, inexpressivo.
UN.FAIR.NESS, *s.*, injustiça, deslealdade, infidelidade.
UN.FAL.TER.ING, *adj.*, firme, decidido, resoluto.
UN.FASH.ION.ABLE, *adj.*, fora de moda.
UN.FAS.TEN, *v.*, desatar.

UN.FA.VOUR.ABLE, *adj.*, desfavorável.
UN.FEEL.ING, *adj.*, insensível.
UN.FET.TER, *v.*, soltar, colocar em liberdade.
UN.FIN.ISHED, *adj.*, incompleto, inacabado, não lapidado.
UN.FOLD, *v.*, desdobrar.
UN.FORE.SEEN, *adj.*, imprevisto.
UN.FOR.GET.TA.BLE, *adj.*, inesquecível.
UN.FORMED, *adj.*, não formado, informe.
UN.FOR.TU.NATE, *adj.*, infortunado, infeliz.
UN.FOUND.ED, *adj.*, infundado.
UN.FRUIT.FUL, *adj.*, infrutífero, estéril.
UN.FURL, *v.*, estender, desdobrar, esticar.
UN.GEN.ER.OUS, *adj.*, mesquinho.
UN.GLOR.I.OUS, *adj.*, inglório, modesto.
UN.GOD.LY, *adj.*, ímpio, ateu, malvado.
UN.GOV.ERN.ABLE, *adj.*, ingovernável.
UN.GRACE.FUL, *adj.*, sem graça, desgracioso, insosso.
UN.GRATE.FUL, *adj.*, ingrato, desagradável, mal-agradecido.
UN.GUENT, *s.*, unguento.
UN.GUAL, *s.*, unha, garra.
UN.HAP.PY, *adj.*, infeliz, triste, tristonho, infortunado, desgraçado.
UN.HARMED, *adj.*, ileso, indene.
UN.HEALTHY, *adj.*, insalubre, doentio, doente.
UN.HEED.ING, *adj.*, negligente, descuidado, despreocupado, relapso.
UN.HOPED, *adj.*, inesperado.
UN.HOUSE, *v.*, desalojar, despejar.
UNI.CY.CLE, *s.*, monociclo.
UNI.FI.CA.TION, *s.*, unificação.
UNI.FORM, *adj., s.*, uniforme.
UNI.FOR.MI.TY, *s.*, uniformidade.
UNI.FY, *v.*, unificar, unir, reunir.
UNI.LAT.ER.AL, *adj.*, unilateral.
UN.IN.FORMED, *adj.*, incauto, imprudente.
UN.IN.TEL.LI.GENT, *adj.*, imbecil, não inteligente.
UN.IN.TER.EST.ED, *adj.*, desinteressado, indiferente.
UN.IN.TER.RUPT.ED, *adj.*, contínuo, ininterrupto.
UNION, *s.*, união.
UNIQUE, *adj.*, único, ímpar.
UNI.SEX, *adj.*, unissexo.
UNIT, *s.*, unidade, equipe, grupo.
UNI.TARY, *adj.*, unitário, total.
UNITE, *v.*, unir, ligar, reunir.
UNI.TY, *s.*, unidade.
UNI.VER.SAL, *adj.*, universal.
UNI.VER.SAL.ISM, *s.*, universalismo.
UNI.VER.SAL.I.TY, *s.*, universalidade.
UNI.VER.SAL.IZE, *v.*, universalizar.
UNI.VERSE, *s.*, universo.
UNI.VER.SI.TY, *s.*, universidade.
UN.JUST, *adj.*, injusto.
UN.JUS.TI.FI.ABLE, *adj.*, injustificável.
UN.JUST.NESS, *s.*, injustiça.
UN.KIND, *adj.*, maldoso, cruel, perverso.
UN.KNOW.ING, *adj.*, ignorante, iletrado, estúpido.
UN.KNOWN, *adj.*, desconhecido; ignoto.
UN.LACE, *v.*, desatar, desamarrar.
UN.LAW.FUL, *adj.*, ilegal.
UN.LEARN, *v.*, desaprender.
UN.LESS, *conj.*, a menos que.
UN.LIKE, *adj.*, diferente, diverso; *prep.*, ao contrário de, ao invés de.
UN.LIM.IT.ED, *adj.*, ilimitado, infinito.
UN.LOCK, *v.*, abrir, destrancar, destravar.
UN.LUCKY, *adj.*, infeliz, mal-humorado, taciturno.
UN.MAKE, *v.*, destruir, arruinar, depor.
UN.MARKED, *adj.*, sem marca.
UN.MAR.RIED, *adj.*, solteiro.
UN.MEA.SUR.ABLE, *adj.*, imensurável.
UN.MER.CI.FUL, *adj.*, cruel, impiedoso, perverso.
UN.MIND.FUL, *adj.*, descuidado, insensível, indiferente.
UN.MIXED, *adj.*, puro, não misturado.
UN.MOV.ABLE, *adj.*, imóvel, inarredável.
UN.NAMED, *adj.*, anônimo.
UN.NEC.ES.SARY, *adj.*, desnecessário.
UN.NERVE, *v.*, enervar, enfraquecer.
UN.NUM.BERED, *adj.*, inumerável.
UN.OB.SERV.ANCE, *s.*, inobservância, descuido.
UN.OC.CU.PIED, *adj.*, vago, desocupado, livre.
UN.OF.FEN.SIVE, *adj.*, inofensivo.

UN.OPENED, *adj.*, fechado.
UN.OWNED, *adj.*, sem dono.
UN.PAID, *adj.*, não pago, não ressarcido.
UN.PAR.DON.ABLE, *adj.*, imperdoável.
UN.PEO.PLE, *v.*, despovoar.
UN.PER.TURBED, *adj.*, calmo, sossegado, impassível.
UN.PICK, *v.*, desfazer, desmanchar, desatar.
UN.PIT.Y.ING, *adj.*, cruel, malvado, maldoso, perverso.
UN.PLUG, *v.*, desligar, desconectar, desarrolhar, destampar.
UN.PO.LITE, *adj.*, descortês, malcriado, grosseiro.
UN.POP.U.LAR, *adj.*, impopular.
UN.PRE.TEN.TIOUS, *adj.*, despretensioso.
UN.PRICED, *adj.*, sem preço.
UN.PRINTED, *adj.*, não impresso.
UN.PRO.DUC.TIVE, *adj.*, improdutivo.
UN.PROF.IT.ABLE, *adj.*, inútil.
UN.PRO.PI.TIOUS, *adj.*, desfavorável, não propício.
UN.PROVED, *adj.*, não provado.
UN.PUNC.TU.AL.I.TY, *s.*, impontualidade.
UN.PUN.ISHED, *adj.*, impune.
UN.READ, *adj.*, iletrado, não lido, ignorante.
UN.REAL, *adj.*, irreal, ilusório.
UN.RE.AL.I.TY, *s.*, irrealidade.
UN.REA.SON, *s.*, absurdo.
UN.RE.CLAIMED, *adj.*, não reclamado.
UN.REC.ON.CIL.ABLE, *adj.*, irreconciliável.
UN.RE.LAXED, *adj.*, não relaxado.
UN.RE.LIEVED, *adj.*, não socorrido.
UN.RE.MEM.BERED, *adj.*, esquecido.
UN.RE.PAID, *adj.*, não reembolsado.
UN.RE.PAIR.ABLE, *adj.*, irreparável.
UN.REST, *s.*, inquietação, distúrbio, confusão.
UN.RE.STORED, *adj.*, não recuperado.
UN.RIGHT.FUL, *adj.*, injusto, perverso, malvado.
UN.RIPE, *adj.*, verde, imaturo, não maduro.
UN.ROBE, *v.*, desnudar, tirar a roupa, pelar.
UN.ROLL, *v.*, desenrolar.
UN.RUL.I.NESS, *s.*, indisciplina, desordem.
UN.SAFE, *adj.*, perigoso.
UN.SALE.ABLE, *adj.*, não vendável.
UN.SAT.IS.FAC.TO.RY, *adj.*, insatisfatório.
UN.SAT.IS.FIED, *adj.*, insatisfeito.
UN.SA.VOUR.I.NESS, *s.*, insipidez.
UN.SAY, *v.*, desdizer, desmentir.
UN.SCREW, *v.*, desparafusar.
UN.SEAT, *v.*, derrubar, depor.
UN.SEA.WOR.THY, *adj.*, inegável.
UN.SEEING, *adj.*, invisível, oculto, escondido.
UN.SHAK.EN, *adj.*, firme, imóvel.
UN.SHOD, *adj.*, descalço.
UN.SO.CIA.BIL.I.TY, *s.*, insociabilidade.
UN.SOLD, *adj.*, não vendido.
UN.SO.LIC.IT.ED, *adj.*, não solicitado, não pedido.
UN.SPAR.ING, *adj.*, generoso, bondoso.
UN.SPENT, *adj.*, não gasto.
UN.SPO.KEN, *adj.*, não falado.
UN.STA.BIL.I.TY, *s.*, instabilidade.
UN.SUC.CESS.FUL, *adj.*, frustrado, mal sucedido.
UN.SUP.PORT.ABLE, *adj.*, insuportável.
UN.SURE, *adj.*, inseguro, incerto.
UN.SUS.PECT.ED, *adj.*, insuspeito.
UN.SYM.PA.THET.IC, *adj.*, antipático, insensível.
UN.TAPPED, *adj.*, inexplorado.
UN.TAUGHT, *adj.*, ignorante, analfabeto, iletrado.
UN.TEN.A.BLE, *adj.*, insustentável.
UN.THANK.FUL, *adj.*, ingrato, mal-agradecido.
UN.THRIFTY, *adj.*, pródigo.
UN.TIE, *v.*, soltar, desatar, desmanchar.
UN.TIL, *prep.*, até; *conj.*, até que.
UN.TOLD, *adj.*, inédito, inestimável.
UN.TOUCHED, *adj.*, intato, inteiro, ileso, intocado.
UN.TRAINED, *adj.*, indisciplinado, desordeiro.
UN.TRANS.FER.ABLE, *adj.*, intransferível.
UN.TROU.BLED, *adj.*, calmo, inquieto, tranquilo.
UN.TRUE, *adj.*, falso, errado.
UN.TRUE.NESS, *s.*, mentira, falsidade.
UN.TRUTH, *s.*, mentira, falsidade.
UN.USED, *adj.*, sem uso, novo, completo.
UN.VAR.I.ABLE, *adj.*, invariável.
UN.VARY.ING, *adj.*, invariável.
UN.VERSED, *adj.*, inexperiente, ignorante,

desconhecedor.
UN.WANT.ED, *adj.*, indesejado, indesejável, malquisto.
UN.WAR.RANT.ED, *adj.*, não garantido.
UN.WASHED, *adj.*, sujo, imundo, não lavado.
UN.WEL.COME, *adj.*, inoportuno, aborrecido.
UN.WHOLE.SOME, *adj.*, insalubre, doentio.
UN.WISE, *adj.*, imprudente, desavisado.
UN.WIT.TING, *adj.*, inconsciente, involuntário.
UN.WOR.THY, *adj.*, indigno, desprezível.
UN.WRIT.TEN, *adj.*, não escrito, tácito, presumido, oral.
UN.YOKE, *v.*, libertar-se, liberar-se, sair do jugo.
UP, *prep.*, para cima, em cima, em, sobre, através de; *adv.*, para cima, para o alto.
UP.BRAID, *v.*, advertir, censurar, criticar, admoestar.
UP.CAST, *adj.*, erguido, levantado, alçado.
UP.DATE, *v.*, atualizar, pôr em dia.
UP.GRADE, *s.*, upgrade, subida, elevação; *v.*, melhorar, remodelar, atualizar.
UP.HEAV.AL, *s.*, transtorno, confusão.
UP.HOLD.ER, *s.*, apoio, sustentáculo, reforço.
UP.HOL.STER, *v.*, acolchoar, estofar.
UP.KEEP, *s.*, manutenção, cuidado.
UP.LAND.ER, *s.*, terreno montanhoso, elevado; *adj.*, montanhoso.
UP.ON, *prep.*, em cima, sobre, por cima de.
UP.PER, *s.*, superior, parte superior; *adj.*, superior, mais alto.
UPPER-CLASS, *adj.*, referente à classe alta.
UP.PER.MOST, *adj.*, o mais alto.
UP.RAISE, *v.*, levantar, erguer, exaltar, louvar.
UP.RIGHT, *adj.*, ereto, reto, vertical.
UP.RIS.ING, *s.*, revolta, rebeldia, revolução.
UP.SET, *s.*, reviravolta, revés, contrariedade; *v.*, virar, perturbar, incomodar.
UP.SHOT, *s.*, conclusão, resultado, arremate, finalização.
UP.STAIRS, *s.*, andar superior; *adv.*, em cima, na parte superior; *adj.*, superior.
UP.START, *s.*, novo-rico, tipo indigesto.

UP.TIGHT, *adj.*, nervoso.
URAE.MIA, *s.*, uremia.
URA.NI.UM, *s.*, urânio.
UR.BAN, *adj.*, urbano, citadino.
UR.BAN.I.TY, *s.*, urbanidade, gentileza, polidez.
UREA, *s.*, ureia.
URE.THRA, *s.*, uretra.
URET.IC, *adj.*, urético.
UR.GEN.CY, *s.*, urgência, pressa, insistência.
UR.GENT, *adj.*, urgente.
URI.NAL, *s.*, urinol.
URI.NATE, *v.*, urinar.
URINE, *s.*, urina.
URN, *s.*, urna.
URU.GUAY, *s.*, Uruguai.
URU.GUAY.AN, *adj.*, *s.*, uruguaio.
US, *pron.*, nos; nós.
U.S.A, *s.*, Estados Unidos da América.
US.AGE, *s.*, uso, usança.
USE, *s.*, uso, emprego, utilidade; *v.*, usar, empregar, utilizar.
USE.FUL, *adj.*, útil, proveitoso, utilizado.
USE UP, *v.*, esgotar, terminar, acabar.
USU.AL, *adj.*, usual, corriqueiro, habitual.
USU.AL.NESS, *s.*, uso, emprego, costume.
USU.FRUCT, *s.*, usufruto.
USU.RER, *s.*, usurário.
USURP, *v.*, usurpar, tirar, pegar.
USUR.PA.TION, *s.*, usurpação.
USU.RY, *s.*, usura, sovinice.
UTER.US, *s.*, útero.
UTIL.I.TY, *s.*, utilidade.
UTIL.I.ZA.TION, *s.*, utilização.
UTI.LIZE, *v.*, utilizar, usar.
UT.MOST, *adj.*, maior, superior.
UTO.PIA, *s.*, utopia.
UTO.PI.AN, *adj.*, utópico.
UT.TER.ANCE, *s.*, declaração, dito, fala.
UVU.LA, *s.*, úvula.
UX.OR.I.CIDE, *s.*, uxoricida.
UX.O.RI.OUS, *adj.*, submisso à mulher; maricas, afeminado.

V

V, *s.*, vigésima segunda letra do alfabeto inglês; **V**, número romano - 5.
VA.CAN.CY, *s.*, vacância, vaga, lacuna, quarto de hotel desocupado.
VA.CANT, *adj.*, vago, vazio, livre, desocupado, abandonado.
VA.CATE, *v.*, desocupar, esvaziar, liberar.
VA.CA.TION, *s.*, férias, feriado, período de descanso.
VAC.CI.NATE, *v.*, vacinar.
VAC.CINE, *s.*, vacina.
VAC.IL.LATE, *v.*, vacilar, hesitar, titubear.
VAC.IL.LA.TION, *s.*, vacilação, hesitação, titubeio.
VAC.U.UM, *s.*, vácuo.
VAG.A.BOND, *s.*, vagabundo.
VA.GI.NA, *s.*, vagina.
VAGUE, *adj.*, vago.
VAGUE.NESS, *s.*, incerteza, vagueza, indefinição.
VAIN, *adj.*, vão, vaidoso.
VAIN.GLO.RY, *s.*, vanglória, vaidade, soberba.
VAIN.NESS, *s.*, vaidade, soberba.
VA.LET, *s.*, camareiro, criado, aio, pagem.
VAL.ID, *adj.*, válido.
VAL.I.DATE, *v.*, validar, valorizar.
VA.LID.I.TY, *s.*, validade.
VAL.LEY, *s.*, vale.
VAL.OUR, *s.*, valor, valentia, denodo.
VAL.UE, *s.*, valor, importância, preço, valia; *v.*, valorizar, avaliar.
VALVE, *s.*, válvula.
VAMP, *s.*, mulher fascinante.
VAM.PIRE, *s.*, vampiro.
VAN, *s.*, camioneta, furgão, van.
VAN.DAL, *s.*, vândalo.
VAN.DAL.ISE, *v.*, vandalizar.
VAN.GUARD, *s.*, vanguarda.
VA.NIL.LA, *s.*, baunilha.
VAN.I.TY, *s.*, vaidade, soberba.
VAN.TAGE, *s.*, vantagem.
VA.POR.I.ZA.TION, *s.*, vaporização.
VA.POR.IZE, *v.*, vaporizar.
VA.POUR, *s.*, vapor.
VA.POURY, *adj.*, vaporoso.
VAR.I.ABIL.I.TY, *s.*, variabilidade.
VAR.I.ANT, *adj.*, *s.*, variante.
VAR.I.A.TION, *s.*, variação.
VAR.I.CEL.LA, *s.*, varicela.
VAR.I.CES, *s.*, varizes.
VAR.IED, *adj.*, vário, variado.
VA.RI.E.TY, *s.*, variedade, diversidade.
VA.RI.O.LA, *s.*, varíola.
VAR.NISH, *s.*, verniz; *v.*, envernizar.
VARY, *v.*, variar, mudar, trocar.
VAS.CU.LAR, *adj.*, vascular.
VASE, *s.*, vaso.
VAS.E.LINE, *s.*, vaselina.
VAST, *adj.*, vasto, amplo, enorme.
VAT, *s.*, tina, cuba, vaza.
VAT.I.CAN, *s.*, Vaticano.
VEER, *v.*, virar, tornar.
VEG.E.TA.BLE, *s.*, vegetal, legume, hortaliça; *adj.*, vegetal.
VEG.E.TA.TION, *s.*, vegetação.
VE.HE.MENCE, *s.*, veemência.
VE.HI.CLE, *s.*, veículo.
VEIN, *s.*, veia; nervura.
VEINY, *adj.*, venenoso, detentor de veias.
VE.LOC.I.PEDE, *s.*, velocípede.
VE.LOC.I.TY, *s.*, velocidade.
VE.LUM, *s.*, véu.
VEL.VET, *s.*, veludo; *adj.*, aveludado.
VE.NAL, *adj.*, venal.
VE.NAL.I.TY, *s.*, venalidade, corrupção.
VEND, *v.*, vender.
VEN.ER.ATE, *v.*, venerar.

VEN.ER.A.TION, s., veneração.
VEN.ERY, s., caça, caçada.
VEN.GEANCE, s., vingança, vendeta.
VE.NIAL, adj., venial.
VEN.OM, s., veneno.
VEN.TI.LATE, v., ventilar, arejar.
VEN.TI.LA.TION, s., ventilação, arejamento.
VEN.TRI.CLE, s., ventrículo.
VEN.TRIL.O.QUIST, s., ventríloquo.
VEN.TURE, s., empreendimento, atuação comercial; v., arriscar, tentar.
VE.RA.CIOUS, adj., verídico, verdadeiro, veraz.
VE.RAC.I.TY, s., veracidade.
VE.RAN.DA, s., varanda.
VERB, s., verbo.
VER.BAL, adj., verbal, oral.
VER.DAN.CY, s., verdura.
VER.DICT, s., veredicto, sentença, decisão judicial.
VER.DURE, s., verdura.
VER.I.FI.CA.TION, s., verificação, exame.
VER.I.FY, v., verificar, inspecionar, vistoriar.
VER.I.TY, s., verdade.
VER.MI.CEL.LI, s., aletria.
VER.MIN.OUS, adj., verminoso.
VER.MOUTH, s., vermute.
VER.NAC.U.LAR, s., vernáculo, língua-mãe.
VER.RU.CA, s., verruga.
VER.SA.TILE, adj., versátil, plástico.
VERSE, s., verso, estrofe.
VER.SI.CLE, s., versículo.
VER.SI.FY, v., versificar, fazer versos.
VER.SION, s., versão.
VER.TE.BRA, s., vértebra.
VER.TE.BRATE, s., vertebrado.
VER.TI.CAL, adj., vertical.
VER.TI.CAL.I.TY, s., verticalidade.
VER.TIG.I.NOUS, adj., vertiginoso.
VER.TI.GO, s., vertigem.
VERY, adv., muito, bastante.
VES.I.CA, s., bexiga.
VES.I.CLE, s., vesícula.
VES.PER.TINE, adj., vespertino.
VES.PI.ARY, s., vespeiro.
VES.TI.BULE, s., vestíbulo, saguão, átrio.
VEST.MENT, s., veste, vestimenta, roupas.
VET.E.RAN, s., veterano de guerra.
VET.ER.I.NARY, s., veterinário.
VE.TO, s., veto; v., vetar, proibir.
VEX.A.TION, s., vexação, irritação.
VI.A.BLE, adj., viável.
VIA.DUCT, s., viaduto.
VI.AND, s., vianda, carne.
VI.BRANT, adj., vibrante, entusiasmado, animado.
VI.BRATE, v., vibrar, festejar.
VI.BRA.TOR, s., vibrador.
VICE, s., vício, defeito, vezo; torno mecânico.
VI.CIOUS, adj., vicioso, violento, cruel.
VIC.TIM, s., vítima.
VIC.TO.RI.OUS, adj., vitorioso, vencedor.
VIC.TO.RY, s., vitória.
VIEW, s., vista, ponto de vista, perspectiva, parecer.
VIEW.ER, s., telespectador.
VIEW.POINT, s., ponto de vista.
VIG.IL, s., vigília.
VIG.I.LANCE, s., vigilância.
VIG.OUR, s., vigor, força, robustez.
VILE, adj., vil, infame, repulsivo.
VIL.I.FY, v., envilecer, aviltar, difamar.
VIL.LAGE, s., aldeia, povoado, localidade.
VIL.LAIN, s., vilão, biltre, patife, safado.
VIN.DI.CATE, v., vingar, justiçar, justificar.
VIN.DI.CA.TION, s., vingança.
VIN.E.GAR, s., vinagre.
VINE.YARD, s., vinhedo, vinha.
VIN.TAGE, s., vindima, colheita de uva.
VI.NYL, s., vinil.
VI.O.LATE, v., violar.
VI.O.LA.TION, s., violação.
VI.O.LENCE, s., violência.
VI.O.LET, s., violeta; adj., violeta, da cor de violeta.
VI.O.LIN, s., violino.
VI.O.LIN.IST, s., violinista.
VI.PER, s., víbora, serpente, cobra.
VIR.GIN, adj., s., virgem.

VI.RID.I.TY, *s.*, verdor, verdura, viço.
VIR.ILE, *adj.*, viril.
VI.RIL.I.TY, *s.*, virilidade.
VIR.TUE, *s.*, virtude, vantagem.
VIR.U.LENCE, *s.*, virulência.
VI.RUS, *s.*, vírus.
VI.SA, *s.*, visto, sinal.
VIS.CERA, *s.*, vísceras, intestinos.
VIS.COS.I.TY, *s.*, viscosidade.
VIS.COUNT, *s.*, visconde.
VIS.COUS, *adj.*, viscoso, pegajoso.
VIS.I.BIL.I.TY, *s.*, visibilidade.
VI.SION, *s.*, vista, visão, panorama.
VIS.IT, *s.*, visita; *v.*, visitar, fazer visitas.
VIS.I.TOR, *s.*, visitante, turista.
VI.SU.AL, *adj.*, visual.
VI.SU.AL.ISE, *v.*, visualizar.
VI.TAL, *adj.*, vital, essencial, fundamental.
VI.TAL.I.TY, *s.*, vitalidade, vigor, energia.
VI.TAL.IZE, *v.*, vitalizar, revigorar.
VI.TA.MIN, *s.*, vitamina.
VI.TI.ATE, *v.*, viciar, corromper.
VI.TI.CUL.TURE, *s.*, viticultura.
VIT.RI.FI.CA.TION, *s.*, vitrificação.
VIT.RI.FY, *v.*, vitrificar.
VI.TU.PER.A.TION, *s.*, vituperação, advertência.
VI.VAC.I.TY, *s.*, vivacidade, ânimo.
VIV.ID, *adj.*, vívido, claro, evidente.
VIV.I.FI.CA.TION, *s.*, vivificação.
VIV.I.FY, *v.*, vivificar.
VO.CA.BLE, *s.*, vocábulo, termo, palavra.
VO.CAB.U.LARY, *s.*, vocabulário.
VO.CAL.ISM, *s.*, vocalismo.
VO.CAL.IZE, *v.*, vocalizar, pronunciar.
VO.CA.TION, *s.*, vocação.
VOC.A.TIVE, *adj.*, *s.*, vocativo.

VO.CIF.ER.ATE, *v.*, vociferar.
VOGUE, *s.*, moda, voga, evidência.
VOID, *s.*, vazio, vácuo; *adj.*, nulo, vazio.
VOL.A.TILE, *adj.*, volátil.
VOL.A.TIL.I.SE, *v.*, volatilizar.
VOL.CA.NIC, *adj.*, vulcânico.
VOL.CA.NO, *s.*, vulcão.
VOL.LEY.BALL, *s.*, vôlei, voleibol.
VOLT, *s.*, volt.
VOLT.AGE, *s.*, voltagem.
VOL.U.BIL.I.TY, *s.*, volubilidade, loquacidade.
VOL.UME, *s.*, volume, peso; capacidade.
VOL.UN.TARY, *adj.*, voluntário, que trabalha de graça.
VOL.UN.TEER, *s.*, voluntário; *v.*, oferecer gratuitamente.
VOM.IT, *s.*, vômito; *v.*, vomitar.
VO.RAC.I.TY, *s.*, voracidade, rapacidade.
VOR.TEX, *s.*, turbilhão.
VOTE, *s.*, voto, votação, sufrágio; *v.*, votar, sufragar.
VOT.ER, *s.*, eleitor, votante.
VOT.ING, *s.*, votação, sufrágio.
VOUCH, *v.*, garantir, dar garantia, assegurar.
VOUCH.ER, *s.*, garantia, tíquete, senha, cartão, vale.
VOW, *s.*, voto.
VOY.AGE, *s.*, viagem, itinerário.
VOY.AG.ER, *s.*, viajante.
VUL.GAR, *adj.*, vulgar, ordinário, popular.
VUL.GAR.I.TY, *s.*, vulgaridade, grosseria.
VUL.GAR.IZE, *v.*, vulgarizar, popularizar.
VUL.NER.A.BIL.I.TY, *s.*, vulnerabilidade.
VUL.TURE, *s.*, abutre.
VUL.VA, *s.*, vulva.

W

W, *s.*, vigésima terceira letra do alfabeto inglês.
WAD.DING, *s.*, forro, entretela.
WADE, *v.*, andar com dificuldade, caminhar.
WA.FER, *s.*, bolacha doce.
WAG, *v.*, sacudir, menear, mexer.
WAGE, *s.*, salário, vencimento.
WA.GER, *s.*, aposta.
WAG.GON-LIT, *s.*, vagão-dormitório.
WAG.GON, *s.*, vagão.
WAIL, *s.*, lamento, queixa, gemido; *v.*, lamentar-se, gemer.
WAIN, *s.*, carro, carroça, veículo.
WAIST.COAT, *s.*, colete.
WAIT, *s.*, espera; *v.*, esperar, aguardar.
WAIT.ING, *s.*, espera, serviço.
WAK.ING, *s.*, vigilância, vigília.
WALES, *s.*, País de Gales.
WALK, *s.*, passeio, excursão, caminhada, andada, passo; *v.*, andar, caminhar.
WALK.ER, *s.*, caminhante, pedestre, andante.
WALK.ING, *s.*, andar, caminhada, andada.
WALL, *s.*, muro, parede.
WALLED, *adj.*, murado, cercado por muros.
WALL.PA.PER, *s.*, papel de parede.
WAL.NUT, *s.*, noz; nogueira.
WAL.RUS, *s.*, morsa.
WALTZ, *s.*, valsa; *v.*, valsar, dançar valsa.
WAN.DER.ER, *s.*, vagabundo.
WANE, *v.*, diminuir, decrescer.
WAN.NESS, *s.*, palidez.
WANT, *v.*, desejar, querer, necessitar, exigir.
WANT.AGE, *s.*, falta, carência.
WAN.TON, *adj.*, gratuito, irresponsável.
WAN.TON.NESS, *s.*, lascívia.
WAR, *s.*, guerra.
WAR.DEN, *s.*, administrador de hotel, diretor.
WAR.DER, *s.*, carcereiro.
WARD.ROBE, *s.*, guarda-roupas.
WARE, *s.*, mercadoria, gêneros alimentícios.
WARE.HOUSE, *s.*, armazém, depósito.
WARES, *s.*, mercadorias.
WARI.NESS, *s.*, cautela, cuidado, precaução.
WAR.LOCK, *s.*, bruxo, feiticeiro, mago.
WARM, *adj.*, quente.
WARMTH, *s.*, calor, quentura, calor humano.
WARN, *v.*, avisar, prevenir, acautelar.
WARN.ING, *s.*, advertência, aviso, chamada de atenção.
WAR.RANT, *s.*, autorização, mandado judicial, patente.
WAR.RANT.ER, *s.*, fiador.
WAR.RAN.TY, *s.*, garantia.
WAR.RIOR, *s.*, guerreiro.
WAR.SHIP, *s.*, navio de guerra.
WART, *s.*, verruga.
WASH, *v.*, lavar, limpar; *s.*, lavagem, limpeza.
WASH.BA.SIN, *s.*, lavatório.
WASH.CLOTH, *s.*, toalha de rosto.
WASHY, *adj.*, úmido, molhado, lavado.
WASP, *s.*, vespa.
WAST.AGE, *s.*, desgaste, desperdício, perda.
WAST.ER, *s.*, gastador, pródigo, esbanjador.
WATCH.ER, *s.*, vigia, vigilante, guarda.
WATCH.MA.KER, *s.*, relojoeiro.
WATCH.STRAP, *s.*, pulseira de relógio.
WA.TER, *s.*, água; *v.*, regar, molhar, lacrimejar.
WA.TER.COL.OUR, *s.*, aquarela.
WA.TER.CRESS, *s.*, agrião.
WA.TER.MAN, *s.*, barqueiro.
WA.TER.MEL.ON, *s.*, melancia.
WA.TER.PROOF, *adj.*, *s.*, impermeável; *adj.*, à prova d'água.
WA.TERY, *adj.*, úmido, molhado, aquoso.
WAVE, *s.*, onda, sinal, ondulação; *v.*, acenar com a mão.
WAVED, *adj.*, ondulado, cheio de ondas.

WA.VER.ING, *adj.*, indeciso, hesitante.
WAX, *s.*, cera; *v.*, passar cera.
WAX.WORKS, *s.*, museu de cera.
WAXY, *adj.*, de cera.
WAY, *s.*, caminho, via, estrada, percurso, direção, hábito.
WAY.FAR.ER, *s.*, viajante.
W.C., *s.*, banheiro, privada, toalete.
WE, *pron.*, nós.
WEALTH, *s.*, riqueza, abundância, copiosidade.
WEAP.ON, *s.*, arma.
WEAR, *s.*, uso, desgaste, perda; *v.*, vestir, desgastar, calçar.
WEA.RI.NESS, *s.*, cansaço, aborrecimento.
WEARY, *adj.*, cansado, deprimido.
WEATH.ER, *s.*, tempo.
WEATH.ER.MAN, *s.*, meteorologista.
WEAV.ING, *s.*, tecelagem.
WEB.STER, *s.*, tecelão.
WED.DING, *s.*, casamento.
WED.LOCK, *s.*, casamento, matrimônio.
WEDNES.DAY, *s.*, quarta-feira.
WEEK.DAY, *s.*, dia de semana.
WEEK.END, *s.*, fim de semana.
WEIGHT, *s.*, peso.
WEIGHTY, *adj.*, pesado.
WEIR, *s.*, represa, açude, dique.
WEL.COME, *s.*, acolhida, recepção; *adj.*, bem-vindo.
WEL.COM.ING, *s.*, acolhida, acolhimento.
WELL, *s.*, poço.
WELL-BE.ING, *s.*, bem-estar.
WELSH, *adj.*, galês.
WERE.WOLF, *s.*, lobisomem.
WEST, *s.*, oeste; *adv.*, para oeste.
WEST.ERN, *s.*, filme americano de ação dos tempos da colonização; *adj.*, ocidental.
WEST.ERN.MOST, *adj.*, o mais ocidental.
WEST.WARD *adv.*, para o oeste, em direção ao oeste.
WET, *s.*, chuva, umidade; *adj.*, úmido, molhado, ensopado ; *v.*, molhar, umedecer.
WHALE, *s.*, baleia.
WHAT, *pron.*, que, o que, aquilo; quê? o quê?

WHAT.EV.ER, *pron.*, tudo aquilo que, qualquer coisa que.
WHEAT, *s.*, trigo.
WHEE.DLE, *v.*, obter por astúcia, conseguir por logro, conseguir por adulação.
WHEEL, *s.*, roda, roda do leme; *v.*, dar voltas, girar, empurrar algo com rodas.
WHEEL.BAR.ROW, *s.*, carrinho de mão.
WHEN, *adv.*, quando; *conj.*, ao passo que.
WHENCE, *adv.*, donde, de que lugar.
WHENCE.SO.EV.ER, *adv.*, de qualquer lugar.
WHERE, *s.*, cenário, lugar; *adv.* e *conj.*, onde?, onde, aonde.
WHERE.BY, *pron.*, pelo qual.
WHERE.OF, *adv.*, do que.
WHER.EV.ER, *adv.* e *conj.*, para onde quer que; seja onde for; onde? para onde?
WER.RY, *s.*, barco.
WHETH.ER, *conj.*, se.
WHICH, *pron.*, que, qual, quais, o qual, a qual.
WHICH.EV.ER, *pron.*, qualquer, quaisquer.
WHILE, *s.*, tempo, período; *conj.*, enquanto, ao mesmo tempo que, contanto.
WHIM.PER, *s.*, queixa, lamento, lamúria; *v.*, chorar, lamuriar-se, soluçar.
WHIM.SY, *s.*, capricho, teimosia, mania.
WHIP, *s.*, chicote; *v.*, chicotear, bater, espancar, sovar.
WHIP.PING, *s.*, açoite, espancamento.
WHIRL.POOL, *s.*, remoinho.
WHIRL.WIND, *s.*, furacão, tornado.
WHISK, *s.*, batedeira; *v.*, mover com rapidez.
WHIS.KY, *s.*, uísque.
WHIS.PER, *s.*, murmúrio, sussurro; *v.*, murmurar.
WHITE, *adj.*, branco, pálido, alvo, cândido.
WHITE.WASH, *s.*, cal.
WHIT.SUN, *s.*, Pentecostes.
WHIT.TLE, *v.*, cortar, cortar com faca.
WHIZ, *s.*, zumbido, zunido, ruído estridente.
WHO, *pron.*, quem?, que; o qual, os quais.
WHO.EV.ER, *pron.*, quem quer que.
WHOLE, *s.*, totalidade; *adj.*, todo, integral, completo; *pron.*, todo.
WHOLE.MEAL, *adj.*, integral, completo, total.

WHOLE.SALE, s., venda por atacado, venda em grande quantidade.
WHOLE.SOME, adj., saudável, sadio, são.
WHOM, pron., quem?; quem.
WHOM.SO.EV.ER, pron., quem quer que seja.
WHORE, s., prostituta, meretriz, rameira.
WHOSE, pron., de quem, do qual, da qual.
WHY, pron., por que, por quê?; conj., porque.
WICK.ER, s., vime.
WIDE, adj., largo, vasto, grande, amplo.
WID.EN, v., alargar, ampliar, aumentar.
WIDE.NESS, s., largura, amplitude.
WID.OW, s., viúva.
WID.OW.ER, s., viúvo.
WID.OW.HOOD, s., viuvez.
WIDTH, s., largura.
WIFE, s., esposa, consorte.
WIG, s., peruca.
WILD, adj., selvagem, silvestre, furioso, bárbaro, insensato.
WIL.DER.NESS, s., sertão, terra inculta e bravia, local ermo.
WILL, s., desejo, vontade, testamento; v., querer, desejar.
WILLED, adj., com boa vontade, pronto, propenso.
WILL.ING.NESS, s., boa vontade, disposição, prontidão.
WIL.LOW, s., salgueiro.
WILY, adj., esperto, sagaz, astuto, inteligente.
WIN, s., vitória; v., vencer, superar, ganhar.
WIND, s., vento, fôlego, aragem.
WIND.FALL, s., golpe de sorte.
WIND.MILL, s., moinho de vento.
WIN.DOW, s., janela.
WIND.SCREEN, s., para-brisa.
WINDY, adj., com vento, cheio de vento.
WINE, s., vinho.
WING, s., asa, para-lama.
WIN.NER, s., vencedor, conquistador.
WIN.TER, s., inverno.
WIN.TRY, adj., invernal, hibernal, invernoso.
WIPE, s., limpeza, higiene; v., limpar, higienizar.
WIRE, s., arame, fio, telegrama; v., colocar fios elétricos.
WIR.ING, s., instalação elétrica.
WIS.DOM, s., sabedoria, prudência, ciência.
WISE, adj., prudente, sábio, sensato, erudito.
WISH, s., desejo, vontade; v., querer, desejar.
WISH.FUL, adj., desejoso.
WITCH, s., bruxa.
WITCH.CRAFT, s., bruxaria, feitiçaria.
WITH, prep., com.
WITHE, s., vime, junco.
WITH.HOLD, v., reter, conservar; negar.
WITH.IN, prep., dentro de.
WITH.OUT, prep., sem.
WIT.NESS, s., testemunha; testemunho; v., testemunhar, presenciar.
WIZ.ARD, s., feiticeiro.
WOE, s., mágoa, dor, sofrimento.
WOLD, s., bosque.
WOLF, s., lobo.
WOM.AN, s., mulher.
WOM.AN.HOOD, s., sexo feminino, feminilidade.
WOM.AN.LY, adj., feminino.
WOMB, s., útero.
WON.DER, s., maravilha, espetáculo; v., maravilhar, admirar, desejar.
WON.DER.FUL, adj., maravilhoso, espetacular, prodigioso.
WON.DROUS, adj., maravilhoso, prodigioso.
WOO, v., namorar, flertar, fazer a corte.
WOOD, s., madeira, floresta, mata.
WOOD.LAND, s., mata, floresta, bosque.
WOOD.MAN, s., guarda-florestal.
WOOD.PECK.ER, s., pica-pau.
WOOD.WORK, s., carpintaria.
WOOL, s., lã.
WORD, s., palavra, termo, notícia, comentário; v., redigir, escrever.
WORD.ING, s., palavreado, fraseado.
WORK, s., trabalho, labuta, emprego, serviço; v., trabalhar, funcionar, moldar.
WORK.ER, s., trabalhador, operário.
WORK.SHOP, s., oficina, lição prática.
WORLD, s., mundo, globo; adj., mundial, global.

WOR.RY, *s.*, preocupação; *v.*, preocupar.
WORSE, *adj.*, *adv.*, pior; o pior, péssimo.
WOR.SHIP, *s.*, adoração, veneração.
WORTH, *s.*, valor, merecimento.
WOR.THY, *adj.*, merecedor, justo, digno.
WOUND, *v.*, ferir, machucar, lesar.
WRAITH, *s.*, fantasma, espírito, espectro.
WRAN.GLE, *s.*, briga, luta, pugilato.
WRAP, *s.*, xale, capa.
WRATH, *s.*, raiva, ira, cólera.
WRATH.FUL, *adj.*, raivoso, irritado, furioso.
WRECK, *s.*, destroços, restos, ruína; *v.*, destruir, destroçar.
WRENCH, *s.*, chave inglesa, puxada; *v.*, separar, separar com dor.
WREST, *v.*, arrancar, extrair.
WRES.TLING, *s.*, luta livre.

WRETCH, *adj.*, desgraçado, infeliz, desditoso, safado.
WRING, *v.*, torcer, apertar, sufocar.
WRING.ING, *s.*, torcedura, aperto.
WRIST, *s.*, pulso.
WRIST.WATCH, *s.*, relógio de pulso.
WRIT, *s.*, mandado judicial.
WRITE, *v.*, escrever, redigir.
WRITE OFF, *v.*, cancelar.
WRIT.ER, *s.*, escritor.
WRITE UP, *v.*, redigir.
WRIT.ING, *s.*, escrita, letra, caligrafia.
WRONG, *s.*, injustiça; *adj.*, errado, mau, injusto, equivocado; *adv.*, mal, erradamente.
WRONG.NESS, *s.*, injustiça, safadeza.
WRY, *adj.*, irônico, mordaz.

X, *s.*, vigésima quarta letra do alfabeto inglês;
X, número romano – 10.
XANT.HOUS, *adj.*, mongólico, amarelo.
XE.NO.PHO.BIA, *s.*, xenofobia.

X-RAY, *s.*, radiografia; *v.*, radiografar.
XY.LO.GRAPH *s.*, xilogravura.
XY.LO.NITE, *s.*, celuloide.
XY.LO.PHONE, *s.*, xilofone.

Y

Y, *s.*, vigésima quinta letra do alfabeto inglês.
YACHT, *s.*, iate.
YANK, *adj.*, *s.*, ianque.
YAP, *v.*, ganir, gemer.
YARD, *s.*, jarda, medida de 91,4cm.
YAWN, *s.*, bocejo; *v.*, bocejar.
YAWN.ER, *s.*, bocejador.
YEAN.LING, *s.*, cordeirinho, cabritinho ou ovelhinha.
YEAR, *s.*, ano.
YEAR.LY, *adj.*, anual.
YEARN, *v.*, ansiar por, aspirar a, pretender, desejar.
YEAST, *s.*, fermento, levedura.
YELL, *s.*, grito, berro, urro; *v.*, gritar, berrar.
YEL.LOW, *adj.*, amarelo.
YEL.LOW.ISH, *adj.*, amarelado.
YEO.MAN, *s.*, sitiante, dono de pequena propriedade agrícola.
YES, *adv.*, sim.
YES.TER, *adj.*, passado, ido, transcorrido, último; *adv.*, ontem.
YES.TER.DAY, *s.*, ontem; *adv.*, ontem.
YET, *adv.*, ainda; *conj.*, contudo, porém, mas.
YIELD, *s.*, colheita; *v.*, produzir, render, ceder.
YO.GURT, *s.*, iogurte.
YOKE, *s.*, junta de bois, junta, jugo.
YOLK, *s.*, gema de ovo.
YOU, *pron.*, tu, você, senhor; vós, vocês, o, os, a, as, lhe, contigo, convosco.
YOUNG, *s.*, juventude; *adj.*, jovem, moço; *s.*, filhote, cria de bicho.
YOUN.GER, *adj.*, mais novo.
YOUNG.STER, *s.*, moço, jovem, rapaz.
YOUR, *pron.*, seu, sua, teu, tua, vosso, vossa.
YOUR.SELF, *pron.*, tu mesmo, você mesmo, si mesmo.
YOUR.SELVES, *pron.*, vós mesmos, vocês mesmos.
YOUTH, *s.*, juventude, mocidade.
YOUTH.FUL, *adj.*, jovem, moço.
YU.GO.SLAV, *adj.*, *s.*, iugoslavo.
YUP.PIE, *s.*, iupi.

Z

Z, *s.*, vigésima sexta letra do alfabeto inglês.
ZA.NY, *s.*, palhaço, tolo, pateta; *adj.*, bobo, tolo, imbecil.
ZEAL, *s.*, fervor, entusiasmo, ânimo.
ZEAL.OT, *s.*, zelote, fanático, entusiasta.
ZE.BRA, *s.*, zebra.
ZE.NITH, *s.*, zênite, cume, cimo, pico.
ZEPH.YR, *s.*, zéfiro, aura, aragem, vento brando.
ZE.RO, *s.*, zero.
ZEST, *s.*, sabor, entusiasmo, prazer, deleite.
ZEUG.MA, *s.*, zeugma, silepse.
ZIG.ZAG, *s.*, zigue-zague; *v.*, zigue-zaguear.
ZINC, *s.*, zinco; *v.*, zincar.
ZIP, *s.*, zunido, silvo, fecho, zíper; fechar o zíper.
ZIP.PER, *s.*, zíper.
ZO.DI.AC, *s.*, zodíaco.
ZONE, *s.*, zona, região, localidade.
ZOO, *s.*, zoo, zoológico.
ZO.OL.O.GIST, *s.*, zoólogo.
ZO.OL.O.GY, *s.*, zoologia.
ZOOM, *v.*, zunir, zumbir, subir um aclive com rapidez.
ZO.RIL, *s.*, zorrilho.
ZU.LU, *adj.*, *s.*, zulu, povo africano.
ZUC.CHI.NI, *s.*, abobrinha.
ZY.GO.MA, *s.*, zigoma